Organizational Behavior

Organizational Behavior

15

Stephen P. Robbins
—San Diego State University

Timothy A. Judge
—University of Notre Dame

Boston Columbus Indianapolis New York San Francisco Upper Saddle River
Amsterdam Cape Town Dubai London Madrid Milan Munich Paris Montréal Toronto
Delhi Mexico City São Paulo Sydney Hong Kong Seoul Singapore Taipei Tokyo

Editorial Director: Sally Yagan
Director of Editorial Services:
 Ashley Santora
Acquisitions Editor: Brian Mickelson
Editorial Project Manager: Sarah Holle
Editorial Assistant: Ashlee Bradbury
VP Director of Marketing:
 Patrice Lumumba Jones
Senior Marketing Manager:
 Nikki Ayana Jones
Senior Managing Editor: Judy Leale
Production Project Manager:
 Becca Groves
Senior Operations Supervisor:
 Arnold Vila
Operations Specialist: Cathleen Petersen
Senior Art Director: Janet Slowik

Art Director: Kenny Beck
Text and Cover Designer: Wanda Espana
OB Poll Graphics: Electra Graphics
Cover Art: honey comb and a bee working /
 Shutterstock / LilKar
Sr. Media Project Manager, Editorial:
 Denise Vaughn
Media Project Manager, Production:
 Lisa Rinaldi
Full-Service Project Management:
 Christian Holdener, S4Carlisle Publishing
 Services
Composition: S4Carlisle Publishing
 Services
Printer/Binder: Courier/Kendallville
Cover Printer: Courier/Kendalville
Text Font: 10.5/12 ITC New Baskerville Std

Credits and acknowledgments borrowed from other sources and reproduced, with permission, in this textbook appear on the appropriate page within text.

Library of Congress Cataloging-in-Publication Data
Robbins, Stephen P.
 Organizational behavior / Stephen P. Robbins, Timothy A. Judge. — 15th ed.
  p. cm.
 Includes indexes.
 ISBN-13: 978-0-13-283487-2
 ISBN-10: 0-13-283487-1
 1. Organizational behavior. I. Judge, Tim. II. Title.

HD58.7.R62 2012
658.3—dc23

2011038674

10 9 8 7 6 5 4 3 2 1

ISBN 10:   0-13-283487-1
ISBN 13: 978-0-13-283487-2

Brief Contents

v

4   The Organization System

Contents

2 The Individual

Values 144

The Importance of Values 144 • Terminal versus Instrumental Values 144 • Generational Values 145

Linking an Individual's Personality and Values to the Workplace 148

Person–Job Fit 148 • Person–Organization Fit 150

International Values 150

Summary and Implications for Managers 154

 Self-Assessment Library Am I a Narcissist? 132

Myth or Science? Personality Predicts the Performance of Entrepreneurs 142

glOBalization! The Right Personality for a Global Workplace 143

An Ethical Choice Should You Try to Change Someone's Personality? 147

Point/Counterpoint Millennials Are More Narcissistic 155

Questions for Review 156
Experiential Exercise What Organizational Culture Do You Prefer? **156**
Ethical Dilemma Freedom or Lack of Commitment? **156**
Case Incident 1 Is There a Price for Being Too Nice? **157**
Case Incident 2 Leadership from an Introvert's Perspective **158**

6 *Perception and Individual Decision Making* 165

What Is Perception? 166
Factors That Influence Perception 167

Person Perception: Making Judgments About Others 168
Attribution Theory 168 • Common Shortcuts in Judging Others 170 • Specific Applications of Shortcuts in Organizations 173

The Link Between Perception and Individual Decision Making 174

Decision Making in Organizations 175
The Rational Model, Bounded Rationality, and Intuition 175 • Common Biases and Errors in Decision Making 177

Influences on Decision Making: Individual Differences and Organizational Constraints 184
Individual Differences 184 • Organizational Constraints 186

What About Ethics in Decision Making? 187
Three Ethical Decision Criteria 187 • Improving Creativity in Decision Making 188

Summary and Implications for Managers 190

Self-Assessment Library What Are My Gender Role Perceptions? 166
glOBalization! Chinese Time, North American Time 171
Myth or Science? Creative Decision Making Is a Right-Brain Activity 181
Self-Assessment Library Am I A Deliberate Decision Maker? 183
An Ethical Choice Whose Ethical Standards to Follow? 185
Self-Assessment Library How Creative Am I? 190
Point/Counterpoint Checklists Lead to Better Decisions 191

7 *Motivation Concepts*   201

8 *Motivation: From Concepts to Applications*   239

3 | The Group

12 *Leadership* 367

13 *Power and Politics* 411

4 The Organization System

17 *Human Resource Policies and Practices* 543

18 *Organizational Change and Stress Management* 577

Stephen P. Robbins

Education
Ph.D. University of Arizona

Professional Experience

Academic Positions: Professor, San Diego State University, Southern Illinois University at Edwardsville, University of Baltimore, Concordia University in Montreal, and University of Nebraska at Omaha.

Research: Research interests have focused on conflict, power, and politics in organizations, behavioral decision making, and the development of effective interpersonal skills.

Books Published: World's best-selling author of textbooks in both management and organizational behavior. His books have sold more than 5 million copies and have been translated into 20 languages; editions have been adapted for Canada, Australia, South Africa, and India, such as these:

- *Essentials of Organizational Behavior*, 11th ed. (Prentice Hall, 2012)
- *Management*, 11th ed. with Mary Coulter (Prentice Hall, 2012)
- *Fundamentals of Human Resource Management*, 10th ed., with David DeCenzo (Wiley, 2010)
- *Prentice Hall's Self-Assessment Library 3.4* (Prentice Hall, 2010)
- *Fundamentals of Management*, 8th ed., with David DeCenzo and Mary Coulter (Prentice Hall, 2013)
- *Supervision Today!* 7th ed., with David DeCenzo and Robert Wolter (Prentice Hall, 2013)
- *Training in Interpersonal Skills: TIPS for Managing People at Work*, 6th ed., with Phillip Hunsaker (Prentice Hall, 2012)
- *Managing Today!* 2nd ed. (Prentice Hall, 2000)
- *Organization Theory*, 3rd ed. (Prentice Hall, 1990)
- *The Truth About Managing People*, 2nd ed. (Financial Times/Prentice Hall, 2008)
- *Decide and Conquer: Make Winning Decisions and Take Control of Your Life* (Financial Times/Prentice Hall, 2004).

Other Interests

In his "other life," Dr. Robbins actively participates in masters' track competition. Since turning 50 in 1993, he has won 18 national championships and 12 world titles. He is the current world record holder at 100 meters (12.37 seconds) and 200 meters (25.20 seconds) for men 65 and over.

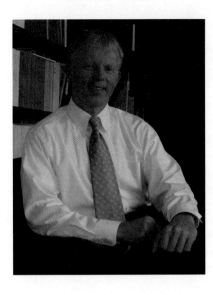

Timothy A. Judge

Education

Ph.D., University of Illinois at Urbana-Champaign

Professional Experience

Academic Positions: Franklin D. Schurz Chair, Department of Management, Mendoza College of Business, University of Notre Dame; Matherly-McKethan Eminent Scholar in Management, Warrington College of Business Administration, University of Florida; Stanley M. Howe Professor in Leadership, Henry B. Tippie College of Business, University of Iowa; Associate Professor (with tenure), Department of Human Resource Studies, School of Industrial and Labor Relations, Cornell University; Lecturer, Charles University, Czech Republic, and Comenius University, Slovakia; Instructor, Industrial/Organizational Psychology, Department of Psychology, University of Illinois at Urbana-Champaign.

Research: Dr. Judge's primary research interests are in (1) personality, moods, and emotions; (2) job attitudes; (3) leadership and influence behaviors; and (4) careers (person–organization fit, career success). Dr. Judge has published more than 140 articles on these and other major topics in journals such as *Journal of Organizational Behavior, Personnel Psychology, Academy of Management Journal, Journal of Applied Psychology, European Journal of Personality,* and *European Journal of Work and Organizational Psychology.*

Fellowship: Dr. Judge is a fellow of the American Psychological Association, the Academy of Management, the Society for Industrial and Organizational Psychology, and the American Psychological Society.

Awards: In 1995, Dr. Judge received the Ernest J. McCormick Award for Distinguished Early Career Contributions from the Society for Industrial and Organizational Psychology. In 2001, he received the Larry L. Cummings Award for mid-career contributions from the Organizational Behavior Division of the Academy of Management. In 2007, he received the Professional Practice Award from the Institute of Industrial and Labor Relations, University of Illinois.

Books Published: H. G. Heneman III, T. A. Judge, and J. D. Kammeyer-Mueller, *Staffing Organizations,* 7th ed. (Madison, WI: Mendota House/Irwin, 2011)

Other Interests

Although he cannot keep up (literally!) with Dr. Robbin's accomplishments on the track, Dr. Judge enjoys golf, cooking and baking, literature (he's a particular fan of Thomas Hardy and is a member of the Thomas Hardy Society), and keeping up with his three children, who range in age from 23 to 9.

Preface

Welcome to the fifteenth edition of *Organizational Behavior!* Long considered the standard for all organizational behavior textbooks, this edition continues its tradition of making current, relevant research come alive for students. While maintaining its hallmark features—clear writing style, cutting-edge content, and engaging pedagogy—the fourteenth edition has been updated to reflect the most recent research within the field of organizational behavior. This is one of the most comprehensive and thorough revisions of *Organizational Behavior* we've undertaken, and while we've preserved the core material, we're confident that this edition reflects the most important research and topical issues facing organizations, managers, and employees.

Key Changes to the Fifteenth Edition

- The **most substantial updating ever.** The following sections of each chapter are new to the fifteenth edition:
  - *Opening Vignette*
  - *Myth or Science?*
  - *Ethical Choice*
  - *Point/Counterpoint*
  - *Case Incident*

- In addition, the following material is substantially revised and updated:
  - *Case Incident* (those not entirely new are revised and updated)
  - *OB Poll* (more than half are new to this edition)
  - *Ethical Dilemma* (more than half are new to this edition)
  - *Photos/captions* (more than half are new to this edition)

- New feature: **glOBalization!,** which features organizational behavior in an international context.

- Improved integration of **global implications:** With the explosion of international research, global OB research is now woven into each chapter, rather than in a stand-alone section at the end of the chapter.

- Revision to **Summary and Implications for Managers** section, with more focus on practical ways to apply the material on the job.

- NEW videos—up-to-date videos showing management topics in action, access to the complete management video library, as well as instructional materials for integrating clips from popular movies into your class, are at **www.mymanagementlab.com**.

Chapter-by-Chapter Changes

Chapter 1: What Is Organizational Behavior?
- Entirely new *Opening Vignette* (The New Normal?)
- New feature: **glOBalization!**
- New *Myth or Science?* ("Most Acts of Workplace Bullying Are Men Attacking Women")
- New *OB Model,* with better integration with pedagogy (structure) of book

- New *Point–Counterpoint* (Lost in Translation?)
- New *An Ethical Choice* (Can You Learn from Failure?)
- New *Case Incident* (Lessons for 'Undercover' Bosses)
- New *Case Incident* (Era of the Disposable Worker?)

Chapter 2: Diversity in Organizations
- Entirely new *Opening Vignette* (The Rise and Fall of Erin Callan)
- New feature: **glOBalization!**
- New *Myth or Science?* ("Dual-Career Couples Divorce Less")
- Enhanced coverage of stereotyping and discrimination research
- Revised content regarding age discrimination and implications of an aging workforce
- Updates to discussion of disability in the workplace
- Expanded coverage of sexual orientation discrimination
- New material and integration of diversity with international/cultural diversity
- New *Point–Counterpoint* (Men Have More Mathematical Ability Than Women)
- New *An Ethical Choice* (Religious Tattoos)
- New *Case Incident* (Increasing Age Diversity in the Workplace)
- Updated *Case Incident* (The Flynn Effect)

Chapter 3: Attitudes and Job Satisfaction
- Entirely new *Opening Vignette* (What Does SAS Stand For?)
- New feature: **glOBalization!**
- New *Myth or Science?* ("Favorable Job Attitudes Make Organizations More Profitable")
- Review of recent studies on within-person variation in job attitudes
- New developments in organizational commitment
- Updated material on organizational citizenship behaviors
- New perspectives on attitudes and organizational performance
- New ethical dilemma
- New *Point–Counterpoint* (Employer–Employee Loyalty Is an Outdated Concept)
- New *An Ethical Choice* (Do Employers Owe Workers More Satisfying Jobs?)
- New *Case Incident* (Crafting a Better Job)
- Updated *Case Incident* (Long Hours, Hundreds of E-Mails, and No Sleep: Does This Sound Like a Satisfying Job?)

Chapter 4: Emotions and Moods
- Entirely new *Opening Vignette* (Love at Work: Taboo No More?)
- New feature: **glOBalization!**
- New *Myth or Science?* ("We Are Better Judges of When Others Are Happy Than When They Are Sad")
- Revised introduction to the topic
- Review of research on moods and employee attachment
- New section on "moral emotions"
- Discussion of emotion regulation strategies and their consequences
- New research on gender and emotions
- Updated content on emotional displays at work
- New section on *Emotional Intelligence,* with substantially more coverage and a new exhibit
- New *Point–Counterpoint* (Sometimes Blowing Your Top Is a Good Thing)
- New *An Ethical Choice* (Schadenfreude)
- New *Case Incident* (Is It Okay to Cry at Work?)
- Updated *Case Incident* (Can You Read Emotions from Faces?)

Chapter 5: Personality and Values

- Entirely new *Opening Vignette* (Changing of the Guard in Japan: Is it the Economy, or the Values?)
- New feature: **glOBalization!**
- New *Myth or Science?* ("Personality Predicts the Performance of Entrepreneurs")
- Introduces concepts related to dispositional self- and other-orientation
- New material regarding vocational choices
- New discussion of values and reactions to violations of employee values
- Major revision regarding Hofstede's model of culture and its consequences
- Updated information on personality and expatriate success
- New *Point–Counterpoint* (Millennials Are More Narcissistic)
- New *An Ethical Choice* (Should You Try to Change Someone's Personality?)
- New *Case Incident* (Leadership from an Introvert's Perspective)
- Updated *Case Incident* (Is There a Price for Being Too Nice?)

Chapter 6: Perception and Individual Decision Making

- Entirely new *Opening Vignette* (Do Machines Make Better Decisions?)
- New feature: **glOBalization!**
- New *Myth or Science?* ("Creative Decision Making Is a Right-Brain Activity")
- Review of recent work on self-serving biases
- New information on stereotyping processes
- Discussion of latest trends in decision errors research
- Updated discussion of culture and perceptions
- New section on *Financial Decision Making* and how it informs to understand recent and current crises
- New Experiential Exercise
- New *Point–Counterpoint* (Checklists Lead to Better Decisions)
- New *An Ethical Choice* (Whose Ethical Standards to Follow?)
- New *Case Incident* (Computerized Decision Making)
- Updated *Case Incident* (Predictions That Didn't Quite Pan Out)

Chapter 7: Motivation Concepts

- Entirely new *Opening Vignette* (The Motivations of the 99ers)
- New feature: **glOBalization!**
- New *Myth or Science?* ("The Support of Others Improves Our Chances of Accomplishing Our Goals")
- New material on psychological need theories
- Increased discussion of employee engagement
- Updates to the discussion on goal-setting theory
- New perspectives on equity and organizational justice
- New *Point–Counterpoint* (Fear Is a Powerful Motivator)
- New *An Ethical Choice* (Motivated to Behave Unethically)
- New *Case Incident* (It's Not Fair!)
- Updated *Case Incident* (Bullying Bosses)

Chapter 8: Motivation: From Concepts to Applications

- Entirely new *Opening Vignette* (Motivation Minus the Moolah)
- New feature: **glOBalization!**
- New *Myth or Science?* ("CEO Pay Can't Be Measured")
- Updated discussion of job characteristics
- New coverage of flextime, telecommuting, and related work practices
- Revised discussion of employee empowerment and its effects
- Discussion of innovations in gainsharing practices

- New *Point–Counterpoint* ("If Money Doesn't Make You Happy, You Aren't Spending It Right")
- New *Case Incident* (Bonuses Can Backfire)
- Updated *Case Incident* (Multitasking: A Good Use of Your Time?)

Chapter 9: Foundations of Group Behavior
- Entirely new *Opening Vignette* (To the Clickers Go the Spoils)
- New feature: **glOBalization!**
- New *Myth or Science?* ("Asians Have Less Ingroup Bias Than Americans")
- New material on dysfunctional behavior in teams
- Discussion of minority influence on group decision making
- Introduces material on team mental models
- Updated information on group decision errors and groupthink
- New information on international variations in group behavior
- New *Point–Counterpoint* (Affinity Groups Fuel Business Success)
- New *An Ethical Choice* (Should You Use Group Peer Pressure?)
- New *Case Incident* (Negative Aspects of Collaboration?)
- Updated *Case Incident* (Herd Behavior and the Housing Bubble [and Collapse])

Chapter 10: Understanding Work Teams
- Entirely new *Opening Vignette* (Killing bin Laden)
- New feature: **glOBalization!**
- New *Myth or Science?* ("Teams Work Best Under Angry Leaders")
- Updated discussion of strategies to improve team performance
- Review of research on team decision-making strategies
- New perspectives on creativity in teams
- New material on team proactivity
- Presents new literature on work teams in international contexts
- New *Point–Counterpoint* (We Can Learn Much about Work Teams from Studying Sports Teams)
- New *An Ethical Choice* (Using Global Virtual Teams as an Environmental Choice)
- New *Case Incident* (Why Don't Teams Work Like They're Supposed To?)
- Updated *Case Incident* (Multicultural Multinational Teams at IBM)

Chapter 11: Communication
- Entirely new *Opening Vignette* (Goldman Rules)
- New feature: **glOBalization!**
- New *Myth or Science?* ("We Know What Makes Good Liars Good")
- New section on *Social Networking*
- New section on *Persuasive Communication* strategies
- Discussion of how to frame messages for maximum impact
- Discussion of the effects of authority, expertise, and liking on communication effectiveness
- Updated discussion of body language in communication
- Introduces new ideas about the effects of electronic communications
- New *Point–Counterpoint* (Social Networking Is Good Business)
- New *An Ethical Choice* (The Ethics of Gossip at Work)
- New *Case Incident* (Using Social Media to Your Advantage)
- Updated *Case Incident* (Should Companies That Fire Shoot First?)

Chapter 12: Leadership
- Entirely new *Opening Vignette* (Making Google's Leaders)
- New feature: **glOBalization!**
- New *Myth or Science?* ("Power Helps Leaders Perform Better")
- Expanded discussion of leader effects on employee attitudes
- New perspectives on culture and leadership
- New material regarding emotional intelligence and leadership
- Increased consideration of contemporary theories of leadership
- Consideration of "servant leadership"
- Discussion of how leaders can increase employee creativity
- New *Point–Counterpoint* (Heroes Are Made, Not Born)
- New *An Ethical Choice* (Do Leaders Have a Responsibility to Protect Followers?)
- New *Case Incident* (Leadership Mettle Forged in Battle)
- Updated *Case Incident* (Leadership Factories)

Chapter 13: Power and Politics
- Entirely new *Opening Vignette* (Appearances Can Be Deceiving)
- New feature: **glOBalization!**
- New *Myth or Science?* ("Corporate Political Activity Pays")
- Coverage of latest research on influence tactics
- Revised discussion of sexual harassment
- Updated discussion of political behavior in organizations
- Revision to international issues in power and politics
- New *Point–Counterpoint* (Power Corrupts People)
- New *An Ethical Choice* (Should All Sexual Behavior Be Prohibited at Work?)
- New *Case Incident* (Delegate Power, or Keep it Close?)
- Updated *Case Incident* (The Persuasion Imperative)

Chapter 14: Conflict and Negotiation
- Entirely new *Opening Vignette* (No Conflict at the Post Office. . . Is That Good?)
- New feature: **glOBalization!**
- New *Myth or Science?* ("Communicating Well Is More Important in Cross-Cultural Negotiations")
- Updated material on gender and negotiation styles
- New material on individual differences in negotiation styles
- Discussion of emotions in negotiation
- New information on suspicion and deception in negotiation
- Updates to discussion on conflict and conflict management processes
- New *Point–Counterpoint* (Player–Owner Disputes Are Unnecessary)
- New *An Ethical Choice* (Using Empathy to Negotiate More Ethically)
- New *Case Incident* (Choosing Your Battles)
- Updated *Case Incident* (Mediation: Master Solution to Employment Disputes?)

Chapter 15: Foundations of Organization Structure
- Entirely new *Opening Vignette* (Dismantling a Bureaucracy)
- New feature: **glOBalization!**
- New *Myth or Science?* ("Employees Resent Outsourcing")
- Latest research on boundaryless organizations and their functioning
- Discussion of technology's influence on organizational structure

- Updated review of the relationship between organizational structure and attitudes
- New *An Ethical Choice* (Downsizing with a Conscience)
- New *Case Incident* (Creative Deviance: Bucking the Hierarchy?)
- Updated *Case Incident* (Siemens' Simple Structure—Not)

Chapter 16: Organizational Culture
- Entirely new *Opening Vignette* (Ursula M. Burns and the Culture of Xerox)
- New feature: **glOBalization!**
- New *Myth or Science?* ("Employees Treat Customers the Same Way the Organization Treats Them")
- New review of basic issues in organizational culture and subcultures
- Enhanced discussion of ethical culture
- Review of culture and organizational performance
- Revised discussion of organizational socialization practices and outcomes
- New *Point–Counterpoint* (Organizations Should Strive to Create a Positive Organizational Culture)
- New *An Ethical Choice* (Designing a Culture of Ethical Voice)
- New *Case Incident* (Did Toyota's Culture Cause Its Problems?)
- Updated *Case Incident* (Mergers Don't Always Lead to Culture Clashes)

Chapter 17: Human Resource Policies and Practices
- Entirely new *Opening Vignette* (Testing NFL Quarterbacks)
- New feature: **glOBalization!**
- New *Myth or Science?* ("Work Is Making Us Fat")
- Discussion of the implications of the Great Recession
- New material on legal issues
- Updated discussion of the effects of high performance work practice on employee attitudes and behavior
- Expanded discussion of the effects of staffing decisions on employee turnover
- New section on *Job Performance and Workplace Civility*
- New material related to performance appraisals and rater goals
- New *Point–Counterpoint* (Social Media Is a Great Source of New Hires)
- New *An Ethical Choice* (Recruiting the Unemployed)
- New *Case Incident* (The End of the Performance Appraisal?)
- Updated *Case Incident* (Job Candidates Without Strong SAT Scores Need Not Apply)

Chapter 18: Organizational Change and Stress Management
- Entirely new *Opening Vignette* (Sweet Changes at Cadbury?)
- New feature: **glOBalization!**
- New *Myth or Science?* ("Men Experience More Job Stress Than Women")
- Updated review of research on individual readiness for organizational change
- Discussion of maladaptive behavioral response to stress at work
- Updated discussion of coping strategies
- Implications of the stress-health relationship
- New *Point–Counterpoint* (Responsible Managers Relieve Stress on Their Employees)
- New *An Ethical Choice* (Responsibly Managing Your Own Stress)
- New *Case Incident* (Starbucks Returns to Its Roots)
- Updated *Case Incident* (The Rise of Extreme Jobs)

Teaching and Learning Support

MyManagementLab (www.mymanagementlab.com) is an easy-to-use online tool that personalizes course content and provides robust assessment and reporting to measure student and class performance. All the resources you need for course success are in one place—flexible and easily adapted for your course experience.

Instructor's Resource Center

At www.pearsonhighered.com/irc, instructors can access a variety of print, digital, and presentation resources available with this text in downloadable format. Registration is simple and gives you immediate access to new titles and new editions. As a registered faculty member, you can download resource files and receive immediate access and instructions for installing course management content on your campus server.

If you need assistance, our dedicated technical support team is ready to help with the media supplements that accompany this text. Visit 247pearsoned.custhelp.com for answers to frequently asked questions and toll-free user support phone numbers.

The following supplements are available to adopting instructors (for detailed descriptions, please visit www.pearsonhighered.com/irc):

- Instructor's Manual—updated and revised to provide ideas and resources in the classroom.
- Test Item File—Revised and updated to include questions that require students to apply the knowledge that they've read about in the text through Learning Objectives and Learning Outcomes. Questions are also tagged to reflect the AACSB Learning Standards.
- TestGen Test Generating Software—Test management software that contains all material from the Test Item File. This software is completely user-friendly and allows instructors to view, edit, and add test questions with just a few mouse clicks. All of our TestGens are converted for use in Blackboard and WebCT and are available for download from www.pearsonhighered.com/irc.
- PowerPoint Presentation—A ready-to-use PowerPoint slideshow designed for classroom presentation. Use it as is, or edit content to fit your individual classroom needs.
- Image Library—includes all the charts, tables, and graphs that are found in the text.

Videos on DVD

Adopters can access the 48 videos on the 2013 Organizational Behavior Video Library DVD. These videos have been produced to depict real-world OB issues and give students a taste of the multi-faceted nature of OB in real companies.

Learning Management Systems

BlackBoard and WebCT Course Cartridges are available for download from www.pearsonhighered.com/irc. These standard course cartridges contain the Instructor's Manual, TestGen, Instructor PowerPoints, and when available, Student PowerPoints and Student Data Files.

CourseSmart eTextbooks Online

Developed for students looking to save money on required or recommended textbooks, CourseSmart eTextbooks online save students money compared with the suggested list price of the print text. Students simply select their eText by title or author and purchase immediate access to the content for the duration of the course using any major credit card. With CourseSmart eText, students can search for specific keywords or page numbers, make notes online, print reading assignments that incorporate lecture notes, and bookmark important passages for later review. For more information, or to purchase a CourseSmart eTextbook, visit www.coursesmart.com.

Pearson's Self-Assessment Library (S.A.L.)

A hallmark of the Robbins series, S.A.L. is a unique learning tool that allows you to assess your knowledge, beliefs, feelings, and actions in regard to a wide range of personal skills, abilities, and interests. Self-assessments have been integrated into each chapter, including a self-assessment at the beginning of each chapter. S.A.L. helps students better understand their interpersonal and behavioral skills as they relate to the theoretical concepts presented in each chapter.

Highlights

- **69 research-based self-assessments**—All 69 instruments of our collection are from sources such as *Journal of Social Behavior and Personality, Harvard Business Review, Organizational Behavior: Experiences and Cases, Journal of Experimental Education, Journal of Applied Measurement,* and more.
- **Work–life and career focused**—All self-assessments are focused to help individuals better manage their work lives or careers. Organized in four parts, these instruments offer you one source from which to learn more about yourself.
- **Choice of formats**—The Prentice Hall Self-Assessment Library is available in CD-ROM, online, or print format.
- **Save feature**—Students can take the self-assessments an unlimited number of times, and they can save and print their scores for class discussion.
- **Scoring key**—The key to the self-assessments has been edited by Steve Robbins to allow students to quickly make sense of the results of their score.
- **Instructor's manual**—An *Instructor's Manual* guides instructors in interpreting self-assessments and helps facilitate better classroom discussion.

Acknowledgments

Getting this book into your hands was a team effort. It took faculty reviewers and a talented group of designers and production specialists, editorial personnel, and marketing and sales staff.

More than one hundred instructors reviewed parts or all of *Organizational Behavior*, Fifteenth Edition. Their comments, compliments, and suggestions have significantly improved the final product. The authors wish to thank John D. Kammeyer-Mueller of the University of Florida for help with several key aspects of this revision. The authors would also like to extend their sincerest thanks to the following instructors:

Lee Boam, University of Utah

Andres Johnson, Santa Clara University

Edward Lisoski, Northeastern University

Douglas Mahony, Lehigh University

Douglas McCabe, Georgetown University

Bradley Norris, Baylor University

Jonelle Roth, Michigan State University

Philip Roth, Clemson University

Dale Rude, University of Houston

Holly Schroth, University of California at Berkeley

Jody Tolan, University of Southern California

Debra Schneck, Indiana University

Marilyn Wesner, George Washington University

Over the last editions this text has grown stronger with the contribution and feedback of the following instructors:

David Abramis, California State University

Chris Adalikwu, Concordia College

Basil Adams, Notre Dame de Namur University

Janet Adams, Kennesaw State University

Cheryl Adkins, Longwood College

Vicky Aitken, St. Louis Community College

David Albritton, Northern Arizona University

Bradley Alge, Purdue University

Lois Antonen, CSUS

Lucy Arendt, University of Wisconsin, Green Bay

Anke Arnaud, University of Central Florida

Mihran Aroian, University of Texas, Austin

Gary Ballinger, Purdue University

Deborah Balser, University of Missouri at St. Louis

Christopher Barlow, DePaul University

Joy Benson, University of Wisconsin at Green Bay

Lehman Benson III, University of Arizona

Jacqui Bergman, Appalachian State University

Anne Berthelot, University of Texas at El Paso

David Bess, Shidler College of Business at the University of Hawaii

Bruce Bikle, California State University, Sacramento

Richard Blackburn, University of North Carolina–Chapel Hill

Weldon Blake, Bethune-Cookman College

Carl Blencke, University of Central Florida

Michael Bochenek, Elmhurst College

Alicia Boisnier, State University of New York

William H. Bommer, Cleveland State University

Bryan Bonner, University of Utah

Jessica Bradley, Clemson University

Dr. Jerry Bream, Empire State College/ Niagara Frontier Center

Jim Breaugh, University of Missouri

Peggy Brewer, Eastern Kentucky University

Deborah Brown, North Carolina State University

Reginald Bruce, University of Louisville

Jeff Bruns, Bacone College

Pamela Buckle, Adelphi University

Patricia Buhler, Goldey-Beacom College

Allen Bures, Radford University

Edith Busija, University of Richmond

Holly Buttner, University of North Carolina at Greensboro

Michael Cafferky, Southern Adventist University

Scott Campbell, Francis Marion University

Elena Capella, University of San Francisco

Don Capener, Monmouth University

Dan Caprar, University of Iowa

David Carmichael, Oklahoma City University

Carol Carnevale, SUNY Empire State College

Donald W. Caudill, Bluefield College

Suzanne Chan, Tulane University

Anthony Chelte, Midwestern State University

Bongsoon Cho, State University of New York—Buffalo

Savannah Clay, Central Piedmont Community College

David Connelly, Western Illinois State University

Jeffrey Conte, San Diego State University

Jane Crabtree, Benedictine University

Suzanne Crampton, Grand Valley State University

Douglas Crawford, Wilson College

Michael Cruz, San Jose State University

Robert Cyr, Northwestern University

Evelyn Dadzie, Clark Atlanta University

Joseph Daly, Appalachian State University

Denise Daniels, Seattle Pacific University

Marie Dasborough, Oklahoma State University

Nancy Da Silva, San Jose State University

Christine Day, Eastern Michigan University

Emmeline de Pillis, University of Hawaii, Hilo

Kathy Lund Dean, Idaho State University

Roger Dean, Washington & Lee University

Robert DelCampo, University of New Mexico

Kristen Detienne, Brigham Young University

Doug Dierking, University of Texas at Austin

Cynthia Doil, Southern Illinois University

Jennifer Dose, Messiah College

Ceasar Douglas, Florida State University

David Duby, Liberty University

Ken Dunegan, Cleveland State University

Michael Dutch, Greensboro College

Kathleen Edwards, University of Texas at Austin

Berrin Erdogan, Portland State University

Ellen Fagenson Eland, George Mason University

Lenny Favara, Central Christian College

Claudia Ferrante, U.S. Air Force Academy

Andy Fitorre, Nyack College

Kathleen Fleming, Averett University

Erin Fluegge, University of Florida

Edward Fox, Wilkes University

Alison Fragale, University of North Carolina at Chapel Hill

Lucy Franks, Bellevue University

Dean Frear, Wilkes University

Jann Freed, Central College

Crissie Frye, Eastern Michigan University

Diane Galbraith, Slippery Rock University

Carolyn Gardner, Radford University

Janice Gates, Western Illinois University

Ellen Kaye Gehrke, Alliant International University

James Gelatt, University of Maryland University College

Joe Gerard, University of Wisconsin at Milwaukee

Matthew Giblin, Southern Illinois University

Donald Gibson, Fairfield University

Cindi Gilliland, The University of Arizona

Mary Giovannini, Truman State University

David Glew, University of North Carolina at Wilmington

Leonard Glick, Northeastern University

Reginald Goodfellow, California State University

Jeffrey Goldstein, Adelphi University

Jodi Goodman, University of Connecticut

Claude Graeff, Illinois State University

Richard Grover, University of Southern Maine

W. Lee Grubb III, East Carolina University

John Guarino, Averett University

Rebecca Guidice, University of Nevada at Las Vegas

Andra Gumbus, Sacred Heart University

Linda Hackleman, Concordia University Austin

Deniz Hackner, Tidewater Community College

Michael Hadani, Long Island University

Jonathon Halbesleben, University of Missouri-Columbia

Dan Hallock, University of North Alabama

Tracey Rockett Hanft, University of Texas at Dallas

Edward Hampton, University of Central Florida

Vernard Harrington, Radford University

Nell Hartley, Robert Morris University

Barbara Hassell, Indiana University, Kelley School of Business

Erin Hayes, George Washington University

Tom Head, Roosevelt University

Douglas Heeter, Ferris State University

David Henderson, University of Illinois at Chicago

Scott Henley, Oklahoma City University

Ted Herbert, Rollins College

Susan Herman, University of Alaska Fairbanks

James Hess, Ivy Tech Community College

Ronald Hester, Marymount University

Patricia Hewlin, Georgetown University

Chad Higgins, University of Washington

Kim Hinrichs, Minnesota State University Mankato

Kathie Holland, University of Central Florida

Elaine Hollensbe, University of Cincinnati

Kristin Holmberg-Wright, University of Wisconsin at Parkside

Brooks Holtom, Georgetown University

Lisa Houts, California State University Fullerton

Abigail Hubbard, University of Houston

Paul Hudec, Milwaukee School of Engineering

Stephen Humphrey, Florida State University

Charlice Hurst, University of Florida

Warren Imada, Leeward Community College

Gazi Islam, Tulane University

Alan Jackson, Peru State College

Christine Jackson, Purdue University

Marsha Jackson, Bowie State University

Kathryn Jacobson, Arizona State University

Paul Jacques, Western Carolina University

David Jalajas, Long Island University

Elizabeth Jamison, Radford University

Stephen Jenner, California State University, Dominguez Hills

John Jermier, University of South Florida

Jack Johnson, Consumnes River College

Michael Johnson, University of Washington

David Jones, South University

Ray Jones, University of Pittsburgh

Anthony Jost, University of Delaware

Louis Jourdan, Clayton College

Rusty Juban, Southeastern Illinois University

Carole L. Jurkiewicz, Louisiana State University

John Kammeyer-Mueller, University of Florida

Edward Kass, Saint Joseph's University

Marsha Katz, Governors State College

James Katzenstein, California State University

John Keiser, SUNY College at Brockport

Mark Kendrick, Methodist University

Mary Kern, Baruch College

Robert Key, University of Phoenix

Sigrid Khorram, University of Texas at El Paso

Hal Kingsley, Erie Community College

Jeffrey Kobles, California State University San Marcos

Jack Kondrasuk, University of Portland

Leslie A. Korb, University of Nebraska at Kearney

Glen Kreiner, University of Cincinnati

James Kroeger, Cleveland State University

Frederick Lane, Baruch College

Rebecca Lau, Virginia Polytechnic Institute and State University

David Leuser, Plymouth State College

Julia Levashina, Indiana State University Kokomo

Benyamin Lichtenstein, University of Massachusetts at Boston

Robert Liden, University of Illinois at Chicago

Don Lifton, Ithaca College

Ginamarie Ligon, Villanova University

Beth Livingston, University of Florida

Barbara Low, Dominican University

Doyle Lucas, Anderson University

Alexandra Luong, University of Minnesota

Rick Maclin, Missouri Baptist University

Peter Madsen, Brigham Young University

Lou Marino, University of Alabama

Catherine Marsh, Northpark University

J. David Martin, Midwestern State University

Timothy A. Matherly, Florida State University

John Mattoon, State University of New York

Paul Maxwell, Saint Thomas University

Brenda McAleer, University of Maine at Augusta

Christina McCale, Regis College

Don McCormick, California State University Northridge

James McElroy, Iowa State University

Bonnie McNeely, Murray State University

Melony Mead, University of Phoenix

Steven Meisel, La Salle University

Nancy Meyer-Emerick, Cleveland State University

Catherine Michael, St. Edwards University

Sandy Miles, Murray State University

Janice Miller, University of Wisconsin at Milwaukee

Leann Mischel, Susquehanna University

Atul Mitra, University of Northern Iowa

Linda Morable, Richland College

Paula Morrow, Iowa State University

Mark Mortensen, Massachusetts Institute of Technology

Lori Muse, Western Michigan University

Padmakumar Nair, University of Texas at Dallas

Judy Nixon, University of Tennessee at Chattanooga

Jeffrey Nystrom, University of Colorado at Denver

Alison O'Brien, George Mason University

Heather Odle-Dusseau, Clemson University

Miguel Olivas-Lujan, Lujan Clarion University

Kelly Ottman, University of Wisconsin at Milwaukee

Cynthia Ozeki, California State University, Dominguez Hills

Peg Padgett, Butler University

Jennifer Palthe, Western Michigan University

Dennis Passovoy, University of Texas at Austin

Karen Paul, Florida International University

Laura Finnerty Paul, Skidmore College

Anette Pendergrass, Arkansas State University at Mountain Home

Bryan Pesta, Cleveland State University

Jeff Peterson, University of Washington

Nanette Philibert, Missouri Southern State University

Larry Phillips, Indiana University South Bend

William Pinchuk, Rutgers University at Camden

Eric Popkoff, Brooklyn College

Paul Preston, University of Montevallo

Scott Quatro, Grand Canyon University

Aarti Ramaswami, Indiana University Bloomington

Jere Ramsey, Cal Poly at San Luis Obispo

Amy Randel, San Diego State University

Anne Reilly, Loyola University Chicago

Clint Relyea, Arkansas State University

Herbert Ricardo, Indian River Community College

David Ritchey, University of Texas at Dallas

Chris Roberts, University of Massachusetts Amherst

Sherry Robinson, Pennsylvania State University Hazleton

Christopher Ann Robinson-Easley, Governors State University

Joe Rode, Miami University

Bob Roller, LeTourneau University

Andrea Roofe, Florida International University

Craig Russell, University of Oklahoma at Norman

Manjula Salimath, University of North Texas

Mary Saunders, Georgia Gwinnett College

Andy Schaffer, North Georgia College and State University

Elizabeth Scott, Elizabeth City University

Mark Seabright, Western Oregon University

Joseph Seltzer, LaSalle University

John Shaw, Mississippi State University

John Sherlock, Western Carolina University

Daniel Sherman, University of Alabama, Huntsville

Heather Shields, Texas Tech University

Ted Shore, California State University at Long Beach

Stuart Sidle, University of New Haven

Bret Simmons, University of Nevada Reno

Randy Sleeth, Virginia Commonwealth University

William Smith, Emporia State University

Kenneth Solano, Northeastern University

Shane Spiller, Morehead State University

Lynda St. Clair, Bryant University

John B. Stark, California State University, Bakersfield

Merwyn Strate, Purdue University

Joo-Seng Tan, Cornell University

Karen Thompson, Sonoma State University

Linda Tibbetts, Antioch University McGregor

Ed Tomlinson, John Carroll University

Bob Trodella, Webster University

Tom Tudor, University of Arkansas at Little Rock

William D. Tudor, Ohio State University

Daniel Turban, University of Missouri

Albert Turner, Webster University

Jim Turner, Morehead State University

Leslie Tworoger, Nova Southeastern University

M. A. Viets, University of Vermont

Roger Volkema, American University

William Walker, University of Houston

Ian Walsh, Boston College

Charles F. Warren, Salem State College

Christa Washington, Saint Augustine's College

Jim Westerman, Appalachian State University

William J. White, Northwestern University

David Whitlock, Southwest Baptist University

Dan Wiljanen, Grand Valley State University

Dean Williamson, Brewton-Parker College

Hilda Williamson, Hampton University

Alice Wilson, Cedar Crest College

Barry Wisdom, Southeast Missouri State University

Craig Wishart, Fayetteville State University

Laura Wolfe, Louisiana State University

Melody Wollan, Eastern Illinois University

Evan Wood, Taylor University Fort Wayne

Chun-Sheng Yu, University of Houston-Victoria

Jun Zhao, Governors State University

Lori Ziegler, University of Texas at Dallas

Mary Ellen Zuckerman, State University of New York at Geneseo

Gail Zwart, Riverside Community College

We owe a debt of gratitude to all those at Pearson Education who have supported this text over the past 30 years and who have worked so hard on the development of this latest edition. On the development and editorial side, we want to thank Elisa Adams, Development Editor; Steve Deitmer, Director of Development; Ashley Santora, Director of Editorial Services; Brian Mickelson, Acquisitions Editor; and Sally Yagan, Editorial Director. On the design and production side, Judy Leale, Senior Managing Editor, did an outstanding job, as did Becca Groves, Production Project Manager, and Nancy Moudry, Photo Development Editor. Last but not least, we would like to thank Nikki Ayana Jones, Senior Marketing Manager; Patrice Lumumba Jones, Vice President Director of Marketing; and their sales staff, who have been selling this book over its many editions. Thank you for the attention you've given to this book.

Organizational Behavior

MyManagementLab

Access a host of interactive learning aids to help strengthen your understanding of the chapter concepts at **www.mymanagementlab.com**

THE NEW NORMAL?

Scott Nicholson sits alone in his parents' house in suburban Boston. His parents have long since left for work. He lifts his laptop from a small table on which his mother used to have a vase with flowers. This day will be like tomorrow, and tomorrow will be like today.

On his laptop, Scott searches corporate Web sites for job openings. Today, he finds one, and he mails off a résumé and cover letter. It's a routine he repeats nearly every day, applying to four to five jobs a week, week after week.

Despite graduating from Colgate University with a 4.0 GPA, Scott has been job-hunting for 5 months. His myriad applications have produced only one offer: A $40,000-a-year job as an associate claims adjuster at Hanover Insurance Group in Worcester. He turned the offer down. "The conversation I'm going to have with my parents now that I've turned down this job is more of a concern to me than turning down the job," Scott said.

Why is Scott more concerned with his parents' reaction than he is with finding a job? To some degree, this is a reflection of the job offer (too low a salary, too small a company, too limited a job description). However, it also suggests a generational shift in thinking. While the job market for new entrants is perhaps the most sluggish in memory, new college graduates remain committed to following their dreams and holding out high hopes for their careers.

Scott's father, David Nicholson, 57, has an established managerial career, with a household income of $175,000/year. Early in his career, David said, he was less concerned with starting off with the right job than his son is now. "You maneuvered and you did not worry what the maneuvering would lead to," David said. "You know it would lead to something good." Scott's grandfather, William Nicholson, a retired stock broker, has even more trouble understanding Scott's travails. "I view what is happening to Scott with dismay," the grandfather said. Despite feeling pressure from his parents to find a job ("I am beginning to realize that refusal is going to have repercussions"), Scott remains undaunted: "I am absolutely certain that my job hunt will eventually pay off."

Scott is not alone. In the past 5 years, millions of U.S. workers have lost their jobs, and millions of new entrants—many of them, like Scott, under 30—have had trouble finding suitable work.

Sources: L. Uchitelle, "A New Generation, an Elusive American Dream" *New York Times* (July 7, 2010), pp. A1, A11; B. Levin, "Sending Out an S.O.S.: Who Will Give This a Handout/Job?" *Dealbreaker* (July 7, 2010), http://dealbreaker.com/tag/scott-nicholson/.

What Is Organizational Behavior?

The stellar universe is not so difficult of comprehension as the real actions of other people. —Marcel Proust

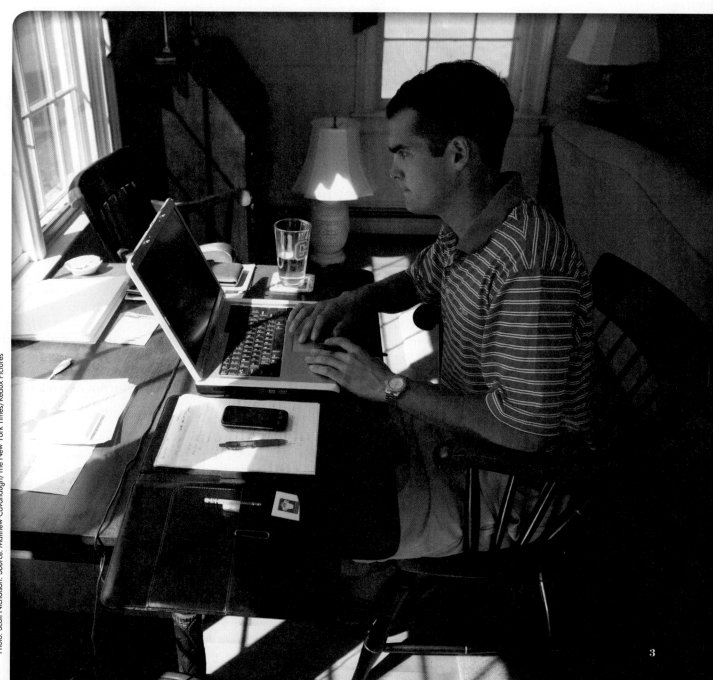

The details of this story might be disheartening to read, but they accurately reflect some of the problems faced by the contemporary workforce. The story also highlights several issues of interest to organizational behavior researchers, including motivation, emotions, personality, and communication. Through the course of this book, you'll learn how all these elements can be studied systematically.

You've probably made many observations about people's behavior in your life. In a way, you are already proficient at seeing some of the major themes in organizational behavior. At the same time, you probably have not had the tools to make these observations systematically. This is where organizational behavior comes into play. And, as we'll learn, it is much more than common sense, intuition, and soothsaying.

To see how far common sense gets you, try the following from the Self-Assessment Library.

SELF-ASSESSMENT LIBRARY

How Much Do I Know About Organizational Behavior?

In the Self-Assessment Library (available on CD and online), take assessment IV.G.1 (How Much Do I Know About OB?) and answer the following questions:

1. How did you score? Are you surprised by your score?
2. How much of effective management do you think is common sense? Did your score on the test change your answer to this question?

The Importance of Interpersonal Skills

1 Demonstrate the importance of interpersonal skills in the workplace.

Until the late 1980s, business school curricula emphasized the technical aspects of management, focusing on economics, accounting, finance, and quantitative techniques. Course work in human behavior and people skills received relatively less attention. Over the past three decades, however, business faculty have come to realize the role that understanding human behavior plays in determining a manager's effectiveness, and required courses on people skills have been added to many curricula. As the director of leadership at MIT's Sloan School of Management put it, "M.B.A. students may get by on their technical and quantitative skills the first couple of years out of school. But soon, leadership and communication skills come to the fore in distinguishing the managers whose careers really take off."[1]

Developing managers' interpersonal skills also helps organizations attract and keep high-performing employees. Regardless of labor market conditions, outstanding employees are always in short supply.[2] Companies known as good places to work—such as Starbucks, Adobe Systems, Cisco, Whole Foods, Google, American Express, Amgen, Pfizer, and Marriott—have a big advantage. A recent survey of hundreds of workplaces, and more than 200,000 respondents, showed the social relationships among co-workers and supervisors were strongly related to overall job satisfaction. Positive social relationships also were associated with lower stress at work and lower intentions to quit.[3] So having managers with good interpersonal skills is likely to make the workplace more pleasant, which in turn makes it easier to hire and keep qualified people. Creating a pleasant workplace also appears to make good economic sense. Companies with reputations

Succeeding in management today requires good interpersonal skills. Communication and leadership skills distinguish managers such as John Chambers, who rise to the top of their profession. Chambers is CEO of Cisco Systems, the world's largest maker of networking equipment. He is respected as a visionary leader and innovator who has the ability to drive an entrepreneurial culture. As an effective communicator, Chambers is described as warmhearted and straight talking. In this photo Chambers speaks during a launch ceremony of a green technology partnership Cisco formed with a university in China.

Source: China Photos / Getty Images, Inc.

as good places to work (such as *Forbes'* "100 Best Companies to Work For in America") have been found to generate superior financial performance.[4]

We have come to understand that in today's competitive and demanding workplace, managers can't succeed on their technical skills alone. They also have to have good people skills. This book has been written to help both managers and potential managers develop those people skills.

What Managers Do

2 Describe the manager's functions, roles, and skills.

MyManagementLab
For an interactive application of this topic, check out this chapter's simulation activity at **www.mymanagementlab.com**.

Let's begin by briefly defining the terms *manager* and *organization*—the place where managers work. Then let's look at the manager's job; specifically, what do managers do?

Managers get things done through other people. They make decisions, allocate resources, and direct the activities of others to attain goals. Managers do their work in an **organization**, which is a consciously coordinated social unit, composed of two or more people, that functions on a relatively continuous basis to achieve a common goal or set of goals. By this definition, manufacturing and service firms are organizations, and so are schools, hospitals, churches, military units, retail stores, police departments, and local, state, and federal government agencies. The people who oversee the activities of

manager   *An individual who achieves goals through other people.*

organization   *A consciously coordinated social unit, composed of two or more people, that functions on a relatively continuous basis to achieve a common goal or set of goals.*

others and who are responsible for attaining goals in these organizations are managers (sometimes called *administrators,* especially in not-for-profit organizations).

Management Functions

In the early part of the twentieth century, French industrialist Henri Fayol wrote that all managers perform five management functions: planning, organizing, commanding, coordinating, and controlling.[5] Today, we have condensed these to four: planning, organizing, leading, and controlling.

Because organizations exist to achieve goals, someone has to define those goals and the means for achieving them; management is that someone. The **planning** function encompasses defining an organization's goals, establishing an overall strategy for achieving those goals, and developing a comprehensive set of plans to integrate and coordinate activities. Evidence indicates this function increases the most as managers move from lower-level to mid-level management.[6]

Managers are also responsible for designing an organization's structure. We call this function **organizing**. It includes determining what tasks are to be done, who is to do them, how the tasks are to be grouped, who reports to whom, and where decisions are to be made.

Every organization contains people, and it is management's job to direct and coordinate those people. This is the **leading** function. When managers motivate employees, direct their activities, select the most effective communication channels, or resolve conflicts among members, they're engaging in leading.

To ensure things are going as they should, management must monitor the organization's performance and compare it with previously set goals. If there are any significant deviations, it is management's job to get the organization back on track. This monitoring, comparing, and potential correcting is the **controlling** function.

So, using the functional approach, the answer to the question "What do managers do?" is that they plan, organize, lead, and control.

Management Roles

In the late 1960s, Henry Mintzberg, then a graduate student at MIT, undertook a careful study of five executives to determine what they did on their jobs. On the basis of his observations, Mintzberg concluded that managers perform ten different, highly interrelated roles—or sets of behaviors.[7] As shown in Exhibit 1-1, these ten roles are primarily (1) interpersonal, (2) informational, or (3) decisional.

Interpersonal Roles   All managers are required to perform duties that are ceremonial and symbolic in nature. For instance, when the president of a college hands out diplomas at commencement or a factory supervisor gives a group of high school students a tour of the plant, he or she is acting in a *figurehead* role. All managers also have a *leadership* role. This role includes hiring, training, motivating, and disciplining employees. The third role within the interpersonal grouping is the *liaison* role, or contacting others who provide the manager with information. The sales manager who obtains information from the quality-control manager in his or her own company has an internal liaison relationship. When that sales manager has contacts with other sales executives through a marketing trade association, he or she has an outside liaison relationship.

Exhibit **1-1**	Minztberg's Managerial Roles

Role	Description
Interpersonal	
Figurehead	Symbolic head; required to perform a number of routine duties of a legal or social nature
Leader	Responsible for the motivation and direction of employees
Liaison	Maintains a network of outside contacts who provide favors and information
Informational	
Monitor	Receives a wide variety of information; serves as nerve center of internal and external information of the organization
Disseminator	Transmits information received from outsiders or from other employees to members of the organization
Spokesperson	Transmits information to outsiders on organization's plans, policies, actions, and results; serves as expert on organization's industry
Decisional	
Entrepreneur	Searches organization and its environment for opportunities and initiates projects to bring about change
Disturbance handler	Responsible for corrective action when organization faces important, unexpected disturbances
Resource allocator	Makes or approves significant organizational decisions
Negotiator	Responsible for representing the organization at major negotiations

Source: Adapted from *The Nature of Managerial Work* by H. Mintzberg. Copyright © 1973 by H. Mintzberg. MINTZBERG, HENRY, THE NATURE OF MANAGERIAL WORK, 1st Edition, © 1980, pp. 92–93. Reprinted with permission of Pearson Education, Inc., Upper Saddle River, NJ.

Informational Roles   All managers, to some degree, collect information from outside organizations and institutions, typically by scanning the news media (including the Internet) and talking with other people to learn of changes in the public's tastes, what competitors may be planning, and the like. Mintzberg called this the *monitor* role. Managers also act as a conduit to transmit information to organizational members. This is the *disseminator* role. In addition, managers perform a *spokesperson* role when they represent the organization to outsiders.

Decisional Roles   Mintzberg identified four roles that require making choices. In the *entrepreneur* role, managers initiate and oversee new projects that will improve their organization's performance. As *disturbance handlers,* managers take corrective action in response to unforeseen problems. As *resource allocators,*

planning   *A process that includes defining goals, establishing strategy, and developing plans to coordinate activities.*

organizing   *Determining what tasks are to be done, who is to do them, how the tasks are to be grouped, who reports to whom, and where decisions are to be made.*

leading   *A function that includes motivating employees, directing others, selecting the most effective communication channels, and resolving conflicts.*

controlling   *Monitoring activities to ensure they are being accomplished as planned and correcting any significant deviations.*

managers are responsible for allocating human, physical, and monetary resources. Finally, managers perform a *negotiator* role, in which they discuss issues and bargain with other units to gain advantages for their own unit.

Management Skills

Still another way of considering what managers do is to look at the skills or competencies they need to achieve their goals. Researchers have identified a number of skills that differentiate effective from ineffective managers.[8]

Technical Skills   **Technical skills** encompass the ability to apply specialized knowledge or expertise. When you think of the skills of professionals such as civil engineers or oral surgeons, you typically focus on the technical skills they have learned through extensive formal education. Of course, professionals don't have a monopoly on technical skills, and not all technical skills have to be learned in schools or other formal training programs. All jobs require some specialized expertise, and many people develop their technical skills on the job.

Human Skills   The ability to understand, communicate with, motivate, and support other people, both individually and in groups, defines **human skills**. Many people are technically proficient but poor listeners, unable to understand the needs of others, or weak at managing conflicts. Because managers get things done through other people, they must have good human skills.

Conceptual Skills   Managers must have the mental ability to analyze and diagnose complex situations. These tasks require **conceptual skills**. Decision making, for instance, requires managers to identify problems, develop alternative solutions to correct those problems, evaluate those alternative solutions, and select the best one. After they have selected a course of action, managers must be able to organize a plan of action and then execute it. The ability to integrate new ideas with existing processes and innovate on the job are also crucial conceptual skills for today's managers.

Effective versus Successful Managerial Activities

Fred Luthans and his associates looked at what managers do from a somewhat different perspective.[9] They asked, "Do managers who move up the quickest in an organization do the same activities and with the same emphasis as managers who do the best job?" You might think the answer is yes, but that's not always the case.

Luthans and his associates studied more than 450 managers. All engaged in four managerial activities:

1. **Traditional management.**   Decision making, planning, and controlling.
2. **Communication.**   Exchanging routine information and processing paperwork.
3. **Human resource management.**   Motivating, disciplining, managing conflict, staffing, and training.
4. **Networking.**   Socializing, politicking, and interacting with outsiders.

The "average" manager spent 32 percent of his or her time in traditional management activities, 29 percent communicating, 20 percent in human resource management activities, and 19 percent networking. However, the time and effort different *individual* managers spent on those activities varied a great deal. As shown in Exhibit 1-2, among managers who were *successful* (defined in terms of speed of promotion within their organization), networking made

Exhibit **1-2**   Allocation of Activities by Time

Source: Based on F. Luthans, R. M. Hodgetts, and S. A. Rosenkrantz, *Real Managers* (Cambridge, MA: Ballinger, 1988).

the largest relative contribution to success, and human resource management activities made the least relative contribution. Among *effective* managers (defined in terms of quantity and quality of their performance and the satisfaction and commitment of employees), communication made the largest relative contribution and networking the least. More recent studies in Australia, Israel, Italy, Japan, and the United States confirm the link between networking and social relationships and success within an organization.[10] And the connection between communication and effective managers is also clear. A study of 410 U.S. managers indicates those who seek information from colleagues and employees—even if it's negative—and who explain their decisions are the most effective.[11]

This research offers important insights. Successful managers give almost the opposite emphases to traditional management, communication, human resource management, and networking as do effective managers. This finding challenges the historical assumption that promotions are based on performance, and it illustrates the importance of networking and political skills in getting ahead in organizations.

A Review of the Manager's Job

One common thread runs through the functions, roles, skills, activities, and approaches to management: Each recognizes the paramount importance of managing people, whether it is called "the leading function," "interpersonal roles," "human skills," or "human resource management, communication, and networking activities." It's clear managers must develop their people skills to be effective and successful.

technical skills *The ability to apply specialized knowledge or expertise.*

human skills *The ability to work with, understand, and motivate other people, both individually and in groups.*

conceptual skills *The mental ability to analyze and diagnose complex situations.*

Enter Organizational Behavior

3 Define *organizational behavior (OB)*.

We've made the case for the importance of people skills. But neither this book nor the discipline on which it is based is called "people skills." The term that is widely used to describe the discipline is *organizational behavior.*

Organizational behavior (often abbreviated OB) is a field of study that investigates the impact that individuals, groups, and structure have on behavior within organizations, for the purpose of applying such knowledge toward improving an organization's effectiveness. That's a mouthful, so let's break it down.

Organizational behavior is a field of study, meaning that it is a distinct area of expertise with a common body of knowledge. What does it study? It studies three determinants of behavior in organizations: individuals, groups, and structure. In addition, OB applies the knowledge gained about individuals, groups, and the effect of structure on behavior in order to make organizations work more effectively.

To sum up our definition, OB is the study of what people do in an organization and how their behavior affects the organization's performance. And because OB is concerned specifically with employment-related situations, you should not be surprised that it emphasizes behavior as related to concerns such as jobs, work, absenteeism, employment turnover, productivity, human performance, and management.

Although debate exists about the relative importance of each, OB includes the core topics of motivation, leader behavior and power, interpersonal communication, group structure and processes, learning, attitude development and perception, change processes, conflict, work design, and work stress.[12]

Online shoe retailer Zappos.com understands how organizational behavior affects an organization's performance. Zappos maintains good employee relationships by providing generous benefits, extensive customer service training, and a positive, fun-loving work environment. Employees are empowered to make decisions that increase customer satisfaction and are encouraged to create fun and a little weirdness." At Zappos, employee loyalty, job satisfaction, and productivity are high, contributing to the company's growth. In this photo, employees view a line of shoes in one of the company's quirky offices.

Source: Isaac Brekken/The New York Times/Redux Pictures

Complementing Intuition with Systematic Study

4 Show the value to OB of systematic study.

Each of us is a student of behavior. Whether you've explicitly thought about it before, you've been "reading" people almost all your life, watching their actions and trying to interpret what you see or predict what people might do under different conditions. Unfortunately, the casual or common sense approach to reading others can often lead to erroneous predictions. However, you can improve your predictive ability by supplementing intuition with a more systematic approach.

The systematic approach in this book will uncover important facts and relationships and provide a base from which to make more accurate predictions of behavior. Underlying this systematic approach is the belief that behavior is not random. Rather, we can identify fundamental consistencies underlying the behavior of all individuals and modify them to reflect individual differences.

These fundamental consistencies are very important. Why? Because they allow predictability. Behavior is generally predictable, and the *systematic study* of behavior is a means to making reasonably accurate predictions. When we use the term **systematic study**, we mean looking at relationships, attempting to attribute causes and effects, and basing our conclusions on scientific evidence—that is, on data gathered under controlled conditions and measured and interpreted in a reasonably rigorous manner. (See Appendix A for a basic review of research methods used in studies of organizational behavior.)

Evidence-based management (EBM) complements systematic study by basing managerial decisions on the best available scientific evidence. For example, we want doctors to make decisions about patient care based on the latest available evidence, and EBM argues that managers should do the same, becoming more scientific in how they think about management problems. A manager might pose a managerial question, search for the best available evidence, and apply the relevant information to the question or case at hand. You might think it difficult to argue against this (what manager would say decisions shouldn't be based on evidence?), but the vast majority of management decisions are still made "on the fly," with little or systematic study of available evidence.[13]

Systematic study and EBM add to **intuition**, or those "gut feelings" about what makes others (and ourselves) "tick." Of course, the things you have come to believe in an unsystematic way are not necessarily incorrect. Jack Welch (former CEO of GE) noted, "The trick, of course, is to know when to go with your gut." But if we make *all* decisions with intuition or gut instinct, we're likely working with incomplete information—like making an investment decision with only half the data.

Relying on intuition is made worse because we tend to overestimate the accuracy of what we think we know. In a recent survey, 86 percent of managers thought their organization was treating their employees well, but only 55 percent of the employees thought so. Surveys of human resource managers have also

organizational behavior (OB) *A field of study that investigates the impact that individuals, groups, and structure have on behavior within organizations, for the purpose of applying such knowledge toward improving an organization's effectiveness.*

systematic study *Looking at relationships, attempting to attribute causes and effects, and drawing conclusions based on scientific evidence.*

evidence-based management (EBM) *The basing of managerial decisions on the best available scientific evidence.*

intuition *A gut feeling not necessarily supported by research.*

"Most Acts of Workplace Bullying Are Men Attacking Women"

This statement is true in the broad sense that most research indicates men are more likely to engage in workplace bullying, and women are more likely to be targets of bullying behavior.

However, the full picture of gender and workplace bullying is more complicated than that.

First, the gender differences are narrowing. A recent study of workplace bullying by the Workplace Bullying Institute (WBI) suggested that 60 percent of workplace bullies are men and 40 percent are women. That is still a significant gender difference. But it is not as large as was once the case. Some of the narrowing in the gender of bullies is due to the ascension of women up their organizations' ladders. Evidence indicates that the vast majority of incidents of workplace bullying are "top-down": the supervisor is intimidating the subordinate. As more women are becoming supervisors, this is changing, to some degree, the gender balance of workplace bullies.

A second complication is that when women bully others at work, other women are overwhelmingly their targets. The same WBI study of workplace bullying revealed that 58 percent of victims of bullying are women. However, almost all of this gender difference in victims is due to *who women bullies target;* in 80 percent of the cases, it was other women. Male bullies are actually more likely to target their own sex, though to a less dramatic degree than female bullies do.

Finally, it does appear that women are more adversely affected by bullying. A recent study of 183 victims of bullying found that the prevalence of trauma was higher for women (49 percent) than men (35 percent). The complexity of these relationships shows us that gaining a true understanding of organizational behavior phenomena often means understanding that the causes and consequences of work behavior are complex.

Back to bullying, experts suggest some ways to cope with workplace bullies regardless of your sex.

1. **Talk to your bully.** "Perhaps your boss is one of those people who aren't aware of how they come across," says Stanford's Robert Sutton, author of several books on bullying in the workplace.
2. **Get help.** Keep a diary of the behavior. Be specific and focus more on actions than feelings. At some point, it might be necessary to involve others, such as human resources.
3. **Ignore it.** This is often easier said than done, but sometimes the only thing you can do is to try to ignore the bully. "Try not to let it touch your soul," says Sutton.
4. **Polish your résumé.** Bullies sometimes go away, and sometimes they listen. But if they aren't going to change and aren't going away, you may want to plan your exit strategy. Take your time and don't panic. But not every workplace is filled with bullies, and you'll likely be happier if you're in one of those.

Source: L. Petrecca, "Bullying in Workplace Is Common, Hard to Fix," *USA Today* (December 28, 2010), pp. 1B–2B; R. I. Sutton, *Good Boss, Bad Boss: How to Be the Best…and Learn from the Worst* (New York: Business Plus, 2010); A. Rodríguez-Muñoz, B. Moreno-Jiménez, A. Vergel, and E. G. Hernández, "Post-Traumatic Symptoms Among Victims of Workplace Bullying: Exploring Gender Differences and Shattered Assumptions," *Journal of Applied Social Psychology* 40, no. 10 (2010), pp. 2616–2635.

shown many managers hold "common sense" opinions regarding effective management that have been flatly refuted by empirical evidence.

We find a similar problem in chasing the business and popular media for management wisdom. The business press tends to be dominated by fads. As a writer for *The New Yorker* put it, "Every few years, new companies succeed, and they are scrutinized for the underlying truths they might reveal. But often there is no underlying truth; the companies just happened to be in the right place at the right time."[14] Although we try to avoid it, we might also fall into this trap. It's not that the business press stories are all wrong; it's that without a systematic approach, it's hard to separate the wheat from the chaff.

We're not advising that you throw your intuition, or all the business press, out the window. Nor are we arguing that research is always right.

Researchers make mistakes, too. What we are advising is to use evidence as much as possible to inform your intuition and experience. That is the promise of OB.

Disciplines That Contribute to the OB Field

5 Identify the major behavioral science disciplines that contribute to OB.

Organizational behavior is an applied behavioral science built on contributions from a number of behavioral disciplines, mainly psychology and social psychology, sociology, and anthropology. Psychology's contributions have been mainly at the individual or micro level of analysis, while the other disciplines have contributed to our understanding of macro concepts such as group processes and organization. Exhibit 1-3 is an overview of the major contributions to the study of organizational behavior.

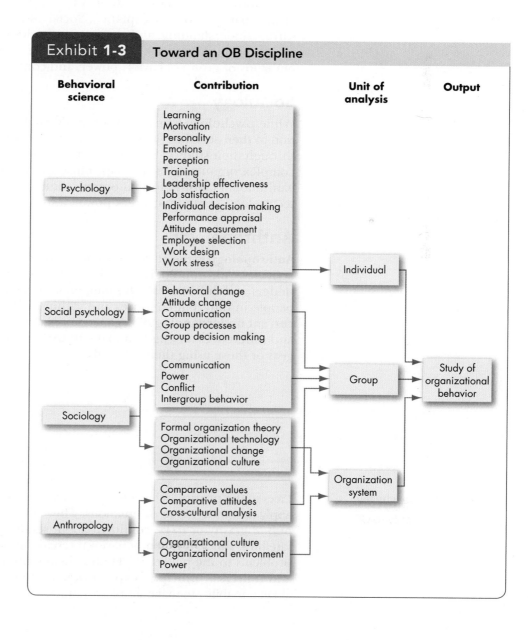

Exhibit 1-3   Toward an OB Discipline

Psychology

Psychology seeks to measure, explain, and sometimes change the behavior of humans and other animals. Those who have contributed and continue to add to the knowledge of OB are learning theorists, personality theorists, counseling psychologists, and, most important, industrial and organizational psychologists.

Early industrial/organizational psychologists studied the problems of fatigue, boredom, and other working conditions that could impede efficient work performance. More recently, their contributions have expanded to include learning, perception, personality, emotions, training, leadership effectiveness, needs and motivational forces, job satisfaction, decision-making processes, performance appraisals, attitude measurement, employee-selection techniques, work design, and job stress.

Social Psychology

Social psychology, generally considered a branch of psychology, blends concepts from both psychology and sociology to focus on peoples' influence on one another. One major study area is *change*—how to implement it and how to reduce barriers to its acceptance. Social psychologists also contribute to measuring, understanding, and changing attitudes; identifying communication patterns; and building trust. Finally, they have made important contributions to our study of group behavior, power, and conflict.

Sociology

While psychology focuses on the individual, **sociology** studies people in relation to their social environment or culture. Sociologists have contributed to OB through their study of group behavior in organizations, particularly formal and complex organizations. Perhaps most important, sociologists have studied organizational culture, formal organization theory and structure, organizational technology, communications, power, and conflict.

Anthropology

Anthropology is the study of societies to learn about human beings and their activities. Anthropologists' work on cultures and environments has helped us understand differences in fundamental values, attitudes, and behavior between people in different countries and within different organizations. Much of our current understanding of organizational culture, organizational environments, and differences among national cultures is a result of the work of anthropologists or those using their methods.

There Are Few Absolutes in OB

6   Demonstrate why few absolutes apply to OB.

Laws in the physical sciences—chemistry, astronomy, physics—are consistent and apply in a wide range of situations. They allow scientists to generalize about the pull of gravity or to be confident about sending astronauts into space to repair satellites. But as a noted behavioral researcher observed, "God gave all the easy problems to the physicists." Human beings are complex, and few, if any, simple and universal principles explain organizational behavior. Because we are not alike, our ability to make simple, accurate, and sweeping generalizations is limited.

Two people often act very differently in the same situation, and the same person's behavior changes in different situations. Not everyone is motivated by money, and people may behave differently at a religious service than they do at a party.

That doesn't mean, of course, that we can't offer reasonably accurate explanations of human behavior or make valid predictions. It does mean that OB concepts must reflect situational, or contingency, conditions. We can say x leads to y, but only under conditions specified in z—the **contingency variables**. The science of OB was developed by applying general concepts to a particular situation, person, or group. For example, OB scholars would avoid stating that everyone likes complex and challenging work (the general concept). Why? Because not everyone wants a challenging job. Some people prefer routine over varied, or simple over complex. A job attractive to one person may not be to another; its appeal is contingent on the person who holds it.

As you proceed through this book, you'll encounter a wealth of research-based theories about how people behave in organizations. But don't expect to find a lot of straightforward cause-and-effect relationships. There aren't many! organizational behavior theories mirror the subject matter with which they deal, and people are complex and complicated.

Challenges and Opportunities for OB

7 Identify the challenges and opportunities managers have in applying OB concepts.

Understanding organizational behavior has never been more important for managers. Take a quick look at the dramatic changes in organizations. The typical employee is getting older; more women and people of color are in the workplace; corporate downsizing and the heavy use of temporary workers are severing the bonds of loyalty that tied many employees to their employers; global competition requires employees to become more flexible and cope with rapid change. The global recession has brought to the forefront the challenges of working with and managing people during uncertain times.

In short, today's challenges bring opportunities for managers to use OB concepts. In this section, we review some of the most critical issues confronting managers for which OB offers solutions—or at least meaningful insights toward solutions.

Responding to Economic Pressures

When the U.S. economy plunged into a deep and prolonged recession in 2008, virtually all other large economies around the world followed suit. Layoffs and job losses were widespread, and those who survived the ax were often asked to accept pay cuts.

During difficult economic times, effective management is often at a premium. Anybody can run a company when business is booming, because the difference

---

psychology   *The science that seeks to measure, explain, and sometimes change the behavior of humans and other animals.*

social psychology   *An area of psychology that blends concepts from psychology and sociology and that focuses on the influence of people on one another.*

sociology   *The study of people in relation to their social environment or culture.*

anthropology   *The study of societies to learn about human beings and their activities.*

contingency variables   *Situational factors: variables that moderate the relationship between two or more variables.*

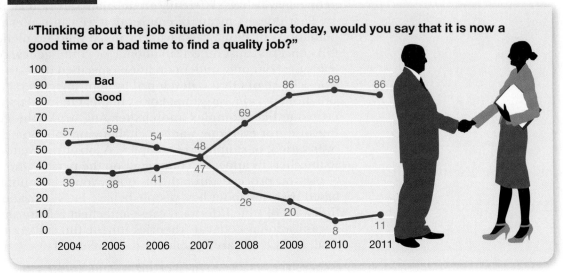

OB Poll   Working in Good Times—and Bad

"Thinking about the job situation in America today, would you say that it is now a good time or a bad time to find a quality job?"

Source: Gallup tracking polls of random samples of roughly 1,000 adults, aged 18 and older, living in the continental U.S., selected using random-digit telephone sampling. See F. Newport, "Americans' Views of Job Market Improve; Still Mostly Negative" (April 18, 2011), www.gallup.com.

between good and bad management reflects the difference between making a lot of money and making a lot more money. When times are bad, though, managers are on the front lines with employees who must be fired, who are asked to make do with less, and who worry about their futures. The difference between good and bad management can be the difference between profit and loss or, ultimately, between survival and failure.

Consider Enterprise Rent-A-Car. The company prided itself on never having laid off a U.S. employee in its 51-year history. Even in the 2001–2002 recession after the 9/11 terrorist attacks, Enterprise kept hiring. In 2008–2009, however, Enterprise was forced to lay off more than a thousand employees. "These types of declines are unprecedented," said Patrick Farrell, Enterprise's vice president of corporate responsibility. Gentex Corp, a Michigan-based auto parts supplier, had never had a layoff in its 34-year history—until 2008–2009. "We didn't even have a layoff policy," said Gentex's vice president of human resources.[15]

Managing employees well when times are tough is just as hard as when times are good—if not more so. But the OB approaches sometimes differ. In good times, understanding how to reward, satisfy, and retain employees is at a premium. In bad times, issues like stress, decision making, and coping come to the fore.

Responding to Globalization

Organizations are no longer constrained by national borders. Burger King is owned by a British firm, and McDonald's sells hamburgers in Moscow. ExxonMobil, a so-called U.S. company, receives almost 75 percent of its revenues from sales outside the United States. New employees at Finland-based phone maker Nokia are increasingly being recruited from India, China, and other developing countries—non-Finns now outnumber Finns at Nokia's renowned research center in Helsinki. And all major automobile makers now manufacture cars outside their borders; Honda builds cars in Ohio, Ford in Brazil, Volkswagen in Mexico, and both Mercedes and BMW in South Africa.

The world has become a global village. In the process, the manager's job has changed.

Increased Foreign Assignments   If you're a manager, you are increasingly likely to find yourself in a foreign assignment—transferred to your employer's operating division or subsidiary in another country. Once there, you'll have to manage a workforce very different in needs, aspirations, and attitudes from those you are used to back home.

Working with People from Different Cultures   Even in your own country, you'll find yourself working with bosses, peers, and other employees born and raised in different cultures. What motivates you may not motivate them. Or your communication style may be straightforward and open, which others may find uncomfortable and threatening. To work effectively with people from different cultures, you need to understand how their culture, geography, and religion have shaped them and how to adapt your management style to their differences.

Managers at global companies such as McDonald's, Disney, and Coca-Cola have come to realize that economic values are not universally transferable. Management practices need to be modified to reflect the values of the different countries in which an organization operates.

Overseeing Movement of Jobs to Countries with Low-Cost Labor   It's increasingly difficult for managers in advanced nations, where minimum wages are typically $6 or more an hour, to compete against firms that rely on workers from China and other developing nations where labor is available for 30 cents an hour. It's not by chance that many in the United States wear clothes made in China, work on computers whose microchips came from Taiwan, and watch movies filmed in Canada. In a global economy, jobs tend to flow where lower costs give businesses a comparative advantage, though labor groups, politicians, and local community leaders see the exporting of jobs as undermining the job market at home. Managers face the difficult task of balancing the interests of their organization with their responsibilities to the communities in which they operate.

In the global economy, jobs tend to shift from developed nations to countries where lower labor costs give firms a comparative advantage. In this photo, an employee wearing a sign on his head reading "Capital Interests" joins co-workers at a Nokia factory in Germany to protest the company's decision of terminating mobile phone production at the plant, resulting in the loss of 2,300 jobs. Nokia announced plans to shift production from Germany to Romania, where labor costs are lower.

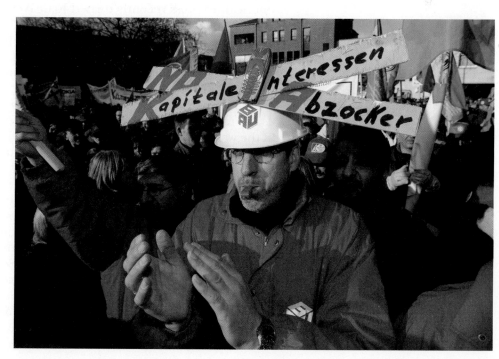

Source: Henning Kaiser/Getty Images

Managing Workforce Diversity

One of the most important challenges for organizations is adapting to people who are different. We describe this challenge as *workforce diversity*. Whereas globalization focuses on differences among people *from* different countries, workforce diversity addresses differences among people *within* given countries.

Workforce diversity acknowledges a workforce of women and men; many racial and ethnic groups; individuals with a variety of physical or psychological abilities; and people who differ in age and sexual orientation. Managing this diversity is a global concern. Most European countries have experienced dramatic growth in immigration from the Middle East, Argentina and Venezuela host a significant number of migrants from other South American countries, and nations from India to Iraq to Indonesia find great cultural diversity within their borders.

The most significant change in the U.S. labor force during the last half of the twentieth century was the rapid increase in the number of female workers. In 1950, for instance, only 29.6 percent of the workforce was female. By 2008, it was 46.5 percent. The first half of the twenty-first century will be notable for changes in racial and ethnic composition and an aging baby boom generation. By 2050, Hispanics will grow from today's 11 percent of the workforce to 24 percent, blacks will increase from 12 to 14 percent, and Asians from 5 to 11 percent. Meanwhile, in the near term the labor force will be aging. The 55-and-older age group, currently 13 percent of the labor force, will increase to 20 percent by 2014.

Though we have more to say about workforce diversity in the next chapter, suffice it to say here that it presents great opportunities and poses challenging questions for managers and employees in all countries. How can we leverage differences within groups for competitive advantage? Should we treat all employees alike? Should we recognize individual and cultural differences? How can we foster cultural awareness in employees without lapsing into political correctness? What are the legal requirements in each country? Does diversity even matter?

Improving Customer Service

American Express recently turned Joan Weinbel's worst nightmare into a non-event. It was 10:00 P.M. Joan was home in New Jersey, packing for a weeklong trip, when she suddenly realized she had left her AmEx Gold card at a restaurant in New York City earlier in the evening. The restaurant was 30 miles away. She had a flight to catch at 7:30 the next morning, and she wanted her card for the trip. She called American Express. The phone was quickly answered by a courteous and helpful AmEx customer service representative who told Ms. Weinbel not to worry. He asked her a few questions and told her, "Help is on the way." To say Joan was flabbergasted when her doorbell rang at 11:45 P.M. is an understatement—it was less than 2 hours after her call. At the door was a courier with a new card. How the company was able to produce the card and get it to her so quickly still puzzles Joan, but she said the experience made her a customer for life.

Today, the majority of employees in developed countries work in service jobs, including 80 percent in the United States. In Australia, 73 percent work in service industries. In the United Kingdom, Germany, and Japan, the percentages are 69, 68, and 65, respectively. Service jobs include technical support representatives, fast-food counter workers, sales clerks, waiters and waitresses, nurses, automobile repair technicians, consultants, credit representatives, financial planners, and flight attendants. The common characteristic of these jobs is substantial interaction with an organization's customers. And because an organization can't exist without customers—whether it is American

The Ritz Carlton Hotel Company is recognized worldwide as the gold standard of the hospitality industry. Its motto—"We are ladies and gentlemen serving ladies and gentlemen"—is exemplified by the employee shown here serving a guest on the summer terrace of the Ritz-Carlton Moscow. The Ritz-Carlton's customer-responsive culture, which is articulated in the company's motto, credo, and service values, is designed to build strong relationships that create guests for life.

Source: ITAR - TASS / Anton Tushin / Newscom

Express, L. L. Bean, a law firm, a museum, a school, or a government agency— management needs to ensure employees do what it takes to please customers.[16] At Patagonia—a retail outfitter for climbers, mountain bikers, skiers and boarders, and other outdoor fanatics—customer service is the store manager's most important general responsibility: "Instill in your employees the meaning and importance of customer service as outlined in the retail philosophy, 'Our store is a place where the word "no" does not exist'; empower staff to 'use their best judgment' in all customer service matters."[17] OB can help managers at Patagonia achieve this goal and, more generally, can contribute to improving an organization's performance by showing managers how employee attitudes and behavior are associated with customer satisfaction.

Many an organization has failed because its employees failed to please customers. Management needs to create a customer-responsive culture. OB can provide considerable guidance in helping managers create such cultures—in which employees are friendly and courteous, accessible, knowledgeable, prompt in responding to customer needs, and willing to do what's necessary to please the customer.[18]

Improving People Skills

As you proceed through the chapters of this book, we'll present relevant concepts and theories that can help you explain and predict the behavior of people at work. In addition, you'll gain insights into specific people skills that you

workforce diversity   *The concept that organizations are becoming more heterogeneous in terms of gender, age, race, ethnicity, sexual orientation, and inclusion of other diverse groups.*

can use on the job. For instance, you'll learn ways to design motivating jobs, techniques for improving your listening skills, and how to create more effective teams.

Stimulating Innovation and Change

Whatever happened to Montgomery Ward, Woolworth, Smith Corona, TWA, Bethlehem Steel, and WorldCom? All these giants went bust. Why have other giants, such as General Motors, Sears, Boeing, and Lucent Technologies, implemented huge cost-cutting programs and eliminated thousands of jobs? The answer is to avoid going broke.

Today's successful organizations must foster innovation and master the art of change, or they'll become candidates for extinction. Victory will go to the organizations that maintain their flexibility, continually improve their quality, and beat their competition to the marketplace with a constant stream of innovative products and services. Domino's single-handedly brought on the demise of small pizza parlors whose managers thought they could continue doing what they had been doing for years. Amazon.com is putting a lot of independent bookstores out of business as it proves you can successfully sell books (and most anything else) from a Web site. After years of lackluster performance, Boeing realized it needed to change its business model. The result was its 787 Dreamliner and a return to being the world's largest airplane manufacturer.

An organization's employees can be the impetus for innovation and change, or they can be a major stumbling block. The challenge for managers is to stimulate their employees' creativity and tolerance for change. The field of OB provides a wealth of ideas and techniques to aid in realizing these goals.

Coping with "Temporariness"

Globalization, expanded capacity, and advances in technology have required organizations to be fast and flexible if they are to survive. The result is that most managers and employees today work in a climate best characterized as "temporary."

Workers must continually update their knowledge and skills to perform new job requirements. Production employees at companies such as Caterpillar, Ford, and Alcoa now need to operate computerized production equipment. That was not part of their job descriptions 20 years ago. In the past, employees were assigned to a specific work group, gaining a considerable amount of security working with the same people day in and day out. That predictability has been replaced by temporary work groups, with members from different departments, and the increased use of employee rotation to fill constantly changing work assignments. Finally, organizations themselves are in a state of flux. They continually reorganize their various divisions, sell off poorly performing businesses, downsize operations, subcontract noncritical services and operations to other organizations, and replace permanent employees with temporary workers.

Today's managers and employees must learn to cope with temporariness, flexibility, spontaneity, and unpredictability. The study of OB can help you better understand a work world of continual change, overcome resistance to change, and create an organizational culture that thrives on change.

Working in Networked Organizations

Networked organizations allow people to communicate and work together even though they may be thousands of miles apart. Independent contractors can telecommute via computer to workplaces around the globe and change employers as the demand for their services changes. Software programmers, graphic designers, systems analysts, technical writers, photo researchers, book

Dr. Orit Wimpfheimer performs her job by linking to others through networks. Shown here at her home office near Jerusalem, Israel, she is a radiologist who analyzes test results from hospitals in the United States over the Internet. Networked organizations that use e-mail, the Internet, and video-conferencing allow Dr. Orit Wimpfheimer and other telecommuters to communicate and work together even though they are thousands of miles apart. The manager's job in a networked organization requires different techniques from those used when workers are physically present in a single location.

Source: AP Photo/Emilio Morenatti

and media editors, and medical transcribers are just a few examples of people who can work from home or other nonoffice locations.

The manager's job is different in a networked organization. Motivating and leading people and making collaborative decisions online requires different techniques than when individuals are physically present in a single location. As more employees do their jobs by linking to others through networks, managers must develop new skills. OB can provide valuable insights to help with honing those skills.

Helping Employees Balance Work–Life Conflicts

The typical employee in the 1960s or 1970s showed up at a specified workplace Monday through Friday and worked for clearly defined 8- or 9-hour chunks of time. That's no longer true for a large segment of today's workforce. Employees are increasingly complaining that the line between work and nonwork time has become blurred, creating personal conflicts and stress.[19] At the same time, today's workplace presents opportunities for workers to create and structure their own roles.

How do work–life conflicts come about? First, the creation of global organizations means the world never sleeps. At any time on any day, thousands of General Electric employees are working somewhere. The need to consult with colleagues or customers eight or ten time zones away means many employees of global firms are "on call" 24 hours a day. Second, communication technology allows many technical and professional employees to do their work at home, in their cars, or on the beach in Tahiti—but it also means many feel like they never really get away from the office. Third, organizations are asking employees to put in longer hours. Over a recent 10-year period, the average U.S. workweek increased from 43 to 47 hours; and the number of people working 50 or more hours a week jumped from 24 to 37 percent. Finally, the rise of the dual-career couple makes it difficult for married employees to find time to fulfill commitments to home, spouse, children, parents, and friends. Millions of single-parent households and employees with dependent parents have even more significant challenges in balancing work and family responsibilities.

Employees increasingly recognize that work infringes on their personal lives, and they're not happy about it. Recent studies suggest employees want jobs that give them flexibility in their work schedules so they can better manage work–life conflicts.[20] In fact, balancing work and life demands now surpasses job security as an employee priority.[21] The next generation of employees is likely to show similar concerns.[22] Most college and university students say attaining a balance between personal life and work is a primary career goal; they want "a life" as well as a job. Organizations that don't help their people achieve work–life balance will find it increasingly difficult to attract and retain the most capable and motivated employees.

As you'll see in later chapters, the field of OB offers a number of suggestions to guide managers in designing workplaces and jobs that can help employees deal with work–life conflicts.

Creating a Positive Work Environment

Although competitive pressures on most organizations are stronger than ever, some organizations are trying to realize a competitive advantage by fostering a positive work environment. Jeff Immelt and Jim McNerney, both disciples of Jack Welch, have tried to maintain high-performance expectations (a characteristic of GE's culture) while fostering a positive work environment in their organizations (GE and Boeing). "In this time of turmoil and cynicism about business, you need to be passionate, positive leaders," Mr. Immelt recently told his top managers.

A real growth area in OB research is **positive organizational scholarship** (also called *positive organizational behavior*), which studies how organizations develop human strengths, foster vitality and resilience, and unlock potential. Researchers in this area say too much of OB research and management practice has been targeted toward identifying what's wrong with organizations and their employees. In response, they try to study what's *good* about them.[23] Some key independent variables in positive OB research are engagement, hope, optimism, and resilience in the face of strain.

Positive organizational scholars have studied a concept called "reflected best-self"—asking employees to think about when they were at their "personal best" in order to understand how to exploit their strengths. The idea is that we all have things at which we are unusually good, yet too often we focus on addressing our limitations and too rarely think about how to exploit our strengths.[24]

Although positive organizational scholarship does not deny the value of the negative (such as critical feedback), it does challenge researchers to look at OB through a new lens and pushes organizations to exploit employees' strengths rather than dwell on their limitations.

Improving Ethical Behavior

In an organizational world characterized by cutbacks, expectations of increasing productivity, and tough competition, it's not surprising many employees feel pressured to cut corners, break rules, and engage in other questionable practices.

Increasingly they face **ethical dilemmas and ethical choices**, in which they are required to identify right and wrong conduct. Should they "blow the whistle" if they uncover illegal activities in their company? Do they follow orders with which they don't personally agree? Should they give an inflated performance evaluation to an employee they like, knowing it could save that employee's job? Do they "play politics" to advance their career?

What constitutes good ethical behavior has never been clearly defined, and, in recent years, the line differentiating right from wrong has blurred. Employees see people all around them engaging in unethical practices—elected officials pad expense accounts or take bribes; corporate executives inflate profits so they can cash in lucrative stock options; and university administrators look the other way when winning coaches encourage scholarship athletes to take easy courses. When caught, these people give excuses such as "Everyone does it" or "You have to seize every advantage nowadays." Determining the ethically correct way to behave is especially difficult in a global economy because different cultures have different perspectives on certain ethical issues.[25] Fair treatment of employees in an economic downturn varies considerably across cultures, for instance. As we'll see in Chapter 2, perceptions of religious, ethnic, and gender diversity differ across countries. Is it any wonder employees are expressing decreased confidence in management and increasing uncertainty about what is appropriate ethical behavior in their organizations?[26]

Managers and their organizations are responding to the problem of unethical behavior in a number of ways.[27] They're writing and distributing codes of ethics to guide employees through ethical dilemmas. They're offering seminars, workshops, and other training programs to try to improve ethical behaviors. They're providing in-house advisors who can be contacted, in many cases anonymously, for assistance in dealing with ethical issues, and they're creating protection mechanisms for employees who reveal internal unethical practices.

Today's manager must create an ethically healthy climate for his or her employees, where they can do their work productively with minimal ambiguity about what right and wrong behaviors are. Companies that promote a strong ethical mission, encourage employees to behave with integrity, and provide strong ethical leadership can influence employee decisions to behave ethically.[28] In upcoming chapters, we'll discuss the actions managers can take to create an ethically healthy climate and help employees sort through ethically ambiguous situations. We'll also present ethical-dilemma exercises at the end of each chapter that allow you to think through ethical issues and assess how you would handle them.

Coming Attractions: Developing an OB Model

8 Compare the three levels of analysis in this book's OB model.

We conclude this chapter by presenting a general model that defines the field of OB, stakes out its parameters, and identifies inputs, processes, and outcomes. The result will be "coming attractions" of the topics in the remainder of this book.

An Overview

A **model** is an abstraction of reality, a simplified representation of some real-world phenomenon. Exhibit 1-4 presents the skeleton on which we will construct our OB model. It proposes three types of variables (inputs, processes, and

---

positive organizational scholarship *An area of OB research that concerns how organizations develop human strength, foster vitality and resilience, and unlock potential.*

ethical dilemmas and ethical choices *Situations in which individuals are required to define right and wrong conduct.*

model *An abstraction of reality. A simplified representation of some real-world phenomenon.*

Can You Learn from Failure?

Mistakes happen in business all the time, but most people have a powerful motivation to try to cover up their errors as much as possible. However, not recognizing and learning from failures might be the most dangerous failure of all because it means the problem is likely to occur again. This means that, even though it might be hard to admit it, doing the right thing often means admitting when you've done the wrong thing. Most people would say that we have an ethical obligation to learn from mistakes, but how can we do that? In a recent special issue in *Harvard Business Review* on failures, experts argued that learning from mistakes relies on several strategies, which include:

1. **Heed pressure.** High pressure often provokes faulty thinking. BP faced enormous pressure from cost overruns—roughly $1 million a day—in its deepwater oil explorations. This led its managers to miss warning signs that led to the catastrophic explosion in the Gulf of Mexico in 2010. Similar time and cost pressures precipitated the ill-fated Challenger and Columbia space shuttle launches. In high-pressure situations, ask yourself,

"If I had more time and resources, would I make the same decision?"

2. **Recognize that failure is not always bad.** Most of us would agree that we have learned more in life from our mistakes than from our successes. So, we need to realize that while we don't want to fail, it does have a hidden gift if we're willing to receive—a chance to learn something important. Eli Lilly holds "failure parties" to honor drug trials and experiments that fail to achieve the desired results. The rationale for these parties is to recognize that when little is ventured, little is lost, but little is gained too. Procter & Gamble CEO A. G. Lafley argues that very high success rates show incremental innovation—but what he wants are game changers. He has celebrated P&G's 11 most expensive product failures, focusing on what the company learned from each. So don't be afraid to admit mistakes—and ask "What can I learn" from each.

3. **Understand and address the root cause.** When Apple introduced the iPhone 4 in 2010, many customers complained about dropped calls. Apple first responded by suggesting the problem lay in the way customers held the phones, suggested

they "avoid gripping [the phone] in the lower left corner." Steve Jobs called the problem a "non-issue." Only later did Apple address the root cause of the problem—and fix it. When you make an error, try to understand what caused it.

4. **Reward owning up.** If you make a mistake, be willing to speak up and admit it. Too often we dig ourselves deeper into a hole by being defensive about mistakes. That also keeps us from learning from our failures. If we all make mistakes, what are we being so defensive about?

Given the complexity of human behavior, we'll never avoid making mistakes entirely. Indeed, a healthy appreciation for how mistake-prone we are is one of the points of this chapter (and of Chapter 6). But we *can* do a better job of admitting our mistakes and learning from them when they occur.

Sources: A. C. Edmondson, "Strategies for Learning from Failure," *Harvard Business Review* 89, no. 4 (2011), pp. 48–55; R. G. Mcgrath, "Failing by Design," *Harvard Business Review* 89, no. 4 (2011), pp. 76–83; C. H. Tinsley, R. L. Dillon, and P. M. Madsen, "How to Avoid Catastrophe," *Harvard Business Review* 89, no. 4 (2011), pp. 90–97.

outcomes) at three levels of analysis (individual, group, and organizational). The model proceeds from left to right, with inputs leading to processes and processes leading to outcomes. Notice that the model also shows that outcomes can influence inputs in the future.

Inputs

Inputs are the variables like personality, group structure, and organizational culture that lead to processes. These variables set the stage for what will occur in an organization later. Many are determined in advance of the employment relationship. For example, individual diversity characteristics, personality, and values are shaped by a combination of an individual's genetic inheritance and childhood environment. Group structure, roles, and team responsibilities are

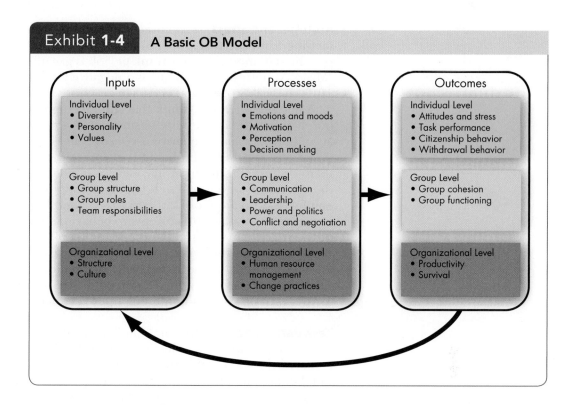

Exhibit 1-4   A Basic OB Model

Inputs	Processes	Outcomes
Individual Level • Diversity • Personality • Values	**Individual Level** • Emotions and moods • Motivation • Perception • Decision making	**Individual Level** • Attitudes and stress • Task performance • Citizenship behavior • Withdrawal behavior
Group Level • Group structure • Group roles • Team responsibilities	**Group Level** • Communication • Leadership • Power and politics • Conflict and negotiation	**Group Level** • Group cohesion • Group functioning
Organizational Level • Structure • Culture	**Organizational Level** • Human resource management • Change practices	**Organizational Level** • Productivity • Survival

typically assigned immediately before or after a group is formed. Finally, organizational structure and culture are usually the result of years of development and change as the organization adapts to its environment and builds up customs and norms.

Processes

If inputs are like the nouns in organizational behavior, processes are like verbs. **Processes** are actions that individuals, groups, and organizations engage in as a result of inputs and that lead to certain outcomes. At the individual level, processes include emotions and moods, motivation, perception, and decision making. At the group level, they include communication, leadership, power and politics, and conflict and negotiation. Finally, at the organizational level, processes include human resource management and change practices.

Outcomes

Outcomes are the key variables that you want to explain or predict, and that are affected by some other variables. What are the primary outcomes in OB? Scholars have emphasized individual-level outcomes like attitudes and satisfaction, task performance, citizenship behavior, and withdrawal behavior. At the group level, cohesion and functioning are the dependent variables. Finally, at the organizational level we look at overall profitability and survival. Because these outcomes will be covered in all the chapters, we'll briefly discuss each here so you can understand what the "goal" of OB will be.

input *Variables that lead to processes.*

processes *Actions that individuals, groups, and organizations engage in as a result of inputs and that lead to certain outcomes.*

outcomes *Key factors that are affected by some other variables.*

Attitudes and Stress   Employee attitudes are the evaluations employees make, ranging from positive to negative, about objects, people, or events. For example, the statement, "I really think my job is great," is a positive job attitude, and "My job is boring and tedious" is a negative job attitude. Stress is an unpleasant psychological process that occurs in response to environmental pressures.

Some people might think that influencing employee attitudes and stress is purely soft stuff, and not the business of serious managers, but as we will show, attitudes often have behavioral consequences that directly relate to organizational effectiveness. The belief that satisfied employees are more productive than dissatisfied employees has been a basic tenet among managers for years, though only now has research begun to support it. Ample evidence shows that employees who are more satisfied and treated fairly are more willing to engage in the above-and-beyond citizenship behavior so vital in the contemporary business environment. A study of more than 2,500 business units also found that those scoring in the top 25 percent on the employee opinion survey were, on average, 4.6 percent above their sales budget for the year, while those scoring in the bottom 25 percent were 0.8 percent below budget. In real numbers, this was a difference of $104 million in sales per year between the two groups.

Task Performance   The combination of effectiveness and efficiency at doing your core job tasks is a reflection of your level of **task performance**. If we think about the job of a factory worker, task performance could be measured by the number and quality of products produced in an hour. The task performance of a teacher would be the level of education that students obtain. The task performance of a consultant might be measured by the timeliness and quality of the presentations they offer to the client firm. All these types of performance relate to the core duties and responsibilities of a job and are often directly related to the functions listed on a formal job description.

Obviously task performance is the most important human output contributing to organizational effectiveness, so in every chapter we devote considerable time to detailing how task performance is affected by the topic in question.

Task performance is one of the primary individual-level outcomes in organizational behavior. For these women who install wiring in car doors at the General Motors' assembly plant in Lordstown, Ohio, task performance is measured by the number and quality of the work they produce. Their level of task performance is related to the duties of their job and how effectively and efficiently they perform them. Task performance is the most important human output contributing to organizational effectiveness.

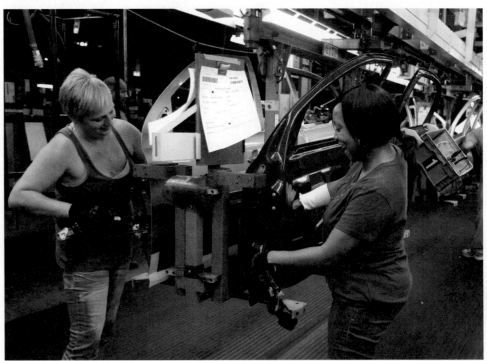

Citizenship Behavior   The discretionary behavior that is not part of an employee's formal job requirements, and that contributes to the psychological and social environment of the workplace, is called **citizenship behavior**. Successful organizations need employees who will do more than their usual job duties—who will provide performance *beyond* expectations. In today's dynamic workplace, where tasks are increasingly performed by teams and flexibility is critical, employees who engage in "good citizenship" behaviors help others on their team, volunteer for extra work, avoid unnecessary conflicts, respect the spirit as well as the letter of rules and regulations, and gracefully tolerate occasional work-related impositions and nuisances.

Organizations want and need employees who will do things that aren't in any job description. Evidence indicates organizations that have such employees outperform those that don't. As a result, OB is concerned with citizenship behavior as an outcome variable.

Withdrawal Behavior   We've already mentioned behavior that goes above and beyond task requirements, but what about behavior that in some way is below task requirements? **Withdrawal behavior** is the set of actions that employees take to separate themselves from the organization. There are many forms of withdrawal, ranging from showing up late or failing to attend meetings to absenteeism and turnover.

Employee withdrawal can have a very negative effect on an organization. The cost of employee turnover alone has been estimated to run into the thousands of dollars, even for entry-level positions. Absenteeism also costs organizations significant amounts of money and time every year. For instance, a recent survey found the average direct cost to U.S. employers of unscheduled absences is 8.7 percent of payroll.[29] In Sweden, an average of 10 percent of the country's workforce is on sick leave at any given time.[30]

It's obviously difficult for an organization to operate smoothly and attain its objectives if employees fail to report to their jobs. The work flow is disrupted, and important decisions may be delayed. In organizations that rely heavily on assembly-line production, absenteeism can be considerably more than a disruption; it can drastically reduce the quality of output or even shut down the facility. Levels of absenteeism beyond the normal range have a direct impact on any organization's effectiveness and efficiency. A high rate of turnover can also disrupt the efficient running of an organization when knowledgeable and experienced personnel leave and replacements must be found to assume positions of responsibility.

All organizations, of course, have some turnover. The U.S. national turnover rate averages about 3 percent per month, about a 36 percent turnover per year. This average varies a lot by occupation, of course; the monthly turnover rate for government jobs is less than 1 percent, versus 5 to 7 percent in the construction industry.[31] If the "right" people are leaving the organization—the marginal and submarginal employees—turnover can actually be positive. It can create an opportunity to replace an underperforming individual with someone who has higher skills or motivation, open up increased opportunities for promotions,

task performance   *The combination of effectiveness and efficiency at doing your core job tasks.*

citizenship behavior   *Discretionary behavior that contributes to the psychological and social environment of the workplace.*

withdrawal behavior   *The set of actions employee take to separate themselves from the organization.*

and bring new and fresh ideas to the organization.[32] In today's changing world of work, reasonable levels of employee-initiated turnover improve organizational flexibility and employee independence, and they can lessen the need for management-initiated layoffs.

So why do employees withdraw from work? As we will show later in the book, reasons include negative job attitudes, emotions and moods, and negative interactions with co-workers and supervisors.

Group Cohesion   Although many outcomes in our model can be conceptualized as individual level phenomena, some relate to how groups operate. **Group cohesion** is the extent to which members of a group support and validate one another at work. In other words, a cohesive group is one that sticks together. When employees trust one another, seek common goals, and work together to achieve these common ends, the group is cohesive; when employees are divided among themselves in terms of what they want to achieve and have little loyalty to one another, the group is not cohesive.

There is ample evidence showing that cohesive groups are more effective.[33] These results are found both for groups that are studied in highly controlled laboratory settings and also for work teams observed in field settings. This fits with our intuitive sense that people tend to work harder in groups that have a common purpose. Companies attempt to increase cohesion in a variety of ways ranging from brief icebreaker sessions to social events like picnics, parties, and outdoor adventure-team retreats. Throughout the book we will try to assess whether these specific efforts are likely to result in increases in group cohesiveness. We'll also consider ways that picking the right people to be on the team in the first place might be an effective way to enhance cohesion.

Group Functioning   In the same way that positive job attitudes can be associated with higher levels of task performance, group cohesion should lead to positive group functioning. **Group functioning** refers to the quantity and quality of a group's work output. In the same way that the performance of a sports team is more than the sum of individual players' performance, group functioning in work organizations is more than the sum of individual task performances.

What does it mean to say that a group is functioning effectively? In some organizations, an effective group is one that stays focused on a core task and achieves its ends as specified. Other organizations look for teams that are able to work together collaboratively to provide excellent customer service. Still others put more of a premium on group creativity and the flexibility to adapt to changing situations. In each case, different types of activities will be required to get the most from the team.

Productivity   The highest level of analysis in organizational behavior is the organization as a whole. An organization is productive if it achieves its goals by transforming inputs into outputs at the lowest cost. Thus **productivity** requires both **effectiveness** and **efficiency**.

A hospital is *effective* when it successfully meets the needs of its clientele. It is *efficient* when it can do so at a low cost. If a hospital manages to achieve higher output from its present staff by reducing the average number of days a patient is confined to bed or increasing the number of staff–patient contacts per day, we say the hospital has gained productive efficiency. A business firm is effective when it attains its sales or market share goals, but its productivity also depends on achieving those goals efficiently. Popular measures of organizational efficiency include return on investment, profit per dollar of sales, and output per hour of labor.

Service organizations must include customer needs and requirements in assessing their effectiveness. Why? Because a clear chain of cause and effect runs

Exhibit 1-5   The Plan of the Book

The Individual

Inputs
- Diversity in Organizations (ch.2)
- Personality and Values (ch. 5)

Processes
- Emotions and moods (ch. 4)
- Motivation (Ch. 7 and 8)
- Perception and decision making (Ch. 6)

Outcomes
- Attitudes (ch. 3) & stress (ch. 18)
- Task performance (all)
- Citizenship behavior (all)
- Withdrawal behavior (all)

The Group

Inputs
- Group structures (Ch. 9 & 10)
- Group roles (Ch. 9 & 10)
- Team responsibilities (Ch. 9 & 10)

Processes
- Communication (Ch. 11)
- Leadership (Ch. 12)
- Power and polities (Ch. 13)
- Conflict and negotiation (Ch. 14)

Outcomes
- Group collesion (Ch. 9 & 10)
- Group functioning (Ch. 9 & 10)

The Organization

Inputs
- Structure (Ch. 15)
- Culture (Ch. 16)

Processes
- Human resource management (Ch. 17)
- Change practices (Ch. 18)

Outcomes
- Profitability (Ch. 16 & 17)
- Survival (Ch. 16 & 17)

from employee attitudes and behavior to customer attitudes and behavior to a service organization's productivity. Sears has carefully documented this chain.[34] The company's management found that a 5 percent improvement in employee attitudes leads to a 1.3 percent increase in customer satisfaction, which in turn translates into a 0.5 percent improvement in revenue growth. By training employees to improve the employee–customer interaction, Sears was able to improve customer satisfaction by 4 percent over a 12-month period, generating an estimated $200 million in additional revenues.

Survival   The final outcome we will consider is **organizational survival**, which is simply evidence that the organization is able to exist and grow over the long term. The survival of an organization depends not just on how productive the organization is, but also on how well it fits with its environment. A company that is very productively making goods and services of little value to the market is unlikely to survive for long, so survival factors in things like perceiving the market successfully, making good decisions about how and when to pursue opportunities, and engaging in successful change management to adapt to new business conditions.

Having reviewed the input, process, and outcome model, we're going to change the figure up a little bit by grouping topics together based on whether we study them at the individual, group, or organizational level. As you can seen in Exhibit 1-5, we will deal with inputs, processes, and outcomes at all three levels of

group cohesion   The extent to which members of a group support and validate one another while at work.

group functioning   The quantity and quality of a work group's output.

productivity   The combination of the effectiveness and efficiency of an organization.

effectiveness   The degree to which an organization meets the needs of its clientele or customers.

efficiency   The degree to which an organization can achieve its ends at a low cost.

organizational survival   The degree to which an organization is able to exist and grow over the long term.

glOBalization!

Does National Culture Affect Organizational Practices?

Companies that operate in more than one country face a challenging dilemma: how much should they tailor organizational practices like leadership style, rewards, and communication to each country's culture? To some extent, it is necessary to change the way a company does business because of differences in regulations, institutions, and labor force characteristics. For example, a U.S. company that operates in Germany will have to contend with laws requiring greater worker participation in decision making, and an Australian company operating in China will have to match the knowledge and skills found in the Chinese workforce. Despite certain limitations imposed by law and situational factors, managers still need to make many decisions about adjusting their organizational culture to match the culture of the countries in which they operate.

There are no simple responses to this dilemma. Some researchers propose that managers need to make a concerted effort to adapt their organizational culture to match the culture of the countries in which they operate. These authors note that within any country, there is a great deal of similarity in management practices that is likely the result of culture or values. If a country's basic outlook is highly individualistic, then organizational culture should also emphasize individual contributions and efforts. Conversely, if national culture values collectivism, then organizational culture should emphasize group contributions and cohesiveness. From this perspective, successful international management is all about tailoring management practices and values to fit with the cultural values of each country in which the company operates.

On the other hand, some propose that national culture should not, and does not, make much difference in shaping organizational culture. These researchers note that even within a single country, there can be a great deal of variation in values and norms. The development of practices to match a culture is fraught with problems of stereotyping and over-generalizing about the degree to which everyone in a given country shares the same values. These authors also note that in tailoring practices to each country, a firm loses the potential value of having a unifying organizational culture. From this perspective, companies should try as much as possible to create a strong culture that operates across borders to create a unified global workforce.

Sources: Based on B. Gerhart, "How Much Does National Culture Constrain Organizational Culture," *Management and Organization Review 5,* no. 2 (2009), pp. 241–259; A. S. Tsui, S. S. Nifadkar, and A. Y. Ou, "Cross-national, Cross-cultural Organizational Behavior Research: Advances, Gaps, and Recommendations," *Journal of Management* 33, no. 3 (2007), pp. 426-478; G. Johns, "The Essential Impact of Context on Organizational Behavior," *Academy of Management Review* 31, no. 2 (2006), pp. 386–408.

analysis, but we group the chapters as shown here to correspond with the typical ways that research has been done in these areas. It is easier to understand one unified presentation about how personality leads to motivation which leads to performance, than to jump around levels of analysis. Because each level builds on the one that precedes it, after going through them in sequence you will have a good idea of how the human side of organizations functions.

Summary and Implications for Managers

Managers need to develop their interpersonal, or people, skills to be effective in their jobs. Organizational behavior (OB) investigates the impact that individuals, groups, and structure have on behavior within an organization, and it applies that knowledge to make organizations work more effectively. Specifically, OB focuses on how to improve productivity; reduce absenteeism,

Lost in Translation?

Walk into your nearest major bookstore. You'll undoubtedly find a large selection of books devoted to management and managing. Consider the following recent titles:

- *Tough Cookies: What 100 Years of the Girl Scouts Can Teach You* (Wiley, 2011)
- *From Wags to Riches: How Dogs Teach Us to Succeed in Business & Life* (BenBella Books, 2011)
- *All I Know About Management I Learned from My Dog: The Real Story of Angel, a Rescued Golden Retriever, Who Inspired the New Four Golden Rules of Management* (Skyhorse Publishing, 2011)
- *Mother Teresa, CEO: Unexpected Principles for Practical Leadership* (Berrett-Koehler Publishers, 2011)
- *Polar Bear Pirates and Their Quest to Engage the Sleepwalkers: Motivate Everyday People to Deliver Extraordinary Results* (Capstone, 2011)
- *Winnie-the-Pooh on Management: In Which a Very Important Bear and His Friends Are Introduced to a Very Important Subject* (Penguin, 2011)
- *Chicken Lips, Wheeler-Dealer, and the Beady-Eyed M.B.A.: An Entrepreneurs Wild Adventures on the New Silk Road* (Wiley, 2011)
- *Bodybuilders in Tutus: and 35 Other Obscure Business-Boosting Observations* (Robinwood Press, 2011)
- *I'll Make You an Offer You Can't Refuse: Insider Business Tips from a Former Mob Boss* (Thomas Nelson, 2011)
- *The Art of War from SmarterComics: How to be Successful in Any Competition* (Writers of The Round Table Press, 2011)

Popular books on organizational behavior often have cute titles and are fun to read, but they make the job of managing people seem much simpler than it is. Most are based on the author's opinions rather than substantive research, and it is doubtful that one person's experience translates into effective management practice for everyone. Why do we waste our time on "fluff" when, with a little effort, we can access knowledge produced from thousands of scientific studies on human behavior in organizations?

Organizational behavior is a complex subject. Few, if any, simple statements about human behavior are generalizable to all people in all situations. Should you really try to apply leadership insights you got from a book about Geronimo or Tony Soprano to managing software engineers in the twenty-first century?

Organizations are always looking for leaders, and managers and manager-wannabes are continually looking for ways to hone their leadership skills. Publishers respond to this demand by offering hundreds of titles that promise insights into managing people. Books like these can provide people with the secrets to management that others know about. Moreover, isn't it better to learn about management from people in the trenches, as opposed to the latest esoteric musings from the "Ivory Tower"? Many of the most important insights we gain from life aren't necessarily the product of careful empirical research studies.

It is true there are some bad books out there. But do they outnumber the esoteric research studies published every year? For example, a couple of recent management and organizational behavior studies were published in 2011 with the following titles:

- *Training for Fostering Knowledge Co-Construction from Collaborative Inference-Drawing*
- *The Factor Structure and Cross-Test Convergence of the Mayer–Salovey–Caruso Model of Emotional Intelligence*
- *Refining Value-Based Differentiation in Business Relationships: A Study of the Higher Order Relationship Building Blocks that Influence Behavioural Intentions*
- *A Dialogical Approach to the Creation of New Knowledge in Organizations*

We don't mean to poke fun at these studies. Rather, our point is that you can't judge a book by its cover any more than you can a research study by its title.

There is no one right way to learn the science and art of managing people in organizations. The most enlightened managers are those who gather insights from multiple sources: their own experience, research findings, observations of others, and, yes, business press books, too. If great management were produced by carefully gleaning results from research studies, academicians would make the best managers. How often do we see that?

Research and academics have an important role to play in understanding effective management. But it isn't fair to condemn all business books by citing the worst (or, at least, the worse-sounding ones).

turnover, and deviant workplace behavior; and increase organizational citizenship behavior and job satisfaction. Here are a few specific implications for managers:

- Some generalizations provide valid insights into human behavior, but many are erroneous. Organizational behavior uses systematic study to improve predictions of behavior over intuition alone.
- Because people are different, we need to look at OB in a contingency framework, using situational variables to explain cause-and-effect relationships.
- Organizational behavior offers specific insights to improve a manager's people skills.
- It helps managers to see the value of workforce diversity and practices that may need to be changed in different countries.
- It can improve quality and employee productivity by showing managers how to empower their people, design and implement change programs, improve customer service, and help employees balance work–life conflicts.
- It can help managers cope in a world of temporariness and learn how to stimulate innovation.
- Finally, OB can guide managers in creating an ethically healthy work climate.

MyManagementLab

Now that you have finished this chapter, go back to **www.mymanagementlab.com** to continue practicing and applying the concepts you've learned.

QUESTIONS FOR REVIEW

1 What is the importance of interpersonal skills?

2 What do managers do in terms of functions, roles, and skills?

3 What is organizational behavior (OB)?

4 Why is it important to complement intuition with systematic study?

5 What are the major behavioral science disciplines that contribute to OB?

6 Why are there few absolutes in OB?

7 What are the challenges and opportunities for managers in using OB concepts?

8 What are the three levels of analysis in this book's OB model?

EXPERIENTIAL EXERCISE Workforce Diversity

Purpose
To learn about the different needs of a diverse workforce.

Time Required
Approximately 40 minutes.

Participants and Roles
Divide the class into six groups of approximately equal size. Assign each group one of the following roles:

Nancy is 28 years old. The divorced mother of three children ages 3, 5, and 7, she is the department head.

She earns $40,000 per year at her job and receives another $3,600 per year in child support from her ex-husband.

Ethel is a 72-year-old widow. She works 25 hours per week at an hourly wage of $8.50 to supplement her $8,000 annual pension and earns a total of $19,000 per year.

John is a 34-year-old born in Trinidad who is now a U.S. resident. He is married and the father of two small children. John attends college at night and is within a year of earning his bachelor's degree. His salary is $27,000 per year. His wife is an attorney and earns approximately $50,000 per year.

Lu is 26 years old and single with a master's degree in education. He is paralyzed and confined to a wheelchair as a result of an auto accident. He earns $32,000 per year.

Maria is a single, 22-year-old woman born and raised in Mexico. She came to the United States only 3 months ago, and her English needs considerable improvement. She earns $20,000 per year.

Mike is a 16-year-old high school sophomore who works 15 hours per week after school and during vacations. He earns $7.20 per hour, or approximately $5,600 per year.

The members of each group are to assume the character consistent with their assigned role.

Background
The six participants work for a company that has recently installed a flexible benefits program. Instead of the traditional "one benefit package fits all," the company is allocating an additional 25 percent of each employee's annual pay to be used for discretionary benefits. Those benefits and their annual cost are as follows:

- Supplementary health care for employee:
  Plan A (no deductible and pays 90 percent) = $3,000
  Plan B ($200 deductible and pays 80 percent) = $2,000
  Plan C ($1,000 deductible and pays 70 percent) = $500
- Supplementary health care for dependents (same deductibles and percentages as above):
  Plan A = $2,000
  Plan B = $1,500
  Plan C = $500
- Supplementary dental plan = $500

- Life insurance:
  Plan A ($25,000 coverage) = $500
  Plan B ($50,000 coverage) = $1,000
  Plan C ($100,000 coverage) = $2,000
  Plan D ($250,000 coverage) = $3,000
- Mental health plan = $500
- Prepaid legal assistance = $300
- Vacation = 2 percent of annual pay for each week, up to 6 weeks a year
- Pension at retirement equal to approximately 50 percent of final annual earnings = $1,500
- 4-day workweek during the 3 summer months (available only to full-time employees) = 4 percent of annual pay
- Day care services (after company contribution) = $2,000 for all of an employee's children, regardless of number
- Company-provided transportation to and from work = $750
- College tuition reimbursement = $1,000
- Language class tuition reimbursement = $500

The Task
1. Each group has 15 minutes to develop a flexible benefits package that consumes 25 percent (and no more!) of its character's pay.
2. After completing step 1, each group appoints a spokesperson who describes to the entire class the benefits package the group has arrived at for its character.
3. The entire class then discusses the results. How did the needs, concerns, and problems of each participant influence the group's decision? What do the results suggest for trying to motivate a diverse workforce?

Source: Special thanks to Professor Penny Wright (San Diego State University) for her suggestions during the development of this exercise.

ETHICAL DILEMMA **Jekyll and Hyde**

Let's assume you have been offered a job by Jekyll Corporation, a company in the consumer products industry. The job is in your chosen career path.

Jekyll Corporation has offered you a position that would begin 2 weeks after you graduate. The job responsibilities are appealing to you, make good use of your training, and are intrinsically interesting. The company seems well positioned financially, and you have met the individual who would be your supervisor, who assures you that the future prospects for your position and career are

bright. Several other graduates of your program work at Jekyll Corporation, and they speak quite positively of the company and promise to socialize and network with you once you start.

As a company, Jekyll Corporation promotes itself as a fair-trade and sustainable organization. Fair trade is a trading partnership—based on dialogue, transparency, and respect—that seeks greater equity in international trade. It contributes to sustainable development by offering better trading conditions to, and securing the rights of, local producers and businesses. Fair-trade organizations are actively engaged in supporting producers and sustainable environmental farming practices, and fair-trade practices prohibit child or forced labor.

Yesterday, Gabriel Utterson—a human resources manager at Jekyll Corporation—called you to discuss initial terms of the offer, which seemed reasonable and standard for the industry. However, one aspect was not mentioned, your starting salary. Gabriel said Jekyll is an internally transparent organization—there are no secrets. While the firm very much wants to hire you, there are limits to what it can afford to offer, and before it makes a formal offer, it was reasonable to ask what you would expect. Gabriel wanted you to think about this and call back tomorrow.

Before calling Gabriel, you thought long and hard about what it would take to accept Jekyll Corporation's offer. You have a number in mind, which may or may not be the same number you give Gabriel. What starting salary would it take for you to accept Jekyll Corporation's offer?

Questions

1. What starting salary will you give Gabriel? What salary represents the minimum offer you would accept? If these two numbers are different, why? Does giving

Gabriel a different number than your "internal" number violate Jekyll Corporation's transparent culture? Why or why not?

2. Assume you've received another offer, this one from Hyde Associates. Like the Jekyll job, this position is on your chosen career path and in the consumer products industry. Assume, however, that you've read in the news that *"Hyde Associates has been criticized for unsustainable manufacturing practices that may be harmful to the environment. It has further been criticized for unfair trade practices and for employing underage children."* Would that change whether you'd be willing to take the job? Why or why not?

3. These scenarios are based on studies of Corporate Social Responsibility (CSR) practices that show consumers generally charge a kind of rent to companies that do not practice CSR. In other words, they generally expect a substantial discount in order to buy a product from Hyde rather than from Jekyll. For example, if Jekyll and Hyde sold coffee, people would pay a premium of $1.40 to buy coffee from Jekyll and demand a discount of $2.40 to buy Hyde coffee. Do you think this preference translates into job choice decisions? Why or why not?

CASE INCIDENT 1 "Lessons for 'Undercover' Bosses"

Executive offices in major corporations are often far removed from the day-to-day work that most employees perform. While top executives might enjoy the perquisites found in the executive suite, and separation from workday concerns can foster a broader perspective on the business, the distance between management and workers can come at a real cost: top managers often fail to understand the ways most employees do their jobs every day. The dangers of this distant approach are clear. Executives sometimes make decisions without recognizing how difficult or impractical they are to implement. Executives can also lose sight of the primary challenges their employees face.

The practice of "management by walking around" (MBWA) works against the insularity of the executive suite. To practice MBWA, managers reserve time to walk through departments regularly, form networks of acquaintances in the organization, and get away from their desks to talk to individual employees. The practice was exemplified by Bill Hewlett and Dave Packard, who used this management style at HP to learn more about the challenges and opportunities their employees were encountering. Many other organizations followed suit and found that this style of management had advantages over a typical desk-bound approach to management. A recent study

of successful Swedish organizations revealed that MBWA was an approach common to several firms that received national awards for being great places to work.

The popular television program *Undercover Boss* took MBWA to the next level by having top executives from companies like Chiquita Brands, DirecTV, Great Wolf Resorts, and NASCAR work incognito among line employees. Executives reported that this process taught them how difficult many of the jobs in their organizations were, and just how much skill was required to perform even the lowest-level tasks. They also said the experience taught them a lot about the core business in their organizations and sparked ideas for improvements.

Although MBWA has long had its advocates, it does present certain problems. First, the time managers spend directly observing the workforce is time they are not doing their core job tasks like analysis, coordination, and strategic planning. Second, management based on subjective impressions gathered by walking around runs counter to a research and data-based approach to making managerial decisions. Third, it is also possible that executives who wander about will be seen as intruders and overseers. Implementing the MBWA style requires a great deal of foresight to avoid these potential pitfalls.

Questions

1. What are some of the things managers can learn by walking around and having daily contact with line employees that they might not be able to learn from looking at data and reports?

2. As an employee, would you appreciate knowing your supervisor regularly spent time with workers? How would knowing top executives routinely interact with line employees affect your attitudes toward the organization?

3. What ways can executives and other organizational leaders learn about day-to-day business operations besides going "undercover?"

4. Are there any dangers in the use of a management by walking around strategy? Could this strategy lead employees to feel they are being spied on? What actions on the part of managers might minimize these concerns?

Sources: Based on T. Peters and N. Austin, "Management by Walking About," *Economist* (September 8, 2008), www.economist.com; F. Aguirre, M. White, K. Schaefer, and S. Phelps, "Secrets of an Undercover Boss," *Fortune* (August 27, 2010), pp. 41–44; J. Larsson, I. Backstrom, and H. Wiklund, "Leadership and Organizational Behavior: Similarities between Three Award-Winning Organizations," *International Journal of Management Practice 3* (2009), pp. 327–345.

CASE INCIDENT 2 Era of the Disposable Worker?

The great global recession has claimed many victims. In many countries, unemployment is at near-historic highs, and even those who have managed to keep their jobs have often been asked to accept reduced work hours or pay cuts. Another consequence of the current business and economic environment is an increase in the number of individuals employed on a temporary or contingent basis.

The statistics on U.S. temporary workers are grim. Many, like single mother Tammy Smith, have no health insurance, no retirement benefits, no vacation, no severance, and no access to unemployment insurance. Increases in layoffs mean that many jobs formerly considered safe have become "temporary" in the sense that they could disappear at any time with little warning. Forecasts suggest that the next 5 to 10 years will be similar, with small pay increases, worse working conditions, and low levels of job security. As Peter Cappelli of the University of Pennsylvania's Wharton School notes, "Employers are trying to get rid of all fixed costs. First they did it with employment benefits. Now they're doing it with the jobs themselves. Everything is variable."

We might suppose these corporate actions are largely taking place in an era of diminishing profitability. However, data from the financial sector is not consistent with this explanation. Among *Fortune* 500 companies, 2009 saw the second-largest jump in corporate earnings in the list's 56-year history. Moreover, many of these gains do not appear to be the result of increases in revenue. Rather, they reflect dramatic decreases in labor costs. One equity market researcher noted, "The largest part of the gain came from lower payrolls rather than the sluggish rise in sales . . ." Wages also rose only slightly during this period of rapidly increasing corporate profitability.

Some observers suggest the very nature of corporate profit monitoring is to blame for the discrepancy between corporate profitability and outcomes for workers. Some have noted that teachers whose evaluations are based on standardized test scores tend to "teach to the test," to the detriment of other areas of learning. In the same way, when a company is judged primarily by the single metric of a stock price, executives naturally try their best to increase this number, possibly to the detriment of other concerns like employee well-being or corporate culture. On the other hand, others defend corporate actions that increase the degree to which they can treat labor flexibly, noting that in an increasingly competitive global marketplace, it might be necessary to sacrifice some jobs to save the organization as a whole.

The issues of how executives make decisions about workforce allocation, how job security and corporate loyalty influence employee behavior, and how emotional reactions come to surround these issues are all core components of organizational behavior research.

Questions

1. To what extent can individual business decisions (as opposed to economic forces) explain deterioration in working conditions for many workers?

2. Do business organizations have a responsibility to ensure that employees have secure jobs with good

working conditions, or is their primary responsibility to shareholders?

3. What alternative measures of organizational performance, besides share prices, do you think might change the focus of business leaders?

4. What do you think the likely impact of the growth of temporary employment relationships will be for employee attitudes and behaviors? How would you develop a measurement system to evaluate the impact of corporate downsizing and temporary job assignments on employees?

Sources: Based on P. Coy, M. Conlin, and M. Herbst, "The Disposable Worker," *Bloomberg Businessweek* (January 7, 2010), www.businessweek.com; S. Tully, "Fortune 500: Profits Bounce Back," *Fortune* (May 3, 2010), pp. 140–144; D. Ariely, "You Are What You Measure," *Harvard Business Review* (June 2010), p. 38.

ENDNOTES

1. Cited in R. Alsop, "Playing Well with Others," *Wall Street Journal* (September 9, 2002).
2. See, for instance, C. Penttila, "Hiring Hardships," *Entrepreneur* (October 2002), pp. 34–35.
3. S. E. Humphrey, J. D. Nahrgang, and F. P. Morgeson, "Integrating Motivational, Social, and Contextual Work Design Features: A Meta-Analytic Summary and Theoretical Extension of the Work Design Literature," *Journal of Applied Psychology* 92, no. 5 (2007), pp. 1332–1356.
4. I. S. Fulmer, B. Gerhart, and K. S. Scott, "Are the 100 Best Better? An Empirical Investigation of the Relationship Between Being a 'Great Place to Work' and Firm Performance," *Personnel Psychology* (Winter 2003), pp. 965–993.
5. H. Fayol, *Industrial and General Administration* (Paris: Dunod, 1916).
6. A. I. Kraut, P. R. Pedigo, D. D. McKenna, and M. D. Dunnette, "The Role of the Manager: What's Really Important in Different Management Jobs," *Academy of Management Executive* 19, no. 4 (2005), pp. 122–129.
7. H. Mintzberg, *The Nature of Managerial Work* (Upper Saddle River, NJ: Prentice Hall, 1973).
8. R. L. Katz, "Skills of an Effective Administrator," *Harvard Business Review* (September–October 1974), pp. 90–102; D. Bartram, "The Great Eight Competencies: A Criterion-Centric Approach to Validation," *Journal of Applied Psychology* 90, no. 6 (2005), pp. 1185–1203; and S. E. Scullen, M. K. Mount, and T. A. Judge, "Evidence of the Construct Validity of Developmental Ratings of Managerial Performance," *Journal of Applied Psychology* 88, no. 1 (2003), pp. 50–66.
9. F. Luthans, "Successful vs. Effective Real Managers," *Academy of Management Executive* (May 1988), pp. 127–132; and F. Luthans, R. M. Hodgetts, and S. A. Rosenkrantz, *Real Managers* (Cambridge, MA: Ballinger, 1988). See also F. Shipper and J. Davy, "A Model and Investigation of Managerial Skills, Employees' Attitudes, and Managerial Performance," *Leadership Quarterly* 13 (2002), pp. 95–120.
10. P. Wu, M. Foo, and D. B. Turban, "The Role of Personality in Relationship Closeness, Developer Assistance, and Career Success," *Journal of Vocational Behavior* 73, no. 3 (2008), pp. 440–448; and A. M. Konrad, R. Kashlak, I. Yoshioka, R. Waryszak, and N. Toren, "What Do Managers Like to Do? A Five-Country Study," *Group & Organization Management* (December 2001), pp. 401–433.
11. A. S. Tsui, S. J. Ashford, L. St. Clair, and K. R. Xin, "Dealing with Discrepant Expectations: Response Strategies and Managerial Effectiveness," *Academy of Management Journal* (December 1995), pp. 1515–1543.
12. See, for instance, C. Heath and S. B. Sitkin, "Big-B Versus Big-O: What Is *Organizational* about Organizational Behavior?" *Journal of Organizational Behavior* (February 2001), pp. 43–58. For a review of what one eminent researcher believes *should* be included in organizational behavior, based on survey data, see J. B. Miner, "The Rated Importance, Scientific Validity, and Practical Usefulness of Organizational Behavior Theories: A Quantitative Review," *Academy of Management Learning & Education* (September 2003), pp. 250–268.
13. D. M. Rousseau and S. McCarthy, "Educating Managers from an Evidence-Based Perspective," *Academy of Management Learning & Education* 6, no. 1 (2007), pp. 84–101; and S. L. Rynes, T. L. Giluk, and K. G. Brown, "The Very Separate Worlds of Academic and Practitioner Periodicals in Human Resource Management: Implications for Evidence-Based Management," *Academy of Management Journal* 50, no. 5 (2007), pp. 987–1008.
14. J. Surowiecki, "The Fatal-Flaw Myth," *The New Yorker* (July 31, 2006), p. 25.
15. C. Tuna, "No-Layoff Policies Crumble," *The Wall Street Journal* (December 29, 2008), p. B2.
16. See, for instance, S. D. Pugh, J. Dietz, J. W. Wiley, and S. M. Brooks, "Driving Service Effectiveness through Employee-Customer Linkages," *Academy of Management Executive* (November 2002), pp. 73–84; and H. Liao and A. Chuang, "A Multilevel Investigation of Factors Influencing Employee Service Performance and Customer Outcomes," *Academy of Management Journal* (February 2004), pp. 41–58.
17. See www.patagonia.com/jobs/retail_asst_mgr.shtml; and "Patagonia Sets the Pace for Green Business," *Grist Magazine* (October 22, 2004), www.grist.org.
18. See, for instance, M. Workman and W. Bommer, "Redesigning Computer Call Center Work: A Longitudinal Field Experiment," *Journal of Organizational Behavior* (May 2004), pp. 317–337.
19. See, for instance, V. S. Major, K. J. Klein, and M. G. Ehrhart, "Work Time, Work Interference with Family, and Psychological Distress," *Journal of Applied Psychology* (June 2002), pp. 427–436; D. Brady, "Rethinking the Rat Race," *BusinessWeek* (August 26, 2002), pp. 142–143; J. M. Brett and L. K. Stroh, "Working 61

Plus Hours a Week: Why Do Managers Do It?" *Journal of Applied Psychology* (February 2003), pp. 67–78.

20. See, for instance, *The 2002 National Study of the Changing Workforce* (New York: Families and Work Institute, 2002); and W. J. Casper and L. C. Buffardi, "Work-Life Benefits and Job Pursuit Intentions: The Role of Anticipated Organizational Support," *Journal of Vocational Behavior* 65, no. 3 (2004), pp. 391–410.

21. Cited in S. Armour, "Workers Put Family First Despite Slow Economy, Jobless Fear" (citation number 21) is: S. Armour, "Workers Put Family First Despite Slow Economy, Jobless Fears," USA Today, (June 6, 2002), p. 38.

22. S. Shellenbarger, "What Job Candidates Really Want to Know: Will I Have a Life?" *The Wall Street Journal* (November 17, 1999), p. B1; and "U.S. Employers Polish Image to Woo a Demanding New Generation," *Manpower Argus* (February 2000), p. 2.

23. F. Luthans and C. M. Youssef, "Emerging Positive Organizational Behavior," *Journal of Management* (June 2007), pp. 321–349; C. M. Youssef and F. Luthans, "Positive Organizational Behavior in the Workplace: The Impact of Hope, Optimism, and Resilience," *Journal of Management* 33, no. 5 (2007), pp. 774–800; and J. E. Dutton and S. Sonenshein, "Positive Organizational Scholarship," in C. Cooper and J. Barling (eds.), *Encyclopedia of Positive Psychology* (Thousand Oaks, CA: Sage, 2007).

24. L. M. Roberts, G. Spreitzer, J. Dutton, R. Quinn, E. Heaphy, and B. Barker, "How to Play to Your Strengths," *Harvard Business Review* (January 2005), pp. 1–6; and L. M. Roberts, J. E. Dutton, G. M. Spreitzer, E. D. Heaphy, and R. E. Quinn, "Composing the Reflected Best-Self Portrait: Becoming Extraordinary in Work Organizations," *Academy of Management Review* 30, no. 4 (2005), pp. 712–736.

25. W. Bailey and A. Spicer, "When Does National Identity Matter? Convergence and Divergence in International Business Ethics," *Academy of Management Journal* 50, no. 6 (2007), pp. 1462–1480; and A. B. Oumlil and J. L. Balloun,

"Ethical Decision-Making Differences between American and Moroccan Managers," *Journal of Business Ethics* 84, no. 4 (2009), pp. 457–478.

26. J. Merritt, "For MBAs, Soul-Searching 101," *BusinessWeek* (September 16, 2002), pp. 64–66; and S. Greenhouse, "The Mood at Work: Anger and Anxiety," *The New York Times* (October 29, 2002), p. E1.

27. See, for instance, G. R. Weaver, L. K. Trevino, and P. L. Cochran, "Corporate Ethics Practices in the Mid-1990's: An Empirical Study of the Fortune 1000," *Journal of Business Ethics* (February 1999), pp. 283–294; and C. De Mesa Graziano, "Promoting Ethical Conduct: A Review of Corporate Practices," *Strategic Investor Relations* (Fall 2002), pp. 29–35.

28. D. M. Mayer, M. Kuenzi, R. Greenbaum, M. Bardes, and R. Salvador, "How Low Does Ethical Leadership Flow? Test of a Trickle-Down Model," *Organizational Behavior and Human Decision Processes* 108, no. 1 (2009), pp. 1–13; and A. Ardichvili, J. A. Mitchell, and D. Jondle, "Characteristics of Ethical Business Cultures," *Journal of Business Ethics* 85, no. 4 (2009), pp. 445–451.

29. "Unplanned Absence Costs Organizations 8.7 Percent of Payroll, Mercer/Kronos Study" (June 28, 2010), www.mercer.com/press-releases/1383785.

30. W. Hoge, "Sweden's Cradle-to-Grave Welfare Starts to Get Ill," *International Herald Tribune* (September 25, 2002), p. 8.

31. See www.bls.gov/data (May 11, 2005).

32. See, for example, M. C. Sturman and C. O. Trevor, "The Implications of Linking the Dynamic Performance and Turnover Literatures," *Journal of Applied Psychology* (August 2001), pp. 684–696.

33. M. Casey-Campbell and M. L. Martens, "Sticking It All Together: A Critical Assessment of the Group Cohesion-Performance Literature," *International Journal of Management Reviews* 11, (2008), pp. 223–246.

34. A. J. Rucci, S. P. Kirn, and R. T. Quinn, "The Employee–Customer–Profit Chain at Sears," *Harvard Business Review* (January–February 1998), pp. 83–97.

LEARNING OBJECTIVES

After studying this chapter, you should be able to:

1 Describe the two major forms of workforce diversity.

2 Recognize stereotypes and understand how they function in organizational settings.

3 Identify the key biographical characteristics and describe how they are relevant to OB.

4 Define *intellectual ability* and demonstrate its relevance to OB.

5 Contrast intellectual and physical ability.

6 Describe how organizations manage diversity effectively.

THE RISE AND FALL OF ERIN CALLAN

Erin Callan was one of those rare individuals who seemed to master everything she undertook. Due to her precocious intelligence and athletic prowess (at 13 she was one of the top gymnasts in New York), people called her Wonder Child. She graduated magna cum laude from Harvard, earned her law degree from New York University, and went to work for one of the most prestigious law firms in New York City. In 1995, she went into banking, eventually rising to be chief financial officer (CFO) of one of the largest and most prestigious U.S. investment banks, Lehman Brothers. At 41—young for a CFO of such a large organization—Callan seemed to have it all. She was the first woman ever to serve on the 158-year-old company's executive committee. One newspaper labeled her "Rising Star Erin Callan, now one of the most powerful women on Wall Street."

Now Callan is jobless and living in virtual exile on Long Island.

What happened?

The story of Erin Callan's fall has a lot to do with the meltdown in the financial services industry. Lehman, after all, went bankrupt in 2008, and most senior executives lost their jobs. Most of its managers and executives, however, have found work elsewhere. Why not Callan? The answer depends on which narrative you accept. Callan refuses to discuss the issue with the media. To some, she brought about her own downfall with her outsized ambition and desire for attention. To others, she is the victim of a gender double standard that is alive and well on Wall Street and elsewhere.

From one point of view, Callan caused her own demise. She lacked background in accounting, treasury, or operations—unusual for a CFO. According to *Fortune,* many at Lehman disapproved of her brash style and provocative wardrobe. "I don't subordinate my feminine side," she says. "I'm very open about it. I have no problem talking about my shopper or my outfit." When Callan was named CFO, one of Lehman's female senior executives went to the CEO to rescind the promotion. Later, in the early days of the financial meltdown, investors thought Callan's responses were unimpressive. A few months later, she was removed. Currently, the Securities and Exchange Commission (SEC) is investigating whether her "forward looking statements" regarding Lehman's finances constitute civil fraud.

Read this way, Callan's is the typical story of a Wall Street executive caught unprepared for a crisis his or her decisions helped create. Is the story so simple, though? After all, nearly all Callan's male counterparts at Lehman are now employed, including ex-CEO Richard Fuld (now managing member of Matrix Advisors and advisor with Legend Securities). Many have landed at Barclays, the British Bank that bought Lehman in bankruptcy.

Diversity in Organizations

I think that God in creating Man somewhat overestimated his ability.

— Oscar Wilde

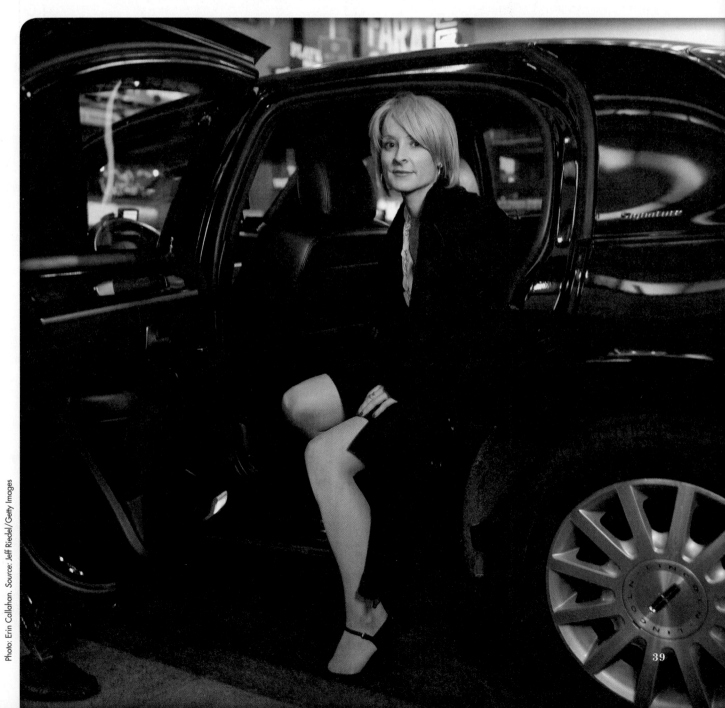

Does Callan's sex have a role in this? Does an interest in fashion serve to stigmatize women more than men? Does an interest in the media ("She was a media hound," said one Lehman executive) cast women in a harsher light?

Even National Public Radio (NPR) seemed to emphasize Callan's looks over her intellect. "Blonde, beautiful and outspoken, the spotlight loved Erin Callan. *Fortune* magazine called her one of four women to watch," said NPR. "Callan cut a striking figure in her crochet-style dress, gold dangling earrings and high-heeled boots." *Fortune* said, "She arrived like a flash—a bright, glamorous figure." Were such descriptions applied to the male CFOs of Goldman Sachs, Morgan Stanley, Merrill Lynch, or Bear Stearns?

As for Callan, friends say she is at peace with herself and her situation. "I'm living a different life," she recently told a reporter.

Sources: P. Sellers, "The Fall of a Wall Street Highflier," *Fortune* (March 22, 2010), pp. 140–148; P. Sellers, "Erin Callan, Lehman's Ex-CFO, Goes Public," *CNN Money* (February 22, 2011), www .cnnmoney.com/; J. Quinn, "Goldman Outshines Rival Bear Stearns," *The Telegraph* (September 21, 2007), www.telegraph.co.uk/; and C. Gasparino, "Lehman Probe Begins to Square in on Former CFO," *FOXBusiness* (June 10, 2010), www.foxbusiness.com/.

Sex is but one characteristic people bring with them when they join an organization. In this chapter, we look at how organizations work to maximize the potential contributions of a diverse workforce. We also show how demographic characteristics such as ethnicity and individual differences in the form of ability affect employee performance and satisfaction.

But first check out the following Self-Assessment Library, where you can assess your views on one of the characteristics we'll discuss in this chapter: age.

SELF-ASSESSMENT LIBRARY

What's My Attitude Toward Older People?

In the Self-Assessment Library (available on CD or online), take assessment IV.C.1 (What's My Attitude Toward Older People?) and answer the following questions:

1. Are you surprised by your results?
2. How do your results compare to those of others?

Diversity

1 Describe the two major forms of workforce diversity.

We aren't all the same. This is obvious enough, but managers sometimes forget that they need to recognize and capitalize on these differences to get the most from their employees. Effective diversity management increases an organization's access to the widest possible pool of skills, abilities, and ideas. Managers also need to recognize that differences among people can lead to miscommunication, misunderstanding, and conflict. In this chapter, we'll learn about how individual characteristics like age, gender, race, ethnicity, and abilities can influence employee performance. We'll also see how managers can develop awareness about these characteristics and manage a diverse workforce effectively.

Demographic Characteristics of the U.S. Workforce

In the past, OB textbooks noted that rapid change was about to occur as the predominantly white, male managerial workforce gave way to a gender-balanced, multiethnic workforce. Today, that change is no longer happening: it has happened, and it is increasingly reflected in the makeup of managerial and professional jobs. Compared to 1976, women today are much more likely to be employed full-time, have more education, and earn wages comparable to those of men.[1] In addition, over the past 50 years the earnings gap between Whites and other racial and ethnic groups has decreased significantly; past differences between Whites and Asians have disappeared or been reversed.[2] Workers over the age of 55 are an increasingly large portion of the workforce as well. This permanent shift toward a diverse workforce means organizations need to make diversity management a central component of their policies and practices. At the same time, however, differences in wages across genders and racial and ethnic groups persist, and executive positions in *Fortune* 500 corporations continue to be held by white males in numbers far beyond their representation in the workforce in general.

A survey by the Society for Human Resources Management shows some major employer concerns and opportunities resulting from the demographic makeup of the U.S. workforce.[3] The aging of the workforce was consistently the most significant concern of HR managers. The loss of skills resulting from the retirement of many baby boomers, increased medical costs due to an aging workforce, and many employees' needs to care for elderly relatives topped the list of issues. Other issues include developing multilingual training materials and providing work–life benefits for dual-career couples.

Progress Energy reflects the demographic characteristics of the U.S. workforce today. It is gender balanced, multiethnic, and engaged in learning about diversity issues and putting them into practice. Progress, which recently merged with Duke Energy, encourages employees to participate in various network groups, diversity councils, and training workshops, such as the one shown here. The company believes that recognizing and embracing diversity maximize employee potential, customer satisfaction, and business success.

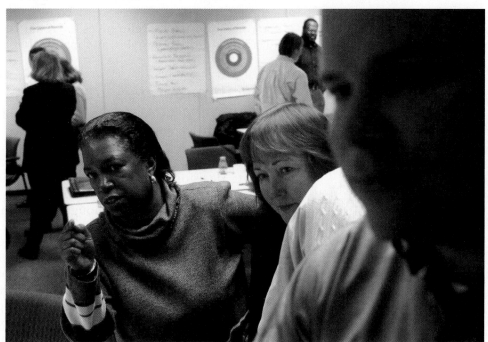

Source: Robert Willett / Raleigh News & Observer/Newscom

Levels of Diversity

Although much has been said about diversity in age, race, gender, ethnicity, religion, and disability status, experts now recognize that these demographic characteristics are just the tip of the iceberg.[4] Demographics mostly reflect **surface-level diversity**, not thoughts and feelings, and can lead employees to perceive one another through stereotypes and assumptions. However, evidence has shown that as people get to know one another, they become less concerned about demographic differences if they see themselves as sharing more important characteristics, such as personality and values, that represent **deep-level diversity**.[5]

To understand this difference between surface- and deep-level diversity, consider a few examples. Luis and Carol are co-workers who seem to have little in common at first glance. Luis is a young, recently hired male college graduate with a business degree, raised in a Spanish-speaking neighborhood in Miami. Carol is an older, long-tenured woman raised in rural Kansas, who achieved her current level in the organization by starting as a high school graduate and working her way through the hierarchy. At first, these co-workers may experience some differences in communication based on their surface-level differences in education, ethnicity, regional background, and gender. However, as they get to know one another, they may find they are both deeply committed to their families, share a common way of thinking about important work problems, like to work collaboratively, and are interested in international assignments in the future. These deep-level similarities will overshadow the more superficial differences between them, and research suggests they will work well together.

On the other hand, Steve and Dave are two unmarried white male college graduates from Oregon who recently started working together. Superficially, they seem well matched. But Steve is highly introverted, prefers to avoid risks, solicits the opinions of others before making decisions, and likes the office quiet, while Dave is extroverted, risk-seeking, and assertive and likes a busy, active, and energetic work environment. Their surface-level similarity will not necessarily lead to positive interactions because they have such fundamental, deep-level differences. It will be a challenge for them to collaborate regularly at work, and they'll have to make some compromises to get things done together.

Throughout this book, we will encounter differences between deep- and surface-level diversity in various contexts. Individual differences in personality and culture shape preferences for rewards, communication styles, reactions to leaders, negotiation styles, and many other aspects of behavior in organizations.

Discrimination

2 Recognize stereotypes and understand how they function in organizational settings.

Although diversity does present many opportunities for organizations, effective diversity management also means working to eliminate unfair **discrimination**. To discriminate is to note a difference between things, which in itself isn't necessarily bad. Noticing one employee is more qualified is necessary for making hiring decisions; noticing another is taking on leadership responsibilities exceptionally well is necessary for making promotion decisions. Usually when we talk about discrimination, though, we mean allowing our behavior to be influenced by stereotypes about *groups* of people. Rather than looking at individual characteristics, unfair discrimination assumes everyone in a group is the same. This discrimination is often very harmful to organizations and employees.

Exhibit 2-1 provides definitions and examples of some forms of discrimination in organizations. Although many of these actions are prohibited by law, and therefore aren't part of almost any organization's official policies, thousands of cases of employment discrimination are documented every year, and many more go unreported. As discrimination has increasingly come under both

Exhibit 2-1   Forms of Discrimination

Type of Discrimination	Definition	Examples from Organizations
Discriminatory policies or practices	Actions taken by representatives of the organization that deny equal opportunity to perform or unequal rewards for performance	Older workers may be targeted for layoffs because they are highly paid and have lucrative benefits.
Sexual harassment	Unwanted sexual advances and other verbal or physical conduct of a sexual nature that create a hostile or offensive work environment	Salespeople at one company went on company-paid visits to strip clubs, brought strippers into the office to celebrate promotions, and fostered pervasive sexual rumors.
Intimidation	Overt threats or bullying directed at members of specific groups of employees	African-American employees at some companies have found nooses hanging over their work stations.
Mockery and insults	Jokes or negative stereotypes; sometimes the result of jokes taken too far	Arab-Americans have been asked at work whether they were carrying bombs or were members of terrorist organizations.
Exclusion	Exclusion of certain people from job opportunities, social events, discussions, or informal mentoring; can occur unintentionally	Many women in finance claim they are assigned to marginal job roles or are given light workloads that don't lead to promotion.
Incivility	Disrespectful treatment, including behaving in an aggressive manner, interrupting the person, or ignoring his or her opinions	Female lawyers note that male attorneys frequently cut them off or do not adequately address their comments.

Sources: J. Levitz and P. Shishkin, "More Workers Cite Age Bias after Layoffs," *The Wall Street Journal* (March 11, 2009), pp. D1–D2; W. M. Bulkeley, "A Data-Storage Titan Confronts Bias Claims," *The Wall Street Journal* (September 12, 2007), pp. A1, A16; D. Walker, "Incident with Noose Stirs Old Memories," *McClatchy-Tribune Business News* (June 29, 2008); D. Solis, "Racial Horror Stories Keep EEOC Busy," *Knight-Ridder Tribune Business News,* July 30, 2005, p. 1; H. Ibish and A. Stewart, *Report on Hate Crimes and Discrimination Against Arab Americans: The Post-September 11 Backlash, September 11, 2001—October 11, 2001* (Washington, DC: American-Arab Anti-Discrimination Committee, 2003); A. Raghavan, "Wall Street's Disappearing Women," *Forbes* (March 16, 2009), pp. 72–78; and L. M. Cortina, "Unseen Injustice: Incivility as Modern Discrimination in Organizations," *Academy of Management Review* 33, no. 1 (2008), pp. 55–75.

legal scrutiny and social disapproval, most overt forms have faded, which may have resulted in an increase in more covert forms like incivility or exclusion.[6]

As you can see, discrimination can occur in many ways, and its effects can be just as varied depending on the organizational context and the personal biases of its members. Some forms, like exclusion or incivility, are especially hard to root out because they are impossible to observe and may occur simply because the actor isn't aware of the effects of his or her actions. Whether intentional or not, discrimination can lead to serious negative consequences for employers, including reduced productivity and citizenship behavior, negative conflicts, and increased turnover. Unfair discrimination also leaves qualified job candidates out of initial hiring and promotions. Even if an employment discrimination lawsuit is never filed, a strong business case can be made for aggressively working to eliminate unfair discrimination.

Diversity is a broad term, and the phrase *workplace diversity* can refer to any characteristic that makes people different from one another. The following section covers some important surface-level characteristics that differentiate members of the workforce.

surface-level diversity *Differences in easily perceived characteristics, such as gender, race, ethnicity, age, or disability, that do not necessarily reflect the ways people think or feel but that may activate certain stereotypes.*

deep-level diversity *Differences in values, personality, and work preferences that become progressively more important for determining similarity as people get to know one another better.*

discrimination *Noting of a difference between things; often we refer to unfair discrimination, which means making judgments about individuals based on stereotypes regarding their demographic group.*

Biographical Characteristics

3 Identify the key biographical characteristics and describe how they are relevant to OB.

Biographical characteristics such as age, gender, race, disability, and length of service are some of the most obvious ways employees differ. As discussed in Chapter 1, this textbook is essentially concerned with finding and analyzing the variables that affect employee productivity, absence, turnover, deviance, citizenship, and satisfaction (refer back to Exhibit 1-4). Many organizational concepts—motivation, say, or power and politics or organizational culture—are hard to assess. Let's begin, then, by looking at factors that are easily definable and readily available—data that can be obtained, for the most part, from an employee's human resources (HR) file. Variations in these surface-level characteristics may be the basis for discrimination against classes of employees, so it is worth knowing how closely related they actually are to important work outcomes. Many are not as important as people believe, and far more variation occurs *within* groups sharing biographical characteristics than between them.

Age

The relationship between age and job performance is likely to be an issue of increasing importance during the next decade for at least three reasons. First, belief is widespread that job performance declines with increasing age. Regardless of whether this is true, a lot of people believe it and act on it. Second, as noted in Chapter 1, the workforce is aging. Many employers recognize that older workers represent a huge potential pool of high-quality applicants. Companies such as Borders and the Vanguard Group have sought to increase their attractiveness to older workers by providing targeted training that meets their needs, and by offering flexible work schedules and part-time work to draw in those who are semi-retired.[7] The third reason is U.S. legislation that, for all intents and purposes, outlaws mandatory retirement. Most U.S. workers today no longer have to retire at age 70.

Older employees are an integral part of the workforce at Publix Supermarkets, where one in five employees is over the age of 50. The company values the work ethic and maturity of its senior associates like the man shown here preparing salmon pinwheels for customers to sample. Publix is known for its employment of senior citizens and actively recruits older workers as part of its corporate philosophy of providing a diverse work place. The company believes that older workers have a strong work ethic, many skills, and job knowledge that they can share with younger co-workers.

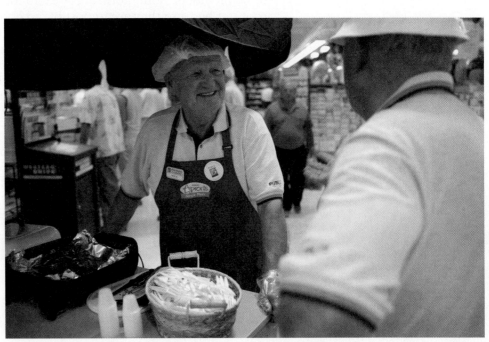

What is the perception of older workers? Employers hold mixed feelings.[8] They see a number of positive qualities older workers bring to their jobs, such as experience, judgment, a strong work ethic, and commitment to quality. But older workers are also perceived as lacking flexibility and resisting new technology. And when organizations are actively seeking individuals who are adaptable and open to change, the negatives associated with age clearly hinder the initial hiring of older workers and increase the likelihood they will be let go during cutbacks.

Now let's take a look at the evidence. What effect does age actually have on turnover, absenteeism, productivity, and satisfaction? The older you get, the less likely you are to quit your job. That conclusion is based on studies of the age–turnover relationship.[9] Of course, this shouldn't be too surprising. As workers get older, they have fewer alternative job opportunities as their skills have become more specialized to certain types of work. Their long tenure also tends to provide them with higher wage rates, longer paid vacations, and more attractive pension benefits.

It's tempting to assume that age is also inversely related to absenteeism. After all, if older workers are less likely to quit, won't they also demonstrate higher stability by coming to work more regularly? Not necessarily. Most studies do show an inverse relationship, but close examination finds it is partially a function of whether the absence is avoidable or unavoidable.[10] In general, older employees have lower rates of avoidable absence than do younger employees. However, they have equal rates of unavoidable absence, such as sickness absences.

How does age affect productivity? Many believe productivity declines with age. It is often assumed that skills like speed, agility, strength, and coordination decay over time and that prolonged job boredom and lack of intellectual stimulation contribute to reduced productivity. The evidence, however, contradicts those assumptions. During a 3-year period, a large hardware chain staffed one of its stores solely with employees over age 50 and compared its results with those of five stores with younger employees. The store staffed by the over-50 employees was significantly more productive (in terms of sales generated against labor costs) than two of the stores and held its own against the other three.[11] Other reviews of the research find that age and job task performance are unrelated and that older workers are more likely to engage in citizenship behavior.[12]

Our final concern is the relationship between age and job satisfaction, where the evidence is mixed. A review of more than 800 studies found that older workers tend to be more satisfied with their work, report better relationships with co-workers, and are more committed to their employing organizations.[13] Other studies, however, have found a U-shaped relationship.[14] Several explanations could clear up these results, the most plausible being that these studies are intermixing professional and nonprofessional employees. When we separate the two types, satisfaction tends to continually increase among professionals as they age, whereas it falls among nonprofessionals during middle age and then rises again in the later years.

biographical characteristics   *Personal characteristics—such as age, gender, race, and length of tenure—that are objective and easily obtained from personnel records. These characteristics are representative of surface-level diversity.*

What are the effects of discrimination against individuals on the basis of age? One large-scale study of more than 8,000 employees in 128 companies found that an organizational climate favoring age discrimination was associated with lower levels of commitment to the company. This lower commitment was, in turn, related to lower levels of organizational performance.[15] Such results suggest that combating age discrimination may be associated with higher levels of organizational performance.

Sex

Few issues initiate more debates, misconceptions, and unsupported opinions than whether women perform as well on jobs as men do.

The best place to begin to consider this is with the recognition that few, if any, important differences between men and women affect job performance. There are no consistent male–female differences in problem-solving ability, analytical skills, competitive drive, motivation, sociability, or learning ability.[16] Psychological studies have found women are more agreeable and willing to conform to authority, whereas men are more aggressive and more likely to have expectations of success, but those differences are minor. Given the significantly increased female participation in the workforce over the past 40 years and the rethinking of what constitutes male and female roles, we can assume no significant difference in job productivity between men and women.[17]

Unfortunately, sex roles still affect our perceptions. For example, women who succeed in traditionally male domains are perceived as less likable, more hostile, and less desirable as supervisors.[18] Interestingly, research also suggests that women believe sex-based discrimination is more prevalent than do male employees, and these beliefs are especially pronounced among women who work with a large proportion of men.[19]

One issue that does seem to differ between men and women, especially when the employee has preschool-age children, is preference for work schedules.[20] Working mothers are more likely to prefer part-time work, flexible work schedules, and telecommuting in order to accommodate their family responsibilities. Women also prefer jobs that encourage work–life balance, which has the effect of limiting their options for career advancement. An interview study showed many of the work–life issues found in U.S. business contexts are also common in France, despite government subsidies for child care.[21]

What about absence and turnover rates? Are women less stable employees than men? First, evidence from a study of nearly 500,000 professional employees indicates significant differences, with women more likely to turn over than men.[22] Women also have higher rates of absenteeism than men do.[23] The most logical explanation is that the research was conducted in North America, and North American culture has historically placed home and family responsibilities on women. When a child is ill or someone needs to stay home to wait for a plumber, the woman has traditionally taken time from work. However, this research is also undoubtedly time-bound.[24] The role of women has definitely changed over the past generation. Men are increasingly sharing responsibility for child care, and an increasing number report feeling a conflict between their home responsibilities and their work lives.[25] One interesting finding is that regardless of sex, parents were rated lower in job commitment, achievement striving, and dependability than individuals without children, but mothers were rated especially low in competence.[26]

Again, it is worth asking what the implications of sex discrimination are for individuals. Research has shown that workers who experience sexual harassment

OB Poll   ## Sexual Harassment Claims by Men

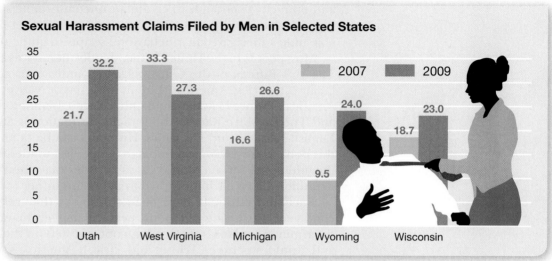

Sexual Harassment Claims Filed by Men in Selected States

	2007	2009
Utah	21.7	32.2
West Virginia	33.3	27.3
Michigan	16.6	26.6
Wyoming	9.5	24.0
Wisconsin	18.7	23.0

Sources: Equal Employment Opportunity Commission; D. Mattioli, "More Men Make Harassment Claims," *The Wall Street Journal* (March 23, 2010), p. D4.

have higher levels of psychological stress, and these feelings in turn are related to lower levels of organizational commitment and job satisfaction, and higher intentions to turn over.[27] As with age discrimination, the evidence suggests that combating sex discrimination may be associated with better performance for the organization as a whole.

Myth or Science?

"Dual-Career Couples Divorce Less"

This statement is mostly false.

A recent large-scale study of married couples in the United States, the United Kingdom, and Germany found that in all three countries whether a wife worked outside the home, and what she earned if she did, had no effect on divorce rates. The authors of this study conclude: "In no country did a wife's employment or relative earnings significantly increase the risk of dissolution." Thus, it appears that social critics on both the left (dual-career couples have healthier, happier marriages) and the right (a traditional male working, wife at home family structure is best) are wrong. Still,

this is a complex issue, and research on it continues.

What about whether the *husband* works outside the home? Historically, this was quite unusual, but it is becoming increasingly common—wives are now the primary breadwinner in 22 percent of U.S. couples, up from 7 percent in 1970. There is some evidence that men are less healthy and marriages are more likely to fail when men do not work outside the home, or when they become unemployed while their wives continue to work. As one researcher noted, many married men ask themselves, "What is my value here if I'm not bringing in money?" One

Canadian working mother, the primary breadwinner in her family, says, "There is a part of me that wonders if I can trust, if it's safe for me to take my foot off the gas, to hold back and relax, not be thinking and working all the time."

Sources: L. P. P. Cooke, "Wives' Part-time Employment and Marital Stability in Great Britain, West Germany and the United States," *Sociology* 44, no. 6 (2010), pp. 1091–1108; T. Parker-Pope, "She Works. They're Happy." *The New York Times* (January 24, 2010), pp. ST1, ST10; and S. Proudfoot, "More Women Bringing Home the Bacon, More Men Cooking It," *National Post* (October 7, 2010), www.canada.com/.

Race and Ethnicity

Race is a controversial issue. In many cases, even bringing up the topic of race and ethnicity is enough to create an uncomfortable silence. Indeed, evidence suggests that some people find interacting with other racial groups uncomfortable unless there are clear behavioral scripts to guide their behavior.[28]

Most people in the United States identify themselves according to racial group. The U.S. Bureau of the Census classifies individuals according to seven broad racial categories: American Indian and Alaska Native, Asian, Black or African American, Native Hawaiian and Other Pacific Islander, Some Other Race, White, and Two or More Races. An ethnicity distinction is also made between native English speakers and Hispanics: Hispanics can be of any race. We define *race* in this book as the biological heritage people use to identify themselves; *ethnicity* is the additional set of cultural characteristics that often overlaps with race. This definition allows each individual to define his or her race and ethnicity.

Race and ethnicity have been studied as they relate to employment outcomes such as hiring decisions, performance evaluations, pay, and workplace discrimination. Most research has concentrated on the differences in outcomes and attitudes between Whites and African Americans, with little study of issues relevant to Asian, Native American, and Hispanic populations. Doing justice to all this research isn't possible here, so let's summarize a few points.

First, in employment settings, individuals tend to slightly favor colleagues of their own race in performance evaluations, promotion decisions, and pay raises, although such differences are not found consistently, especially when highly structured methods of decision making are employed.[29] Second, substantial racial differences exist in attitudes toward affirmative action, with African Americans approving of such programs to a greater degree than Whites.[30] This difference may reflect the fact that African Americans and Hispanics perceive discrimination to be more prevalent in the workplace.[31] Third, African Americans generally fare worse than Whites in employment decisions. They receive lower ratings in employment interviews, receive lower job performance ratings, are paid less, and are promoted less frequently.[32] Yet there are no statistically significant differences between African Americans and Whites in observed absence rates, applied social skills at work, or accident rates. African Americans and Hispanics also have higher turnover rates than Whites.

Employers' major concern about using mental-ability tests for selection, promotion, training, and similar employment decisions is that they may have a negative impact on racial and ethnic groups.[33] However, evidence suggests that "despite group differences in mean test performance, there is little convincing evidence that well-constructed tests are more predictive of educational, training, or occupational performance for members of the majority group than for members of minority groups."[34] Observed differences in IQ test scores by racial or ethnic group are smaller in more recent samples.[35] The issue of racial differences in general mental-ability tests continues to be hotly debated.[36]

Does racial and ethnic discrimination lead to negative workplace outcomes? As noted earlier, most research shows that members of racial and ethnic minorities report higher levels of discrimination in the workplace.[37] Some research suggests that having a positive climate for diversity overall can lead to increased sales.[38]

Disability

With the passage of the Americans with Disabilities Act (ADA) in 1990, the representation of individuals with disabilities in the U.S. workforce rapidly increased.[39] According to the ADA, employers are required to make reasonable

Microsoft views employees with disabilities as valuable assets because they help ensure that the company's products and services meet all customer needs. At the Microsoft Accessibility Lab, employees can experience assistive technologies and ergonomic hardware designs that enable them to be more productive. Kelly Ford, who has been blind since birth, is shown here in the lab testing accessibility features of the Windows operating system. Ford also manages a team that is working on improving Web page browsing for all users, not just for people with disabilities.

Source: AP Photo/Ted S. Warren

accommodations so their workplaces will be accessible to individuals with physical or mental disabilities.

Making inferences about the relationship between disability and employment outcomes is difficult because the term *disability* is so broad. The U.S. Equal Employment Opportunity Commission classifies a person as disabled who has any physical or mental impairment that substantially limits one or more major life activities. Examples include missing limbs, seizure disorder, Down Syndrome, deafness, schizophrenia, alcoholism, diabetes, and chronic back pain. These conditions share almost no common features, so there's no generalization about how each condition is related to employment. Some jobs obviously cannot be accommodated to some disabilities—the law and common sense recognize that a blind person could not be a bus driver, a person with severe cerebral palsy could not be a surgeon, and a person with profound mobility constraints probably could not be a police patrol officer. However, the increasing presence of computer technology and other adaptive devices is shattering many traditional barriers to employment.

One of the most controversial aspects of the ADA is the provision that requires employers to make reasonable accommodations for people with psychiatric disabilities.[40] Most people have very strong biases against those with mental illnesses, who are therefore reluctant to disclose this information to employers. Many who do, report negative consequences.

The impact of disabilities on employment outcomes has been explored from a variety of perspectives. On the one hand, a review of the evidence suggests workers with disabilities receive higher performance evaluations. However, this same review found that despite their higher performance, individuals with disabilities tend to encounter lower performance expectations and are less likely to be hired.[41] These negative effects are much stronger for individuals with mental disabilities, and there is some evidence to suggest mental disabilities may impair performance more than physical disabilities: Individuals with such common mental health issues as depression and anxiety are significantly more likely to be absent from work.[42]

Several studies have examined participants who received résumés that were identical, except that some mentioned a disability. The résumés that mentioned mental illness or a physical disability were associated with much lower ratings for perceived employability, especially in jobs requiring a great deal of personal contact with the public.[43] Employability ratings for individuals with mental illnesses were especially low. Similarly, when given randomly manipulated academic portfolios, students preferred not to work with individuals who had a learning disability even though there were no effects of disability on performance ratings or expectations.[44]

Contrast these selection-oriented results with studies showing that the accomplishments of those with disabilities are often rated as more impressive than the same accomplishments in people without disabilities. Participants watched three individuals completing a carpentry task, one of whom was described as having recently been hospitalized for a debilitating mental illness.[45] The raters consistently gave that person higher performance ratings. In this case, it may be that disabled individuals were being treated as an outgroup in need of special help. Similarly, when disability status is randomly manipulated among hypothetical candidates, disabled individuals are rated as having superior personal qualities like dependability and potency.[46]

Other Biographical Characteristics: Tenure, Religion, Sexual Orientation, and Gender Identity

The last set of biographical characteristics we'll look at includes tenure, religion, sexual orientation, and gender identity.

Tenure   Except for gender and racial differences, few issues are more subject to misconceptions and speculations than the impact of seniority on job performance.

Extensive reviews have been conducted of the seniority–productivity relationship.[47] If we define *seniority* as time on a particular job, the most recent evidence demonstrates a positive relationship between seniority and job productivity. So *tenure*, expressed as work experience, appears to be a good predictor of employee productivity.

The research relating tenure to absence is quite straightforward. Studies consistently show seniority to be negatively related to absenteeism.[48] In fact, in terms of both frequency of absence and total days lost at work, tenure is the single most important explanatory variable.[49]

Tenure is also a potent variable in explaining turnover. The longer a person is in a job, the less likely he or she is to quit.[50] Moreover, consistent with research suggesting past behavior is the best predictor of future behavior, evidence indicates tenure at an employee's previous job is a powerful predictor of that employee's future turnover.[51]

Evidence indicates tenure and job satisfaction are positively related.[52] In fact, when age and tenure are treated separately, tenure appears a more consistent and stable predictor of job satisfaction than age.

Religion   Not only do religious and nonreligious people question each other's belief systems; often people of different religious faiths conflict. As the war in Iraq and the past conflict in Northern Ireland demonstrate, violent differences can erupt among sects of the same religion. U.S. federal law prohibits employers from discriminating against employees based on their religion, with very few exceptions. However, that doesn't mean religion is a nonissue in OB.

Perhaps the greatest religious diversity issue in the United States today revolves around Islam. There are nearly 2 million Muslims in the United States,

Religious Tattoos

Considering the following situation . . .

Edward practices the Kemetic religion, based on ancient Egyptian faith, and affiliates himself with a tribe numbering fewer than ten members. He states that he believes in various deities and follows the faith's concept of Ma'at, a guiding principle regarding truth and order that represents physical and moral balance in the universe. During a religious ceremony he received small tattoos encircling his wrist, written in the Coptic language, which express his servitude to Ra, the Egyptian god of the sun. When his employer asks him to cover the tattoos, he explains

that it is a sin to cover them intentionally because doing so would signify a rejection of Ra.

If you were Edward's employer, how would you respond to his request? If several valued customers objected to Edward's tattoos, would it affect your response?

It may surprise you to learn that the Equal Employment Opportunity Commission (EEOC), the chief regulatory agency that enforces laws against workplace discrimination, holds that Edward's employer may not ask him to cover his tattoos. The seeming strangeness of Edward's religious views is not legally relevant. The EEOC notes,

"These can be religious beliefs and practices even if no one else or few other people subscribe to them." If Edward's tattoos did not emanate from sincere religious beliefs, however, the employer could ask him to cover them.

The upshot: Diversity, ethics, and legal compliance are not always the same thing. Sometimes what is legal is not what you might do, and sometimes what you might do is not legal.

Source: N. C. Earp, "Unique Belief Can Be Religious," *EEOC Compliance Manual* (downloaded April 27, 2011), www.eeoc.gov/policy/docs/religion.html.

and across the world Islam is one of the most popular religions. There are a wide variety of perspectives on Islam. As one Islamic scholar has noted, "There is no such thing as a single American Muslim community, much as there is no single Christian community. Muslims vary hugely by ethnicity, faith, tradition, education, income, and degree of religious observance."[53] For the most part, U.S. Muslims have attitudes similar to those of other U.S. citizens (though the differences tend to be greater for younger U.S. Muslims). Still, there are both perceived and real differences. Nearly four in ten U.S. adults admit they harbor negative feelings or prejudices toward U.S. Muslims, and 52 percent believe U.S. Muslims are not respectful of women. Some take these general biases a step further. Motaz Elshafi, a 28-year-old software engineer for Cisco Systems, born and raised in New Jersey, received an e-mail from a co-worker addressed "Dear Terrorist." Research has shown that job applicants in Muslim-identified religious attire who applied for hypothetical retail jobs in the United States had shorter, more interpersonally negative interviews than applicants who did not wear Muslim-identified attire.[54]

Faith can be an employment issue when religious beliefs prohibit or encourage certain behaviors. Based on their religious beliefs, some pharmacists refuse to hand out RU-486, the "morning after" abortion pill. Many Christians do not believe they should work on Sundays, and many conservative Jews believe they should not work on Saturdays. Religious individuals may also believe they have an obligation to express their beliefs in the workplace, and those who do not share those beliefs may object. Perhaps as a result of different perceptions of religion's role in the workplace, religious discrimination claims have been a growing source of discrimination claims in the United States.

Sexual Orientation and Gender Identity   Employers differ widely in their treatment of sexual orientation. Federal law does not prohibit discrimination against employees based on sexual orientation, though many states and municipalities do. In general, observers note that even in the absence of federal legislation requiring nondiscrimination, many organizations have implemented policies and procedures protecting employees on the basis of sexual orientation.[55]

Raytheon, builder of Tomahawk cruise missiles and other defense systems, offers domestic-partner benefits, supports a wide array of gay rights groups, and wants to be an employer of choice for gays. The firm believes these policies give it an advantage in the ever-competitive market for engineers and scientists. Raytheon is not alone. More than half the *Fortune* 500 companies offer domestic-partner benefits for gay couples, including American Express, IBM, Intel, Morgan Stanley, Motorola, and Walmart. Some companies oppose domestic-partner benefits or nondiscrimination clauses for gay employees. Among these are Alltel, ADM, ExxonMobil, H. J. Heinz, Nissan, Nestlé, and Rubbermaid.[56] Despite some gains, many lesbian, gay, and bisexual employees keep their gender identity from their co-workers for fear of being discriminated against.[57]

As for gender identity, companies are increasingly putting in place policies to govern how their organization treats employees who change genders (often called *transgender employees*). In 2001, only eight companies in the *Fortune* 500 had policies on gender identity. By 2006, that number had swelled to 124. IBM is one of them. Brad Salavich, a diversity manager for IBM, says, "We believe that having strong transgender and gender identification policies is a natural extension of IBM's corporate culture." Dealing with transgender employees requires some special considerations, such as for bathrooms, employee names, and so on.[58]

Ability

We've so far covered surface characteristics unlikely, on their own, to directly relate to job performance. Now we turn to deep-level abilities that *are* closely related to job performance. Contrary to what we were taught in grade school, we weren't all created equal in our abilities. Most people are to the left or the right of the median on some normally distributed ability curve. For example, regardless of how motivated you are, it's unlikely you can act as well as Scarlett Johansson, play basketball as well as LeBron James, write as well as J. K. Rowling, or play the guitar as well as Pat Metheny. Of course, just because we aren't all equal in abilities does not imply that some individuals are inherently inferior. Everyone has strengths and weaknesses that make him or her relatively superior or inferior to others in performing certain tasks or activities. From management's standpoint, the issue is not whether people differ in terms of their abilities. They clearly do. The issue is using the knowledge that people differ to increase the likelihood an employee will perform his or her job well.

What does *ability* mean? As we use the term, **ability** is an individual's current capacity to perform the various tasks in a job. Overall abilities are essentially made up of two sets of factors: intellectual and physical.

Intellectual Abilities

4   Define *intellectual ability* and demonstrate its relevance to OB.

Intellectual abilities are abilities needed to perform mental activities—thinking, reasoning, and problem solving. Most societies place a high value on intelligence, and for good reason. Smart people generally earn more money and attain higher levels of education. They are also more likely to emerge as leaders of

Exhibit 2-2	Dimensions of Intellectual Ability	

Dimension	Description	Job Example
Number aptitude	Ability to do speedy and accurate arithmetic	Accountant: Computing the sales tax on a set of items
Verbal comprehension	Ability to understand what is read or heard and the relationship of words to each other	Plant manager: Following corporate policies on hiring
Perceptual speed	Ability to identify visual similarities and differences quickly and accurately	Fire investigator: Identifying clues to support a charge of arson
Inductive reasoning	Ability to identify a logical sequence in a problem and then solve the problem	Market researcher: Forecasting demand for a product in the next time period
Deductive reasoning	Ability to use logic and assess the implications of an argument	Supervisor: Choosing between two different suggestions offered by employees
Spatial visualization	Ability to imagine how an object would look if its position in space were changed	Interior decorator: Redecorating an office
Memory	Ability to retain and recall past experiences	Salesperson: Remembering the names of customers

groups. Intelligence quotient (IQ) tests, for example, are designed to ascertain a person's general intellectual abilities. So, too, are popular college admission tests, such as the SAT and ACT and graduate admission tests in business (GMAT), law (LSAT), and medicine (MCAT). Testing firms don't claim their tests assess intelligence, but experts know they do.[59] The seven most frequently cited dimensions making up intellectual abilities are number aptitude, verbal comprehension, perceptual speed, inductive reasoning, deductive reasoning, spatial visualization, and memory.[60] Exhibit 2-2 describes these dimensions.

Intelligence dimensions are positively related, so if you score high on verbal comprehension, for example, you're more likely to also score high on spatial visualization. The correlations aren't perfect, meaning people do have specific abilities that predict important work-related outcomes when considered individually.[61] However, they are high enough that researchers also recognize a general factor of intelligence, **general mental ability (GMA)**. Evidence strongly supports the idea that the structures and measures of intellectual abilities generalize across cultures. Thus, someone in Venezuela or Sudan does not have a different set of mental abilities than a U.S. or Czech worker. There is some evidence that IQ scores vary to some degree across cultures, but those differences are much smaller when we take into account educational and economic differences.[62]

Jobs differ in the demands they place on intellectual abilities. The more complex a job in terms of information-processing demands, the more general intelligence and verbal abilities will be necessary to perform successfully.[63]

---

ability An individual's capacity to perform the various tasks in a job.

intellectual abilities The capacity to do mental activities—thinking, reasoning, and problem solving.

general mental ability (GMA) An overall factor of intelligence, as suggested by the positive correlations among specific intellectual ability dimensions.

glOBalization!

Images of Diversity from Around the Globe

As economic globalization continues to expand, the very idea of diversity management must expand to include a diversity of cultures and situations. Attitudes toward diversity programs range greatly across countries, with the idea of what constitutes a "diverse" workforce differing by culture and the demography of the country. The role of women in the workplace also varies, with some countries valuing sexual equality more than others. Other categories of diversity, like sexual orientation, are not recognized in some countries but are important elements of the diversity picture in others. A consideration of three international examples helps illustrate how diverse diversity programs can be.

In Singapore, diversity has become part of the national agenda. On "Racial Harmony Day," street carnivals are held to celebrate the nation's unique status as a crossroads of Chinese, Malay, Indian, and other cultures. Besides applauding these distinct national identities, the country's leaders have also prioritized these celebrations as a moment to emphasize the shared identity of being Singaporean. Brazil is a similarly diverse country; the major demographic groups addressed by Brazilian diversity policies include African descendant, European descendant, and Asian descendant, as well as disability status. Research suggests that diversity programs are relatively new to Brazil compared to Europe and North America, but companies are coming to see diversity management as a major component of their human resources systems. In India, diversity management often means addressing differences in social class and caste that do not arise in other countries, with affirmative action programs mandating the number of individuals from lower castes who must be included in management positions for some types of organizations.

Multinational organizations will have to carefully consider how to create diversity strategies given the variety of perspectives on diversity across countries. Many countries require specific targets and quotas for achieving affirmative action goals, whereas the legal framework in the United States specifically forbids their use. Some countries have strong prohibitions on sexual harassment, whereas in other countries behavior unacceptable in U.S. workplaces is common. Effectively managing diversity in multinational organizations is clearly a challenge of the global marketplace.

Sources: Based on D. P. S. Goh, "State Carnivals and the Subvention of Multiculturalism in Singapore," *The British Journal of Sociology* 62 (2011), pp. 111–133; C. J. C. Jabbour, F. S. Gordono, J. H. C. de Olivera, J. C. Martinez, and R. A. G. Battistelle, "Diversity Management: Challenges, Benefits, and the Role of Human Resource Management in Brazilian Organizations," *Equality, Diversity, and Inclusion: An International Journal* 30 (2011), pp. 58–74; and F. L. Cooke and D. S. Saini, "Diversity Management in India: A Study of Organizations in Different Ownership Forms and Industrial Sectors," *Human Resource Management* 49 (2010), pp. 477–500.

Where employee behavior is highly routine and there are few or no opportunities to exercise discretion, a high IQ is not as important to performing well. However, that does not mean people with high IQs cannot have an impact on traditionally less complex jobs.

It might surprise you that the most widely used intelligence test in hiring decisions takes only 12 minutes to complete. It's the Wonderlic Cognitive Ability Test. There are different forms, and each has 50 questions. Here are a few examples:

- When rope is selling at $0.10 a foot, how many feet can you buy for $0.60?
- Assume the first two statements are true. Is the final one:
    1. True.
    2. False.
    3. Not certain.
        a. The boy plays baseball.
        b. All baseball players wear hats.
        c. The boy wears a hat.

The Wonderlic measures both speed (almost nobody has time to answer every question) and power (questions get harder as you go along), so the average score is pretty low—about 21/50. And because it is able to provide valid information cheaply (for $5 to $10/applicant), more companies are using the Wonderlic in hiring decisions. The Factory Card & Party Outlet, with 182 stores nationwide, uses it. So do Subway, Peoples Flowers, Security Alarm, Workforce Employment Solutions, and many others. Most of these companies don't give up other hiring tools, such as application forms or interviews. Rather, they add the Wonderlic for its ability to provide valid data on applicants' intelligence levels.

Interestingly, while intelligence is a big help in performing a job well, it doesn't make people happier or more satisfied with their jobs. The correlation between intelligence and job satisfaction is about zero. Why? Research suggests that although intelligent people perform better and tend to have more interesting jobs, they are also more critical when evaluating their job conditions. Thus, smart people have it better, but they also expect more.[64]

Physical Abilities

5 Contrast intellectual and physical ability.

Though the changing nature of work suggests intellectual abilities are increasingly important for many jobs, **physical abilities** have been and will remain valuable. Research on hundreds of jobs has identified nine basic abilities needed in the performance of physical tasks.[65] These are described in Exhibit 2-3. Individuals differ in the extent to which they have each of these abilities. Not surprisingly, there is also little relationship among them: a high score on one is no assurance of a high score on others. High employee performance is likely to be achieved when management has ascertained the extent to which a job requires each of the nine abilities and then ensures that employees in that job have those abilities.

Exhibit 2-3	Nine Basic Physical Abilities
Strength Factors	
1. Dynamic strength	Ability to exert muscular force repeatedly or continuously over time
2. Trunk strength	Ability to exert muscular strength using the trunk (particularly abdominal) muscles
3. Static strength	Ability to exert force against external objects
4. Explosive strength	Ability to expend a maximum of energy in one or a series of explosive acts
Flexibility Factors	
5. Extent flexibility	Ability to move the trunk and back muscles as far as possible
6. Dynamic flexibility	Ability to make rapid, repeated flexing movements
Other Factors	
7. Body coordination	Ability to coordinate the simultaneous actions of different parts of the body
8. Balance	Ability to maintain equilibrium despite forces pulling off balance
9. Stamina	Ability to continue maximum effort requiring prolonged effort over time

physical abilities *The capacity to do tasks that demand stamina, dexterity, strength, and similar characteristics.*

The Role of Disabilities

The importance of ability at work obviously creates problems when we attempt to formulate workplace policies that recognize diversity in terms of disability status. As we have noted, recognizing that individuals have different abilities that can be taken into account when making hiring decisions is not problematic. However, it is discriminatory to make blanket assumptions about people on the basis of a disability. It is also possible to make accommodations for disabilities.

Implementing Diversity Management Strategies

MyManagementLab
For an interactive application of this topic, check out this chapter's simulation activity at
www.mymanagementlab.com.

Having discussed a variety of ways in which people differ, we now look at how a manager can and should manage these differences. **Diversity management** makes everyone more aware of and sensitive to the needs and differences of others. This definition highlights the fact that diversity programs include and are meant for everyone. Diversity is much more likely to be successful when we see it as everyone's business than if we believe it helps only certain groups of employees.

Attracting, Selecting, Developing, and Retaining Diverse Employees

One method of enhancing workforce diversity is to target recruiting messages to specific demographic groups underrepresented in the workforce. This means placing advertisements in publications geared toward specific demographic groups; recruiting at colleges, universities, and other institutions with significant numbers of underrepresented minorities; and forming partnerships with associations like the Society for Women Engineers or the Graduate Minority Business Association. These efforts can be successful, and research has shown that women and minorities do have greater interest in employers that make special efforts to highlight a commitment to diversity in their recruiting materials. Advertisements depicting groups of diverse employees are seen as more attractive to women and racioethnic minorities, which is probably why most organizations depict workforce diversity prominently in their recruiting materials. Diversity advertisements that fail to show women and minorities in positions of organizational leadership send a negative message about the diversity climate at an organization.[66]

The selection process is one of the most important places to apply diversity efforts. Managers who hire need to value fairness and objectivity in selecting employees and focus on the productive potential of new recruits. Fortunately, ensuring that hiring is bias-free does appear to work. Where managers use a well-defined protocol for assessing applicant talent and the organization clearly prioritizes nondiscrimination policies, qualifications become far more important in determining who gets hired than demographic characteristics.[67] Organizations that do not discourage discriminatory behavior are more likely to see problems.

Similarity in personality appears to affect career advancement. Those whose personality traits are similar to those of their co-workers are more likely to be promoted than those whose personalities are different.[68] There's an important qualifier to these results: in collectivistic cultures, similarity to supervisors is more important for predicting advancement, whereas in individualistic cultures,

In Japan, Nissan Motor Company is helping female employees develop their careers at the firm's manufacturing plants and car dealerships. Nissan provides women, such as the assembly-line worker shown here, with training programs to develop skills and the one-on-one counseling services of career advisors. Nissan also posts career interviews on its corporate intranet with women who have made significant contributions to the company and serve as role models for other female employees. For Nissan, developing the talents of women is a strategic imperative for its business success.

Source: AP Photo/Katsumi Kasahara

similarity to peers is more important. Once again, deep-level diversity factors appear to be more important in shaping people's reactions to one another than surface-level characteristics.

Evidence from a study of more than 6,000 workers in a major retail organization indicated that in stores with a less supportive diversity climate, African Americans or Hispanics made significantly fewer sales than White employees, but when the diversity climate was positive, Hispanics and Whites sold about the same amount and African Americans made more sales than Whites.[69] Whites sold about the same amount whether there was a positive diversity climate or not, but African Americans and Hispanics sold far more when there was. There are obvious bottom-line implications of this research: stores that fostered a positive diversity climate were able to capitalize on their diverse workforce and make more money.

Some data suggest individuals who are demographically different from their co-workers are more likely to feel low commitment and to turn over: women are more likely to turn over from predominantly male work groups and men from predominantly female work groups; non-Whites are more likely to turn over from predominantly White work groups and Whites from predominantly non-White work groups.[70] However, this behavior is more prominent among new hires. After people become better acquainted with one another, demographic differences are less consistently related to turnover. One very large-scale study showed a positive diversity climate was related to higher organizational commitment and lower turnover intentions among African-American, Hispanic, *and* White managers.[71] In other words, all workers appeared to prefer an organization that values diversity.

diversity management   *The process and programs by which managers make everyone more aware of and sensitive to the needs and differences of others.*

Diversity in Groups

Most contemporary workplaces require extensive work in group settings. When people work in groups, they need to establish a common way of looking at and accomplishing the major tasks, and they need to communicate with one another often. If they feel little sense of membership and cohesion in their groups, all these group attributes are likely to suffer.

Does diversity help or hurt group performance? The answer is "yes." In some cases, diversity in traits can hurt team performance, whereas in others it can facilitate it.[72] Whether diverse or homogeneous teams are more effective depends on the characteristic of interest. Demographic diversity (in gender, race, and ethnicity) does not appear to either help or hurt team performance in general. On the other hand, teams of individuals who are highly intelligent, conscientious, and interested in working in team settings are more effective. Thus diversity on these variables is likely to be a bad thing—it makes little sense to try to form teams that mix in members who are lower in intelligence, conscientiousness, and uninterested in teamwork. In other cases, differences can be a strength. Groups of individuals with different types of expertise and education are more effective than homogeneous groups. Similarly, a group made entirely of assertive people who want to be in charge, or a group whose members all prefer to follow the lead of others, will be less effective than a group that mixes leaders and followers.

Regardless of the composition of the group, differences can be leveraged to achieve superior performance. The most important way is to emphasize the higher-level similarities among members.[73] In other words, groups of diverse individuals will be much more effective if leaders can show how members have a common interest in the group's success. Evidence also shows transformational leaders (who emphasize higher-order goals and values in their leadership style) are more effective in managing diverse teams.[74]

Effective Diversity Programs

6 Describe how organizations manage diversity effectively.

Organizations use a variety of efforts to capitalize on diversity, including the recruiting and selection policies we have already discussed, as well as training and development practices. Effective, comprehensive workforce programs encouraging diversity have three distinct components. First, they teach managers about the legal framework for equal employment opportunity and encourage fair treatment of all people regardless of their demographic characteristics. Second, they teach managers how a diverse workforce will be better able to serve a diverse market of customers and clients. Third, they foster personal development practices that bring out the skills and abilities of all workers, acknowledging how differences in perspective can be a valuable way to improve performance for everyone.[75]

Much concern about diversity has to do with fair treatment.[76] Most negative reactions to employment discrimination are based on the idea that discriminatory treatment is unfair. Regardless of race or gender, people are generally in favor of diversity-oriented programs, including affirmative action, if they believe the policies ensure everyone a fair opportunity to show their skills and abilities.

A major study of the consequences of diversity programs came to what might seem a surprising conclusion.[77] Organizations that provided diversity training were not consistently more likely to have women and minorities in upper management positions than organizations that did not. On closer examination though, these results are not surprising. Experts have long known that one-shot training sessions without strategies to encourage effective diversity management back on the job are not likely to be very effective. Some diversity programs

NASCAR, an American sport with a worldwide following, promotes diversity within its organization and throughout the motorsports industry. Through its Drive to Diversity program, NASCAR ensures that everyone is given a fair opportunity to show and develop his or her skills and abilities. The program seeks to develop minority and female drivers and crew members as shown in this photo. Drivers participate in a scouting combine and earn the chance to compete with an established NASCAR team for a full season. And after completing their training, crew member trainees can compete with a racing team.

Source: Chuck Burton/AP Images

are truly effective in improving representation in management. They include strategies to measure the representation of women and minorities in managerial positions, and they hold managers accountable for achieving more demographically diverse management teams. Researchers also suggest that diversity experiences are more likely to lead to positive adaptation for all parties if (1) the diversity experience undermines stereotypical attitudes, (2) if the perceiver is motivated and able to consider a new perspective on others, (3) if the perceiver engages in stereotype suppression and generative thought in response to the diversity experience, and (4) if the positive experience of stereotype undermining is repeated frequently.[78] Diversity programs based on these principles are likely to be more effective than traditional classroom learning.

Organizational leaders should examine their workforce to determine whether target groups have been underutilized. If groups of employees are not proportionally represented in top management, managers should look for any hidden barriers to advancement. They can often improve recruiting practices, make selection systems more transparent, and provide training for those employees who have not had adequate exposure to certain material in the past. The organization should also clearly communicate its policies to employees so they can understand how and why certain practices are followed. Communications should focus as much as possible on qualifications and job performance; emphasizing certain groups as needing more assistance could well backfire. A case study of the multinational Finnish company TRANSCO found it was possible to develop a consistent global philosophy for diversity management. However, differences in legal and cultural factors across nations forced TRANSCO to develop unique policies to match the cultural and legal frameworks of each country in which it operated.[79]

To ensure the top-level management team represents the diversity of its workforce and client base, Safeway implemented the Retail Leadership Development (RLD) Program, a formal career development program. This program is open to all employees, so it is inclusive, but women and underrepresented racial or ethnic groups are particularly encouraged to participate. Interested individuals take a series of examinations to determine whether they have management potential. Those who perform well on the tests are provided with work in roles that expose them to managerial opportunities. The program's comprehensive nature is underscored by its additional support activities: All managers attend workshops that help them bring diversity concerns front and center in their staff meetings. They are also charged with providing promising RLD participants with additional training and development opportunities to ensure they have the skills needed for advancement. The program incorporates the type of accountability we have said is crucial to the success of diversity efforts; performance bonuses are provided to managers who meet concrete diversity goals. This program has shown real success: the number of White women store managers has increased by 31 percent since its inception, and the number of women-of-color store managers has increased by 92 percent.[80]

MyManagementLab

Now that you have finished this chapter, go back to **www.mymanagementlab.com** to continue practicing and applying the concepts you've learned.

Summary and Implications for Managers

This chapter looked at diversity from many perspectives. We paid particular attention to three variables—biographical characteristics, ability, and diversity programs. Let's summarize what we found and consider its importance for a manager trying to understand organizational behavior.

- We can readily observe biographical characteristics, but that doesn't mean we should explicitly use them in management decisions. Most research shows fairly minimal effects of biographical characteristics on job performance. We also need to be aware of implicit biases we or other managers may have.
- An effective selection process will improve the fit between employees and job requirements. A job analysis will provide information about jobs currently being done and the abilities individuals need to perform the jobs adequately. Applicants can then be tested, interviewed, and evaluated on the degree to which they possess the necessary abilities.
- Promotion and transfer decisions affecting individuals already in the organization's employ should reflect candidates' abilities. As with new employees, care should be taken to assess critical abilities incumbents will need in the job and match those with the organization's human resources.
- To accommodate employees with disabilities, managers can improve the fit by fine-tuning the job to better match an incumbent's abilities. Often, modifications with no significant impact on the job's basic activities, such as changing equipment or reorganizing tasks within a group, can better adapt work to the specific talents of a given employee.
- Diversity management must be an ongoing commitment that crosses all levels of the organization. Group management, recruiting, hiring, retention, and development practices can all be designed to leverage diversity for the organization's competitive advantage.
- Policies to improve the climate for diversity can be effective, so long as they are designed to acknowledge all employees' perspectives. One-shot diversity training sessions are less likely to be effective than comprehensive programs that address the climate for diversity at multiple levels.

Men Have More Mathematical Ability Than Women

Harvard's Larry Summers was forced to resign from his job as president of the university for claiming that women have different abilities than men, but there is some truth to the claim. Evidence reliability indicates significant gender differences in mathematical test scores.

To be sure, there are many, many women whose mathematical and scientific prowess far surpasses that of many men. The distributions overlap to a considerable degree.

It is also true that most research shows that overall intelligence doesn't differ between genders: women are as smart as men. But the fact of the matter is, the *way* in which men and women are smart is, on average, different. Women tend to have significantly higher scores on verbal ability measures and men tend to have significantly higher scores on measures of mathematical ability.

Many sociologists and educational psychologists argue that these differences are explained by socialization: boys are socialized toward and rewarded for mathematical prowess, whereas girls are pointed toward and expected to excel in writing and reading.

These socialization arguments, however, ignore some cold, hard truths that have been uncovered in the latest research. We know from neural imaging research that men's and women's brains differ. Men tend to show higher activation in the area of the brain responsible for mathematical and for spatial operations. Women, in contrast, tend to have better bilateral communication (the right and left sides of their brain communicate better), which is vital to reading comprehension and written and oral expression. Do we really think a child's third-grade teacher caused these differences?

No reasonable person suggests that boys and girls should be steered into different occupations based on these findings. Men and women should pursue the occupations that suit their abilities and that they will find rewarding. But should our pursuit of egalitarianism blind us to scientific findings that suggest the obvious: men and women are not exactly alike?

Women make up about half the new entrants in the professions of law, medicine, and dentistry. They are the vast majority of veterinarians. Yet they remain woefully underrepresented in science, mathematics, and technology positions. For example, only about one in five of recent entrants into engineering graduate programs are women, and in natural sciences and computer science departments at the top universities, fewer than one in ten tenured professors are women. If women are at such a disadvantage in terms of math and science abilities, why are they better represented in some occupations than others? Differing motivations produced by teacher and parent expectations are the answer. If we think women aren't natural engineers, then we learn to steer girls away from such career choices.

It is true there are gender differences in math test scores, but those differences are not large. And often ignored is a widely documented phenomenon: among the very young, girls *outperform* boys on math (as well as on other) tests. By adolescence, this advantage reverses and boys outperform girls. If socialization and school experiences do not explain this result, what does?

Moreover, we know that a large part of the reason fewer women enter science, technology, engineering, and mathematical (STEM) positions is not ability but motivation. Research indicates that women perceive careers in STEM fields to be less interpersonally fulfilling, and this explains their gravitation toward other fields. If we are concerned about sex differences in participation in these fields, we need to be concerned with the motivational effects of these perceptions, not with any presumed differences in male and female abilities.

Sources: Based on A. B. Diekman, E. R. Brown, A. M. Johnston, and E. K. Clark, "Seeking Congruity between Goals and Roles: A New Look at Why Women Opt Out of Science, Technology, Engineering, and Mathematics Careers," *Psychological Science* 21, no. 8 (2010), pp. 1051–1057; S. J. Ceci and W. Williams, "Sex Differences in Math-Intensive Fields," *Current Directions in Psychological Science* 19, no. 5 (2010), pp. 275–279; and J. Tierney, "Legislation Won't Close Gender Gap in Sciences," *The New York Times* (June 14, 2010), pp. 1–4.

QUESTIONS FOR REVIEW

1 What are the two major forms of workforce diversity?

2 What are stereotypes and how do they function in organizational settings?

3 What are the key biographical characteristics and how are they relevant to OB?

4 What is *intellectual ability* and how is it relevant to OB?

5 How can you contrast intellectual and physical ability?

6 How do organizations manage diversity effectively?

EXPERIENTIAL EXERCISE Feeling Excluded

This six-step exercise takes approximately 20 minutes.

Individual Work (Steps 1 and 2)

1. All participants are asked to recall a time when they have felt uncomfortable or targeted because of their demographic status. Ideally, situations at work should be used, but if no work situations come to mind, any situation will work. Encourage students to use any demographic characteristic they think is most appropriate, so they can write about feeling excluded on the basis of race, ethnicity, gender, age, disability status, religion, or any other characteristic. They should briefly describe the situation, what precipitated the event, how they felt at the time, how they reacted, and how they believe the other party could have made the situation better.

2. The instructor asks the students to then think about a time when they might have either deliberately or accidentally done something that made someone else feel excluded or targeted because of their demographic status. Once again, they should briefly describe the situation, what precipitated the event, how they felt at the time, how the other person reacted, and how they could have made the situation better.

Small Groups (Steps 3 and 4)

3. Once everyone has written their descriptions, divide the class into small groups of not more than four

people. If at all possible, try to compose groups that are somewhat demographically diverse, to avoid intergroup conflicts in the class review discussion. Students should be encouraged to discuss their situations and consider how their experiences were similar or different.

4. After reading through everyone's reactions, each group should develop a short list of principles for how they personally can avoid excluding or targeting people in the future. Encourage them to be as specific as possible, and also ask each group to find solutions that work for everyone. Solutions should focus on both avoiding these situations in the first place and resolving them when they do occur.

Class Review (Steps 5 and 6)

5. Members of each group are invited to provide a very brief summary of the major principles of how they've felt excluded or targeted, and then to describe their groups' collective decisions regarding how these situations can be minimized in the future.

6. The instructor should lead a discussion on how companies might be able to develop comprehensive policies that will encourage people to be sensitive in their interactions with one another.

ETHICAL DILEMMA Board Quotas

That women are underrepresented on boards of directors is an understatement. In the United States, only 15 percent of board members among the *Fortune* 500 are women. Among the 100 largest companies in Great Britain, women hold approximately 12 percent of board seats, a representation that has changed little over the past 5 years. In the European Union (EU) more generally, only 9.7 percent of the directors of the 300 largest companies are women. In China and India, the figure is roughly half that.

In response to such underrepresentation, many EU countries—including France, Spain, and Norway—have instituted compulsory quotas for female representation on boards. Great Britain has guidelines and recommendations. A 2011 official British government report recommended that women make up at least 25 percent of the boards of the largest British companies. Under the recommended guidelines, companies would be required to announce their board composition goals to their shareholders and state clearly how they plan on meeting them. France passed a law in 2011 that requires large companies to fill at least 40 percent of board seats with female members within the next six years. Spain has a similar quota in place.

Questions

1. Given that women participate in the labor force in roughly the same proportion as men, why do you think women occupy so few seats on boards of directors?

2. Do you agree with the quotas established in many EU countries? Why or why not?

3. Beyond legal remedies, what do you think can be done to increase women's representations on boards of directors?

4. One recent study found no link between female representation on boards of directors and these companies' corporate sustainability or environmental policies. The study's author expressed surprise at the findings. Do the findings surprise you? Why or why not?

Sources: J. Werdigier, "In Britain, a Push for More Women on Boards of Large Companies," *The New York Times* (February 25, 2011), p. B3; and J. Galbreath, "Are There Gender-Related Influences on Corporate Sustainability? A Study of Women on Boards of Directors," *Journal of Management & Organization* 17, no. 1 (2011), pp. 17–38.

CASE INCIDENT 1 The Flynn Effect

Given that a substantial amount of intellectual ability is inherited, it might surprise you to learn that intelligence test scores are rising. In fact, scores have risen so dramatically that today's great-grandparents seem mentally deficient by comparison. First, let's review the evidence for rising test scores. Then we'll review explanations for the results.

On an IQ scale where 100 is the average, scores have been rising about 3 points per decade, meaning if your grandparent scored 100, the average score for your generation would be around 115. That's a pretty big difference—about a standard deviation, meaning someone from your grandparent's generation whose score was at the 84th percentile would be only average (50th percentile) by today's norms.

James Flynn is a New Zealand researcher credited with first documenting the rising scores. He reported the results in 1984, when he found that almost everyone who took a well-validated IQ test in the 1970s did better than those who took one in the 1940s. The results appear to hold up across cultures. Test scores are rising not only in the United States but in most other countries in which the effect has been tested, too.

What explains the Flynn effect? Researchers are not entirely sure, but some of the explanations offered are these:

1. **Education.** Students today are better educated than their ancestors, and education leads to higher test scores.

2. **Smaller families.** In 1900, the average couple had four children; today the number is fewer than two. We know firstborns tend to have higher IQs than other children, probably because they receive more attention than their later-born siblings.

3. **Test-taking savvy.** Today's children have been tested so often that they are test-savvy: they know how to take tests and how to do well on them.

4. **Genes.** Although smart couples tend to have fewer, not more, children (which might lead us to expect intelligence in the population to drop over time), it's possible that due to better education, tracking, and testing, those who do have the right genes are better able to exploit those advantages. Some genetics researchers also have argued that if genes for intelligence carried by both parents are dominant, they win out, meaning the child's IQ will be as high as or higher than those of the parents.

Despite the strong heritability of IQ, researchers continue to pursue mechanisms that might raise IQ scores. Factors like brain exercises (even video games) and regular physical exercise seem to at least temporarily boost brain power. Other recent research in neuroscience has had difficulty pinpointing physical mechanisms that can lead to a boost in IQ, although researchers propose that a focus on brain chemicals like dopamine may lead, in time, to drugs that can boost IQ chemically.

Questions

1. Do you believe people are really getting smarter? Why or why not?

2. Which of the factors explaining the Flynn effect do you accept?

3. If the Flynn effect is true, does this undermine the theory that IQ is mostly inherited? Why or why not?

Sources: Based on S. Begley, "Sex, Race, and IQ: Off Limits?" *Newsweek* (April 20, 2009), www.newsweek.com; M. A. Mingroni, "Resolving the IQ Paradox: Heterosis as a Cause of the Flynn Effect and Other Trends," *Psychological Review* (July 2007), pp. 806–829; and S. Begley, "Can You Build a Better Brain?" *Newsweek* (January 10, 2011), www.newsweek.com.

CASE INCIDENT 2 Increasing Age Diversity in the Workplace

Over the past century, the average age of the workforce has continually increased as medical science continues to enhance longevity and vitality. The fastest-growing segment of the workforce is individuals over the age of 55. Recent medical research is exploring techniques that could extend human life to 100 years or more. In addition, the combination of laws prohibiting age discrimination and elimination of defined-benefit pension plans means that many individuals continue to work well past the traditional age of retirement.

Unfortunately, older workers face a variety of discriminatory attitudes in the workplace. Researchers scanned more than 100 publications on age discrimination to determine what types of age stereotypes were most prevalent across studies. They found that stereotypes suggested job performance declined with age, counter to empirical evidence presented earlier in this chapter that relationships between age and core task performance are essentially nil. Stereotypes also suggest that older workers are less adaptable, less flexible, and incapable of learning new concepts. Research, on the other hand, suggests they are capable of learning and adapting to new situations when these are framed appropriately.

Organizations can take steps to limit age discrimination and ensure that employees are treated fairly regardless of age. Many of the techniques to limit age discrimination come down to fundamentally sound management practices relevant for all employees: set clear expectations for performance, deal with problems directly, communicate with workers frequently, and follow clear policies and procedures consistently. In particular, management professionals note that clarity and consistency can help ensure all employees are treated equally regardless of age.

Questions

1. What changes in employment relationships are likely to occur as the population ages?

2. Do you think increasing age diversity will create new challenges for managers? What types of challenges do you expect will be most profound?

3. How can organizations cope with differences related to age discrimination in the workplace?

4. What types of policies might lead to charges of age discrimination, and how can they be changed to eliminate these problems?

Sources: Based on D. Stipp, "The Anti-Aging Revolution," *Fortune* (June 14, 2010), pp. 124–130; R. A. Posthuma and M. A. Campion, "Age Stereotypes in the Workplace: Common Stereotypes, Moderators, and Future Research Directions," *Journal of Management* 35 (2009), pp. 158–188; and H. Perlowski, "With an Aging Workforce, a Rising Risk of Discrimination Claims," *Workforce Management Online* (July 2008), www.workforce.com.

ENDNOTES

1. M. DiNatale and S. Boraas, "The Labor Force Experience of Women from Generation X," *Monthly Labor Review* (March 2002), pp. 1–15.

2. See, for example, F. Welch, "Catching Up: Wages of Black Men," *The American Economic Review* 93, no. 2 (2003), pp. 320–325; A. Sakamoto, H. Wu, and J. M. Tzeng, "The Declining Significance of Race Among American Men During the Latter Half of the Twentieth Century," *Demography* 37 (January 2000), pp. 41–51; and A Sakomoto, K. A. Goyette, and C. Kim, "Socioeconomic Attainments of Asian Americans," *Annual Review of Sociology* 35, (2009), pp. 255–276.

3. J. Schram, *SHRM Workplace Forecast* (Alexandria, VA: Society for Human Resource Management, 2006).

4. D. A. Harrison, K. H. Price, J. H. Gavin, and A. T. Florey, "Time, Teams, and Task Performance: Changing Effects of Surface- and Deep-Level Diversity on Group Functioning," *Academy of Management Journal* 45, no. 5 (2002), pp. 1029–1045; and A. H. Eagly and J. L. Chin, "Are Memberships in Race, Ethnicity, and Gender Categories Merely Surface Characteristics?" *American Psychologist* 65 (2010), pp. 934–935.

5. P. Chattopadhyay, M. Tluchowska, and E. George, "Identifying the Ingroup: A Closer Look at the Influence of Demographic Dissimilarity on Employee Social Identity," *Academy of Management Review* 29, no. 2 (2004), pp. 180–202; and P. Chattopadhyay, "Beyond Direct and Symmetrical Effects: The Influence of Demographic Dissimilarity on Organizational Citizenship Behavior," *Academy of Management Journal* 42, no. 3 (1999), pp. 273–287.

6. L. M. Cortina, "Unseen Injustice: Incivility as Modern Discrimination in Organizations," *Academy of Management Review* 33, no. 1 (2008), pp. 55–75.

7. R. J. Grossman, "Keep Pace with Older Workers," *HR Magazine* (May 2008), pp. 39–46.

8. K. A. Wrenn and T. J. Maurer, "Beliefs About Older Workers' Learning and Development Behavior in Relation to Beliefs About Malleability of Skills, Age-Related Decline, and Control," *Journal of Applied Social Psychology* 34, no. 2 (2004), pp. 223–242; and R. A. Posthuma and M. A. Campion, "Age Stereotypes in the Workplace: Common Stereotypes,

Moderators, and Future Research Directions," *Journal of Management* 35 (2009), pp. 158–188.

9. T. W. H. Ng and D. C. Feldman, "Re-examining the Relationship Between Age and Voluntary Turnover," *Journal of Vocational Behavior* 74 (2009), pp. 283–294.

10. T. W. H. Ng and D. C. Feldman, "The Relationship of Age to Ten Dimensions of Job Performance," *Journal of Applied Psychology* 93 (2008), pp. 392–423.

11. Cited in K. Labich, "The New Unemployed," *Fortune* (March 8, 1993), p. 43.

12. See Ng and Feldman, "The Relationship of Age to Ten Dimensions of Job Performance."

13. T. W. H. Ng and D. C. Feldman, "The Relationship of Age with Job Attitudes: A Meta-Analysis," *Personnel Psychology* 63 (2010), pp. 677–718.

14. K. M. Kacmar and G. R. Ferris, "Theoretical and Methodological Considerations in the Age–Job Satisfaction Relationship," *Journal of Applied Psychology* (April 1989), pp. 201–207; and W. A. Hochwarter, G. R. Ferris, P. L. Perrewe, L. A. Witt, and C. Kiewitz, "A Note on the Nonlinearity of the Age–Job Satisfaction Relationship," *Journal of Applied Social Psychology* (June 2001), pp. 1223–1237.

15. F. Kunze, S. A. Boehm, and H. Bruch, "Age Diversity, Age Discrimination Climate and Performance Consequences—A Cross Organizational Study," *Journal of Organizational Behavior* 32 (2011), pp. 264–290.

16. See E. M. Weiss, G. Kemmler, E. A. Deisenhammer, W. W. Fleischhacker, and M. Delazer, "Sex Differences in Cognitive Functions," *Personality and Individual Differences* (September 2003), pp. 863–875; and A. F. Jorm, K. J. Anstey, H. Christensen, and B. Rodgers, "Gender Differences in Cognitive Abilities: The Mediating Role of Health State and Health Habits," *Intelligence* (January 2004), pp. 7–23.

17. See M. M. Black and E. W. Holden, "The Impact of Gender on Productivity and Satisfaction Among Medical School Psychologists," *Journal of Clinical Psychology in Medical Settings* (March 1998), pp. 117–131.

18. M. E. Heilman and T. G. Okimoto, "Why Are Women Penalized for Success at Male Tasks? The Implied Communality Deficit," *Journal of Applied Psychology* 92, no. 1 (2007), pp. 81–92.

19. D. R. Avery, P. F. McKay, and D. C. Wilson "What are the Odds? How Demographic Similarity Affects the Prevalence of Perceived Employment Discrimination," *Journal of Applied Psychology* 93 (2008), pp. 235–249.

20. C. Kirchmeyer, "The Different Effects of Family on Objective Career Success Across Gender: A Test of Alternative Explanations," *Journal of Vocational Behavior* 68, no. 2 (2006), pp. 323–346; and C. Guillaume and S. Pochic, "What Would You Sacrifice? Access to Top Management and the Work-Life Balance," *Gender, Work & Organization* 16, no. 1 (2009), pp. 14–36.

21. Guillaume and Pochic, "What Would You Sacrifice? Access to Top Management and the Work-Life Balance."

22. P. W. Hom, L. Roberson, and A. D. Ellis, "Challenging Conventional Wisdom About Who Quits: Revelations from Corporate America," *Journal of Applied Psychology* 93, no. 1 (2008), pp. 1–34.

23. See, for instance, K. D. Scott and E. L. McClellan, "Gender Differences in Absenteeism," *Public Personnel Management* (Summer 1990), pp. 229–253; and A. VandenHeuvel and

M. Wooden, "Do Explanations of Absenteeism Differ for Men and Women?" *Human Relations* (November 1995), pp. 1309–1329.

24. See, for instance, M. Tait, M. Y. Padgett, and T. T. Baldwin, "Job and Life Satisfaction: A Reevaluation of the Strength of the Relationship and Gender Effects as a Function of the Date of the Study," *Journal of Applied Psychology* (June 1989), pp. 502–507; and M. B. Grover, "Daddy Stress," *Forbes* (September 6, 1999), pp. 202–208.

25. S. Halrynjo, "Men's Work-Life Conflict: Career, Care and Self-Realization: Patterns of Privileges and Dilemmas," *Gender, Work & Organization* 16, no. 1 (2009), pp. 98–125; and S. Jayson, "Gender Roles See a 'Conflict' Shift," *USA Today* (March 26, 2009), p. 1A.

26. M. E. Heilman and T. G. Okimoto, "Motherhood: A Potential Source of Bias in Employment Decisions," *Journal of Applied Psychology* 93, no. 1 (2008), pp. 189–198.

27. J. L. Raver and L. H. Nishii, "Once, Twice, or Three Times as Harmful? Ethnic Harassment, Gender Harassment, and Generalized Workplace Harassment," *Journal of Applied Psychology* 95 (2010), pp. 236–254.

28. D. R. Avery, J. A. Richeson, M R. Hebl, and N. Ambady, "It Does Not Have to Be Uncomfortable: The Role of Behavioral Scripts in Black-White Interracial Interactions," *Journal of Applied Psychology* 94 (2009), pp. 1382–1393.

29. J. M. McCarthy, C. H. Van Iddekinge, and M. A. Campion, "Are Highly Structured Job Interviews Resistant to Demographic Similarity Effects?" *Personnel Psychology* 63 (2010), pp. 325–359; and G. N. Powell and D. A. Butterfield, "Exploring the Influence of Decision Makers' Race and Gender on Actual Promotions to Top Management," *Personnel Psychology* 55, no. 2 (2002), pp. 397–428.

30. D. A. Kravitz, D. M. Mayer, L. M. Leslie, and D. Lev-Arey, "Understanding Attitudes Toward Affirmative Action Programs in Employment: Summary and Meta-Analysis of 35 Years of Research," *Journal of Applied Psychology* 91 (2006), pp. 1013–1036.

31. D. R. Avery, P F. McKay, and D. C. Wilson "What Are the Odds? How Demographic Similarity Affects the Prevalence of Perceived Employment Discrimination," *Journal of Applied Psychology* 93 (2008), pp. 235–249.

32. J. M. Sacco, C. R. Scheu, A. M. Ryan, and N. Schmitt, "An Investigation of Race and Sex Similarity Effects in Interviews: A Multilevel Approach to Relational Demography," *Journal of Applied Psychology* 88, no. 5 (2003), pp. 852–865; and P. F. McKay and M. A. McDaniel, "A Reexamination of Black-White Mean Differences in Work Performance: More Data, More Moderators," *Journal of Applied Psychology* 91, no. 3 (2006), pp. 538–554.

33. P. Bobko, P. L. Roth, and D. Potosky, "Derivation and Implications of a Meta-Analytic Matrix Incorporating Cognitive Ability, Alternative Predictors, and Job Performance," *Personnel Psychology* (Autumn 1999), pp. 561–589.

34. M. J. Ree, T. R. Carretta, and J. R. Steindl, "Cognitive Ability," in N. Anderson, D. S. Ones, H. K. Sinangil, and C. Viswesvaran (eds.), *Handbook of Industrial, Work, and Organizational Psychology*, vol. 1 (London: Sage Publications, 2001), pp. 219–232.

35. W. T. Dickens and J. R. Flynn, "Black Americans Reduce the Racial IQ Gap: Evidence from Standardization Samples,"

Psychological Science 17 (2006), pp. 913–920; and C. Murray, "The Magnitude and Components of Change in the Black-White IQ Difference from 1920 to 1991: A Birth Cohort Analysis of the Woodcock-Johnson Standardizations," *Intelligence* 35, no. 44 (2007), pp. 305–318.

36. See J. P. Rushton and A. R. Jenson, "Thirty Years of Research on Race Differences in Cognitive Ability," *Psychology, Public Policy, and the Law* 11, no. 2 (2005), pp. 235–295; and R. E. Nisbett, "Heredity, Environment, and Race Differences in IQ: A Commentary on Rushton and Jensen (2005)," *Psychology, Public Policy, and the Law* 11, no. 2 (2005), pp. 302–310.

37. Avery, McKay, and Wilson, "What Are the Odds? How Demographic Similarity Affects the Prevalence of Perceived Employment Discrimination"; and Raver and Nishii, "Once, Twice, or Three Times as Harmful? Ethnic Harassment, Gender Harassment, and Generalized Workplace Harassment."

38. P. F. McKay, D. R. Avery, and M. A. Morris, "Mean Racial-Ethnic Differences in Employee Sales Performance: The Moderating Role of Diversity Climate," *Personnel Psychology* 61, no. 2 (2008), pp. 349–374.

39. *Americans with Disabilities Act,* 42 U.S.C. § 12101, et seq. (1990).

40. S. G. Goldberg, M. B. Killeen, and B. O'Day, "The Disclosure Conundrum: How People with Psychiatric Disabilities Navigate Employment," *Psychology, Public Policy, and Law* 11, no. 3 (2005), pp. 463–500; M. L. Ellison, Z. Russinova, K. L. MacDonald-Wilson, and A. Lyass, "Patterns and Correlates of Workplace Disclosure Among Professionals and Managers with Psychiatric Conditions," *Journal of Vocational Rehabilitation* 18, no. 1 (2003), pp. 3–13.

41. L. R. Ren, R. L. Paetzold, and A. Colella, "A Meta-Analysis of Experimental Studies on the Effects of Disability on Human Resource Judgments," *Human Resource Management Review* 18, no. 3 (2008), pp. 191–203.

42. S. Almond and A. Healey, "Mental Health and Absence from Work: New Evidence from the UK Quarterly Labour Force Survey," *Work, Employment, and Society* 17, no. 4 (2003), pp. 731–742.

43. E. Louvet, "Social Judgment Toward Job Applicants with Disabilities: Perception of Personal Qualities and Competences," *Rehabilitation Psychology* 52, no. 3 (2007), pp. 297–303; and W. D. Gouvier, S. Sytsma-Jordan, and S. Mayville, "Patterns of Discrimination in Hiring Job Applicants with Disabilities: The Role of Disability Type, Job Complexity, and Public Contact," *Rehabilitation Psychology* 48, no. 3 (2003), pp. 175–181.

44. A. Colella, A. S. DeNisi, and A. Varma, "The Impact of Ratee's Disability on Performance Judgments and Choice as Partner: The Role of Disability-Job Fit Stereotypes and Interdependence of Rewards," *Journal of Applied Psychology* 83, no. 1 (1998), pp. 102–111.

45. J. M. Czajka and A. S. DeNisi, "Effects of Emotional Disability and Clear Performance Standards on Performance Ratings," *Academy of Management Journal* 31, no. 2 (1988), pp. 394–404.

46. B. S. Bell and K. J. Klein, "Effect of Disability, Gender, and Job Level on Ratings of Job Applicants," *Rehabilitation Psychology* 46, no. 3 (2001), pp. 229–246; and Louvet, "Social Judgment Toward Job Applicants with Disabilities: Perception of Personal Qualities and Competences."

47. T. W. H. Ng and D. C. Feldman, "Organizational Tenure and Job Performance," *Journal of Management* 36, (2010), pp. 1220–1250.

48. I. R. Gellatly, "Individual and Group Determinants of Employee Absenteeism: Test of a Causal Model," *Journal of Organizational Behavior* (September 1995), pp. 469–485.

49. P. O. Popp and J. A. Belohlav, "Absenteeism in a Low Status Work Environment," *Academy of Management Journal* (September 1982), p. 681.

50. R. W. Griffeth, P. W. Hom, and S. Gaertner, "A Meta-analysis of Antecedents and Correlates of Employee Turnover: Update, Moderator Tests, and Research Implications for the Next Millennium," *Journal of Management* 26, no. 3 (2000), pp. 463–488.

51. M. R. Barrick and R. D. Zimmerman, "Hiring for Retention and Performance," *Human Resource Management* 48 (2009), pp. 183–206.

52. W. van Breukelen, R. van der Vlist, and H. Steensma, "Voluntary Employee Turnover: Combining Variables from the 'Traditional' Turnover Literature with the Theory of Planned Behavior," *Journal of Organizational Behavior* 25, no. 7 (2004), pp. 893–914.

53. M. Elias, "USA's Muslims Under a Cloud," *USA Today* (August 10, 2006), pp. 1D, 2D; and R. R. Hastings, "Muslims Seek Acknowledgement of Mainstream Americans," *HRWeek* (May 11, 2007), p. 1.

54. E. B. King and A. S. Ahmad, "An Experimental Field Study of Interpersonal Discrimination Toward Muslim Job Applicants," *Personnel Psychology* 63 (2010), pp. 881–906.

55. See, for example, E. B. King and J. M. Cortina, "The Social and Economic Imperative of Lesbian, Gay, Bisexual, and Transgendered Supportive Organizational Policies," *Industrial and Organizational Psychology: Perspectives on Science and Practice* 3 (2010), pp. 69–78.

56. *HRC Corporate Equality Index,* 2011, www.hrc.org/documents/HRC-CEI-2011-Final.pdf; and R. R. Hastings, "Necessity Breeds Inclusion: Reconsidering 'Don't Ask, Don't Tell,'" *HRWeek* (January 2007), pp. 1–2.

57. B. R. Ragins, "Disclosure Disconnects: Antecedents and Consequences of Disclosing Invisible Stigmas Across Life Domains," *Academy of Management Review* 33 (2008), pp. 194–215.

58. B. Leonard, "Transgender Issues Test Diversity Limits," *HRMagazine* (June 2007), pp. 32–34.

59. L. S. Gottfredson, "The Challenge and Promise of Cognitive Career Assessment," *Journal of Career Assessment* 11, no. 2 (2003), pp. 115–135.

60. M. D. Dunnette, "Aptitudes, Abilities, and Skills," in M. D. Dunnette (ed.), *Handbook of Industrial and Organizational Psychology* (Chicago: Rand McNally, 1976), pp. 478–483.

61. J. W. B. Lang, M. Kersting, U. R. Hülscheger, and J. Lang, "General Mental Ability, Narrower Cognitive Abilities, and Job Performance: The Perspective of the Nested-Factors Model of Cognitive Abilities" *Personnel Psychology* 63 (2010), pp. 595–640.

62. N. Barber, "Educational and Ecological Correlates of IQ: A Cross-National Investigation," *Intelligence* (May–June 2005), pp. 273–284.

63. J. F. Salgado, N. Anderson, S. Moscoso, C. Bertua, F. de Fruyt, and J. P. Rolland, "A Meta-analytic Study of General Mental

Ability Validity for Different Occupations in the European Community," *Journal of Applied Psychology* (December 2003), pp. 1068–1081; and F. L. Schmidt and J. E. Hunter, "Select on Intelligence," in E. A. Locke (ed.), *Handbook of Principles of Organizational Behavior* (Malden, MA: Blackwell, 2004).

64. Y. Ganzach, "Intelligence and Job Satisfaction," *Academy of Management Journal* 41, no. 5 (1998), pp. 526–539; and Y. Ganzach, "Intelligence, Education, and Facets of Job Satisfaction," *Work and Occupations* 30, no. 1 (2003), pp. 97–122.

65. E. A. Fleishman, "Evaluating Physical Abilities Required by Jobs," *Personnel Administrator* (June 1979), pp. 82–92.

66. D. R. Avery, "Reactions to Diversity in Recruitment Advertising: Are the Differences Black and White?" *Journal of Applied Psychology* 88, no. 4 (2003), pp. 672–679; P. F. McKay and D. R. Avery, "What Has Race Got to Do with It? Unraveling the Role of Racioethnicity in Job Seekers' Reactions to Site Visits," *Personnel Psychology* 59, no. 2 (2006), pp. 395–429; and D. R. Avery and P. F. McKay, "Target Practice: An Organizational Impression Management Approach to Attracting Minority and Female Job Applicants," *Personnel Psychology* 59, no. 1 (2006), pp. 157–187.

67. M. R. Buckley, K. A. Jackson, M. C. Bolino, J. G. Veres, and H. S. Field, "The Influence of Relational Demography on Panel Interview Ratings: A Field Experiment," *Personnel Psychology* 60 (2007), pp. 627–646; J. M. Sacco, C. R. Scheu, A. M. Ryan, and N. Schmitt, "An Investigation of Race and Sex Similarity Effects in Interviews: A Multilevel Approach to Relational Demography," *Journal of Applied Psychology* 88 (2003), pp. 852–865; and J. C. Ziegert and P. J. Hanges, "Employment Discrimination: The Role of Implicit Attitudes, Motivation, and a Climate for Racial Bias," *Journal of Applied Psychology* 90 (2005), pp. 553–562.

68. J. Schaubroeck and S. S. K. Lam, "How Similarity to Peers and Supervisor Influences Organizational Advancement in Different Cultures," *Academy of Management Journal* 45 (2002), pp. 1120–1136.

69. P. F. McKay, D. R. Avery, and M. A. Morris, "Mean Racial-Ethnic Differences in Employee Sales Performance: The Moderating Role of Diversity Climate," *Personnel Psychology* 61, no. 2 (2008), pp. 349–374.

70. A. S. Tsui, T. D. Egan, and C. A. O'Reilly, "Being Different: Relational Demography and Organizational Attachment," *Administrative Science Quarterly* 37 (1992), pp. 547–579; and J. M. Sacco and N. Schmitt, "A Dynamic Multilevel Model of Demographic Diversity and Misfit Effects," *Journal of Applied Psychology* 90 (2005), pp. 203–231.

71. P. F. McKay, D. R. Avery, S. Tonidandel, M. A. Morris, M. Hernandez, and M. R. Hebl, "Racial Differences in Employee Retention: Are Diversity Climate Perceptions the Key?" *Personnel Psychology* 60, no. 1 (2007), pp. 35–62.

72. S. T. Bell, "Deep-Level Composition Variables as Predictors of Team Performance: A Meta–Analysis," *Journal of Applied Psychology* 92, no. 3 (2007), pp. 595–615; S. K. Horwitz and I. B. Horwitz, "The Effects of Team Diversity on Team Outcomes: A Meta-Analytic Review of Team Demography," *Journal of Management* 33, no. 6 (2007), pp. 987–1015; G. L. Stewart, "A Meta-Analytic Review of Relationships Between Team Design Features and Team Performance," *Journal of Management* 32, no. 1 (2006), pp. 29–54; and A. Joshi and H. Roh, "The Role of Context in Work Team Diversity Research: A Meta-Analytic Review," *Academy of Management Journal* 52, no. 3 (2009), pp. 599–627.

73. A. C. Homan, J. R. Hollenbeck, S. E. Humphrey, D. Van Knippenberg, D. R. Ilgen, and G. A. Van Kleef, "Facing Differences with an Open Mind: Openness to Experience, Salience of Intragroup Differences, and Performance of Diverse Work Groups," *Academy of Management Journal* 51, no. 6 (2008), pp. 1204–1222.

74. E. Kearney and D. Gebert, "Managing Diversity and Enhancing Team Outcomes: The Promise of Transformational Leadership," *Journal of Applied Psychology* 94, no. 1 (2009), pp. 77–89.

75. C. L. Holladay and M. A. Quiñones, "The Influence of Training Focus and Trainer Characteristics on Diversity Training Effectiveness," *Academy of Management Learning and Education* 7, no. 3 (2008), pp. 343–354; and R. Anand and M. Winters, "A Retrospective View of Corporate Diversity Training from 1964 to the Present," *Academy of Management Learning and Education* 7, no. 3 (2008), pp. 356–372.

76. Q. M. Roberson and C. K. Stevens, "Making Sense of Diversity in the Workplace: Organizational Justice and Language Abstraction in Employees' Accounts of Diversity-Related Incidents," *Journal of Applied Psychology* 91 (2006), pp. 379–391; and D. A. Harrison, D. A. Kravitz, D. M. Mayer, L. M. Leslie, and D. Lev-Arey, "Understanding Attitudes Toward Affirmative Action Programs in Employment: Summary and Meta-Analysis of 35 Years of Research," *Journal of Applied Psychology* 91 (2006), pp. 1013–1036.

77. A. Kalev, F. Dobbin, and E. Kelly, "Best Practices or Best Guesses? Assessing the Efficacy of Corporate Affirmative Action and Diversity Policies," *American Sociological Review* 71, no. 4 (2006), pp. 589–617.

78. R. J. Crisp and R. N. Turner, "Cognitive Adaptation to the Experience of Social and Cultural Diversity," *Psychological Bulletin* 137 (2011), pp. 242–266.

79. A. Sippola and A. Smale, "The Global Integration of Diversity Management: A Longitudinal Case Study," *International Journal of Human Resource Management* 18, no. 11 (2007), pp. 1895–1916.

80. A. Pomeroy, "Cultivating Female Leaders," *HR Magazine* (February 2007), pp. 44–50.

LEARNING OBJECTIVES

After studying this chapter, you should be able to:

1 Contrast the three components of an attitude.

2 Summarize the relationship between attitudes and behavior.

3 Compare and contrast the major job attitudes.

4 Define *job satisfaction* and show how we can measure it.

5 Summarize the main causes of job satisfaction.

6 Identify four employee responses to dissatisfaction.

WHAT DOES SAS STAND FOR?

Most of you probably are not familiar with SAS Institute, Inc. Is it a think-tank? An educational program to teach children manners? No, SAS (originally Statistical Analysis System) is a Cary, North Carolina–based software company, and one that happens to be the best place to work in the United States in 2011 (as it was in 2010), according to *Fortune* magazine.

Founded by North Carolina State University graduate student Anthony J. Barr, SAS quickly established itself as one of the largest developers of statistical software (where its main rival was and continues to be Chicago-based SPSS, now a division of IBM). Part of the secret of SAS's growth and success is that it has branched off into other software markets, such as business planning and support, quality improvement, data storage, and others. Today, the firm employs more than 11,000 people.

However, another distinguishing characteristic of SAS is its highly employee-friendly culture. As a result of being given "the Royal Treatment" (in the words of *60 Minutes*), SAS employees turn over at a rate under 4 percent, roughly a tenth that of their firm's competitors.

So what is this royal treatment? SAS provides a host of benefits employees love, including:

- Free onsite health care.
- Subsidized onsite child care.
- Summer camp for kids.
- "M&M Wednesdays," when employees are given free candy.
- Soda fountains and snacks in every break room.
- A beauty salon.
- A 66,000-ft^2 recreation and fitness center.
- Car cleaning.

To be sure, these benefits are one reason SAS is a desirable place to work. However, the firm's commitment to its employees goes beyond nice perks. Even in the economic downturn, SAS has refused to lay off employees and has even expanded its benefits. "In a tough economy, SAS did not waiver from our commitment to our employees and the innovative culture that keeps them challenged and provides work–life balance," said Jenn Mann, Vice President of Human Resources at SAS. "SAS's continued success proves our core belief: Happy, healthy employees are more productive."

Says one SAS employee: "People stay at SAS in large part because they are happy, but to dig a little deeper, I would argue that people don't leave

Attitudes and Job Satisfaction

3

Attitude isn't everything, but it's close.

—*New York Times* headline, August 6, 2006

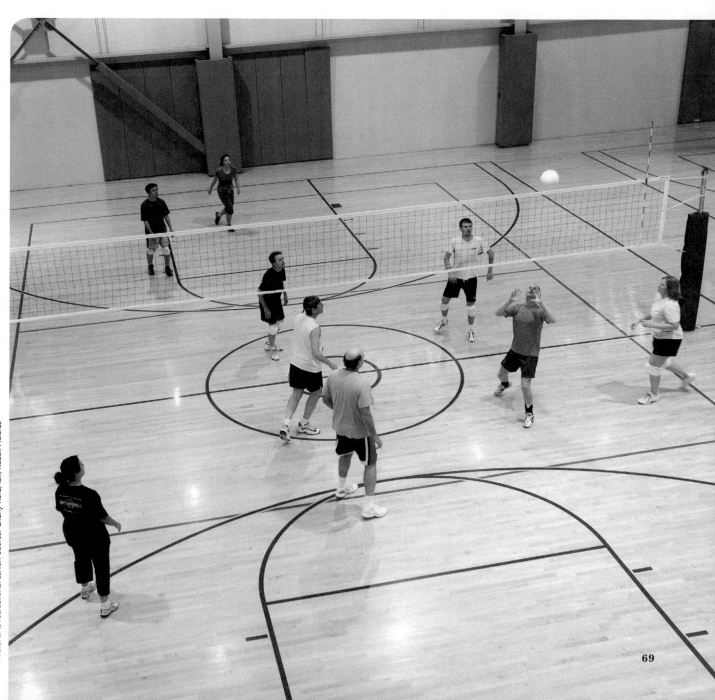

Photo: SAS recreational center. Source: Charly Kurz/laif/Redux Pictures

SAS because they feel regarded—seen, attended to and cared for. I have stayed for that reason, and love what I do for that reason."

Sources: "100 Best Companies to Work For 2011," *Fortune* (January 7, 2011), http://money .cnn.com/; D. Bracken, "SAS Again Tops Fortune List of Best Places to Work," *Charlotte Observer* (January 20, 2011), www.charlotteobserver.com/; and S. Rezvani, "What Makes a 'Best Workplace?' " *Washington Post* (January 21, 2011), http://views.washingtonpost.com/.

Though most will not go as far as SAS to promote employee satisfaction, many organizations are very concerned with the attitudes of their employees. In this chapter, we look at attitudes, their link to behavior, and how employees' satisfaction or dissatisfaction with their jobs affects the workplace.

What are your attitudes toward your job? Use the following Self-Assessment Library to determine your level of satisfaction with your current or past jobs.

SELF-ASSESSMENT LIBRARY

How Satisfied Am I with My Job?

In the Self-Assessment Library (available on CD or online), take assessment I.B.3 (How Satisfied Am I with My Job?) and then answer the following questions. If you currently do not have a job, answer the questions for your most recent job.

1. How does your job satisfaction compare to that of others in your class who have taken the assessment?
2. Why do you think your satisfaction is higher or lower than average?

Attitudes

1 Contrast the three components of an attitude.

Attitudes are evaluative statements—either favorable or unfavorable—about objects, people, or events. They reflect how we feel about something. When I say "I like my job," I am expressing my attitude about work.

Attitudes are complex. If you ask people about their attitude toward religion, Lady Gaga, or the organization they work for, you may get a simple response, but the reasons underlying it are probably complicated. In order to fully understand attitudes, we must consider their fundamental properties or components.

What Are the Main Components of Attitudes?

Typically, researchers have assumed that attitudes have three components: cognition, affect, and behavior.[1] Let's look at each.

The statement "My pay is low" is the **cognitive component** of an attitude—a description of or belief in the way things are. It sets the stage for the more critical part of an attitude—its **affective component**. Affect is the emotional or feeling segment of an attitude and is reflected in the statement "I am angry over how little I'm paid." Finally, affect can lead to behavioral outcomes. The **behavioral component** of an attitude describes an intention to behave in a certain way toward someone or something—to continue the example, "I'm going to look for another job that pays better."

Viewing attitudes as having three components—cognition, affect, and behavior—is helpful in understanding their complexity and the potential

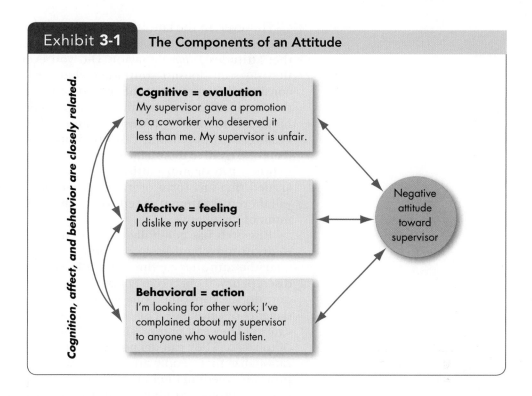

Exhibit 3-1   The Components of an Attitude

Cognition, affect, and behavior are closely related.

Cognitive = evaluation
My supervisor gave a promotion to a coworker who deserved it less than me. My supervisor is unfair.

Affective = feeling
I dislike my supervisor!

Behavioral = action
I'm looking for other work; I've complained about my supervisor to anyone who would listen.

Negative attitude toward supervisor

relationship between attitudes and behavior. Keep in mind that these components are closely related, and cognition and affect in particular are inseparable in many ways. For example, imagine you realized that someone has just treated you unfairly. Aren't you likely to have feelings about that, occurring virtually instantaneously with the realization? Thus, cognition and affect are intertwined.

Exhibit 3-1 illustrates how the three components of an attitude are related. In this example, an employee didn't get a promotion he thought he deserved; a co-worker got it instead. The employee's attitude toward his supervisor is illustrated as follows: the employee thought he deserved the promotion (cognition), he strongly dislikes his supervisor (affect), and he is looking for another job (behavior). As we've noted, although we often think cognition causes affect, which then causes behavior, in reality these components are often difficult to separate.

In organizations, attitudes are important for their behavioral component. If workers believe, for example, that supervisors, auditors, bosses, and time-and-motion engineers are all in conspiracy to make employees work harder for the same or less money, it makes sense to try to understand how these attitudes formed, how they relate to actual job behavior, and how they might be changed.

Does Behavior Always Follow from Attitudes?

2 Summarize the relationship between attitudes and behavior.

Early research on attitudes assumed they were causally related to behavior—that is, the attitudes people hold determine what they do. Common sense, too, suggests a relationship. Isn't it logical that people watch television programs they like, or that employees try to avoid assignments they find distasteful?

---

attitudes *Evaluative statements or judgments concerning objects, people, or events.*

cognitive component *The opinion or belief segment of an attitude.*

affective component *The emotional or feeling segment of an attitude.*

behavioral component *An intention to behave in a certain way toward someone or something.*

However, in the late 1960s, a review of the research challenged this assumed effect of attitudes on behavior.[2] One researcher—Leon Festinger—argued that attitudes *follow* behavior. Did you ever notice how people change what they say so it doesn't contradict what they do? Perhaps a friend of yours has consistently argued that the quality of U.S. cars isn't up to that of imports and that he'd never own anything but a Japanese or German car. But his dad gives him a late-model Ford Mustang, and suddenly he says U.S. cars aren't so bad. Festinger proposed that cases of attitude following behavior illustrate the effects of **cognitive dissonance**,[3] any incompatibility an individual might perceive between two or more attitudes or between behavior and attitudes. Festinger argued that any form of inconsistency is uncomfortable and that individuals will therefore attempt to reduce it. They will seek a stable state, which is a minimum of dissonance.

Research has generally concluded that people do seek consistency among their attitudes and between their attitudes and their behavior.[4] They either alter the attitudes or the behavior, or they develop a rationalization for the discrepancy. Tobacco executives provide an example.[5] How, you might wonder, do these people cope with the continuing revelations about the health dangers of smoking? They can deny any clear causation between smoking and cancer. They can brainwash themselves by continually articulating the benefits of tobacco. They can acknowledge the negative consequences of smoking but rationalize that people are going to smoke and that tobacco companies merely promote freedom of choice. They can accept the evidence and make cigarettes less dangerous or reduce their availability to more vulnerable groups, such as teenagers. Or they can quit their job because the dissonance is too great.

No individual, of course, can completely avoid dissonance. You know cheating on your income tax is wrong, but you fudge the numbers a bit every year and hope you're not audited. Or you tell your children to floss their teeth, but you don't do it yourself. Festinger proposed that the desire to reduce dissonance depends on moderating factors, including the *importance* of the elements creating it and the degree of *influence* we believe we have over them. Individuals

Marriott International strives for consistency between employee attitudes and behavior through its motto "Spirit to Serve." CEO and chairman J. W. Marriott, Jr., models the behavior of service by visiting hotel employees throughout the year. "I want our associates to know that there really is a guy named Marriott who cares about them," he says. The company honors employees with job excellence awards for behavior that exemplifies an attitude of service to customers and co-workers.

will be more motivated to reduce dissonance when the attitudes or behavior are important or when they believe the dissonance is due to something they can control. A third factor is the *rewards* of dissonance; high rewards accompanying high dissonance tend to reduce the tension inherent in the dissonance.

While Festinger argued that attitudes follow behavior, other researchers asked whether there was any relationship at all. More recent research shows that attitudes predict future behavior and confirmed Festinger's idea that "moderating variables" can strengthen the link.[6]

Moderating Variables The most powerful moderators of the attitudes relationship are the *importance* of the attitude, its *correspondence to behavior,* its *accessibility,* the presence of *social pressures,* and whether a person has *direct experience* with the attitude.[7]

Important attitudes reflect our fundamental values, self-interest, or identification with individuals or groups we value. These attitudes tend to show a strong relationship to our behavior.

Specific attitudes tend to predict specific behaviors, whereas general attitudes tend to best predict general behaviors. For instance, asking someone about her intention to stay with an organization for the next 6 months is likely to better predict turnover for that person than asking her how satisfied she is with her job overall. On the other hand, overall job satisfaction would better predict a general behavior, such as whether the individual was engaged in her work or motivated to contribute to her organization.[8]

Attitudes that our memories can easily access are more likely to predict our behavior. Interestingly, you're more likely to remember attitudes you frequently express. So the more you talk about your attitude on a subject, the more likely you are to remember it, and the more likely it is to shape your behavior.

Discrepancies between attitudes and behavior tend to occur when social pressures to behave in certain ways hold exceptional power, as in most organizations. This may explain why an employee who holds strong anti-union attitudes attends pro-union organizing meetings, or why tobacco executives, who are not smokers themselves and who tend to believe the research linking smoking and cancer, don't actively discourage others from smoking.

Finally, the attitude–behavior relationship is likely to be much stronger if an attitude refers to something with which we have direct personal experience. Asking college students with no significant work experience how they would respond to working for an authoritarian supervisor is far less likely to predict actual behavior than asking that same question of employees who have actually worked for such an individual.

What Are the Major Job Attitudes?

3 Compare and contrast the major job attitudes.

We each have thousands of attitudes, but OB focuses our attention on a very limited number of work-related attitudes. These tap positive or negative evaluations that employees hold about aspects of their work environment. Most of the research in OB has looked at three attitudes: job satisfaction, job involvement, and organizational commitment.[9] A few other important attitudes are perceived organizational support and employee engagement; we'll also briefly discuss these.

cognitive dissonance *Any incompatibility between two or more attitudes or between behavior and attitudes.*

Do Employers Owe Workers More Satisfying Jobs?

Research by the Conference Board suggests that job satisfaction for U.S. employees is at a 23-year low. This appears to be occurring in the midst of a dramatic growth in information technology that was supposed to make work easier for employees. What is going on here? Are employers failing to consider an ethical responsibility to employees by providing a satisfying, fulfilling experience at work?

When Professor James Heskett of Harvard posted information about these low job satisfaction rates on his blog, respondents provided a variety of different explanations for why U.S. workers are less satisfied than they were in the past. They included economic pressures, instability in the business environment, and increased competition to get the best jobs. Others believe businesses have

become so focused on stock prices and profitability that the personal relationship that used to exist between employers and employees has been lost. Still others proposed that in a poor economic environment, employees who wanted to switch to a new job aren't always able to find alternatives, leaving them "hostages" to a dissatisfying work situation.

Whatever the explanation, there is cause for concern. Survey data from Towers Watson's global workforce study of 20,000 employees in 22 markets around the world found that employees are especially concerned about job security and feel they are entirely responsible for ensuring their long-term career prospects work out. In the current economic environment, it seems that in employers' minds, employee well-being and

security have taken a back seat to coping with workplace realities.

What can managers do to ensure they are making ethical decisions about protecting the quality of the workplace in their organizations? As we have shown, managers can enact a variety of concrete steps—including improving working conditions and providing a positive social environment—that will make work more enjoyable for employees. Employers may also want to think about whether their efforts to achieve efficiency and productivity are creating a work environment that is not very satisfying for employees.

Sources: Based on J. Heskett, "Why Are Fewer and Fewer U.S. Employees Satisfied with Their Jobs?" *Harvard Business School Working Knowledge* (April 2, 2010), hbswk .hbs.edu; and Towers Watson, *2010 Global Workforce Study* (New York: Author, 2010).

Job Satisfaction   When people speak of employee attitudes, they usually mean **job satisfaction**, which describes a positive feeling about a job, resulting from an evaluation of its characteristics. A person with a high level of job satisfaction holds positive feelings about his or her job, while a person with a low level holds negative feelings. Because OB researchers give job satisfaction high importance, we'll review this attitude in detail later in the chapter.

Job Involvement   Related to job satisfaction is **job involvement**,[10] which measures the degree to which people identify psychologically with their job and consider their perceived performance level important to self-worth.[11] Employees with a high level of job involvement strongly identify with and really care about the kind of work they do. Another closely related concept is **psychological empowerment**, employees' beliefs in the degree to which they influence their work environment, their competence, the meaningfulness of their job, and their perceived autonomy.[12] One study of nursing managers in Singapore found that good leaders empower their employees by involving them in decisions, making them feel their work is important, and giving them discretion to "do their own thing."[13]

High levels of both job involvement and psychological empowerment are positively related to organizational citizenship and job performance.[14] High job involvement is also related to reduced absences and lower resignation rates.[15]

Organizational Commitment   In **organizational commitment**, an employee identifies with a particular organization and its goals and wishes to remain a

At Veterinary Cancer Group in Tustin, California, employees are committed to their company because they identify with their organization and its goals and want to remain part of the small business. The client care specialists shown in this photo and their co-workers share the cancer clinic's goal of improving the quality of life for patients and giving support to the families of patients. Veterinarian Mona Rosenberg, who founded the practice, has created a positive work environment at the clinic by hiring kind and compassionate people and by valuing the work of each employee, resulting in the favorable employee attitude of organizational commitment.

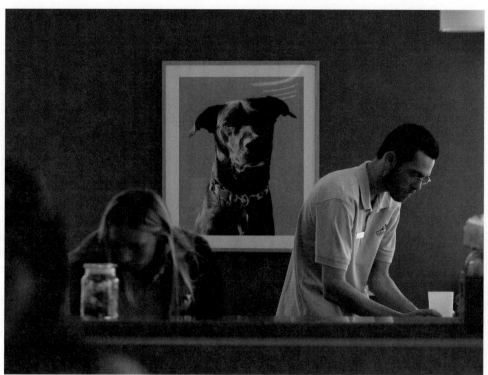

Source: 044/Zums Press/Newscom

member. Most research has focused on emotional attachment to an organization and belief in its values as the "gold standard" for employee commitment.[16]

A positive relationship appears to exist between organizational commitment and job productivity, but it is a modest one.[17] A review of 27 studies suggested the relationship between commitment and performance is strongest for new employees and considerably weaker for more experienced employees.[18] Interestingly, research indicates that employees who feel their employers fail to keep promises to them feel less committed, and these reductions in commitment, in turn, lead to lower levels of creative performance.[19] And, as with job involvement, the research evidence demonstrates negative relationships between organizational commitment and both absenteeism and turnover.[20]

Theoretical models propose that employees who are committed will be less likely to engage in work withdrawal even if they are dissatisfied, because they have a sense of organizational loyalty. On the other hand, employees who are not committed, who feel less loyal to the organization, will tend to show lower levels of attendance at work across the board. Research confirms this theoretical proposition.[21] It does appear that even if employees are not currently happy with their work, they are willing to make sacrifices for the organization if they are committed enough.

job satisfaction   *A positive feeling about one's job resulting from an evaluation of its characteristics.*

job involvement   *The degree to which a person identifies with a job, actively participates in it, and considers performance important to self-worth.*

psychological empowerment   *Employees' belief in the degree to which they affect their work environment, their competence, the meaningfulness of their job, and their perceived autonomy in their work.*

organizational commitment   *The degree to which an employee identifies with a particular organization and its goals and wishes to maintain membership in the organization.*

glOBalization!

Culture and Work–Life Balance

The increased time pressures of the always-connected workplace are eroding the boundary between work life and personal life, and many individuals in postindustrial economies struggle to balance the two. Is this striving for work–life balance unique to the North American and European context, or is it a global phenomenon?

One possible reason for variations in work–life balance across countries is differences in the structure and functioning of the family. Some research suggests that countries with stronger differences in expectations for men and women have different levels and types of work–life conflict. Other research suggests that work–life balance will be different in an individualistic country like the United States than in a country that is more collectivist in its orientation. In individualist countries, employers might expect more sacrifice from their employees in terms of their family lives, whereas collectivist nations where family has a higher priority will have fewer work–life balance issues. Conversely, collectivists' higher value on family may mean they feel more conflicted if there are competing demands from the workplace and home.

There are other reasons to suspect that research based on the U.S. context will not generalize to other countries. Data from a study by Harvard and McGill University researchers found that work–life balance policies like paid maternity leave, paternity leave, and paid time off in the United States are far less generous than in other wealthy nations. The study's lead author, Jody Heymann, notes, "More countries are providing the workplace protections that millions of Americans can only dream of." The research interest in work–life balance may at least partially be a reflection of an unusually strong conflict between work and family life in the United States.

At the same time, many of the same issues that contribute to work–life imbalance *are* present in other countries. Globally, the rise of the dual-earner couple has meant that both partners now have family responsibilities that must be met. Always-connected technology that blurs the line between personal and work time have become standard for managers in every part of the world. The institution of "siesta," or a midday break, used to be much more common in Hispanic cultures than it is today as the globalized workplace puts greater demands on workers. Concerns about overwork have also become very prevalent in the rapidly growing economic sphere of East Asia. The Japanese even have a term, *karoshi,* referring to death from overwork.

Research to date does suggest that work–life concerns are present in other cultures. For example, most studies find that feelings of conflict between work and personal life are related to lower levels of satisfaction and higher levels of psychological strain. The magnitude of these relationships varies across countries, but it appears that concerns about work interfering with family are present around the world. There is also evidence that translated U.S. surveys about work–life conflicts are equally good measures of work–life conflicts in Europe and East Asia.

Even with the growth of international research, most studies to date have been designed and conducted entirely within the United States, and many others have been conducted in cultures with marked similarities to the United States, like Canada and Great Britain. As the number of international studies continues to increase, we will develop a better understanding of how different cultures relate to work–life challenges.

Sources: Based on G. N. Powell, A. M. Francesco, and Y. Ling, "Toward Culture-Sensitive Theories of the Work–Family Interface," *Journal of Organizational Behavior* 30 (2009), pp. 597–616; "Survey: U.S. Workplace Not Family-Oriented." *MSNBC.com,* (May 22, 2007), www.msnbc.msn.com/id/16907584/; and J. Lu, O. Siu, P. E. Spector, and K. Shi, "Antecedents and Outcomes of a Fourfold Taxonomy of Work-Family Balance in Chinese Employed Parents," *Journal of Occupational Health Psychology* 14 (2009), pp. 182–192.

Perceived Organizational Support   Perceived organizational support (POS) is the degree to which employees believe the organization values their contribution and cares about their well-being (for example, an employee believes his organization would accommodate him if he had a child care problem or would forgive an honest mistake on his part). Research shows that people perceive their organization as supportive when rewards are deemed fair, when employees have a voice in decisions, and when they see their supervisors as supportive.[22] Employees with strong POS perceptions have been found more likely to have higher levels of organizational citizenship behaviors, lower levels of tardiness, and better customer

Employee engagement is high at Genentech, a biotechnology firm where employees share a serious commitment to science and patients and are passionate about the work they do. Genentech employees discover, develop, manufacture, and commercialize medicines that treat patients with serious or life-threatening medical conditions. Feeling that their contributions are important and meaningful, employees cite the chance to make a difference in the lives of patients as the number one reason they enjoy working at Genentech.

Source: Paul Sakuma/AP Images

service.[23] Though little cross-cultural research has been done, one study found POS predicted only the job performance and citizenship behaviors of untraditional or low power-distance Chinese employees—in short, those more likely to think of work as an exchange rather than a moral obligation.[24]

Employee Engagement   A new concept is **employee engagement**, an individual's involvement with, satisfaction with, and enthusiasm for, the work she does. We might ask employees whether they have access to resources and the opportunities to learn new skills, whether they feel their work is important and meaningful, and whether their interactions with co-workers and supervisors are rewarding.[25] Highly engaged employees have a passion for their work and feel a deep connection to their company; disengaged employees have essentially checked out—putting time but not energy or attention into their work. A study of nearly 8,000 business units in 36 companies found that those whose employees had high-average levels of engagement had higher levels of customer satisfaction, were more productive, brought in higher profits, and had lower levels of turnover and accidents than at other companies.[26] Molson Coors found engaged employees were five times less likely to have safety incidents, and when one did occur it was much less serious and less costly for the engaged employee than for a disengaged one ($63 per incident versus $392). Engagement becomes a real concern for most organizations because surveys indicate that few employees—between 17 percent and 29 percent—are highly engaged by their work. Caterpillar set out to increase employee engagement and recorded a resulting 80 percent drop in grievances and a 34 percent increase in highly satisfied customers.[27]

perceived organizational support (POS)   *The degree to which employees believe an organization values their contribution and cares about their well-being.*

employee engagement   *An individual's involvement with, satisfaction with, and enthusiasm for the work he or she does.*

Such promising findings have earned employee engagement a following in many business organizations and management consulting firms. However, the concept is relatively new and still generates active debate about its usefulness. One review of the literature concluded, "The meaning of employee engagement is ambiguous among both academic researchers and among practitioners who use it in conversations with clients." Another reviewer called engagement "an umbrella term for whatever one wants it to be."[28] More recent research has set out to clarify the dimensions of employee engagement. This work has demonstrated that engagement is distinct from job satisfaction and job involvement and incrementally predicts job behaviors after we take these traditional job attitudes into account.

SELF-ASSESSMENT LIBRARY

Am I Engaged?

In the Self-Assessment Library (available on CD or online), take assessment IV.B.1 (Am I Engaged?). (Note: If you do not currently have a job, answer the questions for your most recent job.)

Are These Job Attitudes Really All That Distinct?   You might wonder whether these job attitudes are really distinct. If people feel deeply engaged by their job (high job involvement), isn't it probable they like it too (high job satisfaction)? Won't people who think their organization is supportive (high perceived organizational support) also feel committed to it (strong organizational commitment)?

Evidence suggests these attitudes *are* highly related, perhaps to a troubling degree. For example, the correlation between perceived organizational support and affective commitment is very strong.[29] That means the variables may be redundant—if you know someone's affective commitment, you know her perceived organizational support. Why is redundancy troubling? Because it is inefficient and confusing. Why have two steering wheels on a car when you need only one? Why have two concepts—going by different labels—when you need only one?

Although we OB researchers like proposing new attitudes, often we haven't been good at showing how they compare and contrast with each other. There is some distinctiveness among them, but they overlap greatly, for various reasons including the employee's personality. Some people are predisposed to be positive or negative about almost everything. If someone tells you she loves her company, it may not mean a lot if she is positive about everything else in her life. Or the overlap may mean some organizations are just all-around better places to work than others. Then if you as a manager know someone's level of job satisfaction, you know most of what you need to know about how that person sees the organization.

Job Satisfaction

4   Define *job satisfaction* and show how we can measure it.

We have already discussed job satisfaction briefly. Now let's dissect the concept more carefully. How do we measure job satisfaction? What causes an employee to have a high level of job satisfaction? How do dissatisfied and satisfied employees affect an organization?

Measuring Job Satisfaction

Our definition of job satisfaction—a positive feeling about a job resulting from an evaluation of its characteristics—is clearly broad.[30] Yet that breadth is appropriate. A job is more than just shuffling papers, writing programming code, waiting on customers, or driving a truck. Jobs require interacting with co-workers and bosses, following organizational rules and policies, meeting performance standards, living with less than ideal working conditions, and the like.[31] An employee's assessment of his satisfaction with the job is thus a complex summation of many discrete elements. How, then, do we measure it?

Two approaches are popular. The single global rating is a response to one question, such as "All things considered, how satisfied are you with your job?" Respondents circle a number between 1 and 5 on a scale from "highly satisfied" to "highly dissatisfied." The second method, the summation of job facets, is more sophisticated. It identifies key elements in a job such as the nature of the work, supervision, present pay, promotion opportunities, and relationships with co-workers.[32] Respondents rate these on a standardized scale, and researchers add the ratings to create an overall job satisfaction score.

Is one of these approaches superior? Intuitively, summing up responses to a number of job factors seems likely to achieve a more accurate evaluation of job satisfaction. Research, however, doesn't support the intuition.[33] This is one of those rare instances in which simplicity seems to work as well as complexity, making one method essentially as valid as the other. The best explanation is that the concept of job satisfaction is so broad a single question captures its essence. The summation of job facets may also leave out some important data. Both methods are helpful. The single global rating method isn't very time consuming, thus freeing time for other tasks, and the summation of job facets helps managers zero in on problems and deal with them faster and more accurately.

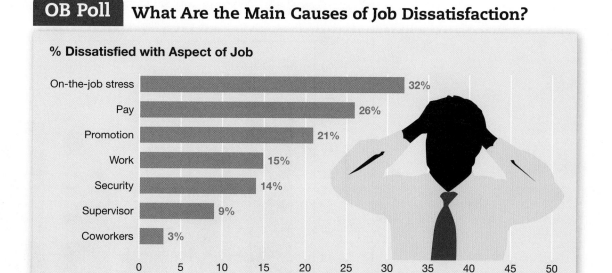

OB Poll   **What Are the Main Causes of Job Dissatisfaction?**

% Dissatisfied with Aspect of Job

Aspect	%
On-the-job stress	32%
Pay	26%
Promotion	21%
Work	15%
Security	14%
Supervisor	9%
Coworkers	3%

Source: L. Saad, "On-the-Job Stress Is U.S. Workers' Biggest Complaint," *Gallup Poll* (August 30, 2010), www.gallup.com/.

How Satisfied Are People in Their Jobs?

Are most people satisfied with their jobs? The answer seems to be a qualified "yes" in the United States and most other developed countries. Independent studies conducted among U.S. workers over the past 30 years generally indicate more workers are satisfied with their jobs than not. But a caution is in order. Recent data show a dramatic drop-off in average job satisfaction levels during the economic contraction that started in late 2007, so much so that only about half of workers report being satisfied with their jobs now.[34]

Research also shows satisfaction levels vary a lot, depending on which facet of job satisfaction you're talking about. As shown in Exhibit 3-2, people have typically been more satisfied with their jobs overall, with the work itself, and with their supervisors and co-workers than they have been with their pay and with promotion opportunities. It's not really clear why people dislike their pay and promotion possibilities more than other aspects of their jobs.[35]

Although job satisfaction appears relevant across cultures, that doesn't mean there are no cultural differences in job satisfaction. Evidence suggests employees in Western cultures have higher levels of job satisfaction than those in Eastern cultures.[36] Exhibit 3-3 provides the results of a global study of job satisfaction levels of workers in 15 countries. (This study included 23 countries, but for presentation purposes we report the results for only the largest.) As the exhibit shows, the highest levels appear in the United States and western Europe. Do employees in Western cultures have better jobs? Or are they simply more positive (and less self critical)? Although both factors are probably at play, evidence suggests that individuals in Eastern cultures find negative emotions less aversive more than do individuals in Western cultures, who tend to emphasize positive emotions and individual happiness.[37] That may be why employees in Western cultures such as the United States and Scandinavia are more likely to have higher levels of satisfaction.

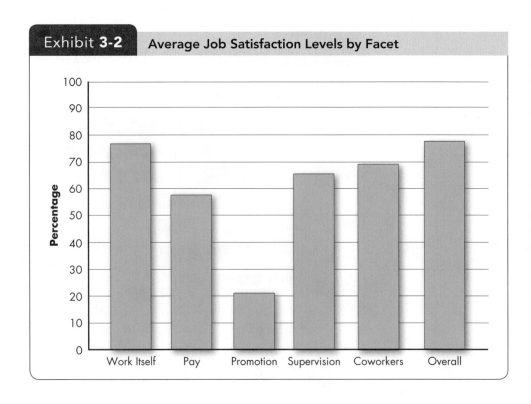

Exhibit 3-2   Average Job Satisfaction Levels by Facet

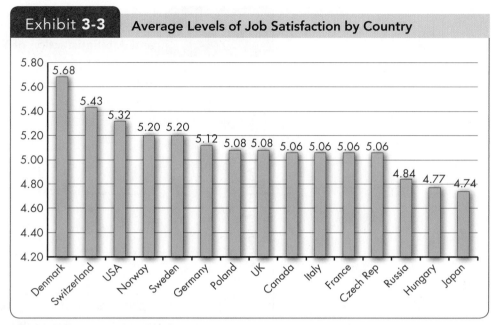

| Exhibit **3-3** | Average Levels of Job Satisfaction by Country |

Note: Scores represent average job-satisfaction levels in each country as rated on a 1 = very dissatisfied to 10 = very satisfied scale.

Source: M. Benz and B. S. Frey, "The Value of Autonomy: Evidence from the Self-Employed in 23 Countries," working paper 173, Institute for Empirical Research in Economics, University of Zurich, November 2003 (ssrn.com/abstract=475140).

What Causes Job Satisfaction?

5 Summarize the main causes of job satisfaction.

Think about the best job you've ever had. What made it so? Chances are you liked the work you did and the people with whom you worked. Interesting jobs that provide training, variety, independence, and control satisfy most employees.[38] There is also a strong correspondence between how well people enjoy the social context of their workplace and how satisfied they are overall. Interdependence, feedback, social support, and interaction with co-workers outside the workplace are strongly related to job satisfaction even after accounting for characteristics of the work itself.[39]

You've probably noticed that pay comes up often when people discuss job satisfaction. For people who are poor or who live in poor countries, pay does correlate with job satisfaction and overall happiness. But once an individual reaches a level of comfortable living (in the United States, that occurs at about $40,000 a year, depending on the region and family size), the relationship between pay and job satisfaction virtually disappears. People who earn $80,000 are, on average, no happier with their jobs than those who earn closer to $40,000. Take a look at Exhibit 3-4. It shows the relationship between the average pay for a job and the average level of job satisfaction. As you can see, there isn't much of a relationship there. Handsomely compensated jobs have average satisfaction levels no higher than those that pay much less. One researcher even found no significant difference when he compared the overall well-being of the richest people on the *Forbes* 400 list with that of Maasai herders in East Africa.[40]

Money does motivate people, as we will discover in Chapter 6. But what motivates us is not necessarily the same as what makes us happy. A recent poll by UCLA and the American Council on Education found that entering college freshmen rated becoming "very well off financially" first on a list of 19 goals, ahead of choices such as helping others, raising a family, or becoming proficient in an academic pursuit. Maybe your goal isn't to be happy. But if it is, money's probably not going to do much to get you there.[41]

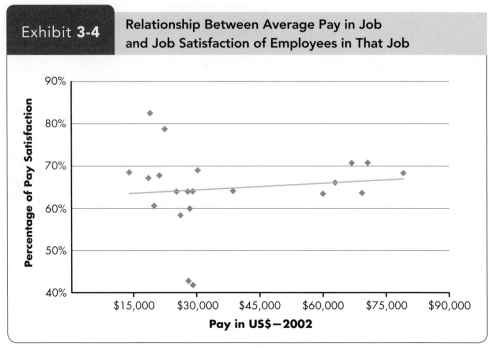

Exhibit **3-4** | **Relationship Between Average Pay in Job and Job Satisfaction of Employees in That Job**

Source: T. A. Judge, R. F. Piccolo, N. P. Podsakoff, J. C. Shaw, and B. L. Rich, "Can Happiness Be 'Earned'? The Relationship Between Pay and Job Satisfaction," working paper, University of Florida, 2005.

Job satisfaction is not just about job conditions. Personality also plays a role. Research has shown that people who have positive **core self-evaluations**—who believe in their inner worth and basic competence—are more satisfied with their jobs than those with negative core self-evaluations. Not only do they see their work as more fulfilling and challenging, they are more likely to gravitate toward challenging jobs in the first place. Those with negative core self-evaluations set less ambitious goals and are more likely to give up when confronting difficulties. Thus, they're more likely to be stuck in boring, repetitive jobs than those with positive core self-evaluations.[42]

The Impact of Satisfied and Dissatisfied Employees on the Workplace

6   Identify four employee responses to dissatisfaction.

What happens when employees like their jobs, and when they dislike their jobs? One theoretical model—the exit–voice–loyalty–neglect framework—is helpful in understanding the consequences of dissatisfaction. Exhibit 3-5 illustrates the framework's four responses, which differ along two dimensions: constructive/destructive and active/passive. The responses are as follows:[43]

- **Exit.** The **exit** response directs behavior toward leaving the organization, including looking for a new position as well as resigning.
- **Voice.** The **voice** response includes actively and constructively attempting to improve conditions, including suggesting improvements, discussing problems with superiors, and undertaking some forms of union activity.
- **Loyalty.** The **loyalty** response means passively but optimistically waiting for conditions to improve, including speaking up for the organization in the face of external criticism and trusting the organization and its management to "do the right thing."
- **Neglect.** The **neglect** response passively allows conditions to worsen and includes chronic absenteeism or lateness, reduced effort, and increased error rate.

Exhibit 3-5	Responses to Dissatisfaction

	Constructive	Destructive
Active	VOICE	EXIT
Passive	LOYALTY	NEGLECT

"Favorable Job Attitudes Make Organizations More Profitable"

This statement appears to be true. A recent study of 2,178 business units suggested that job attitudes measured at one point in time predicted organizational financial performance roughly six months later. In the study, job attitudes were measured through employees' responses to 12 questions (such as, "At work, my opinions seem to count") and financial performance was measured in terms of revenue and profit margin.

Why does employee job satisfaction appear to pay off? The authors of this study uncovered two explanations:

satisfied employees are less likely to quit, and they engender stronger customer loyalty. Low turnover and high customer loyalty both helped make organizations more profitable.

This study also found some evidence for what might be called a virtuous cycle: having satisfied employees tends to improve subsequent financial performance, which tends to improve later employee satisfaction even further.

No organization can be all things to all employees, but this study does suggest that attention to improving employee attitudes is well rewarded.

The authors of this study conclude, "Improving employee work perceptions can improve business competitiveness while positively impacting the well-being of employees."

Sources: Based on Anonymous, "Happy Employees May Be the Key to Success for Organizations," *Science Daily* (August 4, 2010), www.sciencedaily.com; J. K. Harter and F. L. Schmidt, "What Really Drives Financial Success?" *Gallup Management Journal* (September 2, 2010), http://gmj .gallup.com/content/142733/really-drives-financial-success.aspx.

core self-evaluations *Bottom-line conclusions individuals have about their capabilities, competence, and worth as a person.*

exit *Dissatisfaction expressed through behavior directed toward leaving the organization.*

voice *Dissatisfaction expressed through active and constructive attempts to improve conditions.*

loyalty *Dissatisfaction expressed by passively waiting for conditions to improve.*

neglect *Dissatisfaction expressed through allowing conditions to worsen.*

Exit and neglect behaviors encompass our performance variables—productivity, absenteeism, and turnover. But this model expands employee response to include voice and loyalty—constructive behaviors that allow individuals to tolerate unpleasant situations or revive satisfactory working conditions. It helps us understand situations, such as we sometimes find among unionized workers, for whom low job satisfaction is coupled with low turnover.[44] Union members often express dissatisfaction through the grievance procedure or formal contract negotiations. These voice mechanisms allow them to continue in their jobs while convincing themselves they are acting to improve the situation.

As helpful as this framework is, it's quite general. We now discuss more specific outcomes of job satisfaction and dissatisfaction in the workplace.

Job Satisfaction and Job Performance   As several studies have concluded, happy workers are more likely to be productive workers. Some researchers used to believe the relationship between job satisfaction and job performance was a myth. But a review of 300 studies suggested the correlation is pretty strong.[45] As we move from the individual to the organizational level, we also find support for the satisfaction–performance relationship.[46] When we gather satisfaction and productivity data for the organization as a whole, we find organizations with more satisfied employees tend to be more effective than organizations with fewer.

Job Satisfaction and OCB   It seems logical to assume job satisfaction should be a major determinant of an employee's organizational citizenship behavior (OCB).[47] Satisfied employees would seem more likely to talk positively about the organization, help others, and go beyond the normal expectations in their job, perhaps because they want to reciprocate their positive experiences. Consistent with this thinking, evidence suggests job satisfaction *is* moderately correlated with OCBs; people who are more satisfied with their jobs are more likely to engage in OCBs.[48] Why? Fairness perceptions help explain the relationship.[49] Those who feel their co-workers support them are more likely to engage in helpful behaviors, whereas those who have antagonistic relationships with co-workers are less likely to do so.[50] Individuals with certain personality traits are

Customers of CSN Stores appreciate the excellent service provided by the online retailer's customer representatives shown here at the company's offices in Boston. Service firms like CSN understand that satisfied employees increase customer satisfaction and loyalty. CSN believes that customers deserve exceptional service and is dedicated to hiring people who are friendly and willing to help others. The company helps shape a positive on-the-job attitude by giving employees product knowledge training and teaching them how to assess customer needs and how to guide buyers in making well-informed decisions.

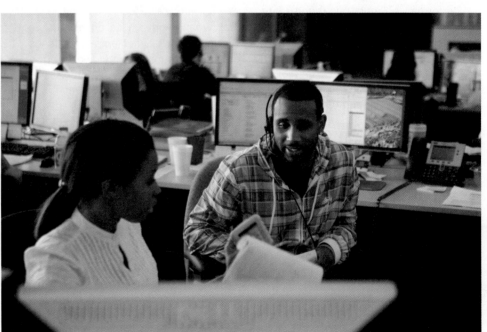

Source: Melanie Stetson Freeman/CSM/Newscom

also more satisfied with their work, which in turn leads them to engage in more OCBs.[51] Finally, research shows that when people are in a good mood, they are more likely to engage in OCBs.[52]

Job Satisfaction and Customer Satisfaction   As we noted in Chapter 1, employees in service jobs often interact with customers. Because service organization managers should be concerned with pleasing those customers, it is reasonable to ask, Is employee satisfaction related to positive customer outcomes? For frontline employees who have regular customer contact, the answer is "yes." Satisfied employees increase customer satisfaction and loyalty.[53]

A number of companies are acting on this evidence. The first core value of online retailer Zappos, "Deliver WOW through service," seems fairly obvious, but the way in which Zappos does it is not. Employees are encouraged to "create fun and a little weirdness" and are given unusual discretion in making customers satisfied; they are encouraged to use their imaginations, including sending flowers to disgruntled customers, and Zappos even offers a $2,000 bribe to quit the company after training (to weed out the half-hearted).[54] Other organizations seem to work the other end of the spectrum. Two independent reports—one on the Transportation Security Administration (TSA) and the other on airline passenger complaints—argue that low employee morale was a major factor undermining passenger satisfaction. At US Airways, employees have posted comments on blogs such as "Our planes (sic) smell filthy" and, from another, "How can I take pride in this product?"[55]

Job Satisfaction and Absenteeism   We find a consistent negative relationship between satisfaction and absenteeism, but it is moderate to weak.[56] While it certainly makes sense that dissatisfied employees are more likely to miss work, other factors affect the relationship. Organizations that provide liberal sick leave benefits are encouraging all their employees—including those who are highly satisfied—to take days off. You can find work satisfying yet still want to enjoy a 3-day weekend if those days come free with no penalties. When numerous alternative jobs are available, dissatisfied employees have high absence rates, but when there are few they have the same (low) rate of absence as satisfied employees.[57]

Job Satisfaction and Turnover   The relationship between job satisfaction and turnover is stronger than between satisfaction and absenteeism.[58] The satisfaction–turnover relationship also is affected by alternative job prospects. If an employee is presented with an unsolicited job offer, job dissatisfaction is less predictive of turnover because the employee is more likely leaving in response to "pull" (the lure of the other job) than "push" (the unattractiveness of the current job). Similarly, job dissatisfaction is more likely to translate into turnover when employment opportunities are plentiful because employees perceive it is easy to move. Finally, when employees have high "human capital" (high education, high ability), job dissatisfaction is more likely to translate into turnover because they have, or perceive, many available alternatives.[59]

Job Satisfaction and Workplace Deviance   Job dissatisfaction and antagonistic relationships with co-workers predict a variety of behaviors organizations find undesirable, including unionization attempts, substance abuse, stealing at work, undue socializing, and tardiness. Researchers argue these behaviors are indicators of a broader syndrome called *deviant behavior in the workplace* (or *counterproductive behavior* or *employee withdrawal*).[60] If employees don't like their work environment, they'll respond somehow, though it is not always easy to forecast exactly *how*. One worker might quit. Another might use work time to

When employees do not like their work environment, they will respond in some way. An attempt to form a union is one specific behavior that may stem from job dissatisfaction. At several different Wal-Mart locations throughout the United States, dissatisfied employees have tried, unsuccessfully, to organize a union as a way to receive better pay and more affordable health insurance. Joined by supporters, the employees shown here from a Wal-Mart warehouse and distribution center in California are protesting low wages and no health care or other benefits.

Source: Robyn Beck/Getty Images

surf the Internet or take work supplies home for personal use. In short, workers who don't like their jobs "get even" in various ways—and because those ways can be quite creative, controlling only one behavior, such as with an absence control policy, leaves the root cause untouched. To effectively control the undesirable consequences of job dissatisfaction, employers should attack the source of the problem—the dissatisfaction—rather than try to control the different responses.

Managers Often "Don't Get It"   Given the evidence we've just reviewed, it should come as no surprise that job satisfaction can affect the bottom line. One study by a management consulting firm separated large organizations into high morale (more than 70 percent of employees expressed overall job satisfaction) and medium or low morale (fewer than 70 percent). The stock prices of companies in the high-morale group grew 19.4 percent, compared with 10 percent for the medium- or low-morale group. Despite these results, many managers are unconcerned about employee job satisfaction. Still others overestimate how satisfied employees are with their jobs, so they don't think there's a problem when there is. In one study of 262 large employers, 86 percent of senior managers believed their organization treated its employees well, but only 55 percent of employees agreed. Another study found 55 percent of managers thought morale was good in their organization, compared to only 38 percent of employees.[61]

Regular surveys can reduce gaps between what managers *think* employees feel and what they *really* feel. Jonathan McDaniel, manager of a KFC restaurant in Houston, surveys his employees every 3 months. Some results led him to make changes, such as giving employees greater say about which workdays they have off. However, McDaniel believes the process itself is valuable. "They really love giving their opinions," he says. "That's the most important part of it—that they have a voice and that they're heard." Surveys are no panacea, but if job attitudes are as important as we believe, organizations need to find out where they can be improved.[62]

Employer–Employee Loyalty Is an Outdated Concept

POINT | **COUNTERPOINT**

The word *loyalty* is so outdated it is practically laughable. Long gone are the days when an employer would keep an employee for life, as are the days when an employee would work for a single company for his or her entire career.

Workplace guru Linda Gratton says, "Loyalty is dead—killed off through shortening contracts, outsourcing, automation and multiple careers. Faced with what could be 50 years of work, who honestly wants to spend that much time with one company? Serial monogamy is the order of the day."

Right or wrong, the commitment on each side of the equation is weak. Take the example of Renault. The company ended the 31-year career of employee Michel Balthazard (and two others) on charges of espionage. The problem? The charges were proved false. When the falseness of the charges became public, Renault halfheartedly offered the employees their jobs back and a lame apology: "Renault thanks them for the quality of their work at the group and wishes them every success in the future."

As for employee's loyalty to their employers, that too is worth little nowadays. One manager with Deloitte says the current employee attitude is, "I'm leaving, I had a great experience, and I'm taking that with me."

Employers tend to cut commitments to an employee, and reduce his or her benefits, the minute they perceive they can do so. Employees tend to jump at the best available job offer as soon as they see it.

The sooner we see the employment experience for what it is (mostly transactional, mostly short to medium term), the better off we'll be. The workplace is no place for fantasies.

There are employers and employees who show little regard for each other. That each side can be uncaring or cavalier is hardly a revelation. No doubt such cynical attitudes are as old as the employment relationship itself.

But is that the norm? And is it desirable? The answer to both these questions is "no."

Says management guru Tom Peters, "Bottom line: loyalty matters. A lot. Yesterday. Today. Tomorrow." University of Michigan's Dave Ulrich says, "Leaders who encourage loyalty want employees who are not only committed to and engaged in their work but who also find meaning from it."

It is true that the employer–employee relationship has changed. For example, (largely) gone are the days when employers provide guaranteed payout pensions to which employees contribute nothing. But is that such a bad thing? There is a big difference between asking employees to contribute to their pension plans and abandoning plans altogether (or firing without cause).

Moreover, it's not that loyalty is dead, but rather that employers are loyal to a different kind of employee. Gone are the days when an employer would refuse to fire a long-tenured but incompetent employee. But is that the kind of loyalty most employees expect today anyway? Companies are loyal to employees who do their jobs well, and that too is as it should be.

In short, employees still expect certain standards of decency and loyalty from their employers, and employers want engaged, committed employees in return. That is a good thing—and not so different from yesterday. Says workplace psychologist Binna Kandola, "Workplaces may have changed but loyalty is not dead—the bonds between people are too strong."

Sources: P. Korkki, "The Shifting Definition of Worker Loyalty," *The New York Times* (April 24, 2011), p. BU8; "Is Workplace Loyalty an Outmoded Concept?" *Financial Times* (March 8, 2011), www.ft.com/; and O. Gough and S. Arkani, "The Impact of the Shifting Pensions Landscape on the Psychological Contract," *Personnel Review* 40, no. 2 (2011), pp. 173–184.

Summary and Implications for Managers

Managers should be interested in their employees' attitudes because attitudes give warnings of potential problems and influence behavior. Creating a satisfied workforce is hardly a guarantee of successful organizational performance, but evidence strongly suggests that whatever managers can do to improve employee attitudes will likely result in heightened organizational effectiveness. Some take-away lessons from the study of attitudes include the following:

- Satisfied and committed employees have lower rates of turnover, absenteeism, and withdrawal behaviors. They also perform better on the job. Given that managers want to keep resignations and absences down—especially among their most productive employees—they'll want to do things that generate positive job attitudes.
- Managers will also want to measure job attitudes effectively so they can tell how employees are reacting to their work. As one review put it, "A sound measurement of overall job attitude is one of the most useful pieces of information an organization can have about its employees."[63]
- The most important thing managers can do to raise employee satisfaction is focus on the intrinsic parts of the job, such as making the work challenging and interesting.
- Although paying employees poorly will likely not attract high-quality employees to the organization or keep high performers, managers should realize that high pay alone is unlikely to create a satisfying work environment.

QUESTIONS FOR REVIEW

1 What are the main components of attitudes? Are these components related or unrelated?

2 Does behavior always follow from attitudes? Why or why not? Discuss the factors that affect whether behavior follows from attitudes.

3 What are the major job attitudes? In what ways are these attitudes alike? What is unique about each?

4 How do we measure job satisfaction?

5 What causes job satisfaction? For most people, is pay or the work itself more important?

6 What outcomes does job satisfaction influence? What implications does this have for management?

EXPERIENTIAL EXERCISE What Factors Are Most Important to Your Job Satisfaction?

Most of us probably want a job we think will satisfy us. But because no job is perfect, we often have to trade off job attributes. One job may pay well but provide limited opportunities for advancement or skill development. Another may offer work we enjoy but have poor benefits. The following is a list of 21 job factors or attributes:

- Autonomy and independence.
- Benefits.
- Career advancement opportunities.
- Career development opportunities.
- Compensation/pay.
- Communication between employees and management.
- Contribution of work to organization's business goals.
- Feeling safe in the work environment.
- Flexibility to balance life and work issues.
- Job security.
- Job-specific training.
- Management recognition of employee job performance.
- Meaningfulness of job.
- Networking.
- Opportunities to use skills/abilities.
- Organization's commitment to professional development.
- Overall corporate culture.
- Relationship with co-workers.
- Relationship with immediate supervisor.
- The work itself.
- The variety of work.

On a sheet of paper, rank-order these job factors from top to bottom so number 1 is the job factor you think is most important to your job satisfaction, number 2 is the second most important factor to your job satisfaction, and so on.

Next, gather in teams of three or four people and try the following:

1. Appoint a spokesperson who will take notes and report the answers to the following questions, on behalf of your group, back to the class.
2. Averaging across all members in your group, generate a list of the top five job factors.
3. Did most people in your group seem to value the same job factors? Why or why not?
4. Your instructor will provide you the results of a study of a random sample of 600 employees conducted by the Society for Human Resource Management (SHRM). How do your group's rankings compare with the SHRM results?
5. The chapter says pay doesn't correlate all that well with job satisfaction, but in the SHRM survey, people say it is relatively important. Can your group suggest a reason for the apparent discrepancy?
6. Now examine your own list again. Does your list agree with the group list? Does your list agree with the SHRM study?

ETHICAL DILEMMA Bounty Hunters

His SUV carefully obscured behind a row of trees, Rick Raymond, private investigator, was on another case. This case was not to catch the unfaithful spouse or petty criminal in action. Instead, Raymond was tracking an employee, at the request of an employer, to determine whether an Orlando repairman was sick as he claimed today and as he had claimed to be several times recently.

As we have seen, absenteeism is a huge problem for organizations that has left them desperate for solutions. One solution is to investigate. In the typical routine, when an employee calls in sick, the employer asks for the reason. If the reason is illness, and illness has been the reason for an

abnormal number of times in the past, the employer hires a P.I. to follow the employee and photograph or videotape his or her activity outside the house. Private investigators also are used to ascertain whether individuals filing injury claims (and drawing worker's compensation benefits) are in fact injured.

It may surprise you to learn that a recent court decision indicated hiring a private investigator to follow an employee is legal. In this particular case, Diana Vail was fired by Raybestos Products, an automotive parts manufacturer in Crawfordsville, Indiana, after an off-duty police officer hired by Raybestos produced evidence that she was abusing her sick-leave benefits. The U.S. Court of Appeals ruled that such investigations were legal.

Despite their legality, such investigations are controversial. Oracle and Hewlett-Packard have reportedly used private investigators to follow managers or uncover the source of leaks. Both actions spawned negative media coverage.

There is no doubt, though, that some employees do abuse their sick-leave benefits. In an earlier case, Raymond investigated an employee who called in sick with the flu for 3 days. Raymond discovered that she actually visited Orlando theme parks on each of those days. When Raymond showed her three time-stamped pictures of herself on rides, the employee's first response was, "That's not me!" In another case, Raymond caught a worker

constructing an elaborate scheme to call in sick and go on a cruise. "When he was shown the video surveillance I'd done, he actually said to his boss, 'I can't believe you'd be so sneaky.'" Raymond said. "The hypocrisy is amazing."

Questions

1. If you had reason to believe someone was lying about an absence from work, do you think it would be appropriate to investigate?

2. If excessive absenteeism is a real problem in an organization, are there alternatives to surveillance? If so, what are they, and do they have any limitations of their own?

Sources: E. Spitznagel, "The Sick-Day Bounty Hunters," *Businessweek* (December 6, 2010), pp. 93–95; D. Levine, "Oracle Enlists Private Eyes to Find HP CEO," *Reuters* (November 9, 2010), http://in.reuters .com/; and K. Gullo, "HP's Apotheker, Like Carmen Sandiego, Focus at Trial," *Businessweek* (November 10, 2010), www.businessweek.com/.

CASE INCIDENT 1 Long Hours, Hundreds of E-Mails, and No Sleep: Does This Sound Like a Satisfying Job?

In the 1970s, futurists were predicting that increases in technology would dramatically shorten the workweek for most people. But in the wired work world of today, where employees can reach "the office" from wherever they are, many managers are finding it extremely difficult to get away from their jobs. In fact, one employment firm estimated that 30 percent of professionals take less than their allotted vacation time, and 42 percent said they have to cancel vacation plans regularly. Consider a few examples:

- Gian Paolo Lombardo might work for a firm that manufactures luggage for luxury travel, but he's had precious little time for vacationing himself. During his last "faux-cation" 3 years ago, he spent most of the time in his hotel room in the resort town of Carmel, California, with his BlackBerry, while his wife Ellen chatted with other guests, hoping he'd finally finish with work. Ellen notes that no meal or movie goes by without her husband being hunched over his smartphone. She says, "I think he needs to go into rehab." He agrees.

- Irene Tse heads the government bond-trading division at Goldman Sachs. For 10 years, she has seen the stock market go from all-time highs to recession levels. Such fluctuations can mean millions of dollars in either profits or losses. "There are days when you can make a lot, and other days where you lose so much you're just stunned by what you've done," says Tse. She says she

hasn't slept through the night in years and often wakes up several times to check the global market status. Her average workweek? Eighty hours. "I've done this for 10 years, and I can count on the fingers of one hand the number of days in my career when I didn't want to come to work. Every day I wake up and I can't wait to get here."

- Tony Kurz is a managing director at Capital Alliance Partners, and he raises funds for real estate investments. However, these are not your average properties. Kurz often flies to exotic locations such as Costa Rica and Hawaii to woo prospective clients. He travels more than 300,000 miles per year, often sleeping on planes and coping with jet lag. Kurz is not the only one he knows with such a hectic work schedule. His girlfriend, Avery Baker, logs around 400,000 miles a year as the senior vice president of marketing for Tommy Hilfiger. "It's not easy to maintain a relationship like this," says Kurz. But do Kurz and Baker like their jobs? You bet.

- David Clark is the vice president of global marketing for MTV. His job often consists of traveling around the globe to promote the channel as well as to keep up with the global music scene. If he is not traveling (Clark typically logs 200,000 miles a year), a typical day consists of waking at 6:30 A.M. and immediately responding to numerous messages that have accumulated over the course of the night. He then goes to his office, where throughout the day he responds to another 500 or so messages from clients around the world. If he's lucky, he gets to spend an hour a day with his son, but then it's back to work until he finally goes to bed around midnight. Says Clark, "There are plenty of people who would love to have this job. They're knocking on the door all the time. So that's motivating."

Many individuals would balk at the prospect of a 60-hour or more workweek with constant traveling and little time for anything else. Some individuals are exhilarated by it. But the demands of such jobs are clearly not for everyone. Many quit, with turnover levels at 55 percent for consultants and 30 percent for investment bankers, according to Vault.com. However, clearly such jobs, while time-consuming and often stressful, can be satisfying to some individuals.

Sources: Based on L. Golden, "A Brief History of Long Work Time and the Contemporary Sources of Overwork," *Journal of Business Ethics* 84, (2009), pp. 217–227; L. Tischler, "Extreme Jobs (And the People Who Love Them)," *Fast Company*, April 2005, pp. 55–60, www.glo-jobs.com/article.php?article_no=87; M. Conlin, "Do Us a Favor, Take a Vacation," *Bloomberg Businessweek*, May 21, 2007, www.businessweek.com.

Questions

1. Do you think only certain individuals are attracted to these types of jobs, or is it the characteristics of the jobs themselves that are satisfying?

2. What characteristics of these jobs might contribute to increased levels of job satisfaction?

3. Given that the four individuals we just read about tend to be satisfied with their jobs, how might this satisfaction relate to their job performance, citizenship behavior, and turnover?

4. Recall David Clark's statement that "There are plenty of people who would love to have this job. They're knocking on the door all the time." How might Clark's perceptions that he has a job many others desire contribute to his job satisfaction?

CASE INCIDENT 2 Crafting a Better Job

Consider for a moment a midlevel manager at a multinational foods company, Fatima, who would seem to be at the top of her career. She's consistently making her required benchmarks and goals, she has built successful relationships with colleagues, and senior management have identified her as "high potential." But she isn't happy with her work. She'd be much more interested in understanding how her organization can use social media in marketing efforts. Ideally, she'd like to quit and find something that better suits her passions, but in the current economic environment this may not be an option. So she has decided to proactively reconfigure her current job.

Fatima is part of a movement toward job "crafting," which is the process of deliberately reorganizing your job so that it better fits your motives, strengths, and passions. The core of job crafting is creating diagrams of day-to-day activities with a coach. Then you and the coach collaboratively identify which tasks fit with your personal passions, and which tend to drain motivation and satisfaction. Next the client and coach work together to imagine ways to emphasize preferred activities and de-emphasize those that are less interesting. Many people engaged in job crafting find that upon deeper consideration, they have more control over their work than they thought.

So how did Fatima craft her job? She first noticed that she was spending too much of her time monitoring her team's performance and answering team questions, and not enough time working on the creative projects that inspire her. She then considered how to modify her relationship with the team so that these activities incorporated her passion for social media strategies, with team activities more centered around developing new marketing. She also identified members of her team who might be able to help her implement these new strategies and directed her interactions with these individuals toward her new goals. As a result, not only has her engagement in her work increased, but she has also developed new ideas that are being recognized and advanced within the organization. In sum, she has found that by actively and creatively examining her work, she has been able to craft her current job into one that is truly satisfying.

Questions

1. Why do you think many people are in jobs that are not satisfying? Do organizations help people craft satisfying and motivating jobs, and if not, why not?

2. Think about how you might reorient yourself to your own job. Are the principles of job crafting described above relevant to your work? Why or why not?

3. Some contend that job crafting sounds good in principle but is not necessarily available to everyone. What types of jobs are probably not amenable to job crafting activities?

4. Are there any potential drawbacks to the job crafting approach? How can these concerns be minimized?

Sources: Based on A. Wrzesniewski, J. M. Berg, and J. E. Dutton, "Turn the Job You Have into the Job You Want," *Harvard Business Review* (June 2010), pp. 114–117; A. Wrzesniewski and J. E. Dutton, "Crafting a Job: Revisioning Employees as Active Crafters of Their Work," *Academy of Management Review* 26 (2010), pp. 179–201; and J. Caplan, "Hate Your Job? Here's How to Reshape It," *Time* (December 4, 2009), www.time.com.

ENDNOTES

1. S. J. Breckler, "Empirical Validation of Affect, Behavior, and Cognition as Distinct Components of Attitude," *Journal of Personality and Social Psychology* (May 1984), pp. 1191–1205.
2. A. W. Wicker, "Attitude Versus Action: The Relationship of Verbal and Overt Behavioral Responses to Attitude Objects," *Journal of Social Issues* (Autumn 1969), pp. 41–78.
3. L. Festinger, *A Theory of Cognitive Dissonance* (Stanford, CA: Stanford University Press, 1957).
4. See, for instance, L. R. Fabrigar, R. E. Petty, S. M. Smith, and S. L. Crites, "Understanding Knowledge Effects on Attitude-Behavior Consistency: The Role of Relevance, Complexity, and Amount of Knowledge," *Journal of Personality and Social Psychology* 90, no. 4 (2006), pp. 556–577; and D. J. Schleicher, J. D. Watt, and G. J. Greguras, "Reexamining the Job Satisfaction-Performance Relationship: The Complexity of Attitudes," *Journal of Applied Psychology* 89, no. 1 (2004), pp. 165–177.
5. See, for instance, J. Nocera, "If It's Good for Philip Morris, Can It Also Be Good for Public Health?" *The New York Times* (June 18, 2006).
6. See L. R. Glasman and D. Albarracín, "Forming Attitudes That Predict Future Behavior: A Meta-Analysis of the Attitude–Behavior Relation," *Psychological Bulletin* (September 2006), pp. 778–822; I. Ajzen, "Nature and Operation of Attitudes," in S. T. Fiske, D. L. Schacter, and C. Zahn-Waxler (eds.), *Annual Review of Psychology*, vol. 52 (Palo Alto, CA: Annual Reviews, Inc., 2001), pp. 27–58; and M. Riketta, "The Causal Relation Between Job Attitudes and Performance: A Meta-Analysis of Panel Studies," *Journal of Applied Psychology*, 93, no. 2 (2008), pp. 472–481.
7. Ibid.
8. D. A. Harrison, D. A. Newman, and P. L. Roth, "How Important Are Job Attitudes? Meta-Analytic Comparisons of Integrative Behavioral Outcomes and Time Sequences," *Academy of Management Journal* 49, no. 2 (2006), pp. 305–325.
9. D. P. Moynihan and S. K. Pandey, "Finding Workable Levers Over Work Motivation: Comparing Job Satisfaction, Job Involvement, and Organizational Commitment," *Administration & Society* 39, no. 7 (2007), pp. 803–832.
10. See, for example, J. M. Diefendorff, D. J. Brown, and A. M. Kamin, "Examining the Roles of Job Involvement and Work Centrality in Predicting Organizational Citizenship Behaviors and Job Performance," *Journal of Organizational Behavior* (February 2002), pp. 93–108.
11. Based on G. J. Blau and K. R. Boal, "Conceptualizing How Job Involvement and Organizational Commitment Affect Turnover and Absenteeism," *Academy of Management Review* (April 1987), p. 290.
12. G. Chen and R. J. Klimoski, "The Impact of Expectations on Newcomer Performance in Teams as Mediated by Work Characteristics, Social Exchanges, and Empowerment," *Academy of Management Journal* 46, no. 5 (2003), pp. 591–607; A. Ergeneli, G. Saglam, and S. Metin, "Psychological Empowerment and Its Relationship to Trust in Immediate Managers," *Journal of Business Research* (January 2007), pp. 41–49; and S. E. Seibert, S. R. Silver, and W. A. Randolph, "Taking Empowerment to the Next Level: A Multiple-Level Model of Empowerment, Performance, and Satisfaction," *Academy of Management Journal* 47, no. 3 (2004), pp. 332–349.
13. B. J. Avolio, W. Zhu, W. Koh, and P. Bhatia, "Transformational Leadership and Organizational Commitment: Mediating Role of Psychological Empowerment and Moderating Role of Structural Distance," *Journal of Organizational Behavior* 25, no. 8 (2004), pp. 951–968.
14. J. M. Diefendorff, D. J. Brown, A. M. Kamin, and R. G. Lord, "Examining the Roles of Job Involvement and Work Centrality in Predicting Organizational Citizenship Behaviors and Job Performance," *Journal of Organizational Behavior* (February 2002), pp. 93–108.
15. M. R. Barrick, M. K. Mount, and J. P. Strauss, "Antecedents of Involuntary Turnover Due to a Reduction in Force," *Personnel Psychology* 47, no. 3 (1994), pp. 515–535.
16. O. N. Solinger, W. van Olffen, and R. A. Roe, "Beyond the Three-Component Model of Organizational Commitment," *Journal of Applied Psychology* 93 (2008), pp. 70–83.
17. B. J. Hoffman, C. A. Blair, J. P. Meriac, and D. J. Woehr, "Expanding the Criterion Domain? A Quantitative Review of the OCB Literature," *Journal of Applied Psychology* 92, no. 2 (2007), pp. 555–566.
18. T. A. Wright and D. G. Bonett, "The Moderating Effects of Employee Tenure on the Relation Between Organizational Commitment and Job Performance: A Meta-Analysis," *Journal of Applied Psychology* (December 2002), pp. 1183–1190.
19. T. W. H. Ng, D. C. Feldman, and S. S. K. Lam, "Psychological Contract Breaches, Organizational Commitment, and Innovation-Related Behaviors: A Latent Growth Modeling

Approach," *Journal of Applied Psychology* 95 (2010), pp. 744–751.

20. See, for instance, K. Bentein, C. Vandenberghe, R. Vandenberg, and F. Stinglhamber, "The Role of Change in the Relationship between Commitment and Turnover: A Latent Growth Modeling Approach," *Journal of Applied Psychology* 90 (2005), pp. 468–482; and J. D. Kammeyer-Mueller, C. R. Wanberg, T. M. Glomb, and D. Ahlburg, "The Role of Temporal Shifts in Turnover Processes: It's About Time." *Journal of Applied Psychology* 90 (2005), pp. 644–658.

21. J. P. Hausknecht, N. J. Hiller, and R. J. Vance, "Work-Unit Absenteeism: Effects of Satisfaction, Commitment, Labor Market Conditions, and Time," *Academy of Management Journal* 51 (2008), pp. 1223–1245.

22. L. Rhoades, R. Eisenberger, and S. Armeli, "Affective Commitment to the Organization: The Contribution of Perceived Organizational Support," *Journal of Applied Psychology* 86, no. 5 (2001), pp. 825–836.

23. C. Vandenberghe, K. Bentein, R. Michon, J. Chebat, M. Tremblay, and J. Fils, "An Examination of the Role of Perceived Support and Employee Commitment in Employee–Customer Encounters," *Journal of Applied Psychology* 92, no. 4 (2007), pp. 1177–1187; and P. Eder and R. Eisenberger, "Perceived Organizational Support: Reducing the Negative Influence of Coworker Withdrawal Behavior," *Journal of Management* 34, no. 1 (2008), pp. 55–68.

24. J. Farh, R. D. Hackett, and J. Liang, "Individual-Level Cultural Values as Moderators of Perceived Organizational Support—Employee Outcome Relationships in China: Comparing the Effects of Power Distance and Traditionality," *Academy of Management Journal* 50, no. 3 (2007), pp. 715–729.

25. B. L. Rich, J. A. Lepine, and E. R. Crawford, "Job Engagement: Antecedents and Effects on Job Performance," *Academy of Management Journal* 53 (2010), pp. 617–635.

26. J. K. Harter, F. L. Schmidt, and T. L. Hayes, "Business-Unit-Level Relationship Between Employee Satisfaction, Employee Engagement, and Business Outcomes: A Meta-Analysis," *Journal of Applied Psychology* 87, no. 2 (2002), pp. 268–279.

27. N. R. Lockwood, *Leveraging Employee Engagement for Competitive Advantage* (Alexandria, VA: Society for Human Resource Management, 2007); and R. J. Vance, *Employee Engagement and Commitment* (Alexandria, VA: Society for Human Resource Management, 2006).

28. W. H. Macey and B. Schneider, "The Meaning of Employee Engagement," *Industrial and Organizational Psychology* 1 (2008), pp. 3–30; A. Saks, "The Meaning and Bleeding of Employee Engagement: How Muddy Is The Water?" *Industrial and Organizational Psychology* 1 (2008), pp. 40–43.

29. L. Rhoades and R. Eisenberger, "Perceived Organizational Support: A Review of the Literature," *Journal of Applied Psychology* 87, no. 4 (2002), pp. 698–714; and R. L. Payne and D. Morrison, "The Differential Effects of Negative Affectivity on Measures of Well-Being Versus Job Satisfaction and Organizational Commitment," *Anxiety, Stress & Coping: An International Journal* 15, no. 3 (2002), pp. 231–244.

30. For problems with the concept of job satisfaction, see R. Hodson, "Workplace Behaviors," *Work and Occupations* (August 1991), pp. 271–290; and H. M. Weiss and R. Cropanzano, "Affective Events Theory: A Theoretical Discussion of the Structure, Causes and Consequences of Affective Experiences at Work," in B. M. Staw and L. L. Cummings (eds.), *Research in Organizational Behavior*, vol. 18 (Greenwich, CT: JAI Press, 1996), pp. 1–3.

31. The Wyatt Company's 1989 national WorkAmerica study identified 12 dimensions of satisfaction: Work organization, working conditions, communications, job performance and performance review, co-workers, supervision, company management, pay, benefits, career development and training, job content and satisfaction, and company image and change.

32. See E. Spector, *Job Satisfaction: Application, Assessment, Causes, and Consequences* (Thousand Oaks, CA: Sage, 1997), p. 3.

33. J. Wanous, A. E. Reichers, and M. J. Hudy, "Overall Job Satisfaction: How Good Are Single-Item Measures?" *Journal of Applied Psychology* (April 1997), pp. 247–252.

34. A. F. Chelte, J. Wright, and C. Tausky, "Did Job Satisfaction Really Drop During the 1970s?" *Monthly Labor Review* (November 1982), pp. 33–36; "Job Satisfaction High in America, Says Conference Board Study," *Monthly Labor Review* (February 1985), p. 52; K. Bowman, "Attitudes About Work, Chores, and Leisure in America," *AEI Opinion Studies* (August 25, 2003); and J. Pepitone, "U.S. Job Satisfaction Hits 22-Year Low," *CNNMoney.com* (January 5, 2010).

35. W. K. Balzer, J. A. Kihm, P. C. Smith, J. L. Irwin, P. D. Bachiochi, C. Robie, E. F. Sinar, and L. F. Parra, *Users' Manual for the Job Descriptive Index (JDI; 1997 Revision) and the Job in General Scales* (Bowling Green, OH: Bowling Green State University, 1997).

36. M. J. Gelfand, M. Erez, and Z. Aycan, "Cross-Cultural Organizational Behavior," *Annual Review of Psychology* 58 (2007), pp. 479–514; and A. S. Tsui, S. S. Nifadkar, and A. Y. Ou, "Cross-National, Cross-Cultural Organizational Behavior Research: Advances, Gaps, and Recommendations," *Journal of Management* (June 2007), pp. 426–478.

37. M. Benz and B. S. Frey, "The Value of Autonomy: Evidence from the Self-Employed in 23 Countries," working paper 173, Institute for Empirical Research in Economics, University of Zurich, November 2003 (ssrn.com/abstract=475140); and P. Warr, *Work, Happiness, and Unhappiness* (Mahwah, NJ: Laurence Erlbaum, 2007).

38. J. Barling, E. K. Kelloway, and R. D. Iverson, "High-Quality Work, Job Satisfaction, and Occupational Injuries," *Journal of Applied Psychology* 88, no. 2 (2003), pp. 276–283; and F. W. Bond and D. Bunce, "The Role of Acceptance and Job Control in Mental Health, Job Satisfaction, and Work Performance," *Journal of Applied Psychology* 88, no. 6 (2003), pp. 1057–1067.

39. S. E. Humphrey, J. D. Nahrgang, and F. P. Morgeson, "Integrating Motivational, Social, and Contextual Work Design Features: A Meta-Analytic Summary and Theoretical Extension of the Work Design Literature," *Journal of Applied Psychology* 92, no. 5 (2007), pp. 1332–1356; and D. S. Chiaburu and D. A. Harrison, "Do Peers Make the Place? Conceptual Synthesis and Meta-Analysis of Coworker Effect

on Perceptions, Attitudes, OCBs, and Performance," *Journal of Applied Psychology* 93, no. 5 (2008), pp. 1082–1103.

40. E. Diener, E. Sandvik, L. Seidlitz, and M. Diener, "The Relationship Between Income and Subjective Well-Being: Relative or Absolute?" *Social Indicators Research* 28 (1993), pp. 195–223.

41. E. Diener and M. E. P. Seligman, "Beyond Money: Toward an Economy of Well-Being," *Psychological Science in the Public Interest* 5, no. 1 (2004), pp. 1–31; and A. Grant, "Money = Happiness? That's Rich: Here's the Science Behind the Axiom," *The (South Mississippi) Sun Herald* (January 8, 2005).

42. T. A. Judge and C. Hurst, "The Benefits and Possible Costs of Positive Core Self-Evaluations: A Review and Agenda for Future Research," in D. Nelson and C. L. Cooper (eds.), *Positive Organizational Behavior* (London, UK: Sage Publications, 2007), pp. 159–174.

43. See D. Farrell, "Exit, Voice, Loyalty, and Neglect as Responses to Job Dissatisfaction: A Multidimensional Scaling Study," *Academy of Management Journal* (December 1983), pp. 596–606; C. E. Rusbult, D. Farrell, G. Rogers, and A. G. Mainous III, "Impact of Exchange Variables on Exit, Voice, Loyalty, and Neglect: An Integrative Model of Responses to Declining Job Satisfaction," *Academy of Management Journal* (September 1988), pp. 599–627; M. J. Withey and W. H. Cooper, "Predicting Exit, Voice, Loyalty, and Neglect," *Administrative Science Quarterly* (December 1989), pp. 521–539; J. Zhou and J. M. George, "When Job Dissatisfaction Leads to Creativity: Encouraging the Expression of Voice," *Academy of Management Journal* (August 2001), pp. 682–696; J. B. Olson-Buchanan and W. R. Boswell, "The Role of Employee Loyalty and Formality in Voicing Discontent," *Journal of Applied Psychology* (December 2002), pp. 1167–1174; and A. Davis-Blake, J. P. Broschak, and E. George, "Happy Together? How Using Nonstandard Workers Affects Exit, Voice, and Loyalty Among Standard Employees," *Academy of Management Journal* 46, no. 4 (2003), pp. 475–485.

44. R. B. Freeman, "Job Satisfaction as an Economic Variable," *American Economic Review* (January 1978), pp. 135–141.

45. T. A. Judge, C. J. Thoresen, J. E. Bono, and G. K. Patton, "The Job Satisfaction–Job Performance Relationship: A Qualitative and Quantitative Review," *Psychological Bulletin* (May 2001), pp. 376–407.

46. C. Ostroff, "The Relationship Between Satisfaction, Attitudes, and Performance: An Organizational Level Analysis," *Journal of Applied Psychology* (December 1992), pp. 963–974; A. M. Ryan, M. J. Schmit, and R. Johnson, "Attitudes and Effectiveness: Examining Relations at an Organizational Level," *Personnel Psychology* (Winter 1996), pp. 853–882; and J. K. Harter, F. L. Schmidt, and T. L. Hayes, "Business-Unit Level Relationship Between Employee Satisfaction, Employee Engagement, and Business Outcomes: A Meta-Analysis," *Journal of Applied Psychology* (April 2002), pp. 268–279.

47. See P. Podsakoff, S. B. MacKenzie, J. B. Paine, and D. G. Bachrach, "Organizational Citizenship Behaviors: A Critical Review of the Theoretical and Empirical Literature and Suggestions for Future Research," *Journal of Management* 26, no. 3 (2000), pp. 513–563.

48. B. J. Hoffman, C. A. Blair, J. P. Maeriac, and D. J. Woehr, "Expanding the Criterion Domain? A Quantitative Review of the OCB Literature," *Journal of Applied Psychology* 92, no. 2 (2007), pp. 555–566.

49. S. L. Blader and T. R. Tyler, "Testing and Extending the Group Engagement Model: Linkages Between Social Identity, Procedural Justice, Economic Outcomes, and Extrarole Behavior," *Journal of Applied Psychology* 94, no. 2 (2009), pp. 445–464.

50. D. S. Chiaburu and D. A. Harrison, "Do Peers Make the Place? Conceptual Synthesis and Meta-Analysis of Coworker Effect on Perceptions, Attitudes, OCBs, and Performance," *Journal of Applied Psychology* 93, no. 5 (2008), pp. 1082–1103.

51. R. Ilies, I. S. Fulmer, M. Spitzmuller, and M. D. Johnson, "Personality and Citizenship Behavior: The Mediating Role of Job Satisfaction," *Journal of Applied Psychology* 94 (2009), pp. 945–959.

52. R. Ilies, B. A. Scott, and T. A. Judge, "The Interactive Effects of Personal Traits and Experienced States on Intraindividual Patterns of Citizenship Behavior," *Academy of Management Journal* 49 (2006), pp. 561–575.

53. See, for instance, D. J. Koys, "The Effects of Employee Satisfaction, Organizational Citizenship Behavior, and Turnover on Organizational Effectiveness: A Unit-Level, Longitudinal Study," *Personnel Psychology* (Spring 2001), pp. 101–114; and C. Vandenberghe, K. Bentein, R. Michon, J. Chebat, M. Tremblay, and J. Fils, "An Examination of the Role of Perceived Support and Employee Commitment in Employee-Customer Encounters," *Journal of Applied Psychology* 92, no. 4 (2007), pp. 1177–1187; and M. Schulte, C. Ostroff, S. Shmulyian, and A. Kinicki, "Organizational Climate Configurations: Relationships to Collective Attitudes, Customer Satisfaction, and Financial Performance," *Journal of Applied Psychology* 94 (2009), pp. 618–634.

54. J. M. O'Brien, "Zappos Knows How to Kick It," *Fortune* (February 2, 2009), pp. 55–60.

55. T. Frank, "Report: Low Morale May Hurt Airport Security," *USA Today* (June 25, 2008), p. 3A; and J. Bailey, "Fliers Fed Up? The Employees Feel the Same," *The New York Times* (December 22, 2007), pp. A1, A18.

56. E. A. Locke, "The Nature and Causes of Job Satisfaction," in M. D. Dunnette (ed.), *Handbook of Industrial and Organizational Psychology* (Chicago: Rand McNally, 1976), p. 1331; K. D. Scott and G. S. Taylor, "An Examination of Conflicting Findings on the Relationship Between Job Satisfaction and Absenteeism: A Meta-Analysis," *Academy of Management Journal* (September 1985), pp. 599–612; and R. Steel and J. R. Rentsch, "Influence of Cumulation Strategies on the Long-Range Prediction of Absenteeism," *Academy of Management Journal* (December 1995), pp. 1616–1634.

57. J. P. Hausknecht, N. J. Hiller, and R. J. Vance, "Work-Unit Absenteeism: Effects of Satisfaction, Commitment, Labor Market Conditions, and Time," *Academy of Management Journal* 51, no. 6 (2008), pp. 1123–1245.

58. W. Hom and R. W. Griffeth, *Employee Turnover* (Cincinnati, OH: South-Western Publishing, 1995); R. W. Griffeth, P. W. Hom, and S. Gaertner, "A Meta-Analysis of Antecedents and Correlates of Employee Turnover: Update, Moderator

Tests, and Research Implications for the Next Millennium," *Journal of Management* 26, no. 3 (2000), p. 479.

59. T. H. Lee, B. Gerhart, I. Weller, and C. O. Trevor, "Understanding Voluntary Turnover: Path-Specific Job Satisfaction Effects and the Importance of Unsolicited Job Offers," *Academy of Management Journal* 51, no. 4 (2008), pp. 651–671.

60. P. E. Spector, S. Fox, L. M. Penney, K. Bruursema, A. Goh, and S. Kessler, "The Dimensionality of Counterproductivity: Are All Counterproductive Behaviors Created Equal?" *Journal of Vocational Behavior* 68, no. 3 (2006), pp. 446–460; and D. S. Chiaburu and D. A. Harrison, "Do Peers Make the Place? Conceptual Synthesis and Meta-Analysis of Coworker Effect on Perceptions, Attitudes, OCBs, and Performance," *Journal of Applied Psychology* 93, no. 5 (2008), pp. 1082–1103.

61. K. Holland, "Inside the Minds of Your Employees," *The New York Times* (January 28, 2007), p. B1; "Study Sees Link Between Morale and Stock Price," *Workforce Management* (February 27, 2006), p. 15; and "The Workplace as a Solar System," *The New York Times* (October 28, 2006), p. B5.

62. E. White, "How Surveying Workers Can Pay Off," *The Wall Street Journal* (June 18, 2007), p. B3.

63. Harrison, D. A., Newman, D. A., & Roth, P. L., How important are job attitudes?: Meta-analytic comparisons for integrative behavioral outcomes and time sequences. *Academy of Management Journal*, no. 49 (2006), pp. 320–321.

LOVE AT WORK: TABOO NO MORE?

At one time, workplace romances were a taboo topic. When they *were* discussed by organizations, it was often by means of a memo outlining the policy against such liaisons among co-workers. Though the motivations behind such policies were not evil—mostly, it was a desire to avoid sexual harassment lawsuits emanating from one employee's amorous pursuit of another—they also overlooked a real problem: a large percentage of couples first met in the workplace, and for many reasons, work is a great place to meet a future mate.

In one 2011 survey of 3,900 workers, nearly 20 percent indicated they had dated co-workers at least twice in their working career, and about one-third of those who did ended up marrying a person they dated at work. What's more—65 percent of those who date someone at work say they are open about it at work.

Nathan Shaw and Maiko Sato met at a Cisco training program. For two years, they dated openly as fellow employees. When Nathan decided to propose to Maiko, he asked his boss to help with a ruse. During a fake test of teleconferencing equipment, Nathan's proposal flashed on the screen. Maiko said yes, and they remain happily married and working at Cisco's San Jose, CA, headquarters.

To Stacie Taylor, who has been dating Cary Costello, a fellow employee of Zoot Enterprises (a Bozeman, Montana, technical services provider), for more than 3 years, finding a mate at work is logical. "People spend so much of their time working that it's unavoidable," she said. Cary adds, "If you're around a bunch of like-minded people who have similar interests, it's bound to happen."

There are risks. When 27-year-old Arti Banerjee's relationship with her co-worker went sour, her ex-boyfriend started spreading rumors about her in the office and on Facebook. He forwarded some of her text messages to co-workers. After two months, Banerjee quit.

Another risk is violations of privacy. Some employees—to protect their privacy or from fear of their organization's reaction—try to keep their relationship under wraps. It generally doesn't work. When GMR Marketing co-workers Michelle Walters and Ryan Scholz began dating, they hid their relationship, only to be found out. As it turns out, they had nothing to fear. Their boss, Gary Reynolds, says GMR has no dating policy: "Why try to mandate behavior and develop policy when you don't need it?"

Sources: S. Shallenbarger, "For Office Romance, The Secret's Out," *The Wall Street Journal* (February 10, 2010), pp. D1–D2; "Survey: Workplace Dating Losing Stigma," *UPI* (February 13, 2011), www.upi.com; R. T. Sharma, "How to Handle an Office Romance, Especially after a Messy Breakup," *Economic Times* (May 1, 2011), http://economictimes.indiatimes.com/.

Emotions and Moods

Time cools, time clarifies; no mood can be maintained quite unaltered through the course of hours. —Mark Twain

As the preceding stories illustrate, emotions can be an important part of the way people behave at work. Given the obvious role emotions play in our lives, it might surprise you that, until recently, the field of OB has given the topic of emotions little attention.[1] Why? We offer two possible explanations.

First is the *myth of rationality*.[2] Until very recently, the protocol of the work world kept a damper on emotions. A well-run organization didn't allow employees to express frustration, fear, anger, love, hate, joy, grief, or similar feelings thought to be the antithesis of rationality. Though researchers and managers knew emotions were an inseparable part of everyday life, they tried to create organizations that were emotion-free. Of course, that wasn't possible.

The second explanation is that many believed emotions of any kind were disruptive.[3] Researchers looked at strong negative emotions—especially anger—that interfered with an employee's ability to work effectively. They rarely viewed emotions as constructive or contributing to enhanced performance.

Certainly some emotions, particularly exhibited at the wrong time, can hinder performance. But employees do bring their emotions to work every day, and no study of OB would be comprehensive without considering their role in workplace behavior.

SELF-ASSESSMENT LIBRARY

How Are You Feeling Right Now?

In the Self-Assessment Library (available on CD or online), take assessment IV.D.1 (How Are You Feeling Right Now?) and answer the following questions.

1. What was higher—your positive mood score or negative mood score? How do these scores compare with those of your classmates?
2. Did your score surprise you? Why or why not?
3. What sorts of things influence your positive moods, your negative moods?

What Are Emotions and Moods?

1 Differentiate emotions from moods and list the basic emotions and moods.

In our analysis, we'll need three terms that are closely intertwined: *affect, emotions,* and *moods.*

Affect is a generic term that covers a broad range of feelings people experience, including both emotions and moods.[4] **Emotions** are intense feelings directed at someone or something.[5] **Moods** are less intense feelings than emotions and often (though not always) arise without a specific event acting as a stimulus.[6]

Most experts believe emotions are more fleeting than moods.[7] For example, if someone is rude to you, you'll feel angry. That intense feeling probably comes and goes fairly quickly, maybe even in a matter of seconds. When you're in a bad mood, though, you can feel bad for several hours.

Emotions are reactions to a person (seeing a friend at work may make you feel glad) or an event (dealing with a rude client may make you feel frustrated). You show your emotions when you're "happy about something, angry at someone, afraid of something."[8] Moods, in contrast, aren't usually directed at a person or an event. But emotions can turn into moods when you lose focus on the event or object that started the feeling. And, by the same token, good or bad moods can make you more emotional in response to an event. So when a colleague criticizes how you spoke to a client, you might show emotion (anger) toward a specific object (your colleague). But as the specific emotion dissipates, you might just feel generally dispirited. You can't attribute this feeling to any single event; you're just not your normal self. You might then overreact to other events. This affect state describes a mood. Exhibit 4-1 shows the relationships among affect, emotions, and mood.

First, as the exhibit shows, affect is a broad term that encompasses emotions and moods. Second, there are differences between emotions and moods. Some of these differences—that emotions are more likely to be caused by a specific event, and emotions are more fleeting than moods—we just discussed. Other differences are subtler. For example, unlike moods, emotions like anger and disgust tend to be more clearly revealed by facial expressions. Also, some researchers speculate that emotions may be more action-oriented—they may lead us to some immediate action—while moods may be more cognitive, meaning they may cause us to think or brood for a while.[9]

Finally, the exhibit shows that emotions and moods are closely connected and can influence each other. Getting your dream job may generate the emotion of joy, which can put you in a good mood for several days. Similarly, if you're in a good or bad mood, it might make you experience a more intense positive or negative emotion than otherwise. In a bad mood, you might blow up in response to a co-worker's comment that would normally have generated only a mild reaction.

Affect, emotions, and moods are separable in theory; in practice the distinction isn't always crystal-clear. In some areas, researchers have studied mostly moods, in other areas mainly emotions. So, when we review the OB topics on emotions and moods, you may see more information about emotions in one area and about moods in another. This is simply the state of the research.

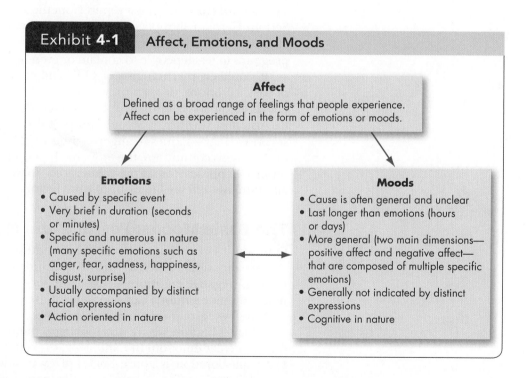

Exhibit 4-1   Affect, Emotions, and Moods

Affect
Defined as a broad range of feelings that people experience. Affect can be experienced in the form of emotions or moods.

Emotions
- Caused by specific event
- Very brief in duration (seconds or minutes)
- Specific and numerous in nature (many specific emotions such as anger, fear, sadness, happiness, disgust, surprise)
- Usually accompanied by distinct facial expressions
- Action oriented in nature

Moods
- Cause is often general and unclear
- Last longer than emotions (hours or days)
- More general (two main dimensions—positive affect and negative affect—that are composed of multiple specific emotions)
- Generally not indicated by distinct expressions
- Cognitive in nature

---

affect *A broad range of feelings that people experience.*

emotions *Intense feelings that are directed at someone or something.*

moods *Feelings that tend to be less intense than emotions and that lack a contextual stimulus.*

The Basic Emotions

How many emotions are there? There are dozens, including anger, contempt, enthusiasm, envy, fear, frustration, disappointment, embarrassment, disgust, happiness, hate, hope, jealousy, joy, love, pride, surprise, and sadness. Numerous researchers have tried to limit them to a fundamental set.[10] But some argue that it makes no sense to think in terms of "basic" emotions because even emotions we rarely experience, such as shock, can have a powerful effect on us.[11] Other researchers, even philosophers, say there are universal emotions common to all. René Descartes, often called the founder of modern philosophy, identified six "simple and primitive passions"—wonder, love, hatred, desire, joy, and sadness—and argued that "all the others are composed of some of these six or are species of them."[12] Although other philosophers like Hume, Hobbes, and Spinoza identified categories of emotions, proof of the existence of a basic set of emotions still waits for contemporary researchers.

Psychologists have tried to identify basic emotions by studying facial expressions.[13] One problem is that some emotions are too complex to be easily represented on our faces. Many think of love as the most universal of all emotions,[14] for example, yet it's not easy to express it through only a facial expression. Cultures also have norms that govern emotional expression, so the way we *experience* an emotion isn't always the same as the way we *show* it. People in the United States and the Middle East recognize a smile as indicating happiness, but in the Middle East a smile is also more likely to be seen as a sign of sexual attraction, so women have learned not to smile at men.[15] In collectivist countries people are more likely to believe another's emotional displays have something to do with the relationship between them, while people in individualistic cultures don't think others' emotional expressions are directed at them. French retail clerks, in contrast, are infamous for being surly toward customers (as a report from the French government itself confirmed). Serious German shoppers have reportedly been turned off by Walmart's friendly greeters and helpful staff.[16] And many companies today offer anger-management programs to teach people to contain or even hide their inner feelings.[17]

It's unlikely psychologists or philosophers will ever completely agree on a set of basic emotions, or even on whether there is such a thing. Still, many researchers agree on six essentially universal emotions—anger, fear, sadness, happiness, disgust, and surprise.[18] Some even plot them along a continuum: happiness—surprise—fear—sadness—anger—disgust.[19] The closer two emotions are to each other on this continuum, the more likely people will confuse them. We sometimes mistake happiness for surprise, but rarely do we confuse happiness and disgust. In addition, as we'll see later on, cultural factors can also influence interpretations.

The Basic Moods: Positive and Negative Affect

One way to classify emotions is by whether they are positive or negative.[20] Positive emotions—such as joy and gratitude—express a favorable evaluation or feeling. Negative emotions—such as anger or guilt—express the opposite. Keep in mind that emotions can't be neutral. Being neutral is being nonemotional.[21]

When we group emotions into positive and negative categories, they become mood states because we are now looking at them more generally instead of isolating one particular emotion. In Exhibit 4-2, excited is a pure marker of high positive affect, while boredom is a pure marker of low positive affect. Nervous is a pure marker of high negative affect; relaxed is a pure marker of low negative affect. Finally, some emotions—such as contentment (a mixture of high positive affect and low negative affect) and sadness (a mixture of low positive affect and high negative affect)—are in between. You'll notice this model does not include all emotions. Some, such as surprise, don't fit well because they're not as clearly positive or negative.

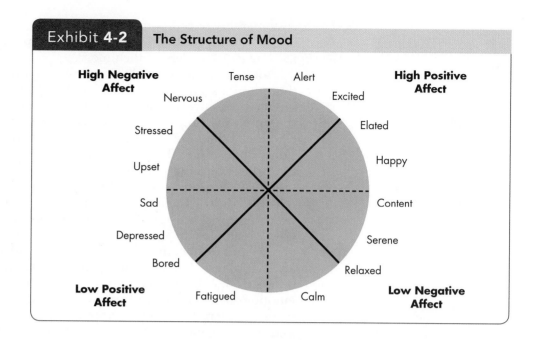

Exhibit **4-2**   The Structure of Mood

So, we can think of **positive affect** as a mood dimension consisting of positive emotions such as excitement, self-assurance, and cheerfulness at the high end and boredom, sluggishness, and tiredness at the low end. **Negative affect** is a mood dimension consisting of nervousness, stress, and anxiety at the high end and relaxation, tranquility, and poise at the low end. (*Note:* Positive and negative affect *are* moods. We're using these labels, rather than *positive mood* and *negative mood,* because that's how researchers label them.)

Positive affect and negative affect play out at work and beyond in that they color our perceptions, and these perceptions can become their own reality. One flight attendant posted an anonymous blog on the Web that said, "I work in a pressurized aluminum tube and the environment outside my 'office' cannot sustain human life. That being said, the human life inside is not worth sustaining sometimes . . . in fact, the passengers can be jerks, and idiots. I am often treated with no respect, nobody listens to me . . . until I threaten to kick them off the plane."[22] Clearly, if a flight attendant is in a bad mood, it's going to influence his perceptions of passengers, which will, in turn, influence his behavior.

Negative emotions are likely to translate into negative moods. People think about events that created strong negative emotions five times as long as they do about events that created strong positive ones.[23] So, we should expect people to recall negative experiences more readily than positive ones. Perhaps one reason is that, for most of us, negative experiences also are more unusual. Indeed, research finds a **positivity offset**, meaning that at zero input (when nothing in particular is going on), most individuals experience a mildly positive mood.[24] So, for most people, positive moods are somewhat more common than negative moods. The positivity offset also appears to operate at work. One study of

---

positive affect   *A mood dimension that consists of specific positive emotions such as excitement, self-assurance, and cheerfulness at the high end and boredom, sluggishness, and tiredness at the low end.*

negative affect   *A mood dimension that consists of emotions such as nervousness, stress, and anxiety at the high end and relaxation, tranquility, and poise at the low end.*

positivity offset   *The tendency of most individuals to experience a mildly positive mood at zero input (when nothing in particular is going on).*

customer-service representatives in a British call center (a job where it's probably pretty difficult to feel positive) revealed people reported experiencing positive moods 58 percent of the time.[25]

Does the degree to which people experience these positive and negative emotions vary across cultures? Yes. In China, people report experiencing fewer positive and negative emotions than people in other cultures, and the emotions they experience are less intense. Compared with Mainland Chinese, Taiwanese are more like U.S. workers in their experience of emotions: on average, they report more positive and fewer negative emotions than their Chinese counterparts.[26] People in most cultures appear to experience certain positive and negative emotions, but the frequency and intensity varies to some degree.[27] Despite these differences, people from all over the world interpret negative and positive emotions in much the same way. We all view negative emotions, such as hate, terror, and rage, as dangerous and destructive, and we desire positive emotions, such as joy, love, and happiness. However, some cultures value certain emotions more than others. U.S. culture values enthusiasm, while the Chinese consider negative emotions more useful and constructive than do people in the United States. Pride is generally a positive emotion in Western individualistic cultures such as the United States, but Eastern cultures such as China and Japan view pride as undesirable.[28]

The Function of Emotions

2 Discuss whether emotions are rational and what functions they serve.

Do Emotions Make Us Irrational?   How often have you heard someone say "Oh, you're just being emotional"? You might have been offended. The famous astronomer Carl Sagan once wrote, "Where we have strong emotions, we're liable to fool ourselves." These observations suggest rationality and emotion are in conflict, and that if you exhibit emotion you are likely to act irrationally. One team of authors argues that displaying emotions such as sadness to the point of crying is so toxic to a career that we should leave the room rather than allow others to witness it.[29] These perspectives suggest the demonstration or even experience of emotions can make us seem weak, brittle, or irrational. However, research is increasingly showing that emotions are actually critical to rational thinking.[30] There has been evidence of such a link for a long time.

Consider Phineas Gage, a railroad worker in Vermont. One September day in 1848, while Gage was setting an explosive charge at work, a 3-foot 7-inch iron bar flew into his lower-left jaw and out through the top of his skull. Remarkably, Gage survived his injury. He was still able to read and speak, and he performed well above average on cognitive ability tests. However, it became clear he had lost his ability to experience emotion; he was emotionless at even the saddest misfortunes or the happiest occasions. Gage's inability to express emotion eventually took away his ability to reason. He started making irrational choices about his life, often behaving erratically and against his self-interests. Despite being an intelligent man whose intellectual abilities were unharmed by the accident, Gage drifted from job to job, eventually taking up with a circus. In commenting on Gage's condition, one expert noted, "Reason may not be as pure as most of us think it is or wish it were . . . emotions and feelings may not be intruders in the bastion of reason at all: they may be enmeshed in its networks, for worse *and* for better."[31]

The example of Phineas Gage and many other brain injury studies show emotions are critical to rational thinking. We must have the ability to experience emotions to be rational. Why? Because our emotions provide important information about how we understand the world around us. Would we really want a manager to make a decision about firing an employee without regarding either his or the employee's emotions? The key to good decision making is to employ both thinking *and* feeling in our decisions.

Do Emotions Make Us Ethical? A growing body of research has begun to examine the relationship between emotions and moral attitudes.[32] It was previously believed that, like decision making in general, most ethical decision making was based on higher-order cognitive processes, but research on moral emotions increasingly questions this perspective. Examples of moral emotions include sympathy for the suffering of others, guilt about our own immoral behavior, anger about injustice done to others, contempt for those who behave unethically, and disgust at violations of moral norms. Numerous studies suggest that these reactions are largely based on feelings rather than cold cognition.

You can think about this research in your own life to see how the emotional model of ethics operates. Consider the massive earthquake that struck Japan in 2011. When you heard about it, did you feel emotionally upset about the suffering of others, or did you make more of a rational calculation about their unfortunate situation? Consider a time when you have done something that hurt someone else. Did you feel angry or upset with yourself? Or think about a time when you have seen someone else treated unfairly. Did you feel contempt for the person acting unfairly, or did you engage in a cool rational calculation of the justice of the situation? Most people who think about these situations do have at least some sense of an emotional stirring that might prompt them to engage in ethical actions like donating money to help others, apologizing and attempting to make amends, or intervening on behalf of those who have been mistreated. In sum, we can conclude that people who are behaving ethically are at least partially making decisions based on their emotions and feelings, and this emotional reaction will often be a good thing.

Sources of Emotions and Moods

Have you ever said "I got up on the wrong side of the bed today"? Have you ever snapped at a co-worker or family member for no particular reason? If you have, it probably makes you wonder where emotions and moods come from. Here we discuss some of the primary influences.

Personality Moods and emotions have a trait component: most people have built-in tendencies to experience certain moods and emotions more frequently than others do. People also experience the same emotions with different intensities. Contrast Texas Tech basketball coach Bobby Knight to Microsoft CEO Bill Gates. The first is easily moved to anger, while the other is relatively distant and unemotional. Knight and Gates probably differ in **affect intensity**, or how strongly they experience their emotions.[33] Affectively intense people experience both positive and negative emotions more deeply: when they're sad, they're really sad, and when they're happy, they're really happy.

By studying brain injuries, such as the one experienced by Phineas Gage and whose skull is illustrated here, researchers discovered an important link between emotions and rational thinking. They found that losing the ability to emote led to loss of the ability to reason. From this discovery, researchers learned that our emotions provide us with valuable information that helps our thinking process.

3 Identify the sources of emotions and moods.

---

affect intensity *Individual differences in the strength with which individuals experience their emotions.*

What's My Affect Intensity?

In the Self-Assessment Library (available on CD or online), take assessment IV.D.2 (What's My Affect Intensity?).

Day of the Week and Time of the Day   Are people in their best moods on the weekends? As Exhibit 4-3 shows, people tend to be in their worst moods (highest negative affect and lowest positive affect) early in the week, and in their best moods (highest positive affect and lowest negative affect) late in the week.[34]

What about time of the day? (See Exhibit 4-4.) We often think we are either "morning" or "evening" people. However, most of us actually follow the same pattern. Regardless of what time we go to bed at night or get up in the morning, levels of positive affect tend to peak at around the halfway point between waking and sleeping. Negative affect, however, shows little fluctuation throughout the day.

What does this mean for organizational behavior? Monday morning is probably not the best time to ask someone for a favor or convey bad news. Our workplace interactions will probably be more positive from midmorning onward and also later in the week.

Weather   When do you think you would be in a better mood—when it's 70 degrees and sunny, or on a gloomy, cold, rainy day? Many people believe their mood is tied to the weather. However, a fairly large and detailed body of evidence conducted by multiple researchers suggests weather has little effect on mood.[35] One expert concluded, "Contrary to the prevailing cultural view, these data indicate that people do not report a better mood on bright and sunny days (or, conversely, a worse mood on dark and rainy days)."[36] **Illusory correlation** explains why people tend to *think* nice weather improves their mood. It occurs when people associate two events that in reality have no connection.

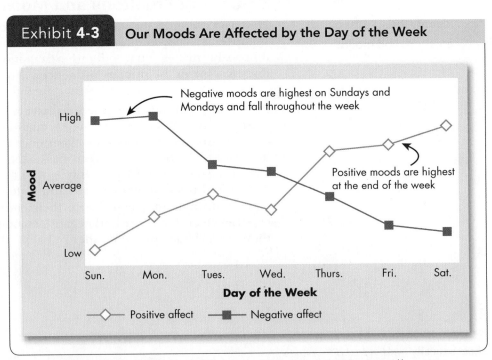

Exhibit 4-3   Our Moods Are Affected by the Day of the Week

Source: "Our Moods Are Affected by the Day of the Week" from Mood and Temperament, by D. Watson. Reprinted by permission of Guilford Publications, Inc.

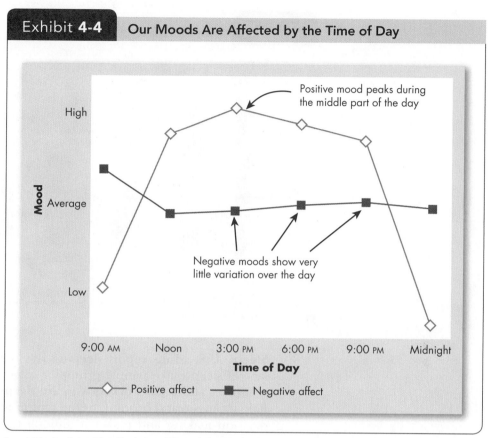

Exhibit 4-4   **Our Moods Are Affected by the Time of Day**

Source: "Our Moods Are Affected by the Day of the Week" from Mood and Temperament, *by D. Watson. Reprinted by permission of Guilford Publications, Inc.*

Stress   As you might imagine, stressful daily events at work (a nasty e-mail, an impending deadline, the loss of a big sale, a reprimand from the boss) negatively affect moods. The effects of stress also build over time. As the authors of one study note, "a constant diet of even low-level stressful events has the potential to cause workers to experience gradually increasing levels of strain over time."[37] Mounting levels of stress can worsen our moods, and we experience more negative emotions. Consider the following entry from a worker's blog: "I'm in a bit of a blah mood today . . . physically, I feel funky, though, and the weather out combined with the amount of personal and work I need to get done are getting to me." Although sometimes we thrive on stress, most of us, like this blogger, find stress takes a toll on our mood.[38]

Social Activities   Do you tend to be happiest when out with friends? For most people, social activities increase positive mood and have little effect on negative mood. But do people in positive moods seek out social interactions, or do social interactions cause people to be in good moods? It seems both are true.[39] Does the *type* of social activity matter? Indeed it does. Research suggests activities that are physical (skiing or hiking with friends), informal (going to a party), or epicurean (eating with others) are more strongly associated with increases in positive mood than events that are formal (attending a meeting) or sedentary (watching TV with friends).[40]

illusory correlation   *The tendency of people to associate two events when in reality there is no connection.*

OB Poll   Moods of the Unemployed

Mood	Unemployed	Employed
Thriving	34	55
Worried	50	28
Sad	36	17
Stressed	54	35
Angry	25	12
Depressed	27	16

Source: E. Mendes and L. Saad, "For Unemployed, Length, Scale of Job Search Affects Well Being, Life Ratings," *Gallup News* (February 25, 2011), http://www.gallup.com/. Reprinted with permission.

Sleep   U.S. adults report sleeping less than adults a generation ago.[41] Does lack of sleep make people grumpier? Sleep quality does affect mood. Undergraduates and adult workers who are sleep-deprived report greater feelings of fatigue, anger, and hostility.[42] One reason is that poor or reduced sleep impairs decision making and makes it difficult to control emotions.[43] A recent study suggests poor sleep also impairs job satisfaction because people feel fatigued, irritable, and less alert.[44]

Exercise and social activities are two of the primary sources of emotions and moods. For most people, working out and participating in social activities that are informal and physical increase positive moods. Shown here are employees of Blizzard Entertainment taking a break from work to play volleyball. Blizzard, a developer of entertainment software, offers employees yoga classes, a sand volleyball court, basketball court, bike track, and fitness center where they can exercise and socialize. Like many other organizations, Blizzard believes these activities result in happier, healthier, and more productive employees.

Source: 044/ZUMA Press/Newscomm

We Are Better Judges of When Others Are Happy Than When They Are Sad

This statement is generally true. Consider the following scenario: Assume you work with three other people: Jane, Blake, and Morgan. Jane received several calls from customers unhappy with a product made by her company. Blake broke up with his fiancé. Morgan has had a recurrence of depression. Yet at lunch today all three seemed pretty happy. There were smiles, laughter, and in general good humor for all to see. Yet each person, in his or her own way, is weathering tough times. If you had to gauge the moods of Jane, Blake, and Morgan, you might say they were in relatively good moods. If you asked each of them, however, they might attribute their seeming good humor to impression management, "putting on a good face," or the effects of the social environment.

This hypothetical scenario reflects a phenomenon recent research supports: we typically underestimate the negative emotions experienced by others. In other words, people often feel worse than we believe they do. To some extent, the same is true of positive emotions: We estimate people to experience more positive emotions than they do. Why do we think people are in better moods than they really are, and what are the implications?

There are two reasons we see others as experiencing more positive and fewer negative emotions than they do:

1. People generally experience more negative emotions when they are by themselves than when they are in the company of others. So we tend to see others not at their lowest, but at their highest.
2. Most people are reluctant to divulge negative feelings in social situations. Thus, when we're feeling low, we tend to avoid showing others how bad we feel.

The upshot? First, we should appreciate that in social situations like work, people probably feel less happy than they appear. Second, we should be less afraid to disclose negative emotions to friends, close coworkers, and significant others, given the costs of "keeping it all in." Often the strongest emotional links we form with others occur when someone reports experiencing something negative that we too have experienced.

Sources: Based on: A. H. Jordan, B. Monin, C. S. Dweck, B. J. Lovett, O. P. John, and J. J. Gross, "Misery Has More Company Than People Think: Underestimating the Prevalence of Others' Negative Emotions," *Personality and Social Psychology Bulletin* 37, no. 1 (2011), pp. 120–135; M. Szalavitz, "Misery Has More Company Than You Think, Especially on Facebook," *Time* (January 27, 2011), http://healthland.time.com; and C. Jarrett, "Other People May Experience More Misery Than You Realize," *Research Digest* (January 24, 2011), http://bps-research-digest.blogspot.com.

Exercise You often hear people should exercise to improve their mood. Does "sweat therapy" really work? It appears so. Research consistently shows exercise enhances peoples' positive mood.[45] While not terribly strong overall, the effects are strongest for those who are depressed. So exercise may help put you in a better mood, but don't expect miracles.

Age Do young people experience more extreme positive emotions (so-called youthful exuberance) than older people? If you answered "yes," you were wrong. One study of people ages 18 to 94 revealed that negative emotions seem to occur less as people get older. Periods of highly positive moods lasted longer for older individuals, and bad moods faded more quickly.[46] The study implies emotional experience improves with age; as we get older, we experience fewer negative emotions.

Sex Many believe women are more emotional than men. Is there any truth to this? Evidence does confirm women are more emotionally expressive than men;[47] they experience emotions more intensely, they tend to "hold onto" emotions longer than men, and they display more frequent expressions of both positive and negative emotions, except anger.[48] Evidence from a study of participants from 37 different countries found that men consistently report higher levels of powerful emotions like anger, whereas women report more powerless emotions like sadness and fear. Thus, there are some sex differences in the experience and expression of emotions.[49]

Should You Expect "Service with a Smile" All Around the World?

In most customer service jobs in the United States, there is a strong social pressure for employees to display an upbeat demeanor at all times, demonstrating happy and friendly emotions in an effort to make customers feel pleasant and at ease. Experts on emotional labor have found that these rules encouraging "service with a smile" are also found in many other countries, but that doesn't mean they are followed to the same extent everywhere.

One study examined international differences in emotional displays by having participants from Israel, France, Singapore, and the United States explain how they would behave in a variety of emotionally charged situations as customer service agents. Their results showed that although there was a strongly consistent tendency for respondents to report they would try to show happiness and suppress anger toward customers, there were differences in the extent to which people would engage in these forms of emotional labor. Respondents from Singapore were especially negatively disposed toward expressing anger at customers, while the French found it more acceptable. U.S. respondents were especially likely to display happiness toward customers, while French respondents were most reserved in their expressions of happiness.

This is not to say there aren't cross-cultural similarities in customer service expectations and customer reactions. There are no cultures in which smiling is seen as an expression of hostility or in which a grimace or frown is seen as a sign of friendliness. There also appear to be consistently positive reactions to others who display positive emotions. However, companies that operate in multiple markets should expect to see differences in the types of emotions customer service employees will display.

Sources: A. Grandey, A Rafaeli, S. Ravid, J. Wirtz, and D. D. Steiner, "Emotion Display Rules at Work in the Global Service Economy: The Special Case of the Customer," *Journal of Service Management* 21, (2010), pp. 388–412; and D. Matsumoto, "Culture and Emotional Expression," in R. S. Wyer, C. Chiu, and Y. Hong (Eds.), *Understanding Culture: Theory, Research, and Application* (New York: Taylor and Francis, 2009), pp. 271–288.

People also tend to attribute men's and women's emotions in ways that might be based on stereotypes of what typical emotional reactions are. One study showed that experimental participants who read about emotional expressions interpreted women's reactions as being dispositional (related to personality), whereas men's reactions were interpreted as being due to the situation around them.[50] For example, a picture of a sad woman led observers to believe she was acting consistently with an emotional personality type, whereas a picture of a sad man was more likely to be attributed to his having a bad day. Another study showed that participants were faster at detecting angry expressions on male faces and happy expressions on female faces; neutral faces in men were attributed as more angry and neutral faces in women were interpreted as happy.[51]

Emotional Labor

4 Show the impact emotional labor has on employees.

If you've ever had a job in retail sales or waited on tables in a restaurant, you know the importance of projecting a friendly demeanor and smiling. Even though there were days when you didn't feel cheerful, you knew management expected you to be upbeat when dealing with customers. So you faked it. Every employee expends physical and mental labor by putting body and mind, respectively, into the job. But jobs also require **emotional labor**, an employee's expression of organizationally desired emotions during interpersonal transactions at work.

In addition to physical and mental labor, jobs also require emotional labor. Emerging from studies of service jobs, the concept of emotional labor involves an employee's expression of emotions that an organization requires during interpersonal transactions. Employees of this new Apple store in Scottsdale, Arizona, greeted shoppers standing in line and waiting to get into the store with a warm reception. Employees' smiles and high fives are expressions of emotional labor that Apple requires and considers appropriate for their jobs.

Source: K94/ZUMA Press/Newscom

The concept of emotional labor emerged from studies of service jobs. Airlines expect their flight attendants to be cheerful; we expect funeral directors to be sad and doctors emotionally neutral. But emotional labor is relevant to almost every job. At the least your managers expect you to be courteous, not hostile, in your interactions with co-workers. The true challenge arises when employees have to project one emotion while feeling another.[52] This disparity is **emotional dissonance**, and it can take a heavy toll. Bottled-up feelings of frustration, anger, and resentment can eventually lead to emotional exhaustion and burnout.[53] It's from the increasing importance of emotional labor as a key component of effective job performance that we have come to understand the relevance of emotion within the field of OB.

Emotional labor creates dilemmas for employees. There are people with whom you have to work that you just plain don't like. Maybe you consider their personality abrasive. Maybe you know they've said negative things about you behind your back. Regardless, your job requires you to interact with these people on a regular basis. So you're forced to feign friendliness.

It can help you, on the job especially, if you separate emotions into *felt* or *displayed emotions*.[54] **Felt emotions** are an individual's actual emotions. In contrast, **displayed emotions** are those that the organization requires workers to show and considers appropriate in a given job. They're not innate; they're learned. "The ritual look of delight on the face of the first runner-up as the new Miss America is announced is a product of the display rule that losers should mask their sadness with an expression of joy for the winner."[55] Similarly, most of us know we're expected to act sad at funerals, regardless of whether we consider the person's death a loss, and to appear happy at weddings even if we don't feel like celebrating.

---

emotional labor   *A situation in which an employee expresses organizationally desired emotions during interpersonal transactions at work.*

emotional dissonance   *Inconsistencies between the emotions people feel and the emotions they project.*

felt emotions   *An individual's actual emotions.*

displayed emotions   *Emotions that are organizationally required and considered appropriate in a given job.*

Research suggests that at U.S. workplaces, it is expected that we should typically display positive emotions like happiness and excitement and suppress negative emotions like fear, anger, disgust, and contempt.[56] Effective managers have learned to be serious when giving an employee a negative performance evaluation and to hide their anger when they've been passed over for promotion. A salesperson who hasn't learned to smile and appear friendly, despite his or her true feelings at the moment, typically won't last long in the job. How we *experience* an emotion isn't always the same as how we *show* it.[57]

Displaying fake emotions requires us to suppress real ones. **Surface acting** is hiding inner feelings and forgoing emotional expressions in response to display rules. A worker who smiles at a customer even when he doesn't feel like it is surface acting. **Deep acting** is trying to modify our true inner feelings based on display rules. A health care provider trying to genuinely feel more empathy for her patients is deep acting.[58] Surface acting deals with *displayed* emotions, and deep acting deals with *felt* emotions. Research shows that surface acting is more stressful to employees because it entails denying their true emotions.[59] Displaying emotions we don't really feel is exhausting, so it is important to give employees who engage in surface displays a chance to relax and recharge. A study that looked at how cheerleading instructors spent their breaks from teaching found those who used their breaks to rest and relax were more effective instructors after their breaks.[60] Instructors who did chores during their breaks were only about as effective after their break as they were before. Another study found that in hospital work groups where there were heavy emotional display demands, burnout was higher than in other hospital work groups.[61]

Affective Events Theory

5 Describe affective events theory and identify its applications.

We've seen that emotions and moods are an important part of our lives and our work lives. But how do they influence our job performance and satisfaction? A model called **affective events theory (AET)** demonstrates that employees react emotionally to things that happen to them at work, and this reaction influences their job performance and satisfaction.[62]

Exhibit 4-5 summarizes AET. The theory begins by recognizing that emotions are a response to an event in the work environment. The work environment includes everything surrounding the job—the variety of tasks and degree of autonomy, job demands, and requirements for expressing emotional labor. This environment creates work events that can be hassles, uplifting events, or both. Examples of hassles are colleagues who refuse to carry their share of work, conflicting directions from different managers, and excessive time pressures. Uplifting events include meeting a goal, getting support from a colleague, and receiving recognition for an accomplishment.[63]

These work events trigger positive or negative emotional reactions, to which employees' personalities and moods predispose them to respond with greater or lesser intensity. People who score low on emotional stability are more likely to react strongly to negative events. And our emotional response to a given event can change depending on mood. Finally, emotions influence a number of performance and satisfaction variables, such as organizational citizenship behavior, organizational commitment, level of effort, intention to quit, and workplace deviance.

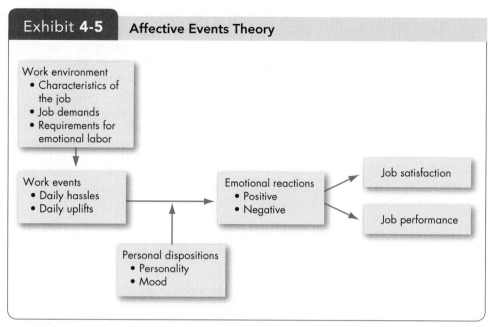

Exhibit **4-5** | **Affective Events Theory**

Source: Based on N. M. Ashkanasy and C. S. Daus, "Emotion in the Workplace: The New Challenge for Managers," *Academy of Management Executive* (February 2002), p. 77.

Tests of affective events theory suggest the following:

1. An emotional episode is actually a series of emotional experiences, precipitated by a single event and containing elements of both emotions and mood cycles.
2. Current emotions influence job satisfaction at any given time, along with the history of emotions surrounding the event.
3. Because moods and emotions fluctuate over time, their effect on performance also fluctuates.
4. Emotion-driven behaviors are typically short in duration and of high variability.
5. Because emotions, even positive ones, tend to be incompatible with behaviors required to do a job, they typically have a negative influence on job performance.[64]

Consider an example.[65] Say you work as an aeronautical engineer for Boeing. Because of the downturn in demand for commercial jets, you've just learned the company is considering laying off 10,000 employees, possibly including you. This event is likely to make you feel negative emotions, especially fear that you might lose your primary source of income. And because you're prone to worry a lot and obsess about problems, this event increases your feelings of insecurity. The layoff also sets in motion a series of smaller events that create an episode: you talk with your boss and he assures you your job is safe; you hear rumors your department is high on the list to be eliminated; and you run into a former colleague who was laid off 6 months ago and still hasn't found work. These events,

surface acting *Hiding one's inner feelings and forgoing emotional expressions in response to display rules.*

deep acting *Trying to modify one's true inner feelings based on display rules.*

affective events theory (AET) *A model that suggests that workplace events cause emotional reactions on the part of employees, which then influence workplace attitudes and behaviors.*

in turn, create emotional ups and downs. One day, you're feeling upbeat that you'll survive the cuts. The next, you might be depressed and anxious. These emotional swings take your attention away from your work and lower your job performance and satisfaction. Finally, your response is magnified because this is the fourth-largest layoff Boeing has initiated in the past 3 years.

In summary, AET offers two important messages.[66] First, emotions provide valuable insights into how workplace hassles and uplifting events influence employee performance and satisfaction. Second, employees and managers shouldn't ignore emotions or the events that cause them, even when they appear minor, because they accumulate.

Emotional Intelligence

6   Contrast the evidence for and against the existence of emotional intelligence.

Diane Marshall is an office manager. Her awareness of her own and others' emotions is almost nil. She's moody and unable to generate much enthusiasm or interest in her employees. She doesn't understand why employees get upset with her. She often overreacts to problems and chooses the most ineffectual responses to emotional situations.[67] Diane has low emotional intelligence. **Emotional intelligence (EI)** is a person's ability to (1) perceive emotions in the self and others, (2) understand the meaning of these emotions, and (3) regulate one's emotions accordingly in a cascading model, as shown in Exhibit 4-6. People who know their own emotions and are good at reading emotional cues—for instance, knowing why they're angry and how to express themselves without violating norms—are most likely to be effective.[68]

Several studies suggest EI plays an important role in job performance. One study that used functional magnetic resonance imaging (fMRI) technology found executive MBA students who performed best on a strategic decision making task were more likely to incorporate emotion centers of the brain into their choice process. The students also de-emphasized the use of the more cognitive parts of their brains.[69] Another study looked at the successes and failures of 11 U.S. presidents—from Franklin Roosevelt to Bill Clinton—and evaluated them on six qualities: communication, organization, political skill, vision, cognitive style, and emotional intelligence. The key quality that differentiated

Exhibit 4-6   A Cascading Model of Emotional Intelligence

Conscientiousness → Perceive Emotions in Self and Others

Cognitive → Understand the Meaning of Emotions

Emotional Stability → Regulate Emotions

Diane Hoskins, a top leader at Gensler, a global architectural firm, has high emotional intelligence. She is one of three executive directors who operate the firm along with the management committee. Hoskins is a star performer in a job that demands interacting with employees and developing their careers to ensure that Gensler has the talent it needs to serve clients. Hoskins is shown here discussing a new internship program that could help Gensler build its global business.

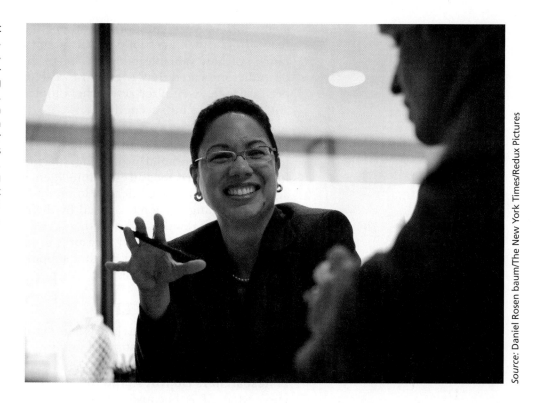

Source: Daniel Rosen baum/The New York Times/Redux Pictures

the successful (such as Roosevelt, Kennedy, and Reagan) from the unsuccessful (such as Johnson, Carter, and Nixon) was emotional intelligence.[70] One simulation study also showed that students who were good at identifying and distinguishing among their own feelings were able to make more profitable investment decisions.[71]

EI has been a controversial concept in OB, with supporters and detractors. In the following sections, we review the arguments for and against its viability.

The Case for EI

The arguments in favor of EI include its intuitive appeal, the fact that it predicts criteria that matter, and the idea that it is biologically based.

Intuitive Appeal   Almost everyone agrees it is good to possess social intelligence. Intuition suggests people who can detect emotions in others, control their own emotions, and handle social interactions well have a powerful leg up in the business world. Partners in a multinational consulting firm who scored above the median on an EI measure delivered $1.2 million more in business than did the other partners.[72]

EI Predicts Criteria That Matter   Evidence suggests a high level of EI means a person will perform well on the job. One study found EI predicted the performance of employees in a cigarette factory in China.[73] Another study found the

emotional intelligence (EI)   *The ability to detect and to manage emotional cues and information.*

ability to recognize emotions in others' facial expressions and to emotionally "eavesdrop" (pick up subtle signals about peoples' emotions) predicted peer ratings of how valuable people were to their organization.[74] Finally, a review of studies indicated that, overall, EI weakly but consistently correlated with job performance, even after researchers took cognitive ability, conscientiousness, and neuroticism into account.[75]

EI Is Biologically Based   In one study, people with damage to the brain area that governs emotional processing (part of the prefrontal cortex) scored no lower on standard measures of intelligence than people without similar damage. But they scored significantly lower on EI tests and were impaired in normal decision making, as demonstrated by their poor performance in a card game with monetary rewards. This study suggests EI is neurologically based in a way that's unrelated to standard measures of intelligence.[76] There is also evidence EI is genetically influenced, further supporting the idea that it measures a real underlying biological factor.[77]

The Case Against EI

For all its supporters, EI has just as many critics who say it is vague and impossible to measure, and they question its validity.

EI Researchers Do Not Agree on Definitions   To many researchers, it's not clear what EI is because researchers use different definitions of the construct.[78] Some researchers have focused on emotional intelligence via tests with right and wrong answers, scoring the ability to recognize and control emotions. This is the ability-based perspective on EI. Others focus on emotional intelligence as a broad variety of constructs that can be measured by self-reports and are connected primarily by the fact that they are not redundant with cognitive intelligence. Not only are these two definitions different, but the measures used by each perspective are barely correlated with one another.[79]

EI Can't Be Measured   Many critics have raised questions about measuring EI. Because EI is a form of intelligence, they argue, there must be right and wrong answers for it on tests. Some tests do have right and wrong answers, although the validity of some questions is doubtful. One measure asks you to associate feelings with colors, as if purple always makes us feel cool and not warm. Other measures are self-reported, such as "I'm good at 'reading' other people," and have no right or wrong answers. However, these self-report measures could reflect a variety of non-ability related constructs like general self-esteem or self-efficacy. The measures of EI are diverse, and researchers have not subjected them to as much rigorous study as they have measures of personality and general intelligence.[80]

EI Is Nothing but Personality with a Different Label   Some critics argue that because EI is so closely related to intelligence and personality, once you control for these factors, it has nothing unique to offer. There is some foundation to this argument. EI appears to be correlated with measures of personality, especially emotional stability.[81] If this is true, then the evidence for a biological component to EI is spurious, and biological markers like brain activity and heritability are attributable to other well-known and much better researched psychological constructs. To some extent, researchers have resolved this issue by noting that EI is a construct partially determined by traits like cognitive intelligence, conscientiousness, and neuroticism, as shown in Exhibit 4-6, so it makes sense that EI is correlated with these characteristics.[82]

Although the field is progressing in its understanding of EI, many questions have not been answered. Still, EI is wildly popular among consulting firms and in the popular press. One company's promotional materials for an EI measure claimed, "EI accounts for more than 85 percent of star performance in top leaders."[83] To say the least, it's difficult to validate this statement with the research literature.

Emotion Regulation

Have you ever tried to cheer yourself up when you're feeling down, or calm yourself when you're feeling angry? If so, you have engaged in *emotion regulation,* which is part of the EI literature but has also been studied as an independent concept.[84] The central idea behind emotion regulation is to identify and modify the emotions you feel. Strategies to change your emotions include thinking about more pleasant things, suppressing negative thoughts, distracting yourself, reappraising the situation, or engaging in relaxation techniques.

As you might suspect based on our discussion up to this point, not everyone is equally good at regulating their emotions. Individuals who are higher in the personality trait of neuroticism have more trouble doing so and often find their moods are beyond their ability to control. Individuals who have lower levels of self-esteem are also less likely to try to improve their sad moods, perhaps because they are less likely than others to feel like they deserve to be in a good mood.[85]

While it might seem in some ways desirable to regulate your emotions, research suggests there is a downside to trying to change the way you feel. Changing your emotions takes effort, and this effort can be exhausting. Sometimes attempts to change an emotion actually make the emotion stronger; for example, trying to talk yourself out of being afraid can make you focus more on what scares you, which makes you more afraid.[86] Emotion suppression appears to be especially difficult to do effectively and can lead to more negative emotions; reappraising situations is usually more effective in increasing positive emotions and limiting negative emotions.[87] From another perspective, research suggests that avoiding negative emotional experiences is less likely to lead to positive moods than seeking out positive emotional experiences.[88] For example, you're more likely to experience a positive mood if you have a pleasant conversation with a friend than you would be if you avoided an unpleasant conversation with a hostile co-worker.

SELF-ASSESSMENT LIBRARY

What's My Emotional Intelligence Score?

In the Self-Assessment Library (available on CD or online), take assessment I.E.1 (What's My Emotional Intelligence Score?).

OB Applications of Emotions and Moods

7 Identify strategies for emotion regulation and their likely effects.

In this section, we assess how an understanding of emotions and moods can improve our ability to explain and predict the selection process in organizations, decision making, creativity, motivation, leadership, interpersonal conflict, negotiation, customer service, job attitudes, and deviant workplace behaviors. We also look at how managers can influence our moods.

Hiring employees with high emotional intelligence is important for companies such as Starbucks, whose baristas have frequent social interactions with customers. In keeping with Starbucks mission "to inspire and nurture the human spirit," the company selects baristas who relate well to customers, connect with them, and uplift their lives. At Starbucks, emotional intelligence plays an important role in job performance, as the company enjoys a loyal customer base and a reputation as one of the most admired companies in America.

Source: C.W. McKeen/Syracuse Newspapers/The Image Works

Selection

One implication from the evidence on EI to date is that employers should consider it a factor in hiring employees, especially in jobs that demand a high degree of social interaction. In fact, more employers *are* starting to use EI measures to hire people. A study of U.S. Air Force recruiters showed that top-performing recruiters exhibited high levels of EI. Using these findings, the Air Force revamped its selection criteria. A follow-up investigation found future hires who had high EI scores were 2.6 times more successful than those who didn't. At L'Oreal, salespersons selected on EI scores outsold those hired using the company's old selection procedure. On an annual basis, salespeople selected for their emotional competence sold $91,370 more than other salespeople did, for a net revenue increase of $2,558,360.[89]

Decision Making

As you will see in Chapter 6, traditional approaches to the study of decision making in organizations have emphasized rationality. But OB researchers are increasingly finding that moods and emotions have important effects on decision making.

Positive moods and emotions seem to help. People in good moods or experiencing positive emotions are more likely than others to use heuristics, or rules of thumb,[90] to help make good decisions quickly. Positive emotions also enhance problem-solving skills, so positive people find better solutions to problems.[91]

OB researchers continue to debate the role of negative emotions and moods in decision making. Although one often-cited study suggested depressed people reach more accurate judgments,[92] more recent evidence hints they make poorer decisions. Why? Because depressed people are slower at processing information and tend to weigh all possible options rather than the most likely ones.[93] They search for the perfect solution, when there rarely is one.

Creativity

People in good moods tend to be more creative than people in bad moods.[94] They produce more ideas and more options, and others think their ideas are original.[95] It seems people experiencing positive moods or emotions are more flexible and open in their thinking, which may explain why they're more creative.[96] Supervisors should actively try to keep employees happy because doing so creates more good moods (employees like their leaders to encourage them and provide positive feedback on a job well done), which in turn leads people to be more creative.[97]

Some researchers, however, do not believe a positive mood makes people more creative. They argue that when people are in positive moods, they may relax ("If I'm in a good mood, things must be going okay, and I must not need to think of new ideas") and not engage in the critical thinking necessary for some forms of creativity.[98] The answer may lie in thinking of moods somewhat differently. Rather than looking at positive or negative affect, it's possible to conceptualize moods as active feelings like anger, fear, or elation and contrast these with deactivating moods like sorrow, depression, or serenity. All the activating moods, whether positive *or* negative, seem to lead to more creativity, whereas deactivating moods lead to less.[99]

Motivation

Several studies have highlighted the importance of moods and emotions on motivation. One study set two groups of people to solving word puzzles. The first group saw a funny video clip, intended to put the subjects in a good mood first. The other group was not shown the clip and started working on the puzzles right away. The results? The positive-mood group reported higher expectations of being able to solve the puzzles, worked harder at them, and solved more puzzles as a result.[100]

The second study found that giving people performance feedback—whether real or fake—influenced their mood, which then influenced their motivation.[101] So a cycle can exist in which positive moods cause people to be more creative, which leads to positive feedback from those observing their work. This positive feedback further reinforces the positive mood, which may make people perform even better, and so on.

Another study looked at the moods of insurance sales agents in Taiwan.[102] Agents in a good mood were more helpful toward their co-workers and also felt better about themselves. These factors in turn led to superior performance in the form of higher sales and better supervisor reports of performance.

Leadership

Effective leaders rely on emotional appeals to help convey their messages.[103] In fact, the expression of emotions in speeches is often the critical element that makes us accept or reject a leader's message. "When leaders feel excited, enthusiastic, and active, they may be more likely to energize their subordinates and convey a sense of efficacy, competence, optimism, and enjoyment."[104] Politicians, as a case in point, have learned to show enthusiasm when talking about their chances of winning an election, even when polls suggest otherwise.

Corporate executives know emotional content is critical if employees are to buy into their vision of the company's future and accept change. When higher-ups offer new visions, especially with vague or distant goals, it is often difficult for employees to accept the changes they'll bring. By arousing emotions and linking them to an appealing vision, leaders increase the likelihood that managers and employees alike will accept change.[105] Leaders who focus on inspirational goals also generate greater optimism and enthusiasm in employees, leading to more positive social interactions with co-workers and customers.[106]

Negotiation

Negotiation is an emotional process; however, we often say a skilled negotiator has a "poker face." The founder of Britain's Poker Channel, Crispin Nieboer, stated, "It is a game of bluff and there is fantastic human emotion and tension,

The general manager of a professional sports team is the organizational leader responsible for developing a winning team. As general manager of the Los Angeles Dodgers, Ned Colletti is shown here delivering an inspirational talk to employees right before a game between the Dodgers and the San Diego Padres. Colletti relies on emotional appeals to employees of all the individual divisions of the team, from administrative affairs to public relations, to work well together in achieving a victorious season.

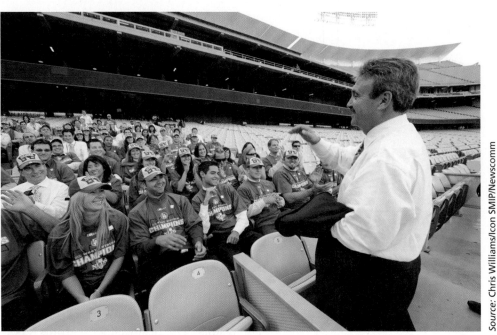

Source: Chris Williams/Icon SMIP/Newscomm

seeing who can bluff the longest."[107] Several studies have shown that a negotiator who feigns anger has an advantage over the opponent. Why? Because when a negotiator shows anger, the opponent concludes the negotiator has conceded all she can and so gives in.[108] Anger should be used selectively in negotiation: angry negotiators who have less information or less power than their opponents have significantly worse outcomes.[109] It appears that a powerful, better-informed individual will be less willing to share information or meet an angry opponent halfway.

Displaying a negative emotion (such as anger) can be effective, but feeling bad about your performance appears to impair future negotiations. Individuals who do poorly in a negotiation experience negative emotions, develop negative perceptions of their counterpart, and are less willing to share information or be cooperative in future negotiations.[110] Interestingly, then, while moods and emotions have benefits at work, in negotiation—unless we're putting up a false front like feigning anger—emotions may impair negotiator performance. A 2005 study found people who suffered damage to the emotional centers of their brains (the same part that was injured in Phineas Gage) may be the *best* negotiators, because they're not likely to overcorrect when faced with negative outcomes.[111]

Customer Service

A worker's emotional state influences customer service, which influences levels of repeat business and of customer satisfaction.[112] Providing high-quality customer service makes demands on employees because it often puts them in a state of emotional dissonance. Over time, this state can lead to job burnout, declines in job performance, and lower job satisfaction.[113]

Employees' emotions can transfer to the customer. Studies indicate a matching effect between employee and customer emotions called **emotional contagion**—the "catching" of emotions from others.[114] How does it work? The primary explanation is that when someone experiences positive emotions and laughs and smiles at you, you tend to respond positively. Emotional contagion is important because customers who catch the positive moods or emotions of employees shop longer. But are negative emotions and moods contagious, too? Absolutely. When an employee feels unfairly treated by a customer, for example, it's harder for him to display the positive emotions his organization expects of him.[115]

Job Attitudes

Ever hear the advice "Never take your work home with you," meaning you should forget about work once you go home? That's easier said than done. Several studies have shown people who had a good day at work tend to be in a better mood at home that evening, and vice versa.[116] People who have a stressful day at work also have trouble relaxing after they get off work.[117] One study had married couples describing their moods when responding to timed cell-phone surveys through the course of the day. As most married readers might suspect, if one member of the couple was in a negative mood during the workday, that mood spilled over to the spouse at night.[118] In other words, if you've had a bad day at work, your spouse is likely to have an unpleasant evening. Even though people do emotionally take their work home with them, however, by the next day the effect is usually gone.[119]

Deviant Workplace Behaviors

Anyone who has spent much time in an organization realizes people often behave in ways that violate established norms and threaten the organization, its members, or both. As we saw in Chapter 1, these actions are called *workplace deviant behaviors*.[120] Many can be traced to negative emotions.

For instance, envy is an emotion that occurs when you resent someone for having something you don't have but strongly desire—such as a better work assignment, larger office, or higher salary.[121] It can lead to malicious deviant behaviors. An envious employee could backstab another employee, negatively distort others' successes, and positively distort his own accomplishments.[122] Angry people look for other people to blame for their bad mood, interpret other people's behavior as hostile, and have trouble considering others' point of view.[123] It's not hard to see how these thought processes, too, can lead directly to verbal or physical aggression.

Evidence suggests people who feel negative emotions, particularly anger or hostility, are more likely than others to engage in deviant behavior at work.[124] Once aggression starts, it's likely that other people will become angry and aggressive, so the stage is set for a serious escalation of negative behavior.

Safety and Injury at Work

Research relating negative affectivity to increased injuries at work suggests employers might improve health and safety (and reduce costs) by ensuring workers aren't engaged in potentially dangerous activities when they're in a bad mood. Bad moods can contribute to injury at work in several ways.[125] Individuals in negative moods tend to be more anxious, which can make them less able to cope effectively with hazards. A person who is always scared will be more pessimistic about the effectiveness of safety precautions because she feels she'll just get hurt anyway, or she might panic or freeze up when confronted with a threatening

emotional contagion *The process by which peoples' emotions are caused by the emotions of others.*

Schadenfreude

English may be a robust language, but sometimes a word from another language expresses something that English misses. Such is the case with a particular and interesting emotional sentiment known by a German name.

"Taking delight in the misery of others," or *schadenfreude*, has recently been studied by psychologists whose findings have implications for work. Neuropsychological research shows that when we experience *schadenfreude*, it is the pleasure centers of our brains that light up, similar to what happens when we enjoy good food or win a contest. It may explain why we take a special interest in reading about the misfortunes of Bernie Madoff, Lindsay Lohan, Charlie Sheen, and others.

As you might experience, we are more likely to experience *schadenfreude* when the misfortune happens to someone we envy or dislike, or, as a recent study showed, to someone we see as a rival, such as a co-worker with whom we have a competitive relationship. This effect persisted even when researchers controlled for how much the person liked the other.

What are the ethical and work implications of *schadenfreude*?

1. Don't judge yourself too harshly for experiencing *schadenfreude*. As one review noted, "it seems almost inherent to social being." If we expect ourselves to never experience *schadenfreude* toward a disliked co-worker, it's a standard we're bound to fail to meet.

2. At the same time, try to recognize that while social comparisons are natural, they're not particularly healthy. As eminent psychologist Susan Fiske noted, "Comparison emotions can corrupt the comparer." Perhaps we can't avoid some comparisons to our coworkers or friends, but we can control how much we do it. *Schadenfreude* can keep us from empathizing not only with one individual, but with those experiencing misfortune more generally.

Sources: W. van Dijk, J. W. Ouwerkerk, Y. M. Wesseling, and G. M. van Koningsbruggen, "Towards Understanding Pleasure at the Misfortunes of Others: The Impact of Self-Evaluation Threat on Schadenfreude," *Cognition and Emotion* 25, no. 2 (2011), pp. 360–368; R. H. Smith, C. A. Powell, D. J. Combs, and D. R. Schurtz, "Exploring the When and Why of Schadenfreude," *Social and Personality Psychology Compass* 3, no. 4 (2009), pp. 530–546; S. T. Fiske, "Envy Up, Scorn Down: How Comparison Divides Us," *American Psychologist* 65, no. 8 (2010), pp. 698–706; and D. Rakoff, "When Bad Things Happen To Do-Good People," *The New York Times* (May 1, 2011), p. WK12.

situation. Negative moods also make people more distractable, and distractions can obviously lead to careless behaviors.

How Managers Can Influence Moods

8 Apply concepts about emotions and moods to specific OB issues.

You can usually improve a friend's mood by sharing a funny video clip, giving the person a small bag of candy, or even offering a pleasant beverage.[126] But what can companies do to improve employees' moods? Managers can use humor and give their employees small tokens of appreciation for work well done. Also, when leaders themselves are in good moods, group members are more positive, and as a result they cooperate more.[127]

Finally, selecting positive team members can have a contagion effect because positive moods transmit from team member to team member. One study of professional cricket teams found players' happy moods affected the moods of their team members and positively influenced their performance.[128] It makes sense, then, for managers to select team members predisposed to experience positive moods.

MyManagementLab

Now that you have finished this chapter, go back to **www.mymanagementlab.com** to continue practicing and applying the concepts you've learned.

Summary and Implications for Managers

Emotions and moods are similar in that both are affective in nature. But they're also different—moods are more general and less contextual than emotions. And events do matter. The time of day and day of the week, stressful events, social activities, and sleep patterns are some of the factors that influence emotions and moods. Emotions and moods have proven relevant for virtually every OB topic we study, and they have implications for managerial practice.

- Increasingly, organizations are selecting employees they believe have high levels of emotional intelligence. Research has helped to refine theory related to emotional intelligence in recent years, which should lead to superior tools for assessing ability-based EI.
- Emotions and positive moods appear to facilitate effective decision making and creativity.
- Recent research suggests mood is linked to motivation, especially through feedback.
- Leaders rely on emotions to increase their effectiveness.
- The display of emotions is important to social behavior like negotiation and customer service.
- The experience of emotions is closely linked to job attitudes and behaviors that follow from attitudes, such as deviant workplace behavior.
- Our final managerial implication is a question: can managers control colleagues' and employees' emotions and moods? Certainly there are limits, practical and ethical. Emotions and moods are a natural part of an individual's makeup. Where managers err is in ignoring co-workers' and employees' emotions and assessing others' behavior as if it were completely rational. As one consultant aptly put it, "You can't divorce emotions from the workplace because you can't divorce emotions from people."[129] Managers who understand the role of emotions and moods will significantly improve their ability to explain and predict their co-workers' and employees' behavior.

QUESTIONS FOR REVIEW

1 What is the difference between emotions and moods? What are the basic emotions and moods?

2 Are emotions rational? What functions do they serve?

3 What are the sources of emotions and moods?

4 What impact does emotional labor have on employees?

5 What is affective events theory? What are its applications?

6 What is the evidence for and against the existence of emotional intelligence?

7 What are some strategies for emotion regulation and their likely effects?

8 How do you apply concepts about emotions and moods to specific OB issues?

Sometimes Blowing Your Top Is a Good Thing

POINT

Anger is discussed throughout this chapter for a reason: it's an important emotion. However, what about our responses to feeling anger? Work cultures teach us to avoid showing any anger at all, lest we be seen as poor service providers or, worse, unprofessional or even deviant or violent. While, of course, there *are* times when the expression of anger is harmful or unprofessional, we've taken this view so far that we now teach people to suppress perfectly normal emotions. It is inappropriate to ask people to behave in abnormal ways, and there is even more evidence about the organizational and personal costs of such suppression.

Emerging research shows that suppressing anger takes a terrible toll on individuals. One Stanford University study showed, for example, that when individuals were asked to wear a poker face during the showing of the atomic bombings of Japan during World War II, they were much more stressful conversation partners once the video was over. Other research shows that college students who suppress emotions like anger have more trouble making friends and are more likely to be depressed, and that employees who suppress anger feel more stressed by work.

There is a better way. One recent study showed that even when employees displayed anger deemed inappropriate by co-workers, if co-workers responded supportively to the anger (for example, by listening to the angry employee), favorable responses such as constructive work changes were the result.

Yes, managers must work to maintain a positive, respectful, and nonviolent culture. However, asking employees to suppress their anger not only is an ineffective and costly strategy, it ultimately may backfire if appropriate ways to express and release anger are blocked.

COUNTERPOINT

Yes, anger is a common emotion. But it's also a toxic one. The experience of anger and its close correlate, hostility, is linked to many counterproductive behaviors in organizations. That is why many organizations have developed anger management programs—to blunt the harmful effects of anger in the workplace.

The Bureau of Labor Statistics estimates that 16 percent of fatal workplace injuries resulted from workplace violence. Do we think the individuals who committed these acts were feeling joyful and contented?

To reduce anger in the workplace, many companies develop policies that govern conduct such as yelling, shouting profanities, and making hostile gestures. Others institute anger management programs. For example, one organization conducted mandatory in-house workshops that showed individuals how to deal with conflicts in the workplace before they boil over. The director who instituted the training said it "gave people specific tools for opening a dialogue to work things out." MTS Systems, an Eden Prairie, Minnesota, engineering firm, engages an outside consulting firm to conduct anger management programs for its organization. Typically, MTS holds an eight-hour seminar that discusses sources of anger, conflict resolution techniques, and organizational policies. This is followed by one-on-one sessions with individual employees that focus on cognitive behavioral techniques to manage their anger. The outside trainer charges $7,000–$10,000 for the seminar and one-on-one sessions. "You want people to get better at communicating with each other," says MTS manager Karen Borre.

In the end, everyone wins when organizations seek to diminish both the experience and, yes, the expression of anger at work. The work environment is less threatening and stressful to employees and customers. Employees are likely to feel safer. And the angry employee is often helped as well.

Sources: B. Carey, "The Benefits of Blowing Your Top," *The New York Times* (July 6, 2010), p. D1; R. Y. Cheung and I. J. Park, "Anger Suppression, Interdependent Self-Construal, and Depression Among Asian American and European American College Students," *Cultural Diversity and Ethnic Minority Psychology* 16, no. 4 (2010), pp. 517–525; D. Geddes and L. T. Stickney, "The Trouble with Sanctions: Organizational Responses to Deviant Anger Displays at Work," *Human Relations* 64, no. 2 (2011), pp. 201–230; and J. Fairley, "Taking Control of Anger Management," *Workforce Management* (October 2010), p. 10.

EXPERIENTIAL EXERCISE Who Can Catch a Liar?

We mentioned earlier in the chapter that emotion researchers are highly interested in facial expressions as a window into individuals' emotional worlds. Research has also studied whether people can tell someone is lying based on signs of guilt or nervousness in their facial expressions. Let's see who is good at catching liars.

Split up into teams and follow these instructions.

1. Randomly choose someone to be the team organizer. Have this person write down on a piece of paper "T" for truth and "L" for lie. If there are, say, six people in the group (other than the organizer), then three people will get a slip with a "T" and three a slip with an "L." It's important that all team members keep what's on their paper a secret.

2. Each team member who holds a T slip needs to come up with a true statement, and each team member who holds an L slip needs to come up with a false statement. Try not to make the statement so outrageous that no one would believe it (for example, "I have flown to the moon").

3. The organizer will have each member make his or her statement. Group members should then examine the person making the statement closely to try to determine whether he or she is telling the truth or lying. Once each person has made his or her statement, the organizer will ask for a vote and record the tallies.

4. Each person should now indicate whether the statement was the truth or a lie.

5. How good was your group at catching the liars? Were some people good liars? What did you look for to determine whether someone was lying?

ETHICAL DILEMMA Happiness Coaches for Employees

We know there is considerable spillover from personal unhappiness to negative emotions at work. Moreover, those who experience negative emotions in life and at work are more likely to engage in counterproductive behaviors with customers, clients, or fellow employees.

Increasingly, organizations such as American Express, UBS, and KPMG are turning to happiness coaches to address this spillover from personal unhappiness to work emotions and behaviors.

Srikumar Rao is a former college professor who has the nickname, "the happiness guru." Rao teaches people to analyze negative emotions to prevent them from becoming overwhelming. If your job is restructured, for example, Rao suggests avoiding negative thoughts and feelings about it. Instead, he advises, tell yourself it could turn out well in the long run, and there is no way to know at present.

Beyond reframing the emotional impact of work situations, some happiness coaches attack the negative emotional spillover from life to work (and from work to life). A working mother found that a happiness talk by Shawn Actor helped her stop focusing on her stressed-out life and instead look for chances to smile, laugh, and be grateful.

In some cases, the claims made by happiness coaches seem a bit trite. Jim Smith, who labels himself "The Executive Happiness Coach," asks: "What if I told you that there are secrets nobody told you as a kid—or as an adult, for that matter—that can unlock for you all sorts of positive emotional experiences? What if the only thing that gets in the way of you feeling more happiness is—YOU?! What if you can change your experience of the world by shifting a few simple things in your life, and then practicing them until they become second nature?"

Then again, if employees leave their experiences with a happiness coach feeling happier about their jobs and their lives, is that not better for everyone? Says one individual, Ivelisse Rivera, who felt she benefitted from a happiness coach, "If I assume a negative attitude and complain all the time, whoever is working with me is going to feel the same way."

Questions

1. Do you think happiness coaches are effective? How might you assess their effectiveness?

2. Would you welcome happiness training in your workplace? Why or why not?

3. Some argue that happiness coaches are a way for organizations to avoid solving real work problems—a diversion, if you will. How might we make this determination?

4. Under what circumstances—if any—is it ethically appropriate for a supervisor to suggest a happiness coach for a subordinate?

Sources: S. Shellenbarger, "Thinking Happy Thoughts at Work," *The Wall Street Journal* (January 27, 2010), p. D2; S. Sharma and D. Chatterjee, "Cos Are Keenly Listening to 'Happiness Coach'," *Economic Times* (July 16, 2010), http://articles.economictimes.indiatimes.com; and J. Smith, *The Executive Happiness Coach*, www.lifewithhappiness.com/ (Downloaded May 3, 2011).

CASE INCIDENT 1 Is It Okay to Cry at Work?

As this chapter has shown, emotions are an inevitable part of people's behavior at work. At the same time, it's not entirely clear that we've reached a point where people feel comfortable expressing *all* emotions at work. The reason might be that business culture and etiquette remain poorly suited to handling overt emotional displays. The question is, can organizations become more intelligent about emotional management? Is it ever appropriate to yell, laugh, or cry at work?

Some people are skeptical about the virtues of more emotional displays at the workplace. As the chapter notes, emotions are automatic physiological responses to the environment, and as such, they can be difficult to control appropriately. One 22-year-old customer service representative named Laura who was the subject of a case study noted that fear and anger were routinely used as methods to control employees, and employees deeply resented this use of emotions to manipulate them. In another case, the chairman of a major television network made a practice of screaming at employees whenever anything went wrong, leading to badly hurt feelings and a lack of loyalty to the organization. Like Laura, workers at this organization were hesitant to show their true reactions to these emotional outbursts for fear of being branded as "weak" or "ineffectual." It might seem like these individuals worked in heavily emotional workplaces, but in fact, only a narrow range of emotions was deemed acceptable. Anger appears to be more acceptable than sadness in many organizations, and anger can have serious maladaptive consequences.

Others believe organizations that recognize and work with emotions effectively are more creative, satisfying, and productive. For example, Laura noted that if she could express her hurt feelings without fear, she would be much more satisfied with her work. In other words, the problem with Laura's organization is not that emotions are displayed, but that emotional displays are handled poorly. Others note that use of emotional knowledge, like being able to read and understand the reactions of others, is crucial for workers ranging from salespeople and customer service agents all the way to managers and executives. One survey even found that 88 percent of workers feel being sensitive to the emotions of others is an asset. Management consultant Erika Anderson notes, "Crying at work is transformative and can open the door to change." The question then is, can organizations take specific steps to become better at allowing emotional displays without opening a Pandora's Box of outbursts?

Questions

1. What factors do you think make some organizations ineffective at managing emotions?

2. Do you think the strategic use and display of emotions serve to protect employees, or does covering your true emotions at work lead to more problems than it solves?

3. Have you ever worked where emotions were used as part of a management style? Describe the advantages and disadvantages of this approach in your experience.

4. Research shows that acts of co-workers (37 percent) and management (22 percent) cause more negative emotions for employees than do acts of customers (7 percent).[130] What can Laura's company do to change its emotional climate?

Sources: A. Kreamer, "Go Ahead—Cry at Work," *Time* (April 4, 2010), www.time.com; J. S. Lerner and K. Shonk, "How Anger Poisons Decision Making," *Harvard Business Review* (September 2010), p. 26; and J. Perrone and M. H. Vickers, "Emotions as Strategic Game in a Hostile Workplace: An Exemplar Case," *Employee Responsibilities and Rights Journal* 16, no. 3 (2004), pp. 167–178.

CASE INCIDENT 2 Can You Read Emotions from Faces?

We mentioned previously that some researchers—the psychologist Paul Ekman is the best known—have studied whether facial expressions reveal true emotions. These researchers have distinguished real smiles (so-called Duchenne smiles, named after French physician Guillaume Duchenne) from "fake" smiles. Duchenne found genuine smiles raised not only the corners of the mouth (easily faked) but also cheek and eye muscles (much more difficult to fake). So, one way to determine whether someone is genuinely happy or amused is to look at the muscles around the upper cheeks and eyes—if the person's eyes are smiling or twinkling, the smile is genuine. Ekman and his associates have developed similar methods to detect other emotions, such as anger, disgust, and distress. According to Ekman, the key to identifying real emotions is to focus on micro-expressions, or those facial muscles we cannot easily manipulate.

Dan Hill has used these techniques to study the facial expressions of CEOs and found they vary dramatically not only in their Duchenne smiles but also in the degree to which they display positive versus negative facial expressions. The accompanying table shows Hill's analysis of the facial expressions of some prominent male executives:

Jeff Bezos, Amazon	51% positive
Warren Buffet, Berkshire Hathaway	69% positive
Michael Dell, Dell Computers	47% positive
Larry Ellison, Oracle	0% positive
Bill Gates, Microsoft	73% positive
Steve Jobs, Apple	48% positive
Phil Knight, Nike	67% positive
Donald Trump, The Trump Organization	16% positive

It's interesting to note that these individuals, all of whom are successful in various ways, have such different levels of positive facial expressions. It also raises the question: is a smile from Larry Ellison worth more than a smile from Bill Gates?

Sources: Based on P. Ekman, *Telling Lies: Clues to Deceit in the Marketplace, Politics, and Marriage* (New York: W. W. Norton & Co., 2009); D. Jones, "It's Written All Over Their Faces," *USA Today* (February 25, 2008), pp. 1B–2B; and N. O. Rule and N. Ambady, "The Face of Success," *Psychological Science* 19, no. 2 (2008), pp. 109–111.

Questions

1. Most research suggests we are not very good at detecting fake emotions, and we think we're much better at it than we are. Do you believe training would improve your ability to detect emotional displays in others?

2. Do you think the information in this case could help you tell whether someone's smile is genuine?

3. Is your own impression of the facial expressions of the eight business leaders consistent with what the researcher found? If not, why do you think your views might be at odds with his?

4. One research study found people's ratings of the positive affect displayed in CEO's faces had very little correlation to their company's profits. Does that suggest to you that Hill's analysis is immaterial?

5. Assuming you could become better at detecting the real emotions in facial expressions, do you think it would help your career? Why or why not?

ENDNOTES

1. See, for instance, C. D. Fisher and N. M. Ashkanasy, "The Emerging Role of Emotions in Work Life: An Introduction," *Journal of Organizational Behavior*, Special Issue 2000, pp. 123–129; N. M. Ashkanasy, C. E. J. Hartel, and W. J. Zerbe (eds.), *Emotions in the Workplace: Research, Theory, and Practice* (Westport, CT: Quorum Books, 2000); N. M. Ashkanasy and C. S. Daus, "Emotion in the Workplace: The New Challenge for Managers," *Academy of Management Executive* (February 2002), pp. 76–86; and N. M. Ashkanasy, C. E. J. Hartel, and C. S. Daus, "Diversity and Emotion: The New Frontiers in Organizational Behavior Research," *Journal of Management* 28, no. 3 (2002), pp. 307–338.

2. See, for example, L. L. Putnam and D. K. Mumby, "Organizations, Emotion and the Myth of Rationality," in S. Fineman (ed.), *Emotion in Organizations* (Thousand Oaks, CA: Sage, 1993), pp. 36–57; and J. Martin, K. Knopoff, and C. Beckman, "An Alternative to Bureaucratic Impersonality and Emotional Labor: Bounded Emotionality at the Body Shop," *Administrative Science Quarterly* (June 1998), pp. 429–469.

3. B. E. Ashforth and R. H. Humphrey, "Emotion in the Workplace: A Reappraisal," *Human Relations* (February 1995), pp. 97–125.

4. S. G. Barsade and D. E. Gibson, "Why Does Affect Matter in Organizations?" *Academy of Management Perspectives* (February 2007), pp. 36–59.

5. See N. H. Frijda, "Moods, Emotion Episodes and Emotions," in M. Lewis and J. M. Haviland (eds.), *Handbook of Emotions* (New York: Guilford Press, 1993), pp. 381–403.

6. H. M. Weiss and R. Cropanzano, "Affective Events Theory: A Theoretical Discussion of the Structure, Causes and Consequences of Affective Experiences at Work," in B. M. Staw and L. L. Cummings (eds.), *Research in Organizational Behavior*, vol. 18 (Greenwich, CT: JAI Press, 1996), pp. 17–19.

7. See P. Ekman and R. J. Davidson (eds.), *The Nature of Emotions: Fundamental Questions* (Oxford, UK: Oxford University Press, 1994).

8. Frijda, "Moods, Emotion Episodes and Emotions," p. 381.

9. See Ekman and Davidson (eds.), *The Nature of Emotions*.

10. See, for example, P. Ekman, "An Argument for Basic Emotions," *Cognition and Emotion* (May/July 1992), pp. 169–200; C. E. Izard, "Basic Emotions, Relations Among Emotions, and Emotion–Cognition Relations," *Psychological Bulletin* (November 1992), pp. 561–565; and J. L. Tracy and R. W. Robins, "Emerging Insights into the Nature and Function of Pride," *Current Directions in Psychological Science* 16, no. 3 (2007), pp. 147–150.

11. R. C. Solomon, "Back to Basics: On the Very Idea of 'Basic Emotions,'" *Journal for the Theory of Social Behaviour* 32, no. 2 (June 2002), pp. 115–144.

12. R. Descartes, *The Passions of the Soul* (Indianapolis: Hackett, 1989).

13. P. Ekman, *Emotions Revealed: Recognizing Faces and Feelings to Improve Communication and Emotional Life* (New York: Times Books/Henry Holt and Co., 2003).

14. P. R. Shaver, H. J. Morgan, and S. J. Wu, "Is Love a 'Basic' Emotion?" *Personal Relationships* 3, no. 1 (March 1996), pp. 81–96.

15. Ibid.

16. Ashforth and Humphrey, "Emotion in the Workplace," p. 104; B. Plasait, "Accueil des Touristes Dans les Grands Centres de Transit Paris," *Rapport du Bernard Plasait* (October 4, 2004), www.tourisme.gouv.fr/fr/navd/presse/dossiers/att00005767/dp_ plasait.pdf; B. Mesquita, "Emotions in Collectivist and Individualist Contexts," *Journal of Personality and Social Psychology* 80, no. 1 (2001), pp. 68–74; and D. Rubin, "Grumpy German Shoppers Distrust the Wal-Mart Style," *Seattle Times* (December 30, 2001), p. A15.

17. Solomon, "Back to Basics."

18. Weiss and Cropanzano, "Affective Events Theory," pp. 20–22.

19. Cited in R. D. Woodworth, *Experimental Psychology* (New York: Holt, 1938).

20. D. Watson, L. A. Clark, and A. Tellegen, "Development and Validation of Brief Measures of Positive and Negative Affect: The PANAS Scales," *Journal of Personality and Social Psychology* (1988), pp. 1063–1070.

21. A. Ben-Ze'ev, *The Subtlety of Emotions* (Cambridge, MA: MIT Press, 2000), p. 94.

22. "Flight Attendant War Stories . . . Stewardess," AboutMyJob.com, www.aboutmyjob.com/?p=2111.

23. A. Ben-Ze'ev, *The Subtlety of Emotions*, p. 99.

24. J. T. Cacioppo and W. L. Gardner, "Emotion," in *Annual Review of Psychology*, vol. 50 (Palo Alto, CA: Annual Reviews, 1999), pp. 191–214.

25. D. Holman, "Call Centres," in D. Holman, T. D. Wall, C. Clegg, P. Sparrow, and A. Howard (eds.), *The Essentials of the New Work Place: A Guide to the Human Impact of Modern Working Practices* (Chichester, UK: Wiley, 2005), pp. 111–132.

26. M. Eid and E. Diener, "Norms for Experiencing Emotions in Different Cultures: Inter- and International Differences," *Journal of Personality & Social Psychology* 81, no. 5 (2001), pp. 869–885.

27. S. Oishi, E. Diener, and C. Napa Scollon, "Cross-Situational Consistency of Affective Experiences Across Cultures," *Journal of Personality & Social Psychology* 86, no. 3 (2004), pp. 460–472.

28. Eid and Diener, "Norms for Experiencing Emotions in Different Cultures."

29. L. M. Poverny and S. Picascia, "There Is No Crying in Business," *Womensmedia.com*, October 20, 2009, www.womensmedia.com/new/Crying-at-Work.shtml.

30. A. R. Damasio, *Descartes' Error: Emotion, Reason, and the Human Brain* (New York: Quill, 1994).

31. Ibid.

32. J. Haidt, "The New Synthesis in Moral Psychology," *Science* 316 (May 18, 2007), pp. 998, 1002; I. E. de Hooge, R. M. A. Nelissen, S. M. Breugelmans, and M. Zeelenberg, "What is Moral about Guilt? Acting 'Prosocially' at the Disadvantage of Others," *Journal of Personality and Social Psychology* 100 (2011), pp. 462–473; and C. A. Hutcherson and J. J. Gross, "The Moral Emotions: A Social-Functionalist Account of Anger, Disgust, and Contempt," *Journal of Personality and Social Psychology* 100 (2011), pp. 719–737.

33. R. J. Larsen and E. Diener, "Affect Intensity as an Individual Difference Characteristic: A Review," *Journal of Research in Personality* 21 (1987), pp. 1–39.

34. D. Watson, *Mood and Temperament* (New York: Guilford Press, 2000).

35. J. J. A. Denissen, L. Butalid, L. Penke, and M. A. G. van Aken, "The Effects of Weather on Daily Mood: A Multilevel Approach," *Emotion* 8, no. 5 (2008), pp. 662–667; M. C. Keller, B. L. Fredrickson, O. Ybarra, S. Côté, K. Johnson, J. Mikels, A. Conway, and T. Wagner, "A Warm Heart and a Clear Head: The Contingent Effects of Weather on Mood and Cognition," *Psychological Science* 16 (2005) pp. 724–731; and Watson, *Mood and Temperament*.

36. Watson, *Mood and Temperament*, p. 100.

37. J. A. Fuller, J. M. Stanton, G. G. Fisher, C. Spitzmüller, S. S. Russell, and P. C. Smith, "A Lengthy Look at the Daily Grind: Time Series Analysis of Events, Mood, Stress, and Satisfaction," *Journal of Applied Psychology* 88, no. 6 (December 2003), pp. 1019–1033.

38. See "Monday Blahs," May 16, 2005, www.ashidome.com/blogger/housearrest.asp?c=809&m=5&y=2005.

39. A. M. Isen, "Positive Affect as a Source of Human Strength," in L. G. Aspinwall and U. Staudinger (eds.), *The Psychology of Human Strengths* (Washington, DC: American Psychological Association, 2003), pp. 179–195.

40. Watson, *Mood and Temperament*.

41. *Sleep in America Poll* (Washington, DC: National Sleep Foundation, 2005), www.kintera.org/atf/cf/%7Bf6bf2668-a1b4-4fe8-8d1a-a5d39340d9cb%7D/2005_summary_of_findings.pdf.

42. M. Lavidor, A. Weller, and H. Babkoff, "How Sleep Is Related to Fatigue," *British Journal of Health Psychology* 8 (2003), pp. 95–105; and J. J. Pilcher and E. Ott, "The Relationships Between Sleep and Measures of Health and Well-Being in College Students: A Repeated Measures Approach," *Behavioral Medicine* 23 (1998), pp. 170–178.

43. E. K. Miller and J. D. Cohen, "An Integrative Theory of Prefrontal Cortex Function," *Annual Review of Neuroscience* 24 (2001), pp. 167–202.

44. B. A. Scott and T. A. Judge, "Insomnia, Emotions, and Job Satisfaction: A Multilevel Study," *Journal of Management* 32, no. 5 (2006), pp. 622–645.

45. P. R. Giacobbi, H. A. Hausenblas, and N. Frye, "A Naturalistic Assessment of the Relationship Between Personality, Daily Life Events, Leisure-Time Exercise, and Mood," *Psychology of Sport & Exercise* 6, no. 1 (January 2005), pp. 67–81.

46. L. L. Carstensen, M. Pasupathi, M. Ulrich, and J. R. Nesselroade, "Emotional Experience in Everyday Life Across the Adult Life Span," *Journal of Personality and Social Psychology* 79, no. 4 (2000), pp. 644–655.

47. M. LaFrance and M. Banaji, "Toward a Reconsideration of the Gender–Emotion Relationship," in M. Clark (ed.), *Review of Personality and Social Psychology*, vol. 14 (Newbury Park, CA: Sage, 1992), pp. 178–197; and A. M. Kring and A. H. Gordon, "Sex Differences in Emotion: Expression, Experience, and Physiology," *Journal of Personality and Social Psychology* (March 1998), pp. 686–703.

48. M. G. Gard and A. M. Kring, "Sex Differences in the Time Course of Emotion," *Emotion* 7, no. 2 (2007), pp. 429–437; M. Jakupcak, K. Salters, K. L. Gratz, and L. Roemer, "Masculinity and Emotionality: An Investigation of Men's Primary and Secondary Emotional Responding," *Sex Roles* 49 (2003), pp. 111–120; and M. Grossman and W. Wood, "Sex Differences in Intensity of Emotional Experience: A Social Role Interpretation," *Journal of Personality and Social Psychology* (November 1992), pp. 1010–1022.

49. A. H. Fischer, P. M. Rodriguez Mosquera, A. E. M. van Vianen, and A. S. R. Manstead, "Gender and Culture Differences in Emotion," *Emotion* 4 (2004), pp. 84–87.

50. L. F. Barrett and E. Bliss-Moreau, "She's Emotional. He's Having a Bad Day: Attributional Explanations for Emotion Stereotypes," *Emotion* 9 (2009), pp. 649–658.

51. D. V. Becker, D. T. Kenrick, S. L. Neuberg, K. C. Blackwell, and D. M. Smith, "The Confounded Nature of Angry Men and Happy Women," *Journal of Personality and Social Psychology* 92 (2007), pp. 179–190.

52. P. Ekman, W. V. Friesen, and M. O'Sullivan, "Smiles When Lying," in P. Ekman and E. L. Rosenberg (eds.), *What the Face Reveals: Basic and Applied Studies of Spontaneous Expression Using the Facial Action Coding System (FACS)* (London: Oxford University Press, 1997), pp. 201–216.

53. A. Grandey, "Emotion Regulation in the Workplace: A New Way to Conceptualize Emotional Labor," *Journal of Occupational Health Psychology* 5, no. 1 (2000), pp. 95–110; and R. Cropanzano, D. E. Rupp, and Z. S. Byrne, "The Relationship of Emotional Exhaustion to Work Attitudes, Job Performance, and Organizational Citizenship Behavior," *Journal of Applied Psychology* (February 2003), pp. 160–169.

54. A. R. Hochschild, "Emotion Work, Feeling Rules, and Social Structure," *American Journal of Sociology* (November 1979), pp. 551–575; W.-C. Tsai, "Determinants and Consequences of Employee Displayed Positive Emotions," *Journal of Management* 27, no. 4 (2001), pp. 497–512; M. W. Kramer and J. A. Hess, "Communication Rules for the Display of Emotions in Organizational Settings," *Management Communication Quarterly* (August 2002), pp. 66–80; and J. M. Diefendorff and E. M. Richard, "Antecedents and Consequences of Emotional Display Rule Perceptions," *Journal of Applied Psychology* (April 2003), pp. 284–294.

55. B. M. DePaulo, "Nonverbal Behavior and Self-Presentation," *Psychological Bulletin* (March 1992), pp. 203–243.

56. J. M. Diefendorff and G. J. Greguras, "Contextualizing Emotional Display Rules: Examining the Roles of Targets and Discrete Emotions in Shaping Display Rule Perceptions," *Journal of Management* 35 (2009), pp. 880–898.

57. Solomon, "Back to Basics."

58. C. M. Brotheridge and R. T. Lee, "Development and Validation of the Emotional Labour Scale," *Journal of Occupational & Organizational Psychology* 76 (2003), pp. 365–379.

59. A. A. Grandey, "When 'The Show Must Go On': Surface Acting and Deep Acting as Determinants of Emotional Exhaustion and Peer-Rated Service Delivery," *Academy of Management Journal* (February 2003), pp. 86–96; and A. A. Grandey, D. N. Dickter, and H. Sin, "The Customer Is Not Always Right: Customer Aggression and Emotion Regulation of Service Employees," *Journal of Organizational Behavior* 25 (2004), pp. 397–418.

60. J. P. Trougakos, D. J. Beal, S. G. Green, and H. M. Weiss, "Making the Break Count: An Episodic Examination of Recovery Activities, Emotional Experiences, and Positive Affective Displays," *Academy of Management Journal* 51 (2008), pp. 131–146.

61. J. M. Diefendorff, R. J. Erickson, A. A. Grandey, and J. J. Dahling, "Emotional Display Rules as Work Unit Norms: A Multilevel Analysis of Emotional Labor among Nurses," *Journal of Occupational Health Psychology* 16 (2011), pp. 170–186.

62. H. M. Weiss and R. Cropanzano, "An Affective Events Approach to Job Satisfaction," *Research in Organizational Behavior* 18 (1996), pp. 1–74.

63. J. Basch and C. D. Fisher, "Affective Events–Emotions Matrix: A Classification of Work Events and Associated Emotions," in N. M. Ashkanasy, C. E. J. Hartel, and W. J. Zerbe (eds.), *Emotions in the Workplace* (Westport, CT: Quorum Books, 2000), pp. 36–48.

64. See, for example, H. M. Weiss and R. Cropanzano, "Affective Events Theory"; and C. D. Fisher, "Antecedents and Consequences of Real-Time Affective Reactions at Work," *Motivation and Emotion* (March 2002), pp. 3–30.

65. Based on Weiss and Cropanzano, "Affective Events Theory," p. 42.

66. N. M. Ashkanasy, C. E. J. Hartel, and C. S. Daus, "Diversity and Emotion: The New Frontiers in Organizational Behavior Research," *Journal of Management* 28, no. 3 (2002), p. 324.

67. Based on D. R. Caruso, J. D. Mayer, and P. Salovey, "Emotional Intelligence and Emotional Leadership," in R. E. Riggio, S. E. Murphy, and F. J. Pirozzolo (eds.), *Multiple Intelligences and Leadership* (Mahwah, NJ: Lawrence Erlbaum, 2002), p. 70.

68. This section is based on Daniel Goleman, *Emotional Intelligence* (New York: Bantam, 1995); P. Salovey and D. Grewal, "The Science of Emotional Intelligence," *Current Directions in Psychological Science* 14, no. 6 (2005), pp. 281–285; M. Davies, L. Stankov, and R. D. Roberts, "Emotional Intelligence: In Search of an Elusive Construct," *Journal of Personality and Social Psychology* (October 1998), pp. 989–1015; D. Geddes and R. R. Callister, "Crossing the Line(s): A Dual Threshold Model of Anger in Organizations," *Academy of Management Review* 32, no. 3 (2007), pp. 721–746.

69. R. Gilkey, R. Caceda, and C. Kilts, "When Emotional Reasoning Trumps IQ," *Harvard Business Review* (September 2010), p. 27.

70. F. I. Greenstein, *The Presidential Difference: Leadership Style from FDR to Clinton* (Princeton, NJ: Princeton University Press, 2001).

71. M. Seo and L. F. Barrett, "Being Emotional During Decision Making—Good or Bad? An Empirical Investigation," *Academy of Management Journal* 50, no. 4 (2007), pp. 923–940.

72. C. Cherniss, "The Business Case for Emotional Intelligence," *Consortium for Research on Emotional Intelligence in Organizations,* 1999, www.eiconsortium.org/reports/business_case_for_ei.html.

73. K. S. Law, C. Wong, and L. J. Song, "The Construct and Criterion Validity of Emotional Intelligence and Its Potential Utility for Management Studies," *Journal of Applied Psychology* 89, no. 3 (2004), pp. 483–496.

74. H. A. Elfenbein and N. Ambady, "Predicting Workplace Outcomes from the Ability to Eavesdrop on Feelings," *Journal of Applied Psychology* 87, no. 5 (October 2002), pp. 963–971.

75. D. L. Joseph and D. A. Newman, "Emotional Intelligence: An Integrative Meta-Analysis and Cascading Model," *Journal of Applied Psychology* 95 (2010), pp. 54–78.

76. R. Bar-On, D. Tranel, N. L. Denburg, and A. Bechara, "Exploring the Neurological Substrate of Emotional and Social Intelligence," *Brain* 126, no. 8 (August 2003), pp. 1790–1800.

77. P. A. Vernon, K. V. Petrides, D. Bratko, and J. A. Schermer, "A Behavioral Genetic Study of Trait Emotional Intelligence," *Emotion* 8, no. 5 (2008), pp. 635–642.

78. E. A. Locke, "Why Emotional Intelligence Is an Invalid Concept," *Journal of Organizational Behavior* 26, no. 4 (June 2005), pp. 425–431.

79. J. D. Mayer, R. D. Roberts, and S. G. Barsade, "Human Abilities: Emotional Intelligence," *Annual Review of Psychology* 59 (2008), pp. 507–536; H. A. Elfenbein, "Emotion in Organizations: A Review and Theoretical Integration," *Academy of Management Annals* 1 (2008), pp. 315–386; and D. L. Joseph and D. A. Newman, "Emotional Intelligence: An Integrative Meta-Analysis and Cascading Model," *Journal of Applied Psychology* 95 (2010), pp. 54–78.

80. J. M. Conte, "A Review and Critique of Emotional Intelligence Measures," *Journal of Organizational Behavior* 26, no. 4 (June 2005), pp. 433–440; and M. Davies, L. Stankov, and R. D. Roberts, "Emotional Intelligence," pp. 989–1015.

81. T. Decker, "Is Emotional Intelligence a Viable Concept?" *Academy of Management Review* 28, no. 2 (April 2003), pp. 433–440; and Davies, Stankov, and Roberts, "Emotional Intelligence."

82. D. L. Joseph and D. A. Newman, "Emotional Intelligence: An Integrative Meta-Analysis and Cascading Model," *Journal of Applied Psychology* 95 (2010), pp. 54–78.

83. F. J. Landy, "Some Historical and Scientific Issues Related to Research on Emotional Intelligence," *Journal of Organizational Behavior* 26, no. 4 (June 2005), pp. 411–424.

84. S. L. Koole, "The Psychology of Emotion Regulation: An Integrative Review," *Cognition and Emotion* 23 (2009), pp. 4–41; H. A. Wadlinger and D. M. Isaacowitz, "Fixing Our Focus: Training Attention to Regulate Emotion," *Personality and Social Psychology Review* 15 (2011), pp. 75–102.

85. J. V. Wood, S. A. Heimpel, L. A. Manwell, and E. J. Whittington, "This Mood Is Familiar and I Don't Deserve to Feel Better Anyway: Mechanisms Underlying Self-Esteem Differences in Motivation to Repair Sad Moods," *Journal of Personality and Social Psychology* 96 (2009), pp. 363–380.

86. S. L. Koole, "The Psychology of Emotion Regulation: An Integrative Review," *Cognition and Emotion* 23 (2009), pp. 4–41.

87. S. Srivastava, M. Tamir, K. M. McGonigal, O. P. John, and J. J. Gross, "The Social Costs of Emotional Suppression: A Prospective Study of the Transition to College," *Journal of Personality and Social Psychology* 96 (2009), pp. 883–897; Y. Liu, L. M. Prati, P. L. Perrewé, and R. A. Brymer, "Individual Differences in Emotion Regulation, Emotional Experiences at Work, and Work-Related Outcomes: A Two-Study Investigation," *Journal of Applied Social Psychology* 40 (2010), pp. 1515–1538; and H. A. Wadlinger and D. M. Isaacowitz, "Fixing our Focus: Training Attention to Regulate Emotion," *Personality and Social Psychology Review* 15 (2011), pp. 75–102.

88. L. K. Barber, P. G. Bagsby, and D. C. Munz, "Affect Regulation Strategies for Promoting (or Preventing) Flourishing Emotional Health," *Personality and Individual Differences* 49 (2010), pp. 663–666.

89. L. M. J. Spencer, D. C. McClelland, and S. Kelner, *Competency Assessment Methods: History and State of the Art* (Boston: Hay/McBer, 1997).

90. J. Park and M. R. Banaji, "Mood and Heuristics: The Influence of Happy and Sad States on Sensitivity and Bias in Stereotyping," *Journal of Personality and Social Psychology* 78, no. 6 (2000), pp. 1005–1023.

91. See A. M. Isen, "Positive Affect and Decision Making," in M. Lewis and J. M. Haviland-Jones (eds.), *Handbook of Emotions*, 2nd ed. (New York: Guilford, 2000), pp. 261–277.

92. L. B. Alloy and L. Y. Abramson, "Judgment of Contingency in Depressed and Nondepressed Students: Sadder but Wiser?" *Journal of Experimental Psychology: General* 108 (1979), pp. 441–485.

93. N. Ambady and H. M. Gray, "On Being Sad and Mistaken: Mood Effects on the Accuracy of Thin-Slice Judgments," *Journal of Personality and Social Psychology* 83, no. 4 (2002), pp. 947–961.

94. S. Lyubomirsky, L. King, and E. Diener, "The Benefits of Frequent Positive Affect: Does Happiness Lead to Success?" *Psychological Bulletin* 131, no. 6 (2005), pp. 803–855; and M. Baas, C. K. W. De Dreu, and B. A. Nijstad, "A Meta-Analysis of 25 Years of Mood-Creativity Research: Hedonic Tone, Activation, or Regulatory Focus," *Psychological Bulletin* 134 (2008), pp. 779–806.

95. M. J. Grawitch, D. C. Munz, and E. K. Elliott, "Promoting Creativity in Temporary Problem-Solving Groups: The Effects of Positive Mood and Autonomy in Problem Definition on Idea-Generating Performance," *Group Dynamics* 7, no. 3 (September 2003), pp. 200–213.

96. S. Lyubomirsky, L. King, and E. Diener, "The Benefits of Frequent Positive Affect: Does Happiness Lead to Success?" *Psychological Bulletin* 131, no. 6 (2005), pp. 803–855.

97. N. Madjar, G. R. Oldham, and M. G. Pratt, "There's No Place Like Home? The Contributions of Work and Nonwork Creativity Support to Employees' Creative Performance," *Academy of Management Journal* 45, no. 4 (2002), pp. 757–767.

98. J. M. George and J. Zhou, "Understanding When Bad Moods Foster Creativity and Good Ones Don't: The Role of Context and Clarity of Feelings," *Journal of Applied Psychology* 87, no. 4 (August 2002), pp. 687–697; and J. P. Forgas and J. M. George, "Affective Influences on Judgments and Behavior in Organizations: An Information Processing Perspective," *Organizational Behavior and Human Decision Processes* 86, no. 1 (2001), pp. 3–34.

99. C. K. W. De Dreu, M. Baas, and B. A. Nijstad, "Hedonic Tone and Activation Level in the Mood-Creativity Link: Toward a Dual Pathway to Creativity Model," *Journal of Personality and Social Psychology* 94, no. 5 (2008), pp. 739–756; J. M. George and J. Zhou, "Dual Tuning in a Supportive Context: Joint Contributions of Positive Mood, Negative Mood, and Supervisory Behaviors to Employee Creativity," *Academy of Management Journal* 50, no. 3 (2007), pp. 605–622.

100. A. Erez and A. M. Isen, "The Influence of Positive Affect on the Components of Expectancy Motivation," *Journal of Applied Psychology* 87, no. 6 (2002), pp. 1055–1067.

101. R. Ilies and T. A. Judge, "Goal Regulation Across Time: The Effect of Feedback and Affect," *Journal of Applied Psychology* 90, no. 3 (May 2005), pp. 453–467.

102. W. Tsai, C. Chen, and H. Liu, "Test of a Model Linking Employee Positive Moods and Task Performance," *Journal of Applied Psychology* 92, no. 6 (2007), pp. 1570–1583.

103. K. M. Lewis, "When Leaders Display Emotion: How Followers Respond to Negative Emotional Expression of Male and Female Leaders," *Journal of Organizational Behavior*,

March 2000, pp. 221–234; and J. M. George, "Emotions and Leadership: The Role of Emotional Intelligence," *Human Relations* (August 2000), pp. 1027–1055.

104. J. M. George, "Trait and State Affect," In K. Murphy (ed.), *Individual Differences and Behavior in Organizations* (San Francisco: Jossey Bass, 1996), pp. 145–171.

105. Ashforth and Humphrey, "Emotion in the Workplace," p. 116.

106. J. E. Bono, H. J. Foldes, G. Vinson, and J. P. Muros, "Workplace Emotions: The Role of Supervision and Leadership," *Journal of Applied Psychology* 92, no. 5 (2007), pp. 1357–1367.

107. N. Reynolds, "Whiz-Kids Gamble on TV Channel for Poker," *telegraph.co.uk* (April 16, 2005), www.telegraph.co.uk/news/uknews/1487949/Whiz-kids-gamble-on-TV-channel-for-poker.html.

108. G. A. Van Kleef, C. K. W. De Dreu, and A. S. R. Manstead, "The Interpersonal Effects of Emotions in Negotiations: A Motivated Information Processing Approach," *Journal of Personality and Social Psychology* 87, no. 4 (2004), pp. 510–528; and G. A. Van Kleef, C. K. W. De Dreu, and A. S. R. Manstead, "The Interpersonal Effects of Anger and Happiness in Negotiations," *Journal of Personality and Social Psychology* 86, no. 1 (2004), pp. 57–76.

109. E. van Dijk, G. A. Van Kleef, W. Steinel, and I. van Beest, "A Social Functional Approach to Emotions in Bargaining: When Communicating Anger Pays and When It Backfires," *Journal of Personality and Social Psychology* 94, no. 4 (2008), pp. 600–614.

110. K. M. O'Connor and J. A. Arnold, "Distributive Spirals: Negotiation Impasses and the Moderating Role of Disputant Self-Efficacy," *Organizational Behavior and Human Decision Processes* 84, no. 1 (2001), pp. 148–176.

111. B. Shiv, G. Loewenstein, A. Bechara, H. Damasio, and A. R. Damasio, "Investment Behavior and the Negative Side of Emotion," *Psychological Science* 16, no. 6 (2005), pp. 435–439.

112. W.-C. Tsai and Y.-M. Huang, "Mechanisms Linking Employee Affective Delivery and Customer Behavioral Intentions," *Journal of Applied Psychology* (October 2002), pp. 1001–1008.

113. Grandey, "When 'The Show Must Go On.' "

114. See P. B. Barker and A. A. Grandey, "Service with a Smile and Encounter Satisfaction: Emotional Contagion and Appraisal Mechanisms," *Academy of Management Journal* 49, no. 6 (2006), pp. 1229–1238; and S. D. Pugh, "Service with a Smile: Emotional Contagion in the Service Encounter," *Academy of Management Journal* (October 2001), pp. 1018–1027.

115. D. E. Rupp and S. Spencer, "When Customers Lash Out: The Effects of Customer Interactional Injustice on Emotional Labor and the Mediating Role of Emotions, *Journal of Applied Psychology* 91, no. 4 (2006), pp. 971–978; and Tsai and Huang, "Mechanisms Linking Employee Affective Delivery and Customer Behavioral Intentions."

116. R. Ilies and T. A. Judge, "Understanding the Dynamic Relationships Among Personality, Mood, and Job Satisfaction: A Field Experience Sampling Study," *Organizational Behavior and Human Decision Processes* 89 (2002), pp. 1119–1139.

117. R. Rau, "Job Strain or Healthy Work: A Question of Task Design," *Journal of Occupational Health Psychology* 9, no. 4 (October 2004), pp. 322–338; and R. Rau and A. Triemer, "Overtime in Relation to Blood Pressure and Mood During Work, Leisure, and Night Time," *Social Indicators Research* 67, no. 1–2 (June 2004), pp. 51–73.

118. Z. Song, M. Foo, and M. A. Uy, "Mood Spillover and Crossover Among Dual-Earner Couples: A Cell Phone Event Sampling Study," *Journal of Applied Psychology* 93, no. 2 (2008), pp. 443–452.

119. T. A. Judge and R. Ilies, "Affect and Job Satisfaction: A Study of Their Relationship at Work and at Home," *Journal of Applied Psychology* 89 (2004), pp. 661–673.

120. See R. J. Bennett and S. L. Robinson, "Development of a Measure of Workplace Deviance," *Journal of Applied Psychology,* June 2000, pp. 349–360; see also P. R. Sackett and C. J. DeVore, "Counterproductive Behaviors at Work," in N. Anderson, D. S. Ones, H. K. Sinangil, and C. Viswesvaran (eds.), *Handbook of Industrial, Work & Organizational Psychology,* vol. 1 (Thousand Oaks, CA: Sage, 2001), pp. 145–164.

121. A. G. Bedeian, "Workplace Envy," *Organizational Dynamics* (Spring 1995), p. 50; and Ben-Ze'ev, *The Subtlety of Emotions,* pp. 281–326.

122. Bedeian, "Workplace Envy," p. 54.

123. S. C. Douglas, C. Kiewitz, M. Martinko, P. Harvey, Y. Kim, and J. U. Chun, "Cognitions, Emotions, and Evaluations: An Elaboration Likelihood Model for Workplace Aggression," *Academy of Management Review* 33, no. 2 (2008), pp. 425–451.

124. K. Lee and N. J. Allen, "Organizational Citizenship Behavior and Workplace Deviance: The Role of Affect and Cognition," *Journal of Applied Psychology* 87, no. 1 (2002), pp. 131–142; T. A. Judge, B. A. Scott, and R. Ilies, "Hostility, Job Attitudes, and Workplace Deviance: Test of a Multilevel Model," *Journal of Applied Psychology* 91, no. 1 (2006), 126–138; and S. Kaplan, J. C. Bradley, J. N. Luchman, and D. Haynes, "On the Role of Positive and Negative Affectivity in Job Performance: A Meta-Analytic Investigation," *Journal of Applied Psychology* 94, no. 1 (2009), pp. 162–176.

125. R. D. Iverson and P. J. Erwin, "Predicting Occupational Injury: The Role of Affectivity," *Journal of Occupational and Organizational Psychology* 70, no. 2 (1997), pp. 113–128; and Kaplan, Bradley, Luchman, and Haynes, "On the Role of Positive and Negative Affectivity in Job Performance: A Meta-Analytic Investigation."

126. A. M. Isen, A. A. Labroo, and P. Durlach, "An Influence of Product and Brand Name on Positive Affect: Implicit and Explicit Measures," *Motivation & Emotion* 28, no. 1 (March 2004), pp. 43–63.

127. T. Sy, S. Côté, and R. Saavedra, "The Contagious Leader: Impact of the Leader's Mood on the Mood of Group Members, Group Affective Tone, and Group Processes," *Journal of Applied Psychology* 90, no. 2 (2005), pp. 295–305.

128. P. Totterdell, "Catching Moods and Hitting Runs: Mood Linkage and Subjective Performance in Professional Sports Teams," *Journal of Applied Psychology* 85, no. 6 (2000), pp. 848–859.

129. S. Nelton, "Emotions in the Workplace," *Nation's Business* (February 1996), p. 25.

130. Kruml and Geddes, "Catching Fire Without Burning Out."

CHANGING OF THE GUARD IN JAPAN: IS IT THE ECONOMY, OR THE VALUES?

Among the world's largest economies, none has been more frustratingly stuck in neutral than Japan. Until 2010, when it was surpassed by China, Japan was the world's second-largest economy (after the United States). However, it has now experienced two "lost decades" in a row, spanning 1990 to 2010, and many recent college graduates have no memory of the halcyon days of the 1980s, when Japan was the most envied economy in the world. The horrendous aftermath of the earthquake and tsunami that struck in March 2011, sending Japan into another recession, has only added to the misery. Many now fear the Japanese economy will forever remain stuck in the doldrums.

Perhaps it will rebound sooner than expected; Japan has been underestimated before. However, two decades of stagnant economic growth seem to have had a permanent effect on new entrants' work values.

At one time, Japan was famous for the close psychological and behavioral bond between company and worker. Most employees expected to remain with their employer for their entire career, based on the belief that if they took care of their company, their company would take care of them. To these individuals, quitting, or taking a side job, would be an unthinkable act of disloyalty.

How things have changed. While unemployment in Japan remains low in comparison to the United States, it is at historic highs. Moreover, earnings continue to shrink—down more than 12 percent over the past decade. The Japanese Ministry of Health, Labor and Welfare estimates that 56 percent of workers age 15 to 34 need another form of income to pay living expenses.

Hiroko Yokogawa, 32, makes one-third of her income from her second job. "It's not that I hate my main job, but I want to have a stable income without being completely dependent on the company," she said.

At first, Kirito Nakano, 28, followed the traditional career path, expecting to remain forever in his job as a Web engineer with a large Japanese multinational. Soon, however, he found that his salary, and lack of salary growth, began to crimp his lifestyle. He began moonlighting, developing affiliate marketing programs. As his side job grew, Kirito quit his main job. He felt he was left with little choice. "The Japanese economy is not just stagnant, it's in retreat," he said. "When people believe the future is going to be better than the present, they are happy. But if they think that the future holds no hope, then they become unhappy. It's that unhappiness that people are trying to negate with side jobs."

Personality and Values

5

I am driven by fear of failure.
It is a strong motivator for me.
—Dennis Manning, CEO of Guardian Life Insurance Co.

Photo: University students at a job fair in Koto Ward, Tokyo. Source: The Yomiuri Shimbun via AP Images.

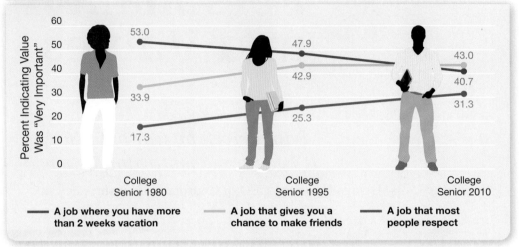

Source: Based on "What Millennial Workers Want: How to Attract and Retain Gen Y Employees," Robert Half International web interviews of 1,007 individuals age 21–28, 2008.

The choice of young Japanese employees to work more hours is an interesting contrast to workers in the United States and Europe, who express a preference to work fewer hours. As for the hours she works—generally her side job takes 25 hours a week— Hiroko Yokogawa remains undeterred. "I wouldn't say I want to leave my main job—rather, I'd like to have a couple of different jobs at once."

A s the opening vignette indicates, employees with different values may enact different behaviors to achieve their work goals, and these differences can be a reflection of culture. In the first half of this chapter, we review the research on personality and its relationship to behavior. In the latter half, we look at how values shape many of our work-related behaviors.

Although we focus much of our discussion on the Big Five personality traits, they are not the only traits that describe people. One of the others we'll discuss is narcissism. Check out the Self-Assessment Library to see how you score on narcissism (remember: be honest!).

SELF-ASSESSMENT LIBRARY

Am I a Narcissist?

In the Self-Assessment Library (available on CD or online), take assessment IV.A.1 (Am I a Narcissist?) and answer the following questions.

1. How did you score? Did your scores surprise you? Why or why not?
2. On which facet of narcissism did you score highest? Lowest?
3. Do you think this measure is accurate? Why or why not?

Personality

1 Define *personality,* describe how it is measured, and explain the factors that determine an individual's personality.

Why are some people quiet and passive, while others are loud and aggressive? Are certain personality types better adapted than others for certain job types? Before we can answer these questions, we need to address a more basic one: What is personality?

What Is Personality?

When we talk of personality, we don't mean a person has charm, a positive attitude toward life, or a constantly smiling face. When psychologists talk of personality, they mean a dynamic concept describing the growth and development of a person's whole psychological system.

Defining Personality   The definition of *personality* we most frequently use was produced by Gordon Allport nearly 70 years ago. Allport said personality is "the dynamic organization within the individual of those psychophysical systems that determine his unique adjustments to his environment."[1] For our purposes, you should think of **personality** as the sum total of ways in which an individual reacts to and interacts with others. We most often describe it in terms of the measurable traits a person exhibits.

Measuring Personality   The most important reason managers need to know how to measure personality is that research has shown personality tests are useful in hiring decisions and help managers forecast who is best for a job.[2] The most common means of measuring personality is through self-report surveys, with which individuals evaluate themselves on a series of factors, such as "I worry a lot about the future." Though self-report measures work well when well constructed, one weakness is that the respondent might lie or practice impression management to create a good impression. When people know their personality scores are going to be used for hiring decisions, they rate themselves as about half a standard deviation more conscientious and emotionally stable than if they are taking the test just to learn more about themselves.[3] Another problem is accuracy. A perfectly good candidate could have been in a bad mood when taking the survey, and that will make the scores less accurate.

Observer-ratings surveys provide an independent assessment of personality. Here, a co-worker or another observer does the rating (sometimes with the subject's knowledge and sometimes not). Though the results of self-report surveys and observer-ratings surveys are strongly correlated, research suggests observer-ratings surveys are a better predictor of success on the job.[4] However, each can tell us something unique about an individual's behavior in the workplace. An analysis of a large number of observer-reported personality studies shows that a combination of self-report and observer-reports predicts performance better than any one type of information. The implication is clear: use both observer ratings and self-report ratings of personality when making important employment decisions.

personality   *Enduring characteristics that describe an individual's behavior.*

Personality Determinants   An early debate in personality research centered on whether an individual's personality was the result of heredity or of environment. It appears to be a result of both. However, it might surprise you that research tends to support the importance of heredity over the environment.

Heredity refers to factors determined at conception. Physical stature, facial attractiveness, gender, temperament, muscle composition and reflexes, energy level, and biological rhythms are generally considered to be either completely or substantially influenced by who your parents are—that is, by their biological, physiological, and inherent psychological makeup. The heredity approach argues that the ultimate explanation of an individual's personality is the molecular structure of the genes, located in the chromosomes.

Researchers in many different countries have studied thousands of sets of identical twins who were separated at birth and raised separately.[5] If heredity played little or no part in determining personality, you would expect to find few similarities between the separated twins. But twins raised apart have much in common, and a significant part of the behavioral similarity between them turns out to be associated with genetic factors. One set of twins separated for 39 years and raised 45 miles apart were found to drive the same model and color car. They chain-smoked the same brand of cigarette, owned dogs with the same name, and regularly vacationed within three blocks of each other in a beach community 1,500 miles away. Researchers have found that genetics accounts for about 50 percent of the personality similarities between twins and more than 30 percent of the similarities in occupational and leisure interests.

Interestingly, twin studies have suggested parents don't add much to our personality development. The personalities of identical twins raised in different households are more similar to each other than to the personalities of siblings with whom the twins were raised. Ironically, the most important contribution our parents may make to our personalities is giving us their genes!

This is not to suggest that personality never changes. People's scores on measures of dependability tend to increase over time, as when young adults take on roles like starting a family and establishing a career that require great responsibility. However, strong individual differences in dependability remain;

Personality traits are enduring characteristics that describe an individual's behavior. British entrepreneur Richard Branson, chairman of Virgin Group, is described as energetic, enthusiastic, charismatic, decisive, ambitious, adaptable, courageous, and industrious. These traits helped Branson build one of the most recognized and respected global brands for products and services in the areas of business travel, entertainment, and lifestyle. In this photo Branson is joined by his daughter Holly during the promotional launch of a new venture—the Marussia Virgin racing partnership with Disney's *Cars 2* film. Identifying personality traits helps organizations select employees and match workers to job.

Source: Eric Best/Landmark Media Landmark Media/Newscom.

everyone tends to change by about the same amount, so their rank order stays roughly the same.[6] An analogy to intelligence may make this clearer. Children become smarter as they age, so nearly everyone is smarter at age 20 than at age 10. Still, if Madison is smarter than Blake at age 10, she is likely to be so at age 20, too. Consistent with the notion that the teenage years are periods of great exploration and change, research has shown that personality is more changeable in adolescence and more stable among adults.[7]

Early work on the structure of personality tried to identify and label enduring characteristics that describe an individual's behavior, including shy, aggressive, submissive, lazy, ambitious, loyal, and timid. When someone exhibits these characteristics in a large number of situations, we call them **personality traits** of that person.[8] The more consistent the characteristic over time, and the more frequently it occurs in diverse situations, the more important that trait is in describing the individual.

Early efforts to identify the primary traits that govern behavior[9] often resulted in long lists that were difficult to generalize from and provided little practical guidance to organizational decision makers. Two exceptions are the Myers-Briggs Type Indicator and the Big Five Model, now the dominant frameworks for identifying and classifying traits.

The Myers-Briggs Type Indicator

The **Myers-Briggs Type Indicator (MBTI)** is the most widely used personality-assessment instrument in the world.[10] It is a 100-question personality test that asks people how they usually feel or act in particular situations. Respondents are classified as extraverted or introverted (E or I), sensing or intuitive (S or N), thinking or feeling (T or F), and judging or perceiving (J or P). These terms are defined as follows:

- *Extraverted (E) versus Introverted (I).* Extraverted individuals are outgoing, sociable, and assertive. Introverts are quiet and shy.
- *Sensing (S) versus Intuitive (N).* Sensing types are practical and prefer routine and order. They focus on details. Intuitives rely on unconscious processes and look at the "big picture."
- *Thinking (T) versus Feeling (F).* Thinking types use reason and logic to handle problems. Feeling types rely on their personal values and emotions.
- *Judging (J) versus Perceiving (P).* Judging types want control and prefer their world to be ordered and structured. Perceiving types are flexible and spontaneous.

These classifications together describe 16 personality types, identifying every person by one trait from each of the four pairs. For example, Introverted/Intuitive/Thinking/Judging people (INTJs) are visionaries with original minds and great drive. They are skeptical, critical, independent, determined, and often stubborn. ESTJs are organizers. They are realistic, logical, analytical, and decisive and have a natural head for business or mechanics. The ENTP type is a conceptualizer, innovative, individualistic, versatile, and attracted to entrepreneurial ideas. This person tends to be resourceful in solving challenging problems but may neglect routine assignments.

The MBTI has been widely used by organizations including Apple Computer, AT&T, Citigroup, GE, 3M Co., many hospitals and educational institutions, and

2 Describe the Myers-Briggs Type Indicator personality framework and assess its strengths and weaknesses.

---

heredity *Factors determined at conception; one's biological, physiological, and inherent psychological makeup.*

personality traits *Enduring characteristics that describe an individual's behavior.*

Myers-Briggs Type Indicator (MBTI) *A personality test that taps four characteristics and classifies people into 1 of 16 personality types.*

even the U.S. Armed Forces. Evidence is mixed about its validity as a measure of personality, however; most of the evidence is against it.[11] One problem is that it forces a person into one type or another; that is, you're either introverted or extraverted. There is no in-between, though in reality people can be both extraverted and introverted to some degree. The best we can say is that the MBTI can be a valuable tool for increasing self-awareness and providing career guidance. But because results tend to be unrelated to job performance, managers probably shouldn't use it as a selection test for job candidates.

The Big Five Personality Model

3 Identify the key traits in the Big Five personality model.

The MBTI may lack strong supporting evidence, but an impressive body of research supports the thesis of the **Big Five Model**—that five basic dimensions underlie all others and encompass most of the significant variation in human personality.[12] Moreover, test scores of these traits do a very good job of predicting how people behave in a variety of real-life situations.[13] The following are the Big Five factors:

- *Extraversion.* The **extraversion** dimension captures our comfort level with relationships. Extraverts tend to be gregarious, assertive, and sociable. Introverts tend to be reserved, timid, and quiet.
- *Agreeableness.* The **agreeableness** dimension refers to an individual's propensity to defer to others. Highly agreeable people are cooperative, warm, and trusting. People who score low on agreeableness are cold, disagreeable, and antagonistic.
- *Conscientiousness.* The **conscientiousness** dimension is a measure of reliability. A highly conscientious person is responsible, organized, dependable, and persistent. Those who score low on this dimension are easily distracted, disorganized, and unreliable.
- *Emotional stability.* The **emotional stability** dimension—often labeled by its converse, neuroticism—taps a person's ability to withstand stress. People with positive emotional stability tend to be calm, self-confident, and secure. Those with high negative scores tend to be nervous, anxious, depressed, and insecure.
- *Openness to experience.* The **openness to experience** dimension addresses range of interests and fascination with novelty. Extremely open people are creative, curious, and artistically sensitive. Those at the other end of the category are conventional and find comfort in the familiar.

Source: Kristin Callahan/Photoshot.

Andrea Jung, chairman and CEO of Avon, scores high on all personality dimensions of the Big Five Model. She is sociable, agreeable, conscientious, emotionally stable, and open to experiences. These personality traits have contributed to Jung's high job performance and career success. Since joining Avon in 1994, Jung has led a dramatic turnaround of a company that had a poor image, slow growth, and decline in sales to one of the world's top cosmetics companies and the world's leading direct sales brand. She transformed Avon by developing and executing growth strategies, launching new brand initiatives, and developing earnings opportunities for women worldwide.

How Do the Big Five Traits Predict Behavior at Work?   Research has found relationships between these personality dimensions and job performance.[14] As the authors of the most-cited review put it, "The preponderance of evidence shows that individuals who are dependable, reliable, careful, thorough, able to plan, organized, hardworking, persistent, and achievement-oriented tend to have higher job performance in most if not all occupations."[15] In addition, employees who score higher in conscientiousness develop higher levels of job knowledge, probably because highly conscientious people learn more (a review of 138 studies revealed conscientiousness was rather strongly related to GPA).[16] Higher levels of job knowledge then contribute to higher levels of job performance. Conscientious individuals who are more interested in learning than in just performing on the job are also exceptionally good at maintaining performance in the face of negative feedback.[17] There can be "too much of a good thing," however, as extremely conscientious individuals typically do not perform better than those who are simply above average in conscientiousness.[18]

Exhibit **5-1**	Traits That Matter Most to Business Success at Buyout Companies

Most Important	**Less Important**
Persistence	Strong oral communication
Attention to detail	Teamwork
Efficiency	Flexibility/adaptability
Analytical skills	Enthusiasm
Setting high standards	Listening skills

Conscientiousness is as important for managers as for front-line employees. As Exhibit 5-1 shows, a study of the personality scores of 313 CEO candidates in private equity companies (of whom 225 were hired, and their company's performance later correlated with their personality scores) found conscientiousness—in the form of persistence, attention to detail, and setting of high standards—was more important than other traits. These results attest to the importance of conscientiousness to organizational success.

Interestingly, conscientious people live longer because they take better care of themselves (they eat better and exercise more) and engage in fewer risky behaviors like smoking, drinking and drugs, and risky sexual or driving behavior.[19] Still, probably because they're so organized and structured, conscientious people don't adapt as well to changing contexts. They are generally performance oriented and have more trouble learning complex skills early in the training process because their focus is on performing well rather than on learning. Finally, they are often less creative than less conscientious people, especially artistically.[20]

4 Demonstrate how the Big Five traits predict behavior at work.

Although conscientiousness is most consistently related to job performance, the other Big Five traits are also related to aspects of performance and have other implications for work and for life. Let's look at them one at a time. Exhibit 5-2 summarizes.

Of the Big Five traits, emotional stability is most strongly related to life satisfaction, job satisfaction, and low stress levels. This is probably true because high scorers are more likely to be positive and optimistic and experience fewer negative emotions. They are happier than those who score low. People low on emotional stability are hypervigilant (looking for problems or impending signs of danger) and are especially vulnerable to the physical and psychological effects of stress. Extraverts tend to be happier in their jobs and in their lives as a whole. They experience more positive emotions than do introverts, and they more freely express these feelings. They also tend to perform better in jobs that require significant interpersonal interaction, perhaps because they have more social skills—they usually have more friends and spend more time in social

---

Big Five Model *A personality assessment model that taps five basic dimensions.*

extraversion *A personality dimension describing someone who is sociable, gregarious, and assertive.*

agreeableness *A personality dimension that describes someone who is good natured, cooperative, and trusting.*

conscientiousness *A personality dimension that describes someone who is responsible, dependable, persistent, and organized.*

emotional stability *A personality dimension that characterizes someone as calm, self-confident, secure (positive) versus nervous, depressed, and insecure (negative).*

openness to experience *A personality dimension that characterizes someone in terms of imagination, sensitivity, and curiosity.*

Exhibit **5-2** — Model of How Big Five Traits Influence OB Criteria

BIG FIVE TRAITS	WHY IS IT RELEVANT?	WHAT DOES IT AFFECT?
Emotional stability	• Less negative thinking and fewer negative emotions • Less hyper-vigilant	• Higher job & life satisfaction • Lower stress levels
Extroversion	• Better interpersonal skills • Greater social dominance • More emotionally expressive	• Higher performance* • Enhanced leadership • Higher job & life satisfaction
Openness	• Increased learning • More creative • More flexible & autonomous	• Training performance • Enhanced leadership • More adaptable to change
Agreeableness	• Better liked • More compliant and conforming	• Higher performance* • Lower levels of deviant behavior
Conscientiousness	• Greater effort & persistence • More drive and discipline • Better organized & planning	• Higher performance • Enhanced leadership • Greater longevity

* In jobs requiring significant teamwork or frequent interpersonal interactions.

situations than introverts. Finally, extraversion is a relatively strong predictor of leadership emergence in groups; extraverts are more socially dominant, "take charge" sorts of people, and they are generally more assertive than introverts.[21] One downside is that extraverts are more impulsive than introverts; they are more likely to be absent from work and engage in risky behavior such as unprotected sex, drinking, and other impulsive or sensation-seeking acts.[22] One study also found extraverts were more likely than introverts to lie during job interviews.[23]

Individuals who score high on openness to experience are more creative in science and art than those who score low. Because creativity is important to leadership, open people are more likely to be effective leaders, and more comfortable with ambiguity and change. They cope better with organizational change and are more adaptable in changing contexts. Recent evidence also suggests, however, that they are especially susceptible to workplace accidents.[24]

You might expect agreeable people to be happier than disagreeable people. They are, but only slightly. When people choose romantic partners, friends, or organizational team members, agreeable individuals are usually their first choice. Agreeable individuals are better liked than disagreeable people, which explains why they tend to do better in interpersonally oriented jobs such as customer service. They also are more compliant and rule abiding and less likely to get into accidents as a result. People who are agreeable are more satisfied in their jobs and contribute to organizational performance by engaging in citizenship behavior.[25] They are also less likely to engage in organizational deviance. One downside is that agreeableness is associated with lower levels of career success (especially earnings).

The five personality factors identified in the Big Five model appear in almost all cross-cultural studies.[26] These studies have included a wide variety of diverse cultures—such as China, Israel, Germany, Japan, Spain, Nigeria, Norway, Pakistan, and the United States. Differences are complex but tend to be primarily about whether countries are predominantly individualistic or collectivistic. Chinese managers use the category of conscientiousness more often and agreeableness less often than do U.S. managers. And the Big Five appear to predict a bit better in individualistic than in collectivist cultures.[27] But there is a surprisingly high amount of agreement, especially across individuals from developed countries. A comprehensive review of studies covering people from what was then the 15-nation European Community found conscientiousness a valid predictor of performance across jobs and occupational groups.[28] This is exactly what U.S. studies have found.

Other Personality Traits Relevant to OB

5 Identify other personality traits relevant to OB.

Although the Big Five traits have proven highly relevant to OB, they don't exhaust the range of traits that can describe someone's personality. Now we'll look at other, more specific, attributes that are powerful predictors of behavior in organizations. The first relates to our core self-evaluation. The others are Machiavellianism, narcissism, self-monitoring, propensity for risk taking, proactive personality, and other-orientation.

Core Self-Evaluation People who have positive **core self-evaluations** like themselves and see themselves as effective, capable, and in control of their environment. Those with negative core self-evaluations tend to dislike themselves, question their capabilities, and view themselves as powerless over their environment.[29] We discussed in Chapter 3 that core self-evaluations relate to job satisfaction because people positive on this trait see more challenge in their job and actually attain more complex jobs.

But what about job performance? People with positive core self-evaluations perform better than others because they set more ambitious goals, are more committed to their goals, and persist longer in attempting to reach these goals. One study of life insurance agents found core self-evaluations were critical predictors of performance. Ninety percent of life insurance sales calls end in rejection, so an agent has to believe in him- or herself to persist. In fact, this study showed the majority of successful salespersons did have positive core self-evaluations.[30] Such people also provide better customer service, are more popular co-workers, and have careers that both begin on better footing and ascend more rapidly over time.[31] Some evidence suggests that individuals high in core self-evaluations perform especially well if they also feel their work provides meaning and is helpful to others.[32]

Can we be *too* positive? What happens when someone thinks he is capable but is actually incompetent? One study of *Fortune* 500 CEOs showed that many are overconfident, and their perceived infallibility often causes them to make bad decisions.[33] Teddy Forstmann, chairman of the sports marketing giant

Source: Ric Francis/AP Images.

The personality trait of positive core self-evaluation helps Satoru Iwata meet the challenges and complexity of his job as CEO of Nintendo. Confident and capable, Iwata has applied his years of experience and innovation as a game developer to introducing new products, such as the Wii gaming console and the 3DS portable console. Iwata views his job as an opportunity to cultivate new customers by widening the appeal of video games to new market segments in developed nations and by introducing products to developing countries.

core self-evaluation *Bottom-line conclusions individuals have about their capabilities, competence, and worth as a person.*

IMG, said of himself, "I know God gave me an unusual brain. I can't deny that. I have a God-given talent for seeing potential."[34] We might say people like Forstmann are overconfident, but very often we humans sell ourselves short and are less happy and effective than we could be because of it. If we decide we can't do something, for example, we won't try, and not doing it only reinforces our self-doubts.

Machiavellianism   Kuzi is a young bank manager in Taiwan. He's had three promotions in the past 4 years and makes no apologies for the aggressive tactics he's used to propel his career upward. "I'm prepared to do whatever I have to do to get ahead," he says. Kuzi would properly be called Machiavellian.

The personality characteristic of **Machiavellianism** (often abbreviated *Mach*) is named after Niccolo Machiavelli, who wrote in the sixteenth century on how to gain and use power. An individual high in Machiavellianism is pragmatic, maintains emotional distance, and believes ends can justify means. "If it works, use it" is consistent with a high-Mach perspective. A considerable amount of research has found high Machs manipulate more, win more, are persuaded less, and persuade others more than do low Machs.[35] They like their jobs less, are more stressed by their work, and engage in more deviant work behaviors.[36] Yet high-Mach outcomes are moderated by situational factors. High Machs flourish (1) when they interact face to face with others rather than indirectly; (2) when the situation has minimal rules and regulations, allowing latitude for improvisation; and (3) when emotional involvement with details irrelevant to winning distracts low Machs.[37] Thus, in jobs that require bargaining skills (such as labor negotiation) or that offer substantial rewards for winning (such as commissioned sales), high Machs will be productive. But if ends can't justify the means, there are absolute standards of behavior, or the three situational factors we noted are not in evidence, our ability to predict a high Mach's performance will be severely curtailed.

Narcissism   Hans likes to be the center of attention. He looks at himself in the mirror a lot, has extravagant dreams, and considers himself a person of many talents. Hans is a narcissist. The term is from the Greek myth of Narcissus, a man so vain and proud he fell in love with his own image. In psychology, **narcissism** describes a person who has a grandiose sense of self-importance, requires excessive admiration, has a sense of entitlement, and is arrogant. Evidence suggests that narcissists are more charismatic and thus more likely to emerge as leaders, and they may even display better psychological health (at least as they self-report).[38]

Despite having some advantages, most evidence suggests that narcissism is undesirable. A study found that while narcissists thought they were *better* leaders than their colleagues, their supervisors actually rated them as *worse.* An Oracle executive described that company's CEO Larry Ellison as follows: "The difference between God and Larry is that God does not believe he is Larry."[39] Because narcissists often want to gain the admiration of others and receive affirmation of their superiority, they tend to "talk down" to those who threaten them, treating others as if they were inferior. Narcissists also tend to be selfish and exploitive and believe others exist for their benefit.[40] Their bosses rate them as less effective at their jobs than others, particularly when it comes to helping people.[41] Subsequent research using data compiled over 100 years has shown that narcissistic CEOs of baseball organizations tend to generate higher levels of manager turnover, although curiously, members of external organizations see them as more influential.[42]

Self-Monitoring Joyce McIntyre is always in trouble at work. Though she's competent, hardworking, and productive, in performance reviews she is rated no better than average, and she seems to have made a career of irritating bosses. Joyce's problem is that she's politically inept. She's unable to adjust her behavior to fit changing situations. As she puts it, "I'm true to myself. I don't remake myself to please others." We would describe Joyce as a low self-monitor.

Self-monitoring refers to an individual's ability to adjust his or her behavior to external, situational factors.[43] Individuals high in self-monitoring show considerable adaptability in adjusting their behavior to external situational factors. They are highly sensitive to external cues and can behave differently in different situations, sometimes presenting striking contradictions between their public persona and their private self. Low self-monitors, like Joyce, can't disguise themselves in that way. They tend to display their true dispositions and attitudes in every situation; hence, there is high behavioral consistency between who they are and what they do.

Evidence indicates high self-monitors pay closer attention to the behavior of others and are more capable of conforming than are low self-monitors.[44] They also receive better performance ratings, are more likely to emerge as leaders, and show less commitment to their organizations.[45] In addition, high self-monitoring managers tend to be more mobile in their careers, receive more promotions (both internal and cross-organizational), and are more likely to occupy central positions in an organization.[46]

Risk Taking Donald Trump stands out for his willingness to take risks. He started with almost nothing in the 1960s. By the mid-1980s, he had made a fortune by betting on a resurgent New York City real estate market. Then, trying to capitalize on his successes, Trump overextended himself. By 1994, he had a *negative* net worth of $850 million. Never fearful of taking chances, "The Donald" leveraged the few assets he had left on several New York, New Jersey, and Caribbean real estate ventures and hit it big again. In 2011, when Trump was contemplating a presidential run, *The Atlantic* estimated his net worth at more than $7 billion.[47]

People differ in their willingness to take chances, a quality that affects how much time and information they need to make a decision. For instance, 79 managers worked on simulated exercises that required them to make hiring decisions.[48] High risk-taking managers made more rapid decisions and used less information than did the low risk takers. Interestingly, decision accuracy was the same for both groups.

Although previous studies have shown managers in large organizations to be more risk averse than growth-oriented entrepreneurs who actively manage small businesses, recent findings suggest managers in large organizations may actually be more willing to take risks than entrepreneurs.[49] The work population as a whole also differs in risk propensity.[50] It makes sense to recognize these differences and even consider aligning them with specific job demands. A high risk-taking propensity may lead to more effective performance for a stock trader in a brokerage firm because that type of job demands rapid decision

Machiavellianism *The degree to which an individual is pragmatic, maintains emotional distance, and believes that ends can justify means.*

narcissism *The tendency to be arrogant, have a grandiose sense of self-importance, require excessive admiration, and have a sense of entitlement.*

self-monitoring *A personality trait that measures an individual's ability to adjust his or her behavior to external, situational factors.*

making. On the other hand, a willingness to take risks might prove a major obstacle to an accountant who performs auditing activities.

Proactive Personality   Did you ever notice that some people actively take the initiative to improve their current circumstances or create new ones? These are proactive personalities.[51] Those with a **proactive personality** identify opportunities, show initiative, take action, and persevere until meaningful change occurs, compared to others who passively react to situations. Proactives create positive change in their environment, regardless of, or even in spite of, constraints or obstacles.[52] Not surprisingly, they have many desirable behaviors that organizations covet. They are more likely than others to be seen as leaders and to act as change agents.[53] Proactive individuals are more likely to be satisfied with work and help others more with their tasks, largely because they build more relationships with others.[54]

Proactives are also more likely to challenge the status quo or voice their displeasure when situations aren't to their liking.[55] If an organization requires people with entrepreneurial initiative, proactives make good candidates; however, they're also more likely to leave an organization to start their own business.[56] As individuals, proactives are more likely than others to achieve career success.[57] They select, create, and influence work situations in their favor. They seek out job and organizational information, develop contacts in high places, engage in career planning, and demonstrate persistence in the face of career obstacles.

Other-orientation   Some people just naturally seem to think about other people a lot, being concerned about their well-being and feelings. Others behave like "economic actors," primarily rational and self-interested. These differences

Personality Predicts the Performance of Entrepreneurs

This statement is true.

Studies of identical twins reared apart suggest striking career similarities—if one twin became an entrepreneur, the other twin was more likely to do the same. The explanation may lie in personality.

One recent analysis of 60 studies linked individuals' personalities to their intentions to undertake an entrepreneurial career, and to the performance of their ventures once they made that decision. The Big Five personality traits—except agreeableness, which didn't matter—significantly predicted entrepreneurial

intentions and, more significantly, entrepreneurial firm performance. Especially important were openness to experience and conscientiousness, both of which also predicted firm growth over time. Interestingly, risk propensity—the tendency to take and be comfortable with taking risks—was not associated with entrepreneurial performance.

What are the implications of these findings? Traditionally, people who saw themselves as risk averse were steered away from entrepreneurship. However, these results suggest it is more important to steer low scorers on openness

and conscientiousness away. The best entrepreneurs appear not to be the swashbuckling risk-takers, but rather the methodical ones who have the discipline to turn their open thinking and creative ideas into reality.

Sources: H. Zhao, S. E. Seibert, and G. T. Lumpkin, "The Relationship of Personality to Entrepreneurial Intentions and Performance: A Meta-Analytic Review," *Journal of Management* 36, no. 2 (2010), pp. 381–404; M. Herper, "Could We Invent an Antibody to Make You an Entrepreneur?" *Forbes* (May 5, 2011), downloaded on May 23, 2011, from http://blogs.forbes.com/.

The Right Personality for a Global Workplace

As work becomes increasingly international in focus, successful managers need to be able to operate across cultures easily. Obviously, expatriate managers working in other countries will need personality traits that make them better able to work overseas, but managers at home who order parts and services from overseas or prepare marketing plans for other countries, for example, will also conduct cross-cultural communications. In the workforce of the future, everyone from mechanics to customer service representatives to advertisers will need to understand the global market. What is the right personality for a global workplace?

You might suspect that, of the Big Five traits, openness to experience would be most important to effectiveness in international assignments. Open people are more likely to be culturally flexible—to "go with the flow" when things are different in another country. Research is not fully consistent on the issue, but most does suggest that managers who score high on openness perform better than others in international assignments. Other evidence suggests that employees who are more agreeable and extraverted have an easier time with international assignments. They may be better at establishing new relationships and developing social networks in unfamiliar contexts.

What do these results imply for organizations? Given continuing globalization in the future, organizations should select employees with traits related to better performance in international assignments. Managers will need to foster an open-minded perspective about other cultures among their employees.

Sources: Based on M. A. Shaffer, D. A. Harrison, and H. Gregersen, "You Can Take It with You: Individual Differences and Expatriate Effectiveness," *Journal of Applied Psychology* 91, no. 1 (2006), pp. 109–125; M. van Woerkom and R. S. M. de Reuver, "Predicting Excellent Management Performance in an Intercultural Context: A Study of the Influence of Multicultural Personality on Transformational Leadership and Performance," *International Journal of Human Resource Management* 20, no. 10 (2009), pp. 2013–2029; and M. Downes, I. I. Varner, and M. Hemmasi, "Individual Profiles as Predictors of Expatriate Effectiveness," *Competitiveness Review* 20, no. 3 (2010), pp. 235–247.

reflect varying levels of other-orientation, a personality trait that reflects the extent to which decisions are affected by social influences and concerns vs. our own well-being and outcomes.[58]

What are the consequences of having a high level of other-orientation? Those who are other-oriented feel more obligated to help others who have helped them (pay me back), whereas those who are more self-oriented will help others when they expect to be helped in the future (pay me forward).[59] Employees high in other-orientation also exert especially high levels of effort when engaged in helping work or prosocial behavior.[60] In sum, it appears that having a strong orientation toward helping others does affect some behaviors that actually matter for organizations. However, research is still needed to clarify this emerging construct and its relationship with agreeableness.

Having discussed personality traits—the enduring characteristics that describe a person's behavior—we now turn to values. Values are often very specific and describe belief systems rather than behavioral tendencies. Some beliefs or values don't say much about a person's personality, and we don't always act consistently with our values.

proactive personality　*People who identify opportunities, show initiative, take action, and persevere until meaningful change occurs.*

Values

6   Define *values*, demonstrate the importance of values, and contrast terminal and instrumental values.

Is capital punishment right or wrong? If a person likes power, is that good or bad? The answers to these questions are value laden. Some might argue capital punishment is right because it is an appropriate retribution for crimes such as murder and treason. Others might argue, just as strongly, that no government has the right to take anyone's life.

Values represent basic convictions that "a specific mode of conduct or end-state of existence is personally or socially preferable to an opposite or converse mode of conduct or end-state of existence."[61] They contain a judgmental element in that they carry an individual's ideas as to what is right, good, or desirable. Values have both content and intensity attributes. The content attribute says a mode of conduct or end-state of existence is *important*. The intensity attribute specifies *how important* it is. When we rank an individual's values in terms of their intensity, we obtain that person's **value system**. All of us have a hierarchy of values that forms our value system. We find it in the relative importance we assign to values such as freedom, pleasure, self-respect, honesty, obedience, and equality.

Are values fluid and flexible? Generally speaking, no. They tend to be relatively stable and enduring.[62] A significant portion of the values we hold is established in our early years—by parents, teachers, friends, and others. As children, we are told certain behaviors or outcomes are *always* desirable or *always* undesirable, with few gray areas. You were never taught to be just a little bit honest or a little bit responsible, for example. It is this absolute, or "black-or-white," learning of values that ensures their stability and endurance. If we question our values, of course, they may change, but more often they are reinforced. There is also evidence linking personality to values, implying our values may be partly determined by our genetically transmitted traits.[63]

The Importance of Values

Values lay the foundation for our understanding of people's attitudes and motivation and influence our perceptions. We enter an organization with preconceived notions of what "ought" and "ought not" to be. These notions are not value-free; on the contrary, they contain our interpretations of right and wrong and our preference for certain behaviors or outcomes over others. As a result, values cloud objectivity and rationality; they influence attitudes and behavior.[64]

Suppose you enter an organization with the view that allocating pay on the basis of performance is right, while allocating pay on the basis of seniority is wrong. How will you react if you find the organization you've just joined rewards seniority and not performance? You're likely to be disappointed—and this can lead to job dissatisfaction and a decision not to exert a high level of effort because "It's probably not going to lead to more money anyway." Would your attitudes and behavior be different if your values aligned with the organization's pay policies? Most likely.

Terminal versus Instrumental Values

Can we classify values? Yes. In this section, we review two approaches to developing value typologies.

Rokeach Value Survey Milton Rokeach created the Rokeach Value Survey (RVS).[65] It consists of two sets of values, each containing 18 individual value items. One set, called **terminal values**, refers to desirable end-states. These are the goals a person would like to achieve during his or her lifetime. The other set, called **instrumental values**, refers to preferable modes of behavior, or means of achieving the terminal values. Some examples of terminal values in the Rokeach Value Survey are: Prosperity and economic success, Freedom, Health and well-being, World peace, Social recognition, and Meaning in life. The types of instrumental values illustrated in RVS are Self-improvement, Autonomy and self-reliance, Personal discipline, kindness, Ambition, and Goal-orientation.

Several studies confirm that RVS values vary among groups.[66] People in the same occupations or categories (corporate managers, union members, parents, students) tend to hold similar values. One study compared corporate executives, members of the steelworkers' union, and members of a community activist group. Although there was a good deal of overlap among them,[67] there were also significant differences (see Exhibit 5-3). The activists ranked "equality" as their most important terminal value; executives and union members ranked this value 12 and 13, respectively. Activists ranked "helpful" as their second-highest instrumental value. The other two groups both ranked it 14. Because executives, union members, and activists all have a vested interest in what corporations do, these differences can create serious conflicts when groups contend with each other over an organization's economic and social policies.[68]

7 Compare generational differences in values and identify the dominant values in today's workforce.

Generational Values

Contemporary Work Cohorts Researchers have integrated several recent analyses of work values into four groups that attempt to capture the unique values

Exhibit **5-3**	Mean Value Ranking Executives, Union Members, and Activists (Top Five Only)

EXECUTIVES		UNION MEMBERS		ACTIVISTS	
Terminal	Instrumental	Terminal	Instrumental	Terminal	Instrumental
1. Self-respect	1. Honest	1. Family security	1. Responsible	1. Equality	1. Honest
2. Family security	2. Responsible	2. Freedom	2. Honest	2. A world of peace	2. Helpful
3. Freedom	3. Capable	3. Happiness	3. Courageous	3. Family security	3. Courageous
4. A sense of accomplishment	4. Ambitious	4. Self-respect	4. Independent	4. Self-respect	4. Responsible
5. Happiness	5. Independent	5. Mature love	5. Capable	5. Freedom	5. Capable

Source: Based on W. C. Frederick and J. Weber, "The Values of Corporate Managers and Their Critics: An Empirical Description and Normative Implications," in W. C. Frederick and L. E. Preston (eds.), Business Ethics: Research Issues and Empirical Studies (Greenwich, CT: JAI Press, 1990), pp. 123–144.

values *Basic convictions that a specific mode of conduct or end-state of existence is personally or socially preferable to an opposite or converse mode of conduct or end-state of existence.*

value system *A hierarchy based on a ranking of an individual's values in terms of their intensity.*

terminal values *Desirable end-states of existence; the goals a person would like to achieve during his or her lifetime.*

instrumental values *Preferable modes of behavior or means of achieving one's terminal values.*

	Entered the	Approximate	
Cohort	Workforce	Current Age	Dominant Work Values
Boomers	1965–1985	Mid-40s to mid-60s	Success, achievement, ambition, dislike of authority; loyalty to career
Xers	1985–2000	Late 20s to early 40s	Work/life balance, team-oriented, dislike of rules; loyalty to relationships
Nexters	2000 to present	Under 30	Confident, financial success, self-reliant but team-oriented; loyalty to both self and relationships

Exhibit 5-4   Dominant Work Values in Today's Workforce

of different cohorts or generations in the U.S. workforce.[69] Exhibit 5-4 segments employees by the era during which they entered the workforce. Because most people start work between the ages of 18 and 23, the eras also correlate closely with employee age.

Let's start with some limitations of this analysis. First, we make no assumption that the framework applies across all cultures. Second, despite a steady stream of press coverage, there is very little rigorous research on generational values, so we have to rely on an intuitive framework. Finally, these are imprecise categories. There is no law that someone born in 1985 can't have values similar to those of someone born in 1955. Despite these limitations, values do change over generations,[70] and we can gain some useful insights from analyzing values this way.

Boomers (*Baby Boomers*) are a large cohort born after World War II when veterans returned to their families and times were good. Boomers entered the workforce from the mid-1960s through the mid-1980s. They brought with them a large measure of the "hippie ethic" and distrust of authority. But they place a great deal of emphasis on achievement and material success. Pragmatists who believe ends can justify means, they work hard and want to enjoy the fruits of their labors. Boomers see the organizations that employ them merely as vehicles for their careers. Terminal values such as a sense of accomplishment and social recognition rank high with them.

The lives of *Xers* (*Generation Xers*) have been shaped by globalization, two-career parents, MTV, AIDS, and computers. Xers value flexibility, life options, and the achievement of job satisfaction. Family and relationships are very important. Xers are skeptical, particularly of authority. They also enjoy team-oriented work. In search of balance in their lives, Xers are less willing to make personal sacrifices for the sake of their employer than previous generations were. On the RVS, they rate high on true friendship, happiness, and pleasure.

The most recent entrants to the workforce, the *Millennials* (also called *Netters, Nexters, Generation Yers,* and *Generation Nexters*) grew up during prosperous times. They have high expectations and seek meaning in their work. Millennials have life goals more oriented toward becoming rich (81 percent) and famous (51 percent) than do Generation Xers (62 percent and 29 percent, respectively), but they also see themselves as socially responsible. At ease with diversity, Millennials are the first generation to take technology for granted. More than other generations, they tend to be questioning, electronically networked, and entrepreneurial. At the same time, some have described Millennials as entitled and needy. They may clash

Should You Try to Change Someone's Personality?

As we have noted, individuals differ in terms of their personality scores, and these differences contribute to effective performance. It isn't always possible to identify personality traits successfully during the hiring process, and sometimes there simply aren't enough people with the "right" personality traits available. So should organizations try to shape their employees to make them more conscientious, agreeable, open, emotionally stable, and extraverted? Is there a potential ethical problem with exercising this type of control over workers?

Some evidence suggests that people's basic temperament is largely fixed by biology, and in this case, attempts to change personality will mostly lead to frustration and dissatisfaction. An employee who tends to see things negatively is unlikely to suddenly become an optimist just because a manager pushes him or her to read self-help books and

take up meditation. Moreover, such efforts may send a strong message of disapproval—who would want a manager saying, "We don't like you the way you are, you need to change!" Employees who are forced into working environments that don't fit their dispositions will also likely experience high levels of psychological strain.

On the other hand, it *is* possible to change the way personality is expressed. Biological anthropologist Helen Fisher notes that despite the importance of biology, "the environment always molds your biology." Someone who isn't particularly open to experience might be comfortable with new work assignments if they're framed appropriately, and someone who isn't very conscientious can display organization and dutifulness if the right environmental supports like checklists and formalized goal-setting are in place. And personality does change somewhat over time. As people age, their scores on conscientiousness and

agreeableness increase rather dramatically, and neuroticism decreases substantially (the results for openness and extraversion are more complex).

So what might employers do to accommodate employee personality differences while still obtaining maximum performance? One strategy is to focus on outcomes and allow employees to determine their own way to achieve them. An extrovert and an introvert might both be able to produce a very high quality report, even if the extrovert will want to collaborate and discuss during the process of writing whereas the introvert will prefer to work out problems alone. Employers can also try to assign employees to activities that best match their personality types.

Sources: B. W. Roberts and D. Mroczek, "Personality Trait Change in Adulthood," *Current Directions in Psychological Science,* no. 1, Vol. 17 (2008), pp. 31–35; "Five Ways to Change Your Personality," *CBS News* (August 21, 2010), www.cbsnews.com.

EBay's young employees rank their employer as one of the best places to work for millennials. The company's culture of fun, casual dress, and flexible work schedules that provide for a work/life balance appeal to Generation Y employees like those shown here at eBay's offices in San Jose, California. Young employees say that eBay managers give them job responsibility quickly, generous recognition for their achievements, and learning opportunities to advance their careers. They also admire eBay's "Social Venture" initiatives such as WorldofGood.com, eBay Giving Works, and MicroPlace that make a positive difference in the lives of people throughout the world.

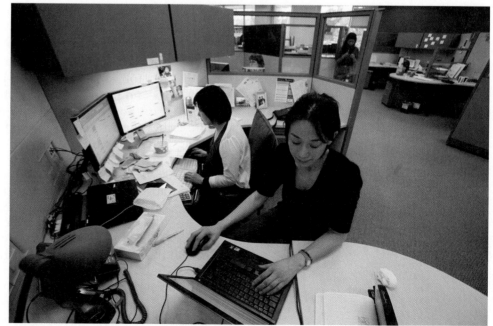

with other generations over work attire and communication. They also like feedback. An Ernst & Young survey found that 85 percent of Millennials want "frequent and candid performance feedback," compared to only half of Boomers.[71]

Though it is fascinating to think about generational values, remember these classifications lack solid research support. Recent reviews suggest many of the generalizations are either overblown or incorrect.[72] Studies that have found differences across generations do not support the popular conceptions of how generations differ, and most are plagued with methodological problems that make it difficult to assess whether differences actually exist. One study that used an appropriate longitudinal design did find the value placed on leisure increased over generations from the Baby Boomers to the Millennials and work centrality has declined, but it did not find that Millennials had higher altruistic work values as expected.[73] Generational classifications may help us understand our own and other generations better, but we must also appreciate their limits.

Linking an Individual's Personality and Values to the Workplace

Thirty years ago, organizations were concerned only with personality because their primary focus was to match individuals to specific jobs. That concern has expanded to include how well the individual's personality *and* values match the organization. Why? Because managers today are less interested in an applicant's ability to perform a *specific* job than with his or her *flexibility* to meet changing situations and commitment to the organization.

We'll now discuss person–job fit and person–organization fit in more detail.

Person–Job Fit

The effort to match job requirements with personality characteristics is best articulated in John Holland's **personality–job fit theory**.[74] Holland presents six personality types and proposes that satisfaction and the propensity to leave a position depend on how well individuals match their personalities to a job. Exhibit 5-5 describes the six types, their personality characteristics, and examples of the congruent occupations for each.

Holland developed the Vocational Preference Inventory questionnaire, which contains 160 occupational titles. Respondents indicate which they like or dislike, and their answers form personality profiles. Research strongly supports the resulting hexagonal diagram shown in Exhibit 5-6.[75] The closer two fields or orientations are in the hexagon, the more compatible they are. Adjacent categories are quite similar, whereas diagonally opposite ones are highly dissimilar.

What does all this mean? The theory argues that satisfaction is highest and turnover lowest when personality and occupation are in agreement. A realistic person in a realistic job is in a more congruent situation than a realistic person in an investigative job. A realistic person in a social job is in the most incongruent situation possible. The key points of this model are that (1) there do appear to

| Exhibit 5-5 | Holland's Typology of Personality and Congruent Occupations |

Type	Personality Characteristics	Congruent Occupations
Realistic: Prefers physical activities that require skill, strength, and coordination	Shy, genuine, persistent, stable, conforming, practical	Mechanic, drill press operator, assembly-line worker, farmer
Investigative: Prefers activities that involve thinking, organizing, and understanding	Analytical, original, curious, independent	Biologist, economist, mathematician, news reporter
Social: Prefers activities that involve helping and developing others	Sociable, friendly, cooperative, understanding	Social worker, teacher, counselor, clinical psychologist
Conventional: Prefers rule-regulated, orderly, and unambiguous activities	Conforming, efficient, practical, unimaginative, inflexible	Accountant, corporate manager, bank teller, file clerk
Enterprising: Prefers verbal activities in which there are opportunities to influence others and attain power	Self-confident, ambitious, energetic, domineering	Lawyer, real estate agent, public relations specialist, small business manager
Artistic: Prefers ambiguous and unsystematic activities that allow creative expression	Imaginative, disorderly, idealistic, emotional, impractical	Painter, musician, writer, interior decorator

be intrinsic differences in personality among individuals, (2) there are different types of jobs, and (3) people in jobs congruent with their personality should be more satisfied and less likely to voluntarily resign than people in incongruent jobs. Evidence supports the value of assessing vocational interests in the selection process, with a match between interests and job requirements predicting job knowledge, performance, and low likelihood of turnover.[76]

| Exhibit 5-6 | Relationships Among Occupational Personality Types |

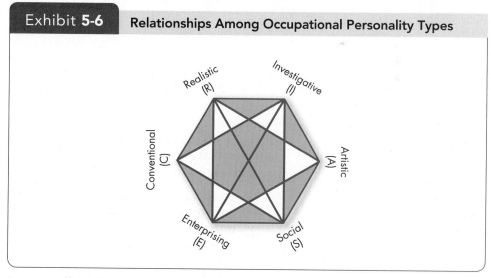

Source: Reprinted by special permission of the publisher, Psychological Assessment Resources, Inc., from *Making Vocational Choices*, copyright 1973, 1985, 1992 by Psychological Assessment Resources, Inc. All rights reserved.

personality–job fit theory *A theory that identifies six personality types and proposes that the fit between personality type and occupational environment determines satisfaction and turnover.*

As you might expect, Holland types relate to personality scales. One study found individuals higher in openness to experience as children were more likely to take jobs high on the investigative and artistic dimensions as adults, and those higher in conscientiousness as children were more likely to work in conventional jobs as adults.[77]

Person–Organization Fit

We've noted that researchers have looked at matching people to organizations as well as to jobs. If an organization faces a dynamic and changing environment and requires employees able to readily change tasks and move easily between teams, it's more important that employees' personalities fit with the overall organization's culture than with the characteristics of any specific job.

The person–organization fit essentially argues that people are attracted to and selected by organizations that match their values, and they leave organizations that are not compatible with their personalities.[78] Using the Big Five terminology, for instance, we could expect that people high on extraversion fit well with aggressive and team-oriented cultures, that people high on agreeableness match up better with a supportive organizational climate than one focused on aggressiveness, and that people high on openness to experience fit better in organizations that emphasize innovation rather than standardization.[79] Following these guidelines at the time of hiring should identify new employees who fit better with the organization's culture, which should, in turn, result in higher employee satisfaction and reduced turnover. Research on person–organization fit has also looked at whether people's values match the organization's culture. This match predicts job satisfaction, commitment to the organization, and low turnover.[80] Interestingly, some research found that person-organization fit was more important in predicting turnover in a collectivistic nation (India) than in a more individualistic nation (the United States).[81]

International Values

8 Identify Hofstede's five value dimensions of national culture.

MyManagementLab
For an interactive application of this topic, check out this chapter's simulation activity at
www.mymanagementlab.com.

One of the most widely referenced approaches for analyzing variations among cultures was done in the late 1970s by Geert Hofstede.[82] He surveyed more than 116,000 IBM employees in 40 countries about their work-related values and found that managers and employees vary on five value dimensions of national culture:

- *Power distance.* **Power distance** describes the degree to which people in a country accept that power in institutions and organizations is distributed unequally. A high rating on power distance means that large inequalities of power and wealth exist and are tolerated in the culture, as in a class or caste system that discourages upward mobility. A low power distance rating characterizes societies that stress equality and opportunity.
- *Individualism versus collectivism.* **Individualism** is the degree to which people prefer to act as individuals rather than as members of groups and believe in individual rights above all else. **Collectivism** emphasizes a tight social framework in which people expect others in groups of which they are a part to look after them and protect them.
- *Masculinity versus femininity.* Hofstede's construct of **masculinity** is the degree to which the culture favors traditional masculine roles such as achievement, power, and control, as opposed to viewing men and women as equals. A high masculinity rating indicates the culture has separate roles

for men and women, with men dominating the society. A high **femininity** rating means the culture sees little differentiation between male and female roles and treats women as the equals of men in all respects.

- *Uncertainty avoidance.* The degree to which people in a country prefer structured over unstructured situations defines their **uncertainty avoidance**. In cultures that score high on uncertainty avoidance, people have an increased level of anxiety about uncertainty and ambiguity and use laws and controls to reduce uncertainty. People in cultures low on uncertainty avoidance are more accepting of ambiguity, are less rule oriented, take more risks, and more readily accept change.
- *Long-term versus short-term orientation.* This newest addition to Hofstede's typology measures a society's devotion to traditional values. People in a culture with **long-term orientation** look to the future and value thrift, persistence, and tradition. In a **short-term orientation**, people value the here and now; they accept change more readily and don't see commitments as impediments to change.

How do different countries score on Hofstede's dimensions? Exhibit 5-7 shows the ratings for the countries for which data are available. For example, power distance is higher in Malaysia than in any other country. The United States is very individualistic; in fact, it's the most individualistic nation of all (closely followed by Australia and Great Britain). The United States also tends to be short term in orientation and low in power distance (people in the United States tend not to accept built-in class differences between people). It is also relatively low on uncertainty avoidance, meaning most adults are relatively tolerant of uncertainty and ambiguity. The United States scores relatively high on masculinity; most people emphasize traditional gender roles (at least relative to countries such as Denmark, Finland, Norway, and Sweden).

You'll notice regional differences. Western and northern nations such as Canada and the Netherlands tend to be more individualistic. Poorer countries such as Mexico and the Philippines tend to be higher on power distance. South American nations tend to be higher than other countries on uncertainty avoidance, and Asian countries tend to have a long-term orientation.

Hofstede's culture dimensions have been enormously influential on OB researchers and managers. Nevertheless, his research has been criticized. First, although the data have since been updated, the original work is more than 30 years old and was based on a single company (IBM). A lot has happened on the world scene since then. Some of the most obvious changes include the fall of the Soviet Union, the transformation of central and eastern Europe, the end of apartheid in South Africa, and the rise of China as a global power. Second, few researchers have read the details of Hofstede's methodology closely and are

power distance *A national culture attribute that describes the extent to which a society accepts that power in institutions and organizations is distributed unequally.*

individualism *A national culture attribute that describes the degree to which people prefer to act as individuals rather than as members of groups.*

collectivism *A national culture attribute that describes a tight social framework in which people expect others in groups of which they are a part to look after them and protect them.*

masculinity *A national culture attribute that describes the extent to which the culture favors traditional masculine work roles of achievement, power, and control. Societal values are characterized by assertiveness and materialism.*

femininity *A national culture attribute that indicates little differentiation between male and female roles; a high rating indicates that women are treated as the equals of men in all aspects of the society.*

uncertainty avoidance *A national culture attribute that describes the extent to which a society feels threatened by uncertain and ambiguous situations and tries to avoid them.*

long-term orientation *A national culture attribute that emphasizes the future, thrift, and persistence.*

short-term orientation *A national culture attribute that emphasizes the past and present, respect for tradition, and fulfillment of social obligations.*

Exhibit **5-7**   Hofstede's Cultural Values by Nation

Country	Power Distance		Individualism versus Collectivism		Masculinity versus Femininity		Uncertainty Avoidance		Long- versus Short-Term Orientation	
	Index	Rank	Index	Rank	Index	Rank	Index	Rank	Index	Rank
Argentina	49	35–36	46	22–23	56	20–21	86	10–15		
Australia	36	41	90	2	61	16	51	37	31	22–24
Austria	11	53	55	18	79	2	70	24–25	31	22–24
Belgium	65	20	75	8	54	22	94	5–6	38	18
Brazil	69	14	38	26–27	49	27	76	21–22	65	6
Canada	39	39	80	4–5	52	24	48	41–42	23	30
Chile	63	24–25	23	38	28	46	86	10–15		
Colombia	67	17	13	49	64	11–12	80	20		
Costa Rica	35	42–44	15	46	21	48–49	86	10–15		
Denmark	18	51	74	9	16	50	23	51	46	10
Ecuador	78	8–9	8	52	63	13–14	67	28		
El Salvador	66	18–19	19	42	40	40	94	5–6		
Finland	33	46	63	17	26	47	59	31–32	41	14
France	68	15–16	71	10–11	43	35–36	86	10–15	39	17
Germany	35	42–44	67	15	66	9–10	65	29	31	22–24
Great Britain	35	42–44	89	3	66	9–10	35	47–48	25	28–29
Greece	60	27–28	35	30	57	18–19	112	1		
Guatemala	95	2–3	6	53	37	43	101	3		
Hong Kong	68	15–16	25	37	57	18–19	29	49–50	96	2
India	77	10–11	48	21	56	20–21	40	45	61	7
Indonesia	78	8–9	14	47–48	46	30–31	48	41–42		
Iran	58	29–30	41	24	43	35–36	59	31–32		
Ireland	28	49	70	12	68	7–8	35	47–48	43	13
Israel	13	52	54	19	47	29	81	19		
Italy	50	34	76	7	70	4–5	75	23	34	19
Jamaica	45	37	39	25	68	7–8	13	52		
Japan	54	33	46	22–23	95	1	92	7	80	4
Korea (South)	60	27–28	18	43	39	41	85	16–17	75	5
Malaysia	104	1	26	36	50	25–26	36	46		
Mexico	81	5–6	30	32	69	6	82	18		
The Netherlands	38	40	80	4–5	14	51	53	35	44	11–12
New Zealand	22	50	79	6	58	17	49	39–40	30	25–26
Norway	31	47–48	69	13	8	52	50	38	44	11–12
Pakistan	55	32	14	47–48	50	25–26	70	24–25	0	34
Panama	95	2–3	11	51	44	34	86	10–15		
Peru	64	21–23	16	45	42	37–38	87	9		
Philippines	94	4	32	31	64	11–12	44	44	19	31–32
Portugal	63	24–25	27	33–35	31	45	104	2	30	25–26
Singapore	74	13	20	39–41	48	28	8	53	48	9
South Africa	49	35–36	65	16	63	13–14	49	39–40		
Spain	57	31	51	20	42	37–38	86	10–15	19	31–32
Sweden	31	47–48	71	10–11	5	53	29	49–50	33	20
Switzerland	34	45	68	14	70	4–5	58	33	40	15–16
Taiwan	58	29–30	17	44	45	32–33	69	26	87	3
Thailand	64	21–23	20	39–41	34	44	64	30	56	8
Turkey	66	18–19	37	28	45	32–33	85	16–17		
United States	40	38	91	1	62	15	46	43	29	27
Uruguay	61	26	36	29	38	42	100	4		
Venezuela	81	5–6	12	50	73	3	76	21–22		
Yugoslavia	76	12	27	33–35	21	48–49	88	8		
Regions:										
Arab countries	80	7	38	26–27	53	23	68	27		
East Africa	64	21–23	27	33–35	41	39	52	36	25	28–29
West Africa	77	10–11	20	39–41	46	30–31	54	34	16	33

Scores range from 0 5 extremely low on dimension to 100 5 extremely high.

Note: 1 5 highest rank. LTO ranks: 1 5 China; 15–16 5 Bangladesh; 21 5 Poland; 34 5 lowest.

Source: Copyright Geert Hofstede BV, hofstede@bart.nl. Reprinted with permission.

Understanding differences in values across cultures helps explain the behavior of employees from different countries. According to Hofstede's framework for assessing cultures, China, like all Asian nations, ranks high in long-term orientation. China also ranks high in power distance, where the inequality of power and wealth within the country is accepted by citizens as part of their cultural heritage. Ranking low in individualism, China has a strong collectivist culture that fosters relationships where everyone takes responsibility for group members. Using these and other ratings can help organizations considering doing business in China to predict the behavior of employees shown here at a glassware factory.

Source: Imaginechina via AP Images.

therefore unaware of the many decisions and judgment calls he had to make (for example, reducing the number of cultural values to just five). Some results are unexpected. Japan, which is often considered a highly collectivist nation, is considered only average on collectivism under Hofstede's dimensions.[83] Despite these concerns, Hofstede has been one of the most widely cited social scientists ever, and his framework has left a lasting mark on OB.

Recent research across 598 studies with more than 200,000 respondents has investigated the relationship of cultural values and a variety of organizational criteria at both the individual and national level of analysis.[84] Overall, the four original culture dimensions were equally strong predictors of relevant outcomes, meaning researchers and practicing managers need to think about culture holistically and not just focus on one or two dimensions. Cultural values were more strongly related to organizational commitment, citizenship behavior, and team-related attitudes than were personality scores. On the other hand, personality was more strongly related to behavioral criteria like performance, absenteeism, and turnover. The researchers also found that individual scores were much better predictors of most outcomes than assigning all people in a country the same cultural values. In sum, this research suggests that Hofstede's value framework may be a valuable way of thinking about differences among people, but we should be cautious about assuming all people from a country have the same values.

The GLOBE Framework for Assessing Cultures   Begun in 1993, the Global Leadership and Organizational Behavior Effectiveness (GLOBE) research program is an ongoing cross-cultural investigation of leadership and national culture. Using data from 825 organizations in 62 countries, the GLOBE team identified nine dimensions on which national cultures differ.[85] Some—such as power distance, individualism/collectivism, uncertainty avoidance, gender differentiation (similar to masculinity versus femininity), and future orientation (similar to long-term versus short-term orientation)—resemble the Hofstede dimensions. The main difference is that the GLOBE framework added dimensions, such as humane orientation (the degree to which a society rewards individuals for being altruistic, generous, and kind to others) and performance orientation (the degree to which a society encourages and rewards group members for performance improvement and excellence).

Which framework is better? That's hard to say, and each has its adherents. We give more emphasis to Hofstede's dimensions here because they have stood the test of time and the GLOBE study confirmed them. However, researchers continue to debate the differences between them, and future studies may favor the more nuanced perspective of the GLOBE study.[86]

MyManagementLab

Now that you have finished this chapter, go back to **www.mymanagementlab.com** to continue practicing and applying the concepts you've learned.

Summary and Implications for Managers

Personality   What value, if any, does the Big Five model provide to managers? From the early 1900s through the mid-1980s, researchers sought a link between personality and job performance. "The outcome of those 80-plus years of research was that personality and job performance were not meaningfully related across traits or situations."[87] However, the past 20 years have been more promising, largely due to the findings about the Big Five.

- Screening job candidates for high conscientiousness—as well as the other Big Five traits, depending on the criteria an organization finds most important—should pay dividends. Of course, managers still need to take situational factors into consideration.[88]
- Factors such as job demands, the degree of required interaction with others, and the organization's culture are examples of situational variables that moderate the personality–job performance relationship.
- You need to evaluate the job, the work group, and the organization to determine the optimal personality fit.
- Other traits, such as core self-evaluation or narcissism, may be relevant in certain situations, too.
- Although the MBTI has been widely criticized, it may have a place in organizations. In training and development, it can help employees better understand themselves, help team members better understand each other, and open up communication in work groups and possibly reduce conflicts.

Values   Why is it important to know an individual's values? Values often underlie and explain attitudes, behaviors, and perceptions. So knowledge of an individual's value system can provide insight into what makes the person "tick."

- Employees' performance and satisfaction are likely to be higher if their values fit well with the organization. The person who places great importance on imagination, independence, and freedom is likely to be poorly matched with an organization that seeks conformity from its employees.

Millennials Are More Narcissistic

POINT   **COUNTERPOINT**

Those in college today have many good qualities: they are more technologically savvy, more socially tolerant, and more balanced in their work and family priorities than previous generations. Thus, those poised to enter the workforce today do so with some important virtues. Humility, however, is not one of them.

A large-scale, longitudinal study found that those graduating from college in 2010 were more likely than those from previous generations to have seemingly inflated views of themselves. The 2010 graduates were more likely than 1980 graduates to agree they would be "very good" spouses (56 percent of 2010 graduates, compared to 37 percent among 1980 graduates), parents (54 percent of 2010 graduates, 36 percent among 1980 graduates), and workers (65 percent of 2010 graduates, 49 percent among 1980 graduates).

Studies measuring narcissism suggests that scores are rising, especially among younger generations. For example, by presenting a choice between two statements—"I try not to be a show-off" versus "I will usually show off if I get the chance"—psychologists have found that narcissism has been growing since the early 1980s.

A 2011 study by University of Kentucky researcher Dr. Nathan DeWall even found that popular songs are becoming more narcissistic. Analyzing the lyrics of songs on the *Billboard Hot 100 Chart* from 1980 to 2007, DeWall found a clear trend toward narcissism. The words "I" and "me" have replaced "we" and "us." Two recent examples: *"I'm bringing sexy back. Yeah. Them other boys don't know how to act. Yeah"* (Justin Timberlake), and *"I am the greatest man that ever lived. I was born to give and give and give"* (Weezer).

Narcissism's rise is all around us. The sooner we admit it, the sooner we can begin to address the problem in families, in education, and at work.

Speaking of music, this argument is like a broken record that seems to play over and over: "THE YOUTH OF TODAY ARE LOST!" Every generation tends to think the new generation is without values, and the new generation thinks the older generation is hopelessly judgmental and out of touch. Wasn't the "Me generation" supposedly a generation ago? Let's send the broken record to the recycling bin and review the evidence.

One recent study that tracked nearly half a million young people on measures of egotistic traits such as self-perceived intelligence, self-esteem, and self-enhancement found little evidence to suggest changes since the 1970s. In short, Millennials aren't any more narcissistic than young people were in the 1970s or 1980s. The authors of this study conclude, "Today's youth seem no more egotistical than previous generations . . . In fact, today's youth seem to have psychological profiles that are remarkably similar to youth from the past 30 years."

Another study offered an interesting explanation for why people *think* Millennials are more narcissistic. Specifically, young people in general are more self-focused, but as people age, they become more "other" focused. So we think young people are different when in fact they're just the way older folks were when *they* were younger. As these authors conclude, "Every generation is Generation Me." Our level of narcissism appears to be one of the many things that change as we get older.

More broadly, narcissistic folks exist in every generation. We need to be careful when generalizing about entire groups (whether one sex, one race, one culture, or one generation). While generalizations have caused no small amount of trouble, we still like to simplify the world, sometimes for good reason. In this case, however, the good reason isn't there, especially considering the latest evidence.

Sources: N. Wolchover, "Song Lyrics Suggest Narcissism Is on the Rise," *LiveScience* (April, 26, 2011), downloaded May 16, 2011, from www.livescience.com; M. Norris, "Study: Narcissism on Rise in Pop Lyrics," *All Things Considered* (April 26, 2011), downloaded May 15 from www.npr.org/; K. H. Trzesniewski and M. B. Donnellan, "Rethinking 'Generation Me': A Study of Cohort Effects from 1976–2006," *Perspectives on Psychological Science* 5, no. 1 (2010), pp. 58–75; and B. W. Roberts, G. Edmonds, and E. Grijalva, "It Is Developmental Me, Not Generation Me: Developmental Changes Are More Important Than Generational Changes in Narcissism—Comment on Trzesniewski & Donnellon (2010)," *Perspectives on Psychological Science* 5, No. 1 (2010), pp. 97–102.

- Managers are more likely to appreciate, evaluate positively, and allocate rewards to employees who fit in, and employees are more likely to be satisfied if they perceive they do fit in. This argues for management to seek job candidates who have not only the ability, experience, and motivation to perform but also a value system compatible with the organization's.

QUESTIONS FOR REVIEW

1 What is personality? How do we typically measure it? What factors determine personality?

2 What is the Myers-Briggs Type Indicator (MBTI), and what does it measure?

3 What are the Big Five personality traits?

4 How do the Big Five traits predict work behavior?

5 Besides the Big Five, what other personality traits are relevant to OB?

6 What are values, why are they important, and what is the difference between terminal and instrumental values?

7 Do values differ across generations? How so?

8 Do values differ across cultures? How so?

EXPERIENTIAL EXERCISE   What Organizational Culture Do You Prefer?

The Organizational Culture Profile (OCP) can help assess whether an individual's values match the organization's.[89] The OCP helps individuals sort their characteristics in terms of importance, which indicates what a person values.

1. Working on your own, complete the OCP found at www.jstor.org/stable/256404.

2. Your instructor may ask you the following questions individually or as a group of three or four students (with a spokesperson appointed to speak to the class for each group):

a. What were your most preferred and least preferred values? Do you think your most preferred and least preferred values are similar to those of other class or group members?

b. Do you think there are generational differences in the most preferred and least preferred values?

c. Research has shown that individuals tend to be happier, and perform better, when their OCP values match those of their employer. How important do you think a "values match" is when you're deciding where you want to work?

ETHICAL DILEMMA   Freedom or Lack of Commitment?

Lifelong commitment to one employer is a thing of the past. An analysis by Princeton economist Henry Farber revealed that the percentage of private-sector employees who remained with the same employer for 10 or more years has dropped from 50 percent in 1973 to less than 35 percent today. Those with 20 or more years with the same employer dropped from 35 percent to 20 percent.

To be sure, some of this movement is employer-driven. Lifetime job security is long gone for most positions. So are benefit packages that would keep employees secure, such as rock-solid pensions and generous health benefits. But does a generational shift in values also explain the drop?

According to Pew Research, 66 percent of Millennials say they want to switch careers some time in their life,

while 62 percent of Generation X members and 84 percent of Baby Boomers say they would prefer to stay at their current job for the rest of their lives. Another study suggested that while 64 percent of Baby Boomers "really care about the fate" of their organization, this figure is only 47 percent for Millennials. Yet another study indicated that two-thirds of Millennials had plans to move or "surf" from one job to another as a means of gaining desired skills and increasing their pay.

One Millennial, Rebecca Thorman, notes that mobility makes sense only because if you aren't mobile, you limit your options. She says you can't expect your pay to grow "by staying at the same job . . . You just can't."

These values don't sit well with some employers. "We prefer long tenured employees who have stuck with us and been loyal," says Dave Foster, CEO of AvreaFoster, an advertising agency in Dallas. "It appears that a lot of Millennials don't think that one path is the answer. This is a problem because the commitment isn't there."

To attitudes like that, Thorman retorts, "We're not going to settle."

Questions

1. In your experience, do younger individuals differ from older individuals in their plans to remain with one employer for a long time? Do you think these differences, if you believe they exist, are due to shifting economic realities or to changing work values?

2. Do you think you should feel free to "job surf"— purposely moving from job to job as soon as the desire strikes? Do you think employers have a right to ask about "job surfing" plans when they interview you?

3. If you had an interview with Foster or someone with his views of Millennials, how might you combat his preconceptions?

Sources: S. Collins, "Millennials Take on the Workforce," *SHIFT Magazine* (May 3, 2011), downloaded May 12, 2011, from www.smudailymustang.com; and R. Wartzman, "Generation Mobility," *Los Angeles Times* (July 16, 2010), downloaded May 12, 2011, from www.dailytidings.com/.

CASE INCIDENT 1 Is There a Price for Being Too Nice?

Agreeable people tend to be kinder and more accommodating in social situations, which you might think could add to their success in life. However, we've already noted that one downside of agreeableness is potentially lower earnings. We're not sure why this is so, but agreeable individuals may be less aggressive in negotiating starting salaries and pay raises.

Yet there is clear evidence that agreeableness is something employers value. Several recent books argue in favor of "leading with kindness" (Baker & O'Malley, 2008) and "capitalizing on kindness" (Tillquist, 2008). Other articles in the business press have argued that the sensitive, agreeable CEO—such as GE's Jeffrey Immelt and Boeing's James McNerney—signals a shift in business culture (Brady, 2007). In many circles, individuals desiring success in their careers are exhorted to be "complimentary," "kind," and "good" (for example, Schillinger, 2007).

Take the example of 500-employee Lindblad Expeditions. It emphasizes agreeableness in its hiring decisions. The VP of HR commented, "You can teach people any technical skill, but you can't teach them how to be a kindhearted, generous-minded person with an open spirit."

So, while employers want agreeable employees, agreeable employees are not better job performers, and they are *less* successful in their careers. We might explain this apparent contradiction by noting that employers value agreeable employees for other reasons: they are more pleasant to be around, and they may help others in ways that aren't reflected in their job performance. Most evidence suggests that agreeable people like agreeable people, which you might expect because people like those who are similar to themselves. However, even disagreeable people like agreeable people, perhaps because they are easier to manipulate than individuals who are lower in agreeableness. Perhaps everyone wants to hire agreeable people just because everyone likes to be around them.

Moreover, a 2008 study of CEO and CEO candidates revealed that this contradiction applies to organizational leaders as well. Using ratings made by an executive search firm, researchers studied the personalities and abilities of 316 CEO candidates for companies involved in buyout and venture capital transactions. They found that what gets a CEO candidate hired is not what makes him or her effective. Specifically, CEO candidates who were rated high on "nice" traits such as respecting others, developing others, and teamwork were more likely to be hired. However, these same characteristics—especially teamwork and respecting others for venture capital CEOs—made the organizations they led less successful.

Questions

1. Do you think there is a contradiction between what employers want in employees (agreeable employees) and what employees actually do best (disagreeable employees)? Why or why not?

2. Often, the effects of personality depend on the situation. Can you think of some job situations in which

agreeableness is an important virtue? And in which it is harmful?

3. In some research we've conducted, we've found that the negative effects of agreeableness on earnings is stronger for men than for women (that is, being agreeable hurt men's earnings more than women's). Why do you think this might be the case?

Sources: T. A. Judge, B. A. Livingston, and C. Hurst, "Do Nice Guys—and Gals—Really Finish Last? The Joint Effects of Sex and Agreeableness on Earnings," working paper, University of Florida (2009); S. N. Kaplan, M. M. Klebanov, and M. Sorensen, "Which CEO Characteristics and Abilities Matter?" working paper, University of Chicago Graduate School of Business (2008), faculty.chicagobooth.edu/steven.kaplan/research/kks.pdf; W. F. Baker and M. O'Malley, *Leading with Kindness: How Good People Consistently Get Superior Results* (New York: AMACOM, 2008); K. Tillquist, *Capitalizing on Kindness: When 21st Century Professionals Need to Be Nice* (Pompton Plains, NJ: Career Press, 2008); D. Brady, "Being Mean Is So Last Millennium," *BusinessWeek* (January 15, 2007), p. 61; and L. Schillinger, "Nice and Ambitious: Either, Neither, or Both?" *The New York Times* (January 14, 2007), p. 1.

CASE INCIDENT 2   Leadership from an Introvert's Perspective

When people think of a stereotypical leader, they often conjure up the image of a dynamic public speaker, a forceful and dominant personality, and someone who can cultivate relationships with a broad number of people. These are all hallmarks of the extroverted personality type, so it's often been the case that extroverts rise to leadership positions more readily than introverts.

However, some question whether the social dominance and ability to command attention shown by extraverts might make them less effective leaders in certain ways. In particular, extroverts may be less likely to take advice from followers. One study investigated how quickly groups of college students could fold shirts in 10 minutes. Each group had a leader who was cued to be either extroverted or introverted. The introverted leaders took more advice from their proactive followers, and this led the groups with introverted leaders to be more effective. Thus, even though there are cases where introverts are less successful as leaders, in some conditions they are more effective. Others note that introverted leaders can be better than extroverts at one-on-one interactions, empathy, and deliberate decision making.

Are there business executives who break the extroverted leader mold? One is Google co-founder Larry Page, well-known for developing a small number of close relationships and being an excellent listener. Colgate-Palmolive

chief Ian Cook might feel uncomfortable in front of large groups of people he doesn't know, but he has learned to partner with more extroverted colleagues for presentations to offset his natural shyness. Wal-Mart Stores CEO Mike Duke is famously low-key and reserved, but he has utilized his natural introvert skills of managing details and engineering solutions to maintain the retail giant's dominant market position. These examples show that although extroverts might get all the attention, introverts can still make effective leaders.

Questions

1. Are you more of an introverted or extraverted leader? What can you do to leverage your personality to be a more effective leader?

2. Under what conditions do you think extraverts make more effective leaders than introverts? What unique abilities of introverts could make them more effective in some situations?

3. The case describes some problems introverts might have in leadership situations. What techniques might they employ to help them overcome these?

4. What types of developmental experiences do you think would be especially valuable for introverted leaders?

Sources: A. M. Grant, F. Gino, and D. A. Hofman, "The Hidden Advantages of Quiet Bosses," *Harvard Business Review* (December 2010), p. 28; B. O'Keefe and D. Burke, "Meet the CEO of the Biggest Company on Earth," *Fortune* (September 27, 2010), pp. 80–94; and J. S. Lubin, "Introverted Execs Find Ways to Shine," *The Wall Street Journal* (April 14, 2011), online.wsj.com.

ENDNOTES

1. G. W. Allport, *Personality: A Psychological Interpretation* (New York: Holt, Rinehart & Winston, 1937), p. 48. For a brief critique of current views on the meaning of personality, see R. T. Hogan and B. W. Roberts, "Introduction: Personality and Industrial and Organizational Psychology," in B. W. Roberts and R. Hogan (eds.), *Personality Psychology in the Workplace* (Washington, DC: American Psychological Association, 2001), pp. 11–12.

2. K. I. van der Zee, J. N. Zaal, and J. Piekstra, "Validation of the Multicultural Personality Questionnaire in the Context of Personnel Selection," *European Journal of Personality* 17, Supl. 1 (2003), pp. S77–S100.

3. S. A. Birkeland, T. M. Manson, J. L. Kisamore, M. T. Brannick, and M. A. Smith, "A Meta-Analytic Investigation of Job Applicant Faking on Personality Measures," *International Journal of Selection and Assessment* 14, no. 14 (2006), pp. 317–335.

4. T. A. Judge, C. A. Higgins, C. J. Thoresen, and M. R. Barrick, "The Big Five Personality Traits, General Mental Ability, and Career Success Across the Life Span," *Personnel Psychology* 52, no. 3 (1999), pp. 621–652; I. Oh, G. Wang, and M. K. Mount, "Validity of Observer Ratings of the Five-Factor Model of Personality Traits: A Meta-Analysis," *Journal of Applied Psychology* 96, No. 4 (2011), pp. 762-773.

5. See R. Illies, R. D. Arvey, and T. J. Bouchard, "Darwinism, Behavioral Genetics, and Organizational Behavior: A Review and Agenda for Future Research," *Journal of Organizational Behavior* 27, no. 2 (2006), pp. 121–141; and W. Johnson, E. Turkheimer, I. I. Gottesman, and T. J. Bouchard, Jr., "Beyond Heritability: Twin Studies in Behavioral Research," *Current Directions in Psychological Science* 18, no. 4 (2009), pp. 217–220.

6. S. Srivastava, O. P. John, and S. D. Gosling, "Development of Personality in Early and Middle Adulthood: Set Like Plaster or Persistent Change?" *Journal of Personality and Social Psychology* 84, no. 5 (2003), pp. 1041–1053; and B. W. Roberts, K. E. Walton, and W. Viechtbauer, "Patterns of Mean-Level Change in Personality Traits Across the Life Course: A Meta-Analysis of Longitudinal Studies," *Psychological Bulletin* 132, no. 1 (2006), pp. 1–25.

7. S. E. Hampson and L. R. Goldberg, "A First Large Cohort Study of Personality Trait Stability Over the 40 Years Between Elementary School and Midlife," *Journal of Personality and Social Psychology* 91, no. 4 (2006), pp. 763–779.

8. See A. H. Buss, "Personality as Traits," *American Psychologist* 44, no. 11 (1989), pp. 1378–1388; R. R. McCrae, "Trait Psychology and the Revival of Personality and Culture Studies," *American Behavioral Scientist* 44, no. 1 (2000), pp. 10–31; and L. R. James and M. D. Mazerolle, *Personality in Work Organizations* (Thousand Oaks, CA: Sage, 2002).

9. See, for instance, G. W. Allport and H. S. Odbert, "Trait Names, A Psycholexical Study," *Psychological Monographs*, no. 47 (1936); and R. B. Cattell, "Personality Pinned Down," *Psychology Today* (July 1973), pp. 40–46.

10. R. B. Kennedy and D. A. Kennedy, "Using the Myers-Briggs Type Indicator in Career Counseling," *Journal of Employment Counseling* 41, no. 1 (2004), pp. 38–44.

11. See, for instance, D. J. Pittenger, "Cautionary Comments Regarding the Myers-Briggs Type Indicator," *Consulting Psychology Journal: Practice and Research* 57, no. 3 (2005), pp. 10–221; L. Bess and R. J. Harvey, "Bimodal Score Distributions and the Myers-Briggs Type Indicator: Fact or Artifact?" *Journal of Personality Assessment* 78, no. 1 (2002), pp. 176–186; R. M. Capraro and M. M. Capraro, "Myers-Briggs Type Indicator Score Reliability Across Studies: A Meta-Analytic Reliability Generalization Study," *Educational & Psychological Measurement* 62, no. 4 (2002), pp. 590–602; and R. C. Arnau, B. A. Green, D. H. Rosen, D. H. Gleaves, and J. G. Melancon, "Are Jungian Preferences Really Categorical? An Empirical Investigation Using Taxometric Analysis," *Personality & Individual Differences* 34, no. 2 (2003), pp. 233–251.

12. See, for example, I. Oh, G. Wang, and M. K. Mount, "Validity of Observer Ratings of the Five-Factor Model of Personality Traits: A Meta-Analysis," *Journal of Applied Psychology* 96, No. 4 (2011), pp. 762–773; and M. R. Barrick and M. K. Mount, "Yes, Personality Matters: Moving On to More Important Matters," *Human Performance* 18, no. 4 (2005), pp. 359–372.

13. W. Fleeson and P. Gallagher, "The Implications of Big Five Standing for the Distribution of Trait Manifestation in Behavior: Fifteen Experience-Sampling Studies and a Meta-Analysis," *Journal of Personality and Social Psychology* 97, no. 6 (2009), pp. 1097–1114.

14. See, for instance, I. Oh and C. M. Berry, "The Five-Factor Model of Personality and Managerial Performance: Validity Gains Through the Use of 360 Degree Performance Ratings," *Journal of Applied Psychology* 94, no. 6 (2009), pp. 1498–1513; G. M. Hurtz and J. J. Donovan, "Personality and Job Performance: The Big Five Revisited," *Journal of Applied Psychology* 85, no. 6 (2000), pp. 869–879; J. Hogan and B. Holland, "Using Theory to Evaluate Personality and Job-Performance Relations: A Socioanalytic Perspective," *Journal of Applied Psychology* 88, no. 1 (2003), pp. 100–112; and M. R. Barrick and M. K. Mount, "Select on Conscientiousness and Emotional Stability," in E. A. Locke (ed.), *Handbook of Principles of Organizational Behavior* (Malden, MA: Blackwell, 2004), pp. 15–28.

15. M. K. Mount, M. R. Barrick, and J. P. Strauss, "Validity of Observer Ratings of the Big Five Personality Factors," *Journal of Applied Psychology* 79, no. 2 (1994), p. 272. Additionally confirmed by G. M. Hurtz and J. J. Donovan, "Personality and Job Performance: The Big Five Revisited"; and Oh and Berry, "The Five-Factor Model of Personality and Managerial Performance."

16. A. E. Poropat, "A Meta-Analysis of the Five-Factor Model of Personality and Academic Performance," *Psychological Bulletin* 135, no. 2 (2009), pp. 322–338.

17. A. M. Cianci, H. J. Klein, and G. H. Seijts, "The Effect of Negative Feedback on Tension and Subsequent Performance: The Main and Interactive Effects of Goal Content and Conscientiousness," *Journal of Applied Psychology* 95, no. 4 (2010), pp. 618–630.

18. H. Le, I. Oh, S. B. Robbins, R. Ilies, E. Holland, and P. Westrick, "Too Much of a Good Thing: Curvilinear Relationships

Between Personality Traits and Job Performance," *Journal of Applied Psychology* 96, no. 1 (2011), pp. 113–133.

19. T. Bogg and B. W. Roberts, "Conscientiousness and Health-Related Behaviors: A Meta-Analysis of the Leading Behavioral Contributors to Mortality," *Psychological Bulletin* 130, no. 6 (2004), pp. 887–919.

20. G. J. Feist, "A Meta-Analysis of Personality in Scientific and Artistic Creativity," *Personality and Social Psychology Review* 2, no. 4 (1998), pp. 290–309; C. Robert and Y. H. Cheung, "An Examination of the Relationship Between Conscientiousness and Group Performance on a Creative Task," *Journal of Research in Personality* 44, no. 2 (2010), pp. 222–231; and M. Batey, T. Chamorro-Premuzic, and A. Furnham, "Individual Differences in Ideational Behavior. Can the Big Five and Psychometric Intelligence Predict Creativity Scores?" *Creativity Research Journal* 22, no. 1 (2010), pp. 90-97.

21. R. J. Foti and M. A. Hauenstein, "Pattern and Variable Approaches in Leadership Emergence and Effectiveness," *Journal of Applied Psychology* 92, no. 2 (2007), pp. 347–355.

22. L. I. Spirling and R. Persaud, "Extraversion as a Risk Factor," *Journal of the American Academy of Child & Adolescent Psychiatry* 42, no. 2 (2003), p. 130.

23. B. Weiss, and R. S. Feldman, "Looking Good and Lying to Do It: Deception as an Impression Management Strategy in Job Interviews," *Journal of Applied Social Psychology* 36, no. 4 (2006), pp. 1070–1086.

24. J. A. LePine, J. A. Colquitt, and A. Erez, "Adaptability to Changing Task Contexts: Effects of General Cognitive Ability, Conscientiousness, and Openness to Experience," *Personnel Psychology* 53, no. 3 (2000), pp. 563–595; S. Clarke and I. Robertson, "An Examination of the Role of Personality in Accidents Using Meta-Analysis," *Applied Psychology: An International Review* 57, no. 1 (2008), pp. 94–108; M. Baer, "The Strength-of-Weak-Ties Perspective on Creativity: A Comprehensive Examination and Extension," *Journal of Applied Psychology* 95, no. 3 (2010), pp. 592–601.

25. R. Ilies, I. S. Fulmer, M. Spitzmuller, and M. D. Johnson, "Personality and Citizenship Behavior: The Mediating Role of Job Satisfaction," *Journal of Applied Psychology* 94, no. 4 (2009), pp. 945–959.

26. See, for instance, S. Yamagata, A. Suzuki, J. Ando, Y. Ono, K. Yutaka, N. Kijima, et al., "Is the Genetic Structure of Human Personality Universal? A Cross-Cultural Twin Study from North America, Europe, and Asia," *Journal of Personality and Social Psychology* 90, no. 6 (2006), pp. 987–998; H. C. Triandis and E. M. Suh, "Cultural Influences on Personality," *Annual Review of Psychology* 53, no. 1 (2002), pp. 133–160; and R. R. McCrae, P. T. Costa Jr., T. A. Martin, V. E. Oryol, A. A. Rukavishnikov, I. G. Senin, et al., "Consensual Validation of Personality Traits Across Cultures," *Journal of Research in Personality* 38, no. 2 (2004), pp. 179–201.

27. A. T. Church and M. S. Katigbak, "Trait Psychology in the Philippines," *American Behavioral Scientist* 44, no. 1, (2000), pp. 73–94.

28. J. F. Salgado, "The Five Factor Model of Personality and Job Performance in the European Community," *Journal of Applied Psychology* 82, no. 1 (1997), pp. 30–43.

29. T. A. Judge and J. E. Bono, "A Rose by Any Other Name . . . Are Self-Esteem, Generalized Self-Efficacy, Neuroticism, and Locus of Control Indicators of a Common Construct?" in B. W. Roberts and R. Hogan (eds.), *Personality Psychology in the Workplace* (Washington, DC: American Psychological Association, 2001), pp. 93–118.

30. A. Erez and T. A. Judge, "Relationship of Core Self-Evaluations to Goal Setting, Motivation, and Performance," *Journal of Applied Psychology* 86, no. 6 (2001), pp. 1270–1279.

31. A. N. Salvaggio, B. Schneider, L. H. Nishi, D. M. Mayer, A. Ramesh, and J. S. Lyon, "Manager Personality, Manager Service Quality Orientation, and Service Climate: Test of a Model," *Journal of Applied Psychology* 92, no. 6 (2007), pp. 1741–1750; B. A. Scott and T. A. Judge, "The Popularity Contest at Work: Who Wins, Why, and What Do They Receive?" *Journal of Applied Psychology* 94, no. 1 (2009), pp. 20–33; and T. A. Judge and C. Hurst, "How the Rich (and Happy) Get Richer (and Happier): Relationship of Core Self-Evaluations to Trajectories in Attaining Work Success," *Journal of Applied Psychology* 93, no. 4 (2008), pp. 849–863.

32. A. M. Grant and A. Wrzesniewksi, "I Won't Let You Down . . . or Will I? Core Self-Evaluations, Other-Orientation, Anticipated Guilt and Gratitude, and Job Performance," *Journal of Applied Psychology* 95, no. 1 (2010), pp. 108–121.

33. U. Malmendier and G. Tate, "CEO Overconfidence and Corporate Investment," *Journal of Finance* 60, no. 6 (2005), pp. 2661–2700.

34. R. Sandomir, "Star Struck," *The New York Times* (January 12, 2007), pp. C10, C14.

35. R. Christie and F. L. Geis, *Studies in Machiavellianism* (New York: Academic Press, 1970), p. 312; and S. R. Kessler, A. C. Bandelli, P. E. Spector, W. C. Borman, C. E. Nelson, L. M. Penney, "Re-Examining Machiavelli: A Three-Dimensional Model of Machiavellianism in the Workplace," *Journal of Applied Social Psychology* 40, no. 8 (2010), pp. 1868–1896.

36. J. J. Dahling, B. G. Whitaker, and P. E. Levy, "The Development and Validation of a New Machiavellianism Scale," *Journal of Management* 35, no. 2 (2009), pp. 219–257.

37. Christie and Geis, *Studies in Machiavellianism*.

38. P. Cramer and C. J. Jones, "Narcissism, Identification, and Longitudinal Change in Psychological Health: Dynamic Predictions," *Journal of Research in Personality* 42, no. 5 (2008), pp. 1148–1159; B. M. Galvin, D. A. Waldman, and P. Balthazard, "Visionary Communication Qualities as Mediators of the Relationship between Narcissism and Attributions of Leader Charisma," *Personnel Psychology* 63, no. 3 (2010), pp. 509–537; and T. A. Judge, R. F. Piccolo, and T. Kosalka, "The Bright and Dark Sides of Leader Traits: A Review and Theoretical Extension of the Leader Trait Paradigm," *The Leadership Quarterly* 20, no. 6 (2009), pp. 855–875.

39. M. Maccoby, "Narcissistic Leaders: The Incredible Pros, the Inevitable Cons," *The Harvard Business Review* (January–February 2000), pp. 69–77, www.maccoby.com/Articles/NarLeaders.shtml.

40. W. K. Campbell and C. A. Foster, "Narcissism and Commitment in Romantic Relationships: An Investment Model Analysis," *Personality and Social Psychology Bulletin* 28, no. 4 (2002), pp. 484–495.

41. T. A. Judge, J. A. LePine, and B. L. Rich, "The Narcissistic Personality: Relationship with Inflated Self-Ratings of Leadership and with Task and Contextual Performance," *Journal of Applied Psychology* 91, no. 4 (2006), pp. 762–776.

42. C. J. Resick, D. S. Whitman, S. M. Weingarden, and N. J. Hiller, "The Bright-Side and Dark-Side of CEO Personality: Examining Core Self-Evaluations, Narcissism, Transformational Leadership, and Strategic Influence," *Journal of Applied Psychology* 94, no. 6 (2009), pp. 1365–1381.

43. See M. Snyder, *Public Appearances/Private Realities: The Psychology of Self-Monitoring* (New York: W. H. Freeman, 1987); and S. W. Gangestad and M. Snyder, "Self-Monitoring: Appraisal and Reappraisal," *Psychological Bulletin* 126, no. 4 (2000), pp. 530–555.

44. F. J. Flynn and D. R. Ames, "What's Good for the Goose May Not Be as Good for the Gander: The Benefits of Self-Monitoring for Men and Women in Task Groups and Dyadic Conflicts," *Journal of Applied Psychology* 91, no. 2 (2006), pp. 272–281; and Snyder, *Public Appearances/ Private Realities*.

45. D. V. Day, D. J. Shleicher, A. L. Unckless, and N. J. Hiller, "Self-Monitoring Personality at Work: A Meta-Analytic Investigation of Construct Validity," *Journal of Applied Psychology* 87, no. 2 (2002), pp. 390–401.

46. H. Oh and M. Kilduff, "The Ripple Effect of Personality on Social Structure: Self-monitoring Origins of Network Brokerage," *Journal of Applied Psychology* 93, no. 5 (2008), pp. 1155–1164; and A. Mehra, M. Kilduff, and D. J. Brass, "The Social Networks of High and Low Self-Monitors: Implications for Workplace Performance," *Administrative Science Quarterly* 46, no. 1 (2001), pp. 121–146.

47. E. Reeve, "A History of Donald Trump's Net Worth Publicity," The Atlantic, (April 21, 2011), www.theatlanticwire.com.

48. R. N. Taylor and M. D. Dunnette, "Influence of Dogmatism, Risk-Taking Propensity, and Intelligence on Decision-Making Strategies for a Sample of Industrial Managers," *Journal of Applied Psychology* 59, no. 4 (1974), pp. 420–423.

49. I. L. Janis and L. Mann, *Decision Making: A Psychological Analysis of Conflict, Choice, and Commitment* (New York: The Free Press, 1977); W. H. Stewart Jr. and L. Roth, "Risk Propensity Differences Between Entrepreneurs and Managers: A Meta-Analytic Review," *Journal of Applied Psychology* 86, no. 1 (2001), pp. 145–153; J. B. Miner and N. S. Raju, "Risk Propensity Differences Between Managers and Entrepreneurs and Between Low- and High-Growth Entrepreneurs: A Reply in a More Conservative Vein," *Journal of Applied Psychology* 89, no. 1 (2004), pp. 3–13; and W. H. Stewart Jr. and P. L. Roth, "Data Quality Affects Meta-Analytic Conclusions: A Response to Miner and Raju (2004) Concerning Entrepreneurial Risk Propensity," *Journal of Applied Psychology* 89, no. 1 (2004), pp. 14–21.

50. J. K. Maner, J. A. Richey, K. Cromer, M. Mallott, C. W. Lejuez, T. E. Joiner, and N. B. Schmidt, "Dispositional Anxiety and Risk-Avoidant Decision Making," *Personality and Individual Differences* 42, no. 4 (2007), pp. 665–675.

51. J. M. Crant, "Proactive Behavior in Organizations," *Journal of Management* 26, no. 3 (2000), p. 436.

52. S. E. Seibert, M. L. Kraimer, and J. M. Crant, "What Do Proactive People Do? A Longitudinal Model Linking Proactive Personality and Career Success," *Personnel Psychology* 54, no. 4 (2001), pp. 845–874.

53. T. S. Bateman and J. M. Crant, "The Proactive Component of Organizational Behavior: A Measure and Correlates," *Journal of Organizational Behavior* 14, no. 2 (1993), pp. 103–118; and J. M. Crant and T. S. Bateman, "Charismatic Leadership Viewed from Above: The Impact of Proactive Personality," *Journal of Organizational Behavior* 21, no. 1 (2000), pp. 63–75.

54. N. Li, J. Liang, and J. M. Crant, "The Role of Proactive Personality in Job Satisfaction and Organizational Citizenship Behavior: A Relational Perspective," *Journal of Applied Psychology* 95, no. 2 (2010), pp. 395–404.

55. Crant, "Proactive Behavior in Organizations," p. 436.

56. See, for instance, R. C. Becherer and J. G. Maurer, "The Proactive Personality Disposition and Entrepreneurial Behavior Among Small Company Presidents," *Journal of Small Business Management* 37, no. 1 (1999), pp. 28–36.

57. S. E. Seibert, J. M. Crant, and M. L. Kraimer, "Proactive Personality and Career Success," *Journal of Applied Psychology* 84, no. 3 (1999), pp. 416–427; Seibert, Kraimer, and Crant, "What Do Proactive People Do?" p. 850; D. J. Brown, R. T. Cober, K. Kane, P. E. Levy, and J. Shalhoop, "Proactive Personality and the Successful Job Search: A Field Investigation with College Graduates," *Journal of Applied Psychology* 91, no. 3 (2006), pp. 717–726; and J. D. Kammeyer-Mueller and C. R. Wanberg, "Unwrapping the Organizational Entry Process: Disentangling Multiple Antecedents and Their Pathways to Adjustment," *Journal of Applied Psychology* 88, no. 5 (2003), pp. 779–794.

58. B. M. Meglino and M. A. Korsgaard, "Considering Situational and Dispositional Approaches to Rational Self-Interest: An Extension and Response to De Dreu (2006)," *Journal of Applied Psychology* 91, no. 6 (2006), pp. 1253-1259; and B. M. Meglino and M. A. Korsgaard, "Considering Rational Self-Interest as a Disposition: Organizational Implications of Other Orientation," *Journal of Applied Psychology* 89, no. 6 (2004), pp. 946–959.

59. M. A. Korsgaard, B. M. Meglino, S. W. Lester, and S. S. Jeong, "Paying You Back or Paying Me Forward: Understanding Rewarded and Unrewarded Organizational Citizenship Behavior," *Journal of Applied Psychology* 95, no. 2 (2010), pp. 277–290.

60. Grant and Wrzesniewski, "I Won't Let You Down . . . Or Will I?; C. K. W. De Dreu, "Self-Interest and Other-Orientation in Organizational Behavior: Implications for Job Performance, Prosocial Behavior, and Personal Initiative," *Journal of Applied Psychology* 94, no. 4 (2009), pp. 913–926.

61. M. Rokeach, *The Nature of Human Values* (New York: The Free Press, 1973), p. 5.

62. M. Rokeach and S. J. Ball-Rokeach, "Stability and Change in American Value Priorities, 1968–1981," *American Psychologist* 44, no. 5 (1989), pp. 775–784; and A. Bardi, J. A. Lee, N. Hofmann-Towfigh, and G. Soutar, "The Structure of Intraindividual Value Change," *Journal of Personality and Social Psychology* 97, no. 5 (2009), pp. 913–929.

63. S. Roccas, L. Sagiv, S. H. Schwartz, and A. Knafo, "The Big Five Personality Factors and Personal Values," *Personality and Social Psychology Bulletin* 28, no. 6 (2002), pp. 789–801.

64. See, for instance, B. M. Meglino and E. C. Ravlin, "Individual Values in Organizations: Concepts, Controversies, and Research," *Journal of Management* 24, no. 3 (1998), p. 355.

65. Rokeach, *The Nature of Human Values*, p. 6.

66. J. M. Munson and B. Z. Posner, "The Factorial Validity of a Modified Rokeach Value Survey for Four Diverse Samples," *Educational and Psychological Measurement* 40, no. 4 (1980), pp. 1073–1079; and W. C. Frederick and J. Weber, "The Values of Corporate Managers and Their Critics: An Empirical Description and Normative Implications," in W. C. Frederick and L. E. Preston (eds.), *Business Ethics: Research Issues and Empirical Studies* (Greenwich, CT: JAI Press, 1990), pp. 123–144.

67. Frederick and Weber, "The Values of Corporate Managers and Their Critics," pp. 123–144.

68. Ibid., p. 132.

69. See, for example, N. R. Lockwood, F. R. Cepero, and S. Williams, *The Multigenerational Workforce* (Alexandria, VA: Society for Human Resource Management, 2009).

70. K. W. Smola and C. D. Sutton, "Generational Differences: Revisiting Generational Work Values for the New Millennium," *Journal of Organizational Behavior* 23, Special Issue (2002), pp. 363–382; and R. F. Inglehart, "Changing Values Among Western Publics from 1970 to 2006," *West European Politics* 31, no. 1 & 2 (2008), pp. 130–146.

71. B. Hite, "Employers Rethink How They Give Feedback," *The Wall Street Journal* (October 13, 2008), p. B5.

72. E. Parry and P. Urwin, "Generational Differences in Work Values: A Review of Theory and Evidence," *International Journal of Management Reviews* 13, no. 1 (2011), pp. 79–96.

73. J. M. Twenge, S. M. Campbell, B. J. Hoffman, and C. E. Lance, "Generational Differences in Work Values: Leisure and Extrinsic Values Increasing, Social and Intrinsic Values Decreasing," *Journal of Management* 36, no. 5 (2010), pp. 1117–1142.

74. J. L. Holland, *Making Vocational Choices: A Theory of Vocational Personalities and Work Environments* (Odessa, FL: Psychological Assessment Resources, 1997).

75. See, for example, J. L. Holland and G. D. Gottfredson, "Studies of the Hexagonal Model: An Evaluation (or, The Perils of Stalking the Perfect Hexagon)," *Journal of Vocational Behavior* 40, no. 2 (1992), pp. 158–170; and T. J. Tracey and J. Rounds, "Evaluating Holland's and Gati's Vocational-Interest Models: A Structural Meta-Analysis," *Psychological Bulletin* 113, no. 2 (1993), pp. 229–246.

76. C. H. Van Iddekinge, D. J. Putka, and J. P. Campbell, "Reconsidering Vocational Interests for Personnel Selection: The Validity of an Interest-Based Selection Test in Relation to Job Knowledge, Job Performance, and Continuance Intentions," *Journal of Applied Psychology* 96, no. 1 (2011), pp. 13–33.

77. S. A. Woods and S. E. Hampson, "Predicting Adult Occupational Environments from Gender and Childhood Personality Traits," *Journal of Applied Psychology* 95, no. 6 (2010), pp. 1045–1057.

78. See B. Schneider, H. W. Goldstein, and D. B. Smith, "The ASA Framework: An Update," *Personnel Psychology* 48, no. 4 (1995), pp. 747–773; B. Schneider, D. B. Smith, S. Taylor, and J. Fleenor, "Personality and Organizations: A Test of the Homogeneity of Personality Hypothesis," *Journal of Applied Psychology* 83, no. 3 (1998), pp. 462–470; W. Arthur Jr., S. T. Bell, A. J. Villado, and D. Doverspike, "The Use of Person-Organization Fit in Employment Decision-Making: An Assessment of Its Criterion-Related Validity," *Journal of Applied Psychology* 91, no. 4 (2006), pp. 786–801; and J. R. Edwards, D. M. Cable, I. O. Williamson, L. S. Lambert, and A. J. Shipp, "The Phenomenology of Fit: Linking the Person and Environment to the Subjective Experience of Person–Environment Fit," *Journal of Applied Psychology* 91, no. 4 (2006), pp. 802–827.

79. Based on T. A. Judge and D. M. Cable, "Applicant Personality, Organizational Culture, and Organization Attraction," *Personnel Psychology* 50, no. 2 (1997), pp. 359–394.

80. M. L. Verquer, T. A. Beehr, and S. E. Wagner, "A Meta-Analysis of Relations Between Person–Organization Fit and Work Attitudes," *Journal of Vocational Behavior* 63, no. 3 (2003), pp. 473–489; and J. C. Carr, A. W. Pearson, M. J. Vest, and S. L. Boyar, "Prior Occupational Experience, Anticipatory Socialization, and Employee Retention, *Journal of Management* 32, no. 32 (2006), pp. 343–359.

81. A. Ramesh and M. J. Gelfand, "Will They Stay or Will They Go? The Role of Job Embeddedness in Predicting Turnover in Individualistic and Collectivistic Cultures," *Journal of Applied Psychology* 95, no. 5 (2010), pp. 807–823.

82. G. Hofstede, *Cultures and Organizations: Software of the Mind* (London: McGraw-Hill, 1991); G. Hofstede, "Cultural Constraints in Management Theories," *Academy of Management Executive* 7, no. 1 (1993), pp. 81–94; G. Hofstede and M. F. Peterson, "National Values and Organizational Practices," in N. M. Ashkanasy, C. M. Wilderom, and M. F. Peterson (eds.), *Handbook of Organizational Culture and Climate* (Thousand Oaks, CA: Sage, 2000), pp. 401–416; and G. Hofstede, *Culture's Consequences: Comparing Values, Behaviors, Institutions, and Organizations Across Nations*, 2nd ed. (Thousand Oaks, CA: Sage, 2001). For criticism of this research, see B. McSweeney, "Hofstede's Model of National Cultural Differences and Their Consequences: A Triumph of Faith—A Failure of Analysis," *Human Relations* 55, no. 1 (2002), pp. 89–118.

83. G. Ailon, "Mirror, Mirror on the Wall: *Culture's Consequences* in a Value Test of Its Own Design," *Academy of Management Review* 33, no. 4 (2008), pp. 885–904; M. H. Bond, "Reclaiming the Individual from Hofstede's Ecological Analysis—A 20-Year Odyssey: Comment on Oyserman et al. (2002), *Psychological Bulletin* 128, no. 1 (2002), pp. 73–77; and G. Hofstede, "The Pitfalls of Cross-National Survey Research: A Reply to the Article by Spector et al. on the Psychometric Properties of the Hofstede Values Survey Module 1994," *Applied Psychology: An International Review* 51, no. 1 (2002), pp. 170–178.

84. V. Taras, B. L. Kirkman, and P. Steel, "Examining the Impact of Culture's Consequences: A Three-Decade, Multilevel,

Meta-Analytic Review of Hofstede's Cultural Value Dimensions," *Journal of Applied Psychology* 95, no. 5 (2010), pp. 405–439.

85. M. Javidan and R. J. House, "Cultural Acumen for the Global Manager: Lessons from Project GLOBE," *Organizational Dynamics* 29, no. 4 (2001), pp. 289–305; and R. J. House, P. J. Hanges, M. Javidan, and P. W. Dorfman (eds.), *Leadership, Culture, and Organizations: The GLOBE Study of 62 Societies* (Thousand Oaks, CA: Sage, 2004).

86. P. C. Early, "Leading Cultural Research in the Future: A Matter of Paradigms and Taste," *Journal of International Business Studies* 37, no. 6 (2006), pp. 922–931; G. Hofstede, "What Did GLOBE Really Measure? Researchers' Minds Versus Respondents' Minds," *Journal of International Business Studies* 37, no. 6 (2006), pp. 882–896; and M. Javidan, R. J. House, P. W. Dorfman, P. J. Hanges, and M. S. de Luque, "Conceptualizing and Measuring Cultures and Their Consequences: A Comparative Review of GLOBE's and Hofstede's Approaches,"

Journal of International Business Studies 37, no. 6 (2006), pp. 897–914.

87. L. A. Witt, "The Interactive Effects of Extraversion and Conscientiousness on Performance," *Journal of Management* 28, no. 6 (2002), p. 836.

88. R. P. Tett and D. D. Burnett, "A Personality Trait–Based Interactionist Model of Job Performance," *Journal of Applied Psychology* 88, no. 3 (2003), pp. 500–517.

89. B. Adkins and D. Caldwell, "Firm or Subgroup Culture: Where Does Fitting in Matter Most?" *Journal of Organizational Behavior* 25, no. 8 (2004), pp. 969–978; H. D. Cooper-Thomas, A. van Vianen, and N. Anderson, "Changes in Person–Organization Fit: The Impact of Socialization Tactics on Perceived and Actual P–O Fit," *European Journal of Work & Organizational Psychology* 13, no. 1 (2004), pp. 52–78; and C. A. O'Reilly, J. Chatman, and D. F. Caldwell, "People and Organizational Culture: A Profile Comparison Approach to Assessing Person–Organization Fit," *Academy of Management Journal* 34, no. 3 (1991), pp. 487–516.

LEARNING OBJECTIVES

After studying this chapter, you should be able to:

1 Define *perception* and explain the factors that influence it.

2 Explain attribution theory and list the three determinants of attribution.

3 Identify the shortcuts individuals use in making judgments about others.

4 Explain the link between perception and decision making.

5 Apply the rational model of decision making and contrast it with bounded rationality and intuition.

6 List and explain the common decision biases or errors.

7 Explain how individual differences and organizational constraints affect decision making.

8 Contrast the three ethical decision criteria.

9 Define *creativity* and discuss the three-component model of creativity.

MyManagementLab

Access a host of interactive learning aids to help strengthen your understanding of the chapter concepts at **www.mymanagementlab.com**.

DO MACHINES MAKE BETTER DECISIONS?

Hedge fund managers are unlike other people in ways that are fairly obvious. Typically, they are unusually quantitatively oriented and not made uncomfortable with the thought of losing thousands or even millions of dollars on a bet gone bad. Their careers may rise or fall based on factors over which they have little control.

Even in this unusual group, Spencer Greenberg is unusual. Only 27, he is chief executive and co-chair of a Manhattan investment firm. After graduating from Columbia Business School, Greenberg founded Rebellion Research Technologies with two other recent Amherst College graduates (Alexander Fleiss and Jonathan Sturges) and another partner (Jeremy Newton) who was still in college. Greenberg and his compatriots are, of course, very young to be leading a New York investment firm. What is even more interesting is the way they're doing it.

All investment bankers and hedge fund managers are comfortable with analytics. What makes Rebellion unusual is the degree to which the firm has taken them. The firm uses computers to actually make buy, sell, or hold decisions and to learn from its mistakes. "It's pretty clear that human beings aren't improving," says Greenberg. "But computers and algorithms are only getting more robust."

Based on the returns Rebellion has been able to generate, other companies, including Cerebellum Capital and RGM Advisors, have followed suit. The computers outperform humans, their advocates say, because they can crunch numbers more quickly, "learn" what works, and adapt more readily and objectively. Rebellion's program analyzes more than a decade of financial activity and the latest market results to evaluate stocks. When buy, sell, or hold decisions stop working, the computer adjusts by automatically incorporating new information. Rebellion's leaders have faith in their artificial intelligence (AI). "I've learned not to question the AI," says Fleiss.

Machines are not only taking over financial decision making. From flying airplanes to making medical decisions to running nuclear power plants, computers are gradually supplanting and even replacing human judgment.

Not everyone is convinced that AI always improves on human judgment and decision making. Some argue that reliance on computers makes complex systems more susceptible to errors because no computer can anticipate every scenario, and humans function less well as the passive monitors

Perception and Individual Decision Making

*Indecision may or may not
be my problem.*

—Jimmy Buffett

into which AI makes them. Says an observer of one complex system—airline piloting, "When the person has no role in the task, there's a much greater risk of complacency."

Sources: A. Shell, "Wall Street Traders Mine Tweets to Gain a Trading Edge," *USA Today* (May 4, 2011), downloaded May 23, 2011, from www.usatoday.com/money/; "Soon, Your Computer Will Have Emotions Like You," *The Economic Times* (April 20, 2011), downloaded May 23, 2011, from http://articles.economictimes.indiatimes.com; S. Patterson, "Letting the Machines Decide," *The Wall Street Journal* (July 14, 2010), p. C1; and C. Negroni, "As Attention Wanders, Second Thoughts About the Autopilot," *The New York Times* (May 18, 2010), pp. B1, B5.

The preceding example illustrates some of the issues that arise when people look for techniques to improve their decision making. One reason some like computerized decision making is that human decision makers can be incorrect or biased in many ways. This chapter will review some of these biases in human decision making, but it also explores how human decision makers can outperform machines, especially in the area of creativity. The Case Incident 1 (at the end of the chapter) considers computerized decision making further.

In the following Self-Assessment Library, consider one perception—that of appropriate gender roles.

SELF-ASSESSMENT LIBRARY

What Are My Gender Role Perceptions?

In the Self-Assessment Library (available on CD or online), take assessment IV.C.2 (What Are My Gender Role Perceptions?) and answer the following questions.

1. Did you score as high as you thought you would?
2. Do you think a problem with measures like this is that people aren't honest in responding?
3. If others, such as friends, classmates, and family members, rated you, would they rate you differently? Why or why not?
4. Research has shown that people's gender role perceptions are becoming less traditional over time. Why do you suppose this is so?

What Is Perception?

1 Define *perception* and explain the factors that influence it.

Perception is a process by which individuals organize and interpret their sensory impressions in order to give meaning to their environment. However, what we perceive can be substantially different from objective reality. For example, all employees in a firm may view it as a great place to work—favorable working conditions, interesting job assignments, good pay, excellent benefits, understanding and responsible management—but, as most of us know, it's very unusual to find such agreement.

Why is perception important in the study of OB? Simply because people's behavior is based on their perception of what reality is, not on reality itself. *The world as it is perceived is the world that is behaviorally important.*

Factors That Influence Perception

How do we explain the fact that individuals may look at the same thing yet perceive it differently? A number of factors operate to shape and sometimes distort perception. These factors can reside in the *perceiver;* in the object, or *target,* being perceived; or in the context of the *situation* in which the perception is made (see Exhibit 6-1).

When you look at a target and attempt to interpret what you see, your interpretation is heavily influenced by your personal characteristics—your attitudes, personality, motives, interests, past experiences, and expectations. For instance, if you expect police officers to be authoritative or young people to be lazy, you may perceive them as such, regardless of their actual traits.

Characteristics of the target also affect what we perceive. Loud people are more likely to be noticed in a group than quiet ones. So, too, are extremely attractive or unattractive individuals. Because we don't look at targets in isolation, the relationship of a target to its background also influences perception, as does our tendency to group close things and similar things together. We often perceive women, men, Whites, African Americans, Asians, or members of any other group that has clearly distinguishable characteristics as alike in other, unrelated ways as well.

Context matters too. The time at which we see an object or event can influence our attention, as can location, light, heat, or any number of situational factors. At a nightclub on Saturday night, you may not notice a young guest "dressed to the nines." Yet that same person so attired for your Monday morning management class would certainly catch your attention (and that of the rest of the class). Neither the perceiver nor the target has changed between Saturday night and Monday morning, but the situation is different.

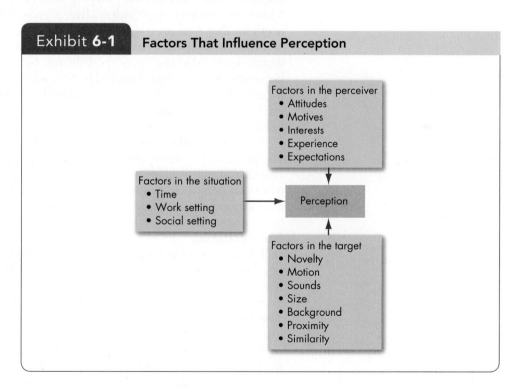

Exhibit 6-1　**Factors That Influence Perception**

perception　*A process by which individuals organize and interpret their sensory impressions in order to give meaning to their environment.*

Person Perception: Making Judgments About Others

Now we turn to the application of perception concepts most relevant to OB—*person perception,* or the perceptions people form about each other.

Attribution Theory

2 Explain attribution theory and list the three determinants of attribution.

Nonliving objects such as desks, machines, and buildings are subject to the laws of nature, but they have no beliefs, motives, or intentions. People do. That's why when we observe people, we attempt to explain why they behave in certain ways. Our perception and judgment of a person's actions, therefore, will be significantly influenced by the assumptions we make about that person's internal state.

Attribution theory tries to explain the ways in which we judge people differently, depending on the meaning we attribute to a given behavior.[1] It suggests that when we observe an individual's behavior, we attempt to determine whether it was internally or externally caused. That determination, however, depends largely on three factors: (1) distinctiveness, (2) consensus, and (3) consistency. First, let's clarify the differences between internal and external causation, and then we'll elaborate on each of the three determining factors.

Internally caused behaviors are those we believe to be under the personal control of the individual. *Externally* caused behavior is what we imagine the situation forced the individual to do. If one of your employees is late for work, you might attribute that to his partying into the wee hours and then oversleeping. This is an internal attribution. But if you attribute lateness to an automobile accident that tied up traffic, you are making an external attribution.

Now let's discuss the three determining factors. *Distinctiveness* refers to whether an individual displays different behaviors in different situations. Is the employee who arrives late today also one who regularly "blows off" commitments? What we want to know is whether this behavior is unusual. If it is, we are likely to give it an external attribution. If it's not, we will probably judge the behavior to be internal.

If everyone who faces a similar situation responds in the same way, we can say the behavior shows *consensus.* The behavior of our tardy employee meets this criterion if all employees who took the same route were also late. From an attribution perspective, if consensus is high, you would probably give an external attribution to the employee's tardiness, whereas if other employees who took the same route made it to work on time, you would attribute his lateness to an internal cause.

Finally, an observer looks for *consistency* in a person's actions. Does the person respond the same way over time? Coming in 10 minutes late for work is not perceived in the same way for an employee who hasn't been late for several months as it is for an employee who is late two or three times a week. The more consistent the behavior, the more we are inclined to attribute it to internal causes.

Exhibit 6-2 summarizes the key elements in attribution theory. It tells us, for instance, that if an employee, Kim Randolph, generally performs at about the same level on related tasks as she does on her current task (low distinctiveness), other employees frequently perform differently—better or worse—than Kim on that task (low consensus), and Kim's performance on this current task is consistent over time (high consistency), anyone judging Kim's work will likely hold her primarily responsible for her task performance (internal attribution).

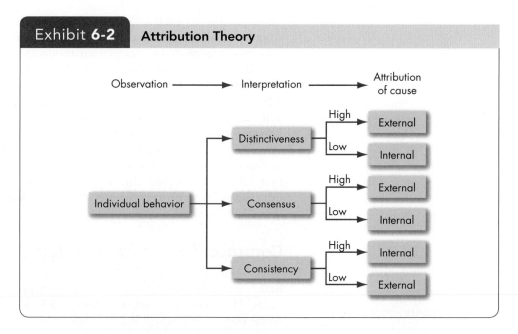

One of the most interesting findings from attribution theory research is that errors or biases distort attributions. When we make judgments about the behavior of other people, we tend to underestimate the influence of external factors and overestimate the influence of internal or personal factors.[2] This **fundamental attribution error** can explain why a sales manager is prone to attribute the poor performance of her sales agents to laziness rather than to the innovative product line introduced by a competitor. Individuals and organizations also tend to attribute their own successes to internal factors such as ability or effort, while blaming failure on external factors such as bad luck or unproductive co-workers. People also tend to attribute ambiguous information as relatively flattering and accept positive feedback while rejecting negative feedback. This is the **self-serving bias**.[3] A *U.S. News & World Report* study showed its power. Researchers asked one group of people "If someone sues you and you win the case, should he pay your legal costs?" Eighty-five percent responded "yes." Another group was asked "If you sue someone and lose the case, should you pay his costs?" Only 44 percent answered "yes."[4]

The evidence on cultural differences in perception is mixed, but most suggest there *are* differences across cultures in the attributions people make.[5] One study found Korean managers less likely to use the self-serving bias—they tended to accept responsibility for group failure "because I was not a capable leader" instead of attributing failure to group members.[6] On the other hand, Asian managers are more likely to blame institutions or whole organizations, whereas Western observers believe individual managers should get blame or praise.[7] That probably explains why U.S. newspapers prominently report the names of individual executives when firms do poorly, whereas Asian media cover how the firm as a whole has failed. This tendency to make group-based attributions also explains why individuals from Asian cultures are more likely to make group-based stereotypes.[8] Attribution theory was developed largely based

attribution theory   *An attempt to determine whether an individual's behavior is internally or externally caused.*

fundamental attribution error   *The tendency to underestimate the influence of external factors and overestimate the influence of internal factors when making judgments about the behavior of others.*

self-serving bias   *The tendency for individuals to attribute their own successes to internal factors and put the blame for failures on external factors.*

on experiments with U.S. and Western European workers. But these studies suggest caution in making attribution theory predictions in non-Western societies, especially in countries with strong collectivist traditions.

Differences in attribution tendencies don't mean the basic concepts of attribution and blame completely differ across cultures, though. Self-serving biases may be less common in East Asian cultures, but evidence suggests they still operate across cultures.[9] Recent studies indicate Chinese managers assess blame for mistakes using the same distinctiveness, consensus, and consistency cues Western managers use.[10] They also become angry and punish those deemed responsible for failure, a reaction shown in many studies of Western managers. This means the basic process of attribution applies across cultures, but that it takes more evidence for Asian managers to conclude someone else should be blamed.

Common Shortcuts in Judging Others

3 Identify the shortcuts individuals use in making judgments about others.

The shortcuts we use in judging others are frequently valuable: they allow us to make accurate perceptions rapidly and provide valid data for making predictions. However, they are not foolproof. They can and do get us into trouble when they result in significant distortions.

Selective Perception   Any characteristic that makes a person, an object, or an event stand out will increase the probability we will perceive it. Why? Because it is impossible for us to assimilate everything we see; we can take in only certain stimuli. This explains why you're more likely to notice cars like your own, or why a boss may reprimand some people and not others doing the same thing. Because we can't observe everything going on about us, we engage in **selective perception**. A classic example shows how vested interests can significantly influence which problems we see.

Dearborn and Simon asked 23 business executives (6 in sales, 5 in production, 4 in accounting, and 8 in miscellaneous functions) to read a comprehensive case describing the organization and activities of a steel company.[11] Each manager was asked to write down the most important problem in the case. Eighty-three percent of the sales executives rated sales important; only 29 percent of the others did so. The researchers concluded that participants perceived as important the aspects of a situation specifically related to their own unit's activities and goals. A group's perception of organizational activities is selectively altered to align with the vested interests the group represents.

Because we cannot assimilate all that we observe, we take in bits and pieces. But we don't choose randomly; rather, we select according to our interests, background, experience, and attitudes. Selective perception allows us to speed-read others, but not without the risk of drawing an inaccurate picture. Seeing what we want to see, we can draw unwarranted conclusions from an ambiguous situation.

We find another example of selective perception in financial analysis. From 2007 to 2009, the U.S. stock market lost roughly half its value. Yet during that time, analysts' sell ratings (typically, analysts rate a company's stock with three recommendations: buy, sell, or hold) actually *decreased* slightly. Although there are several reasons analysts are reluctant to put sell ratings on stocks, one is selective perception. When prices are going down, analysts often attend to the past (saying the stock is a bargain relative to its prior price), rather than the future (the downward trend may well continue). As one money manager noted, "Each time the market went down was a new opportunity to buy the stock even cheaper."[12] That much is true, of course, but it shows the dangers of selective perception: by looking only at the past price, analysts were relying on a false reference point and failing to recognize that what has fallen can fall further still.

glOBalization!

Chinese Time, North American Time

We realize just how much we take our perceptions of the world for granted when we try to see through the eyes of someone who grew up in a culture totally different from our own.

For instance, people see the passage of time quite differently in different cultures. Some cultures tend to focus more on the past, others on the future. Li-Jun Ji and colleagues investigated how Chinese perceive events relative to Canadians' perceptions. Participants read a description of a theft, along with descriptions of events that occurred in the distant past, recent past, or present. When attempting to solve the case, Chinese participants were more likely to rely on events from the distant past and recent past, whereas Canadians were more attentive to recent events.

Even the way we visualize the passage of time differs across cultures. Lera Boroditsky, Orly Fuhrman, and Kelly McCormick from Stanford University examined how American English speakers and Mandarin (Chinese) speakers differed in their perception of time. Because English uses phrases like "looking forward to" events or "putting the past behind us," English speakers tend to think about time as a horizontal timeline. Mandarin however uses words like *shàng* (up) and *xià* (down) to refer to time, so events accumulate in a stack. Could this difference in language structure explain why Chinese speakers pay more attention to history when thinking about events? Do Chinese think more about events "piling up" on top of one another (making them more

relevant), whereas North Americans think about events moving away in time so that what is in the past is over and done? Further research will have to examine whether this is the case, but it remains an interesting possibility.

Sources: L. Ji, Z. Zhang, and D. Messervey, "Looking Into the Past: Cultural Differences in Perception and Representation of Past Information," *Journal of Personality and Social Psychology* 96, no. 4 (2009), pp. 761–769; L. Boroditsky, O. Fuhrman, and K. McCormick, "Do English and Mandarin Speakers Think about Time Differently?" *Cognition* 118, no. 1 (2011), pp. 123–129; and A. J. Shipp, J. R. Edwards, and L. S. Lambert, "Conceptualization and Measurement of Temporal Focus: The Subjective Experience of Past, Present, and Future," *Organizational Behavior and Human Decision Processes* 110, no. 1 (2009), pp. 1–22.

Halo Effect When we draw a general impression about an individual on the basis of a single characteristic, such as intelligence, sociability, or appearance, a **halo effect** is operating.[13] If you're a critic of President Obama, try listing 10 things you admire about him. If you're an admirer, try listing 10 things you dislike about him. No matter which group describes you, odds are you won't find this an easy exercise! That's the halo effect: our general views contaminate our specific ones.

The reality of the halo effect was confirmed in a classic study in which subjects were given a list of traits such as intelligent, skillful, practical, industrious, determined, and warm and asked to evaluate the person to whom those traits applied.[14] Subjects judged the person to be wise, humorous, popular, and imaginative. When the same list was modified to include "cold" instead of "warm," a completely different picture emerged. Clearly, the subjects were allowing a single trait to influence their overall impression of the person they were judging.

Contrast Effects An old adage among entertainers is "Never follow an act that has kids or animals in it." Why? Audiences love children and animals so much that you'll look bad in comparison. This example demonstrates how a **contrast effect** can distort perceptions. We don't evaluate a person in isolation. Our reaction is influenced by other persons we have recently encountered.

selective perception *The tendency to selectively interpret what one sees on the basis of one's interests, background, experience, and attitudes.*

halo effect *The tendency to draw a general impression about an individual on the basis of a single characteristic.*

contrast effect *Evaluation of a person's characteristics that is affected by comparisons with other people recently encountered who rank higher or lower on the same characteristics.*

In a series of job interviews, for instance, interviewers can make distortions in any given candidate's evaluation as a result of his or her place in the interview schedule. A candidate is likely to receive a more favorable evaluation if preceded by mediocre applicants and a less favorable evaluation if preceded by strong applicants.

Stereotyping   When we judge someone on the basis of our perception of the group to which he or she belongs, we are using the shortcut called **stereotyping**.[15]

We rely on generalizations every day because they help us make decisions quickly; they are a means of simplifying a complex world. It's less difficult to deal with an unmanageable number of stimuli if we use *heuristics* or stereotypes. For example, it does make sense to assume that Tre, the new employee from accounting, is going to know something about budgeting, or that Allie from finance will be able to help you figure out a forecasting problem. The problem occurs, of course, when we generalize inaccurately or too much. In organizations, we frequently hear comments that represent stereotypes based on gender, age, race, religion, ethnicity, and even weight (see Chapter 2):[16] "Men aren't interested in child care," "Older workers can't learn new skills," "Asian immigrants are hardworking and conscientious." A growing body of research suggests stereotypes operate emotionally and often below the level of conscious awareness, making them particularly hard to challenge and change.[17]

Stereotypes can be deeply ingrained and powerful enough to influence life-and-death decisions. One study, controlling for a wide array of factors (such as aggravating or mitigating circumstances), showed that the degree to which black defendants in murder trials looked "stereotypically black" essentially doubled their odds of receiving a death sentence if convicted.[18] Another experimental study found that students who read scenarios describing leaders tended to assign higher scores for leadership potential and effective leadership to Whites than to minorities even though the content of the scenarios was equivalent, supporting the idea of a stereotype of Whites as better leaders.[19]

These young women are taking part in a running test for employment in a police force in Peshawar, Pakistan. But women in America and European, Eastern European, Asian, and Latin American countries report that gender stereotyping makes it difficult for them to enter the profession because it is largely regarded as a job strictly for men. Even in countries like the United States where the law requires hiring police officers without regard to gender, the stereotypical view of women inaccurately generalizes them as lacking the mental, physical, and emotional fitness required to perform police work. But women who want to do police work contend that they satisfy the fitness requirements and even bring special qualities to the job such as compassion and good communication skills.

Source: Pakistan Press International Photo/Newscom

One problem of stereotypes is that they *are* widespread and often useful generalizations, though they may not contain a shred of truth when applied to a particular person or situation. So we constantly have to check ourselves to make sure we're not unfairly or inaccurately applying a stereotype in our evaluations and decisions. Stereotypes are an example of the warning "The more useful, the more danger from misuse."

Specific Applications of Shortcuts in Organizations

People in organizations are always judging each other. Managers must appraise their employees' performances. We evaluate how much effort our co-workers are putting into their jobs. Team members immediately "size up" a new person. In many cases, our judgments have important consequences for the organization. Let's look at the most obvious applications.

Employment Interview Few people are hired without an interview. But interviewers make perceptual judgments that are often inaccurate[20] and draw early impressions that quickly become entrenched. Research shows we form impressions of others within a tenth of a second, based on our first glance.[21] If these first impressions are negative, they tend to be more heavily weighted in the interview than if that same information came out later.[22] Most interviewers' decisions change very little after the first 4 or 5 minutes of an interview. As a result, information elicited early in the interview carries greater weight than does information elicited later, and a "good applicant" is probably characterized more by the absence of unfavorable characteristics than by the presence of favorable ones.

Performance Expectations People attempt to validate their perceptions of reality even when these are faulty.[23] The terms **self-fulfilling prophecy** and *Pygmalion effect* describe how an individual's behavior is determined by others' expectations. If a manager expects big things from her people, they're not likely to let her down. Similarly, if she expects only minimal performance, they'll likely meet those low expectations. Expectations become reality. The self-fulfilling prophecy has been found to affect the performance of students, soldiers, and even accountants.[24]

Performance Evaluation We'll discuss performance evaluations more fully in Chapter 17, but note for now that they very much depend on the perceptual process.[25] An employee's future is closely tied to the appraisal—promotion, pay raises, and continuation of employment are among the most obvious outcomes. Although the appraisal can be objective (for example, a sales-person is appraised on how many dollars of sales he generates in his territory), many jobs are evaluated in subjective terms. Subjective evaluations, though often necessary, are problematic because all the errors we've discussed thus far—selective perception, contrast effects, halo effects, and so on—affect them. Ironically, sometimes performance ratings say as much about the evaluator as they do about the employee!

stereotyping *Judging someone on the basis of one's perception of the group to which that person belongs.*

self-fulfilling prophecy *A situation in which a person inaccurately perceives a second person, and the resulting expectations cause the second person to behave in ways consistent with the original perception.*

The Link Between Perception and Individual Decision Making

4 Explain the link between perception and decision making.

MyManagementLab

For an interactive application of this topic, check out this chapter's simulation activity at **www.mymanagementlab.com**.

Individuals in organizations make **decisions**, choices from among two or more alternatives. Top managers determine their organization's goals, what products or services to offer, how best to finance operations, or where to locate a new manufacturing plant. Middle- and lower-level managers set production schedules, select new employees, and decide how to allocate pay raises. Nonmanagerial employees decide how much effort to put forth at work and whether to comply with a boss's request. Organizations have begun empowering their nonmanagerial employees with decision-making authority historically reserved for managers alone. Individual decision making is thus an important part of organizational behavior. But the way individuals make decisions and the quality of their choices are largely influenced by their perceptions.

Decision making occurs as a reaction to a **problem**.[26] That is, a discrepancy exists between the current state of affairs and some desired state, requiring us to consider alternative courses of action. If your car breaks down and you rely on it to get to work, you have a problem that requires a decision on your part. Unfortunately, most problems don't come neatly labeled "problem." One person's *problem* is another person's *satisfactory state of affairs*. One manager may view her division's 2 percent decline in quarterly sales to be a serious problem requiring immediate action on her part. In contrast, her counterpart in another division, who also had a 2 percent sales decrease, might consider that quite acceptable. So awareness that a problem exists and that a decision might or might not be needed is a perceptual issue.

Every decision requires us to interpret and evaluate information. We typically receive data from multiple sources and need to screen, process, and interpret them. Which data are relevant to the decision, and which are not? Our perceptions will answer that question. We also need to develop alternatives and evaluate their strengths and weaknesses. Again, our perceptual

Delta Airlines management made a decision in reaction to the problem of negative publicity resulting from a growing number of customer complaints about poor service. To improve service, Delta reinstated the personal assistance of its elite Red Coat airport agents that it started in the 1960s but eliminated in 2005 due to budget cuts. The primary mission of the Red Coats, such as Charmaine Gordon shown here helping customers at Kennedy International Airport in New York, is to fix customer problems. Today, Delta has about 800 Red Coats who walk around airports and use hand-held devices to give one-on-one, on-the-spot help to customers in everything ranging from printing boarding passes to directing passengers to the right concourse.

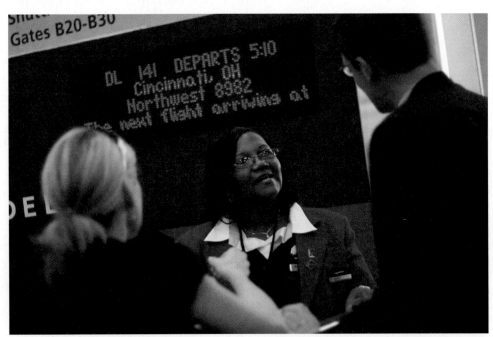

Source: Jessica Ebelhar / The New York Times / Redux Pictures

process will affect the final outcome. Finally, throughout the entire decision-making process, perceptual distortions often surface that can bias analysis and conclusions.

Decision Making in Organizations

5 Apply the rational model of decision making and contrast it with bounded rationality and intuition.

Business schools generally train students to follow rational decision-making models. While models have considerable merit, they don't always describe how people actually make decisions. This is where OB enters the picture: to improve the way we make decisions in organizations, we must understand the decision-making errors people commit (in addition to the perception errors we've discussed). Next we describe these errors, beginning with a brief overview of the rational decision-making model.

The Rational Model, Bounded Rationality, and Intuition

Rational Decision Making   We often think the best decision maker is **rational** and makes consistent, value-maximizing choices within specified constraints.[27] These decisions follow a six-step **rational decision-making model**.[28] The six steps are listed in Exhibit 6-3.

The rational decision-making model relies on a number of assumptions, including that the decision maker has complete information, is able to identify all the relevant options in an unbiased manner, and chooses the option with the highest utility.[29] As you might imagine, most decisions in the real world don't follow the rational model. People are usually content to find an acceptable or reasonable solution to a problem rather than an optimal one. Choices tend to be limited to the neighborhood of the problem symptom and the current alternative. As one expert in decision making put it, "Most significant decisions are made by judgment, rather than by a defined prescriptive model."[30] What's more, people are remarkably unaware of making suboptimal decisions.[31]

Exhibit **6-3**	Steps in the Rational Decision-Making Model

1. Define the problem.
2. Identify the decision criteria.
3. Allocate weights to the criteria.
4. Develop the alternatives.
5. Evaluate the alternatives.
6. Select the best alternative.

decisions   *Choices made from among two or more alternatives.*

problem   *A discrepancy between the current state of affairs and some desired state.*

rational   *Characterized by making consistent, value-maximizing choices within specified constraints.*

rational decision-making model   *A decision-making model that describes how individuals should behave in order to maximize some outcome.*

Bounded Rationality   Our limited information-processing capability makes it impossible to assimilate and understand all the information necessary to optimize.[32] So most people respond to a complex problem by reducing it to a level at which they can readily understand it. Also many problems don't have an optimal solution because they are too complicated to fit the rational decision-making model. So people *satisfice;* they seek solutions that are satisfactory and sufficient.

When you considered which college to attend, did you look at every viable alternative? Did you carefully identify all the criteria that were important in your decision? Did you evaluate each alternative against the criteria in order to find the optimal college? The answers are probably "no." Well, don't feel bad. Few people made their college choice this way. Instead of optimizing, you probably satisficed.

Because the human mind cannot formulate and solve complex problems with full rationality, we operate within the confines of **bounded rationality**. We construct simplified models that extract the essential features from problems without capturing all their complexity.[33] We can then behave rationally within the limits of the simple model.

How does bounded rationality work for the typical individual? Once we've identified a problem, we begin to search for criteria and alternatives. But the criteria are unlikely to be exhaustive. We identify choices that are easy to find and highly visible and that usually represent familiar criteria and tried-and-true solutions. Next, we begin reviewing them, focusing on alternatives that differ little from the choice currently in effect until we identify one that is "good enough"—that meets an acceptable level of performance. That ends our search. So the solution represents a satisficing choice—the first *acceptable* one we encounter—rather than an optimal one.

Satisficing is not always a bad idea—a simple process may frequently be more sensible than the traditional rational decision-making model.[34] To use the rational model in the real world, you need to gather a great deal of information about all the options, compute applicable weights, and then calculate values across a huge number of criteria. All these processes can cost time, energy,

Top managers of Nike, Inc. operated within the confines of bounded rationality in making a decision about its operations in China. To reinforce its future development and rapid growth in China, Nike decided to invest $99 million to build the China Logistics Center, a new distribution facility in Jiangsu for the company's footwear, apparel, and equipment products. With China overtaking Japan as Nike's second largest market after the United States, the new distribution center is expected to reduce product delivery times by up to 14 percent to the more than 3,000 Nike retail stores in China.

and money. And if there are many unknown weights and preferences, the fully rational model may not be any more accurate than a best guess. Sometimes a fast-and-frugal process of solving problems might be your best option. Returning to your college choice, would it really be smarter to fly around the country to visit dozens of potential campuses, paying application fees for all these options? Can you really even know what type of college is "best" for you when you're just graduating from high school, or is there a lot of unknown information about how your interests are going to develop over time? Maybe you won't major in the same subject you started with. It might be much smarter to find a few colleges that match most of your preferences and then focus your attention on differentiating between those.

Intuition   Perhaps the least rational way of making decisions is **intuitive decision making**, an unconscious process created from distilled experience.[35] It occurs outside conscious thought; it relies on holistic associations, or links between disparate pieces of information; it's fast; and it's *affectively charged,* meaning it usually engages the emotions.[36]

While intuition isn't rational, it isn't necessarily wrong. Nor does it always contradict rational analysis; rather, the two can complement each other. But nor is intuition superstition, or the product of some magical or paranormal sixth sense. As one recent review noted, "Intuition is a highly complex and highly developed form of reasoning that is based on years of experience and learning."[37]

For most of the twentieth century, experts believed decision makers' use of intuition was irrational or ineffective. That's no longer the case.[38] We now recognize that rational analysis has been overemphasized and, in certain instances, relying on intuition can improve decision making.[39] But we can't rely on it too much. Because it is so unquantifiable, it's hard to know when our hunches are right or wrong. The key is neither to abandon nor rely solely on intuition, but to supplement it with evidence and good judgment.

Common Biases and Errors in Decision Making

6 List and explain the common decision biases or errors.

Decision makers engage in bounded rationality, but they also allow systematic biases and errors to creep into their judgments.[40] To minimize effort and avoid difficult trade-offs, people tend to rely too heavily on experience, impulses, gut feelings, and convenient rules of thumb. These shortcuts can be helpful. However, they can also distort rationality. Following are the most common biases in decision making. Exhibit 6-4 provides some suggestions for how to avoid falling into these biases and errors.

Overconfidence Bias   It's been said that "no problem in judgment and decision making is more prevalent and more potentially catastrophic than overconfidence."[41] When we're given factual questions and asked to judge the probability that our answers are correct, we tend to be far too optimistic. When people say they're 90 percent confident about the range a certain number might take, their estimated ranges contain the correct answer only about 50 percent of the time—and experts are no more accurate in setting up confidence intervals than are

---

bounded rationality   *A process of making decisions by constructing simplified models that extract the essential features from problems without capturing all their complexity.*

intuitive decision making   *An unconscious process created out of distilled experience.*

Exhibit 6-4	Reducing Biases and Errors

Focus on Goals. Without goals, you can't be rational, you don't know what information you need, you don't know which information is relevant and which is irrelevant, you'll find it difficult to choose between alternatives, and you're far more likely to experience regret over the choices you make. Clear goals make decision making easier and help you eliminate options that are inconsistent with your interests.

Look for Information That Disconfirms Your Beliefs. One of the most effective means for counteracting overconfidence and the confirmation and hindsight biases is to actively look for information that contradicts your beliefs and assumptions. When we overtly consider various ways we could be wrong, we challenge our tendencies to think we're smarter than we actually are.

Don't Try to Create Meaning out of Random Events. The educated mind has been trained to look for cause-and-effect relationships. When something happens, we ask why. And when we can't find reasons, we often invent them. You have to accept that there are events in life that are outside your control. Ask yourself if patterns can be meaningfully explained or whether they are merely coincidence. Don't attempt to create meaning out of coincidence.

Increase Your Options. No matter how many options you've identified, your final choice can be no better than the best of the option set you've selected. This argues for increasing your decision alternatives and for using creativity in developing a wide range of diverse choices. The more alternatives you can generate, and the more diverse those alternatives, the greater your chance of finding an outstanding one.

Source: S. P. Robbins, Decide & Conquer: *Making Winning Decisions and Taking Control of Your Life* (Upper Saddle River, NJ: Financial Times/Prentice Hall, 2004), pp. 164–168.

novices.[42] When people say they're 100 percent sure of an outcome, they tend to be 70 to 85 percent correct.[43] Here's another interesting example. In one random-sample national poll, 90 percent of U.S. adults said they expected to go to heaven. But in another random-sample national poll, only 86 percent thought Mother Teresa was in heaven. Talk about an overconfidence bias!

Individuals whose intellectual and interpersonal abilities are *weakest* are most likely to overestimate their performance and ability.[44] There's also a negative relationship between entrepreneurs' optimism and the performance of their new ventures: the more optimistic, the less successful.[45] The tendency to be too confident about their ideas might keep some from planning how to avoid problems that arise.

Investor overconfidence operates in a variety of ways.[46] Finance professor Terrance Odean says "people think they know more than they do, and it costs them." Investors, especially novices, overestimate not just their own skill in processing information, but also the quality of the information they're working with. Test your own confidence level with investments: compare the long-term returns of your stock market picks relative to index funds. You'll find an overall index performs as well as, or better than, carefully hand-picked stocks. The main reason many people resist index funds is that they think they're better at picking stocks than the average person, but most investors will actually do only as well as or only slightly better than the market as a whole.

Anchoring Bias   The **anchoring bias** is a tendency to fixate on initial information and fail to adequately adjust for subsequent information.[47] It occurs because our mind appears to give a disproportionate amount of emphasis to the first information it receives. Anchors are widely used by people in professions in which persuasion skills are important—advertising, management, politics, real estate, and law. Assume two pilots—Jason and Glenda—have been laid off their current jobs, and after an extensive search their best offers are from Delta Airlines. Each would earn the average annual pay of Delta's narrow-body jet pilots: $126,000. Jason was a pilot for Pinnacle, a regional airline where the average annual salary is $82,000. Glenda was a pilot for FedEx, where the average annual salary is $200,000. Which pilot is most likely to accept, or be happiest with, Delta's offer? Obviously Jason, because he is anchored by the lower salary.[48]

Any time a negotiation takes place, so does anchoring. When a prospective employer asks how much you made in your prior job, your answer typically anchors the employer's offer. (Remember this when you negotiate your salary, but set the anchor only as high as you realistically can.) Finally, the more precise your anchor, the smaller the adjustment. Some research suggests people think of making an adjustment after an anchor is set as rounding off a number. If you suggest a target salary of $55,000, your boss will consider $50,000 to $60,000 a reasonable range for negotiation, but if you mention $55,650, your boss is more likely to consider $55,000 to $56,000 the range of likely values.[49]

Confirmation Bias   The rational decision-making process assumes we objectively gather information. But we don't. We *selectively* gather it. The **confirmation bias** represents a specific case of selective perception: we seek out information that reaffirms our past choices, and we discount information that contradicts them.[50] We also tend to accept at face value information that confirms our preconceived views, while we are critical and skeptical of information that challenges them. Therefore, the information we gather is typically biased toward supporting views we already hold. We even tend to seek sources most likely to tell us what we want to hear, and we give too much weight to supporting information and too little to contradictory. Interestingly, we are most prone to the confirmation bias when we believe we have good information and strongly believe in our opinions. Fortunately, those who feel there is a strong need to be accurate in making a decision are less prone to the confirmation bias.

Availability Bias   More people fear flying than fear driving in a car. But if flying on a commercial airline really were as dangerous as driving, the equivalent of two 747s filled to capacity would crash every week, killing all aboard. Because the media give much more attention to air accidents, we tend to overstate the risk of flying and understate the risk of driving.

The **availability bias** is our tendency to base judgments on information readily available.[51] Events that evoke emotions, are particularly vivid, or are more recent tend to be more available in our memory, leading us to overestimate the chances of unlikely events such as an airplane crash. The availability bias can also explain why managers doing performance appraisals give more weight to recent employee behaviors than to behaviors of 6 or 9 months earlier, or why credit-rating agencies such as Moody's or Standard & Poor's may issue overly positive ratings by relying on information presented by debt issuers, who have an incentive to offer data favorable to their case.[52]

anchoring bias   *A tendency to fixate on initial information, from which one then fails to adequately adjust for subsequent information.*

confirmation bias   *The tendency to seek out information that reaffirms past choices and to discount information that contradicts past judgments.*

availability bias   *The tendency for people to base their judgments on information that is readily available to them.*

Escalation of Commitment   Another distortion that creeps into decisions is a tendency to escalate commitment.[53] **Escalation of commitment** refers to staying with a decision even when there is clear evidence it's wrong. Consider a friend who has been dating someone for several years. Although he admits things aren't going too well, he says he is still going to marry her. His justification: "I have a lot invested in the relationship!"

Individuals escalate commitment to a failing course of action when they view themselves as responsible for the failure.[54] They "throw good money after bad" to demonstrate their initial decision wasn't wrong and to avoid admitting they made a mistake.[55] In fact, people who carefully gather and consider information consistent with the rational decision-making model are *more* likely to engage in escalation of commitment than those who spend less time thinking about their choices.[56] Perhaps they have invested so much time and energy in making their decisions that they have convinced themselves they're taking the right course of action and don't update their knowledge in the face of new information. Many an organization has suffered because a manager determined to prove his or her original decision right continued to commit resources to a lost cause.

Randomness Error   Most of us like to think we have some control over our world and our destiny. Our tendency to believe we can predict the outcome of random events is the **randomness error**.

Decision making suffers when we try to create meaning in random events, particularly when we turn imaginary patterns into superstitions.[57] These can be completely contrived ("I never make important decisions on Friday the 13th") or can evolve from a reinforced past pattern of behavior (Tiger Woods often wears a red shirt during a golf tournament's final round because he won many junior tournaments wearing red shirts). Superstitious behavior can be debilitating when it affects daily judgments or biases major decisions.

Risk Aversion   Mathematically, we should find a 50–50 flip of the coin for $100 to be worth as much as a sure promise of $50. After all, the expected value of the gamble over a number of trials is $50. However, nearly everyone but committed gamblers would rather have the sure thing than a risky prospect.[58] For many people, a 50–50 flip of a coin even for $200 might not be worth as much as a sure promise of $50, even though the gamble is mathematically worth twice as much! This tendency to prefer a sure thing over a risky outcome is **risk aversion**.

Risk aversion has important implications. To offset the risks inherent in a commission-based wage, companies pay commissioned employees considerably more than they do those on straight salaries. Risk-averse employees will stick with the established way of doing their jobs, rather than taking a chance on innovative or creative methods. Sticking with a strategy that has worked in the past does minimize risk, but in the long run it will lead to stagnation. Ambitious people with power that can be taken away (most managers) appear to be especially risk averse, perhaps because they don't want to lose on a gamble everything they've worked so hard to achieve.[59] CEOs at risk of being terminated are also exceptionally risk averse, even when a riskier investment strategy is in their firms' best interests.[60]

Because people are less likely to escalate commitment where there is a great deal of uncertainty, the implications of risk aversion aren't all bad.[61] When a risky investment isn't paying off, most people would rather play it safe and cut their losses, but if they think the outcome is a sure thing, they'll keep escalating.

Risk preference is sometimes reversed: people prefer to take their chances when trying to prevent a negative outcome.[62] They would rather take a 50–50 gamble on

Creative Decision Making Is a Right-Brain Activity

One article of faith in creativity research and practice is that whereas the left brain governs analytical, rational thinking, the right brain underlies creative thinking. However, judging from a recent review of neuropsychology research, this accepted wisdom is false.

Neuropsychologists study creativity by asking people to engage in creative thinking, which they measure in different ways. In the Remote Associates Test, individuals indicate what word links a series of three words (such as Falling Actor Dust; Salt Deep Foam). Other tests ask individuals to compose creative stories, write captions for cartoons, or provide unique solutions to unusual hypothetical problems. While participants are thinking creatively, the researchers assess their brain activity using various techniques, including MRI.

A recent review of 72 studies found right brain activity was *not* associated with creative thinking. The authors conclude, "Creativity, or any alleged stage of it, is not particularly associated with the right brain or any part of the right brain." Indeed, the review showed it was difficult to isolate creative thinking in any one region of the brain.

Another review of 45 studies reached the same conclusion, noting that the diverse ways in which creativity and brain activity were measured made generalizations difficult.

These results do not discourage all neuropsychologists. One neuroscientist, Oshin Vartanian, summed up the literature as follows: "Initially, a lot of people were looking for the holy grail. They were searching for the creativity module in the brain. Now we know it is more complicated."

Sources: A. Dietrich and R. Kanso, "A Review of EEG, ERP, and Neuroimaging Studies of Creativity and Insight," *Psychological Bulletin* 136, no. 5 (2010), pp. 822–848; R. Ardena, R. S. Chavez, R. Grazioplene, & R. E. Jung, "Neuroimaging Creativity: A Psychometric View," *Behavioural Brain Research* 214, no. 2 (2010), pp. 143–156; and A. McIlroy, "Neuroscientists Try to Unlock the Origins of Creativity," *Globe and Mail* (January 28, 2011), downloaded May 20, 2011, from www.theglobeandmail.com/.

losing $100 than accept the certain loss of $50. Thus they will risk losing a lot of money at trial rather than settle out of court. Trying to cover up wrongdoing instead of admitting a mistake, despite the risk of truly catastrophic press coverage or even jail time, is another example. Stressful situations can make these risk preferences stronger. People will more likely engage in risk-seeking behavior for negative outcomes, and risk-averse behavior for positive outcomes, when under stress.[63]

Hindsight Bias   The **hindsight bias** is the tendency to believe falsely, after the outcome is known, that we'd have accurately predicted it.[64] When we have accurate feedback on the outcome, we seem pretty good at concluding it was obvious.

Over the past 10 years, the home video rental industry has been collapsing fast as online distribution outlets have eaten away at the market.[65] Hollywood Video declared bankruptcy in May 2010 and began liquidating its assets; Blockbuster filed for bankruptcy in September 2010. Some have suggested that if only these organizations had leveraged their brand and distribution resources

escalation of commitment *An increased commitment to a previous decision in spite of negative information.*

randomness error *The tendency of individuals to believe that they can predict the outcome of random events.*

risk aversion *The tendency to prefer a sure gain of a moderate amount over a riskier outcome, even if the riskier outcome might have a higher expected payoff.*

hindsight bias *The tendency to believe falsely, after an outcome of an event is actually known, that one would have accurately predicted that outcome.*

effectively and sooner to develop web-based delivery, as Netflix does, and low-cost distribution in grocery and convenience stores, which Redbox offers, they could have been avoided failure. While that might seem obvious now, many experts with good information failed to see these two major trends that would upend the industry.

Of course, after the fact, it is easy to see that a combination of automated and mail-order distribution would outperform the traditional brick-and-mortar movie rental business. Similarly, former Merrill Lynch CEO John Thain—and many other Wall Street executives—took blame for failing to see what now seems obvious (that housing prices were inflated, too many risky loans were made, and the values of many "securities" were based on fragile assumptions). Though the criticisms may have merit, things are often all too clear in hindsight. As Malcolm Gladwell, author of *Blink* and *The Tipping Point*, writes, "What is clear in hindsight is rarely clear before the fact."[66]

The hindsight bias reduces our ability to learn from the past. It lets us think we're better predictors than we are and can make us falsely confident. If your actual predictive accuracy is only 40 percent but you think it's 90, you're likely to be less skeptical about your predictive skills.

Application: Financial Decision Making   This discussion of decision making errors may have you thinking about how organizations and individuals make financial decisions. Did decision errors influence capital markets and even lead to crises like the financial meltdown of 2008? How are financial decisions affected by errors and biases? Experts have identified several ways this can occur.[67]

One of the core problems that created the financial crisis was that large loans were made to individuals who could not repay them, and finance companies purchased these bad debts without realizing how poor the prospects of repayment were. Thus, overconfidence bias by both lenders and borrowers

When the U.S.-based global financial services firm Lehman Brothers failed, many people blamed Richard Fuld, the company's chief executive, accusing him of overconfidence, confirmation, and anchoring biases and a lack of knowledge about complicated financial investment instruments. Even as Lehman Brothers continued to post billion-dollar losses, Fuld exuded confidence that the investment bank was sound, and he rebuffed criticism of the bank's failure to value its assets accurately. Comments by former employees and passersby blaming Fuld for the bankruptcy were recorded on an artists' rendering of him placed in front of Lehman's offices in New York City.

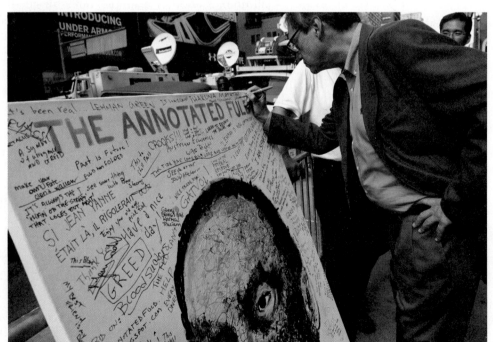

OB Poll   Gloomy Perceptions Return

Percent Indicating Economy Is in Recession or Depression

Depression
Recession

	February, 2008	September, 2008	April, 2011
Depression	12%	33%	29%
Recession	33%	36%	26%

Source: Based on C. Merkle and M. Weber, "True Overconfidence—The Inability of Rational Information Processing to Account for Apparent Overconfidence" (March 2009). Available at SSRN: http://ssrn.com/abstract=1373675

about the ability to pay back loans was clearly a major factor. Most studies suggest that people are more willing to buy on credit and spend more money when they feel confident. Although experts were no more accurate at predicting financial outcomes than were people without knowledge or skills in finance, they *were* more confident in their predictions. Unfortunately, as confidence decreases in the face of poor economic data, businesses and consumers become more conservative in their spending. This further decreases demand for products and services, which deepens the economic crisis in a vicious cycle.

Overconfidence isn't the only decision error implicated in the financial crisis. Investors deliberately avoid negative information about investments, an example of the confirmation bias. Lenders may have overlooked potential problems with borrowers' accounts when making loans, and stock traders may have ignored information about potential problems with complex derivatives when making purchasing decisions. Once a loan has been paid off, lenders also selectively ignore the negative effects of debt, making them more likely to make unwise loans in the future.

What might prevent these situations from occurring in the future? Both investors and consumers may need to more carefully consider whether their confidence level is aligned with their actual future ability to pay. It is also always a good idea to seek information that goes against your initial inclinations, to ensure you're getting the whole picture. Be careful not to commit the hindsight bias and conclude after financial crises have dissipated that it should have been obvious problems were about to occur.

SELF-ASSESSMENT LIBRARY

Am I A Deliberate Decision Maker?

In the Self-Assessment Library (available on CD or online), take assessment IV.A.2 (Am I a Deliberate Decision Maker?). Would it be better to be a more deliberate decision maker? Why or why not?

Influences on Decision Making: Individual Differences and Organizational Constraints

We turn here to factors that influence how people make decisions and the degree to which they are susceptible to errors and biases. We discuss individual differences and organizational constraints.

Individual Differences

7 Explain how individual differences and organizational constraints affect decision making.

Decision making in practice is characterized by bounded rationality, common biases and errors, and the use of intuition. In addition, individual differences create deviations from the rational model. In this section, we look at two such differences: personality and gender.

Personality The little research so far conducted on personality and decision making suggests personality does influence our decisions. Let's look at conscientiousness and self-esteem (both discussed in Chapter 5).

Specific facets of conscientiousness—rather than the broad trait itself—may affect escalation of commitment (above).[68] Two such facets—achievement striving and dutifulness—actually had opposite effects. Achievement-striving people were more likely to escalate their commitment, whereas dutiful people were less likely. Why? Generally, achievement-oriented people hate to fail, so they escalate their commitment, hoping to forestall failure. Dutiful people, however, are more inclined to do what they see as best for the organization. Second, achievement-striving individuals appear more susceptible to the hindsight bias, perhaps because they have a greater need to justify their actions.[69] Unfortunately, we don't have evidence on whether dutiful people are immune to this bias.

Finally, people with high self-esteem are strongly motivated to maintain it, so they use the self-serving bias to preserve it. They blame others for their failures while taking credit for successes.[70]

Gender Research on rumination offers insights into gender differences in decision making.[71] *Rumination* refers to reflecting at length. In terms of decision making, it means overthinking problems. Twenty years of study find women spend much more time than men analyzing the past, present, and future. They're more likely to overanalyze problems before making a decision and to rehash a decision once made. This can lead to more careful consideration of problems and choices. However, it can make problems harder to solve, increase regret over past decisions, and increase depression. Women are nearly twice as likely as men to develop depression.[72]

Why women ruminate more than men is not clear. One view is that parents encourage and reinforce the expression of sadness and anxiety more in girls than in boys. Another theory is that women, more than men, base their self-esteem and well-being on what others think of them. A third idea is that women are more empathetic and more affected by events in others' lives, so they have more to ruminate about.

By age 11, girls are ruminating more than boys. But this gender difference seems to lessen with age. Differences are largest during young adulthood and smallest after age 65, when both men and women ruminate the least.[73]

Whose Ethical Standards to Follow?

As we note in the chapter, different standards identify ethical behavior in different cultures. Managers who work in international contexts frequently run into complex problems when behavior acceptable for the home office is unacceptable in local cultures, and vice versa.

How difficult is it to arrive at a global policy for ethical decision making? Consider these examples. Individuals from countries higher in Hofstede's dimension of power distance, like those in Latin America, were more likely to report that bribery was acceptable than were individuals from lower power distance countries, like the United States and much of Europe. An international scandal ensued after German corporation Siemens set aside money for bribes when working in Africa, but company executives initially defended the actions as consistent with business practices in those countries. Such differences don't mean business ethics are "higher" or "lower" in different countries. Although U.S. executives might frown on bribery, they may view it as ethical and necessary to lay workers off during poor economic times, whereas other cultures view layoffs as a betrayal of the relationship between workers and employers.

So how are managers to decide which ethical standards to observe? Is it better to act consistently with your own culture, or adopt the ethical standards of the countries where you operate? This question isn't easy to answer. Ethics experts suggest leaders should adhere to universal values of human life and welfare as the core of their international codes of ethics, and they note there are few cases where values are directly in conflict (no culture actively encourages bribery as moral; it's just that some societies view it as less of a problem than others do).

Source: Based on L. J. Thompson, "The Global Moral Compass for Business Leaders," *Journal of Business Ethics* 93, no. S1 (2010), pp. 15–32; C. Baughn, N. L. Bodie, M. A. Buchanan, and M. B. Bixby, "Bribery in International Business Transactions," *Journal of Business Ethics* 92, no. 1 (2010), pp. 15–32; and T. Patel and A. Schaefer, "Making Sense of the Diversity of Ethical Decision Making in Business: An Illustration of the Indian Context," *Journal of Business Ethics* 90, no. 2 (2009), pp. 171–186.

Mental Ability   We know people with higher levels of mental ability are able to process information more quickly, solve problems more accurately, and learn faster, so you might expect them also to be less susceptible to common decision errors. However, mental ability appears to help people avoid only some of these.[74] Smart people are just as likely to fall prey to anchoring, overconfidence, and escalation of commitment, probably because just being smart doesn't alert you to the possibility you're too confident or emotionally defensive. That doesn't mean intelligence never matters. Once warned about decision-making errors, more intelligent people learn more quickly to avoid them. They are also better able to avoid logical errors like false syllogisms or incorrect interpretation of data.

Cultural Differences   The rational model makes no acknowledgment of cultural differences, nor does the bulk of OB research literature on decision making. But Indonesians, for instance, don't necessarily make decisions the same way Australians do. Therefore, we need to recognize that the cultural background of a decision maker can significantly influence the selection of problems, the depth of analysis, the importance placed on logic and rationality, and whether organizational decisions should be made autocratically by an individual manager or collectively in groups.[75]

Cultures differ in their time orientation, the importance of rationality, their belief in the ability of people to solve problems, and their preference for collective decision making. Differences in time orientation help us understand why managers in Egypt make decisions at a much slower and more deliberate pace than their U.S. counterparts. While rationality is valued in North America, that's not true elsewhere in the world. A North American manager might make an important decision intuitively but know it's important to appear to proceed in a rational fashion because rationality is highly valued in the West. In countries such as Iran, where rationality is not as paramount as other factors, efforts to appear rational are not necessary.

Some cultures emphasize solving problems, while others focus on accepting situations as they are. The United States falls in the first category; Thailand and Indonesia are examples of the second. Because problem-solving managers believe they can and should change situations to their benefit, U.S. managers might identify a problem long before their Thai or Indonesian counterparts would choose to recognize it as such. Decision making by Japanese managers is much more group-oriented than in the United States. The Japanese value conformity and cooperation. So before Japanese CEOs make an important decision, they collect a large amount of information, which they use in consensus-forming group decisions. In short, there are probably important cultural differences in decision making, but unfortunately not yet much research to identify them.

Organizational Constraints

Organizations can constrain decision makers, creating deviations from the rational model. For instance, managers shape their decisions to reflect the organization's performance evaluation and reward system, to comply with its formal regulations, and to meet organizationally imposed time constraints. Precedent can also limit decisions.

Performance Evaluation   Managers are strongly influenced by the criteria on which they are evaluated. If a division manager believes the manufacturing plants under his responsibility are operating best when he hears nothing negative, we shouldn't be surprised to find his plant managers spending a good part of their time ensuring that negative information doesn't reach him.

Reward Systems   The organization's reward system influences decision makers by suggesting which choices have better personal payoffs. If the organization rewards risk aversion, managers are more likely to make conservative decisions. From the 1930s through the mid-1980s, General Motors consistently gave promotions and bonuses to managers who kept a low profile and avoided controversy. These executives became adept at dodging tough issues and passing controversial decisions on to committees.

Formal Regulations   David Gonzalez, a shift manager at a Taco Bell restaurant in San Antonio, Texas, describes constraints he faces on his job: "I've got rules and regulations covering almost every decision I make—from how to make a burrito to how often I need to clean the restrooms. My job doesn't come with much freedom of choice." David's situation is not unique. All but the smallest organizations create rules and policies to program decisions and get individuals to act in the intended manner. And of course, in so doing, they limit decision choices.

System-Imposed Time Constraints   Almost all important decisions come with explicit deadlines. A report on new-product development may have to be ready for executive committee review by the first of the month. Such conditions often make it difficult, if not impossible, for managers to gather all the information they might like before making a final choice.

Historical Precedents   Decisions aren't made in a vacuum; they have a context. In fact, individual decisions are points in a stream of choice. Those made in the

Formal regulations shape employee decisions at McDonald's restaurants throughout the world. McDonald's standardizes the behavior of restaurant crew members such as the employee shown here preparing the company's specialty coffee, McCafe Mocha. McDonald's requires employees to follow rules and regulations for food preparation and service to meet the company's high standards of food quality and safety and reliable and friendly service. For example, McDonald's requires 72 safety protocols to be conducted every day in each restaurant as part of a daily monitoring routine for restaurant managers.

Source: Newscom

past are like ghosts that haunt and constrain current choices. It's common knowledge that the largest determinant of the size of any given year's budget is last year's budget.[76] Choices made today are largely a result of choices made over the years.

What About Ethics in Decision Making?

8 Contrast the three ethical decision criteria.

Ethical considerations should be an important criterion in all organizational decision making. In this section, we present three ways to frame decisions ethically.[77]

Three Ethical Decision Criteria

The first ethical yardstick is **utilitarianism**, which proposes making decisions solely on the basis of their *outcomes,* ideally to provide the greatest good for the greatest number. This view dominates business decision making. It is consistent with goals such as efficiency, productivity, and high profits.

Another ethical criterion is to make decisions consistent with fundamental liberties and privileges, as set forth in documents such as the Bill of Rights. An emphasis on *rights* in decision making means respecting and protecting the basic rights of individuals, such as the right to privacy, free speech, and due process. This criterion protects **whistle-blowers** when they reveal an organization's unethical practices to the press or government agencies, using their right to free speech.

---

utilitarianism *A system in which decisions are made to provide the greatest good for the greatest number.*

whistle-blowers *Individuals who report unethical practices by their employer to outsiders.*

A third criterion is to impose and enforce rules fairly and impartially to ensure *justice* or an equitable distribution of benefits and costs. Union members typically favor this view. It justifies paying people the same wage for a given job regardless of performance differences and using seniority as the primary determination in layoff decisions.

Each criterion has advantages and liabilities. A focus on utilitarianism promotes efficiency and productivity, but it can sideline the rights of some individuals, particularly those with minority representation. The use of rights protects individuals from injury and is consistent with freedom and privacy, but it can create a legalistic environment that hinders productivity and efficiency. A focus on justice protects the interests of the underrepresented and less powerful, but it can encourage a sense of entitlement that reduces risk taking, innovation, and productivity.

Decision makers, particularly in for-profit organizations, feel comfortable with utilitarianism. The "best interests" of the organization and its stockholders can justify a lot of questionable actions, such as large layoffs. But many critics feel this perspective needs to change.[78] Public concern about individual rights and social justice suggests managers should develop ethical standards based on nonutilitarian criteria. This presents a challenge because satisfying individual rights and social justice creates far more ambiguities than utilitarian effects on efficiency and profits. However, while raising prices, selling products with questionable effects on consumer health, closing down inefficient plants, laying off large numbers of employees, and moving production overseas to cut costs can be justified in utilitarian terms, that may no longer be the single measure by which good decisions are judged.

Improving Creativity in Decision Making

9   Define *creativity* and discuss the three-component model of creativity.

Although the rational decision-making model will often improve decisions, a rational decision maker also needs **creativity**, the ability to produce novel and useful ideas.[79] These are different from what's been done before but appropriate to the problem presented.

Creativity allows the decision maker to more fully appraise and understand the problem, including seeing problems others can't see. L'Oréal puts its managers through creative exercises such as cooking or making music, and the University of Chicago requires MBA students to make short movies about their experiences.

Creative Potential   Most people have useful creative potential. But to unleash it, they have to escape the psychological ruts many of us fall into and learn how to think about a problem in divergent ways.

Exceptional creativity is scarce. We all know of creative geniuses in science (Albert Einstein), art (Pablo Picasso), and business (Steve Jobs). But what about the typical individual? Intelligent people and those who score high on openness to experience (see Chapter 5) are more likely to be creative.[80] Other traits of creative people are independence, self-confidence, risk taking, an internal locus of control, tolerance for ambiguity, a low need for structure, and perseverance.[81] Exposure to a variety of cultures can also improve creativity.[82] So taking an international assignment, or even an international vacation, could jump-start your creative process.

A study of the lifetime creativity of 461 men and women found fewer than 1 percent were exceptionally creative.[83] But 10 percent were highly creative and about 60 percent were somewhat creative. This reinforces that most of us have creative potential; we just need to learn to unleash it.

Three-Component Model of Creativity What can individuals and organizations do to stimulate employee creativity? The best answer lies in the **three-component model of creativity**,[84] which proposes that individual creativity essentially requires expertise, creative thinking skills, and intrinsic task motivation. Studies confirm that the higher the level of each, the higher the creativity.

Expertise is the foundation for all creative work. Film writer, producer, and director Quentin Tarantino spent his youth working in a video rental store, where he built up an encyclopedic knowledge of movies. The potential for creativity is enhanced when individuals have abilities, knowledge, proficiencies, and similar expertise in their field of endeavor. You wouldn't expect someone with minimal knowledge of programming to be very creative as a software engineer.

The second component is *creative-thinking skills*. This encompasses personality characteristics associated with creativity, the ability to use analogies, and the talent to see the familiar in a different light.

A meta-analysis of 102 studies found positive moods increase creativity, but it depends on what sort of positive mood was considered.[85] Moods such as happiness that encourage interaction with the world are more conducive to creativity than passive moods such as calm. This means the common advice to relax and clear your mind to develop creative ideas may be misplaced. It would be better to get in an upbeat mood and then frame your work as an opportunity to have fun and experiment. Negative moods also don't always have the same effects on creativity. Passive negative moods such as sadness doesn't seem to have much effect, but avoidance-oriented negative moods such as fear and anxiety decrease creativity. Feeling threatened reduces your desire to try new activities; risk aversion increases when you're scared. Active negative moods, such as anger, however, do appear to enhance creativity, especially if you are taking your task seriously.

Being around creative others can make us more inspired, especially if we're creatively "stuck."[86] One study found that having "weak ties" to creative people—knowing them but not well—facilitates creativity because the people are there as a resource if we need them but not so close as to stunt our own independent thinking.[87]

Analogies allow decision makers to apply an idea from one context to another. One of the most famous examples was Alexander Graham Bell's observation that it might be possible to apply the way the ear operates to his "talking box." Bell noticed the bones in the ear are operated by a delicate, thin membrane. He wondered why a thicker and stronger membrane shouldn't be able to move a piece of steel. From that analogy, the telephone was conceived. Thinking in terms of analogies is a complex intellectual skill, which helps explain why cognitive ability is related to creativity. Demonstrating this effect, one study found children who got high scores on cognitive ability tests at age 13 were significantly more likely to have made creative achievements in their professional lives 25 years later.[88]

Some people develop creative skills because they see problems in a new way. They're able to make the strange familiar and the familiar strange.[89] For instance, most of us think of hens laying eggs. But how many of us have considered that a hen is only an egg's way of making another egg?

---

creativity *The ability to produce novel and useful ideas.*

three-component model of creativity *The proposition that individual creativity requires expertise, creative thinking skills, and intrinsic task motivation.*

Creative people often love their work, to the point of seeming obsession. The final component in the three-component model of creativity is *intrinsic task motivation*. This is the desire to work on something because it's interesting, involving, exciting, satisfying, or personally challenging. It's what turns creativity *potential* into *actual* creative ideas. Environmental stimulants that foster creativity include a culture that encourages the flow of ideas; fair and constructive judgment of ideas; rewards and recognition for creative work; sufficient financial, material, and information resources; freedom to decide what work is to be done and how to do it; a supervisor who communicates effectively, shows confidence in others, and supports the work group; and work group members who support and trust each other.[90]

International Differences There are no global ethical standards,[91] as contrasts between Asia and the West illustrate.[92] Because bribery is commonplace in countries such as China, a Canadian working in China might face a dilemma: should I pay a bribe to secure business if it is an accepted part of that country's culture? A manager of a large U.S. company operating in China once caught an employee stealing. Following company policy, she fired him and turned him over to the local authorities. Later, she was horrified to learn the employee had been summarily executed.[93]

Although ethical standards may seem ambiguous in the West, criteria defining right and wrong are actually much clearer there than in Asia, where few issues are black and white and most are gray. Global organizations must establish ethical principles for decision makers in countries such as India and China and modify them to reflect cultural norms if they want to uphold high standards and consistent practices.

SELF-ASSESSMENT LIBRARY

How Creative Am I?

In the Self-Assessment Library (available on CD or online), take assessment I.A.5 (How Creative Am I?).

MyManagementLab

Now that you have finished this chapter, go back to **www.mymanagementlab.com** to continue practicing and applying the concepts you've learned.

Summary and Implications for Managers

Perception Individuals base their behavior not on the way their external environment actually is but rather on what they see or believe it to be.

* Whether a manager successfully plans and organizes the work of employees and actually helps them to structure their work more efficiently and effectively is far less important than how employees perceive the manager's efforts.
* Employees judge issues such as fair pay, performance appraisals, and working conditions in very individual ways. To influence productivity, we need to assess how workers perceive their jobs.

Checklists Lead to Better Decisions

POINT

While life and lives sometimes turn on the basis of big decisions, it's often the little ones that matter more. Our failure to follow routine, everyday protocols makes the world a more dangerous place for ourselves, and for others. A few examples . . .

Nearly 100,000 U.S. patients are killed every year by the failure of doctors and nurses to follow simple instructions. Really. Hospital-acquired infections kill that many people every year, and nearly all those deaths are entirely preventable.

Most airline crashes occur because pilots ignore the rules. Pilot failure to follow protocols is a primary contributing factor to the majority of incidents and accidents.

An important way of attacking these errors is to use checklists.

Support for a checklist approach is provided by a new book, *The Checklist Manifesto*. In it, the author, Harvard Medical School surgeon Atul Gawande notes, "The volume and complexity of what we know has exceeded our ability to deliver its benefits correctly, safely, or reliably." Unless, of course, we use checklists.

Dr. Peter Pronovost, a critical care specialist at Johns Hopkins, developed his own operating room checklist, which included some "no brainers" such as wash your hands with soap, put drapes over entire patient, and put sterile dressing over incisions. Within 1 year of the checklist's adoption at Johns Hopkins, the post-op infection rate went from 11 percent to zero.

According to Gawande, in using checklists to improve decisions, we should keep the following guidelines in mind:

- Include all "stupid but critical" tasks so they're not overlooked.
- Make it mandatory for team members to inform others when an item on the list is completed (or not).
- Empower team members to question superiors about the checklist.
- Allow for improvisation in unusual circumstances.
- Thoroughly test-drive the checklist before implementing it.

Gawande notes that checklists aren't important only for medical decision making. Engineering, business, technology, safety, and transportation are all industries that would benefit from greater development and use of checklists in everyday decision making.

As a project manager noted, "Successful checklists detail both the sequence of necessary activities as well as the communication checkpoints to ensure dialog among project participants."

COUNTERPOINT

Checklists work well, except when they don't.

Checklists have a paradox that makes them of dubious usefulness: the more complex the decision making, ostensibly the more important the checklist. But the more complex the decision making, the less likely that a checklist can or should be followed. Checklists can take an impractical amount of time to follow. Driving an automobile is a routine but complex process. Do you keep a checklist in your car for every time you get behind the wheel?

Moreover, by their very nature, complex tasks can pose problems that fall outside the scope of the checklist. The last thing we need to solve unanticipated or complicated problems is rote allegiance to a checklist that is poorly suited to the problem at hand.

Indeed, a problem with many poor decisions is that heuristics are too often followed, with little thought to whether the assumptions behind them still hold true. If we have learned anything from the financial crisis, it is that a model or heuristic is only as good as its assumptions. Assume housing prices are properly valued and likely to continue to increase, and it makes all the sense in the world to be aggressive in making loans. Countrywide and Fannie Mae had all sorts of rules, protocols, and checklists they followed in making catastrophically bad loan decisions.

As for the medical decision making, as another physician and author, Sandeep Jauhar, noted, advocates of checklists often ignore the unintended consequences. Insurers compensate doctors for ticking off boxes on checklists—like prescribing antibiotics—even when there is no evidence they are warranted. Because this protocol encourages the growth of antibiotic-resistant bacteria, we all are endangered by this checklist-adhering behavior.

We want to think we live in a world where decision-making errors can be easily solved. We can mitigate some decisions by learning more about decision-making errors, but one of the main learning points is that we need a healthier respect for the degree to which we're susceptible to errors. Checklists provide a false sense of security and an ignorance about when they cause more problems than they solve.

Sources: S. Jauhar, "One Thing After Another," *New York Times Book Review* (January 24, 2010), p. 7; C. Arnst, "Make a List. Check it Twice," *Bloomberg Businessweek* (February 22, 2010), pp. 78–79; J. Ross, "The Checklist Manifesto and the Digital Divide," *Forbes* (July 27, 2010), downloaded on May 7, 2011, from www.forbes.com.

- Absenteeism, turnover, and job satisfaction are also reactions to an individual's perceptions. Dissatisfaction with working conditions and the belief that an organization lacks promotion opportunities are judgments based on attempts to create meaning in the job.
- The employee's conclusion that a job is good or bad is an interpretation. Managers must spend time understanding how each individual interprets reality and, when there is a significant difference between what someone sees and what exists, try to eliminate the distortions.

Individual Decision Making   Individuals think and reason before they act. This is why an understanding of how people make decisions can be helpful for explaining and predicting their behavior. In some decision situations, people follow the rational decision-making model. But few important decisions are simple or unambiguous enough for the rational model's assumptions to apply. So we find individuals looking for solutions that satisfice rather than optimize, injecting biases and prejudices into the decision process, and relying on intuition.

What can managers do to improve their decision making? We offer four suggestions.

- Analyze the situation. Adjust your decision-making approach to the national culture you're operating in and to the criteria your organization evaluates and rewards. If you're in a country that doesn't value rationality, don't feel compelled to follow the rational decision-making model or to try to make your decisions appear rational. Similarly, organizations differ in the importance they place on risk, the use of groups, and the like. Adjust your decision approach to ensure it's compatible with the organization's culture.
- Second, be aware of biases. Then try to minimize their impact. Exhibit 6-4 offers some suggestions.
- Third, combine rational analysis with intuition. These are not conflicting approaches to decision making. By using both, you can actually improve your decision-making effectiveness. As you gain managerial experience, you should feel increasingly confident in imposing your intuitive processes on top of your rational analysis.
- Finally, try to enhance your creativity. Actively look for novel solutions to problems, attempt to see problems in new ways, and use analogies. Try to remove work and organizational barriers that might impede your creativity.

QUESTIONS FOR REVIEW

1 What is perception, and what factors influence our perception?

2 What is attribution theory? What are the three determinants of attribution? What are its implications for explaining organizational behavior?

3 What shortcuts do people frequently use in making judgments about others?

4 What is the link between perception and decision making? How does one affect the other?

5 What is the rational model of decision making? How is it different from bounded rationality and intuition?

6 What are some of the common decision biases or errors that people make?

7 What are the influences of individual differences, organizational constraints, and culture on decision making?

8 Are unethical decisions more a function of an individual decision maker or the decision maker's work environment? Explain.

9 What is creativity, and what is the three-component model of creativity?

EXPERIENTIAL EXERCISE Biases in Decision Making

Step 1

Answer each of the following problems.

1. *Fortune* magazine ranked the following 10 corporations among the 500 largest U.S.–based firms according to sales volume for 2008:
   Group A: Apple Computer, Hershey Foods, Kellogg, McDonald's, U.S. Airways
   Group B: Altria Group, AmerisourceBergen, Cardinal Health, McKesson, Valero Energy
       Which group would you say had the larger total sales volume—A or B? By what percentage—10 percent, 50 percent, 100 percent?

2. The best student in your introductory MBA class this past semester writes poetry and is rather shy and small in stature. What was the student's undergraduate major—Chinese studies or psychology?

3. Which of the following causes more deaths in the United States each year?
   a. Stomach cancer
   b. Motor vehicle accidents

4. Which would you choose?
   a. A sure gain of $240
   b. A 25 percent chance of winning $1,000 and a 75 percent chance of winning nothing

5. Which would you choose?
   a. A sure loss of $750
   b. A 75 percent chance of losing $1,000 and a 25 percent chance of losing nothing

6. Which would you choose?
   a. A sure loss of $3,000
   b. An 80 percent chance of losing $4,000 and a 20 percent chance of losing nothing

Step 2

Break into groups of three to five students. Compare your answers. Explain why you chose the answers you did.

Step 3

Your instructor will give you the correct answers to each problem. Now discuss the accuracy of your decisions, the biases evident in the decisions you reached, and how you might improve your decision making to make it more accurate.

Source: These problems are based on examples provided in M. H. Bazerman, *Judgment in Managerial Decision Making*, 3rd ed. (New York: Wiley, 1994).

ETHICAL DILEMMA Do Unethical Decisions Come from Bad Character?

Why would former New York Attorney General and then Governor Eliot Spitzer decide to use a prostitution service? Why would highly respected attorney Marc Dreier, with degrees from Harvard and Yale and a successful Park Avenue law firm, decide to impersonate people in order to swindle others? From Tiger Woods to Bernie Madoff, it's not hard to find examples of unethical behavior. But what causes people to make unfortunate choices?

Behavioral genetics research has taught us that virtually every human characteristic has genetic origins and that genetic differences are a central reason people differ in their behavior. Thus, some personality traits probably predispose people toward unethical behavior. One study of white-collar criminals, for example, showed they were significantly lower on a conscientiousness scale than the general population.

On the other hand, recent research shows that all of us perform unethical behavior to some degree while subconsciously fooling ourselves about it. We may bend a rule to help a colleague, overlook information that might damage a case we want to make, or lie to avoid a negative consequence—blithely unaware that others might view this behavior as unethical.

Why do we do this? Evidence suggests that when we fail to notice a decision has an ethical component, it enables us to behave in a self-interested manner without having to feel badly about it. No wonder, then, that people tend to believe they are more ethical than they are.

Many think that transparency and accountability increase ethical behavior. Behavioral ethics research, however, shows us that often these actions increase unethical behavior, because they cause individuals to think disclosure absolves them of ethical responsibilities to be objective, or to deny to an even greater degree the ethical components of their decisions.

The first step toward behaving more ethically is, ironically, admitting to ourselves that we adhere to ethical standards less well than we admit.

Questions

1. Do you think people see themselves as more ethical than they really are? And you?

2. The authors of one study noted that "disclosures can exacerbate [unethical behavior] by causing people to feel absolved of their duty to be objective." Do you agree? Why or why not?

3. Do you think if we admitted it to ourselves times when we behaved unethically we would be less likely to behave unethically in the future?

Sources: M. H. Bazerman and A. E. Tenbrunsel, *Blind Spots: Why We Fail to Do What's Right and What to Do about It* (Princeton, NJ: Princeton University Press, 2011); M. H. Bazerman and A. E. Tenbrunsel, "Stumbling into Bad Behavior," *The New York Times* (April 21, 2011), p. A23); and S. Jayson, "What Propels Us to Do Bad Things?" *USA Today* (May 3, 2011), p. 6D.

CASE INCIDENT 1 Computerized Decision Making

As you saw in the opening vignette, computerized decision making has really taken off in recent years. Some have blamed the financial crisis that began in 2007–2008 on excessive reliance on these computerized decision-making models. Lending officers who used to make individualized decisions about credit worthiness through personal judgment were replaced by computerized and statistical models, which resulted in mechanistic decision making. As a result, large numbers of decisions were tied to a common set of assumptions, and when those assumptions proved to be wrong, the entire credit system fell apart and the economy faltered.

Besides the use of computerized decision models, the use of computerized systems like Twitter for information sharing and the burgeoning number of computer "apps" may be leading to information overload, so facts and figures replace analysis and thought in making human decisions. Eric Kessler from Pace University's Lubin School of Business notes, "What starts driving decisions is the urgent rather than the important." Researchers have begun to find that people using too much information actually make worse decisions than people with less information, or they get so swamped in information that they are unable to reach a decision at all.

Computer decision models do present certain advantages. Computers are capable of amassing and compiling enormous amounts of data and using them to spot trends and patterns a human observer would simply never see. Computers also are not prone to emotional decision making or falling into the heuristics and biases we discussed in this chapter. Finally, computerized decision making systems are generally faster than human beings.

However, computer decision-making systems have certain faults that might severely constrain their usefulness. Although computers can grind through masses of data, they are not capable of intuition or creative thought. As scholar Amar Bhidé notes, "An innovator cannot simply rely on historical patterns in placing bets on future opportunities." People are much more likely to spot opportunities that lie just beyond what the data can tell us directly. Also, groups of people working in collaboration can discuss and question assumptions and conclusions. Computers cannot actively consider whether their programming makes sense or adapt automatically when values change.

Questions

1. What are the specific advantages of using computerized decision making? How can computers be better decision makers than humans?

2. What are the weaknesses of using computers as decision tools? Are computers likely to have any specific problems in making decisions that people wouldn't have?

3. Do you think computer decision making systems can effectively take ethical issues into account? What is the role of human decision makers in creating ethical choices?

4. Are there advantages to completely disconnecting from the wired world when possible? What can you do to try to retain your ability to focus and process information deeply?

Sources: Based on S. Begley, "I Can't Think!" *Newsweek* (March 7, 2011), www.newsweek.com; A. Bhidé, "The Judgment Deficit" *Harvard Business Review* (September 2010), pp. 44–53; and T. H. Davenport and J. H. Snabe, "How Fast and Flexible Do You Want Your Information, Really?" *Sloan Management Review* 52 (Spring 2011), pp. 57–62.

CASE INCIDENT 2 Predictions That Didn't Quite Pan Out

Consider the following examples of predictions:

- **Prediction:** "More people are going to be put to work this summer."—*Vice President Joe Biden* (June 17, 2010)

- **Status:** By August, job growth in the private sector fell by two-thirds and unemployment increased to 9.8 percent in November.

- **Prediction:** "The market is telling you that something is not quite right. . . . The Chinese economy is going to slow down regardless."—Investment analyst Marc Faber (May 3, 2010)

- **Status:** The Chinese economy grew by 9.5 percent over the rest of the year.

- **Prediction:** A quick, prepackaged bankruptcy for General Motors might stall, leading to "a long period of bankruptcy which I believe would result in liquidation of the company."—CEO Rick Wagoner (March 17, 2009)

- **Status:** GM's bankruptcy court lasted a mere 40 days, and by September the company held $43 billion in cash.

- **Prediction:** "My long-term opinion is that the bear market has several years left to run, and stock prices will go a lot lower. . . . So any rally that happens is going to be a bear market rally."—Robert Prechter, CEO at research company Elliot Wave International (February 27, 2009)

- **Status:** The S&P 500 was up 64 percent from its lowest point by the middle of December, and stocks have continued to perform well since.

- **Prediction:** "I think this is a case where Freddie Mac (FRE) and Fannie Mae (FNM) are fundamentally sound. They're not in danger of going under. . . . I think they are in good shape going forward."—Representative Barney Frank (July 14, 2008)

- **Status:** Just 2 months later, the mortgage companies were in conservatorship, and the government had pledged to invest $100 billion in each.

- **Prediction:** "I think Bob Steel's the one guy I trust to turn this bank around, which is why I've told you on weakness to buy Wachovia."—CNBC commentator Jim Cramer (March 11, 2008)

- **Status:** Investors fled Wachovia within the next 2 weeks, and the company nearly failed, with shares losing half their value from September 15 to December 29.

Questions

1. Despite the difficulty of making predictions, many people confidently make assertions about what will happen in the future. Why do you think this is?

2. What perceptual or decision-making errors can you identify in these predictions?

3. Can you think of some predictions you've made that haven't turned out the way you expected?

4. Why do you think it's so hard to make accurate predictions?

Sources: Based on J. E. Keating, "The 10 Worst Predictions for 2010," *Foreign Policy* (December 17, 2010), www.foreignpolicy.com; P. Coy, "Worst Predictions about 2009," *Bloomberg Businessweek* (December 15, 2009), www.businessweek.com; and P. Coy, "Worst Predictions about 2008," *BusinessWeek* (January 12, 2009), pp. 15–16.

ENDNOTES

1. H. H. Kelley, "Attribution in Social Interaction," in E. Jones et al. (eds.), *Attribution: Perceiving the Causes of Behavior* (Morristown, NJ: General Learning Press, 1972); and M. J. Martinko, P. Harvey, and M. T. Dasborough, "Attribution Theory in the Organizational Sciences: A Case of Unrealized Potential," *Journal of Organizational Behavior 32*, no. 1 (2011), pp. 144–149.

2. See L. Ross, "The Intuitive Psychologist and His Shortcomings," in L. Berkowitz (ed.), *Advances in Experimental Social Psychology*, vol. 10 (Orlando, FL: Academic Press, 1977), pp. 174–220; and A. G. Miller and T. Lawson, "The Effect of an Informational Option on the Fundamental Attribution Error," *Personality and Social Psychology Bulletin* 15, no. 2 (1989), pp. 194–204.

3. See, for instance, N. Epley and D. Dunning, "Feeling 'Holier Than Thou': Are Self-Serving Assessments Produced by Errors in Self- or Social Prediction?" *Journal of Personality and Social Psychology* 76, no. 6 (2000), pp. 861–875; M. Goerke, J. Moller, S. Schulz-Hardt, U. Napiersky, and D. Frey, "'It's Not My Fault—But Only I Can Change It': Counterfactual and Prefactual Thoughts of Managers," *Journal of Applied Psychology* 89, no. 2 (2004), pp. 279–292; and E. G. Hepper, R. H. Gramzow, and C. Sedikides, "Individual Differences in Self-Enhancement and Self-Protection Strategies: An Integrative Analysis," *Journal of Personality* 78, no. 2 (2010), pp. 781–814.

4. See D. M. Cain and A. S. Little, "Everyone's a Little Bit Biased (even Physicians)," *JAMA: Journal of the American Medical Association* 299, no. 24 (2008), pp. 2893–2895.

5. See, for instance, A. H. Mezulis, L. Y. Abramson, J. S. Hyde, and B. L. Hankin, "Is There a Universal Positivity

Bias in Attributions: A Meta-Analytic Review of Individual, Developmental, and Cultural Differences in the Self-Serving Attributional Bias," *Psychological Bulletin* 130, no. 5 (2004), pp. 711–747; C. F. Falk, S. J. Heine, M. Yuki, and K. Takemura, "Why Do Westerners Self-Enhance More than East Asians?" *European Journal of Personality* 23, no. 3 (2009), pp. 183–203; and F. F. T. Chiang and T. A. Birtch, "Examining the Perceived Causes of Successful Employee Performance: An East–West Comparison," *International Journal of Human Resource Management* 18, no. 2 (2007), pp. 232–248.

6. S. Nam, "Cultural and Managerial Attributions for Group Performance," unpublished doctoral dissertation, University of Oregon. Cited in R. M. Steers, S. J. Bischoff, and L. H. Higgins, "Cross-Cultural Management Research," *Journal of Management Inquiry*, December 1992, pp. 325–326.

7. T. Menon, M. W. Morris, C. Y. Chiu, and Y. Y. Hong, "Culture and the Construal of Agency: Attribution to Individual Versus Group Dispositions," *Journal of Personality and Social Psychology* 76, no. 5 (1999), pp. 701–717; and R. Friedman, W. Liu, C. C. Chen, and S. S. Chi, "Causal Attribution for Interfirm Contract Violation: A Comparative Study of Chinese and American Commercial Arbitrators," *Journal of Applied Psychology* 92, no. 3 (2007), pp. 856–864.

8. J. Spencer-Rodgers, M. J. Williams, D. L. Hamilton, K. Peng, and L. Wang, "Culture and Group Perception: Dispositional and Stereotypic Inferences about Novel and National Groups," *Journal of Personality and Social Psychology* 93, no. 4 (2007), pp. 525–543.

9. J. D. Brown, "Across the (Not So) Great Divide: Cultural Similarities in Self-Evaluative Processes," *Social and Personality Psychology Compass* 4, no. 5 (2010), pp. 318–330.

10. A. Zhang, C. Reyna, Z. Qian, and G. Yu, "Interpersonal Attributions of Responsibility in the Chinese Workplace: A Test of Western Models in a Collectivistic Context," *Journal of Applied Social Psychology* 38, no. 9 (2008), pp. 2361–2377; and A. Zhang, F. Xia, and C. Li, "The Antecedents of Help Giving in Chinese Culture: Attribution, Judgment of Responsibility, Expectation Change and the Reaction of Affect," *Social Behavior and Personality* 35, no. 1 (2007), pp. 135–142.

11. D. C. Dearborn and H. A. Simon, "Selective Perception: A Note on the Departmental Identification of Executives," *Sociometry* 21, no. 2 (1958), pp. 140–144. Some of the conclusions in this classic study have recently been challenged in J. Walsh, "Selectivity and Selective Perception: An Investigation of Managers' Belief Structures and Information Processing," *Academy of Management Journal* 31, no. 4 (1988), pp. 873–896; M. J. Waller, G. Huber, and W. H. Glick, "Functional Background as a Determinant of Executives' Selective Perception," *Academy of Management Journal* 38, no. 4 (1995), pp. 943–974; and J. M. Beyer, P. Chattopadhyay, E. George, W. H. Glick, D. T. Ogilvie, and D. Pugliese, "The Selective Perception of Managers Revisited," *Academy of Management Journal* 40, no. 3 (1997), pp. 716–737.

12. J. Healy and M. M. Grynbaum, "Why Analysts Keep Telling Investors to Buy," *The New York Times* (February 9, 2009), pp. B1, B7.

13. See P. Rosenzweig, *The Halo Effect* (New York: The Free Press, 2007); I. Dennis, "Halo Effects in Grading Student Projects,"

Journal of Applied Psychology 92, no. 4 (2007), pp. 1169–1176; C. E. Naquin and R. O. Tynan, "The Team Halo Effect: Why Teams Are Not Blamed for Their Failures," *Journal of Applied Psychology* 88, no. 2 (2003), pp. 332–340; and T. M. Bechger, G. Maris, and Y. P. Hsiao, "Detecting Halo Effects in Performance-Based Evaluations," *Applied Psychological Measurement* 34, no. 8 (2010), pp. 607–619.

14. S. E. Asch, "Forming Impressions of Personality," *Journal of Abnormal and Social Psychology* 41, no. 3 (1946), pp. 258–290.

15. J. L. Hilton and W. von Hippel, "Stereotypes," *Annual Review of Psychology* 47 (1996), pp. 237–271.

16. See, for example, C. Ostroff and L. E. Atwater, "Does Whom You Work with Matter? Effects of Referent Group Gender and Age Composition on Managers' Compensation," *Journal of Applied Psychology* 88, no. 4 (2003), pp. 725–740; M. E. Heilman, A. S. Wallen, D. Fuchs, and M. M. Tamkins, "Penalties for Success: Reactions to Women Who Succeed at Male Gender-Typed Tasks," *Journal of Applied Psychology* 89, no. 3 (2004), pp. 416–427; V. K. Gupta, D. B. Turban, and N. M. Bhawe, "The Effect of Gender Stereotype Activation on Entrepreneurial Intentions," *Journal of Applied Psychology* 93, no. 5 (2008), pp. 1053–1061; and R. A. Posthuma and M. A. Campion, "Age Stereotypes in the Workplace: Common Stereotypes, Moderators, and Future Research Directions," *Journal of Management* 35, no. 1 (2009), pp. 158–188.

17. See, for example, N. Dasgupta, D. DeSteno, L. A. Williams, and M. Hunsinger, "Fanning the Flames of Prejudice: The Influence of Specific Incidental Emotions on Implicit Prejudice," *Emotion* 9, no. 4 (2009), pp. 585–591; and J. C. Ziegert and P. C. Hanges, "Strong Rebuttal for Weak Criticisms: Reply to Blanton et al. (2009)," *Journal of Applied Psychology* 94, no. 3 (2009), pp. 590–597.

18. J. L. Eberhardt, P. G. Davies, V. J. Purdic-Vaughns, and S. L. Johnson, "Looking Deathworthy: Perceived Stereotypicality of Black Defendants Predicts Capital-Sentencing Outcomes," *Psychological Science* 17, no. 5 (2006), pp. 383–386.

19. A. S. Rosette, G. J. Leonardelli, and K. W. Phillips, "The White Standard: Racial Bias in Leader Categorization," *Journal of Applied Psychology* 93, no. 4 (2008), pp. 758–777.

20. H. G. Heneman III, T. A. Judge, and J. D. Kammeyer-Mueller, *Staffing Organizations* (Middleton, WI: Mendota House, 2012).

21. J. Willis and A. Todorov, "First Impressions: Making Up Your Mind after a 100ms Exposure to a Face," *Psychological Science* 17, no. 7 (2006), pp. 592–598.

22. See, for example, E. C. Webster, *Decision Making in the Employment Interview* (Montreal: McGill University, Industrial Relations Center, 1964).

23. See, for example, D. B. McNatt, "Ancient Pygmalion Joins Contemporary Management: A Meta-Analysis of the Result," *Journal of Applied Psychology* 85, no. 2 (2000), pp. 314–322; O. B. Davidson and D. Eden, "Remedial Self-Fulfilling Prophecy: Two Field Experiments to Prevent Golem Effects among Disadvantaged Women," *Journal of Applied Psychology* 85, no. 3 (2000), pp. 386–398; and G. Natanovich and D. Eden, "Pygmalion Effects among Outreach Supervisors and Tutors: Extending Sex Generalizability," *Journal of Applied Psychology* 93, no. 6 (2008), pp. 1382–1389.

24. D. Eden and A. B. Shani, "Pygmalion Goes to Boot Camp: Expectancy, Leadership, and Trainee Performance," *Journal*

of Applied Psychology (April 1982), pp. 194–199; D. B. McNatt and T. A. Judge, "Boundary Conditions of the Galatea Effect: A Field Experiment and Constructive Replication," *Academy of Management Journal* (August 2004), pp. 550–565; and X. M. Bezuijen, P. T. van den Berg, K. van Dam, and H. Thierry, "Pygmalion and Employee Learning: The Role of Leader Behaviors," *Journal of Management* 35, (2009), pp. 1248–1267.

25. See, for example, K. F. E. Wong and J. Y. Y. Kwong, "Effects of Rater Goals on Rating Patterns: Evidence from an Experimental Field Study," *Journal of Applied Psychology* 92, no. 2 (2007), pp. 577–585; and S. E. DeVoe and S. S. Iyengar, "Managers' Theories of Subordinates: A Cross-Cultural Examination of Manager Perceptions of Motivation and Appraisal of Performance," *Organizational Behavior and Human Decision Processes* (January 2004), pp. 47–61.

26. R. Sanders, *The Executive Decisionmaking Process: Identifying Problems and Assessing Outcomes* (Westport, CT: Quorum, 1999).

27. See H. A. Simon, "Rationality in Psychology and Economics," *Journal of Business* (October 1986), pp. 209–224; and E. Shafir and R. A. LeBoeuf, "Rationality," *Annual Review of Psychology* 53 (2002), pp. 491–517.

28. For a review of the rational decision-making model, see M. H. Bazerman and D. A. Moore, *Judgment in Managerial Decision Making*, 7th ed. (Hoboken, New Jersey: Wiley, 2008).

29. J. G. March, *A Primer on Decision Making* (New York: The Free Press, 2009); and D. Hardman and C. Harries, "How Rational Are We?" *Psychologist* (February 2002), pp. 76–79.

30. Bazerman and Moore, *Judgment in Managerial Decision Making*.

31. J. E. Russo, K. A. Carlson, and M. G. Meloy, "Choosing an Inferior Alternative," *Psychological Science* 17, no. 10 (2006), pp. 899–904.

32. D. Kahneman, "Maps of Bounded Rationality: Psychology for Behavioral Economics," *The American Economic Review* 93, no. 5 (2003), pp. 1449–1475; and J. Zhang, C. K. Hsee, and Z. Xiao, "The Majority Rule in Individual Decision Making," *Organizational Behavior and Human Decision Processes* 99 (2006), pp. 102–111.

33. See H. A. Simon, *Administrative Behavior*, 4th ed. (New York: The Free Press, 1997); and M. Augier, "Simon Says: Bounded Rationality Matters," *Journal of Management Inquiry* (September 2001), pp. 268–275.

34. G. Gigerenzer, "Why Heuristics Work," *Perspectives on Psychological Science* 3, no. 1 (2008), pp. 20–29; and A. K. Shah and D. M. Oppenheimer, "Heuristics Made Easy: An Effort-Reduction Framework," *Psychological Bulletin* 134, no. 2 (2008), pp. 207–222.

35. See A. W. Kruglanski and G. Gigerenzer, "Intuitive and Deliberate Judgments Are Based on Common Principles," *Psychological Review* 118 (2011), pp. 97–109.

36. E. Dane and M. G. Pratt, "Exploring Intuition and Its Role in Managerial Decision Making," *Academy of Management Review* 32, no. 1 (2007), pp. 33–54; and J. A. Hicks, D. C. Cicero, J. Trent, C. M. Burton, and L. A. King, "Positive Affect, Intuition, and Feelings of Meaning," *Journal of Personality and Social Psychology* 98 (2010), pp. 967–979.

37. P. D. Brown, "Some Hunches About Intuition," *The New York Times* (November 17, 2007), p. B5.

38. See, for instance, L. A. Burke and M. K. Miller, "Taking the Mystery Out of Intuitive Decision Making," *Academy of Management Executive* (November 1999), pp. 91–99; J. A. Andersen, "Intuition in Managers: Are Intuitive Managers More Effective?" *Journal of Managerial Psychology* 15, no. 1–2 (2000), pp. 46–63; and Y. Ibar, J. Cone, and T. Gilovich, "People's Intuitions about Intuitive Insight and Intuitive Choice," *Journal of Personality and Social Psychology* 99 (2010), pp. 232–247.

39. See, for instance, A. W. Kruglanski and G. Gigerenzer, "Intuitive and Deliberate Judgments are Based on Common Principles," *Psychological Review* 118 (2011), pp. 97–109.

40. S. P. Robbins, *Decide & Conquer: Making Winning Decisions and Taking Control of Your Life* (Upper Saddle River, NJ: Financial Times/Prentice Hall, 2004), p. 13.

41. S. Plous, *The Psychology of Judgment and Decision Making* (New York: McGraw-Hill, 1993), p. 217.

42. C. R. M. McKenzie, M. J. Liersch, and I. Yaniv, "Overconfidence in Interval Estimates: What Does Expertise Buy You," *Organizational Behavior and Human Decision Processes* 107 (2008), pp. 179–191.

43. B. Fischhoff, P. Slovic, and S. Lichtenstein, "Knowing with Certainty: The Appropriateness of Extreme Confidence," *Journal of Experimental Psychology: Human Perception and Performance* (November 1977), pp. 552–564.

44. J. Kruger and D. Dunning, "Unskilled and Unaware of It: How Difficulties in Recognizing One's Own Incompetence Lead to Inflated Self-Assessments," *Journal of Personality and Social Psychology* (November 1999), pp. 1121–1134; and R. P. Larrick, K. A. Burson, and J. B. Soll, "Social Comparison and Confidence: When Thinking You're Better than Average Predicts Overconfidence (and When It Does Not)" *Organizational Behavior and Human Decision Processes* 102 (2007), pp. 76–94.

45. K. M. Hmieleski and R. A. Baron, "Entrepreneurs' Optimism and New Venture Performance: A Social Cognitive Perspective," *Academy of Management Journal* 52, no. 3 (2009), pp. 473–488.

46. R. Frick and A. K. Smith, "Overconfidence Game," *Kiplinger's Personal Finance* 64, no. 3 (2010), p. 23.

47. See, for instance, J. P. Simmons, R. A. LeBoeuf, and L. D. Nelson, "The Effect of Accuracy Motivation on Anchoring and Adjustment: Do People Adjust from Their Provided Anchors?" *Journal of Personality and Social Psychology* 99 (2010), pp. 917–932.

48. J. Bailey, "Dreams Fly Into Reality," *The New York Times* (April 10, 2008), pp. B1, B4.

49. C. Janiszewski and D. Uy, "Precision of the Anchor Influences the Amount of Adjustment," *Psychological Science* 19, no. 2 (2008), pp. 121–127.

50. See E. Jonas, S. Schultz-Hardt, D. Frey, and N. Thelen, "Confirmation Bias in Sequential Information Search after Preliminary Decisions," *Journal of Personality and Social Psychology* (April 2001), pp. 557–571; and W. Hart, D. Albarracín, A. H. Eagly, I. Brechan, M. Lindberg, and L. Merrill, "Feeling Validated Versus Being Correct: A Meta-Analysis of Selective Exposure to Information," *Psychological Bulletin* 135 (2009), pp. 555–588.

51. See A. Tversky and D. Kahneman, "Availability: A Heuristic for Judging Frequency and Probability," in D. Kahneman,

P. Slovic, and A. Tversky (eds.), *Judgment Under Uncertainty: Heuristics and Biases* (Cambridge, UK: Cambridge University Press, 1982), pp. 163–178; and B. J. Bushman and G. L. Wells, "Narrative Impressions of Literature: The Availability Bias and the Corrective Properties of Meta-Analytic Approaches," *Personality and Social Psychology Bulletin* (September 2001), pp. 1123–1130.

52. G. Morgenson, "Debt Watchdogs: Tamed or Caught Napping?" *The New York Times* (December 7, 2009), pp. 1, 32.

53. See B. M. Staw, "The Escalation of Commitment to a Course of Action," *Academy of Management Review* (October 1981), pp. 577–587; K. Fai, E. Wong, M. Yik, and J. Y. Y. Kwong, "Understanding the Emotional Aspects of Escalation of Commitment: The Role of Negative Affect," *Journal of Applied Psychology* 91, no. 2 (2006), pp. 282–297; and A. Zardkoohi, "Do Real Options Lead to Escalation of Commitment? Comment," *Academy of Management Review* (January 2004), pp. 111–119.

54. B. M. Staw, "Knee-Deep in the Big Muddy: A Study of Escalating Commitment to a Chosen Course of Action," *Organizational Behavior and Human Performance* 16 (1976), pp. 27–44; and S. Schulz-Hardt, B. Thurow Kröning, and D. Frey, "Preference-Based Escalation: A New Interpretation for the Responsibility Effect in Escalating Commitment and Entrapment," *Organizational Behavior and Human Decision Processes* 108 (2009), pp. 175–186.

55. K. F. E. Wong and J. Y. Y. Kwong, "The Role of Anticipated Regret in Escalation of Commitment," *Journal of Applied Psychology* 92, no. 2 (2007), pp. 545–554.

56. K. F. E. Wong, J. Y. Y. Kwong, and C. K. Ng, "When Thinking Rationally Increases Biases: The Role of Rational Thinking Style in Escalation of Commitment," *Applied Psychology: An International Review* 57, no. 2 (2008), pp. 246–271.

57. See, for instance, A. James and A. Wells, "Death Beliefs, Superstitious Beliefs and Health Anxiety," *British Journal of Clinical Psychology* (March 2002), pp. 43–53; and U. Hahn and P. A. Warren, "Perceptions of Randomness: Why Three Heads Are Better than One," *Psychological Review* 116 (2009), pp. 454–461.

58. See, for example, D. J. Keys and B. Schwartz, "Leaky Rationality: How Research on Behavioral Decision Making Challenges Normative Standards of Rationality," *Psychological Science* 2, no. 2 (2007), pp. 162–180; and U. Simonsohn, "Direct Risk Aversion: Evidence from Risky Prospects Valued Below Their Worst Outcome," *Psychological Science* 20, no. 6 (2009), pp. 686–692.

59. J. K. Maner, M. T. Gailliot, D. A. Butz, and B. M. Peruche, "Power, Risk, and the Status Quo: Does Power Promote Riskier or More Conservative Decision Making," *Personality and Social Psychology Bulletin* 33, no. 4 (2007), pp. 451–462.

60. A. Chakraborty, S. Sheikh, and N. Subramanian, "Termination Risk and Managerial Risk Taking," *Journal of Corporate Finance* 13 (2007), pp. 170–188.

61. X. He and V. Mittal, "The Effect of Decision Risk and Project Stage on Escalation of Commitment," *Organizational Behavior and Human Decision Processes* 103, no. 2 (2007), pp. 225–237.

62. D. Kahneman and A. Tversky, "Prospect Theory: An Analysis of Decisions Under Risk," *Econometrica* 47, no. 2 (1979), pp. 263–291; and P. Bryant and R. Dunford, "The Influence of Regulatory Focus on Risky Decision-Making,"

Applied Psychology: An International Review 57, no. 2 (2008), pp. 335–359.

63. A. J. Porcelli and M. R. Delgado, "Acute Stress Modulates Risk Taking in Financial Decision Making," *Psychological Science* 20, no. 3 (2009), pp. 278–283.

64. R. L. Guilbault, F. B. Bryant, J. H. Brockway, and E. J. Posavac, "A Meta-Analysis of Research on Hindsight Bias," *Basic and Applied Social Psychology* (September 2004), pp. 103–117; and L. Werth, F. Strack, and J. Foerster, "Certainty and Uncertainty: The Two Faces of the Hindsight Bias," *Organizational Behavior and Human Decision Processes* (March 2002), pp. 323–341.

65. J. Bell, "The Final Cut?" *Oregon Business* 33, no. 5 (2010), p. 27.

66. E. Dash and J. Creswell, "Citigroup Pays for a Rush to Risk," *The New York Times* (November 20, 2008), pp. 1, 28; S. Pulliam, S. Ng, and R. Smith, "Merrill Upped Ante as Boom in Mortgage Bonds Fizzled," *The Wall Street Journal* (April 16, 2008), pp. A1, A14; and M. Gladwell, "Connecting the Dots," *The New Yorker* (March 10, 2003).

67. This section is based on T. Gärling, E. Kirchler, A. Lewis, and F. van Raaij, "Psychology, Financial Decision Making, and Financial Crises," *Psychological Science in the Public Interest* 10 (2009), pp.1–47; T. Zaleskiewicz, "Financial Forecasts During the Crisis: Were Experts More Accurate than Laypeople?" *Journal of Economic Psychology* 32 (2011), pp. 384–390; and G. A. Akerlof and R. J. Shiller, *Animal Spirits: How Human Psychology Drives the Economy and Why It Matters for Global Capitalism* (Princeton, NJ: Princeton University Press, 2009).

68. H. Moon, J. R. Hollenbeck, S. E. Humphrey, and B. Maue, "The Tripartite Model of Neuroticism and the Suppression of Depression and Anxiety within an Escalation of Commitment Dilemma," *Journal of Personality* 71 (2003), pp. 347–368; and H. Moon, "The Two Faces of Conscientiousness: Duty and Achievement Striving in Escalation of Commitment Dilemmas," *Journal of Applied Psychology* 86 (2001), pp. 535–540.

69. J. Musch, "Personality Differences in Hindsight Bias," *Memory* 11 (2003), pp. 473–489.

70. W. K. Campbell and C. Sedikides, "Self-Threat Magnifies the Self-Serving Bias: A Meta-Analytic Integration," *Review of General Psychology* 3 (1999), pp. 23–43.

71. This section is based on S. Nolen-Hoeksema, J. Larson, and C. Grayson, "Explaining the Gender Difference in Depressive Symptoms," *Journal of Personality & Social Psychology* (November 1999), pp. 1061–1072; and J. S. Hyde, A. H. Mezulis, and L. Y. Abramson, "The ABCs of Depression: Integrating Affective, Biological, and Cognitive Models to Explain the Emergence of the Gender Difference in Depression," *Psychological Review* 115, no. 2 (2008), pp. 291–313.

72. H. Connery and K. M. Davidson, "A Survey of Attitudes to Depression in the General Public: A Comparison of Age and Gender Differences," *Journal of Mental Health* 15, no. 2 (April 2006), pp. 179–189.

73. M. Elias, "Thinking It Over, and Over, and Over," *USA Today* (February 6, 2003), p. 10D.

74. K. E. Stanovich and R. F. West, "On the Relative Independence of Thinking Biases and Cognitive Ability,"

Journal of Personality and Social Psychology 94, no. 4 (2008), pp. 672–695.

75. N. J. Adler, *International Dimensions of Organizational Behavior*, 4th ed. (Cincinnati, OH: South-Western Publishing, 2002), pp. 182–189.

76. A. Wildavsky, *The Politics of the Budgetary Process* (Boston: Little, Brown, 1964).

77. G. F. Cavanagh, D. J. Moberg, and M. Valasquez, "The Ethics of Organizational Politics," *Academy of Management Journal* (June 1981), pp. 363–374.

78. See, for example, T. Machan, ed., *Commerce and Morality* (Totowa, NJ: Rowman and Littlefield, 1988).

79. T. M. Amabile, "A Model of Creativity and Innovation in Organizations," in B. M. Staw and L. L. Cummings (eds.), *Research in Organizational Behavior*, vol. 10 (Greenwich, CT: JAI Press, 1988), p. 126; and J. E. Perry-Smith and C. E. Shalley, "The Social Side of Creativity: A Static and Dynamic Social Network Perspective," *Academy of Management Review* (January 2003), pp. 89–106.

80. G. J. Feist and F. X. Barron, "Predicting Creativity from Early to Late Adulthood: Intellect, Potential, and Personality," *Journal of Research in Personality* (April 2003), pp. 62–88.

81. R. W. Woodman, J. E. Sawyer, and R. W. Griffin, "Toward a Theory of Organizational Creativity," *Academy of Management Review* (April 1993), p. 298; J. M. George and J. Zhou, "When Openness to Experience and Conscientiousness Are Related to Creative Behavior: An Interactional Approach," *Journal of Applied Psychology* (June 2001), pp. 513–524; and E. F. Rietzschel, C. K. W. de Dreu, and B. A. Nijstad, "Personal Need for Structure and Creative Performance: The Moderating Influence of Fear of Invalidity," *Personality and Social Psychology Bulletin* (June 2007), pp. 855–866.

82. A. K. Leung, W. W. Maddux, A. D. Galinsky, and C. Chiu, "Multicultural Experience Enhances Creativity," *American Psychologist* 63, no. 3 (2008), pp. 169–180.

83. Cited in C. G. Morris, *Psychology: An Introduction*, 9th ed. (Upper Saddle River, NJ: Prentice Hall, 1996), p. 344.

84. This section is based on T. M. Amabile, "Motivating Creativity in Organizations: On Doing What You Love and Loving What You Do," *California Management Review* 40, no. 1 (Fall 1997), pp. 39–58.

85. M. Baas, C. K. W. De Dreu, and B. A. Nijstad, "A Meta-Analysis of 25 Years of Mood-Creativity Research: Hedonic Tone, Activation, or Regulatory Focus?" *Psychological Bulletin* 134, no. 6 (2008), pp. 779–806.

86. J. Zhou, "When the Presence of Creative Coworkers Is Related to Creativity: Role of Supervisor Close Monitoring, Developmental Feedback, and Creative Personality," *Journal of Applied Psychology* 88, no. 3 (June 2003), pp. 413–422.

87. J. E. Perry-Smith, "Social yet Creative: The Role of Social Relationships in Facilitating Individual Creativity," *Academy of Management Journal* 49, no. 1 (2006), pp. 85–101.

88. G. Park, D. Lubinski, and C. P. Benbow, "Contrasting Intellectual Patterns Predict Creativity in the Arts and Sciences," *Psychological Science* 18, no. 11 (2007), pp. 948–952.

89. W. J. J. Gordon, *Synectics* (New York: Harper & Row, 1961).

90. See C. E. Shalley, J. Zhou, and G. R. Oldham, "The Effects of Personal and Contextual Characteristics on Creativity: Where Should We Go from Here?" *Journal of Management* (November 2004), pp. 933–958; G. Hirst, D. Van Knippenberg, and J. Zhou, "A Cross-Level Perspective on Employee Creativity: Goal Orientation, Team Learning Behavior, and Individual Creativity," *Academy of Management Journal* 52, no. 2 (2009), pp. 280–293; and C. E. Shalley, L. L. Gilson, and T. C. Blum, "Interactive Effects of Growth Need Strength, Work Context, and Job Complexity on Self-Reported Creative Performance," *Academy of Management Journal* 52, no. 3 (2009), pp. 489–505.

91. T. Jackson, "Cultural Values and Management Ethics: A 10-Nation Study," *Human Relations* (October 2001), pp. 1267–1302; see also J. B. Cullen, K. P. Parboteeah, and M. Hoegl, "Cross-National Differences in Managers' Willingness to Justify Ethically Suspect Behaviors: A Test of Institutional Anomie Theory," *Academy of Management Journal* (June 2004), pp. 411–421.

92. W. Chow Hou, "To Bribe or Not to Bribe?" *Asia, Inc.* (October 1996), p. 104.

93. P. Digh, "Shades of Gray in the Global Marketplace," *HRMagazine* (April 1997), p. 91.

MyManagementLab

Access a host of interactive learning aids to help strengthen your understanding of the chapter concepts at **www.mymanagementlab.com**.

THE MOTIVATIONS OF THE 99ERS

While the economy shows signs of improving, the sluggish nature of the recovery has left behind more long-term unemployed than anyone has seen since the Great Depression.

Typically, unemployment insurance lasts 6 months. As the great recession continued, Congress extended these benefits—up to 99 weeks for those in 27 states hit hardest by the recession.

The 99ers are those who have been unemployed more than 99 weeks. They number about 2 million, and millions more are underemployed or have withdrawn from the labor market altogether. Among the hardest hit are older workers who struggle to convince employers to hire them.

St. Louis resident Peter Gordon, 53, has been unemployed more than a year. Once he becomes a 99er, his unemployment check will run out. "I will be OK for another 20 weeks," Gordon said. "But I'm going crazy." Akron's Susan Harrell has been jobless more than 2 years and has exhausted her unemployment benefits. Laid off from her $60,000/year telecommunications job, she finds employers unwilling to hire her because she is unemployed, 58, or both. "They look at me and say, 'How long are you really going to work?'"

Should the government help those in need by extending unemployment benefits further? The question is complicated and divides Republicans and Democrats. But put aside ideology for a moment, and consider the motivational dynamics at play. Many have lost their jobs through no fault of their own. Not only are unemployment benefits compassionate, they provide an opportunity for people to retrain for a new occupation. Benefits thus motivate them to move into more viable occupations.

On the other hand, many economists argue that extending benefits provides disincentives for finding employment. One concludes, "Unemployment insurance is not free: It results in less employment and less output, not more." Paying people not to work gives them incentives not to work, this argument goes.

Our nation will probably never agree on the motivational effects of unemployment insurance. However, with or without insurance, there is troubling evidence that some individuals like Peter Gordon and Susan Harrell will remain out of work for a very long time. "This is horrible," says Harrell. "It's embarrassing and humiliating."

Sources: W. M. Welch, "Long-Term Unemployed See Benefits Rolled Back," *USA Today* (May 17, 2011), p. A1; D. Hunsinger, Long-Term Unemployed Face Stigmas in Job Search," *USA Today* (January 23, 2011), downloaded May 2, 2011, from www.usatoday.com/money/; M. Thornton, "99ers and the Long-term Unemployed Are the Elephants in the Economic Recovery Room," *Huffington Post* (May 15, 2011), downloaded May 25, 2011, from www.huffingtonpost.com/; C. B. Mulligan, "Do Jobless Benefits Discourage People From Finding Jobs?" *New York Times* (March 17, 2010), downloaded May 2, 2011, from http://economix.blogs.nytimes.com/.

Motivation Concepts

Luke: *"I don't believe it."*
Yoda: *"That is why you fail."*

—The Empire Strikes Back

Debates about motivation can occupy a central role in important public policy debates, and as we will see, they also rank among the most important questions managers need to answer.

However, motivation is not simply about working hard—it also reflects your view of your own abilities. Try a self-assessment of your confidence in your ability to succeed.

Motivation is one of the most frequently researched topics in OB.[1] A recent Gallup poll revealed one reason—a majority of U.S. employees (54 percent) are not actively engaged in their work, and another portion (17 percent) are actively disengaged.[2] In another study, workers reported wasting roughly 2 hours per day, not counting lunch and scheduled breaks (usually Internet surfing and talking with co-workers).[3] Clearly, motivation is an issue. The good news is that all this research provides useful insights into how to improve it.

In this chapter, we'll review the basics of motivation, assess motivation theories, and provide an integrative model that fits the best of these theories together.

SELF-ASSESSMENT LIBRARY

How Confident Am I in My Abilities to Succeed?

In the Self-Assessment Library (available on CD or online), take assessment IV.A.3 (How Confident Am I in My Abilities to Succeed?) and answer the following questions.

1. How did you score relative to other class members? Does that surprise you?
2. Do you think self-confidence is critical to success? Can a person be too confident?

Defining Motivation

1 Describe the three key elements of motivation.

Some individuals seem driven to succeed. But the same student who struggles to read a textbook for more than 20 minutes may devour a *Harry Potter* book in a day. The difference is the situation. So as we analyze the concept of motivation, keep in mind that the level of motivation varies both between individuals and within individuals at different times.

We define **motivation** as the processes that account for an individual's intensity, direction, and persistence of effort toward attaining a goal.[4] While general motivation is concerned with effort toward *any* goal, we'll narrow the focus to *organizational* goals in order to reflect our singular interest in work-related behavior.

The three key elements in our definition are intensity, direction, and persistence. *Intensity* describes how hard a person tries. This is the element most of us focus on when we talk about motivation. However, high intensity is unlikely to lead to favorable job-performance outcomes unless the effort is channeled in a *direction* that benefits the organization. Therefore, we consider the quality of effort as well as its intensity. Effort directed toward, and consistent with, the organization's goals is the kind of effort we should be seeking. Finally, motivation has a *persistence* dimension. This measures how long a person can maintain effort. Motivated individuals stay with a task long enough to achieve their goal.

Early Theories of Motivation

2 Identify early theories of motivation and evaluate their applicability today.

Four theories of employee motivation formulated during the 1950s, although now of questionable validity, are probably still the best known. We discuss more valid explanations later, but these four represent a foundation on which they have grown, and practicing managers still use them and their terminology.

Hierarchy of Needs Theory

The best-known theory of motivation is Abraham Maslow's **hierarchy of needs**.[5] Maslow hypothesized that within every human being, there exists a hierarchy of five needs:

1. **Physiological.** Includes hunger, thirst, shelter, sex, and other bodily needs.
2. **Safety.** Security and protection from physical and emotional harm.
3. **Social.** Affection, belongingness, acceptance, and friendship.
4. **Esteem.** Internal factors such as self-respect, autonomy, and achievement, and external factors such as status, recognition, and attention.
5. **Self-actualization.** Drive to become what we are capable of becoming; includes growth, achieving our potential, and self-fulfillment.

Although no need is ever fully gratified, a substantially satisfied need no longer motivates. Thus as each becomes substantially satisfied, the next one becomes dominant. So if you want to motivate someone, according to Maslow, you need to understand what level of the hierarchy that person is currently on and focus on satisfying needs at or above that level, moving up the steps in Exhibit 7-1.

Maslow separated the five needs into higher and lower orders. Physiological and safety needs, where the theory says people start, were **lower-order needs**,

Exhibit **7-1**   Maslow's Hierarchy of Needs

Self-actualization
Esteem
Social
Safety
Physiological

Source: A. H. Maslow, Motivation and Personality, 3rd ed., R. D. Frager and J. Fadiman (eds.). © 1997. Adapted by permission of Pearson Education, Inc., Upper Saddle River, New Jersey.

motivation *The processes that account for an individual's intensity, direction, and persistence of effort toward attaining a goal.*

hierarchy of needs *Abraham Maslow's hierarchy of five needs—physiological, safety, social, esteem, and self-actualization—in which, as each need is substantially satisfied, the next need becomes dominant.*

lower-order needs *Needs that are satisfied externally, such as physiological and safety needs.*

"The Support of Others Improves Our Chances of Accomplishing Our Goals"

Surprisingly, this statement appears to be false.

There is some research on how team goals facilitate team performance. However, until recently, we knew very little about whether others help or hinder our individual chances of meeting a goal.

Generally, whether it's reaching a weight loss goal, successfully completing an undergraduate course, or completing a work task, help and support from others actually appears to hinder our chances and make us feel worse rather than better.

Why? First, research has found that help is often, well, unhelpful. Advice and direction from others is seldom well suited for accomplishing our goal. If you're trying to meet a work deadline using your approach, it's not often useful for a co-worker to advise you to use his or her method instead. Second, such advice and assistance generally makes us feel less confident and positive about achieving the goal. The more help is offered, the more negative feelings and stress we have about the goal.

The upshot? Generally, you'll do a better job of meeting your individual work goals if you "just do it" by yourself. Of course, sometimes you do need the help of others. But keep that help focused on specific questions and not on advice for attaining the general goal.

_____

Sources: H. B. Kappes and P. E. Shrout, "When Goal Sharing Produces Support That Is Not Caring," *Personality and Social Psychology Bulletin* 37, no. 5 (2011), pp. 662–673; P. E. Shrout, N. Bolger, M. Iida, C. Burke, M. E. Gleason, and S. P. Lane, "The Effects of Daily Support Transactions During Acute Stress: Results from a Diary Study of Bar Exam Preparation," in K. Sullivan and J. Davila (Eds.), *Support Processes in Intimate Relationships* (New York: Oxford University Press, 2010), pp. 175–199.

and social, esteem, and **self-actualization** were **higher-order needs**. Higher-order needs are satisfied internally (within the person), whereas lower-order needs are predominantly satisfied externally (by things such as pay, union contracts, and tenure).

The hierarchy, if it applies at all, aligns with U.S. culture. In Japan, Greece, and Mexico, where uncertainty-avoidance characteristics are strong, security needs would be on top of the hierarchy. Countries that score high on nurturing characteristics—Denmark, Sweden, Norway, the Netherlands, and Finland—would have social needs on top.[6] Group work will motivate employees more when the country's culture scores high on the nurturing criterion.

Maslow's theory has received wide recognition, particularly among practicing managers. It is intuitively logical and easy to understand. When introduced, it provided a compelling alternative to behaviorist theories that posited only physiological and safety needs as important. Unfortunately, however, research does not validate it. Maslow provided no empirical substantiation, and several studies that sought to validate it found no support for it.[7] There is little evidence that need structures are organized as Maslow proposed, that unsatisfied needs motivate, or that a satisfied need activates movement to a new need level.[8] But old theories, especially intuitively logical ones, apparently die hard.

Some researchers have attempted to revive components of the need hierarchy concept, using principles from evolutionary psychology.[9] They propose that lower-level needs are the chief concern of immature animals or those with primitive nervous systems, whereas higher needs are more frequently observed in mature animals with more developed nervous systems. They also note distinct underlying biological systems for different types of needs. Time will tell whether these revisions to Maslow's hierarchy will be useful to practicing managers.

Theory X and Theory Y

Douglas McGregor proposed two distinct views of human beings: one basically negative, labeled Theory X, and the other basically positive, labeled Theory Y.[10] After studying managers' dealings with employees, McGregor concluded that their views of the nature of human beings are based on certain assumptions that mold their behavior.

Under **Theory X**, managers believe employees inherently dislike work and must therefore be directed or even coerced into performing it. Under **Theory Y**, in contrast, managers assume employees can view work as being as natural as rest or play, and therefore the average person can learn to accept, and even seek, responsibility.

To understand more fully, think in terms of Maslow's hierarchy. Theory Y assumes higher-order needs dominate individuals. McGregor himself believed Theory Y assumptions were more valid than Theory X. Therefore, he proposed such ideas as participative decision making, responsible and challenging jobs, and good group relations to maximize an employee's job motivation.

Unfortunately, no evidence confirms that *either* set of assumptions is valid or that acting on Theory Y assumptions will lead to more motivated workers. OB theories need empirical support before we can accept them. Theory X and Theory Y lack such support as much as the hierarchy of needs.

Two-Factor Theory

Believing an individual's relationship to work is basic, and that attitude toward work can determine success or failure, psychologist Frederick Herzberg wondered, "What do people want from their jobs?" He asked people to describe, in detail, situations in which they felt exceptionally *good* or *bad* about their jobs. The responses differed significantly and led Hertzberg to his **two-factor theory**—also called *motivation-hygiene theory*.[11]

As shown in Exhibit 7-2, intrinsic factors such as advancement, recognition, responsibility, and achievement seem related to job satisfaction. Respondents who felt good about their work tended to attribute these factors to themselves, while dissatisfied respondents tended to cite extrinsic factors, such as supervision, pay, company policies, and working conditions.

To Hertzberg, the data suggest that the opposite of satisfaction is not dissatisfaction, as was traditionally believed. Removing dissatisfying characteristics from a job does not necessarily make the job satisfying. As illustrated in Exhibit 7-3, Herzberg proposed a dual continuum: The opposite of "satisfaction" is "no satisfaction," and the opposite of "dissatisfaction" is "no dissatisfaction."

According to Herzberg, the factors that lead to job satisfaction are separate and distinct from those that lead to job dissatisfaction. Therefore, managers who seek to eliminate factors that can create job dissatisfaction may bring about peace, but not necessarily motivation. They will be placating rather than motivating their workers. As a result, Herzberg characterized conditions such as quality of supervision, pay, company policies, physical working conditions, relationships with others, and job security as **hygiene factors**. When they're

---

self-actualization   *The drive to become what a person is capable of becoming.*

higher-order needs   *Needs that are satisfied internally, such as social, esteem, and self-actualization needs.*

Theory X   *The assumption that employees dislike work, are lazy, dislike responsibility, and must be coerced to perform.*

Theory Y   *The assumption that employees like work, are creative, seek responsibility, and can exercise self-direction.*

two-factor theory   *A theory that relates intrinsic factors to job satisfaction and associates extrinsic factors with dissatisfaction. Also called motivation-hygiene theory.*

hygiene factors   *Factors—such as company policy and administration, supervision, and salary—that, when adequate in a job, placate workers. When these factors are adequate, people will not be dissatisfied.*

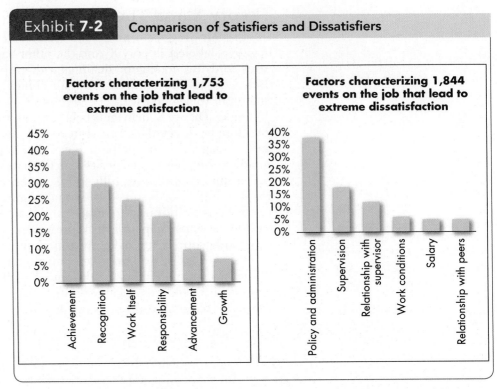

Exhibit **7-2**   Comparison of Satisfiers and Dissatisfiers

Factors characterizing 1,753 events on the job that lead to extreme satisfaction

Factors characterizing 1,844 events on the job that lead to extreme dissatisfaction

Exhibit **7-3**   Contrasting View of Satisfaction and Dissatisfaction

Traditional view

Satisfaction   Dissatisfaction

Herzberg's view

Motivators

Satisfaction   No satisfaction

Hygiene factors

No dissatisfaction   Dissatisfaction

adequate, people will not be dissatisfied; neither will they be satisfied. If we want to *motivate* people on their jobs, Herzberg suggested emphasizing factors associated with the work itself or with outcomes directly derived from it, such as promotional opportunities, personal growth opportunities, recognition, responsibility, and achievement. These are the characteristics people find intrinsically rewarding.

The two-factor theory has not been well supported in the literature, and it has many detractors.[12] Criticisms include the following:

1. Herzberg's methodology is limited because it relies on self-reports. When things are going well, people tend to take credit. Contrarily, they blame failure on the extrinsic environment.
2. The reliability of Herzberg's methodology is questionable. Raters have to make interpretations, so they may contaminate the findings by interpreting one response in one manner while treating a similar response differently.
3. No overall measure of satisfaction was utilized. A person may dislike part of a job yet still think the job is acceptable overall.
4. Herzberg assumed a relationship between satisfaction and productivity, but he looked only at satisfaction. To make his research relevant, we must assume a strong relationship between satisfaction and productivity.

Regardless of the criticisms, Herzberg's theory has been widely read, and few managers are unfamiliar with its recommendations.

McClelland's Theory of Needs

You have one beanbag and five targets set up in front of you, each farther away than the last. Target A sits almost within arm's reach. If you hit it, you get $2. Target B is a bit farther out, but about 80 percent of the people who try can hit it. It pays $4. Target C pays $8, and about half the people who try can hit it. Very few people can hit Target D, but the payoff is $16 for those who do. Finally, Target E pays $32, but it's almost impossible to achieve. Which would you try for? If you selected C, you're likely to be a high achiever. Why? Read on.

McClelland's theory of needs was developed by David McClelland and his associates.[13] It looks at three needs:

- **Need for achievement (nAch)** is the drive to excel, to achieve in relationship to a set of standards.
- **Need for power (nPow)** is the need to make others behave in a way they would not have otherwise.
- **Need for affiliation (nAff)** is the desire for friendly and close interpersonal relationships.

McClelland and subsequent researchers focused most of their attention on nAch. High achievers perform best when they perceive their probability of success as 0.5—that is, a 50–50 chance. They dislike gambling with high odds because they get no achievement satisfaction from success that comes by pure chance. Similarly, they dislike low odds (high probability of success) because then there is no challenge to their skills. They like to set goals that require stretching themselves a little.

Relying on an extensive amount of research, we can predict some relationships between achievement need and job performance. First, when jobs have a high degree of personal responsibility and feedback and an intermediate degree of risk, high achievers are strongly motivated. They are successful in

Source: Seth Wenig/AP Images

As a high achiever, Patricia Woertz is motivated by work that demands a high degree of personal responsibility. Today, she is the CEO, president, and chair of Archer Daniels Midland, an agricultural food processing business. She started her career as a certified public accountant but was attracted to the complexity and opportunity of global energy. For the next 30 years she worked for Gulf Oil and Chevron in refining, marketing, strategic planning, and finance positions. Since joining ADM, Woertz continues to shift company resources toward fuel production in a drive to accelerate ADM's global leadership in bioenergy and has led the company to record financial results.

McClelland's theory of needs *A theory that states achievement, power, and affiliation are three important needs that help explain motivation.*

need for achievement (nAch) *The drive to excel, to achieve in relationship to a set of standards, and to strive to succeed.*

need for power (nPow) *The need to make others behave in a way in which they would not have behaved otherwise.*

need for affiliation (nAff) *The desire for friendly and close interpersonal relationships.*

entrepreneurial activities such as running their own businesses, for example, and managing self-contained units within large organizations.[14] Second, a high need to achieve does not necessarily make someone a good manager, especially in large organizations. People with a high achievement need are interested in how well they do personally, and not in influencing others to do well. High-nAch salespeople do not necessarily make good sales managers, and the good general manager in a large organization does not typically have a high need to achieve.[15] Third, needs for affiliation and power tend to be closely related to managerial success. The best managers are high in their need for power and low in their need for affiliation.[16] In fact, a high power motive may be a requirement for managerial effectiveness.[17]

The view that a high achievement need acts as an internal motivator presupposes two U.S. cultural characteristics—willingness to accept a moderate degree of risk (which excludes countries with strong uncertainty-avoidance characteristics) and concern with performance (which applies to countries with strong achievement characteristics). This combination is found in Anglo-American countries such as the United States, Canada, and Great Britain[18] and much less in Chile and Portugal.

Among the early theories of motivation, McClelland's has had the best research support. Unfortunately, it has less practical effect than the others. Because McClelland argued that the three needs are subconscious—we may rank high on them but not know it—measuring them is not easy. In the most common approach, a trained expert presents pictures to individuals, asks them to tell a story about each, and then scores their responses in terms of the three needs. However, the process is time consuming and expensive, and few organizations have been willing to invest in measuring McClelland's concept.

Contemporary Theories of Motivation

Early theories of motivation either have not held up under close examination or have fallen out of favor. In contrast, contemporary theories have one thing in common: each has a reasonable degree of valid supporting documentation. This doesn't mean they are unquestionably right. We call them "contemporary theories" because they represent the current state of thinking in explaining employee motivation.

Self-Determination Theory

3 Apply the predictions of self-determination theory to intrinsic and extrinsic rewards.

"It's strange," said Marcia. "I started work at the Humane Society as a volunteer. I put in 15 hours a week helping people adopt pets. And I loved coming to work. Then, 3 months ago, they hired me full-time at $11 an hour. I'm doing the same work I did before. But I'm not finding it nearly as much fun."

Does Marcia's reaction seem counterintuitive? There's an explanation for it. It's called **self-determination theory**, which proposes that people prefer to feel they have control over their actions, so anything that makes a previously enjoyed task feel more like an obligation than a freely chosen activity will undermine motivation.[19] Much research on self-determination theory in OB has focused on **cognitive evaluation theory**, which hypothesizes that extrinsic rewards will reduce intrinsic interest in a task. When people are paid for work, it feels less like something they *want* to do and more like something they *have* to do. Self-determination theory also proposes that in addition to being driven

Motivated to Behave Unethically

The popular press often reports about ethical lapses in business by focusing on employees and managers who are "loose cannons," deviating from organizational rules and norms to produce bad consequences for society and business. However, sometimes unethical behavior is not just ignored by organizational leaders but actively encouraged by the company's motivational structures. In fact, one survey found that 56 percent of U.S. workers experience pressure from their superiors to behave in an unethical manner. Craig E. Johnson sums up the problem, noting, "Examine nearly any corporate scandal—AIG Insurance, Arthur Andersen, Enron, Health South, Sotheby's Auction House, Fannie Mae, Hollinger International, Marsh & McLennan, Quest—and you'll find leaders who engaged in immoral behavior and encouraged their followers to do the same."

How do managers create pressure to behave unethically? Management scholar Ben Tepper notes that structures in place in organizations often encourage unethical behavior. Incentives might go to individuals who maximize sales without regard to whether they achieved these ends honestly. Lawyers often are paid in such a way that tacitly encourages them to overbill their clients. Or perhaps rewards might be offered for producing products at low cost without considering the social and environmental impacts of production decisions. In all these cases, the reward systems in place in organizations can serve to motivate unethical behavior.

So what can you do as a manager or employee to confront these powerful motivations to behave unethically? First and foremost, decision makers should consider the unintended consequences of reward systems. Second, top management should foster an organizational culture of honesty and fair dealing and disseminate it through all levels of the organizational hierarchy. Finally, organizations might even consider finding ways to explicitly reward those employees who engage in "above and beyond" instances of ethical behavior.

Sources: B. J. Tepper, "When Managers Pressure Employees to Behave Badly: Toward a Comprehensive Response," *Business Horizons* 53, no. 6 (2010), pp. 591–598; C. E. Johnson, *Meeting the Ethical Challenges of Leadership: Casting Light or Shadow,* 3rd ed. (San Francisco: Sage, 2009).

by a need for autonomy, people seek ways to achieve competence and positive connections to others. A large number of studies support self-determination theory.[20] As we'll show, its major implications relate to work rewards.

When organizations use extrinsic rewards as payoffs for superior performance, employees feel they are doing a good job less because of their own intrinsic desire to excel than because that's what the organization wants. Eliminating extrinsic rewards can also shift an individual's perception of why she works on a task from an external to an internal explanation. If you're reading a novel a week because your English literature instructor requires you to, you can attribute your reading behavior to an external source. However, if you find yourself continuing to read a novel a week after the course is over, your natural inclination is to say, "I must enjoy reading novels because I'm still reading one a week."

Studies examining how extrinsic rewards increased motivation for some creative tasks suggest we might need to place cognitive evaluation theory's predictions in a broader context.[21] Goal-setting is more effective in improving

self-determination theory   *A theory of motivation that is concerned with the beneficial effects of intrinsic motivation and the harmful effects of extrinsic motivation.*

cognitive evaluation theory   *A version of self-determination theory which holds that allocating extrinsic rewards for behavior that had been previously intrinsically rewarding tends to decrease the overall level of motivation if the rewards are seen as controlling.*

glOBalization!

Autonomy Needs Around the Globe

Much of the research we have presented on needs for autonomy and self-determination has been conducted in the United States and Canada, two countries that place a high value on personal independence and freedom of choice. But some researchers question whether a need for autonomy is universal or whether some cultures foster a greater need for relatedness.

Some research does suggest universal needs for autonomy, while other studies find that different cultures see autonomy differently. In a survey of 40 nations, collectivistic countries valued social order, obedience, and respect for tradition more, and within cultures, individuals who value autonomy tend to put less value on social connectedness and vice versa.

In a study with Chinese Canadian and European Canadian participants, those from Chinese culture expressed lower levels of autonomy, but autonomy was related to well-being for both Chinese and European respondents. Although different cultures view their autonomy differently, it appears people across cultures are higher in well-being when they perceive they have freedom of choice.

Sources: C. Vauclair, K. Hanke, R. Fischer, and J. Fontaine, "The Structure of Human Values at the Culture Level: A Meta-Analytical Replication of Schwartz's Value Orientations Using the Rokeach Value Survey," *Journal of Cross-Cultural Psychology* 42, no. 2 (2011), pp. 186–205; and D. Rudy, K. M. Sheldon, T. Awong, and H. H. Tan, "Autonomy, Culture, and Well-Being: The Benefits of Inclusive Autonomy," *Journal of Research in Personality* 41, no. 5 (2007), pp. 983–1007.

motivation, for instance, when we provide rewards for achieving the goals. The original authors of self-determination theory acknowledge that extrinsic rewards such as verbal praise and feedback about competence can improve even intrinsic motivation under specific circumstances. Deadlines and specific work standards do, too, if people believe they are in control of their behavior.[22] This is consistent with the central theme of self-determination theory: rewards and deadlines diminish motivation if people see them as coercive.

What does self-determination theory suggest for providing rewards? If a senior sales representative really enjoys selling and making the deal, a commission indicates she's been doing a good job and increases her sense of competence by providing feedback that could improve intrinsic motivation. On the other hand, if a computer programmer values writing code because she likes to solve problems, a reward for working to an externally imposed standard she does not accept, such as writing a certain number of lines of code every day, could feel coercive, and her intrinsic motivation would suffer. She would be less interested in the task and might reduce her effort.

A recent outgrowth of self-determination theory is **self-concordance**, which considers how strongly peoples' reasons for pursuing goals are consistent with their interests and core values. If individuals pursue goals because of an intrinsic interest, they are more likely to attain their goals and are happy even if they do not. Why? Because the process of striving toward them is fun. In contrast, people who pursue goals for extrinsic reasons (money, status, or other benefits) are less likely to attain their goals and less happy even when they do. Why? Because the goals are less meaningful to them.[23] OB research suggests that people who pursue work goals for intrinsic reasons are more satisfied with their jobs, feel they fit into their organizations better, and may perform better.[24]

What does all this mean? For individuals, it means choose your job for reasons other than extrinsic rewards. For organizations, it means managers should provide intrinsic as well as extrinsic incentives. They need to make the work interesting, provide recognition, and support employee growth and development. Employees who feel what they do is within their control and a result of free choice are likely to be more motivated by their work and committed to their employers.[25]

Job Engagement

When nurse Melissa Jones comes to work, it seems that everything else in her life goes away, and she becomes completely absorbed in what she is doing. Her emotions, her thoughts, and her behavior are all directed toward patient care. In fact, she can get so caught up in her work that she isn't even aware of how long she's been there. As a result of this total commitment, she is more effective in providing patient care and feels uplifted by her time at work.

Melissa has a high level of **job engagement**, the investment of an employee's physical, cognitive, and emotional energies into job performance.[26] Practicing managers and scholars alike have lately become interested in facilitating job engagement, believing something deeper than liking a job or finding it interesting drives performance. Many studies attempt to measure this deeper level of commitment.

The Gallup organization has been using 12 questions to assess the extent to which employee engagement is linked to positive work outcomes for millions of employees over the past 30 years.[27] There are far more engaged employees in highly successful than in average organizations, and groups with more engaged employees have higher levels of productivity, fewer safety incidents, and lower turnover. Academic studies have also found positive outcomes. One examined multiple business units for their level of engagement and found a

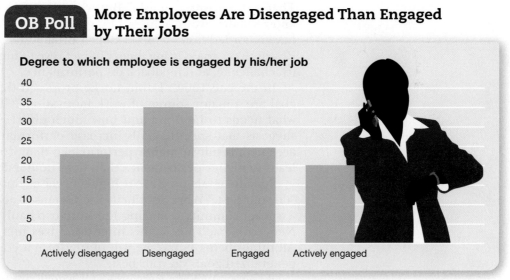

OB Poll   **More Employees Are Disengaged Than Engaged by Their Jobs**

Degree to which employee is engaged by his/her job

Source: A. Fox, "Raising Engagement," *HR Magazine* (May 2010), pp. 35–40; "Gallup's Customer Engagement Index" (March 11, 2010), www.smartKPIs.com.

self-concordance   *The degree to which peoples' reasons for pursuing goals are consistent with their interests and core values.*

job engagement   *The investment of an employee's physical, cognitive, and emotional energies into job performance.*

positive relationship with a variety of practical outcomes.[28] Another reviewed 91 distinct investigations and found higher levels of engagement associated with task performance and citizenship behavior.[29]

What makes people more likely to be engaged in their jobs? One key is the degree to which an employee believes it is meaningful to engage in work. This is partially determined by job characteristics and access to sufficient resources to work effectively.[30] Another factor is a match between the individual's values and those of the organization.[31] Leadership behaviors that inspire workers to a greater sense of mission also increase employee engagement.[32]

One of the critiques of engagement is that the construct is partially redundant with job attitudes like satisfaction or stress.[33] However, engagement questionnaires usually assess motivation and absorption in a task, quite unlike job satisfaction questionnaires. Engagement may also predict important work outcomes better than traditional job attitudes.[34] Other critics note there may be a "dark side" to engagement, as evidenced by positive relationships between engagement and work–family conflict.[35] Individuals might grow so engaged in their work roles that family responsibilities become an unwelcome intrusion. Further research exploring how engagement relates to these negative outcomes may help clarify whether some highly engaged employees might be getting "too much of a good thing."

Goal-Setting Theory

4 Understand the implications of employee engagement for management.

Gene Broadwater, coach of the Hamilton High School cross-country team, gave his squad these last words before they approached the starting line for the league championship race: "Each one of you is physically ready. Now, get out there and do your best. No one can ever ask more of you than that."

You've heard the sentiment a number of times yourself: "Just do your best. That's all anyone can ask." But what does "do your best" mean? Do we ever know whether we've achieved that vague goal? Would the cross-country runners have recorded faster times if Coach Broadwater had given each a specific goal? Research on **goal-setting theory** in fact reveals impressive effects of goal specificity, challenge, and feedback on performance.

In the late 1960s, Edwin Locke proposed that intentions to work toward a goal are a major source of work motivation.[36] That is, goals tell an employee what needs to be done and how much effort is needed.[37] Evidence strongly suggests that specific goals increase performance; that difficult goals, when accepted, result in higher performance than do easy goals; and that feedback leads to higher performance than does nonfeedback.[38]

Specific goals produce a higher level of output than the generalized goal "do your best." Why? Specificity itself seems to act as an internal stimulus. When a trucker commits to making 12 round-trip hauls between Toronto and Buffalo, New York, each week, this intention gives him a specific objective to attain. All things being equal, he will outperform a counterpart with no goals or the generalized goal "do your best."

If factors such as acceptance of the goals are held constant, the more difficult the goal, the higher the level of performance. Of course, it's logical to assume easier goals are more likely to be accepted. But once a hard task is accepted, we can expect the employee to exert a high level of effort to try to achieve it.

But why are people motivated by difficult goals?[39] First, challenging goals get our attention and thus tend to help us focus. Second, difficult goals energize us because we have to work harder to attain them. Do you study as hard for an easy exam as you do for a difficult one? Probably not. Third, when goals are difficult, people persist in trying to attain them. Finally, difficult goals lead us to discover strategies that help us perform the job or task more effectively. If we

Chung Mong-koo, chairman of Hyundai Motor Company, is well known for articulating difficult and specific goals as a potent motivating force. For example, although Hyundai was a latecomer in the development of a hybrid vehicle, the South Korean auto-maker launched its first U.S. hybrid in 2010, with annual sales set at 50,000 units. By 2018, the company expects hybrid sales to balloon to 500,000 units worldwide. Challenging employees to reach high goals has helped Hyundai experience tremendous growth in recent years.

Source: Ahn Young-joon/AP Images

have to struggle to solve a difficult problem, we often think of a better way to go about it.

People do better when they get feedback on how well they are progressing toward their goals, because it helps identify discrepancies between what they have done and what they want to do—that is, feedback guides behavior. But all feedback is not equally potent. Self-generated feedback—with which employees are able to monitor their own progress—is more powerful than externally generated feedback.[40]

If employees can participate in the setting of their own goals, will they try harder? The evidence is mixed.[41] In some cases, participatively set goals yielded superior performance; in others, individuals performed best when assigned goals by their boss. But a major advantage of participation may be that it increases acceptance of the goal as a desirable one toward which to work.[42] Commitment is important. Without participation, the individual assigning the goal needs to clearly explain its purpose and importance.[43]

In addition to feedback, three other factors influence the goals–performance relationship: goal commitment, task characteristics, and national culture.

Goal-setting theory assumes an individual is committed to the goal and determined not to lower or abandon it. The individual (1) believes he or she can achieve the goal and (2) wants to achieve it.[44] Goal commitment is most likely to occur when goals are made public, when the individual has an internal locus of control (see Chapter 4), and when the goals are self-set rather than assigned.[45] Goals themselves seem to affect performance more strongly when tasks are simple rather than complex, well learned rather than novel, and independent rather than interdependent.[46] On interdependent tasks, group goals are preferable.

Finally, setting specific, difficult, individual goals may have different effects in different cultures. Most goal-setting research has been done in the United States and Canada, where individual achievement and performance are most highly valued. To date, research has not shown that group-based

goal-setting theory *A theory that says that specific and difficult goals, with feedback, lead to higher performance.*

goals are more effective in collectivists than in individualist cultures. In collectivistic and high-power-distance cultures, achievable moderate goals can be more highly motivating than difficult ones.[47] Finally, assigned goals appear to generate greater goal commitment in high than in low power-distance cultures.[48] More research is needed to assess how goal constructs might differ across cultures.

Although goal-setting has positive outcomes, some goals may be *too* effective.[49] When learning something is important, goals related to performance undermine adaptation and creativity because people become too focused on outcomes and ignore changing conditions. In this case, a goal to learn and generate alternative solutions will be more effective than a goal to perform. Some authors argue that goals can lead employees to focus on a single standard and exclude all others. Consider the narrow focus on boosting short-term stock prices in many businesses—it may have led organizations to ignore long-term success and even to engage in such unethical behavior as accounting fraud or excessively risky investments. (Of course, organizations can establish goals for ethical performance.) Other studies show that employees low in conscientiousness and emotional stability experience greater emotional exhaustion when their leaders set goals.[50] Despite differences of opinion, most researchers do agree that goals are powerful in shaping behavior. Managers should make sure they are actually aligned with the company's objectives.

Research has begun to examine subconscious goals—that is, goals we are not even aware of setting.[51] One study primed people to think about goals by having them assemble scrambled words into sentences with achievement themes, while other people assembled sentences without achievement themes. The people who made the achievement sentences were subconsciously primed. That might not sound like a very strong manipulation, but this group performed more effectively in a brainstorming task than those given easier goals. Another study found similar results when a picture of a woman winning a race was the subconscious prime rather than assembling sentences. Interestingly, these studies do not find that conscious and subconscious goal-setting are related.

SELF-ASSESSMENT LIBRARY

What Are My Course Performance Goals?

In the Self-Assessment Library (available on CD or online), take assessment I.C.5 (What Are My Course Performance Goals?).

Implementing Goal-Setting   As a manager, how do you make goal-setting theory operational? That's often left up to the individual. Some managers set aggressive performance targets—what General Electric called "stretch goals." Some CEOs, such as Procter & Gamble's A. G. Lafley and SAP AG's Hasso Plattner, are known for the demanding performance goals they set. But many managers don't set goals. When asked whether their job had clearly defined goals, only a minority of employees in a recent survey said yes.[52]

A more systematic way to utilize goal-setting is with **management by objectives (MBO)**, which emphasizes participatively set goals that are tangible, verifiable, and measurable. As in Exhibit 7-4, the organization's overall objectives are translated into specific objectives for each level (divisional,

Exhibit 7-4   Cascading of Objectives

departmental, individual). But because lower-unit managers jointly participate in setting their own goals, MBO works from the bottom up as well as
from the top down. The result is a hierarchy that links objectives at one level
to those at the next. And for the individual employee, MBO provides specific
personal performance objectives.

Four ingredients are common to MBO programs: goal specificity, participation in decision making (including the setting of goals or objectives), an explicit
time period, and performance feedback.[53] Many elements in MBO programs
match propositions of goal-setting theory. For example, having an explicit time
period to accomplish objectives matches goal-setting theory's emphasis on goal
specificity. Similarly, we noted earlier that feedback about goal progress is a
critical element of goal-setting theory. The only area of possible disagreement
between MBO and goal-setting theory is participation: MBO strongly advocates
it, whereas goal-setting theory demonstrates that managers' assigned goals are
usually just as effective.

You'll find MBO programs in many business, health care, educational, government, and nonprofit organizations.[54] Their popularity does not mean they
always work.[55] When MBO fails, the culprits tend to be unrealistic expectations,
lack of commitment by top management, and inability or unwillingness to
allocate rewards based on goal accomplishment.

Self-Efficacy Theory

Self-efficacy (also known as *social cognitive theory* or *social learning theory*) refers
to an individual's belief that he or she is capable of performing a task.[56] The
higher your self-efficacy, the more confidence you have in your ability to succeed. So, in difficult situations, people with low self-efficacy are more likely to
lessen their effort or give up altogether, while those with high self-efficacy will

management by objectives (MBO) *A
program that encompasses specific
goals, participatively set, for an explicit
time period, with feedback on goal
progress.*

self-efficacy *An individual's belief
that he or she is capable of performing
a task.*

try harder to master the challenge.[57] Self-efficacy can create a positive spiral in which those with high efficacy become more engaged in their tasks and then, in turn, increase performance, which increases efficacy further.[58] Changes in self-efficacy over time are related to changes in creative performance as well.[59] Individuals high in self-efficacy also seem to respond to negative feedback with increased effort and motivation, while those low in self-efficacy are likely to lessen their effort after negative feedback.[60] How can managers help their employees achieve high levels of self-efficacy? By bringing goal-setting theory and self-efficacy theory together.

Goal-setting theory and self-efficacy theory don't compete; they complement each other. As Exhibit 7-5 shows, employees whose manager sets difficult goals for them will have a higher level of self-efficacy and set higher goals for their own performance. Why? Setting difficult goals for people communicates your confidence in them. Imagine you learn your boss sets a higher goal for you than for your co-workers. How would you interpret this? As long as you didn't feel you were being picked on, you would probably think, "Well, I guess my boss thinks I'm capable of performing better than others." This sets in motion a psychological process in which you're more confident in yourself (higher self-efficacy) and you set higher personal goals, performing better both inside and outside the workplace.

The researcher who developed self-efficacy theory, Albert Bandura, proposes four ways self-efficacy can be increased:[61]

1. Enactive mastery.
2. Vicarious modeling.
3. Verbal persuasion.
4. Arousal.

According to Bandura, the most important source of increasing self-efficacy is *enactive mastery*—that is, gaining relevant experience with the task or job. If you've been able to do the job successfully in the past, you're more confident you'll be able to do it in the future.

| Exhibit **7-5** | Joint Effects of Goals and Self-Efficacy on Performance |

Source: Based on E. A. Locke and G. P. Latham, "Building a Practically Useful Theory of Goal Setting and Task Motivation: A 35-Year Odyssey," American Psychologist (September 2002), pp. 705–717.

The second source is *vicarious modeling*—becoming more confident because you see someone else doing the task. If your friend slims down, it increases your confidence that you can lose weight, too. Vicarious modeling is most effective when you see yourself as similar to the person you are observing. Watching Tiger Woods play a difficult golf shot might not increase your confidence in being able to play the shot yourself, but if you watch a golfer with a handicap similar to yours, it's persuasive.

The third source is *verbal persuasion:* becoming more confident because someone convinces you that you have the skills necessary to be successful. Motivational speakers use this tactic.

Finally, Bandura argues that *arousal* increases self-efficacy. Arousal leads to an energized state, so the person gets "psyched up" and performs better. But if the task requires a steady, lower-key perspective (say, carefully editing a manuscript), arousal may in fact hurt performance.

What are the OB implications of self-efficacy theory? Well, it's a matter of applying Bandura's sources of self-efficacy to the work setting. Training programs often make use of enactive mastery by having people practice and build their skills. In fact, one reason training works is that it increases self-efficacy.[62] Individuals with higher levels of self-efficacy also appear to reap more benefits from training programs and are more likely to use their training on the job.[63]

The best way for a manager to use verbal persuasion is through the *Pygmalion effect* or the *Galatea effect*. As discussed in Chapter 5, the Pygmalion effect is a form of self-fulfilling prophecy in which believing something can make it true. In some studies, teachers were told their students had very high IQ scores when, in fact, they spanned a range from high to low. Consistent with the Pygmalion effect, the teachers spent more time with the students they *thought* were smart, gave them more challenging assignments, and expected more of them—all of which led to higher student self-efficacy and better grades.[64] This strategy also has been used in the workplace.[65] Sailors who were told convincingly that they would not get seasick were in fact much less likely to do so.[66]

Intelligence and personality are absent from Bandura's list, but they can increase self-efficacy.[67] People who are intelligent, conscientiousness, and

Toyota Motor Corporation applies social learning theory in teaching employees skills they need to meet the company's high standards of quality and efficiency. At its Global Production Center training facilities in Japan, England, and the United States, workers and managers from factories around the world learn production techniques through observation and direct experience. Trainees first watch computerized visual manuals to learn basic skills. Then, under the tutelage of an experienced production master, they practice the skills. In this photo, a trainee practices the skill of bolt tightening at Toyota's training center in Toyota City, Japan.

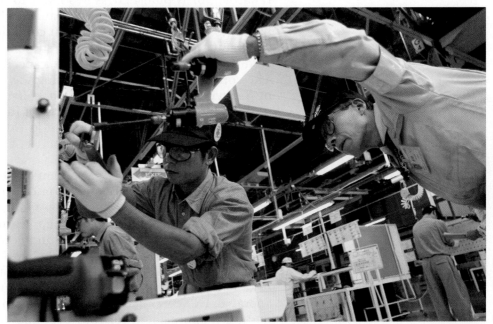

Source: Toru Yamanaka/AFP/Getty Images/Newscom

emotionally stable are so much more likely to have high self-efficacy that some researchers argue self-efficacy is less important than prior research would suggest.[68] They believe it is partially a by-product in a smart person with a confident personality. Although Bandura strongly disagrees with this conclusion, more research is needed.

Reinforcement Theory

5   Compare and contrast goal-setting theory and management by objectives.

Goal-setting is a cognitive approach, proposing that an individual's purposes direct his action. **Reinforcement theory**, in contrast, takes a behavioristic view, arguing that reinforcement conditions behavior. The two theories are clearly at odds philosophically. Reinforcement theorists see behavior as environmentally caused. You need not be concerned, they would argue, with internal cognitive events; what controls behavior is reinforcers—any consequences that, when immediately following responses, increase the probability that the behavior will be repeated.

Reinforcement theory ignores the inner state of the individual and concentrates solely on what happens when he or she takes some action. Because it does not concern itself with what initiates behavior, it is not, strictly speaking, a theory of motivation. But it does provide a powerful means of analyzing what controls behavior, and this is why we typically consider it in discussions of motivation.[69]

Operant conditioning theory, probably the most relevant component of reinforcement theory for management, argues that people learn to behave to get something they want or to avoid something they don't want. Unlike reflexive or unlearned behavior, operant behavior is influenced by the reinforcement or lack of reinforcement brought about by its consequences. Therefore, reinforcement strengthens a behavior and increases the likelihood it will be repeated.[70] B. F. Skinner, one of the most prominent advocates of operant conditioning, argued that creating pleasing consequences to follow specific forms of behavior would increase the frequency of that behavior. He demonstrated that people will most likely engage in desired behaviors if they are positively reinforced for doing so; that rewards are most effective if they immediately follow the desired response; and that behavior that is not rewarded, or is punished, is less likely to be repeated. We know a professor who places a mark by a student's name each time the student makes a contribution to class discussions. Operant conditioning would argue this practice is motivating because it conditions a student to expect a reward (earning class credit) each time she demonstrates a specific behavior (speaking up in class). The concept of operant conditioning was part of Skinner's broader concept of **behaviorism**, which argues that behavior follows stimuli in a relatively unthinking manner. Skinner's form of radical behaviorism rejects feelings, thoughts, and other states of mind as causes of behavior. In short, people learn to associate stimulus and response, but their conscious awareness of this association is irrelevant.[71]

You can see illustrations of operant conditioning everywhere that reinforcements are contingent on some action on your part. Your instructor says if you want a high grade in the course, you must supply correct answers on the test. A commissioned salesperson wanting to earn a sizable income finds doing so is contingent on generating high sales in her territory. Of course, the linkage can also teach individuals to engage in behaviors that work against the best interests of the organization. Assume your boss says if you work overtime during the next 3-week busy season you'll be compensated for it at your next performance appraisal. However, when performance-appraisal time comes, you are given no positive reinforcement for your overtime work. The next time your boss asks you to work overtime, what will you do? You'll probably decline! Your behavior can be explained by operant conditioning: if a behavior fails to be positively reinforced, the probability it will be repeated declines.

Although reinforcers such as pay can motivate people, the process is much more complicated than stimulus–response. In its pure form, reinforcement theory ignores feelings, attitudes, expectations, and other cognitive variables known to affect behavior. In fact, some researchers look at the same experiments reinforcement theorists use to support their position and interpret the findings in a *cognitive* framework.[72]

Reinforcement is undoubtedly an important influence on behavior, but few scholars are prepared to argue it is the only one. The behaviors you engage in at work and the amount of effort you allocate to each task are affected by the consequences that follow. If you're consistently reprimanded for outproducing your colleagues, you'll likely reduce your productivity. But we might also explain your lower productivity in terms of goals, inequity, or expectancies.

Individuals can learn by being told or by observing what happens to other people, as well as through direct experiences. Much of what we have learned comes from watching models—parents, teachers, peers, film and television performers, bosses, and so forth. This view that we can learn through both observation and direct experience is called **social-learning theory**.[73]

Although social-learning theory is an extension of operant conditioning— that is, it assumes behavior is a function of consequences—it also acknowledges the effects of observational learning and perception. People respond to the way they perceive and define consequences, not to the objective consequences themselves.

Models are central to the social-learning viewpoint. Four processes determine their influence on an individual:

1. **Attentional processes.**   People learn from a model only when they recognize and pay attention to its critical features. We tend to be most influenced by models that are attractive, repeatedly available, important to us, or similar to us in our estimation.
2. **Retention processes.**   A model's influence depends on how well the individual remembers the model's action after the model is no longer readily available.
3. **Motor reproduction processes.**   After a person has seen a new behavior by observing the model, watching must be converted to doing. This process demonstrates that the individual can perform the modeled activities.
4. **Reinforcement processes.**   Individuals are motivated to exhibit the modeled behavior if positive incentives or rewards are provided. Positively reinforced behaviors are given more attention, learned better, and performed more often.

Equity Theory/Organizational Justice

6 Contrast reinforcement theory and goal-setting theory.

Jane Pearson graduated from State University last year with a degree in accounting. After interviews with a number of organizations on campus, she accepted a position with a top public accounting firm and was assigned to its Boston office. Jane was very pleased with the offer she received: challenging work with a prestigious firm, an excellent opportunity to gain valuable experience, and

---

reinforcement theory   *A theory that says that behavior is a function of its consequences.*

behaviorism   *A theory that argues that behavior follows stimuli in a relatively unthinking manner.*

social-learning theory   *The view that we can learn through both observation and direct experience.*

the highest salary any accounting major at State was offered last year—$4,550 per month—but Jane was the top student in her class; she was articulate and mature, and she fully expected to receive a commensurate salary.

Twelve months have passed. The work has proved to be as challenging and satisfying as Jane had hoped. Her employer is extremely pleased with her performance; in fact, Jane recently received a $200-per-month raise. However, her motivational level has dropped dramatically in the past few weeks. Why? Jane's employer has just hired a fresh graduate out of State University who lacks the year of experience Jane has gained, for $4,600 per month—$50 more than Jane now makes! Jane is irate. She is even talking about looking for another job.

Jane's situation illustrates the role that equity plays in motivation. Employees perceive what they get from a job situation (salary levels, raises, recognition) in relationship to what they put into it (effort, experience, education, competence), and then they compare their outcome–input ratio with that of relevant others. This is shown in Exhibit 7-6. If we perceive our ratio to be equal to that of the relevant others with whom we compare ourselves, a state of equity exists; we perceive that our situation is fair and justice prevails. When we see the ratio as unequal and we feel underrewarded, we experience equity tension that creates anger. When we see ourselves as overrewarded, tension creates guilt. J. Stacy Adams proposed that this negative state of tension provides the motivation to do something to correct it.[74]

The referent an employee selects adds to the complexity of **equity theory**.[75] There are four referent comparisons:

1. **Self–inside.** An employee's experiences in a different position inside the employee's current organization.
2. **Self–outside.** An employee's experiences in a situation or position outside the employee's current organization.
3. **Other–inside.** Another individual or group of individuals inside the employee's organization.
4. **Other–outside.** Another individual or group of individuals outside the employee's organization.

Employees might compare themselves to friends, neighbors, co-workers, or colleagues in other organizations or compare their present job with past jobs. Which referent an employee chooses will be influenced by the information the employee holds about referents as well as by the attractiveness of the referent. Four moderating variables are gender, length of tenure, level in the organization, and amount of education or professionalism.[76]

Exhibit 7-6 **Equity Theory**

Ratio Comparisons*	Perception
$\dfrac{O}{I_A} < \dfrac{O}{I_B}$	Inequity due to being underrewarded
$\dfrac{O}{I_A} = \dfrac{O}{I_B}$	Equity
$\dfrac{O}{I_A} > \dfrac{O}{I_B}$	Inequity due to being overrewarded

*Where $\dfrac{O}{I_A}$ represents the employee; and $\dfrac{O}{I_B}$ represents relevant others

Women are typically paid less than men in comparable jobs and have lower pay expectations than men for the same work.[77] So a woman who uses another woman as a referent tends to calculate a lower comparative standard. Of course, employers' stereotypes about women (for example, the belief that women are less committed to the organization or that "women's work" is less valuable) also may contribute to the pay gap.[78] While both men and women prefer same-sex comparisons, employees in jobs that are not sex segregated will likely make more cross-sex comparisons than those in jobs that are male or female dominated.

Employees with short tenure in their current organizations tend to have little information about others inside the organization, so they rely on their personal experiences. Employees with long tenure rely more heavily on co-workers for comparison. Upper-level employees, those in the professional ranks, and those with higher amounts of education tend to have better information about people in other organizations and will make more other–outside comparisons.

Based on equity theory, employees who perceive inequity will make one of six choices:[79]

1. Change inputs (exert less effort if underpaid or more if overpaid).
2. Change outcomes (individuals paid on a piece-rate basis can increase their pay by producing a higher quantity of units of lower quality).
3. Distort perceptions of self ("I used to think I worked at a moderate pace, but now I realize I work a lot harder than everyone else.").
4. Distort perceptions of others ("Mike's job isn't as desirable as I thought.").
5. Choose a different referent ("I may not make as much as my brother-in-law, but I'm doing a lot better than my Dad did when he was my age.").
6. Leave the field (quit the job).

In perceiving inequity in pay, these American Airline pilots used an "other-inside" referent comparison when comparing their pay to that of the airline's managers. The pilots agreed to accept wage and benefit cuts after the airline reported an $8 billion loss. When they returned to profitability, the CEO and other top managers received stock bonuses. Marching in protest, the pilots argued that their sacrifices in pay and benefits helped save the airline from bankruptcy and that they deserved to be rewarded with pay increases.

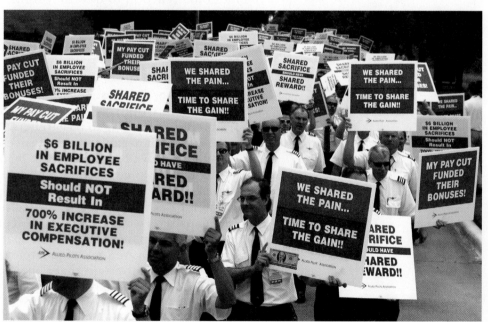

Source: LM Otero/AP Images

equity theory   *A theory that says that individuals compare their job inputs and outcomes with those of others and then respond to eliminate any inequities.*

Some of these propositions have been supported, but others haven't.[80] First, inequities created by overpayment do not seem to significantly affect behavior in most work situations. Apparently, people have more tolerance of overpayment inequities than of underpayment inequities or are better able to rationalize them. It's pretty damaging to a theory when half the equation falls apart. Second, not all people are equity sensitive.[81] A few actually prefer outcome–input ratios lower than the referent comparisons. Predictions from equity theory are not likely to be very accurate about these "benevolent types."

While most research on equity theory has focused on pay, some employees also look for equity in the distribution of other organizational rewards like high-status job titles and large and lavishly furnished offices.[82]

Finally, recent research has expanded the meaning of *equity,* or *fairness.*[83] Historically, equity theory focused on **distributive justice**, the employee's perceived fairness of the *amount* rewards among individuals and who received them. But **organizational justice** draws a bigger picture. Employees perceive their organizations as just when they believe rewards and the *way* they are distributed are fair. In other words, fairness or equity can be subjective; what one person sees as unfair, another may see as perfectly appropriate. In general, people see allocations or procedure favoring themselves as fair.[84] In a recent poll, 61 percent of respondents said they pay their fair share of taxes, but an almost equal number (54 percent) felt the system as a whole is unfair, saying some people skirt it.[85]

Most of the equity theory research we've described proposes a fairly rational, calculative way of estimating what is fair and unfair. But few people really make mathematical calculations of their inputs relative to the outcomes of others. Instead, they base distributive judgments on a feeling or an emotional reaction to how they think they are treated relative to others, and their reactions are often emotional as well.[86] Our discussion has also focused on reactions to personal mistreatment. However, people also react emotionally to injustices committed against others, prompting them to take retributive actions.[87]

Beyond perceptions of fairness, the other key element of organizational justice is the view that justice is multidimensional. How much we get paid relative to what we think we should be paid (distributive justice) is obviously important. But, according to researchers, *how* we get paid is just as important. Thus, the model of organizational justice in Exhibit 7-7 includes **procedural justice**—the perceived fairness of the *process* used to determine the distribution of rewards. Two key elements of procedural justice are process control and explanations. *Process control* is the opportunity to present your point of view about desired outcomes to decision makers. *Explanations* are clear reasons management gives for the outcome. Thus, for employees to see a process as fair, they need to feel they have some control over the outcome and that they were given an adequate explanation about why the outcome occurred. It's also important that a manager is *consistent* (across people and over time), is *unbiased*, makes decisions based on *accurate information*, and is *open to appeals.*[88]

The effects of procedural justice become more important when distributive justice is lacking. This makes sense. If we don't get what we want, we tend to focus on *why*. If your supervisor gives a cushy office to a co-worker instead of to you, you're much more focused on your supervisor's treatment of you than if you had gotten the office. Explanations are beneficial when they take the form of post hoc excuses ("I know this is bad, and I wanted to give you the office, but it wasn't my decision") rather than justifications ("I decided to give the office to Sam, but having it isn't a big deal.").[89]

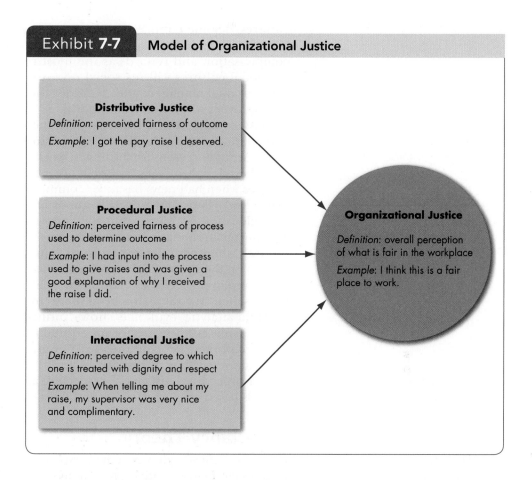

Exhibit 7-7   Model of Organizational Justice

Distributive Justice
Definition: perceived fairness of outcome
Example: I got the pay raise I deserved.

Procedural Justice
Definition: perceived fairness of process used to determine outcome
Example: I had input into the process used to give raises and was given a good explanation of why I received the raise I did.

Interactional Justice
Definition: perceived degree to which one is treated with dignity and respect
Example: When telling me about my raise, my supervisor was very nice and complimentary.

Organizational Justice
Definition: overall perception of what is fair in the workplace
Example: I think this is a fair place to work.

Interactional justice describes an individual's perception of the degree to which she is treated with dignity, concern, and respect. When people are treated in an unjust manner (at least in their own eyes), they retaliate (for example, badmouthing a supervisor).[90] Because people intimately connect interactional justice or injustice to the conveyer of the information, we would expect perceptions of injustice to be more closely related to the supervisor. Generally, that's what the evidence suggests.[91]

Of these three forms of justice, distributive justice is most strongly related to organizational commitment and satisfaction with outcomes such as pay. Procedural justice relates most strongly to job satisfaction, employee trust, withdrawal from the organization, job performance, and citizenship behaviors. There is less evidence about interactional justice.[92]

Equity theory has gained a strong following in the United States because U.S.-style reward systems assume workers are highly sensitive to equity in reward allocations. And in the United States, equity is meant to closely tie pay to performance. However, in collectivist cultures employees expect rewards to reflect their individual needs as well as their performance.[93] Other research suggests that inputs and outcomes are valued differently in various

distributive justice *Perceived fairness of the amount and allocation of rewards among individuals.*
organizational justice *An overall perception of what is fair in the workplace, composed of distributive, procedural, and interactional justice.*

procedural justice *The perceived fairness of the process used to determine the distribution of rewards.*

interactional justice *The perceived degree to which an individual is treated with dignity, concern, and respect.*

cultures.[94] Some cultures emphasize status over individual achievement as a basis for allocating resources. Materialistic cultures are more likely to see cash compensation and rewards as the most relevant outcomes of work, whereas relational cultures will see social rewards and status as important outcomes. International managers must consider the cultural preferences of each group of employees when determining what is "fair" in different contexts.

Studies suggest that managers are indeed motivated to foster employees' perceptions of justice because they wish to ensure compliance, maintain a positive identity, and establish fairness at work.[95] To enhance perceptions of justice, they should realize that employees are especially sensitive to unfairness in procedures when bad news has to be communicated (that is, when distributive justice is low). Thus, it's especially important to openly share information about how allocation decisions are made, follow consistent and unbiased procedures, and engage in similar practices to increase the perception of procedural justice. Second, when addressing perceived injustices, managers need to focus their actions on the source of the problem.

If employees feel they have been treated unjustly, having opportunities to express their frustration has been shown to reduce their desire for retribution.[96]

Meta-analytic evidence shows individuals in both individualistic and collectivistic cultures prefer an equitable distribution of rewards (the most effective workers get paid the most) over an equal division (everyone gets paid the same regardless of performance).[97] Across nations, the same basic principles of procedural justice are respected, and workers around the world prefer rewards based on performance and skills over rewards based on seniority.[98]

Expectancy Theory

One of the most widely accepted explanations of motivation is Victor Vroom's **expectancy theory**.[99] Although it has its critics, most of the evidence supports it.[100]

Expectancy theory argues that the strength of our tendency to act a certain way depends on the strength of our expectation of a given outcome and its attractiveness. In more practical terms, employees will be motivated to exert a high level of effort when they believe it will lead to a good performance appraisal; that a good appraisal will lead to organizational rewards such as bonuses, salary increases, or promotions; and that the rewards will satisfy the employees' personal goals. The theory, therefore, focuses on three relationships (see Exhibit 7-8):

1. **Effort–performance relationship.** The probability perceived by the individual that exerting a given amount of effort will lead to performance.
2. **Performance–reward relationship.** The degree to which the individual believes performing at a particular level will lead to the attainment of a desired outcome.

7 Demonstrate how organizational justice is a refinement of equity theory.

MyManagementLab
For an interactive application of this topic, check out this chapter's simulation activity at **www.mymanagementlab.com**.

Exhibit **7-8**   Expectancy Theory

3. **Rewards–personal goals relationship.** The degree to which organizational rewards satisfy an individual's personal goals or needs and the attractiveness of those potential rewards for the individual.[101]

Expectancy theory helps explain why a lot of workers aren't motivated on their jobs and do only the minimum necessary to get by. Let's frame the theory's three relationships as questions employees need to answer in the affirmative if their motivation is to be maximized.

First, *if I give a maximum effort, will it be recognized in my performance appraisal?* For many employees, the answer is "no." Why? Their skill level may be deficient, which means no matter how hard they try, they're not likely to be high performers. The organization's performance appraisal system may be designed to assess nonperformance factors such as loyalty, initiative, or courage, which means more effort won't necessarily result in a higher evaluation. Another possibility is that employees, rightly or wrongly, perceive the boss doesn't like them. As a result, they expect a poor appraisal, regardless of effort. These examples suggest one possible source of low motivation is employees' belief that, no matter how hard they work, the likelihood of getting a good performance appraisal is low.

Second, *if I get a good performance appraisal, will it lead to organizational rewards?* Many organizations reward things besides performance. When pay is based on factors such as having seniority, being cooperative, or "kissing up" to the boss, employees are likely to see the performance–reward relationship as weak and demotivating.

Finally, *if I'm rewarded, are the rewards attractive to me?* The employee works hard in the hope of getting a promotion but gets a pay raise instead. Or the employee wants a more interesting and challenging job but receives only a few words of praise. Unfortunately, many managers are limited in the rewards they can distribute, which makes it difficult to tailor rewards to individual employee needs. Some incorrectly assume all employees want the same thing, thus overlooking the motivational effects of differentiating rewards. In either case, employee motivation is submaximized.

As a vivid example of how expectancy theory can work, consider stock analysts. They make their living trying to forecast a stock's future price; the accuracy of their buy, sell, or hold recommendations is what keeps them in work or gets them fired. But it's not quite that simple. Analysts place few sell ratings on stocks, although in a steady market, by definition, as many stocks are falling as are rising. Expectancy theory provides an explanation: analysts who place a sell rating on a company's stock have to balance the benefits they receive by being accurate against the risks they run by drawing that company's ire. What are these risks? They include public rebuke, professional blackballing, and exclusion from information. When analysts place a buy rating on a stock, they face no such trade-off because, obviously, companies love it when analysts recommend that investors buy their stock. So the incentive structure suggests the expected outcome of buy ratings is higher than the expected outcome of sell ratings, and that's why buy ratings vastly outnumber sell ratings.[102]

expectancy theory *A theory that says that the strength of a tendency to act in a certain way depends on the strength of an expectation that the act will be followed by a given outcome and on the attractiveness of that outcome to the individual.*

At Mary Kay Cosmetics, the performance-reward relationship is strong. The company offers a generous rewards and recognition program based on the achievement of personal goals set by each employee. Mary Kay also understands the motivational effects of differentiating rewards. For some employees, the best reward is the opportunity to work from home, while other employees are motivated by the opportunity to win a trip, jewelry, or the use of a pink Cadillac. In this photo, a Mary Kay sales director explains career opportunities at a job fair to women interested in joining the company.

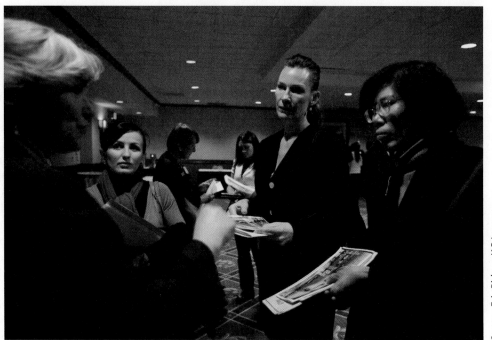

Source: Eric Risberg/AP Images

Does expectancy theory work? Some critics suggest it has only limited use and is more valid where individuals clearly perceive effort–performance and performance–reward linkages.[103] Because few individuals do, the theory tends to be idealistic. If organizations actually rewarded individuals for performance rather than seniority, effort, skill level, and job difficulty, expectancy theory might be much more valid. However, rather than invalidating it, this criticism can explain why a significant segment of the workforce exerts low effort on the job.

Integrating Contemporary Theories of Motivation

8 Apply the key tenets of expectancy theory to motivating employees.

9 Compare contemporary theories of motivation.

Things might be simpler if, after presenting a half dozen theories, we could say only one was found valid. But many of the theories in this chapter are complementary. We now tie them together to help you understand their interrelationships.[104]

Exhibit 7-9 integrates much of what we know about motivation. Its basic foundation is the expectancy model shown in Exhibit 7-8. Let's walk through Exhibit 7-9. (We will look at job design closely in Chapter 8.)

We begin by explicitly recognizing that opportunities can either aid or hinder individual effort. The individual effort box on the left also has another arrow leading into it, from the person's goals. Consistent with goal-setting theory, the goals–effort loop is meant to remind us that goals direct behavior.

Expectancy theory predicts employees will exert a high level of effort if they perceive a strong relationship between effort and performance, performance and rewards, and rewards and satisfaction of personal goals. Each of these relationships is, in turn, influenced by other factors. For

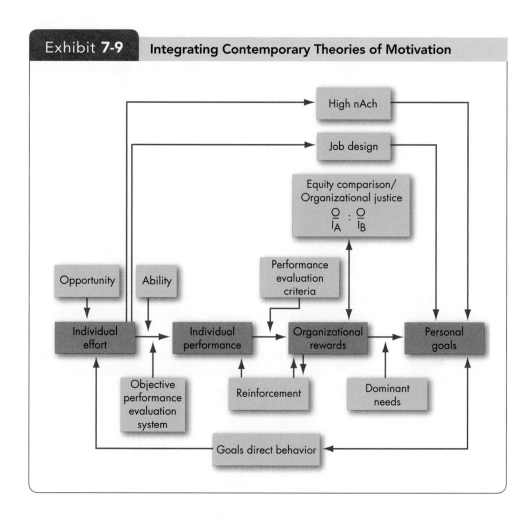

Exhibit 7-9 **Integrating Contemporary Theories of Motivation**

effort to lead to good performance, the individual must have the ability to perform and perceive the performance appraisal system as fair and objective. The performance–reward relationship will be strong if the individual perceives that performance (rather than seniority, personal favorites, or other criteria) is rewarded. If cognitive evaluation theory were fully valid in the actual workplace, we would predict here that basing rewards on performance should decrease the individual's intrinsic motivation. The final link in expectancy theory is the rewards–goals relationship. Motivation is high if the rewards for high performance satisfied the dominant needs consistent with individual goals.

A closer look at Exhibit 7-9 also reveals that the model considers achievement motivation, job design, reinforcement, and equity theories/organizational justice. A high achiever is not motivated by an organization's assessment of performance or organizational rewards, hence the jump from effort to personal goals for those with a high nAch. Remember, high achievers are internally driven as long as their jobs provide them with personal responsibility, feedback, and moderate risks. They are not concerned with the effort–performance, performance–rewards, or rewards–goal linkages.

Reinforcement theory enters the model by recognizing that the organization's rewards reinforce the individual's performance. If employees see a reward system as "paying off" for good performance, the rewards will reinforce and encourage good performance. Rewards also play the key part in organizational justice research. Individuals will judge the favorability of their outcomes (for example, their pay) relative to what others receive but also with respect to how they are treated: when people are disappointed in their rewards, they are likely to be sensitive to the perceived fairness of the procedures used and the consideration given to them by their supervisor.

MyManagementLab

Now that you have finished this chapter, go back to **www.mymanagementlab.com** to continue practicing and applying the concepts you've learned.

Summary and Implications for Managers

The motivation theories in this chapter differ in their predictive strength. Here, we (1) review the most established to determine their relevance in explaining turnover, productivity, and other outcomes and (2) assess the predictive power of each.[105]

- **Need theories.** Maslow's hierarchy, McClelland's needs, and the two-factor theory focus on needs. None has found widespread support, although McClelland's is the strongest, particularly regarding the relationship between achievement and productivity. In general, need theories are not very valid explanations of motivation.
- **Self-determination theory and cognitive evaluation theory.** As research on the motivational effects of rewards has accumulated, it increasingly appears extrinsic rewards can undermine motivation if they are seen as coercive. They can increase motivation if they provide information about competence and relatedness.
- **Goal-setting theory.** Clear and difficult goals lead to higher levels of employee productivity, supporting goal-setting theory's explanation of this dependent variable. The theory does not address absenteeism, turnover, or satisfaction, however.
- **Reinforcement theory.** This theory has an impressive record for predicting quality and quantity of work, persistence of effort, absenteeism, tardiness, and accident rates. It does not offer much insight into employee satisfaction or the decision to quit.
- **Equity theory/organizational justice.** Equity theory deals with productivity, satisfaction, absence, and turnover variables. However, its strongest legacy is that it provided the spark for research on organizational justice, which has more support in the literature.
- **Expectancy theory.** Expectancy theory offers a powerful explanation of performance variables such as employee productivity, absenteeism, and turnover. But it assumes employees have few constraints on decision making, such as bias or incomplete information, and this limits its applicability. Expectancy theory has some validity because, for many behaviors, people consider expected outcomes.

Fear Is a Powerful Motivator

This is a "dark side" topic that no one likes to discuss, but fear works as a motivator. Few of us like the idea of feeling fearful in the workplace. But what we like and what motivates us are not the same.

Ever studied harder for an exam for fear of doing poorly, or worried about doing something that would draw your parents' ire? If you answer "yes," you're on your way to admitting this essential truth: we engage in a lot of behaviors, and refrain from others, out of fear.

Too often in organizational behavior we sing this happy song that when employees are happy, they will give their best effort and the company will sail along in smooth seas.

The truth is that when a manager adopts this philosophy, people often relax. They take off early. They "shoot the breeze" more and work a little less. George Cloutier, founder of American Management Services, is realistic about this. "The concept that if you love your employees they'll perform is on the edge of insanity," he says. "Fear is the best motivator."

Employees should realize that in today's competitive environment, they have to bring their A-game to work each and every day. And managers need to closely monitor them to make sure that's the case. Instilling in employees a fear that if they shirk, they'll lose their jobs, is one way to accomplish that monitoring. Without fear, people would do as they wish, and that rarely includes working hard if they feel they don't have to. Like it or not, that's the cold, hard truth about employee motivation.

How cynical! Fear is a natural emotion, but it generally serves a purpose only in crisis situations. Those unfortunate enough to work under a manager who consciously uses fear to "motivate" behavior will leave as soon as they can or get even in some hidden way. Fear never works as a motivational tool. Various areas of research in psychology and organizational behavior prove the point.

Fear generates a "fight-flight-freeze" response, in which an individual (or animal) experiencing fear or extreme stress is forced to choose one of these behaviors. Any sane manager wants none of them. Imagine supervising Chris, who flees work when fearful or stressed, Sanjay, who fights with others when he feels cornered, and Mercedes, who locks up whenever she is chastised. Does effective management mean eliciting these behaviors?

One workplace expert noted, "Fear motivation always results in inner anger and resentment against the person using the fear tactics . . . Fear motivation is the lowest form of motivation and usually results in 'when the cat is away, the mice will play.'" So, ironically, fear actually undermines performance monitoring, because employees will get even when they know they can't be caught. And they will never go out of their way to help the organization.

As one Canadian manager noted, "Exercising unilateral power [through fear] can be effective for those leaders whose modest ambitions are matched by the modest successes that such tactics bring." Zappos founder Tony Hsieh, who tries to create a happy work environment at Zappos by giving employees the sense that they are part of something bigger, argues that inspiration is a much better motivator than fear.

Fear may motivate short-term performance, but in the long run, it is always a losing motivational tool.

Sources: K. Pattison, "Fire Your Relatives. Scare Your Employees. And Stop Whining," *The New York Times* (February 11, 2010), p. B8; L. Mignone, "How to Build an Army of Happy, Busy Worker Bees," *Fortune* (May 23, 2011), downloaded May 25, 2011, from www.fortune.com; TTI Performance Systems, "Provide a Climate for Motivation," downloaded May 25, 2011, from www.nielsongroup.com/; and J. Wood, "Stories, Not Data, At Heart of Human Motivation," *Vancouver Sun* (May 20, 2011), downloaded May 25, 2011, from www.vancouversun.com/.

QUESTIONS FOR REVIEW

1 What are the three key elements of motivation?

2 What are some early theories of motivation? How applicable are they today?

3 How do the predictions of self-determination theory apply to intrinsic and extrinsic rewards?

4 What are the implications of employee engagement for management?

5 What are the similarities and differences between goal-setting theory and management by objectives?

6 What are the similarities and differences between reinforcement theory and goal-setting theory?

7 How is organizational justice a refinement of equity theory?

8 What are the key tenets of expectancy theory?

9 What are some contemporary theories of motivation and how do they compare to one another?

EXPERIENTIAL EXERCISE Goal-Setting Task

Purpose
This exercise will help you learn how to write tangible, verifiable, measurable, and relevant goals that might evolve from an MBO program.

Time
Approximately 20 to 30 minutes.

Instructions
1. Break into groups of three to five.

2. Spend a few minutes discussing your class instructor's job. What does he or she do? What defines good performance? What behaviors lead to good performance?

3. Each group is to develop a list of five goals that, although not established participatively with your instructor, you believe might be developed in an MBO program at your college. Try to select goals that seem most critical to the effective performance of your instructor's job.

4. Each group will select a leader who will share the group's goals with the entire class. For each group's goals, class discussion should focus on the goals'
(a) specificity, (b) ease of measurement,
(c) importance, and (d) motivational properties.

ETHICAL DILEMMA The Big Easy?

As you know, college is an expensive proposition. Students, parents, donors, and the government invest millions of dollars every year. Thus, there may be an incumbent responsibility on students to ensure they are learning. However, consider the following results from a recent study of time use by more than 3,000 undergraduates:

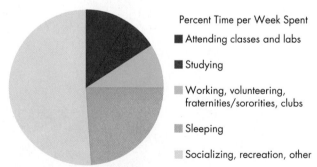

Percent Time per Week Spent
- ■ Attending classes and labs
- ■ Studying
- Working, volunteering, fraternities/sororities, clubs
- Sleeping
- Socializing, recreation, other

Undergraduate Use of Time per Week

Questions
1. One article commented that college students are "frittering away their time at an astonishing rate." Do you agree this is what the data show? Why or why not?

2. Do you think students have an ethical responsibility to spend more time studying? Why or why not?

3. One study suggested that full-time students in 1961 studied an average of 40 hours per week, compared to 27 hours now. Does this apparent trend concern you? Do you think that, as some experts have claimed, our economic competitiveness would increase if college students studied more?

Sources: M. Burns, "What Happened to Academic Rigor?" *Miller-McCune* (March 8, 2011), pp. 47–49; and R. Arum, *Academically Adrift: Limited Learning on College Campuses* (Chicago: University of Chicago Press, 2011).

CASE INCIDENT 1 It's Not Fair!

Few topics in the business press have grabbed more headlines recently than highly lucrative annual bonuses for top management. Critics bemoan the multimillion-dollar compensation packages offered in the financial services industry in particular, following the dire consequences of the meltdown of this sector a few short years ago.

How is executive compensation determined by compensation committees? Some researchers suggest that principles from equity theory (making comparisons to referent others) might explain variations in executive pay. To set what is considered a "fair" level of pay for top executives, members of the board find out how much executives with similar levels of experience in similar firms (similar inputs) are being paid and attempt to adjust compensation (outcomes) to be equitable. In other words, top executives in large oil firms are paid similarly to top executives in other large oil firms, top executives in small hospitals are paid similarly to top executives in other small hospitals. In many cases, simply changing the referent others can change the salary range considered acceptable. According to one view of justice theory, this should be perceived as equitable, although executives may encourage boards to consider specific referent others who are especially well-paid.

Critics of executive compensation change the debate by focusing on the ratio of executive compensation to that of the company's lowest-paid employees. Researcher Cary Cooper notes, "In business, it is important to reward success and not simply status." Cooper believes all employees should share the company's good fortune in profitable periods. He has recommended that CEO compensation be capped at 20 times the salary of the lowest-paid employee. In fact, the average S&P 500 CEO is paid 263 times what the lowest-paid laborer makes. This is eight times more than the ratio from the 1950s, which might serve as another reference point for determining what is considered "fair."

Questions

1. How does the executive compensation issue relate to equity theory? Who do you think should be the referent others in these equity judgments? What are the relevant inputs for top executives?

2. Can you think of procedural justice implications related to the ways pay policies for top executives have been instituted? Do these pay-making decisions follow the procedural justice principles outlined in the chapter?

3. Do you think the government has a legitimate role in controlling executive compensation? How might we use distributive and procedural justice theories to inform this debate?

4. Are there any positive motivational consequences of tying compensation pay closely to firm performance?

Sources: J. Bizjak, M. Lemmon, and T. Nguyen, "Are All CEOs Above Average? An Empirical Analysis of Compensation Peer Groups and Pay Design," *Journal of Financial Economics* 100, no. 3 (2011), pp. 538–555; C. Cooper, "We're All in This Together," *Director* 64 (February 2011), p. 27; and R. Foroohar, "Stuffing Their Pockets: For CEOs, A Lucrative Recession" *Newsweek* (September 13, 2010), www.newsweek.com.

CASE INCIDENT 2 Bullying Bosses

After a long weekend, Kara stared at her computer with a sick feeling in her stomach: her boss had added her as a friend on Facebook. Kara did not feel particularly close to her boss, nor did she like the idea of mixing her social life with her work. Still, it was her boss. Kara reluctantly accepted her boss as a Facebook friend. Little did she know her troubles were only beginning.

Kara's boss soon began using her online information to manipulate her work life. It began with inappropriate innuendos regarding Facebook photos. Eventually, Kara's boss manipulated her work hours, confronted her both on and off Facebook, and repeatedly called Kara's cell phone questioning her whereabouts. "My boss was a gossiping, domineering, contriving megalomaniac, and her behavior dramatically intensified when she used Facebook to pry," Kara said. Eventually, Kara was forced to quit. "I feel like I got my freedom back and can breathe again," she said.

Although many individuals recall bullies from elementary school days, some are realizing bullies can exist in the workplace, too. In a recent poll, 37 percent of employees report being victims of a bullying boss. And these bullies don't pick on just the weakest in the group; any subordinate may fall prey. As Kara found, bullying is not limited to male bosses: 40 percent of bullies are women, and women are their targets 70 percent of the time.

How does bullying affect employee motivation and behavior? Surprisingly, though victims may feel less motivated to go to work every day, they continue performing their required job duties. However, some are less motivated to perform extra-role or citizenship behaviors. Helping others, speaking positively about the organization, and going beyond the call of duty are reduced as a result of bullying. According to Dr. Bennett Tepper, fear may be the reason many workers continue to perform. And not all individuals reduce their citizenship behaviors. Some continue to engage in extra-role behaviors to make themselves look better than their colleagues. Other victims of bullying may be motivated to actively retaliate against their bullying supervisor, or engage in acts of workplace withdrawal.

What should you do if your boss is bullying you? Don't necessarily expect help from co-workers. As Emelise Aleandri, an actress and producer from New York who left her job after being bullied, stated, "Some people were afraid to do anything. But others didn't mind what was happening at all, because they wanted my job." Moreover, according to Dr. Michelle Duffy of the University of Kentucky, co-workers often blame victims of bullying in order to resolve their own guilt. "They do this by wondering whether maybe the person deserved the treatment, that

he or she has been annoying, or lazy, [or] did something to earn it," she says.

Questions

1. How does workplace bullying violate the rules of organizational justice?

2. What aspects of motivation might workplace bullying reduce? For example, are there likely to be effects on an employee's self-efficacy? If so, what might those effects be? Do you think bullying would motivate you to retaliate?

3. If you were a victim of workplace bullying, what steps would you take to try to reduce its occurrence? What strategies would be most effective? Least effective? What would you do if one of your colleagues were a victim?

4. What factors do you believe contribute to workplace bullying? Are bullies a product of the situation, or do they have flawed personalities? What situations and what personality factors might contribute to the presence of bullies?

Sources: Based on M. Wilding, "Is Your Boss Your Friend or Foe?" *Sydney Morning Herald* (May 19, 2009), pp. 1–3; C. Benedict, "The Bullying Boss," *The New York Times* (June 22, 2004), p. F1; and S. Thau and M. S. Mitchell, "Self-Gain or Self-Regulation Impairment? Tests of Competing Explanations of the Supervisor Abuse and Employee Deviance Relationship Through Perceptions of Distributive Justice," *Journal of Applied Psychology* 95, (2010), pp. 1009–1031.

ENDNOTES

1. See, for example, G. P. Latham and C. C. Pinder, "Work Motivation Theory and Research at the Dawn of the Twenty-First Century," *Annual Review of Psychology* 56 (2005), pp. 485–516; and C. Pinder, *Work Motivation in Organizational Behavior*, 2nd ed. (London, UK: Psychology Press, 2008).

2. R. Wagner and J. K. Harter, *12: The Elements of Great Managing* (Washington, DC: Gallup Press, 2006).

3. "The 2008 Wasting Time at Work Survey Reveals a Record Number of People Waste Time at Work," Salary.com (2008), www.salary.com.

4. See, for instance, Pinder, *Work Motivation in Organizational Behavior*.

5. A. Maslow, *Motivation and Personality* (New York: Harper & Row, 1954).

6. G. Hofstede, "Motivation, Leadership, and Organization: Do American Theories Apply Abroad?" *Organizational Dynamics* (Summer 1980), p. 55.

7. See, for example, E. E. Lawler III and J. L. Suttle, "A Causal Correlation Test of the Need Hierarchy Concept," *Organizational Behavior and Human Performance* 7, no. 2 (1972), pp. 265–287; D. T. Hall and K. E. Nougaim, "An Examination of Maslow's Need Hierarchy in an Organizational Setting," *Organizational Behavior and Human Performance* 3, no. 1 (1968), pp. 12–35; and J. Rauschenberger, N. Schmitt, and

J. E. Hunter, "A Test of the Need Hierarchy Concept by a Markov Model of Change in Need Strength," *Administrative Science Quarterly* 25, no. 4 (1980), pp. 654–670.

8. M. A. Wahba and L. G. Bridwell, "Maslow Reconsidered: A Review of Research on the Need Hierarchy Theory," *Organizational Behavior and Human Performance* 15, no. 2 (1976), pp. 212–240.

9. D. T. Kenrick, V. Griskevicius, S. L. Neuberg, and M. Schaller, "Renovating the Pyramid of Needs: Contemporary Extensions Built on Ancient Foundations," *Perspectives on Psychological Science* 5, no. 3 (2010), pp. 292–314.

10. D. McGregor, *The Human Side of Enterprise* (New York: McGraw-Hill, 1960). For an updated analysis of Theory X and Theory Y constructs, see R. E. Kopelman, D. J. Prottas, and D. W. Falk, "Construct Validation of a Theory X/Y Behavior Scale," *Leadership and Organization Development Journal* 31, no. 2 (2010), pp. 120–135.

11. F. Herzberg, B. Mausner, and B. Snyderman, *The Motivation to Work* (New York: Wiley, 1959).

12. R. J. House and L. A. Wigdor, "Herzberg's Dual-Factor Theory of Job Satisfaction and Motivations: A Review of the Evidence and Criticism," *Personnel Psychology* 20, no. 4 (1967), pp. 369–389; D. P. Schwab and L. L. Cummings, "Theories of Performance and Satisfaction: A Review," *Industrial Relations* 9, no. 4 (1970), pp. 403–430; and J. Phillipchuk

and J. Whittaker, "An Inquiry into the Continuing Relevance of Herzberg's Motivation Theory," *Engineering Management Journal* 8 (1996), pp. 15–20.

13. D. C. McClelland, *The Achieving Society* (New York: Van Nostrand Reinhold, 1961); J. W. Atkinson and J. O. Raynor, *Motivation and Achievement* (Washington, DC: Winston, 1974); D. C. McClelland, *Power: The Inner Experience* (New York: Irvington, 1975); and M. J. Stahl, *Managerial and Technical Motivation: Assessing Needs for Achievement, Power, and Affiliation* (New York: Praeger, 1986).

14. D. C. McClelland and D. G. Winter, *Motivating Economic Achievement* (New York: The Free Press, 1969); and J. B. Miner, N. R. Smith, and J. S. Bracker, "Role of Entrepreneurial Task Motivation in the Growth of Technologically Innovative Firms: Interpretations from Follow-up Data," *Journal of Applied Psychology* 79, no. 4 (1994), pp. 627–630.

15. McClelland, *Power;* D. C. McClelland and D. H. Burnham, "Power Is the Great Motivator," *Harvard Business Review* (March–April 1976), pp. 100–110; and R. E. Boyatzis, "The Need for Close Relationships and the Manager's Job," in D. A. Kolb, I. M. Rubin, and J. M. McIntyre, *Organizational Psychology: Readings on Human Behavior in Organizations,* 4th ed. (Upper Saddle River, NJ: Prentice Hall, 1984), pp. 81–86.

16. D. G. Winter, "The Motivational Dimensions of Leadership: Power, Achievement, and Affiliation," in R. E. Riggio, S. E. Murphy, and F. J. Pirozzolo (eds.), *Multiple Intelligences and Leadership* (Mahwah, NJ: Lawrence Erlbaum, 2002), pp. 119–138.

17. J. B. Miner, *Studies in Management Education* (New York: Springer, 1965).

18. Ibid.

19. E. Deci and R. Ryan (eds.), *Handbook of Self-Determination Research* (Rochester, NY: University of Rochester Press, 2002); R. Ryan and E. Deci, "Self-Determination Theory and the Facilitation of Intrinsic Motivation, Social Development, and Well-Being," *American Psychologist* 55, no. 1 (2000), pp. 68–78; and M. Gagné and E. L. Deci, "Self-Determination Theory and Work Motivation," *Journal of Organizational Behavior* 26, no. 4 (2005), pp. 331–362.

20. See, for example, E. L. Deci, R. Koestner, and R. M. Ryan, "A Meta-Analytic Review of Experiments Examining the Effects of Extrinsic Rewards on Intrinsic Motivation," *Psychological Bulletin* 125, no. 6 (1999), pp. 627–668; G. J. Greguras and J. M. Diefendorff, "Different Fits Satisfy Different Needs: Linking Person-Environment Fit to Employee Commitment and Performance Using Self-Determination Theory," *Journal of Applied Psychology* 94, no. 2 (2009), pp. 465–477; and D. Liu, X. Chen, and X. Yao, "From Autonomy to Creativity: A Multilevel Investigation of the Mediating Role of Harmonious Passion," *Journal of Applied Psychology* 96, no. 2 (2011), pp. 294–309.

21. R. Eisenberger and L. Rhoades, "Incremental Effects of Reward on Creativity," *Journal of Personality and Social Psychology* 81, no. 4 (2001), 728–741; and R. Eisenberger, W. D. Pierce, and J. Cameron, "Effects of Reward on Intrinsic Motivation—Negative, Neutral, and Positive: Comment on Deci, Koestner, and Ryan (1999)," *Psychological Bulletin* 125, no. 6 (1999), pp. 677–691.

22. M. Burgess, M. E. Enzle, and R. Schmaltz, "Defeating the Potentially Deleterious Effects of Externally Imposed Deadlines: Practitioners' Rules-of-Thumb," *Personality and Social Psychology Bulletin* 30, no. 7 (2004), pp. 868–877.

23. K. M. Sheldon, A. J. Elliot, and R. M. Ryan, "Self-Concordance and Subjective Well-being in Four Cultures," *Journal of Cross-Cultural Psychology* 35, no. 2 (2004), pp. 209–223.

24. J. E. Bono and T. A. Judge, "Self-Concordance at Work: Toward Understanding the Motivational Effects of Transformational Leaders," *Academy of Management Journal* 46, no. 5 (2003), pp. 554–571.

25. J. P. Meyer, T. E. Becker, and C. Vandenberghe, "Employee Commitment and Motivation: A Conceptual Analysis and Integrative Model," *Journal of Applied Psychology* 89, no. 6 (2004), pp. 991–1007.

26. W. A. Kahn, "Psychological Conditions of Personal Engagement and Disengagement at Work," *Academy of Management Journal* 33, no. 4 (1990), pp. 692–724.

27. www.gallup.com/consulting/52/Employee-Engagement.aspx

28. J. K. Harter, F. L. Schmidt, and T. L. Hayes, "Business-Unit-Level Relationship Between Employee Satisfaction, Employee Engagement, and Business Outcomes: A Meta-Analysis," *Journal of Applied Psychology* 87, no. 2 (2002), pp. 268–279.

29. M. S. Christian, A. S. Garza, and J. E. Slaughter, "Work Engagement: A Quantitative Review and Test of Its Relations with Task and Contextual Performance," *Personnel Psychology* 64, no. 1 (2011), pp. 89–136.

30. W. B. Schaufeli, A. B. Bakker, and W. van Rhenen, "How Changes in Job Demands and Resources Predict Burnout, Work Engagement, and Sickness Absenteeism," *Journal of Organizational Behavior* 30, no. 7 (2009), pp. 893–917; E. R. Crawford, J. A. LePine, and B. L. Rich, "Linking Job Demands and Resources to Employee Engagement and Burnout: A Theoretical Extension and Meta-Analytic Test," *Journal of Applied Psychology* 95, no. 5 (2010), pp. 834–848; and D. Xanthopoulou, A. B. Bakker, E. Demerouti, and W. B. Schaufeli, "Reciprocal Relationships Between job Resources, Personal Resources, and Work Engagement," *Journal of Vocational Behavior* 74, no. 3 (2009), pp. 235–244.

31. B. L. Rich, J. A. LePine, and E. R. Crawford, "Job Engagement: Antecedents and Effects on Job Performance," *Academy of Management Journal* 53, no. 3 (2010), pp. 617–635.

32. M. Tims, A. B. Bakker, and D. Xanthopoulou, "Do Transformational Leaders Enhance Their Followers' Daily Work Engagement?" *Leadership Quarterly* 22, no. 1 (2011), pp. 121–131; and F. O. Walumbwa, P. Wang, H. Wang, J. Schaubroeck, and B. J. Avolio, "Psychological Processes Linking Authentic Leadership to Follower Behaviors," *Leadership Quarterly* 21, no. 5 (2010), pp. 901–914.

33. D. A. Newman and D. A. Harrison, "Been There, Bottled That: Are State and Behavioral Work Engagement New and Useful Construct 'Wines?'" *Industrial and Organizational Psychology* 1, no. 1 (2008), pp. 31–35; A. J. Wefald and R. G. Downey, "Job Engagement in Organizations: Fad, Fashion, or Folderol," *Journal of Organizational Behavior* 30, no. 1 (2009), pp. 141–145.

34. See, for example, Rich, LePine, and Crawford, "Job Engagement: Antecedents and Effects on Job Performance;"

and Christian, Garza, and Slaughter, "Work Engagement: A Quantitative Review and Test of Its Relations with Task and Contextual Performance."

35. J. M. George, "The Wider Context, Costs, and Benefits of Work Engagement," *European Journal of Work and Organizational Psychology* 20, no. 1 (2011), pp. 53–59; and J. R. B. Halbesleben, J. Harvey, and M. C. Bolino, "Too Engaged? A Conservation of Resources View of the Relationship Between Work Engagement and Work Interference with Family," *Journal of Applied Psychology* 94, no. 6 (2009), pp. 1452–1465.

36. E. A. Locke, "Toward a Theory of Task Motivation and Incentives," *Organizational Behavior and Human Performance* 3, no. 2 (1968), pp. 157–189.

37. P. C. Earley, P. Wojnaroski, and W. Prest, "Task Planning and Energy Expended: Exploration of How Goals Influence Performance," *Journal of Applied Psychology* 72, no. 1 (1987), pp. 107–114.

38. See M. E. Tubbs, "Goal Setting: A Meta-Analytic Examination of the Empirical Evidence," *Journal of Applied Psychology* 71, no. 3 (1986), pp. 474–483; and E. A. Locke and G. P. Latham, "New Directions in Goal-Setting Theory," *Current Directions in Psychological Science* 15, no. 5 (2006), pp. 265–268.

39. E. A. Locke and G. P. Latham, "Building a Practically Useful Theory of Goal Setting and Task Motivation," *American Psychologist* 57, no. 2 (2002), pp. 705–717.

40. J. M. Ivancevich and J. T. McMahon, "The Effects of Goal Setting, External Feedback, and Self-Generated Feedback on Outcome Variables: A Field Experiment," *Academy of Management Journal* 25, no. 2 (1982), pp. 359–372; and E. A. Locke, "Motivation Through Conscious Goal Setting," *Applied and Preventive Psychology* 5, no. 2 (1996), pp. 117–124.

41. See, for example, G. P. Latham, M. Erez, and E. A. Locke, "Resolving Scientific Disputes by the Joint Design of Crucial Experiments by the Antagonists: Application to the Erez-Latham Dispute Regarding Participation in Goal Setting," *Journal of Applied Psychology* 73, no. 4 (1988), pp. 753–772; T. D. Ludwig and E. S. Geller, "Assigned Versus Participative Goal Setting and Response Generalization: Managing Injury Control among Professional Pizza Deliverers," *Journal of Applied Psychology* 82, no. 2 (1997), pp. 253–261; and S. G. Harkins and M. D. Lowe, "The Effects of Self-Set Goals on Task Performance," *Journal of Applied Social Psychology* 30, no. 1 (2000), pp. 1–40.

42. M. Erez, P. C. Earley, and C. L. Hulin, "The Impact of Participation on Goal Acceptance and Performance: A Two-Step Model," *Academy of Management Journal* 28, no. 1 (1985), pp. 50–66.

43. E. A. Locke, "The Motivation to Work: What We Know," *Advances in Motivation and Achievement* 10 (1997), pp. 375–412; and Latham, Erez, and Locke, "Resolving Scientific Disputes by the Joint Design of Crucial Experiments by the Antagonists," pp. 753–772.

44. Ibid.

45. J. R. Hollenbeck, C. R. Williams, and H. J. Klein, "An Empirical Examination of the Antecedents of Commitment to Difficult Goals," *Journal of Applied Psychology* 74, no. 1 (1989), pp. 18–23. See also J. C. Wofford, V. L. Goodwin, and S. Premack, "Meta-Analysis of the Antecedents of Personal Goal Level and of the Antecedents and Consequences of Goal Commitment," *Journal of Management* 18, no. 3 (1992), pp. 595–615; M. E. Tubbs, "Commitment as a Moderator of the Goal-Performance Relation: A Case for Clearer Construct Definition," *Journal of Applied Psychology* 78, no. 1 (1993), pp. 86–97; and J. E. Bono and A. E. Colbert, "Understanding Responses to Multi-Source Feedback: The Role of Core Self-evaluations," *Personnel Psychology* 58, no. 1 (2005), pp. 171–203.

46. See R. E. Wood, A. J. Mento, and E. A. Locke, "Task Complexity as a Moderator of Goal Effects: A Meta-Analysis," *Journal of Applied Psychology* 72, no. 3 (1987), pp. 416–425; R. Kanfer and P. L. Ackerman, "Motivation and Cognitive Abilities: An Integrative/Aptitude-Treatment Interaction Approach to Skill Acquisition," *Journal of Applied Psychology* 74, no. 4 (1989), pp. 657–690; T. R. Mitchell and W. S. Silver, "Individual and Group Goals When Workers Are Interdependent: Effects on Task Strategies and Performance," *Journal of Applied Psychology* 75, no. 2 (1990), pp. 185–193; and A. M. O'Leary-Kelly, J. J. Martocchio, and D. D. Frink, "A Review of the Influence of Group Goals on Group Performance," *Academy of Management Journal* 37, no. 5 (1994), pp. 1285–1301.

47. D. F. Crown, "The Use of Group and Groupcentric Individual Goals for Culturally Heterogeneous and Homogeneous Task Groups: An Assessment of European Work Teams," *Small Group Research* 38, no. 4 (2007), pp. 489–508; J. Kurman, "Self-Regulation Strategies in Achievement Settings: Culture and Gender Differences," *Journal of Cross-Cultural Psychology* 32, no. 4 (2001), pp. 491–503; and M. Erez and P. C. Earley, "Comparative Analysis of Goal-Setting Strategies Across Cultures," *Journal of Applied Psychology* 72, no. 4 (1987), pp. 658–665.

48. C. Sue-Chan and M. Ong, "Goal Assignment and Performance: Assessing the Mediating Roles of Goal Commitment and Self-Efficacy and the Moderating Role of Power Distance," *Organizational Behavior and Human Decision Processes* 89, no. 2 (2002), pp. 1140–1161.

49. G. P. Latham and E. A. Locke, "Enhancing the Benefits and Overcoming the Pitfalls of Goal Setting," *Organizational Dynamics* 35, no. 6, pp. 332–340; L. D. Ordóñez, M. E. Schweitzer, A. D. Galinsky, and M. Bazerman, "Goals Gone Wild: The Systematic Side Effects of Overprescribing Goal Setting," *Academy of Management Perspectives* 23, no. 1 (2009), pp. 6–16; and E. A. Locke and G. P. Latham, "Has Goal Setting Gone Wild, or Have Its Attackers Abandoned Good Scholarship?" *Academy of Management Perspectives* 23, no. 1 (2009), pp. 17–23.

50. S. J. Perry, L. A. Witt, L. M. Penney, and L. Atwater, "The Downside of Goal-Focused Leadership: The Role of Personality in Subordinate Exhaustion," *Journal of Applied Psychology* 95, no. 6 (2010), pp. 1145–1153.

51. See, for example, A. D. Sajkovic, E. A. Locke, and E. S. Blair, "A First Examination of the Relationships Between Primed Subconscious Goals, Assigned Conscious Goals, and Task Performance," *Journal of Applied Psychology* 91, no. 5 (2006), pp. 1172–1180; G. P. Latham, A. D. Stajkovic, and E. A. Locke, "The Relevance and Viability of Subconscious Goals in the Workplace," *Journal of Management* 36, no. 1 (2010), pp. 234–255; and A. Schantz

and G. P. Latham, "An Exploratory Field Experiment on the Effect of Subconscious and Conscious Goals on Employee Performance," *Organizational Behavior and Human Decision Processes* 109, no. 1 (2009), pp. 9–17.

52. "KEYGroup Survey Finds Nearly Half of All Employees Have No Set Performance Goals," *IPMA-HR Bulletin* (March 10, 2006), p. 1; S. Hamm, "SAP Dangles a Big, Fat Carrot," *BusinessWeek* (May 22, 2006), pp. 67–68; and "P&G CEO Wields High Expectations but No Whip," *USA Today* (February 19, 2007), p. 3B.

53. See, for instance, S. J. Carroll and H. L. Tosi, *Management by Objectives: Applications and Research* (New York: Macmillan, 1973); and R. Rodgers and J. E. Hunter, "Impact of Management by Objectives on Organizational Productivity," *Journal of Applied Psychology* 76, no. 2 (1991), pp. 322–336.

54. See, for instance, T. H. Poister and G. Streib, "MBO in Municipal Government: Variations on a Traditional Management Tool," *Public Administration Review* (January/February 1995), pp. 48–56; C. Garvey, "Goalsharing Scores," *HRMagazine* (April 2000), pp. 99–106; E. Lindberg and T. L. Wilson, "Management by Objectives: The Swedish Experience in Upper Secondary Schools," *Journal of Educational Administration* 49, no. 1 (2011), pp. 62–75; and A. C. Spaulding, L. D. Gamm, and J. M. Griffith, "Studer Unplugged: Identifying Underlying Managerial Concepts," *Hospital Topics* 88, no. 1 (2010), pp. 1–9.

55. See, for instance, R. Rodgers, J. E. Hunter, and D. L. Rogers, "Influence of Top Management Commitment on Management Program Success," *Journal of Applied Psychology* 78, no. 1 (1993), pp. 151–155; M. Tanikawa, "Fujitsu Decides to Backtrack on Performance-Based Pay," *New York Times* (March 22, 2001), p. W1; and W. F. Roth, "Is Management by Objectives Obsolete?" *Global Business and Organizational Excellence* 28 (May/June 2009), pp. 36–43.

56. A. Bandura, *Self-Efficacy: The Exercise of Control* (New York: Freeman, 1997).

57. A. D. Stajkovic and F. Luthans, "Self-Efficacy and Work-Related Performance: A Meta-Analysis," *Psychological Bulletin* 124, no. 2 (1998), pp. 240–261; and A. Bandura, "Cultivate Self-Efficacy for Personal and Organizational Effectiveness," in E. Locke (ed.), *Handbook of Principles of Organizational Behavior* (Malden, MA: Blackwell, 2004), pp. 120–136.

58. M. Salanova, S. Llorens, and W. B. Schaufeli, "Yes I Can, I Feel Good, and I Just Do It! On Gain Cycles and Spirals of Efficacy Beliefs, Affect, and Engagement," *Applied Psychology* 60, no. 2 (2011), pp. 255–285.

59. P. Tierney and S. M. Farmer, "Creative Self-Efficacy Development and Creative Performance Over Time," *Journal of Applied Psychology* 96, no. 2 (2011), pp. 277–293.

60. A. Bandura and D. Cervone, "Differential Engagement in Self-Reactive Influences in Cognitively-Based Motivation," *Organizational Behavior and Human Decision Processes* 38, no. 1 (1986), pp. 92–113.

61. Bandura, *Self-Efficacy.*

62. C. L. Holladay and M. A. Quiñones, "Practice Variability and Transfer of Training: The Role of Self-Efficacy Generality," *Journal of Applied Psychology* 88, no. 6 (2003), pp. 1094–1103.

63. E. C. Dierdorff, E. A. Surface, and K. G. Brown, "Frame-of-Reference Training Effectiveness: Effects of Goal Orientation and Self-Efficacy on Affective, Cognitive, Skill-Based, and Transfer Outcomes," *Journal of Applied Psychology* 95, no. 6 (2010), pp. 1181–1191; and R. Grossman, and E. Salas, "The Transfer of Training: What Really Matters," *International Journal of Training and Development* 15, no. 2 (2011), pp. 103–120.

64. R. C. Rist, "Student Social Class and Teacher Expectations: The Self-Fulfilling Prophecy in Ghetto Education," *Harvard Educational Review* 70, no. 3 (2000), pp. 266–301.

65. D. Eden, "Self-Fulfilling Prophecies in Organizations," in J. Greenberg (ed.), *Organizational Behavior: The State of the Science,* 2nd ed. (Mahwah, NJ: Lawrence Erlbaum, 2003), pp. 91–122.

66. Ibid.

67. T. A. Judge, C. L. Jackson, J. C. Shaw, B. Scott, and B. L. Rich, "Self-Efficacy and Work-Related Performance: The Integral Role of Individual Differences," *Journal of Applied Psychology* 92, no. 1 (2007), pp. 107–127.

68. Ibid.

69. J. L. Komaki, T. Coombs, and S. Schepman, "Motivational Implications of Reinforcement Theory," in R. M. Steers, L. W. Porter, and G. Bigley (eds.), *Motivation and Work Behavior,* 6th ed. (New York: McGraw-Hill, 1996), pp. 87–107.

70. B. F. Skinner, *Contingencies of Reinforcement* (East Norwalk, CT: Appleton-Century-Crofts, 1971).

71. J. A. Mills, *Control: A History of Behavioral Psychology* (New York: New York University Press, 2000).

72. E. A. Locke, "Latham vs. Komaki: A Tale of Two Paradigms," *Journal of Applied Psychology* 65, no. 1 (1980), pp. 16–23.

73. A. Bandura, *Social Learning Theory* (Upper Saddle River, NJ: Prentice Hall, 1977).

74. J. S. Adams, "Inequity in Social Exchanges," in L. Berkowitz (ed.), *Advances in Experimental Social Psychology* (New York: Academic Press, 1965), pp. 267–300.

75. P. S. Goodman, "An Examination of Referents Used in the Evaluation of Pay," *Organizational Behavior and Human Performance* 12, no. 2 (1974), pp. 170–195; W. Scholl, E. A. Cooper, and J. F. McKenna, "Referent Selection in Determining Equity Perception: Differential Effects on Behavioral and Attitudinal Outcomes," *Personnel Psychology* 40, no. 1 (1987), pp. 113–127; and M. L. Williams, M. A. McDaniel, and N. T. Nguyen, "A Meta-Analysis of the Antecedents and Consequences of Pay Level Satisfaction," *Journal of Applied Psychology* 91, no. 2 (2006), pp. 392–413.

76. C. T. Kulik and M. L. Ambrose, "Personal and Situational Determinants of Referent Choice," *Academy of Management Review* 17, no. 2 (1992), pp. 212–237.

77. C. Ostroff and L. E. Atwater, "Does Whom You Work with Matter? Effects of Referent Group Gender and Age Composition on Managers' Compensation," *Journal of Applied Psychology* 88, no. 4 (2003), pp. 725–740.

78. Ibid.

79. See, for example, E. Walster, G. W. Walster, and W. G. Scott, *Equity: Theory and Research* (Boston: Allyn & Bacon, 1978); and J. Greenberg, "Cognitive Reevaluation of Outcomes in Response to Underpayment Inequity," *Academy of Management Journal,* March 1989, pp. 174–184.

80. P. S. Goodman and A. Friedman, "An Examination of Adams' Theory of Inequity," *Administrative Science Quarterly* 16, no. 3 (1971), pp. 271–288; R. P. Vecchio, "An Individual-Differences Interpretation of the Conflicting Predictions Generated by Equity Theory and Expectancy Theory," *Journal of Applied Psychology* 66, no. 4 (1981), pp. 470–481; R. T. Mowday, "Equity Theory Predictions of Behavior in Organizations," in R. Steers, L. W. Porter, and G. Bigley (eds.), *Motivation and Work Behavior,* 6th ed. (New York: McGraw-Hill, 1996), pp. 111–131; R. W. Griffeth and S. Gaertner, "A Role for Equity Theory in the Turnover Process: An Empirical Test," *Journal of Applied Social Psychology* 31, no. 5 (2001), pp. 1017–1037; and L. K. Scheer, N. Kumar, and J.-B. E. M. Steenkamp, "Reactions to Perceived Inequity in U.S. and Dutch Interorganizational Relationships," *Academy of Management* 46, no. 3 (2003), pp. 303–316.

81. See, for example, R. C. Huseman, J. D. Hatfield, and E. W. Miles, "A New Perspective on Equity Theory: The Equity Sensitivity Construct," *Academy of Management Journal* 12, no. 2 (1987), pp. 222–234; K. S. Sauley and A. G. Bedeian, "Equity Sensitivity: Construction of a Measure and Examination of Its Psychometric Properties," *Journal of Management* 26, no. 5 (2000), pp. 885–910; and J. A. Colquitt, "Does the Justice of One Interact with the Justice of Many? Reactions to Procedural Justice in Teams," *Journal of Applied Psychology* 89, no. 4 (2004), pp. 633–646.

82. J. Greenberg and S. Ornstein, "High Status Job Title as Compensation for Underpayment: A Test of Equity Theory," *Journal of Applied Psychology* 68, no. 2 (1983), pp. 285–297; and J. Greenberg, "Equity and Workplace Status: A Field Experiment," *Journal of Applied Psychology* 73, no. 4 (1988), pp. 606–613.

83. See, for instance, J. A. Colquitt, D. E. Conlon, M. J. Wesson, C. O. L. H. Porter, and K. Y. Ng, "Justice at the Millennium: A Meta-Analytic Review of the 25 Years of Organizational Justice Research," *Journal of Applied Psychology* 86, no. 3 (2001), pp. 425–445; T. Simons and Q. Roberson, "Why Managers Should Care About Fairness: The Effects of Aggregate Justice Perceptions on Organizational Outcomes," *Journal of Applied Psychology* 88, no. 3 (2003), pp. 432–443; and B. C. Holtz and C. M. Harold, "Fair Today, Fair Tomorrow? A Longitudinal Investigation of Overall Justice Perceptions," *Journal of Applied Psychology* 94, no. 5 (2009), pp. 1185–1199.

84. K. Leung, K. Tong, and S. S. Ho, "Effects of Interactional Justice on Egocentric Bias in Resource Allocation Decisions," *Journal of Applied Psychology* 89, no. 3 (2004), pp. 405–415; and L. Francis-Gladney, N. R. Manger, and R. B. Welker, "Does Outcome Favorability Affect Procedural Fairness as a Result of Self-Serving Attributions," *Journal of Applied Social Psychology* 40, no. 1 (2010), pp. 182–194.

85. "Americans Feel They Pay Fair Share of Taxes, Says Poll," NaturalNews.com, May 2, 2005, www.naturalnews.com/007297.html.

86. See, for example, R. Cropanzano, J. H. Stein, and T. Nadisic, *Social Justice and the Experience of Emotion* (New York: Routledge/Taylor and Francis Group, 2011).

87. D. P. Skarlicki and D. E. Rupp, "Dual Processing and Organizational Justice: The Role of Rational Versus Experiential Processing in Third-Party Reactions to Workplace Mistreatment," *Journal of Applied Psychology* 95, no. 5 (2010), pp. 944–952.

88. G. S. Leventhal, "What Should Be Done with Equity Theory? New Approaches to the Study of Fairness in Social Relationships," in K. Gergen, M. Greenberg, and R. Willis (eds.), *Social Exchange: Advances in Theory and Research* (New York: Plenum, 1980), pp. 27–55.

89. J. C. Shaw, E. Wild, and J. A. Colquitt, "To Justify or Excuse? A Meta-Analytic Review of the Effects of Explanations," *Journal of Applied Psychology* 88, no. 3 (2003), pp. 444–458.

90. D. P. Skarlicki and R. Folger, "Retaliation in the Workplace: The Roles of Distributive, Procedural, and Interactional Justice," *Journal of Applied Psychology* 82, no. 3 (1997), pp. 434–443; and D. A. Jones, "Getting Even with One's Supervisor and One's Organization: Relationships Among Types of Injustice, Desires for Revenge, and Counterproductive Work Behavior," *Journal of Organizational Behavior* 30, no. 4 (2009), pp. 525–542.

91. R. Cropanzano, C. A. Prehar, and P. Y. Chen, "Using Social Exchange Theory to Distinguish Procedural from Interactional Justice," *Group & Organization Management* 27, no. 3 (2002), pp. 324–351; and S. G. Roch and L. R. Shanock, "Organizational Justice in an Exchange Framework: Clarifying Organizational Justice Dimensions," *Journal of Management* 32, no. 2 (2006), pp. 299–322.

92. Colquitt, Conlon, Wesson, Porter, and Ng, "Justice at the Millennium," pp. 425–445.

93. J. K. Giacobbe-Miller, D. J. Miller, and V. I. Victorov, "A Comparison of Russian and U.S. Pay Allocation Decisions, Distributive Justice Judgments, and Productivity Under Different Payment Conditions," *Personnel Psychology* 51, no. 1 (1998), pp. 137–163.

94. M. C. Bolino and W. H. Turnley, "Old Faces, New Places: Equity Theory in Cross-Cultural Contexts," *Journal of Organizational Behavior* 29, no. 1 (2008), pp. 29–50.

95. B. A. Scott, J. A. Colquitt, and E. L. Paddock, "An Actor-Focused Model of Justice Rule Adherence and Violation: The Role of Managerial Motives and Discretion," *Journal of Applied Psychology* 94, no. 3 (2009), pp. 756–769.

96. L. J. Barlcay and D. P. Skarlicki, "Healing the Wounds of Organizational Injustice: Examining the Benefits of Expressive Writing," *Journal of Applied Psychology* 94, no. 2 (2009), pp. 511–523.

97. R. Fischer and P. B. Smith, "Reward Allocation and Culture: A Meta-Analysis," *Journal of Cross-Cultural Psychology* 34, no. 3 (2003), pp. 251–268.

98. F. F. T. Chiang and T. Birtch, "The Transferability of Management Practices: Examining Cross-National Differences in Reward Preferences," *Human Relations* 60, no. 9 (2007), pp. 1293–1330; A. E. Lind, T. R. Tyler, and Y. J. Huo, "Procedural Context and Culture: Variation in the Antecedents of Procedural Justice Judgments," *Journal of Personality and Social Psychology* 73, no. 4 (1997), pp. 767–780; M. J. Gelfand, M. Erez, and Z. Aycan, "Cross-Cultural Organizational Behavior," *Annual Review of Psychology* 58, (2007), pp. 479–514.

99. V. H. Vroom, *Work and Motivation* (New York: Wiley, 1964).

100. For criticism, see H. G. Heneman III and D. P. Schwab, "Evaluation of Research on Expectancy Theory Prediction of Employee Performance," *Psychological Bulletin* 78, no. 1 (1972), pp. 1–9; T. R. Mitchell, "Expectancy Models of Job Satisfaction, Occupational Preference and Effort: A Theoretical, Methodological and Empirical Appraisal," *Psychological Bulletin* 81, no. 12 (1974), pp. 1053–1077; and W. Van Eerde and H. Thierry, "Vroom's Expectancy Models and Work-Related Criteria: A Meta-Analysis," *Journal of Applied Psychology* 81, no. 5 (1996), pp. 575–586. For support, see L. W. Porter and E. E. Lawler III, *Managerial Attitudes and Performance* (Homewood, IL: Irwin, 1968); and J. J. Donovan, "Work Motivation," in N. Anderson et al. (eds.), *Handbook of Industrial, Work & Organizational Psychology*, vol. 2 (Thousand Oaks, CA: Sage, 2001), pp. 56–59.

101. Vroom refers to these three variables as expectancy, instrumentality, and valence, respectively.

102. J. Nocera, "The Anguish of Being an Analyst," *The New York Times* (March 4, 2006), pp. B1, B12.

103. R. J. House, H. J. Shapiro, and M. A. Wahba, "Expectancy Theory as a Predictor of Work Behavior and Attitudes: A Re-evaluation of Empirical Evidence," *Decision Sciences* 5, no. 3 (1974), pp. 481–506.

104. For other examples of models that seek to integrate motivation theories, see H. J. Klein, "An Integrated Control Theory Model of Work Motivation," *Academy of Management Review* 14, no. 2 (1989), pp. 150–172; E. A. Locke, "The Motivation Sequence, the Motivation Hub, and the Motivation Core," *Organizational Behavior and Human Decision Processes* 50, no. 2 (1991), pp. 288–299; and T. R. Mitchell, "Matching Motivational Strategies with Organizational Contexts," pp. 60–62.

105. This section is based on F. J. Landy and W. S. Becker, "Motivation Theory Reconsidered," in L. L. Cummings and B. M. Staw (eds.), *Research in Organizational Behavior*, vol. 9 (Greenwich, CT: JAI Press, 1987), pp. 24–35.

MyManagementLab

Access a host of interactive learning aids to help strengthen your understanding of the chapter concepts at **www.mymanagementlab.com**.

MOTIVATION MINUS THE MOOLAH

When Nancy Jackson hired a new full-time salesperson for a company she co-owns, Architectural Systems, she was caught off guard by protests from her 19 employees. "I couldn't believe their reactions," she says. The employees had seen their work hours reduced or their pay trimmed. Why was she hiring someone new amid the retrenchments? "There's been a lot of emotional hand-holding here that we've never had to do before," Jackson says.

Christopher Mills, co-owner of Prime Debt Services, a debt management firm in Dallas, has found it helpful to meet with employees one-on-one more often. "I found the more I listened, the better they pepped up," he says. Mills even has taken to cooking them a breakfast of waffles, bacon, and coffee every Wednesday.

Beyond expressing support and appreciation for their efforts, some employers are being more creative in their approaches to motivation. Elise Lelong, owner of a New York consulting firm, decided to upgrade her employees' job titles. "It doesn't cost anything and it makes them feel good," Lelong says. "You've got to think outside the money box when it comes to motivating your employees in this economic environment." Lelong took other steps too, including giving her employees increased chances to work remotely and with flexible hours. Atlassian, an Australian software company, motivated its employees by allowing them to devote 20 percent of their time to any software idea they liked.

When pay raises aren't possible, sometimes even smaller monetary awards can make a difference. Though Intuit human resource manager Jennifer Lepird spent several weeks working long hours on a big one-time project, she still pulled several "all nighters" toward the end. When the project was finished, what was her reward? The acquisitions team leader sent her a gift certificate worth several hundred dollars. Jennifer was thrilled. "The fact that somebody took the time to recognize the effort," she said, "made the long hours just melt away."

Eric Mosley, founder and CEO of Boston-based Globoforce, is a big fan of this approach. "Even higher earners can appreciate a small award if it is unexpected," he said. "Even billionaires appreciate a Christmas sweater from their mom."

Sources: S. E. Needleman, "Business Owners Try to Motivate Employees," *The Wall Street Journal* (January 14, 2010), p. B5; P. D. Broughton, "More Than a Paycheck," *The Wall Street Journal* (February 2, 2010), p. A17; and T. Demos, "Motivate Without Spending Millions," *Fortune* (April 12, 2010), pp. 37–38.

Motivation: From Concepts to Applications

Money is better than poverty,
if only for financial reasons.

—Woody Allen

Photo: Factory worker receiving certificate. *Source:* Corbis/Glow Images

Employee of the Month
Certificate of Excellence

is hereby granted to:

Richard Lopez

Though pay is one central means of motivation we consider in this chapter—what we call extrinsic motivation—it's not the only one. The other is intrinsic. The following self-assessment will provide some information about how intrinsically motivating *your* job might be.

In Chapter 7, we focused on motivation theories. In this chapter, we start applying motivation concepts to practices such as employee involvement and skill-based pay. Why? Because it's one thing to know specific theories; it's quite another to see how, as a manager, you can use them.

SELF-ASSESSMENT LIBRARY

What's My Job'S Motivating Potential?

In the Self-Assessment Library (available on CD or online), take assessment I.C.9 (What's My Job's Motivating Potential?) and answer the following questions. If you currently do not have a job, answer the questions for your most recent job.

1. How did you score relative to your classmates?
2. Did your score surprise you? Why or why not?
3. How might your results affect your career path?

Motivating by Job Design: The Job Characteristics Model

1 Describe the job characteristics model and evaluate the way it motivates by changing the work environment.

Increasingly, research on motivation focuses on approaches that link motivational concepts to changes in the way work is structured.

Research in **job design** suggests the way the elements in a job are organized can increase or decrease effort and also suggests what those elements are. We'll first review the job characteristics model and then discuss some ways jobs can be redesigned. Finally, we'll explore alternative work arrangements.

The Job Characteristics Model

Developed by J. Richard Hackman and Greg Oldham, the **job characteristics model (JCM)** says we can describe any job in terms of five core job dimensions:[1]

1. **Skill variety** is the degree to which a job requires a variety of different activities so the worker can use a number of different skills and talent. The work of a garage owner-operator who does electrical repairs, rebuilds engines, does bodywork, and interacts with customers scores high on skill variety. The job of a bodyshop worker who sprays paint 8 hours a day scores low on this dimension.
2. **Task identity** is the degree to which a job requires completion of a whole and identifiable piece of work. A cabinetmaker who designs a piece of furniture, selects the wood, builds the object, and finishes it to perfection has a job that scores high on task identity. A job scoring low on this dimension is operating a factory lathe solely to make table legs.
3. **Task significance** is the degree to which a job affects the lives or work of other people. The job of a nurse handling the diverse needs of patients in a hospital intensive care unit scores high on task significance; sweeping floors in a hospital scores low.
4. **Autonomy** is the degree to which a job provides the worker freedom, independence, and discretion in scheduling work and determining the procedures in carrying it out. A salesperson who schedules his or her own

work each day and decides on the most effective sales approach for each customer without supervision has a highly autonomous job. A salesperson who is given a set of leads each day and is required to follow a standardized sales script with each potential customer has a job low on autonomy.

5. **Feedback** is the degree to which carrying out work activities generates direct and clear information about your own performance. A job with high feedback is assembling iPads and testing them to see whether they operate properly. A factory worker who assembles iPads but then routes them to a quality-control inspector for testing and adjustments receives low feedback from his or her activities.

Exhibit 8-1 presents the job characteristics model (JCM). Note how the first three dimensions—skill variety, task identity, and task significance—combine to create meaningful work the incumbent will view as important, valuable, and worthwhile. Note, too, that jobs with high autonomy give incumbents a feeling of personal responsibility for the results and that, if a job provides feedback, employees will know how effectively they are performing. From a motivational standpoint, the JCM proposes that individuals obtain internal rewards when they learn (knowledge of results) that they personally (experienced responsibility)

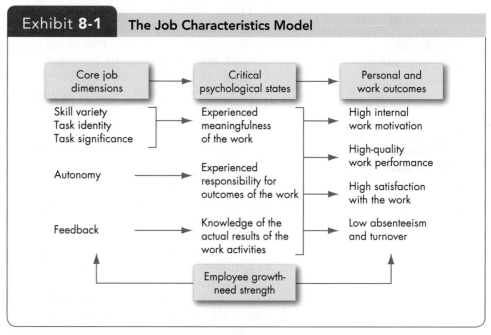

Exhibit 8-1   The Job Characteristics Model

Source: Adaptation of Job Characteristics Model, pp. 78–80 from J. Richard Hackman & Greg R. Oldham, *Work Redesign*, 1st Edition, © 1980. Adapted by permission of Pearson Education, Inc., Upper Saddle River, NJ.

job design *The way the elements in a job are organized.*

job characteristics model (JCM) *A model that proposes that any job can be described in terms of five core job dimensions: skill variety, task identity, task significance, autonomy, and feedback.*

skill variety *The degree to which a job requires a variety of different activities.*

task identity *The degree to which a job requires completion of a whole and identifiable piece of work.*

task significance *The degree to which a job has a substantial impact on the lives or work of other people.*

autonomy *The degree to which a job provides substantial freedom and discretion to the individual in scheduling the work and in determining the procedures to be used in carrying it out.*

feedback *The degree to which carrying out the work activities required by a job results in the individual obtaining direct and clear information about the effectiveness of his or her performance.*

have performed well on a task they care about (experienced meaningfulness).[2] The more these three psychological states are present, the greater will be employees' motivation, performance, and satisfaction, and the lower their absenteeism and likelihood of leaving. As Exhibit 8-1 also shows, individuals with a high growth need are more likely to experience the critical psychological states when their jobs are enriched—and respond to them more positively—than are their counterparts with low growth need.

We can combine the core dimensions into a single predictive index, called the **motivating potential score (MPS)**, and calculated as follows:

$$\text{MPS} = \frac{\text{Skill variety} + \text{Task identity} + \text{Task significance}}{3} \times \text{Autonomy} \times \text{Feedback}$$

To be high on motivating potential, jobs must be high on at least one of the three factors that lead to experienced meaningfulness and high on both autonomy and feedback. If jobs score high on motivating potential, the model predicts motivation, performance, and satisfaction will improve and absence and turnover will be reduced.

Much evidence supports the JCM concept that the presence of a set of job characteristics—variety, identity, significance, autonomy, and feedback—does generate higher and more satisfying job performance.[3] But apparently we can better calculate motivating potential by simply adding the characteristics rather than using the formula.[4] Think about your job. Do you have the opportunity to work on different tasks, or is your day pretty routine? Are you able to work independently, or do you constantly have a supervisor or co-worker looking over your shoulder? What do you think your answers to these questions say about your job's motivating potential? Revisit your answers to the self-assessment at the beginning of this chapter, and then calculate your MPS from the job characteristics model. You might try computing your MPS score two ways: using the traditional MPS formula, or simply adding the dimensions. Then compare.

A few studies have tested the job characteristics model in different cultures, but the results aren't very consistent. One study suggested that when employees are "other oriented" (concerned with the welfare of others at work), the relationship between intrinsic job characteristics and job satisfaction was weaker. The fact that the job characteristics model is relatively individualistic (considering the relationship between the employee and his or her work) suggests job enrichment strategies may not have the same effects in collectivistic cultures as in individualistic cultures (such as the United States).[5] However, another study suggested the degree to which jobs had intrinsic job characteristics predicted job satisfaction and job involvement equally well for U.S., Japanese, and Hungarian employees.[6]

How Can Jobs Be Redesigned?

2   Compare and contrast the main ways jobs can be redesigned.

"Every day was the same thing," Frank Greer said. "Stand on that assembly line. Wait for an instrument panel to be moved into place. Unlock the mechanism and drop the panel into the Jeep Liberty as it moved by on the line. Then I plugged in the harnessing wires. I repeated that for eight hours a day. I don't care that they were paying me twenty-four dollars an hour. I was going crazy. I did it for almost a year and a half. Finally, I just said to my wife that this isn't going to be the way I'm going to spend the rest of my life. My brain was turning to JELL-O on that Jeep assembly line. So I quit. Now I work in a print shop and I make less than fifteen dollars an hour. But let me tell you, the work I do is really interesting. The job changes all the time, I'm continually learning new things, and the work really challenges me! I look forward every morning to going to work again."

"CEO Pay Can't Be Measured"

Anything can be measured. The question is whether it can be measured *well*. As for CEO pay, it seems it can't be measured well, or at least in a way experts agree upon. There is nearly as much disagreement among compensation experts about how to measure CEO pay as about whether CEOs are paid too much.

You may have read that the Dodd-Frank Act of 2010 included "say on pay" rules, whereby shareholders have a vote on executive compensation. But what pay? There is often a big difference between expected pay (bonus targets and value of options at the time granted) and realized pay (bonuses actually received and realized value of options).

Eli Lilly announced the pay of its CEO John Lechleiter as $15.9 million, up 10 percent from the year before. However, independent experts calculated his pay as $20.9 million, a 45 percent increase over the prior year. Occidental Petroleum CEO Ray Irani's expected pay was $58.3 million. His realized pay was $222.6 million.

Says one expert, even if the pay for two CEOs is reported to be the same,

"you can pretty much bet they are not the same."

Why is it so difficult to get an accurate read on CEO pay? A big part of the answer is that, for some time, a CEO's pay has been tied to the company's financial performance, and an organization's finances are quite complex. CEO pay might be based on any number of important financial indicators: stock appreciation, profitability, market share, earnings per share, and equity per share. Many CEOs are granted stocks at a current price, providing an incentive to make the stock price grow. The main principal at play here is to align the CEO's interests with the company's interests, so the CEO's motivation is in line with the company's best interests.

Another complicating factor is time: the value of CEO incentives often depends on measures, like stock price, that are time-sensitive. The worth of a stock option thus depends on when that option is exercised. Timing is everything. When Apple granted CEO Steve Jobs 7.5 million stock options, someone falsified records so the stock was priced low, as if at an earlier time

than when the options were actually granted. This "backdating" allowed Jobs to sell his options at a greater profit when he cashed them in.

Because this type of compensation is complicated, so are the motivational dynamics involved. CEOs have an incentive to "manage to the metric"—such as by making decisions that maximize short-term stock price (and thus increase the value of stock options) at the expense of the long-term interests of the company. Not all CEOs do this, of course, but the incentive is often there.

As one expert concluded, "Assessing CEO compensation is a bit of a black art."

Sources: S. Thurm, "For CEO Pay, A Single Number Never Tells the Whole Story," *The Wall Street Journal* (March 6, 2010), p. A2; B. McClure, "A Guide To CEO Compensation," *San Francisco Chronicle* (May 2, 2011), downloaded May 25, 2011, from www.investopedia.com/; and R. Gopalan, T. Milbourn, F. Song, and A. V. Thakor, "The Optimal Duration of Executive Compensation: Theory and Evidence," Working paper, April 15, 2011, Washington University in St. Louis, http://apps.olin.wustl.edu/faculty/milbourn/duration_ver_apr15.pdf.

The repetitive tasks in Frank Greer's job at the Jeep plant provided little variety, autonomy, or motivation. In contrast, his job in the print shop is challenging and stimulating. Let's look at some of the ways to put JCM into practice to make jobs more motivating.

Job Rotation If employees suffer from overroutinization of their work, one alternative is **job rotation**, or the periodic shifting of an employee from one task to another with similar skill requirements at the same organizational level (also called *cross-training*). At Singapore Airlines, a ticket agent may take on the duties of a baggage handler. Extensive job rotation is among the reasons Singapore Airlines is rated one of the best airlines in the world and a highly desirable place to work. Many manufacturing firms have adopted job rotation as a means

motivating potential score (MPS) *A predictive index that suggests the motivating potential in a job.*

job rotation *The periodic shifting of an employee from one task to another.*

of increasing flexibility and avoiding layoffs.[7] Managers at Apex Precision Technologies, a custom-machine shop in Indiana, train workers on all the company's equipment so they can move around as needed in response to incoming orders. Although job rotation has often been conceptualized as an activity for assembly line and manufacturing employees, many organizations use job rotation for new managers to help them get a picture of the whole business as well.[8]

The strengths of job rotation are that it reduces boredom, increases motivation, and helps employees better understand how their work contributes to the organization. An indirect benefit is that employees with a wider range of skills give management more flexibility in scheduling work, adapting to changes, and filling vacancies.[9] International evidence from Italy, Britain, and Turkey does show that job rotation is associated with higher levels of organizational performance in manufacturing settings.[10] However, job rotation has drawbacks. Training costs increase, and moving a worker into a new position reduces productivity just when efficiency at the prior job is creating organizational economies. Job rotation also creates disruptions when members of the work group have to adjust to the new employee. And supervisors may also have to spend more time answering questions and monitoring the work of recently rotated employees.

Job Enrichment   **Job enrichment** expands jobs by increasing the degree to which the worker controls the planning, execution, and evaluation of the work. An enriched job organizes tasks to allow the worker to do a complete activity, increases the employee's freedom and independence, increases responsibility, and provides feedback so individuals can assess and correct their own performance.[11]

How does management enrich an employee's job? Exhibit 8-2 offers suggested guidelines based on the job characteristics model. *Combining tasks* puts fractionalized tasks back together to form a new and larger module of work. *Forming natural work units* makes an employee's tasks create an identifiable and meaningful whole. *Establishing client relationships* increases the direct relationships between workers and their clients (clients can be internal as well as outside the organization). *Expanding jobs vertically* gives employees responsibilities and control formerly reserved for management. *Opening feedback channels* lets employees know how well they are doing and whether their performance is improving, deteriorating, or remaining constant.

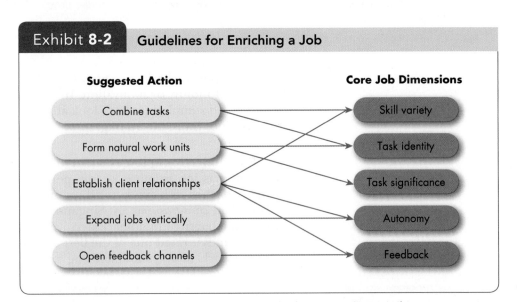

| Exhibit 8-2 | Guidelines for Enriching a Job |

Suggested Action → **Core Job Dimensions**

- Combine tasks
- Form natural work units
- Establish client relationships
- Expand jobs vertically
- Open feedback channels

- Skill variety
- Task identity
- Task significance
- Autonomy
- Feedback

Source: "Guidelines for Enriching a Job" Source: J. R. Hackman and J. L. Suttle (eds.), *Improving Life at Work* (Glenview, IL: Scott Foresman, 1977), p. 138. Reprinted by permission of Richard Hackman and J. Lloyd Suttle.

Some newer versions of job enrichment concentrate specifically on improving the meaningfulness of work. One method is to relate employee experiences to customer outcomes, by providing employees with stories from customers who benefited from the company's products or services. The medical device manufacturer Medtronic invites people to describe how Medtronic products have improved, or even saved, their lives and shares these stories with employees during annual meetings, providing a powerful reminder of the impact of their work. Researchers recently found that when university fund-raisers briefly interacted with the undergraduates who would receive the scholarship money they raised, they persisted 42 percent longer, and raised nearly twice as much money, as those who didn't interact with potential recipients.[12]

Another method for improving the meaningfulness of work is providing employees with mutual assistance programs.[13] Employees who can help each other directly through their work come to see themselves, and the organizations for which they work, in more positive, pro-social terms. This, in turn, can increase employee affective commitment.

Many organizations provide job enrichment through cross-training to learn new skills, and through job rotation to perform new tasks in another position. Employees typically work with managers to set job enrichment goals, identify desired competencies, and find appropriate placement. For example, an employee who usually works in handling client records might receive cross-training to learn about the organization's purchasing and accounting systems. Then an accounting employee might learn about client data processes. These two employees could then rotate through one another's jobs, allowing them to cover for one another and prepare for possible future promotions.

The evidence on job enrichment shows it reduces absenteeism and turnover costs and increases satisfaction, but not all programs are equally effective.[14] A review of 83 organizational interventions designed to improve performance management showed that frequent, specific feedback related to solving problems was linked to consistently higher performance, but infrequent feedback that focused more on past problems than future solutions was much less effective.[15] Some recent evidence suggests job enrichment works best when it compensates for poor feedback and reward systems.[16] Work design may also not affect everyone in the same way. One recent study showed employees with a higher preference for challenging work experienced larger reductions in stress following job redesign than individuals who did not prefer challenging work.[17]

Alternative Work Arrangements

3 Identify three alternative work arrangements and show how they might motivate employees.

Another approach to motivation is to alter work arrangements with flextime, job sharing, or telecommuting. These are likely to be especially important for a diverse workforce of dual-earner couples, single parents, and employees caring for a sick or aging relative.

Flextime   Susan Ross is the classic "morning person." She rises at 5:00 A.M. sharp each day, full of energy. However, as she puts it, "I'm usually ready for bed right after the 7:00 P.M. news."

job enrichment   *The vertical expansion of jobs, which increases the degree to which the worker controls the planning, execution, and evaluation of the work.*

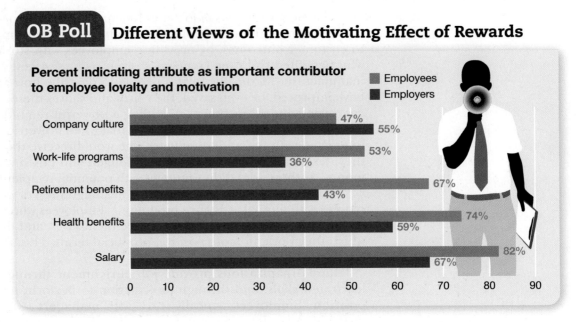

OB Poll   **Different Views of the Motivating Effect of Rewards**

Percent indicating attribute as important contributor to employee loyalty and motivation

- Employees
- Employers

Attribute	Employees	Employers
Company culture	47%	55%
Work-life programs	53%	36%
Retirement benefits	67%	43%
Health benefits	74%	59%
Salary	82%	67%

Sources: Survey of 1,503 employers and 1,305 full-time employees. MetLife, www.metlife.com; and "Loyalty Drivers," *Workforce Management* (October 2010), p. 18.

Susan's work schedule as a claims processor at The Hartford Financial Services Group is flexible. Her office opens at 6:00 A.M. and closes at 7:00 P.M. It's up to her how she schedules her 8-hour day within this 13-hour period. Because Susan is a morning person and also has a 7-year-old son who gets out of school at 3:00 P.M. every day, she opts to work from 6:00 A.M. to 3:00 P.M. "My work hours are perfect. I'm at the job when I'm mentally most alert, and I can be home to take care of my son after he gets out of school."

Susan's schedule is an example of **flextime**, short for "flexible work time." Employees must work a specific number of hours per week but are free to vary their hours of work within certain limits. As in Exhibit 8-3, each day consists of a common core, usually 6 hours, with a flexibility band surrounding it. The core may be 9:00 A.M. to 3:00 P.M., with the office actually opening at 6:00 A.M. and closing at 6:00 P.M. All employees are required to be at their jobs during the common core period, but they may accumulate their other 2 hours before, after, or before *and* after that. Some flextime programs allow employees to accumulate extra hours and turn them into a free day off each month.

Flextime has become extremely popular; according to the Bureau of Labor Statistics, nearly 26 percent of working women with children have flexible work schedules, compared to just 14 percent in 1991.[18] And this is not just a U.S. phenomenon. In Germany, for instance, 29 percent of businesses offer flextime, and such practices are becoming more widespread in Japan as well.[19]

Claimed benefits include reduced absenteeism, increased productivity, reduced overtime expenses, reduced hostility toward management, reduced traffic congestion around work sites, elimination of tardiness, and increased autonomy and responsibility for employees—any of which may increase employee job satisfaction.[20] But what's flextime's actual record?

Most of the evidence stacks up favorably. Flextime tends to reduce absenteeism and frequently improves worker productivity,[21] probably for several reasons. Employees can schedule their work hours to align with personal

Exhibit 8-3	Possible Flextime Staff Schedules

Schedule 1

Percent Time:	100% = 40 hours per week
Core Hours:	9:00 A.M.–5:00 P.M., Monday through Friday (1 hour lunch)
Work Start Time:	Between 8:00 A.M. and 9:00 A.M.
Work End Time:	Between 5:00 P.M. and 6:00 P.M.

Schedule 2

Percent Time:	100% = 40 hours per week
Work Hours:	8:00 A.M.–6:30 P.M., Monday through Thursday (1/2 hour lunch) Friday off
Work Start Time:	8:00 A.M.
Work End Time:	6:30 P.M.

Schedule 3

Percent Time:	90% = 36 hours per week
Work Hours:	8:30 A.M.–5:00 P.M., Monday through Thursday (1/2 hour lunch) 8:00 A.M.–Noon Friday (no lunch)
Work Start Time:	8:30 A.M. (Monday–Thursday); 8:00 A.M. (Friday)
Work End Time:	5:00 P.M. (Monday–Thursday); Noon (Friday)

Schedule 4

Percent Time:	80% = 32 hours per week 8:00 A.M.–6:00 P.M., Monday through Wednesday (1/2 hour lunch)
Work Hours:	8:00 A.M.–11:30 A.M. Thursday (no lunch) Friday off
Work Start Time:	Between 8:00 A.M. and 9:00 A.M.
Work End Time:	Between 5:00 P.M. and 6:00 P.M.

demands, reducing tardiness and absences, and they can work when they are most productive. Flextime can also help employees balance work and family lives; it is a popular criterion for judging how "family friendly" a workplace is.

Flextime's major drawback is that it's not applicable to every job or every worker. It works well with clerical tasks for which an employee's interaction with people outside his or her department is limited. It is not a viable option for receptionists, sales personnel in retail stores, or people whose service jobs require them to be at their workstations at predetermined times. It also appears that people who have a stronger desire to separate their work and family lives are less prone to take advantage of opportunities for flextime.[22] Overall, employers need to consider the appropriateness of both the work and the workers before implementing flextime schedules.

Job Sharing   Job sharing allows two or more individuals to split a traditional 40-hour-a-week job. One might perform the job from 8:00 A.M. to noon and the other from 1:00 P.M. to 5:00 P.M., or the two could work full but alternate

flextime   *Flexible work hours.*

job sharing   *An arrangement that allows two or more individuals to split a traditional 40-hour-a-week job.*

Accounting firm Ernst & Young has created a supportive culture of flexibility that allows employees to control where, when, and how their work gets accomplished. The company encourages employees to utilize flexible work hours to meet their personal and professional goals while still providing the highest quality of service to customers. Employees value their flexible work options that include shorter workweeks, working from home, and varying start and finish times of their work days. Giving employees freedom in scheduling their work helps Ernst & Young attract and retain a satisfied, motivated, and loyal work force. In this photo, Ernst & Young employees work on the process of tabulating ballots for the Golden Globe Awards.

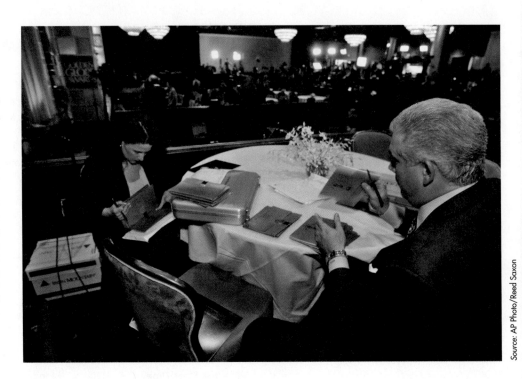

Source: AP Photo/Reed Saxon

days. For example, top Ford engineers Julie Levine and Julie Rocco engage in a job-sharing program that allows both of them to spend time with their families while working on the time-intensive job of redesigning the Explorer crossover. Typically, one of the pair will work late afternoons and evenings while the other works mornings. They both agree that the program has worked well, although making such a relationship work requires a great deal of time and preparation.[23]

Approximately 19 percent of large organizations now offer job sharing.[24] Reasons it is not more widely adopted are likely the difficulty of finding compatible partners to share a job and the historically negative perceptions of individuals not completely committed to their job and employer.

Job sharing allows an organization to draw on the talents of more than one individual in a given job. A bank manager who oversees two job sharers describes it as an opportunity to get two heads but "pay for one."[25] It also opens the opportunity to acquire skilled workers—for instance, women with young children and retirees—who might not be available on a full-time basis.[26] Many Japanese firms are increasingly considering job sharing—but for a very different reason.[27] Because Japanese executives are extremely reluctant to fire people, job sharing is seen as a potentially humanitarian means of avoiding layoffs due to overstaffing.

From the employee's perspective, job sharing increases flexibility and can increase motivation and satisfaction when a 40-hour-a-week job is just not practical. But the major drawback is finding compatible pairs of employees who can successfully coordinate the intricacies of one job.[28]

Telecommuting   It might be close to the ideal job for many people. No commuting, flexible hours, freedom to dress as you please, and few or no interruptions from colleagues. It's called **telecommuting**, and it refers to working at home at least 2 days a week on a computer linked to the employer's office.[29] (A closely related term—the *virtual office*—describes working from home on a relatively permanent basis.)

The U.S. Department of the Census estimated there had been a 25 percent increase in self-employed home-based workers from 1999 to 2005, and a 20 percent increase in employed workers who work exclusively from home.[30] One recent survey of more than 5,000 HR professionals found that 35 percent of organizations allowed employees to telecommute at least part of the time, and 21 percent allowed employees to telecommute full-time.[31] Well-known organizations that actively encourage telecommuting include AT&T, IBM, American Express, Sun Microsystems, and a number of U.S. government agencies.[32]

What kinds of jobs lend themselves to telecommuting? There are three categories: routine information-handling tasks, mobile activities, and professional and other knowledge-related tasks.[33] Writers, attorneys, analysts, and employees who spend the majority of their time on computers or the telephone—such as telemarketers, customer-service representatives, reservation agents, and product-support specialists—are natural candidates. As telecommuters, they can access information on their computers at home as easily as in the company's office.

The potential pluses of telecommuting include a larger labor pool from which to select, higher productivity, less turnover, improved morale, and reduced office-space costs. A positive relationship exists between telecommuting and supervisor performance ratings, but any relationship between telecommuting and potentially lower turnover intentions has not been substantiated in research to date.[34] The major downside for management is less direct supervision of employees. In today's team-focused workplace, telecommuting may make it more difficult to coordinate teamwork and can reduce knowledge transfer in organizations.[35] From the employee's standpoint, telecommuting can offer a considerable increase in flexibility and job satisfaction—but not without costs.[36] For employees with a high social need, telecommuting can increase feelings of isolation and reduce job satisfaction. And all telecommuters are vulnerable to the "out of sight, out of mind" effect.[37] Employees who aren't at their desks, who miss meetings, and who don't share in day-to-day informal workplace interactions may be at a disadvantage when it comes to raises and promotions.

The Social and Physical Context of Work

Robin and Chris both graduated from college a couple years ago with degrees in elementary education and became first-grade teachers in different school districts. Robin immediately confronted a number of obstacles: several long-term employees were hostile to her hiring, there was tension between administrators and teachers, and students had little interest in learning. Chris had a colleague who was excited to work with a new graduate, students who were excited about academics, and a highly supportive principal. Not surprisingly, at the end of the first year, Chris had been a considerably more effective teacher than Robin.

The job characteristics model shows most employees are more motivated and satisfied when their intrinsic work tasks are engaging. However, having the most interesting workplace characteristics in the world may not always lead to satisfaction if you feel isolated from your co-workers, and having good social relationships can make even the most boring and onerous tasks more fulfilling.

telecommuting   *Working from home at least two days a week on a computer that is linked to the employer's office.*

FedEx provides two services: the physical transportation and distribution of packages and the information systems that identify and track the location of packages at any time. Jobs involved in physically transporting packages, such as the employee shown here serving a customer at a FedEx office, are not suitable candidates for telecommuting. But in operating one of the world's largest computer and telecommunications networks for recording and tracking shipments, FedEx provides many computer-based jobs for telecommuters who help the firm process more than 20 million transactions daily.

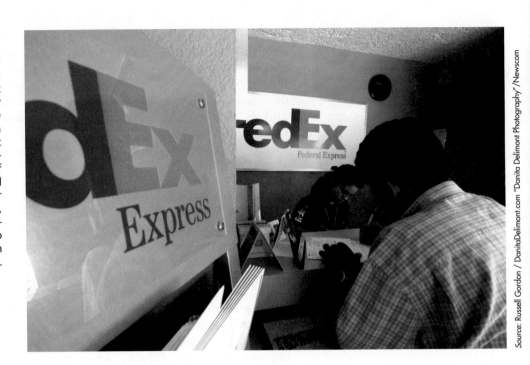

Research demonstrates that social aspects and work context are as important as other job design features.[38] Policies such as job rotation, worker empowerment, and employee participation have positive effects on productivity, at least partially because they encourage more communication and a positive social environment.

Some social characteristics that improve job performance include interdependence, social support, and interactions with other people outside work. Social interactions are strongly related to positive moods and give employees more opportunities to clarify their work role and how well they are performing. Social support gives employees greater opportunities to obtain assistance with their work. Constructive social relationships can bring about a positive feedback loop as employees assist one another in a "virtuous circle."

The work context is also likely to affect employee satisfaction. Hot, loud, and dangerous work is less satisfying than work conducted in climate-controlled, relatively quiet, and safe environments. This is probably why most people would rather work in a coffee shop than a metalworking foundry. Physical demands make people physically uncomfortable, which is likely to show up in lower levels of job satisfaction.

To assess why an employee is not performing to his or her best level, see whether the work environment is supportive. Does the employee have adequate tools, equipment, materials, and supplies? Does the employee have favorable working conditions, helpful co-workers, supportive work rules and procedures, sufficient information to make job-related decisions, and adequate time to do a good job? If not, performance will suffer.

Employee Involvement

Employee involvement is a participative process that uses employees' input to increase their commitment to the organization's success. The logic is that if we engage workers in decisions that affect them and increase their autonomy and control over their work lives, they will become more motivated, more committed to the organization, more productive, and more satisfied with their jobs.[39]

Employee involvement programs differ among countries.[40] A study of four countries, including the United States and India, confirmed the importance of modifying practices to reflect national culture.[41] While U.S. employees readily accepted employee involvement programs, managers in India who tried to empower their employees were rated low by those employees. These reactions are consistent with India's high power–distance culture, which accepts and expects differences in authority. Similarly, Chinese workers who were very accepting of traditional Chinese values showed few benefits from participative decision making, but workers who were less traditional were more satisfied and had higher performance ratings under participative management.[42]

Examples of Employee Involvement Programs

Let's look at two major forms of employee involvement—participative management and representative participation—in more detail.

Participative Management   Common to all **participative management** programs is joint decision making, in which subordinates share a significant degree of decision-making power with their immediate superiors. Participative management has, at times, been promoted as a panacea for poor morale and low productivity. But for it to work, employees must be engaged in issues relevant to their interests so they'll be motivated, they must have the competence and knowledge to make a useful contribution, and trust and confidence must exist among all parties.[43]

Studies of the participation–performance relationship have yielded mixed findings.[44] Organizations that institute participative management do have higher stock returns, lower turnover rates, and higher estimated labor productivity, although these effects are typically not large.[45] A careful review of research at the individual level shows participation typically has only a modest influence on employee productivity, motivation, and job satisfaction. Of course, this doesn't mean participative management can't be beneficial under the right conditions. However, it is not a sure means for improving performance.

Representative Participation   Almost every country in western Europe requires companies to practice **representative participation**, called "the most widely legislated form of employee involvement around the world."[46] Its goal is to redistribute power within an organization, putting labor on a more equal footing with the interests of management and stockholders by letting workers be represented by a small group of employees who actually participate.

The two most common forms are works councils and board representatives.[47] Works councils are groups of nominated or elected employees who must be consulted when management makes decisions about employees. Board representatives are employees who sit on a company's board of directors and represent employees' interests.

Source: AP Photo/Jacquelyn Martin

Empowerment is a corporate value at Wegmans Food Markets Inc., a regional supermarket chain that involves its employees in making decisions that affect their work and please their customers. This family-run company empowers employees, such as the chef shown here at a café within a Wegmans store, to make on-the-spot decisions without consulting their immediate supervisors. For example, if a customer wants a product that Wegmans doesn't stock, any employee can initiate the process of procuring the item for the customer. Wegmans believes that empowering employees leads to higher job satisfaction and productivity.

4   Give examples of employee involvement measures and show how they can motivate employees.

The influence of representative participation on working employees seems to be minimal.[48] Works councils are dominated by management and have little impact on employees or the organization. While participation might increase the motivation and satisfaction of employee representatives, there is little evidence this trickles down to the employees they represent. Overall, "the greatest value of representative participation is symbolic. If one is interested in changing employee attitudes or in improving organizational performance, representative participation would be a poor choice."[49]

Linking Employee Involvement Programs and Motivation Theories

Employee involvement draws on a number of the motivation theories we discussed in Chapter 7. Theory Y is consistent with participative management and Theory X with the more traditional autocratic style of managing people. In terms of two-factor theory, employee involvement programs could provide intrinsic motivation by increasing opportunities for growth, responsibility, and involvement in the work itself. The opportunity to make and implement decisions—and then see them work out—can help satisfy an employee's needs for responsibility, achievement, recognition, growth, and enhanced self-esteem. And extensive employee involvement programs clearly have the potential to increase employee intrinsic motivation in work tasks.

Using Rewards to Motivate Employees

5 Demonstrate how the different types of variable-pay programs can increase employee motivation.

As we saw in Chapter 3, pay is not a primary factor driving job satisfaction. However, it does motivate people, and companies often underestimate its importance in keeping top talent. A 2006 study found that while 45 percent of employers thought pay was a key factor in losing top talent, 71 percent of top performers called it a top reason.[50]

Given that pay is so important, will the organization lead, match, or lag the market in pay? How will individual contributions be recognized? In this section, we consider (1) what to pay employees (decided by establishing a pay structure), (2) how to pay individual employees (decided through variable pay plans and skill-based pay plans), (3) what benefits and choices to offer (such as flexible benefits), and (4) how to construct employee recognition programs.

What to Pay: Establishing a Pay Structure

There are many ways to pay employees. The process of initially setting pay levels entails balancing *internal equity*—the worth of the job to the organization (usually established through a technical process called job evaluation)—and *external equity*—the external competitiveness of an organization's pay relative to pay elsewhere in its industry (usually established through pay surveys). Obviously, the best pay system pays what the job is worth (internal equity) while also paying competitively relative to the labor market.

Some organizations prefer to pay above the market, while some may lag the market because they can't afford to pay market rates, or they are willing to bear the costs of paying below market (namely, higher turnover as people are lured to better-paying jobs). Walmart, for example, pays less than its competitors and often outsources jobs overseas. Chinese workers in Shenzhen earn $120 a month (that's $1,440 per year) to make stereos for Walmart. Of the 6,000 factories that are worldwide suppliers to Walmart, 80 percent are located in China. In fact, one-eighth of all Chinese exports to the United States go to Walmart.[51]

Pay more, and you may get better-qualified, more highly motivated employees who will stay with the organization longer. A study covering 126 large organizations found employees who believed they were receiving a competitive pay level had higher morale and were more productive, and customers were more satisfied as well.[52] But pay is often the highest single operating cost for an organization, which means paying too much can make the organization's products or services too expensive. It's a strategic decision an organization must make, with clear trade-offs.

How to Pay: Rewarding Individual Employees Through Variable-Pay Programs

"Why should I put any extra effort into this job?" asked Anne Garcia, a fourth-grade elementary schoolteacher in Denver, Colorado. "I can excel or I can do the bare minimum. It makes no difference. I get paid the same. Why do anything above the minimum to get by?" Comments like Anne's have been voiced by schoolteachers for decades because pay increases were tied to seniority. Recently, however, a number of states have revamped their compensation systems to motivate people like Anne by tying teacher pay levels to results in the classroom in various ways, and other states are considering such programs.[53]

A number of organizations are moving away from paying solely on credentials or length of service. Piece-rate plans, merit-based pay, bonuses, profit sharing, gainsharing, and employee stock ownership plans are all forms of a **variable-pay program**, which bases a portion of an employee's pay on some individual and/or organizational measure of performance. Earnings therefore fluctuate up and down.[54]

First grade teacher Kim Hemmis at Will Rogers Elementary School in Houston, Texas, is eligible to receive a bonus when her students make progress on state and national achievement tests. The city's school board adopted a merit pay "Teacher Performance Plan" that rewards teachers who work hard and whose students show academic improvement. The plan motivates teachers by basing part of their pay on performance rather than only on seniority or degrees. The move toward rewarding teachers with bonuses for individual performance follows the widespread adoption of variable-pay plans in many businesses and government agencies.

Source: AP Photo/David J. Phillip

variable-pay program   *A pay plan that bases a portion of an employee's pay on some individual and/or organizational measure of performance.*

Variable-pay plans have long been used to compensate salespeople and executives. Some estimates suggest more than 70 percent of U.S. companies have some form of variable-pay plan, up from only about 5 percent in 1970.[55] Moreover, recent research shows that 26 percent of U.S. companies have either increased or plan to increase the proportion of variable pay in employee pay programs, and another 40 percent have already recently increased the proportion of variable pay.[56] Unfortunately, most employees still don't see a strong connection between pay and performance. Only 29 percent say their performance is rewarded when they do a good job.[57]

The fluctuation in variable pay is what makes these programs attractive to management. It turns part of an organization's fixed labor costs into a variable cost, thus reducing expenses when performance declines. When the U.S. economy encountered a recession in 2001 and 2008, companies with variable pay were able to reduce their labor costs much faster than others.[58] When pay is tied to performance, the employee's earnings also recognize contribution rather than being a form of entitlement. Over time, low performers' pay stagnates, while high performers enjoy pay increases commensurate with their contributions.

Let's examine the different types of variable-pay programs in more detail.

Piece-Rate Pay   The **piece-rate pay plan** has long been popular as a means of compensating production workers with a fixed sum for each unit of production completed. A pure piece-rate plan provides no base salary and pays the employee only for what he or she produces. Ballpark workers selling peanuts and soda are frequently paid this way. If they sell 40 bags of peanuts at $1 each, their take is $40. The harder they work and the more peanuts they sell, the more they earn. The limitation of these plans is that they're not feasible for many jobs. Surgeons earn significant salaries regardless of their patients' outcomes. Would it be better to pay them only if their patients fully recover? It seems unlikely that most would accept such a deal, and it might cause unanticipated consequences as well (such as surgeons avoiding patients with complicated or terminal conditions). So, although incentives are motivating and relevant for some jobs, it is unrealistic to think they can constitute the only piece of some employees' pay.

Merit-Based Pay   A **merit-based pay plan** pays for individual performance based on performance appraisal ratings. A main advantage is that people thought to be high performers can get bigger raises. If designed correctly, merit-based plans let individuals perceive a strong relationship between their performance and their rewards.[59]

Most large organizations have merit pay plans, especially for salaried employees. IBM increases employees' base salary based on annual performance evaluations. Since the 1990s, when the economy stumbled badly, an increasing number of Japanese companies have abandoned seniority-based pay in favor of merit-based pay. Koichi Yanashita of Takeda Chemical Industries, commented, "The merit-based salary system is an important means to achieve goals set by the company's top management, not just a way to change wages."[60]

To motivate and retain the best, more companies are increasing the differential between top and bottom performers. The consulting firm Hewitt Associates found that in 2006, employers gave their best performers roughly 10 percent raises, compared to 3.6 percent for average performers and 1.3 percent for below-average performers. These differences have increased over time. Martyn Fisher of Imperial Chemical in the United Kingdom said his company widened the merit pay gap between top and average performers because "as much as we would regret our average performers leaving, we regret more an above-target performer leaving."[61]

Despite their intuitive appeal, merit pay plans have several limitations. One is that they are typically based on an annual performance appraisal and thus are only as valid as the performance ratings. Another limitation is that the pay-raise pool fluctuates on economic or other conditions that have little to do with individual performance. One year, a colleague at a top university who performed very well in teaching and research was given a pay raise of $300. Why? Because the pay-raise pool was very small. Yet that is hardly pay-for-performance. Finally, unions typically resist merit pay plans. Relatively few teachers are covered by merit pay for this reason. Instead, seniority-based pay, where all employees get the same raises, predominates.

Bonuses   An annual **bonus** is a significant component of total compensation for many jobs. Among *Fortune* 100 CEOs, the bonus (mean of $1.01 million) generally exceeds the base salary (mean of $863,000). But bonus plans increasingly include lower-ranking employees; many companies now routinely reward production employees with bonuses in the thousands of dollars when profits improve. The incentive effects of performance bonuses should be higher than those of merit pay because, rather than paying for performance years ago (that was rolled into base pay), bonuses reward recent performance. When times are bad, firms can cut bonuses to reduce compensation costs. Steel company Nucor, for example, guarantees employees only about $10 per hour, but bonuses can be substantial. In 2006, the average Nucor worker made roughly $91,000. When the recession hit, bonuses were cut dramatically: in 2009, total pay had dropped 40 percent.[62]

This example also highlights the downside of bonuses: employees' pay is more vulnerable to cuts. This is problematic when bonuses are a large percentage of

Walmart is an organization that includes hourly workers in the company's bonus plan. In this photo, a Walmart manager distributes bonus checks to store employees. The bonus amount for employees depends on their full- or part-time status and on the amount of profit individual stores earn each year. Hourly workers also have the potential to receive additional quarterly bonuses based on their store's performance. Employees who go above and beyond in helping customers are also eligible for customer satisfaction bonuses. Bonuses give Walmart employees an incentive to increase sales and improve customer service.

Source: s70/ZUMA Press/Newscom

---

piece-rate pay plan   *A pay plan in which workers are paid a fixed sum for each unit of production completed.*

merit-based pay plan   *A pay plan based on performance appraisal ratings.*

bonus   *A pay plan that rewards employees for recent performance rather than historical performance.*

total pay or when employees take bonuses for granted. "People have begun to live as if bonuses were not bonuses at all but part of their expected annual income," said Jay Lorsch, a Harvard Business School professor. KeySpan Corp., a 9,700-employee utility company in New York, tried to combine yearly bonuses with a smaller merit-pay raise. Elaine Weinstein, KeySpan's senior vice president of HR, credits the plan with changing the culture from "entitlement to meritocracy."[63]

Skill-Based Pay   **Skill-based pay** (also called *competency-based* or *knowledge-based pay*) is an alternative to job-based pay that bases pay levels on how many skills employees have or how many jobs they can do.[64] For employers, the lure of skill-based pay plans is increased flexibility of the workforce: staffing is easier when employee skills are interchangeable. Skill-based pay also facilitates communication across the organization because people gain a better understanding of each other's jobs. One study found that across 214 different organizations, skill-based pay was related to higher levels of workforce flexibility, positive attitudes, membership behaviors, and productivity.[65] Another study found that over 5 years, a skill-based pay plan was associated with higher levels of individual skill change and skill maintenance.[66] These results suggest that skill-based pay plans are effective in achieving their stated goals.

What about the downsides? People can "top out"—that is, they can learn all the skills the program calls for them to learn. This can frustrate employees after they've been challenged by an environment of learning, growth, and continual pay raises. IDS Financial Services[67] found itself paying people more even though there was little immediate use for their new skills. IDS eventually dropped its skill-based pay plan for one that equally balances individual contribution and gains in work-team productivity. Finally, skill-based plans don't address level of performance but only whether someone can perform the skill. Perhaps reflecting these weaknesses, one study of 97 U.S. companies using skill-based pay plans found that 39 percent had switched to a more traditional market-based pay plan 7 years later.[68]

Profit-Sharing Plans   A **profit-sharing plan** distributes compensation based on some established formula designed around a company's profitability. Compensation can be direct cash outlays or, particularly for top managers, allocations of stock options. When you read about executives like Oracle's Larry Ellison earning $75.33 million in pay, it almost all (88.8 percent in Ellison's case) comes from cashing in stock options previously granted based on company profit performance. Not all profit-sharing plans are so grand in scale. Jacob Luke, age 13, started his own lawn-mowing business after getting a mower from his uncle. Jacob employs his brother, Isaiah, and friend, Marcel Monroe, and pays them each 25 percent of the profits he makes on each yard. Profit-sharing plans at the organizational level appear to have positive impacts on employee attitudes; employees report a greater feeling of psychological ownership.[69]

Gainsharing   **Gainsharing**[70] is a formula-based group incentive plan that uses improvements in group productivity from one period to another to determine the total amount of money allocated. Its popularity seems narrowly focused among large manufacturing companies, although some health care organizations have experimented with it as a cost-saving mechanism. Gainsharing differs from profit sharing in tying rewards to productivity gains rather than profits, so employees can receive incentive awards even when the organization isn't profitable. Because the benefits accrue to groups of workers, high performers pressure weaker ones to work harder, improving performance for the group as a whole.[71]

Employee Stock Ownership Plans   An **employee stock ownership plan (ESOP)** is a company-established benefit plan in which employees acquire stock, often at below-market prices, as part of their benefits. Companies as varied as Publix Supermarkets and W. L. Gore & Associates are now more than 50 percent employee-owned.[72] But most of the 10,000 or so ESOPs in the United States are in small, privately held companies.[73]

Research on ESOPs indicates they increase employee satisfaction and innovation.[74] But their impact on performance is less clear. ESOPs have the potential to increase employee job satisfaction and work motivation, but employees need to psychologically experience ownership.[75] That is, in addition to their financial stake in the company, they need to be kept regularly informed of the status of the business and have the opportunity to influence it in order to significantly improve the organization's performance.[76]

ESOP plans for top management can reduce unethical behavior. CEOs are more likely to manipulate firm earnings reports to make themselves look good in the short run when they don't have an ownership share, even though this manipulation will eventually lead to lower stock prices. However, when CEOs own a large amount of stock, they report earnings accurately because they don't want the negative consequences of declining stock prices.[77]

Evaluation of Variable Pay   Do variable-pay programs increase motivation and productivity? Studies generally support the idea that organizations with profit-sharing plans have higher levels of profitability than those without them.[78] Profit-sharing plans have also been linked to higher levels of employee affective commitment, especially in small organizations.[79] Similarly, gainsharing has been found to improve productivity in a majority of cases and often has a positive impact on employee attitudes.[80] Another study found that whereas piece-rate pay-for-performance plans stimulated higher levels of productivity, this positive affect was not observed for risk-averse employees. Thus, economist Ed Lazear seems generally right when he says, "Workers respond to prices just as economic theory predicts. Claims by sociologists and others that monetizing incentives may actually reduce output are unambiguously refuted by the data." But that doesn't mean everyone responds positively to variable-pay plans.[81]

You'd probably think individual pay systems such as merit pay or pay-for-performance work better in individualistic cultures such as the United States or that group-based rewards such as gainsharing or profit sharing work better in collectivistic cultures. Unfortunately, there isn't much research on the issue. One recent study did suggest that employee beliefs about the fairness of a group incentive plan were more predictive of pay satisfaction in the United States than in Hong Kong. One interpretation is that U.S. employees are more critical in appraising a group pay plan, and therefore, it's more critical that the plan be communicated clearly and administered fairly.[82]

Flexible Benefits: Developing a Benefits Package

6 Show how flexible benefits turn benefits into motivators.

Todd Evans is married and has three young children; his wife is at home full-time. His Citigroup colleague Allison Murphy is married too, but her husband has a high-paying job with the federal government, and they have no children.

---

skill-based pay   *A pay plan that sets pay levels on the basis of how many skills employees have or how many jobs they can do.*

profit-sharing plan   *An organization-wide program that distributes compensation based on some established formula designed around a company's profitability.*

gainsharing   *A formula-based group incentive plan.*

employee stock ownership plan (ESOP)   *A company-established benefits plan in which employees acquire stock, often at below-market prices, as part of their benefits.*

Identifying Conflicts of Interest

Managers often find themselves needing to take multiple perspectives at the same time, and sometimes they are motivated by rewards to take actions that are unethical. Financial auditors, actuaries, and accountants have a legal responsibility to accurately report on clients' records, but they might also be tempted to present an overly positive picture to please a client and secure commissions for future work. Leading up to the financial collapse of 2008, credit rating agencies gave AAA ratings to collateralized mortgage securities that were of dubious value, possibly because they were paid by the very companies they were supposed to regulate.

It's sometimes tough to recognize conflicts of interest when they occur. Max Bazerman from Harvard University and his colleagues have been exploring the psychological processes that lead to "motivated blindness"—a tendency to only see what you want to see. For example, a car salesperson motivated by a commission to sell as much as possible might subconsciously overlook evidence that a customer won't be able to afford payments. A pharmaceutical researcher might fudge data from clinical trials in hopes of securing a bonus for bringing a new drug to market. In cases like these, financial rewards may amplify conflicts of interest.

What helps minimize conflicts of interest? The most important step is to beware of motivated blindness and be honest about where conflicts exist. Be aware of biases that might creep into your perceptions when money is at stake. Another possibility is to provide explicit rewards for behaviors like producing critical reports or detecting problems with organizational systems, especially if the responsible party has a motivation to obtain a positive result.

Sources: S. Gunz and S. van der Laan, "Actuaries, Conflicts of Interest and Professional Independence: The Case of James Hardie Industries Limited," *Journal of Business Ethics* 98, no. 4 (2011), pp. 583–596; M. H. Bazerman and A. E. Tenbrunsel, "Ethical Breakdowns," *Harvard Business Review* (April 2011), pp. 58–65; and D. A. Moore, L. Tanlu, and M. H. Bazerman, "Conflict of Interest and the Intrusion of Bias," *Judgment and Decision Making* 5, no. 1 (2010), pp. 37–53.

Todd is concerned about having a good medical plan and enough life insurance to support his family in case it's needed. In contrast, Allison's husband already has her medical needs covered on his plan, and life insurance is a low priority. Allison is more interested in extra vacation time and long-term financial benefits such as a tax-deferred savings plan.

A standardized benefits package would be unlikely to meet the needs of Todd and Allison well. Citigroup could, however, cover both sets of needs with flexible benefits.

Consistent with expectancy theory's thesis that organizational rewards should be linked to each individual employee's goals, **flexible benefits** individualize rewards by allowing each employee to choose the compensation package that best satisfies his or her current needs and situation. These plans replace the "one-benefit-plan-fits-all" programs designed for a male with a wife and two children at home that dominated organizations for more than 50 years.[83] Fewer than 10 percent of employees now fit this image: about 25 percent are single, and one-third are part of two-income families with no children. Flexible benefits can accommodate differences in employee needs based on age, marital status, spouses' benefit status, and number and age of dependents.

The three most popular types of benefits plans are modular plans, core-plus options, and flexible spending accounts.[84] *Modular plans* are predesigned packages or modules of benefits, each of which meets the needs of a specific group of employees. A module designed for single employees with no dependents might include only essential benefits. Another, designed for single parents, might have additional life insurance, disability insurance, and expanded health coverage. *Core-plus plans* consist of a core of essential benefits and a menulike selection of others

Employees of software developer Oracle Corporation, shown here in the company's cafeteria, receive a basic benefits package and may also choose coverage levels and additional benefits that meet their specific individual needs and the needs of their dependents. The OracleFlex plan gives employees flex credits they can use to purchase benefits so they can control the amount they spend for each benefit option. Employees with remaining credits may direct them to taxable income or to their 401(k) savings, health care reimbursement, or dependent care reimbursement accounts.

7   Identify the motivational benefits of intrinsic rewards.

from which employees can select. Typically, each employee is given "benefit credits," which allow the purchase of additional benefits that uniquely meet his or her needs. *Flexible spending plans* allow employees to set aside pretax dollars up to the dollar amount offered in the plan to pay for particular benefits, such as health care and dental premiums. Flexible spending accounts can increase take-home pay because employees don't pay taxes on the dollars they spend from these accounts.

Today, almost all major corporations in the United States offer flexible benefits. And they're becoming the norm in other countries, too. A recent survey of 211 Canadian organizations found that 60 percent offer flexible benefits, up from 41 percent in 2005.[85] And a similar survey of firms in the United Kingdom found that nearly all major organizations were offering flexible benefits programs, with options ranging from private supplemental medical insurance to holiday trading, discounted bus travel, and childcare vouchers.[86]

Intrinsic Rewards: Employee Recognition Programs

Laura Schendell makes only $8.50 per hour working at her fast-food job in Pensacola, Florida, and the job isn't very challenging or interesting. Yet Laura talks enthusiastically about the job, her boss, and the company that employs her. "What I like is the fact that Guy [her supervisor] appreciates the effort I make. He compliments me regularly in front of the other people on my shift, and I've been chosen Employee of the Month twice in the past six months. Did you see my picture on that plaque on the wall?"

Organizations are increasingly recognizing what Laura knows: important work rewards can be both intrinsic and extrinsic. Rewards are intrinsic in the form of employee recognition programs and extrinsic in the form of compensation systems. In this section, we deal with ways in which managers can reward and motivate employee performance.

Employee recognition programs range from a spontaneous and private thank-you to widely publicized formal programs in which specific types of behavior are encouraged and the procedures for attaining recognition are clearly identified. Some research suggests financial incentives may be more motivating in the short term, but in the long run it's nonfinancial incentives.[87]

A few years ago, 1,500 employees were surveyed in a variety of work settings to find out what they considered the most powerful workplace motivator. Their response? Recognition, recognition, and more recognition. As illustrated in Exhibit 8-4, Phoenix Inn, a West Coast chain of small hotels, encourages employees to smile by letting customers identify this desirable behavior and then recognizing winning employees with rewards and publicity.

An obvious advantage of recognition programs is that they are inexpensive, since praise is free![88] As companies and government organizations face tighter budgets, nonfinancial incentives become more attractive. Everett Clinic in Washington State uses a combination of local and centralized initiatives to encourage managers to recognize employees.[89] Employees and managers give "Hero Grams" and "Caught in the Act" cards to colleagues for exceptional accomplishments at work. Part of the incentive is simply to receive recognition, but there are also drawings for prizes based on the number of cards a person receives. Managers are trained to use the programs frequently and effectively to reward good performance. Multinational corporations like Symantec

flexible benefits   *A benefits plan that allows each employee to put together a benefits package individually tailored to his or her own needs and situation.*

Exhibit **8-4**

PHOENIX INN SUITES

I GOT CAUGHT SMILING!

WHO WAS THE PHOENIX INN SUITES EMPLOYEE THAT MADE YOUR STAY <u>EXCEPTIONAL</u>?

EMPLOYEE NAME_____

GUEST NAME _____

ROOM # _____

DATE OF STAY _____

PLEASE EITHER LEAVE THIS IN YOUR ROOM OR DROP OFF AT THE FRONT DESK

glOBalization!

Motivated by Individual Goals or Relational Goals?

In previous chapters, we discussed differences between cultures in terms of the level of individualism or collectivism. Do these differences extend to motivation? Most research suggests they do, and differences between self-oriented and collectivistic cultures will affect behavior in meaningful ways.

Psychologists have consistently demonstrated differences in the ways personal or group-based achievements are valued. In cultures that emphasize collective orientation, people strive to achieve goals that benefit the whole group and find processes that isolate individual performance and achievement. People from these cultures admire "team players" and those who help and support one another. Cultures that emphasize individual orientation are marked by striving to achieve personal goals and a lack of attention to what benefits the group as a whole. People from these cultures are more likely to admire "star performers" and those who accomplish their ends independently.

These differences in individual or relational motivation might even affect the type of practices found in organizations and the ways that people behave. Some authors propose that human resource systems can influence whether individualistic or collectivistic motivation is stronger. Collective bargaining structures and group-based decision making are more prevalent in collectivistic countries, whereas more individualistic societies like the United States are noted for individual performance rating and individual rewards. Thus, management systems might well support or even enhance the individualistic or collectivistic nature of a culture.

Sources: C. K. W. De Dreu and A. Nauta, "Self-Interest and Other-Orientation in Organizational Behavior: Implications for Job Performance, Prosocial Behavior, and Personal Initiative," *Journal of Applied Psychology* 94, no. 4 (2009), pp. 913–926; J. S. Gore, S. E. Cross, and C. Kanagawa, "Acting in Our Interests: Relational Self-Construal and Goal Motivation Across Cultures," *Motivation and Emotion* 33, no. 1 (2009), pp. 75–87; and K. W. Mossholder, H. A. Richardson, and R. P. Settoon, "Human Resource Systems and Helping in Organizations: A Relational Perspective," *Academy of Management Review* 36, no. 1 (2011), pp. 33–52.

Corporation have also increased their use of recognition programs. Centralized programs across multiple offices in different countries can help ensure that all employees, regardless of where they work, can be recognized for their contribution to the work environment.[90] Another study found that recognition programs are common in both Canadian and Australian firms as well.[91]

Despite the increased popularity of employee recognition programs, critics argue they are highly susceptible to political manipulation by management. When applied to jobs for which performance factors are relatively objective, such as sales, recognition programs are likely to be perceived by employees as fair. However, in most jobs, the criteria for good performance aren't self-evident, which allows managers to manipulate the system and recognize their favorites. Abuse can undermine the value of recognition programs and demoralize employees.

MyManagementLab

Now that you have finished this chapter, go back to **www.mymanagementlab.com** to continue practicing and applying the concepts you've learned.

Summary and Implications for Managers

Although it's always dangerous to synthesize a large number of complex ideas, the following suggestions summarize what we know about motivating employees in organizations.

- **Recognize individual differences.** Managers should be sensitive to individual differences. For example, employees from Asian cultures prefer not to be singled out as special because it makes them uncomfortable. Spend the time necessary to understand what's important to each employee. This allows you to individualize goals, level of involvement, and rewards to align with individual needs. Design jobs to align with individual needs and maximize their motivation potential.
- **Use goals and feedback.** Employees should have firm, specific goals, and they should get feedback on how well they are faring in pursuit of those goals.
- **Allow employees to participate in decisions that affect them.** Employees can contribute to setting work goals, choosing their own benefits packages, and solving productivity and quality problems. Participation can increase employee productivity, commitment to work goals, motivation, and job satisfaction.
- **Link rewards to performance.** Rewards should be contingent on performance, and employees must perceive the link between the two. Regardless of how strong the relationship is, if individuals perceive it to be weak, the results will be low performance, a decrease in job satisfaction, and an increase in turnover and absenteeism.
- **Check the system for equity.** Employees should perceive that experience, skills, abilities, effort, and other obvious inputs explain differences in performance and hence in pay, job assignments, and other obvious rewards.

"If Money Doesn't Make You Happy, You Aren't Spending It Right"

POINT

As was noted in Chapter 3, some research suggests the relationship between pay and happiness isn't very strong. But pay can be a powerful motivator. It's simply that sometimes we're motivated to pursue things that have a limited ability to make us happy.

However, the story doesn't end there. New research suggests it's what we want to *do* with money that is most important. Specifically, spending money on experiences makes us happier than spending it on possessions. That is, vacations, entertainment, and sports make people happier. Extra money spent on material objects—clothes, jewelry, cars, furniture—did not make these people happier.

One study found that $30,000 spent on leisure over several seasons had as positive an effect on life satisfaction as did getting married.

One of the reasons spending on experiences is money well spent is that experiences build relationships, and evidence reliably shows that relationships make people happier. Other research shows that people tend to look back on experiences sentimentally (you tend to forget that dirty hotel room in Prague and instead remember fondly the Charles Bridge at night); they don't attach this same sentimentality when thinking about their possessions.

One researcher has even calibrated that, in terms of the happiness produced by spending money on something, experiences beat possessions three-to-one.

Thus, it's OK to be motivated by money. Just pay attention to how you spend what you earn.

COUNTERPOINT

Money doesn't do much to improve happiness after existence needs (food, clothing, and shelter) are met. Why worry about what aspects of spending money make us happy when money doesn't appear to matter much at all? Research should instead be directed toward understanding why such a powerful motivator is such a pitiful satisfier.

What should motivate us? We know social relationships are important to happiness and well-being. Keeping in touch with friends, spending meaningful time with family, building positive and supportive relationships at work—those are what really matter, and none of them have a thing to do with making money.

Activity also contributes to happiness—not only physical activity like exercise, but being proactive too. When people reflect back on their lives, they are much more likely to regret actions they never took, as opposed to the ones they did.

Money is not evil. We need it to acquire the basic elements of survival. But after those basic needs are met, we should realize our pursuit of money to make us happy is a fallacy. We can recall an inexpensive camping trip as fondly as a stay at a five-star hotel. Thus, we should take jobs that have interesting and meaningful work, not those that command the highest wages. In managing others, we should create a culture that motivates by building relationships, giving others autonomy and input, and pursing work people see as important and challenging.

Source: S. Rosenbloom, "But Will It Make You Happy?" *The New York Times* (August 8, 2010), pp. B1, B4; J. Axelrod, "Want to Be Happy? Don't Just Sit There," *CBS News* (March 3, 2011), downloaded May 10, 2011, from www.cbsnews.com/; and J. Quoidbach, E. W. Dunn, K. V. Petrides, and M. Mikolajczak, "Money Giveth, Money Taketh Away: The Dual Effect of Wealth on Happiness," *Psychological Science*, in press.

QUESTIONS FOR REVIEW

1 What is the job characteristics model? How does it motivate employees?

2 What are the three major ways that jobs can be redesigned? In your view, in what situations would one of the methods be favored over the others?

3 What are the three alternative work arrangements of flextime, job sharing, and telecommuting? What are the advantages and disadvantages of each?

4 What are employee involvement programs? How might they increase employee motivation?

5 What is variable pay? What are the variable-pay programs that are used to motivate employees? What are their advantages and disadvantages?

6 How can flexible benefits motivate employees?

7 What are the motivational benefits of intrinsic rewards?

EXPERIENTIAL EXERCISE Assessing Employee Motivation and Satisfaction Using the Job Characteristics Model

Purpose

This exercise will help you examine outcomes of the job characteristics model for different professions.

Time

Approximately 30 to 45 minutes.

Background

Data were collected on 6,930 employees in 56 different organizations in the United States, using the Job Diagnostic Survey. The following table contains data on the five core job dimensions of the job characteristics model for several professions. Also included are growth-needs strength, internal motivation, and pay satisfaction for each profession. The values are averages based on a 7-point scale.

Instructions

1. Break into groups of three to five.

2. Calculate the MPS score for each of the professions and compare them. Discuss whether you think these scores accurately reflect your perceptions of the motivating potential of these professions.

3. Graph the relationship between each profession's core job dimensions and its corresponding value for internal motivation and for pay satisfaction, using the core job dimensions as independent variables. What conclusions can you draw about motivation and satisfaction of employees in these professions?

Job Characteristics Averages for Six Professions

Variable	Professional/ Technical	Managerial	Sales	Service	Clerical	Machine Trades
Skill variety	5.4	5.6	4.8	5.0	4.0	5.1
Task identity	5.1	4.7	4.4	4.7	4.7	4.9
Task significance	5.6	5.8	5.5	5.7	5.3	5.6
Autonomy	5.4	5.4	4.8	5.0	4.5	4.9
Feedback	5.1	5.2	5.4	5.1	4.6	4.9
Growth-needs strength	5.6	5.3	5.7	5.4	5.0	4.8
Internal motivation	5.8	5.8	5.7	5.7	5.4	5.6
Pay satisfaction	4.4	4.6	4.2	4.1	4.0	4.2

Source: Adaptation of Job Characteristics Model, pp. 78–80 from J. Richard Hackman & Greg R. Oldham, *Work Redesign*, 1st Edition, © 1980. Adapted by permission of Pearson Education, Inc., Upper Saddle River, NJ.

ETHICAL DILEMMA Spitting Mad

How would you like to be spat at? The answer to that question is pretty obvious, but what may surprise you is that spit is an occupational hazard of New York City bus drivers. The outcomes of these incidents are even more interesting.

In a typical 1-year period, roughly 80 New York City bus drivers are spat upon by disgruntled passengers. These spitting incidents (no other injury was involved) generate an average of 64 days off work—the equivalent of 3 months' pay. In 2009, one spat-upon driver took 191 days of paid leave. The union representing the bus drivers said the leave was justified because being spat upon "is a physically and psychologically traumatic experience."

The causes of passenger spitting are varied, ranging from the MetroCard not working to perceived delays in schedules.

Driver Raul Morales was spat upon by a passenger irate over the fare. After the incident, Morales stopped at a nearby McDonald's, cleaned himself off, then finished his shift. "I just kept on going," he says.

As any watcher of the TV series *World's Toughest Jobs* knows, there is a lot of dangerous work out there, and bus drivers face their own hazards. Some bus drivers have been assaulted by passengers, including one New York City bus driver who was stabbed to death by a passenger in 2008.

Nancy Shevell, chair of the New York City transit authority, questions whether the time off is justified by the injury. "You have to wonder if you can go home and shower off, take a nap, take off the rest of the day and maybe the next day," she said. "When it gets strung out over months, you start to wonder."

Questions

1. Do you think bus drivers should be able to take time off in return for being spit at? If so, how long do you think they should have?

2. People react differently to stressful situations. One of the flight attendants on US Airways Flight 1549 that Captain Chesley "Sully" Sullenberger landed on the Hudson River has not been able to go back to work 3 years after the incident. Yet her two fellow flight attendants have. How do you judge ethical responsibilities and develop policy in situations where different people react differently?

3. What ethical responsibility does New York City's Transit Authority have toward its bus drivers?

Sources: M. M. Grynbaum, "When Angry Passengers Spit, Bus Drivers Take Months Off," *The New York Times* (May 25, 2010), pp. A1, A20; and V. Bishop and H. Hoel, "The Customer Is Always Right?" *Journal of Consumer Culture* 8, no. 3 (2008), pp. 341–367.

CASE INCIDENT 1 Multitasking: A Good Use of Your Time?

Multitasking—doing two or more things at once, or rapidly switching from one task to another—is a characteristic of the Millennial generation. One recent study revealed that during a typical week, 81 percent of young people report "media multitasking" at least some of the time.

Multitasking nicely illustrates our point that motivation is not just effort but also the way you direct your efforts. However, is the direction of efforts in multitasking efficient or inefficient?

Many people who multitask say it makes them more efficient: "Why not do two things at once if I can accomplish about as much as if I only did one thing?" they ask. Research, however, suggests multitasking is inefficient, that it actually takes longer to do two things at once than to do one thing first and then turn to the other. David Meyer, a University of Michigan psychologist who has studied multitasking, argues, "You wind up needing to use the same sorts of mental and physical resources for performing each of the tasks. You're having to switch back and forth between the two tasks as opposed to really doing them simultaneously."

Multitasking appears to result in adverse outcomes beyond inefficiency. Another study found multitaskers absorb material more superficially; they notice more things in their environment but are able to learn material less deeply. "It's not that they can't focus," says one researcher. "It's that they focus on everything. They hear everything—even things they would normally be able to block out—because they are now so used to attending to many things at once." Others note that multitasking can damage productivity and social relationships as individuals devote less concentrated time and attention to the tasks they are working on and conversations they are having. This scattered attention is especially damaging for tasks that require deep insight or creativity.

Questions

1. One expert who has studied multitasking calls it "a big illusion," arguing that multitaskers think they are more motivated and productive even when they aren't. Do you consider yourself a multitasker? If

so, does this case make you reconsider whether multitasking makes you more motivated or productive?

2. The effects of multitasking have been found to be more negative when the tasks are complex. Why do you think this is the case?

3. You might think multitasking makes you happy. While there is less research on this topic, some evidence suggests multitaskers feel more stress in their work. Multitaskers "feel a constant low-level panic." Do you agree? Why or why not?

4. One expert recommends we "recreate boundaries" by training ourselves, while doing something, not to look at other devices like cell phone or television for increasing periods of time. Do you think you could do that? For how long?

Sources: R. A. Clay, "Mini-Multitaskers," *Monitor on Psychology* 40, no. 2 (2009), pp. 38–40; D. Crenshaw, *The Myth of Multitasking: How "Doing It All" Gets Nothing Done* (San Francisco: Jossey Bass, 2008), and A. Tugend, "Multitasking Can Make You Lose . . . Um . . . Focus," *The New York Times* (October 25, 2008), p. B7.

CASE INCIDENT 2 Bonuses Can Backfire

It might seem obvious that people will be motivated by bonuses, but many scholars question this premise. Alfie Kohn has long suggested that workers are "punished by rewards" and urges that organizations avoid tying rewards to performance because of the negative consequences that can result. As an alternative to rewards, some experts recommend that managers foster a positive, upbeat work environment in hopes that enthusiasm will translate into motivation.

Although rewards *can* be motivating, they can reduce employees' intrinsic interest in the tasks they are doing. Along these lines, Mark Lepper of Stanford University found that children rewarded for drawing with felt-tip pens no longer wished to use the pens at all when rewards were removed, whereas children who were not rewarded for using the pens were eager to use them. Similar experiments in which children completed puzzles have also shown that increasing rewards can decrease interest in the rewarded task. Some have questioned the extent to which these results generalize to working adults, but concern about rewards diminishing intrinsic motivation persists.

Rewards can also lead to misbehavior by workers. Psychologist Edward Deci notes, "Once you start making people's rewards dependent on outcomes rather than behaviors, the evidence is people will take the shortest route to those outcomes." Consider factory workers paid purely based on the number of units they produce. Because only quantity is rewarded, workers may neglect quality. Executives rewarded strictly on the basis of quarterly stock price will tend to ignore the long-term profitability and survival of the firm; they might even engage in illegal or unethical behavior to increase their compensation. A review of research on pay-for-performance in medicine found that doctors who were rewarded for treatment outcomes were reluctant to take on the most serious cases, where success was less likely.

Although there might be some problems with providing incentives, the great majority of research cited in this and the previous chapter shows that individuals given rewards for behavior will be more likely to engage in the rewarded behaviors. It is also unlikely that individuals engaged in very boring, repetitive tasks will lose their intrinsic motivation if the task is rewarded, because they never had any intrinsic motivation to begin with. The real issue for managers is finding an appropriate way to reward behaviors so desired behavior is increased while less-desired behavior is reduced.

QUESTIONS

1. Do you think that, as a manager, you would use bonuses regularly? Why or why not?

2. Can you think of a time in your own life when being evaluated and rewarded on a specific goal lead you to engage in negative or unproductive behavior?

3. Do you think providing group bonuses instead of individual bonuses would be more effective or less effective? Why or why not?

4. How would you design a bonus/reward program to avoid the problems mentioned in this case?

Sources: Based on N. Fleming, "The Bonus Myth" *New Scientist* 210 (2011), pp. 40–43; D. Woodward, "Perking Up the Workplace," *Director* (February 2011), pp. 33–34; and G. G. Scott, "How to Create a Motivating Environment," *Nonprofit World* 28 (September/October 2010), p. 9.

ENDNOTES

1. J. R. Hackman and G. R. Oldham, "Motivation Through the Design of Work: Test of a Theory," *Organizational Behavior and Human Performance* 16, no. 2 (1976), pp. 250–279; and J. R. Hackman and G. R. Oldham, *Work Redesign* (Reading, MA: Addison-Wesley, 1980).

2. J. R. Hackman, "Work Design," in J. R. Hackman and J. L. Suttle (eds.), *Improving Life at Work* (Santa Monica, CA: Goodyear, 1977), p. 129.

3. See B. T. Loher, R. A. Noe, N. L. Moeller, and M. P. Fitzgerald, "A Meta-Analysis of the Relation of Job Characteristics to Job Satisfaction," *Journal of Applied Psychology* 70, no. 2 (1985), pp. 280–289; S. J. Zaccaro and E. F. Stone, "Incremental Validity of an Empirically Based Measure of Job Characteristics," *Journal of Applied Psychology* 73, no. 2 (1988), pp. 245–252; J. R. Rentsch and R. P. Steel, "Testing the Durability of Job Characteristics as Predictors of Absenteeism over a Six-Year Period," *Personnel Psychology* 51, no. 2 (1998), pp. 165–190; S. J. Behson, E. R. Eddy, and S. J. Lorenzet, "The Importance of the Critical Psychological States in the Job Characteristics Model: A Meta-Analytic and Structural Equations Modeling Examination," *Current Research in Social Psychology* 51, no. 12 (2000), pp. 170–189; and S. E. Humphrey, J. D. Nahrgang, and F. P. Morgeson, "Integrating Motivational, Social, and Contextual Work Design Features: A Meta-Analytic Summary and Theoretical Extension of the Work Design Literature," *Journal of Applied Psychology* 92, no. 5 (2007), pp. 1332–1356.

4. T. A. Judge, S. K. Parker, A. E. Colbert, D. Heller, and R. Ilies, "Job Satisfaction: A Cross-Cultural Review," in N. Anderson, D. S. Ones (eds.), *Handbook of Industrial, Work and Organizational Psychology*, vol. 2 (Thousand Oaks, CA: Sage Publications, 2002), pp. 25–52.

5. B. M. Meglino and A. M. Korsgaard, "The Role of Other Orientation in Reactions to Job Characteristics," *Journal of Management* 33, no. 1 (2007), pp. 57–83.

6. M. F. Peterson and S. A. Ruiz-Quintanilla, "Cultural Socialization as a Source of Intrinsic Work Motivation," *Group & Organization Management* 28, no. 2 (2003), pp. 188–216.

7. C. Ansberry, "In the New Workplace, Jobs Morph to Suit Rapid Pace of Change," *The Wall Street Journal* (March 22, 2002), p. A1.

8. T. Silver, "Rotate Your Way to Higher Value," *Baseline* (March/April 2010), p. 12; and J. J. Salopek, "Coca-Cola Division Refreshes Its Talent with Diversity Push on Campus," *Workforce Management Online* (March 2011), www.workforce.com.

9. J. Ortega, "Job Rotation as a Learning Mechanism," *Management Science* 47, no. 10 (2001), pp. 1361–1370.

10. A. Christini and D. Pozzoli, "Workplace Practices and Firm Performance in Manufacturing: A Comparative Study of Italy and Britain," *International Journal of Manpower* 31, no. 7 (2010), pp. 818–842; K. Kaymaz, "The Effects of Job Rotation Practices on Motivation: A Research on Managers in the Automotive Organizations," *Business and Economics Research Journal* 1, no. 3 (2010), pp. 69–86.

11. Hackman and Oldham, *Work Redesign.*

12. A. M. Grant, E. M. Campbell, G. Chen, K. Cottone, D. Lapedis, and K. Lee, "Impact and the Art of Motivation Maintenance: The Effects of Contact with Beneficiaries on Persistence Behavior," *Organizational Behavior and Human Decision Processes* 103, no. 1 (2007), pp. 53–67.

13. A. M. Grant, J. E. Dutton, and B. D. Rosso, "Giving Commitment: Employee Support Programs and the Prosocial Sensemaking Process," *Academy of Management Journal* 51, no. 5 (2008), pp. 898–918.

14. See, for example, R. W. Griffin, "Effects of Work Redesign on Employee Perceptions, Attitudes, and Behaviors: A Long-Term Investigation," *Academy of Management Journal* 34, no. 2 (1991), pp. 425–435; and M. Subramony, "A Meta-Analytic Investigation of the Relationship between HRM Bundles and Firm Performance," *Human Resource Management* 48, no. 5 (2009), pp. 745–768.

15. R. D. Pritchard, M. M. Harrell, D. DiazGrandos, and M. J. Guzman, "The Productivity Measurement and Enhancement System: A Meta-Analysis," *Journal of Applied Psychology* 93, no. 3 (2008), pp. 540–567.

16. F. P. Morgeson, M. D. Johnson, M. A. Campion, G. J. Medsker, and T. V. Mumford, "Understanding Reactions to Job Redesign: A Quasi-Experimental Investigation of the Moderating Effects of Organizational Contact on Perceptions of Performance Behavior," *Personnel Psychology* 59, no. 2 (2006), pp. 333–363.

17. F. W. Bond, P. E. Flaxman, and D. Bunce, "The Influence of Psychological Flexibility on Work Redesign: Mediated Moderation of a Work Reorganization Intervention," *Journal of Applied Psychology* 93, no. 3 (2008), pp. 645–654.

18. Cited in K. Palmer, "The New Mommy Track," *U.S. News and World Report* (September 3, 2007), pp. 40–45.

19. Cited in "Flextime Gains in Popularity in Germany," *Manpower Argus* (September 2000), p. 4; and Y. Yanadori and T. Kato, "Work and Family Practices in Japanese Firms: Their Scope, Nature, and Impact on Employee Turnover," *International Journal of Human Resource Management* 20, no. 2 (2009), pp. 439–456.

20. 20 S. Westcott, "Beyond Flextime: Trashing the Workweek," *Inc.* (August 2008), p. 30.

21. See, for example, D. A. Ralston and M. F. Flanagan, "The Effect of Flextime on Absenteeism and Turnover for Male and Female Employees," *Journal of Vocational Behavior* 26, no. 2 (1985), pp. 206–217; B. B. Baltes, T. E. Briggs, J. W. Huff, J. A. Wright, and G. A. Neuman, "Flexible and Compressed Workweek Schedules: A Meta-Analysis of Their Effects on Work-Related Criteria," *Journal of Applied Psychology* 84, no. 4 (1999), pp. 496–513; K. M. Shockley, and T. D. Allen, "When Flexibility Helps: Another Look at the Availability of Flexible Work Arrangements and Work–Family Conflict," *Journal of Vocational Behavior* 71, no. 3 (2007), pp. 479–493; J. G. Grzywacz, D. S. Carlson, and S. Shulkin, "Schedule Flexibility and Stress: Linking Formal Flexible Arrangements and Perceived Flexibility to Employee Health." *Community, Work, and Family* 11, no. 2 (2008), pp. 199–214; and L. A. McNall, A. D. Masuda, and J. M. Nicklin "Flexible Work Arrangements, Job Satisfaction, and Turnover Intentions: The Mediating Role of Work-to-Family Enrichment," *Journal of Psychology* 144, no. 1 (2010), pp. 61–81.

22. K. M. Shockley and T. D. Allen, "Investigating the Missing Link in Flexible Work Arrangement Utilization: An Individual Difference Perspective," *Journal of Vocational Behavior* 76, no. 1 (2010), pp. 131–142.

23. J. LaReau, "Ford's 2 Julies Share Devotion—and Job," *Automotive News* (October 25, 2010), p. 4.

24. Society for Human Resource Management, *2008 Employee Benefits* (Alexandria, VA: Author, 2008).

25. S. Shellenbarger, "Two People, One Job: It Can Really Work," *The Wall Street Journal* (December 7, 1994), p. B1.

26. "Job-Sharing: Widely Offered, Little Used," *Training* (November 1994), p. 12.

27. C. Dawson, "Japan: Work-Sharing Will Prolong the Pain," *BusinessWeek* (December 24, 2001), p. 46.

28. Shellenbarger, "Two People, One Job," p. B1.

29. See, for example, E. J. Hill, M. Ferris, and V. Martinson, "Does It Matter Where You Work? A Comparison of How Three Work Venues (Traditional Office, Virtual Office, and Home Office) Influence Aspects of Work and Personal/Family Life," *Journal of Vocational Behavior* 63, no. 2 (2003), pp. 220–241; B. Williamson, "Managing Virtual Workers," *Bloomberg Businessweek* (July 16, 2009), www.businessweek.com, and B. A. Lautsch and E. E. Kossek, "Managing a Blended Workforce: Telecommuters and Non-Telecommuters," *Organizational Dynamics* 40, no. 1 (2010), pp. 10–17.

30. J. Tozzi, "Home-Based Businesses Increasing," *Bloomberg Businessweek* (January 25, 2010), www.businessweek.com.

31. Society for Human Resource Management, *2008 Employee Benefits*.

32. See, for instance, M. Conlin, "The Easiest Commute of All," *BusinessWeek* (December 12, 2005), p. 78; S. Shellenbarger, "Telework Is on the Rise, but It Isn't Just Done from Home Anymore," *The Wall Street Journal* (January 23, 2001), p. B1; and E. O'Keefe, "Teleworking Grows But Still a Rarity," *The Washington Post* (February 22, 2011), p. B3.

33. Conlin, "The Easiest Commute of All."

34. E. E. Kossek, B. A. Lautsch, S. C. Eaton, "Telecommuting, Control, and Boundary Management: Correlates of Policy Use and Practice, Job Control, and Work-Family Effectiveness," *Journal of Vocational Behavior* 68, no. 2 (2006), pp. 347–367.

35. J. M. Stanton and J. L. Barnes-Farrell, "Effects of Electronic Performance Monitoring on Personal Control, Task Satisfaction, and Task Performance," *Journal of Applied Psychology* 81, no. 6 (1996), pp. 738–745; and L. Taskin and F. Bridoux, "Telework: A Challenge to Knowledge Transfer in Organizations," *International Journal of Human Resource Management* 21, no. 13 (2010), pp. 2503–2520.

36. See, for example, P. Brotherton, "For Teleworkers, Less Is Definitely More," *T+D* 65 (March 2011), p. 29; and M. Virick, N. DaSilva, and K. Arrington, "Moderators of the Curvilinear Relation Between Extent of Telecommuting and Job and Life Satisfaction: The Role of Performance Outcome Orientation and Worker Type," *Human Relations* 63, no. 1 (2010), pp. 137–154.

37. J. Welch and S. Welch, "The Importance of Being There," *BusinessWeek* (April 16, 2007), p. 92; Z. I. Barsness, K. A. Diekmann, and M. L. Seidel, "Motivation and Opportunity: The Role of Remote Work, Demographic Dissimilarity, and Social Network Centrality in Impression Management," *Academy of Management Journal* 48, no. 3 (2005), pp. 401–419.

38. F. P. Morgeson and S. E. Humphrey, "The Work Design Questionnaire (WDQ): Developing and Validating a Comprehensive Measure for Assessing Job Design and the Nature of Work," *Journal of Applied Psychology* 91, no. 6 (2006), pp. 1321–1339; S. E. Humphrey, J. D. Nahrgang, and F. P. Morgeson, "Integrating Motivational, Social, and Contextual Work Design Features: A Meta-Analytic Summary and Theoretical Extension of the Work Design Literature," *Journal of Applied Psychology* 92, no. 5 (2007), pp. 1332–1356; and R. Takeuchi, D. P. Lepak, H. Wang, and K. Takeuchi, "An Empirical Examination of the Mechanisms Mediating Between High-Performance Work Systems and the Performance of Japanese Organizations," *Journal of Applied Psychology* 92, no. 4 (2007), pp. 1069–1083.

39. See, for example, the increasing body of literature on empowerment, such as D. P. Ashmos, D. Duchon, R. R. McDaniel Jr., and J. W. Huonker, "What a Mess! Participation as a Simple Managerial Rule to 'Complexify' Organizations," *Journal of Management Studies* 39, no. 2 (2002), pp. 189–206; S. E. Seibert, S. R. Silver, and W. A. Randolph, "Taking Empowerment to the Next Level: A Multiple-Level Model of Empowerment, Performance, and Satisfaction," *Academy of Management Journal* 47, no. 3 (2004), pp. 332–349; M. M. Butts, R. J. Vandenberg, D. M. DeJoy, B. S. Schaffer, and M. G. Wilson, "Individual Reactions to High Involvement Work Processes: Investigating the Role of Empowerment and Perceived Organizational Support," *Journal of Occupational Health Psychology* 14, no. 2 (2009), pp. 122–136; R. Park, E. Applebaum, and D. Kruse, "Employee Involvement and Group Incentives in Manufacturing Companies: A Multi-Level Analysis," *Human Resource Management Journal* 20, no. 3 (2010), pp. 227–243; and D. C. Jones, P. Kalmi, and A. Kauhanen, "How Does Employee Involvement Stack Up? The Effects of Human Resource Management Policies in a Retail Firm," *Industrial Relations* 49, no. 1 (2010), pp. 1–21.

40. See, for instance, A. Sagie and Z. Aycan, "A Cross-Cultural Analysis of Participative Decision-Making in Organizations," *Human Relations* 56, no. 4 (2003), pp. 453–473; and J. Brockner, "Unpacking Country Effects: On the Need to Operationalize the Psychological Determinants of Cross-National Differences," in R. M. Kramer and B. M. Staw (eds.), *Research in Organizational Behavior*, vol. 25 (Oxford, UK: Elsevier, 2003), pp. 336–340.

41. C. Robert, T. M. Probst, J. J. Martocchio, R. Drasgow, and J. J. Lawler, "Empowerment and Continuous Improvement in the United States, Mexico, Poland, and India: Predicting Fit on the Basis of the Dimensions of Power Distance and Individualism," *Journal of Applied Psychology* 85, no. 5 (2000), pp. 643–658.

42. Z. X. Chen and S. Aryee, "Delegation and Employee Work Outcomes: An Examination of the Cultural Context of Mediating Processes in China," *Academy of Management Journal* 50, no. 1 (2007), pp. 226–238.

43. F. Heller, E. Pusic, G. Strauss, and B. Wilpert, *Organizational Participation: Myth and Reality* (Oxford, UK: Oxford University Press, 1998).

44. See, for instance, K. L. Miller and P. R. Monge, "Participation, Satisfaction, and Productivity: A Meta-Analytic Review," *Academy of Management Journal* (December 1986), pp. 727–753; J. A. Wagner III, "Participation's Effects on Performance and Satisfaction: A Reconsideration of Research Evidence," *Academy of Management Review* 19, no. 2 (1994), pp. 312–330; C. Doucouliagos, "Worker Participation and Productivity in

Labor-Managed and Participatory Capitalist Firms: A Meta-Analysis," *Industrial and Labor Relations Review* 49, no. 1 (1995), pp. 58–77; J. A. Wagner III, C. R. Leana, E. A. Locke, and D. M. Schweiger, "Cognitive and Motivational Frameworks in U.S. Research on Participation: A Meta-Analysis of Primary Effects," *Journal of Organizational Behavior* 18, no. 1 (1997), pp. 49–65; A. Pendleton and A. Robinson, "Employee Stock Ownership, Involvement, and Productivity: An Interaction-Based Approach," *Industrial and Labor Relations Review* 64, no. 1 (2010), pp. 3–29.

45. D. K. Datta, J. P. Guthrie, and P. M. Wright, "Human Resource Management and Labor Productivity: Does Industry Matter? *Academy of Management Journal* 48, no. 1 (2005), pp. 135–145; C. M. Riordan, R. J. Vandenberg, and H. A. Richardson, "Employee Involvement Climate and Organizational Effectiveness." *Human Resource Management* 44, no. 4 (2005), pp. 471–488; and J. Kim, J. P. MacDuffie, and F. K. Pil, "Employee Voice and Organizational Performance: Team Versus Representative Influence," *Human Relations 63*, no. 3 (2010), pp. 371-394.

46. Cotton, *Employee Involvement*, p. 114.

47. See, for example, M. Gilman and P. Marginson, "Negotiating European Works Council: Contours of Constrained Choice," *Industrial Relations Journal* 33, no. 1 (2002), pp. 36–51; J. T. Addison and C. R. Belfield, "What Do We Know About the New European Works Council? Some Preliminary Evidence from Britain," *Scottish Journal of Political Economy* 49, no. 4 (2002), pp. 418–444; and B. Keller, "The European Company Statute: Employee Involvement—and Beyond," *Industrial Relations Journal* 33, no. 5 (2002), pp. 424–445.

48. Cotton, *Employee Involvement*, pp. 129–130, 139–140.

49. Ibid., p. 140.

50. E. White, "Opportunity Knocks, and It Pays a Lot Better," *The Wall Street Journal* (November 13, 2006), p. B3.

51. P. S. Goodman and P. P. Pan, "Chinese Workers Pay for Wal-Mart's Low Prices," *Washington Post* (February 8, 2004), p. A1.

52. M. Sabramony, N. Krause, J. Norton, and G. N. Burns "The Relationship Between Human Resource Investments and Organizational Performance: A Firm-Level Examination of Equilibrium Theory," *Journal of Applied Psychology* 93, no. 4 (2008), pp. 778–788.

53. See, for example, B. Martinez, "Teacher Bonuses Emerge in Newark," *The Wall Street Journal,* (April 21, 2011), p. A.15; and D. Weber, "Seminole Teachers to Get Bonuses Instead of Raises," *Orlando Sentinel* (January 19, 2011), www.orlandosentinel.com.

54. Based on J. R. Schuster and P. K. Zingheim, "The New Variable Pay: Key Design Issues," *Compensation & Benefits Review* (March–April 1993), p. 28; K. S. Abosch, "Variable Pay: Do We Have the Basics in Place?" *Compensation & Benefits Review* (July–August 1998), pp. 12–22; and K. M. Kuhn and M. D. Yockey, "Variable Pay as a Risky Choice: Determinants of the Relative Attractiveness of Incentive Plans," *Organizational Behavior and Human Decision Processes* 90, no. 2 (2003), pp. 323–341.

55. L. Wiener, "Paycheck Plus," *U.S. News & World Report* (February 24/March 3, 2003), p. 58.

56. Hay Group, "Hay Group Research Finds Increased Use of Variable Pay for Employees," *Investment Weekly News,* (July 24, 2010), p. 269.

57. Cited in "Pay Programs: Few Employees See the Pay-for-Performance Connection," *Compensation & Benefits Report,* (June 2003), p. 1.

58. B. Wysocki Jr., "Chilling Reality Awaits Even the Employed," *The Wall Street Journal* (November 5, 2001), p. A1; and J. C. Kovac, "Sour Economy Presents Compensation Challenges," *Employee Benefit News* (July 1, 2008), p. 18.

59. G. D. Jenkins Jr., N. Gupta, A. Mitra, and J. D. Shaw, "Are Financial Incentives Related to Performance? A Meta-Analytic Review of Empirical Research," *Journal of Applied Psychology* 83, no. 5 (1998), pp. 777–787; and S. L. Rynes, B. Gerhart, and L. Parks, "Personnel Psychology: Performance Evaluation and Pay for Performance," *Annual Review of Psychology* 56, no. 1 (2005), pp. 571–600.

60. E. Arita, "Teething Troubles Aside, Merit-Based Pay Catching On," *Japan Times* (April 23, 2004), search.japantimes.co.jp/cgi-bin/nb20040423a3.html.

61. E. White, "The Best vs. the Rest," *The Wall Street Journal* (January 30, 2006), pp. B1, B3.

62. N. Byrnes, "Pain, But No Layoffs at Nucor," *BusinessWeek* (March 26, 2009), www.businessweek.com.

63. E. White, "Employers Increasingly Favor Bonuses to Raises," *The Wall Street Journal* (August 28, 2006), p. B3; and J. S. Lublin, "Boards Tie CEO Pay More Tightly to Performance," *The Wall Street Journal* (February 21, 2006), pp. A1, A14.

64. G. E. Ledford Jr., "Paying for the Skills, Knowledge, and Competencies of Knowledge Workers," *Compensation & Benefits Review,* (July–August 1995), pp. 55–62; B. Murray and B. Gerhart, "An Empirical Analysis of a Skill-Based Pay Program and Plant Performance Outcomes," *Academy of Management Journal* 41, no. 1 (1998), pp. 68–78; J. R. Thompson and C. W. LeHew, "Skill-Based Pay as an Organizational Innovation," *Review of Public Personnel Administration* 20, no. 1 (2000), pp. 20–40; and J. D. Shaw, N. Gupta, A. Mitra, and G. E. Ledford, Jr., "Success and Survival of Skill-Based Pay Plans," *Journal of Management* 31, no. 1 (2005), pp. 28–49.

65. A. Mitra, N. Gupta, and J. D. Shaw, "A Comparative Examination of Traditional and Skill-Based Pay Plans," *Journal of Managerial Psychology* 26, no. 4 (2011), pp. 278–296.

66. E. C. Dierdorff and E. A. Surface, "If You Pay for Skills, Will They Learn? Skill Change and Maintenance under a Skill-Based Pay System," *Journal of Management* 34, no.4 (2008), pp. 721–743.

67. "Tensions of a New Pay Plan," *The New York Times* (May 17, 1992), p. F5.

68. F. Giancola, "Skill-based Pay—Issues for Consideration," *Benefits and Compensation Digest* 44, no. 5 (2007), pp. 1–15.

69. N. Chi and T. Han, "Exploring the Linkages Between Formal Ownership and Psychological Ownership for the Organization: The Mediating Role of Organizational Justice," *Journal of Occupational and Organizational Psychology* 81, no. 4 (2008), pp. 691–711.

70. See, for instance, D. O. Kim, "Determinants of the Survival of Gainsharing Programs," *Industrial & Labor Relations Review* 53, no. 1 (1999), pp. 21–42; "Why Gainsharing Works Even Better Today Than in the Past," *HR Focus* (April 2000), pp. 3–5; L. R. Gomez-Mejia, T. M. Welbourne, and R. M. Wiseman, "The Role of Risk Sharing and Risk Taking Under Gainsharing," *Academy of Management Review* 25, no. 3 (2000),

pp. 492–507; M. Reynolds, "A Cost-Reduction Strategy That May Be Back," *Healthcare Financial Management* (January 2002), pp. 58–64; and M. R. Dixon, L. J. Hayes, and J. Stack, "Changing Conceptions of Employee Compensation," *Journal of Organizational Behavior Management* 23, no. 2–3 (2003), pp. 95–116; I. M. Leitman, R. Levin, M. J. Lipp, L. Sivaprasad, C. J. Karalakulasingam, D. S. Bernard, P. Friedmann, and D. J. Shulkin, "Quality and Financial Outcomes from Gainsharing for Inpatient Admissions: A Three-Year Experience," *Journal of Hospital Medicine* 5, no. 9 (2010), pp. 501–517.

71. T. M. Welbourne and C. J. Ferrante, "To Monitor or Not to Monitor: A Study of Individual Outcomes from Monitoring One's Peers under Gainsharing and Merit Pay," *Group & Organization Management* 33, no. 2 (2008), pp. 139–162.

72. National Center for Employee Ownership, *The Employee Ownership 100* (July 2003), www.nceo.org.

73. Cited in K. Frieswick, "ESOPs: Split Personality," *CFO* (July 7, 2003), p. 1.

74. A. A. Buchko, "The Effects of Employee Ownership on Employee Attitudes: A Test of Three Theoretical Perspectives," *Work and Occupations* 19, no. 1 (1992), 59–78; and R. P. Garrett, "Does Employee Ownership Increase Innovation?" *New England Journal of Entrepreneurship* 13, no. 2, (2010), pp. 37–46.

75. D. McCarthy, E. Reeves, and T. Turner, "Can Employee Share-Ownership Improve Employee Attitudes and Behaviour?" *Employee Relations* 32, no. 4 (2010), pp. 382–395.

76. A. Pendleton and A. Robinson, "Employee Stock Ownership, Involvement, and Productivity: An Interaction-Based Approach," *Industrial and Labor Relations Review* 64, no. 1 (2010), pp. 3–29.

77. X. Zhang, K. M. Bartol, K. G. Smith, M. D. Pfarrer, and D. M. Khanin, "CEOs on the Edge: Earnings Manipulation and Stock-Based Incentive Misalignment," *Academy of Management Journal* 51, no. 2 (2008), pp. 241–258.

78. D. D'Art and T. Turner, "Profit Sharing, Firm Performance, and Union Influence in Selected European Countries," *Personnel Review* 33, no. 3 (2004), pp. 335–350; and D. Kruse, R. Freeman, and J. Blasi, *Shared Capitalism at Work: Employee Ownership, Profit and Gain Sharing, and Broad-Based Stock Options* (Chicago: University of Chicago Press, 2010).

79. A. Bayo-Moriones and M. Larraza-Kintana, "Profit-Sharing Plans and Affective Commitment: Does the Context Matter?" *Human Resource Management* 48, no. 2 (2009), pp. 207–226.

80. T. M. Welbourne and L. R. Gomez-Mejia, "Gainsharing: A Critical Review and a Future Research Agenda," *Journal of Management* 21, no. 3 (1995), pp. 559–609.

81. C. B. Cadsby, F. Song, and F. Tapon, "Sorting and Incentive Effects of Pay for Performance: An Experimental Investigation," *Academy of Management Journal* 50, no. 2 (2007), pp. 387–405.

82. S. C. L. Fong and M. A. Shaffer, "The Dimensionality and Determinants of Pay Satisfaction: A Cross-Cultural Investigation of a Group Incentive Plan," *International Journal of Human Resource Management* 14, no. 4 (2003), pp. 559–580.

83. See, for instance, M. W. Barringer and G. T. Milkovich, "A Theoretical Exploration of the Adoption and Design of Flexible Benefit Plans: A Case of Human Resource Innovation," *Academy of Management Review* 23, no. 2 (1998), pp. 305–324; D. Brown, "Everybody Loves Flex," *Canadian HRReporter* (November 18, 2002), p. 1; J. Taggart, "Putting Flex Benefits Through Their Paces," *Canadian HR Reporter* (December 2, 2002), p. G3; and N. D. Cole and D. H. Flint, "Perceptions of Distributive and Procedural Justice in Employee Benefits: Flexible Versus Traditional Benefit Plans," *Journal of Managerial Psychology* 19, no. 1 (2004), pp. 19–40.

84. D. A. DeCenzo and S. P. Robbins, *Fundamentals of Human Resource Management*, 10th ed. (New York: Wiley, 2009).

85. P. Stephens, "Flex Plans Gain in Popularity," *CA Magazine* (January/February 2010), p. 10.

86. D. Lovewell, "Flexible Benefits: Benefits on Offer," *Employee Benefits* (March 2010), p. S15.

87. S. E. Markham, K. D. Scott, and G. H. McKee, "Recognizing Good Attendance: A Longitudinal, Quasi-Experimental Field Study," *Personnel Psychology* 55, no. 3 (2002), p. 641; and S. J. Peterson and F. Luthans, "The Impact of Financial and Nonfinancial Incentives on Business Unit Outcomes over Time," *Journal of Applied Psychology* 91, no. 1 (2006), pp. 156–165.

88. A. D. Stajkovic and F. Luthans, "Differential Effects of Incentive Motivators on Work Performance," *Academy of Management Journal* 4, no. 3 (2001), p. 587. See also F. Luthans and A. D. Stajkovic, "Provide Recognition for Performance Improvement," in E. A. Locke (ed.), *Handbook of Principles of Organizational Behavior* (Malden, MA: Blackwell, 2004), pp. 166–180.

89. L. Shepherd, "Special Report on Rewards and Recognition: Getting Personal," *Workforce Management* (September 2010), pp. 24–29.

90. L. Shepherd, "On Recognition, Multinationals Think Globally," *Workforce Management* (September 2010), p. 26.

91. R. J. Long and J. L. Shields, "From Pay to Praise? Non-Case Employee Recognition in Canadian and Australian Firms," *International Journal of Human Resource Management* 21, no. 8 (2010), pp. 1145–1172.

LEARNING OBJECTIVES

After studying this chapter, you should be able to:

1 Define *group* and distinguish the different types of groups.

2 Identify the five stages of group development.

3 Show how role requirements change in different situations.

4 Demonstrate how norms and status exert influence on an individual's behavior.

5 Show how group size affects group performance.

6 Contrast the benefits and disadvantages of cohesive groups.

7 Understand the implications of diversity for group effectiveness.

8 Contrast the strengths and weaknesses of group decision making.

9 Compare the effectiveness of interacting, brainstorming, nominal, and electronic meeting groups.

TO THE CLICKERS GO THE SPOILS

"Ability to function well in groups" is often near the top of employer lists of desired skills in new hires. New evidence suggests that being popular or able to "click" with colleagues is more important than we have realized.

Take Heather Moseley. When Heather started her job as an accounting associate, her cubicle was right outside the office of one of her organization's top managers, Kelly McVickers. McVickers mostly kept to herself, but that didn't deter Heather. Over the next few months, Heather struck up a friendship with Kelly and found out they both admired Stevie Wonder.

"I do an accountant's job, which is really administrative," said Heather. "Because of my relationship with Kelly, I now get invited to events, meetings, and conferences that I'd have no business going to as an accountant." Even though she is above Heather in the organization, Kelly finds her friendship with Heather pays benefits, too. "Knowing Heather, I find out what's on people's minds," Kelly said. "As supervisor this is crucial information."

What Heather did was find a way to click with Kelly. Research has emerged that shows other "clickers" have experiences similar to Heather's: they advance further and more quickly in their careers. That is the nature of groups—some people seem to have a natural ability to do well in groups, and they benefit as a result.

One study of health care administrators had employees list co-workers in terms of how popular they thought their co-workers were. Popularity of each worker was measured by summing how often each person was mentioned. Interestingly, not only did popular employees receive more help from their co-workers, they were also subject to less uncivil behaviors at work.

What do you have to do to be a "clicker" and be popular with others in a group? To some degree, it's personality. Those who are agreeable, have high core self-evaluations, and are self-monitors just click more readily in groups. Geographically, clickers also tend to be centrally located. One study of dorm locations found that each dorm room down from the center of the hall decreased popularity by 50 percent.

If you can't change your personality or your office, you might be able to do something else. Harvard researchers found that when someone asks others questions requiring more intimate self-revelation, respondents later feel closer to the person who asked the question. So, without becoming too personal, try to deepen conversations with others. Move beyond, "What did you do this weekend?"

Foundations of Group Behavior

9

*Madness is the exception in individuals
but the rule in groups.*
—Friedrich Nietzsche

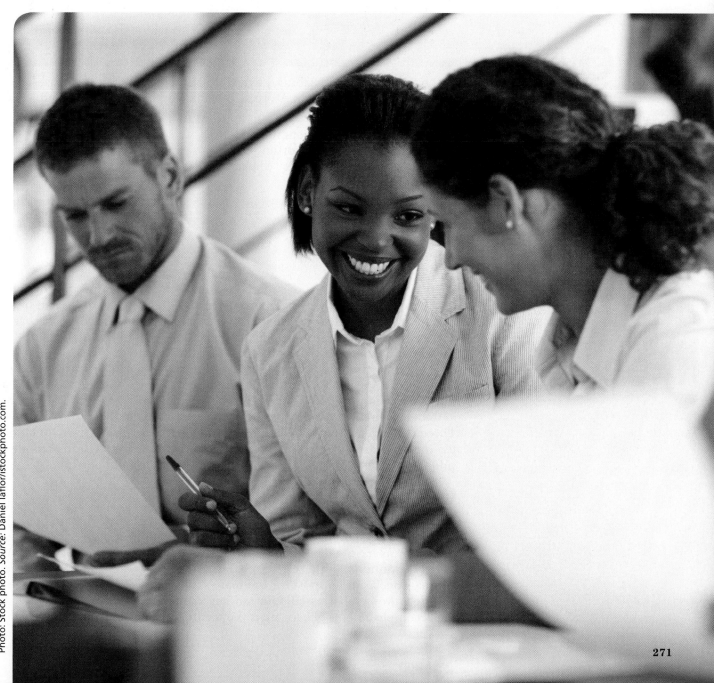

Being popular in groups and "clicking" with others seems to be as important at work as in school. The more things change, the more they stay the same.

Sources: O. Brafman and R. Brafman, "To the Vulnerable Go the Spoils," *Bloomberg Businessweek* (June 20, 2010), pp. 71–73; and B. A. Scott and T. A. Judge, "The Popularity Contest at Work: Who Wins, Why, and What Do They Receive?" *Journal of Applied Psychology* 94, no. 1 (2009), pp. 20–33.

Groups have their place—and their pitfalls. Before we discuss them, examine your own attitude toward working in groups. Take the following self-assessment and answer the accompanying questions.

The objectives of this chapter and Chapter 10 are to introduce you to basic group concepts, provide you with a foundation for understanding how groups work, and show you how to create effective teams. Let's begin by defining *group* and explaining why people join groups.

SELF-ASSESSMENT LIBRARY

Do I Have a Negative Attitude Toward Working in Groups?

In the Self-Assessment Library (available on CD or online), take assessment IV.E.1 (Do I Have a Negative Attitude Toward Working in Groups?) and answer the following questions.

1. Are you surprised by your results? If yes, why? If not, why not?
2. Do you think it is important to always have a positive attitude toward working in groups? Why or why not?

Defining and Classifying Groups

1 Define *group* and distinguish the different types of groups.

We define a **group** as two or more individuals, interacting and interdependent, who have come together to achieve particular objectives. Groups can be either formal or informal. By a **formal group**, we mean one defined by the organization's structure, with designated work assignments establishing tasks. In formal groups, the behaviors team members should engage in are stipulated by and directed toward organizational goals. The six members of an airline flight crew are a formal group. In contrast, an **informal group** is neither formally structured nor organizationally determined. Informal groups are natural formations in the work environment that appear in response to the need for social contact. Three employees from different departments who regularly have lunch or coffee together are an informal group. These types of interactions among individuals, though informal, deeply affect their behavior and performance.

Why Do People Form Groups?

Why do people form groups, and why do they feel so strongly about them? Consider the celebrations that follow a sports team's winning a national championship. Fans have staked their own self-image on the performance of someone else. The winner's supporters are elated, and sales of team-related shirts, jackets, and hats declaring support for the team skyrocket. Fans of the losing team feel dejected, even embarrassed. Our tendency to take personal pride or offense for the accomplishments of a group is the territory of **social identity theory**.

The employees of the Swedish transportation company Scania shown here exercising at a sports complex comprise an informal group. At different company locations, Scania offers employees free access to sports facilities during working hours. The company puts a high priority on employee health and offers employees many opportunities to reinforce an active lifestyle. The informal groups that participate in sports and exercise activities are neither formally structured nor organizationally determined. However, informal groups like these can fulfill employee desires for social interaction at work.

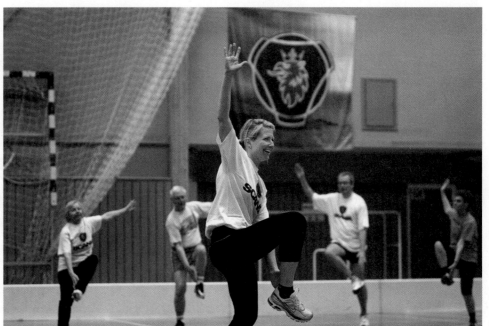

Source: Soren andersson/Afp/Getty/Newscom.

Social identity theory proposes that people have emotional reactions to the failure or success of their group because their self-esteem gets tied into the group's performance.[1] When your group does well, you bask in reflected glory, and your own self-esteem rises. When your group does poorly, you might feel bad about yourself, or you might even reject that part of your identity, like "fair weather fans." Social identities also help people reduce uncertainty about who they are and what they should do.[2]

People develop a lot of identities through the course of their lives. You might define yourself in terms of the organization you work for, the city you live in, your profession, your religious background, your ethnicity, or your gender. A U.S. expatriate working in Rome might be very aware of being from the United States but won't give this national identity a second thought when transferring from Tulsa to Tucson.[3]

Social identities help us understand who we are and where we fit in with other people, but they can have a negative side as well. **Ingroup favoritism** means we see members of our ingroup as better than other people, and people not in our group as all the same. This obviously paves the way for stereotyping.

When do people develop a social identity? Several characteristics make a social identity important to a person:

- **Similarity.** Not surprisingly, people who have the same values or characteristics as other members of their organization have higher levels of group identification.[4] Demographic similarity can also lead to stronger

group *Two or more individuals, interacting and interdependent, who have come together to achieve particular objectives.*
formal group *A designated work group defined by an organization's structure.*

informal group *A group that is neither formally structured nor organizationally determined; such a group appears in response to the need for social contact.*
social identity theory *Perspective that considers when and why individuals consider themselves members of groups.*

ingroup favoritism *Perspective in which we see members of our ingroup as better than other people, and people not in our group as all the same.*

Social identities help Bal Seal Engineering employees interact with co-workers. The company's Spanish-speaking employees gather at the home of a co-worker to participate in an English-as-a-second-language program. Bal Seal, which buys the training materials for the program, reports that it has improved the company's communications, cooperation among fellow workers, and customer service. As social identity theory proposes, program graduates identify with the high performance of a winning team. As a result, graduates who ruled out the option of going back to school are motivated to continue their education by enrolling in GED, community college, and citizenship classes.

Source: O44/Zuma Press/Newscom.

identification for new hires, while those who are demographically different may have a hard time identifying with the group as a whole.[5]

- **Distinctiveness.**   People are more likely to notice identities that show how they are different from other groups. Respondents in one study identified more strongly with those in their work group with whom they shared uncommon or rare demographic characteristics.[6] For example, veterinarians who work in veterinary medicine (where everyone is a veterinarian) identify with their organization, and veterinarians in nonveterinary medicine fields such as animal research or food inspection (where being a veterinarian is a more distinctive characteristic) identify with their profession.[7]

- **Status.**   Because people use identities to define themselves and increase self-esteem, it makes sense that they are most interested in linking themselves to high-status groups. Graduates of prestigious universities will go out of their way to emphasize their links to their alma maters and are also more likely to make donations.[8] People are likely to not identify with a low-status organization and will be more likely to quit in order to leave that identity behind.[9]

- **Uncertainty reduction.**   Membership in a group also helps some people understand who they are and how they fit into the world.[10] One study showed how the creation of a spin-off company created questions about how employees should develop a unique identity that corresponded more closely to what the division was becoming.[11] Managers worked to define and communicate an idealized identity for the new organization when it became clear employees were confused.

Stages of Group Development

2   Identify the five stages of group development.

Groups generally pass through a predictable sequence in their evolution. Although not all groups follow this five-stage model,[12] it is a useful framework for understanding group development. In this section, we describe the five-stage model and an alternative for temporary groups with deadlines.

The Five-Stage Model

As shown in Exhibit 9-1, the **five-stage group-development model** characterizes groups as proceeding through the distinct stages of forming, storming,
norming, performing, and adjourning.[13]

The first stage, **forming stage**, is characterized by a great deal of uncertainty
about the group's purpose, structure, and leadership. Members "test the waters" to determine what types of behaviors are acceptable. This stage is complete when members have begun to think of themselves as part of a group.

The **storming stage** is one of intragroup conflict. Members accept the
existence of the group but resist the constraints it imposes on individuality.
There is conflict over who will control the group. When this stage is complete,
there will be a relatively clear hierarchy of leadership within the group.

In the third stage, close relationships develop and the group demonstrates
cohesiveness. There is now a strong sense of group identity and camaraderie.
This **norming stage** is complete when the group structure solidifies and the
group has assimilated a common set of expectations of what defines correct
member behavior.

The fourth stage is **performing**. The structure at this point is fully functional
and accepted. Group energy has moved from getting to know and understand
each other to performing the task at hand.

For permanent work groups, performing is the last stage in development.
However, for temporary committees, teams, task forces, and similar groups that
have a limited task to perform, the **adjourning stage** is for wrapping up activities
and preparing to disband. Some group members are upbeat, basking in the
group's accomplishments. Others may be depressed over the loss of camaraderie and friendships gained during the work group's life.

Many interpreters of the five-stage model have assumed a group becomes
more effective as it progresses through the first four stages. Although this may
be generally true, what makes a group effective is actually more complex.[14]
First, groups proceed through the stages of group development at different
rates. Those with a strong sense of purpose and strategy rapidly achieve high
performance and improve over time, whereas those with less sense of purpose
actually see their performance worsen over time. Similarly, groups that begin
with a positive social focus appear to achieve the "performing" stage more

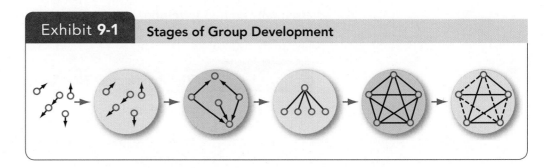

Exhibit **9-1**   Stages of Group Development

**five-stage group-development
model**   *The five distinct stages
groups go through: forming,
storming, norming, performing,
and adjourning.*

forming stage   *The first stage in group
development, characterized by much
uncertainty.*

storming stage   *The second stage in
group development, characterized by
intragroup conflict.*

norming stage   *The third stage
in group development, characterized
by close relationships and
cohesiveness.*

performing stage   *The fourth stage in
group development, during which the
group is fully functional.*

adjourning stage   *The final stage in
group development for temporary
groups, characterized by concern with
wrapping up activities rather than task
performance.*

rapidly. Nor do groups always proceed clearly from one stage to the next. Storming and performing can occur simultaneously, and groups can even regress to previous stages.

An Alternative Model for Temporary Groups with Deadlines

Temporary groups with deadlines don't seem to follow the usual five-stage model. Studies indicate they have their own unique sequencing of actions (or inaction): (1) their first meeting sets the group's direction, (2) this first phase of group activity is one of inertia, (3) a transition takes place exactly when the group has used up half its allotted time, (4) this transition initiates major changes, (5) a second phase of inertia follows the transition, and (6) the group's last meeting is characterized by markedly accelerated activity.[15] This pattern, called the **punctuated-equilibrium model**, is shown in Exhibit 9-2.

The first meeting sets the group's direction, and then a framework of behavioral patterns and assumptions through which the group will approach its project emerges, sometimes in the first few seconds of the group's existence. Once set, the group's direction is solidified and is unlikely to be reexamined throughout the first half of its life. This is a period of inertia—the group tends to stand still or become locked into a fixed course of action even if it gains new insights that challenge initial patterns and assumptions.

One of the most interesting discoveries[16] was that each group experienced its transition precisely halfway between its first meeting and its official deadline—whether members spent an hour on their project or 6 months. The midpoint appears to work like an alarm clock, heightening members' awareness that their time is limited and they need to get moving. This transition ends phase 1 and is characterized by a concentrated burst of changes, dropping of old patterns, and adoption of new perspectives. The transition sets a revised direction for phase 2, a new equilibrium or period of inertia in which the group executes plans created during the transition period.

The group's last meeting is characterized by a final burst of activity to finish its work. In summary, the punctuated-equilibrium model characterizes groups as exhibiting long periods of inertia interspersed with brief revolutionary changes triggered primarily by members' awareness of time and deadlines. Keep in mind, however, that this model doesn't apply to all groups. It's essentially limited to temporary task groups working under a time-constrained completion deadline.[17]

Exhibit **9-2**   **The Punctuated-Equilibrium Model**

3 Show how role requirements change in different situations.

Work groups are not unorganized mobs; they have properties that shape members' behavior and help explain and predict individual behavior within the group as well as the performance of the group itself. Some of these properties are roles, norms, status, size, cohesiveness, and diversity.

Group Property 1: Roles

Shakespeare said, "All the world's a stage, and all the men and women merely players." Using the same metaphor, all group members are actors, each playing a **role**. By this term, we mean a set of expected behavior patterns attributed to someone occupying a given position in a social unit. Our understanding of role behavior would be dramatically simplified if each of us could choose one role and play it regularly and consistently. Instead, we are required to play a number of diverse roles, both on and off our jobs. As we'll see, one of the tasks in understanding behavior is grasping the role a person is currently playing.

Bill Patterson is a plant manager with EMM Industries, a large electrical equipment manufacturer in Phoenix. He fulfills a number of roles—EMM employee, member of middle management, electrical engineer, and primary company spokesperson in the community. Off the job, Bill Patterson finds himself in still more roles: husband, father, Catholic, tennis player, member of the Thunderbird Country Club, and president of his homeowners' association. Many of these roles are compatible; some create conflicts. How does Bill's religious commitment influence his managerial decisions regarding layoffs, expense account padding, and provision of accurate information to government agencies? A recent offer of promotion requires Bill to relocate, yet his family wants to stay in Phoenix. Can the role demands of his job be reconciled with the demands of his husband and father roles?

Like Bill Patterson, we are all required to play a number of roles, and our behavior varies with each. So different groups impose different role requirements on individuals.

Role Perception   Our view of how we're supposed to act in a given situation is a **role perception**. We get role perceptions from stimuli all around us—for example, friends, books, films, television, as when we form an impression of the work of doctors from watching *Grey's Anatomy*. Of course, the primary reason apprenticeship programs exist in many trades and professions is to allow beginners to watch an expert so they can learn to act as they should.

---

punctuated-equilibrium model   *A set of phases that temporary groups go through that involves transitions between inertia and activity.*

role   *A set of expected behavior patterns attributed to someone occupying a given position in a social unit.*

role perception   *An individual's view of how he or she is supposed to act in a given situation.*

Green Bay Packers football player Donald Driver plays a variety of roles. As a wide receiver for the Packers, his principal role is to catch passes from the quarterback and then run the ball downfield. Driver is also a husband, father, author of a children's books series, the host of a statewide TV show in Wisconsin called Inside the Huddle, and a volunteer for Children's Hospital of Wisconsin and Goodwill Industries. Along with his wife, he created the Donald Driver Foundation that offers assistance to ill children with unmanageable hospital bills and provides housing for the homeless. Each of these positions imposes different role requirements on Driver. This photo shows him diving for a first down in his role as a wide receiver.

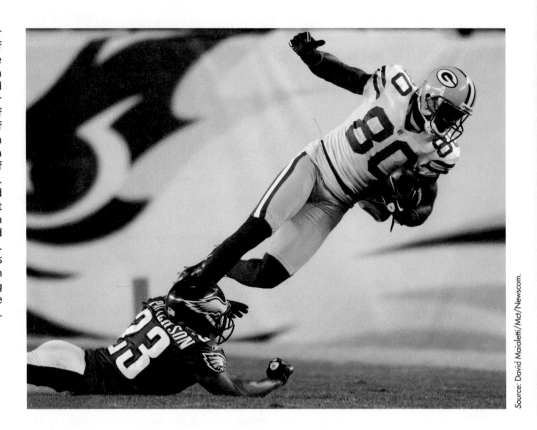

Source: David Maialetti/Mct/Newscom.

Role Expectations   **Role expectations** are the way others believe you should act in a given context. The role of a U.S. federal judge is viewed as having propriety and dignity, while a football coach is seen as aggressive, dynamic, and inspiring to his players.

In the workplace, we look at role expectations through the perspective of the **psychological contract**: an unwritten agreement that exists between employees and employer. This agreement sets out mutual expectations: what management expects from workers and vice versa.[18] Management is expected to treat employees justly, provide acceptable working conditions, clearly communicate what is a fair day's work, and give feedback on how well an employee is doing. Employees are expected to respond by demonstrating a good attitude, following directions, and showing loyalty to the organization.

What happens if management is derelict in keeping its part of the bargain? We can expect negative effects on employee performance and satisfaction. One study among restaurant managers found that psychological contact violations were related to greater intentions to quit the job, while another study of a variety of different industries found they were associated with lower levels of productivity, higher levels of theft, and greater work withdrawal.[19]

Role Conflict   When compliance with one role requirement may make it difficult to comply with another, the result is **role conflict**.[20] At the extreme, two or more role expectations are mutually contradictory.

Bill Patterson had to deal with role conflicts, such as his attempt to reconcile the expectations placed on him as a husband and father with those placed on him as an executive with EMM Industries. Bill's wife and children want to remain in Phoenix, while EMM expects its employees to be responsive to the company's needs and requirements. Although it might be in Bill's financial and career interests to accept a relocation, the conflict comes down to choosing between family and career role expectations. Indeed, a great deal of research demonstrates that conflict between the work and family roles is one of the most significant sources of stress for most employees.[21]

Most employees are simultaneously in occupations, work groups, divisions, and demographic groups, and these different identities can come into conflict when the expectations of one clash with the expectations of another.[22] During mergers and acquisitions, employees can be torn between their identities as members of their original organization and of the new parent company.[23] Organizations structured around multinational operations also have been shown to lead to dual identification, with employees distinguishing between the local division and the international organization.[24]

Zimbardo's Prison Experiment   One of the most illuminating role and identity experiments was done a number of years ago by Stanford University psychologist Philip Zimbardo and his associates.[25] They created a "prison" in the basement of the Stanford psychology building; hired at $15 a day two dozen emotionally stable, physically healthy, law-abiding students who scored "normal average" on extensive personality tests; randomly assigned them the role of either "guard" or "prisoner"; and established some basic rules.

It took the "prisoners" little time to accept the authority positions of the "guards" or for the mock guards to adjust to their new authority roles. Consistent with social identity theory, the guards came to see the prisoners as a negative outgroup, and their comments to researchers showed they had developed stereotypes about the "typical" prisoner personality type. After the guards crushed a rebellion attempt on the second day, the prisoners became increasingly passive. Whatever the guards "dished out," the prisoners took. The prisoners actually began to believe and act as if they were inferior and powerless, as the guards constantly reminded them. And every guard, at some time during the simulation, engaged in abusive, authoritative behavior. One said, "I was surprised at myself. . . . I made them call each other names and clean the toilets out with their bare hands. I practically considered the prisoners cattle, and I kept thinking: 'I have to watch out for them in case they try something.'" Surprisingly, during the entire experiment—even after days of abuse—not one prisoner said, "Stop this. I'm a student like you. This is just an experiment!"

The simulation actually proved *too successful* in demonstrating how quickly individuals learn new roles. The researchers had to stop it after only 6 days because of the participants' pathological reactions. And remember, these were individuals chosen precisely for their normalcy and emotional stability.

What can we conclude from this prison simulation? Like the rest of us, the participants had learned stereotyped conceptions of guard and prisoner roles from the mass media and their own personal experiences in power and powerlessness relationships gained at home (parent–child), in school (teacher–student), and in other situations. This background allowed them easily and rapidly to assume roles very different from their inherent personalities and, with no prior personality pathology or training in the parts they were playing, execute extreme forms of behavior consistent with those roles.

A follow-up reality television show conducted by the BBC that used a lower-fidelity simulated prison setting provides some insights into these results.[26] The

role expectations   *How others believe a person should act in a given situation.*

psychological contract   *An unwritten agreement that sets out what management expects from an employee and vice versa.*

role conflict   *A situation in which an individual is confronted by divergent role expectations.*

results were dramatically different from those of the Stanford experiment. The "guards" were far more careful in their behavior and limited the aggressive treatment of "prisoners." They often described their concerns about how their actions might be perceived. In short, they did not fully take on their roles, possibly because they knew their behavior was being observed by millions of viewers. As shared identity increased among "prisoners," they provided higher levels of social support to one another, and an egalitarian system developed between them and the guards. Philip Zimbardo has contended that the BBC study is not a replication of his study for several reasons, but he acknowledges the results demonstrate how both guards and prisoners act differently when closely monitored. These results suggest abuse of roles can be limited when people are made conscious of their behavior.

SELF-ASSESSMENT LIBRARY

Do I Trust Others?

In the Self-Assessment Library (available on CD or online), take assessment II.B.3 (Do I Trust Others?). You can also check out assessment II.B.4 (Do Others See Me as Trusting?).

Group Property 2: Norms

4 Demonstrate how norms and status exert influence on an individual's behavior.

Did you ever notice that golfers don't speak while their partners are putting on the green or that employees don't criticize their bosses in public? Why not? The answer is norms.

All groups have established **norms**—acceptable standards of behavior shared by their members that express what they ought and ought not to do under certain circumstances. When agreed to and accepted by the group, norms influence members' behavior with a minimum of external controls. Different groups, communities, and societies have different norms, but they all have them.[27]

Norms can cover virtually any aspect of group behavior.[28] Probably the most common is a *performance norm*, providing explicit cues about how hard members should work, what the level of output should be, how to get the job done, what level of tardiness is appropriate, and the like. These norms are extremely powerful and are capable of significantly modifying a performance prediction based solely on ability and level of personal motivation. Other norms include *appearance norms* (dress codes, unspoken rules about when to look busy), *social arrangement norms* (with whom to eat lunch, whether to form friendships on and off the job), and *resource allocation norms* (assignment of difficult jobs, distribution of resources like pay or equipment).

The Hawthorne Studies   Full-scale appreciation of the influence of norms on worker behavior did not occur until the early 1930s, following studies undertaken between 1924 and 1932 at the Western Electric Company's Hawthorne Works in Chicago.[29]

The Hawthorne researchers began by examining the relationship between the physical environment and productivity. As they increased the light level for the experimental group of workers, output rose for that unit and the control group. But to their surprise, as they dropped the light level in the experimental group, productivity continued to increase in both groups. In fact, productivity in the experimental group decreased only when the light intensity had been reduced to that of moonlight.

As a follow-up, the researchers began a second set of experiments at Western Electric. A small group of women assembling telephone relays was isolated from the main work group so their behavior could be more carefully observed. Observations covering a multiyear period found this small group's

From the Hawthorne Studies, researchers gained valuable insights into how individual behavior is influenced by group norms. They observed that a group of workers determined the level of fair output and established norms for individual work rates that conformed to the output. To enforce the group norms, workers used sarcasm, ridicule, and even physical force to influence individual behaviors that were not acceptable to the group. Researchers also learned that money was less a factor in determining worker output than were group standards, sentiments, and security.

Source: Hawthorne Works Factory of Morton College.

output increased steadily. The number of personal and out-sick absences was approximately one-third that recorded by women in the regular production department. It became evident this group's performance was significantly influenced by its status as "special." The members thought being in the experimental group was fun, that they were in an elite group, and that management showed concern about their interests by engaging in such experimentation. In essence, workers in both the illumination and assembly-test-room experiments were really reacting to the increased attention they received.

A third study, in the bank wiring observation room, was introduced to study the effect of a sophisticated wage incentive plan. The most important finding was that employees did not individually maximize their outputs. Rather, their output became controlled by a group norm that determined what was a proper day's work. Interviews determined the group was operating well below its capability and was leveling output to protect itself. Members were afraid that if they significantly increased their output, the unit incentive rate would be cut, the expected daily output would be increased, layoffs might occur, or slower workers would be reprimanded. So the group established its idea of a fair output—neither too much nor too little. Members helped each other ensure their reports were nearly level.

The norms the group established included a number of "don'ts." *Don't* be a rate-buster, turning out too much work. *Don't* be a chiseler, turning out too little work. *Don't* squeal on any of your peers. How did the group enforce these norms? The methods included sarcasm, name-calling, ridicule, and even punches to the upper arm of any member who violated the group's norms. Members also ostracized individuals whose behavior was against the group's interest.

norms *Acceptable standards of behavior within a group that are shared by the group's members.*

Conformity   As a member of a group, you desire acceptance by the group. Thus you are susceptible to conforming to the group's norms. Considerable evidence suggests that groups can place strong pressures on individual members to change their attitudes and behaviors to conform to the group's standard.[30] There are numerous reasons for conformity, with recent research highlighting the importance of a desire to form accurate perceptions of reality based on group consensus, to develop meaningful social relationships with others, and to maintain a favorable self-concept.

The impact that group pressures for **conformity** can have on an individual member's judgment was demonstrated in now-classic studies by Solomon Asch.[31] Asch made up groups of seven or eight people who were asked to compare two cards held by the experimenter. One card had one line, and the other had three lines of varying length, one of which was identical to the line on the one-line card, as Exhibit 9-3 shows. The difference in line length was quite obvious; in fact, under ordinary conditions, subjects made fewer than 1 percent errors in announcing aloud which of the three lines matched the single line. But what happens if members of the group begin giving incorrect answers? Will pressure to conform cause an unsuspecting subject (USS) to alter an answer? Asch arranged the group so only the USS was unaware the experiment was rigged. The seating was prearranged so the USS was one of the last to announce a decision.

The experiment began with several sets of matching exercises. All the subjects gave the right answers. On the third set, however, the first subject gave an obviously wrong answer—for example, saying "C" in Exhibit 9-3. The next subject gave the same wrong answer, and so did the others. Now the dilemma confronting the USS was this: publicly state a perception that differs from the announced position of the others in the group, or give an incorrect answer in order to agree with the others.

The results over many experiments and trials showed 75 percent of subjects gave at least one answer that conformed—that they knew was wrong but was consistent with the replies of other group members—and the average conformer gave wrong answers 37 percent of the time. What meaning can we draw from these results? They suggest group norms press us toward conformity. We desire to be one of the group and therefore avoid being visibly different.

This research was conducted more than 50 years ago. Has time altered the conclusions' validity? And should we consider them generalizable across cultures? Evidence indicates levels of conformity have steadily declined since Asch's studies in the early 1950s, and his findings *are* culture-bound.[32] Conformity to social norms is higher in collectivist cultures, but it is still a powerful force in groups in individualistic countries.

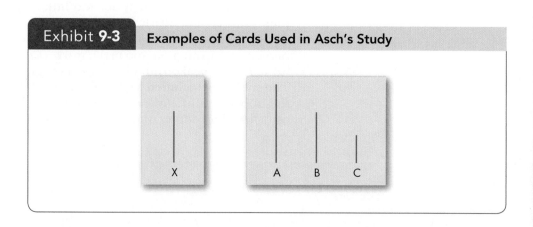

Exhibit 9-3   Examples of Cards Used in Asch's Study

Do individuals conform to the pressures of all the groups to which they belong? Obviously not, because people belong to many groups, and their norms vary and sometimes are contradictory. So what do people do? They conform to the important groups to which they belong or hope to belong. These important groups are **reference groups**, in which a person is aware of other members, defines himself or herself as a member or would like to be a member, and feels group members are significant to him or her. The implication, then, is that all groups do not impose equal conformity pressures on their members.

Deviant Workplace Behavior   LeBron Hunt is frustrated by a co-worker who constantly spreads malicious and unsubstantiated rumors about him. Debra Hundley is tired of a member of her work team who, when confronted with a problem, takes out his frustration by yelling and screaming at her and other members. And Mi-Cha Kim recently quit her job as a dental hygienist after being constantly sexually harassed by her employer.

What do these three episodes have in common? They represent employees exposed to acts of deviant workplace behavior.[33] **Deviant workplace behavior** (also called *antisocial behavior* or *workplace incivility*) is voluntary behavior that violates significant organizational norms and, in doing so, threatens the well-being of the organization or its members. Exhibit 9-4 provides a typology of deviant workplace behaviors, with examples of each.

Few organizations will admit to creating or condoning conditions that encourage and maintain deviant norms. Yet they exist. Employees report an increase in rudeness and disregard toward others by bosses and co-workers in recent years. And nearly half of employees who have suffered this incivility say

Exhibit **9-4**	Typology of Deviant Workplace Behavior

Category	Examples
Production	Leaving early Intentionally working slowly Wasting resources
Property	Sabotage Lying about hours worked Stealing from the organization
Political	Showing favoritism Gossiping and spreading rumors Blaming co-workers
Personal aggression	Sexual harassment Verbal abuse Stealing from co-workers

Source: Based on S. L. Robinson and R. J. Bennett, "A Typology of Deviant Workplace Behaviors: A Multidimensional Scaling Study," *Academy of Management Journal*, April 1995, p. 565. Copyright 1995 by Academy of Management (NY); S. H. Appelbaum, G. D. Iaconi and A. Matousek, "Positive and Negative Deviant Workplace Behaviors: Causes, Impacts, and Solutions," *Corporate Governance* 7, no. 5 (2007), pp. 586–598; and R. W. Griffin, and A. O'Leary-Kelly, *The Dark Side of Organizational Behavior*. (Wiley, New York: 2004).

conformity   *The adjustment of one's behavior to align with the norms of the group.*

reference groups   *Important groups to which individuals belong or hope to belong and with whose norms individuals are likely to conform.*

deviant workplace behavior   *Voluntary behavior that violates significant organizational norms and, in so doing, threatens the well-being of the organization or its members. Also called antisocial behavior or workplace incivility.*

it has led them to think about changing jobs; 12 percent actually quit because of it.[34] A study of nearly 1,500 respondents found that in addition to increasing turnover intentions, incivility at work increased reports of psychological stress and physical illness.[35]

Like norms in general, individual employees' antisocial actions are shaped by the group context within which they work. Evidence demonstrates deviant workplace behavior is likely to flourish where it's supported by group norms.[36] Workers who socialize either at or outside work with people who are frequently absent from work are more likely to be absent themselves.[37] What this means for managers is that when deviant workplace norms surface, employee cooperation, commitment, and motivation are likely to suffer.

What are the consequences of workplace deviance for teams? Some research suggests a chain reaction occurs in a group with high levels of dysfunctional behavior.[38] The process begins with negative behaviors like shirking, undermining co-workers, or being generally uncooperative. As a result of these behaviors, the team collectively starts to have negative moods. These negative moods then result in poor coordination of effort and lower levels of group performance, especially when there is a lot of nonverbal negative communication between members.

One study suggests those working in a group are more likely to lie, cheat, and steal than individuals working alone. As shown in Exhibit 9-5, in this study, no individual working alone lied, but 22 percent of those working in groups did. They also were more likely to cheat on a task (55 percent versus 23 percent of individuals working alone) and steal (29 percent compared to 10 percent working alone).[39] Groups provide a shield of anonymity, so someone who might ordinarily be afraid of getting caught can rely on the fact that other group members had the same opportunity, creating a false sense of confidence that may result in more aggressive behavior. Thus, deviant behavior depends on the accepted norms of the group—or even whether an individual is part of a group.[40]

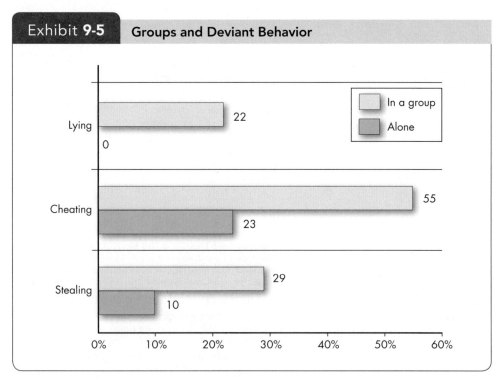

Exhibit 9-5   Groups and Deviant Behavior

Source: From "Lying, Cheating, Stealing: It Happens More in Groups" by A. Erez, H. Elms and E. Fong, paper presented at the European Business Ethics Network Annual Conference, Budapest, August 30, 2003. Reprinted by permission of the author.

Group Property 3: Status

Status   Status—a socially defined position or rank given to groups or group members by others—permeates every society. Even the smallest group will develop roles, rights, and rituals to differentiate its members. Status is a significant motivator and has major behavioral consequences when individuals perceive a disparity between what they believe their status is and what others perceive it to be.

What Determines Status?   According to **status characteristics theory**, status tends to derive from one of three sources:[41]

1. **The power a person wields over others.**   Because they likely control the group's resources, people who control the outcomes tend to be perceived as high status.
2. **A person's ability to contribute to a group's goals.**   People whose contributions are critical to the group's success tend to have high status. Some thought NBA star Kobe Bryant had more say over player decisions than his coaches (though not as much as Bryant wanted!).
3. **An individual's personal characteristics.**   Someone whose personal characteristics are positively valued by the group (good looks, intelligence, money, or a friendly personality) typically has higher status than someone with fewer valued attributes.

Status and Norms   Status has some interesting effects on the power of norms and pressures to conform. High-status individuals are often given more freedom to deviate from norms than are other group members.[42] Physicians actively resist administrative decisions made by lower-ranking insurance company

Earning a brown apron as a winner in Starbucks' Ambassador Cup competitions is a symbol of high status. The company holds Ambassador Cup contests throughout the world, with some contests regional and others countrywide, to determine which employees are the best coffee experts, or "ambassadors." The competitions involve making coffee drinks, identifying coffees in blind taste tests, and testing contestants' knowledge about Starbucks and different aspects of the coffee industry such as growing regions, roasting, purchasing, and fair trade practices. Winning a brown apron signifies achieving the highest level of coffee knowledge. This photo shows coffee ambassadors who won brown aprons during a competition at Starbucks' headquarters.

Source: Erika Schultz/MCT/Newscom.

status   *A socially defined position or rank given to groups or group members by others.*

status characteristics theory   *A theory that states that differences in status characteristics create status hierarchies within groups.*

employees.[43] High-status people are also better able to resist conformity pressures than their lower-status peers. An individual who is highly valued by a group but doesn't need or care about the group's social rewards is particularly able to disregard conformity norms.[44]

These findings explain why many star athletes, celebrities, top-performing salespeople, and outstanding academics seem oblivious to appearance and social norms that constrain their peers. As high-status individuals, they're given a wider range of discretion as long as their activities aren't severely detrimental to group goal achievement.[45]

Status and Group Interaction   High-status people tend to be more assertive group members.[46] They speak out more often, criticize more, state more commands, and interrupt others more often. But status differences actually inhibit diversity of ideas and creativity in groups, because lower-status members tend to participate less actively in group discussions. When they possess expertise and insights that could aid the group, failure to fully utilize them reduces the group's overall performance.

Status Inequity   It is important for group members to believe the status hierarchy is equitable. Perceived inequity creates disequilibrium, which inspires various types of corrective behavior. Hierarchical groups can lead to resentment among those at the lower end of the status continuum. Large differences in status within groups are also associated with poorer individual performance, lower health, and higher intentions to leave the group.[47]

The concept of equity we presented in Chapter 6 applies to status. People expect rewards to be proportionate to costs incurred. If Dana and Anne are the two finalists for the head nurse position in a hospital, and Dana clearly has more seniority and better preparation, Anne will view the selection of Dana as equitable. However, if Anne is chosen because she is the daughter-in-law of the hospital director, Dana will believe an injustice has been committed.

Groups generally agree within themselves on status criteria; hence, there is usually high concurrence in group rankings of individuals. Managers who occupy central positions in their social networks are typically seen as higher in status by their subordinates, and this position translates into greater influence over the group's functioning.[48] However, individuals can find themselves in conflicts when they move between groups whose status criteria are different, or when they join groups whose members have heterogeneous backgrounds. Business executives may use personal income or the growth rate of their companies as determinants of status. Government bureaucrats may use the size of their budgets, and blue-collar workers years of seniority. When groups are heterogeneous or when heterogeneous groups must be interdependent, status differences may initiate conflict as the group attempts to reconcile the differing hierarchies. As we'll see in Chapter 10, this can be a problem when management creates teams of employees from varied functions.

Do cultural differences affect status and the criteria that create it? The answer is a resounding "yes."[49] The French are highly status conscious. Latin Americans and Asians derive status from family position and formal roles in organizations. In the United States and Australia, status is more often conferred for accomplishments.[50]

Group Property 4: Size

5   Show how group size affects group performance.

Does the size of a group affect the group's overall behavior? Yes, but the effect depends on what dependent variables we look at. Smaller groups are faster at completing tasks than larger ones, and individuals perform better in smaller groups.[51] However, in problem solving, large groups consistently get better marks than their smaller counterparts.[52] Translating these results into specific numbers is a bit more hazardous, but groups with a dozen or more members are good for gaining diverse input. So if the goal is fact-finding, larger groups should be more effective. Smaller groups of about seven members are better at doing something productive with that input.

One of the most important findings about the size of a group concerns **social loafing**, the tendency for individuals to expend less effort when working collectively than alone.[53] It directly challenges the assumption that the productivity of the group as a whole should at least equal the sum of the productivity of the individuals in it.

Does team spirit spur individual effort and enhance the group's overall productivity? In the late 1920s, German psychologist Max Ringelmann compared the results of individual and group performance on a rope-pulling task.[54] He expected that three people pulling together should exert three times as much pull on the rope as one person, and eight people eight times as much. But one person pulling on a rope alone exerted an average of 63 kilograms of force. In groups of three, the per-person force dropped to 53 kilograms. And in groups of eight, it fell to only 31 kilograms per person.

Replications of Ringelmann's research with similar tasks have generally supported his findings.[55] Group performance increases with group size, but the addition of new members has diminishing returns on productivity. So more may be better in that total productivity of a group of four is greater than that of three, but the individual productivity of each member declines.

What causes social loafing? It may be a belief that others in the group are not carrying their fair share. If you see others as lazy or inept, you can reestablish equity by reducing your effort. Another explanation is the dispersion of responsibility. Because group results cannot be attributed to any single person, the relationship between an individual's input and the group's output is clouded. Individuals may then be tempted to become free riders and coast on the group's efforts. The implications for OB are significant. When managers use collective work situations to enhance morale and teamwork, they must also be able to identify individual efforts. Otherwise, they must weigh the potential losses in productivity from using groups against the possible gains in worker satisfaction.[56]

Social loafing appears to have a Western bias. It's consistent with individualistic cultures, such as the United States and Canada, that are dominated by self-interest. It is *not* consistent with collective societies, in which individuals are motivated by in-group goals. In studies comparing U.S. employees with employees from the People's Republic of China and Israel (both collectivist societies), the Chinese and Israelis showed no propensity to engage in social loafing and actually performed better in a group than alone.

There are several ways to prevent social loafing: (1) Set group goals, so the group has a common purpose to strive toward; (2) increase intergroup competition, which again focuses on the shared outcome; (3) engage in peer evaluation so each person evaluates each other person's contribution; (4) select members who have high motivation and prefer to work in groups, and (5) if possible, base group rewards in part on each member's unique contributions.[57] Although no magic bullet will prevent social loafing in all cases, these steps should help minimize its effect.

social loafing   *The tendency for individuals to expend less effort when working collectively than when working individually.*

Social loafing is the tendency for individuals to put forth less of an effort when working in a group than when working alone. Studies indicate that the employees shown here producing Spice handsets at a factory in China do not show any propensity to engage in social loafing. In collectivist societies such as China and Israel, employees actually prefer working in a group and are motivated by in-group goals. But in individualistic societies such as the United States and Canada that are dominated by self-interest, social loafing is more likely.

Source: Str/Stringer/Getty Images.

Group Property 5: Cohesiveness

6   Contrast the benefits and disadvantages of cohesive groups.

Groups differ in their **cohesiveness**—the degree to which members are attracted to each other and motivated to stay in the group. Some work groups are cohesive because the members have spent a great deal of time together, or the group's small size facilitates high interaction, or external threats have brought members close together.

Cohesiveness affects group productivity.[58] Studies consistently show that the relationship between cohesiveness and productivity depends on the group's performance-related norms.[59] If norms for quality, output, and cooperation with outsiders, for instance, are high, a cohesive group will be more productive than will a less cohesive group. But if cohesiveness is high and performance norms are low, productivity will be low. If cohesiveness is low and performance norms are high, productivity increases, but less than in the high-cohesiveness/high-norms situation. When cohesiveness and performance-related norms are both low, productivity tends to fall into the low-to-moderate range. These conclusions are summarized in Exhibit 9-6.

What can you do to encourage group cohesiveness? (1) Make the group smaller, (2) encourage agreement with group goals, (3) increase the time members spend together, (4) increase the group's status and the perceived difficulty of attaining membership, (5) stimulate competition with other groups, (6) give rewards to the group rather than to individual members, and (7) physically isolate the group.[60]

Group Property 6: Diversity

The final property of groups we consider is **diversity** in the group's membership, the degree to which members of the group are similar to, or different from, one another. A great deal of research is being done on how diversity influences group performance. Some looks at cultural diversity and some at racial, gender, and other differences. Overall, studies identify both benefits and costs from group diversity.

Diversity appears to increase group conflict, especially in the early stages of a group's tenure, which often lowers group morale and raises dropout rates. One study compared groups that were culturally diverse (composed of people from different countries) and homogeneous (composed of people from the

OB Poll **Working with Others Is Often Irritating**

What causes annoyance and stress when working in groups?

National sample of 1,836 adults working in an office in the United Kingdom.

Source: "The Office--An Annoying Workplace," Opinium Research LLP (February 24, 2010), downloaded May 26, 2011 from http://news. opinium.co.uk. Reprinted with permission from The Gallup Organization.

Exhibit 9-6 | **Relationship Between Group Cohesiveness, Performance Norms, and Productivity**

same country). On a wilderness survival exercise (not unlike the Experiential Exercise at the end of this chapter), the groups performed equally well, but the diverse groups were less satisfied with their groups, were less cohesive, and had more conflict.[61] Another study examined the effect of differences in tenure on the performance of 67 engineering research and development groups.[62] When most people had roughly the same level of tenure, performance was high, but as tenure diversity increased, performance dropped off. There was an important qualifier: higher levels of tenure diversity were not related to lower performance for groups when there were effective team-oriented human resources practices. Teams in which members' values or opinions differ tend

cohesiveness *The degree to which group members are attracted to each other and are motivated to stay in the group.*

diversity *The extent to which members of a group are similar to, or different from, one another.*

to experience more conflict, but leaders who can get the group to focus on the task at hand and encourage group learning are able to reduce these conflicts and enhance discussion of group issues.[63] It seems diversity can be bad for performance even in creative teams, but appropriate organizational support and leadership might offset these problems.

However, culturally and demographically diverse groups may perform better over time—if they can get over their initial conflicts. Why might this be so?

Surface-level diversity—in observable characteristics such as national origin, race, and gender—alerts people to possible deep-level diversity—in underlying attitudes, values, and opinions. One researcher argues, "The mere presence of diversity you can see, such as a person's race or gender, actually cues a team that there's likely to be differences of opinion."[64] Although those differences can lead to conflict, they also provide an opportunity to solve problems in unique ways.

One study of jury behavior found diverse juries more likely to deliberate longer, share more information, and make fewer factual errors when discussing evidence. Two studies of MBA student groups found surface-level diversity led to greater openness even without deep-level diversity. Here, surface-level diversity may subconsciously cue team members to be more open-minded in their views.[65]

The impact of diversity on groups is mixed. It is difficult to be in a diverse group in the short term. However, if members can weather their differences, over time diversity may help them be more open-minded and creative and to do better. But even positive effects are unlikely to be especially strong. As one review stated, "The business case (in terms of demonstrable financial results) for diversity remains hard to support based on the extant research."[66]

Group Decision Making

7 Understand the implications of diversity for group effectiveness.

The belief—characterized by juries—that two heads are better than one has long been accepted as a basic component of the U.S. legal system and those of many other countries. Today, many decisions in organizations are made by groups, teams, or committees.[67]

Groups versus the Individual

Decision-making groups may be widely used in organizations, but are group decisions preferable to those made by an individual alone? The answer depends on a number of factors. Let's begin by looking at the strengths and weaknesses of group decision making.[68]

Strengths of Group Decision Making Groups generate *more complete information and knowledge.* By aggregating the resources of several individuals, groups bring more input as well as heterogeneity into the decision process. They offer *increased diversity of views.* This opens up the opportunity to consider more approaches and alternatives. Finally, groups lead to increased *acceptance of a solution.* Group members who participated in making a decision are more likely to enthusiastically support and encourage others to accept it.

Weaknesses of Group Decision Making Group decisions are time consuming because groups typically take more time to reach a solution. There are *conformity pressures.* The desire by group members to be accepted and considered an asset to the group can squash any overt disagreement. Group discussion can be *dominated*

Forming International Teams in a Virtual World

As more organizations become global entities, the need for work groups that can collaborate across national boundaries grows. Advances in technology that have accompanied globalization lead us to a new type of working relationship: *global virtual teams*. These are groups of individuals working together across national boundaries through electronic communication media. Engineers in Germany might communicate with production teams in China to produce components for assembly and marketing by team members in Canada. Although some global teams occasionally meet in person, geographically dispersed managers often must collaborate virtually.

Virtual global teams have certain liabilities. Traditional teams offer multiple opportunities to work closely with colleagues and develop close personal relationships that can facilitate performance. To be effective, virtual teams need to facilitate these relationships despite numerous barriers. It's easy to misinterpret messages without cues like facial expression and tone of voice. These problems can be even more pronounced among individuals with different cultural backgrounds.

So how can virtual global teams be more effective? Alcoa found it was important to develop regular meeting routines to facilitate collaboration. Groups were also encouraged to review the progress of their own and other teams to identify "best practices" that worked in a variety of situations. Not surprisingly, higher levels of communication and cohesion among members of global virtual teams are associated with shared performance goals, which in turn lead to higher performance. More surprisingly, leaders' efforts to build personal, inspirational relationships can help even teams that don't meet face to face.

Although global virtual teams face many challenges, companies that implement them effectively can realize tremendous rewards through the diverse knowledge they gain.

Sources: Based on A. Joshi, M. B. Lazarova, and H. Liao, "Getting Everyone on Board: The Role of Inspirational Leadership in Geographically Dispersed Teams," *Organization Science* 20, no. 1 (2009), pp. 240–252; J. Cordery, C. Soo, B. Kirkman, B. Rosen, and J. Mathieu, "Leading Parallel Global Virtual Teams: Lessons from Alcoa," *Organizational Dynamics* 38, no. 3 (2009), pp. 204–216; and R. L. Algesheimer, U. M. Dholakia, and C. Gurau, "Virtual Team Performance in a Highly Competitive Environment," *Group and Organization Management* 36, no. 2 (2011), pp. 161–190.

by one or a few members. If they're low- and medium-ability members, the group's overall effectiveness will suffer. Finally, group decisions suffer from *ambiguous responsibility.* In an individual decision, it's clear who is accountable for the final outcome. In a group decision, the responsibility of any single member is diluted.

Effectiveness and Efficiency   Whether groups are more effective than individuals depends on how you define effectiveness. Group decisions are generally more *accurate* than the decisions of the average individual in a group, but less accurate than the judgments of the most accurate.[69] In terms of *speed,* individuals are superior. If *creativity* is important, groups tend to be more effective. And if effectiveness means the degree of *acceptance* the final solution achieves, the nod again goes to the group.[70]

But we cannot consider effectiveness without also assessing efficiency. With few exceptions, group decision making consumes more work hours than an individual tackling the same problem alone. The exceptions tend to be the instances in which, to achieve comparable quantities of diverse input, the single decision maker must spend a great deal of time reviewing files and talking to other people. In deciding whether to use groups, then, managers must assess whether increases in effectiveness are more than enough to offset the reductions in efficiency.

Summary   In summary, groups are an excellent vehicle for performing many steps in the decision-making process and offer both breadth and depth of input for information gathering. If group members have diverse backgrounds, the alternatives generated should be more extensive and the analysis more critical.

"Asians Have Less Ingroup Bias Than Americans"

This statement is true. But first let's review what in-group bias means. When they form groups, members characteristically exhibit an *ingroup bias*—they tend to favor members of their group regardless of whether they deserve it. Race, gender, and nationality are commonly investigated causes of ingroup bias. However, nearly any identity can activate ingroup bias, even when individuals are randomly assigned to groups and given a group identity ("lions," "bears," and so on).

Ingroup bias happens because when group identity is salient to people—which it often is—they tend to simplify; they see themselves as more similar to other group members, and less similar to outgroup members, than is really the case.

Recent research suggests that Asians exhibit less ingroup bias than

Americans. One study asked Chinese students at Peking University and U.S. students at University of California–Berkeley to describe the degree to which a set of 16 favorable–unfavorable characteristics (intelligent/foolish, loyal/undependable) described the family member they were closest to. Chinese students described their closest family members significantly less favorably than did the U.S. students. In another study, when Chinese and Americans were asked to evaluate cultural stereotypes of Chinese and Americans in general (intelligent, hard-working, leaderlike, and so on), Americans were more likely to favor their group than were the Chinese.

Why do Asians appear to demonstrate less ingroup bias? One likely explanation is that Asians score higher on *dialecticism*—the tendency to be more comfortable with contradiction

(yin and yang), change (nothing is permanent), and holism (everything has both good and bad). As one Chinese student noted, "If you ask me about Chinese politics, the culture, the people, I can go on for hours talking about everything that's negative. But I still love that place." This tendency may help Asians see both the good and bad sides of their own ingroups.

Sources: C. Ma-Kellams, J. Spencer-Rodgers, and K. Peng, "I Am Against Us? Unpacking Cultural Differences in Ingroup Favoritism Via Dialecticism," *Personality and Social Psychology Bulletin* 37, no. 1 (2011), pp. 15–27; A. E. Giannakakis and I. Fritsche, "Social Identities, Group Norms, and Threat: On the Malleability of Ingroup Bias," *Personality and Social Psychology Bulletin* 37, no. 1 (2011), pp. 82–93; and T. E. DiDonato, J. Ullrich, and J. I. Krueger, "Social Perception as Induction and Inference: An Integrative Model of Intergroup Differentiation, Ingroup Favoritism, and Differential Accuracy," *Journal of Personality and Social Psychology* 100, no. 1 (2011), pp. 66–83.

When the final solution is agreed on, there are more people in a group decision to support and implement it. These pluses, however, can be more than offset by the time consumed by group decisions, the internal conflicts they create, and the pressures they generate toward conformity. In some cases, therefore, we can expect individuals to make better decisions than groups.

Groupthink and Groupshift

Two by-products of group decision making have the potential to affect a group's ability to appraise alternatives objectively and arrive at high-quality solutions.

The first, called **groupthink**, relates to norms. It describes situations in which group pressures for conformity deter the group from critically appraising unusual, minority, or unpopular views. Groupthink is a disease that attacks many groups and can dramatically hinder their performance. The second phenomenon is **groupshift**, which describes the way group members tend to exaggerate the initial positions they hold when discussing a given set of alternatives and arriving at a solution. In some situations, caution dominates and there is a conservative shift, while in other situations groups tend toward a risky shift. Let's look at each phenomenon in detail.

Groupthink Have you ever felt like speaking up in a meeting, a classroom, or an informal group but decided against it? One reason may have been shyness. Or you may have been a victim of groupthink, which occurs when the norm for consensus overrides the realistic appraisal of alternative courses and the full expression of deviant, minority, or unpopular views. The individual's mental efficiency, reality testing, and moral judgment deteriorate as a result of group pressures.[71]

We have all seen the symptoms of groupthink:

1. Group members rationalize any resistance to the assumptions they've made. No matter how strongly the evidence may contradict their basic assumptions, they behave so as to reinforce them.
2. Members apply direct pressures on those who momentarily express doubts about any of the group's shared views, or who question the validity of arguments supporting the alternative favored by the majority.
3. Members who have doubts or differing points of view seek to avoid deviating from what appears to be group consensus by keeping silent about misgivings and even minimizing to themselves the importance of their doubts.
4. There is an illusion of unanimity. If someone doesn't speak, it's assumed he or she is in full accord. Abstention becomes a "yes" vote.[72]

Groupthink appears closely aligned with the conclusions Solomon Asch drew in his experiments with a lone dissenter. Individuals who hold a position different from that of the dominant majority are under pressure to suppress, withhold, or modify their true feelings and beliefs. As members of a group, we find it more pleasant to be in agreement—to be a positive part of the group—than to be a disruptive force, even if disruption is necessary to improve the effectiveness of the group's decisions. Groups that are more focused on performance than on learning are especially likely to fall victim to groupthink and to suppress the opinions of those who do not agree with the majority.[73]

Does groupthink attack all groups? No. It seems to occur most often when there is a clear group identity, when members hold a positive image of their group that they want to protect, and when the group perceives a collective threat to this positive image.[74] So groupthink is not a dissenter-suppression mechanism as much as it's a means for a group to protect its positive image. One study also showed that those influenced by groupthink were more confident about their course of action early on.[75] Groups that believe too strongly in the correctness of their course of action are more likely to suppress dissent and encourage conformity than are groups that are more skeptical about their course of action.

What can managers do to minimize groupthink?[76] First, they can monitor group size. People grow more intimidated and hesitant as group size increases, and although there is no magic number that will eliminate groupthink, individuals are likely to feel less personal responsibility when groups get larger than about 10 members. Managers should also encourage group leaders to play an impartial role. Leaders should actively seek input from all members and avoid expressing their own opinions, especially in the early stages of deliberation. In addition, managers should appoint one group member to play the role of devil's advocate, overtly challenging the majority position and offering divergent perspectives. Still another suggestion is to use exercises that stimulate active discussion of diverse alternatives without threatening the group or intensifying identity protection. Have group members delay discussion of possible gains so they can first talk about the dangers or risks inherent in a decision. Requiring

groupthink   *A phenomenon in which the norm for consensus overrides the realistic appraisal of alternative courses of action.*

groupshift   *A change between a group's decision and an individual decision that a member within the group would make; the shift can be toward either conservatism or greater risk but it generally is toward a more extreme version of the group's original position.*

An Ethical Choice

Should You Use Group Peer Pressure?

We've all experienced peer pressure, and it can be hard to behave differently from your friends and co-workers. As more work in organizations is performed in groups and teams, the possibilities and pitfalls of such pressure have become an increasingly important ethical issue for managers.

Peer pressure can be a positive force in some ways. If one member of a group or team is not performing to full potential, pressure from co-workers can encourage better performance. A team with a norm toward behaving ethically might even use peer pressure directly to minimize negative

behavior. Peer pressure can increase all sorts of ethical behavior ranging from donating to charity to working for the Salvation Army.

However, as the chapter has shown, peer pressure can also be more destructive. It can create a feeling of exclusion in those who do not go along with group norms and can be very stressful and hurtful for those who don't see eye-to-eye with the rest of the group. Peer pressure itself might become an unethical practice that unduly influences workers' behavior and thoughts.

So should you use group peer pressure? It depends on what type and why. If you are using peer pressure to

encourage individuals to work toward team goals and behave consistently with organizational values, it can enhance ethical performance. But it should emphasize acceptance and rewarding of positive behavior, rather than rejection and exclusion, as a means of getting everyone to behave consistently in a group.

Sources: Based on: A. Verghese, "The Healing Power of Peer Pressure," *Newsweek* (March 14, 2011), www .newsweek.com; T. Rosenberg, *Join the Club: How Peer Pressure Can Transform the World* (New York: W. W. Norton & Company, 2011); and J. Meer, "Brother, Can You Spare a Dime? Peer Pressure in Charitable Solicitation," *Journal of Public Economics* 95, no. 7–8 (2011), pp. 926–941.

members to first focus on the negatives of an alternative makes the group less likely to stifle dissenting views and more likely to gain an objective evaluation.

Group Shift or Group Polarization   There are differences between group decisions and the individual decisions of group members.[77] What appears to happen in groups is that the discussion leads members toward a more extreme view of the position they already held. Conservatives become more cautious, and more aggressive types take on more risk. The group discussion tends to exaggerate the initial position of the group.

We can view group polarization as a special case of groupthink. The group's decision reflects the dominant decision-making norm that develops during discussion. Whether the shift in the group's decision is toward greater caution or more risk depends on the dominant pre-discussion norm.

The shift toward polarization has generated several explanations.[78] It's been argued, for instance, that discussion makes the members more comfortable with each other and, thus, more willing to express extreme versions of their original positions. Another argument is that the group diffuses responsibility. Group decisions free any single member from accountability for the group's final choice, so a more extreme position can be taken. It's also likely that people take on extreme positions because they want to demonstrate how different they are from the outgroup.[79] People on the fringes of political or social movements take on ever-more extreme positions just to prove they are really committed to the cause, whereas those who are more cautious tend to take exceptionally moderate positions to demonstrate how reasonable they are.

So how should you use the findings on groupshift? Recognize that group decisions exaggerate the initial position of the individual members, that the shift has been shown more often to be toward greater risk, and that which way a group will shift is a function of the members' pre-discussion inclinations.

We now turn to the techniques by which groups make decisions. These reduce some of the dysfunctional aspects of group decision making.

Group Decision-Making Techniques

8 Contrast the strengths and weaknesses of group decision making.

The most common form of group decision making takes place in **interacting groups**. Members meet face to face and rely on both verbal and nonverbal interaction to communicate. But as our discussion of groupthink demonstrated, interacting groups often censor themselves and pressure individual members toward conformity of opinion. Brainstorming, the nominal group technique, and electronic meetings can reduce problems inherent in the traditional interacting group.

Brainstorming can overcome the pressures for conformity that dampen creativity[80] by encouraging any and all alternatives while withholding criticism. In a typical brainstorming session, a half-dozen to a dozen people sit around a table. The group leader states the problem in a clear manner so all participants understand. Members then freewheel as many alternatives as they can in a given length of time. To encourage members to "think the unusual," no criticism is allowed, even of the most bizarre suggestions, and all ideas are recorded for later discussion and analysis.

Brainstorming may indeed generate ideas—but not in a very efficient manner. Research consistently shows individuals working alone generate more ideas than a group in a brainstorming session. One reason for this is "production blocking." When people are generating ideas in a group, many are talking at once, which blocks the thought process and eventually impedes the sharing of ideas.[81] The following two techniques go further than brainstorming by helping groups arrive at a preferred solution.[82]

The **nominal group technique** restricts discussion or interpersonal communication during the decision-making process, hence the term *nominal*. Group members are all physically present, as in a traditional committee meeting, but they operate independently. Specifically, a problem is presented and then the group takes the following steps:

1. Before any discussion takes place, each member independently writes down ideas on the problem.
2. After this silent period, each member presents one idea to the group. No discussion takes place until all ideas have been presented and recorded.
3. The group discusses the ideas for clarity and evaluates them.
4. Each group member silently and independently rank-orders the ideas. The idea with the highest aggregate ranking determines the final decision.

The chief advantage of the nominal group technique is that it permits a group to meet formally but does not restrict independent thinking, as does an interacting group. Research generally shows nominal groups outperform brainstorming groups.[83]

The most recent approach to group decision making blends the nominal group technique with sophisticated computer technology.[84] It's called a computer-assisted group, or an **electronic meeting**. Once the required technology is in

interacting groups *Typical groups in which members interact with each other face to face.*

brainstorming *An idea-generation process that specifically encourages any and all alternatives while withholding any criticism of those alternatives.*

nominal group technique *A group decision-making method in which individual members meet face to face to pool their judgments in a systematic but independent fashion.*

electronic meeting *A meeting in which members interact on computers, allowing for anonymity of comments and aggregation of votes.*

Exhibit 9-7	Evaluating Group Effectiveness			

| | Type of Group | | | |
Effectiveness Criteria	Interacting	Brainstorming	Nominal	Electronic
Number and quality of ideas	Low	Moderate	High	High
Social pressure	High	Low	Moderate	Low
Money costs	Low	Low	Low	High
Speed	Moderate	Moderate	Moderate	Moderate
Task orientation	Low	High	High	High
Potential for interpersonal conflict	High	Low	Moderate	Low
Commitment to solution	High	Not applicable	Moderate	Moderate
Development of group cohesiveness	High	High	Moderate	Low

place, the concept is simple. Up to 50 people sit around a horseshoe-shaped table, empty except for a series of networked laptops. Issues are presented to them, and they type their responses into their computers. These individual but anonymous comments, as well as aggregate votes, are displayed on a projection screen. This technique also allows people to be brutally honest without penalty. And it's fast because chitchat is eliminated, discussions don't digress, and many participants can "talk" at once without stepping on one another's toes. Early evidence, however, suggests electronic meetings don't achieve most of their proposed benefits. They actually lead to *decreased* group effectiveness, require *more* time to complete tasks, and result in *reduced* member satisfaction compared with face-to-face groups.[85] Nevertheless, current enthusiasm for computer-mediated communications suggests this technology is here to stay and is likely to increase in popularity in the future.

9 Compare the effectiveness of interacting, brainstorming, nominal, and electronic meeting groups.

Each of the four group-decision techniques has its own set of strengths and weaknesses. The choice depends on what criteria you want to emphasize and the cost–benefit trade-off. As Exhibit 9-7 indicates, an interacting group is good for achieving commitment to a solution, brainstorming develops group cohesiveness, the nominal group technique is an inexpensive means for generating a large number of ideas, and electronic meetings minimize social pressures and conflicts.

MyManagementLab

Now that you have finished this chapter, go back to **www.mymanagementlab.com** to continue practicing and applying the concepts you've learned.

Summary and Implications for Managers

Several implications can be drawn from our discussion of groups. The next chapter will explore several of these in greater depth.

- Role perception and an employee's performance evaluation are positively related.[86] The degree of congruence between the employee's and the boss's perception of the employee's job influences the degree to which the boss will judge that employee effective. An employee whose role perception fulfills the boss's role expectations will receive a higher performance evaluation.

- Norms control behavior by establishing standards of right and wrong. The norms of a given group can help explain members' behaviors for managers. When norms support high output, managers can expect markedly higher individual performance than when they aim to restrict output. Norms that support antisocial behavior increase the likelihood that individuals will engage in deviant workplace activities.

- Status inequities create frustration and can adversely influence productivity and willingness to remain with an organization. Incongruence is likely to reduce motivation and motivate a search for ways to bring about fairness (say, by taking another job). Because lower-status people tend to participate less in group discussions, groups with high status differences are likely to inhibit input from lower-status members and reduce their potential.

- The impact of size on a group's performance depends on the type of task. Larger groups are more effective at fact-finding activities, smaller groups at action-taking tasks. Our knowledge of social loafing suggests that managers using larger groups should also provide measures of individual performance.

- Cohesiveness can influence a group's level of productivity or not, depending on the group's performance-related norms.

- Diversity appears to have a mixed impact on group performance, with some studies suggesting that diversity can help performance and others suggesting it can hurt it. It appears the situation makes a difference in whether positive or negative results predominate.

- High congruence between a boss's and an employee's perception of the employee's job correlates strongly with high employee satisfaction.[87] Role conflict is associated with job-induced tension and job dissatisfaction.[88]

- Most people prefer to communicate with others at their own status level or a higher one rather than with those below them.[89] As a result, we should expect satisfaction to be greater among employees whose job minimizes interaction with individuals lower in status than themselves.

- The group size–satisfaction relationship is what we would intuitively expect: larger groups are associated with lower satisfaction.[90] As size increases, opportunities for participation and social interaction decrease, as does the ability of members to identify with the group's accomplishments. At the same time, having more members also prompts dissension, conflict, and the formation of subgroups, which all act to make the group a less pleasant entity of which to be a part.

QUESTIONS FOR REVIEW

1 Define *group*. What are the different types of groups?

2 What are the five stages of group development?

3 Do role requirements change in different situations? If so, how?

4 How do group norms and status influence an individual's behavior?

5 How does group size affect group performance?

6 What are the advantages and limitations of cohesive groups?

7 What are the implications of diversity for group effectiveness?

8 What are the strengths and weaknesses of group (versus individual) decision making?

9 How effective are interacting, brainstorming, nominal, and electronic meeting groups?

Affinity Groups Fuel Business Success

POINT

Employee resource groups (ERGs), also known as affinity groups, have become part of nearly all large organizations' cultures. ERGs are voluntary networking groups that provide forums for employees to gather socially and share ideas outside their particular business units. Many ERGs are organized around surface characteristics such as gender, age, disability, sexual orientation, race, and ethnic background. However, they can be formed around any issue.

The rationale for ERGs is obvious. Large organizations often are very decentralized, leading many employees to feel disconnected and isolated. That's especially true for employees who are or feel different. So large companies such as Best Buy, Ford, Intuit, Prudential, Wells Fargo, Johnson & Johnson, and Macy's have found that their ERGs lead to greater feelings of inclusiveness. When employees of a large organization realize they're hardly alone, ERGs are a great way to foster commitment by joining employees to others in the organization, often in a way that's independent of their work unit. Why not tie employees to one another in as many ways as possible?

Finally, many ERGs solve organizational problems in unique ways. Cisco's Asian Affinity Network played a key role in forging a bond between Cisco and Shui On Group, the largest publicly traded real estate company in China, by proposing that Cisco hold a business development event during a Silicon Valley visit by Shui On Group's founder and chairman.

Many thought the decline in the economy and the growth of social networking sites would spell the end for ERGs. However, it seems the opposite is true. ERGs are growing. When a company like Northrop Grumman has 125,000 employees spread across 25 countries and all 50 states, it needs a way to join them together. That's exactly what ERGs do best.

ERGs make great business sense. Ford executive Rosalind Cox says of Ford's ERGs: "At the end of the day, we want to build a diverse and inclusive culture that drives business results."

COUNTERPOINT

ERGs may sound like a good idea with few drawbacks, but that's not the case. They have some real problems, few of which you'll hear about in the rah-rah press generated about them, much of it put forth by companies' PR departments.

First, there's cost. These affinity groups can cost a lot of money. One study estimated that the budget for affinity groups was $7,203 for each 100 group members. That doesn't even include the cost of technology, facilities, and staff support (on average, about 1.5 staff employees for each group). Costlier still is the time ERG members spend on their groups, coaching, training, meeting, and planning events oriented around a very small slice of the company's workforce—on average, only 8 percent of an organization's employees. In these competitive times, that doesn't sound like the most efficient and fair use of an organization's resources.

Then there are the legal issues. Affinity groups have been subject to significant legal action, often by excluded employees. Most employers also don't realize that ERGs can be viewed as "sweetheart unions" by the National Labor Relations Board. "The National Labor Relations Act controls collective actions between employers and employees whether a union is present or not," says one employment law expert. Most companies resist unions trying to organize their employees. Why do they form them by their own hand?

Organizations should do everything they can to encourage all employees to feel they are included and heard. Networking is a wonderful way to do that. But organizations that endorse, establish, and fund segmented groups that exclude some employees are asking for trouble. The best way to fight feelings of isolation is by drawing employees in and giving them a voice. It's not by slicing the organizations into groups, including some and excluding others.

Sources: R. R. Hastings, "Employee Resource Groups Drive Business Results," *HR Magazine* (February 15, 2011), downloaded June 10, 2011, from www.shrm.org/; R. R. Hastings, "Employee Resource Groups Can Create Labor Issues, "*HR Magazine* (June 25, 2009), downloaded June 10, 2011, from www.shrm.org/; and "Affinity and Networking Groups," *The New York Times*, downloaded June 11, 2011 from www.nytimes.com/.

EXPERIENTIAL EXERCISE Wilderness Survival

You are a member of a hiking party. After reaching base camp on the first day, you decide to take a quick sunset hike by yourself. After a few exhilarating miles, you decide to return to camp. On your way back, you realize you are lost. You have shouted for help, to no avail. It is now dark. And getting cold.

Your Task

Without communicating with anyone else in your group, read the following scenarios and choose the best answer. Keep track of your answers on a sheet of paper. You have 10 minutes to answer the 10 questions.

1. The first thing you decide to do is to build a fire. However, you have no matches, so you use the bow-and-drill method. What is the bow-and-drill method?
   a. A dry, soft stick is rubbed between the hands against a board of supple green wood.
   b. A soft green stick is rubbed between the hands against a hardwood board.
   c. A straight stick of wood is quickly rubbed back and forth against a dead tree.
   d. Two sticks (one being the bow, the other the drill) are struck to create a spark.

2. It occurs to you that you can also use the fire as a distress signal. How do you form the international distress signal with fire?
   a. 2 fires
   b. 4 fires in a square
   c. 4 fires in a cross
   d. 3 fires in a line

3. You are very thirsty. You go to a nearby stream and collect some water in the small metal cup you have in your backpack. How long should you boil the water?
   a. 15 minutes
   b. A few seconds
   c. 1 hour
   d. It depends on the altitude.

4. You are very hungry, so you decide to eat what appear to be edible berries. When performing the universal edibility test, what should you do?
   a. Do not eat for 2 hours before the test.
   b. If the plant stings your lip, confirm the sting by holding it under your tongue for 15 minutes.
   c. If nothing bad has happened 2 hours after digestion, eat half a cup of the plant and wait again.
   d. Separate the plant into its basic components and eat each component, one at a time.

5. Next, you decide to build a shelter for the evening. In selecting a site, what do you *not* have to consider?
   a. It must contain material to make the type of shelter you need.
   b. It must be free of insects, reptiles, and poisonous plants.
   c. It must be large enough and level enough for you to lie down comfortably.
   d. It must be on a hill so you can signal rescuers and keep an eye on your surroundings.

6. In the shelter that you built, you notice a spider. You heard from a fellow hiker that black widow spiders populate the area. How do you identify a black widow spider?
   a. Its head and abdomen are black; its thorax is red.
   b. It is attracted to light.
   c. It runs away from light.
   d. It is a dark spider with a red or orange marking on the female's abdomen.

7. After getting some sleep, you notice that the night sky has cleared, so you decide to try to find your way back to base camp. You believe you should travel north and can use the North Star for navigation. How do you locate the North Star?
   a. Hold your right hand up as far as you can and look between your index and middle fingers.
   b. Find Sirius and look 60 degrees above it and to the right.
   c. Look for the Big Dipper and follow the line created by its cup end.
   d. Follow the line of Orion's belt.

8. You come across a fast-moving stream. What is the best way to cross it?
   a. Find a spot downstream from a sandbar, where the water will be calmer.
   b. Build a bridge.
   c. Find a rocky area, as the water will be shallow and you will have hand- and footholds.
   d. Find a level stretch where it breaks into a few channels.

9. After walking for about an hour, you feel several spiders in your clothes. You don't feel any pain, but you know some spider bites are painless. Which of these spider bites is painless?
   a. Black widow
   b. Brown recluse
   c. Wolf spider
   d. Harvestman (daddy longlegs)

10. You decide to eat some insects. Which insects should you avoid?
    a. Adults that sting or bite
    b. Caterpillars and insects that have a pungent odor
    c. Hairy or brightly colored ones
    d. All the above

Group Task

Break into groups of five or six people. Now imagine that your whole group is lost. Answer each question as a group, employing a consensus approach to reach each decision. Once the group comes to an agreement, write down the decision on the same sheet of paper that you used for your individual answers. You will have approximately 20 minutes for the group task.

Scoring Your Answers

Your instructor will provide you with the correct answers, which are based on expert judgments in these situations. Once you have received the answers, calculate (A) your individual score; (B) your group's score; (C) the average individual score in the group; and (D) the best individual score in the group. Write these down and consult with your group to ensure that these scores are accurate.

A. Your individual score _____

B. Your group's score _____

C. Average individual score in group _____

D. Best individual score in group _____

Discussion Questions

1. How did your group (B) perform relative to yourself (A)?
2. How did your group (B) perform relative to the average individual score in the group (C)?
3. How did your group (B) perform relative to the best individual score in the group (D)?
4. Compare your results with those of other groups. Did some groups do a better job of outperforming individuals than others?
5. What do these results tell you about the effectiveness of group decision making?
6. What can groups do to make group decision making more effective?

ETHICAL DILEMMA Is Social Loafing Shirking?

As you now know, social loafing is one disadvantage of working in groups. Regardless of the type of task—from games of Tug of War to working on a group projects—research suggests that when working in a group, most individuals contribute less than if they were working on their own. We might call those who do social loafing "shirkers" because they are not living up to their responsibilities as group members.

Most of us have experienced social loafing, or shirking, in groups. And we may even admit to times when we shirked ourselves. We discussed earlier in this chapter some ways of discouraging social loafing, such as limiting group size, holding individuals responsible for their contributions, setting group goals, and providing "hybrid" incentives that reward both individual and group performance. While these tactics may be effective, in our experience many students simply work around shirkers. "We just did it ourselves—it was easier that way," says one group member.

Questions

1. If group members end up "working around" shirkers, do you think this information should be communicated to the instructor so that each individual's contribution to the project is judged more fairly? If so, does the group have an ethical responsibility to communicate this to the shirking group member?

2. Do you think social loafing is always shirking (failing to live up to one's responsibilities)? Is social loafing always unethical? Why or why not?

3. Social loafing has been found to be higher in Western, more individualist, nations than in other countries. Do you think this means we should tolerate shirking on the part of U.S. students and workers to a greater degree than if it occurred with someone from Asia?

CASE INCIDENT 1 Negative Aspects of Collaboration?

Throughout this chapter we've discussed ways that groups can perform well or perform poorly, which leaves an overriding question: are the negative aspects of collaboration so severe that we should avoid making decisions and working in groups?

Groups and teams need more time to process multiple piece of information and coordinate what they know. Daniel Kaheman and colleagues also warn that when committees and groups make recommendations, they've often "fallen in love" with a particular idea and are no longer thinking rationally. These problems of heuristics and biases (introduced earlier in the book) can be magnified when a group of people are making a decision collectively. Look no further than the U.S. Congress in recent years to see instances in which a group decision-making process might lead to a worse outcome than if one consistent course of action were pursued.

So what can managers do to minimize these biases? The problems of coordination and collaboration suggest that we should invoke group decision making only when it appears that pooling information will lead to better decisions than individual decision making. Experts advise that decision makers receiving advice from teams should always ask whether the team's recommendations contain any self-interested biases. It's also important to see whether the team has developed an emotional attachment to one course of action or has succumbed to groupthink. Finally, run down a checklist of the heuristics and biases we've described earlier in the book to see whether the group might be prone to making these decision errors.

Questions

1. Think about a time when you've been in a group that had to make a collective decision that didn't turn out well. Can you identify any specific decision-making errors the team made?

2. In the situation you encountered, can you think of any strategies that would have helped make the group decision-making process more efficient and accurate?

3. Can you think of a type of decision that is probably better made by an individual than a group? What types of decisions need to be made by groups?

Sources: M. T. Hansen, "When Internal Collaboration Is Bad for Your Company," *Harvard Business Review* (April 2009), pp. 82–88; D. Kahneman, D. Lovallo, and O. Sibony, "Before You Make that Big Decision," *Harvard Business Review* (June 2011), pp. 50–60; and E. Klein, "Washington's Suicide Pact" *Newsweek* (March 21, 2011), www.newsweek.com.

CASE INCIDENT 2 Herd Behavior and the Housing Bubble (and Collapse)

It is sometimes easy to forget that humans are not unlike other animals. Economist John Maynard Keynes recognized this when he commented, "Most, probably, of our decisions to do something positive, the full consequences of which will be drawn out over many days to come, can only be taken as the result of animal spirits—a spontaneous urge to action rather than inaction, and not as the outcome of a weighted average of quantitative benefits multiplied by quantitative probabilities."

Such "animal spirits" are particularly dangerous at the collective level. One animal's decision to charge over a cliff is a tragedy for the animal, but it may also lead the entire herd over the cliff.

You may be wondering how this is applicable to organizational behavior. Consider the recent housing bubble and its subsequent and enduring collapse, or the dot-com implosion of the turn of the century. As housing prices rose ever higher, people discounted risk. Homeowners and investors rushed to buy properties because everyone else was doing it. Banks rushed to provide loans with little due diligence because, well, everyone else was doing it. "Banks didn't want to get left behind. Everybody lowered their underwriting standards, no matter who they are," said Regions Bank executive Michael Menk. "As bankers that's who we are; we follow the herd." Similar problems led to a run up in prices for internet-based companies during the early twenty-first century, and some wonder whether the current valuations of social networking sites are following a similar trend of overpricing.

Yale Economist Robert Shiller called this "herd behavior" and cited research showing people often rely heavily on the behavior of groups in formulating decisions about what they should do. A recent study in behavioral finance confirmed herd behavior in investment decisions and showed that analysts were especially likely to follow other analysts' behavior when they had private information that was less accurate or reliable.

Questions

1. Some research suggests herd behavior increases as the size of the group increases. Why do you think this might be the case?

2. One researcher argues that "pack behavior" comes about because it has benefits. What is the upside of such behavior?

3. Shiller argues that herd behavior can go both ways: It explains the housing bubble, but it also explains the bust. As he notes, "Rational individuals become excessively pessimistic as they see others bidding down home prices to abnormally low levels." Do you agree with Shiller?

4. How might organizations combat the problems resulting from herd behavior?

Sources: Based on R. J. Shiller, "How a Bubble Stayed Under the Radar," *The New York Times* (March 2, 2008), p. BU6; W. Hobson, "Reversal of Fortune," *Panama City News Herald* (March 22, 2009), www.newsherald.com; P. Leoni, "Pack Behavior," *Journal of Mathematical Psychology* 52, no. 6 (2008), pp. 348–351; and J. Reiczigel, Z. Lang, L. Rózsa, and B. Tóthmérész, "Measures of Sociality: Two Different Views of Group Size," *Animal Behaviour* 75, no. 2 (2008), pp. 715–721.

ENDNOTES

1. B. E. Ashforth and F. Mael, "Social Identity Theory and the Organization," *Academy of Management Review* 14, no. 1 (1989), pp. 20–39; and M. A. Hogg and D. J. Terry, "Social Identity and Self-Categorization Processes in Organizational Contexts," *Academy of Management Review* 25, no. 1 (2000), pp. 121–140.

2. M. A. Hogg and B. A. Mullin, "Joining Groups to Reduce Uncertainty: Subjective Uncertainty Reduction and Group Identification," in D. Abrams and M. A. Hogg (eds.), *Social Identity and Social Cognition* (Maiden MA: Blackwell, 1999), pp. 249–279.

3. O. Yakushko, M. M. Davidson, and E. N. Williams, "Identity Salience Model: A Paradigm for Integrating Multiple Identities in Clinical Practice." *Psychotherapy* 46, no. 2 (2009), pp. 180-192; and S. M. Toh and A. S. Denisi, "Host Country Nationals as Socializing Agents: A Social Identity Approach," *Journal of Organizational Behavior* 28, no. 3 (2007), pp. 281–301.

4. D. M. Cable and D. S. DeRue, "The Convergent and Discriminant Validity of Subjective Fit Perceptions," *Journal of Applied Psychology* 87, no. 5 (2002), pp. 875–884; E. George and P. Chattopadhyay, "One Foot in Each Camp: The Dual Identification of Contract Workers," *Administrative Science Quarterly* 50, no. 1 (2005), pp. 68–99; and D. M. Cable and J. R. Edwards, "Complementary and Supplementary Fit: A Theoretical and Empirical Integration," *Journal of Applied Psychology* 89, no. 5 (2004), pp. 822–834.

5. P. F. McKay and D. R. Avery, "What Has Race Got to Do with It? Unraveling the Role of Racioethnicity in Job Seekers' Reactions to Site Visits," *Personnel Psychology* 59, no. 2 (2006), pp. 395–429; A. S. Leonard, A. Mehra, and R. Katerberg, "The Social Identity and Social Networks of Ethnic Minority Groups in Organizations: A Crucial Test of Distinctiveness Theory," *Journal of Organizational Behavior* 29, no. 5 (2008), pp. 573–589.

6. A. Mehra, M. Kilduff, and D. J. Brass, "At the Margins: A Distinctiveness Approach to the Social Identity and Social Networks of Underrepresented Groups," *Academy of Management Journal* 41, no. 4 (1998), pp. 441–452.

7. M. D. Johnson, F. P. Morgeson, D. R. Ilgen, C. J. Meyer, and J. W. Lloyd, "Multiple Professional Identities: Examining Differences in Identification Across Work-Related Targets," *Journal of Applied Psychology* 91, no. 2 (2006), pp. 498–506.

8. F. Mael and B. E. Ashforth, "Alumni and Their Alma Mater: A Partial Test of the Reformulated Model of Organizational Identification," *Journal of Organizational Behavior* 13, no. 2 (1992), pp. 103–123.

9. K. Mignonac, O. Herrbach, and S. Guerrero, "The Interactive Effects of Perceived External Prestige and Need for Organizational Identification on Turnover Intentions," *Journal of Vocational Behavior* 69, no. 3 (2006), pp. 477–493; A. Carmeli, and A. Shteigman, "Top Management Team Behavioral Integration in Small-Sized Firms: A Social Identity Perspective," *Group Dynamics* 14, no. 4 (2010), pp. 318–331.

10. M. Hogg and D. Abrams, "Towards A Single-Process Uncertainty-Reduction Model of Social Motivation in Groups," In M. Hogg and D. Abrams (eds.), *Group Motivation: Social Psychological Perspectives* (New York: Harvester-Wheatsheaf, 1993), pp. 173–190.

11. D. A. Gioia, K. N. Price, A. L. Hamilton, and J. B. Thomas, "Change Reference to Forging An Identity: An Insider-Outsider Study of Processes Involved in the Formation of Organizational Identity." *Administrative Science Quarterly* 55, no. 1 (2010), pp. 1–46.

12. J. F. McGrew, J. G. Bilotta, and J. M. Deeney, "Software Team Formation and Decay: Extending the Standard Model for Small Groups," *Small Group Research* 30, no. 2 (1999), pp. 209–234.

13. B. W. Tuckman, "Developmental Sequences in Small Groups," *Psychological Bulletin*, June 1965, pp. 384–399; B. W. Tuckman and M. C. Jensen, "Stages of Small-Group Development Revisited," *Group and Organizational Studies*, December 1977, pp. 419–427; M. F. Maples, "Group Development: Extending Tuckman's Theory," *Journal for Specialists in Group Work* (Fall 1988), pp. 17–23; and K. Vroman and J. Kovacich, "Computer-Mediated Interdisciplinary Teams: Theory and Reality," *Journal of Interprofessional Care* 16, no. 2 (2002), pp. 159–170.

14. J. E. Mathieu and T. L. Rapp, "Laying the Foundation for Successful Team Performance Trajectories: The Roles of Team Charters and Performance Strategies," *Journal of Applied Psychology* 94, no. 1 (2009), pp. 90–103; and E. C. Dierdorff, S. T. Bell, and J. A. Belohlav, "The Power of 'We': Effects of Psychological Collectivism on Team Performance Over Time," *Journal of Applied Psychology* 96, no. 2 (2011), pp. 247–262.

15. C. J. G. Gersick, "Time and Transition in Work Teams: Toward a New Model of Group Development," *Academy of Management Journal* (March 1988), pp. 9–41; C. J. G. Gersick, "Marking Time: Predictable Transitions in Task Groups," *Academy of Management Journal* (June 1989), pp. 274–309; M. J. Waller, J. M. Conte, C. B. Gibson, and M. A. Carpenter, "The Effect of Individual Perceptions of Deadlines on Team Performance," *Academy of Management Review* (October 2001), pp. 586–600; and A. Chang, P. Bordia, and J. Duck, "Punctuated Equilibrium and Linear Progression: Toward a New Understanding of Group Development," *Academy of Management Journal* (February 2003), pp. 106–117.

16. Gersick, "Time and Transition in Work Teams"; and Gersick, "Marking Time."

17. A. Seers and S. Woodruff, "Temporal Pacing in Task Forces: Group Development or Deadline Pressure?" *Journal of Management* 23, no. 2 (1997), pp. 169–187.

18. See D. M. Rousseau, *Psychological Contracts in Organizations: Understanding Written and Unwritten Agreements* (Thousand Oaks, CA: Sage, 1995); E. W. Morrison and S. L. Robinson, "When Employees Feel Betrayed: A Model of How Psychological Contract Violation Develops," *Academy of Management Review* (April 1997), pp. 226–256; L. Sels, M. Janssens, and I. Van den Brande, "Assessing the Nature of Psychological Contracts: A Validation of Six Dimensions," *Journal of Organizational Behavior* (June 2004), pp. 461–488; and C. Hui, C. Lee, and D. M. Rousseau, "Psychological Contract and Organizational Citizenship Behavior in China: Investigating Generalizability and Instrumentality," *Journal of Applied Psychology* (April 2004), pp. 311–321.

19. M. D. Collins, "The Effect of Psychological Contract Fulfillment on Manager Turnover Intentions and Its Role As a Mediator in a Casual, Limited-Service Restaurant Environment," *International Journal of Hospitality Management* 29, no. 4 (2010), pp. 736–742; J. M. Jensen, R. A. Opland, and A. M. Ryan, "Psychological Contracts and Counterproductive Work Behaviors: Employee Responses to Transactional and

Relational Breach," *Journal of Business and Psychology* 25, no. 4 (2010), pp. 555–568.

20. See M. F. Peterson et al., "Role Conflict, Ambiguity, and Overload: A 21-Nation Study," *Academy of Management Journal* (April 1995), pp. 429–452; and I. H. Settles, R. M. Sellers, and A. Damas Jr., "One Role or Two? The Function of Psychological Separation in Role Conflict," *Journal of Applied Psychology* (June 2002), pp. 574–582.

21. See, for example, F. T. Amstad, L. L. Meier, U. Fasel, A. Elfering, and N. K. Semmer, "A Meta-Analysis of Work-Family Conflict and Various Outcomes with a Special Emphasis on Cross-Domain Versus Matching-Domain Relations," *Journal of Occupational Health Psychology* 16, no. 2 (2011), pp. 151–169.

22. M. A. Hogg and D. J. Terry, "Social Identity and Self-Categorization Processes in Organizational Contexts," *Academy of Management Review* 25, no. 1 (2000), pp. 121–140.

23. D. Vora and T. Kostova. "A Model of Dual Organizational Identification in the Context of the Multinational Enterprise," *Journal of Organizational Behavior* 28 (2007), pp. 327–350.

24. C. Reade, "Dual Identification in Multinational Corporations: Local Managers and Their Psychological Attachment to the Subsidiary Versus the Global Organization," *International Journal of Human Resource Management,* 12, no. 3 (2001), pp. 405–424.

25. P. G. Zimbardo, C. Haney, W. C. Banks, and D. Jaffe, "The Mind Is a Formidable Jailer: A Pirandellian Prison," *The New York Times* (April 8, 1973), pp. 38–60; and C. Haney and P. G. Zimbardo, "Social Roles and Role-Playing: Observations from the Stanford Prison Study," *Behavioral and Social Science Teacher* (January 1973), pp. 25–45.

26. S. A. Haslam and S. Reicher, "Stressing the Group: Social Identity and the Unfolding Dynamics of Responses to Stress," *Journal of Applied Psychology* 91, no. 5 (2006), pp. 1037–1052; S. Reicher and S. A. Haslam, "Rethinking the Psychology of Tyranny: The BBC Prison Study," *British Journal of Social Psychology* 45, no. 1 (2006), pp. 1–40; and P. G. Zimbardo, "On Rethinking the Psychology of Tyranny: The BBC Prison Study," *British Journal of Social Psychology* 45, no. 1 (2006), pp. 47–53.

27. For a review of the research on group norms, see J. R. Hackman, "Group Influences on Individuals in Organizations," in M. D. Dunnette and L. M. Hough (eds.), *Handbook of Industrial & Organizational Psychology,* 2nd ed., vol. 3 (Palo Alto, CA: Consulting Psychologists Press, 1992), pp. 235–250. For a more recent discussion, see M. G. Ehrhart and S. E. Naumann, "Organizational Citizenship Behavior in Work Groups: A Group Norms Approach," *Journal of Applied Psychology* (December 2004), pp. 960–974.

28. Adapted from P. S. Goodman, E. Ravlin, and M. Schminke, "Understanding Groups in Organizations," in L. L. Cummings and B. M. Staw (eds.), *Research in Organizational Behavior,* vol. 9 (Greenwich, CT: JAI Press, 1987), p. 159.

29. E. Mayo, *The Human Problems of an Industrial Civilization* (New York: Macmillan, 1933); and F. J. Roethlisberger and W. J. Dickson, *Management and the Worker* (Cambridge, MA: Harvard University Press, 1939).

30. C. A. Kiesler and S. B. Kiesler, *Conformity* (Reading, MA: Addison-Wesley, 1969); R. B. Cialdini and N. J. Goldstein, "Social Influence: Compliance and Conformity," *Annual Review of Psychology* 55 (2004), pp. 591–621.

31. S. E. Asch, "Effects of Group Pressure upon the Modification and Distortion of Judgments," in H. Guetzkow (ed.), *Groups, Leadership and Men* (Pittsburgh: Carnegie Press, 1951), pp. 177–190; and S. E. Asch, "Studies of Independence and Conformity: A Minority of One Against a Unanimous Majority," *Psychological Monographs: General and Applied* 70, no. 9 (1956), pp. 1–70.

32. R. Bond and P. B. Smith, "Culture and Conformity: A Meta-Analysis of Studies Using Asch's (1952, 1956) Line Judgment Task," *Psychological Bulletin* (January 1996), pp. 111–137.

33. See S. L. Robinson and A. M. O'Leary-Kelly, "Monkey See, Monkey Do: The Influence of Work Groups on the Antisocial Behavior of Employees," *Academy of Management Journal* (December 1998), pp. 658–672; R. J. Bennett and S. L. Robinson, "The Past, Present, and Future of Workplace Deviance," in J. Greenberg (ed.), *Organizational Behavior: The State of the Science,* 2nd ed. (Mahwah, NJ: Erlbaum, 2003), pp. 237–271; and C. M. Berry, D. S. Ones, and P. R. Sackett, "Interpersonal Deviance, Organizational Deviance, and Their Common Correlates: A Review and Meta-Analysis," *Journal of Applied Psychology* 92, no. 2 (2007), pp. 410–424.

34. C. M. Pearson, L. M. Andersson, and C. L. Porath, "Assessing and Attacking Workplace Civility," *Organizational Dynamics* 29, no. 2 (2000), p. 130; see also C. Pearson, L. M. Andersson, and C. L. Porath, "Workplace Incivility," in S. Fox and P. E. Spector (eds.), *Counterproductive Work Behavior: Investigations of Actors and Targets* (Washington, DC: American Psychological Association, 2005), pp. 177–200.

35. S. Lim, L. M. Cortina, V. J. Magley, "Personal and Workgroup Incivility: Impact on Work and Health Outcomes," *Journal of Applied Psychology* 93, no. 1 (2008), pp. 95–107.

36. Robinson and O'Leary-Kelly, "Monkey See, Monkey Do"; and T. M. Glomb and H. Liao, "Interpersonal Aggression in Workgroups: Social Influence, Reciprocal, and Individual Effects," *Academy of Management Journal* 46 (2003), pp. 486–496.

37. P. Bamberger and M. Biron, "Group Norms and Excessive Absenteeism: The Role of Peer Referent Others," *Organizational Behavior and Human Decision Processes* 103, no. 2 (2007), pp. 179–196; and A. Väänänen, N. Tordera, M. Kivimäki, A. Kouvonen, J. Pentti, A. Linna, and J. Vahtera, "The Role of Work Group in Individual Sickness Absence Behavior," *Journal of Health & Human Behavior* 49, no. 4 (2008), pp. 452–467.

38. M. S. Cole, F. Walter, and H. Bruch, "Affective Mechanisms Linking Dysfunctional Behavior to Performance in Work Teams: A Moderated Mediation Study," *Journal of Applied Psychology* 93, no. 5 (2008), pp. 945–958.

39. A. Erez, H. Elms, and E. Fong, "Lying, Cheating, Stealing: It Happens More in Groups," paper presented at the European Business Ethics Network Annual Conference, Budapest, Hungary, August 30, 2003.

40. S. L. Robinson and M. S. Kraatz, "Constructing the Reality of Normative Behavior: The Use of Neutralization Strategies by Organizational Deviants," in R. W. Griffin and A. O'Leary-Kelly (eds.), *Dysfunctional Behavior in Organizations: Violent and Deviant Behavior* (Greenwich, CT: JAI Press, 1998), pp. 203–220.

41. See J. Berger, M. H. Fisek, R. Z. Norman, and M. Zelditch, *Status Characteristics and Social Interaction: An Expected States Approach* (New York: Elsevier, 1977).

42. Cited in Hackman, "Group Influences on Individuals in Organizations," p. 236.

43. R. R. Callister and J. A. Wall Jr., "Conflict Across Organizational Boundaries: Managed Care Organizations Versus Health Care Providers," *Journal of Applied Psychology* 86, no. 4 (2001), pp. 754–763; and P. Chattopadhyay, W. H. Glick, and G. P. Huber, "Organizational Actions in Response to Threats and Opportunities," *Academy of Management Journal* 44, no. 5 (2001), pp. 937–955.

44. P. F. Hewlin, "Wearing the Cloak: Antecedents and Consequences of Creating Facades of Conformity," *Journal of Applied Psychology* 94, no. 3 (2009), pp. 727–741.

45. J. A. Wiggins, F. Dill, and R. D. Schwartz, "On 'Status-Liability,'" *Sociometry* (April–May 1965), pp. 197–209.

46. See J. M. Levine and R. L. Moreland, "Progress in Small Group Research," in J. T. Spence, J. M. Darley, and D. J. Foss (eds.), *Annual Review of Psychology*, vol. 41 (Palo Alto, CA: Annual Reviews, 1990), pp. 585–634; S. D. Silver, B. P. Cohen, and J. H. Crutchfield, "Status Differentiation and Information Exchange in Face-to-Face and Computer-Mediated Idea Generation," *Social Psychology Quarterly* (1994), pp. 108–123; and J. M. Twenge, "Changes in Women's Assertiveness in Response to Status and Roles: A Cross-Temporal Meta-Analysis, 1931–1993," *Journal of Personality and Social Psychology* (July 2001), pp. 133–145.

47. A. M. Christie and J. Barling, "Beyond Status: Relating Status Inequality to Performance and Health in Teams," *Journal of Applied Psychology* 95, no. 5 (2010), pp. 920–934; and L. H. Nishii and D. M. Mayer, "Do Inclusive Leaders Help to Reduce Turnover in Diverse Groups? The Moderating Role of Leader-Member Exchange in the Diversity to Turnover Relationship," *Journal of Applied Psychology* 94, no. 6 (2009), pp. 1412–1426.

48. V. Venkataramani, S. G. Green, and D. J. Schleicher, "Well-Connected Leaders: The Impact of Leaders' Social Network Ties on LMX and Members' Work Attitudes," *Journal of Applied Psychology* 95, no. 6 (2010), pp. 1071–1084.

49. See G. Hofstede, *Cultures and Organizations: Software of the Mind* (New York: McGraw-Hill, 1991).

50. This section is based on P. R. Harris and R. T. Moran, *Managing Cultural Differences*, 5th ed. (Houston: Gulf Publishing, 1999).

51. G. H. Seijts and G. P. Latham, "The Effects of Goal Setting and Group Size on Performance in a Social Dilemma," *Canadian Journal of Behavioural Science* 32, no. 2 (2000), pp. 104–116.

52. M. E. Shaw, *Group Dynamics: The Psychology of Small Group Behavior*, 3rd ed. (New York: McGraw-Hill, 1981).

53. See, for instance, D. R. Comer, "A Model of Social Loafing in Real Work Groups," *Human Relations* (June 1995), pp. 647–667; S. M. Murphy, S. J. Wayne, R. C. Liden, and B. Erdogan, "Understanding Social Loafing: The Role of Justice Perceptions and Exchange Relationships," *Human Relations* (January 2003), pp. 61–84; and R. C. Liden, S. J. Wayne, R. A. Jaworski, and N. Bennett, "Social Loafing: A Field Investigation," *Journal of Management* (April 2004), pp. 285–304.

54. W. Moede, "Die Richtlinien der Leistungs-Psychologie," *Industrielle Psychotechnik* 4 (1927), pp. 193–207. See also D. A. Kravitz and B. Martin, "Ringelmann Rediscovered: The Original Article," *Journal of Personality and Social Psychology* (May 1986), pp. 936–941.

55. See, for example, J. A. Shepperd, "Productivity Loss in Performance Groups: A Motivation Analysis," *Psychological Bulletin* (January 1993), pp. 67–81; and S. J. Karau and K. D. Williams, "Social Loafing: A Meta-Analytic Review and Theoretical Integration," *Journal of Personality and Social Psychology* (October 1993), pp. 681–706.

56. S. G. Harkins and K. Szymanski, "Social Loafing and Group Evaluation," *Journal of Personality and Social Psychology* (December 1989), pp. 934–941.

57. A. Gunnthorsdottir and A. Rapoport, "Embedding Social Dilemmas in Intergroup Competition Reduces Free-Riding," *Organizational Behavior and Human Decision Processes* 101 (2006), pp. 184–199; and E. M. Stark, J. D. Shaw, and M. K. Duffy, "Preference for Group Work, Winning Orientation, and Social Loafing Behavior in Groups," *Group and Organization Management* 32, no. 6 (2007), pp. 699–723.

58. B. Mullen and C. Cooper, "The Relation Between Group Cohesiveness and Performance: An Integration," *Psychological Bulletin* (March 1994), pp. 210–227; P. M. Podsakoff, S. B. MacKenzie, and M. Ahearne, "Moderating Effects of Goal Acceptance on the Relationship Between Group Cohesiveness and Productivity," *Journal of Applied Psychology* (December 1997), pp. 974–983; and D. J. Beal, R. R. Cohen, M. J. Burke, and C. L. McLendon, "Cohesion and Performance in Groups: A Meta-Analytic Clarification of Construct Relations," *Journal of Applied Psychology* (December 2003), pp. 989–1004.

59. Ibid.

60. Based on J. L. Gibson, J. M. Ivancevich, and J. H. Donnelly Jr., *Organizations*, 8th ed. (Burr Ridge, IL: Irwin, 1994), p. 323.

61. D. S. Staples and L. Zhao, "The Effects of Cultural Diversity in Virtual Teams Versus Face-to-Face Teams," *Group Decision and Negotiation* (July 2006), pp. 389–406.

62. N. Chi, Y. Huang, and S. Lin, "A Double-Edged Sword? Exploring the Curvilinear Relationship Between Organizational Tenure Diversity and Team Innovation: The Moderating Role of Team-Oriented HR Practices," *Group and Organization Management* 34, no. 6 (2009), pp. 698–726.

63. K. J. Klein, A. P. Knight, J. C. Ziegert, B. C. Lim, and J. L. Saltz, "When Team Members' Values Differ: The Moderating Role of Team Leadership," *Organizational Behavior and Human Decision Processes* 114, no. 1 (2011), pp. 25–36; and G. Park and R. P. DeShon, "A Multilevel Model of Minority Opinion Expression and Team Decision-Making Effectiveness," *Journal of Applied Psychology* 95, no. 5 (2010), pp. 824–833.

64. M. Rigoglioso, "Diverse Backgrounds and Personalities Can Strengthen Groups," *Standford Knowledgebase*, (August 15, 2006), http://www.stanford.edu/group/knowledgebase/

65. K. W. Phillips and D. L. Loyd, "When Surface and Deep-Level Diversity Collide: The Effects on Dissenting Group Members," *Organizational Behavior and Human Decision Processes* 99 (2006), pp. 143–160; and S. R. Sommers, "On Racial Diversity and Group Decision Making: Identifying Multiple Effects of Racial Composition on Jury Deliberations," *Journal of Personality and Social Psychology* (April 2006), pp. 597–612.

66. E. Mannix and M. A. Neale, "What Differences Make a Difference? The Promise and Reality of Diverse Teams in Organizations," *Psychological Science in the Public Interest* (October 2005), pp. 31–55.

67. N. Foote, E. Matson, L. Weiss, and E. Wenger, "Leveraging Group Knowledge for High-Performance Decision-Making," *Organizational Dynamics* 31, no. 2 (2002), pp. 280–295.

68. See N. R. F. Maier, "Assets and Liabilities in Group Problem Solving: The Need for an Integrative Function," *Psychological*

Review (April 1967), pp. 239–249; G. W. Hill, "Group Versus Individual Performance: Are *N*+1 Heads Better Than One?" *Psychological Bulletin* (May 1982), pp. 517–539; M. D. Johnson and J. R. Hollenbeck, "Collective Wisdom as an Oxymoron: Team-Based Structures as Impediments to Learning," in J. Langan-Fox, C. L. Cooper, and R. J. Klimoski (eds), *Research Companion to the Dysfunctional Workplace: Management Challenges and Symptoms* (Northampton, MA: Edward Elgar Publishing, 2007), pp. 319–331; and R. F. Martell and M. R. Borg, "A Comparison of the Behavioral Rating Accuracy of Groups and Individuals," *Journal of Applied Psychology* (February 1993), pp. 43–50.

69. D. Gigone and R. Hastie, "Proper Analysis of the Accuracy of Group Judgments," *Psychological Bulletin* (January 1997), pp. 149–167; and B. L. Bonner, S. D. Sillito, and M. R. Baumann, "Collective Estimation: Accuracy, Expertise, and Extroversion as Sources of Intra-Group Influence," *Organizational Behavior and Human Decision Processes* 103 (2007), pp. 121–133.

70. See, for example, W. C. Swap and Associates, *Group Decision Making* (Newbury Park, CA: Sage, 1984).

71. I. L. Janis, *Groupthink* (Boston: Houghton Mifflin, 1982); W. Park, "A Review of Research on Groupthink," *Journal of Behavioral Decision Making* (July 1990), pp. 229–245; J. N. Choi and M. U. Kim, "The Organizational Application of Groupthink and Its Limits in Organizations," *Journal of Applied Psychology* (April 1999), pp. 297–306; and W. W. Park, "A Comprehensive Empirical Investigation of the Relationships Among Variables of the Groupthink Model," *Journal of Organizational Behavior* (December 2000), pp. 873–887.

72. Janis, *Groupthink*.

73. G. Park and R. P. DeShon, "A Multilevel Model of Minority Opinion Expression and Team Decision-Making Effectiveness," *Journal of Applied Psychology* 95, no. 5 (2010), pp. 824–833.

74. M. E. Turner and A. R. Pratkanis, "Mitigating Groupthink by Stimulating Constructive Conflict," in C. De Dreu and E. Van de Vliert (eds.), *Using Conflict in Organizations* (London: Sage, 1997), pp. 53–71.

75. J. A. Goncalo, E. Polman, and C. Maslach, "Can Confidence Come Too Soon? Collective Efficacy, Conflict, and Group Performance over Time," *Organizational Behavior and Human Decision Processes* 113, no. 1 (2010), pp. 13–24.

76. See N. R. F. Maier, *Principles of Human Relations* (New York: Wiley, 1952); I. L. Janis, *Groupthink: Psychological Studies of Policy Decisions and Fiascoes*, 2nd ed. (Boston: Houghton Mifflin, 1982); N. Richardson Ahlfinger and J. K. Esser, "Testing the Groupthink Model: Effects of Promotional Leadership and Conformity Predisposition," *Social Behavior & Personality* 29, no. 1 (2001), pp. 31–41; and S. Schultz-Hardt, F. C. Brodbeck, A. Mojzisch, R. Kerschreiter, and D. Frey, "Group Decision Making in Hidden Profile Situations: Dissent as a Facilitator for Decision Quality," *Journal of Personality and Social Psychology* 91, no. 6 (2006), pp. 1080–1093.

77. See D. J. Isenberg, "Group Polarization: A Critical Review and Meta-Analysis," *Journal of Personality and Social Psychology* (December 1986), pp. 1141–1151; J. L. Hale and F. J. Boster, "Comparing Effect Coded Models of Choice Shifts," *Communication Research Reports* (April 1988), pp. 180–186; and P. W. Paese, M. Bieser, and M. E. Tubbs, "Framing Effects and Choice Shifts in Group Decision Making,"

Organizational Behavior and Human Decision Processes (October 1993), pp. 149–165.

78. R. D. Clark III, "Group-Induced Shift Toward Risk: A Critical Appraisal," *Psychological Bulletin* (October 1971), pp. 251–270; M. Brauer and C. M. Judd, "Group Polarization and Repeated Attitude Expression: A New Take on an Old Topic," *European Review of Social Psychology* 7, (1996), pp. 173–207; and M. P. Brady and S. Y. Wu, "The Aggregation of Preferences in Groups: Identity, Responsibility, and Polarization," *Journal of Economic Psychology* 31, no. 6 (2010), pp. 950–963.

79. Z. Krizan and R. S. Baron, "Group Polarization and Choice-Dilemmas: How Important Is Self-Categorization?" *European Journal of Social Psychology* 37, no. 1 (2007), pp. 191–201.

80. A. F. Osborn, *Applied Imagination: Principles and Procedures of Creative Thinking*, 3rd ed. (New York: Scribner, 1963). See also R. P. McGlynn, D. McGurk, V. S. Effland, N. L. Johll, and D. J. Harding, "Brainstorming and Task Performance in Groups Constrained by Evidence," *Organizational Behavior and Human Decision Processes* (January 2004), pp. 75–87; and R. C. Litchfield, "Brainstorming Reconsidered: A Goal-Based View," *Academy of Management Review* 33, no. 3 (2008), pp. 649–668.

81. N. L. Kerr and R. S. Tindale, "Group Performance and Decision-Making," *Annual Review of Psychology* 55 (2004), pp. 623–655.

82. See A. L. Delbecq, A. H. Van deVen, and D. H. Gustafson, *Group Techniques for Program Planning: A Guide to Nominal and Delphi Processes* (Glenview, IL: Scott Foresman, 1975); and P. B. Paulus and H.-C. Yang, "Idea Generation in Groups: A Basis for Creativity in Organizations," *Organizational Behavior and Human Decision Processing* (May 2000), pp. 76–87.

83. C. Faure, "Beyond Brainstorming: Effects of Different Group Procedures on Selection of Ideas and Satisfaction with the Process," *Journal of Creative Behavior* 38 (2004), pp. 13–34.

84. See, for instance, A. B. Hollingshead and J. E. McGrath, "Computer-Assisted Groups: A Critical Review of the Empirical Research," in R. A. Guzzo and E. Salas (eds.), *Team Effectiveness and Decision Making in Organizations* (San Francisco: Jossey-Bass, 1995), pp. 46–78.

85. B. B. Baltes, M. W. Dickson, M. P. Sherman, C. C. Bauer, and J. LaGanke, "Computer-Mediated Communication and Group Decision Making: A Meta-Analysis," *Organizational Behavior and Human Decision Processes* (January 2002), pp. 156–179.

86. T. P. Verney, "Role Perception Congruence, Performance, and Satisfaction," in D. J. Vredenburgh and R. S. Schuler (eds.), *Effective Management: Research and Application*, Proceedings of the 20th Annual Eastern Academy of Management, Pittsburgh, PA (May 1983), pp. 24–27.

87. Ibid.

88. A. G. Bedeian and A. A. Armenakis, "A Path-Analytic Study of the Consequences of Role Conflict and Ambiguity," *Academy of Management Journal* (June 1981), pp. 417–424; and P. L. Perrewe, K. L. Zellars, G. R. Ferris, A. M. Rossi, C. J. Kacmar, and D. A. Ralston, "Neutralizing Job Stressors: Political Skill as an Antidote to the Dysfunctional Consequences of Role Conflict," *Academy of Management Journal* (February 2004), pp. 141–152.

89. Shaw, *Group Dynamics*.

90. B. Mullen, C. Symons, L. Hu, and E. Salas, "Group Size, Leadership Behavior, and Subordinate Satisfaction," *Journal of General Psychology* (April 1989), pp. 155–170.

LEARNING OBJECTIVES

After studying this chapter, you should be able to:

1 Analyze the growing popularity of teams in organizations.

2 Contrast groups and teams.

3 Compare and contrast four types of teams.

4 Identify the characteristics of effective teams.

5 Show how organizations can create team players.

6 Decide when to use individuals instead of teams.

7 Show how our understanding of teams differs in a global context.

MyManagementLab

Access a host of interactive learning aids to help strengthen your understanding of the chapter concepts at **www.mymanagementlab.com**.

KILLING BIN LADEN

The decision by the U.S. government on May 1, 2011, to send SEAL Team Six to hunt and capture or kill Osama bin Laden was, by all accounts, not an easy one. Appreciating the team dynamics of this decision helps us understand how teams make key decisions.

The decision of a government to deploy military force to capture or kill is obviously among the most serious, and often controversial, decisions leaders and teams can make. Keep in mind that our focus here is not on the merits of the decision, but on how the decision was made.

In 2010, U.S. intelligence identified and located a man whom captured al Qaeda operatives had named as Osama bin Laden's courier. After spending months tracking him and analyzing the compound in Pakistan, Central Intelligence Agency (CIA) analysts were convinced there was a "strong possibility" that bin Laden was also hiding there. At that point, Navy SEAL teams began training to take the compound. But no one knew for sure whether bin Laden was actually there.

The mission carried considerable risk. The members of the administration's national security team brought up past failed missions: the U.S. Army battle in Mogadishu, Somalia (depicted in the movie, *Black Hawk Down*), and the attempted rescue of U.S. hostages in Iran. "There wasn't a meeting when someone didn't mention 'Black Hawk Down,'" said one team member. The United States might be sending troops into hostile territory with no proof that the target of their efforts was even there. The president later said military commanders put the odds of a successful mission at 55–45.

Over the next 2 months, the administration's national security team met at least six times. Some members were against the operation, pending more definitive proof that bin Laden was actually there. None came. After a final meeting between the president and his national security team at 2 P.M. on Sunday, May 1, the 40 elite SEAL Team Six commandos departed in four helicopters from an undisclosed location in Afghanistan, the eastern border of which is about 120 miles west of bin Laden's compound. A White House photo shows Obama and his national security team anxiously watching as the mission played out on the situation room monitor. Obama is tieless and grim-faced, his eyes fixed on the screen. Hillary Clinton, holding a hand to her mouth, and Robert Gates, his arms folded across his chest, gaze at the same point. After the "minutes passed like days," the team received confirmation that the mission was over. "Geronimo"—the code name given bin Laden—was dead.

That many members of the decision-making team were willing to voice their reservations probably aided the decision-making process. President Obama later told *60 Minutes:* "The fact that there were some who voiced doubts about this approach was invaluable, because it meant the plan was

Understanding Work Teams

We're going to turn this team around 360 degrees. —Jason Kidd sharper, it meant that we had thought through all of our options, it meant that when I finally did make the decision, I was making it based on the very best information."

Sources: A. Kruglanski, "Obama's Choice and the Social Psychology of Group Decision Making," *Huffington Post* (May 12, 2011), downloaded June 1, 2011, from www.huffingtonpost.com/; B. Steiden, "Bin Laden Dead," *The Atlanta Journal-Constitution* (May 3, 2011), downloaded June 2, 2011, from www.ajc.com/; and M. Mazzetti, H. Cooper, and P. Baker, "Behind the Hunt for Bin Laden," *The New York Times* (May 2, 2011), downloaded June 2, 2011, from www.nytimes.com/.

Teams are increasingly the primary means for organizing work in contemporary business firms. In fact, there are few more damaging insults than "not a team player." Do you think you're a team player? Take the following self-assessment to find out.

SELF-ASSESSMENT LIBRARY

How Good Am I at Building and Leading a Team?

In the Self-Assessment Library (available on CD or online), take assessment II.B.6 (How Good Am I at Building and Leading a Team?) and answer the following questions.

1. Did you score as high as you thought you would? Why or why not?
2. Do you think you can improve your score? If so, how? If not, why not?
3. Do you think there is such a thing as team players? If yes, what are their behaviors?

Why Have Teams Become So Popular?

1 Analyze the growing popularity of teams in organizations.

Decades ago, when companies such as W. L. Gore, Volvo, and General Foods introduced teams into their production processes, it made news because no one else was doing it. Today, it's just the opposite. The organization that *doesn't* use teams has become newsworthy. Teams are everywhere.

How do we explain the current popularity of teams? As organizations have restructured themselves to compete more effectively and efficiently, they have turned to teams as a better way to use employee talents. Teams are more flexible and responsive to changing events than traditional departments or other forms of permanent groupings. They can quickly assemble, deploy, refocus, and disband. But don't overlook the motivational properties of teams. Consistent with our discussion in Chapter 7 of employee involvement as a motivator, teams facilitate employee participation in operating decisions. So another explanation for their popularity is that they are an effective means for management to democratize organizations and increase employee motivation.

The fact that organizations have turned to teams doesn't necessarily mean they're always effective. Decision makers, as humans, can be swayed by fads and herd mentality. Are teams truly effective? What conditions affect their potential? How do members work together? These are some of the questions we'll answer in this chapter.

Differences Between Groups and Teams

2   Contrast groups and teams.

Groups and teams are not the same thing. In this section, we define and clarify the difference between work groups and work teams.[1]

In Chapter 9, we defined a *group* as two or more individuals, interacting and interdependent, who have come together to achieve particular objectives. A **work group** is a group that interacts primarily to share information and make decisions to help each member perform within his or her area of responsibility.

Work groups have no need or opportunity to engage in collective work that requires joint effort. So their performance is merely the summation of each group member's individual contribution. There is no positive synergy that would create an overall level of performance greater than the sum of the inputs.

A **work team**, on the other hand, generates positive synergy through coordinated effort. The individual efforts result in a level of performance greater than the sum of those individual inputs. Exhibit 10-1 highlights the differences between work groups and work teams.

These definitions help clarify why so many organizations have recently restructured work processes around teams. Management is looking for positive synergy that will allow the organizations to increase performance. The extensive use of teams creates the *potential* for an organization to generate greater outputs with no increase in inputs. Notice, however, that we said *potential*. There is nothing inherently magical that ensures the achievement of positive synergy in the creation of teams. Merely calling a *group* a *team* doesn't automatically improve its performance. As we show later in this chapter, effective teams have certain common characteristics. If management hopes to gain increases in organizational performance through the use of teams, its teams must possess these.

Exhibit 10-1   **Comparing Work Groups and Work Teams**

Work Groups		**Work Teams**
Share information	←— Goal —→	Collective performance
Neutral (sometimes negative)	←—Synergy—→	Positive
Individual	←—Accountability—→	Individual and mutual
Random and varied	←— Skills —→	Complementary

work group   *A group that interacts primarily to share information and to make decisions to help each group member perform within his or her area of responsibility.*

work team   *A group whose individual efforts result in performance that is greater than the sum of the individual inputs.*

Types of Teams

3 Compare and contrast four types of teams.

Teams can make products, provide services, negotiate deals, coordinate projects, offer advice, and make decisions.[2] In this section, we describe the four most common types of teams in an organization: *problem-solving teams, self-managed work teams, cross-functional teams,* and *virtual teams* (see Exhibit 10-2).

Problem-Solving Teams

In the past, teams were typically composed of 5 to 12 hourly employees from the same department who met for a few hours each week to discuss ways of improving quality, efficiency, and the work environment.[3] These **problem-solving teams** rarely have the authority to unilaterally implement any of their suggestions. Merrill Lynch created a problem-solving team to figure out ways to reduce the number of days it took to open a new cash management account.[4] By suggesting cutting the number of steps from 46 to 36, the team reduced the average number of days from 15 to 8.

Self-Managed Work Teams

Problem-solving teams only make recommendations. Some organizations have gone further and created teams that not only solve problems but implement solutions and take responsibility for outcomes.

Self-managed work teams are groups of employees (typically 10 to 15 in number) who perform highly related or interdependent jobs and take on many of the responsibilities of their former supervisors.[5] Typically, these tasks are planning and scheduling work, assigning tasks to members, making operating decisions, taking action on problems, and working with suppliers and customers. Fully self-managed work teams even select their own members and evaluate each other's performance. Supervisory positions take on decreased importance and are sometimes even eliminated.

But research on the effectiveness of self-managed work teams has not been uniformly positive.[6] Self-managed teams do not typically manage conflicts well. When disputes arise, members stop cooperating and power struggles ensue, which leads to lower group performance.[7] Moreover, although individuals on these teams report higher levels of job satisfaction than other individuals, they also sometimes have higher absenteeism and turnover rates. One large-scale study of labor productivity in British establishments found that although using teams in general does improve labor productivity, no evidence supported the

Exhibit 10-2   Four Types of Teams

Problem-solving   Self-managed   Cross-functional   Virtual

Sprig Toys, Inc. uses cross-functional teamwork in creating toys that are made of recycled products to keep the planet healthy and kids off the couch. The Sprig Dream Team includes toy designers and toy industry-specific expertise in the areas of product design, patent development, supply chain strategy, market research, vendor sourcing, merchandising, branding, packaging, and marketing. Team members are dedicated to Sprig's mission of creating fun toys that encourage active play for kids and are battery-free, eco-friendly, and paint-free. Shown here with some Sprig toys are chief executive Craig Storey (standing, left) and the firm's co-founders.

Source: AP Photo/The Coloradoan, V. Richard Haro.

claim that self-managed teams performed better than traditional teams with less decision-making authority.[8]

Cross-Functional Teams

Starbucks created a team of individuals from production, global PR, global communications, and U.S. marketing to develop its Via brand of instant coffee. The team's suggestions resulted in a product that would be cost-effective to produce and distribute and that was marketed through a tightly integrated, multifaceted strategy.[9] This example illustrates the use of **cross-functional teams**, made up of employees from about the same hierarchical level but different work areas, who come together to accomplish a task.

Many organizations have used horizontal, boundary-spanning groups for decades. In the 1960s, IBM created a large task force of employees from across departments to develop its highly successful System 360. Today cross-functional teams are so widely used it is hard to imagine a major organizational undertaking without one. All the major automobile manufacturers—Toyota, Honda, Nissan, BMW, GM, Ford, and Chrysler—currently use this form of team to coordinate complex projects. Cisco relies on specific cross-functional teams to identify and capitalize on new trends in several areas of the software market. The teams are the equivalent of social-networking groups that collaborate in real time to identify new business opportunities in the field and then implement them from the bottom up.[10]

problem-solving teams   *Groups of 5 to 12 employees from the same department who meet for a few hours each week to discuss ways of improving quality, efficiency, and the work environment.*

self-managed work teams   *Groups of 10 to 15 people who take on responsibilities of their former supervisors.*

cross-functional teams   *Employees from about the same hierarchical level, but from different work areas, who come together to accomplish a task.*

Cross-functional teams are an effective means of allowing people from diverse areas within or even between organizations to exchange information, develop new ideas, solve problems, and coordinate complex projects. Of course, cross-functional teams are no picnic to manage. Their early stages of development are often long, as members learn to work with diversity and complexity. It takes time to build trust and teamwork, especially among people from different backgrounds with different experiences and perspectives.

Virtual Teams

The teams described in the preceding section do their work face to face. **Virtual teams** use computer technology to unite physically dispersed members and achieve a common goal.[11] They collaborate online—using communication links such as wide-area networks, videoconferencing, or e-mail—whether they're a room away or continents apart. Virtual teams are so pervasive, and technology has advanced so far, that it's probably a bit of a misnomer to call them "virtual." Nearly all teams today do at least some of their work remotely.

Despite their ubiquity, virtual teams face special challenges. They may suffer because there is less social rapport and direct interaction among members. Evidence from 94 studies entailing more than 5,000 groups found that virtual teams are better at sharing unique information (information held by individual members but not the entire group), but they tend to share less information overall.[12] As a result, low levels of virtuality in teams results in higher levels of information sharing, but high levels of virtuality hinder it. For virtual teams to be effective, management should ensure that (1) trust is established among members (one inflammatory remark in an e-mail can severely undermine team trust), (2) team progress is monitored closely (so the team doesn't lose sight of its goals and no team member "disappears"), and (3) the efforts and products of the team are publicized throughout the organization (so the team does not become invisible).[13]

Creating Effective Teams

4   Identify the characteristics of effective teams.

Many have tried to identify factors related to team effectiveness.[14] However, some studies have organized what was once a "veritable laundry list of characteristics"[15] into a relatively focused model.[16] Exhibit 10-3 summarizes what we currently know about what makes teams effective. As you'll see, it builds on many of the group concepts introduced in Chapter 9.

The following discussion is based on the model in Exhibit 10-3. Keep in mind two points. First, teams differ in form and structure. The model attempts to generalize across all varieties of teams, but avoid rigidly applying its predictions to all teams.[17] Use it as a guide. Second, the model assumes teamwork is preferable to individual work. Creating "effective" teams when individuals can do the job better is like perfectly solving the wrong problem.

We can organize the key components of effective teams into three general categories. First are the resources and other *contextual* influences that make teams effective. The second relates to the team's *composition*. Finally, *process* variables are events within the team that influence effectiveness. What does *team effectiveness* mean in this model? Typically, it has included objective measures of the team's productivity, managers' ratings of the team's performance, and aggregate measures of member satisfaction.

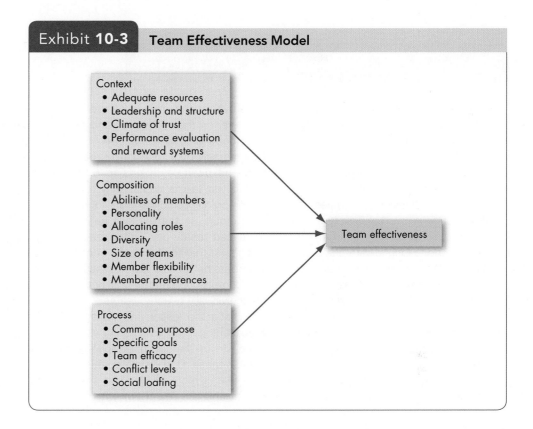

Exhibit 10-3 Team Effectiveness Model

Context
- Adequate resources
- Leadership and structure
- Climate of trust
- Performance evaluation and reward systems

Composition
- Abilities of members
- Personality
- Allocating roles
- Diversity
- Size of teams
- Member flexibility
- Member preferences

Process
- Common purpose
- Specific goals
- Team efficacy
- Conflict levels
- Social loafing

Team effectiveness

Context: What Factors Determine Whether Teams Are Successful

The four contextual factors most significantly related to team performance are adequate resources, effective leadership, a climate of trust, and a performance evaluation and reward system that reflects team contributions.

Adequate Resources   Teams are part of a larger organization system; every work team relies on resources outside the group to sustain it. A scarcity of resources directly reduces the ability of a team to perform its job effectively and achieve its goals. As one study concluded, after looking at 13 factors related to group performance, "perhaps one of the most important characteristics of an effective work group is the support the group receives from the organization."[18] This support includes timely information, proper equipment, adequate staffing, encouragement, and administrative assistance.

Leadership and Structure   Teams can't function if they can't agree on who is to do what and ensure all members share the workload. Agreeing on the specifics of work and how they fit together to integrate individual skills requires leadership and structure, either from management or from the team members themselves. It's true in self-managed teams that team members absorb many of the

virtual teams *Teams that use computer technology to tie together physically dispersed members in order to achieve a common goal.*

Group Cohesiveness across Cultures

As you might suspect, researchers have paid a great deal of attention to the differences between individualists and collectivists in terms of team orientation. As we learned from Chapter 5 on personality and values, people from collectivist societies—like those found in much of East Asia, Latin America, and Africa—are generally more prone to look toward group goals as important and to emphasize collaborative processes. Individualist cultures like the United States, Canada, and the UK, on the other hand, emphasize individual achievement and performance.

Individualist cultures may have greater difficulty implementing team-based work processes for a variety of reasons. Collectivists appear more sensitive to the moods of their co-workers, so the motivation and positive mood of one group member is likely to spill over to increase motivation and positive moods in others. Collectivist teams also already have a strong predisposition to work together as a group, so there's less need for increased teamwork. Other research suggests that collectively oriented teams are better able to pool resources and correct one another's errors than are individually oriented teams.

What's the lesson for managers? Managers in individualist cultures may need to work harder to increase team cohesiveness. One way to do this is to give teams more challenging assignments and provide them with more independence. Alternatively, managers may find it useful to promote a collectivist orientation for team processes even when working with groups of individualists.

Sources: Based on R. Ilies, D. T. Wagner, and F. P. Morgeson, "Explaining Affective Linkages in Teams: Individual Differences in Susceptibility to Contagion and Individualism-Collectivism," *Journal of Applied Psychology* 92, no. 4 (2007), pp. 1140–1148; E. C. Dierdorff, S. T. Bell, and J. A. Belohlav, "The Power of 'We': Effects of Psychological Collectivism on Team Performance Over Time," *Journal of Applied Psychology* 96, no. 2 (2011), pp. 247–262; and J. E. Driskell, E. Salas, and S. Hughes, "Collective Orientation and Team Performance: Development of an Individual Differences Measure," *Human Factors* 52, no. 2 (2010), pp. 316–328.

duties typically assumed by managers. However, a manager's job then becomes managing *outside* (rather than inside) the team.

Leadership is especially important in **multiteam systems**, in which different teams coordinate their efforts to produce a desired outcome. Here, leaders need to empower teams by delegating responsibility to them, and they play the role of facilitator, making sure the teams work together rather than against one another.[19] Teams that establish shared leadership by effectively delegating it are more effective than teams with a traditional single-leader structure.[20]

Climate of Trust   Members of effective teams trust each other. They also exhibit trust in their leaders.[21] Interpersonal trust among team members facilitates cooperation, reduces the need to monitor each others' behavior, and bonds members around the belief that others on the team won't take advantage of them. Team members are more likely to take risks and expose vulnerabilities when they believe they can trust others on their team. And, as we will discuss in Chapter 12, trust is the foundation of leadership. It allows a team to accept and commit to its leader's goals and decisions.

Performance Evaluation and Reward Systems   How do you get team members to be both individually and jointly accountable? Individual performance evaluations and incentives may interfere with the development of high-performance teams. So, in addition to evaluating and rewarding employees for their individual contributions, management should modify the traditional, individually oriented evaluation and reward system to reflect team performance and focus on hybrid systems that recognize individual members for their exceptional

Using Global Virtual Teams as an Environmental Choice

Many teams in geographically dispersed organizations have turned to electronic media to improve communication across locations. However, there may be an equally strong *ethical* argument for using global virtual teams: it may be a more environmentally responsible choice than having team members travel internationally when they need to communicate. A very large proportion of airline, rail, and car transport is for business purposes and contributes greatly to global carbon dioxide emissions. When teams are able to meet virtually rather than face-to-face, they dramatically reduce the amount of energy consumed.

In a globally connected world, what sorts of actions might you take to minimize your organization's environmental impact from business travel? Several tips might help to get you started thinking about ways that global virtual teams can be harnessed for greater sustainability:

1. Encourage all team members to think about whether a face-to-face meeting is really necessary, and to try to utilize alternative communication methods whenever possible.
2. Communicate as much information as possible through virtual means, including e-mail, telephone calls, and teleconferencing.
3. When traveling to team meetings, choose the most environmentally responsible methods possible, such as flying in coach rather than business class. Also, check the environmental profile of hotels prior to booking rooms.
4. Make the business case for sustainable business travel alternatives. Most experts agree that teleconferencing and environmentally responsible travel arrangements not only help the environment but are more cost-effective as well.

Sources: P. Tilstone, "Cut Carbon... and Bills," *Director* (May 2009), p. 54; and L. C. Latimer, "6 Strategies for Sustainable Business Travel," *Greenbiz* (February 11, 2011), www.greenbiz.com.

contributions and reward the entire group for positive outcomes.[22] Group-based appraisals, profit sharing, gainsharing, small-group incentives, and other system modifications can reinforce team effort and commitment.

Team Composition

The team composition category includes variables that relate to how teams should be staffed—the ability and personality of team members, allocation of roles and diversity, size of the team, and members' preference for teamwork.

Abilities of Members   Part of a team's performance depends on the knowledge, skills, and abilities of its individual members.[23] It's true we occasionally read about an athletic team of mediocre players who, because of excellent coaching, determination, and precision teamwork, beat a far more talented group. But such cases make the news precisely because they are unusual. A team's performance is not merely the summation of its individual members' abilities. However, these abilities set limits on what members can do and how effectively they will perform on a team.

Research reveals some insights into team composition and performance. First, when the task entails considerable thought (solving a complex problem

multiteam systems   *Systems in which different teams need to coordinate their efforts to produce a desired outcome.*

such as reengineering an assembly line), high-ability teams—composed of mostly intelligent members—do better than lower-ability teams, especially when the workload is distributed evenly. That way, team performance does not depend on the weakest link. High-ability teams are also more adaptable to changing situations; they can more effectively apply existing knowledge to new problems.

Finally, the ability of the team's leader also matters. Smart team leaders help less-intelligent team members when they struggle with a task. But a less intelligent leader can neutralize the effect of a high-ability team.[24]

Personality of Members   We demonstrated in Chapter 5 that personality significantly influences individual employee behavior. Many of the dimensions identified in the Big Five personality model are also relevant to team effectiveness; a review of the literature identified three.[25] Specifically, teams that rate higher on mean levels of conscientiousness and openness to experience tend to perform better, and the minimum level of team member agreeableness also matters: teams did worse when they had one or more highly disagreeable members. Perhaps one bad apple *can* spoil the whole bunch!

Research has also provided us with a good idea about why these personality traits are important to teams. Conscientious people are good at backing up other team members, and they're also good at sensing when their support is truly needed. One study found that specific behavioral tendencies such as personal organization, cognitive structuring, achievement orientation, and endurance were all related to higher levels of team performance.[26] Open team members communicate better with one another and throw out more ideas, which makes teams composed of open people more creative and innovative.[27]

Suppose an organization needs to create 20 teams of 4 people each and has 40 highly conscientious people and 40 who score low on conscientiousness. Would the organization be better off (1) forming 10 teams of highly conscientious people and 10 teams of members low on conscientiousness, or

British Chief Inspector of Nuclear Installations Mike Weightman is the leader of an 18-member global team created by the International Atomic Energy Commission to study the Fukushima nuclear power station accident triggered by the 2011 earthquake in Japan. This high-ability team with members from 12 countries includes experts with experience across a wide range of nuclear specialties. Team members apply their technical expertise, problem-solving and decision-making skills, and interpersonal skills to their mission of identifying lessons learned from the accident that can help improve nuclear safety around the world. In this photo, Weightman (left) shakes hands with the Fukushima plant chief after the team inspected the crippled nuclear power plant.

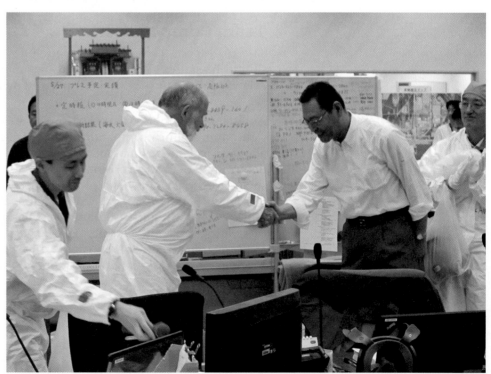

Source: HO/AFP/Getty Images/Newscom.

(2) "seeding" each team with 2 people who scored high and 2 who scored low on conscientiousness? Perhaps surprisingly, evidence suggests option 1 is the best choice; performance across the teams will be higher if the organization forms 10 highly conscientious teams and 10 teams low in conscientiousness.[28]

Allocation of Roles   Teams have different needs, and members should be selected to ensure all the various roles are filled. A study of 778 major league baseball teams over a 21-year period highlights the importance of assigning roles appropriately.[29] As you might expect, teams with more experienced and skilled members performed better. However, the experience and skill of those in core roles who handle more of the workflow of the team, and who are central to all work processes (in this case, pitchers and catchers), were especially vital. In other words, put your most able, experienced, and conscientious workers in the most central roles in a team.

We can identify nine potential team roles (see Exhibit 10-4). Successful work teams have selected people to play all these roles based on their skills and preferences.[30] (On many teams, individuals will play multiple roles.) To increase the likelihood the team members will work well together, managers need to understand the individual strengths each person can bring to a team, select members with their strengths in mind, and allocate work assignments that fit with members' preferred styles.

Diversity of Members   In Chapter 9, we discussed research on the effect of diversity on groups. How does *team* diversity affect *team* performance? The degree to which members of a work unit (group, team, or department) share a common demographic attribute, such as age, sex, race, educational level, or

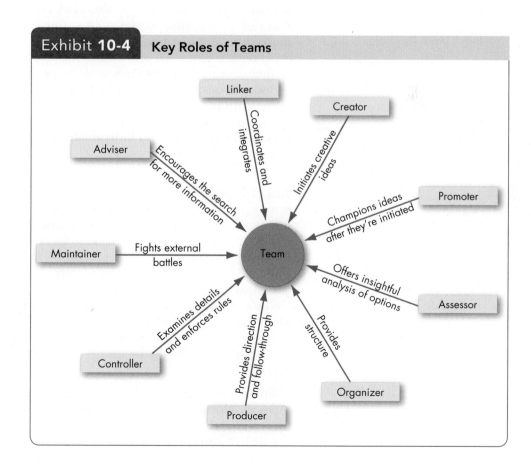

Exhibit **10-4**   Key Roles of Teams

length of service in the organization, is the subject of **organizational demography**. Organizational demography suggests that attributes such as age or the date of joining should help us predict turnover. The logic goes like this: turnover will be greater among those with dissimilar experiences because communication is more difficult and conflict is more likely. Increased conflict makes membership less attractive, so employees are more likely to quit. Similarly, the losers in a power struggle are more apt to leave voluntarily or be forced out.[31]

Many of us hold the optimistic view that diversity should be a good thing—diverse teams should benefit from differing perspectives. Two meta-analytic reviews of the research literature show, however, that demographic diversity is essentially unrelated to team performance overall, while a third actually suggests that race and gender diversity are negatively related to team performance.[32] One qualifier is that gender and ethnic diversity have more negative effects in occupations dominated by white or male employees, but in more demographically balanced occupations, diversity is less of a problem. Diversity in function, education, and expertise are positively related to group performance, but these effects are quite small and depend on the situation.

Proper leadership can also improve the performance of diverse teams.[33] When leaders provide an inspirational common goal for members with varying types of education and knowledge, teams are very creative. When leaders don't provide such goals, diverse teams fail to take advantage of their unique skills and are actually *less* creative than teams with homogeneous skills. Even teams with diverse values can perform effectively, however, if leaders provide a focus on work tasks rather than leading based on personal relationships.

We have discussed research on team diversity in race or gender. But what about diversity created by national differences? Like the earlier research, evidence here indicates these elements of diversity interfere with team processes, at least in the short term.[34] Cultural diversity does seem to be an asset for tasks that call for a variety of viewpoints. But culturally heterogeneous teams have more difficulty learning to work with each other and solving problems. The good news is that these difficulties seem to dissipate with time. Although newly formed culturally diverse teams underperform newly formed culturally homogeneous teams, the differences disappear after about 3 months.[35] Fortunately, some team performance-enhancing strategies seem to work well in many cultures. One study found that teams in the European Union made up of members from collectivist and individualist countries benefited equally from having group goals.[36]

Size of Teams   Most experts agree, keeping teams small is a key to improving group effectiveness.[37] Generally speaking, the most effective teams have five to nine members. And experts suggest using the smallest number of people who can do the task. Unfortunately, managers often err by making teams too large. It may require only four or five members to develop diversity of views and skills, while coordination problems can increase exponentially as team members are added. When teams have excess members, cohesiveness and mutual accountability decline, social loafing increases, and more people communicate less. Members of large teams have trouble coordinating with one another, especially under time pressure. If a natural working unit is larger and you want a team effort, consider breaking the group into subteams.[38]

Member Preferences   Not every employee is a team player. Given the option, many employees will select themselves *out* of team participation. When people who prefer to work alone are required to team up, there is a direct threat to the team's morale and to individual member satisfaction.[39] This result suggests

Members of Wells Fargo's ethnography teams are diversified in function and expertise. Working in the bank's strategic account-management group, team members possess a variety of banking experiences and skills in treasury management, investments, credit cards, and relationship management. The teams visit clients to interview their key managers and observe how employees perform various financial workflows such as payroll and accounts payable. From these studies, the ethnography teams help clients improve their work processes and use of technology. Wells Fargo benefits by gaining a deeper understanding of customer needs and improving customer responsiveness.

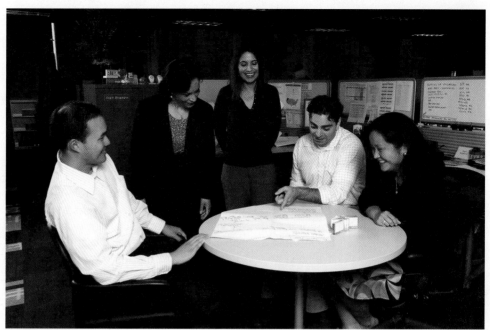

Source: Cindy Charles / PhotoEdit

that, when selecting team members, managers should consider individual preferences along with abilities, personalities, and skills. High-performing teams are likely to be composed of people who prefer working as part of a group.

Team Processes

The final category related to team effectiveness is process variables such as member commitment to a common purpose, establishment of specific team goals, team efficacy, a managed level of conflict, and minimized social loafing. These will be especially important in larger teams and in teams that are highly interdependent.[40]

Why are processes important to team effectiveness? Let's return to the topic of social loafing. We found that 1 + 1 + 1 doesn't necessarily add up to 3. When each member's contribution is not clearly visible, individuals tend to decrease their effort. Social loafing, in other words, illustrates a process loss from using teams. But teams should create outputs greater than the sum of their inputs, as when a diverse group develops creative alternatives. Exhibit 10-5 illustrates how group processes can have an impact on a group's actual effectiveness.[41] Teams are often used in research laboratories because they can draw on the diverse skills of various individuals to produce more meaningful research than researchers working independently—that is, they produce positive synergy, and their process gains exceed their process losses.

Common Plan and Purpose Effective teams begin by analyzing the team's mission, developing goals to achieve that mission, and creating strategies for

organizational demography *The degree to which members of a work unit share a common demographic attribute, such as age, sex, race, educational level, or length of service in an organization, and the impact of this attribute on turnover.*

Myth or Science?

"Teams Work Best Under Angry Leaders"

This statement is false as a general rule. However, there *are* situations when teams perform their best when their leader is angry.

If you have ever seen an episode of one of celebrity chef Gordon Ramsay's reality television shows (*Hell's Kitchen*, *The F Word*, *Kitchen Nightmares*)—where Ramsay regularly terrorizes culinary teams with outbursts, threats, and intimidation—you have seen how angry leaders motivate. But does this approach really get results? Many of us would be skeptical. A harsh, temperamental approach to leading teams would seem to be reliably counterproductive. Who would want to work for such a leader?

As it turns out, the angry team leader may, in fact, have his or her place. A recent study found that whereas teams filled with relatively agreeable members were the most

motivated and performed the best when their leader showed happiness, teams filled with relatively disagreeable members were the most motivated and did best when their leader expressed anger.

Why do disagreeable teams do their best when their leader is angry? If you recall our discussion of agreeableness in Chapter 5, disagreeable individuals are more direct, more argumentative, and less conflict-averse than their more agreeable counterparts. Disagreeable teams may react better to an angry leader because the leader is speaking a language the team can understand, or the disagreeable team members may be less sensitive to inconsiderate behavior (of which the display of anger is a prime example).

Asked to reflect on his angry approach to leading teams, Ramsay said, "When there's no adrenaline

flying high and there's very little pressure created, you don't get results." For some types of teams (those filled with team members as disagreeable as their leader), it appears he is right. Tough love seems to work best with tough teams.

Sources: G. A. Van Kleef, A. C. Homan, B. Beersma, and D. van Knippenberg, "On Angry Leaders and Agreeable Followers: How Leaders' Emotions and Followers' Personalities Shape Motivation and Team Performance," *Psychological Science* 21, no. 12 (2010), pp. 1827–1834; G. A. Van Kleef, A. C. Homan, B. Beersma, D. van Knippenberg, B. van Knippenberg, and F. Damen, "Searing Sentiment or Cold Calculation? The Effects of Leader Emotional Displays on Team Performance Depend on Follower Epistemic Motivation," *Academy of Management Journal* 52, no. 3 (2009), pp. 562–580; and S. Lyall, "The Terrible-Tempered Star Chef of London," *The New York Times* (February 23, 2005), downloaded June 3, 2011, from http://select.nytimes.com/.

achieving the goals. Teams that consistently perform better have established a clear sense of what needs to be done and how.[42]

Members of successful teams put a tremendous amount of time and effort into discussing, shaping, and agreeing on a purpose that belongs to them both collectively and individually. This common purpose, when accepted by the team, becomes what celestial navigation is to a ship captain: it provides direction and guidance under any and all conditions. Like a ship following the wrong course, teams that don't have good planning skills are doomed; perfectly executing the wrong plan is a lost cause.[43] Teams should also agree on whether their goal is to learn about and master a task or simply to perform the task; evidence suggest that different perspectives on learning versus performance goals lead to lower levels of team performance overall.[44] It appears that these differences in goal orientation have their effects by reducing discussion and sharing

Exhibit 10-5   **Effects of Group Processes**

Team members of NASCAR race car driver Danica Patrick's pit crew shown here work toward the common goal of winning the race. Providing direction, momentum, and commitment, the pit crew's plan is to function at top speed with no errors in checking the car, fixing parts, changing tires, and pumping gas. Each member of the pit crew has a specific job and a clear sense of what needs to be done. And each member continuously fine-tunes his job to shave time off the pit stops, which are so important because they may win or lose a race.

Source: Brandon Wade/MCT/Newscom.

of information. In sum, having all employees on a team strive for the same *type* of goal is important.

Effective teams also show **reflexivity**, meaning they reflect on and adjust their master plan when necessary. A team has to have a good plan, but it also has to be willing and able to adapt when conditions call for it.[45] Interestingly, some evidence does suggest that teams high in reflexivity are better able to adapt to conflicting plans and goals among team members.[46]

Specific Goals   Successful teams translate their common purpose into specific, measurable, and realistic performance goals. Specific goals facilitate clear communication. They also help teams maintain their focus on getting results.

Consistent with the research on individual goals, team goals should also be challenging. Difficult but achievable goals raise team performance on those criteria for which they're set. So, for instance, goals for quantity tend to raise quantity, goals for accuracy raise accuracy, and so on.[47]

Team Efficacy   Effective teams have confidence in themselves; they believe they can succeed. We call this *team efficacy*.[48] Teams that have been successful raise their beliefs about future success, which, in turn, motivates them to work harder. What can management do to increase team efficacy? Two options are helping the team achieve small successes that build confidence and providing training to improve members' technical and interpersonal skills. The greater the abilities of team members, the more likely the team will develop confidence and the ability to deliver on that confidence.

Mental Models   Effective teams share accurate **mental models**—organized mental representations of the key elements within a team's environment that team members share.[49] If team members have the wrong mental models, which is particularly likely with teams under acute stress, their performance suffers.[50]

reflexivity   *A team characteristic of reflecting on and adjusting the master plan when necessary.*

mental models   *Team members' knowledge and beliefs about how the work gets done by the team.*

In the Iraq War, for instance, many military leaders said they underestimated the power of the insurgency and the infighting among Iraqi religious sects. The similarity of team members' mental models matters, too. If team members have different ideas about how to do things, the team will fight over methods rather than focus on what needs to be done.[51] One review of 65 independent studies of team cognition found that teams with shared mental models engaged in more frequent interactions with one another, were more motivated, had more positive attitudes toward their work, and had higher levels of objectively rated performance.[52]

Conflict Levels   Conflict on a team isn't necessarily bad. As we discuss in Chapter 15, conflict has a complex relationship with team performance. Relationship conflicts—those based on interpersonal incompatibilities, tension, and animosity toward others—are almost always dysfunctional. However, when teams are performing nonroutine activities, disagreements about task content (called *task conflicts*) stimulate discussion, promote critical assessment of problems and options, and can lead to better team decisions. A study conducted in China found that moderate levels of task conflict during the initial phases of team performance were positively related to team creativity, but both very low and very high levels of task conflict were negatively related to team performance.[53] In other words, both too much and too little disagreement about how a team should initially perform a creative task can inhibit performance.

The way conflicts are resolved can also make the difference between effective and ineffective teams. A study of ongoing comments made by 37 autonomous work groups showed that effective teams resolved conflicts by explicitly discussing the issues, whereas ineffective teams had conflicts focused more on personalities and the way things were said.[54]

Social Loafing   As we noted earlier, individuals can engage in social loafing and coast on the group's effort because their particular contributions can't be identified. Effective teams undermine this tendency by making members individually and jointly accountable for the team's purpose, goals, and approach.[55] Therefore, members should be clear on what they are individually responsible for and what they are jointly responsible for on the team.

SELF-ASSESSMENT LIBRARY

What Is My Team Efficacy?

In the Self-Assessment Library (available on CD or online), take assessment IV.E.2 (What Is My Team Efficacy?).

Turning Individuals into Team Players

5   Show how organizations can create team players.

We've made a strong case for the value and growing popularity of teams. But many people are not inherently team players, and many organizations have historically nurtured individual accomplishments. Finally, teams fit well in countries that score high on collectivism. But what if an organization wants

OB Poll **Different Views on the Importance of Teamwork**

Percent indicating teamwork as high priority skill in workplace

- Employers: 79%
- Employees: 58%

Source: Based on "New Study Sheds Light on Chicago's Employment Landscape," PR Newswire (May 4, 2011). Reprinted with permission from The Gallup Organization.

to introduce teams into a work population of individuals born and raised in an individualistic society? A veteran employee of a large company, who had done well working in an individualistic company in an individualist country, described the experience of joining a team: "I'm learning my lesson. I just had my first negative performance appraisal in 20 years."[56]

So what can organizations do to enhance team effectiveness—to turn individual contributors into team members? Here are options for managers trying to turn individuals into team players.

Selecting: Hiring Team Players

Some people already possess the interpersonal skills to be effective team players. When hiring team members, be sure candidates can fulfill their team roles as well as technical requirements.[57]

When faced with job candidates who lack team skills, managers have three options. First, don't hire them. If you have to hire them, assign them to tasks or positions that don't require teamwork. If that is not feasible, the candidates can undergo training to make them into team players. In established organizations that decide to redesign jobs around teams, some employees will resist being team players and may be untrainable. Unfortunately, they typically become casualties of the team approach.

Creating teams often means resisting the urge to hire the best talent no matter what. The Los Angeles Galaxy professional soccer team paid enormously for British star David Beckham's talents, seemingly without considering whether he was a team player.[58] The result was low levels of coordination and cooperation with the team. Personal traits also appear to make some people better candidates for working in diverse teams. Teams made up of members who like to work through difficult mental puzzles also seem more effective and capitalizing on the multiple points of view that arise from diversity in age and education.[59]

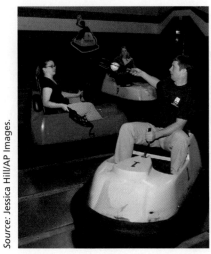

Source: Jessica Hill/AP Images.

Employees of Cigna, a global health services corporation, learn how to become team players by participating in WhirlyBall competitions. Organizations like Cigna use the team sport as a team-building exercise in which two teams maneuver WhirlyBugs on a court while using scoops to toss a ball back and forth among team members in trying to score a goal. WhirlyBall is one of many team-building activities that employees participate in to build their teamwork skills and experience the satisfaction that teamwork can provide.

MyManagementLab
For an interactive application of this topic, check out this chapter's simulation activity at **www.mymanagementlab.com.**

Training: Creating Team Players

Training specialists conduct exercises that allow employees to experience the satisfaction teamwork can provide. Workshops help employees improve their problem-solving, communication, negotiation, conflict-management, and coaching skills. L'Oréal, for example, found that successful sales teams required much more than being staffed with high-ability salespeople: management had to focus much of its efforts on team building. "What we didn't account for was that many members of our top team in sales had been promoted because they had excellent technical and executional skills," said L'Oréal's senior VP of sales, David Waldock. As a result of the focus on team training, Waldock says, "We are no longer a team just on paper, working independently. We have a real group dynamic now, and it's a good one."[60] Employees also learn the five-stage group development model described in Chapter 9. Developing an effective team doesn't happen overnight—it takes time.

Rewarding: Providing Incentives to Be a Good Team Player

An organization's reward system must be reworked to encourage cooperative efforts rather than competitive ones.[61] Hallmark Cards Inc. added to its basic individual-incentive system an annual bonus based on achievement of team goals. Whole Foods directs most of its performance-based rewards toward team performance. As a result, teams select new members carefully so they will contribute to team effectiveness (and thus team bonuses).[62] It is usually best to set a cooperative tone as soon as possible in the life of a team. As we already noted, teams that switch from a competitive to a cooperative system do not immediately share information, and they still tend to make rushed, poor-quality decisions.[63] Apparently, the low trust typical of the competitive group will not be readily replaced by high trust with a quick change in reward systems. These problems are not seen in teams that have consistently cooperative systems.

Promotions, pay raises, and other forms of recognition should be given to individuals who work effectively as team members by training new colleagues, sharing information, helping resolve team conflicts, and mastering needed new skills. This doesn't mean individual contributions should be ignored; rather, they should be balanced with selfless contributions to the team.

Finally, don't forget the intrinsic rewards, such as camaraderie, that employees can receive from teamwork. It's exciting and satisfying to be part of a successful team. The opportunity for personal development of self and teammates can be a very satisfying and rewarding experience.

Beware! Teams Aren't Always the Answer

6   Decide when to use individuals instead of teams.

Teamwork takes more time and often more resources than individual work. Teams have increased communication demands, conflicts to manage, and meetings to run. So, the benefits of using teams have to exceed the costs, and that's not always the case.[64] Before you rush to implement teams, carefully assess whether the work requires or will benefit from a collective effort.

How do you know whether the work of your group would be better done in teams? You can apply three tests.[65] First, can the work be done better by more than one person? A good indicator is the complexity of the work and the need for different perspectives. Simple tasks that don't require diverse input are probably better left to individuals. Second, does the work create a common purpose or set of goals for the people in the group that is more than the aggregate of individual goals? Many service departments of new-vehicle dealers have introduced teams that link customer-service people, mechanics, parts specialists, and sales representatives. Such teams can better manage collective responsibility for ensuring customer needs are properly met.

The final test is to determine whether the members of the group are interdependent. Using teams makes sense when there is interdependence among tasks—the success of the whole depends on the success of each one, *and* the success of each one depends on the success of the others. Soccer, for instance, is an obvious *team* sport. Success requires a great deal of coordination between interdependent players. Conversely, except possibly for relays, swim teams are not really teams. They're groups of individuals performing individually, whose total performance is merely the aggregate summation of their individual performances.

MyManagementLab

Now that you have finished this chapter, go back to **www.mymanagementlab.com** to continue practicing and applying the concepts you've learned.

Summary and Implications for Managers

7 Show how our understanding of teams differs in a global context.

Few trends have influenced jobs as much as the massive movement to introduce teams into the workplace. The shift from working alone to working on teams requires employees to cooperate with others, share information, confront differences, and sublimate personal interests for the greater good of the team.

- Effective teams have common characteristics. They have adequate resources, effective leadership, a climate of trust, and a performance evaluation and reward system that reflects team contributions. These teams have individuals with technical expertise as well as problem-solving, decision-making, and interpersonal skills and the right traits, especially conscientiousness and openness.

- Effective teams also tend to be small—with fewer than 10 people, preferably of diverse backgrounds. They have members who fill role demands and who prefer to be part of a group. And the work that members do provides freedom and autonomy, the opportunity to use different skills and talents, the ability to complete a whole and identifiable task or product, and work that has a substantial impact on others.

- Finally, effective teams have members who believe in the team's capabilities and are committed to a common plan and purpose, an accurate shared mental model of what is to be accomplished, specific team goals, a manageable level of conflict, and a minimal degree of social loafing.

- Because individualistic organizations and societies attract and reward individual accomplishments, it can be difficult to create team players in these environments. To make the conversion, management should try to select individuals who have the interpersonal skills to be effective team players, provide training to develop teamwork skills, and reward individuals for cooperative efforts.

We Can Learn Much About Work Teams from Studying Sports Teams

POINT

In nearly every nation on earth, sports teams are looked upon as examples of teamwork and collective achievement. We celebrate when our favorite teams win and commiserate with others when they lose. Individual sports like golf or singles tennis can be enjoyable to play and, depending on your taste, to watch, but nothing compares to the exhilaration of seeing teams—whether it is football (soccer or American football), basketball, or baseball—band together and succeed.

Of course, it only stands to reason that we seek to draw leadership lessons from these teams. After all, they won at the highest levels of competition, and sometimes they can provide a unique window into team dynamics because their actions are so visible. There is nothing wrong in seeing what we can learn from these teams in terms of making our teams at work more effective. We learn from examples, and if the examples are good ones, the learning is good, too.

Interestingly, some research suggests that, more than those in other cultures, U.S. individuals tend to use team metaphors rather than references to family, the military, or other institutions. Hewlett-Packard's Susie Wee writes:

> Every so often someone asks me what I learned in grad school that helped me in the working world. I can say that many of my most important learnings from school came from playing team sports. My school had a women's club ice hockey team that I played on for 10 years (as an undergrad and grad student). Over these 10 years, my role on the team evolved from a benchwarmer . . . to a player . . . to a captain . . . back to a player . . . and to an assistant coach. Many of my everyday experiences with the team turned into learnings that stayed with me and help me at work.
>
> A perhaps more subtle learning comes from how you make yourself a part of the team when you are the "worst skilled" player or a bench warmer. You can still make important contributions by having a great attitude, [and] by working hard to improve your skills. This directly carries over to the working world, as no matter what your skill or experience level, you can always find a way to make an important contribution to your team.
>
> My advice to people? Students—get involved in a team sport! Workers—treat your career like a team sport!

COUNTERPOINT

Susie Wee's story is a nice one, but that fact that she found her athletic experience helpful doesn't prove much, because that experience may be specific to Susie Wee. A lot of mischief is created in our understanding of organizational behavior when folks try to over-generalize from their past experience.

There certainly is no shortage of athletes and coaches hawking books they propose have organizational implications. In fact, such books are a veritable cottage industry for current and former NFL coaches. Tony Dungy can tell you how to be a "mentor leader" of your team. Rex Ryan can tell you how to use passion and humor to lead teams. Even Bill Walsh (who died in 2007) has a 2010 team leadership book whose theme is "the score takes care of itself." Vince Lombardi (who died in 1970) seems to have a book on team leadership published every year. In all these books, the coaches spend a lot of time discussing how their approach is relevant in the business world. These are all good coaches, some of them are great coaches, but there is little reason to believe athletic teams function like work teams. How many coaches go on to successful careers in organizations outside the athletic context?

In fact, some in-depth reporting on the 2010 U.S. Winter Olympic Team, which won more medals in Vancouver than have ever been won by a U.S. team, demonstrate it was not really a team. The hockey team didn't have much to do with the figure skating team, which didn't have much interaction with the curling team. However, even within the teams organized by sport, there often was no team effort in any real sense of the word. Speedskater Shani Davis, winner of a gold and a silver medal, neither lived nor practiced with the team. He didn't even allow his biography to be posted on the team's Web site. Skier Lindsey Vonn, snowboarder Shaun White, and many others were similarly and rather defiantly "on their own."

There are not many organizations in which a member of a team could get by with that kind of behavior. It often happens, and in fact may be the norm, in sports teams where winning is the only thing that matters. That is one of many differences between sports teams and work teams.

Source: G. B. Gibson and D. M. McDaniel, "Moving Beyond Conventional Wisdom: Advancements in Cross-Cultural Theories of Leadership, Conflict, and Teams," *Perspectives on Psychological Science* 5, no. 4 (2010), pp. 450–462; K. Thomas, "U.S. Olympic Glory, From Stars Hardly on Team," *The New York Times* (February 28, 2010), pp. 1, 4; and S. Schomer, "HP's Susie Wee and the "Wall of Touch," *Fast Company* (May 1, 2010), downloaded June 3, 2011, from www.fastcompany.com/.

QUESTIONS FOR REVIEW

1 How do you explain the growing popularity of teams in organizations?

2 What is the difference between a group and a team?

3 What are the four types of teams?

4 What conditions or context factors determine whether teams are effective?

5 How can organizations create team players?

6 When is work performed by individuals preferred over work performed by teams?

7 What are three ways in which our understanding of teams differs in a global context?

EXPERIENTIAL EXERCISE FIXED VERSUS VARIABLE FLIGHT CREWS

Break into teams of five. Assume that you've been hired by AJet, a startup airline based in St. Louis. Your team has been formed to consider the pros and cons of using variable flight crews and to arrive at a recommendation on whether to follow this industry practice at AJet.

Variable flight crews are crews formed when pilots, co-pilots, and flight attendants typically bid for schedules on specific planes (for instance, Boeing 737s, 757s, or 767s) based on seniority. Then they're given a monthly schedule made up of 1- to 4-day trips. Thus, any given flight crew on a plane is rarely together for more than a few days at a time. A complicated system is required to complete the schedules. Because of this system, it's not unusual for a senior pilot at a large airline to fly with a different co-pilot on every trip during any given month. And a pilot and co-pilot who work together for 3 days in

January may never work together again the rest of the year. (In contrast, a fixed flight crew consists of the same group of pilots and attendants who fly together for a period of time.)

In considering whether to use variable flight crews, your team is to answer the following questions:

1. What are the primary advantages of variable flight crews?

2. If you were to recommend some version of fixed flight crews, drawing from the material in this chapter, on what criteria would you assign AJet crews?

When your team has considered the advantages and disadvantages of variable flight crews and answered these questions, be prepared to present to the class your recommendations and justification.

ETHICAL DILEMMA Unethical Teams

We often think of unethical behavior as individual behavior. However, in many cases, unethical behavior is a team effort. The Enron, Adelphia, and WorldCom corporate scandals were brewed by members of the top management teams in these organizations. The BP oil disaster implicated several teams that failed to ensure construction and safety guidelines were followed. Do these examples show that team unethical behavior is limited to top management teams, or can it also occur with "ordinary" work teams?

A study of 126 three-member teams of undergraduates suggests that unethical team behavior can occur beyond top management teams. In this study, teams were given a problem on which to work, with the following instructions:

> You are assigned a team project in one of your finance courses. Your team waits until the last minute to being working. To save time, a friend suggests using an old project out of his fraternity files. Does your team go along with this plan?

How many of the teams decided to cheat? About 37 percent decided to use the old project.

Because this exercise was hypothetical, the authors also studied team cheating in another way—by allowing teams to self-grade a "decoy" assignment (an aspect of their assignment that did not in reality exist) that counted as 2 percent of their course grade. How many teams cheated here? About one in four.

This study found that team cheating was greater when a team was composed of utilitarian members (those who think the ends justify the means). However, utilitarian attitudes were more likely to translate into team cheating when team members felt interpersonally "safe"—when they felt there was little risk within the team of being attacked or ridiculed for propositions or arguments they made.

The upshot? It appears that in the right circumstances, all types of teams are capable of behaving unethically.

By holding individual team members accountable, and by providing a climate of "voice" where dissenting team members feel free to speak up, managers can discourage team unethical behavior.

Questions

1. Do you know for certain that you would have refused to agree to the unethical behavior in the experiment?

2. Do you think the team nature of the decision makes it more likely or less likely that individuals will choose to behave unethically?

3. In this study, all team members were required to sign a response form indicating they agreed with the decision. Do you think the results would change if consensus or a signature was not required?

Sources: M. J. Pearsall and A. P. J. Ellis, "Thick as Thieves: The Effects of Ethical Orientation and Psychological Safety on Unethical Team Behavior," *Journal of Applied Psychology* 96, no. 2 (2011), pp. 401–411; and D. W. White and E. Lean, "The Impact of Perceived Leader Integrity on Subordinates in a Work Team Environment," *Journal of Business Ethics* 81, no. 4 (2008), pp. 765–778.

CASE INCIDENT 1 Why Don't Teams Work Like They're Supposed to?

Despite years of promises that teamwork will serve as a cure-all for the problems of business, many managers have found that even teams with highly motivated, skilled, and committed members can fail to achieve the expected results. Professor Richard Hackman from Harvard University has been studying teams for years and believes that more often than not, failing to establish the groundwork for effective team performance leads teams to be less effective than if the leader simply divided up tasks and had each individual work on his or her assigned part. As Hackman notes, "I have no question that a team can generate magic. But don't count on it."

What are the main factors Hackman has identified that lead to effective teams? Teams should be kept small and have consistent membership to minimize the types of coordination tasks that take up valuable time. Too often, organizations set up project-based teams and then reconfigure them, without considering the stages of group development that might have to occur before the team can achieve full performance. Supports need to be in place, like group-based rewards and clearly defined group responsibilities. Surprisingly, in his study of 120 senior management teams, Hackman found fewer than 10 percent of members agreed about who was even on the team!

Successful teams also have assertive, courageous leaders who can invoke authority even when the team resists direction. Similar lessons were derived from the failure of Ghana Airways, a state-run organization that experienced frequent changes in top management that were disruptive to establishing a consistent leadership team. As a result of excessive turbulence and lack of strategic vision, the 40-year-old air carrier that was once an emblem for the country went bankrupt.

Do these weaknesses mean teams are never the answer to a business problem? Obviously, it is often necessary to bring together and coordinate individuals with a diverse set of skills and abilities to solve a problem. It would be impossible for all the management tasks of a complex organization like Ghana Airways to be done by disconnected individuals. And often there is more work to be done in a compressed time period than any one individual can possibly accomplish. In these cases, it is wise to consider how to best heed the advice provided above and ensure your team isn't less than the sum of its parts.

Questions

1. What do you think of the elements of successful teamwork Hackman has identified? Do you believe these elements are necessary for effective team performance?

2. Can you think of other conditions necessary for teams to be effective?

3. Imagine you've been asked to assemble and lead a team of high-potential new hires to work on the development of an international marketing campaign. What specific steps might you take early in the team's life to ensure that the new team is able to avoid some of the problems Hackman identified? Is there any way to break down the overall group goal into subtasks so individual accountability can be enhanced?

Sources: D. Coutu, "Why Teams Don't Work" *Harvard Business Review* (May 2009), pp. 99–105; G. Gregory, "Why All-Star Teams Fail," *Lab Manager Magazine* (January 11, 2011), www.labmanager.com; and J. Amankwah-Amoah and Y. A. Debrah, "The Protracted Collapse of Ghana Airways: Lessons in Organizational Failure," *Group and Organization Management* 35, no. 5 (2010), pp. 636–665.

CASE INCIDENT 2 Multicultural Multinational Teams at IBM

When many people think of a traditional, established company, they think of IBM. IBM has been famous for its written and unwritten rules—such as its no-layoff policy, its focus on individual promotions and achievement, the expectation of lifetime service at the company, and its requirement of suits and white shirts at work. The firm was one of the mainstays of the "man in a gray flannel suit" corporate culture in the United States.

Times have certainly changed.

IBM has clients in 170 countries and now does two-thirds of its business outside the United States. As a result, it has overturned virtually all aspects of its old culture. One relatively new focus is on teamwork. While IBM uses work teams extensively, like almost all large organizations, the way it does so is unique.

To foster appreciation of a variety of cultures and open up emerging markets, IBM sends hundreds of its employees to month-long volunteer project teams in regions of the world where most big companies don't do business. Al Chakra, a software development manager located in Raleigh, North Carolina, was sent to join GreenForest, a furniture manufacturing team in Timisoara, Romania. With Chakra were IBM employees from five other countries. Together, the team helped GreenForest become more computer-savvy to increase its business. In return for the IBM team's assistance, GreenForest was charged nothing.

This is hardly altruism at work. IBM firmly believes these multicultural, multinational teams are good investments. First, they help lay the groundwork for uncovering business in emerging economies, many of which might be expected to enjoy greater future growth than mature markets. Stanley Litow, the IBM VP who oversees the program, also thinks it helps IBMers develop multicultural team skills and an appreciation of local markets. He notes, "We want to build a leadership cadre that learns about these places and also learns to exchange their diverse backgrounds and skills." Among the countries where IBM has sent its multicultural teams are Turkey, Tanzania, Vietnam, Ghana, and the Philippines.

As for Chakra, he was thrilled to be selected for the team. "I felt like I won the lottery," he said. He advised GreenForest on how to become a paperless company in 3 years and recommended computer systems to boost productivity and increase exports to western Europe.

Another team member, Bronwyn Grantham, an Australian who works at IBM in London, advised GreenForest about sales strategies. Describing her team experience, Grantham said, "I've never worked so closely with a team of IBMers from such a wide range of competencies."

Questions

1. If you calculate the person-hours devoted to IBM's team projects, they amount to more than 180,000 hours of management time each year. Do you think this is a wise investment of IBM's human resources? Why or why not?

2. Why do you think IBM's culture changed from formal, stable, and individualistic to informal, impermanent, and team-oriented?

3. Would you like to work on one of IBM's multicultural, multinational project teams? Why or why not?

4. Multicultural project teams often face problems with communication, expectations, and values. How do you think some of these challenges can be overcome?

Sources: Based on C. Hymowitz, "IBM Combines Volunteer Service, Teamwork to Cultivate Emerging Markets," *The Wall Street Journal* (August 4, 2008), p. B6; S. Gupta, "Mine the Potential of Multicultural Teams," *HR Magazine* (October 2008), pp. 79–84; and H. Aguinis and K. Kraiger, "Benefits of Training and Development for Individuals and Teams, Organizations, and Society," *Annual Review of Psychology* 60, no. 1 (2009), pp. 451–474.

ENDNOTES

1. This section is based on J. R. Katzenbach and D. K. Smith, *The Wisdom of Teams* (Cambridge, MA: Harvard University Press, 1993), pp. 21, 45, 85; and D. C. Kinlaw, *Developing Superior Work Teams* (Lexington, MA: Lexington Books, 1991), pp. 3–21.
2. J. Mathieu, M. T. Maynard, T. Rapp, and L. Gilson, "Team Effectiveness 1997–2007: A Review of Recent Advancements and a Glimpse into the Future," *Journal of Management* 34, no. 3 (2008), pp. 410–476.
3. J. H. Shonk, *Team-Based Organizations* (Homewood, IL: Business One Irwin, 1992); and M. A. Verespej, "When Workers Get New Roles," *IndustryWeek* (February 3, 1992), p. 11.
4. G. Bodinson and R. Bunch, "AQP's National Team Excellence Award: Its Purpose, Value and Process," *The Journal for Quality and Participation* (Spring 2003), pp. 37–42.

5. See, for example, A. Erez, J. A. LePine, and H. Elms, "Effects of Rotated Leadership and Peer Evaluation on the Functioning and Effectiveness of Self-Managed Teams: A Quasi-experiment," *Personnel Psychology* (Winter 2002), pp. 929–948.

6. See, for instance, C. W. Langfred, "Too Much of a Good Thing? Negative Effects of High Trust and Individual Autonomy in Self-Managing Teams," *Academy of Management Journal* (June 2004), pp. 385–399.

7. C. W. Langfred, "The Downside of Self-Management: A Longitudinal Study of the Effects of Conflict on Trust, Autonomy, and Task Interdependence in Self-Managing Teams," *Academy of Management Journal* 50, no. 4 (2007), pp. 885–900.

8. J. Devaro, "The Effects of Self-Managed and Closely Managed Teams on Labor Productivity and Product Quality: An Empirical Analysis of a Cross-Section of Establishments," *Industrial Relations* 47, no. 4 (2008), pp. 659–698.

9. A. Shah, "Starbucks Strives for Instant Gratification with Via Launch," *PRWeek* (December 2009), p. 15.

10. B. Freyer and T. A. Stewart, "Cisco Sees the Future," *Harvard Business Review* (November 2008), pp. 73–79.

11. See, for example, L. L. Martins, L. L. Gilson, and M. T. Maynard, "Virtual Teams: What Do We Know and Where Do We Go from Here?" *Journal of Management* (November 2004), pp. 805–835; and B. Leonard, "Managing Virtual Teams," *HRMagazine* (June 2011), pp. 39–42.

12. J. R. Mesmer-Magnus, L. A. DeChurch, M. Jimenez-Rodriguez, J. Wildman, and M. Shuffler, "A Meta-Analytic Investigation of Virtuality and Information Sharing in Teams," *Organizational Behavior and Human Decision Processes* 115, no. 2 (2011), pp. 214–225.

13. A. Malhotra, A. Majchrzak, and B. Rosen, "Leading Virtual Teams," *Academy of Management Perspectives* (February 2007), pp. 60–70; and J. M. Wilson, S. S. Straus, and B. McEvily, "All in Due Time: The Development of Trust in Computer-Mediated and Face-to-Face Teams," *Organizational Behavior and Human Decision Processes* 19 (2006), pp. 16–33.

14. See, for instance, J. R. Hackman, "The Design of Work Teams," in J. W. Lorsch (ed.), *Handbook of Organizational Behavior* (Upper Saddle River, NJ: Prentice Hall, 1987), pp. 315–342; and M. A. Campion, G. J. Medsker, and C. A. Higgs, "Relations Between Work Group Characteristics and Effectiveness: Implications for Designing Effective Work Groups," *Personnel Psychology* (Winter 1993), pp. 823–850.

15. D. E. Hyatt and T. M. Ruddy, "An Examination of the Relationship Between Work Group Characteristics and Performance: Once More into the Breech," *Personnel Psychology* (Autumn 1997), p. 555.

16. This model is based on M. A. Campion, E. M. Papper, and G. J. Medsker, "Relations Between Work Team Characteristics and Effectiveness: A Replication and Extension," *Personnel Psychology* (Summer 1996), pp. 429–452; Hyatt and Ruddy, "An Examination of the Relationship Between Work Group Characteristics and Performance," pp. 553–585; S. G. Cohen and D. E. Bailey, "What Makes Teams Work: Group Effectiveness Research from the Shop Floor to the Executive Suite," *Journal of Management* 23, no. 3 (1997), pp. 239–290; L. Thompson, *Making the Team* (Upper Saddle River, NJ: Prentice Hall, 2000), pp. 18–33; and J. R. Hackman, *Leading Teams: Setting the Stage for Great Performance* (Boston: Harvard Business School Press, 2002).

17. See G. L. Stewart and M. R. Barrick, "Team Structure and Performance: Assessing the Mediating Role of Intrateam Process and the Moderating Role of Task Type," *Academy of Management Journal* (April 2000), pp. 135–148.

18. Hyatt and Ruddy, "An Examination of the Relationship Between Work Group Characteristics and Performance," p. 577.

19. P. Balkundi and D. A. Harrison, "Ties, Leaders, and Time in Teams: Strong Inference About Network Structure's Effects on Team Viability and Performance," *Academy of Management Journal* 49, no. 1 (2006), pp. 49–68; G. Chen, B. L. Kirkman, R. Kanfer, D. Allen, and B. Rosen, "A Multilevel Study of Leadership, Empowerment, and Performance in Teams," *Journal of Applied Psychology* 92, no. 2 (2007), pp. 331–346; L. A. DeChurch and M. A. Marks, "Leadership in Multiteam Systems," *Journal of Applied Psychology* 91, no. 2 (2006), pp. 311–329; A. Srivastava, K. M. Bartol, and E. A. Locke, "Empowering Leadership in Management Teams: Effects on Knowledge Sharing, Efficacy, and Performance," *Academy of Management Journal* 49, no. 6 (2006), pp. 1239–1251; and J. E. Mathieu, K. K. Gilson, and T. M. Ruddy, "Empowerment and Team Effectiveness: An Empirical Test of an Integrated Model," *Journal of Applied Psychology* 91, no. 1 (2006), pp. 97–108.

20. J. B. Carson, P. E. Tesluk, and J. A. Marrone, "Shared Leadership in Teams: An Investigation of Antecedent Conditions and Performance," *Academy of Management Journal* 50, no. 5 (2007), pp. 1217–1234.

21. K. T. Dirks, "Trust in Leadership and Team Performance: Evidence from NCAA Basketball," *Journal of Applied Psychology* (December 2000), pp. 1004–1012; M. Williams, "In Whom We Trust: Group Membership as an Affective Context for Trust Development," *Academy of Management Review* (July 2001), pp. 377–396; and J. Schaubroeck, S. S. K. Lam, and A. C. Peng, "Cognition-Based and Affect-Based Trust as Mediators of Leader Behavior Influences on Team Performance," *Journal of Applied Psychology,* Online First Publication (February 7, 2011), doi: 10.1037/a0022625.

22. See F. Aime, C. J. Meyer, and S. E. Humphrey, "Legitimacy of Team Rewards: Analyzing Legitimacy as a Condition for the Effectiveness of Team Incentive Designs," *Journal of Business Research* 63, no. 1 (2010), pp. 60–66; and P. A. Bamberger and R. Levi, "Team-Based Reward Allocation Structures and the Helping Behaviors of Outcome-Interdependent Team Members," *Journal of Managerial Psychology* 24, no. 4 (2009), pp. 300–327; and M. J. Pearsall, M. S. Christian, and A. P. J. Ellis, "Motivating Interdependent Teams: Individual Rewards, Shared Rewards, or Something in Between?" *Journal of Applied Psychology* 95, no. 1 (2010), pp. 183–191.

23. R. R. Hirschfeld, M. H. Jordan, H. S. Feild, W. F. Giles, and A. A. Armenakis, "Becoming Team Players: Team Members' Mastery of Teamwork Knowledge as a Predictor of Team Task Proficiency and Observed Teamwork Effectiveness,"

Journal of Applied Psychology 91, no. 2 (2006), pp. 467–474; and K. R. Randall, C. J. Resick, and L. A. DeChurch, "Building Team Adaptive Capacity: The Roles of Sensegiving and Team Composition," *Journal of Applied Psychology* 96, no. 3 (2011), pp. 525–540.

24. H. Moon, J. R. Hollenbeck, and S. E. Humphrey, "Asymmetric Adaptability: Dynamic Team Structures as One-Way Streets," *Academy of Management Journal* 47, no. 5 (October 2004), pp. 681–695; A. P. J. Ellis, J. R. Hollenbeck, and D. R. Ilgen, "Team Learning: Collectively Connecting the Dots," *Journal of Applied Psychology* 88, no. 5 (October 2003), pp. 821–835; C. L. Jackson and J. A. LePine, "Peer Responses to a Team's Weakest Link: A Test and Extension of LePine and Van Dyne's Model," *Journal of Applied Psychology* 88, no. 3 (June 2003), pp. 459–475; and J. A. LePine, "Team Adaptation and Postchange Performance: Effects of Team Composition in Terms of Members' Cognitive Ability and Personality," *Journal of Applied Psychology* 88, no. 1 (February 2003), pp. 27–39.

25. S. T. Bell, "Deep-Level Composition Variables as Predictors of Team Performance: A Meta-Analysis," *Journal of Applied Psychology* 92, no. 3 (2007), pp. 595–615; and M. R. Barrick, G. L. Stewart, M. J. Neubert, and M. K. Mount, "Relating Member Ability and Personality to Work-Team Processes and Team Effectiveness," *Journal of Applied Psychology* (June 1998), pp. 377–391.

26. T. A. O'Neill and N. J. Allen, "Personality and the Prediction of Team Performance," *European Journal of Personality* 25, no. 1 (2011), pp. 31–42.

27. Ellis, Hollenbeck, and Ilgen, "Team Learning"; C. O. L. H. Porter, J. R. Hollenbeck, and D. R. Ilgen, "Backing Up Behaviors in Teams: The Role of Personality and Legitimacy of Need," *Journal of Applied Psychology* 88, no. 3 (June 2003), pp. 391–403; A. Colquitt, J. R. Hollenbeck, and D. R. Ilgen, "Computer-Assisted Communication and Team Decision-Making Performance: The Moderating Effect of Openness to Experience," *Journal of Applied Psychology* 87, no. 2 (April 2002), pp. 402–410; J. A. LePine, J. R. Hollenbeck, D. R. Ilgen, and J. Hedlund, "The Effects of Individual Differences on the Performance of Hierarchical Decision Making Teams: Much More Than G," *Journal of Applied Psychology* 82 (1997), pp. 803–811; Jackson and LePine, "Peer Responses to a Team's Weakest Link"; and LePine, "Team Adaptation and Postchange Performance."

28. Barrick, Stewart, Neubert, and Mount, "Relating Member Ability and Personality to Work-Team Processes and Team Effectiveness," p. 388; and S. E. Humphrey, J. R. Hollenbeck, C. J. Meyer, and D. R. Ilgen, "Trait Configurations in Self-Managed Teams: A Conceptual Examination of the Use of Seeding for Maximizing and Minimizing Trait Variance in Teams," *Journal of Applied Psychology* 92, no. 3 (2007), pp. 885–892.

29. S. E. Humphrey, F. P. Morgeson, and M. J. Mannor, "Developing a Theory of the Strategic Core of Teams: A Role Composition Model of Team Performance," *Journal of Applied Psychology* 94, no. 1 (2009), pp. 48–61.

30. C. Margerison and D. McCann, *Team Management: Practical New Approaches* (London: Mercury Books, 1990).

31. K. Y. Williams and C. A. O'Reilly III, "Demography and Diversity in Organizations: A Review of 40 Years of Research," in B. M. Staw and L. L. Cummings (eds.), *Research in Organizational Behavior*, vol. 20, (Stamford, CT: Jai Press, 1998) pp. 77–140; and A. Joshi, "The Influence of Organizational Demography on the External Networking Behavior of Teams," *Academy of Management Review* (July 2006), pp. 583–595.

32. A. Joshi and H. Roh, "The Role of Context in Work Team Diversity Research: A Meta-Analytic Review," *Academy of Management Journal* 52, no. 3 (2009), pp. 599–627; S. K. Horwitz and I. B. Horwitz, "The Effects of Team Diversity on Team Outcomes: A Meta-Analytic Review of Team Demography," *Journal of Management* 33, no. 6 (2007), pp. 987–1015; and S. T. Bell, A. J. Villado, M. A. Lukasik, L. Belau, and A. L. Briggs, "Getting Specific about Demographic Diversity Variable and Team Performance Relationships: A Meta-Analysis," *Journal of Management* 37, no. 3 (2011), pp. 709–743.

33. S. J. Shin and J. Zhou, "When Is Educational Specialization Heterogeneity Related to Creativity in Research and Development Teams? Transformational Leadership as a Moderator," *Journal of Applied Psychology* 92, no. 6 (2007), pp. 1709–1721; and K. J. Klein, A. P. Knight, J. C. Ziegert, B. C. Lim, and J. L. Saltz, "When Team Members' Values Differ: The Moderating Role of Team Leadership," *Organizational Behavior and Human Decision Processes* 114, no. 1 (2011), pp. 25–36.

34. W. E. Watson, K. Kumar, and L. K. Michaelsen, "Cultural Diversity's Impact on Interaction Process and Performance: Comparing Homogeneous and Diverse Task Groups," *Academy of Management Journal* (June 1993), pp. 590–602; P. C. Earley and E. Mosakowski, "Creating Hybrid Team Cultures: An Empirical Test of Transnational Team Functioning," *Academy of Management Journal* (February 2000), pp. 26–49; and S. Mohammed and L. C. Angell, "Surface- and Deep-Level Diversity in Workgroups: Examining the Moderating Effects of Team Orientation and Team Process on Relationship Conflict," *Journal of Organizational Behavior* (December 2004), pp. 1015–1039.

35. Watson, Kumar, and Michaelsen, "Cultural Diversity's Impact on Interaction Process and Performance."

36. D. F. Crown, "The use of Group and Groupcentric Individual Goals for Culturally Heterogeneous and Homogeneous Task Groups: An Assessment of European Work Teams," *Small Group Research* 38, no. 4 (2007), pp. 489–508.

37. D. Coutu, "Why Teams Don't Work" *Harvard Business Review* (May 2009), pp. 99–105. The evidence in this section is described in Thompson, *Making the Team*, pp. 65–67. See also L. A. Curral, R. H. Forrester, and J. F. Dawson, "It's What You Do and the Way That You Do It: Team Task, Team Size, and Innovation-Related Group Processes," *European Journal of Work & Organizational Psychology* 10, no. 2 (June 2001), pp. 187–204; R. C. Liden, S. J. Wayne, and R. A. Jaworski, "Social Loafing: A Field Investigation," *Journal of Management* 30, no. 2 (2004), pp. 285–304; and J. A. Wagner, "Studies of Individualism–Collectivism: Effects on Cooperation in Groups," *Academy of Management Journal* 38, no. 1 (February 1995), pp. 152–172.

38. "Is Your Team Too Big? Too Small? What's the Right Number? *Knowledge@Wharton* (June 14, 2006), pp. 1–5.

39. Hyatt and Ruddy, "An Examination of the Relationship Between Work Group Characteristics and Performance"; J. D. Shaw, M. K. Duffy, and E. M. Stark, "Interdependence and Preference for Group Work: Main and Congruence Effects on the Satisfaction and Performance of Group Members," *Journal of Management* 26, no. 2 (2000), pp. 259–279; and S. A. Kiffin-Peterson and J. L. Cordery, "Trust, Individualism, and Job Characteristics of Employee Preference for Teamwork," *International Journal of Human Resource Management* (February 2003), pp. 93–116.

40. J. A. LePine, R. F. Piccolo, C. L. Jackson, J. E. Mathieu, and J. R. Saul, "A Meta-Analysis of Teamwork Processes: Tests of a Multidimensional Model and Relationships with Team Effectiveness Criteria," *Personnel Psychology* 61 (2008), pp. 273–307.

41. I. D. Steiner, *Group Processes and Productivity* (New York: Academic Press, 1972).

42. J. A. LePine, R. F. Piccolo, C. L. Jackson, J. E. Mathieu, and J. R. Saul, "A Meta-Analysis of Teamwork Processes: Tests of a Multidimensional Model and Relationships with Team Effectiveness Criteria"; and J. E. Mathieu and T. L. Rapp, "Laying the Foundation for Successful Team Performance Trajectories: The Roles of Team Charters and Performance Strategies," *Journal of Applied Psychology* 94, no. 1 (2009), pp. 90–103.

43. J. E. Mathieu and W. Schulze, "The Influence of Team Knowledge and Formal Plans on Episodic Team Process—Performance Relationships," *Academy of Management Journal* 49, no. 3 (2006), pp. 605–619.

44. A. N. Pieterse, D. van Knippenberg, and W. P. van Ginkel, "Diversity in Goal Orientation, Team Reflexivity, and Team Performance," *Organizational Behavior and Human Decision Processes* 114, no. 2 (2011), pp. 153–164.

45. A. Gurtner, F. Tschan, N. K. Semmer, and C. Nagele, "Getting Groups to Develop Good Strategies: Effects of Reflexivity Interventions on Team Process, Team Performance, and Shared Mental Models," *Organizational Behavior and Human Decision Processes* 102 (2007), pp. 127–142; M. C. Schippers, D. N. Den Hartog, and P. L. Koopman, "Reflexivity in Teams: A Measure and Correlates," *Applied Psychology: An International Review* 56, no. 2 (2007), pp. 189–211; and C. S. Burke, K. C. Stagl, E. Salas, L. Pierce, and D. Kendall, "Understanding Team Adaptation: A Conceptual Analysis and Model," *Journal of Applied Psychology* 91, no. 6 (2006), pp. 1189–1207.

46. A. N. Pieterse, D. van Knippenberg, and W. P. van Ginkel, "Diversity in Goal Orientation, Team Reflexivity, and Team Performance," *Organizational Behavior and Human Decision Processes* 114, no. 2 (2011), pp. 153–164.

47. E. Weldon and L. R. Weingart, "Group Goals and Group Performance," *British Journal of Social Psychology* (Spring 1993), pp. 307–334. See also R. P. DeShon, S. W. J. Kozlowski, A. M. Schmidt, K. R. Milner, and D. Wiechmann, "A Multiple-Goal, Multilevel Model of Feedback Effects on the Regulation of Individual and Team Performance," *Journal of Applied Psychology* (December 2004), pp. 1035–1056.

48. K. Tasa, S. Taggar, and G. H. Seijts, "The Development of Collective Efficacy in Teams: A Multilevel and Longitudinal Perspective," *Journal of Applied Psychology* 92, no. 1 (2007),
pp. 17–27; D. I. Jung and J. J. Sosik, "Group Potency and Collective Efficacy: Examining Their Predictive Validity, Level of Analysis, and Effects of Performance Feedback on Future Group Performance," *Group & Organization Management* (September 2003), pp. 366–391; and R. R. Hirschfeld and J. B. Bernerth, "Mental Efficacy and Physical Efficacy at the Team Level: Inputs and Outcomes Among Newly Formed Action Teams," *Journal of Applied Psychology* 93, no. 6 (2008), pp. 1429–1437.

49. S. Mohammed, L. Ferzandi, and K. Hamilton, "Metaphor No More: A 15-Year Review of the Team Mental Model Construct," *Journal of Management* 36, no. 4 (2010), pp. 876–910.

50. A. P. J. Ellis, "System Breakdown: The Role of Mental Models and Transactive Memory on the Relationships Between Acute Stress and Team Performance," *Academy of Management Journal* 49, no. 3 (2006), pp. 576–589.

51. S. W. J. Kozlowski and D. R. Ilgen, "Enhancing the Effectiveness of Work Groups and Teams," *Psychological Science in the Public Interest* (December 2006), pp. 77–124; and B. D. Edwards, E. A. Day, W. Arthur Jr., and S. T. Bell, "Relationships Among Team Ability Composition, Team Mental Models, and Team Performance," *Journal of Applied Psychology* 91, no. 3 (2006), pp. 727–736.

52. L. A. DeChurch and J. R. Mesmer-Magnus, "The Cognitive Underpinnings of Effective Teamwork: A Meta-Analysis," *Journal of Applied Psychology* 95, no. 1 (2010), pp. 32–53.

53. J. Farh, C. Lee, and C.I.C. Farh, "Task Conflict and Team Creativity: A Question of How Much and When," *Journal of Applied Psychology* 95, no. 6 (2010), pp. 1173–1180.

54. K. J. Behfar, R. S. Peterson, E. A. Mannix, and W. M. K. Trochim, "The Critical Role of Conflict Resolution in Teams: A Close Look at the Links Between Conflict Type, Conflict Management Strategies, and Team Outcomes," *Journal of Applied Psychology* 93, no. 1 (2008), pp. 170–188.

55. K. H. Price, D. A. Harrison, and J. H. Gavin, "Withholding Inputs in Team Contexts: Member Composition, Interaction Processes, Evaluation Structure, and Social Loafing," *Journal of Applied Psychology* 91, no. 6 (2006), pp. 1375–1384.

56. See, for instance, B. L. Kirkman and D. L. Shapiro, "The Impact of Cultural Values on Employee Resistance to Teams: Toward a Model of Globalized Self-Managing Work Team Effectiveness," *Academy of Management Review*, July 1997, pp. 730–757; and B. L. Kirkman, C. B. Gibson, and D. L. Shapiro, "'Exporting' Teams: Enhancing the Implementation and Effectiveness of Work Teams in Global Affiliates," *Organizational Dynamics* 30, no. 1 (2001), pp. 12–29.

57. G. Hertel, U. Konradt, and K. Voss, "Competencies for Virtual Teamwork: Development and Validation of a Web-Based Selection Tool for Members of Distributed Teams," *European Journal of Work and Organizational Psychology* 15, no. 4 (2006), pp. 477–504.

58. I. Galarcep, "Beckham Loan Makes No Sense for the Galaxy," *ESPNsoccernet* (October 24, 2008), soccernet.espn.go.com.

59. E. Kearney, D. Gebert, and S. C. Voelpel, "When and How Diversity Benefits Teams: The Importance of Team Members' Need for Cognition," *Academy of Management Journal* 52, no. 3 (2009), pp. 581–598.

60. H. M. Guttman, "The New High-Performance Player," *The Hollywood Reporter* (October 27, 2008), www .hollywoodreporter.com.

61. J. S. DeMatteo, L. T. Eby, and E. Sundstrom, "Team-Based Rewards: Current Empirical Evidence and Directions for Future Research," in B. M. Staw and L. L. Cummings (eds.), *Research in Organizational Behavior,* vol. 20, (Stamford CT: JAI Press), pp. 141–183 (1998).

62. T. Erickson and L. Gratton, "What It Means to Work Here," *BusinessWeek* (January 10, 2008), www.businessweek.com.

63. M. D. Johnson, J. R. Hollenbeck, S. E. Humphrey, D. R. Ilgen, D. Jundt, and C. J. Meyer, "Cutthroat Cooperation: Asymmetrical Adaptation to Changes in Team Reward Structures," *Academy of Management Journal* 49, no. 1 (2006), pp. 103–119.

64. C. E. Naquin and R. O. Tynan, "The Team Halo Effect: Why Teams Are Not Blamed for Their Failures," *Journal of Applied Psychology,* April 2003, pp. 332–340.

65. A. B. Drexler and R. Forrester, "Teamwork—Not Necessarily the Answer," *HRMagazine* (January 1998), pp. 55–58.

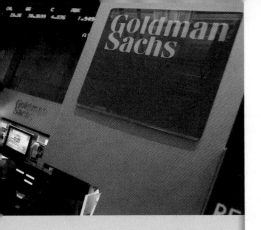

GOLDMAN RULES

Large organizations have policies governing many aspects of employee behavior, including e-mail communication. But few have e-mail rules more elaborate than Goldman Sachs.

Goldman is one of the oldest, largest, and most respected U.S. investment banks. While some of its competitors either went bankrupt during the recent subprime mortgage meltdown (Lehman Brothers, Bear Stearns) or required massive government assistance (especially Citigroup, Bank of America, JPMorgan Chase, and Wells Fargo), Goldman fared better. It did take $10 billion from the government's Troubled Asset Relief Program (TARP), but it paid the money back (with 23 percent interest) before any other investment bank.

What makes Goldman great? One factor surely is management. *BusinessWeek* ranked Goldman sixth on its 2010 list of best places to start a career. One review commented, "MBAs perennially rank Goldman Sachs as one of the most desired places to work, and it's foremost among financial services firms. Once in the door, people still love the firm."

But do they love its e-mail policies? Goldman's e-mail manual, ominously titled *United States Policies for the Preparation, Supervision, Distribution and Retention of Written and Electronic Communications*, is so intricate that it has two rules for the uses of "and."

Some of the more interesting e-mail rules are:

- "The level of detail or explanation necessary to make a communication clear, accurate, and understandable will depend, in part, on the breadth and sophistication of the intended audience . . . the lack of financial sophistication of the recipient will often warrant a more detailed presentation."
- "All sales correspondence from or to employees working from home offices must be routed through regional offices for purposes of review, approval, distribution, and retention."
- "Each individual's correspondence must be sampled no less often than annually."

As elaborate as Goldman's rules are, they didn't keep the company out of hot water when it came to light that Goldman was recommending clients make mortgage investments while the company itself was betting against—"shorting"—those very same mortgage obligations. Several e-mails were particularly damning, calling the strategy "The Big Short." Another e-mail string showed that while being instructed to "be aggressive distributing these things" (positive mortgage positions), a Goldman manager wrote to his girlfriend, "That business is dead, and the poor little subprime borrowers will not last long."

Communication

Constantly talking isn't necessarily communicating. —Joel in *Eternal Sunshine of the Spotless Mind*

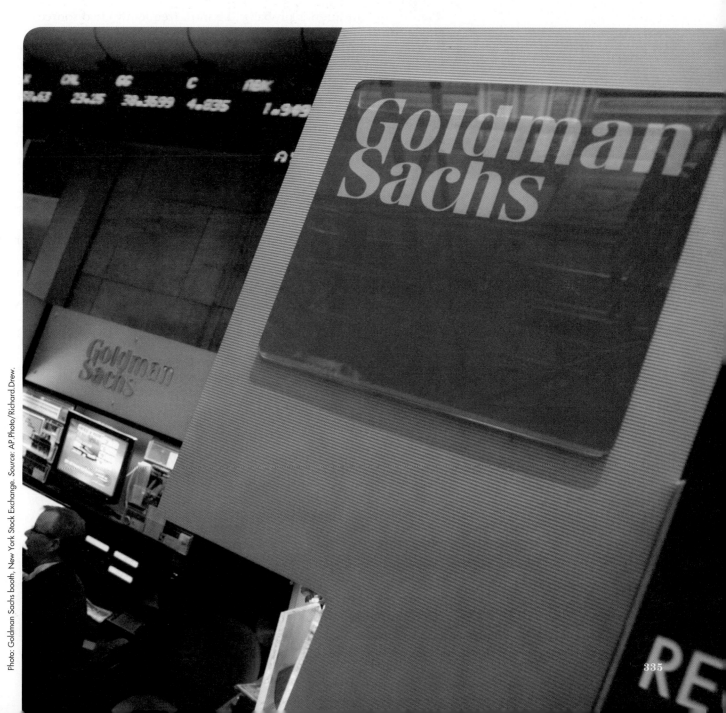

It's unlikely these messages would be consistent with Goldman's elaborate e-mail policies. But the firm did make some serious profit.

Source: M. Abelson and C. Winter, "The Goldman Rules," *Bloomberg Businessweek* (April 25, 2011), pp. 90–91; L Lavelle, "Best Places to Launch a Career," *Bloomberg Businessweek* (June 2010), downloaded June 10, 2011, from http://images.businessweek.com/; and L. Story and S. Chan, "Goldman Cited 'Serious' Profit on Mortgages," *The New York Times* (April 25, 2010), pp. Y1, Y25.

This example illustrates the profound consequences of communication. In this chapter, we'll analyze the power of communication and ways in which it can be more effective. One of the topics we'll discuss is gossip. Consider the following self-assessment, and see how you score on your attitudes toward gossip at work.

Poor communication is probably the most frequently cited source of interpersonal conflict.[1] Because individuals spend nearly 70 percent of their waking hours communicating—writing, reading, speaking, listening—it seems reasonable that one of the biggest inhibitors of group performance is lack of effective communication. Good communication skills are critical to career success. Polls of recruiters nearly always show communication skills among the most desired characteristics.[2]

No individual, group, or organization can exist without sharing meaning among its members. It is only thus that we can convey information and ideas. Communicating, however, is more than merely imparting meaning; that meaning must also be understood. If one group member speaks only German and the others do not know the language, the German speaker will not be fully understood. Therefore, **communication** must include both the *transfer and the understanding of meaning*.

Perfect communication, if it existed, would occur when a thought or idea was transmitted so the receiver perceived exactly the same mental picture as the sender. Though it sounds elementary, perfect communication is never achieved in practice, for reasons we shall see later in this chapter.

First let's briefly review the functions communication performs and describe the communication process.

SELF-ASSESSMENT LIBRARY

Am I A Gossip?

In the Self-Assessment Library (available on CD or online), take assessment IV.E.3 (Am I a Gossip?) and answer the following questions.

1. How did you score relative to your classmates?
2. Do you think gossiping is morally wrong? Why or why not?

Functions of Communication

1 Identify the main functions of communication.

Communication serves four major functions within a group or organization: control, motivation, emotional expression, and information.[3]

Communication acts to *control* member behavior in several ways. Organizations have authority hierarchies and formal guidelines employees

Many communication interactions that take place in an organization perform the function of providing for the emotional expression of feelings and fulfillment of social needs. In this photo, Rene Brookbank, marketing consultant and director of client relations at Cummins & White law firm, jokes with her co-workers during a corporate fashion event. The law firm staged a show for female lawyers and staffers as a fun way for them to view fashion trends in business attire and then treated them all to new outfits. Throughout the social event, cheerful communication among employees allowed them to express their emotions of happiness and gratitude.

Source: o44/ZUMA Press/Newscom.

are required to follow. When employees must communicate any job-related grievance to their immediate boss, follow their job description, or comply with company policies, communication is performing a control function. Informal communication controls behavior too. When work groups tease or harass a member who produces too much (and makes the rest of the group look bad), they are informally communicating, and controlling, the member's behavior.

Communication fosters *motivation* by clarifying to employees what they must do, how well they are doing it, and how they can improve if performance is subpar. We saw this operating in our review of goal-setting theory in Chapter 7. The formation of specific goals, feedback on progress toward the goals, and reward for desired behavior all stimulate motivation and require communication.

Their work group is a primary source of social interaction for many employees. Communication within the group is a fundamental mechanism by which members show their satisfaction and frustrations. Communication, therefore, provides for the *emotional expression* of feelings and fulfillment of social needs.

The final function of communication is to facilitate decision making. Communication provides the *information* individuals and groups need to make decisions by transmitting the data needed to identify and evaluate choices.

Almost every communication interaction that takes place in a group or organization performs one or more of these functions, and none of the four is more important than the others. To perform effectively, groups need to maintain some form of control over members, stimulate members to perform, allow emotional expression, and make decision choices.

communication   *The transfer and understanding of meaning.*

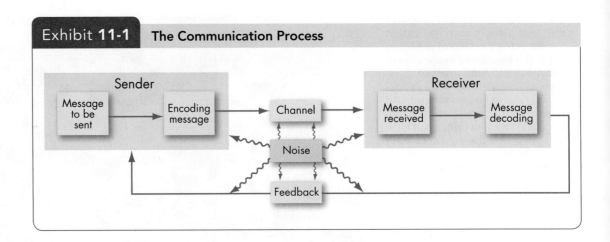

Exhibit **11-1**   The Communication Process

The Communication Process

2 Describe the communication process and distinguish between formal and informal communication.

Before communication can take place it needs a purpose, a message to be conveyed between a sender and a receiver. The sender encodes the message (converts it to a symbolic form) and passes it through a medium (channel) to the receiver, who decodes it. The result is transfer of meaning from one person to another.[4]

Exhibit 11-1 depicts this **communication process**. The key parts of this model are (1) the sender, (2) encoding, (3) the message, (4) the channel, (5) decoding, (6) the receiver, (7) noise, and (8) feedback.

The *sender* initiates a message by encoding a thought. The *message* is the actual physical product of the sender's *encoding*. When we speak, the speech is the message. When we write, the writing is the message. When we gesture, the movements of our arms and the expressions on our faces are the message. The *channel* is the medium through which the message travels. The sender selects it, determining whether to use a formal or informal channel. **Formal channels** are established by the organization and transmit messages related to the professional activities of members. They traditionally follow the authority chain within the organization. Other forms of messages, such as personal or social, follow **informal channels**, which are spontaneous and emerge as a response to individual choices.[5] The *receiver* is the person(s) to whom the message is directed, who must first translate the symbols into understandable form. This step is the *decoding* of the message. *Noise* represents communication barriers that distort the clarity of the message, such as perceptual problems, information overload, semantic difficulties, or cultural differences. The final link in the communication process is a feedback loop. *Feedback* is the check on how successful we have been in transferring our messages as originally intended. It determines whether understanding has been achieved.

Direction of Communication

3 Contrast downward, upward, and lateral communication, and provide examples of each.

Communication can flow vertically or laterally. We further subdivide the vertical dimension into downward and upward directions.[6]

Downward Communication

Communication that flows from one level of a group or organization to a lower level is *downward communication*. Group leaders and managers use it to assign goals, provide job instructions, explain policies and procedures, point out problems that need attention, and offer feedback about performance.

When engaging in downward communication, managers must explain the reasons *why* a decision was made. One study found employees were twice as likely to be committed to changes when the reasons behind them were fully explained. Although this may seem like common sense, many managers feel they are too busy to explain things or that explanations will "open up a big can of worms." Evidence clearly indicates, though, that explanations increase employee commitment and support of decisions.[7] Moreover, although managers might think that sending a message one time is enough to get through to lower-level employees, most research suggests managerial communications must be repeated several times and through a variety of different media to be truly effective.[8]

Another problem in downward communication is its one-way nature; generally, managers inform employees but rarely solicit their advice or opinions. A study revealed that nearly two-thirds of employees say their boss rarely or never asks their advice. The study noted, "Organizations are always striving for higher employee engagement, but evidence indicates they unnecessarily create fundamental mistakes. People need to be respected and listened to." Companies like cell phone maker Nokia actively listen to employee's suggestions, a practice the company thinks is especially important to innovation.[9]

The best communicators explain the reasons behind their downward communications but also solicit communication from the employees they supervise. That leads us to the next direction: upward communication.

Upward Communication

Upward communication flows to a higher level in the group or organization. It's used to provide feedback to higher-ups, inform them of progress toward goals, and relay current problems. Upward communication keeps managers aware of how employees feel about their jobs, co-workers, and the organization in general. Managers also rely on upward communication for ideas on how conditions can be improved.

Given that most managers' job responsibilities have expanded, upward communication is increasingly difficult because managers are overwhelmed and easily distracted. To engage in effective upward communication, try to reduce distractions (meet in a conference room if you can, rather than your boss's office or cubicle), communicate in headlines not paragraphs (your goal is to get your boss's attention, not to engage in a meandering discussion), support your headlines with actionable items (what you believe should happen), and prepare an agenda to make sure you use your boss's attention well.[10]

Lateral Communication

When communication takes place among members of the same work group, members of work groups at the same level, managers at the same level, or any other horizontally equivalent workers, we describe it as *lateral communication*.

communication process *The steps between a source and a receiver that result in the transfer and understanding of meaning.*

formal channels *Communication channels established by an organization to transmit messages related to the professional activities of members.*

informal channels *Communication channels that are created spontaneously and that emerge as responses to individual choices.*

As president of Home Depot's southern division, Ann-Marie Campbell demonstrates the text concept of downward communication when speaking with the manager and employees of a store in St. Petersburg, Florida. Serving as a member of Home Depot's senior leadership team, Campbell oversees 100,000 workers at 640 stores in 15 states, Puerto Rico, and the Virgin Islands. During her store visits, Campbell communicates the retailer's goals of focusing on clean warehouses, stocked shelves, and excellent customer service. Her personal, face-to-face meetings with employees give her the opportunity to solicit upward communication from them.

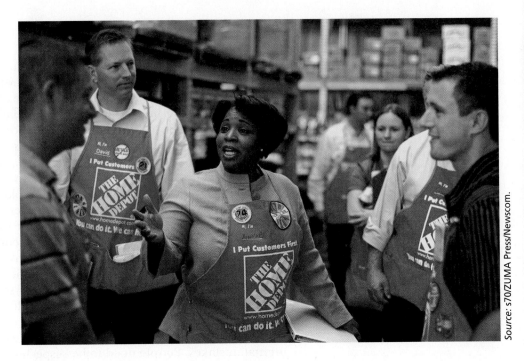

Source: s70/ZUMA Press/Newscom.

Why is lateral communication needed if a group or an organization's vertical communications are effective? Lateral communication saves time and facilitates coordination. Some lateral relationships are formally sanctioned. More often, they are informally created to short-circuit the vertical hierarchy and expedite action. So from management's viewpoint, lateral communications can be good or bad. Because strictly adhering to the formal vertical structure for all communications can be inefficient, lateral communication occurring with management's knowledge and support can be beneficial. But it can create dysfunctional conflicts when the formal vertical channels are breached, when members go above or around their superiors to get things done, or when bosses find actions have been taken or decisions made without their knowledge.

Interpersonal Communication

4 Contrast oral, written, and nonverbal communication.

How do group members transfer meaning between and among each other? They essentially rely on oral, written, and nonverbal communication.

Oral Communication

The chief means of conveying messages is oral communication. Speeches, formal one-on-one and group discussions, and the informal rumor mill or grapevine are popular forms of oral communication.

The advantages of oral communication are speed and feedback. We can convey a verbal message and receive a response in minimal time. If the receiver is unsure of the message, rapid feedback allows the sender to quickly detect and correct it. As one professional put it, "Face-to-face communication on a consistent basis is still the best way to get information to and from employees."[11]

The major disadvantage of oral communication surfaces whenever a message has to pass through a number of people: the more people, the greater the potential distortion. If you've ever played the game "Telephone," you know the problem. Each person interprets the message in his or her own way. The message's content, when it reaches its destination, is often very different from the original. In an organization, where decisions and other communiqués are verbally passed up and down the authority hierarchy, considerable opportunities arise for messages to become distorted.

Written Communication

Written communications include memos, letters, fax transmissions, e-mail, instant messaging, organizational periodicals, notices placed on bulletin boards (including electronic ones), and any other device that transmits via written words or symbols.

Why would a sender choose written communication? It's often tangible and verifiable. Both the sender and receiver have a record of the communication; and the message can be stored for an indefinite period. If there are questions about its content, the message is physically available for later reference. This feature is particularly important for complex and lengthy communications. The marketing plan for a new product, for instance, is likely to contain a number of tasks spread out over several months. By putting it in writing, those who have to initiate the plan can readily refer to it over its lifespan. A final benefit of all written communication comes from the process itself. People are usually forced to think more thoroughly about what they want to convey in a written message than in a spoken one. Thus, written communications are more likely to be well thought out, logical, and clear.

Of course, written messages have drawbacks. They're time consuming. You could convey far more information to a college instructor in a 1-hour oral exam than in a 1-hour written exam. In fact, what you can say in 10 to 15 minutes might take you an hour to write. The other major disadvantage is lack of a built-in feedback mechanism. Oral communication allows the receiver to respond rapidly to what he thinks he hears. But emailing a memo or sending an instant message provides no assurance it has been received or that the recipient will interpret it as the sender intended.

Nonverbal Communication

Every time we deliver a verbal message, we also impart a nonverbal message.[12] Sometimes the nonverbal component may stand alone. In a singles bar, a glance, a stare, a smile, a frown, and a provocative body movement all convey meaning. No discussion of communication would thus be complete without consideration of *nonverbal communication*—which includes body movements, the intonations or emphasis we give to words, facial expressions, and the physical distance between the sender and receiver.

We could argue that every *body movement* has meaning, and no movement is accidental (though some are unconscious). Through body language, we say, "Help me, I'm lonely"; "Take me, I'm available"; and "Leave me alone, I'm depressed." We act out our state of being with nonverbal body language. We lift one eyebrow for disbelief. We rub our noses for puzzlement. We clasp our arms to isolate ourselves or to protect ourselves. We shrug our shoulders for indifference, wink for intimacy, tap our fingers for impatience, slap our forehead for forgetfulness.[13]

The two most important messages body language conveys are (1) the extent to which we like another and are interested in his or her views and (2) the perceived status between a sender and receiver.[14] We're more likely to position ourselves closer to people we like and touch them more often. Similarly, if you feel you're of higher status than another, you're more likely to display body movements—such as crossed legs or a slouched seated position—that reflect a casual and relaxed manner.[15]

Exhibit **11-2**	Intonations: It's the Way You Say It!

Change your tone and you change your meaning:

Placement of the Emphasis	What It Means
Why don't I take **you** to dinner tonight?	I was going to take someone else.
Why don't **I** take you to dinner tonight?	Instead of the guy you were going with.
Why **don't** I take you to dinner tonight?	I'm trying to find a reason why I **shouldn't** take you.
Why don't I take you to dinner tonight?	Do you have a problem with me?
Why don't I **take** you to dinner tonight?	Instead of going on your own.
Why don't I take you to **dinner** tonight?	Instead of lunch tomorrow.
Why don't I take you to dinner **tonight**?	Not tomorrow night.

Source: Based on M. Kiely, "when 'No' Means 'Yes,'" *Marketing* (October 1993), pp. 7–9. Reproduced in A. Huczynski and D. Buchanan, *Organizational Behavior*, 4th ed. (Essex, UK: Pearson Education, 2001), p. 194.

Body language adds to, and often complicates, verbal communication. A body position or movement can communicate something of the emotion behind a message, but when it is linked with spoken language, it gives fuller meaning to a sender's message.

If you read the verbatim minutes of a meeting, you wouldn't grasp the impact of what was said the same way as if you had been there or could see the meeting on video. Why? There is no record of nonverbal communication. The emphasis given to words or phrases is missing. Exhibit 11-2 illustrates how *intonations* can change the meaning of a message. *Facial expressions* also convey meaning. A snarling face says something different from a smile. Facial expressions, along with intonations, can show arrogance, aggressiveness, fear, shyness, and other characteristics.

Physical distance also has meaning. What is considered proper spacing between people largely depends on cultural norms. A businesslike distance in some European countries feels intimate in many parts of North America. If someone stands closer to you than is considered appropriate, it may indicate aggressiveness or sexual interest; if farther away, it may signal disinterest or displeasure with what is being said.

It's important to be alert to these nonverbal aspects of communication and look for nonverbal cues as well as the literal meaning of a sender's words. You should particularly be aware of contradictions between the messages. Someone who frequently glances at her wristwatch is giving the message that she would prefer to terminate the conversation no matter what she actually says. We misinform others when we express one message verbally, such as trust, but nonverbally communicate a contradictory message that reads, "I don't have confidence in you."

Organizational Communication

5 Analyze the advantages and challenges of electronic communication.

In this section, we move from interpersonal communication to organizational communication. Our first focus will be to describe and distinguish formal networks and the grapevine. Then we discuss technological innovations in communication.

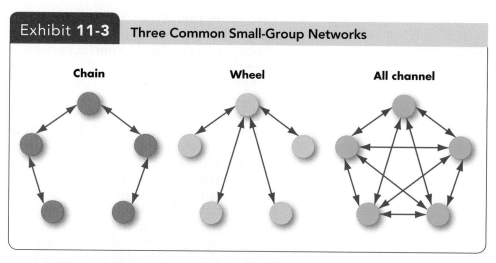

Exhibit **11-3**   Three Common Small-Group Networks

Chain   Wheel   All channel

MyManagementLab
For an interactive application of this
topic, check out this chapter's
simulation activity at
www.mymanagementlab.com.

Formal Small-Group Networks

Formal organizational networks can be very complicated, including hundreds of people and a half-dozen or more hierarchical levels. To simplify our discussion, we've condensed these networks into three common small groups of five people each (see Exhibit 11-3): chain, wheel, and all channel.

The *chain* rigidly follows the formal chain of command; this network approximates the communication channels you might find in a rigid three-level organization. The *wheel* relies on a central figure to act as the conduit for all the group's communication; it simulates the communication network you would find on a team with a strong leader. The *all-channel* network permits all group members to actively communicate with each other; it's most often characterized in practice by self-managed teams, in which all group members are free to contribute and no one person takes on a leadership role.

As Exhibit 11-4 demonstrates, the effectiveness of each network depends on the dependent variable that concerns you. The structure of the wheel facilitates the emergence of a leader, the all-channel network is best if you desire high member satisfaction, and the chain is best if accuracy is most important. Exhibit 11-4 leads us to the conclusion that no single network will be best for all occasions.

The Grapevine

The informal communication network in a group or organization is called the **grapevine**.[16] Although the rumors and gossip transmitted through the grapevine may be informal, it's still an important source of information.

Exhibit **11-4**   Small-Group Networks and Effective Criteria

Criteria	Chain	Networks Wheel	All Channel
Speed	Moderate	Fast	Fast
Accuracy	High	High	Moderate
Emergence of a leader	Moderate	High	None
Member satisfaction	Moderate	Low	High

grapevine *An organization's informal communication network.*

One survey found it's where 75 percent of employees hear news first.[17] A recent report shows that grapevine or word-of-mouth information from peers about a company has important effects on whether job applicants join an organization.[18]

One of the most famous studies of the grapevine investigated communication patterns among 67 managers in a small manufacturing firm.[19] The study asked each communication recipient how he or she first received a given piece of information and then traced it back to its source. While the grapevine was important, only 10 percent of the executives acted as liaison individuals (that is, passed the information to more than one other person). When one executive decided to resign to enter the insurance business, 81 percent of the others knew about it, but only 11 percent told someone else. This lack of spreading information through the grapevine is interesting in light of how often individuals claim to receive information that way.

It's frequently assumed rumors start because they make good gossip. This is rarely the case. Rumors emerge as a response to situations that are *important* to us, when there is *ambiguity*, and under conditions that arouse *anxiety*.[20] The fact that work situations frequently contain these three elements explains why rumors flourish in organizations. The secrecy and competition that typically prevail in large organizations—around the appointment of new bosses, the relocation of offices, downsizing decisions, or the realignment of work assignments—encourage and sustain rumors on the grapevine. A rumor will persist until either the wants and expectations creating the uncertainty are fulfilled or the anxiety has been reduced.

What can we conclude about the grapevine? Certainly it's an important part of any group or organization communication network and is well worth understanding. It gives managers a feel for the morale of their organization, identifies issues employees consider important, and helps tap into employee anxieties. The grapevine also serves employees' needs: small talk creates a sense of closeness and friendship among those who share information, although research suggests it often does so at the expense of those in the "out" group.[21] There is also evidence that gossip is driven largely by employee social networks that managers can study to learn more about how positive and negative information is flowing through their organization.[22] Thus, while the grapevine may not be sanctioned or controlled by the organization, it can be understood.

Can managers entirely eliminate rumors? no. What they should do, however, is minimize the negative consequences of rumors by limiting their range and impact. Exhibit 11-5 offers a few practical suggestions.

Exhibit 11-5   Suggestions for Reducing the Negative Consequences of Rumors

1. **Provide** information—in the long run, the best defense against rumors is a good offense (in other words, rumors tend to thrive in the absence of formal communication).
2. **Explain** actions and decisions that may appear inconsistent, unfair, or secretive.
3. **Refrain** from shooting the messenger—rumors are a natural fact of organizational life, so respond to them calmly, rationally, and respectfully.
4. **Maintain** open communication channels—constantly encourage employees to come to you with concerns, suggestions, and ideas.

Source: Based on L. Hirschhorn, "Managing Rumors," in L. Hirschhorn (ed.), Cutting Back (San Francisco: Jossey-Bass, 1983), pp. 54–56.

The Ethics of Gossip at Work

Experts define gossip as "the exchange of information between two people about a third, absent person." It's tempting to gossip about others at work. We all want to know about what's going on with our co-workers, even if it isn't necessarily our concern. But there is a real possibility that gossip can change from harmless chat about other people's lives to truly destructive words that can spread animosity and anger.

So is gossip necessarily bad? Not according to Joe Labianca at the University of Kentucky. He notes, "If a few people know what's really going on, gossip becomes the means of spreading that information to everyone else. What's more, research shows that gossip often reduces individuals'

anxiety and helps them cope with uncertainty." How? Labianca and colleagues have found that gossip allows people to make personal connections with co-workers and facilitates social support. Managers tend not to like gossip because it subverts their authority, but at the same time, it can level the playing field for those who do not otherwise have access to power. Gossip can also be a means to identify individuals who are free riders, bullies, or difficult to work with. In this way, gossip can even facilitate productive performance.

Does this mean that anything goes when it comes to gossip? Hardly. There are several guidelines for keeping gossip a positive source of information. First, don't pass on any information without checking that it's

accurate. Second, don't share personally sensitive information about someone else that violates that person's privacy. Finally, whenever possible, let the person you are talking about to have a chance to enter the discussion at some later point so his or her view can be explicitly taken into account.

Sources: Based on G. Michelson, A. van Iterson, and K. Waddington, "Gossip in Organizations: Contexts, Consequences, and Controversies," *Group and Organization Management* 35, no. 4 (2010), pp. 371–390; K. M. Kniffin and D. S. Wilson, "Evolutionary Perspectives on Workplace Gossip: Why and How Gossip Can Serve Groups," *Group and Organization Management* 35, no. 2 (2010), pp. 150–176; and J. Labianca, "It's Not 'Unprofessional' to Gossip at Work," *Harvard Business Review* (September 2010), pp. 28–29.

Electronic Communications

An indispensable—and in about 71 percent of cases, the primary—medium of communication in today's organizations is electronic. Electronic communications include e-mail, text messaging, networking software, blogs, and video conferencing. Let's discuss each.

E-mail   E-mail uses the Internet to transmit and receive computer-generated text and documents. Its growth has been spectacular, and its use is now so pervasive it's hard to imagine life without it. E-mail messages can be quickly written, edited, and stored. They can be distributed to one person or thousands with a click of a mouse. And the cost of sending formal e-mail messages to employees is a fraction of the cost of printing, duplicating, and distributing a comparable letter or brochure.[23]

E-mail is not without drawbacks. The following are some of its most significant limitations and what organizations should do to reduce or eliminate them:

- **Risk of misinterpreting the message.**   It's true we often misinterpret verbal messages, but the potential to misinterpret e-mail is even greater. One research team at New York University found we can accurately decode an e-mail's intent and tone only 50 percent of the time, yet most of us vastly overestimate our ability to send and interpret clear messages. If you're sending an important message, make sure you reread it for clarity.[24]
- **Drawbacks for communicating negative messages.**   E-mail may not be the best way to communicate negative information. When Radio Shack

decided to lay off 400 employees, it drew an avalanche of scorn inside and outside the company by doing it via e-mail. Employees need to be careful when communicating negative messages via e-mail, too. Justen Deal, 22, wrote an e-mail critical of some strategic decisions made by his employer, pharmaceutical giant Kaiser Permanente, and questioned the financing of several information technology projects. Within hours, Deal's computer was seized; he was later fired.[25]

- **Time-consuming nature.** An estimated 62 trillion e-mails are sent every year, of which approximately 60 percent, or 36 trillion, are non-spam messages that someone has to answer![26] Some people, such as venture capitalist and Dallas Mavericks owner Mark Cuban, receive more than a thousand messages a day (Cuban says 10 percent are of the "I want" variety). Although you probably don't receive *that* many, most of us have trouble keeping up with all e-mail, especially as we advance in our career. Experts suggest the following strategies:

  - **Don't check e-mail in the morning.** Take care of important tasks before getting ensnared in e-mails. Otherwise, you may never get to those tasks.

  - **Check e-mail in batches.** Don't check e-mail continually throughout the day. Some experts suggest twice a day. "You wouldn't want to do a new load of laundry every time you have a dirty pair of socks," says one expert.

  - **Unsubscribe.** Stop newsletters and other subscriptions you don't really need.

  - **Stop sending e-mail.** The best way to receive lots of e-mail is to send lots of e-mail, so send less. Shorter e-mails garner shorter responses. "A well-written message can and should be as concise as possible," says one expert.

  - **Declare e-mail bankruptcy.** Some people, like recording artist Moby and venture capitalist Fred Wilson, become so overwhelmed by e-mail they declare "e-mail bankruptcy." They wipe out their entire inbox and start over.

  Although some of these steps may not work for you, keep in mind that e-mail can be less productive than it seems: we often seem busy but get less accomplished through e-mail than we might think.[27]

- **Limited expression of emotions.** We tend to think of e-mail as a sort of sterile, faceless form of communication. Some researchers say the lack of visual and vocal cues means emotionally positive messages, like those including praise, will be seen as more emotionally neutral than the sender intended.[28] But as you no doubt know, e-mails are often highly emotional. E-mail tends to have a disinhibiting effect on people; without the recipient's facial expression to temper their emotional expression, senders write things they'd never be comfortable saying in person. When others send flaming messages, remain calm and try not to respond in kind. And, as hard as it might sometimes be, try to see the flaming message from the other party's point of view. That in itself may calm your nerves.[29]

- **Privacy concerns.** There are two privacy issues with e-mail.[30] First, your e-mails may be, and often are, monitored. You can't always trust the recipient of your e-mail to keep it confidential, either. For these reasons, you shouldn't write anything you wouldn't want made public. Second, you need to exercise caution in forwarding e-mail from your company's e-mail account to a personal or "public" e-mail account (for example, Gmail, Yahoo!, MSN). These accounts often aren't as secure as corporate accounts, so when you forward a company e-mail to them, you may be violating your organization's policy or unintentionally disclosing confidential data. Many employers hire vendors to sift through e-mails, using software to catch not only obvious key words ("insider trading") but also the vague ("that thing we talked about") or the guilt-ridden ("regret"). Another survey revealed nearly 40 percent of companies have employees whose only job is to read other employees' e-mail.[31]

Instant Messaging and Text Messaging   Like e-mail, instant messaging (IM) and text messaging (TM) use electronic media. Unlike e-mail, though, IM and TM either occur in real time (IM) or use portable communication devices (TM). In just a few years, IM and TM have become pervasive. As you no doubt know from experience, IM is usually sent via computer, whereas TM is transmitted via cellphones or handheld devices such as BlackBerrys and iPhones.

Despite their advantages, IM and TM aren't going to replace e-mail. E-mail is still probably a better device for conveying long messages that must be saved. IM is preferable for one- or two-line messages that would just clutter up an e-mail inbox. On the downside, some IM and TM users find the technology intrusive and distracting. Its continual presence can make it hard for employees to concentrate and stay focused. A survey of managers revealed that in 86 percent of meetings, at least some participants checked TM, and another survey revealed 20 percent of managers report having been scolded for using wireless devices during meetings.[32] Finally, because instant messages can be intercepted easily, many organizations are concerned about the security of IM and TM.[33]

One other point: it's important to not let the informality of text messaging ("omg! r u serious? brb") spill over into business e-mails. Many prefer to keep business communication relatively formal. A survey of employers revealed that 58 percent rate grammar, spelling, and punctuation as "very important" in e-mail messages.[34] By making sure your professional communications are, well, professional, you'll show yourself to be mature and serious. Avoid jargon and slang, use formal titles, use formal e-mail addresses for yourself (lose thatpartygirl@yahoo.com), and take care to make your message concise and well written. None of this means, of course, that you have to give up TM or IM; you just need to maintain the differences between the way you communicate with your friends and the way you communicate professionally.

Social Networking   Nowhere has communication been more transformed than in the rise of social networking. You are doubtless familiar with and perhaps a user of social networking platforms such as Facebook and LinkedIn. Rather than being one huge site, Facebook, which has more than 600 million active users, is actually composed of separate networks based on schools, companies, or regions. Individuals older than age 25 are now its fastest-growing group of users. In a desire to maintain control over employee use of social networking for professional purposes, many organizations have developed their own in-house social networking applications. The research and advisory firm Gartner Inc. estimates that social networking will soon replace e-mail as the primary form of business communication for 20 percent or more of business users.[35]

To get the most from social networks and avoid irritating your contacts, reserve them for high-value items only—not as an everyday or even every-week tool. Remember that a prospective employer might check your Facebook entries. Some entrepreneurs have developed software that mines such Web sites on behalf of companies (or individuals) that want to check up on a job applicant

Malaysia's airline AirAsia is taking advantage of the flexibility of text messaging to make it more convenient for travelers to book flights. AirAsia flight attendants are shown here with a mobile phone billboard during the launch of the world's first airline booking through a short messaging service (SMS) on cell phones. The SMS makes it easier for travelers to book their seats as the service allows them to choose their flights, confirm their booking, and pay for their seats by text messaging from the convenience of their mobile phone wherever they are.

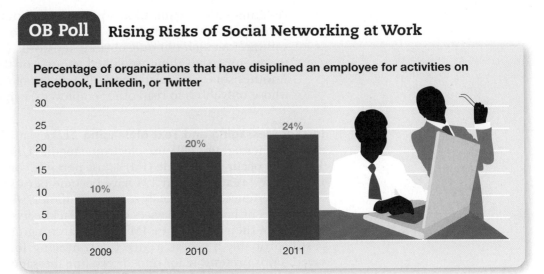

OB Poll   **Rising Risks of Social Networking at Work**

Percentage of organizations that have disiplined an employee for activities on Facebook, Linkedin, or Twitter

- 2009: 10%
- 2010: 20%
- 2011: 24%

Source: Based on Studylogic poll for Starwood Hotels and Resorts/Sheraton.

Source: Deshakalyan Chowdhury/Getty Images.

Sunita Williams, a NASA astronaut commander and the woman who has spent the longest time in space, used videoconferencing to speak to students and journalists at The American Center in Kolkata, India. The videoconferencing technology allowed the students and journalists to interact with Williams as she discussed her experiences aboard the Space Station Atlantis. The interactive meeting gave Williams the opportunity to answer questions about her job as a U.S. Navy experimental test pilot and as a helicopter pilot during the Gulf War.

(or potential date). So keep in mind that what you post may be read by people other than your intended contacts.[36]

Blogs   A **blog (Web log)** is a Web site about a single person or company. Experts estimate that more than 156 million blogs now exist. Millions of U.S. workers have blogs. And, of course, many organizations and organizational leaders have blogs that speak for the organization.

Twitter is a hybrid social networking service that allows users to post "microblog" entries to their subscribers about any topic, including work. Many organizational leaders send Twitter messages ("tweets"), but they can also come from any employee about any work topic, leaving organizations with less control over the communication of important or sensitive information.

Although some companies have policies governing the content of blogs and Twitter feeds, many don't, and many posters say they have blogged or tweeted comments that could be construed as harmful to their company's reputation. Many think their personal blogs are outside their employer's purview, but if someone else in the company happens to read a critical or negative blog entry or post, there is nothing to keep him or her from sharing that information with others, and the employee could be dismissed as a result.

One legal expert notes, "Employee bloggers mistakenly believe the First Amendment gives them the right to say whatever they want on their personal blogs. Wrong!" Also, beware of posting personal blog entries from work. More than three-quarters of employers actively monitor employees' Web site connections. In short, if you are going to have a personal blog, maintain a strict work–personal "firewall."[37]

Video Conferencing   *Video conferencing* permits employees in an organization to have real-time meetings with people at different locations. Live audio and video images let participants see, hear, and talk with each other without being physically in the same location.

Peter Quirk, a program manager with EMC Corporation, uses video conferencing to hold monthly meetings of employees at various locations and many other meetings as well. Doing so saves travel expenses and time. However, Quirk notes it's especially important to stimulate questions and involve all participants in order to avoid someone who is linked in but disengaged. Sun Microsystem's Karen Rhode agrees special efforts must be made to engage remote participants, suggesting, "You can poll people, people can ask questions, you can do an engaging presentation."[38]

Managing Information

We all have more information at our disposal than ever. It brings us many benefits, but also two important challenges: information overload and threats to information security. We consider each in turn.

Dealing with Information Overload   Do you find yourself bombarded with information—from e-mail, blogs, Internet surfing, IMs, cell phones, and televisions? You're not alone. Basex, a company that looks at worker efficiency, found the largest part of an average worker's day—43 percent—is spent on matters that are neither important nor urgent, such as responding to noncrucial e-mails and surfing the Web. (In fairness to e-mail, Basex also found 25 percent of an employee's time was spent composing and responding to *important* e-mail.)

Intel designed an 8-month experiment to see how limiting this **information overload** might aid productivity. One group of employees was told to limit both digital and in-person contact for 4 hours on Tuesdays, while another group followed its usual routine. The first group was more productive, and 75 percent of its members suggested the program be expanded. "It's huge. We were expecting less," remarked Nathan Zeldes, an Intel engineer who led the experiments. "When people are uninterrupted they can sit back and design chips and really think."[39]

We have already reviewed some ways of reducing the time sunk into e-mails. More generally, as the Intel study shows, it may make sense to connect to technology less frequently, to, in the words of one article, "avoid letting the drumbeat of digital missives constantly shake up and reorder to-do lists." Lynaia Lutes, an account supervisor for a small Texas company, was able to think much more strategically by taking a break from digital information each day. In the past, she said, "I basically completed an assignment" but didn't approach it strategically. By creating such breaks for yourself, you may be better able to prioritize, think about the big picture, and thereby be more effective.[40]

As information technology and immediate communication have become a more prevalent component of modern organizational life, more employees find they are never able to get offline. Some business travelers were disappointed when airlines began offering wireless Internet connections in flight because they could no longer use their travel time as a rare opportunity to relax without a constant barrage of organizational communications. The negative impacts of these communication devices can spill over into employees' personal lives as well. Both workers and their spouses relate the use of electronic communication technologies outside work to higher levels of work–life conflict.[41] Employees must balance the need for constant communication with their own

---

blog (Web log)   *A Web site where entries are written, and generally displayed in reverse chronological order, about news, events, and personal diary entries.*

Twitter   *A free blogging and networking service where users send and read messages known as tweets, many of which concern OB issues.*

information overload   *A condition in which information inflow exceeds an individual's processing capacity.*

personal need for breaks from work, or they risk burnout from being on call 24 hours a day.

Threats to Information Security   Security is a huge concern for nearly all organizations with private or proprietary information about clients, customers, and employees. A Merrill Lynch survey of 50 executives found 52 percent rated leaks of company information as their number-one information security concern, topping viruses and hackers. Most companies actively monitor employee Internet use and e-mail records, and some even use video surveillance and record phone conversations. Necessary though they may be, such practices can seem invasive to employees. An organization can relieve employee concerns by engaging them in the creation of information-security policies and giving them some control over how their personal information is used.[42]

Choice of Communication Channel

6   Show how channel richness underlies the choice of communication channel.

Why do people choose one channel of communication over another—say, a phone call instead of a face-to-face talk? A model of media richness helps explain channel selection among managers.[43]

Channels differ in their capacity to convey information. Some are *rich* in that they can (1) handle multiple cues simultaneously, (2) facilitate rapid feedback, and (3) be very personal. Others are *lean* in that they score low on these factors. As Exhibit 11-6 illustrates, face-to-face conversation scores highest in **channel richness** because it transmits the most information per communication episode—multiple information cues (words, postures, facial expressions, gestures, intonations), immediate feedback (both verbal and nonverbal), and

Exhibit 11-6   Information Richness and Communication Channels

Source: Based on R. H. Lengel and R. L. Daft, "The Selection of Communication Media as an Executive Skill," *Academy of Management Executive* (August 1988), pp. 225–232; and R. L. Daft and R. H. Lengel, "Organizational Information Requirements, Media Richness, and Structural Design," *Managerial Science* (May 1996), pp. 554–572. Reproduced from R. L. Daft and R. A. Noe, *Organizational Behavior* (Fort Worth, TX: Harcourt, 2001), p. 311.

the personal touch of being present. Impersonal written media such as formal reports and bulletins rate lowest in richness.

The choice of channel depends on whether the message is routine. Routine messages tend to be straightforward and have minimal ambiguity; channels low in richness can carry them efficiently. Nonroutine communications are likely to be complicated and have the potential for misunderstanding. Managers can communicate them effectively only by selecting rich channels.

When tough times hit Manpower Business Solutions during the recent economic contraction, the company elected to communicate with employees daily in a variety of media to ensure that everyone remained informed.[44] Employees were given updates about the company's plans for dealing with economic problems, including advance warning before layoffs. The company believes its strategy of using rich communication channels for nonroutine information has paid off by reducing employee anxiety and increasing engagement with the organization.

Persuasive Communications

7 Differentiate between automatic and controlled processing of persuasive messages.

We've discussed a number of methods for communication up to this point. Now we turn our attention to one of the functions of communication and the features that might make messages more or less persuasive to an audience.

Automatic and Controlled Processing

To understand the process of communication, it is useful to consider two relatively different ways that we process information.[45] Think about the last time you bought a can of soda. Did you carefully research brands and engage in your own double-blind taste test to see which types you actually prefer? Or did you reach for the can that had the most appealing advertising images? If we're honest, we'll admit glitzy ads and catchy slogans do indeed have an influence on our choices as consumers. We often rely on **automatic processing**, a relatively superficial consideration of evidence and information making use of heuristics like those we discussed in Chapter 6. Automatic processing takes little time and low effort, so it makes sense to use it for processing persuasive messages related to topics you don't care much about. The disadvantage is that it lets us be easily fooled by a variety of tricks, like a cute jingle or glamorous photo.

Now consider the last time you chose a place to live. For this more important decision, you probably did do some independent research among experts who know something about the area, gathered information about prices from a variety of sources, and considered the costs and benefits of renting versus buying. Here, you're relying on more effortful **controlled processing**, a detailed consideration of evidence and information relying on facts, figures, and logic. Controlled processing requires effort and energy, but it's harder to fool

channel richness *The amount of information that can be transmitted during a communication episode.*

automatic processing *A relatively superficial consideration of evidence and information making use of heuristics.*

controlled processing *A detailed consideration of evidence and information relying on facts, figures, and logic.*

someone who has taken the time and effort to engage in it. So what makes someone engage in either shallow or deep processing? There are a few rules of thumb for determining what types of processing an audience will use.

Interest Level

One of the best predictors of whether people will use an automatic or controlled process for reacting to a persuasive message is their level of interest in it.[46] Interest levels reflect the impact a decision is going to have on your life. When people are very interested in the outcome of a decision, they're more likely to process information carefully. That's probably why people look for so much more information when deciding about something important (like where to live) than something relatively unimportant (like which soda to drink).

Prior Knowledge

People who are very well informed about a subject area are also more likely to use controlled processing strategies. They have already thought through various arguments for or against a specific course of action, and therefore they won't readily change their position unless very good, thoughtful reasons are provided. On the other hand, people who are poorly informed about a topic can change their minds more readily, even in the face of fairly superficial arguments presented without a great deal of evidence. In other words, a better informed audience is likely to be much harder to persuade.

Personality

Are you the type of person who always likes to read at least five reviews of a movie before deciding whether to see it? Do you carefully consider several movies before making a choice? Perhaps you even research recent films by the same stars and director. If so, you are probably high in *need for cognition,* a personality trait of individuals who are most likely to be persuaded by evidence and facts.[47] Those who are lower in need for cognition are more likely to use automatic processing strategies, relying on intuition and emotion to guide their evaluation of persuasive messages.

Message Characteristics

Another factor that influences whether people use an automatic or controlled processing strategy is the characteristics of the message itself. Messages provided through relatively lean communication channels, with little opportunity for users to interact with the content of the message, tend to encourage automatic processing. For example, most television advertisements go by too fast for really deliberative thought; we automatically process these. Conversely, messages provided through richer communication channels, like a long magazine article, tend to encourage more deliberative processing.

The most important implication of all this research is to match your persuasive message to the type of processing your audience is likely to use. When the audience is not especially interested in a persuasive message topic, when they are poorly informed, when they are low in need for cognition, and when information is transmitted through relatively lean channels, they'll be more likely to use automatic processing. In these cases, use messages that are more emotion-laden and associate positive images with your preferred outcome. On the other hand, when the audience is interested in a topic, when they are high in need for cognition, or when the information is transmitted through rich channels, then it is a better idea to focus on rational arguments and evidence to make your case.

Barriers to Effective Communication

8 Identify common barriers to effective communication.

A number of barriers can retard or distort effective communication. In this section, we highlight the most important.

Filtering

Filtering refers to a sender's purposely manipulating information so the receiver will see it more favorably. A manager who tells his boss what he feels the boss wants to hear is filtering information.

The more vertical levels in the organization's hierarchy, the more opportunities there are for filtering. But some filtering will occur wherever there are status differences. Factors such as fear of conveying bad news and the desire to please the boss often lead employees to tell their superiors what they think they want to hear, thus distorting upward communications.

Selective Perception

We have mentioned selective perception before in this book. It appears again here because the receivers in the communication process selectively see and hear based on their needs, motivations, experience, background, and other personal characteristics. Receivers also project their interests and expectations into communications as they decode them. An employment interviewer who expects a female job applicant to put her family ahead of her career is likely to see that in all female applicants, regardless of whether they actually feel that way. As we said in Chapter 6, we don't see reality; we interpret what we see and call it reality.

Information Overload

Individuals have a finite capacity for processing data. When the information we have to work with exceeds our processing capacity, the result is information overload. We've seen that dealing with it has become a huge challenge for individuals and for organizations. It's a challenge you can manage—to some degree—by following the steps outlined earlier in this chapter.

What happens when individuals have more information than they can sort and use? They tend to select, ignore, pass over, or forget. Or they may put off further processing until the overload situation ends. In any case, lost information and less effective communication results, making it all the more important to deal well with overload.

Emotions

You may interpret the same message differently when you're angry or distraught than when you're happy. For example, individuals in positive moods are more confident about their opinions after reading a persuasive message, so well-crafted arguments have stronger impacts on their opinions.[48] People in negative moods are more likely to scrutinize messages in greater detail, whereas those in positive moods tend to accept communications at face value.[49] Extreme

filtering *A sender's manipulation of information so that it will be seen more favorably by the receiver.*

Managers of Hochtief, Germany's largest construction firm, relied on controlled processing when addressing employees during a supervisory board meeting at company headquarters in Essen, Germany, shown here. In response to a takeover bid by the Spanish construction firm Actividades de Construccion & Servicios (ACS), Hochtief management focused on rational evidence and arguments in presenting its defense against the takeover bid and its plans to fend off the bid. Employees' level of interest in the takeover attempt is high, because they fear that an ACS takeover would result in a major downsizing of Hochtief's workforce and would put their jobs at risk.

Source: Bernd Thissen/dpa/picture-alliance/Newscom.

emotions such as jubilation or depression are most likely to hinder effective communication. In such instances, we are most prone to disregard our rational and objective thinking processes and substitute emotional judgments.

Language

Even when we're communicating in the same language, words mean different things to different people. Age and context are two of the biggest factors that influence such differences.

When Michael Schiller, a business consultant, was talking with his 15-year-old daughter about where she was going with her friends, he told her, "You need to recognize your KPIs and measure against them." Schiller said that in response, his daughter "looked at him like he was from outer space." (For the record, KPI stands for key performance indicators.) Those new to corporate lingo may find acronyms such as *KPI*, words such as *deliverables* (verifiable outcomes of a project), and phrases such as *get the low-hanging fruit* (deal with the easiest parts first) bewildering, in the same way parents may be mystified by teen slang.[50]

In short, our use of language is far from uniform. If we knew how each of us modified the language, we could minimize communication difficulties, but we usually don't know. Senders tend to assume the words and terms they use mean the same to the receiver as to them. This assumption is often incorrect.

Silence

It's easy to ignore silence or lack of communication, precisely because it is defined by the absence of information. However, research suggests silence and withholding communication are both common and problematic.[51] One survey found that more than 85 percent of managers reported remaining silent about at least one issue of significant concern.[52] Employee silence means managers lack information about ongoing operational problems. And silence regarding discrimination, harassment, corruption, and misconduct means top management cannot take action to eliminate this behavior. Finally, employees who are silent about important issues may also experience psychological stress.

Silence is less likely where minority opinions are treated with respect, workgroup identification is high, and high procedural justice prevails.[53] Practically, this means managers must make sure they behave in a supportive manner when employees voice divergent opinions or concerns, and they must take these under advisement. One act of ignoring or belittling an employee for expressing concerns may well lead the employee to withhold important future communication.

Communication Apprehension

An estimated 5 to 20 percent of the population suffers debilitating **communication apprehension**, or social anxiety.[54] These people experience undue tension and anxiety in oral communication, written communication, or both.[55] They may find it extremely difficult to talk with others face-to-face or may become extremely anxious when they have to use the phone, relying on memos or e-mails when a phone call would be faster and more appropriate.

Studies show oral-communication apprehensives avoid situations, such as teaching, for which oral communication is a dominant requirement.[56] But almost all jobs require *some* oral communication. Of greater concern is evidence that high oral-communication apprehensives distort the communication demands of their jobs in order to minimize the need for communication. So be aware that some people severely limit their oral communication and rationalize their actions by telling themselves communicating isn't necessary for them to do their job effectively.

Lying

The final barrier to effective communication is outright misrepresentation of information, or lying. People differ in their definition of what constitutes a lie. For example, is deliberately withholding information about a mistake you made a lie, or do you have to actively deny your role in the mistake to pass the threshold of deceit? While the definition of a lie will continue to befuddle both ethicists and social scientists, there is no denying the prevalence of lying. In one diary study, the average person reported telling one to two lies per day, with some individuals telling considerably more.[57] Compounded across a large organization, this is an enormous amount of deception happening every single day! Evidence also shows that people are more comfortable lying over the phone than face-to-face and more comfortable lying in e-mails than when they have to write with pen and paper.[58]

Can you detect liars? Despite a great deal of investigation, research generally suggests most people are not very good at detecting deception in others.[59] The problem is, there are no nonverbal or verbal cues unique to lying—averting your gaze, pausing, and shifting your posture can also be signals of nervousness, shyness, or doubt. Moreover, most people who lie take a number of steps to guard against being detected, so they might deliberately look a person in the eye when lying because they know that direct eye contact is (incorrectly) assumed to be a sign of truthfulness. Finally, many lies are embedded in truths; liars usually give a somewhat true account with just enough details changed to avoid detection.

In sum, the frequency of lying and the difficulty in detecting liars makes this an especially strong barrier to effective communication in organizations.

communication apprehension   *Undue tension and anxiety about oral communication, written communication, or both.*

"We Know What Makes Good Liars Good"

This statement is true, though we still have more to learn about the characteristics of proficient liars.

As we have noted in this chapter, it is not easy to detect whether liars are telling the truth. We have reviewed some of the reasons for this, but recent research has uncovered an obvious but only recently tested explanation for why it's hard to catch a liar: some people are just good at lying, and we're beginning to understand why.

What causes people to be good liars? A major review of the literature identified six features of good liars:

1. Their natural behavior is disarming—they smile, make eye contact, mimic the gestures of their target, and avoid "ums" and "ehs."
2. They do their homework—they have thought up plausible cover stories before they are demanded.
3. They don't let their emotions get in the way—good liars are unusually calm and composed when lying.
4. They are good-looking—good liars are physically attractive; we are more likely to trust stories told by attractive people.
5. They have good insights into others' thought processes.
6. They tend to believe their own lies—this has been established by studies that ask people to lie and later find many of them believe their original lies to be true.

A sad truth of organizational behavior is that people are better liars than we think, and we are worse at unveiling them than we realize.

Sources: A. Vrij, P. A. Granhag, and S. Porter, "Pitfalls and Opportunities in Nonverbal and Verbal Lie Detection," _Psychological Science in the Public Interest_ 11, no. 3 (2010), pp. 89–121; E. F. Loftus, "Catching Liars," _Psychological Science in the Public Interest_ 11, no. 3 (2010), pp. 87–88; and A. Vrij, P. A. Granhag, and S. Mann, "Good Liars," Unpublished manuscript, University of Portsmouth, 2011, www.port.ac.uk/departments/academic/psychology/staff/downloads/filetodownload,89132,en.pdf.

Global Implications

9 Show how to overcome the potential problems in cross-cultural communication.

Effective communication is difficult under the best of conditions. Cross-cultural factors clearly create the potential for increased communication problems. A gesture that is well understood and acceptable in one culture can be meaningless or lewd in another. Only 18 percent of companies have documented strategies for communicating with employees across cultures, and only 31 percent require that corporate messages be customized for consumption in other cultures. Procter & Gamble seems to be an exception; more than half the company's employees don't speak English as their first language, so the company focuses on simple messages to make sure everyone knows what's important.[60]

Cultural Barriers

Researchers have identified a number of problems related to language difficulties in cross-cultural communications.[61]

First are _barriers caused by semantics._ Words mean different things to different people, particularly people from different national cultures. Some words don't translate between cultures. The Finnish word _sisu_ means something akin to "guts" or "dogged persistence" but is essentially untranslatable into English. The new capitalists in Russia may have difficulty communicating with British or Canadian counterparts because English terms such as _efficiency, free market,_ and _regulation_ have no direct Russian equivalents.

Second are _barriers caused by word connotations._ Words imply different things in different languages. Negotiations between U.S. and Japanese executives can be difficult because the Japanese word _hai_ translates as "yes," but its connotation is "Yes, I'm listening" rather than "Yes, I agree."

Third are *barriers caused by tone differences.* In some cultures, language is formal; in others, it's informal. In some cultures, the tone changes depending on the context: People speak differently at home, in social situations, and at work. Using a personal, informal style when a more formal style is expected can be embarrassing.

Fourth are *differences in tolerance for conflict and methods for resolving conflicts.* Individuals from individualist cultures tend to be more comfortable with direct conflicts and will make the source of their disagreements overt. Collectivists are more likely to acknowledge conflict only implicitly and avoid emotionally charged disputes. They may attribute conflicts to the situation more than to the individuals and therefore may not require explicit apologies to repair relationships, whereas individualists prefer explicit statements accepting responsibility for conflicts and public apologies to restore relationships.

Cultural Context

Cultures tend to differ in the degree to which context influences the meaning individuals take from communication.[62] In **high-context cultures** such as China, Korea, Japan, and Vietnam, people rely heavily on nonverbal and subtle situational cues in communicating with others, and a person's official status, place in society, and reputation carry considerable weight. What is *not* said may be more significant than what *is* said. In contrast, people from Europe and North America reflect their **low-context cultures**. They rely essentially on spoken and written words to convey meaning; body language and formal titles are secondary (see Exhibit 11-7).

These contextual differences actually mean quite a lot in terms of communication. Communication in high-context cultures implies considerably more trust by both parties. What may appear to be casual and insignificant conversation in fact reflects the desire to build a relationship and create trust. Oral agreements imply strong commitments in high-context cultures. And who you are—your age, seniority, rank in the organization—is highly valued and heavily influences your credibility. But in low-context cultures, enforceable contracts tend to be in writing, precisely worded, and highly legalistic. Similarly, low-context cultures value directness. Managers are expected to be explicit and precise in conveying intended meaning. It's quite different in high-context cultures, in which managers tend to "make suggestions" rather than give orders.

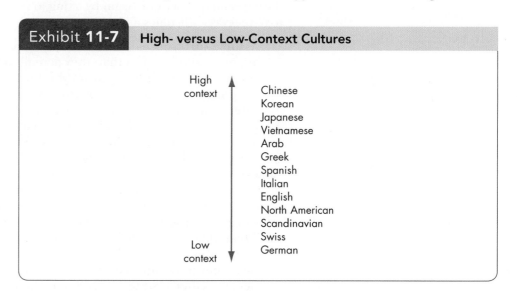

Exhibit **11-7** High- versus Low-Context Cultures

high-context cultures *Cultures that rely heavily on nonverbal and subtle situational cues in communication.*

low-context cultures *Cultures that rely heavily on words to convey meaning in communication.*

How Direct Should You Be?

Those who have traveled or done business internationally are often advised to be careful about how directly they communicate with people from different cultures. The popular advice suggests that U.S. citizens prefer upbeat, positive communication; the English prefer formal communication; central Europeans are more interested in direct communication even if information is negative; and East Asians prefer to minimize disagreements and emphasize shared perspectives. Although there is more advice than research on this particular issue, some preliminary work does suggest some reliable differences in how cultures value direct and indirect communication.

One study examined cultural differences in values, beliefs, and personality data to see whether any consistent patterns in communication could be found. A group of East Asian countries, including China, Taiwan, Singapore, and Japan, were marked by a bias for low levels of both agreement *and* disagreement in communication, preferring moderate discussions with respondents not taking strong sides on an issue. Conversely, countries like Morocco, Iraq, Israel, and Saudi Arabia prefer high levels of both agreement and disagreement in their communications; in these countries, the preferred communication style meant directly taking a stand on issues whether positive or negative. "Dissent" cultures like Germany, the United Kingdom, Sweden, and Greece favored high levels of disagreement in communication with relatively low levels of agreement. Nigeria, India, and Vietnam were found to be high in agreement and low in disagreement in communication.

The results of studies of this nature should always be considered carefully in light of the large differences we also find within cultures. Some individuals from India may well value negative opinions and active disagreement from others, whereas some Germans might prefer to focus on areas of shared values. However, some patterning of responses across cultures does indicate a real difference in preferences for communication styles.

Sources: P. B. Smith, "Communication Styles as Dimensions of National Culture," *Journal of Cross-Cultural Psychology* 42, no. 2 (2011), pp. 216–233; and M. G. Kittler, D. Rygl, and A. Mackinnon, "Beyond Culture or Beyond Control? Reviewing the Use of Hall's High-/Low-Context Concept," *International Journal of Cross Cultural Management* 11, no. 1 (2011), pp. 63–82.

A Cultural Guide

When communicating with people from a different culture, what can you do to reduce misinterpretations? Begin by trying to assess the cultural context. You're likely to have fewer difficulties if it's similar to yours. The following rules can be helpful:[63]

1. **Assume differences until similarity is proven.**   Most of us assume others are more similar to us than they actually are. You are less likely to err if you assume they are different from you until proven otherwise.
2. **Emphasize description rather than interpretation or evaluation.** Interpreting or evaluating what someone has said or done draws more on your own culture and background than on the observed situation. So delay judgment until you've had sufficient time to observe and interpret the situation from the differing perspectives of all concerned.
3. **Practice empathy.**   Before sending a message, put yourself in the recipient's shoes. What are his or her values, experiences, and frames of reference? What do you know about his or her education, upbringing, and background that can give you added insight? Try to see the other person as he or she really is.
4. **Treat your interpretations as a working hypothesis.**   Once you've developed an explanation for a new situation or think you empathize with someone from a foreign culture, treat your interpretation as a hypothesis that needs further testing rather than as a certainty. Carefully assess the feedback recipients provide you, to see whether it confirms your hypothesis. For important decisions or communiqués, check with other foreign and home-country colleagues to make sure your interpretations are on target.

Social Networking Is Good Business

POINT

Facebook has passed a half a billion users for a reason. It's an inspired idea that serves many useful purposes for organizations and employees alike. Other social networking and media sites like Twitter are not far behind.

Employers can learn a lot about prospective hires by examining their Facebook (or other social networking) page. UPS recently ramped up its use of social networking to recruit. "Our reason for using social media is because that's where we think the applicants are," says a UPS manager in charge of recruitment. Applicants likewise can learn a lot about an organization by analyzing its online presence.

Facebook and other social networks are also great ways for employees to communicate with one another, particularly when they work in geographically dispersed locales and do an increasing amount of their work remotely. Banning or discouraging employees from using social media needlessly places each employee in a communications silo. One social media expert said the Millennial generation "is horrified at how unconnected people in many organizations are." Many firms, like UPS, are embracing social networking, though. IBM developed its own social networking software—called w3—to link its 400,000 employees across the world. IBM manager John Rooney says the software "contributes to the integration of our company on a global basis. It's seen as part of our ability to succeed."

In some companies, teams create Facebook groups around their projects to foster teamwork and open the lines of communication. Pushed to its full potential, social networking can even change a company's culture given its open, democratic, and transparent nature. "You better believe it can democratize a company," said one workplace expert. Isn't that what we want?"

COUNTERPOINT

There's no doubt social networking has exploded. There is significant doubt, however, that this explosion is beneficial to employees and to organizations. Although there are many dangers in social networking, let's focus on three.

First, companies can get into legal hot water by looking into applicants' social networking profiles. Equal Employment Opportunity laws require companies to hire without respect to race, sex, age, religion, national origin, or disability. Yet you can learn all these things from someone's profile. And that's not the only legal minefield. Recently, when a Chicago-area employee was reprimanded for posting her frustrations with her boss on her Facebook page, the National Labor Relations Board ruled against the company.

Second, social networks are risky for employees and applicants too. They were originally established to connect friends— and that remains their primary purpose. When employers snoop into an employee or applicant's Facebook page, fairly or not, they won't judge the information and its informality as dialogue among friends. Rather, they'll use it to draw the wrong conclusions. As one employment expert says, "While employers shouldn't use affiliations with social networks or your personal posts as reasons not to hire you, why take the risk?"

Finally, and perhaps most important, today nearly all of us suffer from communication overload, and social networking only adds to it. "There are so many things coming at you," says 29-year-old manager Jose Huitron. "Sometimes it can be so overwhelming," says George Washington University student Ben Yarmis. Scores of research studies show that the growth in social networking has limited people's attention spans and increased distractions. Says one neuroscientist who has studied the effect of social networking on how the mind works: "We are exposing our brains to an environment and asking them to do things we weren't necessarily evolved to do. We know already there are consequences."

Sources: J. A. Segal, "Dancing on the Edge of a Volcano," HR Magazine (April 2011), pp. 83–86; T. L. Griffith, "Tapping Into Social-Media Smarts," The Wall Street Journal (April 25, 2011), p. R6; L. Petrecca, "More Grads Use Social Media to Job Hunt," USA Today (April 5, 2011), p. B1; J. Swartz, "Communications Overload," USA Today (February 2, 2011), pp. 1B–2B; S. Ladika, "Socially Evolved," Workforce Management (September 2010), pp. 18–22; M. Richtel, "Hooked on Gadgets, and Paying a Mental Price," The New York Times (June 6, 2010), pp. A1, A12, A13; and A. Clark, "Watch What You're Posting: Your Boss May Be Watching," Gainesville Sun (February 19, 2011), pp. 1B, 5B.

How Good Are My Listening Skills?

In the Self-Assessment Library (available on CD or online), take assessment II.A.2 (How Good Are My Listening Skills?).

MyManagementLab

Now that you have finished this chapter, go back to **www.mymanagementlab.com** to continue practicing and applying the concepts you've learned.

Summary and Implications for Managers

You've probably discovered the link between communication and employee satisfaction in this chapter: the less uncertainty, the greater the satisfaction. Distortions, ambiguities, and incongruities between verbal and nonverbal messages all increase uncertainty and reduce satisfaction.[64]

- The less distortion, the more employees will receive goals, feedback, and other management messages as intended.[65] This, in turn, should reduce ambiguities and clarify the group's task.
- Extensive use of vertical, lateral, and informal channels also increases communication flow, reduces uncertainty, and improves group performance and satisfaction.
- Perfect communication is unattainable. Yet a positive relationship exists between effective communication and worker productivity.[66] Choosing the correct channel, being an effective listener, and using feedback can make for more effective communication.
- Whatever the sender's expectations, the message as decoded in the receiver's mind represents his or her reality. And this reality will determine performance, along with the individual's level of motivation and degree of satisfaction.
- Because we gather so much meaning from the way a message is communicated, the potential for misunderstanding in electronic communication is great despite its advantages .
- We sometimes process messages relatively automatically, while at other times we use a more effortful, controlled process. Make sure you use communication strategies appropriate to your audience and the type of message you're sending.
- Finally, by keeping in mind communication barriers such as gender and culture, we can overcome them and increase our communication effectiveness.

QUESTIONS FOR REVIEW

1 What are the primary functions of the communication process in organizations?

2 What are the key parts of the communication process, and how do you distinguish formal and informal communication?

3 What are the differences among downward, upward, and lateral communication?

4 What are the unique challenges to oral, written, and nonverbal communication?

5 What are the advantages and challenges of electronic communication?

6 What are the main forms of electronic communication? What are their unique benefits and challenges?

7 What is the difference between automatic and controlled processing of persuasive messages?

8 What are some common barriers to effective communication?

9 What unique problems underlie cross-cultural communication?

EXPERIENTIAL EXERCISE An Absence of Nonverbal Communication

This exercise will help you to see the value of nonverbal communication to interpersonal relations.

1. The class is to split up into pairs (party A and party B).
2. Party A is to select a topic from the following list:
   a. Managing in the Middle East is significantly different from managing in North America.
   b. Employee turnover in an organization can be functional.
   c. Some conflict in an organization is good.
   d. Whistle-blowers do more harm than good for an organization.
   e. An employer has a responsibility to provide every employee with an interesting and challenging job.
   f. Everyone should register to vote.
   g. Organizations should require all employees to undergo regular drug tests.
   h. Individuals who have majored in business or economics make better employees than those who have majored in history or English.
   i. The place where you get your college degree is more important in determining your career success than what you learn while you're there.
   j. It's unethical for a manager to purposely distort communications to get a favorable outcome.
3. Party B is to choose a position on this topic (for example, arguing *against* the view "Some conflict in an organization is good"). Party A now must automatically take the opposite position.
4. The two parties have 10 minutes in which to debate their topic. The catch is that the individuals can only communicate verbally. They may *not* use gestures, facial movements, body movements, or any other nonverbal communication. It may help for each party to sit on their hands to remind them of their restrictions and to maintain an expressionless look.
5. After the debate is over, form groups of six to eight and spend 15 minutes discussing the following:
   a. How effective was communication during these debates?
   b. What barriers to communication existed?
   c. What purposes does nonverbal communication serve?
   d. Relate the lessons learned in this exercise to problems that might occur when communicating on the telephone or through e-mail.

ETHICAL DILEMMA Pitfalls of E-Mail

While e-mail may be a very useful—even indispensable—form of communication in organizations, it certainly has its limits and dangers. Indeed, e-mail can get you into trouble with more people, more quickly, than almost any other form of communication.

Ask Bill Cochran. Cochran, 44, is a manager at Richmond Group, a Dallas-based advertising agency. As Richmond was gearing up to produce a Superbowl ad for one its clients—Bridgestone—Cochran's boss sent an e-mail to 200 people describing the internal competition to determine which ad idea would be presented. Cochran chose the occasion to give a pep talk to his team. Using "locker room talk," he composed an e-mail criticizing the other Richmond teams, naming employees he thought would provide them real competition—and those who wouldn't.

What Cochran did next—hit the Send key—seemed so innocuous. But it was a keystroke he would soon wish he could undo. Shortly after he sent the e-mail, a co-worker, Wendy Mayes, wrote to him: "Oh God . . . Bill. You just hit REPLY ALL!"

Questions

1. After realizing what he had done, how should Cochran have responded to this situation?
2. After the incident, Mayes says of Cochran: "His name soon became synonymous with 'idiotic behavior' such as 'don't pull a Cochran.'" Is it unethical to participate in such ribbing?
3. Kaspar Rorsted, CEO of Henkil, a consumer and industrial products company based in Germany, says that copying others on e-mails is overused. "It's

a waste of time," he said. "If they want to write me, they can write me. People often copy me to cover their back." Do you agree? How can you decide when copying others is necessary vs. "a waste of time"?

Sources: E. Bernstein, "Reply All: The Button Everyone Loves to Hate," *The Wall Street Journal* (March 8, 2011), pp. D1, D4; and A. Bryant, "No Need to Hit The 'Send' Key. Just Talk to Me," *The New York Times* (August 29, 2010), p. 2.

CASE INCIDENT 1   Using Social Media to Your Advantage

As you know, social media have transformed the way we interact. The transparent, rapid-fire communication they make possible means people can spread information about companies more rapidly than ever.

Do organizations understand yet how to use social media effectively? Perhaps not. As recently as 2010, only 19 of the top 50 chief executives in the world had Facebook accounts, only 6 had LinkedIn pages, and only 2 regularly used Twitter or blogs to communicate. Many executives are wary of these new technologies because they cannot always control the outcomes of their communications. However, whether they are directly involved with social media or not, companies should recognize that these messages are out there, so it behooves them to make their voices heard. And social media can be an important way to learn about emerging trends. André Schneider, chief operating officer of the World Economic Forum, uses feedback from LinkedIn discussion groups and Facebook friends to discover emerging trends and issues worldwide. Padmasree Warrior, chief technology officer of Cisco, has used social media to refine her presentations before a "test" audience.

The first step in developing a social media strategy is establishing a brand for your communications—define what you want your social media presence to express. Experts recommend that companies begin their social media strategy by leveraging their internal corporate networks to test their strategy in a medium that's easier to control. Most companies already have the technology to use social media through their corporate Web sites. Begin by using these platforms for communicating with employees and facilitating social networks for general information sharing.

As social networking expert Soumitra Dutta from Insead notes, "My advice is to build your audience slowly and be selective about your contacts."

Despite the potential advantages, companies also need to be aware of significant drawbacks to social media. First, it's very difficult to control social media communications. Microsoft found this out when the professional blogger it hired spent more time promoting himself than getting positive information out about the company. Second, important intellectual capital might leak out. Companies need to establish very clear policies and procedures to ensure that sensitive information about ongoing corporate strategies is not disseminated via social media. Finally, managers should maintain motivation and interest beyond their initial forays into social media. A site that's rarely updated can send a very negative message about the organization's level of engagement with the world.

Questions

1. Do you think organizations need to have a social media presence today? Are the drawbacks sufficient to make you think it's better for them to avoid certain media?

2. What features would you look for in a social media outlet? What types of information would you avoid making part of your social media strategy?

3. Which social media sources do you think are most useful for organizations to send communications to external stakeholders, like stockholders or customers? Are different social media more appropriate for communicating with employees?

4. What do you think is the future direction of social media? How might emerging technologies change them?

Sources: S. Dutta, "What's Your Personal Social Media Strategy," *Harvard Business Review* (November 2010), pp. 127–130; and G. Connors, "10 Social Media Commandments for Employers," *Workforce Management Online* (February 2010), www.workforce.com.

CASE INCIDENT 2   Should Companies That Fire Shoot First?

In the recessions in the early 1990s and after the 2001 terrorist attacks, layoffs were fairly private affairs. News often leaked out to local and national media outlets, but companies did their best to keep it as quiet as possible. Given the growth of the Internet in general, and of social networking sites in particular, that's no longer possible.

When Starbucks laid off employees in 2008 and 2009, the Web site StarbucksGossip.com received a barrage of posts from disgruntled employees. One 10-year employee wrote, "This company is going to lose every great partner that it has. I am sick and tired of being blamed for not meeting my budget when the economy is in a recession.

I used to be proud of my company . . . now I am embarrassed and feel physically ill every time I have to go to work."

Some companies are taking a proactive approach. When Tesla Motors laid off employees, its CEO Elon Musk posted a blog entry about it just before announcing the layoffs internally. "We had to say something to prevent articles being written that were not accurate," he said.

"Today, whatever you say inside a company will end up in a blog," says Rusy Rueff, a former executive at PepsiCo. "So, you have a choice as a company—you can either be proactive and say, 'Here's what's going on,' or you can allow someone else to write the story for you."

Illustrating the perils of *ignoring* the blogosphere, when newspaper giant Gannett announced it was laying off 10 percent of its employees, it posted no blog entries and made no statement. Jim Hopkins, a 20-year veteran who left the company just before the layoffs, writes the unofficial Gannett Blog. "I try to give the unvarnished truth. I don't think the company offers the same level of candor

to employees," he said. Gannett spokeswoman Tara Connell replied, "We attempt to make those personal communications happen as quickly as possible."

Says blog expert Andy Sernovitz, "There are hold-out companies that still wish there was traditional P.R. control of the message, but that day is long over."

Questions

1. Do you think Tesla CEO Elon Musk did the right thing when he blogged about impending layoffs just before announcing them to employees? Why or why not?

2. Do you think employees have a responsibility to be careful when they blog about their company? Why or why not?

3. Do you think employees who blog about their companies have an ethical responsibility to disclose their identities?

4. How can a company develop a policy for handling communication of sensitive issues inside, and outside, the company?

Sources: Based on C. C. Miller, "In Era of Blog Sniping, Companies Shoot First," *The New York Times* (November 5, 2008), pp. B1, B11; M. Allison, "More Layoffs Expected at Starbucks," *Seattle Times* (January 24, 2009), seattletimes.nwsource.com; and C. Hirschman, "Giving Voice to Employee Concerns," *HR Magazine* (August 2008), pp. 51–53.

ENDNOTES

1. See, for example, R. S. Lau and A. T. Cobb, "Understanding the Connections between Relationship Conflict and Performance: The Intervening Roles of Trust and Exchange," *Journal of Organizational Behavior* 31, no. 6 (2010), pp. 898–917; and M. Olekalns, L. L. Putnam, L. R. Weingart, and L. Metcalf, "Communication Processes and Conflict Management: The Psychology of Conflict and Conflict Management in Organizations," in C. K. W. De Dreu and M. J. Gelfand, (eds.), *The Psychology of Conflict and Conflict Management in Organizations.* (New York: Taylor & Francis Group, 2008) pp. 81–114.

2. "Employers Cite Communication Skills, Honesty/Integrity as Key for Job Candidates," *IPMA-HR Bulletin* (March 23, 2007), p. 1.

3. W. G. Scott and T. R. Mitchell, *Organization Theory: A Structural and Behavioral Analysis* (Homewood, IL: Irwin, 1976).

4. D. K. Berlo, *The Process of Communication* (New York: Holt, Rinehart & Winston, 1960), pp. 30–32; see also K. Byron, "Carrying Too Heavy a Load? The Communication and Miscommunication of Emotion by Email," *The Academy of Management Review* 33, no. 2 (2008), pp. 309–327.

5. J. Langan-Fox, "Communication in Organizations: Speed, Diversity, Networks, and Influence on Organizational Effectiveness, Human Health, and Relationships," in N. Anderson, D. S. Ones, H. K. Sinangil, and C. Viswesvaran (Eds.), *Handbook of Industrial, Work and Organizational Psychology*, vol. 2 (Thousand Oaks, CA: Sage, 2001), p. 190.

6. R. L. Simpson, "Vertical and Horizontal Communication in Formal Organizations," *Administrative Science Quarterly* (September 1959), pp. 188–196; A. G. Walker and J. W. Smither,

"A Five-Year Study of Upward Feedback: What Managers Do with Their Results Matter," *Personnel Psychology* (Summer 1999), pp. 393–424; and J. W. Smither and A. G. Walker, "Are the Characteristics of Narrative Comments Related to Improvement in Multirater Feedback Ratings Over Time?" *Journal of Applied Psychology* 89, no. 3 (June 2004), pp. 575–581.

7. P. Dvorak, "How Understanding the 'Why' of Decisions Matters," *The Wall Street Journal* (March 19, 2007), p. B3.

8. T. Neeley and P. Leonardi, "Effective Managers Say the Same Thing Twice (or More)," *Harvard Business Review* (May 2011), pp. 38–39.

9. J. Ewing, "Nokia: Bring on the Employee Rants," *BusinessWeek* (June 22, 2009), p. 50.

10. E. Nichols, "Hyper-Speed Managers," *HRMagazine* (April 2007), pp. 107–110.

11. L. Dulye, "Get Out of Your Office," *HRMagazine* (July 2006), pp. 99–101.

12. L. S. Rashotte, "What Does That Smile Mean? The Meaning of Nonverbal Behaviors in Social Interaction," *Social Psychology Quarterly* (March 2002), pp. 92–102.

13. J. Fast, *Body Language* (Philadelphia: M. Evan, 1970), p. 7.

14. A. Mehrabian, *Nonverbal Communication* (Chicago: Aldine-Atherton, 1972).

15. N. M. Henley, "Body Politics Revisited: What Do We Know Today?" in P. J. Kalbfleisch and M. J. Cody (eds.), *Gender, Power, and Communication in Human Relationships* (Hillsdale, NJ: Lawrence Erlbaum, 1995), pp. 27–61.

16. See, for example, N. B. Kurland and L. H. Pelled, "Passing the Word: Toward a Model of Gossip and Power in the Workplace," *Academy of Management Review* (April 2000), pp. 428–438; and G. Michelson, A. van Iterson,

and K. Waddington, "Gossip in Organizations: Contexts, Consequences, and Controversies," *Group and Organization Management* 35, no. 4 (2010), pp. 371–390.

17. Cited in "Heard It Through the Grapevine," *Forbes* (February 10, 1997), p. 22.

18. G. Van Hoye and F. Lievens, "Tapping the Grapevine: A Closer Look at Word-of-Mouth as a Recruitment Source," *Journal of Applied Psychology* 94, no. 2 (2009), pp. 341–352.

19. K. Davis, "Management Communication and the Grapevine," *Harvard Business Review* (September–October 1953), pp. 43–49.

20. R. L. Rosnow and G. A. Fine, *Rumor and Gossip: The Social Psychology of Hearsay* (New York: Elsevier, 1976).

21. J. K. Bosson, A. B. Johnson, K. Niederhoffer, and W. B. Swann, Jr., "Interpersonal Chemistry Through Negativity: Bonding by Sharing Negative Attitudes About Others," *Personal Relationships* 13 (2006), pp. 135–150.

22. T. J. Grosser, V. Lopez-Kidwell, and G. Labianca, "A Social Network Analysis of Positive and Negative Gossip in Organizational Life," *Group and Organization Management* 35, no. 2 (2010), pp. 177–212.

23. B. Gates, "How I Work," *Fortune* (April 17, 2006), money.cnn.com.

24. D. Brady, "*!#?@ the E-mail. Can We Talk?" *BusinessWeek* (December 4, 2006), p. 109.

25. E. Binney, "Is E-mail the New Pink Slip?" *HR Magazine* (November 2006), pp. 32–33; and R. L. Rundle, "Critical Case: How an Email Rant Jolted a Big HMO," *The Wall Street Journal* (April 24, 2007), pp. A1, A16.

26. S. Hourigan, "62 Trillion Spam Emails Cause Huge Carbon Footprint," *Courier Mail* (April 17, 2009), www.news.com.au/couriermail.

27. R. Stross, "The Daily Struggle to Avoid Burial by E-Mail," *New York Times* (April 21, 2008), p. BU5; and H. Rhodes, "You've Got Mail . . . Again," *Gainesville Sun* (September 29, 2008), pp. 1D, 6D.

28. C. Byron, "Carrying Too Heavy a Load? The Communication and Miscommunication of Emotion by Email," *Academy of Management Review* 33, no. 2 (2008), pp. 309–327.

29. D. Goleman, "Flame First, Think Later: New Clues to E-mail Misbehavior," *The New York Times* (February 20, 2007), p. D5; and E. Krell, "The Unintended Word," *HRMagazine* (August 2006), pp. 50–54.

30. J. E. Hall, M. T. Kobata, and M. Denis, "Employees and E-mail Privacy Rights," *Workforce Management* (June 2010), p. 10.

31. R. Zeidner, "Keeping E-mail in Check," *HRMagazine* (June 2007), pp. 70–74; "E-mail May Be Hazardous to Your Career," *Fortune* (May 14, 2007), p. 24; and J. D. Glater, "Open Secrets," *The New York Times* (June 27, 2008), pp. B1, B5.

32. A. Williams, "Mind Your BlackBerry or Mind Your Manners," *The New York Times* (June 21, 2009), www.nytimes.com.

33. "Survey Finds Mixed Reviews on Checking E-mail During Meetings," *IPMA-HR Bulletin* (April 27, 2007), p. 1.

34. K. Gurchiek, "Shoddy Writing Can Trip Up Employees, Organizations," *SHRM Online* (April 27, 2006), pp. 1–2.

35. T. Henneman, "Companies Making Friends with Social Media," *Workforce Management*, (April 2010), p. 4.

36. D. Lidsky, "It's Not Just Who You Know," *Fast Company* (May 2007), p. 56.

37. "Bosses Battle Risk by Firing E-mail, IM & Blog Violators," *IPMA-HR Bulletin* (January 12, 2007), pp. 1–2; G. Krants, "Blogging with a Vendetta," *Workforce Week* 8, no. 25 (June 10, 2007), www.workforce.com/section/quick_takes/49486_3.html; B. Leonard, "Blogs Can Present New Challenges to Employers," *SHRM Online* (March 13, 2006), pp. 1–2; and J. Greenwald, "Monitoring Communications? Know Legal Pitfalls," *Workforce Management Online* (February 2011), www.workforce.com.

38. E. Agnvall, "Meetings Go Virtual," *HR Magazine* (January 2009), pp. 74–77.

39. C. Huff, "Staying Afloat in a Digital Flood," *Workforce Management Online* (July 2008), www.workforce.com.

40. M. Richtel, "Lost in E-mail, Tech Firms Face Self-Made Beast," *The New York Times* (June 14, 2008), pp. A1, A14; and M. Johnson, "Quelling Distraction," *HR Magazine* (August 2008), pp. 43–46.

41. W. R. Boswell and J. B. Olson-Buchanan, "The Use of Communication Technologies After Hours: The Role of Work-Attitudes and Work-Life Conflict," *Journal of Management* 33, no. 4 (2007), pp. 592–610.

42. "At Many Companies, Hunt for Leakers Expands Arsenal of Monitoring Tactics," *The Wall Street Journal* (September 11, 2006), pp. B1, B3; and B. J. Alge, G. A. Ballinger, S. Tangirala, and J. L. Oakley, "Information Privacy in Organizations: Empowering Creative and Extrarole Performance," *Journal of Applied Psychology* 91, No. 1 (2006), pp. 221–232.

43. See R. L. Daft and R. H. Lengel, "Information Richness: A New Approach to Managerial Behavior and Organization Design," in B. M. Staw and L. L. Cummings (eds.), *Research in Organizational Behavior*, vol. 6 (Greenwich, CT: JAI Press, 1984), pp. 191–233; R. L. Daft and R. H. Lengel, "Organizational Information Requirements, Media Richness, and Structural Design," *Managerial Science* (May 1986), pp. 554–572; R. E. Rice, "Task Analyzability, Use of New Media, and Effectiveness," *Organization Science* (November 1992), pp. 475–500; S. G. Straus and J. E. McGrath, "Does the Medium Matter? The Interaction of Task Type and Technology on Group Performance and Member Reaction," *Journal of Applied Psychology* (February 1994), pp. 87–97; L. K. Trevino, J. Webster, and E. W. Stein, "Making Connections: Complementary Influences on Communication Media Choices, Attitudes, and Use," *Organization Science* (March–April 2000), pp. 163–182; and N. Kock, "The Psychobiological Model: Towards a New Theory of Computer-Mediated Communication Based on Darwinian Evolution," *Organization Science* 15, no. 3 (May–June 2004), pp. 327–348.

44. E. Frauenheim, "Communicating For Engagement During Tough Times," *Workforce Management Online* (April 2010), www.workforce.com.

45. R. E. Petty and P. Briñol, "Persuasion: From Single to Multiple to Metacognitive Processes," *Perspectives on Psychological Science* 3, no. 2 (2008), pp. 137–147; F. A. White, M. A. Charles, and J. K. Nelson, "The Role of Persuasive Arguments in Changing Affirmative Action Attitudes and Expressed Behavior in Higher Education," *Journal of Applied Psychology* 93, no. 6 (2008), pp. 1271–1286.

46. B. T. Johnson, and A. H. Eagly, "Effects of Involvement on Persuasion: A Meta-Analysis," *Psychological Bulletin* 106, no. 2 (1989), pp. 290–314; and K. L. Blankenship and D. T. Wegener, "Opening the Mind to Close It: Considering a Message in Light of Important Values Increases Message Processing and Later Resistance to Change," *Journal of Personality and Social Psychology* 94, no. 2 (2008), pp. 196–213.

47. See, for example, Y. H. M. See, R. E. Petty, and L. R. Fabrigar, "Affective and Cognitive Meta-Bases of Attitudes: Unique Effects of Information Interest and Persuasion," *Journal of Personality and Social Psychology* 94, no. 6 (2008), pp. 938–955; M. S. Key, J. E. Edlund, B. J. Sagarin, and G. Y. Bizer, "Individual Differences in Susceptibility to Mindlessness," *Personality and Individual Differences* 46, no. 3 (2009), pp. 261–264 and M. Reinhard and M. Messner, "The Effects of Source Likeability and Need for Cognition on Advertising Effectiveness Under Explicit Persuasion," *Journal of Consumer Behavior* 8, no. 4 (2009), pp. 179–191.

48. P. Briñol, R. E. Petty, and J. Barden, "Happiness Versus Sadness as a Determinant of Thought Confidence in Persuasion: A Self-Validation Analysis," *Journal of Personality and Social Psychology* 93, no. 5 (2007), pp. 711–727.

49. R. C. Sinclair, S. E. Moore, M. M. Mark, A. S. Soldat, and C. A. Lavis, "Incidental Moods, Source Likeability, and Persuasion: Liking Motivates Message Elaboration in Happy People," *Cognition and Emotion* 24, no. 6 (2010), pp. 940–961; and V. Griskevicius, M. N. Shiota, and S. L. Neufeld, "Influence of Different Positive Emotions on Persuasion Processing: A Functional Evolutionary Approach," *Emotion* 10, no. 2 (2010), pp. 190–206.

50. J. Sandberg, "The Jargon Jumble," *The Wall Street Journal* (October 24, 2006), p. B1.

51. E. W. Morrison and F. J. Milliken, "Organizational Silence: A Barrier to Change and Development in a Pluralistic World," *Academy of Management Review* 25, no. 4 (2000), pp. 706–725; and B. E. Ashforth and V. Anand, "The Normalization of Corruption in Organizations," *Research in Organizational Behavior* 25 (2003), pp. 1–52.

52. F. J. Milliken, E. W. Morrison, and P. F. Hewlin, "An Exploratory Study of Employee Silence: Issues That Employees Don't Communicate Upward and Why," *Journal of Management Studies* 40, no. 6 (2003), pp. 1453–1476.

53. S. Tangirala and R. Ramunujam, "Employee Silence on Critical Work Issues: The Cross-Level Effects of Procedural Justice Climate," *Personnel Psychology* 61, no. 1 (2008), pp. 37–68; and F. Bowen and K. Blackmon, "Spirals of Silence: The Dynamic Effects of Diversity on Organizational Voice," *Journal of Management Studies* 40, no. 6 (2003), pp. 1393–1417.

54. B. R. Schlenker and M. R. Leary, "Social Anxiety and Self-Presentation: A Conceptualization and Model," *Psychological Bulletin* 92 (1982), pp. 641–669; and L. A. Withers, and L. L. Vernon, "To Err Is Human: Embarrassment, Attachment, and Communication Apprehension," *Personality and Individual Differences* 40, no. 1 (2006), pp. 99–110.

55. See, for instance, S. K. Opt and D. A. Loffredo, "Rethinking Communication Apprehension: A Myers-Briggs Perspective," *Journal of Psychology* (September 2000), pp. 556–570; and B. D. Blume, G. F. Dreher, and T. T. Baldwin, "Examining the Effects of Communication Apprehension within Assessment Centres," *Journal of Occupational and Organizational Psychology* 83, no. 3 (2010), pp. 663–671.

56. See, for example, J. A. Daly and J. C. McCroskey, "Occupational Desirability and Choice as a Function of Communication Apprehension," *Journal of Counseling Psychology* 22, no. 4 (1975), pp. 309–313; and T. L. Rodebaugh, "I Might Look OK, But I'm Still Doubtful, Anxious, and Avoidant: The Mixed Effects of Enhanced Video Feedback on Social Anxiety Symptoms," *Behaviour Research & Therapy* 42, no. 12 (December 2004), pp. 1435–1451.

57. B. M. Depaulo, D. A. Kashy, S. E. Kirkendol, M. M. Wyer, and J. A. Epstein, "Lying in Everyday Life," *Journal of Personality and Social Psychology* 70, No. 5 (1996), pp. 979–995; and K. B. Serota, T. R. Levine, and F. J. Boster, "The Prevalence of Lying in America: Three Studies of Self-Reported Lies," *Human Communication Research* 36, No. 1. (2010), pp. 2–25.

58. DePaulo, Kashy, Kirkendol, Wyer, and Epstein, "Lying in Everyday Life"; and C. E. Naguin, T. R. Kurtzberg, and L. Y. Belkin, "The Finer Points of Lying Online: E-Mail Versus Pen and Paper," *Journal of Applied Psychology* 95, No. 2 (2010), pp. 387–394.

59. A. Vrij, P. A. Granhag, and S. Porter, "Pitfalls and Opportunities in Nonverbal and Verbal Lie Detection," *Psychological Science in the Public Interest* 11, No. 3 (2010), pp. 89–121.

60. R. E. Axtell, *Gestures: The Do's and Taboos of Body Language Around the World* (New York: Wiley, 1991); Watson Wyatt Worldwide, "Effective Communication: A Leading Indicator of Financial Performance—2005/2006 Communication ROI Study," www.watsonwyatt.com/research/resrender .asp?id=w-868; and A. Markels, "Turning the Tide at P&G," *U.S. News & World Report* (October 30, 2006), p. 69.

61. See M. Munter, "Cross-Cultural Communication for Managers," *Business Horizons* (May–June 1993), pp. 75–76; and H. Ren and B. Gray, "Repairing Relationship Conflict: How Violation Types and Culture Influence the Effectiveness of Restoration Rituals," *Academy of Management Review* 34, no. 1 (2009), pp. 105–126.

62. See E. T. Hall, *Beyond Culture* (Garden City, NY: Anchor Press/Doubleday, 1976); W. L. Adair, "Integrative Sequences and Negotiation Outcome in Same- and Mixed-Culture Negotiations," *International Journal of Conflict Management* 14, no. 3–4 (2003), pp. 1359–1392; W. L. Adair and J. M. Brett, "The Negotiation Dance: Time, Culture, and Behavioral Sequences in Negotiation," *Organization Science* 16, no. 1 (2005), pp. 33–51; E. Giebels and P. J. Taylor, "Interaction Patterns in Crisis Negotiations: Persuasive Arguments and Cultural Differences," *Journal of Applied Psychology* 94, no. 1 (2009), pp. 5–19; and M. G. Kittler, D. Rygl, and A. Mackinnon, "Beyond Culture or Beyond Control? Reviewing the Use of Hall's High-/Low-Context Concept," *International Journal of Cross-Cultural Management* 11, no. 1 (2011), pp. 63–82.

63. N. Adler, *International Dimensions of Organizational Behavior*, 4th ed. (Cincinnati, OH: South-Western Publishing, 2002), p. 94.

64. See, for example. R. S. Schuler, "A Role Perception Transactional Process Model for Organizational Communication-Outcome Relationships," *Organizational Behavior and Human Performance* (April 1979), pp. 268–291.

65. J. P. Walsh, S. J. Ashford, and T. E. Hill, "Feedback Obstruction: The Influence of the Information Environment on Employee Turnover Intentions," *Human Relations* (January 1985), pp. 23–46.

66. S. A. Hellweg and S. L. Phillips, "Communication and Productivity in Organizations: A State-of-the-Art Review," in *Proceedings of the 40th Annual Academy of Management Conference*, Detroit, 1980, pp. 188–192. See also B. A. Bechky, "Sharing Meaning Across Occupational Communities: The Transformation of Understanding on a Production Floor," *Organization Science* 14, no. 3 (May–June 2003), pp. 312–330.

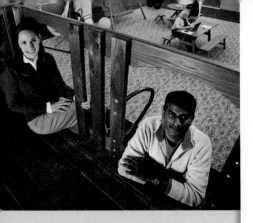

MAKING GOOGLE'S LEADERS

In its 14-year history, Google has established a strong culture around some simple principles: Hire smart people. Leave them alone. Allow the engineers and programmers to do their job. If they are stuck, they can turn to their boss, whose technical expertise put him or her into that position in the first place.

In the past few years, however, Google has been studying its leader selection and development programs. The results of that study, called Project Oxygen, challenge some of Google's founding principles.

Project Oxygen analyzed more than 10,000 observations about managers across more than 100 variables. Michelle Donovan and Prasad Setty were closely involved in it, as was Google's Vice President for People Operations, Laszio Bock. "We want to understand what works at Google rather than what worked in any other organization" says Setty.

But there was a more strategic reason. "The starting point was that our best managers have teams that perform better, are retained better, are happier—they do everything better," says Bock. "So the biggest controllable factor that we could see was the quality of the manager, and how they sort of made things happen."

Project Oxygen uncovered eight competencies that separated effective from ineffective leaders. That technical competence was one of those eight wasn't surprising to Google. That it finished dead last on the list, however, was.

What finished first? The top three leadership competencies were:

1. **Be a good coach.** Provide specific, constructive feedback; have regular one-on-ones.
2. **Empower your team and don't micromanage.** Balance giving freedom with being available for advice.
3. **Express interest in team members' success and personal well-being.** Get to know your employees as people; make new members feel welcome.

What is Google doing with its list? It is using it for both leadership selection and development. Already some Google managers feel the training has helped them become better leaders. To make their case, Project Oxygen's team found an analytical approach invaluable. "The thing that moves or nudges Google is facts; they like information," says Donovan.

Sources: A. Bryant, "Google's Quest to Build a Better Boss," *The New York Times* (March 13, 2011), p. BU1–BU6; E. A. Cevallos, "Project Oxygen: Building Better Bosses," *BIZ-THINK* (April 13, 2011), downloaded from http://biz-think.blogspot.com/2011/04/project-oxygen-building-better-bosses.html on July 26, 2011; and R. L. Brandt, "Google Project Oxygen: Rules for Good Management," *Entrepreneur Watch* (March 12, 2011), downloaded July 26, 2011, from http://richardbrandt.blogs.com/entrepreneurwatch/2011/03/google-project-oxygen-rules-for-good-management.html.

LEARNING OBJECTIVES

After studying this chapter, you should be able to:

1 Define *leadership* and contrast leadership and management.

2 Summarize the conclusions of trait theories of leadership.

3 Identify the central tenets and main limitations of behavioral theories.

4 Assess contingency theories of leadership by their level of support.

5 Compare and contrast *charismatic* and *transformational leadership*.

6 Define *authentic leadership* and show why effective leaders exemplify ethics and trust.

7 Demonstrate the role mentoring plays in our understanding of leadership.

8 Address challenges to the effectiveness of leadership.

MyManagementLab

Access a host of interactive learning aids to help strengthen your understanding of the chapter concepts at **www.mymanagementlab.com**.

Leadership

12

*I am more afraid of an army of 100 sheep
led by a lion than an army of 100 lions
led by a sheep.* —Talleyrand

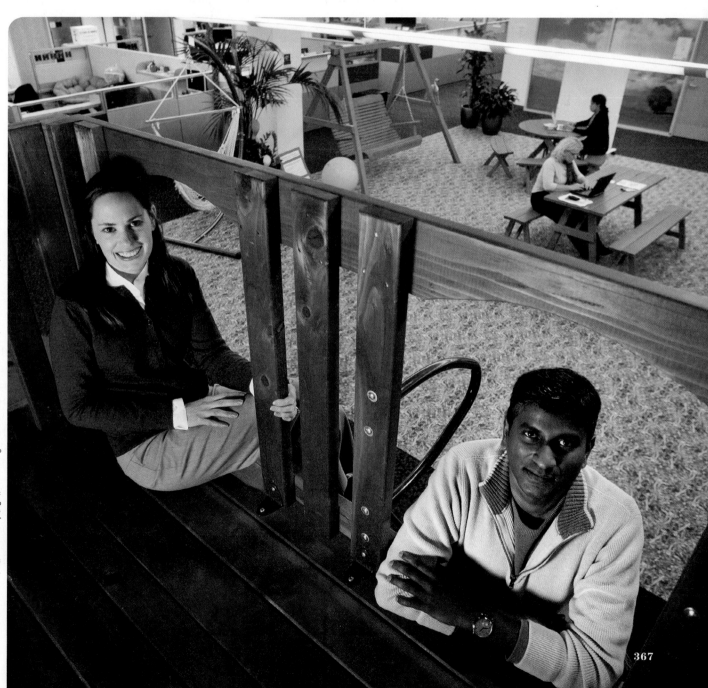

Photo: Michelle Donovan (left), Prasad Setty (right), at the Google HR offices. *Source:* Peter Dasilva/The New York Times/Redux Pictures.

367

A s the Google example shows, leadership styles differ considerably. So which styles, and which people, are most effective? These are some of the questions we'll tackle in this chapter. To assess yourself on a specific set of qualities that we'll discuss shortly, take the following self-assessment.

In this chapter, we look at what makes an effective leader and what differentiates leaders from nonleaders. First, we present trait theories, which dominated the study of leadership until the late 1940s. Then we discuss behavioral theories, popular until the late 1960s. Next, we introduce contingency and interactive theories. Finally, we discuss the most contemporary approaches: charismatic, transformational, and authentic leadership. Most of the research discussed in this chapter was conducted in English-speaking countries. We know very little about how culture might influence the validity of the theories, particularly in Eastern cultures. However, analysis of the Global Leadership and Organizational Behavior Effectiveness (GLOBE) research project has produced some useful preliminary insights that we discuss throughout.[1] But first, let's clarify what we mean by *leadership*.

SELF-ASSESSMENT LIBRARY

What's My Leadership Style?

In the Self-Assessment Library (available on CD and online) take assessment II.B.1 (What's My Leadership Style?) and answer the following questions.

1. How did you score on the two scales?
2. Do you think a leader can be both task oriented and people oriented? Do you think there are situations in which a leader has to make a choice between the two styles?
3. Do you think your leadership style will change over time? Why or why not?

What Is Leadership?

1 Define *leadership* and contrast leadership and management.

We define **leadership** as the ability to influence a group toward the achievement of a vision or set of goals. The source of this influence may be formal, such as that provided by managerial rank in an organization. But not all leaders are managers, nor, for that matter, are all managers leaders. Just because an organization provides its managers with certain formal rights is no assurance they will lead effectively. Nonsanctioned leadership—the ability to influence that arises outside the formal structure of the organization—is often as important or more important than formal influence. In other words, leaders can emerge from within a group as well as by formal appointment.

Organizations need strong leadership *and* strong management for optimal effectiveness. We need leaders today to challenge the status quo, create visions of the future, and inspire organizational members to want to achieve the visions. We also need managers to formulate detailed plans, create efficient organizational structures, and oversee day-to-day operations.

Trait Theories

2 Summarize the conclusions of trait theories of leadership.

Throughout history, strong leaders—Buddha, Napoleon, Mao, Churchill, Roosevelt, Reagan—have been described in terms of their traits. **Trait theories of leadership** thus focus on personal qualities and characteristics. We recognize leaders like South Africa's Nelson Mandela, Virgin Group CEO Richard Branson, Apple co-founder Steve Jobs, and American Express chairman Ken Chenault as *charismatic, enthusiastic,* and *courageous.* The search for personality, social, physical, or intellectual attributes that differentiate leaders from non-leaders goes back to the earliest stages of leadership research.

Early research efforts to isolate leadership traits resulted in a number of dead ends. A review in the late 1960s of 20 different studies identified nearly 80 leadership traits, but only 5 were common to 4 or more of the investigations.[2] By the 1990s, after numerous studies and analyses, about the best we could say was that most leaders "are not like other people," but the particular traits that characterized them varied a great deal from review to review.[3] It was a pretty confusing state of affairs.

A breakthrough, of sorts, came when researchers began organizing traits around the Big Five personality framework (see Chapter 5).[4] Most of the dozens of traits in various leadership reviews fit under one of the Big Five (ambition and energy are part of extraversion, for instance), giving strong support to traits as predictors of leadership.

The personal qualities and traits of Indra Nooyi make her a great leader. Nooyi is CEO and board chairman of PepsiCo, the second largest food and beverage firm in the world. She is described as fun-loving, sociable, agreeable, conscientious, emotionally stable, and open to experiences. Nooyi's personality traits have contributed to her job performance and career success. She joined PepsiCo in 1994 as head of corporate strategy and was promoted to president and chief financial officer before moving into the firm's top management position. Nooyi has been named one of the most powerful women in business and one of the most powerful women in the world.

Source: PRNewsFoto/PepsiCo, Ray Hand.

leadership *The ability to influence a group toward the achievement of a vision or set of goals.*

trait theories of leadership *Theories that consider personal qualities and characteristics that differentiate leaders from nonleaders.*

A comprehensive review of the leadership literature, when organized around the Big Five, has found extraversion to be the most important trait of effective leaders,[5] but it is more strongly related to the way leaders emerge than to their effectiveness. Sociable and dominant people are more likely to assert themselves in group situations, but leaders need to make sure they're not too assertive—one study found leaders who scored very high on assertiveness were less effective than those who were moderately high.[6]

Unlike agreeableness and emotional stability, conscientiousness and openness to experience also showed strong relationships to leadership, though not quite as strong as extraversion. Overall, the trait approach does have something to offer. Leaders who like being around people and are able to assert themselves (extraverted), who are disciplined and able to keep commitments they make (conscientious), and who are creative and flexible (open) do have an apparent advantage when it comes to leadership, suggesting good leaders do have key traits in common.

One reason is that conscientiousness and extraversion are positively related to leaders' self-efficacy, which explained most of the variance in subordinates' ratings of leader performance.[7] People are more likely to follow someone who is confident she's going in the right direction.

Another trait that may indicate effective leadership is emotional intelligence (EI), discussed in Chapter 4. Advocates of EI argue that without it, a person can have outstanding training, a highly analytical mind, a compelling vision, and an endless supply of terrific ideas but still not make a great leader. This may be especially true as individuals move up in an organization.[8] Why is EI so critical to effective leadership? A core component of EI is empathy. Empathetic leaders can sense others' needs, listen to what followers say (and don't say), and read the reactions of others. A leader who effectively displays and manages emotions will find it easier to influence the feelings of followers, by both expressing genuine sympathy and enthusiasm for good performance and by using irritation for those who fail to perform.[9]

The link between EI and leadership effectiveness may be worth investigating in greater detail.[10] Some recent research has demonstrated that people high in EI are more likely to emerge as leaders, even after taking cognitive ability and personality into account, which helps to answer some of the most significant criticisms of this research.[11]

Based on the latest findings, we offer two conclusions. First, contrary to what we believed 20 years ago and thanks to the Big Five, we can say that traits can predict leadership. Second, traits do a better job predicting the emergence of leaders and the appearance of leadership than actually distinguishing between *effective* and *ineffective* leaders.[12] The fact that an individual exhibits the traits and that others consider him or her a leader does not necessarily mean the leader is successful at getting the group to achieve its goals.

Behavioral Theories

3   Identify the central tenets and main limitations of behavioral theories.

The failures of early trait studies led researchers in the late 1940s through the 1960s to wonder whether there was something unique in the way effective leaders *behave*. Trait research provides a basis for *selecting* the right people for leadership. In contrast, **behavioral theories of leadership** implied we could *train* people to be leaders.

Morgan Smith is an employee-oriented leader. As owner and managing partner of Boneheads Restaurant in Lake Forest, California, Smith (left) takes a personal interest in the needs of his employees. Described as generous, kind, and cheerful, he shows respect for his employees and invests a great deal of time in helping them at work and assisting them in their personal lives such as donating food for their weddings. Smith's goal for his employees is for them to reach their full potential. During bi-weekly one-on-one meetings with employees, Smith serves as their leader, trainer, role model, and advisor. He also provides quarterly training for employees and includes them in reviewing the restaurant's profit and loss statement.

Source: o44/ZUMA Press/Newscom.

The most comprehensive theories resulted from the Ohio State Studies in the late 1940s,[13] which sought to identify independent dimensions of leader behavior. Beginning with more than a thousand dimensions, the studies narrowed the list to two that substantially accounted for most of the leadership behavior described by employees: *initiating structure* and *consideration*.

Initiating structure is the extent to which a leader is likely to define and structure his or her role and those of employees in the search for goal attainment. It includes behavior that attempts to organize work, work relationships, and goals. A leader high in initiating structure is someone who "assigns group members to particular tasks," "expects workers to maintain definite standards of performance," and "emphasizes the meeting of deadlines."

Consideration is the extent to which a person's job relationships are characterized by mutual trust, respect for employees' ideas, and regard for their feelings. A leader high in consideration helps employees with personal problems, is friendly and approachable, treats all employees as equals, and expresses appreciation and support. In a recent survey, when asked to indicate what most motivated them at work, 66 percent of employees mentioned appreciation.[14]

Leadership studies at the University of Michigan's Survey Research Center had similar objectives: to locate behavioral characteristics of leaders that appeared related to performance effectiveness. The Michigan group also came up with two behavioral dimensions: the **employee-oriented leader** emphasized

---

behavioral theories of leadership *Theories proposing that specific behaviors differentiate leaders from nonleaders.*

initiating structure *The extent to which a leader is likely to define and structure his or her role and those of subordinates in the search for goal attainment.*

consideration *The extent to which a leader is likely to have job relationships characterized by mutual trust, respect for subordinates' ideas, and regard for their feelings.*

employee-oriented leader *A leader who emphasizes interpersonal relations, takes a personal interest in the needs of employees, and accepts individual differences among members.*

interpersonal relationships by taking a personal interest in the needs of employees and accepting individual differences among them, and the **production-oriented leader** emphasized the technical or task aspects of the job, focusing on accomplishing the group's tasks. These dimensions are closely related to the Ohio State dimensions. Employee-oriented leadership is similar to consideration, and production-oriented leadership is similar to initiating structure. In fact, most leadership researchers use the terms synonymously.[15]

At one time, the results of testing behavioral theories were thought to be disappointing. However, a more recent review of 160 studies found the followers of leaders high in consideration were more satisfied with their jobs, were more motivated, and had more respect for their leader. Initiating structure was more strongly related to higher levels of group and organization productivity and more positive performance evaluations.

Some research from the GLOBE study suggests there are international differences in preference for initiating structure and consideration.[16] Based on the values of Brazilian employees, a U.S. manager leading a team in Brazil would need to be team oriented, participative, and humane. Leaders high in consideration would succeed best in this culture. As one Brazilian manager said in the GLOBE study, "We do not prefer leaders who take self-governing decisions and act alone without engaging the group. That's part of who we are." Compared to U.S. employees, the French have a more bureaucratic view of leaders and are less likely to expect them to be humane and considerate. A leader high in initiating structure (relatively task-oriented) will do best and can make decisions in a relatively autocratic manner. A manager who scores high on consideration (people oriented) may find that style backfiring in France. According to the GLOBE study, Chinese culture emphasizes being polite, considerate, and unselfish, but it also has a high performance orientation. Thus, consideration and initiating structure may both be important.

Summary of Trait Theories and Behavioral Theories

Leaders who have certain traits and who display consideration and structuring behaviors do appear to be more effective. Perhaps you're wondering whether conscientious leaders (trait) are more likely to be structuring (behavior) and extraverted leaders (trait) to be considerate (behavior). Unfortunately, we can't be sure there is a connection. Future research is needed to integrate these approaches.

Some leaders may have the right traits or display the right behaviors and still fail. As important as traits and behaviors are in identifying effective or ineffective leaders, they do not guarantee success. The context matters, too.

Contingency Theories

4   Assess contingency theories of leadership by their level of support.

Some tough-minded leaders seem to gain a lot of admirers when they take over struggling companies and help lead them out of the doldrums. Home Depot and Chrysler didn't hire former CEO Bob Nardelli for his winning personality. However, such leaders also seem to be quickly dismissed when the situation stabilizes.

The rise and fall of leaders like Bob Nardelli illustrate that predicting leadership success is more complex than isolating a few traits or behaviors. In their cases, what worked in very bad times and in very good times didn't seem to translate into long-term success. When researchers looked at situational influences, it appeared that under condition *a*, leadership style *x* would be appropriate, whereas style *y* was more suitable for condition *b*, and style *z* for condition *c*. But what *were* conditions *a, b, c?* We next consider three approaches to isolating situational variables: the Fiedler model, situational theory, path–goal theory, and the leader-participation model.

The Fiedler Model

Fred Fiedler developed the first comprehensive contingency model for leadership.[17] The **Fiedler contingency model** proposes that effective group performance depends on the proper match between the leader's style and the degree to which the situation gives the leader control.

Identifying Leadership Style   Fiedler believes a key factor in leadership success is the individual's basic leadership style. He created the **least preferred co-worker (LPC) questionnaire** to identify that style by measuring whether a person is task or relationship oriented. The LPC questionnaire asks respondents to think of all the co-workers they have ever had and describe the one they *least enjoyed* working with by rating that person on a scale of 1 to 8 for each of 16 sets of contrasting adjectives (such as pleasant–unpleasant, efficient–inefficient, open–guarded, supportive–hostile). If you describe the person you are least able to work with in favorable terms (a high LPC score), Fiedler would label you *relationship oriented*. If you see your least-preferred co-worker in unfavorable terms (a low LPC score), you are primarily interested in productivity and are *task oriented*. About 16 percent of respondents score in the middle range[18] and thus fall outside the theory's predictions. The rest of our discussion relates to the 84 percent who score in either the high or low range of the LPC questionnaire.

Fiedler assumes an individual's leadership style is fixed. This means if a situation requires a task-oriented leader and the person in the leadership position is relationship oriented, either the situation has to be modified or the leader has to be replaced to achieve optimal effectiveness.

SELF-ASSESSMENT LIBRARY

What's My LPC Score?

In the Self-Assessment Library (available on CD and online) take assessment IV.E.5 (What's My LPC Score?).

Defining the Situation   After assessing an individual's basic leadership style through the LPC questionnaire, we match the leader with the situation. Fiedler has identified three contingency or situational dimensions:

1. **Leader–member relations** is the degree of confidence, trust, and respect members have in their leader.

---

production-oriented leader   *A leader who emphasizes technical or task aspects of the job.*

Fiedler contingency model   *The theory that effective groups depend on a proper match between a leader's style of interacting with subordinates and the degree to which the situation gives control and influence to the leader.*

least preferred co-worker (LPC) questionnaire   *An instrument that purports to measure whether a person is task or relationship oriented.*

leader–member relations   *The degree of confidence, trust, and respect subordinates have in their leader.*

2. **Task structure** is the degree to which the job assignments are procedurized (that is, structured or unstructured).
3. **Position power** is the degree of influence a leader has over power variables such as hiring, firing, discipline, promotions, and salary increases.

The next step is to evaluate the situation in terms of these three variables. Fiedler states that the better the leader–member relations, the more highly structured the job, and the stronger the position power, the more control the leader has. A very favorable situation (in which the leader has a great deal of control) might include a payroll manager who is well respected and whose employees have confidence in her (good leader–member relations); activities that are clear and specific—such as wage computation, check writing, and report filing (high task structure); and provision of considerable freedom to reward and punish employees (strong position power). An unfavorable situation might be that of the disliked chairperson of a volunteer United Way fundraising team. In this job, the leader has very little control.

Matching Leaders and Situations   Combining the three contingency dimensions yields eight possible situations in which leaders can find themselves (Exhibit 12-1). The Fiedler model proposes matching an individual's LPC score and these eight situations to achieve maximum leadership effectiveness.[19] Fiedler concluded that task-oriented leaders perform better in situations very favorable to them and very unfavorable. So, when faced with a category I, II, III, VII, or VIII situation, task-oriented leaders perform better. Relationship-oriented leaders, however, perform better in moderately favorable situations—categories IV, V, and VI. In recent years, Fiedler has condensed these eight situations down to three.[20] He now says task-oriented leaders perform best in

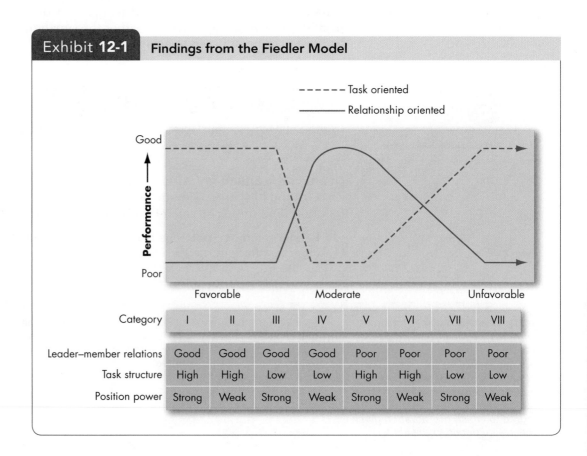

Exhibit 12-1   **Findings from the Fiedler Model**

Category	I	II	III	IV	V	VI	VII	VIII
Leader–member relations	Good	Good	Good	Good	Poor	Poor	Poor	Poor
Task structure	High	High	Low	Low	High	High	Low	Low
Position power	Strong	Weak	Strong	Weak	Strong	Weak	Strong	Weak

situations of high and low control, while relationship-oriented leaders perform best in moderate control situations.

How would you apply Fiedler's findings? You would match leaders—in terms of their LPC scores—with the type of situation—in terms of leader–member relationships, task structure, and position power—for which they were best suited. But remember that Fiedler views an individual's leadership style as fixed. Therefore, there are only two ways to improve leader effectiveness.

First, you can change the leader to fit the situation—as a baseball manager puts a right- or left-handed pitcher into the game depending on the hitter. If a group situation rates highly unfavorable but is currently led by a relationship-oriented manager, the group's performance could be improved under a manager who is task-oriented. The second alternative is to change the situation to fit the leader by restructuring tasks or increasing or decreasing the leader's power to control factors such as salary increases, promotions, and disciplinary actions.

Evaluation   Studies testing the overall validity of the Fiedler model find considerable evidence to support substantial parts of it.[21] If we use only three categories rather than the original eight, ample evidence supports Fiedler's conclusions.[22] But the logic underlying the LPC questionnaire is not well understood, and respondents' scores are not stable.[23] The contingency variables are also complex and difficult for practitioners to assess.[24]

Other Contingency Theories

Although LPC theory is the most widely researched contingency theory, three others deserve mention.

When Yahoo's growth and revenues slowed for several years, the company hired Carol Bartz as its new chief executive. Known as a task-oriented leader, Bartz previously led a successful turnaround at software maker Autodesk where, under her leadership, the company's revenues grew from $300 million to more than $1.5 billion. But after two and a half years at Yahoo, Bartz was fired as CEO for failing to revive the company's revenues and stock price. According to Fiedler's contingency model, Bartz's task-oriented style was not effective in improving Yahoo's performance. Observers noted that Bartz failed to provide the visionary leadership and focused strategic direction and execution needed to position the company for growth.

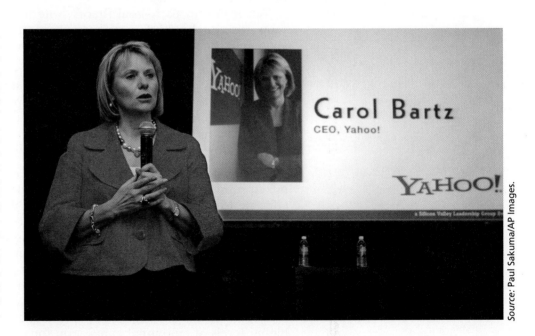

Source: Paul Sakuma/AP Images.

task structure   *The degree to which job assignments are procedurized.*

position power   *Influence derived from one's formal structural position in the organization; includes power to hire, fire, discipline, promote, and give salary increases.*

Situational Leadership Theory   **Situational leadership theory (SLT)** focuses on the followers. It says successful leadership depends on selecting the right leadership style contingent on the followers' *readiness,* or the extent to which they are willing and able to accomplish a specific task. A leader should choose one of four behaviors depending on follower readiness.

If followers are *unable* and *unwilling* to do a task, the leader needs to give clear and specific directions; if they are *unable* and *willing,* the leader needs to display high task orientation to compensate for followers' lack of ability and high relationship orientation to get them to "buy into" the leader's desires. If followers are *able* and *unwilling,* the leader needs to use a supportive and participative style; if they are both *able* and *willing,* the leader doesn't need to do much.

SLT has intuitive appeal. It acknowledges the importance of followers and builds on the logic that leaders can compensate for their limited ability and motivation. Yet research efforts to test and support the theory have generally been disappointing.[25] Why? Possible explanations include internal ambiguities and inconsistencies in the model itself as well as problems with research methodology in tests. So, despite its intuitive appeal and wide popularity, any endorsement must be cautious for now.

Path–Goal Theory   Developed by Robert House, **path–goal theory** extracts elements from the Ohio State leadership research on initiating structure and consideration and the expectancy theory of motivation.[26] It says it's the leader's job to provide followers with the information, support, or other resources necessary to achieve their goals. (The term *path–goal* implies effective leaders clarify followers' paths to their work goals and make the journey easier by reducing roadblocks.)

According to path–goal theory, whether a leader should be directive or supportive or should demonstrate some other behavior depends on complex analysis of the situation. It predicts the following:

- Directive leadership yields greater satisfaction when tasks are ambiguous or stressful than when they are highly structured and well laid out.
- Supportive leadership results in high performance and satisfaction when employees are performing structured tasks.
- Directive leadership is likely to be perceived as redundant among employees with high ability or considerable experience.

Testing path–goal theory has not been easy. A review of the evidence found mixed support for the proposition that removing obstacles is a component of effective leadership. Another review found the lack of support "shocking and disappointing."[27] Others argue that adequate tests of the theory have yet to be conducted.[28] Thus, the jury is still out. Because path–goal theory is so complex to test, that may remain the case for some time.

In a study of 162 workers in a document-processing organization, researchers found workers' conscientiousness was related to higher levels of performance only when supervisors set goals and defined roles, responsibilities, and priorities.[29] Other research has found that goal-focused leadership can lead to higher levels of emotional exhaustion for subordinates who are low in conscientiousness and emotional stability.[30] These studies demonstrate that leaders who set goals enable conscientious followers to achieve higher performance and may cause stress for workers who are low in conscientiousness.

Leader-Participation Model   The final contingency theory we cover argues that *the way* the leader makes decisions is as important as *what* she or he decides.

Victor Vroom and Phillip Yetton's **leader-participation model** relates leadership behavior and participation in decision making.[31] Like path–goal theory, it says leader behavior must adjust to reflect the task structure. The model is normative—it provides a decision tree of seven contingencies and five leadership styles for determining the form and amount of participation in decision making.

Research testing both the original and revised leader-participation models has not been encouraging, although the revised model rates higher in effectiveness.[32] Criticism focuses on the model's complexity and the variables it omits.[33] Although Vroom and Jago have developed a computer program to guide managers through all the decision branches in the revised model, it's not very realistic to expect practicing managers to consider 12 contingency variables, eight problem types, and five leadership styles to select the decision process for a problem.

As one leadership scholar noted, "Leaders do not exist in a vacuum"; leadership is a symbiotic relationship between leaders and followers.[34] But the theories we've covered to this point assume leaders use a fairly homogeneous style with everyone in their work unit. Think about your experiences in groups. Did leaders often act very differently toward different people? Our next theory considers differences in the relationships leaders form with different followers.

Leader–Member Exchange (LMX) Theory

Think of a leader you know. Did this leader have favorites who made up his or her ingroup? If you answered "yes," you're acknowledging the foundation of leader–member exchange theory.[35] **Leader–member exchange (LMX) theory** argues that, because of time pressures, leaders establish a special relationship with a small group of their followers. These individuals make up the ingroup—they are trusted, get a disproportionate amount of the leader's attention, and are more likely to receive special privileges. Other followers fall into the toutgroup.

The theory proposes that early in the history of the interaction between a leader and a given follower, the leader implicitly categorizes the follower as an "in" or an "out" and that relationship is relatively stable over time. Leaders induce LMX by rewarding those employees with whom they want a closer linkage and punishing those with whom they do not.[36] But for the LMX relationship to remain intact, the leader and the follower must invest in the relationship.

Just how the leader chooses who falls into each category is unclear, but there is evidence ingroup members have demographic, attitude, and personality characteristics similar to those of their leader or a higher level of competence

---

situational leadership theory (SLT) *A contingency theory that focuses on followers' readiness.*

path–goal theory *A theory that states that it is the leader's job to assist followers in attaining their goals and to provide the necessary direction and/or support to ensure that their goals are compatible with the overall objectives of the group or organization.*

leader-participation model *A leadership theory that provides a set of rules to determine the form and amount of participative decision making in different situations.*

leader–member exchange (LMX) theory *A theory that supports leaders' creation of in-groups and out-groups; subordinates with in-group status will have higher performance ratings, less turnover, and greater job satisfaction.*

Cross-Cultural Leadership Styles

While a great deal has been said about international differences in leadership styles and their effectiveness, another issue probably matters more for most organizations: How can we develop leaders who are effective across cultural boundaries? Is it possible to create a truly global leadership style that will extend across cultures? Some recent forays into the field of cross-cultural leadership highlight possibilities for how global organizations might proceed.

Some of the leadership styles we have described in this chapter do seem to generalize across cultures. For example, research suggests charismatic leadership is effective in a variety of national contexts. In many cultures, terms like *visionary, symbolizer,* and *self-sacrificer* appear as descriptors of

effective leaders, and positive leader–member exchanges also are associated with high performance across a variety of cultures. Culturally intelligent leaders are flexible and adaptable, tailoring their leadership styles to the specific and changing needs of the global workforce.

Researchers agree that learning to be a global leader requires gaining active experience in dealing with multiple cultures simultaneously. These experiences give leaders a chance to observe how different leadership styles work with different groups of people and build confidence in working across cultural boundaries. Leadership development programs can also use 360-degree feedback from supervisors, colleagues, and subordinates to help leaders recognize when their

behavior is not effective with certain populations of employees. Companies like PepsiCo and Ford have their most effective global leaders provide seminars to emerging leaders so they can describe practices that have been especially effective.

Sources: K. Ng, L. Van Dyne, and S. Ang, "From Experience to Experiential Learning: Cultural Intelligence as a Learning Capacity for Global Leader Development," *Academy of Management Learning and Education* 9, no. 4 (2009), pp. 511–526; C. B. Gibson and D. M. McDaniel, "Moving Beyond Conventional Wisdom: Advancements in Cross-Cultural Theories of Leadership, Conflict, and Teams," *Perspectives on Psychological Science* 5, no. 4 (2010), pp. 450–462; and D. Simmonds and O. Tsui, "Effective Design of a Global Leadership Programme," *Human Resource Development International* 13, no. 5 (2010), pp. 519–540.

than outgroup members[37] (see Exhibit 12-2). Leaders and followers of the same gender tend to have closer (higher LMX) relationships than those of different genders.[38] Even though the leader does the choosing, the follower's characteristics drive the categorizing decision.

Research to test LMX theory has been generally supportive, with substantive evidence that leaders do differentiate among followers; these disparities are far from random; and followers with ingroup status will have higher performance ratings, engage in more helping or "citizenship" behaviors at work, and report greater satisfaction with their superior.[39] One study conducted in both Portugal

Exhibit 12-2 Leader–Member Exchange Theory

and the United States found that leader–member exchange was associated especially strongly with followers' commitment to the organization when the leaders were seen as embodying the values and identity of the organization.[40] These positive findings for ingroup members shouldn't be surprising, given our knowledge of self-fulfilling prophecy (see Chapter 6). Leaders invest their resources with those they expect to perform best. And believing ingroup members are the most competent, leaders treat them as such and unwittingly fulfill their prophecy. Conversely, a study in Turkey demonstrated that when leaders differentiated strongly among their followers in terms of their relationships (some followers had very positive leader–member exchange, others very poor), employees responded with more negative work attitudes and higher levels of withdrawal behavior.[41] Leader–follower relationships may be stronger when followers have a more active role in shaping their own job performance. Research on 287 software developers and 164 supervisors showed leader–member relationships have a stronger impact on employee performance and attitudes when employees have higher levels of autonomy and a more internal locus of control.[42]

Charismatic Leadership and Transformational Leadership

5 Compare and contrast *charismatic* and *transformational leadership*.

In this section, we present two contemporary leadership theories—charismatic leadership and transformational leadership—with a common theme: they view leaders as individuals who inspire followers through their words, ideas, and behaviors.

Charismatic Leadership

John F. Kennedy, Martin Luther King Jr., Ronald Reagan, Bill Clinton, Mary Kay Ash (founder of Mary Kay Cosmetics), and Steve Jobs (co-founder of Apple Computer) are frequently cited as charismatic leaders. What do they have in common?

What Is Charismatic Leadership?   Max Weber, a sociologist, defined *charisma* (from the Greek for "gift") more than a century ago as "a certain quality of an individual personality, by virtue of which he or she is set apart from ordinary people and treated as endowed with supernatural, superhuman, or at least specifically exceptional powers or qualities. These are not accessible to the ordinary person and are regarded as of divine origin or as exemplary, and on the basis of them the individual concerned is treated as a leader."[43] Weber argued that charismatic leadership was one of several ideal types of authority.

The first researcher to consider charismatic leadership in terms of OB was Robert House. According to House's **charismatic leadership theory**, followers attribute heroic or extraordinary leadership abilities when they observe certain behaviors.[44] A number of studies have attempted to identify the characteristics of charismatic leaders: they have a vision, they are willing to take personal

charismatic leadership theory   *A leadership theory that states that followers make attributions of heroic or extraordinary leadership abilities when they observe certain behaviors.*

Exhibit 12-3	Key Characteristics of a Charismatic Leader

1. *Vision and articulation.* Has a vision—expressed as an idealized goal—that proposes a future better than the status quo; and is able to clarify the importance of the vision in terms that are understandable to others.
2. *Personal risk.* Willing to take on high personal risk, incur high costs, and engage in self-sacrifice to achieve the vision.
3. *Sensitivity to follower needs.* Perceptive of others' abilities and responsive to their needs and feelings.
4. *Unconventional behavior.* Engages in behaviors that are perceived as novel and counter to norms.

Source: Based on J. A. Conger and R. N. Kanungo, *Charismatic Leadership in Organizations* (Thousand Oaks, CA: Sage, 1998), p. 94.

risks to achieve that vision, they are sensitive to follower needs, and they exhibit extraordinary behaviors[45] (see Exhibit 12-3).

Are Charismatic Leaders Born or Made?   Are charismatic leaders born with their qualities? Or can people actually learn to be charismatic leaders? Yes, and yes.

Individuals *are* born with traits that make them charismatic. In fact, studies of identical twins have found they score similarly on charismatic leadership measures, even if they were raised in different households and had never met. Personality is also related to charismatic leadership; charismatic leaders are likely to be extraverted, self-confident, and achievement oriented.[46] Consider Presidents Barack Obama and Ronald Reagan: like them or not, they are often compared because both possess the qualities of charismatic leaders.

Most experts believe individuals can be trained to exhibit charismatic behaviors.[47] After all, just because we inherit certain tendencies doesn't mean we can't learn to change. One set of authors proposes a three-step process.[48] First, develop an aura of charisma by maintaining an optimistic view; using passion as a catalyst for generating enthusiasm; and communicating with the whole body, not just with words. Second, draw others in by creating a bond that inspires them to follow. Third, bring out the potential in followers by tapping into their emotions.

The approach seems to work, according to researchers who have asked undergraduate business students to "play" charismatic.[49] The students were taught to articulate an overarching goal, communicate high performance expectations, exhibit confidence in the ability of followers to meet these expectations, and empathize with the needs of their followers; they learned to project a powerful, confident, and dynamic presence; and they practiced using a captivating and engaging voice. They were also trained to evoke charismatic nonverbal characteristics: they alternated between pacing and sitting on the edges of their desks, leaned toward the subjects, maintained direct eye contact, and had relaxed postures and animated facial expressions. Their followers had higher task performance, task adjustment, and adjustment to the leader and the group than did followers of noncharismatic leaders.

How Charismatic Leaders Influence Followers   How do charismatic leaders actually influence followers? Evidence suggests a four-step process.[50] It begins with articulating an appealing **vision**, a long-term strategy for attaining a goal by linking the present with a better future for the organization. Desirable visions fit the times and circumstances and reflect the uniqueness of the organization. Steve Jobs championed the iPod at Apple, noting, "It's as Apple as anything

Apple has ever done." People in the organization must also believe the vision is challenging yet attainable.

Second, a vision is incomplete without an accompanying **vision statement**, a formal articulation of an organization's vision or mission. Charismatic leaders may use vision statements to imprint on followers an overarching goal and purpose. They build followers' self-esteem and confidence with high performance expectations and belief that followers can attain them. Next, through words and actions the leader conveys a new set of values and sets an example for followers to imitate. One study of Israeli bank employees showed charismatic leaders were more effective because their employees personally identified with them. Charismatic leaders also set a tone of cooperation and mutual support. A study of 115 government employees found they had a stronger sense of personal belonging at work when they had charismatic leaders, increasing their willingness to engage in helping and compliance-oriented behavior.[51]

Finally, the charismatic leader engages in emotion-inducing and often unconventional behavior to demonstrate courage and conviction about the vision. Followers "catch" the emotions their leader is conveying.[52]

Does Effective Charismatic Leadership Depend on the Situation? Research shows impressive correlations between charismatic leadership and high performance and satisfaction among followers.[53] People working for charismatic leaders are motivated to exert extra effort and, because they like and respect their leader, express greater satisfaction. Organizations with charismatic CEOs are also more profitable, and charismatic college professors enjoy higher course evaluations.[54] However, charisma appears most successful when the follower's task has an ideological component or the environment includes a high degree of stress and uncertainty.[55] Even in laboratory studies, when people are psychologically aroused, they are more likely to respond to charismatic leaders.[56] This may explain why, when charismatic leaders surface, it's likely to be in politics or religion, or during wartime, or when a business is in its infancy or facing a life-threatening crisis. Franklin D. Roosevelt offered a vision to get the United States out of the Great Depression in the 1930s. In 1997, when Apple Computer was floundering and lacking direction, the board persuaded charismatic co-founder Steve Jobs to return as interim CEO and return the company to its innovative roots.

Another situational factor apparently limiting charisma is level in the organization. Top executives create vision; it's more difficult to utilize a person's charismatic leadership qualities in lower-level management jobs or to align his or her vision with the larger goals of the organization.

Finally, people are especially receptive to charismatic leadership when they sense a crisis, when they are under stress, or when they fear for their lives. Charismatic leaders are able to reduce stress for their employees, perhaps because they help make work seem more meaningful and interesting.[57] And some peoples' personalities are especially susceptible to charismatic leadership.[58] Consider self-esteem. An individual who lacks self-esteem and questions his or her self-worth is more likely to absorb a leader's direction rather than establish his or her own way of leading or thinking.

The Dark Side of Charismatic Leadership   Charismatic business leaders like AIG's Hank Greenberg, GE's Jack Welch, Tyco's Dennis Kozlowski, Southwest Airlines' Herb Kelleher, Disney's Michael Eisner, and HP's Carly Fiorina became

vision   *A long-term strategy for attaining a goal or goals.*

vision statement   *A formal articulation of an organization's vision or mission.*

celebrities on the order of David Beckham and Madonna. Every company wanted a charismatic CEO, and to attract them boards of directors gave them unprecedented autonomy and resources—the use of private jets and multimillion-dollar penthouses, interest-free loans to buy beach homes and artwork, security staffs, and similar benefits befitting royalty. One study showed charismatic CEOs were able to leverage higher salaries even when their performance was mediocre.[59]

Unfortunately, charismatic leaders who are larger than life don't necessarily act in the best interests of their organizations.[60] Many have allowed their personal goals to override the goals of the organization. The results at companies such as Enron, Tyco, WorldCom, and HealthSouth were leaders who recklessly used organizational resources for their personal benefit and executives who violated laws and ethical boundaries to inflate stock prices and allow leaders to cash in millions of dollars in stock options. It's little wonder research has shown that individuals who are narcissistic are also higher in some behaviors associated with charismatic leadership.[61]

It's not that charismatic leadership isn't effective; overall, it is. But a charismatic leader isn't always the answer. Success depends, to some extent, on the situation and on the leader's vision. Some charismatic leaders—Hitler, for example—are all too successful at convincing their followers to pursue a vision that can be disastrous.

SELF-ASSESSMENT LIBRARY

How Charismatic Am I?

In the Self-Assessment Library (available on CD and online), take assessment II.B.2 (How Charismatic Am I?).

Transformational Leadership

A stream of research has focused on differentiating transformational from transactional leaders.[62] The Ohio State studies, Fiedler's model, and path–goal theory describe **transactional leaders**, who guide their followers toward established goals by clarifying role and task requirements. **Transformational leaders** inspire followers to transcend their self-interests for the good of the organization and can have an extraordinary effect on their followers. Andrea Jung at Avon, Richard Branson of the Virgin Group, and Jim McNerney of Boeing are all transformational leaders. They pay attention to the concerns and needs of individual followers; they change followers' awareness of issues by helping them look at old problems in new ways; and they excite and inspire followers to put out extra effort to achieve group goals. Exhibit 12-4 briefly identifies and defines the characteristics that differentiate these two types of leaders.

Transactional and transformational leadership complement each other; they aren't opposing approaches to getting things done.[63] Transformational leadership *builds on* transactional leadership and produces levels of follower effort and performance beyond what transactional leadership alone can do. But the reverse isn't true. So if you are a good transactional leader but do not have transformational qualities, you'll likely only be a mediocre leader. The best leaders are transactional *and* transformational.

Full Range of Leadership Model   Exhibit 12-5 shows the full range of leadership model. Laissez-faire is the most passive and therefore least effective of leader behaviors.[64] Management by exception—active or passive—is slightly better, but it's still considered ineffective. Management-by-exception leaders tend to be available only when there is a problem, which is often too late. Contingent reward leadership can be an effective style of leadership but will not get employees to go above and beyond the call of duty.

Exhibit **12-4**	**Characteristics of Transactional and Transformational Leaders**

Transactional Leader

Contingent Reward: Contracts exchange of rewards for effort, promises rewards for good performance, recognizes accomplishments.

Management by Exception (active): Watches and searches for deviations from rules and standards, takes correct action.

Management by Exception (passive): Intervenes only if standards are not met.

Laissez-Faire: Abdicates responsibilities, avoids making decisions.

Transformational Leader

Idealized Influence: Provides vision and sense of mission, instills pride, gains respect and trust.

Inspirational Motivation: Communicates high expectations, uses symbols to focus efforts, expresses important purposes in simple ways.

Intellectual Stimulation: Promotes intelligence, rationality, and careful problem solving.

Individualized Consideration: Gives personal attention, treats each employee individually, coaches, advises.

Source: Based on A. H. Eagly, M. C. Johannesen-Schmidt, and M. L. Van Engen, "Transformational, Transactional, and Laissez-faire Leadership Styles: A Meta-Analysis Comparing Women and Men," *Psychological Bulletin* 129, no. 4 (2003), pp. 569–591; and T. A. Judge and J. E. Bono, "Five Factor Model of Personality and Transformational Leadership," *Journal of Applied Psychology* 85, no. 5 (2000), pp. 751–765.

Only with the four remaining styles—all aspects of transformational leadership—are leaders able to motivate followers to perform above expectations and transcend their self-interest for the sake of the organization. Individualized consideration, intellectual stimulation, inspirational motivation, and idealized influence all result in extra effort from workers, higher productivity, higher morale and satisfaction, higher organizational effectiveness, lower turnover, lower absenteeism, and greater organizational adaptability. Based on this model, leaders are generally most effective when they regularly use each of the four transformational behaviors.

How Transformational Leadership Works   Transformational leaders are more effective because they are more creative, but also because they encourage those who follow them to be creative, too.[65] Companies with transformational leaders have greater decentralization of responsibility, managers have more propensity to take risks, and compensation plans are geared toward long-term results—all of which facilitate corporate entrepreneurship.[66] One study of information technology workers in China found empowering leadership behavior led to feelings of positive personal control among workers, which increased their creativity at work.[67]

Companies with transformational leaders also show greater agreement among top managers about the organization's goals, which yields superior organizational performance.[68] The Israeli military has seen similar results, showing

transactional leaders *Leaders who guide or motivate their followers in the direction of established goals by clarifying role and task requirements.*

transformational leaders *Leaders who inspire followers to transcend their own self-interests and who are capable of having a profound and extraordinary effect on followers.*

| Exhibit 12-5 | Full Range of Leadership Model |

that transformational leaders improve performance by building consensus among group members.[69] Transformational leaders are able to increase follower self-efficacy, giving the group a "can do" spirit.[70] Followers are more likely to pursue ambitious goals, agree on the strategic goals of the organization, and believe the goals they are pursuing are personally important.[71]

Just as vision helps explain how charismatic leadership works, it also explains part of the effect of transformational leadership. One study found vision was even more important than a charismatic (effusive, dynamic, lively) communication style in explaining the success of entrepreneurial firms.[72] Finally, transformational leadership engenders commitment on the part of followers and instills greater trust in the leader.[73]

Evaluation of Transformational Leadership   Transformational leadership has been impressively supported at diverse job levels and occupations (school principals, teachers, marine commanders, ministers, presidents of MBA associations, military cadets, union shop stewards, sales reps). One study of R&D firms found teams whose project leaders scored high on transformational leadership produced better-quality products as judged 1 year later and higher profits 5 years later.[74] Another study looking at employee creativity and transformational leadership more directly found employees with transformational leaders had more confidence in their ability to be creative at work and higher levels of creative performance.[75] A review of 117 studies testing transformational leadership found it was related to higher levels of individual follower performance, team performance, and organizational performance.[76]

Transformational leadership isn't equally effective in all situations. It has a greater impact on the bottom line in smaller, privately held firms than in more complex organizations.[77] The personal nature of transformational leadership may be most effective when leaders can directly interact with the workforce and make decisions than when they report to an external board of directors or deal with a complex bureaucratic structure. Another study showed transformational leaders were more effective in improving group potency in teams higher in power distance and collectivism.[78] Other recent research using a sample of employees both in China and the United States found that transformational leadership had a more positive relationship with perceived procedural justice among individuals who were lower in power-distance orientation, which in turn related to a stronger transformational leadership-citizenship behavior relationship among those higher in power distance.[79] Transformational leaders also obtain higher levels of trust, which reduces stress for followers.[80] In short, transformational leadership works through a number of different processes.

One study examined how different types of transformational leadership can be effective depending on whether work is evaluated at the team or the individual level.[81] Individual-focused transformational leadership is behavior that empowers individual followers to develop, enhance their abilities, and increase self-efficacy. Team-focused transformational leadership emphasizes group goals, shared values and beliefs, and unified efforts. Evidence from a sample of 203 team members and 60 leaders in a business unit found individual transformational leadership associated with higher individual-level performance, whereas team-focused transformational leadership drew higher group-level performance.

Transformational leadership theory is not perfect. Contingent reward leadership may not characterize transactional leaders only. And contrary to the full range of leadership model, the four I's in transformational leadership are not always superior in effectiveness to transactional leadership (contingent reward leadership sometimes works as well as transformational leadership).

In summary, transformational leadership is more strongly correlated than transactional leadership with lower turnover rates, higher productivity, lower employee stress and burnout, and higher employee satisfaction.[82] Like charisma, it can be learned. One study of Canadian bank managers found branches managed by those who underwent transformational leadership training performed significantly better than branches whose managers did not receive training. Other studies show similar results.[83]

The GLOBE study—of 18,000 leaders from 825 organizations in 62 countries—links a number of elements of transformational leadership with effective leadership, regardless of country.[84] This conclusion is very important because it disputes the contingency view that leadership style needs to adapt to cultural differences.

What elements of transformational leadership appear universal? Vision, foresight, providing encouragement, trustworthiness, dynamism, positiveness, and proactiveness top the list. The GLOBE team concluded that "effective business leaders in any country are expected by their subordinates to provide a powerful and proactive vision to guide the company into the future, strong motivational skills to stimulate all employees to fulfill the vision, and excellent planning skills to assist in implementing the vision."[85]

A vision is important in any culture, then, but the way it is formed and communicated may need to vary by culture. A GE executive who used his U.S. leadership style in Japan recalls, "Nothing happened. I quickly realized that I had to adapt my approach, to act more as a consultant to my colleagues and to adopt a team-based motivational decision-making process rather than the more vocal style which tends to be common in the West. In Japan the silence of a leader means far more than a thousand words uttered by somebody else."[86]

Authentic Leadership: Ethics and Trust

6 Define *authentic leadership* and show why effective leaders exemplify ethics and trust.

Although theories have increased our understanding of effective leadership, they do not explicitly deal with the role of ethics and trust, which some argue is essential to complete the picture. Here, we consider these two concepts under the rubric of authentic leadership.[87]

What Is Authentic Leadership?

Mike Ullman, JCPenney CEO, argues that leaders have to be selfless, listen well, and be honest. Campbell Soup's CEO Douglas R. Conant is decidedly understated. When asked to reflect on the strong performance of Campbell Soup, he says, "We're hitting our stride a little bit more (than our peers)." He regularly admits mistakes and often says, "I can do better." Ullman and Conant appear to be good exemplars of authentic leadership.[88]

Authentic leaders know who they are, know what they believe in and value, and act on those values and beliefs openly and candidly. Their followers consider them ethical people. The primary quality produced by authentic leadership, therefore, is trust. Authentic leaders share information, encourage open communication, and stick to their ideals. The result: people come to have faith in them.

Because the concept is new, there has been little research on authentic leadership. However, it's a promising way to think about ethics and trust in leadership because it focuses on the moral aspects of being a leader. Transformational or charismatic leaders can have a vision and communicate it persuasively, but sometimes the vision is wrong (as in the case of Hitler), or the leader is more concerned with his or her own needs or pleasures, as were Dennis Kozlowski (ex-CEO of Tyco), Jeff Skilling (ex-CEO of Enron), and Raj Rajaratnam (founder of the Galleon Group).[89]

SELF-ASSESSMENT LIBRARY

Am I an Ethical Leader?

In the Self-Assessment Library (available on CD and online), take assessment IV.E.4 (Am I an Ethical Leader?).

Ethics and Leadership

Only recently have researchers begun to consider the ethical implications in leadership.[90] Why now? One reason may be the growing interest in ethics throughout the field of management. Another may be the discovery that many past leaders—such as Martin Luther King Jr., John F. Kennedy, and Thomas Jefferson—suffered ethical shortcomings. Some companies, like Boeing, are tying executive compensation to ethics to reinforce the idea that, in CEO Jim McNerney's words, "there's no compromise between doing things the right way and performance."[91]

Ethics and leadership intersect at a number of junctures. We can think of transformational leaders as fostering moral virtue when they try to change the attitudes and behaviors of followers.[92] Charisma, too, has an ethical component. Unethical leaders use their charisma to enhance power over followers, directed toward self-serving ends. Ethical leaders use it in a socially constructive way to serve others.[93] Leaders who treat their followers with fairness, especially by providing honest, frequent, and accurate information, are seen as more effective.[94] Leaders rated highly ethical tend to have followers who engage in more organizational citizenship behaviors and who are more willing to bring problems to the leaders' attention.[95] Because top executives set the moral tone for an organization, they need to set high ethical standards, demonstrate them through their own behavior, and encourage and reward integrity in others while avoiding abuses of power such as giving themselves large raises and bonuses while seeking to cut costs by laying off longtime employees.

Leadership is not value-free. In assessing its effectiveness, we need to address the *means* a leader uses in trying to achieve goals, as well as the content of those goals. Scholars have tried to integrate ethical and charismatic leadership by advancing the idea of **socialized charismatic leadership**—leadership that conveys other-centered (not self-centered) values by leaders who model ethical conduct.[96] Socialized charismatic leaders are able to bring employee values in line with their own values through their words and actions.[97]

Servant Leadership

Scholars have recently considered ethical leadership from a new angle by examining **servant leadership**.[98] Servant leaders go beyond their own self-interest and focus on opportunities to help followers grow and develop. They don't use power to achieve ends; they emphasize persuasion. Characteristic behaviors include listening, empathizing, persuading, accepting stewardship, and actively developing followers' potential. Because servant leadership focuses on serving the needs of others, research has focused on its outcomes for the well-being of followers.

What are the effects of servant leadership? One study of 123 supervisors found it resulted in higher levels of commitment to the supervisor, self-efficacy, and perceptions of justice, which all were related to organizational citizenship behavior.[99] This relationship between servant leadership and follower OCB appears to be stronger when followers are focused on being dutiful and responsible.[100] Second, servant leadership increases team potency (a belief that one's team has above-average skills and abilities), which in turn leads to higher levels of group performance.[101] Third, a study with a nationally representative sample of 250 workers found higher levels of citizenship associated with a focus on growth and advancement, which in turn was associated with higher levels of creative performance.[102]

Servant leadership may be more prevalent and more effective in certain cultures.[103] When asked to draw images of leaders, U.S. subjects tend to draw them in front of the group, giving orders to followers. Singaporeans tend to draw leaders at the back of the group, acting more to gather a group's opinions together and then unify them from the rear. This suggests the East Asian prototype is more like a servant leader, which might mean servant leadership is more effective in these cultures.

Trust and Leadership

Trust is a psychological state that exists when you agree to make yourself vulnerable to another because you have positive expectations about how things are going to turn out.[104] Even though you aren't completely in control of the

---

authentic leaders *Leaders who know who they are, know what they believe in and value, and act on those values and beliefs openly and candidly. Their followers would consider them to be ethical people.*

socialized charismatic leadership *A leadership concept that states that leaders convey values that are other centered versus self centered and who role-model ethical conduct.*

servant leadership *A leadership style marked by going beyond the leader's own self-interest and instead focusing on opportunities to help followers grow and develop.*

trust *A positive expectation that another will not act opportunistically.*

Do Leaders Have a Responsibility to Protect Followers?

Leaders are expected to monitor performance and assign work tasks. But do they also have a responsibility to protect their followers as well? Should they "take the heat" so employees can be more productive? Former research and development head at 3M William Coyne felt one of his most significant contributions as a manager of creative employees was to prevent them from being bombarded with questions and suggestions from higher-ups. Especially in creative fields, leaders need to make the environment safe for employees to express their ideas, even if it means generating conflict with upper levels in the organization. Leaders may also need to protect up-and-coming employees from longer-tenured employees who see them as a threat.

Important components of servant leadership include putting subordinates first, helping them grow, and empowering them. We might thus expect servant leaders to protect their followers from negative pressures in the organization. Studies also show

that higher levels of servant leadership are associated with more citizenship behavior, higher performance, and greater creativity in work groups. As our review of the literature shows, acting to protect workers has a demonstrated impact on effective performance in the real world.

Still, shielding workers may not be in the organization's best interest all the time. Close personal relationships with subordinates can make it difficult to provide negative feedback when it's needed. A leader might be coddling a poor performer rather than protecting him or her from excess scrutiny. Thus, leaders need to take care when exercising their protecting role and be objective about what function it is serving.

So what should leaders do to effectively protect workers without falling into the trap of protecting the incompetent? Here are a few suggestions:

1. Try to identify barriers to effective performance in the work environment and protect employees from

these unnecessary sources of political infighting, distraction, and delay.
2. Assess employee contributions realistically. Try to separate your feelings about an employee from your desire to protect him or her from outside scrutiny.
3. Sometimes the best thing to do is let an employee handle problems independently and wait for him or her to ask for help. This can be surprisingly hard for many leaders who are used to seeing themselves in a proactive role.

Sources: Based on R. I. Sutton, "The Boss as Human Shield," *Harvard Business Review* (September, 2010), pp. 106–109; J. Hu and R. C. Liden, "Antecedents of Team Potency and Team Effectiveness: An Examination of Goal and Process Clarity and Servant Leadership," *Journal of Applied Psychology*, Online first publication (February 14, 2011), doi: 10.1037/a0022465; and F. O. Walumbwa, C. A. Hartnell, and A. Oke, "Servant Leadership, Procedural Justice Climate, Service Climate, Employee Attitudes, and Organizational Citizenship Behavior: A Cross-Level Investigation," *Journal of Applied Psychology* 95, no. 3 (2010), pp. 517–529.

situation, you are willing to take a chance that the other person will come through for you.

Trust is a primary attribute associated with leadership; breaking it can have serious adverse effects on a group's performance.[105] As one author noted, "Part of the leader's task has been, and continues to be, working with people to find and solve problems, but whether leaders gain access to the knowledge and creative thinking they need to solve problems depends on how much people trust them. Trust and trust-worthiness modulate the leader's access to knowledge and cooperation."[106]

Followers who trust a leader are confident their rights and interests will not be abused.[107] Transformational leaders create support for their ideas in part by arguing that their direction will be in everyone's best interests. People are unlikely to look up to or follow someone they perceive as dishonest or likely to take advantage of them. Thus, as you might expect, transformational leaders do generate higher levels of trust from their followers, which in turn is related to higher levels of team confidence and, ultimately, higher levels of team performance.[108]

In a simple contractual exchange of goods and services, your employer is legally bound to pay you for fulfilling your job description. But today's rapid reorganizations, diffusion of responsibility, and collaborative team-based work style mean employment relationships are not stable long-term contracts with explicit terms. Rather, they are more fundamentally based on trusting relationships than ever before. You have to trust that if you show your supervisor a creative project you've been working on, she won't steal the credit behind your back. You have to trust that extra work you've been doing will be recognized in your performance appraisal. In contemporary organizations, where less work is closely documented and specified, voluntary employee contribution based on trust is absolutely necessary. And only a trusted leader will be able to encourage employees to reach beyond themselves to a transformational goal.

How Is Trust Developed?

Trust isn't just about the leader; the characteristics of followers also influence its development. What key characteristics lead us to believe a leader is trustworthy? Evidence has identified three: integrity, benevolence, and ability (see Exhibit 12-6).[109]

Integrity refers to honesty and truthfulness. It seems the most critical characteristic in assessing another's trustworthiness.[110] When 570 white-collar employees were given a list of 28 attributes related to leadership, they rated honesty the most important by far.[111] Integrity also means having consistency between what you do and say. "Nothing is noticed more quickly . . . than a discrepancy between what executives preach and what they expect their associates to practice."[112]

Benevolence means the trusted person has your interests at heart, even if yours aren't necessarily in line with theirs. Caring and supportive behavior is part of the emotional bond between leaders and followers.

Ability encompasses an individual's technical and interpersonal knowledge and skills. Even a highly principled person with the best intentions in the world won't be trusted to accomplish a positive outcome for you if you don't have faith in his or her ability to get the job done. Does the person know what he or she is talking about? You're unlikely to listen to or depend on someone whose abilities you don't respect.

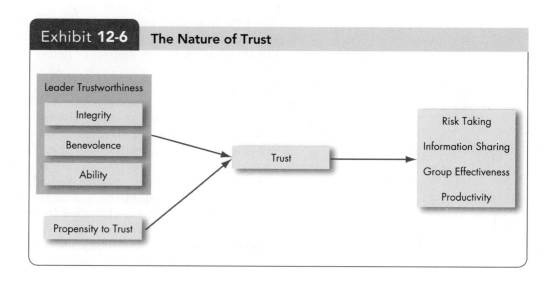

Exhibit 12-6   The Nature of Trust

Leader Trustworthiness
- Integrity
- Benevolence
- Ability

Propensity to Trust

Trust

- Risk Taking
- Information Sharing
- Group Effectiveness
- Productivity

Trust as a Process

Trust propensity refers to how likely a particular employee is to trust a leader. Some people are simply more likely to believe others can be trusted.[113] Those who carefully document every promise or conversation with their supervisors aren't very high in trust propensity, and they probably aren't going to take a leader's word for anything. Those who think most people are basically honest and forthright will be much more likely to seek out evidence that their leaders have behaved in a trustworthy manner. Trust propensity is closely linked to the personality trait of agreeableness, while people with lower self-esteem are less likely to trust others.[114]

Time is the final ingredient in the recipe for trust. We come to trust people based on observing their behavior over a period of time.[115] Leaders need to demonstrate they have integrity, benevolence, and ability in situations where trust is important—say, where they could behave opportunistically or let employees down but don't. Trust can also be won in the ability domain simply by demonstrating competence.

Leaders who break the psychological contract with workers, demonstrating they aren't trustworthy, will find employees are less satisfied and less committed, have a higher intent toward turnover, engage in less citizenship behavior, and have lower task performance.[116] Leaders who betray trust are especially likely to be evaluated negatively by followers if there is already a low level of leader–member exchange.[117] Once it is violated, trust can be regained, but only in certain situations that depend on the type of violation.[118] If the cause is lack of ability, it's usually best to apologize and recognize you should have done better. When lack of integrity is the problem, though, apologies don't do much good. Regardless of the violation, simply saying nothing or refusing to confirm or deny guilt is never an effective strategy for regaining trust. Trust can be restored when we observe a consistent pattern of trustworthy behavior by the transgressor. However, if the transgressor used deception, trust never fully returns, not even after apologies, promises, or a consistent pattern of trustworthy actions.[119]

What Are the Consequences of Trust?

Trust between supervisors and employees has a number of important advantages. Here are just a few that research has shown:

- **Trust encourages taking risks.** Whenever employees decide to deviate from the usual way of doing things, or to take their supervisors' word on a new direction, they are taking a risk. In both cases, a trusting relationship can facilitate that leap.
- **Trust facilitates information sharing.** One big reason employees fail to express concerns at work is that they don't feel psychologically safe revealing their views. When managers demonstrate they will give employees' ideas a fair hearing and actively make changes, employees are more willing to speak out.[120]
- **Trusting groups are more effective.** When a leader sets a trusting tone in a group, members are more willing to help each other and exert extra effort, which further increases trust. Conversely, members of mistrusting groups tend to be suspicious of each other, constantly guard against exploitation, and restrict communication with others in the group. These actions tend to undermine and eventually destroy the group.
- **Trust enhances productivity.** The bottom-line interest of companies also appears positively influenced by trust. Employees who trust their supervisors tend to receive higher performance ratings.[121] People respond to mistrust by concealing information and secretly pursuing their own interests.

Leading for the Future: Mentoring

7 Demonstrate the role mentoring plays in our understanding of leadership.

Leaders often take responsibility for developing future leaders. Let's consider what makes mentoring valuable as well as its potential pitfalls.

Mentoring

A **mentor** is a senior employee who sponsors and supports a less-experienced employee, a protégé. Successful mentors are good teachers. They present ideas clearly, listen well, and empathize with protégés' problems. Mentoring relationships serve both career functions and psychosocial functions (see Exhibit 12-7).[122]

Traditional informal mentoring relationships develop when leaders identify a less experienced, lower-level employee who appears to have potential for future development.[123] The protégé will often be tested with a particularly challenging assignment. If he or she performs acceptably, the mentor will develop the relationship, informally showing the protégé how the organization *really* works outside its formal structures and procedures.

Why would a leader want to be a mentor?[124] Many feel they have something to share with the younger generation and want to provide a legacy. Mentoring also provides unfiltered access to the attitudes of lower-ranking employees, and protégés can be an excellent source of early warning signals that identify potential organizational problems.

Are all employees in an organization equally likely to participate in a mentoring relationship? Unfortunately, no.[125] In the United States, upper managers in most organizations have traditionally been white males, and because mentors tend to select protégés similar to themselves in background, education, gender,

---

Exhibit 12-7   **Career and Psychological Functions of the Mentoring Relationship**

Career Functions	Psychosocial Functions
• Lobbying to get the protégé challenging and visible assignments	• Counseling the protégé to bolster his or her self-confidence
• Coaching the protégé to help develop his or her skills and achieve work objectives	• Sharing personal experiences with the protégé
• Providing exposure to influential individuals within the organization	• Providing friendship and acceptance
• Protecting the protégé from possible risks to his or her reputation	• Acting as a role model
• Sponsoring the protégé by nominating him or her for potential advances or promotions	
• Acting as a sounding board for ideas the protégé might be hesitant to share with a direct supervisor	

---

mentor   *A senior employee who sponsors and supports a less-experienced employee, called a protégé.*

"Power Helps Leaders Perform Better"

Somewhat surprisingly, this statement appears to be partly true.

All leaders, of course, have some power (we'll consider power in the next chapter). But how do differences in power between leaders affect how they do their jobs? Most of us probably think that when leaders obtain *more* power, they relax and "rest on their laurels"—or worse, they abuse it.

Several recent studies, however, suggest that this is not quite the case. Power actually can help a leader do his or her job more effectively. In a series of experiments, researchers found that when individuals were given power as leaders, they performed more effectively. Why? Power gives leaders a greater sense of responsibility toward their group—as a result, powerful leaders were more likely to exert effort and make sacrifices than those with less power. If you're powerless (or *think* you're powerless), after all, why bother?

Interestingly, though, the research also suggested that if leaders happen to see a task as beneath them, they will disregard it. Thus, if leaders are given more power, it's important that they don't use it to dismiss as trivial the duties that truly matter.

Of course, we don't really know whether these experimental results generalize to more realistic settings, or whether power has long-term corrupting effects. But the findings do suggest that giving leaders more power is not always a bad idea.

Source: C. N. DeWall, R. F. Baumeister, N. L. Mead, and K. D. Vohs, "How Leaders Self-Regulate Their Task Performance: Evidence That Power Promotes Diligence, Depletion, and Disdain," *Journal of Personality and Social Psychology* 100, no. 1 (2010), pp. 47–65.

---

race, ethnicity, and religion, minorities and women are less likely to be chosen. "People naturally move to mentor and can more easily communicate with those with whom they most closely identify."[126] Senior male managers may also select male protégés to minimize problems such as sexual attraction or gossip.

Many organizations have created formal programs to ensure mentoring relationships are equally available to minorities and women.[127] Although begun with the best intentions, these formal relationships are not as effective as informal ones.[128]

Poor planning and design may often be the reason. Mentor commitment is critical to a program's effectiveness; mentors must see the relationship as beneficial to themselves and the protégé. The protégé, too, must feel he or she has input into the relationship; someone who feels it's foisted on him or her will just go through the motions.[129] Formal mentoring programs are also most likely to succeed if they appropriately match the work style, needs, and skills of protégé and mentor.[130]

You might assume mentoring is valuable for objective outcomes like compensation and job performance, but research suggests the gains are primarily psychological. One review concluded, "Though mentoring may not be properly labeled an utterly useless concept to careers, neither can it be argued to be as important as the main effects of other influences on career success such as ability and personality."[131] It may *feel* nice to have a mentor, but it doesn't appear that having a good mentor, or any mentor, is critical to your career. Mentors may be effective not because of the functions they provide, but because of the resources they can obtain: a mentor connected to a powerful network can build relationships that will help the protégé advance. Most evidence suggests that network ties, whether built through a mentor or not, are a significant predictor of career success.[132] If a mentor is not well connected or not a very strong performer, the best mentoring advice in the world will not be very beneficial.

Challenges to the Leadership Construct

8 Address challenges to the effectiveness of leadership.

"In the 1500s, people ascribed all events they didn't understand to God. Why did the crops fail? God. Why did someone die? God. Now our all-purpose explanation is leadership."[133] But much of an organization's success or failure is due to factors outside the influence of leadership. Sometimes it's just a matter of being in the right or wrong place at a given time. In this section, we present two perspectives and one technological change that challenge accepted beliefs about the value of leadership.

Leadership as an Attribution

As you may remember from Chapter 6, attribution theory examines how people try to make sense of cause-and-effect relationships. The **attribution theory of leadership** says leadership is merely an attribution people make about other individuals.[134] Thus we attribute to leaders intelligence, outgoing personality, strong verbal skills, aggressiveness, understanding, and industriousness.[135] At the organizational level, we tend to see leaders, rightly or wrongly, as responsible for extremely negative or extremely positive performance.[136]

One longitudinal study of 128 major U.S. corporations found that whereas perceptions of CEO charisma did not lead to objective company performance, company performance did lead to perceptions of charisma.[137] Employee perceptions of their leaders' behaviors are significant predictors of whether they blame the leader for failure, regardless of how the leader assesses him- or

Elements of transformational leadership such as vision and foresight appear to be universal. In China, for example, Wang Jianzhou is the CEO of China Mobile, the world's largest mobile phone operator with more than 600 million subscribers. With vision and foresight, Jianzhou is expanding mobile service throughout China's vast rural areas and plans to expand in emerging markets such as Africa, Asia, and Latin America. Proactive and positive, Jianzhou's leadership draws from his extensive knowledge of and more than 30 years of experience in the telecommunications industry. Jianzhou is shown here during the launch of the firm's OPhone operating system platform.

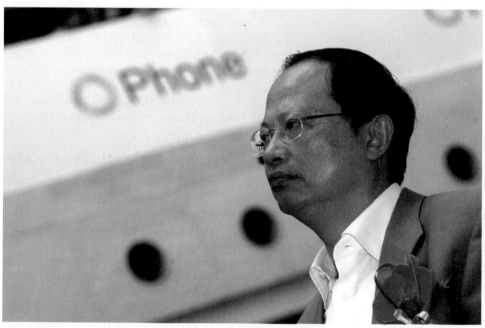

Source: Bao fan / Imaginechina/AP Images.

attribution theory of leadership *A leadership theory that says that leadership is merely an attribution that people make about other individuals.*

herself.[138] A study of more than 3,000 employees from western Europe, the United States, and the Middle East found people who tended to "romanticize" leadership in general were more likely to believe their own leaders were transformational.[139]

When Merrill Lynch began to lose billions in 2008 as a result of its investments in mortgage securities, it wasn't long before CEO Stan O'Neal lost his job. He appeared before the House Oversight and Government Reform Committee of the U.S. Congress for what one committee member termed "a public flogging." Some called him a "criminal," and still others suggested Merrill's losses represented "attempted destruction."[140]

Whether O'Neal was responsible for the losses at Merrill or deserved his nine-figure severance package are difficult questions to answer. However, it is not difficult to argue that he probably changed very little between 2004 when *Fortune* described him as a "turnaround genius" and 2009 when he was fired. What did change was the performance of the organization he led. It's not necessarily wrong to terminate a CEO for failing or flagging financial performance. However, O'Neal's story illustrates the power of the attribution approach to leadership: hero and genius when things are going well, villain when they aren't.

We also make demographic assumptions about leaders. Respondents in a study assumed a leader described with no identifying racial information was white at a rate beyond the base rate of white employees in a company. In scenarios where identical leadership situations are described but the leaders' race is manipulated, white leaders are rated as more effective than leaders of other racial groups.[141] One large-scale summary study (a meta-analysis) found that many individuals hold stereotypes of men as having more leader characteristics than women, although as you might expect, this tendency to equate leadership with masculinity has decreased over time.[142] Other data suggest women's perceived success as transformational leaders may be based on demographic characteristics. Teams prefer male leaders when aggressively competing against other teams, but they prefer female leaders when the competition is within teams and calls for improving positive relationships within the group.[143]

Attribution theory suggests what's important is projecting the *appearance* of being a leader rather than focusing on *actual accomplishments*. Leader-wannabes who can shape the perception that they're smart, personable, verbally adept, aggressive, hardworking, and consistent in their style can increase the probability their bosses, colleagues, and employees will view them as effective leaders.

Substitutes for and Neutralizers of Leadership

One theory of leadership suggests that in many situations leaders' actions are irrelevant.[144] Experience and training are among the **substitutes** that can replace the need for a leader's support or ability to create structure. Organizational characteristics such as explicit formalized goals, rigid rules and procedures, and cohesive work groups can also replace formal leadership, while indifference to organizational rewards can neutralize its effects. **Neutralizers** make it impossible for leader behavior to make any difference to follower outcomes (see Exhibit 12-8).

This observation shouldn't be too surprising. After all, we've introduced a number of variables—such as attitudes, personality, ability, and group norms—that affect employee performance and satisfaction. It's simplistic to think employees are guided to goal accomplishments solely by the actions of their leader. Leadership is simply another independent variable in our overall OB model.

Sometimes the difference between substitutes and neutralizers is fuzzy. If I'm working on a task that's intrinsically enjoyable, theory predicts leadership

Exhibit 12-8	Substitutes for and Neutralizers of Leadership		

Defining Characteristics	Relationship-Oriented Leadership	Task-Oriented Leadership
Individual		
Experience/training	No effect on	Substitutes for
Professionalism	Substitutes for	Substitutes for
Indifference to rewards	Neutralizes	Neutralizes
Job		
Highly structured task	No effect on	Substitutes for
Provides its own feedback	No effect on	Substitutes for
Intrinsically satisfying	Substitutes for	No effect on
Organization		
Explicit formalized goals	No effect on	Substitutes for
Rigid rules and procedures	No effect on	Substitutes for
Cohesive work groups	Substitutes for	Substitutes for

Source: Based on S. Kerr and J. M. Jermier, "Substitutes for Leadership: Their Meaning and Measurement," *Organizational Behavior and Human Performance* (December 1978), p. 378.

will be less important because the task itself provides enough motivation. But does that mean intrinsically enjoyable tasks neutralize leadership effects, or substitute for them, or both? Another problem is that while substitutes for leadership (such as employee characteristics, the nature of the task, and so forth) matter to performance, that doesn't necessarily mean leadership doesn't.[145]

Online Leadership

How do you lead people who are physically separated from you and with whom you communicate electronically? This question needs attention from OB researchers.[146] Today's managers and employees are increasingly linked by networks rather than geographic proximity.

We propose that online leaders have to think carefully about what actions they want their digital messages to initiate. They confront unique challenges, the greatest of which appears to be developing and maintaining trust. **Identification-based trust**, based on a mutual understanding of each other's intentions and appreciation of the other's wants and desires, is particularly difficult to achieve without face-to-face interaction.[147] And online negotiations can also be hindered because parties express lower levels of trust.[148]

We tentatively conclude that good leadership skills will soon include the abilities to communicate support, trust, and inspiration through keyboarded words and accurately read emotions in others' messages. In electronic communication, writing skills are likely to become an extension of interpersonal skills.

substitutes *Attributes, such as experience and training, that can replace the need for a leader's support or ability to create structure.*

neutralizers *Attributes that make it impossible for leader behavior to make any difference to follower outcomes.*

identification-based trust *Trust based on a mutual understanding of each other's intentions and appreciation of each other's wants and desires.*

Finding and Creating Effective Leaders

Source: Carlos Osorio/AP Images.

Richard Wagoner was fired as CEO and chairman of General Motors. His leadership was faulted for playing a part in the automaker's bankruptcy, with critics saying that he did not force much-needed radical change in reducing debt, cutting costs, and investing in fuel-efficient cars. Wagoner, however, inherited a messy situation and accomplished much in fixing GM during his 9 years as CEO. He cut GM's U.S. workforce from 177,000 to 92,000, closed factories, saved billions of dollars by globalizing engineering, manufacturing, and design, and led a resurgence in quality and performance. But the attribution approach to leadership would suggest a reverse causality: that GM's failures caused people to question his leadership, and not the other way around.

How can organizations find or create effective leaders? Let's try to answer that question.

Selecting Leaders

The entire process organizations go through to fill management positions is essentially an exercise in trying to identify effective leaders. You might begin by reviewing the knowledge, skills, and abilities needed to do the job effectively. Personality tests can identify traits associated with leadership—extraversion, conscientiousness, and openness to experience. High self-monitors are better at reading situations and adjusting their behavior accordingly. Candidates with high emotional intelligence should have an advantage, especially in situations requiring transformational leadership.[149] Experience is a poor predictor of leader effectiveness, but situation-specific experience is relevant.

Because nothing lasts forever, the most important event an organization needs to plan for is a change in leadership. Recently, Apple's board of directors has been very concerned with identifying a successor to Steve Jobs. Other organizations seem to spend no time on leadership succession and are surprised when their picks turn out poorly. University of Kentucky chose its men's basketball coach, Billy Gillispie, within 2 weeks of the departure of Tubby Smith. Yet within 2 years Gillispie had been fired, causing observers to wonder whether Kentucky had done its homework in leadership succession.

Training Leaders

Organizations spend billions of dollars on leadership training and development.[150] These efforts take many forms—from $50,000 executive leadership programs offered by universities such as Harvard to sailing experiences offered by the Outward Bound program. Business schools, including some elite programs such as those at Dartmouth, MIT, and Stanford, are placing renewed emphasis on leadership development. Some companies, too, place a lot of emphasis on leadership development. Goldman Sachs is well known for developing leaders; *BusinessWeek* called it the "Leadership Factory."[151]

How can managers get maximum effect from their leadership-training budgets?[152] First, let's recognize the obvious. Leadership training of any kind is likely to be more successful with high self-monitors. Such individuals have the flexibility to change their behavior.

Second, what can organizations teach that might be related to higher leader effectiveness? Probably not "vision creation" but, likely, implementation skills. We can train people to develop "an understanding about content themes critical to effective visions."[153] We can also teach skills such as trust building and mentoring. And leaders can be taught situational-analysis skills. They can learn how to evaluate situations, modify them to better fit their style, and assess which leader behaviors might be most effective in given situations. BHP Billiton, Best Buy, Nokia, and Adobe have hired coaches to help top executives one on one to improve their interpersonal skills and act less autocratically.[154]

Behavioral training through modeling exercises can increase an individual's ability to exhibit charismatic leadership qualities. Recall the researchers who scripted undergraduate business students to "play" charismatic.[155] Finally, leaders can be trained in transformational leadership skills that have bottom-line results, whether in the financial performance of Canadian banks or the effectiveness of soldiers in the Israeli Defense Forces.[156]

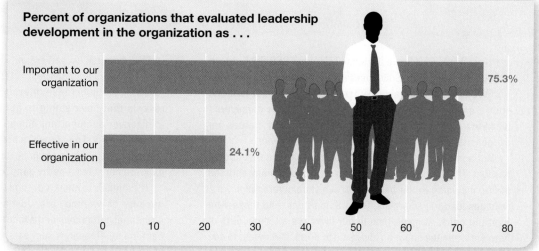

OB Poll   The Leadership Gap

Percent of organizations that evaluated leadership development in the organization as . . .

- Important to our organization: 75.3%
- Effective in our organization: 24.1%

(scale: 0, 10, 20, 30, 40, 50, 60, 70, 80)

Source: G. Kranz, "Special Report: Leadership Development," *Workforce Management* (May 2011), pp. 28–32; and P. J. Kiger, "The Leadership Formula," *Workforce Management* (May 2010), pp. 25–31.

MyManagementLab

Now that you have finished this chapter, go back to **www.mymanagementlab.com** to continue practicing and applying the concepts you've learned.

Summary and Implications for Managers

9 Assess whether charismatic and transformational leadership generalize across cultures.

Leadership plays a central part in understanding group behavior, because it's the leader who usually directs us toward our goals. Knowing what makes a good leader should thus be valuable in improving group performance.

- The early search for a set of universal leadership traits failed. However, recent efforts using the Big Five personality framework show strong and consistent relationships between leadership and extraversion, conscientiousness, and openness to experience.
- The behavioral approach's major contribution was narrowing leadership into task-oriented (initiating structure) and people-oriented (consideration) styles. By considering the situation in which the leader operates, contingency theories promised to improve on the behavioral approach, but only LPC theory has fared well in leadership research.
- Research on charismatic and transformational leadership has made major contributions to our understanding of leadership effectiveness. Organizations want managers who can exhibit transformational leadership qualities and who have vision and the charisma to carry it out.
- Effective managers must develop trusting relationships with followers because, as organizations have become less stable and predictable, strong bonds of trust are replacing bureaucratic rules in defining expectations and relationships.
- Tests and interviews help identify people with leadership qualities. Managers should also consider investing in leadership training such as formal courses, workshops, rotating job responsibilities, coaching, and mentoring.

Heroes Are Made, Not Born

POINT   **COUNTERPOINT**

From Apple CEO Steve Jobs and Microsoft CEO Bill Gates to US Air Pilot Sully Sullenberger and Walmart founder Sam Walton, we often ascribe heroic qualities to our leaders. They are courageous in the face of great risk. They persevered when few would. They take action when most sit by. Heroes are exceptional people who display exceptional behavior.

But some social psychologists question this conventional wisdom. They note that heroism can be found in many spheres of life, including in the behavior of whistleblowers, explorers, religious leaders, scientists, Good Samaritans, and those who beat the odds. At some time in our lives, we all show acts of heroism when the situation allows us to do so. If we want to see more heroic behavior, we need to create more situations that produce it.

Stanford psychologist Phil Zimbardo goes even further to argue that our romantic, inborn, trait-based view of heroic behavior is misplaced:

> "The banality of evil is matched by the banality of heroism. Neither is the consequence of dispositional tendencies. . . . Both emerge in particular situations at particular times, when situational forces play a compelling role in moving individuals across the line from inaction to action."

People exhibit brave behavior every day. The workers who risked their lives to contain Japan's earthquake-ravaged nuclear reactors are a great example. Thus, we err when we think leaders are uniquely positioned to behave heroically. We all can be heroes in the right situation.

Of course heroes are not like everyone else. That's what makes them heroes.

A generation of evidence from behavioral genetics reveals that "everything is genetic," meaning we have yet to discover an important human behavior that does not have genetic origins. Though we're not aware of any such study with respect to heroism, it would be surprising if courageous behavior were not at least partly genetic.

It's foolish to think courageous people aren't exceptional because of who they are. Just as we know there is an entrepreneurial personality and a leader personality, there is a heroic personality. Research suggests, for example, that people who score high on conscientiousness are more likely to engage in courageous behavior.

Not all leaders are heroes, but many have exhibited courageous behavior. When Richard Branson launches his latest attempt to set the world record for an around-the-world balloon flight or sloop sailing, he is the same leader who also exhibits courageous behavior as CEO of Virgin Group. Virgin Group now includes more than 400 companies, including Virgin Galactic, a space tourism company, and Virgin Fuels, whose goal is to revolutionize the industry by providing sustainable fuels for automobiles and aircraft. Same leader, same heroic behavior—in work and in life.

Are we really to believe that Richard Branson and other courageous leaders are just like everyone else?

Sources: Z. E. Franco, K. Blau, and P. G. Zimbardo, "Heroism: A Conceptual Analysis and Differentiation Between Heroic Action and Altruism," *Review of General Psychology* 15, no. 2 (2011), pp. 99–113; O. Dorell, "At Nuke Plant, Heroes Emerge," *USA Today* (March 25, 2011), pp. 1A, 2A; L. J. Walker, J. A. Frimer, and W. L. Dunlop, "Varieties of Moral Personality: Beyond the Banality of Heroism," *Journal of Personality* 78, no. 3 (2010), pp. 907–942; and J. Lehrer, "Are Heroes Born, or Can They Be Made?" *The Wall Street Journal* (December 11, 2010), p. C12.

QUESTIONS FOR REVIEW

1 Are leadership and management different from one another? If so, how?

2 What is the difference between trait and behavioral theories? Are the theories valid?

3 What are the main limitations of behavioral theories of leadership?

4 What is Fiedler's contingency model? Has it been supported in research?

5 How do charismatic and transformational leadership compare and contrast? Are they valid?

6 What is authentic leadership? Why do ethics and trust matter to leadership?

7 How is mentoring valuable to leadership? What are the keys to effective mentoring?

8 How can organizations select and develop effective leaders?

EXPERIENTIAL EXERCISE What Is a Leader?

1. Working on your own, write down 12 adjectives that describe an effective business leader.
2. Break into groups of four or five. Appoint a note-taker and spokesperson. Compare your lists of adjectives, making a new list of those common across two or more persons' lists. (Count synonyms—steadfast and unwavering, for example—as the same.)

3. Each spokesperson should present the group's list to the class.
4. Are there many similarities among the lists? What does this tell you about the nature of leadership?

ETHICAL DILEMMA Undercover Leaders

As you saw in one of the Chapter 1 cases, the television show *Undercover Boss* features a leader working undercover in his or her own company to find out how the organization really works. In Chapter 1, we considered the show as an example of management by walking around (MBWA). Here, we consider the ethical leadership lessons it might offer.

Executives from DirecTV, Hooters, 7-Eleven, NASCAR, Chiquita, and Choice Hotels have been featured on the show. Typically, the executive works undercover for a week. Then the employees with whom and under whom the leader has worked are summoned to company headquarters and rewarded, or punished, for their actions.

In one episode, Waste Management's president Larry O'Donnell, sporting gray stubble and work clothes, works the back of a trash truck. Later, he sorts recyclables from a fast-moving conveyor belt. Under the barking orders of a supervisor, he even cleans a long line of portable toilets.

Some criticize the show for its faux realism. The CEOs know they are on camera, so every word and facial expression is for the cameras. Many employees know they are on camera too. One critic commented, "Because the series' very existence requires cooperation from the executives that it purports to make suffer for their sins, it has to raise them higher, in the end, than it found them at the start."

Realistic or not, the series continues to be popular. After all, haven't you sometimes wondered what it would be like to do someone else's job?

The idea has moved beyond television too. Recently, the Australian government created a program that places CEOs undercover in their own workplaces. One CEO, Phil Smith of clothing retailer Fletcher Jones, said in tears of the experience, "I learnt a lot from this that I wouldn't have found out any other way."

Questions

1. Do you think it is ethical for a leader to go undercover in his or her organization? Why or why not?

2. Do you think leaders who work undercover are really changed as a result of their experiences?

3. Would you support a government program that gave companies incentives to send leaders undercover?

Sources: K. Jones, "CEOs Go Undercover Over Workplace Safety," *SafetyAtWorkBlog* (February 5, 2011), downloaded June 10, 2011, from http://safetyatworkblog.wordpress.com/; W. Kern, "The Fakery of CEOs Undercover," *Bloomberg Businessweek* (February 15, 2010), pp. 78–79.

CASE INCIDENT 1 Leadership Mettle Forged in Battle

In 2008, facing a serious shortage of leadership-ready employees at the store management level, Walmart decided to recruit from the U.S. military. The company sent recruiters to military job fairs and hired 150 junior military officers, pairing them with store mentors to learn on the job. The result: Walmart claims that it's been able to bring in world-class leaders who were ready to take over once they had learned the retail business that Walmart could easily teach them. Other organizations that have heavily recruited from the military in recent years include GE, Home Depot, Lowe's, State Farm Insurance, Merck, and Bank of America.

It's not really surprising to see companies turn to the military for leadership potential. A long tradition of books and seminars advises leaders to think like military leaders ranging from Sun Tzu to Norman Schwarzkopf. And military veterans do have a variety of valuable skills learned through experience. General David Petraeus notes, "Tell me anywhere in the business world where a 22- or 23-year-old is responsible for 35 or 40 other individuals on missions that involve life and death... They're under enormous scrutiny, on top of everything else. These are pretty formative experiences. It's a bit of a crucible-like experience that they go through." Military leaders are also used to having to make due in less than optimal conditions, negotiate across cultures, and operate under extreme stress.

However, they do have to relearn some lessons from the service. Some may not be used to leading someone like an eccentric computer programmer who works strange hours and dresses like a slob, but who brings more to the company's bottom line than a conventional employee would. Indeed, in some companies like Google, there is nothing like the chain of command military leaders are used to. Still, most forecasts suggest there will be an ample supply of battle-tested military leaders ready to report for corporate duty in the near future, and many companies are eager to have them.

Questions

1. Do you think leaders in military contexts exhibit the same qualities as organizational leaders? Why or why not?

2. In what ways not mentioned in the case would military leadership lessons *not* apply in the private sector? What might military leaders have to re-learn to work in business?

3. Are specific types of work or situations more likely to benefit from the presence of "battle-tested" leaders? List a few examples.

Sources: B. O'Keefe, J. Birger, and D. Burke, "Battle Tested," *Fortune* (March 22, 2010), p. 108–118; B. Whitmore, "Hiring Military Veterans Is Good Business," *Huntington WV Herald-Dispatch* (November 6, 2010), www.herald-dispatch.com; and B. Wansink, C. R. Payne, and K. van Ittersum, "Profiling the Heroic Leader: Empirical Lessons from Combat-Decorated Veterans of World War II," *Leadership Quarterly* 19, no. 5 (2008), pp. 547–555.

CASE INCIDENT 2 Leadership Factories

Companies differ markedly in their ability to produce future leaders, as several recent analyses of the 1,187 largest publicly traded U.S. companies revealed. Among the CEOs in one study, a remarkable total of 26 once worked at General Electric (GE).

However, as the following table shows, on a per-employee basis, that ability earns GE only tenth place in terms of the likelihood of a current or former employee becoming CEO of a large company. Top on the list is management consulting firm McKinsey & Company. Amazingly, if we extrapolate into the future from the current stock of McKinsey alums who are CEOs, of every 1,060 McKinsey employees, one will become CEO of a *Fortune* 1000 company.

Company	Size (employees)	CEOs Produced	Odds
McKinsey & Co.	17,000	16	1,060:1
Baxter International	48,500	11	4,410:1
Motorola	60,000	7	8,570:1
Intel	82,500	8	10,310:1
Procter & Gamble (P&G)	127,000	12	10,580:1
General Electric (GE)	287,000	26	11,040:1
Ernst & Young	144,000	12	12,000:1

Some companies did not fare nearly as well, such as Citigroup (odds: 30,180:1), AT&T (odds: 23,220:1) and Johnson & Johnson (odds: 15,275:1).

While some might dismiss the results, not surprisingly, the companies at the top of the list do not. "We are a leadership engine and a talent machine," said retiring Procter & Gamble CEO A. G. Lafley.

Questions

1. Management consulting firms did very well on a per-employee basis, partly because they are mostly made up of managers (as opposed to blue-collar or entry-level workers). How big a factor do you think composition of the workforce is in likelihood of producing a CEO?

2. Do you think so-called leadership factories are also better places for nonleaders to work? Why or why not?

3. Assume you had job offers from two companies that differed only in how often they produced CEOs. Would this difference affect your decision?

4. Do these data support the value of leader selection and leader development? Why or why not?

Source: Based on D. McCarthy, "The 2008 Best Companies for Leaders," *Great Leadership* (February 17, 2009), www.greatleadership bydan.com/2009/02/2008-best-companies-for-leaders.html; D. Jones, "Some Firms' Fertile Soil Grows Crop of Future CEOs," *USA Today* (January 9, 2008), pp. 1B, 2B; and P. O'Connell, "How Companies Develop Great Leaders," *Bloomberg Businessweek* (February 16, 2010), www.businessweek.com.

ENDNOTES

1. M. Javidan, P. W. Dorfman, M. S. de Luque, and R. J. House, "In the Eye of the Beholder: Cross Cultural Lessons in Leadership from Project Globe," *Academy of Management Perspectives* (February 2006), pp. 67–90.

2. J. G. Geier, "A Trait Approach to the Study of Leadership in Small Groups," *Journal of Communication* (December 1967), pp. 316–323.

3. S. A. Kirkpatrick and E. A. Locke, "Leadership: Do Traits Matter?" *Academy of Management Executive* (May 1991), pp. 48–60; and S. J. Zaccaro, R. J. Foti, and D. A. Kenny, "Self-Monitoring and Trait-Based Variance in Leadership: An Investigation of Leader Flexibility Across Multiple Group Situations," *Journal of Applied Psychology* (April 1991), pp. 308–315.

4. See T. A. Judge, J. E. Bono, R. Ilies, and M. W. Gerhardt, "Personality and Leadership: A Qualitative and Quantitative Review," *Journal of Applied Psychology* (August 2002), pp. 765–780.

5. Judge, Bono, Ilies, and Gerhardt, "Personality and Leadership."

6. D. R. Ames and F. J. Flynn, "What Breaks a Leader: The Curvilinear Relation Between Assertiveness and Leadership," *Journal of Personality and Social Psychology* 92, no. 2 (2007), pp. 307–324.

7. K. Ng, S. Ang, and K. Chan, "Personality and Leader Effectiveness: A Moderated Mediation Model of Leadership Self-Efficacy, Job Demands, and Job Autonomy," *Journal of Applied Psychology* 93, no. 4 (2008), pp. 733–743.

8. This section is based on J. M. George, "Emotions and Leadership: The Role of Emotional Intelligence," *Human Relations* (August 2000), pp. 1027–1055; C.-S. Wong and K. S. Law, "The Effects of Leader and Follower Emotional Intelligence on Performance and Attitude: An Exploratory Study," *Leadership Quarterly* (June 2002), pp. 243–274; and J. Antonakis, N. M. Ashkanasy, and M. T. Dasborough, "Does Leadership Need Emotional Intelligence?" *Leadership Quarterly* 20 (2009), pp. 247–261.

9. R. H. Humphrey, J. M. Pollack, and T. H. Hawver, "Leading with Emotional Labor," *Journal of Managerial Psychology* 23 (2008), pp. 151–168.

10. F. Walter, M. S. Cole, and R. H. Humphrey, "Emotional Intelligence: Sine Qua Non of Leadership or Folderol?"

Academy of Management Perspectives (February 2011), pp. 45–59.

11. S. Côté, P. N. Lopez, P. Salovey, and C. T. H. Miners, "Emotional Intelligence and Leadership Emergence in Small Groups," *Leadership Quarterly* 21 (2010), pp. 496–508.

12. R. G. Lord, C. L. DeVader, and G. M. Alliger, "A Meta-Analysis of the Relation Between Personality Traits and Leadership Perceptions: An Application of Validity Generalization Procedures," *Journal of Applied Psychology* (August 1986), pp. 402–410; and J. A. Smith and R. J. Foti, "A Pattern Approach to the Study of Leader Emergence," *Leadership Quarterly* (Summer 1998), pp. 147–160.

13. R. M. Stogdill and A. E. Coons (eds.), *Leader Behavior: Its Description and Measurement*, Research Monograph no. 88 (Columbus: Ohio State University, Bureau of Business Research, 1951). This research is updated in C. A. Schriesheim, C. C. Cogliser, and L. L. Neider, "Is It 'Trustworthy'? A Multiple-Levels-of-Analysis Reexamination of an Ohio State Leadership Study, with Implications for Future Research," *Leadership Quarterly* (Summer 1995), pp. 111–145; and T. A. Judge, R. F. Piccolo, and R. Ilies, "The Forgotten Ones? The Validity of Consideration and Initiating Structure in Leadership Research," *Journal of Applied Psychology* (February 2004), pp. 36–51.

14. D. Akst, "The Rewards of Recognizing a Job Well Done," *The Wall Street Journal* (January 31, 2007), p. D9.

15. Judge, Piccolo, and Ilies, "The Forgotten Ones?"

16. M. Javidan, P. W. Dorfman, M. S. de Luque, and R. J. House, "In the Eye of the Beholder: Cross Cultural Lessons in Leadership from Project GLOBE," *Academy of Management Perspectives* (February 2006), pp. 67–90.

17. F. E. Fiedler, *A Theory of Leadership Effectiveness* (New York: McGraw-Hill, 1967).

18. S. Shiflett, "Is There a Problem with the LPC Score in LEADER MATCH?" *Personnel Psychology* (Winter 1981), pp. 765–769.

19. F. E. Fiedler, M. M. Chemers, and L. Mahar, *Improving Leadership Effectiveness: The Leader Match Concept* (New York: Wiley, 1977).

20. Cited in R. J. House and R. N. Aditya, "The Social Scientific Study of Leadership," *Journal of Management* 23, no. 3 (1997), p. 422.

21. L. H. Peters, D. D. Hartke, and J. T. Pohlmann, "Fiedler's Contingency Theory of Leadership: An Application of the Meta-Analysis Procedures of Schmidt and Hunter," *Psychological Bulletin* (March 1985), pp. 274–285; C. A. Schriesheim, B. J. Tepper, and L. A. Tetrault, "Least Preferred Coworker Score, Situational Control, and Leadership Effectiveness: A Meta-Analysis of Contingency Model Performance Predictions," *Journal of Applied Psychology* (August 1994), pp. 561–573; and R. Ayman, M. M. Chemers, and F. Fiedler, "The Contingency Model of Leadership Effectiveness: Its Levels of Analysis," *Leadership Quarterly* (Summer 1995), pp. 147–167.

22. House and Aditya, "The Social Scientific Study of Leadership."

23. See, for instance, R. W. Rice, "Psychometric Properties of the Esteem for the Least Preferred Coworker (LPC) Scale," *Academy of Management Review* (January 1978), pp. 106–118; C. A. Schriesheim, B. D. Bannister, and W. H. Money, "Psychometric Properties of the LPC Scale: An Extension of Rice's Review," *Academy of Management Review* (April 1979), pp. 287–290; and J. K. Kennedy, J. M. Houston, M. A. Korgaard, and D. D. Gallo, "Construct Space of the Least Preferred Coworker (LPC) Scale," *Educational & Psychological Measurement* (Fall 1987), pp. 807–814.

24. See E. H. Schein, *Organizational Psychology*, 3rd ed. (Upper Saddle River, NJ: Prentice Hall, 1980), pp. 116–117; and B. Kabanoff, "A Critique of Leader Match and Its Implications for Leadership Research," *Personnel Psychology* (Winter 1981), pp. 749–764.

25. See, for instance, Ibid., pp. 67–84; C. L. Graeff, "Evolution of Situational Leadership Theory: A Critical Review," *Leadership Quarterly* 8, no. 2 (1997), pp. 153–170; and R. P. Vecchio and K. J. Boatwright, "Preferences for Idealized Styles of Supervision," *Leadership Quarterly* (August 2002), pp. 327–342.

26. R. J. House, "A Path-Goal Theory of Leader Effectiveness," *Administrative Science Quarterly* (September 1971), pp. 321–338; R. J. House and T. R. Mitchell, "Path-Goal Theory of Leadership," *Journal of Contemporary Business* (Autumn 1974), pp. 81–97; and R. J. House, "Path-Goal Theory of Leadership: Lessons, Legacy, and a Reformulated Theory," *Leadership Quarterly* (Fall 1996), pp. 323–352.

27. J. C. Wofford and L. Z. Liska, "Path-Goal Theories of Leadership: A Meta-Analysis," *Journal of Management* (Winter 1993), pp. 857–876; and P. M. Podsakoff, S. B. MacKenzie, and M. Ahearne, "Searching for a Needle in a Haystack: Trying to Identify the Illusive Moderators of Leadership Behaviors," *Journal of Management* 21 (1995), pp. 423–470.

28. J. R. Villa, J. P. Howell, and P. W. Dorfman, "Problems with Detecting Moderators in Leadership Research Using Moderated Multiple Regression," *Leadership Quarterly* 14 (2003), pp. 3–23; C. A. Schriesheim and L. Neider, "Path-Goal Leadership Theory: The Long and Winding Road," *Leadership Quarterly* 7 (1996), pp. 317–321; and M. G. Evans, "R. J. House's 'A Path-Goal Theory of Leader Effectiveness,'" *Leadership Quarterly* 7 (1996), pp. 305–309.

29. A. E. Colbert and L. A. Witt, "The Role of Goal-Focused Leadership in Enabling the Expression of Conscientiousness," *Journal of Applied Psychology* 94, no. 3 (2009), pp. 790–796.

30. S. J. Perry, L. A. Witt, L. M. Penney, and L. Atwater, "The Downside of Goal-Focused Leadership: The Role of Personality in Subordinate Exhaustion," *Journal of Applied Psychology* 95, no. 6 (2010), pp. 1145–1153.

31. See V. H. Vroom and P. W. Yetton, *Leadership and Decision-Making* (Pittsburgh: University of Pittsburgh Press, 1973); and V. H. Vroom and A. G. Jago, "The Role of the Situation in Leadership," *American Psychologist* (January 2007), pp. 17–24.

32. See, for example, R. H. G. Field, "A Test of the Vroom-Yetton Normative Model of Leadership," *Journal of Applied*

Psychology (October 1982), pp. 523–532; C. R. Leana, "Power Relinquishment Versus Power Sharing: Theoretical Clarification and Empirical Comparison of Delegation and Participation," *Journal of Applied Psychology* (May 1987), pp. 228–233; J. T. Ettling and A. G. Jago, "Participation Under Conditions of Conflict: More on the Validity of the Vroom-Yetton Model," *Journal of Management Studies* (January 1988), pp. 73–83; R. H. G. Field and R. J. House, "A Test of the Vroom-Yetton Model Using Manager and Subordinate Reports," *Journal of Applied Psychology* (June 1990), pp. 362–366; and R. H. G. Field and J. P. Andrews, "Testing the Incremental Validity of the Vroom-Jago Versus Vroom-Yetton Models of Participation in Decision Making," *Journal of Behavioral Decision Making* (December 1998), pp. 251–261.

33. House and Aditya, "The Social Scientific Study of Leadership," p. 428.

34. W. Bennis, "The Challenges of Leadership in the Modern World," *American Psychologist* (January 2007), pp. 2–5.

35. X. Zhou and C. A. Schriesheim, "Supervisor–Subordinate Convergence in Descriptions of Leader–Member Exchange (LMX) Quality: Review and Testable Propositions." *Leadership Quarterly* 20, no. 6 (2009), pp. 920–932; G. B. Graen and M. Uhl-Bien, "Relationship-Based Approach to Leadership: Development of Leader–Member Exchange (LMX) Theory of Leadership Over 25 Years: Applying a Multi-Domain Perspective," *Leadership Quarterly* (Summer 1995), pp. 219–247; R. C. Liden, R. T. Sparrowe, and S. J. Wayne, "Leader–Member Exchange Theory: The Past and Potential for the Future," in G. R. Ferris (ed.), *Research in Personnel and Human Resource Management,* vol. 15 (Greenwich, CT: JAI Press, 1997), pp. 47–119; and C. A. Schriesheim, S. L. Castro, X. Zhou, and F. J. Yammarino, "The Folly of Theorizing 'A' but Testing 'B': A Selective Level-of-Analysis Review of the Field and a Detailed Leader–Member Exchange Illustration," *Leadership Quarterly* (Winter 2001), pp. 515–551.

36. B. Erdogan and T. N. Bauer, "Differentiated Leader–Member Exchanges: The Buffering Role of Justice Climate," *Journal of Applied Psychology* 95, no. 6 (2010), pp. 1104–1120; R. C. Liden, S. J. Wayne, and D. Stilwell, "A Longitudinal Study of the Early Development of Leader–Member Exchanges," *Journal of Applied Psychology* (August 1993), pp. 662–674; S. J. Wayne, L. M. Shore, W. H. Bommer, and L. E. Tetrick, "The Role of Fair Treatment and Rewards in Perceptions of Organizational Support and Leader–Member Exchange," *Journal of Applied Psychology* 87, no. 3 (June 2002), pp. 590–598; and S. S. Masterson, K. Lewis, and B. M. Goldman, "Integrating Justice and Social Exchange: The Differing Effects of Fair Procedures and Treatment on Work Relationships," *Academy of Management Journal* 43, no. 4 (August 2000), pp. 738–748.

37. D. Duchon, S. G. Green, and T. D. Taber, "Vertical Dyad Linkage: A Longitudinal Assessment of Antecedents, Measures, and Consequences," *Journal of Applied Psychology* (February 1986), pp. 56–60; Liden, Wayne, and Stilwell, "A Longitudinal Study on the Early Development of Leader–Member

Exchanges"; and M. Uhl-Bien, "Relationship Development as a Key Ingredient for Leadership Development," in S. E. Murphy and R. E. Riggio (eds.), *Future of Leadership Development* (Mahwah, NJ: Lawrence Erlbaum, 2003) pp. 129–147.

38. R. Vecchio and D. M. Brazil, "Leadership and Sex-Similarity: A Comparison in a Military Setting," *Personnel Psychology* 60 (2007), pp. 303–335.

39. See, for instance, C. R. Gerstner and D. V. Day, "Meta-Analytic Review of Leader–Member Exchange Theory: Correlates and Construct Issues," *Journal of Applied Psychology* (December 1997), pp. 827–844; R. Ilies, J. D. Nahrgang, and F. P. Morgeson, "Leader–Member Exchange and Citizenship Behaviors: A Meta-Analysis," *Journal of Applied Psychology* 92, no. 1 (2007), pp. 269–277; and Z. Chen, W. Lam, and J. A. Zhong, "Leader–Member Exchange and Member Performance: A New Look at Individual-Level Negative Feedback-Seeking Behavior and Team-Level Empowerment Culture," *Journal of Applied Psychology* 92, no. 1 (2007), pp. 202–212.

40. R. Eisenberger, G. Karagonlar, F. Stinglhamber, P. Neves, T. E. Becker, M. G. Gonzalez-Morales, and M. Steiger-Mueller, "Leader-Member Exchange and Affective Organizational Commitment: The Contribution of Supervisor's Organizational Embodiment," *Journal of Applied Psychology* 95, no. 6 (2010), pp. 1085–1103.

41. B. Erdogan and T. N. Bauer, "Differentiated Leader-Member Exchanges: The Buffering Role of Justice Climate," *Journal of Applied Psychology* 95, no. 6 (2010), pp. 1104–1120.

42. M. Ozer, "Personal and Task-Related Moderators of Leader-Member Exchange Among Software Developers," *Journal of Applied Psychology* 93, no. 5 (2008), pp. 1174–1182.

43. M. Weber, *The Theory of Social and Economic Organization,* A. M. Henderson and T. Parsons (trans.) (New York: The Free Press, 1947).

44. J. A. Conger and R. N. Kanungo, "Behavioral Dimensions of Charismatic Leadership," in J. A. Conger, R. N. Kanungo, and Associates (eds.), *Charismatic Leadership* (San Francisco: Jossey-Bass, 1988), p. 79.

45. J. A. Conger and R. N. Kanungo, *Charismatic Leadership in Organizations* (Thousand Oaks, CA: Sage, 1998); and R. Awamleh and W. L. Gardner, "Perceptions of Leader Charisma and Effectiveness: The Effects of Vision Content, Delivery, and Organizational Performance," *Leadership Quarterly* (Fall 1999), pp. 345–373.

46. R. J. House and J. M. Howell, "Personality and Charismatic Leadership," *Leadership Quarterly* 3 (1992), pp. 81–108; D. N. Den Hartog and P. L. Koopman, "Leadership in Organizations," in N. Anderson and D. S. Ones (eds.), *Handbook of Industrial, Work and Organizational Psychology,* vol. 2 (Thousand Oaks, CA: Sage, 2002), pp. 166–187.

47. See J. A. Conger and R. N. Kanungo, "Training Charismatic Leadership: A Risky and Critical Task," *Charismatic Leadership* (San Francisco: Jossey-Bass, 1988), pp. 309–323; A. J. Towler, "Effects of Charismatic Influence Training on Attitudes, Behavior, and Performance," *Personnel Psychology* (Summer 2003), pp. 363–381; and M. Frese, S. Beimel, and S. Schoenborn, "Action Training for Charismatic Leadership: Two Evaluations of Studies of a Commercial

Training Module on Inspirational Communication of a Vision," *Personnel Psychology* (Autumn 2003), pp. 671–697.

48. R. J. Richardson and S. K. Thayer, *The Charisma Factor: How to Develop Your Natural Leadership Ability* (Upper Saddle River, NJ: Prentice Hall, 1993).

49. J. M. Howell and P. J. Frost, "A Laboratory Study of Charismatic Leadership," *Organizational Behavior and Human Decision Processes* (April 1989), pp. 243–269. See also Frese, Beimel, and Schoenborn, "Action Training for Charismatic Leadership."

50. B. Shamir, R. J. House, and M. B. Arthur, "The Motivational Effects of Charismatic Leadership: A Self-Concept Theory," *Organization Science* (November 1993), pp. 577–594.

51. D. N. Den Hartog, A. H. B. De Hoogh, and A. E. Keegan, "The Interactive Effects of Belongingness and Charisma on Helping and Compliance," *Journal of Applied Psychology* 92, no. 4 (2007), pp. 1131–1139.

52. A. Erez, V. F. Misangyi, D. E. Johnson, M. A. LePine, and K. C. Halverson, "Stirring the Hearts of Followers: Charismatic Leadership as the Transferal of Affect," *Journal of Applied Psychology* 93, no. 3 (2008), pp. 602–615. For reviews on the role of vision in leadership, see S. J. Zaccaro, "Visionary and Inspirational Models of Executive Leadership: Empirical Review and Evaluation," in S. J. Zaccaro (ed.), *The Nature of Executive Leadership: A Conceptual and Empirical Analysis of Success* (Washington, DC: American Psychological Association, 2001), pp. 259–278; and M. Hauser and R. J. House, "Lead Through Vision and Values," in E. A. Locke (ed.), *Handbook of Principles of Organizational Behavior* (Malden, MA: Blackwell, 2004), pp. 257–273.

53. D. A. Waldman, B. M. Bass, and F. J. Yammarino, "Adding to Contingent-Reward Behavior: The Augmenting Effect of Charismatic Leadership," *Group & Organization Studies*, December 1990, pp. 381–394; and S. A. Kirkpatrick and E. A. Locke, "Direct and Indirect Effects of Three Core Charismatic Leadership Components on Performance and Attitudes," *Journal of Applied Psychology* (February 1996), pp. 36–51.

54. A. H. B. de Hoogh, D. N. Den Hartog, P. L. Koopman, H. Thierry, P. T. van den Berg, and J. G. van der Weide, "Charismatic Leadership, Environmental Dynamism, and Performance," *European Journal of Work & Organizational Psychology* (December 2004), pp. 447–471; S. Harvey, M. Martin, and D. Stout, "Instructor's Transformational Leadership: University Student Attitudes and Ratings," *Psychological Reports* (April 2003), pp. 395–402; and D. A. Waldman, M. Javidan, and P. Varella, "Charismatic Leadership at the Strategic Level: A New Application of Upper Echelons Theory," *Leadership Quarterly* (June 2004), pp. 355–380.

55. R. J. House, "A 1976 Theory of Charismatic Leadership," in J. G. Hunt and L. L. Larson (eds.), *Leadership: The Cutting Edge* (Carbondale: Southern Illinois University Press, 1977), pp. 189–207; and House and Aditya, "The Social Scientific Study of Leadership," p. 441.

56. J. C. Pastor, M. Mayo, and B. Shamir, "Adding Fuel to Fire: The Impact of Followers' Arousal on Ratings of Charisma," *Journal of Applied Psychology* 92, no. 6 (2007), pp. 1584–1596.

57. A. H. B. De Hoogh and D. N. Den Hartog, "Neuroticism and Locus of Control as Moderators of the Relationships of Charismatic and Autocratic Leadership with Burnout," *Journal of Applied Psychology* 94, no. 4 (2009), pp. 1058–1067.

58. F. Cohen, S. Solomon, M. Maxfield, T. Pyszczynski, and J. Greenberg, "Fatal Attraction: The Effects of Mortality Salience on Evaluations of Charismatic, Task-Oriented, and Relationship-Oriented Leaders," *Psychological Sciences* (December 2004), pp. 846–851; and M. G. Ehrhart and K. J. Klein, "Predicting Followers' Preferences for Charismatic Leadership: The Influence of Follower Values and Personality," *Leadership Quarterly* (Summer 2001), pp. 153–179.

59. H. L. Tosi, V. Misangyi, A. Fanelli, D. A. Waldman, and F. J. Yammarino, "CEO Charisma, Compensation, and Firm Performance," *Leadership Quarterly* (June 2004), pp. 405–420.

60. See, for instance, R. Khurana, *Searching for a Corporate Savior: The Irrational Quest for Charismatic CEOs* (Princeton, NJ: Princeton University Press, 2002); and J. A. Raelin, "The Myth of Charismatic Leaders," *Training & Development* (March 2003), pp. 47–54.

61. B. M. Galvin, D. A. Waldman, and P. Balthazard, "Visionary Communication Qualities as Mediators of the Relationship between Narcissism and Attributions of Leader Charisma," *Personnel Psychology* 63, no. 3 (2010), pp. 509–537.

62. See, for instance, B. M. Bass, B. J. Avolio, D. I. Jung, and Y. Berson, "Predicting Unit Performance by Assessing Transformational and Transactional Leadership," *Journal of Applied Psychology* (April 2003), pp. 207–218; and T. A. Judge and R. F. Piccolo, "Transformational and Transactional Leadership: A Meta-Analytic Test of Their Relative Validity," *Journal of Applied Psychology* (October 2004), pp. 755–768.

63. B. M. Bass, "Leadership: Good, Better, Best," *Organizational Dynamics* (Winter 1985), pp. 26–40; and J. Seltzer and B. M. Bass, "Transformational Leadership: Beyond Initiation and Consideration," *Journal of Management* (December 1990), pp. 693–703.

64. T. R. Hinkin and C. A. Schriesheim, "An Examination of 'Nonleadership': From Laissez-Faire Leadership to Leader Reward Omission and Punishment Omission," *Journal of Applied Psychology* 93, no. 6 (2008), pp. 1234–1248.

65. S. J. Shin and J. Zhou, "Transformational Leadership, Conservation, and Creativity: Evidence from Korea," *Academy of Management Journal* (December 2003), pp. 703–714; V. J. García-Morales, F. J. Lloréns-Montes, and A. J. Verdú-Jover, "The Effects of Transformational Leadership on Organizational Performance Through Knowledge and Innovation," *British Journal of Management* 19, no. 4 (2008), pp. 299–313; and S. A. Eisenbeiss, D. van Knippenberg, and S. Boerner, "Transformational Leadership and Team Innovation: Integrating Team Climate Principles," *Journal of Applied Psychology* 93, no. 6 (2008), pp. 1438–1446.

66. Y. Ling, Z. Simsek, M. H. Lubatkin, and J. F. Veiga, "Transformational Leadership's Role in Promoting Corporate Entrepreneurship: Examining the CEO-TMT Interface," *Academy of Management Journal* 51, no. 3 (2008), pp. 557–576.

67. X. Zhang and K. M. Bartol, "Linking Empowering Leadership and Employee Creativity: The Influence of Psychological Empowerment, Intrinsic Motivation, and Creative Process Engagement," *Academy of Management Journal* 53, no. 1 (2010), pp. 107–128.

68. A. E. Colbert, A. E. Kristof-Brown, B. H. Bradley, and M. R. Barrick, "CEO Transformational Leadership: The Role of Goal Importance Congruence in Top Management Teams," *Academy of Management Journal* 51, no. 1 (2008), pp. 81–96.

69. D. Zohar and O. Tenne-Gazit, "Transformational Leadership and Group Interaction as Climate Antecedents: A Social Network Analysis," *Journal of Applied Psychology* 93, no. 4 (2008), pp. 744–757.

70. F. O. Walumbwa, B. J. Avolio, and W. Zhu, "How Transformational Leadership Weaves Its Influence on Individual Job Performance: The Role of Identification and Efficacy Beliefs," *Personnel Psychology* 61, no. 4 (2008), pp. 793–825.

71. J. E. Bono and T. A. Judge, "Self-Concordance at Work: Toward Understanding the Motivational Effects of Transformational Leaders," *Academy of Management Journal* (October 2003), pp. 554–571; Y. Berson and B. J. Avolio, "Transformational Leadership and the Dissemination of Organizational Goals: A Case Study of a Telecommunication Firm," *Leadership Quarterly* (October 2004), pp. 625–646; and J. Schaubroeck, S. S. K. Lam, and S. E. Cha, "Embracing Transformational Leadership: Team Values and the Impact of Leader Behavior on Team Performance," *Journal of Applied Psychology* 92, no. 4 (2007), pp. 1020–1030.

72. J. R. Baum, E. A. Locke, and S. A. Kirkpatrick, "A Longitudinal Study of the Relation of Vision and Vision Communication to Venture Growth in Entrepreneurial Firms," *Journal of Applied Psychology* (February 2000), pp. 43–54.

73. B. J. Avolio, W. Zhu, W. Koh, and P. Bhatia, "Transformational Leadership and Organizational Commitment: Mediating Role of Psychological Empowerment and Moderating Role of Structural Distance," *Journal of Organizational Behavior* (December 2004), pp. 951–968; and T. Dvir, N. Kass, and B. Shamir, "The Emotional Bond: Vision and Organizational Commitment Among High-Tech Employees," *Journal of Organizational Change Management* 17, no. 2 (2004), pp. 126–143.

74. R. T. Keller, "Transformational Leadership, Initiating Structure, and Substitutes for Leadership: A Longitudinal Study of Research and Development Project Team Performance," *Journal of Applied Psychology* 91, no. 1 (2006), pp. 202–210.

75. Y. Gong, J. Huang, and J. Farh, "Employee Learning Orientation, Transformational Leadership, and Employee Creativity: The Mediating Role of Employee Creative Self-Efficacy," *Academy of Management Journal* 52, no. 4 (2009), pp. 765–778.

76. G. Wang, I. Oh, S. H. Courtright, and A. E. Colbert, "Transformational Leadership and Performance Across Criteria and Levels: A Meta-Analytic Review of 25 Years of Research," *Group and Organization Management* 36, no. 2 (2011), pp. 223–270.

77. Y. Ling, Z. Simsek, M. H. Lubatkin, and J. F. Veiga, "The Impact of Transformational CEOs on the Performance of Small- to Medium-Sized Firms: Does Organizational Context Matter?" *Journal of Applied Psychology* 93, no. 4 (2008), pp. 923–934.

78. Schaubroeck, Lam, and Cha, "Embracing Transformational Leadership."

79. B. L. Kirkman, G. Chen, J. Farh, Z. X. Chen, and K. B. Lowe, "Individual Power Distance Orientation and Follower Reactions to Transformational Leaders: A Cross-Level, Cross-Cultural Examination," *Academy of Management Journal* 52, no. 4 (2009), pp. 744–764.

80. J. Liu, O. Siu, and K. Shi, "Transformational Leadership and Employee Well-Being: The Mediating Role of Trust in the Leader and Self-Efficacy," *Applied Psychology: An International Review* 59, no. 3 (2010), pp. 454–479.

81. X. Wang and J. M. Howell, "Exploring the Dual-Level Effects of Transformational Leadership on Followers," *Journal of Applied Psychology* 95, no. 6 (2010), pp. 1134–1144.

82. H. Hetland, G. M. Sandal, and T. B. Johnsen, "Burnout in the Information Technology Sector: Does Leadership Matter?" *European Journal of Work and Organizational Psychology* 16, no. 1 (2007), pp. 58–75; and K. B. Lowe, K. G. Kroeck, and N. Sivasubramaniam, "Effectiveness Correlates of Transformational and Transactional Leadership: A Meta-Analytic Review of the MLQ Literature," *Leadership Quarterly* (Fall 1996), pp. 385–425.

83. See, for instance, J. Barling, T. Weber, and E. K. Kelloway, "Effects of Transformational Leadership Training on Attitudinal and Financial Outcomes: A Field Experiment," *Journal of Applied Psychology* (December 1996), pp. 827–832; and T. Dvir, D. Eden, and B. J. Avolio, "Impact of Transformational Leadership on Follower Development and Performance: A Field Experiment," *Academy of Management Journal* (August 2002), pp. 735–744.

84. R. J. House, M. Javidan, P. Hanges, and P. Dorfman, "Understanding Cultures and Implicit Leadership Theories Across the Globe: An Introduction to Project GLOBE," *Journal of World Business* (Spring 2002), pp. 3–10.

85. D. E. Carl and M. Javidan, "Universality of Charismatic Leadership: A Multi-Nation Study," paper presented at the National Academy of Management Conference, Washington, DC (August 2001), p. 29.

86. N. Beccalli, "European Business Forum Asks: Do Companies Get the Leaders They Deserve?" *European Business Forum* (2003), www.pwcglobal.com/extweb/pwcpublications.nsf/DocID/D1EC3380F589844585256D7300346A1B.

87. See B. J. Avolio, W. L. Gardner, F. O. Walumbwa, F. Luthans, and D. R. May, "Unlocking the Mask: A Look at the Process by Which Authentic Leaders Impact Follower Attitudes and Behaviors," *Leadership Quarterly* (December 2004), pp. 801–823; W. L. Gardner and J. R. Schermerhorn Jr., "Performance Gains Through Positive Organizational Behavior and Authentic Leadership," *Organizational Dynamics* (August 2004), pp. 270–281; and M. M. Novicevic, M. G. Harvey, M. R. Buckley, J. A. Brown-Radford, and R. Evans, "Authentic Leadership: A Historical Perspective,"

Journal of Leadership and Organizational Behavior 13, no. 1 (2006), pp. 64–76.

88. C. Tan, "CEO Pinching Penney in a Slowing Economy," *The Wall Street Journal* (January 31, 2008), pp. 1–2; and A. Carter, "Lighting a Fire Under Campbell," *BusinessWeek* (December 4, 2006), pp. 96–101.

89. R. Ilies, F. P. Morgeson, and J. D. Nahrgang, "Authentic Leadership and Eudaemonic Wellbeing: Understanding Leader-follower Outcomes," *Leadership Quarterly* 16 (2005), pp. 373–394; B. Levin, "Raj Rajaratnam Did Not Appreciate Rajat Gupta's Attempt to Leave The Goldman Board, Join 'The Billionaire circle,'" *NetNet with John Carney* (March 14, 2011), downloaded July 26, 2011, from http://www.cnbc.com/.

90. This section is based on E. P. Hollander, "Ethical Challenges in the Leader–Follower Relationship," *Business Ethics Quarterly* (January 1995), pp. 55–65; J. C. Rost, "Leadership: A Discussion About Ethics," *Business Ethics Quarterly* (January 1995), pp. 129–142; L. K. Treviño, M. Brown, and L. P. Hartman, "A Qualitative Investigation of Perceived Executive Ethical Leadership: Perceptions from Inside and Outside the Executive Suite," *Human Relations* (January 2003), pp. 5–37; and R. M. Fulmer, "The Challenge of Ethical Leadership," *Organizational Dynamics* 33, no. 3 (2004), pp. 307–317.

91. J. L. Lunsford, "Piloting Boeing's New Course," *The Wall Street Journal* (June 13, 2006), pp. B1, B3.

92. J. M. Burns, *Leadership* (New York: Harper & Row, 1978).

93. J. M. Howell and B. J. Avolio, "The Ethics of Charismatic Leadership: Submission or Liberation?" *Academy of Management Executive* (May 1992), pp. 43–55.

94. D. van Knippenberg, D. De Cremer, and B. van Knippenberg, "Leadership and Fairness: The State of the Art," *European Journal of Work and Organizational Psychology* 16, no. 2 (2007), pp. 113–140.

95. K. M. Kacmar, D. G. Bachrach, K. J. Harris, and S. Zivnuska, "Fostering Good Citizenship Through Ethical Leadership: Exploring the Moderating Role of Gender and Organizational Politics," *Journal of Applied Psychology*, Advance Online Publication (December 13, 2010), doi: 10.1037/a0021872; F. O. Walumbwa and J. Schaubroeck, "Leader Personality Traits and Employee Voice Behavior: Mediating Roles of Ethical Leadership and Work Group Psychological Safety," *Journal of Applied Psychology* 94, no. 5 (2009), pp. 1275–1286.

96. M. E. Brown and L. K. Treviño, "Socialized Charismatic Leadership, Values Congruence, and Deviance in Work Groups," *Journal of Applied Psychology* 91, no. 4 (2006), pp. 954–962.

97. M. E. Brown and L. K. Treviño, "Leader-Follower Values Congruence: Are Socialized Charismatic Leaders Better Able to Achieve It?" *Journal of Applied Psychology* 94, no. 2 (2009), pp. 478–490.

98. D. van Dierendonck, "Servant Leadership: A Review and Synthesis," *Journal of Management* 37, no. 4 (2011), pp. 1228–1261.

99. F. Walumbwa, C. A. Hartnell, and A. Oke, "Servant Leadership, Procedural Justice Climate, Service Climate, Employee Attitudes, and Organizational Citizenship Behavior: A Cross-Level Investigation," *Journal of Applied Psychology* 95, no. 3 (2010), pp. 517–529.

100. D. De Cremer, D. M. Mayer, M. van Dijke, B. C. Schouten, and M. Bardes, "When Does Self-Sacrificial Leadership Motivate Prosocial Behavior? It Depends on Followers' Prevention Focus," *Journal of Applied Psychology* 2009, no. 4 (2009), pp. 887–899.

101. J. Hu and R. C. Liden, "Antecedents of Team Potency and Team Effectiveness: An Examination of Goal and Process Clarity and Servant Leadership," *Journal of Applied Psychology*, Online first publication (February 14, 2011), doi: 10.1037/a0022465.

102. M. J. Neubert, K. M. Kacmar, D. S. Carlson, L. B. Chonko, and J. A. Roberts, "Regulatory Focus as a Mediator of the Influence of Initiating Structure and Servant Leadership on Employee Behavior," *Journal of Applied Psychology* 93, no. 6 (2008), pp. 1220–1233.

103. T. Menon, J. Sim, J. Ho-Ying Fu, C. Chiu, and Y. Hong, "Blazing the Trail Versus Trailing the Group: Culture and Perceptions of the Leader's Position," *Organizational Behavior and Human Decision Processes* 113, no. 1 (2010), pp. 51–61.

104. D. M. Rousseau, S. B. Sitkin, R. S. Burt, and C. Camerer, "Not So Different After All: A Cross-Discipline View of Trust," *Academy of Management Review* (July 1998), pp. 393–404; and J. A. Simpson, "Psychological Foundations of Trust," *Current Directions in Psychological Science* 16, no. 5 (2007), pp. 264–268.

105. See, for instance, K. Dirks and D. Ferrin, "Trust in Leadership: Meta-Analytic Findings and Implications for Research and Practice," *Journal of Applied Psychology* 87, no.4, (2002), pp. 611–628; D. I. Jung and B. J. Avolio, "Opening the Black Box: An Experimental Investigation of the Mediating Effects of Trust and Value Congruence on Transformational and Transactional Leadership," *Journal of Organizational Behavior* (December 2000), pp. 949–964; and A. Zacharatos, J. Barling, and R. D. Iverson, "High-Performance Work Systems and Occupational Safety," *Journal of Applied Psychology* (January 2005), pp. 77–93.

106. D. E. Zand, *The Leadership Triad: Knowledge, Trust, and Power* (New York: Oxford University Press, 1997), p. 89.

107. Based on L. T. Hosmer, "Trust: The Connecting Link Between Organizational Theory and Philosophical Ethics," *Academy of Management Review* (April 1995), p. 393; R. C. Mayer, J. H. Davis, and F. D. Schoorman, "An Integrative Model of Organizational Trust," *Academy of Management Review* (July 1995), pp. 709–734; and F. D. Schoorman, R. C. Mayer, and J. H. Davis, "An Integrative Model of Organizational Trust: Past, Present, and Future," *Academy of Management Review* 32, no. 2 (2007), pp. 344–354.

108. J. Schaubroeck, S. S. K. Lam, and A. C. Peng, "Cognition-Based and Affect-Based Trust as Mediators of Leader

Behavior Influences on Team Performance." *Journal of Applied Psychology,* Advance online publication (February 7, 2011), doi: 10.1037/a0022625.

109. Mayer, Davis, and Schoorman, "An Integrative Model of Organizational Trust"; and J. A. Colquitt, B. A. Scott, and J. A. LePine, "Trust, Trustworthiness, and Trust Propensity: A Meta-Analytic Test of Their Unique Relationships with Risk Taking and Job Performance," *Journal of Applied Psychology* 92, no. 4 (2007), pp. 909–927.

110. H. H. Tan and C. S. F. Tan, "Toward the Differentiation of Trust in Supervisor and Trust in Organization," *Genetic, Social, and General Psychology Monographs* (May 2000), pp. 241–260.

111. Cited in D. Jones, "Do You Trust Your CEO?" *USA Today* (February 12, 2003), p. 7B.

112. B. Nanus, *The Leader's Edge: The Seven Keys to Leadership in a Turbulent World* (Chicago: Contemporary Books, 1989), p. 102.

113. R. C. Mayer and J. H. Davis, "The Effect of the Performance Appraisal System on Trust for Management: A Quasi-Experiment," *Journal of Applied Psychology* 84, no. 1 (1999), pp. 123–136; and R. C. Mayer and M. B. Gavin, "Trust in Management and Performance: Who Minds the Shop While the Employees Watch the Boss?" *Academy of Management Journal* 38 (2005), pp. 874–888.

114. J. A. Simpson, "Foundations of Interpersonal Trust," in A. W. Kruglanski and E. T. Higgins (eds.), *Social Psychology: Handbook of Basic Principles,* 2nd ed. (New York: Guilford, 2007), pp. 587–607.

115. Ibid.

116. H. Zhao, S. J. Wayne, B. C. Glibkowski, and J. Bravo, "The Impact of Psychological Contract Breach on Work-Related Outcomes: A Meta-Analysis," *Personnel Psychology* 60 (2007), pp. 647–680.

117. D. L. Shapiro, A. D. Boss, S. Salas, S. Tangirala, and M. A. Von Glinow, "When Are Transgressing *Leaders* Punitively Judged? An Empirical Test," *Journal of Applied Psychology* 96, no. 2 (2011), pp. 412–422.

118. D. L. Ferrin, P. H. Kim, C. D. Cooper, and K. T. Dirks, "Silence Speaks Volumes: The Effectiveness of Reticence in Comparison to Apology and Denial for Responding to Integrity- and Competence-Based Trust Violations," *Journal of Applied Psychology* 92, no. 4 (2007), pp. 893–908.

119. M. E. Schweitzer, J. C. Hershey, and E. T. Bradlow, "Promises and Lies: Restoring Violated Trust," *Organizational Behavior and Human Decision Processes* 101, no. 1 (2006), pp. 1–19.

120. J. R. Detert and E. R. Burris, "Leadership Behavior and Employee Voice: Is the Door Really Open?" *Academy of Management Journal* 50, no. 4 (2007), pp. 869–884.

121. Colquitt, Scott, and LePine, "Trust, Trustworthiness, and Trust Propensity."

122. See, for example, M. Murray, *Beyond the Myths and Magic of Mentoring: How to Facilitate an Effective Mentoring Process,* rev. ed. (New York: Wiley, 2001); K. E. Kram, "Phases of the Mentor Relationship," *Academy of Management Journal* (December 1983), pp. 608–625; R. A. Noe, "An Investigation of the Determinants of Successful Assigned Mentoring Relationships," *Personnel Psychology* (Fall 1988), pp. 559–580; and L. Eby, M. Butts, and A. Lockwood, "Protégés' Negative Mentoring Experiences: Construct Development and Nomological Validation," *Personnel Psychology* (Summer 2004), pp. 411–447.

123. B. R. Ragins and J. L. Cotton, "Easier Said than Done: Gender Differences in Perceived Barriers to Gaining a Mentor," *Academy of Management Journal* 34, no. 4 (1993), pp. 939–951; C. R. Wanberg, E. T. Welsh, and S. A. Hezlett, "Mentoring Research: A Review and Dynamic Process Model," in G. R. Ferris and J. J. Martocchio (eds.), *Research in Personnel and Human Resources Management,* vol. 22 (Greenwich, CT: Elsevier Science, 2003), pp. 39–124; and T. D. Allen, "Protégé Selection by Mentors: Contributing Individual and Organizational Factors," *Journal of Vocational Behavior* 65, no. 3 (2004), pp. 469–483.

124. T. D. Allen, M. L. Poteet, J. E. A. Russell, and G. H. Dobbins, "A Field Study of Factors Related to Supervisors' Willingness to Mentor Others," *Journal of Vocational Behavior* 50, no. 1 (1997), pp. 1–22; S. Aryee, Y. W. Chay, and J. Chew, "The Motivation to Mentor Among Managerial Employees in the Maintenance Career Stage: An Interactionist Perspective," *Group and Organization Management* 21, no. 3 (1996), pp. 261–277; L. T. Eby, A. L. Lockwood, and M. Butts, "Perceived Support for Mentoring: A Multiple Perspectives Approach," *Journal of Vocational Behavior* 68, no. 2 (2006), pp. 267–291; and T. D. Allen, E. Lentz, and R. Day, "Career Success Outcomes Associated with Mentoring Others: A Comparison of Mentors and Nonmentors," *Journal of Career Development* 32, no. 3 (2006), pp. 272–285.

125. See, for example, K. E. Kram and D. T. Hall, "Mentoring in a Context of Diversity and Turbulence," in E. E. Kossek and S. A. Lobel (eds.), *Managing Diversity* (Cambridge, MA: Blackwell, 1996), pp. 108–136; B. R. Ragins and J. L. Cotton, "Mentor Functions and Outcomes: A Comparison of Men and Women in Formal and Informal Mentoring Relationships," *Journal of Applied Psychology* (August 1999), pp. 529–550; and D. B. Turban, T. W. Dougherty, and F. K. Lee, "Gender, Race, and Perceived Similarity Effects in Developmental Relationships: The Moderating Role of Relationship Duration," *Journal of Vocational Behavior* (October 2002), pp. 240–262.

126. J. A. Wilson and N. S. Elman, "Organizational Benefits of Mentoring," *Academy of Management Executive* 4, no. 4 (1990), p. 90.

127. See, for instance, K. Houston-Philpot, "Leadership Development Partnerships at Dow Corning Corporation," *Journal of Organizational Excellence* (Winter 2002), pp. 13–27.

128. Ragins and Cotton, "Mentor Functions and Outcomes"; and C. M. Underhill, "The Effectiveness of Mentoring Programs in Corporate Settings: A Meta-Analytical Review of the Literature," *Journal of Vocational Behavior* 68, no. 2 (2006), pp. 292–307.

129. T. D. Allen, E. T. Eby, and E. Lentz, "The Relationship Between Formal Mentoring Program Characteristics and

Perceived Program Effectiveness," *Personnel Psychology* 59 (2006), pp. 125–153; T. D. Allen, L. T. Eby, and E. Lentz, "Mentorship Behaviors and Mentorship Quality Associated with Formal Mentoring Programs: Closing the Gap Between Research and Practice," *Journal of Applied Psychology* 91, no. 3 (2006), pp. 567–578; and M. R. Parise and M. L. Forret, "Formal Mentoring Programs: The Relationship of Program Design and Support to Mentors' Perceptions of Benefits and Costs," *Journal of Vocational Behavior* 72, no. 2 (2008), pp. 225–240.

130. L. T. Eby and A. Lockwood, "Protégés' and Mentors' Reactions to Participating in Formal Mentoring Programs: A Qualitative Investigation," *Journal of Vocational Behavior* 67, no. 3 (2005), pp. 441–458; G. T. Chao, "Formal Mentoring: Lessons Learned from Past Practice," *Professional Psychology: Research and Practice* 40, no. 3 (2009), pp. 314–320; and C. R. Wanberg, J. D. Kammeyer-Mueller, and M. Marchese, "Mentor and Protégé Predictors and Outcomes of Mentoring in a Formal Mentoring Program," *Journal of Vocational Behavior* 69 (2006), pp. 410–423.

131. T. D. Allen, L. T. Eby, M. L. Poteet, E. Lentz, and L. Lima, "Career Benefits Associated with Mentoring for Protégés: A Meta-Analysis," *Journal of Applied Psychology* (February 2004), pp. 127–136; and J. D. Kammeyer-Mueller and T. A. Judge, "A Quantitative Review of the Mentoring Literature: Test of a Model," *Journal of Vocational Behavior* 72 (2008), pp. 269–283.

132. M. K. Feeney and B. Bozeman, "Mentoring and Network Ties," *Human Relations* 61, no. 12 (2008), pp. 1651–1676; N. Bozionelos, "Intra-Organizational Network Resources: How They Relate to Career Success and Organizational Commitment," *Personnel Review* 37, no. 3 (2008), pp. 249–263; and S. A. Hezlett and S. K. Gibson, "Linking Mentoring and Social Capital: Implications for Career and Organization Development," *Advances in Developing Human Resources* 9, no. 3 (2007), pp. 384–412.

133. Comment by Jim Collins, cited in J. Useem, "Conquering Vertical Limits," *Fortune* (February 19, 2001), p. 94.

134. See, for instance, J. R. Meindl, "The Romance of Leadership as a Follower-centric Theory: A Social Constructionist Approach," *Leadership Quarterly* (Fall 1995), pp. 329–341; and B. Schyns, J. Felfe, and H. Blank, "Is Charisma Hyper-Romanticism? Empirical Evidence from New Data and a Meta-Analysis," *Applied Psychology: An International Review* 56, no. 4 (2007), pp. 505–527.

135. R. G. Lord, C. L. DeVader, and G. M. Alliger, "A Meta-Analysis of the Relation Between Personality Traits and Leadership Perceptions: An Application of Validity Generalization Procedures," *Journal of Applied Psychology* (August 1986), pp. 402–410.

136. J. R. Meindl, S. B. Ehrlich, and J. M. Dukerich, "The Romance of Leadership," *Administrative Science Quarterly* (March 1985), pp. 78–102; and M. C. Bligh, J. C. Kohles, C. L. Pearce, J. E. Justin, and J. F. Stovall, "When the Romance Is Over: Follower Perspectives of Aversive Leadership," *Applied Psychology: An International Review* 56, no. 4 (2007), pp. 528–557.

137. B. R. Agle, N. J. Nagarajan, J. A. Sonnenfeld, and D. Srinivasan, "Does CEO Charisma Matter?" *Academy of Management Journal* 49, no. 1 (2006), pp. 161–174.

138. Bligh, Kohles, Pearce, Justin, and Stovall, "When the Romance Is Over."

139. Schyns, Felfe, and Blank, "Is Charisma Hyper-Romanticism?"

140. J. Cassidy, "Subprime Suspect: The Rise and Fall of Wall Street's First Black C.E.O.," *The New Yorker* (March 31, 2008), pp. 78–91.

141. A. S. Rosette, G. J. Leonardelli, and K. W. Phillips, "The White Standard: Racial Bias in Leader Categorization," *Journal of Applied Psychology* 93, no. 4 (2008), pp. 758–777.

142. A. M. Koenig, A. H. Eagly, A. A. Mitchell, and T. Ristikari, "Are Leader Stereotypes Masculine? A Meta-Analysis of Three Research Paradigms," *Psychological Bulletin* 137, no. 4 (2011), pp. 616–642.

143. M. Van Vugt and B. R. Spisak, "Sex Differences in the Emergence of Leadership During Competitions Within and Between Groups," *Psychological Science* 19, no. 9 (2008), pp. 854–858.

144. M. Van Vugt and B. R. Spisak, "Sex Differences in the Emergence of Leadership During Competitions Within and Between Groups," *Psychological Science* 19, no. 9 (2008), pp. 854–858.

145. S. D. Dionne, F. J. Yammarino, L. E. Atwater, and L. R. James, "Neutralizing Substitutes for Leadership Theory: Leadership Effects and Common-Source Bias," *Journal of Applied Psychology*, 87 (2002), pp. 454–464; and J. R. Villa, J. P. Howell, P. W. Dorfman, and D. L. Daniel, "Problems with Detecting Moderators in Leadership Research Using Moderated Multiple Regression," *Leadership Quarterly* 14 (2002), pp. 3–23.

146. L. A. Hambley, T. A. O'Neill, and T. J. B. Kline, "Virtual Team Leadership: The Effects of Leadership Style and Communication Medium on Team Interaction Styles and Outcomes," *Organizational Behavior and Human Decision Processes* 103 (2007), pp. 1–20; and B. J. Avolio and S. S. Kahai, "Adding the 'E' to E-Leadership: How It May Impact Your Leadership," *Organizational Dynamics* 31, no. 4 (2003), pp. 325–338.

147. S. J. Zaccaro and P. Bader, "E-Leadership and the Challenges of Leading E-Teams: Minimizing the Bad and Maximizing the Good," *Organizational Dynamics* 31, no. 4 (2003), pp. 381–385.

148. C. E. Naquin and G. D. Paulson, "Online Bargaining and Interpersonal Trust," *Journal of Applied Psychology* (February 2003), pp. 113–120.

149. B. M. Bass, "Cognitive, Social, and Emotional Intelligence of Transformational Leaders," in R. E. Riggio, S. E. Murphy, and F. J. Pirozzolo (eds.), *Multiple Intelligences and Leadership* (Mahwah, NJ: Lawrence Erlbaum, 2002), pp. 113–114.

150. See, for instance, P. Dvorak, "M.B.A. Programs Hone 'Soft Skills,'" *The Wall Street Journal* (February 12, 2007), p. B3.

151. J. Weber, "The Leadership Factor," *BusinessWeek* (June 12, 2006), pp. 60–64.

152. See, for instance, Barling, Weber, and Kelloway, "Effects of Transformational Leadership Training on Attitudinal and Financial Outcomes"; and D. V. Day, "Leadership Development: A Review in Context," *Leadership Quarterly* (Winter 2000), pp. 581–613.

153. M. Sashkin, "The Visionary Leader," in J. A. Conger, R. N. Kanungo, et al. (eds.), *Charismatic Leadership* (San Francisco: Jossey-Bass, 1988), p. 150.

154. D. Brady, "The Rising Star of CEO Consulting" *Bloomberg Businessweek* (November 24, 2010), www.businessweek.com.

155. Howell and Frost, "A Laboratory Study of Charismatic Leadership."

156. Dvir, Eden, and Avolio, "Impact of Transformational Leadership on Follower Development and Performance"; B. J. Avolio and B. M. Bass, *Developing Potential Across a Full Range of Leadership: Cases on Transactional and Transformational Leadership* (Mahwah, NJ: Lawrence Erlbaum, 2002); A. J. Towler, "Effects of Charismatic Influence Training on Attitudes, Behavior, and Performance," *Personnel Psychology* (Summer 2003), pp. 363–381; and Barling, Weber, and Kelloway, "Effects of Transformational Leadership Training on Attitudinal and Financial Outcomes."

LEARNING OBJECTIVES

After studying this chapter, you should be able to:

1 Define *power* and contrast leadership and power.

2 Contrast the five bases of power.

3 Explain the role of dependence in power relationships.

4 Identify nine power or influence tactics and their contingencies.

5 Show the connection between sexual harassment and the abuse of power.

6 Identify the causes and consequences of political behavior.

7 Apply impression management techniques.

8 Determine whether a political action is ethical.

MyManagementLab

Access a host of interactive learning aids to help strengthen your understanding of the chapter concepts at **www.mymanagementlab.com**.

APPEARANCES CAN BE DECEIVING

He led one of the world's most trusted and prestigious consulting firms, McKinsey & Company. As a philanthropist, he raised tens of millions of dollars for health care, education, and AIDS. He was often mentioned as a business executive-to-philanthropist role model in the same breath as Warren Buffett and Bill Gates. He collaborated with some of the world's most famous leaders, including Gates, former President Bill Clinton, and leading CEOs.

He served on the boards of directors of some of the world's most respected companies, including Goldman Sachs, Procter & Gamble, and American Airlines, often as chair. He was advisor to many of the world's leading business schools, including Harvard Business School, Tsinghua University, IIT, MIT Sloan School of Management, Wharton's Lauder Institute, and Northwestern's Kellogg School of Management. When President Obama hosted the Indian Prime minister at a state dinner, he was at the White House.

People described him as "humble" and "egoless." His colleagues at McKinsey admired him for the value he placed on family. He described himself as a "servant leader." *Bloomberg Businessweek* noted that he was "that rare businessman whose integrity was beyond reproach."

Yet this man—Rajat Gupta—appears to have led a double life.

When the FBI and SEC were investigating Galleon Group founder and CEO Raj Rajaratnam (convicted in 2011 on 14 charges of fraud and insider trading), they uncovered a "flurry" of phone conversations between Rajaratnam and Gupta. In wiretapped calls, Gupta appears to have alerted Rajaratnam to an upcoming $5 billion investment in Goldman by Berkshire Hathaway. On another occasion, 23 seconds after hanging up on a Goldman conference call, Gupta called Rajaratnam with news that Goldman would report a quarterly loss. All the while, Gupta was investing in and profiting from Galleon's profits on these and other trades. Rajaratnam also "loaned" Gupta millions so he could increase his investments in Galleon.

When these facts became public in 2010 and 2011, the companies with whom Gupta had a relationship—from McKinsey to Goldman Sachs to Proctor & Gamble—quietly ended their associations with him. By mid-2011, not a single company or university still listed Gupta as an advisor.

As of this writing, Gupta has not yet been convicted of insider trading. Even if he is acquitted, however, the damage has been done. A CEO who once was as powerful, networked, and admired as any whose names aren't Gates, Buffett, or Jobs, Gupta is now a pariah and his power is gone.

Power and Politics

*Power is not revealed by striking hard
or often, but by striking true.*

—Honoré de Balzac

411

Why did a man with such power decide to risk it all? Only Gupta knows for certain.

———————

Source: S. Andrews, "How Gupta Came Undone," *Bloomberg Businessweek* (May 19, 2011), pp. 56– 63; M. Gordon and L. Neumeister, "Ex-Goldman Sachs Director Rajat Gupta Charged with Insider Trading," *Washington Post* (March 1, 2011), downloaded June 18, 2011 from www.washingtonpost .com/; W. Pavlo, "Goldman's Boardroom Meetings—Less Proprietary Than Computer Code?" *Forbes* (March 17, 2011), downloaded June 21, 2011, from http://blogs.forbes.com/.

In both research and practice, *power* and *politics* have been described as the last dirty words. It is easier for most of us to talk about sex or money than about power or political behavior. People who have power deny it, people who want it try not to look like they're seeking it, and those who are good at getting it are secretive about how they do so.[1] To see whether you think your work environment is political, take the accompanying self-assessment.

A major theme of this chapter is that power and political behavior are natural processes in any group or organization. Given that, you need to know how power is acquired and exercised if you are to fully understand organizational behavior. Although you may have heard that "Power corrupts, and absolute power corrupts absolutely," power is not always bad. As one author noted, most medicines can kill if taken in the wrong amount, and thousands die each year in automobile accidents, but we don't abandon chemicals or cars because of the dangers associated with them. Rather, we consider danger an incentive to get training and information that will help us to use these forces productively.[2] The same applies to power. It's a reality of organizational life, and it's not going to go away. By learning how power works in organizations, you'll be better able to use your knowledge to become a more effective manager.

SELF-ASSESSMENT LIBRARY

Is My Workplace Political?

In the Self-Assessment Library (available on CD and online), take assessment IV.F.1 (Is My Workplace Political?). If you don't currently have a job, answer for your most recent job. Then answer the following questions.

1. How does your score relate to those of your classmates? Do you think your score is accurate? Why or why not?
2. Do you think a political workplace is a bad thing? If yes, why? If no, why not?
3. What factors cause your workplace to be political?

A Definition of Power

1 Define *power* and contrast leadership and power.

Power refers to a capacity that *A* has to influence the behavior of *B* so *B* acts in accordance with *A*'s wishes.[3]

Someone can thus have power but not use it; it is a capacity or potential. Probably the most important aspect of power is that it is a function of **dependence**. The greater *B*'s dependence on *A*, the greater *A*'s power in the relationship. Dependence, in turn, is based on alternatives that *B* perceives and the importance *B* places on the alternative(s) *A* controls. A person can have power over you only if he or she controls something you desire. If you want a college degree and have to pass a certain course to get it, and your current instructor is the only faculty member in the college who teaches that course, he or she has power over you. Your alternatives are highly limited, and you place a high degree of importance on obtaining a passing grade. Similarly, if you're attending college on funds totally provided by your parents, you probably recognize the power they hold over you. You're dependent on them for financial support. But once you're out of school, have a job, and are making a good income, your parents' power is reduced significantly. Who among us, though, has not known or heard of a rich relative who is able to control a large number of family members merely through the implicit or explicit threat of "writing them out of the will"?

One study even suggests that powerful people might be better liars because they are more confident in their status. Researchers gave one group of research subjects bigger offices and more authority, while another group received smaller offices and less authority. Then half the subjects in each condition were told to steal a $100 bill and convince an interviewer they hadn't taken it. If they were able to fool the interviewer, they could keep the money. In the interviews, those in positions of power showed fewer signs of dishonesty and stress like shoulder shrugs and stuttering when lying—perhaps because they felt less dependent on others. Recall that this simulation involved only hypothetical, experimentally manipulated power, so imagine the effects when real power is on the line.[4]

One study investigated how people respond to the poor performance of a subordinate dependent on them in a work context.[5] To study this, a laboratory mockup of a performance review was developed, and participants acted the part of either powerful or unpowerful managers. The result? Powerful managers were more likely to respond to poor performers by either directly confronting them or frankly encouraging them to get training to improve. Less powerful managers enacted strategies not to confront the poor performer, like compensating for poor performance or avoiding the individual altogether. In other words, they were less likely to actively engage in a potential conflict with the subordinate, possibly because they would be more vulnerable if the subordinate wanted to "get revenge" for the negative feedback.

Contrasting Leadership and Power

A careful comparison of our description of power with our description of leadership in Chapter 12 reveals the concepts are closely intertwined. Leaders use power as a means of attaining group goals.

How are the two terms different? Power does not require goal compatibility, merely dependence. Leadership, on the other hand, requires some congruence between the goals of the leader and those being led. A second difference relates to the direction of influence. Leadership focuses on the downward influence on followers. It minimizes the importance of lateral and upward influence patterns. Power does not. In still another difference, leadership research, for the most

---

power   *A capacity that* A *has to influence the behavior of* B *so that* B *acts in accordance with* A *'s wishes.*

dependence   B *'s relationship to* A *when* A *possesses something that* B *requires.*

part, emphasizes style. It seeks answers to questions such as these: How supportive should a leader be? How much decision making should be shared with followers? In contrast, the research on power focuses on tactics for gaining compliance. It goes beyond the individual as the exerciser of power, because groups as well as individuals can use power to control other individuals or groups.

Bases of Power

2 Contrast the five bases of power.

Where does power come from? What gives an individual or a group influence over others? We answer by dividing the bases or sources of power into two general groupings—formal and personal—and then breaking each of these down into more specific categories.[6]

Formal Power

Formal power is based on an individual's position in an organization. It can come from the ability to coerce or reward, or from formal authority.

Coercive Power The **coercive power** base depends on fear of the negative results from failing to comply. It rests on the application, or the threat of application, of physical sanctions such as the infliction of pain, frustration through restriction of movement, or the controlling by force of basic physiological or safety needs.

At the organizational level, *A* has coercive power over *B* if *A* can dismiss, suspend, or demote *B,* assuming *B* values his or her job. If *A* can assign *B* work activities *B* finds unpleasant, or treat *B* in a manner *B* finds embarrassing, *A* possesses coercive power over *B.* Coercive power can also come from withholding key information. People in an organization who have data or knowledge others need can make those others dependent on them.

Reward Power The opposite of coercive power is **reward power**, with which people comply because it produces positive benefits; someone who can distribute rewards others view as valuable will have power over them. These rewards can be either financial—such as controlling pay rates, raises, and bonuses—or nonfinancial, including recognition, promotions, interesting work assignments, friendly colleagues, and preferred work shifts or sales territories.[7]

Legitimate Power In formal groups and organizations, probably the most common access to one or more of the power bases is through **legitimate power**. It represents the formal authority to control and use organizational resources based on structural position in the organization.

Legitimate power is broader than the power to coerce and reward. Specifically, it includes members' acceptance of the authority of a position. We associate power so closely with the concept of hierarchy that just drawing longer lines in an organization chart leads people to infer the leaders are especially powerful, and when a powerful executive is described, people tend to put the person at a higher position when drawing an organization chart.[8] When school principals, bank presidents, or army captains speak (assuming their directives are viewed as within the authority of their positions), teachers, tellers, and first lieutenants listen and usually comply.

Personal Power

Many of the most competent and productive chip designers at Intel have power, but they aren't managers and have no formal power. What they have is **personal power**, which comes from an individual's unique characteristics. There are two bases of personal power: expertise and the respect and admiration of others.

Expert Power   **Expert power** is influence wielded as a result of expertise, special skill, or knowledge. As jobs become more specialized, we become increasingly dependent on experts to achieve goals. It is generally acknowledged that physicians have expertise and hence expert power: Most of us follow our doctor's advice. Computer specialists, tax accountants, economists, industrial psychologists, and other specialists wield power as a result of their expertise.

Referent Power   **Referent power** is based on identification with a person who has desirable resources or personal traits. If I like, respect, and admire you, you can exercise power over me because I want to please you.

Referent power develops out of admiration of another and a desire to be like that person. It helps explain, for instance, why celebrities are paid millions of dollars to endorse products in commercials. Marketing research shows people such as LeBron James and Tom Brady have the power to influence your choice of athletic shoes and credit cards. With a little practice, you and I could probably deliver as smooth a sales pitch as these celebrities, but the buying public doesn't identify with you and me. Some people who are not in formal leadership positions nonetheless have referent power and exert influence over others because of their charismatic dynamism, likability, and emotional effects on us.

Nike CEO Mark Parker has expert power. Since joining Nike in 1979 as a footwear designer, Parker has been involved in many of Nike's most significant design innovations. His primary responsibilities and leadership positions at Nike have been in product research, design, and development. Nike depends on Parker's expertise in leading the company's innovation initiatives and in setting corporate strategy to achieve the growth of its global business portfolio that includes Converse, Nike Golf, and Cole Haan. Parker is shown here introducing Nike's Considered Design during a news conference about the company's latest products that combine sustainability and innovation.

Source: Mark Lennihan/AP Images.

Which Bases of Power Are Most Effective?

Of the three bases of formal power (coercive, reward, legitimate) and two bases of personal power (expert, referent), which is most important to have? Research suggests pretty clearly that the personal sources of power are most effective. Both expert and referent power are positively related to employees' satisfaction with supervision, their organizational commitment, and their performance, whereas reward and legitimate power seem to be unrelated to these outcomes. One source of formal power—coercive power—actually can backfire in that it is negatively related to employee satisfaction and commitment.[9]

Consider Steve Stoute's company, Translation, which matches pop-star spokespersons with corporations that want to promote their brands. Stoute has paired Gwen Stefani with HP, Justin Timberlake with McDonald's, Beyoncé Knowles with Tommy Hilfiger, and Jay-Z with Reebok. Stoute's business seems to be all about referent power. His firm's work aims to use the credibility of these artists and performers to reach youth culture.[10] In other words, people buy products associated with cool figures because they wish to identify with and emulate them.

Power and Perceived Justice

Individuals in positions of power tend to be blamed for their failures and credited for their successes to a greater degree than those who have less power. In the same way, studies suggest that leaders and managers in positions of power pay greater costs for unfairness and reap greater benefits for fairness.[11] Specifically, authorities are given greatest trust when they have a lot of power and their organizations are seen as operating fairly, and the least trust when they have a lot of power and their organizations are seen as operating unfairly. Thus, it appears that people think powerful leaders should have the discretion to shape organizational policies and change unfair rules, and if they fail to do so, they will be seen especially negatively.

Dependence: The Key to Power

The most important aspect of power is that it is a function of dependence. In this section, we show how understanding dependence helps us understand power itself.

The General Dependence Postulate

Let's begin with a general postulate: *the greater* B*'s dependence on* A, *the more power* A *has over* B. When you possess anything others require that you alone control, you make them dependent on you, and therefore you gain power over them.[12] If something is plentiful, possessing it will not increase your power. But as the old saying goes, "In the land of the blind, the one-eyed man is king!" Conversely, the more you can expand your own options, the less power you place in the hands of others. This explains why most organizations develop multiple suppliers rather than give their business to only one. It also explains why so many aspire to financial independence. Independence reduces the power others can wield who can limit our access to opportunities and resources.

What Creates Dependence?

Dependence increases when the resource you control is important, scarce, and nonsubstitutable.[13]

Importance   If nobody wants what you have, it's not going to create dependence. Because organizations, for instance, actively seek to avoid uncertainty,[14] we should expect that individuals or groups that can absorb uncertainty will be perceived as controlling an important resource. A study of industrial organizations found their marketing departments were consistently rated the most powerful.[15] The researcher concluded that the most critical uncertainty facing these firms was selling their products, suggesting that engineers, as a group, would be more powerful at technology company Matsushita than at consumer products giant Procter & Gamble. These inferences appear to be generally valid. Matsushita, which is heavily technologically oriented, depends heavily on its engineers to maintain its products' technical advantages and quality, and so they are a powerful group. At Procter & Gamble, marketing is the name of the game, and marketers are the most powerful occupational group.

Scarcity   Ferruccio Lamborghini, who created the exotic supercars that still carry his name, understood the importance of scarcity and used it to his advantage during World War II. Lamborghini was in Rhodes with the Italian army. His superiors were impressed with his mechanical skills, as he demonstrated an almost uncanny ability to repair tanks and cars no one else could fix. After the war, he admitted his ability was largely due to his having been the first person on the island to receive the repair manuals, which he memorized and then destroyed so as to become indispensable.[16]

We see the scarcity–dependence relationship in the power of occupational categories. Where the supply of labor is low relative to demand, workers can negotiate compensation and benefits packages far more attractive than can

Mary Pochobradsky (center) is in a position of power at Procter & Gamble. She is the North American marketing director for P&G's fabric enhancing products that include the Downy brand, one of 24 company brands that each generate more than $1 billion in sales a year. Mary is shown here announcing a new marketing campaign for the 50-year-old Downy brand that includes TV ads, social networks, and a live window display at Macy's retail store featuring comedian Mike Birbiglia. At consumer product firms like P&G, marketers are the most powerful occupational group because they control the important resource of selling products.

Source: AP Photo/Al Behrman.

those in occupations with an abundance of candidates. College administrators have no problem today finding English instructors. The market for network systems analysts, in contrast, is comparatively tight, with demand high and supply limited. The bargaining power of computer-engineering faculty allows them to negotiate higher salaries, lighter teaching loads, and other benefits.

Nonsubstitutability   The fewer viable substitutes for a resource, the more power control over that resource provides. At universities with strong pressures on the faculty to publish, the more recognition the faculty member receives through publication, the more mobile he or she is, because other universities want faculty who are highly published and visible. Although tenure can alter this relationship by restricting the department head's alternatives, faculty members with few or no publications have the least mobility and are subject to the greatest influence from their superiors.

Power Tactics

3 Explain the role of dependence in power relationships.

What **power tactics** do people use to translate power bases into specific action? What options do they have for influencing their bosses, co-workers, or employees? In this section, we review popular tactical options and the conditions that may make one more effective than another.

Research has identified nine distinct influence tactics:[17]

- **Legitimacy.**   Relying on your authority position or saying a request accords with organizational policies or rules.
- **Rational persuasion.**   Presenting logical arguments and factual evidence to demonstrate a request is reasonable.
- **Inspirational appeals.**   Developing emotional commitment by appealing to a target's values, needs, hopes, and aspirations.
- **Consultation.**   Increasing the target's support by involving him or her in deciding how you will accomplish your plan.
- **Exchange.**   Rewarding the target with benefits or favors in exchange for following a request.
- **Personal appeals.**   Asking for compliance based on friendship or loyalty.
- **Ingratiation.**   Using flattery, praise, or friendly behavior prior to making a request.
- **Pressure.**   Using warnings, repeated demands, and threats.
- **Coalitions.**   Enlisting the aid or support of others to persuade the target to agree.

Some tactics are more effective than others. Rational persuasion, inspirational appeals, and consultation tend to be the most effective, especially when the audience is highly interested in the outcomes of a decision process. Pressure tends to backfire and is typically the least effective of the nine tactics.[18] You can also increase your chance of success by using two or more tactics together or sequentially, as long as your choices are compatible.[19] Using both ingratiation and legitimacy can lessen negative reactions to your appearing to dictate outcomes, but only when the audience does not really care about the outcome of a decision process or the policy is routine.[20]

Let's consider the most effective way of getting a raise. You can start with rational persuasion: figure out how your pay compares to that of peers, or land a competing job offer, or show objective results that testify to your performance. Kitty Dunning, a vice president at Don Jagoda Associates, landed a 16 percent raise when she e-mailed her boss numbers showing she had increased sales.[21] You can also make good use of salary calculators such as Salary.com to compare your pay with comparable others.

But the effectiveness of some influence tactics depends on the direction of influence.[22] As Exhibit 13-1 shows, rational persuasion is the only tactic effective across organizational levels. Inspirational appeals work best as a downward-influencing tactic with subordinates. When pressure works, it's generally downward only. Personal appeals and coalitions are most effective as lateral influence. Other factors that affect the effectiveness of influence include the sequencing of tactics, a person's skill in using the tactic, and the organizational culture.

You're more likely to be effective if you begin with "softer" tactics that rely on personal power, such as personal and inspirational appeals, rational persuasion, and consultation. If these fail, you can move to "harder" tactics, such as exchange, coalitions, and pressure, which emphasize formal power and incur greater costs and risks.[23] Interestingly, a single soft tactic is more effective than a single hard tactic, and combining two soft tactics or a soft tactic and rational persuasion is more effective than any single tactic or combination of hard tactics.[24] The effectiveness of tactics depends on the audience.[25] People especially likely to comply with soft power tactics tend to be more reflective and intrinsically motivated; they have high self-esteem and greater desire for control. Those likely to comply with hard power tactics are more action-oriented and extrinsically motivated and are more focused on getting along with others than on getting their own way.

People in different countries prefer different power tactics.[26] Those from individualistic countries tend to see power in personalized terms and as a legitimate means of advancing their personal ends, whereas those in collectivistic countries see power in social terms and as a legitimate means of helping others.[27] A study comparing managers in the United States and China found that U.S. managers prefer rational appeal, whereas Chinese managers preferred coalition tactics.[28] These differences tend to be consistent with the values in these two countries. Reason is consistent with the U.S. preference for direct confrontation and rational persuasion to influence others and resolve differences, while coalition tactics align with the Chinese preference for meeting

Exhibit **13-1**	Preferred Power Tactics by Influence Direction	
Upward Influence	**Downward Influence**	**Lateral Influence**
Rational persuasion	Rational persuasion	Rational persuasion
	Inspirational appeals	Consultation
	Pressure	Ingratiation
	Consultation	Exchange
	Ingratiation	Legitimacy
	Exchange	Personal appeals
	Legitimacy	Coalitions

power tactics *Ways in which individuals translate power bases into specific actions.*

Power Distance and Innovation

Throughout this book, you may have noticed a lot of international research into the differences between individualistic and collectivistic countries. Differences in power distance between countries are also likely to affect organizational behavior. *Power distance* is the extent to which people with low levels of power in society accept and expect that power will be distributed unequally. Cultures high in power distance tend to have greater differentiation between leaders and followers in organizations, and less power sharing between employees and upper management.

How does power distance affect the development and implementation of new ideas in organizations? One study that looked at data from 212 Chinese firms found control mechanisms and strict rules in higher power-distance organizations to be associated with lower levels of information exchange and experimentation. This implies fewer opportunities for creation of new knowledge when power distance is great.

Power distance might also restrict the implementation of new workplace practices. A study across 16 European countries with different levels of power distance showed that innovative work practices like job rotation, autonomous teams, job autonomy, and upward communication were less common in countries with higher power distance. Similar results were obtained in a study of 743 workers in Turkey. This tendency toward less empowerment in high power distance cultures probably reflects the stronger preferences among workers and managers alike for hierarchical social relationships. However, it may come with a price, because power sharing and autonomy-enhancing practices are most likely to lead to greater innovation.

Source: Based on A. Ollo-López, A. Bayo-Moriones, and M. Larraza-Kintana, "The Impact of Country Level Factors on the Use of New Work Practices," *Journal of World Business* 46, no. 3 (2011), pp. 394–403; D. Wang, Z. Su, and D. Yang, "Organizational Culture and Knowledge Creation Capability," *Journal of Knowledge Management* 15, no. 3 (2011), pp. 363–373; and N. D. Cakar and A. Ertürk, "Comparing Innovation Capability of Small and Medium-Sized Enterprises: Examining the Effects of Organizational Culture and Empowerment," *Journal of Small Business Management* 48, no. 3 (2010), pp. 325–359.

difficult or controversial requests with indirect approaches. Research also has shown that individuals in Western, individualistic cultures tend to engage in more self-enhancement behaviors (such as self-promotion) than individuals in more collectivistic Eastern cultures.[29]

People differ in their **political skill**, or their ability to influence others to enhance their own objectives. The politically skilled are more effective users of all the influence tactics. Political skill also appears more effective when the stakes are high—such as when the individual is accountable for important organizational outcomes. Finally, the politically skilled are able to exert their influence without others detecting it, a key element in being effective (it's damaging to be labeled political).[30] However, these individuals also appear most able to use their political skills in environments marked by low levels of procedural and distributive justice. When an organization is run with open and fairly applied rules, free of favoritism or biases, political skill is actually negatively related to job performance ratings.[31]

Finally, we know cultures within organizations differ markedly—some are warm, relaxed, and supportive; others are formal and conservative. Some encourage participation and consultation, some encourage reason, and still others rely on pressure. People who fit the culture of the organization tend to obtain more influence.[32] Specifically, extraverts tend to be more influential in team-oriented organizations, and highly conscientious people are more influential in organizations that value working alone on technical tasks. People who fit the culture are influential because they can perform especially well in the domains deemed most important for success. In other words, they are influential because they are competent. Thus, the organization itself will influence which subset of power tactics is viewed as acceptable for use.

Sexual Harassment: Unequal Power in the Workplace

4 Identify nine power or influence tactics and their contingencies.

Source: Bill Greeblatt/UPI/Newscom.

A federal jury awarded this young woman a $95 million judgment in a sexual harassment lawsuit against her employer Aaron's Rents. She reported that her supervisor, the store's general manager, sexually harassed her with hostile and abusive behavior that included lewd propositions and unwanted physical sexual contact. She alleged that she called a company harassment hotline but that an investigator never contacted her and that she was denied a promotion for complaining about her boss's behavior. In their verdicts, the jurors found the supervisor guilty of assault and battery and the company liable for negligent supervision, sexual harassment, and intentional infliction of emotional distress.

Sexual harassment is wrong. It can also be costly to employers. Just ask executives at Walmart, the World Bank, and the United Nations.[33] Mitsubishi paid $34 million to settle a sexual harassment case. And a former UPS manager won an $80 million suit against UPS on her claims it fostered a hostile work environment when it failed to listen to her complaints of sexual harassment. Of course, it's not only big organizations that run into trouble: A jury awarded Janet Bianco, a nurse at New York's Flushing Hospital, $15 million for harassment she suffered at the hands of Dr. Matthew Miller. After the verdict, Bianco said, "I think that people take it lightly when you say sexual harassment. They don't understand how it affects your life, not only in your job, but in your home, with your friends."[34]

In addition to the legal dangers to sexual harassment, obviously it can have a negative impact on the work environment, too. Sexual harassment negatively affects job attitudes and leads those who feel harassed to withdraw from the organization. In many cases, reporting sexual harassment doesn't improve the situation because the organization responds in a negative or unhelpful way. When organizational leaders make honest efforts to stop the harassment, the outcomes are much more positive.[35]

Sexual harassment is defined as any unwanted activity of a sexual nature that affects an individual's employment and creates a hostile work environment. The U.S. Supreme Court helped to clarify this definition by adding a key test for determining whether sexual harassment has occurred—when comments or behavior in a work environment "would reasonably be perceived, and [are] perceived, as hostile or abusive."[36] But disagreement continues about what *specifically* constitutes sexual harassment. Organizations have generally made progress toward limiting overt forms of sexual harassment. This includes unwanted physical touching, recurring requests for dates when it is made clear the person isn't interested, and coercive threats that a person will lose his or her job for refusing a sexual proposition. Problems today are likely to surface around more subtle forms of sexual harassment—unwanted looks or comments, off-color jokes, sexual artifacts like pinups posted in the workplace, or misinterpretations of where the line between being friendly ends and harassment begins.

A recent review concluded that 58 percent of women report having experienced potentially harassing behaviors, and 24 percent report having experienced sexual harassment at work.[37] Other research suggests that despite increased media attention and training, perceptions of sexual harassment levels have been fairly stable since the 1990s.[38] One problem with reporting is that sexual harassment is, to some degree, in the eye of the beholder. Women are more likely than men to see a given behavior or set of behaviors as constituting sexual harassment. Men are less likely to see harassment in such behaviors as kissing someone, asking for a date, or making sex-stereotyped jokes. As the authors of one study note, "Although progress has been made at defining sexual harassment, it is still unclear as to whose perspective should be taken."[39] Witnesses offering sexual harassment testimony also find that victims who took

political skill *The ability to influence others in such a way as to enhance one's objectives.*

sexual harassment *Any unwanted activity of a sexual nature that affects an individual's employment and creates a hostile work environment.*

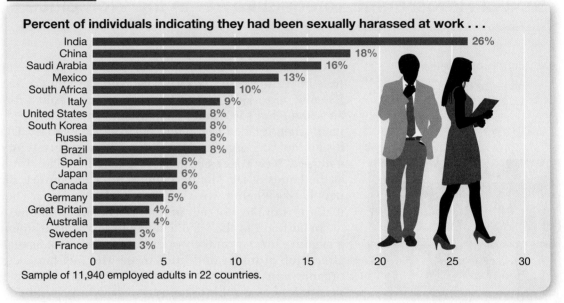

OB Poll   **Reports of Sexual Harassment Differ by Country**

Percent of individuals indicating they had been sexually harassed at work . . .

Country	Percent
India	26%
China	18%
Saudi Arabia	16%
Mexico	13%
South Africa	10%
Italy	9%
United States	8%
South Korea	8%
Russia	8%
Brazil	8%
Spain	6%
Japan	6%
Canada	6%
Germany	5%
Great Britain	4%
Australia	4%
Sweden	3%
France	3%

Sample of 11,940 employed adults in 22 countries.

Note: Sample of 11,940 employed adults in 22 countries.

Source: J. Wright, "Physical Assault and Sexual Harassment in the Workplace" *Ipsos Global @dvisory* (August 12, 2010), downloaded June 20, 2011, from www.ipsos-na.com/.

either an aggressive or a passive tone in making their complaints were seen as less plausible than victims who took a more neutral tone.[40] This research suggests that people may not be able to be entirely objective when listening to sexual harassment complaints, taking the tone of the victim into account when making judgments rather than simply relying on the facts of the case at hand. The best approach is to be careful—refrain from any behavior that may be taken as harassing, even if that was not the intent. Realize that what you see as an innocent joke or hug may be seen as harassment by the other party.

Most studies confirm that the concept of power is central to understanding sexual harassment.[41] This seems true whether the harassment comes from a supervisor, a co-worker, or an employee. And sexual harassment is more likely to occur when there are large power differentials. The supervisor–employee dyad best characterizes an unequal power relationship, where formal power gives the supervisor the capacity to reward and coerce. Because employees want favorable performance reviews, salary increases, and the like, supervisors control resources most employees consider important and scarce. Thus, sexual harassment by the boss typically creates the greatest difficulty for those being harassed. If there are no witnesses, it is the victim's word against the harasser's. Has this boss harassed others, and, if so, will they come forward or fear retaliation? Male respondents in one study in Switzerland who were high in hostile sexism reported higher intentions to sexually harass in organizations that had low levels of justice, suggesting that failure to have consistent policies and procedures for all employees might actually increase levels of sexual harassment.[42]

Women in positions of power in an organization can be subjected to sexual harassment from males who occupy less powerful positions, although this situation doesn't get nearly as much attention as harassment by a supervisor. The employee devalues the woman in power by highlighting traditional gender stereotypes that reflect negatively on her (such as helplessness, passivity, or lack of career commitment), usually in an attempt to gain power over her or minimize power differentials. Increasingly, too, there are cases of women in positions of power harassing male employees.

Should All Sexual Behavior Be Prohibited at Work?

The difficulty in monitoring and defining sexual harassment at work has led some organizations to go beyond discouraging overt sexually harassing behaviors. Companies ranging from Walmart to Staples to Xerox have disciplined employees for workplace romances and upheld policies that ban hierarchical romantic relationships, such as between a supervisor and subordinate. The idea is that such relationships are so fraught with potential for abuse of power that they cannot possibly be consensual for extended periods of time. Surveys by the Society of Human Resource Management suggest that concerns about both potential sexual harassment and lowered productivity have motivated prohibitions on workplace romances. However, ethicists and legal scholars have thrown some "no romance" policies into question on the grounds they are patronizing or invade employee privacy.

What does organizational behavior research have to say about *consensual* sexual behavior at work? One study of more than 1,000 respondents found 40 percent were exposed to sexual behavior in some form in the past year. Counter to the idea that all sexual behavior at work is negative, some female and many male respondents reported enjoying the experience. However, exposure to sexual behavior at work was negatively related to performance and psychological well-being. People may report enjoying it, but it might be hurting their productivity and well-being anyway.

When thinking about a sexual harassment policy for your own organization that might prohibit all workplace romances, consider the following questions:

1. Are there potential problems in monitoring and enforcing such a comprehensive policy on all employees?

2. Does the organization have the right to actively determine what types of behaviors consenting employees engage in outside the work environment?

3. Can the policy be written in a less restrictive manner, such as by prohibiting employees who work together closely from having workplace romances? In this way, the organization might be able to transfer employees who are in a relationship so they don't work directly with one another, and thus they can be retained in the organization and their personal privacy respected.

Source: Based on J. L. Berdahl and K. Aquino, "Sexual Behavior at Work: Fun or Folly?" *Journal of Applied Psychology* 94, no. 1 (2009), pp. 34–47; and C. Boyd, "The Debate over the Prohibition of Romance in the Workplace," *Journal of Business Ethics* 97, no. 2 (2010), pp. 325–338.

A recent review of the literature shows the damage caused by sexual harassment. As you would expect, victims report lower job satisfaction and diminished organizational commitment as a result. Sexual harassment undermines their mental and physical health, as well as lowering productivity in the group in which they work. The authors of this study conclude that sexual harassment "is significantly and substantively associated with a host of harms."[43]

Sexual harassment can wreak havoc on an organization, not to mention on the victims themselves, but it can be avoided. The manager's role is critical. Here are some ways managers can protect themselves and their employees from sexual harassment:

1. Make sure an active policy defines what constitutes sexual harassment, informs employees they can be fired for sexually harassing another employee, and establishes procedures for making complaints.
2. Reassure employees they will not encounter retaliation if they file a complaint.
3. Investigate every complaint, and inform the legal and human resource departments.
4. Make sure offenders are disciplined or terminated.
5. Set up in-house seminars to raise employee awareness of sexual harassment issues.

The bottom line is that managers have a responsibility to protect their employees from a hostile work environment, but they also need to protect themselves. Managers may be unaware that one of their employees is being sexually harassed. But being unaware does not protect them or their organization. If investigators believe a manager could have known about the harassment, both the manager and the company can be held liable.

Politics: Power in Action

5 Show the connection between sexual harassment and the abuse of power.

Source: Kyodo News/AP Images.

After police officer Toshiro Semba (center) blew the whistle on his bosses in the police department, they took his gun away, claiming he was too emotionally unstable to carry a weapon, and reassigned him as a dispatcher. Semba revealed that for decades his superiors wrote false reports to secure public funds and then used the funds for their personal benefit. A district court in Japan ruled that Semba's treatment was retaliation for his exposure of corruption. Traditionally, whistleblowers in Japan have been viewed as traitors, and their exposure of wrongdoing as a betrayal of their superiors. But this perception of whistleblowing as a political behavior is changing as employees like Semba are now being recognized for doing the right thing by exposing illegal, corrupt, or unethical conduct in the workplace.

When people get together in groups, power will be exerted. People want to carve out a niche from which to exert influence, earn rewards, and advance their careers. When employees in organizations convert their power into action, we describe them as being engaged in politics. Those with good political skills have the ability to use their bases of power effectively.[44]

Definition of Organizational Politics

There is no shortage of definitions of *organizational politics*. Essentially, this type of politics focuses on the use of power to affect decision making in an organization, or on self-serving and organizationally unsanctioned behaviors.[45] For our purposes, **political behavior** in organizations consists of activities that are not required as part of an individual's formal role but that influence, or attempt to influence, the distribution of advantages and disadvantages within the organization.[46]

This definition encompasses what most people mean when they talk about organizational politics. Political behavior is outside specified job requirements. It requires some attempt to use power bases. It includes efforts to influence the goals, criteria, or processes used for decision making. Our definition is broad enough to include varied political behaviors such as withholding key information from decision makers, joining a coalition, whistleblowing, spreading rumors, leaking confidential information to the media, exchanging favors with others in the organization for mutual benefit, and lobbying on behalf of or against a particular individual or decision alternative.

The Reality of Politics

Interviews with experienced managers show that most believe political behavior is a major part of organizational life.[47] Many managers report some use of political behavior is both ethical and necessary, as long as it doesn't directly harm anyone else. They describe politics as a necessary evil and believe someone who *never* uses political behavior will have a hard time getting things done. Most also indicate they had never been trained to use political behavior effectively. But why, you may wonder, must politics exist? Isn't it possible for an organization to be politics free? It's *possible*—but unlikely.

Organizations are made up of individuals and groups with different values, goals, and interests.[48] This sets up the potential for conflict over the allocation of limited resources, such as departmental budgets, space, project responsibilities, and salary adjustments.[49] If resources were abundant, then all constituencies within the organization could satisfy their goals. But because they are limited, not everyone's interests can be satisfied. Furthermore, gains by one individual or group are often *perceived* as coming at the expense of others within the organization (whether they are or not). These forces create real competition among members for the organization's limited resources.

Maybe the most important factor leading to politics within organizations is the realization that most of the "facts" used to allocate the limited resources are open to interpretation. What, for instance, is *good* performance? What's an *adequate* improvement? What constitutes an *unsatisfactory* job? One person's "selfless effort to benefit the organization" is seen by another as a "blatant attempt to further one's interest."[50] The manager of any major league baseball team knows a .400 hitter is a high performer and a .125 hitter is a poor performer. You don't need to be a baseball genius to know you should play your .400 hitter and send the .125 hitter back to the minors. But what if you have to choose between players who hit .280 and .290? Then less objective factors come into play: fielding expertise, attitude, potential, ability to perform in a clutch, loyalty to the team, and so on. More managerial decisions resemble the choice between a .280 and a .290 hitter than between a .125 hitter and a .400 hitter. It is in this large and ambiguous middle ground of organizational life—where the facts *don't* speak for themselves—that politics flourish (see Exhibit 13-2).

Exhibit 13-2 Politics Is in the Eye of the Beholder

A behavior one person labels as "organizational politics" is very likely to seem like "effective management" to another. The fact is not that effective management is necessarily political, although in some cases it might be. Rather, a person's reference point determines what he or she classifies as organizational politics. For example, one experimental study showed that power-oriented behavior performed by a permanent, tenured employee is seen as more legitimate and less harsh than the same behavior performed by a temporary employee.[43] Take a look at the following labels used to describe the same phenomenon. These suggest that politics, like beauty, is in the eye of the beholder.

"Political" Label		"Effective Management" Label
1. Blaming others	vs.	Fixing responsibility
2. "Kissing up"	vs.	Developing working relationships
3. Apple polishing	vs.	Demonstrating loyalty
4. Passing the buck	vs.	Delegating authority
5. Covering your rear	vs.	Documenting decisions
6. Creating conflict	vs.	Encouraging change and innovation
7. Forming coalitions	vs.	Facilitating teamwork
8. Whistle-blowing	vs.	Improving efficiency
9. Scheming	vs.	Planning ahead
10. Overachieving	vs.	Competent and capable
11. Ambitious	vs.	Career minded
12. Opportunistic	vs.	Astute
13. Cunning	vs.	Practical minded
14. Arrogant	vs.	Confident
15. Perfectionist	vs.	Attentive to detail

Source: Based on T. C. Krell, M. E. Mendenhall, and J. Sendry, "Doing Research in the Conceptual Morass of Organizational Politics," paper presented at the Western Academy of Management Conference, Hollywood, CA, April 1987.

political behavior *Activities that are not required as part of a person's formal role in the organization but that influence, or attempt to influence, the distribution of advantages and disadvantages within the organization.*

Finally, because most decisions have to be made in a climate of ambiguity—where facts are rarely fully objective and thus are open to interpretation—people within organizations will use whatever influence they can to taint the facts to support their goals and interests. That, of course, creates the activities we call *politicking*.

Therefore, to answer the question whether it is possible for an organization to be politics-free, we can say "yes"—if all members of that organization hold the same goals and interests, if organizational resources are not scarce, and if performance outcomes are completely clear and objective. But that doesn't describe the organizational world in which most of us live.

Causes and Consequences of Political Behavior

6 Identify the causes and consequences of political behavior.

Factors Contributing to Political Behavior

Not all groups or organizations are equally political. In some organizations, for instance, politicking is overt and rampant, while in others politics plays a small role in influencing outcomes. Why this variation? Recent research and observation have identified a number of factors that appear to encourage political behavior. Some are individual characteristics, derived from the unique qualities of the people the organization employs; others are a result of the organization's culture or internal environment. Exhibit 13-3 illustrates how both individual and organizational factors can increase political behavior and provide favorable outcomes (increased rewards and averted punishments) for both individuals and groups in the organization.

Individual Factors   At the individual level, researchers have identified certain personality traits, needs, and other factors likely to be related to political

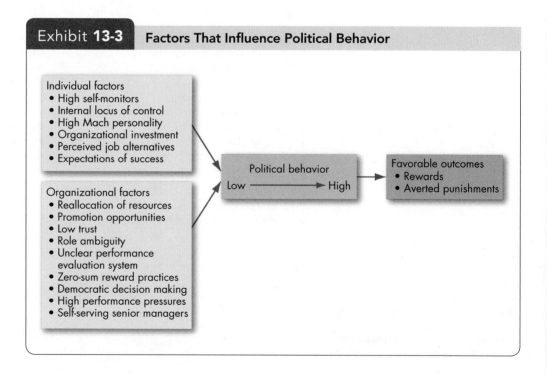

Exhibit 13-3   **Factors That Influence Political Behavior**

Individual factors
• High self-monitors
• Internal locus of control
• High Mach personality
• Organizational investment
• Perceived job alternatives
• Expectations of success

Organizational factors
• Reallocation of resources
• Promotion opportunities
• Low trust
• Role ambiguity
• Unclear performance evaluation system
• Zero-sum reward practices
• Democratic decision making
• High performance pressures
• Self-serving senior managers

Political behavior
Low ⟶ High

Favorable outcomes
• Rewards
• Averted punishments

behavior. In terms of traits, we find that employees who are high self-monitors, possess an internal locus of control, and have a high need for power are more likely to engage in political behavior.[51] The high self-monitor is more sensitive to social cues, exhibits higher levels of social conformity, and is more likely to be skilled in political behavior than the low self-monitor. Because they believe they can control their environment, individuals with an internal locus of control are more prone to take a proactive stance and attempt to manipulate situations in their favor. Not surprisingly, the Machiavellian personality—characterized by the will to manipulate and the desire for power—is comfortable using politics as a means to further his or her self-interest.

In addition, an individual's investment in the organization, perceived alternatives, and expectations of success influence the degree to which he or she will pursue illegitimate means of political action.[52] The more a person expects increased future benefits from the organization, the more that person has to lose if forced out and the less likely he or she is to use illegitimate means. The more alternative job opportunities an individual has—due to a favorable job market or the possession of scarce skills or knowledge, a prominent reputation, or influential contacts outside the organization—the more likely that individual is to risk illegitimate political actions. Finally, an individual with low expectations of success from illegitimate means is unlikely to use them. High expectations from such measures are most likely to be the province of both experienced and powerful individuals with polished political skills and inexperienced and naïve employees who misjudge their chances.

Organizational Factors Although we acknowledge the role individual differences can play, the evidence more strongly suggests that certain situations and cultures promote politics. Specifically, when an organization's resources are declining, when the existing pattern of resources is changing, and when there is opportunity for promotions, politicking is more likely to surface.[53] When organizations downsize to improve efficiency, resources must be reduced, and people may engage in political actions to safeguard what they have. But *any* changes, especially those that imply significant reallocation of resources within the organization, are likely to stimulate conflict and increase politicking. The opportunity for promotions or advancement has consistently been found to encourage competition for a limited resource as people try to positively influence the decision outcome.

Cultures characterized by low trust, role ambiguity, unclear performance evaluation systems, zero-sum reward allocation practices, democratic decision making, high pressures for performance, and self-serving senior managers will also create breeding grounds for politicking.[54] The less trust within the organization, the higher the level of political behavior and the more likely it will be of the illegitimate kind. So, high trust should suppress political behavior in general and inhibit illegitimate actions in particular.

Role ambiguity means the prescribed employee behaviors are not clear. There are, therefore, fewer limits to the scope and functions of the employee's political actions. Because political activities are defined as those not required as part of the employee's formal role, the greater the role ambiguity, the more employees can engage in unnoticed political activity.

Performance evaluation is far from a perfect science. The more organizations use subjective criteria in the appraisal, emphasize a single outcome measure, or allow significant time to pass between the time of an action and its appraisal, the greater the likelihood that an employee can get away with politicking. Subjective performance criteria create ambiguity. The use of a single outcome measure encourages individuals to do whatever is necessary to "look good" on

"Corporate Political Activity Pays"

This statement appears to be true. Political influence behavior certainly appears to pay in some situations. According to a recent review of the literature, that applies to *organizational* political influence as well.

Much organizational political activity takes the form of exchange, such as when favorable government treatment is exchanged for political support or donations to political candidates. A different kind of political activity takes place when competitors collude against a common adversary. For example, major league sports team owners often join forces to obtain more favorable labor settlements.

Unions that normally compete for union members may do the same.

A review of 78 studies on the link between organizational political activity and firm performance found a significant positive relationship. The authors conclude that their finding "explains why more business interests are engaged in [political activity] than at any other time in recorded history."

In 2011, it came to light that General Electric (GE) paid no taxes in 2010, despite earning global profits of $14.2 billion, including $5.1 billion from U.S. operations. Although GE disputes the charge, many credited the firm's political activities with its favorable

treatment (GE CEO Jeff Immelt chairs President Obama's Jobs and Competitiveness Council). GE spokesman Gary Sheffer defended the company's political activity, saying, "We want to be sure our voice is heard."

Sources: S. Lux, T. R. Crook, and D. J. Woehr, "Mixing Business with Politics: A Meta-Analysis of the Antecedents and Outcomes of Corporate Political Activity," *Journal of Management* 37, no. 1 (2011), pp. 223–247; J. D. McKinnon, "New Fight Brews Over Corporate Taxes," *The Wall Street Journal* (May 26, 2011), downloaded on June 17, 2011, from http://blogs.wsj.com/; and D. Kocieniewski, "G.E.'s Strategies Let It Avoid Taxes Altogether," *The New York Times* (March 24, 2011), p. A1.

that measure, but that often occurs at the cost of good performance on other important parts of the job that are not being appraised. The longer the time between an action and its appraisal, the more unlikely it is that the employee will be held accountable for political behaviors.

The more an organization's culture emphasizes the zero-sum or win–lose approach to reward allocations, the more employees will be motivated to

Organizations foster politicking when they reduce resources in order to improve performance. As part of a restructuring program, Germany's Allianz AG announced plans to eliminate 5,000 jobs at its insurance operation and 2,500 jobs at its banking subsidiary. Allianz stated that the job cuts were necessary to improve efficiency and to increase its competitiveness and would result in savings of between $600 and $750,000 million. The company's cost-cutting measures stimulated conflict and political activity, as trade union workers joined Allianz employees in staging a token strike to safeguard their jobs.

Source: Winfried Rothermel/AP Images.

engage in politicking. The zero-sum approach treats the reward "pie" as fixed, so any gain one person or group achieves has to come at the expense of another person or group. If $15,000 in annual raises is to be distributed among five employees, any employee who gets more than $3,000 takes money away from one or more of the others. Such a practice encourages making others look bad and increasing the visibility of what you do.

Finally, when employees see the people on top engaging in political behavior, especially doing so successfully and being rewarded for it, a climate is created that supports politicking. Politicking by top management in a sense gives those lower in the organization permission to play politics by implying that such behavior is acceptable.

How Do People Respond to Organizational Politics?

Trish O'Donnell loves her job as a writer on a weekly television comedy series but hates the internal politics. "A couple of the writers here spend more time kissing up to the executive producer than doing any work. And our head writer clearly has his favorites. While they pay me a lot and I get to really use my creativity, I'm sick of having to be on alert for backstabbers and constantly having to self-promote my contributions. I'm tired of doing most of the work and getting little of the credit." Are Trish O'Donnell's comments typical of people who work in highly politicized workplaces? We all know friends or relatives who regularly complain about the politics at their job. But how do people in general react to organizational politics? Let's look at the evidence.

In our earlier discussion in this chapter of factors that contribute to political behavior, we focused on the favorable outcomes. But for most people—who have modest political skills or are unwilling to play the politics game—outcomes tend to be predominantly negative. Exhibit 13-4 summarizes the extensive research (mostly conducted in the United States) on the relationship between organizational politics and individual outcomes.[55] Very strong evidence indicates, for instance, that perceptions of organizational politics are negatively related to job satisfaction.[56] The perception of politics also tends to increase job anxiety and stress, possibly because people believe they may be losing ground

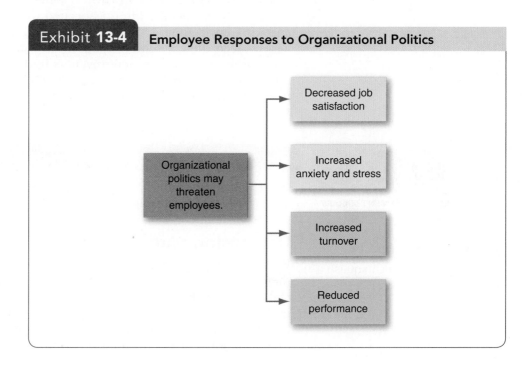

Exhibit **13-4**   **Employee Responses to Organizational Politics**

to others who are active politickers or, conversely, because they feel additional pressures from entering into and competing in the political arena.[57] Politics may lead to self-reported declines in employee performance, perhaps because employees perceive political environments to be unfair, which demotivates them.[58] Not surprisingly, when politicking becomes too much to handle, it can lead employees to quit.[59]

When employees of two agencies in a recent study in Nigeria viewed their work environments as political, they reported higher levels of job distress and were less likely to help their co-workers. Thus, although developing countries such as Nigeria are perhaps more ambiguous and more political environments in which to work, the negative consequences of politics appear to be the same as in the United States.[60]

Researchers have also noted several interesting qualifiers. First, the politics–performance relationship appears to be moderated by an individual's understanding of the "hows" and "whys" of organizational politics. "An individual who has a clear understanding of who is responsible for making decisions and why they were selected to be the decision makers would have a better understanding of how and why things happen the way they do than someone who does not understand the decision-making process in the organization."[61] When both politics and understanding are high, performance is likely to increase because the individual will see political actions as an opportunity. This is consistent with what you might expect among individuals with well-honed political skills. But when understanding is low, individuals are more likely to see politics as a threat, which can have a negative effect on job performance.[62]

Second, political behavior at work moderates the effects of ethical leadership.[63] One study found that male employees were more responsive to ethical leadership and showed the most citizenship behavior when levels of both politics and ethical leadership were high. Women, on the other hand, appear most likely to engage in citizenship behavior when the environment is consistently ethical and *apolitical*.

Third, when employees see politics as a threat, they often respond with **defensive behaviors**—reactive and protective behaviors to avoid action, blame, or change.[64] (Exhibit 13-5 provides some examples of these behaviors.) And defensive behaviors are often associated with negative feelings toward the job and work environment.[65] In the short run, employees may find that defensiveness protects their self-interest, but in the long run it wears them down. People who consistently rely on defensiveness find that, eventually, it is the only way they know how to behave. At that point, they lose the trust and support of their peers, bosses, employees, and clients.

SELF-ASSESSMENT LIBRARY

How Good Am I at Playing Politics?

In the Self-Assessment Library (available on CD and online), take assessment II.C.3 (How Good Am I at Playing Politics?).

7 Apply impression management techniques.

Impression Management

We know people have an ongoing interest in how others perceive and evaluate them. For example, North Americans spend billions of dollars on diets, health club memberships, cosmetics, and plastic surgery—all intended to make them more attractive to others.[66] Being perceived positively by others should have benefits for people in organizations. It might, for instance, help them initially to get the jobs they want in an organization and, once hired, to get favorable

Exhibit **13-5**	Defensive Behaviors

Avoiding Action

Overconforming. Strictly interpreting your responsibility by saying things like "The rules clearly state . . . " or "This is the way we've always done it."

Buck passing. Transferring responsibility for the execution of a task or decision to someone else.

Playing dumb. Avoiding an unwanted task by falsely pleading ignorance or inability.

Stretching. Prolonging a task so that one person appears to be occupied—for example, turning a two-week task into a 4-month job.

Stalling. Appearing to be more or less supportive publicly while doing little or nothing privately.

Avoiding Blame

Buffing. This is a nice way to refer to "covering your rear." It describes the practice of rigorously documenting activity to project an image of competence and thoroughness.

Playing safe. Evading situations that may reflect unfavorably. It includes taking on only projects with a high probability of success, having risky decisions approved by superiors, qualifying expressions of judgment, and taking neutral positions in conflicts.

Justifying. Developing explanations that lessen one's responsibility for a negative outcome and/or apologizing to demonstrate remorse, or both.

Scapegoating. Placing the blame for a negative outcome on external factors that are not entirely blameworthy.

Misrepresenting. Manipulation of information by distortion, embellishment, deception, selective presentation, or obfuscation.

Avoiding Change

Prevention. Trying to prevent a threatening change from occurring.

Self-protection. Acting in ways to protect one's self-interest during change by guarding information or other resources.

evaluations, superior salary increases, and more rapid promotions. In a political context, it might help sway the distribution of advantages in their favor. The process by which individuals attempt to control the impression others form of them is called **impression management (IM)**.[67]

Who might we predict will engage in IM? No surprise here. It's our old friend, the high self-monitor.[68] Low self-monitors tend to present images of themselves that are consistent with their personalities, regardless of the beneficial or detrimental effects for them. In contrast, high self-monitors are good at reading situations and molding their appearances and behavior to fit each situation. If you want to control the impression others form of you, what IM techniques can you use? Exhibit 13-6 summarizes some of the most popular and provides an example of each.

Keep in mind that when people engage in IM, they are sending a false message that might be true under other circumstances.[69] Excuses, for instance, may be offered with sincerity. Referring to the example in Exhibit 13-6, you can *actually* believe that ads contribute little to sales in your region. But misrepresentation can have a high cost. If you "cry wolf" once too often, no one is likely to believe you when the wolf really comes. So the impression manager must be

---

defensive behaviors *Reactive and protective behaviors to avoid action, blame, or change.*

impression management (IM) *The process by which individuals attempt to control the impression others form of them.*

| Exhibit 13-6 | Impression Management (IM) Techniques |

Conformity

Agreeing with someone else's opinion to gain his or her approval is a *form of ingratiation.*

Example: A manager tells his boss, "You're absolutely right on your reorganization plan for the western regional office. I couldn't agree with you more."

Favors

Doing something nice for someone to gain that person's approval is a *form of ingratiation.*

Example: A salesperson says to a prospective client, "I've got two tickets to the theater tonight that I can't use. Take them. Consider it a thank-you for taking the time to talk with me."

Excuses

Explanations of a predicament-creating event aimed at minimizing the apparent severity of the predicament is a *defensive IM technique.*

Example: A sales manager says to her boss, "We failed to get the ad in the paper on time, but no one responds to those ads anyway."

Apologies

Admitting responsibility for an undesirable event and simultaneously seeking to get a pardon for the action is a *defensive IM technique.*

Example: An employee says to his boss, "I'm sorry I made a mistake on the report. Please forgive me."

Self-Promotion

Highlighting one's best qualities, downplaying one's deficits, and calling attention to one's achievements is a *self-focused IM technique.*

Example: A salesperson tells his boss, "Matt worked unsuccessfully for three years to try to get that account. I sewed it up in six weeks. I'm the best closer this company has."

Enhancement

Claiming that something you did is more valuable than most other members of the organizations would think is a *self-focused IM technique.*

Example: A journalist tells his editor, "My work on this celebrity divorce story was really a major boost to our sales" (even though the story only made it to page 3 in the entertainment section).

Flattery

Complimenting others about their virtues in an effort to make oneself appear perceptive and likeable is an *assertive IM technique.*

Example: A new sales trainee says to her peer, "You handled that client's complaint so tactfully! I could never have handled that as well as you did."

Exemplification

Doing more than you need to in an effort to show how dedicated and hard working you are is an *assertive IM technique.*

Example: An employee sends e-mails from his work computer when he works late so that his supervisor will know how long he's been working.

Source: Based on B. R. Schlenker, Impression Management s(Monterey, CA: Brooks/Cole, 1980); M. C. Bolino, K. M. Kacmar, W. H. Turnley, and J. B. Gilstrap, "A Multi-Level Review of Impression Management Motives and Behaviors," *Journal of Management* 34, no. 6 (2008), pp. 1080–1109; and R. B. Cialdini, "Indirect Tactics of Image Management Beyond Basking," in R. A. Giacalone and P. Rosenfeld (eds.), *Impression Management in the Organization* (Hillsdale, NJ: Lawrence Erlbaum, 1989), pp. 45–71.

cautious not to be perceived as insincere or manipulative.[70] Consider the effect of implausible name-dropping as an example of this principle. Participants in a study in Switzerland disliked an experimental confederate who claimed to be a personal friend of the well-liked Swiss tennis star Roger Federer, but they generally liked confederates who just said they were fans.[71] Another study found that when managers attributed an employee's citizenship behaviors to impression management, they actually felt angry (probably because they felt manipulated) and gave subordinates lower performance ratings. When managers attributed the same behaviors to prosocial values and concern about the organization, they felt happy and gave higher performance ratings.[72] In sum, people don't like to feel others are manipulating them through impression management, so such tactics should be employed with caution.

Are there *situations* in which individuals are more likely to misrepresent themselves or more likely to get away with it? Yes—situations characterized by high uncertainty or ambiguity provide relatively little information for challenging a fraudulent claim and reduce the risks associated with misrepresentation.[73] The increasing use of telework may be increasing the use of IM. Individuals who work remotely from their supervisors engage in high levels of IM relative to those who work closely with their supervisors.[74]

Most of the studies undertaken to test the effectiveness of IM techniques have related it to two criteria: interview success and performance evaluations. Let's consider each of these.

The evidence indicates most job applicants use IM techniques in interviews[75] and that it works.[76] In one study, for instance, interviewers felt applicants for a position as a customer service representative who used IM techniques performed better in the interview, and they seemed somewhat more inclined to hire these people.[77] Moreover, when the researchers considered applicants' credentials, they concluded it was the IM techniques alone that influenced the interviewers—that is, it didn't seem to matter whether applicants were well or poorly qualified. If they used IM techniques, they did better in the interview.

Some IM techniques work better in interviews than others. Researchers have compared applicants whose IM techniques focused on promoting their accomplishments (called *self-promotion*) to those who focused on complimenting the interviewer and finding areas of agreement (referred to as *ingratiation*). In general, applicants appear to use self-promotion more than ingratiation.[78] What's more, self-promotion tactics may be more important to interviewing success. Applicants who work to create an appearance of competence by enhancing their accomplishments, taking credit for successes, and explaining away failures do better in interviews. These effects reach beyond the interview: applicants who use more self-promotion tactics also seem to get more follow-up job-site visits, even after adjusting for grade-point average, gender, and job type. Ingratiation also works well in interviews; applicants who compliment the interviewer, agree with his or her opinions, and emphasize areas of fit do better than those who don't.[79]

In terms of performance ratings, the picture is quite different. Ingratiation is positively related to performance ratings, meaning those who ingratiate with their supervisors get higher performance evaluations. However, self-promotion appears to backfire: those who self-promote actually seem to receive *lower* performance evaluations.[80] There is an important qualifier to this general result. It appears that individuals high in political skill are able to translate IM into higher performance appraisals, whereas those lower in political skill are more likely to be hurt by their IM attempts.[81] Another study of 760 boards of directors found that individuals who ingratiate themselves to current board members (express agreement with the director, point out shared attitudes and opinions, compliment the director) increase their chances of landing on a board.[82]

What explains these results? If you think about them, they make sense. Ingratiating always works because everyone—both interviewers and supervisors—likes to be treated nicely. However, self-promotion may work only in interviews and backfire on the job because, whereas the interviewer has little idea whether you're blowing smoke about your accomplishments, the supervisor knows because it's his or her job to observe you. Thus, if you're going to self-promote, remember that what works in an interview won't always work once you're on the job.

Are our conclusions about responses to politics globally valid? Should we expect employees in Israel, for instance, to respond the same way to workplace politics that employees in the United States do? Almost all our conclusions on employee reactions to organizational politics are based on studies conducted in North America. The few studies that have included other countries suggest some minor modifications.[83] One study of managers in U.S. culture and three Chinese cultures (People's Republic of China, Hong Kong, and Taiwan) found U.S. managers evaluated "gentle persuasion" tactics such as consultation and inspirational appeal as more effective than did their Chinese counterparts.[84] Other research suggests that effective U.S. leaders achieve influence by focusing on personal goals of group members and the tasks at hand (an analytical approach), whereas influential East Asian leaders focus on relationships among group members and meeting the demands of the people around them (a holistic approach).[85]

As another example, Israelis and the British seem to generally respond as do North Americans—that is, their perception of organizational politics relates to decreased job satisfaction and increased turnover.[86] But in countries that are more politically unstable, such as Israel, employees seem to demonstrate greater tolerance of intense political processes in the workplace, perhaps because they are used to power struggles and have more experience in coping with them.[87] This suggests that people from politically turbulent countries in the Middle East or Latin America might be more accepting of organizational politics, and even more willing to use aggressive political tactics in the workplace, than people from countries such as Great Britain or Switzerland.

The Ethics of Behaving Politically

8 Determine whether a political action is ethical.

Although there are no clear-cut ways to differentiate ethical from unethical politicking, there are some questions you should consider. For example, what is the utility of engaging in politicking? Sometimes we do it for little good reason. Major league baseball player Al Martin claimed he played football at USC when in fact he never did. As a baseball player, he had little to gain by pretending to have played football. Outright lies like this may be a rather extreme example of impression management, but many of us have at least distorted information to make a favorable impression. One thing to keep in mind is whether it's really worth the risk. Another question to ask is this: how does the utility of engaging in the political behavior balance out any harm (or potential harm) it will do to others? Complimenting a supervisor on his or her appearance in order to curry favor is probably much less harmful than grabbing credit for a project that others deserve.

Finally, does the political activity conform to standards of equity and justice? Sometimes it is difficult to weigh the costs and benefits of a political action, but its ethicality is clear. The department head who inflates the performance evaluation of a favored employee and deflates the evaluation of a disfavored employee—and then uses these evaluations to justify giving the former a big raise and nothing to the latter—has treated the disfavored employee unfairly.

Unfortunately, powerful people can become very good at explaining self-serving behaviors in terms of the organization's best interests. They can persuasively argue that unfair actions are really fair and just. Our point is that immoral people can justify almost any behavior. Those who are powerful, articulate, and persuasive are most vulnerable to ethical lapses because they are likely to be able to get away with unethical practices successfully. When faced with an ethical dilemma regarding organizational politics, try to consider whether playing politics is worth the risk and whether others might be harmed in the process. If you have a strong power base, recognize the ability of power to corrupt. Remember that it's a lot easier for the powerless to act ethically, if for no other reason than they typically have very little political discretion to exploit.

MyManagementLab

Now that you have finished this chapter, go back to **www.mymanagementlab.com** to continue practicing and applying the concepts you've learned.

Summary and Implications for Managers

If you want to get things done in a group or an organization, it helps to have power. Here are several suggestions for how to deal with power in your own work life:

- As a manager who wants to maximize your power, you will want to increase others' dependence on you. You can, for instance, increase your power in relation to your boss by developing knowledge or a skill she needs and for which she perceives no ready substitute. But you will not be alone in attempting to build your power bases. Others, particularly employees and peers, will be seeking to increase your dependence on them, while you are trying to minimize it and increase their dependence on you. The result is a continual battle.
- Few employees relish being powerless in their job and organization. Try to avoid putting others in a position where they feel they have no power.
- People respond differently to the various power bases. Expert and referent power are derived from an individual's personal qualities. In contrast, coercion, reward, and legitimate power are essentially organizationally derived. Competence especially appears to offer wide appeal, and its use as a power base results in high performance by group members. The message for managers seems to be "Develop and use your expert power base!"
- An effective manager accepts the political nature of organizations. By assessing behavior in a political framework, you can better predict the actions of others and use that information to formulate political strategies that will gain advantages for you and your work unit.
- Some people are significantly more politically astute than others, meaning that they are aware of the underlying politics and can manage impressions. Those who are good at playing politics can be expected to get higher performance evaluations and, hence, larger salary increases and more promotions than the politically naïve or inept. The politically astute are also likely to exhibit higher job satisfaction and be better able to neutralize job stressors.
- Employees who have poor political skills or are unwilling to play the politics game generally relate perceived organizational politics to lower job satisfaction and self-reported performance, increased anxiety, and higher turnover.

Power Corrupts People

POINT	COUNTERPOINT

POINT

Lord Acton famously wrote: "All power tends to corrupt and absolute power corrupts absolutely." Most of us probably believe that leaders with more power are more likely to abuse their power to the detriment of others and, ultimately, of the entity they lead. For this reason, most organizations—including governments and corporations—put checks and balances in place to keep leaders from amassing too much power. If we look at the history of corruption and malfeasance among government, business, and other organizational leaders, rarely would we conclude that the core reason for corruption was that the leader had *too little* power.

Why is power so toxic? As one expert plainly states, "Power quickly turns us into hypocrites." In one study, researchers found that the more powerful people felt, the more likely they were to see misreporting travel expenses as unethical. But these researchers next studied how these same people self-reported the results of a game of chance, when it was in their self-interest to lie about their results. What did they find? You guessed it: the more powerful the people felt, the more likely they were to self-report results significantly better than chance. Power really does seem to breed hypocrisy. The powerful are more likely to see behavior as unethical, but more likely to behave unethically themselves. Researchers speculate that power allows people to better rationalize away ethical lapses. "They're important people, with important things to do," says one expert.

The study of the corrupting effects of power is not limited to laboratory studies. A fascinating study of 1,000 Supreme Court decisions found that as justices gained power on the court, their opinions tended to become less complex and nuanced. They considered fewer perspectives and possible outcomes. The really bad news is that as their power increased, of course, their opinions were more likely to become majority opinions, and thus the law of the land.

Power may be effective in allowing us to get our way. But that power, while good for the individual getting it, is bad for almost everyone else.

COUNTERPOINT

Power may help leaders do some aspects of their jobs more effectively, but that isn't the whole story.

Most of the great deeds in history required great power. Do you really think George Washington would have been of more use to the Continental Army if he was a private rather a general? Would Steven Jobs have had more impact on computer technology innovations if he remained a technician with video-game maker Atari? We want our best and brightest in positions where their qualities can do the most good, and that means we want them to be in power.

When Bill Gates used his wealth and power to start the Bill & Melinda Gates Foundation, and when Warren Buffett announced his intention to give 85 percent of his wealth to the foundation, they were using their wealth and power to do acts of good the rest of us can only dream about. You may not think Gates or Buffett is any better than the rest of us, but can you imagine starting your own philanthropic foundation or giving away 85 percent of your wealth? Yes, it is easier for them to do good because they're rich and powerful, but that's the point: they could still be good without their wealth and power, but they couldn't do as much good.

Yes, power is dangerous. But so is electricity. Just because something can be misused in the wrong hands does not mean we abandon it. Nor should we mistake the real cause of corrupt behavior. The only difference between a petty thief and billion-dollar swindler Bernie Madoff is scale—a petty thief in Madoff's shoes with Madoff's talents would do the same thing Madoff did. Power is therefore a conduit—of both good and bad motives.

Most of the great acts in history were done by people with power. And, yes, many of the most evil acts were done by people with power. But the issue isn't power itself; it's what we do with it.

Sources: J. Lehrer, "The Power Trip," *The Wall Street Journal* (August 14, 2010), pp. W1–2; J. Lehrer, "How Power Corrupts," *The Frontal Cortex* (May 18, 2011), downloaded June 7, 2011, from www.wired.com/; and K. Heim, "The New Gates Foundation Headquarters Reflects Charity's Roots—and Reach," *Seattle Times* (May 21, 2011), downloaded on June 7, 2011, from http://seattletimes.nwsource.com/.

QUESTIONS FOR REVIEW

1 What is *power*? How is leadership different from power?

2 What are the similarities and differences among the five bases of power?

3 What is the role of dependence in power relationships?

4 What are the nine most often identified power or influence tactics and their contingencies?

5 What is the connection between sexual harassment and the abuse of power?

6 What are the causes and consequences of political behavior?

7 What are some examples of impression management techniques?

8 What standards can you use to determine whether a political action is ethical?

EXPERIENTIAL EXERCISE Understanding Power Dynamics

Create Groups

Each student is to turn in a dollar bill (or similar value of currency) to the instructor, and students are then divided into three groups (based on criteria given by the instructor), assigned to their workplaces, and instructed to read the following rules and tasks. The money is divided into thirds, and two-thirds of it is given to the top group, one-third to the middle group, and none to the bottom group.

Conduct Exercise

Groups go to their assigned workplaces and have 30 minutes to complete their tasks.

Rules

Members of the top group are free to enter the space of either of the other groups and to communicate whatever they wish, whenever they wish. Members of the middle group may enter the space of the lower group when they wish but must request permission to enter the top group's space (which the top group can refuse). Members of the lower group may not disturb the top group in any way unless specifically invited by the top. The lower group does have the right to knock on the door of the middle group and request permission to communicate with them (which can also be refused).

The members of the top group have the authority to make any change in the rules that they wish, at any time, with or without notice.

Tasks

- **Top group.** Responsible for the overall effectiveness and learning from the exercise and to decide how to use its money.

- **Middle group.** Assist the top group in providing for the overall welfare of the organization and deciding how to use its money.

- **Bottom group.** Identify the organization's resources and decide how best to provide for learning and the overall effectiveness of the organization.

Debriefing

Each of the three groups chooses two representatives to go to the front of the class and discuss the following:

1. Summarize what occurred within and among the three groups.

2. What are some of the differences between being in the top group and being in the bottom group?

3. What can we learn about power from this experience?

4. How accurate do you think this exercise is in reflecting the reality of resource allocation decisions in large organizations?

Source: Adapted from L. Bolman and T. E. Deal, *Exchange* 3, no. 4 (1979), pp. 38–42. Reprinted by permission of Sage Publications Inc.

ETHICAL DILEMMA Corporate Spying

In a conference call with investors and financial analysts, the chief financial officer (CFO) for a major corporation outlines the company's positive expected earnings for the next quarter despite some serious economic challenges. Unknown to the CFO, party to this conference call is an ex-CIA interrogator trained in "tactical behavioral assessment." The investigator detects nervousness and evasiveness in the CFO's hurried answers to questions. In his report, he concludes that the CFO is probably lying.

Who is the recipient of the report? A hedge fund. Based on the report, the fund shorts the company's stock—selling borrowed shares in anticipation that the price will drop—and when the company's earnings do fall short of expectations, the hedge fund buys the shares back at the lower price and profits greatly.

Whatever trust you may place in the ability of investigators to detect lying, this sort of espionage happens. And it goes further. When Swiss chocolatier Nestlé was trying to sell a chocolate-covered toy in the United States, its U.S. competitor, Mars, covertly used consultants to prod government officials with misinformation that the toy was a safety hazard. The strategy worked. Learning of Mars'

activities, Nestlé paid former Secret Service agents to bribe garbage collectors so it could acquire Mars' corporate trash and counterspy.

Chinese companies hacked into Google's website, gaining access to corporate premises using night-vision glasses stolen from a U.S. military contractor. Hewlett-Packard used "pretexting" by investigators who impersonated HP board members in order to obtain their phone records as a means to investigate it own board members.

These stories are all true.

Questions

1. One corporate spy said, "Companies do this in order to stay in front of problems." Can you envision a business problem so dangerous that you would approve a spy mission if you were in charge?

2. Are there ever circumstances in which corporate spying is ethical? If so, what are they?

3. Recently, LinkedIn reposted a tweet that questioned whether Facebook was appropriate for public schools. Is it ever ethical for a company to attempt to undermine another in this way?

Source: J. J. Fialka, "Hugger-Mugger in the Executive Suite," *The Wall Street Journal* (February 5, 2010), p. W10; E. Javers, *Broker, Trader, Lawyer, Spy* (New York: Harper, 2010); and J. Scott, "Is Corporate Spying Legal?" *Forbes* (May 31, 2011), downloaded June 15, 2011, from http://blogs.forbes.com/.

CASE INCIDENT 1 Delegate Power, or Keep It Close?

Samantha Parks is the owner and CEO of Sparks, a small New York agency that develops advertising, promotions, and marketing materials for high-fashion firms. Parks has tended to keep a tight rein on her business, overseeing most projects from start to finish. However, as the firm has grown, she has found it necessary to delegate more and more decisions to her associates. She's recently been approached by a hairstyling chain that wants a comprehensive redefinition of its entire marketing and promotions look. Should Samantha try to manage this project in her traditional way, or should she delegate major parts to her employees?

Most managers confront this question at some point in their careers. Some experts propose that top executives need to stay very close to the creative core of their business, which means that even if their primary responsibility is to manage, CEOs should never cede too much control to committees of creative individuals or they can lose sight of the firm's overall future direction. Moreover, executives who do fall out of touch with the creative process risk being passed over by a new generation of "plugged in" employees who better understand how the business really works.

Others offer the opposite advice, saying it's not a good idea for a CEO to "sweat the small stuff" like managing individual client accounts or projects. These experts advise executives to identify everything they can "outsource" to other employees and to delegate as much as possible. By eliminating trivial tasks, executives will be better able to focus their attention on the most important decision-making and control aspects of their jobs, which will help the business and also ensure that the top executive maintains control over the functions that really matter.

These pieces of advice are not necessarily in conflict with one another. The real challenge is to identify what you can delegate effectively without ceding too much power and control away from the person with the unifying vision. That is certainly easier said than done, though.

Questions

1. If you were Samantha Parks, how would you prioritize which projects or parts of projects to delegate?

2. In explaining what makes her decisions hard, Parks said, "I hire good people, creative people, to run

these projects, and I worry that they will see my oversight and authority as interfering with their creative process." How can she deal with these concerns without giving up too much control?

3. Should executives try to control projects to maintain their position of authority? Do they have a right to

control projects and keep in the loop on important decisions just so they can remain in charge?

4. What are some tasks in an organization that a top executive should never delegate to others?

Source: Based on M. L. Tushman, W. K. Smith, and A. Binns, "The Ambidextrous CEO," *Harvard Business Review* (June 2011), pp. 74–79; and S. Bogan, "Find Your Focus," *Financial Planning* (February 2011), p. 72.

CASE INCIDENT 2 The Persuasion Imperative

At one point in time, bosses gave orders and subordinates followed them without question. Those of you who have seen the AMC series *Mad Men*—based on Madison Avenue marketing executives in the 1960s—will know this image of deference to authority, obedience to those higher up in the hierarchy, and relationships between supervisors and employees that are highly paternalistic.

With time comes change. The male-dominated organization with rampant sexual harassment portrayed in *Mad Men* is far less prevalent than it was in the 1960s. Laws and policies are in place that better protect employees against the sometimes-capricious whims of supervisors.

Another sign of shifting cultural values is the way managers use their power. Commandments are out. Persuasion is in.

When IBM manager Kate Riley Tenant needed to reassign managers and engineers to form a database software team, she had to persuade IBM employees from all corners of the globe, none of whom directly reported to her. According to Tenant, it's a big change from when she started in the field 20 years ago. "You just decided things, and people went off and executed," she said. Now, "not everybody reports to you, and so there's much more negotiation and influence."

John Churchill, a manager with Florida-based Gerdau Ameristeel Corporation, agrees. The question now, he says, is, "How do I influence this group and gain credibility?"

At IBM, the challenge of persuading employees across reporting relationships has become so significant that the firm developed a 2-hour online course to help managers persuade other employees to help with projects crucial to is business. IBM's tips for managers include the following:

- Build a shared vision.
- Negotiate collaboratively.
- Make trade-offs.
- Build and maintain your network.

Despite meeting initial resistance, after completing the training program, Tenant was able to persuade most IBM managers and engineers to join the team.

This doesn't mean authority has lost all its power. Robert Cialdini, a social psychologist who has studied persuasion for decades, lists authority as one of his keys to influence. Even more important may be "social proof"—Cialdini and others have found that people are often deeply persuaded by observing what others are doing. From his research, no message more effectively got hotel guests to reuse their towels than citing statistics that others were reusing their towels.

So, if you're a manager who needs to persuade, present the vision behind the request and be collaborative, but it also wouldn't hurt to tell those you're trying to persuade about others who have already agreed to your request.

Questions

1. Are the precepts of the IBM training program consistent with the concepts in this chapter? Why or why not?

2. Again based on the chapter, are there other keys to persuasion and influence that might be added to the IBM program?

3. If you had a manager who wanted you to do something against your initial inclination, which of IBM's elements would work best on you? Why?

4. Drawing from Chapter 5, do you think generational values explain the changing nature of the employer–employee relationship? Why or why not?

Source: Based on E. White, "Art of Persuasion Becomes Key," *The Wall Street Journal* (May 19, 2008), p. B5; B. Tsui, "Greening with Envy," *The Atlantic* (July/August 2009), www.theatlantic.com; and R. Cialdini, *Influence: The Psychology of Persuasion* (New York: HarperBusiness, 2007).

ENDNOTES

1. R. M. Kanter, "Power Failure in Management Circuits," *Harvard Business Review* (July–August 1979), p. 65.
2. J. Pfeffer, "Understanding Power in Organizations," *California Management Review* (Winter 1992), p. 35.
3. Based on B. M. Bass, *Bass & Stogdill's Handbook of Leadership*, 3rd ed. (New York: The Free Press, 1990).
4. D. Carney, "Powerful People Are Better Liars," *Harvard Business Review* (May 2010), pp. 32–33.
5. A. J. Ferguson, M. E. Ormiston, and H. Moon, "From Approach to Inhibition: The Influence of Power on Responses to Poor Performers," *Journal of Applied Psychology* 95, no. 2 (2010), pp. 305–320.
6. J. R. P. French Jr. and B. Raven, "The Bases of Social Power," in D. Cartwright (ed.), *Studies in Social Power* (Ann Arbor, MI: University of Michigan, Institute for Social Research, 1959), pp. 150–167; B. J. Raven, "The Bases of Power: Origins and Recent Developments," *Journal of Social Issues* (Winter 1993), pp. 227–251; and G. Yukl, "Use Power Effectively," in E. A. Locke (ed.), *Handbook of Principles of Organizational Behavior* (Malden, MA: Blackwell, 2004), pp. 242–247.
7. E. A. Ward, "Social Power Bases of Managers: Emergence of a New Factor," *Journal of Social Psychology* (February 2001), pp. 144–147.
8. S. R. Giessner and T. W. Schubert, "High in the Hierarchy: How Vertical Location and Judgments of Leaders' Power Are Interrelated," *Organizational Behavior and Human Decision Processes* 104, no. 1 (2007), pp. 30–44.
9. P. M. Podsakoff and C. A. Schriesheim, "Field Studies of French and Raven's Bases of Power: Critique, Reanalysis, and Suggestions for Future Research," *Psychological Bulletin* (May 1985), pp. 387–411; T. R. Hinkin and C. A. Schriesheim, "Development and Application of New Scales to Measure the French and Raven (1959) Bases of Social Power," *Journal of Applied Psychology* (August 1989), pp. 561–567; and P. P. Carson, K. D. Carson, and C. W. Roe, "Social Power Bases: A Meta-Analytic Examination of Interrelationships and Outcomes," *Journal of Applied Social Psychology* 23, no. 14 (1993), pp. 1150–1169.
10. S. Perman, "Translation Advertising: Where Shop Meets Hip Hop," *Time* (August 30, 2010), www.time.com.
11. M. van Dijke, D. De Cremer, and D. M. Mayer, "The Role of Authority Power in Explaining Procedural Fairness Effects," *Journal of Applied Psychology* 95, no. 3 (2010), pp. 488–502.
12. R. E. Emerson, "Power–Dependence Relations," *American Sociological Review* (February 1962), pp. 31–41.
13. H. Mintzberg, *Power In and Around Organizations* (Upper Saddle River, NJ: Prentice Hall, 1983), p. 24.
14. R. M. Cyert and J. G. March, *A Behavioral Theory of the Firm* (Upper Saddle River, NJ: Prentice Hall, 1963).
15. C. Perrow, "Departmental Power and Perspective in Industrial Firms," in M. N. Zald (ed.), *Power in Organizations* (Nashville, TN: Vanderbilt University Press, 1970).
16. N. Foulkes, "Tractor Boy," *High Life* (October 2002), p. 90.
17. See, for example, D. Kipnis and S. M. Schmidt, "Upward-Influence Styles: Relationship with Performance Evaluations, Salary, and Stress," *Administrative Science Quarterly* (December 1988), pp. 528–542; G. Yukl and J. B. Tracey, "Consequences of Influence Tactics Used with Subordinates, Peers, and the Boss," *Journal of Applied Psychology* (August 1992), pp. 525–535; G. Blickle, "Influence Tactics Used by Subordinates: An Empirical Analysis of the Kipnis and Schmidt Subscales," *Psychological Reports* (February 2000), pp. 143–154; and G. Yukl, "Use Power Effectively," pp. 249–252.
18. G. Yukl, *Leadership in Organizations*, 5th ed. (Upper Saddle River, NJ: Prentice Hall, 2002), pp. 141–174; G. R. Ferris, W. A. Hochwarter, C. Douglas, F. R. Blass, R. W. Kolodinksy, and D. C. Treadway, "Social Influence Processes in Organizations and Human Resource Systems," in G. R. Ferris and J. J. Martocchio (eds.), *Research in Personnel and Human Resources Management*, vol. 21 (Oxford, UK: JAI Press/Elsevier, 2003), pp. 65–127; and C. A. Higgins, T. A. Judge, and G. R. Ferris, "Influence Tactics and Work Outcomes: A Meta-Analysis," *Journal of Organizational Behavior* (March 2003), pp. 89–106.
19. C. M. Falbe and G. Yukl, "Consequences for Managers of Using Single Influence Tactics and Combinations of Tactics," *Academy of Management Journal* (July 1992), pp. 638–653.
20. R. E. Petty and P. Briñol, "Persuasion: From Single to Multiple to Metacognitive Processes," *Perspectives on Psychological Science* 3, no. 2 (2008), pp. 137–147.
21. J. Badal, "Getting a Raise from the Boss," *The Wall Street Journal* (July 8, 2006), pp. B1, B5.
22. Yukl, *Leadership in Organizations*.
23. Ibid.
24. Falbe and Yukl, "Consequences for Managers of Using Single Influence Tactics and Combinations of Tactics."
25. A. W. Kruglanski, A. Pierro, and E. T. Higgins, "Regulatory Mode and Preferred Leadership Styles: How Fit Increases Job Satisfaction," *Basic and Applied Social Psychology* 29, no. 2 (2007), pp. 137–149; and A. Pierro, L. Cicero, and B. H. Raven, "Motivated Compliance with Bases of Social Power," *Journal of Applied Social Psychology* 38, no. 7 (2008), pp. 1921–1944.
26. P. P. Fu and G. Yukl, "Perceived Effectiveness of Influence Tactics in the United States and China," *Leadership Quarterly* (Summer 2000), pp. 251–266; O. Branzei, "Cultural Explanations of Individual Preferences for Influence Tactics in Cross-Cultural Encounters," *International Journal of Cross Cultural Management* (August 2002), pp. 203–218; G. Yukl, P. P. Fu, and R. McDonald, "Cross-Cultural Differences in Perceived Effectiveness of Influence Tactics for Initiating or Resisting Change," *Applied Psychology: An International Review* (January 2003), pp. 66–82; and P. P. Fu, T. K. Peng, J. C. Kennedy, and G. Yukl, "Examining the Preferences of Influence Tactics in Chinese Societies: A Comparison of Chinese Managers in Hong Kong, Taiwan, and Mainland China," *Organizational Dynamics* 33, no. 1 (2004), pp. 32–46.
27. C. J. Torelli and S. Shavitt, "Culture and Concepts of Power," *Journal of Personality and Social Psychology* 99, no. 4 (2010), pp. 703–723.
28. Fu and Yukl, "Perceived Effectiveness of Influence Tactics in the United States and China."
29. S. J. Heine, "Making Sense of East Asian Self-Enhancement," *Journal of Cross-Cultural Psychology* (September 2003), pp. 596–602.
30. G. R. Ferris, D. C. Treadway, P. L. Perrewé, R. L. Brouer, C. Douglas, and S. Lux, "Political Skill in Organizations,"

Journal of Management (June 2007), pp. 290–320; K. J. Harris, K. M. Kacmar, S. Zivnuska, and J. D. Shaw, "The Impact of Political Skill on Impression Management Effectiveness," *Journal of Applied Psychology* 92, no. 1 (2007), pp. 278–285; W. A. Hochwarter, G. R. Ferris, M. B. Gavin, P. L. Perrewé, A. T. Hall, and D. D. Frink," Political Skill as Neutralizer of Felt Accountability–Job Tension Effects on Job Performance Ratings: A Longitudinal Investigation," *Organizational Behavior and Human Decision Processes* 102 (2007), pp. 226–239; and D. C. Treadway, G. R. Ferris, A. B. Duke, G. L. Adams, and J. B. Tatcher, "The Moderating Role of Subordinate Political Skill on Supervisors' Impressions of Subordinate Ingratiation and Ratings of Subordinate Interpersonal Facilitation," *Journal of Applied Psychology* 92, no. 3 (2007), pp. 848–855.

31. M. C. Andrews, K. M. Kacmar, and K. J. Harris, "Got Political Skill? The Impact of Justice on the Importance of Political Skills for Job Performance." *Journal of Applied Psychology* 94, no. 6 (2009), pp. 1427–1437.

32. C. Anderson, S. E. Spataro, and F. J. Flynn, "Personality and Organizational Culture as Determinants of Influence," *Journal of Applied Psychology* 93, no. 3 (2008), pp. 702–710.

33. S. Stecklow, "Sexual-Harassment Cases Plague U.N.," *The Wall Street Journal* (May 21, 2009), p. A1.

34. N. Bode, "Flushing Hospital Nurse Gets $15 Million Award in Sexual Harassment Suit," *New York Daily News* (February 23, 2009), www.nydailynews.com.

35. L. J. Munson, C. Hulin, and F. Drasgow, "Longitudinal Analysis of Dispositional Influences and Sexual Harassment: Effects on Job and Psychological Outcomes," *Personnel Psychology* (Spring 2000), pp. 21–46; T. M. Glomb, L. J. Munson, C. L. Hulin, M. E. Bergman, and F. Drasgow, "Structural Equation Models of Sexual Harassment: Longitudinal Explorations and Cross-Sectional Generalizations," *Journal of Applied Psychology* (February 1999), pp. 14–28; M. E. Bergman, R. D. Langhout, P. A. Palmieri, L. M. Cortina, and L. F. Fitzgerald, "The (Un)reasonableness of Reporting: Antecedents and Consequences of Reporting Sexual Harassment," *Journal of Applied Psychology* (April 2002), pp. 230–242; and L. R. Offermann and A. B. Malamut, "When Leaders Harass: The Impact of Target Perceptions of Organizational Leadership and Climate on Harassment Reporting and Outcomes," *Journal of Applied Psychology* (October 2002), pp. 885–893.

36. S. Silverstein and S. Christian, "Harassment Ruling Raises Free-Speech Issues," *Los Angeles Times* (November 11, 1993), p. D2.

37. R. Ilies, N. Hauserman, S. Schwochau, and J. Stibal, "Reported Incidence Rates of Work-Related Sexual Harassment in the United States: Using Meta-Analysis to Explain Reported Rate Disparities," *Personnel Psychology* (Fall 2003), pp. 607–631.

38. K. Bursik and J. Gefter, "Still Stable After All These Years: Perceptions of Sexual Harassment in Academic Contexts," *The Journal of Social Psychology* 151, no. 3 (2011), pp. 331–349.

39. M. Rotundo, D. Nguyen, and P. R. Sackett, "A Meta-Analytic Review of Gender Differences in Perceptions of Sexual Harassment," *Journal of Applied Psychology* (October 2001), pp. 914–922.

40. R. L. Weiner, R. Reiter-Palmon, R. J. Winter, E. Richter, A. Humke, and E. Maeder, "Complaint Behavioral Tone, Ambivalent Sexism, and Perceptions of Sexual Harassment," *Psychology, Public Policy, and Law* 16, no. 1 (2010), pp. 56–84.

41. Ilies, Hauserman, Schwochau, and Stibal, "Reported Incidence Rates of Work-Related Sexual Harassment in the United States; A. B. Malamut and L. R. Offermann, "Coping with Sexual Harassment: Personal, Environmental, and Cognitive Determinants," *Journal of Applied Psychology* (December 2001), pp. 1152–1166; L. M. Cortina and S. A. Wasti, "Profiles in Coping: Responses to Sexual Harassment Across Persons, Organizations, and Cultures," *Journal of Applied Psychology* (February 2005), pp. 182–192; and J. W. Kunstman, "Sexual Overperception: Power, Mating Motives, and Biases in Social Judgment," *Journal of Personality and Social Psychology* 100, no. 2 (2011), pp. 282–294.

42. F. Krings and S. Facchin, "Organizational Justice and Men's Likelihood to Sexually Harass: The Moderating Role of Sexism and Personality," *Journal of Applied Psychology* 94, no. 2 (2009), pp. 501–510.

43. C. R. Willness, P. Steel, and K. Lee, "A Meta-Analysis of the Antecedents and Consequences of Workplace Sexual Harassment," *Personnel Psychology* 60 (2007), pp. 127–162.

44. Mintzberg, *Power In and Around Organizations*, p. 26. See also K. M. Kacmar and R. A. Baron, "Organizational Politics: The State of the Field, Links to Related Processes, and an Agenda for Future Research," in G. R. Ferris (ed.), *Research in Personnel and Human Resources Management*, vol. 17 (Greenwich, CT: JAI Press, 1999), pp. 1–39; and G. R. Ferris, D. C. Treadway, R. W. Kolokinsky, W. A. Hochwarter, C. J. Kacmar, and D. D. Frink, "Development and Validation of the Political Skill Inventory," *Journal of Management* (February 2005), pp. 126–152.

45. S. B. Bacharach and E. J. Lawler, "Political Alignments in Organizations," in R. M. Kramer and M. A. Neale (eds.), *Power and Influence in Organizations* (Thousand Oaks, CA: Sage, 1998), pp. 68–69.

46. A. Drory and T. Romm, "The Definition of Organizational Politics: A Review," *Human Relations* (November 1990), pp. 1133–1154; and R. S. Cropanzano, K. M. Kacmar, and D. P. Bozeman, "Organizational Politics, Justice, and Support: Their Differences and Similarities," in R. S. Cropanzano and K. M. Kacmar (eds.), *Organizational Politics, Justice and Support: Managing Social Climate at Work* (Westport, CT: Quorum Books, 1995), pp. 1–18; and G. R. Ferris and W. A. Hochwarter, "Organizational Politics," in S. Zedeck (ed.), *APA Handbook of Industrial and Organizational Psychology*, vol. 3 (Washington, DC: American Psychological Association, 2011), pp. 435–459.

47. D. A. Buchanan, "You Stab My Back, I'll Stab Yours: Management Experience and Perceptions of Organization Political Behavior," *British Journal of Management* 19, no. 1 (2008), pp. 49–64.

48. J. Pfeffer, *Power: Why Some People Have It—And Others Don't* (New York: Harper Collins, 2010).

49. Drory and Romm, "The Definition of Organizational Politics."

50. S. M. Rioux and L. A. Penner, "The Causes of Organizational Citizenship Behavior: A Motivational Analysis," *Journal of Applied Psychology* (December 2001), pp. 1306–1314; M. A. Finkelstein and L. A. Penner, "Predicting Organizational Citizenship Behavior: Integrating the Functional and Role

Identity Approaches," *Social Behavior & Personality* 32, no. 4 (2004), pp. 383–398; and J. Schwarzwald, M. Koslowsky, and M. Allouf, "Group Membership, Status, and Social Power Preference," *Journal of Applied Social Psychology* 35, no. 3 (2005), pp. 644–665.

51. See, for example, G. R. Ferris, G. S. Russ, and P. M. Fandt, "Politics in Organizations," in R. A. Giacalone and P. Rosenfeld (eds.), *Impression Management in the Organization* (Hillsdale, NJ: Lawrence Erlbaum, 1989), pp. 155–156; and W. E. O'Connor and T. G. Morrison, "A Comparison of Situational and Dispositional Predictors of Perceptions of Organizational Politics," *Journal of Psychology* (May 2001), pp. 301–312.

52. Farrell and Petersen, "Patterns of Political Behavior in Organizations," *Academy of Management Review* 7, no. 3 (1982), pp. 403–412.

53. G. R. Ferris and K. M. Kacmar, "Perceptions of Organizational Politics," *Journal of Management* (March 1992), pp. 93–116.

54. See, for example, P. M. Fandt and G. R. Ferris, "The Management of Information and Impressions: When Employees Behave Opportunistically," *Organizational Behavior and Human Decision Processes* (February 1990), pp. 140–158; Ferris, Russ, and Fandt, "Politics in Organizations," p. 147; and J. M. L. Poon, "Situational Antecedents and Outcomes of Organizational Politics Perceptions," *Journal of Managerial Psychology* 18, no. 2 (2003), pp. 138–155.

55. Ferris and Hochwarter, "Organizational Politics."

56. W. A. Hochwarter, C. Kiewitz, S. L. Castro, P. L. Perrewe, and G. R. Ferris, "Positive Affectivity and Collective Efficacy as Moderators of the Relationship Between Perceived Politics and Job Satisfaction," *Journal of Applied Social Psychology* (May 2003), pp. 1009–1035; and C. C. Rosen, P. E. Levy, and R. J. Hall, "Placing Perceptions of Politics in the Context of Feedback Environment, Employee Attitudes, and Job Performance," *Journal of Applied Psychology* 91, no. 1 (2006), pp. 211–230.

57. G. R. Ferris, D. D. Frink, M. C. Galang, J. Zhou, K. M. Kacmar, and J. L. Howard, "Perceptions of Organizational Politics: Prediction, Stress-Related Implications, and Outcomes," *Human Relations* (February 1996), pp. 233–266; and E. Vigoda, "Stress-Related Aftermaths to Workplace Politics: The Relationships Among Politics, Job Distress, and Aggressive Behavior in Organizations," *Journal of Organizational Behavior* (August 2002), pp. 571–591.

58. S. Aryee, Z. Chen, and P. S. Budhwar, "Exchange Fairness and Employee Performance: An Examination of the Relationship Between Organizational Politics and Procedural Justice," *Organizational Behavior & Human Decision Processes* (May 2004), pp. 1–14; and K. M. Kacmar, D. P. Bozeman, D. S. Carlson, and W. P. Anthony, "An Examination of the Perceptions of Organizational Politics Model." *Human Relations* 52, no. 3 (1999), pp. 383-416.

59. C. Kiewitz, W. A. Hochwarter, G. R. Ferris, and S. L. Castro, "The Role of Psychological Climate in Neutralizing the Effects of Organizational Politics on Work Outcomes," *Journal of Applied Social Psychology* (June 2002), pp. 1189–1207; and M. C. Andrews, L. A. Witt, and K. M. Kacmar, "The Interactive Effects of Organizational Politics and Exchange Ideology on Manager Ratings of Retention," *Journal of Vocational Behavior* (April 2003), pp. 357–369.

60. O. J. Labedo, "Perceptions of Organisational Politics: Examination of the Situational Antecedent and Consequences Among Nigeria's Extension Personnel," *Applied Psychology: An International Review* 55, no. 2 (2006), pp. 255–281.

61. Kacmar, Bozeman, Carlson, and Anthony, "An Examination of the Perceptions of Organizational Politics Model," p. 389.

62. Ibid., p. 409.

63. K. M. Kacmar, D. G. Bachrach, K. J. Harris, and S. Zivnuska, "Fostering Good Citizenship Through Ethical Leadership: Exploring the Moderating Role of Gender and Organizational Politics," *Journal of Applied Psychology* 96 (2011), pp. 633–642.

64. B. E. Ashforth and R. T. Lee, "Defensive Behavior in Organizations: A Preliminary Model," *Human Relations* (July 1990), pp. 621–648.

65. M. Valle and P. L. Perrewe, "Do Politics Perceptions Relate to Political Behaviors? Tests of an Implicit Assumption and Expanded Model," *Human Relations* (March 2000), pp. 359–386.

66. M. R. Leary and R. M. Kowalski, "Impression Management: A Literature Review and Two-Component Model," *Psychological Bulletin* (January 1990), pp. 34–47.

67. See, for instance, W. L. Gardner and M. J. Martinko, "Impression Management in Organizations," *Journal of Management* (June 1988), pp. 321–338; M. C. Bolino and W. H. Turnley, "More Than One Way to Make an Impression: Exploring Profiles of Impression Management," *Journal of Management* 29, no. 2 (2003), pp. 141–160; S. Zivnuska, K. M. Kacmar, L. A. Witt, D. S. Carlson, and V. K. Bratton, "Interactive Effects of Impression Management and Organizational Politics on Job Performance," *Journal of Organizational Behavior* (August 2004), pp. 627–640; and M. C. Bolino, K. M. Kacmar, W. H. Turnley, and J. B. Gilstrap, "A Multi-Level Review of Impression Management Motives and Behaviors," *Journal of Management* 34, no. 6 (2008), pp. 1080–1109.

68. M. Snyder and J. Copeland, "Self-monitoring Processes in Organizational Settings," in R. A. Giacalone and P. Rosenfeld (eds.), *Impression Management in the Organization* (Hillsdale, NJ: Lawrence Erlbaum, 1989), p. 11; Bolino and Turnley, "More Than One Way to Make an Impression"; and W. H. Turnley and M. C. Bolino, "Achieved Desired Images While Avoiding Undesired Images: Exploring the Role of Self-Monitoring in Impression Management," *Journal of Applied Psychology* (April 2001), pp. 351–360.

69. Leary and Kowalski, "Impression Management," p. 40.

70. J. Ham and R. Vonk, "Impressions of Impression Management: Evidence of Spontaneous Suspicion of Ulterior Motivation." *Journal of Experimental Social Psychology* 47, no. 2 (2011), pp. 466–471; and W. M. Bowler, J. R. B. Halbesleben, and J. R. B. Paul, "If You're Close with the Leader, You Must Be a Brownnose: The Role of Leader–Member Relationships in Follower, Leader, and Coworker Attributions of Organizational Citizenship Behavior Motives." *Human Resource Management Review* 20, no. 4 (2010), pp. 309–316.

71. C. Lebherz, K. Jonas, and B. Tomljenovic, "Are We Known by the Company We Keep? Effects of Name Dropping on First Impressions," *Social Influence* 4, no. 1 (2009), pp. 62–79.

72. J. R. B. Halbesleben, W. M. Bowler, M. C. Bolino, and W. H Turnley, "Organizational Concern, Prosocial Values, or

Impression Management? How Supervisors Attribute Motives to Organizational Citizenship Behavior," *Journal of Applied Social Psychology* 40, no. 6 (2010), pp. 1450–1489.

73. Ferris, Russ, and Fandt, "Politics in Organizations."
74. Z. I. Barsness, K. A. Diekmann, and M. L. Seidel, "Motivation and Opportunity: The Role of Remote Work, Demographic Dissimilarity, and Social Network Centrality in Impression Management," *Academy of Management Journal* 48, no. 3 (2005), pp. 401–419.
75. A. P. J. Ellis, B. J. West, A. M. Ryan, and R. P. DeShon, "The Use of Impression Management Tactics in Structural Interviews: A Function of Question Type?" *Journal of Applied Psychology* (December 2002), pp. 1200–1208.
76. C. K. Stevens and A. L. Kristof, "Making the Right Impression: A Field Study of Applicant Impression Management During Job Interviews," *Journal of Applied Psychology* 80 (1995), pp. 587– 606; L. A. McFarland, A. M. Ryan, and S. D. Kriska, "Impression Management Use and Effectiveness Across Assessment Methods," *Journal of Management* 29, no. 5 (2003), pp. 641–661; C. A. Higgins and T. A. Judge, "The Effect of Applicant Influence Tactics on Recruiter Perceptions of Fit and Hiring Recommendations: A Field Study," *Journal of Applied Psychology* 89, no. 4 (2004), pp. 622–632; and W. C. Tsai, C. C. Chen, and S. F. Chiu, "Exploring Boundaries of the Effects of Applicant Impression Management Tactics in Job Interviews," *Journal of Management* (February 2005), pp. 108– 125.
77. D. C. Gilmore and G. R. Ferris, "The Effects of Applicant Impression Management Tactics on Interviewer Judgments," *Journal of Management* 15, no. 4 (1989), pp. 557–564
78. Stevens and Kristof, "Making the Right Impression."
79. C. A. Higgins, T. A. Judge, and G. R. Ferris, "Influence Tactics and Work Outcomes: A Meta-Analysis," *Journal of Organizational Behavior* (March 2003), pp. 89–106.
80. Ibid.
81. K. J. Harris, K. M. Kacmar, S. Zivnuska, and J. D. Shaw, "The Impact of Political Skill on Impression Management Effectiveness," *Journal of Applied Psychology* 92, no. 1 (2007), pp. 278–285; and D. C. Treadway, G. R. Ferris, A. B. Duke, G. L. Adams, and J. B. Thatcher, "The Moderating Role of Subordinate Political Skill on Supervisors' Impressions of Subordinate Ingratiation and Ratings of Subordinate Interpersonal Facilitation," *Journal of Applied Psychology* 92, no. 3 (2007), pp. 848–855.
82. J. D. Westphal and I. Stern, "Flattery Will Get You Everywhere (Especially if You Are a Male Caucasian): How Ingratiation, Boardroom Behavior, and Demographic Minority Status Affect Additional Board Appointments of U.S. Companies," *Academy of Management Journal* 50, no. 2 (2007), pp. 267–288.
83. See T. Romm and A. Drory, "Political Behavior in Organizations: A Cross-Cultural Comparison," *International Journal of Value Based Management* 1 (1988), pp. 97–113; and E. Vigoda, "Reactions to Organizational Politics: A Cross-Cultural Examination in Israel and Britain," *Human Relations* (November 2001), pp. 1483–1518.
84. J. L. T. Leong, M. H. Bond, and P. P. Fu, "Perceived Effectiveness of Influence Strategies in the United States and Three Chinese Societies," *International Journal of Cross Cultural Management* (May 2006), pp. 101–120.
85. Y. Miyamoto and B. Wilken, "Culturally Contingent Situated Cognition: Influencing Other People Fosters Analytic Perception in the United States but Not in Japan," *Psychological Science* 21, no. 11 (2010), pp. 1616–1622.
86. E. Vigoda, "Reactions to Organizational Politics," p. 1512.
87. Ibid., p. 1510.

NO CONFLICT AT THE POST OFFICE . . . IS THAT GOOD?

LEARNING OBJECTIVES

After studying this chapter, you should be able to:

1   Define *conflict*.

2   Differentiate among the traditional, interactionist, and managed-conflict views of conflict.

3   Outline the conflict process.

4   Define *negotiation*.

5   Contrast distributive and integrative bargaining.

6   Apply the five steps of the negotiation process.

7   Show how individual differences influence negotiations.

8   Assess the roles and functions of third-party negotiations.

MyManagementLab

Access a host of interactive learning aids to help strengthen your understanding of the chapter concepts at **www.mymanagementlab.com**.

Do you remember a strike of U.S. Postal Service (USPS) workers? You probably don't, because the last one was more than 40 years ago—in 1970. USPS leadership and the unions that represent its employees are proud of their cooperation. In March 2011, the USPS reached an agreement with the American Postal Workers Union (APWU) that, among other things:

- Provides a 3.5 percent annual raise for APWU workers.
- Includes seven uncapped cost-of-living increases.
- Extends the no-layoff provision in the contract.

Both union and management are happy with the contract. "The union and management have reached an agreement that is a 'win–win' proposition," says APWU president Cliff Guffey. Postmaster General Patrick R. Donahoe hailed the agreement as well: "By working together we have created a new contract that serves the best interest of our customers, our employees and the future of the Postal Service."

When two sides cooperate and show few signs of conflict, it is usually a sign of a healthy relationship, right? No, say many experts, including the man assigned to review the USPS, Phillip Herr of the Government Accountability Office (GAO).

The problem, according to these experts, is that the business model for the USPS is fatally flawed. The USPS loses billions nearly every year it operates. It has borrowed $12 billion from the U.S. Treasury and is on the verge of defaulting on a $5.5 billion payment to cover future retirees' health care costs. It is asking Congress to waive its debt obligations. (In 2006, Congress already relieved the USPS of a $27 billion pension obligation, shifting the debt to U.S. taxpayers.) Why is the USPS losing so much money even with heavy subsidies?

One fundamental reason is volume. With the growth of e-mail communication, mail volume is down—way down. It plummeted 20 percent from 2006 to 2010, and nearly everyone expects the downward trend to continue, if not accelerate. In anticipation, many other nations have privatized their mail services, which have been faster to adapt. Sweden's largely privatized postal system gives mail recipients the option to receive their mail by scanned copy, it maintains a digital archive of mail going back seven years, and it recently introduced an app that lets users turn cell phone pictures into postcards. USPS continues to charge the same rate per ounce to deliver anywhere—whether it's down the street or by pack mule to the bottom of the Grand Canyon. The majority of USPS's revenue comes from junk mail, which is, of course, mostly mail no one wants to receive.

Conflict and Negotiation

Let us never negotiate out of fear.
But let us never fear to negotiate. —John F. Kennedy

Finally, USPS is not particularly competitive with Federal Express (FedEx) and United Parcel Service (UPS), its rivals in the lucrative overnight and ground shipping business. Though USPS is much larger—it employs 571,566 full-time workers, making it the nation's largest employer after Walmart—FedEx and UPS hold 84 percent of the express and ground shipping market. One reason USPS is not competitive? More than 80 percent of its budget goes to employee wages and benefits, as opposed to 43 percent for FedEx and 61 percent for UPS.

To be fair, USPS does many things well, it has many dedicated workers, and its leaders continue to talk of changing. But change is rarely easy, and it rarely comes without ruffling some feathers. Meanwhile, USPS continues to follow the path of least resistance. Says one expert: "Pretty soon it's going to be a government-run [junk mail] service. Does that make any sense?"

Sources: D. Leonard, "The End of Mail," *Bloomberg Businessweek* (May 30, 2011), pp. 60–65; G. Easterbrook, "The Post Office—Return to Sender," *Reuters* (June 1, 2011), downloaded June 30, 2011, from http://blogs.reuters.com/; and E. O'Keefe, "Postal Union Contract Ratified," *Washington Post* (May 12, 2011), downloaded on July 10, 2011, from www.washingtonpost.com/.

A s we see in the USPS example, both the presence and the absence of conflict and negotiation are often complex—and controversial—interpersonal processes. While we generally see conflict as a negative topic and negotiation as a positive one, each can generate positive and negative outcomes, and what we deem positive or negative often depends on our perspective. Let's first gauge how you handle conflict. Take the following self-assessment.

SELF-ASSESSMENT LIBRARY

What's My Preferred Conflict-Handling Style?

In the Self-Assessment Library (available on CD and online), take assessment II.C.5 (What's My Preferred Conflict-Handling Style?) and answer the following questions.

1. Judging from your highest score, what's your primary conflict-handling style?
2. Do you think your style varies, depending on the situation?
3. Would you like to change any aspects of your conflict-handling style?

A Definition of Conflict

1 Define *conflict.*

There has been no shortage of definitions of *conflict,*[1] but common to most is the idea that conflict is a perception. If no one is aware of a conflict, then it is generally agreed no conflict exists. Also needed to begin the conflict process are opposition or incompatibility and some form of interaction.

We can define **conflict**, then, as a process that begins when one party perceives another party has or is about to negatively affect something the first party cares about.[2] This definition is purposely broad. It describes that point in any ongoing activity when an interaction crosses over to become an interparty conflict. It encompasses the wide range of conflicts people experience in organizations: incompatibility of goals, differences over interpretations of facts, disagreements based on behavioral expectations, and the like. Finally, our definition is flexible enough to cover the full range of conflict levels—from overt and violent acts to subtle forms of disagreement.

Transitions in Conflict Thought

2 Differentiate among the traditional, interactionist, and managed-conflict views of conflict.

It is entirely appropriate to say there has been conflict over the role of conflict in groups and organizations. One school of thought has argued that conflict must be avoided—that it indicates a malfunctioning within the group. We call this the *traditional* view. Another perspective proposes not only that conflict can be a positive force in a group but that some conflict is absolutely necessary for a group to perform effectively. We label this the *interactionist* view. Finally, recent research argues that instead of encouraging "good" or discouraging "bad" conflict, it's more important to resolve naturally occurring conflicts productively. This perspective is the *managed conflict* view. Let's take a closer look at each view.

The Traditional View of Conflict

The early approach to conflict assumed all conflict was bad and to be avoided. Conflict was viewed negatively and discussed with such terms as *violence, destruction,* and *irrationality* to reinforce its negative connotation. This **traditional view of conflict** was consistent with attitudes about group behavior that prevailed in the 1930s and 1940s. Conflict was a dysfunctional outcome resulting from poor communication, a lack of openness and trust between people, and the failure of managers to be responsive to the needs and aspirations of their employees.

The view that all conflict is bad certainly offers a simple approach to looking at the behavior of people who create conflict. We need merely direct our attention to the causes of conflict and correct those malfunctions to improve group and organizational performance. This view of conflict fell out of favor for a long time as researchers came to realize that some level of conflict was inevitable.

The Interactionist View of Conflict

The **interactionist view of conflict** encourages conflict on the grounds that a harmonious, peaceful, tranquil, and cooperative group is prone to becoming static, apathetic, and unresponsive to needs for change and innovation.[3] The major contribution of this view is recognizing that a minimal level of conflict can help keep a group viable, self-critical, and creative.

The interactionist view does not propose that all conflicts are good. Rather, **functional conflict** supports the goals of the group and improves its performance

---

conflict   *A process that begins when one party perceives that another party has negatively affected, or is about to negatively affect, something that the first party cares about.*

traditional view of conflict   *The belief that all conflict is harmful and must be avoided.*

interactionist view of conflict   *The belief that conflict is not only a positive force in a group but also an absolute necessity for a group to perform effectively.*

functional conflict   *Conflict that supports the goals of the group and improves its performance.*

and is, thus, a constructive form of conflict. A conflict that hinders group performance is a destructive or **dysfunctional conflict**. What differentiates functional from dysfunctional conflict? The evidence indicates we need to look at the *type* of conflict—whether it's connected to task, relationship, or process.[4]

Task conflict relates to the content and goals of the work. **Relationship conflict** focuses on interpersonal relationships. **Process conflict** relates to how the work gets done. Studies demonstrate that relationship conflicts are almost always dysfunctional.[5] Why? It appears that the friction and interpersonal hostilities inherent in relationship conflicts increase personality clashes and decrease mutual understanding, which hinders the completion of organizational tasks. Unfortunately, managers spend a lot of effort resolving personality conflicts among staff members; one survey indicated this task consumes 18 percent of their time.[6]

In contrast, low levels of process conflict and low to moderate levels of task conflict can be functional, but only in very specific cases. Recent reviews have shown that task conflicts are usually just as disruptive as relationship conflicts.[7] For conflict to be productive, it must be kept within certain boundaries. For example, one study in China found that moderate levels of task conflict in the early development stage could increase creativity in groups, but high levels of task conflict decreased team performance, and task conflicts were unrelated to performance once the group was in the later stages of group development.[8] Intense arguments about who should do what become dysfunctional when they create uncertainty about task roles, increase the time to complete tasks, and lead members to work at cross-purposes. Low to moderate levels of task conflict stimulate discussion of ideas. This means task conflicts relate positively to creativity and innovation, but they are not related to routine task performance. Groups performing routine tasks that don't require creativity won't benefit from task conflict. Moreover, if the group is already engaged in active discussion of ideas in a nonconfrontational way, adding conflict will not help generate more ideas. Task conflict is also related to these positive outcomes only when all members share the same goals and have high levels of trust.[9] Another way of saying this is that task conflicts are related to increased performance only when all members believe the team is a safe place for taking risks and that members will not deliberately undermine or reject those who speak up.[10]

Task conflict is often functional, but one of its dangers is that it can escalate and become a battle of wills. For example, as a Target Corporation investor, William Ackman tried, unsuccessfully, for many years to convince the retailer to change its business strategy to improve performance and boost shareholder returns. Ackman sought to bring in new board members with a proxy vote. He asked shareholders to elect candidates who would bring new ideas to Target's board, which he claimed was slow in making critical decisions. After a long battle that cost Target millions of dollars in defending itself, the shareholders voted to keep the current board members. Ackman is shown here meeting with the media after losing the proxy battle in which his candidates received less than 20 percent of the vote.

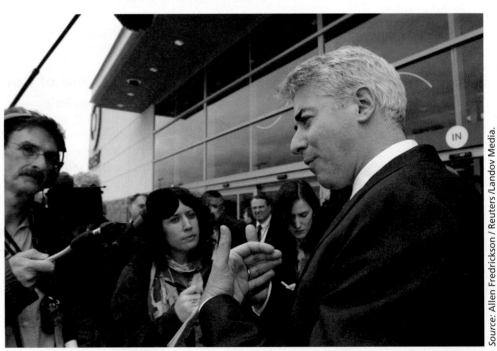

Source: Allen Fredrickson / Reuters /Landov Media.

Resolution-Focused View of Conflict

Researchers, including those who had strongly advocated the interactionist view, have begun to recognize some problems with encouraging conflict.[11] As we will see, there are some very specific cases in which conflict can be beneficial. However, workplace conflicts are not productive, they take time away from job tasks or interacting with customers, and hurt feelings and anger often linger after conflicts appear to be over. People can seldom wall off their feelings into neat categories of "task" or "relationship" disagreements, so task conflicts sometimes escalate into relationship conflicts.[12] A study conducted in Taiwan and Indonesia found that when levels of relationship conflict are high, increases in task conflict are consistently related to lower levels of team performance and team member satisfaction.[13] Conflicts produce stress, which may lead people to become more close minded and adversarial.[14] Studies of conflict in laboratories also fail to take account of the reductions in trust and cooperation that occur even with relationship conflicts. Longer-term studies show that all conflicts reduce trust, respect, and cohesion in groups, which reduces their long-term viability.[15]

In light of these findings, researchers have started to focus more on managing the whole context in which conflicts occur, both before and after the behavioral stage of conflict occurs. A growing body of research, which we review later, suggests we can minimize the negative effects of conflict by focusing on preparing people for conflicts, developing resolution strategies, and facilitating open discussion. Researchers interested in cross-cultural conflicts have also encouraged individuals to recognize impediments to agreement like hidden emotional attachments to a particular course of action and social identities that place people on different "sides" of an issue based on national or cultural variables. Resolving cross-cultural conflicts begins by addressing these emotional and identity-based concerns and building bonds between parties through common interests.[16]

In sum, the traditional view was shortsighted in assuming all conflict should be eliminated. The interactionist view that conflict can stimulate active discussion without spilling over into negative, disruptive emotions is incomplete. The managed conflict perspective does recognize that conflict is probably inevitable in most organizations, and it focuses more on productive conflict resolution. The research pendulum has swung from eliminating conflict, to encouraging limited levels of conflict, and now to finding constructive methods for resolving conflicts productively so their disruptive influence can be minimized.

The Conflict Process

3 Outline the conflict process.

The **conflict process** has five stages: potential opposition or incompatibility, cognition and personalization, intentions, behavior, and outcomes. The process is diagrammed in Exhibit 14-1.

dysfunctional conflict *Conflict that hinders group performance.*
task conflict *Conflict over content and goals of the work.*

relationship conflict *Conflict based on interpersonal relationships.*
process conflict *Conflict over how work gets done.*

conflict process *A process that has five stages: potential opposition or incompatibility, cognition and personalization, intentions, behavior, and outcomes.*

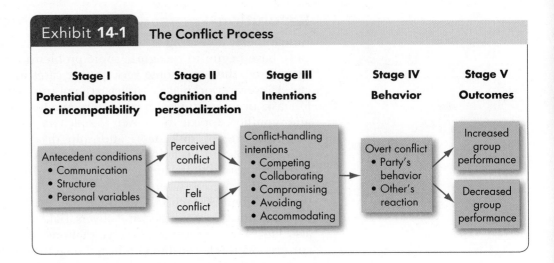

Exhibit **14-1**	The Conflict Process

Stage I	Stage II	Stage III	Stage IV	Stage V
Potential opposition or incompatibility	**Cognition and personalization**	**Intentions**	**Behavior**	**Outcomes**

Antecedent conditions
• Communication
• Structure
• Personal variables

Perceived conflict

Felt conflict

Conflict-handling intentions
• Competing
• Collaborating
• Compromising
• Avoiding
• Accommodating

Overt conflict
• Party's behavior
• Other's reaction

Increased group performance

Decreased group performance

Stage I: Potential Opposition or Incompatibility

The first step in the conflict process is the appearance of conditions that create opportunities for conflict to arise. These conditions *need not* lead directly to conflict, but one of them is necessary if conflict is to surface. For simplicity's sake, we group the conditions (which we can also look at as causes or sources of conflict) into three general categories: communication, structure, and personal variables.

Communication   Susan had worked in supply chain management at Bristol-Myers Squibb for 3 years. She enjoyed her work in large part because her manager, Harry, was a great boss. Then Harry got promoted, and Chuck took his place. Six months later, Susan says her job is a lot more frustrating. "Harry and I were on the same wavelength. It's not that way with Chuck. He tells me something, and I do it. Then he tells me I did it wrong. I think he means one thing but says something else. It's been like this since the day he arrived. I don't think a day goes by when he isn't yelling at me for something. You know, there are some people you just find it easy to communicate with. Well, Chuck isn't one of those!"

Susan's comments illustrate that communication can be a source of conflict.[17] They represent the opposing forces that arise from semantic difficulties, misunderstandings, and "noise" in the communication channels. Recall our comments on communication in Chapter 11.

A review of the research suggests that differing word connotations, jargon, insufficient exchange of information, and noise in the communication channel are all barriers to communication and potential antecedent conditions to conflict. Research has further demonstrated a surprising finding: the potential for conflict increases when either too little or *too much* communication takes place. Apparently, an increase in communication is functional up to a point, after which it is possible to overcommunicate, with a resultant increase in the potential for conflict.

Structure   Charlotte and Mercedes both work at the Portland Furniture Mart—a large discount furniture retailer. Charlotte is a salesperson on the floor, and Mercedes is the company credit manager. The two women have known each other for years and have much in common: they live within two blocks of each other, and their oldest daughters attend the same middle school and are best friends. If Charlotte and Mercedes had different jobs, they might be best friends themselves, but they are constantly fighting battles with each other. Charlotte's job is to sell furniture, and she does it well. But most of her sales are made on credit. Because Mercedes' job is to make sure the company minimizes credit losses, she regularly has to turn down the credit application of a customer with whom Charlotte has just closed a sale. It's nothing personal between the women; the requirements of their jobs just bring them into conflict.

The conflicts between Charlotte and Mercedes are structural in nature. The term *structure* in this context includes variables such as size of the group, degree of specialization in the tasks assigned to group members, jurisdictional clarity, member–goal compatibility, leadership styles, reward systems, and the degree of dependence between groups.

Size and specialization can stimulate conflict. The larger the group and the more specialized its activities, the greater the likelihood of conflict. Tenure and conflict have been found to be inversely related; the potential for conflict is greatest when group members are younger and when turnover is high.

The greater the ambiguity about where responsibility for actions lies, the greater the potential for conflict to emerge. Such jurisdictional ambiguities increase intergroup fighting for control of resources and territory. Diversity of goals among groups is also a major source of conflict. When groups within an organization seek diverse ends, some of which—like sales and credit at Portland Furniture Mart—are inherently at odds, opportunities for conflict increase. Reward systems, too, create conflict when one member's gain comes at another's expense. Finally, if a group is dependent on another group (in contrast to the two being mutually independent), or if interdependence allows one group to gain at another's expense, opposing forces are stimulated.

Personal Variables   Have you ever met someone for whom you felt an immediate dislike? You disagreed with most of the opinions he expressed. Even insignificant characteristics—the sound of his voice, the smirk when he smiled, his personality—annoyed you. We've all met people like that. When you have to work with such individuals, the potential for conflict arises.

Our last category of potential sources of conflict is personal variables, which include personality, emotions, and values. Personality does appear to play a role in the conflict process: some people just tend to get into conflicts a lot. In particular, people high in the personality traits of disagreeableness, neuroticism, or self-monitoring are prone to tangle with other people more often, and to react poorly when conflicts occur.[18] Emotions can also cause conflict. An employee who shows up to work irate from her hectic morning commute may carry that anger with her to her 9:00 a.m. meeting. The problem? Her anger can annoy her colleagues, which can result in a tension-filled meeting.[19]

Stage II: Cognition and Personalization

If the conditions cited in Stage I negatively affect something one party cares about, then the potential for opposition or incompatibility becomes actualized in the second stage.

As we noted in our definition of conflict, one or more of the parties must be aware that antecedent conditions exist. However, because a conflict is a **perceived conflict** does not mean it is personalized. In other words, "A may be aware that B and A are in serious disagreement . . . but it may not make A tense

perceived conflict   *Awareness by one or more parties of the existence of conditions that create opportunities for conflict to arise.*

OB Poll   **Generation Differences Cause Some Workplace Conflict**

To what extent is intergenerational conflict an issue in your workplace?

Source: Based on "Intergenerational Conflict in the Workplace," SHRM News (April 29, 2011).

or anxious, and it may have no effect whatsoever on *A*'s affection toward *B*."[20] It is at the **felt conflict** level, when individuals become emotionally involved, that they experience anxiety, tension, frustration, or hostility.

Keep in mind two points. First, Stage II is important because it's where conflict issues tend to be defined, where the parties decide what the conflict is about.[21] If I define our salary disagreement as a zero-sum situation (if you get the increase in pay you want, there will be just that amount less for me), I am going to be far less willing to compromise than if I frame the conflict as a potential win–win situation (the dollars in the salary pool might be increased so both of us could get the added pay we want). Thus, the definition of a conflict is important because it typically delineates the set of possible settlements.

Our second point is that emotions play a major role in shaping perceptions.[22] Negative emotions allow us to oversimplify issues, lose trust, and put negative interpretations on the other party's behavior.[23] In contrast, positive feelings increase our tendency to see potential relationships among the elements of a problem, to take a broader view of the situation, and to develop more innovative solutions.[24]

Stage III: Intentions

Intentions intervene between people's perceptions and emotions and their overt behavior. They are decisions to act in a given way.[25]

We separate out intentions as a distinct stage because we have to infer the other's intent to know how to respond to his or her behavior. Many conflicts escalate simply because one party attributes the wrong intentions to the other. There is also typically a great deal of slippage between intentions and behavior, so behavior does not always accurately reflect a person's intentions.

Exhibit 14-2 represents one author's effort to identify the primary conflict-handling intentions. Using two dimensions—*cooperativeness* (the degree to which one party attempts to satisfy the other party's concerns) and *assertiveness*

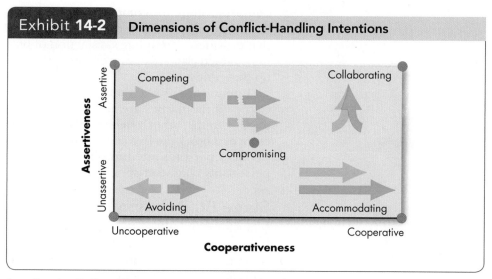

| Exhibit **14-2** | **Dimensions of Conflict-Handling Intentions** |

Source: Figure from "Conflict and Negotiation Processes in Organizations" by K. Thomas in *Handbook of Industrial and Organizational Psychology*, 2/e, Vol. 3, ed. by M. D. Dunnette and L. M. Hough, p. 668 (Palo Alto, CA: Consulting Psychologists Press, 1992). Used with permission.

(the degree to which one party attempts to satisfy his or her own concerns)— we can identify five conflict-handling intentions: *competing* (assertive and unco-operative), *collaborating* (assertive and cooperative), *avoiding* (unassertive and uncooperative), *accommodating* (unassertive and cooperative), and *compromising* (midrange on both assertiveness and cooperativeness).[26]

Competing   When one person seeks to satisfy his or her own interests regard-less of the impact on the other parties to the conflict, that person is **competing**. You compete when you place a bet that only one person can win, for example.

Collaborating   When parties in conflict each desire to fully satisfy the concerns of all parties, there is cooperation and a search for a mutually beneficial out-come. In **collaborating**, the parties intend to solve a problem by clarifying dif-ferences rather than by accommodating various points of view. If you attempt to find a win–win solution that allows both parties' goals to be completely achieved, that's collaborating.

Avoiding   A person may recognize a conflict exists and want to withdraw from or suppress it. Examples of **avoiding** include trying to ignore a conflict and avoiding others with whom you disagree.

Accommodating   A party who seeks to appease an opponent may be willing to place the opponent's interests above his or her own, sacrificing to maintain the relationship. We refer to this intention as **accommodating**. Supporting someone else's opinion despite your reservations about it, for example, is accommodating.

felt conflict   *Emotional involvement in a conflict that creates anxiety, tenseness, frustration, or hostility.*

intentions   *Decisions to act in a given way.*

competing   *A desire to satisfy one's interests, regardless of the impact on the other party to the conflict.*

collaborating   *A situation in which the parties to a conflict each desire to satisfy fully the concerns of all parties.*

avoiding   *The desire to withdraw from or suppress a conflict.*

accommodating   *The willingness of one party in a conflict to place the opponent's interests above his or her own.*

Compromising   In **compromising**, there is no clear winner or loser. Rather, there is a willingness to ration the object of the conflict and accept a solution that provides incomplete satisfaction of both parties' concerns. The distinguishing characteristic of compromising, therefore, is that each party intends to give up something.

Intentions are not always fixed. During the course of a conflict, they might change if the parties are able to see the other's point of view or respond emotionally to the other's behavior. However, research indicates people have preferences among the five conflict-handling intentions we just described.[27] We can predict a person's intentions rather well from a combination of intellectual and personality characteristics.

Stage IV: Behavior

When most people think of conflict situations, they tend to focus on Stage IV because this is where conflicts become visible. The behavior stage includes the statements, actions, and reactions made by the conflicting parties, usually as overt attempts to implement their own intentions. As a result of miscalculations or unskilled enactments, overt behaviors sometimes deviate from these original intentions.[28]

It helps to think of Stage IV as a dynamic process of interaction. For example, you make a demand on me, I respond by arguing, you threaten me, I threaten you back, and so on. Exhibit 14-3 provides a way of visualizing conflict behavior. All conflicts exist somewhere along this continuum. At the lower part are conflicts characterized by subtle, indirect, and highly controlled forms of tension, such as a student questioning in class a point the instructor has just made. Conflict intensities escalate as they move upward along the continuum until they become highly destructive. Strikes, riots, and wars clearly fall in this upper range. Conflicts that reach the upper ranges of the continuum are almost always dysfunctional. Functional conflicts are typically confined to the lower range of the continuum.

If a conflict is dysfunctional, what can the parties do to de-escalate it? Or, conversely, what options exist if conflict is too low and needs to be increased? This brings us to techniques of **conflict management**. Exhibit 14-4 lists the major resolution and stimulation techniques that allow managers to control conflict levels. We have already described several as conflict-handling intentions. This shouldn't be surprising. Under ideal conditions, a person's intentions should translate into comparable behaviors.

Exhibit 14-3   Conflict-Intensity Continuum

Annihilatory conflict — Overt efforts to destroy the other party

Aggressive physical attacks

Threats and ultimatums

Assertive verbal attacks

Overt questioning or challenging of others

Minor disagreements or misunderstandings

No conflict

Sources: Based on S. P. Robbins, *Managing Organizational Conflict: A Nontraditional Approach* (Upper Saddle River, NJ: Prentice Hall, 1974), pp. 93–97; and F. Glasi, "The Process of Conflict Escalation and the Roles of Third Parties," in G. B. J. Bomers and R. Peterson (eds.), *Conflict Management and Industrial Relations* (Boston: Kluwer-Nijhoff, 1982), pp. 119–140.

Exhibit **14-4**	Conflict Management Techniques

Conflict-Resolution Techniques

Problem solving	Face-to-face meeting of the conflicting parties for the purpose of identifying the problem and resolving it through open discussion.
Superordinate goals	Creating a shared goal that cannot be attained without the cooperation of each of the conflicting parties.
Expansion of resources	When a conflict is caused by the scarcity of a resource (for example, money, promotion, opportunities, office space), expansion of the resource can create a win-win solution.
Avoidance	Withdrawal from or suppression of the conflict.
Smoothing	Playing down differences while emphasizing common interests between the conflicting parties.
Compromise	Each party to the conflict gives up something of value.
Authoritative command	Management uses its formal authority to resolve the conflict and then communicates its desires to the parties involved.
Altering the human variable	Using behavioral change techniques such as human relations training to alter attitudes and behaviors that cause conflict.
Altering the structural variables	Changing the formal organization structure and the interaction patterns of conflicting parties through job redesign, transfers, creation of coordinating positions, and the like.

Conflict-Stimulation Techniques

Communication	Using ambiguous or threatening messages to increase conflict levels.
Bringing in outsiders	Adding employees to a group whose backgrounds, values, attitudes, or managerial styles differ from those of present members.
Restructuring the organization	Realigning work groups, altering rules and regulations, increasing interdependence, and making similar structural changes to disrupt the status quo.
Appointing a devil's advocate	Designating a critic to purposely argue against the majority positions held by the group.

Source: Based on S. P. Robbins, Managing Organizational Conflict: A Nontraditional Approach (Upper Saddle River, NJ: Prentice Hall, 1974), pp. 59–89.

Stage V: Outcomes

The action–reaction interplay between the conflicting parties results in consequences. As our model demonstrates (see Exhibit 14-1), these outcomes may be functional, if the conflict improves the group's performance, or dysfunctional, if it hinders performance.

Functional Outcomes   How might conflict act as a force to increase group performance? It is hard to visualize a situation in which open or violent aggression could be functional. But it's possible to see how low or moderate levels of conflict could improve the effectiveness of a group. Let's consider some examples and then review the research evidence. Note that all our examples focus on task and process conflicts and exclude the relationship variety.

Conflict is constructive when it improves the quality of decisions, stimulates creativity and innovation, encourages interest and curiosity among group members, provides the medium through which problems can be aired and tensions released, and fosters an environment of self-evaluation and change. The evidence suggests conflict can improve the quality of decision making by allowing all points to be weighed, particularly those that are unusual or held by a minority.[29] Conflict is an antidote for groupthink. It doesn't allow the group to passively rubber-stamp decisions that may be based on weak assumptions,

compromising   *A situation in which each party to a conflict is willing to give up something.*

conflict management   *The use of resolution and stimulation techniques to achieve the desired level of conflict.*

inadequate consideration of relevant alternatives, or other debilities. Conflict challenges the status quo and therefore furthers the creation of new ideas, promotes reassessment of group goals and activities, and increases the probability that the group will respond to change. An open discussion focused on higher-order goals can make these functional outcomes more likely. Groups that are extremely polarized do not manage their underlying disagreements effectively and tend to accept suboptimal solutions, or they avoid making decisions altogether rather than working out the conflict.[30]

Research studies in diverse settings confirm the functionality of active discussion. Groups whose members have different interests tend to produce higher-quality solutions to a variety of problems than do homogeneous groups.[31] Team members with greater differences in work styles and experience also tend to share more information with one another.[32]

These observations lead us to predict benefits to organizations from the increasing cultural diversity of the workforce. And that's what the evidence indicates, under most conditions. Heterogeneity among group and organization members can increase creativity, improve the quality of decisions, and facilitate change by enhancing member flexibility.[33] Researchers compared decision-making groups composed of all-Caucasian individuals with groups that also contained members from Asian, Hispanic, and Black ethnic groups. The ethnically diverse groups produced more effective and more feasible ideas, and the unique ideas they generated tended to be of higher quality than the unique ideas produced by the all-Caucasian group.

Dysfunctional Outcomes   The destructive consequences of conflict on the performance of a group or an organization are generally well known: uncontrolled opposition breeds discontent, which acts to dissolve common ties and eventually leads to the destruction of the group. And, of course, a substantial body of literature documents how dysfunctional conflicts can reduce group effectiveness.[34] Among the undesirable consequences are poor communication, reductions in group cohesiveness, and subordination of group goals to the primacy

IBM benefits from the diversity of its employees who engage in functional conflict that improves the company's performance. At IBM, diversity drives innovation. Achieving the full potential of its diverse workforce is a business priority fundamental to IBM's competitive success. For innovation to flourish, IBM needs different employee experiences, perspectives, skills, ideas, interests, information, and thinking. It relies on creative tension and opposing ideas that increase creativity, improve the quality of decisions, and facilitate change. IBM employees shown here broaden their diversity experiences and perspectives by participating in overseas assignments in emerging markets.

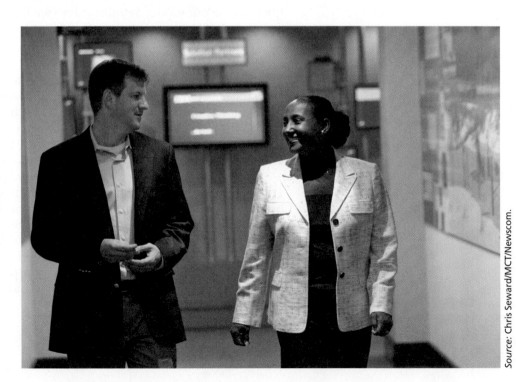

Source: Chris Seward/MCT/Newscom.

of infighting among members. All forms of conflict—even the functional varieties—appear to reduce group member satisfaction and trust.[35] When active discussions turn into open conflicts between members, information sharing between members decreases significantly.[36] At the extreme, conflict can bring group functioning to a halt and threaten the group's survival.

We noted that diversity can usually improve group performance and decision making. However, if differences of opinion open up along demographic fault lines, harmful conflicts result and information sharing decreases.[37] For example, if differences of opinion in a gender-diverse team line up so that men all hold one opinion and women hold another, group members tend to stop listening to one another. They fall into ingroup favoritism and won't take the other side's point of view into consideration. Managers in this situation need to pay special attention to these fault lines and emphasize the shared goals of the team.

The demise of an organization as a result of too much conflict isn't as unusual as you might think. One of New York's best-known law firms, Shea & Gould, closed down solely because the 80 partners just couldn't get along.[38] As one legal consultant familiar with the organization said, "This was a firm that had basic and principled differences among the partners that were basically irreconcilable." That same consultant also addressed the partners at their last meeting: "You don't have an economic problem," he said. "You have a personality problem. You hate each other!"

Managing Functional Conflict   If managers recognize that in some situations conflict can be beneficial, what can they do to manage conflict effectively in their organizations? Let's look at some approaches organizations are using to encourage their people to challenge the system and develop fresh ideas.

One of the keys to minimizing counterproductive conflicts is recognizing when there really is a disagreement. Many apparent conflicts are due to people using different language to discuss the same general course of action. For example, someone in marketing might focus on "distribution problems," while someone from operations will talk about "supply chain management" to describe essentially the same issue. Successful conflict management recognizes these different approaches and attempts to resolve them by encouraging open, frank discussion focused on interests rather than issues (we'll have more to say about this when we contrast distributive and integrative bargaining styles). Another approach is to have opposing groups pick parts of the solution that are most important to them and then focus on how each side can get its top needs satisfied. Neither side may get exactly what it wants, but both sides will get the most important parts of its agenda.[39]

Groups that resolve conflicts successfully discuss differences of opinion openly and are prepared to manage conflict when it arises.[40] The most disruptive conflicts are those that are never addressed directly. An open discussion makes it much easier to develop a shared perception of the problems at hand; it also allows groups to work toward a mutually acceptable solution. Managers need to emphasize shared interests in resolving conflicts, so groups that disagree with one another don't become too entrenched in their points of view and start to take the conflicts personally. Groups with cooperative conflict styles and a strong underlying identification to the overall group goals are more effective than groups with a competitive style.[41]

Differences across countries in conflict resolution strategies may be based on collectivistic tendencies and motives.[42] Collectivist cultures see people as deeply embedded in social situations, whereas individualist cultures see them as autonomous. As a result, collectivists are more likely to seek to preserve relationships and promote the good of the group as a whole. They will avoid direct expression of conflicts, preferring indirect methods for resolving differences of opinion. Collectivists may also be more interested in demonstrations of concern and working through third parties to resolve disputes, whereas individualists will be more likely to confront differences of opinion directly and openly.

Some research does support this theory. Compared to collectivist Japanese negotiators, their more individualist U.S. counterparts are more likely to see offers from their counterparts as unfair and to reject them. Another study revealed that whereas U.S. managers were more likely to use competing tactics in the face of conflicts, compromising and avoiding are the most preferred methods of conflict management in China.[43] Interview data, however, suggests top management teams in Chinese high-technology firms prefer collaboration even more than compromising and avoiding.[44]

Having considered conflict—its nature, causes, and consequences—we now turn to negotiation, which often resolves conflict.

Negotiation

4   Define *negotiation*.

Negotiation permeates the interactions of almost everyone in groups and organizations. There's the obvious: labor bargains with management. There's the not-so-obvious: managers negotiate with employees, peers, and bosses; salespeople negotiate with customers; purchasing agents negotiate with suppliers. And there's the subtle: an employee agrees to cover for a colleague for a few minutes in exchange for some past or future benefit. In today's loosely structured organizations, in which members work with colleagues over whom they have no direct authority and with whom they may not even share a common boss, negotiation skills become critical.

We can define **negotiation** as a process that occurs when two or more parties decide how to allocate scarce resources.[45] Although we commonly think of the outcomes of negotiation in one-shot economic terms, like negotiating over the price of a car, every negotiation in organizations also affects the relationship between the negotiators and the way the negotiators feel about themselves.[46] Depending on how much the parties are going to interact with one another, sometimes maintaining the social relationship and behaving ethically will be just as important as achieving an immediate outcome of bargaining. Note that we use the terms *negotiation* and *bargaining* interchangeably. In this section, we contrast two bargaining strategies, provide a model of the negotiation process, ascertain the role of moods and personality traits on bargaining, review gender and cultural differences in negotiation, and take a brief look at third-party negotiations.

Bargaining Strategies

5   Contrast distributive and integrative bargaining.

There are two general approaches to negotiation—*distributive bargaining* and *integrative bargaining*.[47] As Exhibit 14-5 shows, they differ in their goal and motivation, focus, interests, information sharing, and duration of relationship. Let's define each and illustrate the differences.

Distributive Bargaining   You see a used car advertised for sale online. It appears to be just what you've been looking to buy. You go out to see the car. It's great, and you want it. The owner tells you the asking price. You don't want to pay that much. The two of you then negotiate. The negotiating strategy you're

Exhibit 14-5	Distributive Versus Integrative Bargaining	
Bargaining Characteristic	**Distributive Bargaining**	**Integrative Bargaining**
Goal	Get as much of the pie as possible	Expand the pie so that both parties are satisfied
Motivation	Win–lose	Win–win
Focus	Positions ("I can't go beyond this point on this issue.")	Interests ("Can you explain why this issue is so important to you?")
Interests	Opposed	Congruent
Information sharing	Low (Sharing information will only allow other party to take advantage)	High (Sharing information will allow each party to find ways to satisfy interests of each party)
Duration of relationship	Short term	Long term

engaging in is called **distributive bargaining**. Its identifying feature is that it operates under zero-sum conditions—that is, any gain I make is at your expense and vice versa. Every dollar you can get the seller to cut from the car's price is a dollar you save, and every dollar more the seller can get from you comes at your expense. So the essence of distributive bargaining is negotiating over who gets what share of a fixed pie. By **fixed pie**, we mean a set amount of goods or services to be divvied up. When the pie is fixed, or the parties believe it is, they tend to bargain distributively.

Probably the most widely cited example of distributive bargaining is labor–management negotiations over wages. Typically, labor's representatives come to the bargaining table determined to get as much money as possible from management. Because every cent labor negotiates increases management's costs, each party bargains aggressively and treats the other as an opponent who must be defeated.

The essence of distributive bargaining is depicted in Exhibit 14-6. Parties A and B represent two negotiators. Each has a *target point* that defines what he or she would like to achieve. Each also has a *resistance point,* which marks the lowest acceptable outcome—the point below which the party would break off

Exhibit 14-6	Staking Out the Bargaining Zone

negotiation   *A process in which two or more parties exchange goods or services and attempt to agree on the exchange rate for them.*

distributive bargaining   *Negotiation that seeks to divide up a fixed amount of resources; a win–lose situation.*

fixed pie   *The belief that there is only a set amount of goods or services to be divvied up between the parties.*

negotiations rather than accept a less favorable settlement. The area between these two points makes up each party's aspiration range. As long as there is some overlap between *A*'s and *B*'s aspiration ranges, there exists a settlement range in which each one's aspirations can be met.

When you are engaged in distributive bargaining, research consistently shows one of the best things you can do is make the first offer, and make it an aggressive one. Making the first offer shows power; individuals in power are much more likely to make initial offers, speak first at meetings, and thereby gain the advantage. Another reason this is a good strategy is the anchoring bias, mentioned in Chapter 6. People tend to fixate on initial information. Once that anchoring point is set, they fail to adequately adjust it based on subsequent information. A savvy negotiator sets an anchor with the initial offer, and scores of negotiation studies show that such anchors greatly favor the person who sets them.[48]

Say you have a job offer, and your prospective employer asks you what sort of starting salary you'd want. You've just been given a great gift—you have a chance to set the anchor, meaning you should ask for the highest salary you think the employer could reasonably offer. Asking for a million dollars is only going to make most of us look ridiculous, which is why we suggest being on the high end of what you think is *reasonable*. Too often, we err on the side of caution, afraid of scaring off the employer and thus settling for too little. It *is* possible to scare off an employer, and it's true employers don't like candidates to be assertive in salary negotiations, but liking isn't the same as doing what it takes to hire or retain someone.[49] What happens much more often is that we ask for less than we could have gotten.

Another distributive bargaining tactic is revealing a deadline. Erin is a human resources manager. She is negotiating salary with Ron, who is a highly sought-after new hire. Because Ron knows the company needs him, he decides to play hardball and ask for an extraordinary salary and many benefits. Erin tells Ron the company can't meet his requirements. Ron tells Erin he is going to have to think things over. Worried the company is going to lose Ron to a competitor, Erin decides to tell Ron she is under time pressure and needs to reach an agreement with him immediately, or she will have to offer the job to another candidate. Would you consider Erin to be a savvy negotiator? Well, she is. Why? Negotiators who reveal deadlines speed concessions from their negotiating counterparts, making them reconsider their position. And even though negotiators don't *think* this tactic works, in reality, negotiators who reveal deadlines do better.[50]

Integrative Bargaining   Jake is a 5-year-old Chicago luxury boutique owned by Jim Wetzel and Lance Lawson. In the early days of the business, Wetzel and Lawson had no trouble moving millions of dollars of merchandise from many up-and-coming designers. They developed such a good rapport that many designers would send allotments to Jake without requiring advance payment. When the economy soured in 2008, Jake had trouble selling inventory, and the designers found they were not being paid for what they had shipped to the store. Despite the fact that many designers were willing to work with the store on a delayed payment plan, Wetzel and Lawson stopped returning their calls. Lamented one designer, Doo-Ri Chung, "You kind of feel this familiarity with people who supported you for so long. When they have cash-flow issues, you want to make sure you are there for them as well."[51] Ms. Chung's attitude shows the promise of **integrative bargaining**. In contrast to distributive bargaining, integrative bargaining operates under the assumption that one or more of the possible settlements can create a win–win solution. Of course, as the Jake example shows and we'll highlight later, integrative bargaining takes "two to tango"—both parties must be engaged for it to work.

United Auto Workers officials (left) and Ford Motor Company officials shake hands during a news conference for the start of national negotiations in July 2011. Both UAW and Ford say that they are committed to integrative bargaining in finding mutually acceptable solutions to create a win-win settlement that will help boost their competitiveness with other automakers in the United States and abroad. The negotiations reflect a 70-year history of UAW and Ford working together to share information that will help address difficult business challenges.

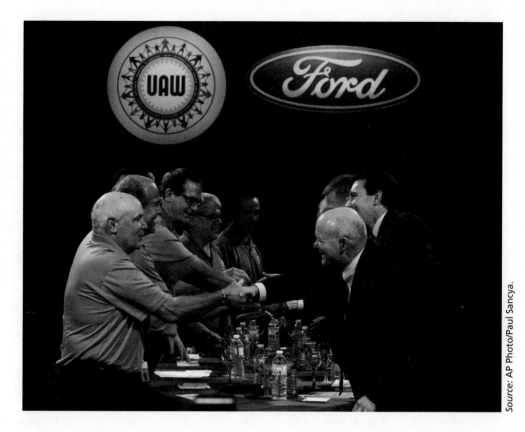

Source: AP Photo/Paul Sancya.

In terms of intraorganizational behavior, all things being equal, integrative bargaining is preferable to distributive bargaining because the former builds long-term relationships. Integrative bargaining bonds negotiators and allows them to leave the bargaining table feeling they have achieved a victory. Distributive bargaining, however, leaves one party a loser. It tends to build animosities and deepen divisions when people have to work together on an ongoing basis. Research shows that over repeated bargaining episodes, a "losing" party who feels positive about the negotiation outcome is much more likely to bargain cooperatively in subsequent negotiations. This points to an important advantage of integrative negotiations: even when you "win," you want your opponent to feel good about the negotiation.[52]

Why, then, don't we see more integrative bargaining in organizations? The answer lies in the conditions necessary for it to succeed. These include opposing parties who are open with information and candid about their concerns, are sensitive to the other's needs and trust, and are willing to maintain flexibility.[53] Because these conditions seldom exist in organizations, it isn't surprising that negotiations often take on a win-at-any-cost dynamic.

There are ways to achieve more integrative outcomes. Individuals who bargain in teams reach more integrative agreements than those who bargain individually because more ideas are generated when more people are at the bargaining table. So, try bargaining in teams.[54] Another way to achieve higher joint-gain settlements is to put more issues on the table. The more negotiable issues introduced into a negotiation, the more opportunity for "logrolling," where issues are traded off because people have different preferences. This

integrative bargaining *Negotiation that seeks one or more settlements that can create a win–win solution.*

"Communicating Well Is More Important in Cross-Cultural Negotiations"

This statement is true.

At no time in human history has the contact between members of different cultures been higher. Supply chains are increasingly multinational networks. Large organizations market their products and services in many nations. Global virtual teams work to make their organizations globally competitive. Most of these supplier/customer/manager/employee relationships include negotiating over something. Only the smallest and most local organization is insulated from the need to negotiate cross-culturally.

Because negotiation is an intense communication process, you might think that globalization has placed a premium on communicating well in negotiations. A recent study supported that view, but it also gave important details about what's necessary to communicate well in cross-cultural negotiations:

Clarity—did each party understand each other?
Responsiveness—did each party respond quickly and smoothly?
Comfort—did each party feel comfortable and trust the other?

The authors found that cross-cultural negotiations did have lower communication quality with respect to all three characteristics than did within-country negotiations. They also found that higher levels of communication quality contributed to success in cross-cultural negotiations—in terms of both the joint gains the parties achieved and their satisfaction with the agreements.

Because communication quality was measured at the end of the negotiation, this study can't determine cause-and-effect (it's possible that negotiation outcomes cause the parties to perceive communication more favorably). However, it does suggest that cross-cultural negotiations need not always result in lower outcomes—if the parties commit themselves to communicating clearly, responsively, and in such a way to make the other side comfortable.

Source: Based on L. A. Liu, C. H. Chua, and G. K. Stahl, "Quality of Communication Experience: Definition, Measurement, and Implications for Intercultural Negotiations," Journal of Applied Psychology 95, No. 3 (2010), pp. 469–487.

---

creates better outcomes for each side than if they negotiated each issue individually.[55] A final piece of advice is to focus on the underlying interests of both sides rather than on issues. In other words, it is better to concentrate on *why* an employee wants a raise rather than focusing just on the raise amount—some unseen potential for integrative outcomes may arise if both sides concentrate on what they really want rather than on the specific items they're bargaining over. Typically, it's easier to concentrate on underlying interests when parties to a negotiation are focused on broad, overall goals rather than on immediate outcomes of a specific decision.[56] Negotiations that occur when both parties are focused on learning and understanding the other side tend to also yield higher joint outcomes than those in which parties are more interested in their individual bottom-line outcomes.[57]

Finally, recognize that compromise may be your worst enemy in negotiating a win–win agreement. Compromising reduces the pressure to bargain integratively. After all, if you or your opponent caves in easily, it doesn't require anyone to be creative to reach a settlement. Thus, people end up settling for less than they could have obtained if they had been forced to consider the other party's interests, trade off issues, and be creative.[58] Think of the classic example in which two sisters are arguing over who gets an orange. Unknown to them, one sister wants the orange to drink the juice, whereas the other wants the orange peel to bake a cake. If one sister simply capitulates and gives the other sister the orange, they will not be forced to explore their reasons for wanting the orange, and thus they will never find the win–win solution: they could *each* have the orange because they want different parts of it!

The Negotiation Process

Exhibit 14-7 provides a simplified model of the negotiation process. It views negotiation as made up of five steps: (1) preparation and planning, (2) definition of ground rules, (3) clarification and justification, (4) bargaining and problem solving, and (5) closure and implementation.[59]

Preparation and Planning Before you start negotiating, you need to do your homework. What's the nature of the conflict? What's the history leading up to this negotiation? Who's involved and what are their perceptions of the conflict? What do you want from the negotiation? What are *your* goals? If you're a supply manager at Dell Computer, for instance, and your goal is to get a significant cost reduction from your supplier of keyboards, make sure this goal stays paramount in your discussions and doesn't get overshadowed by other issues. It often helps to put your goals in writing and develop a range of outcomes—from "most hopeful" to "minimally acceptable"—to keep your attention focused.

You also want to assess what you think are the other party's goals. What are they likely to ask? How entrenched is their position likely to be? What intangible or hidden interests may be important to them? On what might they be willing to settle? When you can anticipate your opponent's position, you are better equipped to counter arguments with the facts and figures that support your position.

Relationships will change as a result of a negotiation, so that's another outcome to take into consideration. If you could "win" a negotiation but push the other side into resentment or animosity, it might be wiser to pursue a more compromising style. If preserving the relationship will make you seem weak and easily exploited, you may want to consider a more aggressive style. As an example of how the tone of a relationship set in negotiations matters, consider that people who feel good about the *process* of a job offer negotiation are more satisfied with their jobs and less likely to turn over a year later regardless of their actual *outcomes* from these negotiations.[60]

Once you've gathered your information, use it to develop a strategy. For example, expert chess players know ahead of time how they will respond to

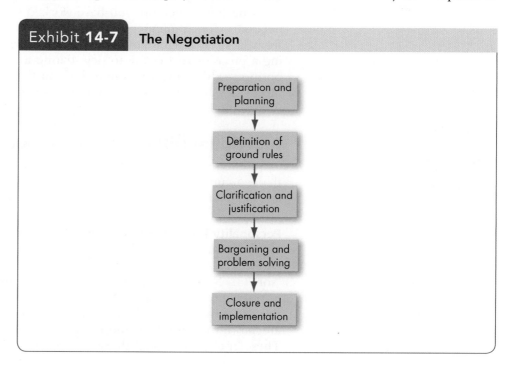

Exhibit **14-7**	The Negotiation

Preparation and planning

↓

Definition of ground rules

↓

Clarification and justification

↓

Bargaining and problem solving

↓

Closure and implementation

any given situation. As part of your strategy, you should determine your and the other side's **b**est **a**lternative **t**o a **n**egotiated **a**greement, or **BATNA**.[61] Your BATNA determines the lowest value acceptable to you for a negotiated agreement. Any offer you receive that is higher than your BATNA is better than an impasse. Conversely, you shouldn't expect success in your negotiation effort unless you're able to make the other side an offer it finds more attractive than its BATNA. If you go into your negotiation having a good idea of what the other party's BATNA is, even if you're not able to meet it you might be able to elicit a change. Think carefully about what the other side is willing to give up. People who underestimate their opponent's willingness to give on key issues before the negotiation even starts end up with lower outcomes from a negotiation.[62]

Definition of Ground Rules   Once you've done your planning and developed a strategy, you're ready to begin defining with the other party the ground rules and procedures of the negotiation itself. Who will do the negotiating? Where will it take place? What time constraints, if any, will apply? To what issues will negotiation be limited? Will you follow a specific procedure if an impasse is reached? During this phase, the parties will also exchange their initial proposals or demands.

Clarification and Justification   When you have exchanged initial positions, both you and the other party will explain, amplify, clarify, bolster, and justify your original demands. This step needn't be confrontational. Rather, it's an opportunity for educating and informing each other on the issues, why they are important, and how you arrived at your initial demands. Provide the other party with any documentation that helps support your position.

Bargaining and Problem Solving   The essence of the negotiation process is the actual give-and-take in trying to hash out an agreement. This is where both parties will undoubtedly need to make concessions.

Closure and Implementation   The final step in the negotiation process is formalizing the agreement you have worked out and developing any procedures necessary for implementing and monitoring it. For major negotiations—from labor–management negotiations to bargaining over lease terms to buying a piece of real estate to negotiating a job offer for a senior management position—this requires hammering out the specifics in a formal contract. For most cases, however, closure of the negotiation process is nothing more formal than a handshake.

Individual Differences in Negotiation Effectiveness

7 Show how individual differences influence negotiations.

Are some people better negotiators than others? The answer is more complex than you might think. Four factors influence how effectively individuals negotiate: personality, mood/emotions, culture, and gender.

Personality Traits in Negotiation   Can you predict an opponent's negotiating tactics if you know something about his or her personality? Because personality and negotiation outcomes are related but only weakly, the answer is, at best, "sort of." Negotiators who are agreeable or extraverted are not very successful in distributive bargaining. Why? Because extraverts are outgoing and friendly, they tend to share more information than they should. And agreeable people are more interested in finding ways to cooperate rather than to butt heads. These traits, while slightly helpful in integrative negotiations, are liabilities when interests are opposed. So the best distributive bargainer appears to be a disagreeable introvert—someone more interested in his or her own outcomes than in pleasing the other party and having a pleasant social exchange. People who are highly interested in having positive relationships with other people, and who are not very concerned about their own outcomes, are especially poor negotiators. These people tend to be very anxious about disagreements and plan to give in quickly to avoid unpleasant conflicts even before negotiations start.[63]

Research also suggests intelligence predicts negotiation effectiveness, but, as with personality, the effects aren't especially strong.[64] In a sense, these weak links are good news because they mean you're not severely disadvantaged, even if you're an agreeable extrovert, when it's time to negotiate. We all can learn to be better negotiators. In fact, people who think so are more likely to do well in negotiations because they persist in their efforts even in the face of temporary setbacks.[65]

Moods/Emotions in Negotiation   Do moods and emotions influence negotiation? They do, but the way they do appears to depend on the type of negotiation. In distributive negotiations, it appears that negotiators in a position of power or equal status who show anger negotiate better outcomes because their anger induces concessions from their opponents. Angry negotiators also feel more focused and assertive in striking a bargain. This appears to hold true even when the negotiators are instructed to show anger despite not being truly angry. On the other hand, for those in a less powerful position, displaying anger leads to worse outcomes. Thus, if you're a boss negotiating with a peer or a subordinate, displaying anger may help you, but if you're an employee negotiating with a boss, it might hurt you.[66] So what happens when two parties have to negotiate and one has shown anger in the past? Does the other try to get revenge and act extra tough, or does this party have some residual fear that the angry negotiator might get angry again? Evidence suggests that being angry has a spillover effect, such that angry negotiators are perceived as "tough" when the parties meet a second time, which leads negotiation partners to give up more concessions again.[67]

Anxiety also appears to have an impact on negotiation. For example, one study found that individuals who experienced more anxiety about a negotiation used more deceptions in dealing with others.[68] Another study found that anxious negotiators expect lower outcomes from negotiations, respond to offers more quickly, and exit the bargaining process more quickly, which leads them to obtain worse outcomes.[69]

All these findings regarding emotions have related to distributive bargains. In integrative negotiations, in contrast, positive moods and emotions appear to lead to more integrative agreements (higher levels of joint gain). This may happen because, as we noted in Chapter 4, positive mood is related to creativity.[70]

Culture in Negotiations   One study compared U.S. and Japanese negotiators and found the generally conflict-avoidant Japanese negotiators tended to communicate indirectly and adapt their behaviors to the situation. A follow-up study showed that, whereas early offers by U.S. managers led to the anchoring effect we noted when discussing distributive negotiation, for Japanese negotiators,

BATNA   *The best alternative to a negotiated agreement; the least the individual should accept.*

early offers led to more information sharing and better integrative outcomes.[71] In another study, managers with high levels of economic power from Hong Kong, which is a high power-distance country, were more cooperative in negotiations over a shared resource than German and U.S. managers, who were lower in power distance.[72] This suggests that in high power-distance countries, those in positions of power might exercise more restraint.

Another study looked at differences between U.S. and Indian negotiators.[73] Indian respondents reported having less trust in their negotiation counterparts than did U.S. respondents. These lower levels of trust were associated with lower discovery of common interests between parties, which occurred because Indian negotiators were less willing to disclose and solicit information. In both cultures, use of question-and-answer methods of negotiation were associated with superior negotiation outcomes, so although there are some cultural differences in negotiation styles, it appears that some negotiation tactics yield superior outcomes across cultures.

Gender Differences in Negotiations   Do men and women negotiate differently? And does gender affect negotiation outcomes? The answer to the first question appears to be no.[74] The answer to the second is a qualified yes.[75]

A popular stereotype is that women are more cooperative and pleasant in negotiations than are men. The evidence doesn't support this belief. However, men have been found to negotiate better outcomes than women, although the difference is relatively small. It's been postulated that men and women place unequal values on outcomes. "It is possible that a few hundred dollars more in salary or the corner office is less important to women than forming and maintaining an interpersonal relationship."[76]

Because women are expected to be "nice" and men "tough," research shows women are penalized when they initiate negotiations.[77] What's more, when women and men actually do conform to these stereotypes—women act "nice" and men "tough"—it becomes a self-fulfilling prophecy, reinforcing the stereotypical gender differences between male and female negotiators.[78] Thus, one of the reasons negotiations favor men is that women are "damned if they do, damned if they don't." Negotiate tough and they are penalized for violating a gender stereotype. Negotiate nice and it only reinforces and lets others take advantage of the stereotype.

In this photo, Japanese labor union leader Hidekazu Kitagawa (right) presents the group's annual wage and benefits demands to Ikuo Mori, president of Fuji Heavy Industries, Ltd., the manufacturer of Subaru automobiles. Studies on how negotiating styles vary across national cultures reveal that the generally conflict-avoidant Japanese negotiators tend to communicate indirectly and use a more polite conversational style. Their style of interaction is less aggressive than other cultures, favoring frequent silent periods and more positive recommendations and commitments and de-emphasizing the use of threats and commands.

Source: */Kyodo/Newscom.

Anger and Conflict Across Cultures

We've discussed anger as a negotiating tactic, but do different cultures view the expression of anger differently? Evidence suggest they do, meaning the use of anger is not a consistently wise negotiation strategy.

One study explicitly compared how U.S. and Chinese negotiators react to an angry counterpart. Chinese negotiators increased their use of distributive negotiating tactics, whereas U.S. negotiators decreased their use of these tactics. That is, Chinese negotiators began to drive a harder bargain once they saw that their negotiation partner was becoming angry, whereas U.S. negotiators actually capitulate somewhat in the face of angry demands.

Why do East Asian negotiators respond more negatively to angry negotiators? In a second study, researchers found that European Americans tended to give larger concessions when faced with an angry negotiation partner, whereas Asian negotiators again gave smaller ones. This difference may occur because individuals from East Asian cultures feel that using anger to get your way in a negotiation is not a legitimate tactic, so they respond by refusing to cooperate when their opponents become upset.

Sources: Based on M. Liu, "The Intrapersonal and Interpersonal Effects of Anger on Negotiation Strategies: A Cross-Cultural Investigation," *Human Communication Research* 35, no. 1 (2009), pp. 148–169; and H. Adam, A. Shirako, and W. W. Maddux, "Cultural Variance in the Interpersonal Effects of Anger in Negotiations," *Psychological Science* 21, no. 6 (2010), pp. 882–889.

SELF-ASSESSMENT LIBRARY

What's My Negotiating Style?

In the Self-Assessment Library (available on CD and online), take assessment II.C.6 (What's My Negotiating Style?).

Evidence also suggests women's own attitudes and behaviors hurt them in negotiations. Managerial women demonstrate less confidence than men in anticipation of negotiating and are less satisfied with their performance afterward, even when their performance and the outcomes they achieve are similar to those for men.[79] Women are also less likely than men to see an ambiguous situation as an opportunity for negotiation. It appears that women may unduly penalize themselves by failing to engage in negotiations that would be in their best interests. Some research suggests that women are less aggressive in negotiations because they are worried about backlash from others. There is an interesting qualifier to this result: women are more likely to engage in assertive negotiation when they are bargaining on behalf of someone else than when they are bargaining on their own behalf.[80]

Third-Party Negotiations

8 Assess the roles and functions of third-party negotiations.

To this point, we've discussed bargaining in terms of direct negotiations. Occasionally, however, individuals or group representatives reach a stalemate and are unable to resolve their differences through direct negotiations. In such cases, they may turn to a third party to help them find a solution. There are three basic third-party roles: mediator, arbitrator, and conciliator.

A **mediator** is a neutral third party who facilitates a negotiated solution by using reasoning and persuasion, suggesting alternatives, and the like.

mediator *A neutral third party who facilitates a negotiated solution by using reasoning, persuasion, and suggestions for alternatives.*

Using Empathy to Negotiate More Ethically

You may have noticed that much of our advice for negotiating effectively depends on understanding the perspective and goals of the person with whom you are negotiating. Preparing checklists of your negotiation partner's interests, likely tactics, and BATNA have all been shown to improve negotiation outcomes. Can these steps make you a more ethical negotiator as well? Studies suggest that it might.

Researchers asked respondents to indicate how much they tended to think about other people's feelings and emotions and to describe the types of tactics they engaged in during a negotiation exercise. More empathetic individuals consistently engaged in fewer unethical negotiation behaviors like making false promises and manipulating information, and

emotions. To put this in terms familiar to you from personality research, it appears that individuals who are higher in agreeableness will be more ethical negotiators.

When considering how to improve your ethical negotiation behavior, follow these guidelines:

1. Try to understand your negotiation partner's perspective, not just by understanding cognitively what the other person wants, but by empathizing with the emotional reaction he or she will have to the possible outcomes.
2. Be aware of your own emotions, because many moral reactions are fundamentally emotional. One study found that engaging in unethical negotiation strategies increased feelings of guilt, so

by extension, feeling guilty in a negotiation may mean you are engaging in behavior you'll regret later.
3. Beware of empathizing so much that you work against your own interests. Just because you try to understand the motives and emotional reactions of the other side does not mean you have to assume the other person is going to be honest and fair in return. So be on guard.

Sources: Based on T. R. Cohen, "Moral Emotions and Unethical Bargaining: The Differential Effects of Empathy and Perspective Taking in Deterring Deceitful Negotiation," *Journal of Business Ethics* 94, no. 4 (2010), pp. 569–579; and R. Volkema, D. Fleck, and A. Hofmeister, "Predicting Competitive-Unethical Negotiating Behavior and Its Consequences," *Negotiation Journal* 26, no. 3 (2010), pp. 263–286.

Mediators are widely used in labor–management negotiations and in civil court disputes. Their overall effectiveness is fairly impressive. The settlement rate is approximately 60 percent, with negotiator satisfaction at about 75 percent. But the situation is the key to whether mediation will succeed; the conflicting parties must be motivated to bargain and resolve their conflict. In addition, conflict intensity can't be too high; mediation is most effective under moderate levels of conflict. Finally, perceptions of the mediator are important; to be effective, the mediator must be perceived as neutral and noncoercive.

An **arbitrator** is a third party with the authority to dictate an agreement. Arbitration can be voluntary (requested by the parties) or compulsory (forced on the parties by law or contract). The big plus of arbitration over mediation is that it always results in a settlement. Whether there is a negative side depends on how heavy-handed the arbitrator appears. If one party is left feeling overwhelmingly defeated, that party is certain to be dissatisfied and the conflict may resurface at a later time.

A **conciliator** is a trusted third party who provides an informal communication link between the negotiator and the opponent. This role was made famous by Robert Duval in the first *Godfather* film. As Don Corleone's adopted son and a lawyer by training, Duval acted as an intermediary between the Corleones and the other Mafioso families. Comparing conciliation to mediation in terms of effectiveness has proven difficult because the two overlap a great deal. In practice, conciliators typically act as more than mere communication conduits. They also engage in fact-finding, interpret messages, and persuade disputants to develop agreements.

Summary and Implications for Managers

While many people assume conflict lowers group and organizational performance, this assumption is frequently incorrect. Conflict can be either constructive or destructive to the functioning of a group or unit. As shown in Exhibit 14-8, levels of conflict can be either too high or too low to be constructive. Either extreme hinders performance. An optimal level is one that prevents stagnation, stimulates creativity, allows tensions to be released, and initiates the seeds of change without being disruptive or preventing coordination of activities.

What advice can we give managers faced with excessive conflict and the need to reduce it? Don't assume one conflict-handling strategy will always be best! Select a strategy appropriate for the situation. Here are some guidelines:[81]

- Use *competition* when quick decisive action is needed (in emergencies), when issues are important, when unpopular actions need to be implemented (in cost cutting, enforcement of unpopular rules, discipline), when the issue is vital to the organization's welfare and you know you're right, and when others are taking advantage of noncompetitive behavior.
- Use *collaboration* to find an integrative solution when both sets of concerns are too important to be compromised, when your objective is to learn, when you want to merge insights from people with different perspectives or gain commitment by incorporating concerns into a consensus, and when you need to work through feelings that have interfered with a relationship.
- Use *avoidance* when an issue is trivial or symptomatic of other issues, when more important issues are pressing, when you perceive no chance of satisfying your concerns, when potential disruption outweighs the benefits of resolution, when people need to cool down and regain perspective, when gathering information supersedes immediate decision, and when others can resolve the conflict more effectively.
- Use *accommodation* when you find you're wrong, when you need to learn or show reasonableness, when you should allow a better position to be heard, when issues are more important to others than to yourself, when you want to satisfy others and maintain cooperation, when you can build social credits for later issues, when you are outmatched and losing (to minimize loss), when harmony and stability are especially important, and when employees can develop by learning from mistakes.

arbitrator *A third party to a negotiation who has the authority to dictate an agreement.*

conciliator *A trusted third party who provides an informal communication link between the negotiator and the opponent.*

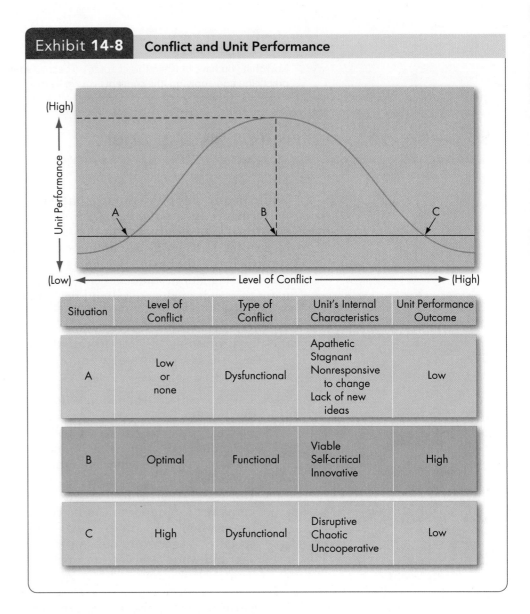

Exhibit **14-8**   **Conflict and Unit Performance**

Situation	Level of Conflict	Type of Conflict	Unit's Internal Characteristics	Unit Performance Outcome
A	Low or none	Dysfunctional	Apathetic Stagnant Nonresponsive to change Lack of new ideas	Low
B	Optimal	Functional	Viable Self-critical Innovative	High
C	High	Dysfunctional	Disruptive Chaotic Uncooperative	Low

- Use *compromise* when goals are important but not worth the effort of potential disruption of more assertive approaches, when opponents with equal power are committed to mutually exclusive goals, when you seek temporary settlements to complex issues, when you need expedient solutions under time pressure, and as a backup when collaboration or competition is unsuccessful.
- Distributive bargaining can resolve disputes, but it often reduces the satisfaction of one or more negotiators because it is confrontational and focused on the short term. Integrative bargaining, in contrast, tends to provide outcomes that satisfy all parties and build lasting relationships.
- Make sure you set aggressive negotiating goals and try to find creative ways to achieve the objectives of both parties, especially when you value the long-term relationship with the other party. That doesn't mean sacrificing your self-interest; rather, it means trying to find creative solutions that give both parties what they really want.

Player–Owner Disputes Are Unnecessary

POINT   **COUNTERPOINT**

It seems there's always a major sports league on the verge of a strike. In the past few years, Major League Baseball (MLB), the National Basketball Association (NBA), the National Hockey League (NHL), and the National Football League (NFL) have had major labor disputes. When greed meets greed, guess who loses? Yes, the fans.

A few years ago, an entire NHL season was canceled due to a labor dispute (NHL owners staged a work stoppage or "lockout" that lasted 311 days). The main issue? How to divide the more than $2 billion in revenues generated by the league. The average NHL player earns an annual salary of $1.35 million, and that doesn't include income from endorsements, appearances, merchandise, and so on. The owners aren't hurting, either. Most are millionaires many times over. Los Angeles Kings owner Philip Anschutz is reported to have a net worth of $7 billion.

The NFL is a variation on the same theme. During the 2011 lockout, during which the player's union temporarily disbanded so it could claim it wasn't a union, the owners and players fought over how to divide $9 billion in revenues. The average player makes $1.9 million a year. The average net worth of an NFL owner is $1.4 billion. And each side squabbles over getting more.

Yes, players get injured. Some lives are permanently damaged. But do you think being a construction worker, farmer, police officer, fisher, or loading-dock worker is a piece of cake? How often do these groups strike? They earn far less than professional athletes (the average fisher earns 2 percent of the average salary of an NHL player!), but they do work year-round, which is much more dangerous.

Meanwhile, ticket prices for sports events continue to soar. In the past 20 years, major league ticket prices have increased at double the rate of inflation. But what are the owners and players focused on? How to line their pockets even further. Was it any surprise when Minnesota Vikings running back Adrian Peterson, fuming over the dispute, called NFL players "modern-day slaves"? (He earns more than $10 million a year.)

Billionaires feuding with millionaires. These are unseemly—and unnecessary—conflicts.

Sports teams are an easy target.

It's true that most major league players are well rewarded for their exceptional talents and the risks they take. It's also true that owners who are able to invest in teams are wealthy—investors usually are. But do the resources on each side mean their conflict should just melt away? The reason these disputes happen is that real interests and real money is at stake.

The operation of major league sports is a complex business. The owners and players can be caricatured, but if you delve a bit deeper, you can see that their disputes are fairly natural. Let's look at hockey. NHL clubs spent 76 percent of their gross revenues on players' salaries and collectively lost $273 million the year before the lockout. The NHL tried to convince players to accept a wage structure that linked player salaries to league revenues, guaranteeing the clubs "cost certainty." Understandably, the players' union resisted, arguing that "cost certainty" was nothing more than another term for a salary cap. They argued in favor of retaining the "market-based" system in which players individually negotiated contracts with teams, and teams had complete control over how much it spent on players.

The NFL lockout hinged on a number of issues that divided the owners and players, including the owners' desire for an 18-game season (with no increase in player compensation), the way costs are considered in revenue sharing, and pensions for retired players. These aren't trivial issues, and neither are they entirely different from issues that arise in other labor–management disputes.

Finally, it's easy to argue that major league sports have an unusual number of labor disputes, but that's not necessarily accurate. Did you hear about the 2011 Saskatchewan Teachers Federation strike? Sports interest us (which is why there's so much money involved), and thus we're more likely to notice major league sports labor disputes, but that doesn't prove they're more common.

Yes, owners are rich and players make a lot of money. We're the ones who helped them do it, and we shouldn't fault them for wanting more of what we gave them.

Sources: A. Benoit, "2010 Jets: What the Film Revealed," *The New York Times* (April 14, 2011), downloaded on July 1, 2011, from http://fifthdown.blogs.nytimes.com/; D. Farrar, "Adrian Peterson Expresses Frustration on Labor Issues," *Yahoo! Sports* (March 15, 2011), downloaded June 30, 2011, from http://sports.yahoo.com/nfl/; and J. Z. Klein and S. Hackel, "SLAP SHOT; A Labor Dispute Still Shapes the N.H.L.," *The New York Times* (January 3, 2010), downloaded July 2, 2011, from http://query.nytimes.com/.

QUESTIONS FOR REVIEW

1 What is conflict?

2 What are the differences among the traditional, interactionist, and managed-conflict views of conflict?

3 What are the steps of the conflict process?

4 What is negotiation?

5 What are the differences between distributive and integrative bargaining?

6 What are the five steps in the negotiation process?

7 How do the individual differences of personality and gender influence negotiations?

8 What are the roles and functions of third-party negotiations?

EXPERIENTIAL EXERCISE A Negotiation Role-Play

This role-play is designed to help you develop your negotiating skills. The class is to break into pairs. One person will play the role of Alex, the department supervisor. The other person will play C. J., Alex's boss. Both participants should read "The Situation," "The Negotiation," and then their role only.

The Situation

Alex and C. J. work for Nike in Beaverton, Oregon. Alex supervises a research laboratory. C. J. is the manager of research and development. Alex and C. J. are former college runners who have worked for Nike for more than 6 years. C. J. has been Alex's boss for 2 years. One of Alex's employees has greatly impressed Alex. This employee is Lisa Roland. Lisa was hired 11 months ago. She is 24 years old and holds a master's degree in mechanical engineering. Her entry-level salary was $57,500 per year. Alex told her that, in accordance with corporation policy, she would receive an initial performance evaluation at 6 months and a comprehensive review after 1 year. Based on her performance record, Lisa was told she could expect a salary adjustment at the time of the 1-year evaluation.

Alex's evaluation of Lisa after 6 months was very positive. Alex commented on the long hours Lisa was putting in, her cooperative spirit, the fact that others in the lab enjoyed working with her, and that she was making an immediate positive impact on the project assigned to her. Now that Lisa's first anniversary is coming up, Alex has again reviewed Lisa's performance. Alex thinks Lisa may be the best new person the R&D group has ever hired. After only a year, Alex has ranked Lisa as the number-3 performer in a department of 11.

Salaries in the department vary greatly. Alex, for instance, has a base salary of $86,000, plus eligibility for a bonus that might add another $7,000 to $12,000 a year. The salary range of the 11 department members is $48,400 to $76,350. The individual with the lowest salary is a recent hire with a bachelor's degree in physics. The two people whom Alex has rated above Lisa earn base salaries of $69,200 and $76,350. They're both 27 years old and have been at Nike for 3 and 4 years, respectively. The median salary in Alex's department is $64,960.

Alex's Role

You want to give Lisa a big raise. Although she's young, she has proven to be an excellent addition to the department. You don't want to lose her. More importantly, she knows in general what other people in the department are earning, and she thinks she's underpaid. The company typically gives 1-year raises of 5 percent, although 10 percent is not unusual, and 20 to 30 percent increases have been approved on occasion. You'd like to get Lisa as large an increase as C. J. will approve.

C. J.'s Role

All your supervisors typically try to squeeze you for as much money as they can for their people. You understand this because you did the same thing when you were a supervisor, but your boss wants to keep a lid on costs. He wants you to keep raises for recent hires generally in the 5 to 8 percent range. In fact, he's sent a memo to all managers and supervisors saying this. He also said that managers will be evaluated on their ability to maintain budgetary control. However, your boss is also concerned with equity and paying people what they're worth. You feel assured that he will support any salary recommendation you make, as long as it can be justified. Your goal, consistent with cost reduction, is to keep salary increases as low as possible.

The Negotiation

Alex has a meeting scheduled with C. J. to discuss Lisa's performance review and salary adjustment. Take a couple of minutes to think through the facts in this exercise and to prepare a strategy. Then take up to 15 minutes to conduct your negotiation. When your negotiation is complete, the class will compare the various strategies used and pair outcomes.

ETHICAL DILEMMA The Lowball Applicant

Consider this real-life scenario:

A freelance project manager, I was hired to find someone to fill a highly specialized job. When I asked an impressive candidate her pay rate, she named a figure far below the industry standard. I could have rejected her for this lack of sophistication or exploited her low bid. Instead, I coached her to a figure nearly twice her bid yet about 30 percent below my client's budget. I did not inform my client about the discrepancy, and she was hired at the rate I recommended. Did I do wrong by either party?

—*NAME WITHHELD, New York*

Questions

1. In coaching the applicant to request a higher salary, did the project manager work against the interests of the client organization by which he or she is employed? Why or why not?

2. Could the manager have avoided this dilemma by proposing a salary figure that was the industry norm? Would that be in the interests of the client organization?

3. If you were in the project manager's situation, would you have handled this negotiation differently? If so, how so?

Source: R. Cohen, "The Ethicist," *New York Times Magazine* (July 18, 2010), p. 19.

CASE INCIDENT 1 Choosing Your Battles

While much of this chapter has discussed methods for achieving harmonious relationships and getting out of conflicts, it's also important to remember there are situations in which too little conflict can be a problem. As we noted, in creative problem-solving teams, some level of task conflict early in the process of formulating a solution can be an important stimulus to innovation.

However, the conditions must be right for productive conflict. In particular, individuals must feel psychologically safe in bringing up issues for discussion. If people fear that what they say is going to be held against them, they may be reluctant to speak up or rock the boat. Experts suggest that effective conflicts have three key characteristics: they should (1) speak to what is possible, (2) be compelling, and (3) involve uncertainty.

So how should a manager "pick a fight?" First, ensure that the stakes are sufficient to actually warrant a disruption. Second, focus on the future, and on how to resolve the conflict rather than on whom to blame. Third, tie the conflict to fundamental values. Rather than concentrating on winning or losing, encourage both parties to see how successfully exploring and resolving the conflict will lead to optimal outcomes for all. If managed successfully, some degree of open disagreement can be an important way for companies to manage simmering and potentially destructive conflicts.

Do these principles work in real organizations? The answer is yes. Dropping its old ways of handling scheduling and logistics created a great deal of conflict at Burlington Northern Santa Fe railroad, but applying these principles to managing the conflict helped the railroad adopt a more sophisticated system and recover its competitive position in the transportation industry. Doug Conant, CEO of Campbell Soup, increased functional conflicts in his organization by emphasizing a higher purpose to the organization's efforts rather than focusing on whose side was winning a conflict. Thus, a dysfunctional conflict environment changed dramatically and the organization was able to move from one of the world's worst-performing food companies to one that was recognized as a top performer by both the Dow Jones Sustainability Index and *Fortune* 500 data on employee morale.

Questions

1. How would you ensure sufficient discussion of contentious issues in a work group? How can managers bring unspoken conflicts into the open without making them worse?

2. How can negotiators utilize conflict management strategies to their advantage so that differences in interests lead not to dysfunctional conflicts but rather to positive integrative solutions?

3. Can you think of situations in your own life in which silence has worsened a conflict between parties? What might have been done differently to ensure that open communication facilitated collaboration instead?

Sources: Based on S. A. Joni and D. Beyer, "How to Pick a Good Fight," *Harvard Business Review* (December 2009), pp. 48–57; and B. H. Bradley, B. E. Postlewaite, A. C. Klotz, M. R. Hamdani, and K. G. Brown., "Reaping the Benefits of Task Conflict in Teams: The Critical Role of Team Psychological Safety Climate," *Journal of Applied Psychology,* Advance publication (July 4, 2011), doi: 10.1037/a0024200.

CASE INCIDENT 2 Mediation: Master Solution to Employment Disputes?

We typically think of mediation as the province of marital counselors and labor strife. More organizations use mediation to resolve conflicts than you might think. In fact, in the United States, Canada, Great Britain, Ireland, and India, mediation is growing rapidly as a means to settle employment disputes. We introduced mediation in this chapter; let's look at some examples when it has succeeded and when it has failed.

Mediation has often succeeded:

- Many states have experimented with mediation as an alternative to traditional trials to resolve legal disputes. The state of Maryland found in a pilot program that 58 percent of appellate cases could be resolved through mediation and that mediation was both cheaper and faster than a traditional courtroom resolution.

- The Equal Employment Opportunity Commission (EEOC), the federal agency that oversees employment discrimination complaints in the United States, uses mediation extensively. Safeway, the third-largest U.S. supermarket chain, uses the EEOC to mediate numerous employment disputes. Says Donna Gwin, Safeway's Director of Human Resources, "Through mediation, we have had the opportunity to proactively resolve issues and avoid potential charges in the future. We have seen the number of charges filed with EEOC against us actually decline. We believe that our participating in mediation and listening to employees' concerns has contributed to that decline."

However, mediation doesn't always work:

- In 2008, the Screen Actors Guild (SAG) and the Alliance of Motion Picture and Television Producers (AMPTP), representing some 350 studios and production companies, engaged in prolonged negotiations over a new labor agreement. The negotiations failed, and the parties agreed to mediation. However, mediation also failed, and in response SAG asked its members to approve a strike authorization.

- When David Kuchinsky, the former driver for New York Knicks center Eddy Curry, sued Curry for sexual harassment, discrimination, and failure to pay $93,000 in wages and reimbursements, the parties agreed to mediation. However, after the sides failed to reach a settlement during mediation, Kuchinsky reinstated his lawsuit, and Curry filed a $50,000 countersuit.

Questions

1. Drawing from these examples, what factors do you think differentiate occasions when mediation was successful and when it failed?

2. One successful mediator, Boston's Paul Finn, argues that if the disputing parties are seeking justice, "It's best to go somewhere else." Why do you think he says that?

3. Do you think a mediator should find out *why* the parties want what they want? Why or why not?

4. The EEOC reports that whereas 85 percent of employees agree to mediate their charges, employers agree to mediate only 30 percent of the time. Why do you think this disparity exists?

Sources: Based on M. Kapko, "Actors Union Seeks Strike Vote After Federal Mediation Fails," *Forbes* (November 23, 2008), www.forbes.com; K. Tyler, "Mediating a Better Outcome," *HR Magazine* (November 2007), pp. 63–66; K. O'Brien, "The Closer," *Boston Globe* (April 12, 2009), www.boston.com; and S. Lash, "Appealing for Appellate Mediation in Maryland," *The Daily Record* (July 4, 2011), www .thedailyrecord.com.

ENDNOTES

1. See, for instance, D. Tjosvold, "Defining Conflict and Making Choices About Its Management: Lighting the Dark Side of Organizational Life," *International Journal of Conflict Management* 17, no. 2 (2006), pp. 87–95; and M. A. Korsgaard, S. S. Jeong, D. M. Mahony, and A. H. Pitariu, "A Multilevel View of Intragroup Conflict," *Journal of Management* 34, no. 6 (2008), pp. 1222–1252.

2. K. W. Thomas, "Conflict and Negotiation Processes in Organizations," in M. D. Dunnette and L. M. Hough (eds.), *Handbook of Industrial and Organizational Psychology*, 2nd ed.,

vol. 3 (Palo Alto, CA: Consulting Psychologists Press, 1992), pp. 651–717.

3. For a comprehensive review of the interactionist approach, see C. De Dreu and E. Van de Vliert (eds.), *Using Conflict in Organizations* (London: Sage, 1997).

4. See K. A. Jehn, "A Multimethod Examination of the Benefits and Detriments of Intragroup Conflict," *Administrative Science Quarterly* (June 1995), pp. 256–282; K. A. Jehn, "A Qualitative Analysis of Conflict Types and Dimensions in Organizational Groups," *Administrative Science Quarterly* (September 1997), pp. 530–557; K. A. Jehn and E. A. Mannix, "The Dynamic Nature of Conflict: A Longitudinal Study of Intragroup

Conflict and Group Performance," *Academy of Management Journal* (April 2001), pp. 238–251; and C. K. W. De Dreu and L. R. Weingart, "Task Versus Relationship Conflict, Team Performance, and Team Member Satisfaction: A Meta-Analysis," *Journal of Applied Psychology* (August 2003), pp. 741–749.

5. J. Yang and K. W. Mossholder, "Decoupling Task and Relationship Conflict: The Role of Intragroup Emotional Processing," *Journal of Organizational Behavior* 25, no. 5 (August 2004), pp. 589–605; and N. Gamero, V. González-Romá, and J. M. Peiró, "The Influence of Intra-Team Conflict on Work Teams' Affective Climate: A Longitudinal Study," *Journal of Occupational and Organizational Psychology* 81, no. 1 (2008), pp. 47–69.

6. "Survey Shows Managers Have Their Hands Full Resolving Staff Personality Conflicts," *IPMA-HR Bulletin* (November 3, 2006).

7. De Dreu and Weingart, "Task Versus Relationship Conflict, Team Performance, and Team Member Satisfaction."

8. J. Farh, C. Lee, and C. I. C. Farh, "Task Conflict and Team Creativity: A Question of How Much and When," *Journal of Applied Psychology* 95, no. 6 (2010), pp. 1173–1180.

9. C. K.W. De Dreu and M. A. West, "Minority Dissent and Team Innovation: The Importance of Participation in Decision Making," *Journal of Applied Psychology* 86, no. 6 (2001), pp. 1191–1201.

10. B. H. Bradley, B. E. Postlewaite, A. C. Klotz, M. R. Hamdani, and K. G. Brown, "Reaping the Benefits of Task Conflict in Teams: The Critical Role of Team Psychological Safety Climate," *Journal of Applied Psychology*, Advance publication, (July 4, 2011), doi: 10.1037/a0024200.

11. C. K. W. De Dreu, "The Virtue and Vice of Workplace Conflict: Food for (Pessimistic) Thought," *Journal of Organizational Behavior* 29, no. 1 (2008), pp. 5–18.

12. R. S. Peterson and K. J. Behfar, "The Dynamic Relationship Between Performance Feedback, Trust, and Conflict in Groups: A Longitudinal Study," *Organizational Behavior and Human Decision Process* 92, no. 1–2 (2003), pp. 102–112.

13. J. D. Shaw, J. Zhu, M. K. Duffy, K. L. Scott, H. Shih, and E. Susanto, "A Contingency Model of Conflict and Team Effectiveness," *Journal of Applied Psychology* 96, no. 2 (2011), pp. 391–400.

14. L. M. Penny and P. E. Spector, "Job Stress, Incivility, and Counterproductive Work Behavior: The Moderating Role of Negative Affectivity," *Journal of Organizational Behavior* 26, no. 7 (2005), pp. 777–796.

15. K. A. Jehn, L. Greer, S. Levine, and G. Szulanski, "The Effects of Conflict Types, Dimensions, and Emergent States on Group Outcomes," *Group Decision and Negotiation* 17, no. 6 (2008), pp. 465–495.

16. D. A. Shapiro, "Relational Identity Theory: A Systematic Approach for Transforming the Emotional Dimension of Conflict," *American Psychologist* (October 2010), pp. 634–645.

17. R. S. Peterson and K. J. Behfar, "The Dynamic Relationship Between Performance Feedback, Trust, and Conflict in Groups: A Longitudinal Study," *Organizational Behavior & Human Decision Processes* (September–November 2003), pp. 102–112.

18. T. M. Glomb and H. Liao, "Interpersonal Aggression in Work Groups: Social Influence, Reciprocal, and Individual

Effects," *Academy of Management Journal* 46, no. 4 (2003), pp. 486–496; and V. Venkataramani and R. S. Dalal, "Who Helps and Harms Whom? Relational Aspects of Interpersonal Helping and Harming in Organizations," *Journal of Applied Psychology* 92, no. 4 (2007), pp. 952–966.

19. R. Friedman, C. Anderson, J. Brett, M. Olekalns, N. Goates, and C. C. Lisco, "The Positive and Negative Effects of Anger on Dispute Resolution: Evidence from Electronically Mediated Disputes," *Journal of Applied Psychology* (April 2004), pp. 369–376.

20. L. R. Pondy, "Organizational Conflict: Concepts and Models," *Administrative Science Quarterly* (September 1967), p. 302.

21. See, for instance, R. L. Pinkley, "Dimensions of Conflict Frame: Disputant Interpretations of Conflict," *Journal of Applied Psychology* (April 1990), pp. 117–126; and R. L. Pinkley and G. B. Northcraft, "Conflict Frames of Reference: Implications for Dispute Processes and Outcomes," *Academy of Management Journal* (February 1994), pp. 193–205.

22. A. M. Isen, A. A. Labroo, and P. Durlach, "An Influence of Product and Brand Name on Positive Affect: Implicit and Explicit Measures," *Motivation & Emotion* (March 2004), pp. 43–63.

23. Ibid.

24. P. J. D. Carnevale and A. M. Isen, "The Influence of Positive Affect and Visual Access on the Discovery of Integrative Solutions in Bilateral Negotiations," *Organizational Behavior and Human Decision Processes* (February 1986), pp. 1–13.

25. Thomas, "Conflict and Negotiation Processes in Organizations."

26. Ibid.

27. See R. A. Baron, "Personality and Organizational Conflict: Effects of the Type A Behavior Pattern and Self-monitoring," *Organizational Behavior and Human Decision Processes* (October 1989), pp. 281–296; R. J. Volkema and T. J. Bergmann, "Conflict Styles as Indicators of Behavioral Patterns in Interpersonal Conflicts," *Journal of Social Psychology* (February 1995), pp. 5–15; and J. A. Rhoades, J. Arnold, and C. Jay, "The Role of Affective Traits and Affective States in Disputants' Motivation and Behavior During Episodes of Organizational Conflict," *Journal of Organizational Behavior* (May 2001), pp. 329–345.

28. Thomas, "Conflict and Negotiation Processes in Organizations."

29. See, for instance, K. A. Jehn, "Enhancing Effectiveness: An Investigation of Advantages and Disadvantages of Value-Based Intragroup Conflict," *International Journal of Conflict Management* (July 1994), pp. 223–238; R. L. Priem, D. A. Harrison, and N. K. Muir, "Structured Conflict and Consensus Outcomes in Group Decision Making," *Journal of Management* 21, no. 4 (1995), pp. 691–710; and K. A. Jehn and E. A. Mannix, "The Dynamic Nature of Conflict: A Longitudinal Study of Intragroup Conflict and Group Performance," *Academy of Management Journal* (April 2001), pp. 238–251.

30. B. A. Nijstad and S. C. Kaps, "Taking the Easy Way Out: Preference Diversity, Decision Strategies, and Decision Refusal in Groups," *Journal of Personality and Social Psychology* 94, no. 5 (2008), pp. 860–870.

31. R. L. Hoffman, "Homogeneity of Member Personality and Its Effect on Group Problem-Solving," *Journal of Abnormal and Social Psychology* (January 1959), pp. 27–32; R. L. Hoffman and N. R. F. Maier, "Quality and Acceptance of Problem Solutions by Members of Homogeneous and Heterogeneous Groups," *Journal of Abnormal and Social Psychology* (March 1961), pp. 401–407; and P. Pitcher and A. D. Smith, "Top Management Team Heterogeneity: Personality, Power, and Proxies," *Organization Science* (January–February 2001), pp. 1–18.

32. M. E. Zellmer-Bruhn, M. M. Maloney, A. D. Bhappu, and R. Salvador, "When and How Do Differences Matter? An Exploration of Perceived Similarity in Teams," *Organizational Behavior and Human Decision Processes* 107, no. 1 (2008), pp. 41–59.

33. See T. H. Cox, S. A. Lobel, and P. L. McLeod, "Effects of Ethnic Group Cultural Differences on Cooperative Behavior on a Group Task," *Academy of Management Journal* (December 1991), pp. 827–847; and D. van Knippenberg, C. K. W. De Dreu, and A. C. Homan, "Work Group Diversity and Group Performance: An Integrative Model and Research Agenda," *Journal of Applied Psychology* (December 2004), pp. 1008–1022.

34. For example, see J. A. Wall Jr. and R. R. Callister, "Conflict and Its Management," *Journal of Management* 21, no. 3 (1995) pp. 523–526, for evidence supporting the argument that conflict is almost uniformly dysfunctional. See also P. J. Hinds and D. E. Bailey, "Out of Sight, Out of Sync: Understanding Conflict in Distributed Teams," *Organization Science* (November–December 2003), pp. 615–632.

35. Jehn, Greer, Levine, and Szulanski, "The Effects of Conflict Types, Dimensions, and Emergent States on Group Outcomes."

36. Zellmer-Bruhn, Maloney, Bhappu, and Salvador, "When and How Do Differences Matter?"

37. K. B. Dahlin, L. R. Weingart, and P. J. Hinds, "Team Diversity and Information Use," *Academy of Management Journal* 48, no. 6 (2005), pp. 1107–1123; and M. J. Pearsall, A. P. J. Ellis, and J. M. Evans, "Unlocking the Effects of Gender Faultlines on Team Creativity: Is Activation the Key?" *Journal of Applied Psychology* 93, no. 1 (2008), pp. 225–234.

38. M. Geyelin and E. Felsenthal, "Irreconcilable Differences Force Shea & Gould Closure," *The Wall Street Journal* (January 31, 1994), p. B1.

39. J. Fried, "I Know You Are, But What Am I?" *Inc.* (July/August 2010), pp. 39–40.

40. K. J. Behfar, R. S. Peterson, E. A. Mannix, and W. M. K. Trochim, "The Critical Role of Conflict Resolution in Teams: A Close Look at the Links Between Conflict Type, Conflict Management Strategies, and Team Outcomes," *Journal of Applied Psychology* 93, no. 1 (2008), pp. 170–188; A. G. Tekleab, N. R. Quigley, and P. E. Tesluk, "A Longitudinal Study of Team Conflict, Conflict Management, Cohesion, and Team Effectiveness," *Group and Organization Management* 34, no. 2 (2009), pp. 170–205; and E. Van de Vliert, M. C. Euwema, and S. E. Huismans, "Managing Conflict with a Subordinate or a Superior: Effectiveness of Conglomerated Behavior," *Journal of Applied Psychology* 80 (1995), pp. 271–281.

41. A. Somech, H. S. Desivilya, and H. Lidogoster, "Team Conflict Management and Team Effectiveness: The Effects of Task Interdependence and Team Identification," *Journal of Organizational Behavior* 30, no. 3 (2009), pp. 359–378.

42. H. R. Markus and S. Kitayama, "Culture and the Self: Implications for Cognition, Emotion, and Motivation," *Psychological Review* 98, no. 2 (1991), pp. 224–253; and H. Ren and B. Gray, "Repairing Relationship Conflict: How Violation Types and Culture Influence the Effectiveness of Restoration Rituals," *Academy of Management Review* 34, no. 1 (2009), pp. 105–126.

43. M. J. Gelfand, M. Higgins, L. H. Nishii, J. L. Raver, A. Dominguez, F. Murakami, S. Yamaguchi, and M. Toyama, "Culture and Egocentric Perceptions of Fairness in Conflict and Negotiation," *Journal of Applied Psychology* (October 2002), pp. 833–845; and Z. Ma, "Chinese Conflict Management Styles and Negotiation Behaviours: An Empirical Test," *International Journal of Cross Cultural Management* (April 2007), pp. 101–119.

44. P. P. Fu, X. H. Yan, Y. Li, E. Wang, and S. Peng, "Examining Conflict-Handling Approaches by Chinese Top Management Teams in IT Firms," *International Journal of Conflict Management* 19, no. 3 (2008), pp. 188–209.

45. M. H. Bazerman, J. R. Curhan, D. A. Moore, and K. L. Valley, "Negotiation," *Annual Review of Psychology* 51 (2000), pp. 279–314.

46. See, for example, D. R. Ames, "Assertiveness Expectancies: How Hard People Push Depends on the Consequences They Predict," *Journal of Personality and Social Psychology* 95, no. 6 (2008), pp. 1541–1557; and J. R. Curhan, H. A. Elfenbein, and H. Xu, "What Do People Value When They Negotiate? Mapping the Domain of Subjective Value in Negotiation," *Journal of Personality and Social Psychology* 91, no. 3 (2006), pp. 493–512.

47. R. Lewicki, D. Saunders, and B. Barry, *Negotiation*, 6th ed. (New York: McGraw-Hill/Irwin, 2009).

48. J. C. Magee, A. D. Galinsky, and D. H. Gruenfeld, "Power, Propensity to Negotiate, and Moving First in Competitive Interactions," *Personality and Social Psychology Bulletin* (February 2007), pp. 200–212.

49. H. R. Bowles, L. Babcock, and L. Lei, "Social Incentives for Gender Differences in the Propensity to Initiative Negotiations: Sometimes It Does Hurt to Ask," *Organizational Behavior and Human Decision Processes* 103 (2007), pp. 84–103.

50. D. A. Moore, "Myopic Prediction, Self-Destructive Secrecy, and the Unexpected Benefits of Revealing Final Deadlines in Negotiation," *Organizational Behavior & Human Decision Processes* (July 2004), pp. 125–139.

51. E. Wilson, "The Trouble with Jake," *The New York Times* (July 15, 2009), www.nytimes.com.

52. J. R. Curhan, H. A. Elfenbein, and H. Xu, "What Do People Value When They Negotiate? Mapping the Domain of Subjective Value in Negotiation," *Journal of Personality and Social Psychology* 91, no. 3 (2006), pp. 493–512.

53. Thomas, "Conflict and Negotiation Processes in Organizations."

54. P. M. Morgan and R. S. Tindale, "Group vs. Individual Performance in Mixed-Motive Situations: Exploring an Inconsistency," *Organizational Behavior & Human Decision Processes* (January 2002), pp. 44–65.

55. C. E. Naquin, "The Agony of Opportunity in Negotiation: Number of Negotiable Issues, Counterfactual Thinking, and Feelings of Satisfaction," *Organizational Behavior & Human Decision Processes* (May 2003), pp. 97–107.

56. M. Giacomantonio, C. K. W. De Dreu, and L. Mannetti, "Now You See It, Now You Don't: Interests, Issues, and Psychological Distance in Integrative Negotiation," *Journal of Personality and Social Psychology* 98, no. 5 (2010), pp. 761–774.

57. F. S. Ten Velden, B. Beersma, and C. K. W. De Dreu, "It Takes One to Tango: The Effect of Dyads' Epistemic Motivation Composition in Negotiation," *Personality and Social Psychology Bulletin* 36, no. 11 (2010), pp. 1454–1466.

58. C. K. W. De Dreu, L. R. Weingart, and S. Kwon, "Influence of Social Motives on Integrative Negotiation: A Meta-Analytic Review and Test of Two Theories," *Journal of Personality & Social Psychology* (May 2000), pp. 889–905.

59. This model is based on R. J. Lewicki, "Bargaining and Negotiation," *Exchange: The Organizational Behavior Teaching Journal* 6, no. 2 (1981), pp. 39–40.

60. J. R. Curhan, H. A. Elfenbein, and G. J. Kilduff, "Getting Off on the Right Foot: Subjective Value Versus Economic Value in Predicting Longitudinal Job Outcomes from Job Offer Negotiations," *Journal of Applied Psychology* 94, no. 2 (2009), pp. 524–534.

61. M. H. Bazerman and M. A. Neale, *Negotiating Rationally* (New York: The Free Press, 1992), pp. 67–68.

62. R. P. Larrick and G. Wu, "Claiming a Large Slice of a Small Pie: Asymmetric Disconfirmation in Negotiation," *Journal of Personality and Social Psychology* 93, no. 2 (2007), pp. 212–233.

63. E. T. Amanatullah, M. W. Morris, and J. R. Curhan, "Negotiators Who Give Too Much: Unmitigated Communion, Relational Anxieties, and Economic Costs in Distributive and Integrative Bargaining," *Journal of Personality and Social Psychology* 95, no. 3 (2008), pp. 723–738; and D. S. DeRue, D. E. Conlon, H. Moon, and H. W. Willaby, "When Is Straightforwardness a Liability in Negotiations? The Role of Integrative Potential and Structural Power," *Journal of Applied Psychology* 94, no. 4 (2009), pp. 1032–1047.

64. B. Barry and R. A. Friedman, "Bargainer Characteristics in Distributive and Integrative Negotiation," *Journal of Personality & Social Psychology* (February 1998), pp. 345–359.

65. L. J. Kray and M. P. Haselhuhn, "Implicit Negotiations Beliefs and Performance: Experimental and Longitudinal Evidence," *Journal of Personality and Social Psychology* 93, no. 1 (2007), pp. 49–64.

66. G. A. Gan Kleef and S. Côté, "Expressing Anger in Conflict: When It Helps and When It Hurts," *Journal of Applied Psychology* 92, no. 6 (2007), pp. 1157–1569; J. M. Brett, M. Olekalns, R. Friedman, N. Goates, C. Anderson, C. C. Lisco, "Sticks and Stones: Language, Face, and Online Dispute Resolution," *Academy of Management Journal* 50, no. 1 (2007), pp. 85–99; and J. R. Overbeck, M. A. Neale, and C. L. Govan, "I Feel, Therefore You Act: Intrapersonal and Interpersonal Effects of Emotion on Negotiations as a Function of Social Power," *Organizational Behavior and Human Decision Processes* 112, no. 2 (2010), pp. 126–139.

67. G. A. Van Kleef and C. K. W. De Dreu, "Longer-Term Consequences of Anger Expression in Negotiation: Retaliation or Spillover?" *Journal of Experimental Social Psychology* 46, no. 5 (2010), pp. 753–760.

68. M. Olekalns and P. L Smith, "Mutually Dependent: Power, Trust, Affect, and the Use of Deception in Negotiation," *Journal of Business Ethics* 85, no. 3 (2009), pp. 347–365.

69. A. W. Brooks and M. E. Schweitzer, "Can Nervous Nellie Negotiate? How Anxiety Causes Negotiators to Make Low First Offers, Exit Early, and Earn Less Profit," *Organizational Behavior and Human Decision Processes* 115, no. 1 (2011), pp. 43–54.

70. S. Kopelman, A. S. Rosette, and L. Thompson, "The Three Faces of Eve: Strategic Displays of Positive, Negative, and Neutral Emotions in Negotiations," *Organizational Behavior and Human Decision Processes* 99 (2006), pp. 81–101.

71. W. L. Adair, T. Okumura, and J. M. Brett, "Negotiation Behavior When Cultures Collide: The United States and Japan," *Journal of Applied Psychology* (June 2001), pp. 371–385; and W. L. Adair, L. Weingart, and J. Brett, "The Timing and Function of Offers in U.S. and Japanese Negotiations," *Journal of Applied Psychology* 92, no. 4 (2007), pp. 1056–1068.

72. S. Kopelman, "The Effect of Culture and Power on Cooperation in Commons Dilemmas: Implications for Global Resource Management," *Organizational Behavior and Human Decision Processes* 108, no. 1 (2009), pp. 153–163.

73. B. C. Gunia, J. M. Brett, A. K. Nandkeolyar, and D. Kamdar, "Paying a Price: Culture, Trust, and Negotiation Consequences," *Journal of Applied Psychology* 96, no. 4 (2010), pp. 774–789.

74. C. Watson and L. R. Hoffman, "Managers as Negotiators: A Test of Power Versus Gender as Predictors of Feelings, Behavior, and Outcomes," *Leadership Quarterly* (Spring 1996), pp. 63–85.

75. A. E. Walters, A. F. Stuhlmacher, and L. L. Meyer, "Gender and Negotiator Competitiveness: A Meta-Analysis," *Organizational Behavior and Human Decision Processes* (October 1998), pp. 1–29; and A. F. Stuhlmacher and A. E. Walters, "Gender Differences in Negotiation Outcome: A Meta-Analysis," *Personnel Psychology* (Autumn 1999), pp. 653–677.

76. Stuhlmacher and Walters, "Gender Differences in Negotiation Outcome," p. 655.

77. Bowles, Babcock, and Lei, "Social Incentives for Gender Differences in the Propensity to Initiative Negotiations."

78. L. J. Kray, A. D. Galinsky, and L. Thompson, "Reversing the Gender Gap in Negotiations: An Exploration of Stereotype Regeneration," *Organizational Behavior & Human Decision Processes* (March 2002), pp. 386–409.

79. D. A. Small, M. Gelfand, L. Babcock, and H. Gettman, "Who Goes to the Bargaining Table? The Influence of Gender and Framing on the Initiation of Negotiation," *Journal of Personality and Social Psychology* 93, no. 4 (2007), pp. 600–613.

80. E. T. Amanatullah and M. W. Morris, "Negotiating Gender Roles: Gender Differences in Assertive Negotiating Are Mediated by Women's Fear of Backlash and Attenuated When Negotiating on Behalf of Others," *Journal of Personality and Social Psychology* 98, no. 2 (2010), pp. 256–267.

81. K. W. Thomas, "Toward Multidimensional Values in Teaching: The Example of Conflict Behaviors," *Academy of Management Review* (July 1977), p. 487.

LEARNING OBJECTIVES

After studying this chapter, you should be able to:

1 Identify the six elements of an organization's structure.

2 Identify the characteristics of a bureaucracy.

3 Describe a matrix organization.

4 Identify the characteristics of a virtual organization.

5 Show why managers want to create boundaryless organizations.

6 Demonstrate how organizational structures differ, and contrast mechanistic and organic structural models.

7 Analyze the behavioral implications of different organizational designs.

MyManagementLab

Access a host of interactive learning aids to help strengthen your understanding of the chapter concepts at **www.mymanagementlab.com**.

DISMANTLING A BUREAUCRACY

Though at one time it was the largest, most successful, and most admired company in the world, today General Motors (GM) serves as a reminder to many of a staid company caught in a bureaucratic structure and culture of mediocrity that it created.

The reasons for GM's decline into bankruptcy are many. The company was heavily unionized and negotiated uncompetitive wage and pension structures for its union members. It was caught off-guard by the rise of Japanese automakers and their emphasis on quality. It was similarly blindsided by rising fuel costs and the push for fuel-efficient cars. Whenever a shock or innovation occurred, it seemed GM was poorly prepared and nearly always lagged behind competitors in anticipating, or even reacting to, a rapidly changing environment.

As in any story of organizational decline, we can't trace these missed opportunities to one cause. However, a source as likely as any is GM's organizational structure. That was the point of attack for Terry J. Woychowski.

Woychowski is vice president of the Global Vehicle Program Management at GM. He was promoted shortly after GM emerged from bankruptcy in 2009. In thinking strategically about GM and its future, Woychowski kept coming back to GM's bureaucracy. It led, he felt, to conservative, risk-averse, and analytical reactions rather than to innovative strategic risk taking. "We measured ourselves ten ways from Sunday," Woychowski says. "But as soon as everything is important, nothing is important."

Woychowski was not alone in his perceptions about the stifling effects of GM's bureaucracy. As far back as 1988, when the firm still dominated the world auto market, a GM senior executive sounded a note of caution about GM's bureaucracy that fell on deaf ears: "We have not achieved the success that we must because of severe limitations on our organization's ability to execute in a timely manner."

Woychowski is committed to changing that. In the past, any design alterations to a car required review by as many as 70 managers, with decisions often taking months and even years to wend their way through the bureaucracy. An ally of Woychowski, Jon Lauckner, head of Global Product Planning, significantly streamlined that process. Decisions that used to take months now take a few weeks.

Other aspects of GM's structure have been changed. Previously, managers were required to rate their tasks as green, yellow, or red, depending on whether the job had been completed, needed work, or should be frozen until a major problem was resolved. Mark Reuss, head of GM's global engineering group, says, "If you had a red issue and stood up, it was very punitive." So GM managers developed a risk-averse attitude and carefully sought approval

Foundations of Organization Structure

15

Every revolution evaporates and leaves behind only the slime of a new bureaucracy. —Franz Kafka

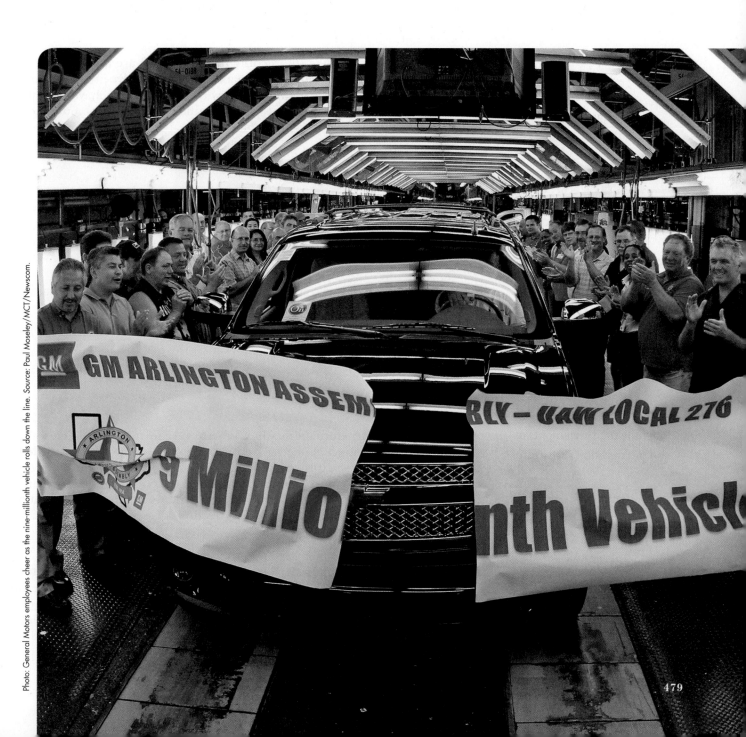

Photo: General Motors employees cheer as the nine-millionth vehicle rolls down the line. *Source:* Paul Moseley/MCT/Newscom.

from as many sources as possible before acting. Woychowski, Lauckner, and Reuss are working hard to make GM less bureaucratic, more informal, and less reactive and risk averse.

Can GM recover? This is not the first transformation it has attempted. Ironically, Reuss' father was dismissed as president of GM in a large restructuring in 1992. "This is an opportunity my dad never had," says Reuss. "I don't want to waste it."

Sources: B. Vlasic, "Culture Shock," *The New York Times* (November 13, 2009), pp. BU1, BU4; P. Brown, "According to Bob: How GM Cars Got Better," *AutoWeek* (May 23, 2011), downloaded June 30, 2011, from www.autoweek.com/; and A. Taylor, "GM vs. Ford: The Hundred-Year War," *Fortune* (March 23, 2011), downloaded June 29, 2011, from http://money.cnn.com/.

S tructural decisions like the reconfiguration of GM are arguably the most fundamental ones a leader has to make. Before we delve into the elements of an organization's structure and how they can affect behavior, consider how you might react to one type of organizational structure—the bureaucratic structure—by taking the following self-assessment.

SELF-ASSESSMENT LIBRARY

Do I Like Bureaucracy?

In the Self-Assessment Library (available on CD and online), take assessment IV.F.2 (Do I Like Bureaucracy?) and answer the following questions.

1. Judging from the results, how willing are you to work in a bureaucratic organization?
2. Do you think scores on this measure matter? Why or why not?
3. Do you think people who score very low (or even very high) on this measure should try to adjust their preferences based on where they are working?

What Is Organizational Structure?

1 Identify the six elements of an organization's structure.

An **organizational structure** defines how job tasks are formally divided, grouped, and coordinated. Managers need to address six key elements when they design their organization's structure: work specialization, departmentalization, chain of command, span of control, centralization and decentralization, and formalization.[1] Exhibit 15-1 presents each of these elements as answers to an important structural question, and the following sections describe them.

Work Specialization

Early in the twentieth century, Henry Ford became rich by building automobiles on an assembly line. Every Ford worker was assigned a specific, repetitive task such as putting on the right-front wheel or installing the right-front door. By dividing jobs into small standardized tasks that could be performed over and over, Ford was able to produce a car every 10 seconds, using employees who had relatively limited skills.

Exhibit 15-1	Key Design Questions and Answers for Designing the Proper Organizational Structure

The Key Question	The Answer Is Provided by
1. To what degree are activities subdivided into separate jobs?	Work specialization
2. On what basis will jobs be grouped together?	Departmentalization
3. To whom do individuals and groups report?	Chain of command
4. How many individuals can a manager efficiently and effectively direct?	Span of control
5. Where does decision-making authority lie?	Centralization and decentralization
6. To what degree will there be rules and regulations to direct employees and managers?	Formalization

Ford demonstrated that work can be performed more efficiently if employees are allowed to specialize. Today, we use the term **work specialization**, or *division of labor,* to describe the degree to which activities in the organization are subdivided into separate jobs. The essence of work specialization is to divide a job into a number of steps, each completed by a separate individual. In essence, individuals specialize in doing part of an activity rather than the entirety.

By the late 1940s, most manufacturing jobs in industrialized countries featured high work specialization. Because not all employees in an organization have the same skills, management saw specialization as a means of making the most efficient use of its employees' skills and even successfully improving them through repetition. Less time is spent in changing tasks, putting away tools and equipment from a prior step, and getting ready for another. Equally important, it's easier and less costly to find and train workers to do specific and repetitive tasks, especially in highly sophisticated and complex operations. Could Cessna produce one Citation jet a year if one person had to build the entire plane alone? Not likely! Finally, work specialization increases efficiency and productivity by encouraging the creation of special inventions and machinery.

Thus, for much of the first half of the twentieth century, managers viewed work specialization as an unending source of increased productivity. And they were probably right. When specialization was not widely practiced, its introduction almost always generated higher productivity. But by the 1960s, it increasingly seemed a good thing can be carried too far. Human diseconomies from specialization began to surface in the form of boredom, fatigue, stress, low productivity, poor quality, increased absenteeism, and high turnover, which more than offset the economic advantages (see Exhibit 15-2). Managers could increase productivity now by enlarging, rather than narrowing, the scope of job activities. Giving employees a variety of activities to do, allowing them to do a whole and complete job, and putting them into teams with interchangeable skills often achieved significantly higher output, with increased employee satisfaction.

organizational structure *The way in which job tasks are formally divided, grouped, and coordinated.*

work specialization *The degree to which tasks in an organization are subdivided into separate jobs.*

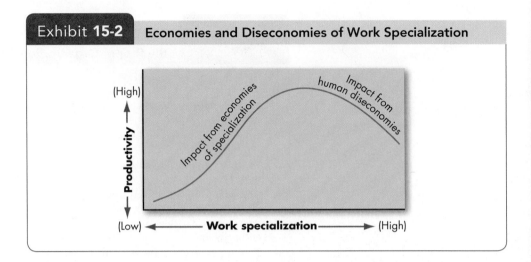

Exhibit **15-2**   Economies and Diseconomies of Work Specialization

Most managers today recognize the economies specialization provides in certain jobs and the problems when it's carried too far. High work specialization helps McDonald's make and sell hamburgers and fries efficiently and aids medical specialists in most health maintenance organizations. Amazon's Mechanical Turk program, TopCoder, and others like it have facilitated a new trend in microspecialization in which extremely small pieces of programming, data processing, or evaluation tasks are delegated to a global network of individuals by a program manager who then assembles the results.[2] For example, a manager who has a complex but routine computer program to write might send a request for specific subcomponents of the code to be written and tested by dozens of subcontracted individuals in the network (which spans the entire globe), enabling the project to be completed far more quickly than if a single programmer were writing the parts. This emerging trend suggests there still may be advantages to be had in specialization.

Departmentalization

Once jobs have been divided through work specialization, they must be grouped so common tasks can be coordinated. The basis by which jobs are grouped is called **departmentalization**.

One of the most popular ways to group activities is by *functions* performed. A manufacturing manager might organize a plant into engineering, accounting, manufacturing, personnel, and supply specialists departments. A hospital might have departments devoted to research, surgery, intensive care, accounting, and so forth. A professional football franchise might have departments entitled player personnel, ticket sales, and travel and accommodations. The major advantage of this type of functional departmentalization is efficiencies gained from putting like specialists together.

We can also departmentalize jobs by the type of *product* or *service* the organization produces. Procter & Gamble places each major product—such as Tide, Pampers, Charmin, and Pringles—under an executive who has complete global responsibility for it. The major advantage here is increased accountability for performance, because all activities related to a specific product or service are under the direction of a single manager.

When a firm is departmentalized on the basis of *geography*, or territory, the sales function, for instance, may have western, southern, midwestern, and eastern regions, each, in effect, a department organized around geography. This form is valuable when an organization's customers are scattered over a large geographic area and have similar needs based on their location.

At Microsoft, customer departmentalization allows the company to better understand customers and respond to their needs. Microsoft is organized by four customer segments: consumers, software developers, small businesses, and large corporations. Products and services the company designs for consumers include Bing, Windows, Windows Phone 7, Xbox 360, and Microsoft retail stores, which give the company direct contact with consumers. This photo shows a boy playing the Kinect for Xbox 360 at a gaming store. Kinect, which has a full-body sensor, allows consumers to play Xbox games without using a controller and to interact with games in a real physical sense.

Source: AP Photo/Nell Redmond.

Process departmentalization works for processing customers as well as products. If you've ever been to a state motor vehicle office to get a driver's license, you probably went through several departments before receiving your license. In one typical state, applicants go through three steps, each handled by a separate department: (1) validation by motor vehicles division, (2) processing by the licensing department, and (3) payment collection by the treasury department.

A final category of departmentalization uses the particular type of *customer* the organization seeks to reach. Microsoft, for example, is organized around four customer markets: consumers, large corporations, software developers, and small businesses. Customers in each department have a common set of problems and needs best met by having specialists for each.

Chain of Command

While the chain of command was once a basic cornerstone in the design of organizations, it has far less importance today.[3] But contemporary managers should still consider its implications. The **chain of command** is an unbroken line of authority that extends from the top of the organization to the lowest echelon and clarifies who reports to whom.

---

departmentalization   *The basis by which jobs in an organization are grouped together.*

chain of command   *The unbroken line of authority that extends from the top of the organization to the lowest echelon and clarifies who reports to whom.*

We can't discuss the chain of command without also discussing *authority* and *unity of command.* **Authority** refers to the rights inherent in a managerial position to give orders and expect them to be obeyed. To facilitate coordination, each managerial position is given a place in the chain of command, and each manager is given a degree of authority in order to meet his or her responsibilities. The principle of **unity of command** helps preserve the concept of an unbroken line of authority. It says a person should have one and only one superior to whom he or she is directly responsible. If the unity of command is broken, an employee might have to cope with conflicting demands or priorities from several superiors.

Times change, and so do the basic tenets of organizational design. A low-level employee today can access information in seconds that was available only to top managers a generation ago. Operating employees are empowered to make decisions previously reserved for management. Add the popularity of self-managed and cross-functional teams and the creation of new structural designs that include multiple bosses, and you can see why authority and unity of command hold less relevance. Many organizations still find they can be most productive by enforcing the chain of command. Indeed, one survey of more than 1,000 managers found that 59 percent of them agreed with the statement, "There is an imaginary line in my company's organizational chart. Strategy is created by people above this line, while strategy is executed by people below the line."[4] However, this same survey found that buy-in to the organization's strategy by lower-level employees was inhibited by too much reliance on hierarchy for decision making.

Span of Control

How many employees can a manager efficiently and effectively direct? This question of **span of control** is important because it largely determines the number of levels and managers an organization has. All things being equal, the wider or larger the span, the more efficient the organization.

Assume two organizations each have about 4,100 operative-level employees. One has a uniform span of four and the other a span of eight. As Exhibit 15-3 illustrates, the wider span will have two fewer levels and approximately 800 fewer managers. If the average manager makes $50,000 a year, the wider span will save

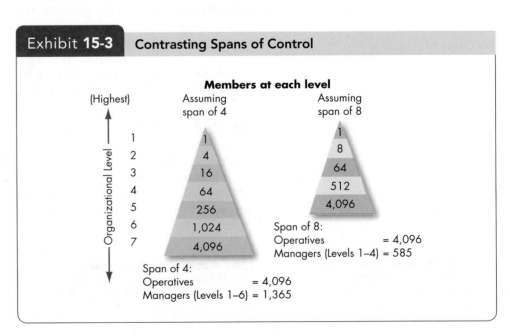

Exhibit 15-3   Contrasting Spans of Control

Members at each level

(Highest) — Organizational Level

Assuming span of 4:

Level	
1	1
2	4
3	16
4	64
5	256
6	1,024
7	4,096

Span of 4:
Operatives = 4,096
Managers (Levels 1–6) = 1,365

Assuming span of 8:

Level	
1	1
2	8
3	64
4	512
5	4,096

Span of 8:
Operatives = 4,096
Managers (Levels 1–4) = 585

$40 million a year in management salaries! Obviously, wider spans are more efficient in terms of cost. However, at some point when supervisors no longer have time to provide the necessary leadership and support, they reduce effectiveness and employee performance suffers.

Narrow or small spans have their advocates. By keeping the span of control to five or six employees, a manager can maintain close control.[5] But narrow spans have three major drawbacks. First, they're expensive because they add levels of management. Second, they make vertical communication in the organization more complex. The added levels of hierarchy slow down decision making and tend to isolate upper management. Third, narrow spans encourage overly tight supervision and discourage employee autonomy.

The trend in recent years has been toward wider spans of control.[6] They're consistent with firms' efforts to reduce costs, cut overhead, speed decision making, increase flexibility, get closer to customers, and empower employees. However, to ensure performance doesn't suffer because of these wider spans, organizations have been investing heavily in employee training. Managers recognize they can handle a wider span best when employees know their jobs inside and out or can turn to co-workers when they have questions.

Centralization and Decentralization

Centralization refers to the degree to which decision making is concentrated at a single point in the organization. In *centralized* organizations, top managers make all the decisions, and lower-level managers merely carry out their directives. In organizations at the other extreme, *decentralized* decision making is pushed down to the managers closest to the action.

The concept of centralization includes only formal authority—that is, the rights inherent in a position. An organization characterized by centralization is inherently different structurally from one that's decentralized. A decentralized organization can act more quickly to solve problems, more people provide input into decisions, and employees are less likely to feel alienated from those who make decisions that affect their work lives.

Management efforts to make organizations more flexible and responsive have produced a recent trend toward decentralized decision making by lower-level managers, who are closer to the action and typically have more detailed knowledge about problems than top managers. Sears and JCPenney have given their store managers considerably more discretion in choosing what merchandise to stock. This allows those stores to compete more effectively against local merchants. Similarly, when Procter & Gamble empowered small groups of employees to make many decisions about new-product development independent of the usual hierarchy, it was able to rapidly increase the proportion of new products ready for market.[7] Research investigating a large number of Finnish organizations demonstrates that companies with decentralized research and development offices in multiple locations were better at producing innovation than companies that centralized all research and development in a single office.[8]

---

authority   *The rights inherent in a managerial position to give orders and to expect the orders to be obeyed.*

unity of command   *The idea that a subordinate should have only one superior to whom he or she is directly responsible.*

span of control   *The number of subordinates a manager can efficiently and effectively direct.*

centralization   *The degree to which decision making is concentrated at a single point in an organization.*

How Willing Am I to Delegate?

In the Self-Assessment Library (available on CD and online), take assessment III.A.2 (How Willing Am I to Delegate?).

Formalization

Formalization refers to the degree to which jobs within the organization are standardized. If a job is highly formalized, the incumbent has a minimal amount of discretion over what to do and when and how to do it. Employees can be expected always to handle the same input in exactly the same way, resulting in a consistent and uniform output. There are explicit job descriptions, lots of organizational rules, and clearly defined procedures covering work processes in organizations in which there is high formalization. Where formalization is low, job behaviors are relatively unprogrammed, and employees have a great deal of freedom to exercise discretion in their work. Standardization not only eliminates the possibility of employees engaging in alternative behaviors, but it even removes the need for employees to consider alternatives.

The degree of formalization can vary widely between and within organizations. Publishing representatives who call on college professors to inform them of their company's new publications have a great deal of freedom in their jobs. They have only a general sales pitch, which they tailor as needed, and rules and procedures governing their behavior may be little more than the requirement to submit a weekly sales report and suggestions on what to emphasize about forthcoming titles. At the other extreme, clerical and editorial employees in the same publishing houses may need to be at their desks by 8:00 a.m. and follow a set of precise procedures dictated by management.

Common Organizational Designs

2 Identify the characteristics of a bureaucracy.

We now turn to three of the more common organizational designs: the *simple structure,* the *bureaucracy,* and the *matrix structure.*

The Simple Structure

What do a small retail store, an electronics firm run by a hard-driving entrepreneur, and an airline's "war room" in the midst of a pilot's strike have in common? They probably all use the **simple structure**.

We can think of the simple structure in terms of what it is *not* rather than what it is. The simple structure is not elaborate.[9] It has a low degree of departmentalization, wide spans of control, authority centralized in a single person, and little formalization. It is a "flat" organization; it usually has only two or three vertical levels, a loose body of employees, and one individual in whom the decision-making authority is centralized.

The simple structure is most widely adopted in small businesses in which the manager and owner are one and the same. Exhibit 15-4 is an organization chart for a retail men's store owned and managed by Jack Gold. Although he employs five full-time salespeople, a cashier, and extra personnel for weekends and holidays, Jack "runs the show." Large companies, in times of crisis, often simplify their structures as a means of focusing their resources. When Anne Mulcahy

Exhibit 15-4 | A Simple Structure (Jack Gold's Men's Store)

Jack Gold, owner-manager

Johnny Moore, salesperson | Edna Joiner, salesperson | Bob Munson, salesperson | Norma Sloman, salesperson | Jerry Plotkin, salesperson | Helen Wright, cashier

took over Xerox, its product mix and management structure were overly complex. She simplified both, cutting corporate overhead by 26 percent. "It's a case of placing your bets in a few areas" she says.[10]

The strength of the simple structure lies in its simplicity. It's fast, flexible, and inexpensive to operate, and accountability is clear. One major weakness is that it becomes increasingly inadequate as an organization grows, because its low formalization and high centralization tend to create information overload at the top. As size increases, decision making typically becomes slower and can eventually come to a standstill as the single executive tries to continue making all the decisions. This proves the undoing of many small businesses. If the structure isn't changed and made more elaborate, the firm often loses momentum and can eventually fail. The simple structure's other weakness is that it's risky—everything depends on one person. One illness can literally destroy the organization's information and decision-making center.

The Bureaucracy

Standardization! That's the key concept that underlies all bureaucracies. Consider the bank where you keep your checking account; the department store where you buy clothes; or the government offices that collect your taxes, enforce health regulations, or provide local fire protection. They all rely on standardized work processes for coordination and control.

The **bureaucracy** is characterized by highly routine operating tasks achieved through specialization, very formalized rules and regulations, tasks grouped into functional departments, centralized authority, narrow spans of control, and decision making that follows the chain of command. As the opening quote to this chapter attests, *bureaucracy* is a dirty word in many people's minds. However, it does have advantages. Its primary strength is its ability to perform standardized activities in a highly efficient manner. Putting like specialties together in functional departments results in economies of scale, minimum duplication of people and equipment, and employees who can speak "the same language" among their peers. Bureaucracies can get by with less talented—and hence less

---

formalization *The degree to which jobs within an organization are standardized.*

simple structure *An organization structure characterized by a low degree of departmentalization, wide spans of control, authority centralized in a single person, and little formalization.*

bureaucracy *An organization structure with highly routine operating tasks achieved through specialization, very formalized rules and regulations, tasks that are grouped into functional departments, centralized authority, narrow spans of control, and decision making that follows the chain of command.*

costly—middle- and lower-level managers because rules and regulations substitute for managerial discretion. Standardized operations and high formalization allow decision making to be centralized. There is little need for innovative and experienced decision makers below the level of senior executives.

Listen in on a dialogue among four executives in one company: "You know, nothing happens in this place until we *produce* something," said the production executive. "Wrong," commented the research and development manager. "Nothing happens until we *design* something!" "What are you talking about?" asked the marketing executive. "Nothing happens here until we *sell* something!" The exasperated accounting manager responded, "It doesn't matter what you produce, design, or sell. No one knows what happens until we *tally up the results!*" This conversation highlights that bureaucratic specialization can create conflicts in which functional-unit goals override the overall goals of the organization.

The other major weakness of a bureaucracy is something we've all witnessed: obsessive concern with following the rules. When cases don't precisely fit the rules, there is no room for modification. The bureaucracy is efficient only as long as employees confront familiar problems with programmed decision rules.

The Matrix Structure

3   Describe a matrix organization.

You'll find the **matrix structure** in advertising agencies, aerospace firms, research and development laboratories, construction companies, hospitals, government agencies, universities, management consulting firms, and entertainment companies.[11] It combines two forms of departmentalization: functional and product. Companies that use matrix-like structures include ABB, Boeing, BMW, IBM, and Procter & Gamble.

The strength of functional departmentalization is putting like specialists together, which minimizes the number necessary while allowing the pooling and sharing of specialized resources across products. Its major disadvantage is the difficulty of coordinating the tasks of diverse functional specialists on time and within budget. Product departmentalization has exactly the opposite benefits and disadvantages. It facilitates coordination among specialties to achieve on-time completion and meet budget targets. It provides clear responsibility for all

Hospitals benefit from standardized work processes and procedures common to a bureaucratic structure because they help employees perform their jobs efficiently. When faced with financial problems, management at Crouse Hospital in Syracuse, New York, decided that its structure was too bureaucratic and hierarchical. Top managers gathered employees from all levels and areas and asked them to find innovative solutions needed to improve every aspect of the hospital, from creating a new mission statement to designing new work processes. With more employee involvement, Crouse raised its revenues and quality, provided more community services, and improved its relationship with employees such as the registered nurse shown here.

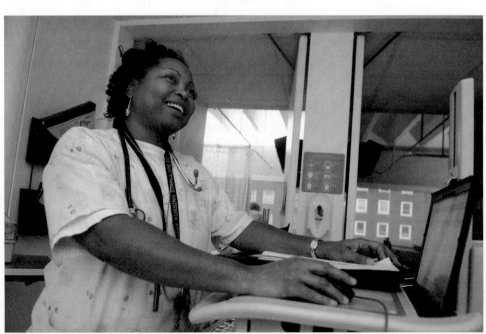

Source: Syracuse Newspapers/H Bragman/The Image Works.

The Global Organization

One of the most significant trends in organizational structure is the emergence of truly global organizations with leadership and development functions located all around the world.

In organizations that offshore many functions, a central office located in one country sends business processes to facilities in another country, like a U.S. computer company (think of Dell or Apple) that designs computers in California, manufactures all the parts in China, and assembles them in Texas. Such companies are global in the sense that their operations span multiple nations, but the central culture of the organization is based in a home country.

In a "stateless" corporation, in contrast, all divisions share a common management culture, and operations are standardized for all locations. Managers are drawn from a variety of national backgrounds and placed wherever their functional expertise will be most valuable. Reckitt Benckiser (maker of Clearasil, Lysol, and Woolite) assigns managers to a variety of global offices to ensure they get a picture of border-spanning trends that might produce innovations in other countries. As a result, an Italian is running the UK business, an American the German business, an Indian the Chinese operation, and a Dutch executive the U.S. business.

Although these international strategies may produce advantages like cost savings and centralization of decision making, some observers feel the future is more likely to belong to truly cosmopolitan organizations that produce and market products and services particular to each country in which they operate. This strategy gives local offices maximal control over their own particular areas and takes the greatest advantage of specialized, local knowledge of markets.

It's not yet clear whether it's better to pursue a strategy based on offshoring, stateless corporations, or cosmopolitan organizations, but it's likely there is no universal best configuration. The best structure is likely to depend heavily on the type of products and market the company is targeting.

Sources: Based on J. Lampel and A. Bhalla, "Living with Offshoring: The Impact of Offshoring on the Evolution of Organizational Configurations," *Journal of World Business* 46, (2011), pp. 346–358; P. Gehmawat, "The Cosmopolitan Corporation," *Harvard Business Review* (May 2011), pp. 92–99; and B. Becht, "Building a Company Without Borders," *Harvard Business Review* (April 2010), pp. 103–106.

activities related to a product, but with duplication of activities and costs. The matrix attempts to gain the strengths of each while avoiding their weaknesses.

The most obvious structural characteristic of the matrix is that it breaks the unity-of-command concept. Employees in the matrix have two bosses: their functional department managers and their product managers.

Exhibit 15-5 shows the matrix form in a college of business administration. The academic departments of accounting, decision and information systems, marketing, and so forth are functional units. Overlaid on them are specific programs (that is, products). Thus, members in a matrix structure have a dual chain of command: to their functional department and to their product groups. A professor of accounting teaching an undergraduate course may report to the director of undergraduate programs as well as to the chairperson of the accounting department.

The strength of the matrix is its ability to facilitate coordination when the organization has a number of complex and interdependent activities. Direct and frequent contacts between different specialties in the matrix can let information permeate the organization and more quickly reach the people who need it. The matrix reduces "bureaupathologies"—the dual lines of authority reduce people's tendency to become so busy protecting their little worlds that

matrix structure *An organization structure that creates dual lines of authority and combines functional and product departmentalization.*

Exhibit 15-5	Matrix Structure for a College of Business Administration

Programs / Academic Departments	Undergraduate	Master's	Ph.D.	Research	Executive Development	Community Service
Accounting						
Finance						
Decision and Information Systems						
Management						
Marketing						

the organization's goals become secondary. A matrix also achieves economies of scale and facilitates the allocation of specialists by providing both the best resources and an effective way of ensuring their efficient deployment.

The major disadvantages of the matrix lie in the confusion it creates, its tendency to foster power struggles, and the stress it places on individuals.[12] Without the unity-of-command concept, ambiguity about who reports to whom is significantly increased and often leads to conflict. It's not unusual for product managers to fight over getting the best specialists assigned to their products. Bureaucracy reduces the potential for power grabs by defining the rules of the game. When those rules are "up for grabs" in a matrix, power struggles between functional and product managers result. For individuals who desire security and absence from ambiguity, this work climate can be stressful. Reporting to more than one boss introduces role conflict, and unclear expectations introduce role ambiguity. The comfort of bureaucracy's predictability is replaced by insecurity and stress.

New Design Options

Senior managers in a number of organizations have been developing new structural options with fewer layers of hierarchy and more emphasis on opening the boundaries of the organization.[13] In this section, we describe two such designs: the *virtual organization* and the *boundaryless organization*. We'll also discuss how efforts to reduce bureaucracy and increase strategic focus have made downsizing routine.

The Virtual Organization

4 Identify the characteristics of a virtual organization.

Why own when you can rent? That question captures the essence of the **virtual organization** (also sometimes called the *network,* or *modular,* organization), typically a small, core organization that outsources its major business functions.[14] In structural terms, the virtual organization is highly centralized, with little or no departmentalization.

The prototype of the virtual structure is today's movie-making organization. In Hollywood's golden era, movies were made by huge, vertically integrated corporations. Studios such as MGM, Warner Brothers, and 20th Century Fox owned large movie lots and employed thousands of full-time specialists—set designers, camera people, film editors, directors, and even actors. Today, most movies are made by a collection of individuals and small companies who come together and make films project by project.[15] This structural form allows each project to be staffed with the talent best suited to its demands, rather than just the people employed by the studio. It minimizes bureaucratic overhead because there is no lasting organization to maintain. And it lessens long-term risks and their costs because there *is* no long term—a team is assembled for a finite period and then disbanded.

Philip Rosedale runs a virtual company called LoveMachine that lets employees send brief electronic messages to one another to acknowledge a job well done that can be then used to facilitate company bonuses. The company has no full-time software development staff—instead, LoveMachine outsources assignments to freelancers who submit bids for projects like debugging software or designing new features. Programmers come from around the world, including Russia, India, Australia, and the United States.[16] Similarly, Newman's Own, the food products company founded by Paul Newman, sells hundreds of millions of dollars in food every year yet employs only 28 people. This is possible because it outsources almost everything: manufacturing, procurement, shipping, and quality control.

Exhibit 15-6 shows a virtual organization in which management outsources all the primary functions of the business. The core of the organization is a small group of executives whose job is to oversee directly any activities done in-house and to coordinate relationships with the other organizations that manufacture, distribute, and perform other crucial functions for the virtual organization. The dotted lines represent the relationships typically maintained under

Exhibit 15-6   A Virtual Organization

Independent research and development consulting firm

Advertising agency

Executive group

Factories in South Korea

Commissioned sales representatives

virtual organization   *A small, core organization that outsources major business functions.*

As a network organization, Boeing outsourced the production of about 70 percent of the components for its new 787 Dreamliner passenger jet aircraft. Boeing used some 100 suppliers at more than 100 sites in different countries, including Alenia Aeronautica of Italy to produce the plane's rear fuselage and Mitsubishi Motors of Japan to create the wings. Although global outsourcing helped Boeing reduce the plane's development and production costs, the extreme complexities of such a structure was also responsible for delays in bringing the cutting-edge aircraft to market. Shown here is the plane's assembly line surrounded by rows of workers at their computers as the planes are built at Boeing's plant in Everett, Washington.

Source: Robert Sorbo/Reuters/Landov Media.

contracts. In essence, managers in virtual structures spend most of their time coordinating and controlling external relations, typically by way of computer network links.

The major advantage of the virtual organization is its flexibility, which allows individuals with an innovative idea and little money to successfully compete against larger, more established organizations. Virtual organizations also save a great deal of money by eliminating permanent offices and hierarchical roles.[17]

Virtual organizations' drawbacks have become increasingly clear as their popularity has grown.[18] They are in a state of perpetual flux and reorganization, which means roles, goals, and responsibilities are unclear, setting the stage for political behavior. Cultural alignment and shared goals can be lost because of the low degree of interaction among members. Team members who are geographically dispersed and communicate infrequently find it difficult to share information and knowledge, which can limit innovation and slow response time. Ironically, some virtual organizations are less adaptable and innovative than those with well-established communication and collaboration networks. A leadership presence that reinforces the organization's purpose and facilitates communication is thus especially valuable.

The Boundaryless Organization

5 Show why managers want to create boundaryless organizations.

General Electric's former chairman, Jack Welch, coined the term **boundaryless organization** to describe what he wanted GE to become: a "family grocery store."[19] That is, in spite of GE's monstrous size (2010 revenues were $150 billion), Welch wanted to eliminate *vertical* and *horizontal* boundaries within it and break down *external* barriers between the company and its customers and suppliers. The boundaryless organization seeks to eliminate the chain of command, have limitless spans of control, and replace departments with empowered teams. Although GE has not yet achieved this boundaryless state—and probably never will—it has made significant progress toward that end. So have other companies, such as Hewlett-Packard, AT&T, Motorola, and 3M. Let's see what a boundaryless organization looks like and what some firms are doing to make it a reality.[20]

By removing vertical boundaries, management flattens the hierarchy and minimizes status and rank. Cross-hierarchical teams (which include top executives, middle managers, supervisors, and operative employees), participative decision-making practices, and the use of 360-degree performance appraisals (in which peers and others above and below the employee evaluate performance) are examples of what GE is doing to break down vertical boundaries. At Oticon A/S, a $160-million-per-year Danish hearing aid manufacturer, all traces of hierarchy have disappeared. Everyone works at uniform mobile workstations, and project teams, not functions or departments, coordinate work.

Functional departments create horizontal boundaries that stifle interaction among functions, product lines, and units. The way to reduce them is to replace functional departments with cross-functional teams and organize activities around processes. Xerox now develops new products through multidisciplinary teams that work on a single process instead of on narrow functional tasks. Some AT&T units prepare annual budgets based not on functions or departments but on processes, such as the maintenance of a worldwide telecommunications network. Another way to lower horizontal barriers is to rotate people through different functional areas using lateral transfers. This approach turns specialists into generalists.

When fully operational, the boundaryless organization also breaks down geographic barriers. Today, most large U.S. companies see themselves as global corporations; many, like Coca-Cola and McDonald's, do as much business overseas as in the United States, and some struggle to incorporate geographic regions into their structure. The boundaryless organization provides one solution because it considers geography more of a tactical, logistical issue than a structural one. In short, the goal is to break down cultural barriers.

BMW Group operates as a boundaryless organization in designing, developing, and producing its BMW, Rolls-Royce, and Mini cars. The automaker uses virtual tools such as computer-aided design and simulation models and a flexible global production network to respond quickly to fluctuations in the market and individual customer preferences. BMW's boundaryless structure drives innovative ideas by eliminating vertical and horizontal barriers among workers and creating an environment of learning and experimentation. From their first day on the job, employees are encouraged to build a network of relationships from all functional areas and across all divisions to speed innovation and problem-solving.

Source: Eckehard Schulz/AP Images.

boundaryless organization *An organization that seeks to eliminate the chain of command, have limitless spans of control, and replace departments with empowered teams.*

One way to do so is through strategic alliances.[21] Firms such as NEC Corporation, Boeing, and Apple each have strategic alliances or joint partnerships with dozens of companies. These alliances blur the distinction between one organization and another as employees work on joint projects. And some companies allow customers to perform functions previously done by management. Some AT&T units receive bonuses based on customer evaluations of the teams that serve them. Finally, telecommuting is blurring organizational boundaries. The security analyst with Merrill Lynch who does her job from her ranch in Montana or the software designer in Boulder, Colorado, who works for a San Francisco firm are just two of the millions of workers operating outside the physical boundaries of their employers' premises.

The Leaner Organization: Downsizing

The goal of the new organizational forms we've described is to improve agility by creating a lean, focused, and flexible organization. *Downsizing* is a systematic effort to make an organization leaner by closing locations, reducing staff, or selling off business units that don't add value.

The radical shrinking of Chrysler and General Motors in recent years was a case of downsizing to survive, due to loss of market share and changes in consumer demand. Other firms, including Research in Motion (makers of the BlackBerry) and Cisco, downsize to direct all their efforts toward their core competencies. After a series of costly acquisitions, VeriSign decided to divest itself of most of its business units and resume its original focus on e-commerce security and online identity protection.[22] Some companies focus on lean management techniques to reduce bureaucracy and speed decision making. Park Nicollet Health Services in Minneapolis eliminated fixed budgets and pushed managers to reduce costs as part of a transformation to lean production; it was able to save at least $15 million per year[23] and adapt to changes in the health care market much more quickly.

Despite the advantages of being a lean organization, the impact of downsizing on organizational performance has been very controversial.[24] Reducing

Foursquare transfers its inputs into outputs by using a location-based mobile platform. The social networking Web site provides a service for consumers and businesses. Founded by Dennis Crowley and Naveen Selvadurai, the service allows people to connect with friends and update their location, and it provides businesses with tools to obtain, engage, and retain customers. Nonroutineness characterizes the work of employees at Foursquare, an organic organization that adapts quickly and flexibly to rapid changes. Foursquare co-founder Selvadurai is shown in this photo presenting an address at an annual digital technology forum in Seoul, South Korea.

Source: Park Jin Hee/Xinhua/Photoshot/Newscom.

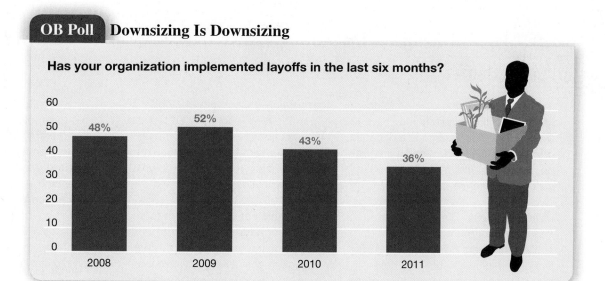

OB Poll   Downsizing Is Downsizing

Has your organization implemented layoffs in the last six months?

Source: Based on E. Frauenheim, "The Thought Police?" *Workforce Management* (March, 2010), pp. 28-31; "Companies Grapple with Viral Vents," *Workforce Management* (December, 2010), p. 6.

the size of the workforce has an immediately positive outcome in the form of lower wage costs. Companies downsizing to improve strategic focus often see positive effects on stock prices after the announcement. On the other hand, among companies that only cut employees but don't restructure, profits and stock prices usually decline. Part of the problem is the effect of downsizing on employee attitudes. Those who remain often feel worried about future layoffs and may be less committed to the organization.[25] Stress reactions can lead to increased sickness absences, lower concentration on the job, and lower creativity. In companies that don't invest much in their employees, downsizing can also lead to more voluntary turnover, so vital human capital is lost. The result is a company that is more anemic than lean.

Companies can reduce negative impacts by preparing in advance, thus alleviating some employee stress and strengthening support for the new direction.[26] Here are some effective strategies for downsizing. Most are closely linked to the principles for organizational justice we've discussed previously:

- **Investment.**   Companies that downsize to focus on core competencies are more effective when they invest in high-involvement work practices afterward.
- **Communication.**   When employers make efforts to discuss downsizing with employees early, employees are less worried about the outcomes and feel the company is taking their perspective into account.
- **Participation.**   Employees worry less if they can participate in the process in some way. Voluntary early-retirement programs or severance packages can help achieve leanness without layoffs.
- **Assistance.**   Severance, extended health care benefits, and job search assistance demonstrate a company cares about its employees and honors their contributions.

In short, companies that make themselves lean can be more agile, efficient, and productive—but only if they make cuts carefully and help employees through the process.

Downsizing with a Conscience

Especially during economic down times, organizations may have to reduce headcount. The negative effects on those who remain are well documented and include increased sickness absence, withdrawal from work tasks, intentions to sue the organization, stress, dissatisfaction, and loss of commitment.

Do employers have a responsibility to help cushion the blow of downsizing? While ethicists debate how much organizations should help laid-off employees, they generally agree that firms that *can* afford to do something probably should. Indeed, this assistance can work in the organization's self-interest, by increasing commitment among those who remain and reducing stress and strain for all. Managing layoffs with an eye to the organization's reputation may also be important for hiring new employees when economic prospects improve.

Here are some suggestions to minimize the negative impact of downsizing on employees:

1. Managers are often reticent to give out information about future company plans, but research clearly suggests that ample advance warning about downsizing can reduce employee distress. Open communication makes it much easier for employees to plan how they will respond.
2. Deliver the news about layoffs in a compassionate, personal manner. Let employees know face-to-face they are being let go. This can be hard for managers who would rather avoid conflict or angry encounters, but most research suggests employees prefer to find out about a job loss in this manner (as opposed to e-mail).
3. Explore ways to help, such as by providing job search assistance or severance pay. This might not always be financially feasible, but it's ethically responsible to do everything you can to help departing employees land on their feet.

Sources: B. Weinstein, "Downsizing 101" *Bloomberg Businessweek* (September 12, 2008), www.businessweek.com; S. Randall, "Attracting Layoff-Wary Millennials," *Workforce Management Online* (February 2010), www.workforce.com; and D. K. Datta, J. P. Guthrie, D. Basuil, and A. Pandey, "Causes and Effects of Employee Downsizing: A Review and Synthesis," *Journal of Management* 36, no. 1 (2010), pp. 281–348.

Why Do Structures Differ?

6 Demonstrate how organizational structures differ, and contrast mechanistic and organic structural models.

We've described organizational designs ranging from the highly structured bureaucracy to the amorphous boundaryless organization. The other designs we discussed exist somewhere in between.

Exhibit 15-7 recaps our discussions by presenting two extreme models of organizational design. One we'll call the **mechanistic model**. It's generally synonymous with the bureaucracy in that it has highly standardized processes for work, high formalization, and more managerial hierarchy. The other extreme, the **organic model**, looks a lot like the boundaryless organization. It's flat, has fewer formal procedures for making decisions, has multiple decision makers, and favors flexible practices.[27]

With these two models in mind, let's ask a few questions: Why are some organizations structured along more mechanistic lines whereas others follow organic characteristics? What forces influence the choice of design? In this section, we present the major causes or determinants of an organization's structure.[28]

Organizational Strategy

Because structure is a means to achieve objectives, and objectives derive from the organization's overall strategy, it's only logical that structure should follow strategy. If management significantly changes the organization's strategy,

Exhibit 15-7   Mechanistic versus Organic Models

The Mechanistic Model

- High specialization
- Rigid departmentalization
- Clear chain of command
- Narrow spans of control
- Centralization
- High formalization

The Organic Model

- Cross-functional teams
- Cross-hierarchical teams
- Free flow of information
- Wide spans of control
- Decentralization
- Low formalization

MyManagementLab
For an interactive application of this topic, check out this chapter's simulation activity at **www.mymanagementlab.com.**

the structure must change to accommodate.[29] Most current strategy frameworks focus on three strategy dimensions—innovation, cost minimization, and imitation—and the structural design that works best with each.[30]

To what degree does an organization introduce major new products or services? An **innovation strategy** strives to achieve meaningful and unique innovations. Obviously, not all firms pursue innovation. Apple and 3M do, but conservative retailer Marks & Spencer doesn't. Innovative firms will use competitive pay and benefits to attract top candidates and motivate employees to take risks. Some degree of mechanistic structure can actually benefit innovation. Well-developed communication channels, policies for enhancing long-term commitment, and clear channels of authority all may make it easier for rapid changes to occur smoothly.

An organization pursuing a **cost-minimization strategy** tightly controls costs, refrains from incurring unnecessary expenses, and cuts prices in selling a basic product. This describes the strategy pursued by Walmart and the makers of generic or store-label grocery products. Cost-minimizing organizations pursue fewer policies meant to develop commitment among their workforce.

Organizations following an **imitation strategy** try to both minimize risk and maximize opportunity for profit, moving new products or entering new markets only after innovators have proven their viability. Mass-market fashion

mechanistic model   *A structure characterized by extensive departmentalization, high formalization, a limited information network, and centralization.*

organic model   *A structure that is flat, uses cross-hierarchical and cross-functional teams, has low formalization, possesses a comprehensive information network, and relies on participative decision making.*

innovation strategy   *A strategy that emphasizes the introduction of major new products and services.*

cost-minimization strategy   *A strategy that emphasizes tight cost controls, avoidance of unnecessary innovation or marketing expenses, and price cutting.*

imitation strategy   *A strategy that seeks to move into new products or new markets only after their viability has already been proven.*

Exhibit 15-8	The Strategy–Structure Relationship

Strategy	Structural Option
Innovation	**Organic:** A loose structure; low specialization, low formalization, decentralized
Cost minimization	**Mechanistic:** Tight control; extensive work specialization, high formalization, high centralization
Imitation	**Mechanistic and organic:** Mix of loose with tight properties; tight controls over current activities and looser controls for new undertakings

manufacturers that copy designer styles follow this strategy, as do firms such as Hewlett-Packard and Caterpillar. They follow smaller and more innovative competitors with superior products, but only after competitors have demonstrated the market is there.

Exhibit 15-8 describes the structural option that best matches each strategy. Innovators need the flexibility of the organic structure, whereas cost minimizers seek the efficiency and stability of the mechanistic structure. Imitators combine the two structures. They use a mechanistic structure to maintain tight controls and low costs in their current activities but create organic subunits in which to pursue new undertakings.

Organization Size

An organization's size significantly affects its structure.[31] Organizations that employ 2,000 or more people tend to have more specialization, more departmentalization, more vertical levels, and more rules and regulations than do small organizations. However, size becomes less important as an organization expands. Why? At around 2,000 employees, an organization is already fairly mechanistic; 500 more employees won't have much impact. But adding 500 employees to an organization of only 300 is likely to significantly shift it toward a more mechanistic structure.

Technology

Technology describes the way an organization transfers inputs into outputs. Every organization has at least one technology for converting financial, human, and physical resources into products or services. Ford Motor Company uses an assembly-line process to make its products. Colleges may use a number of instructional technologies—the ever-popular lecture method, case analysis, the experiential exercise, programmed learning, and online instruction and distance learning. Regardless, organizational structures adapt to their technology.

Numerous studies have examined the technology–structure relationship.[32] What differentiates technologies is their *degree of routineness*. Routine activities are characterized by automated and standardized operations. Examples are injection-mold production of plastic knobs, automated transaction processing of sales transactions, and the printing and binding of this book. Nonroutine activities are customized and require frequent revision and updating. They include furniture restoring, custom shoemaking, genetic research, and the writing and editing of this book. In general, organizations engaged in nonroutine activities tend to prefer organic structures, while those performing routine activities prefer mechanistic structures.

These employees of a restaurant in Urumqi, China, stand in formation while attending a meeting before they start their jobs. It's a common practice in China for employers to gather employees before they begin work to give them a pep talk and instructions for their work day. This daily ritual is acceptable to Chinese employees because power distance is high in China and workers are much more accepting of mechanistic structures than those from lower power-distance cultures. Research suggests that a nation's culture and its employees' preference for structure will influence worker performance and satisfaction.

Source: Li Ziheng /Newscom.

Environment

An organization's **environment** includes outside institutions or forces that can affect its performance, such as suppliers, customers, competitors, government regulatory agencies, and public pressure groups. Dynamic environments create significantly more uncertainty for managers than do static ones. To minimize uncertainty, managers may broaden their structure to sense and respond to threats. For example, most companies, including Pepsi and Southwest Airlines, have added social networking departments to counter negative information posted on blogs. Or companies may form strategic alliances, such as when Microsoft and Yahoo! joined forces to better compete with Google.

Any organization's environment has three dimensions: capacity, volatility, and complexity.[33] *Capacity* refers to the degree to which the environment can support growth. Rich and growing environments generate excess resources, which can buffer the organization in times of relative scarcity.

Volatility describes the degree of instability in the environment. A dynamic environment with a high degree of unpredictable change makes it difficult for management to make accurate predictions. Because information technology changes at such a rapid place, for instance, more organizations' environments are becoming volatile.

Finally, *complexity* is the degree of heterogeneity and concentration among environmental elements. Simple environments—like the tobacco industry—are homogeneous and concentrated. Environments characterized by heterogeneity and dispersion—like the broadband industry—are complex and diverse, with numerous competitors.

technology *The way in which an organization transfers its inputs into outputs.*

environment *Institutions or forces outside an organization that potentially affect the organization's performance.*

Myth or Science?

"Employees Resent Outsourcing"

Surprisingly, this statement appears to be false.

Two relatively new ways organizations restructure themselves are *outsourcing* (moving work to another domestic company) and *offshoring* (moving work to another country). For example, a Denver-based company that contracts with a call center vendor in Cleveland is outsourcing those operations. If the same company decides to contact with a call center in Bangalore, India, it is offshoring.

Like downsizing, outsourcing and offshoring are restructuring efforts primarily pursued for cost-saving

reasons; some companies might undertake all three. All result in job loss for the organization.

Yet, a recent study of 13,683 U.S. employees (all of whom retained their jobs) suggests that employees react differently to these three restructuring efforts. Predictably, where downsizing and offshoring occurred, employees reacted negatively, reporting significantly lower job satisfaction and organizational commitment than in matched organizations where they did not occur. Surprisingly, however, this study found no negative effects of outsourcing on these attitudes.

The authors speculate that employees may view outsourcing less negatively because they see it as less of a threat to their jobs. Future research is needed to test this explanation.

Sources: C. P. Maertz, J. W. Wiley, C. LeRouge, and M. A. Campion, "Downsizing Effects on Survivors: Layoffs, Offshoring, and Outsourcing," *Industrial Relations* 49, no. 2 (2010), pp. 275–285; and L. H. Nishii, D. P. Lepak, and B. Schneider, "Employee Attributions of the 'Why' of HR Practices: Their Effects on Employee Attitudes and Behaviors, and Customer Satisfaction," *Personnel Psychology* 61, no. 3 (2008), pp. 503–545.

Exhibit 15-9 summarizes our definition of the environment along its three dimensions. The arrows indicate movement toward higher uncertainty. Thus, organizations that operate in environments characterized as scarce, dynamic, and complex face the greatest degree of uncertainty because they have high unpredictability, little room for error, and a diverse set of elements in the environment to monitor constantly.

Given this three-dimensional definition of *environment,* we can offer some general conclusions about environmental uncertainty and structural arrangements. The more scarce, dynamic, and complex the environment, the more organic a structure should be. The more abundant, stable, and simple the environment, the more the mechanistic structure will be preferred.

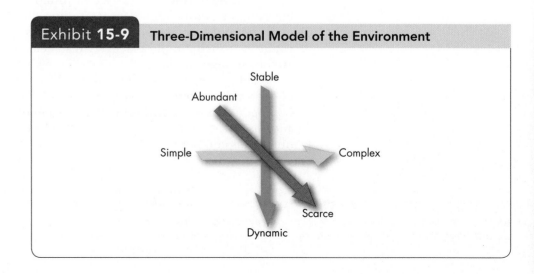
Exhibit 15-9   **Three-Dimensional Model of the Environment**

Organizational Designs and Employee Behavior

7 Analyze the behavioral implications of different organizational designs.

We opened this chapter by implying that an organization's structure can have significant effects on its members. What might those effects be?

A review of the evidence leads to a pretty clear conclusion: you can't generalize! Not everyone prefers the freedom and flexibility of organic structures. Different factors stand out in different structures as well. In highly formalized, heavily structured, mechanistic organizations, the level of fairness in formal policies and procedures is a very important predictor of satisfaction. In more personal, individually adaptive organic organizations, employees value interpersonal justice more.[34] Some people are most productive and satisfied when work tasks are standardized and ambiguity minimized—that is, in mechanistic structures. So, any discussion of the effect of organizational design on employee behavior has to address individual differences. To do so, let's consider employee preferences for work specialization, span of control, and centralization.[35]

The evidence generally indicates that *work specialization* contributes to higher employee productivity—but at the price of reduced job satisfaction. However, work specialization is not an unending source of higher productivity. Problems start to surface, and productivity begins to suffer, when the human diseconomies of doing repetitive and narrow tasks overtake the economies of specialization. As the workforce has become more highly educated and desirous of jobs that are intrinsically rewarding, we seem to reach the point at which productivity begins to decline more quickly than in the past.

There is still a segment of the workforce that prefers the routine and repetitiveness of highly specialized jobs. Some individuals want work that makes minimal intellectual demands and provides the security of routine; for them, high work specialization is a source of job satisfaction. The question, of course, is whether they represent 2 percent of the workforce or 52 percent. Given that some self-selection operates in the choice of careers, we might conclude that negative behavioral outcomes from high specialization are most likely to surface in professional jobs occupied by individuals with high needs for personal growth and diversity.

It is probably safe to say no evidence supports a relationship between *span of control* and employee satisfaction or performance. Although it is intuitively attractive to argue that large spans might lead to higher employee performance because they provide more distant supervision and more opportunity for personal initiative, the research fails to support this notion. Some people like to be left alone; others prefer the security of a boss who is quickly available at all times. Consistent with several of the contingency theories of leadership discussed in Chapter 12, we would expect factors such as employees' experiences and abilities and the degree of structure in their tasks to explain when wide or narrow spans of control are likely to contribute to their performance and job satisfaction. However, some evidence indicates that a *manager's* job satisfaction increases as the number of employees supervised increases.

We find fairly strong evidence linking *centralization* and job satisfaction. In general, less centralized organizations have a greater amount of autonomy. And autonomy appears positively related to job satisfaction. But, again, while one employee may value freedom, another may find autonomous environments frustratingly ambiguous.

Our conclusion: to maximize employee performance and satisfaction, managers must take individual differences, such as experience, personality, and the work task, into account. Culture should factor in, too.

We can draw one obvious insight: other things equal, people don't select employers randomly. They are attracted to, are selected by, and stay with organizations that suit their personal characteristics.[36] Job candidates who prefer predictability are likely to seek out and take employment in mechanistic structures, and those who want autonomy are more likely to end up in an organic structure. Thus, the effect of structure on employee behavior is undoubtedly reduced when the selection process facilitates proper matching of individual characteristics with organizational characteristics.

Although research is slim, it does suggest national culture influences the preference for structure.[37] Organizations that operate with people from high power-distance cultures, such as Greece, France, and most of Latin America, find their employees are much more accepting of mechanistic structures than are employees from low power-distance countries. So consider cultural differences along with individual differences when predicting how structure will affect employee performance and satisfaction.

MyManagementLab

Now that you have finished this chapter, go back to **www.mymanagementlab.com** to continue practicing and applying the concepts you've learned.

Summary and Implications for Managers

The theme of this chapter is that an organization's internal structure contributes to explaining and predicting behavior. That is, in addition to individual and group factors, the structural relationships in which people work has a bearing on employee attitudes and behavior. What's the basis for this argument? To the degree that an organization's structure reduces ambiguity for employees and clarifies concerns such as "What am I supposed to do?" "How am I supposed to do it?" "To whom do I report?" and "To whom do I go if I have a problem?" it shapes their attitudes and facilitates and motivates them to higher levels of performance. Exhibit 15-10 summarizes what we've discussed. There are a few other take-home messages worth considering:

- Although specialization can bring efficiency, excessive specialization also can breed dissatisfaction and reduced motivation.

Exhibit 15-10   Organization Structure: Its Determinants and Outcomes

The End of Management

Management—at least as we know it—is dying. Formal organizational structures are giving way to flatter, less bureaucratic, less formal structures. And that's a good thing.

Today, leaders are celebrated for triumphing *over* structure rather than for working well within it. Innovative companies like Apple, Google, Facebook, Twitter, and Groupon were born and thrive thanks not to a multilayered bureaucracy but to an innovative idea that was creatively executed by a flexible group of people freely collaborating. Management in those companies exists to facilitate, rather than control.

Only 100 of today's *Fortune* 500 companies existed in 1957. Yet management theory and practice continue to hew to a 1957 mode of thinking. As one future-minded expert noted, "The single biggest reason companies fail is that they overinvest in what is, as opposed to what might be." How does a traditional, formal, bureaucratic structure foster "what might be" thinking? It doesn't.

Inertia can cause even innovative companies to become bureaucratized. Google co-founder Larry Page replaced ex-CEO Eric Schmidt when Page's "desire to move quickly on ambitious ideas was stifled by company bureaucracy." Page and co-founder Sergey Brin know traditional, bureaucratic structures are Google's greatest threats.

Some enlightened leaders have learned from their mistakes. Early in his career, says Cristóbal Conde, president and CEO of IT company SunGard, "I was very command-and-control, very top-down. I felt I was smart, and that my decisions would be better." After some of his best people left because they felt constrained, Conde decided to flatten and loosen the structure. He says: "A CEO needs to focus more on the platform that enables collaboration. . . . By having technologies that allow people to see what others are doing, share information, collaborate, brag about their successes—that is what flattens the organization."

There is no "right size fits all" approach to organizational structure. How flat, informal, and collaborative an organization should be depends on many factors. Let's consider two cases.

People lauded how loosely and informally Warren Buffett structured his investment firm, Berkshire Hathaway. Buffett spends most of his day reading and talking informally "with highly gifted people whom he trusts and who trust him." This all sounded wonderful until it was discovered Buffett's CFO and heir apparent David Sokol was on the take. Sokol made $3 million when he successfully lobbied for Berkshire Hathaway to acquire a firm in which he had secretly acquired a significant stake. His insider maneuvers discovered, Sokol was forced to resign. Wouldn't Buffett have known Sokol was compromised if he supervised more closely or had structures in place to check such "freedom"? It's hard to argue with Berkshire Hathaway's past successes, but they don't prove the company is ideally structured.

Berkshire Hathaway is a cautionary example of the perils of a structure that's *too* flat and informal. For the benefits of a formal, complex structure, look no further than Boeing. Boeing's 787 "Dreamliner"—built of composite materials and 20 percent more fuel efficient than comparable passenger planes—is one of the most innovative products in the history of aviation and the fastest-selling ever. How was the Dreamliner invented and produced? Through an enormously complex planning, design, engineering, production, and testing process. To build the Dreamliner, Boeing has contracted with 40 different suppliers at 135 sites around the world—a feat it could not accomplish without an organizational structure to support it. Boeing's organizational structure is quite formal, complex, and even bureaucratic. The Dreamliner proves innovation does not need to come from radical organizational structures.

Sources: A. Bryant, "Structure? The Flatter the Better," *The New York Times* (January 17, 2010), p. BU2; A. R. Sorkin, "Delegator in Chief," *The New York Times* (April 24, 2011), p. B4; A. Murray, "The End of Management," *The Wall Street Journal* (August 21, 2010), p. W3; and A. Efrati and S. Morrison, "Chief Seeks More Agile Google," *The Wall Street Journal* (January 22, 2011), pp. B1, B4.

- Formal hierarchies offer advantages like unification of mission and goals, while employees in excessively rigid hierarchies can feel they have no power or autonomy. As with specialization, the key is striking the right balance.

- Virtual and boundaryless forms are changing the face of many organizations. Contemporary managers should thoroughly understand their implications and recognize advantages and potential pitfalls.

- Organizational downsizing can lead to major cost savings and focus organizations around their core competencies, but it can leave workers dissatisfied and worried about the future of their jobs.

- When determining an appropriate organizational form, managers will need to consider scarcity, dynamism, and complexity of the environment and balance the organic and mechanistic elements appropriate to their organization's environment.

QUESTIONS FOR REVIEW

1 What are the six key elements that define an organization's structure?

2 What is a bureaucracy, and how does it differ from a simple structure?

3 What is a matrix organization?

4 What are the characteristics of a virtual organization?

5 How can managers create a boundaryless organization?

6 Why do organizational structures differ, and what is the difference between a mechanistic structure and an organic structure?

7 What are the behavioral implications of different organizational designs?

EXPERIENTIAL EXERCISE Dismantling a Bureaucracy

Pre-work

In order to understand how to improve an organizational structure, it is important to start with a clear understanding of how an organization is currently structured. For this exercise, you will perform research on the college or university you are attending or another organization that your professor identifies. Using the organization's Web site, find out about different administrative units, paying special attention to different noncore functions like finance, information technology, and human resources. While doing this research, assemble a list of five features that resemble a bureaucracy and five features that you think might be successfully managed by an external partner.

Create Groups

Your instructor will form you into groups of at least four individuals at the start of class.

Assess Bureaucracy

Your initial task will be to share your assessments of the features of the organization that seem bureaucratic in nature. What are the common functions that tend to be run in a bureaucratic manner? Try to identify standardized work practices that enhance coordination and control. In particular, think of systems of rules, regulations, departments, and offices that have highly specific and specialized roles. Collectively, your team will take about 15 minutes to accomplish this task.

Dismantle Bureaucracy

To dismantle a bureaucracy, it is important to consider both the advantages and disadvantages of the current system. Thus, the goal of the second part of the exercise is to employ techniques related to boundaryless and virtual organizations to reduce bureaucracy in a debate format, with one person arguing for why changes can be good, while the other person argues for why changes might be disruptive.

The team will start by dividing into two subgroups and will work in these groups independently for about 10 minutes. One member will have the responsibility to identify alternative mechanisms that might be able to replace the current bureaucratic structure while still keeping all the same functions "in-house" by creating a boundaryless organization. How can the organizations get the same results but with a different set of control systems? Another member will identify reasons it might be difficult to transition from a bureaucracy to the system you advocated in point #2. What are the potential sources of resistance to change? These two members should work together to arrive at a consensus for how bureaucracy might be minimized without damaging organizational productivity and efficiency.

At the same time, the second group of two individuals will work on a different task. One member will consider how each organization can take on elements of a virtual organization as a way to become less bureaucratic. Identify elements of the organization that might be downsized or outsourced. Another member will identify why "going virtual" might be a bad idea, looking to potential loss of control and poor information exchange as possible obstacles. These two members will arrive at a consensus for how the organization can be made as lean as possible without damaging organizational productivity and efficiency.

Finally, all four members of the team will come together to arrive at a consensus for how to limit bureaucracy by either (1) using new systems that are consistent with a boundaryless organization or (2) using elements of a lean, virtual organization to strip off unnecessary bureaucratic layers. This final combination process should take about 10 minutes.

Debriefing

After each group has come to a consensus for how to limit bureaucracy, the instructor will lead an all-class discussion in which each group will describe its eventual approach to minimizing bureaucracy in its organization. Your instructor will provide additional insight into why it may be difficult to change a bureaucracy, as well as suggesting areas where bureaucracy can be effectively limited through either boundarylessness or virtuality.

ETHICAL DILEMMA **Directing the Directors**

One critical structural element of most corporations is the board of directors. In principle, chief executives report to the directors. In practice, however, boards do not always function as you might expect. Boards were implicated in many corporate scandals of the past decade—either because they actively condoned unethical behavior or because they turned a blind eye to it. Many also blamed lax board oversight for the financial meltdown and ensuing recession. Business media have called boards "absolutely useless" and "a sham."

One of the keys to reforming board behavior is ensuring that boards function independently of the CEO. The Securities and Exchange Commission (SEC) and the New York Stock Exchange (NYSE) have set guidelines for the independence of directors—who should not be otherwise affiliated with, employed by, or connected to the organization they direct. The more independent the structure and composition of the board, the better the corporation will be governed, and the more effective it will be.

One example of nonindependence came to light in 2010. In addition to $225,000 in cash and deferred stock he was paid to function as a member of Citibank's board, Robert Joss earned $350,000 in consulting fees for advising the bank on projects "from time to time." When asked to comment, Joss replied, "I'm comfortable that I can handle that."

Such examples seem egregious violations of independence in board structures. Yet, evidence on the link between board independence and firm performance is surprisingly weak. One recent review concluded, "There is no evidence of systematic relationships between board composition and corporate financial performance."

Another structural issue is how the roles of the CEO and chairperson are filled—for instance, whether these positions are held by different people. Most argue that for the board to function independently, the roles must be separate, and *Bloomberg Businessweek* estimates that 37 percent of the 500 largest U.S. corporations do split them. Yet here, too, the evidence is weak: it doesn't appear that corporations with separate CEOs and chairs perform any better than those where the CEO and chairperson are one and the same.

Questions

1. Do you think Citibank's consulting arrangement with Robert Joss was unethical? Or is it possible to justify the arrangement?

2. Why do you think board structure doesn't appear to matter to corporate performance?

3. Do you think the roles of CEO and chairperson of the board of directors should always be separate? Why or why not?

Sources: D. R. Dalton and C. M. Dalton, "Integration of Micro and Macro Studies in Governance Research: CEO Duality, Board Composition, and Financial Performance," *Journal of Management* 37, no. 2 (2011), pp. 404–411; T. J. Neff and R. Charan, "Separating the CEO and Chairman Roles," *Bloomberg Businessweek* (January 15, 2010), downloaded July 5, 2011, from www.businessweek.com/; B. Keoun, "Citigroup to Pay Director $350,000 for Weeks of Consulting," *Bloomberg News* (May 10, 2010), downloaded July 5, 2011, from www.bloomberg.com/news/.

CASE INCIDENT 1 Creative Deviance: Bucking the Hierarchy?

One of the major functions of an organizational hierarchy is to increase standardization and control for top managers. Using the chain of command, managers can direct the activities of subordinates toward a common purpose. If the right person with a creative vision is in charge of a hierarchy, the results can be phenomenal. Until Steve Jobs' regrettable passing in October of 2011, Apple had used a strongly top-down creative process in which most major decisions and innovations flowed directly through Jobs and then were delegated to sub-teams as specific assignments to complete.

Then there is creative deviance, in which individuals create extremely successful products despite being told by senior management to stop working on them. The electrostatic displays used in more than half of Hewlett-Packard's instruments, the tape slitter that was one of the most important process innovations in 3M's history, and Nichia's development of multi-billion-dollar LED bright lighting technology were all officially rejected by the management hierarchy. In all these cases, an approach like Apple's would have shut down some of the most successful products these companies ever produced. Doing "business as usual" can become such an imperative in a hierarchical organization that new ideas are seen as threats rather than opportunities for development.

It's not immediately apparent why top-down decision making works so well for one highly creative company like

Apple, while hierarchy nearly ruined innovations at several other organizations. It may be that Apple's structure is actually quite simple, with relatively few layers and a great deal of responsibility placed on each individual for his or her own outcomes. Or it may be that Apple simply had a very unique leader who was able to rise above the conventional strictures of a CEO to create a culture of constant innovation.

Questions

1. Do you think it's possible for an organization to deliberately create an "anti-hierarchy" to encourage employees to engage in more acts of creative deviance? What steps might a company take to encourage creative deviance?

2. What are the dangers of an approach that encourages creative deviance?

3. Why do you think a company like Apple is able to be creative with a strongly hierarchical structure, whereas other companies find hierarchy limiting?

4. Do you think Apple's success has been entirely dependent upon Steve Jobs' role as head of the hierarchy? What are the potential liabilities of a company that is so strongly connected to the decision-making of a single Individual?

Sources: C. Mainemelis, "Stealing Fire: Creative Deviance in the Evolution of New Ideas," *Academy of Management Review* 35, no. 4 (2010), pp. 558–578; and A. Lashinsky, "Inside Apple," *Fortune* (May 23, 2011), pp. 125–134.

CASE INCIDENT 2 Siemens' Simple Structure—Not

There is perhaps no tougher task for an executive than to restructure a European organization. Ask former Siemens CEO Klaus Kleinfeld.

Siemens—with €76 billion in revenue in financial year 2009/2010, some 405,000 employees, and branches in 190 countries—is one of the largest electronics companies in the world. Although the company has long been respected for its engineering prowess, it's also derided for its sluggishness and mechanistic structure. So when Kleinfeld took over as CEO, he sought to restructure the company, making the structure less bureaucratic so decisions are made more quickly. He spun off underperforming businesses and simplified the company's structure.

One of the challenges of transforming European organizations is the customary participation of employees in executive decisions. Half the seats on the Seimens board of directors are allocated to labor representatives. Not surprisingly, labor did not react positively to Kleinfeld's restructuring efforts, and picket lines became a constant presence outside his corporate offices. In his efforts to speed the restructuring, labor groups alleged, Kleinfeld secretly bankrolled a business-friendly workers' group to try to undermine Germany's main industrial union.

Due to this and other allegations, Kleinfeld was forced out in June 2007 and replaced by Peter Löscher. Löscher has found the same tensions between inertia and the need for restructuring. Only a month after becoming CEO, he faced the decision whether to spin off the firm's underperforming €10 billion auto parts unit, VDO. He had to weigh the forces for stability, which want to protect worker interests, against U.S.-style pressures for financial performance. One of VDO's possible buyers was a U.S. company, TRW, the controlling interest of which is held by Blackstone, a U.S. private equity firm. German labor representatives scorn such firms as "locusts." When Löscher decided to sell VDO to German tire giant Continental Corporation, Continental promptly began to downsize and restructure the unit's operations.

Löscher has continued to restructure Siemens. In mid-2008, he announced elimination of nearly 17,000 jobs worldwide. He also announced plans to consolidate more business units and reorganize the company's operations geographically. "The speed at which business is changing worldwide has increased considerably, and we're orienting Siemens accordingly," Löscher said.

Under Löscher, Siemens has experienced its ups and downs. In 2008, its stock price fell 26 percent on the European stock exchange and 31 percent on the New York Stock Exchange. In 2009, however, Siemens' earnings were up 32 percent, despite an ongoing global recession, and most indicators suggested 2011 would be an equally profitable year.

Though Löscher's restructuring efforts have generated far less controversy than Kleinfeld's, that doesn't mean they went over well with all constituents. Of the 2008 job cuts, Werner Neugebauer, regional director for a union representing many Siemens employees, said, "The planned job cuts are incomprehensible nor acceptable for these reasons, and in this extent, completely exaggerated."

Questions

1. What do Kleinfeld's efforts at Siemens tell you about the difficulties of restructuring organizations?

2. Why do you think Löscher's restructuring decisions have generated less controversy than did Kleinfeld's?

3. Assume a colleague read this case and concluded, "This case proves restructuring efforts do not necessarily improve a company's financial performance." How would you respond?

4. Do you think a CEO who decides to restructure or downsize a company takes the well-being of employees into account? Should he or she do so? Why or why not?

Sources: Based on A. Davidson, "Peter Löscher Makes Siemens Less German," *The Sunday Times* (June 29, 2008), business.timesonline.co.uk; M. Esterl and D. Crawford, "Siemens CEO Put to Early Test," *The Wall Street Journal* (July 23, 2007), p. A8; J. Ewing, "Siemens' Culture Clash," *BusinessWeek* (January 29, 2007), pp. 42–46; and C. C. Williams, "Slimmed-Down Siemens Girds for Growth," *Barron's* (November 29, 2010), pp. 26–27.

ENDNOTES

1. See, for instance, R. L. Daft, *Organization Theory and Design,* 10th ed. (Cincinnati, OH: South-Western Publishing, 2010).

2. T. W. Malone, R. J. Laubacher, and T. Johns, "The Age of Hyperspecialization," *Harvard Business Review* (July–August 2011), pp. 56–65.

3. C. Hymowitz, "Managers Suddenly Have to Answer to a Crowd of Bosses," *The Wall Street Journal* (August 12, 2003), p. B1.

4. See, for instance, "How Hierarchy Can Hurt Strategy Execution," *Harvard Business Review* (July–August 2010), pp. 74–75.

5. See, for instance, J. H. Gittell, "Supervisory Span, Relational Coordination, and Flight Departure Performance: A Reassessment of Postbureaucracy Theory," *Organization Science* (July–August 2001), pp. 468–483.

6. J. Child and R. G. McGrath, "Organizations Unfettered: Organizational Form in an Information-Intensive Economy," *Academy of Management Journal* (December 2001), pp. 1135–1148.

7. B. Brown and S. D. Anthony, "How P&G Tripled Its Innovation Success Rate," *Harvard Business Review* (June 2011), pp. 64–72.

8. A. Leiponen and C. E. Helfat, "Location, Decentralization, and Knowledge Sources for Innovation," *Organization Science* 22, no. 3 (2011), pp. 641–658.

9. H. Mintzberg, *Structure in Fives: Designing Effective Organizations* (Upper Saddle River, NJ: Prentice Hall, 1983), p. 157.

10. W. M. Bulkeley, "Back from the Brink," *The Wall Street Journal* (April 24, 2006), pp. B1, B3.

11. L. R. Burns and D. R. Wholey, "Adoption and Abandonment of Matrix Management Programs: Effects of Organizational Characteristics and Interorganizational Networks," *Academy of Management Journal* (February 1993), pp. 106–138; J. R. Galbraith, *Designing Matrix Organizations that Actually Work: How IBM, Procter & Gamble, and Others Design for Success* (San Francisco: Jossey Bass, 2009); and E. Krell, "Managing the Matrix," *HRMagazine* (April 2011), pp. 69–71.

12. See, for instance, T. Sy and L. S. D'Annunzio, "Challenges and Strategies of Matrix Organizations: Top-Level and Mid-Level Managers' Perspectives," *Human Resource Planning* 28, no. 1 (2005), pp. 39–48; and T. Sy and S. Cote, "Emotional Intelligence: A Key Ability to Succeed in the Matrix Organization," *Journal of Management Development* 23, no. 5 (2004), pp. 437–455.

13. N. Anand and R. L. Daft, "What Is the Right Organization Design?" *Organizational Dynamics* 36, no. 4 (2007), pp. 329–344.

14. See, for instance, R. E. Miles and C. C. Snow, "The New Network Firm: A Spherical Structure Built on Human Investment Philosophy," *Organizational Dynamics* (Spring 1995), pp. 5–18; D. Pescovitz, "The Company Where Everybody's a Temp," *New York Times Magazine* (June 11, 2000), pp. 94–96; B. Hedberg, G. Dahlgren, J. Hansson, and N. Olve, *Virtual Organizations and Beyond* (New York: Wiley, 2001); N. S. Contractor, S. Wasserman, and K. Faust, "Testing Multitheoretical, Multilevel Hypotheses About Organizational Networks: An Analytic Framework and Empirical Example," *Academy of Management Review* 31, no. 3 (2006) pp. 681–703; and Y. Shin, "A Person-Environment Fit Model for Virtual Organizations," *Journal of Management* (October 2004), pp. 725–743.

15. J. Bates, "Making Movies and Moving On," *Los Angeles Times* (January 19, 1998), p. A1.

16. D. Dahl, "Want a Job? Let the Bidding Begin," *Inc.* (March 2011), pp. 94–96.

17. J. Schramm, "At Work in a Virtual World," *HR Magazine* (June 2010), p. 152.

18. C. B. Gibson and J. L. Gibbs, "Unpacking the Concept of Virtuality: The Effects of Geographic Dispersion, Electronic Dependence, Dynamic Structure, and National Diversity on Team Innovation," *Administrative Science Quarterly* 51, no. 3 (2006), pp. 451–495; H. M. Latapie and V. N. Tran, "Subculture Formation, Evolution, and Conflict Between Regional Teams in Virtual Organizations," *The Business Review* (Summer 2007), pp. 189–193; and S. Davenport and U. Daellenbach, "'Belonging' to a Virtual Research Center: Exploring the Influence of Social Capital Formation Processes on Member Identification in a Virtual Organization" *British Journal of Management* 22, no. 1 (2011), pp. 54–76.

19. "GE: Just Your Average Everyday $60 Billion Family Grocery Store," *IndustryWeek* (May 2, 1994), pp. 13–18.

20. The following is based on D. D. Davis, "Form, Function and Strategy in Boundaryless Organizations," in A. Howard (ed.), *The Changing Nature of Work* (San Francisco: Jossey-Bass, 1995), pp. 112–138; R. L. Cross, A. Yan, and M. R. Louis, "Boundary Activities in 'Boundaryless' Organizations: A Case Study of a Transformation to a Team-Based Structure," *Human Relations* (June 2000), pp. 841–868; and R. Ashkenas, D. Ulrich, T. Jick, and S. Kerr, *The Boundaryless Organization: Breaking the Chains of Organizational Structure*, revised and updated (San Francisco: Jossey-Bass, 2002).

21. See, for example, U. Wassmer, "Alliance Portfolios: A Review and Research Agenda," *Journal of Management* 36, no. 1 (2010), pp 141–171; A. M. Hess and F. T. Rothaemel, "When Are Assets Complementary? Star Scientists, Strategic Alliances, and Innovation in the Pharmaceutical Industry," *Strategic Management Journal* 32, no. 8 (2011), pp. 895–909; and J. A. Adegbesan and M. J. Higgins, "The Intra-Alliance Division of Value Created through Collaboration," *Strategic Management Journal* 32, no. 2 (2011), pp. 187–211.

22. B. White, "VeriSign to Slim Down, Sharpen Its Focus," *The Wall Street Journal* (November 14, 2007), p. A12.

23. S. Player, "Leading the Way to Lean," *Business Finance* (May 2007), pp. 13–16.

24. See J. P. Guthrie and D. K. Datta, "Dumb and Dumber: The Impact of Downsizing on Firm Performance as Moderated by Industry Conditions," *Organization Science* 19, no. 1 (2008), pp. 108–123; and K. P. De Meuse, T. J. Bergmann, P. A. Vanderheiden, and C. E. Roraff, "New Evidence Regarding Organizational Downsizing and a Firm's Financial Performance: A Long-Term Analysis," *Journal of Managerial Issues* 16, no. 2 (2004), pp. 155–177.

25. See, for example, C. O. Trevor and A. J. Nyberg, "Keeping Your Headcount When All About You Are Losing Theirs: Downsizing, Voluntary Turnover Rates, and the Moderating Role of HR Practices," *Academy of Management Journal* 51, no. 2 (2008), pp. 259–276; T. M. Probst, S. M. Stewart, M. L. Gruys, and B. W. Tierney, "Productivity, Counterproductivity and Creativity: The Ups and Downs of Job Insecurity," *Journal of Occupational and Organizational Psychology* 80, no. 3 (2007), pp. 479–497; and C. P. Maertz, J. W. Wiley, C. LeRouge, and M. A. Campion, "Downsizing Effects on Survivors: Layoffs, Offshoring, and Outsourcing," *Industrial Relations* 49, no. 2 (2010), pp. 275–285.

26. C. D. Zatzick, and R. D. Iverson, "High-Involvement Management and Workforce Reduction: Competitive Advantage or Disadvantage?" *Academy of Management Journal* 49, no. 5 (2006), pp. 999–1015; A. Travaglione, and B. Cross, "Diminishing the Social Network in Organizations: Does There Need to Be Such a Phenomenon as 'Survivor Syndrome' After Downsizing?" *Strategic Change* 15, no. 1 (2006), pp. 1–13; and J. D. Kammeyer-Mueller, H. Liao, and R. D. Arvey, "Downsizing and Organizational Performance: A Review of the Literature from a Stakeholder Perspective," *Research in Personnel and Human Resources Management* 20 (2001), pp. 269–329.

27. T. Burns and G. M. Stalker, *The Management of Innovation* (London: Tavistock, 1961); and J. A. Courtright, G. T. Fairhurst, and L. E. Rogers, "Interaction Patterns in Organic and Mechanistic Systems," *Academy of Management Journal* (December 1989), pp. 773–802.

28. This analysis is referred to as a contingency approach to organization design. See, for instance, J. M. Pennings, "Structural

Contingency Theory: A Reappraisal," in B. M. Staw and L. L. Cummings (eds.), *Research in Organizational Behavior*, vol. 14 (Greenwich, CT: JAI Press, 1992), pp. 267–309; J. R. Hollenbeck, H. Moon, A. P. J. Ellis, B. J. West, D. R. Ilgen, L. Sheppard, C. O. L. H. Porter, and J. A. Wagner III, "Structural Contingency Theory and Individual Differences: Examination of External and Internal Person-Team Fit," *Journal of Applied Psychology* (June 2002), pp. 599–606; and A. Drach-Zahavy and A. Freund, "Team Effectiveness Under Stress: A Structural Contingency Approach," *Journal of Organizational Behavior* 28, no. 4 (2007), pp. 423–450.

29. The strategy–structure thesis was originally proposed in A. D. Chandler Jr., *Strategy and Structure: Chapters in the History of the Industrial Enterprise* (Cambridge, MA: MIT Press, 1962). For an updated analysis, see T. L. Amburgey and T. Dacin, "As the Left Foot Follows the Right? The Dynamics of Strategic and Structural Change," *Academy of Management Journal* (December 1994), pp. 1427–1452.

30. See R. E. Miles and C. C. Snow, *Organizational Strategy, Structure, and Process* (New York: McGraw-Hill, 1978); D. C. Galunic and K. M. Eisenhardt, "Renewing the Strategy–Structure–Performance Paradigm," in B. M. Staw and L. L. Cummings (eds.), *Research in Organizational Behavior*, vol. 16 (Greenwich, CT: JAI Press, 1994), pp. 215–255; and S. M. Toh, F. P. Morgeson, and M. A. Campion, "Human Resource Configurations: Investigating Fit with the Organizational Context," *Journal of Applied Psychology* 93, no. 4 (2008), pp. 864–882.

31. See, for instance, P. M. Blau and R. A. Schoenherr, *The Structure of Organizations* (New York: Basic Books, 1971); D. S. Pugh, "The Aston Program of Research: Retrospect and Prospect," in A. H. Van de Ven and W. F. Joyce (eds.), *Perspectives on Organization Design and Behavior* (New York: Wiley, 1981), pp. 135–166; R. Z. Gooding and J. A. Wagner III, "A Meta-Analytic Review of the Relationship Between Size and Performance: The Productivity and Efficiency of Organizations and Their Subunits," *Administrative Science Quarterly* (December 1985), pp. 462–481; and A. C. Bluedorn, "Pilgrim's Progress: Trends and Convergence in Research on Organizational Size and Environments," *Journal of Management* (Summer 1993), pp. 163–192.

32. See C. Perrow, "A Framework for the Comparative Analysis of Organizations," *American Sociological Review* (April 1967), pp. 194–208; J. Hage and M. Aiken, "Routine Technology, Social Structure, and Organizational Goals," *Administrative Science Quarterly* (September 1969), pp. 366–377; C. C. Miller, W. H. Glick, Y. Wang, and G. P. Huber, "Understanding Technology-Structure Relationships: Theory Development and Meta-Analytic Theory Testing," *Academy of Management Journal* (June 1991), pp. 370–399; and W. D. Sine, H. Mitsuhashi, and D. A. Kirsch, "Revisiting Burns and Stalker: Formal Structure and New Venture Performance in Emerging Economic Sectors," *Academy of Management Journal* 49, no. 1 (2006), pp. 121–132.

33. G. G. Dess and D. W. Beard, "Dimensions of Organizational Task Environments," *Administrative Science Quarterly* (March 1984), pp. 52–73; E. A. Gerloff, N. K. Muir, and W. D. Bodensteiner, "Three Components of Perceived Environmental Uncertainty: An Exploratory Analysis of the Effects of Aggregation," *Journal of Management* (December 1991), pp. 749–768; and O. Shenkar, N. Aranya, and T. Almor, "Construct Dimensions in the Contingency Model: An Analysis Comparing Metric and Non-metric Multivariate Instruments," *Human Relations* (May 1995), pp. 559–580.

34. C. S. Spell and T. J. Arnold, "A Multi-Level Analysis of Organizational Justice and Climate, Structure, and Employee Mental Health," *Journal of Management* 33, no. 5 (2007), pp. 724–751; and M. L. Ambrose and M. Schminke, "Organization Structure as a Moderator of the Relationship Between Procedural Justice, Interactional Justice, Perceived Organizational Support, and Supervisory Trust," *Journal of Applied Psychology* 88, no. 2 (2003), pp. 295–305.

35. See, for instance, Spell and Arnold, "A Multi-Level Analysis of Organizational Justice Climate, Structure, and Employee Mental Health"; J. D. Shaw and N. Gupta, "Job Complexity, Performance, and Well-Being: When Does Supplies-Values Fit Matter? *Personnel Psychology* 57, no. 4 (2004), 847–879; and C. Anderson and C. E. Brown, "The Functions and Dysfunctions of Hierarchy," *Research in Organizational Behavior* 30 (2010), pp. 55–89.

36. See, for instance, R. E. Ployhart, J. A. Weekley, and K. Baughman, "The Structure and Function of Human Capital Emergence: A Multilevel Examination of the Attraction-Selection-Attrition Model," *Academy of Management Journal* 49, no. 4 (2006), pp. 661–677.

37. See, for example, P. R. Harris and R. T. Moran, *Managing Cultural Differences*, 5th ed. (Houston, TX: Gulf Publishing, 1999).

LEARNING OBJECTIVES

After studying this chapter, you should be able to:

1. Define *organizational culture,* and describe its common characteristics.

2. Compare the functional and dysfunctional effects of organizational culture on people and the organization.

3. Identify the factors that create and sustain an organization's culture.

4. Show how culture is transmitted to employees.

5. Demonstrate how an ethical culture can be created.

6. Describe a positive organizational culture.

7. Identify characteristics of a spiritual culture.

8. Show how national culture may affect the way organizational culture is transported to a different country.

MyManagementLab

Access a host of interactive learning aids to help strengthen your understanding of the chapter concepts at **www.mymanagementlab.com**.

URSULA M. BURNS AND THE CULTURE OF XEROX

Ursula M. Burns is not your typical CEO. She is unusually low key, avoiding the limelight many of her fellow CEOs—from Apple's former CEO Steve Jobs to GE's Jeffrey Immelt—seem to relish. When asked what first surprised her about being CEO, she mentioned the flood of attention. "The accolades I get for doing absolutely nothing are amazing. What have I done?" she asked. "The real story is not Ursula Burns. I just happen to be the person standing up at this point representing Xerox."

We respectfully disagree. Burns is indeed notable as the first African American female CEO of an S&P 100 company. But the real story is the way she is quietly reshaping the culture of the industrial giant.

Historically, Xerox was a photocopying company, so successful that its name became a verb. However, in the 1980s and 1990s, as that business model declined, so did Xerox's profits. When Anne Mulcahy took over Xerox in 2001, some said she won the job no one else wanted. She and Burns planned a bold transformation that included job cuts, but also investing in new technologies.

Since Burns took over in 2009, she has pushed forward two major initiatives. One is product focused: getting Xerox into information technology services. In 2011, Xerox rolled out Xerox Cloud, a set of business services that includes mobile printing and business process management.

Burns' other initiative is cultural: she thinks Xerox's culture is getting in its way. Burns wants Xerox's 130,000 employees to embrace risk-taking, initiative, and frankness. "Terminal niceness" is how Burns describes a key tenet of Xerox's old culture, one she thinks is often counterproductive to growth and innovation.

Maybe, says Burns, Xerox needs to function more like a real family. "When we're in the family, you don't have to be as nice as when you're outside of the family," she says. "I want us to stay civil and kind, but we have to be frank—and the reason we can be frank is because we are all in the same family."

This delicate balance between civility and frankness requires humility. After all, one of the key ways to lead others to be frank is to be honest about your own limits. Burns does that. "I cannot be viewed as the solution to all problems in this company," she notes. She does not expect perfection in herself, or in others. "People actually believe that before they come to you that they have to have perfection," Burns laments. She would much prefer people be honest, open, and decisive. "Decide," she implores. "Do things."

Burns grew up in a gang-infested area of New York City without a father in her life and credits her mother with raising her aspirations and inspiring her humility. Her mother would often bluntly tell Burns to try to be better.

Organizational Culture

When I hear the word culture,
I reach for my Browning.

—Hanns Johst

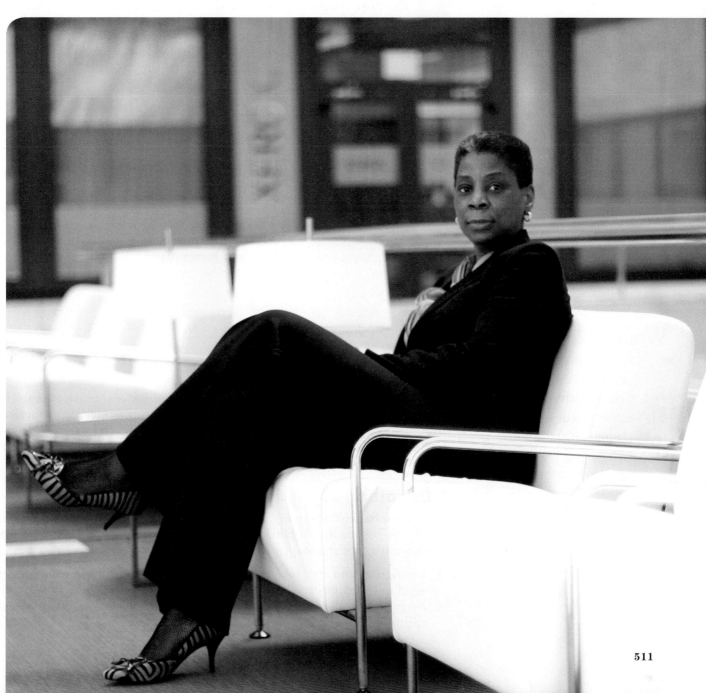

Like every major CEO, Burns is a millionaire. Yet she still shops for groceries. She drives herself to work. She cleans her own house. "Where you are is not who you are," her mother often told her. Burns appears to have lived that credo. With quiet determination, she's trying to make Xerox's culture, in some ways, reflect who she is.

Sources: A. Bryant, "We're Family, So We Can Disagree," *The New York Times* (February 21, 2010), pp. BU1, BU9; K. Damore, "Burns: Blazing A New Trail," *CRN* (May 23, 2011), downloaded on July 15, 2011, from www.crn.com/; and D. Mattioli, "Xerox Makes Push for Faster Services Growth," *The Wall Street Journal* (May 11, 2011), downloaded on July 15, 2011, from http://online.wsj.com/.

A strong organizational culture provides stability to an organization. But as the chapter-opening example shows, it's not for everyone. And for some organizations, it can also be a major barrier to change. In this chapter, we show that every organization has a culture that, depending on its strength, can have a significant influence on the attitudes and behaviors of organization members. First let's figure out what kind of organizational culture you prefer. Take the self-assessment to find out.

SELF-ASSESSMENT LIBRARY

What's the Right Organizational Culture for Me?

In the Self-Assessment Library (available on CD and online), take assessment III.B.1 (What's the Right Organizational Culture for Me?) and answer the following questions.

1. Judging from your results, do you fit better in a more formal and structured culture or in a more informal and unstructured culture?
2. Did your results surprise you? Why do you think you scored as you did?
3. How might your results affect your career path?

What Is Organizational Culture?

1 Define *organizational culture* and describe its common characteristics.

An executive once was asked what he thought *organizational culture* meant. He gave essentially the same answer a U.S. Supreme Court justice once gave in attempting to define pornography: "I can't define it, but I know it when I see it." We, however, need a basic definition of organizational culture to better understand the phenomenon. In this section we propose one and review several related ideas.

A Definition of *Organizational Culture*

Organizational culture refers to a system of shared meaning held by members that distinguishes the organization from other organizations.[1] Seven primary characteristics seem to capture the essence of an organization's culture:[2]

1. **Innovation and risk taking.**   The degree to which employees are encouraged to be innovative and take risks.
2. **Attention to detail.**   The degree to which employees are expected to exhibit precision, analysis, and attention to detail.

3. **Outcome orientation.** The degree to which management focuses on results or outcomes rather than on the techniques and processes used to achieve them.
4. **People orientation.** The degree to which management decisions take into consideration the effect of outcomes on people within the organization.
5. **Team orientation.** The degree to which work activities are organized around teams rather than individuals.
6. **Aggressiveness.** The degree to which people are aggressive and competitive rather than easygoing.
7. **Stability.** The degree to which organizational activities emphasize maintaining the status quo in contrast to growth.

Each of these characteristics exists on a continuum from low to high. Appraising the organization on them, then, gives a composite picture of its culture and a basis for the shared understanding members have about the organization, how things are done in it, and the way they are supposed to behave. Exhibit 16-1

Exhibit **16-1**	Contrasting Organizational Cultures

Organization A

This organization is a manufacturing firm. Managers are expected to fully document all decisions, and "good managers" are those who can provide detailed data to support their recommendations. Creative decisions that incur significant change or risk are not encouraged. Because managers of failed projects are openly criticized and penalized, managers try not to implement ideas that deviate much from the status quo. One lower-level manager quoted an often-used phrase in the company: "If it ain't broke, don't fix it."

There are extensive rules and regulations in this firm that employees are required to follow. Managers supervise employees closely to ensure there are no deviations. Management is concerned with high productivity, regardless of the impact on employee morale or turnover.

Work activities are designed around individuals. There are distinct departments and lines of authority, and employees are expected to minimize formal contact with other employees outside their functional area or line of command. Performance evaluations and rewards emphasize individual effort, although seniority tends to be the primary factor in the determination of pay raises and promotions.

Organization B

This organization is also a manufacturing firm. Here, however, management encourages and rewards risk taking and change. Decisions based on intuition are valued as much as those that are well rationalized. Management prides itself on its history of experimenting with new technologies and its success in regularly introducing innovative products. Managers or employees who have a good idea are encouraged to "run with it." And failures are treated as "learning experiences." The company prides itself on being market driven and rapidly responsive to the changing needs of its customers.

There are few rules and regulations for employees to follow, and supervision is loose because management believes that its employees are hardworking and trustworthy. Management is concerned with high productivity but believes that this comes through treating its people right. The company is proud of its reputation as being a good place to work.

Job activities are designed around work teams, and team members are encouraged to interact with people across functions and authority levels. Employees talk positively about the competition between teams. Individuals and teams have goals, and bonuses are based on achievement of these outcomes. Employees are given considerable autonomy in choosing the means by which the goals are attained.

---

organizational culture *A system of shared meaning held by members that distinguishes the organization from other organizations.*

demonstrates how these characteristics can be mixed to create highly diverse organizations.

Other research has conceptualized culture into four different types based on competing values:[3] the collaborative and cohesive *clan,* the innovative and adaptable *adhocracy,* the controlled and consistent *hierarchy,* and the competitive and customer focused *market.* A review of 94 studies found that job attitudes were especially positive in clan-based cultures, innovation was especially strong in market cultures, and financial performance was especially good in market cultures.[4] Although the competing values framework received some support in this review, the authors noted that further theoretical work needs to ensure it is consistent with the actual cultural values found in organizations.

Culture Is a Descriptive Term

Organizational culture shows how employees perceive the characteristics of an organization's culture, not whether they like them—that is, it's a descriptive term. This is important because it differentiates culture from job satisfaction.

Research on organizational culture has sought to measure how employees see their organization: Does it encourage teamwork? Does it reward innovation? Does it stifle initiative? In contrast, job satisfaction seeks to measure how employees feel about the organization's expectations, reward practices, and the like. Although the two terms have overlapping characteristics, keep in mind that *organizational culture* is descriptive, whereas *job satisfaction* is evaluative.

Do Organizations Have Uniform Cultures?

Organizational culture represents a common perception the organization's members hold. We should therefore expect individuals with different backgrounds or at different levels in the organization to describe its culture in similar terms.[5]

That doesn't mean, however, that there are no subcultures. Most large organizations have a dominant culture and numerous subcultures.[6] A **dominant culture** expresses the **core values** a majority of members share and that give the organization its distinct personality.[7] **Subcultures** tend to develop in large organizations to reflect common problems or experiences members face in the same department or location. The purchasing department can have a subculture that includes the core values of the dominant culture plus additional values unique to members of that department.

If organizations were composed only of numerous subcultures, organizational culture as an independent variable would be significantly less powerful. It is the "shared meaning" aspect of culture that makes it such a potent device for guiding and shaping behavior. That's what allows us to say, for example, that the Zappos culture values customer care and dedication over speed and efficiency and to use that information to better understand the behavior of Zappos executives and employees.[8] But subcultures can influence members' behavior too.

Strong versus Weak Cultures

It's possible to differentiate between strong and weak cultures.[9] If most employees (responding to management surveys) have the same opinions about the organization's mission and values, the culture is strong; if opinions vary widely, the culture is weak.

In a **strong culture,** the organization's core values are both intensely held and widely shared.[10] The more members who accept the core values and the greater their commitment, the stronger the culture and the greater its influence on member behavior, because the high degree of sharedness and intensity creates a climate of high behavioral control. Nordstrom employees know in no *glOBalization!*

Face Culture, Dignity Culture, and Organizational Culture

As we have discussed through-out the book, *culture* can be represented at either the national or the organizational level. Global organizations need to carefully consider the differences in culture across countries to determine which management practices are likely to be most effective with different populations of employees.

Recently, social psychologists have begun to explore the difference between "face" and "dignity" national cultures. In a face culture, individuals use information from others in order to determine who they are, allowing themselves to be defined by social opinions. In a dignity culture, on the other hand, individuals are more eager to define themselves based on their own internal judgments and may be more resistant to outside efforts to define them. Although more research is needed to specify which cultures put more emphasis on social face versus personal dignity in self-definition, most has focused on East Asian countries as face cultures and European countries and the United States and Canada as dignity cultures.

What are the implications of these differences? Individuals from face cultures will be more concerned with the implications of hierarchical judgments on their worth. Thus, organizational cultures in face countries are likely to emphasize roles and titles to give definition to employees and provide them with a secure sense of self. Organizational cultures in dignity countries will be more flexible in providing role definitions, allowing individuals to use self-expression to determine who they are.

Sources: Based on Y. Kim, D. Cohen, and W. Au, "The Jury and Abjury of My Peers: The Self in Face and Dignity Cultures," *Journal of Personality and Social Psychology* 98, no. 6 (2010), pp. 904–916; and Y. Liao and M. H. Bond, "The Dynamics of Face Loss Following Interpersonal Harm for Chinese and Americans," *Journal of Cross-Cultural Psychology* 42, no. 1 (2011), pp. 25–38.

uncertain terms what is expected of them, and these expectations go a long way in shaping their behavior. In contrast, Nordstrom competitor Macy's, which has struggled through an identity crisis, is working to remake its culture.

A strong culture should reduce employee turnover because it demonstrates high agreement about what the organization represents. Such unanimity of purpose builds cohesiveness, loyalty, and organizational commitment. These qualities, in turn, lessen employees' propensity to leave.[11] One study found that the more employees agreed on customer orientation in a service organization, the higher the profitability of the business unit.[12] Another study found that when team managers and team members disagree about perceptions of organizational support, there were more negative moods among team members, and the performance of teams was lower.[13] These negative effects are especially strong when managers believe the organization provides more support than employees think it does.

Culture versus Formalization

We've seen that high formalization creates predictability, orderliness, and consistency. A strong culture achieves the same end without the need for written documentation.[14] Therefore, we should view formalization and culture as two

---

dominant culture   *A culture that expresses the core values that are shared by a majority of the organization's members.*

core values   *The primary or dominant values that are accepted throughout the organization.*

subcultures   *Minicultures within an organization, typically defined by department designations and geographical separation.*

strong culture   *A culture in which the core values are intensely held and widely shared.*

different roads to a common destination. The stronger an organization's culture, the less management need be concerned with developing formal rules and regulations to guide employee behavior. Those guides will be internalized in employees when they accept the organization's culture.

What Do Cultures Do?

2 Compare the functional and dysfunctional effects of organizational culture on people and the organization.

Let's review the role culture performs and whether it can ever be a liability for an organization.

Culture's Functions

First, culture has a boundary-defining role: it creates distinctions between one organization and others. Second, it conveys a sense of identity for organization members. Third, culture facilitates commitment to something larger than individual self-interest. Fourth, it enhances the stability of the social system. Culture is the social glue that helps hold the organization together by providing standards for what employees should say and do. Finally, it is a sense-making and control mechanism that guides and shapes employees' attitudes and behavior. This last function is of particular interest to us.[15] Culture defines the rules of the game.

Today's trend toward decentralized organizations makes culture more important than ever, but ironically it also makes establishing a strong culture more difficult. When formal authority and control systems are reduced, culture's *shared meaning* can point everyone in the same direction. However, employees organized in teams may show greater allegiance to their team and its values than to the organization as a whole. In virtual organizations, the lack of frequent face-to-face contact makes establishing a common set of norms very difficult. Strong leadership that communicates frequently about common goals and priorities is especially important in innovative organizations.[16]

Individual–organization "fit"—that is, whether the applicant's or employee's attitudes and behavior are compatible with the culture—strongly influences who gets a job offer, a favorable performance review, or a promotion. It's no coincidence that Disney theme park employees appear almost universally attractive, clean, and wholesome with bright smiles. The company selects employees who will maintain that image. On the job, a strong culture supported by formal rules and regulations ensures they will act in a relatively uniform and predictable way.

Source: Jonathan Sprague/Redux.

Facebook describes itself as "a cutting-edge technology company, constantly taking on new challenges in the worlds of milliseconds and terabytes." The vast majority of the company's employees are under 40 and enjoy the excitement of working in a fast-paced environment with considerable change and ambiguity. Facebook encourages employees to interact in a creative climate that encourages experimentation and tolerates conflict and risk. The company fosters a fun-loving, casual, and collegial identity in its employees.

Culture Creates Climate

If you've worked with someone whose positive attitude inspired you to do your best, or with a lackluster team that drained your motivation, you've experienced the effects of climate. **Organizational climate** refers to the shared perceptions organizational members have about their organization and work environment.[17] This aspect of culture is like team spirit at the organizational level. When everyone has the same general feelings about what's important or how well things are working, the effect of these attitudes will be more than the sum of the individual parts. One meta-analysis found that across dozens of different samples, psychological climate was strongly related to individuals' level of job satisfaction, involvement, commitment, and motivation.[18] A positive overall workplace climate has been linked to higher customer satisfaction and financial performance as well.[19]

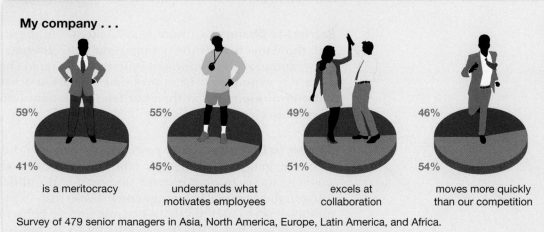

Note: Survey of 479 senior managers in Asia, North America, Europe, Latin America, and Africa.

Source: Based on *Global Firms in 2020* (Economist Intelligence Unit, 2010). Downloaded on July 2, 2011, from www.shrm.org/.

Dozens of dimensions of climate have been studied, including safety, justice, diversity, and customer service.[20] A person who encounters a positive climate for performance will think about doing a good job more often and will believe others support his or her success. Someone who encounters a positive climate for diversity will feel more comfortable collaborating with co-workers regardless of their demographic background. Climates can interact with one another to produce behavior. For example, a positive climate for worker empowerment can lead to higher levels of performance in organizations that also have a climate for personal accountability.[21] Climate also influences the habits people adopt. If the climate for safety is positive, everyone wears safety gear and follows safety procedures even if individually they wouldn't normally think very often about being safe—indeed, many studies have shown that a positive safety climate decreases the number of documented injuries on the job.[22]

Culture as a Liability

Culture can enhance organizational commitment and increase the consistency of employee behavior, clearly benefits to an organization. Culture is valuable to employees too, because it spells out how things are done and what's important. But we shouldn't ignore the potentially dysfunctional aspects of culture, especially a strong one, on an organization's effectiveness.

Institutionalization   When an organization undergoes **institutionalization** and becomes *institutionalized*—that is, it is valued for itself and not for the goods or services it produces—it takes on a life of its own, apart from its founders or members.[23] It doesn't go out of business even if its original goals are no longer relevant. Acceptable modes of behavior become largely self-evident to members,

---

organizational climate   *The shared perceptions organizational members have about their organization and work environment.*

institutionalization   *A condition that occurs when an organization takes on a life of its own, apart from any of its members, and acquires immortality.*

and although this isn't entirely negative, it does mean behaviors and habits that should be questioned and analyzed become taken for granted, which can stifle innovation and make maintaining the organization's culture an end in itself.

Barriers to Change Culture is a liability when the shared values don't agree with those that further the organization's effectiveness. This is most likely when an organization's environment is undergoing rapid change, and its entrenched culture may no longer be appropriate.[24] Consistency of behavior, an asset in a stable environment, may then burden the organization and make it difficult to respond to changes.

Barriers to Diversity Hiring new employees who differ from the majority in race, age, gender, disability, or other characteristics creates a paradox:[25] management wants to demonstrate support for the differences these employees bring to the workplace, but newcomers who wish to fit in must accept the organization's core cultural values. Because diverse behaviors and unique strengths are likely to diminish as people attempt to assimilate, strong cultures can become liabilities when they effectively eliminate these advantages. A strong culture that condones prejudice, supports bias, or becomes insensitive to people who are different can even undermine formal corporate diversity policies.

Barriers to Acquisitions and Mergers Historically, when management looked at acquisition or merger decisions, the key factors were financial advantage and product synergy. In recent years, cultural compatibility has become the primary

Myth or Science?

"Employees Treat Customers the Same Way the Organization Treats Them"

This statement is true to a significant degree. Two studies using different methods for operationalizing organizational treatment have shown that when employees are treated well, they are likely to treat customers well, but when employees are treated poorly, they treat customers poorly. Thus, a culture that shows positive treatment for employees is likely to create a positive culture for treatment of customers.

The first study collected data from 292 managers, 830 employees, and 1,772 bank customers in Japan. The researchers examined whether companies that provided high-performance work practices like service training, information sharing,

self-management teams, and employee autonomy had a superior climate for customer service and whether this climate for service was related to higher levels of organizational performance. The employee-benefiting practices did indeed lead to higher performance through a better climate for customer service.

The second study looked at "internal service," the extent to which employees believe their work unit is treated well by the organization as a whole. More than 600 employees of a Caribbean financial services firm described their internal service, and then quality data were collected from nearly 2,000 customers. The results showed that service climate was more posi-

tively related to customer satisfaction when internal service was high, meaning that having a positive climate for service leads to higher levels of customer satisfaction especially when a company provides positive internal service to its employees.

Sources: H. Liao, K. Toya, D. Lepak, and Y. Hong, "Do They See Eye to Eye? Management and Employee Perspectives of High-Performance Work Systems and Influence Processes on Service Quality," *Journal of Applied Psychology* 94, no. 2 (2009), pp. 371–391; and K. H. Ehrhart, L. A. Witt, B. Schneider, and S. J. Perry, "Service Employees Give as They Get: Internal Service as a Moderator of the Service Climate-Service Outcomes Link," *Journal of Applied Psychology* 96, no. 2 (2011), pp. 423–431.

concern.[26] All things being equal, whether the acquisition actually works seems to have more to do with how well the two organizations' cultures match up.

A survey by consulting firm A. T. Kearney revealed that 58 percent of mergers failed to reach their financial goals.[27] As one expert commented, "Mergers have an unusually high failure rate, and it's always because of people issues"— in other words, conflicting organizational cultures. The $183 billion merger between America Online (AOL) and Time Warner in 2001 was the largest in U.S. corporate history. It was also a disaster. Only 2 years later, the stock had fallen an astounding 90 percent, and the new company reported what was then the largest financial loss in U.S. history. To this day, Time Warner stock— trading around $32 per share in late 2011—remains at a fraction of its former price (around $200 per share before the merger). Culture clash is commonly argued to be one of the causes of AOL Time Warner's problems. As one expert noted, "In some ways the merger of AOL and Time Warner was like the marriage of a teenager to a middle-aged banker. The cultures were vastly different. There were open collars and jeans at AOL. Time Warner was more buttoned-down."[28]

Creating and Sustaining Culture

3 Identify the factors that create and sustain an organization's culture.

An organization's culture doesn't pop out of thin air, and once established it rarely fades away. What influences the creation of a culture? What reinforces and sustains it once it's in place?

How a Culture Begins

An organization's current customs, traditions, and general way of doing things are largely due to what it has done before and how successful it was in doing it. This leads us to the ultimate source of an organization's culture: its founders.[29] Free of previous customs or ideologies, founders have a vision of what the organization should be, and the firm's small size makes it easy to impose that vision on all members.

Culture creation occurs in three ways.[30] First, founders hire and keep only employees who think and feel the same way they do. Second, they indoctrinate and socialize these employees to their way of thinking and feeling. And finally, the founders' own behavior encourages employees to identify with them and internalize their beliefs, values, and assumptions. When the organization succeeds, the founders' personality becomes embedded in the culture.

The fierce, competitive style and disciplined, authoritarian nature of Hyundai, the giant Korean conglomerate, exhibits the same characteristics often used to describe founder Chung Ju-Yung. Other founders with immeasurable impact on their organization's culture include Bill Gates at Microsoft, Ingvar Kamprad at IKEA, Herb Kelleher at Southwest Airlines, Fred Smith at FedEx, and Richard Branson at the Virgin Group.

Keeping a Culture Alive

Once a culture is in place, practices within the organization maintain it by giving employees a set of similar experiences.[31] The selection process, performance evaluation criteria, training and development activities, and promotion procedures (all discussed in Chapter 17) ensure those hired fit in with the culture, reward those who support it, and penalize (or even expel) those who challenge

Source: Brad Swonetz / Redux.

Tony Hsieh, CEO of Zappos.com, is also the architect of the company's culture. Hsieh invited all employees to participate in creating ten core values that define the culture of Zappos and serve as the framework from which all decisions are made. The core values are: deliver WOW through service; embrace and drive change; create fun and a little weirdness; be adventurous, creative, and open minded; pursue growth and learning; build open and honest relationships with communication; build a positive team and family spirit; do more with less; be passionate and determined; and be humble. Hsieh maintains the culture through the company's hiring process and training programs to ensure that employees are committed to the core values.

it. Three forces play a particularly important part in sustaining a culture: selection practices, the actions of top management, and socialization methods. Let's look at each.

Selection   The explicit goal of the selection process is to identify and hire individuals with the knowledge, skills, and abilities to perform successfully. The final decision, because it's significantly influenced by the decision maker's judgment of how well the candidates will fit into the organization, identifies people whose values are essentially consistent with at least a good portion of the organization's.[32] Selection also provides information to applicants. Those who perceive a conflict between their values and those of the organization can remove themselves from the applicant pool. Selection thus becomes a two-way street, allowing employer or applicant to avoid a mismatch and sustaining an organization's culture by selecting out those who might attack or undermine its core values.

W. L. Gore & Associates, the maker of Gore-Tex fabric used in outerwear, prides itself on its democratic culture and teamwork. There are no job titles at Gore, nor bosses or chains of command. All work is done in teams. In Gore's selection process, teams of employees put job applicants through extensive interviews to ensure they can deal with the level of uncertainty, flexibility, and teamwork that's normal in Gore plants. Not surprisingly, W. L. Gore appears regularly on *Fortune*'s list of "100 Best Companies to Work For" (number 31 in 2011).[33]

Top Management   The actions of top management also have a major impact on the organization's culture.[34] Through words and behavior, senior executives establish norms that filter through the organization about, for instance, whether risk taking is desirable, how much freedom managers give employees, what is appropriate dress, and what actions earn pay raises, promotions, and other rewards.

The culture of supermarket chain Wegmans—which believes driven, happy, and loyal employees are more eager to help one another and provide exemplary customer service—is a direct result of the beliefs of the Wegman family. The chain began in 1930 when brothers John and Walter Wegman opened their first grocery store in Rochester, New York. Its focus on fine foods quickly separated it from other grocers—a focus maintained by the company's employees, many of whom are hired based on their interest in food. In 1950, Walter's son Robert became president and added generous employee benefits such as profit sharing and fully paid medical coverage. Now Robert's son Danny is president, and he has continued the Wegmans tradition of taking care of employees. To date, Wegmans has paid more than $54 million in college scholarships for its employees, both full-time and part-time. Pay is well above market average, making annual turnover for full-time employees a mere 6 percent, according to the Food Marketing Institute. (The industry average is 24 percent). Wegman's regularly appears on *Fortune*'s list as well (number 3 in 2011).

Socialization   No matter how good a job the organization does in recruiting and selection, new employees need help adapting to the prevailing culture. That help is **socialization**.[35] For example, all Marines must go through boot camp, where they prove their commitment and learn the "Marine way." The consulting firm Booz Allen Hamilton begins its process of bringing new employees onboard even before they start their first day of work. New recruits go to an internal Web portal to learn about the company and engage in some activities that help them understand the culture of the organization. After they start work, they continue to learn about the organization through an ongoing social

Exhibit **16-2**   A Socialization Model

networking application that links new workers with more established members of the firm and helps ensure that culture is transmitted over time.[36]

We can think of socialization as a process with three stages: prearrival, encounter, and metamorphosis.[37] This process, shown in Exhibit 16-2, has an impact on the new employee's work productivity, commitment to the organization's objectives, and eventual decision to stay with the organization.

The **prearrival stage** recognizes that each individual arrives with a set of values, attitudes, and expectations about both the work and the organization. One major purpose of a business school, for example, is to socialize business students to the attitudes and behaviors business firms want. Newcomers to high-profile organizations with a strong market position will make their own assumptions about what it must be like to work there.[38] Most new recruits will expect Nike to be dynamic and exciting, a prestigious law firm to be high in pressure and rewards, and the Marine Corps to require both discipline and courage. No matter how well managers think they can socialize newcomers, however, the most important predictor of future behavior is past behavior. What people know before they join the organization, and how proactive their personality is, are critical predictors of how well they adjust to a new culture.[39]

One way to capitalize on prehire characteristics in socialization is to use the selection process to inform prospective employees about the organization as a whole. We've also seen how the selection process ensures the inclusion of the "right type"—those who will fit in. "Indeed, the ability of the individual to present the appropriate face during the selection process determines his ability to move into the organization in the first place. Thus, success depends on the degree to which the aspiring member has correctly anticipated the expectations and desires of those in the organization in charge of selection."[40]

On entry into the organization, the new member enters the **encounter stage** and confronts the possibility that expectations—about the job, co-workers, the boss, and the organization in general—may differ from reality. If expectations were fairly accurate, the encounter stage merely cements earlier perceptions. However, this is often not the case. At the extreme, a new member may become disillusioned enough to resign. Proper recruiting and selection should significantly reduce that outcome, along with encouraging friendship ties in the

socialization   *A process that adapts employees to the organization's culture.*

prearrival stage   *The period of learning in the socialization process that occurs before a new employee joins the organization.*

encounter stage   *The stage in the socialization process in which a new employee sees what the organization is really like and confronts the possibility that expectations and reality may diverge.*

Exhibit 16-3   Entry Socialization Options

Formal vs. Informal The more a new employee is segregated from the ongoing work setting and differentiated in some way to make explicit his or her newcomer's role, the more socialization is formal. Specific orientation and training programs are examples. Informal socialization puts the new employee directly into the job, with little or no special attention.

Individual vs. Collective New members can be socialized individually. This describes how it's done in many professional offices. They can also be grouped together and processed through an identical set of experiences, as in military boot camp.

Fixed vs. Variable This refers to the time schedule in which newcomers make the transition from outsider to insider. A fixed schedule establishes standardized stages of transition. This characterizes rotational training programs. It also includes probationary periods, such as the 8- to 10-year "associate" status used by accounting and law firms before deciding on whether or not a candidate is made a partner. Variable schedules give no advance notice of their transition timetable. Variable schedules describe the typical promotion system, in which one is not advanced to the next stage until one is "ready."

Serial vs. Random Serial socialization is characterized by the use of role models who train and encourage the newcomer. Apprenticeship and mentoring programs are examples. In random socialization, role models are deliberately withheld. New employees are left on their own to figure things out.

Investiture vs. Divestiture Investiture socialization assumes that the newcomer's qualities and qualifications are the necessary ingredients for job success, so these qualities and qualifications are confirmed and supported. Divestiture socialization tries to strip away certain characteristics of the recruit. Fraternity and sorority "pledges" go through divestiture socialization to shape them into the proper role.

organization—newcomers are more committed when friends and co-workers help them "learn the ropes."[41]

Finally, to work out any problems discovered during the encounter stage, the new member changes or goes through the **metamorphosis stage**. The options presented in Exhibit 16-3 are alternatives designed to bring about the desired metamorphosis. Most research suggests there are two major "bundles" of socialization practices. The more management relies on formal, collective, sequential, fixed, and serial socialization programs and emphasize divestiture, the more likely newcomers' differences will be stripped away and replaced by standardized predictable behaviors. These *institutional* practices are common in police departments, fire departments, and other organizations that value rule following and order. Programs that are informal, individual, random, variable, and disjunctive and emphasize investiture are more likely to give newcomers an innovative sense of their role and methods of working. Creative fields, such as research and development, advertising, and filmmaking, rely on these *individual* practices. Most research suggests high levels of institutional practices encourage person–organization fit and high levels of commitment, whereas individual practices produce more role innovation.[42]

The three-part entry socialization process is complete when new members have internalized and accepted the norms of the organization and their work group, are confident in their competence, and feel trusted and valued by their peers. They understand the system—not only their own tasks but the rules, procedures, and informally accepted practices as well. Finally, they know what is expected of them and what criteria will be used to measure and evaluate their work. As Exhibit 16-2 showed, successful metamorphosis should have a positive impact on new employees' productivity and their commitment to the organization and reduce their propensity to leave the organization.

Exhibit **16-4**   How Organization Cultures Form

Researchers have begun to examine how employee attitudes change during socialization by measuring at several points over the first few months. One study has documented patterns of "honeymoons" and "hangovers" for new workers, showing that the period of initial adjustment is often marked by decreases in job satisfaction as their idealized hopes come into contact with the reality of organizational life.[43] Other research suggests that role conflict and role overload for newcomers rise over time, and that workers with the largest increases in these role problems experience the largest decreases in commitment and satisfaction.[44] It may be that the initial adjustment period for newcomers presents increasing demands and difficulties, at least in the short term.

Summary: How Cultures Form

Exhibit 16-4 summarizes how an organization's culture is established and sustained. The original culture derives from the founder's philosophy and strongly influences hiring criteria as the firm grows. Top managers' actions set the general climate, including what is acceptable behavior and what is not. The way employees are socialized will depend both on the degree of success achieved in matching new employees' values to those of the organization in the selection process, and on top management's preference for socialization methods.

How Employees Learn Culture

4 Show how culture is transmitted to employees.

Culture is transmitted to employees in a number of forms, the most potent being stories, rituals, material symbols, and language.

Stories

When Henry Ford II was chairman of Ford Motor Company, you would have been hard pressed to find a manager who hadn't heard how he reminded his executives, when they got too arrogant, "It's my name that's on the building." The message was clear: Henry Ford II ran the company.

metamorphosis stage   *The stage in the socialization process in which a new employee changes and adjusts to the job, work group, and organization.*

A number of senior Nike executives spend much of their time serving as corporate storytellers.[45] When they tell how co-founder (and Oregon track coach) Bill Bowerman went to his workshop and poured rubber into his wife's waffle iron to create a better running shoe, they're talking about Nike's spirit of innovation. When new hires hear tales of Oregon running star Steve Prefontaine's battles to make running a professional sport and attain better performance equipment, they learn of Nike's commitment to helping athletes.

Stories such as these circulate through many organizations, anchoring the present in the past and legitimating current practices. They typically include narratives about the organization's founders, rule breaking, rags-to-riches successes, reductions in the workforce, relocation of employees, reactions to past mistakes, and organizational coping.[46] Employees also create their own narratives about how they came to either fit or not fit with the organization during the process of socialization, including first days on the job, early interactions with others, and first impressions of organizational life.[47]

Rituals

Rituals are repetitive sequences of activities that express and reinforce the key values of the organization—what goals are most important and which people are important and which are expendable.[48] One of the best known rituals is Walmart's company chant. Begun by the company's founder, the late Sam Walton, as a way to motivate and unite his workforce, "Gimme a W, gimme an A, gimme an L, gimme a squiggle, give me an M, A, R, T!" has become a ritual that bonds workers and reinforces Walton's belief in the contribution his employees made to the company's success. Similar corporate chants are used by IBM, Ericsson, Novell, Deutsche Bank, and PricewaterhouseCoopers.[49]

Material Symbols

Alcoa headquarters doesn't look like your typical head-office operation. There are few individual offices, even for senior executives. The space is essentially made up of cubicles, common areas, and meeting rooms. This informality conveys to employees that Alcoa values openness, equality, creativity, and flexibility. Some corporations provide their top executives with chauffeur-driven limousines and a corporate jet. Other CEOs drive the company car themselves and travel in the economy section.

The layout of corporate headquarters, the types of automobiles top executives are given, and the presence or absence of corporate aircraft are a few examples of **material symbols**. Others include the size of offices, the elegance of furnishings, executive perks, and attire.[50] These convey to employees who is important, the degree of egalitarianism top management desires, and the kinds of behavior that are appropriate, such as risk taking, conservative, authoritarian, participative, individualistic, or social.

Language

Many organizations and subunits within them use language to help members identify with the culture, attest to their acceptance of it, and help preserve it. Unique terms describe equipment, officers, key individuals, suppliers, customers, or products that relate to the business. New employees may at first be overwhelmed by acronyms and jargon, that, once assimilated, act as a common denominator to unite members of a given culture or subculture.

At Sermo, it's okay for employees to bring their dogs to work and to include them in company meetings, as shown in this photo. Sermo is an online community for physicians where they can collaborate and improve patient care. Sermo's culture derives from the company's founder and CEO Dr. Daniel Palestrant, who wants employees to love coming to work, to be comfortable, to have fun, and to just be themselves in a space that suits them. Sermo's informal work environment and open office plan conveys to employees that the company values openness, individuality, creativity, and flexibility.

Source: Melanie Stetson Freeman/CSM/Newscom.

Creating an Ethical Organizational Culture

5 Demonstrate how an ethical culture can be created.

The organizational culture most likely to shape high ethical standards among its members is high in risk tolerance, low to moderate in aggressiveness, and focused on means as well as outcomes.[51] This type of culture takes a long-term perspective and balances the rights of multiple stakeholders, including employees, stockholders, and the community. Managers are supported for taking risks and innovating, discouraged from engaging in unbridled competition, and guided to heed not just to *what* goals are achieved but also *how*.

If the culture is strong and supports high ethical standards, it should have a very powerful and positive influence on employee behavior. Examples of organizations that have failed to establish proper codes of ethical conduct can be found in the media nearly every day. Some actively deceive customers or clients. Others produce products that harm consumers or the environment, or they harass or discriminate against certain groups of employees. Others are more subtle and cover up or fail to report wrongdoing. The negative consequences of a systematic culture of unethical behavior can be severe and include customer boycotts, fines, lawsuits, and government regulation of an organization's practices.

rituals   *Repetitive sequences of activities that express and reinforce the key values of the organization, which goals are most important, which people are important, and which are expendable.*

material symbols   *What conveys to employees who is important, the degree of egalitarianism top management desires, and the kinds of behavior that are appropriate.*

What can managers do to create a more ethical culture? They can adhere to the following principles:[52]

- **Be a visible role model.**   Employees will look to the actions of top management as a benchmark for appropriate behavior. Send a positive message.
- **Communicate ethical expectations.**   Minimize ethical ambiguities by sharing an organizational code of ethics that states the organization's primary values and ethical rules employees must follow.
- **Provide ethical training.**   Set up seminars, workshops, and training programs to reinforce the organization's standards of conduct, clarify what practices are permissible, and address potential ethical dilemmas.
- **Visibly reward ethical acts and punish unethical ones.**   Appraise managers on how their decisions measure up against the organization's code of ethics. Review the means as well as the ends. Visibly reward those who act ethically and conspicuously punish those who don't.
- **Provide protective mechanisms.**   Provide formal mechanisms so employees can discuss ethical dilemmas and report unethical behavior without fear of reprimand. These might include ethical counselors, ombudsmen, or ethical officers.

The work of setting a positive ethical climate has to start at the top of the organization.[53] A study of 195 managers demonstrated that when top management emphasizes strong ethical values, supervisors are more likely to practice ethical leadership. Positive ethical attitudes transfer down to line employees, who show lower levels of deviant behavior and higher levels of cooperation and assistance. A study involving auditors found perceived pressure from organizational leaders to behave unethically was associated with increased intentions to engage in unethical practices.[54] Clearly the wrong type of organizational

An Ethical Choice

Designing a Culture of Ethical Voice

Much research has emphasized how organizations establish ethical principles that employees are supposed to follow. More recent work examines how organizations can harness employees' inherent sense of right and wrong, so employees will speak up when they feel organizational actions are inconsistent with their own ethical principles.

Saying organizations should establish a culture for ethical behavior is easy enough, but developing a culture where employees feel empowered to speak up is considerably trickier. Here are a few suggestions:

1. Overcome the silence. Employees who know something is wrong may still fail to speak up because they fear reprisals. Both official and unofficial measures must encourage people to bring ethical lapses to the attention of upper management and reward them for doing so.
2. Encourage employees to continually investigate whether their behavior is consistent with organizational values. Many ethical lapses are not so much dishonest or malicious acts but failure to even recognize the moral issue at stake.
3. Develop formal roles for ethical compliance officers, who provide oversight and training to ensure employees are aware of the company's core values and can discuss ethical behavior in practice.

Sources: M. Kaptein, "Ethics Programs and Ethical Culture: A Next Step in Unraveling Their Multi-Faceted Relationship," *Journal of Business Ethics* 89, no. 2 (2009), pp. 261–281; P. Verhezen, "Giving Voice in a Culture of Silence. From a Culture of Compliance to a Culture of Integrity," *Journal of Business Ethics* 96, no. 2 (2010), pp. 187–206; and M. Kaptein, "From Inaction to External Whistleblowing: The Influence of Ethical Culture of Organizations on Employee Responses to Observed Wrongdoing," *Journal of Business Ethics* 98, no. 3 (2011), pp. 513–530.

culture can negatively influence employee ethical behavior. Finally, employees whose ethical values are similar to those of their department are more likely to be promoted, so we can think of ethical culture as flowing from the bottom up as well.[55]

Creating a Positive Organizational Culture

6 Describe a positive organizational culture.

At first blush, creating a positive culture may sound hopelessly naïve or like a Dilbert-style conspiracy. The one thing that makes us believe this trend is here to stay, however, are signs that management practice and OB research are converging.

A **positive organizational culture** emphasizes building on employee strengths, rewards more than it punishes, and emphasizes individual vitality and growth.[56] Let's consider each of these areas.

Building on Employee Strengths   Although a positive organizational culture does not ignore problems, it does emphasize showing workers how they can capitalize on their strengths. As management guru Peter Drucker said, "Most Americans do not know what their strengths are. When you ask them, they look at you with a blank stare, or they respond in terms of subject knowledge, which is the wrong answer." Wouldn't it be better to be in an organizational culture that helped you discover your strengths and learn how to make the most of them?

Larry Hammond used this approach when you'd least expect it: during his firm's darkest days. Hammond is CEO of Auglaize Provico, an agribusiness company based in Ohio. In the midst of the firm's worst financial struggles, when it had to lay off one-quarter of its workforce, Hammond decided to try a different approach. Rather than dwell on what was wrong, he took advantage of what was right. "If you really want to [excel], you have to know yourself—you have to know what you're good at, and you have to know what you're not so good at," says Hammond. With the help of Gallup consultant Barry Conchie, Hammond focused on discovering and using employee strengths and helped the company turn itself around. "You ask Larry [Hammond] what the difference is, and he'll say that it's individuals using their natural talents," says Conchie.[57]

Rewarding More Than Punishing   Although most organizations are sufficiently focused on extrinsic rewards such as pay and promotions, they often forget about the power of smaller (and cheaper) rewards such as praise. Part of creating a positive organizational culture is "catching employees doing something right." Many managers withhold praise because they're afraid employees will coast or because they think praise is not valued. Employees generally don't ask for praise, and managers usually don't realize the costs of failing to give it.

positive organizational culture   *A culture that emphasizes building on employee strengths, rewards more than punishes, and emphasizes individual vitality and growth.*

Employees of Pricewaterhouse Coopers work within a positive organizational culture that emphasizes individuals' vitality and growth. One of the largest global accounting firms, PwC offers employees professional and individual learning opportunities on the job, at clients' workplaces, and in formal training programs. PwC's Learning and Education Group provides access to the latest information on industry standards and best practices, and offers classes to help employees develop their technical skills. Company coaches and mentors guide employees in designing a personalized career path. The PwC team, shown here, counts the Oscars ballots for the Academy of Motion Picture Arts and Sciences, a company client for more than 75 years.

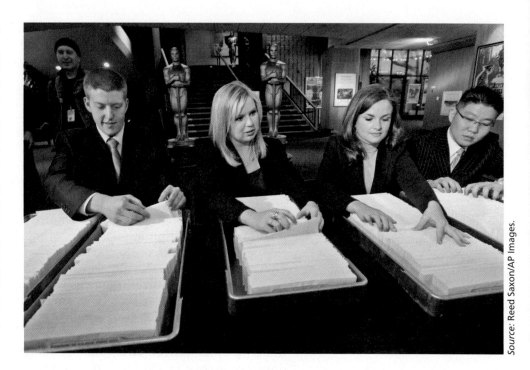

Source: Reed Saxon/AP Images.

Consider El´zbieta Górska-Kolodziejczyk, a plant manager for International Paper's facility in Kwidzyn, Poland. Employees work in a bleak windowless basement. Staffing is roughly one-third its prior level, while production has tripled. These challenges had done in the previous three managers. So when Górska-Kolodziejczyk took over, although she had many ideas about transforming the organization, at the top were recognition and praise. She initially found it difficult to give praise to those who weren't used to it, especially men. "They were like cement at the beginning," she said. "Like cement." Over time, however, she found they valued and even reciprocated praise. One day a department supervisor pulled her over to tell her she was doing a good job. "This I do remember, yes," she said.[58]

Emphasizing Vitality and Growth No organization will get the best from employees who see themselves as mere cogs in the machine. A positive culture recognizes the difference between a job and a career. It supports not only what the employee contributes to organizational effectiveness but also how the organization can make the employee more effective—personally and professionally.

Although it may take more creativity to encourage employee growth in some types of industries, consider the food industry. At Masterfoods in Belgium, Philippe Lescornez leads a team of employees including Didier Brynaert, who works in Luxembourg, nearly 150 miles away. Brynaert was considered a good sales promoter who was meeting expectations when Lescornez decided Brynaert's job could be made more important if he were seen less as just another sales promoter and more as an expert on the unique features of the Luxembourg market. So Lescornez asked Brynaert for information he could share with the home office. He hoped that by raising Brynaert's profile in Brussels, he could create in him a greater sense of ownership for his remote sales territory. "I started to communicate much more what he did to other people [within the company], because there's quite some distance between the Brussels office and the section he's working in. So I started to communicate, communicate, communicate. The more I communicated, the more he started to provide material," says Lescornez. As a result, "Now he's recognized as the specialist for Luxembourg—the guy who is able to build a strong relationship with the Luxembourg clients," says Lescornez. What's good for Brynaert is, of course, also good for Lescornez, who gets credit for helping Brynaert grow and develop.[59]

Limits of Positive Culture   Is a positive culture a cure-all? Though companies such as GE, Xerox, Boeing, and 3M have embraced aspects of a positive organizational culture, it is a new enough idea for us to be uncertain about how and when it works best.

Not all cultures value being positive as much as U.S. culture does, and, even within U.S. culture, there surely are limits to how far we should go to preserve a positive culture. For example, Admiral, a British insurance company, has established a Ministry of Fun in its call centers to organize poem writings, foosball, conker (a British game involving chestnuts), and fancy-dress days. When does the pursuit of a positive culture start to seem coercive or even Orwellian? As one critic notes, "Promoting a social orthodoxy of positiveness focuses on a particular constellation of desirable states and traits but, in so doing, can stigmatize those who fail to fit the template."[60] There may be benefits to establishing a positive culture, but an organization also needs to be objective and not pursue it past the point of effectiveness.

Spirituality and Organizational Culture

What do Southwest Airlines, Hewlett-Packard, Ford, The Men's Wearhouse, Tyson Foods, Wetherill Associates, and Tom's of Maine have in common? They're among a growing number of organizations that have embraced workplace spirituality.

What Is Spirituality?

Workplace spirituality is *not* about organized religious practices. It's not about God or theology. **Workplace spirituality** recognizes that people have an inner life that nourishes and is nourished by meaningful work in the context of community.[61] Organizations that promote a spiritual culture recognize that people seek to find meaning and purpose in their work and desire to connect with other human beings as part of a community. Many of the topics we have discussed—ranging from job design (designing work that is meaningful to employees) to transformational leadership (leadership practices that emphasize a higher-order purpose and self-transcendent goals) are well matched to the concept of organizational spirituality. When a company emphasizes its commitment to paying Third World suppliers a fair (above-market) price for their coffee to facilitate community development—as did Starbucks—or encourages employees to share prayers or inspirational messages through e-mail—as did Interstate Batteries—it is encouraging a more spiritual culture.[62]

workplace spirituality   *The recognition that people have an inner life that nourishes and is nourished by meaningful work that takes place in the context of community.*

Steve Baxter, a Target Corporation employee, tries to comfort a child while serving as a volunteer for Project Homeless Connect, a community program that provides housing, dental, medical, employment, child care, and other services for homeless people and others in need. Baxter and other Target employees are inspired by a strong sense of purpose in showing kindness to, promoting the happiness of, and serving customers, fellow workers, and people in the community. Employees experience the joy and satisfaction that comes from helping others by volunteering in social services programs that feed the hungry, prevent family violence, give shelter to the homeless, and provide disaster relief.

Source: m42/ZUMA Press/Newscom.

Why Spirituality Now?

As we noted in our discussion of emotions in Chapter 4, the myth of rationality assumed the well-run organization eliminated feelings. Concern about an employee's inner life had no role in the perfectly rational model. But just as we've now come to realize that the study of emotions improves our understanding of organizational behavior, an awareness of spirituality can help us better understand employee behavior in the twenty-first century.

Of course, employees have always had an inner life. So why has the search for meaning and purposefulness in work surfaced now? We summarize the reasons in Exhibit 16-5.

Characteristics of a Spiritual Organization

The concept of workplace spirituality draws on our previous discussions of values, ethics, motivation, and leadership. What differentiates spiritual organizations from their nonspiritual counterparts? Although research remains

Exhibit 16-5	Reasons for the Growing Interest in Spirituality

- Spirituality can counterbalance the pressures and stress of a turbulent pace of life. Contemporary lifestyles—single-parent families, geographic mobility, the temporary nature of jobs, new technologies that create distance between people—underscore the lack of community many people feel and increase the need for involvement and connection.

- Formalized religion hasn't worked for many people, and they continue to look for anchors to replace lack of faith and to fill a growing feeling of emptiness.

- Job demands have made the workplace dominant in many people's lives, yet they continue to question the meaning of work.

- People want to integrate personal life values with their professional life.

- An increasing number of people are finding that the pursuit of more material acquisitions leaves them unfulfilled.

preliminary, several cultural characteristics tend to be evident in spiritual organizations:[63]

- **Benevolence.**   Spiritual organizations value showing kindness toward others and promoting the happiness of employees and other organizational stakeholders.
- **Strong sense of purpose.**   Spiritual organizations build their cultures around a meaningful purpose. Although profits may be important, they're not the primary value of the organization.
- **Trust and respect.**   Spiritual organizations are characterized by mutual trust, honesty, and openness. Employees are treated with esteem and value, consistent with the dignity of each individual.
- **Open-mindedness.**   Spiritual organizations value flexible thinking and creativity among employees.

SELF-ASSESSMENT LIBRARY

How Spiritual Am I?

In the Self-Assessment Library (available on CD and online), take assessment IV.A.4 (How Spiritual Am I?). Note: People's scores on this measure vary from time to time, so take that into account when interpreting the results.

Achieving a Spiritual Organization

Many organizations have grown interested in spirituality but have had difficulty putting its principles into practice. Several types of practices can facilitate a spiritual workplace,[64] including those that support work–life balance. Leaders can demonstrate values, attitudes, and behaviors that trigger intrinsic motivation and a sense of calling through work. Encouraging employees to consider how their work provides a sense of purpose through community building also can help achieve a spiritual workplace; often this is achieved through group counseling and organizational development, a topic we take up in Chapter 18.

Criticisms of Spirituality

7 Identify characteristics of a spiritual culture.

Critics of the spirituality movement in organizations have focused on three issues. First is the question of scientific foundation. What really is workplace spirituality? Is it just a new management buzzword? Second, are spiritual organizations legitimate? Specifically, do organizations have the right to impose spiritual values on their employees? Third is the question of economics: are spirituality and profits compatible?

First, as you might imagine, there is comparatively little research on workplace spirituality. We don't know whether the concept will have staying power. Do the cultural characteristics we just identified really separate spiritual organizations? Spirituality has been defined so broadly in some sources that practices from job rotation to corporate retreats at meditation centers have been identified as spiritual. Questions need to be answered before the concept gains full credibility.

On the second point, an emphasis on spirituality can clearly make some employees uneasy. Critics have argued that secular institutions, especially business firms, have no business imposing spiritual values on employees.[65] This criticism is undoubtedly valid when spirituality is defined as bringing religion and God into the workplace. However, it seems less stinging when the goal is limited to helping employees find meaning and purpose in their work lives. If the concerns listed in Exhibit 16-5 truly characterize a large segment of the workforce, then perhaps organizations can do so.

Finally, whether spirituality and profits are compatible objectives is certainly relevant for managers and investors in business. The evidence, although limited, indicates they are. Organizations that provided their employees with opportunities for spiritual development have outperformed those that didn't.[66] Other studies a report that spirituality in organizations was positively related to creativity, employee satisfaction, job involvement, and organizational commitment.[67]

Global Implications

8   Show how national culture may affect the way organizational culture is transported to a different country.

We considered global cultural values (collectivism–individualism, power distance, and so on) in Chapter 5. Here our focus is a bit narrower: how is organizational culture affected by a global context? Organizational culture is so powerful it often transcends national boundaries. But that doesn't mean organizations should, or could, ignore local culture.

Organizational cultures often reflect national culture. The culture at AirAsia, a Malaysian-based airline, emphasizes informal dress so as not to create status differences. The carrier has lots of parties, participative management, and no private offices, reflecting Malaysia's relatively collectivistic culture. The culture of US Airways does not reflect the same degree of informality. If US Airways were to set up operations in Malaysia or merge with AirAsia, it would need to take these cultural differences into account.

One of the primary things U.S. managers can do is to be culturally sensitive. The United States is a dominant force in business and in culture—and with that influence comes a reputation. "We are broadly seen throughout the world as arrogant people, totally self-absorbed and loud," says one U.S. executive. Companies such as American Airlines, Lowe's, Novell, ExxonMobil, and Microsoft have implemented training programs to sensitize their managers to cultural differences. Some ways in which U.S. managers can be culturally sensitive include talking in a low tone of voice, speaking slowly, listening more, and avoiding discussions of religion and politics.

The management of ethical behavior is one area where national culture can rub up against corporate culture.[68] U.S. managers endorse the supremacy of anonymous market forces and implicitly or explicitly view profit maximization as a moral obligation for business organizations. This worldview sees bribery, nepotism, and favoring personal contacts as highly unethical. Any action that deviates from profit maximization may indicate that inappropriate or corrupt behavior may be occurring. In contrast, managers in developing economies are more likely to see ethical decisions as embedded in a social environment. That means doing special favors for family and friends is not only appropriate but possibly even an ethical responsibility. Managers in many nations also view capitalism skeptically and believe the interests of workers should be put on a par with the interests of shareholders.

U.S. employees are not the only ones who need to be culturally sensitive. Three times a week, employees at the Canadian unit of Japanese videogame maker Koei begin the day by standing next to their desks, facing their boss, and saying "Good morning" in unison. Employees then deliver short speeches on topics that range from corporate principles to 3D game engines. Koei also has employees punch a time clock and asks women to serve tea to top executive guests. Although these practices are consistent with Koei's culture, they do not fit Canadian culture very well. "It's kind of like school," says one Canadian employee.[69]

MyManagementLab

Now that you have finished this chapter, go back to **www.mymanagementlab.com** to continue practicing and applying the concepts you've learned.

Summary and Implications for Managers

Exhibit 16-6 depicts organizational culture as an intervening variable. Employees form an overall subjective perception of the organization based on factors such as degree of risk tolerance, team emphasis, and support of people. This overall perception becomes, in effect, the organization's culture or personality and affects employee performance and satisfaction, with stronger cultures having greater impact.

- Just as people's personalities tend to be stable over time, so too do strong cultures. This makes a strong culture difficult for managers to change if it becomes mismatched to its environment. Changing an organization's culture is a long and difficult process. Thus, at least in the short term, managers should treat their organization's culture as relatively fixed.
- One of the most important managerial implications of organizational culture relates to selection decisions. Hiring individuals whose values don't align with those of the organization is likely to yield employees who lack motivation and commitment and are dissatisfied with their jobs and the organization.[70] Not surprisingly, "misfits" have considerably higher turnover rates.
- An employee's performance also depends to a considerable degree on knowing what to do and not do. Understanding the right way to do a job indicates proper socialization.
- As a manager, you can shape the culture of your work environment, sometimes as much as it shapes you. All managers can especially do their part to create an ethical culture and to consider spirituality and its role in creating a positive organizational culture.

Exhibit **16-6** How Organizational Cultures Have an Impact on Employee Performance and Satisfaction

Organizations Should Strive to Create a Positive Organizational Culture

POINT

Organizations should do everything they can to establish a positive culture, because it works. Scores of recent studies have shown that individuals who are in positive states of mind at work and in life lead happier, more productive, and more fulfilling lives. Given the accumulating evidence, researchers are now studying ways to make that happen.

In a recent *Harvard Business Review* article, Wharton faculty member Adam Grant discusses an interesting concept: *outsourcing inspiration*. What does he mean by that? Grant writes: "A growing body of research shows that end users—customers, clients, patients, and others who benefit from a company's products and services—are surprisingly effective in motivating people to work harder, smarter, and more productively."

Some tangible examples of how this can work:

- Northwestern University's "buddy program" introduces Alzheimer's patients to scientists working to develop treatments for the disease.
- At a Merrill Lynch branch, weekly team meetings begin with stories about how the team has made a difference in customers' lives.
- "All Medtronic employees have a 'defining moment' in which they come face-to-face with a patient whose story deeply touches them," writes former CEO Bill George.
- At Wells Fargo, managers show bankers videos of people describing how low-interest loans rescued them from severe debt—a vivid reminder to the bankers that they are striving to serve their customers, not their managers.

Of course, there are other ways of creating a positive organizational culture, including building on strengths and rewarding more than punishing.

Creating a positive organizational culture is not magic, but it tends to have extremely positive benefits for organizations which embrace it. *Outsourcing inspiration* is a great way for employees to feel appreciated, to experience empathy, and to see the impact of their work—all motivating outcomes that will lead organizations to be more effective and individuals more fulfilled in their work.

COUNTERPOINT

There are many unanswered questions about the merits of using positive organizational scholarship to build positive organizational cultures. Let's focus on three.

What is a positive culture? The employment relationship can be amicable and even mutually beneficial. However, glossing over natural differences in interests with the frosting of positive culture is intellectually dishonest and potentially harmful. From time to time, any organization needs to undertake unpopular actions. Can anyone terminate an employee positively (and honestly), or explain to someone why others received a raise? There's a danger in trying to sugarcoat. Positive relationships will develop—or not—on their own. We'd be better off preaching that people, and organizational cultures, should be honest and fair, rather than unabashedly positive.

Is practice ahead of science? Before we start beseeching organizations to build positive cultures, we should make sure these interventions work as we think they do. Many have unintended consequences, and we simply don't have enough research to support the claims put forth. As one reviewer noted, "Everyone wants to believe they could have greater control over their lives by simply changing the way they think. Research that supports this idea gets promoted loudly and widely." But it's not based on a mountain of evidence.

Is building a positive culture manipulative? Psychologist Lisa Aspinwall writes of "saccharine terrorism," where employees are coerced into positive mindsets by Happiness Coaches. You may think this an exaggeration, but companies like UBS, American Express, KPMG, FedEx, Adobe, and IBM use Happiness Coaches to do exactly that. As one critic noted, "Encouraging people to maintain a happy outlook in the face of less-than-ideal conditions is a good way of keeping citizens under control in spite of severe societal problems, or keeping employees productive while keeping pay and benefits low."

Sources: B. Azar, "Positive Psychology Advances, with Growing Pains," *Monitor on Psychology* (April 2011), pp. 32–36; A. Grant, "How Customers Can Rally Your Troops," *Harvard Business Review* (June 2011), downloaded on July 12, 2011, from http://hbr.org/; and J. McCarthy, "5 Big Problems with Positive Thinking (And Why You Should Do It Anyway)," *Positive Psychology* (October 2010), downloaded on July 10, 2011, from http://psychologyofwellbeing.com/.

QUESTIONS FOR REVIEW

1 What is organizational culture, and what are its common characteristics?

2 What are the functional and dysfunctional effects of organizational culture?

3 What factors create and sustain an organization's culture?

4 How is culture transmitted to employees?

5 How can an ethical culture be created?

6 What is a positive organizational culture?

7 What are the characteristics of a spiritual culture?

8 How does national culture affect how organizational culture is transported to a different country?

EXPERIENTIAL EXERCISE Rate Your Classroom Culture

Listed here are 14 statements. Using the 5-item scale (from strongly agree to strongly disagree), respond to each statement by circling the number that best represents your opinion.

	Strongly Agree	Agree	Neutral	Disagree	Strongly Disagree
1. I feel comfortable challenging statements made by my instructor.	1	2	3	4	5
2. My instructor heavily penalizes assignments that are not turned in on time.	1	2	3	4	5
3. My instructor believes that "It's final results that count."	1	2	3	4	5
4. My instructor is sensitive to my personal needs and problems.	1	2	3	4	5
5. A large portion of my grade depends on how well I work with others in the class.	1	2	3	4	5
6. I often feel nervous and tense when I come to class.	1	2	3	4	5
7. My instructor seems to prefer stability over change.	1	2	3	4	5
8. My instructor encourages me to develop new and different ideas.	1	2	3	4	5
9. My instructor has little tolerance for sloppy thinking.	1	2	3	4	5
10. My instructor is more concerned with how I came to a conclusion than with the conclusion itself.	1	2	3	4	5
11. My instructor treats all students alike.	1	2	3	4	5
12. My instructor frowns on class members helping each other with assignments.	1	2	3	4	5
13. Aggressive and competitive people have a distinct advantage in this class.	1	2	3	4	5
14. My instructor encourages me to see the world differently.	1	2	3	4	5

Calculate your total score by adding up the numbers you circled. Your score will fall between 14 and 70.

A high score (49 or above) describes an open, risk-taking, supportive, humanistic, team-oriented, easygoing, growth-oriented culture. A low score (35 or below) describes a closed, structured, task-oriented, individualistic, tense, and stability-oriented culture. Note that differences count, so a score of 60 is a more open culture than one that scores 50. Also, realize that one culture isn't preferable over another. The "right" culture depends on you and your preferences for a learning environment.

Form teams of five to seven members each. Compare your scores. How closely do they align? Discuss and resolve any discrepancies. Based on your team's analysis, what type of student do you think would perform best in this class?

ETHICAL DILEMMA A Bankrupt Culture

Like many newspapers, the *Chicago Tribune* is in trouble. The 165-year-old paper was bought by real estate mogul Sam Zell in 2007, who promptly filed for bankruptcy. That didn't surprise experts. What Zell did next did.

Zell hired Randy Michaels as the Tribune Company's CEO. Soon after Michaels arrived, he launched an attack on the Tribune's culture. In an informal meeting with a group of fellow Tribune executives, Michaels said, "Watch this" and offered the waitress $100 to show her breasts. The group was dumbfounded.

But Michaels hardly stopped there.

Michaels was fond of a culture that included "sexual innuendo, poisonous workplace banter, and profane invective." One press release announced the hiring of Kim Johnson, who, it was said, was "a former waitress at 'Knockers—The Place for Hot Racks and Cold Brews.'" Another executive reporting to Michaels sent links to raunchy Web sites in e-mail messages. Michaels was heard loudly discussing with other executives he had brought with him the "sexual suitability of various employees."

When some complained about the change in the culture, Michaels rewrote the employee handbook. "Working at Tribune means accepting that you might hear a word that you, personally, might not use," the new manual stated. "You might experience an attitude you don't share. You might hear a joke that you don't consider funny. That is because a loose, fun, nonlinear atmosphere is important to the creative process." It then concluded, "This should be understood, should not be a surprise, and not considered harassment."

Eventually Michaels was forced out, but the damage had been done. The Tribune continues to operate in bankruptcy and more than 5,000 employees have lost their jobs. In retrospect, Zell has called his purchase "the deal from hell." It appears he appointed a CEO to match the deal.

Questions

1. What does this story tell you about the effect of top management on organizational culture?

2. Denise Brown, a former member of the Tribune's management, said, "If you spoke up, you were portrayed as a sissy." How would you have reacted if you witnessed some of these behaviors?

3. How can you determine when a line has been crossed between a fun and informal culture, and one that is offensive and inappropriate?

Sources: D. Carr, "At Debt-Ridden Tribune, a Culture Run Amok," *The New York Times* (October 6, 2010), pp. A1, A22; M. Oneal and P. Rosenthal, "Tribune Co. CEO Randy Michaels Resigns Amid Accusations of Crass Behavior," *Chicago Tribune* (October 22, 2010), downloaded July 12, 2011, from http://articles.chicagotribune .com/; and P. Whoriskey, "Former Tribune, Times Mirror Executives, Editors Sue Shareholders," *Washington Post* (June 2, 2011), downloaded on July 11, 2011, from www.washingtonpost.com/.

CASE INCIDENT 1 Mergers Don't Always Lead to Culture Clashes

A lot of mergers lead to culture clashes and, ultimately, failure. So in 2005 when banking giant Bank of America (BOA) announced its $35 billion acquisition of credit card giant MBNA, many thought that in a few years this merger would join the heap of those done in by cultural differences.

MBNA's culture was characterized by a free-wheeling, entrepreneurial spirit that was also quite secretive. MBNA employees also were accustomed to the high life. Their corporate headquarters in Wilmington, Delaware, could be described as lavish, and employees throughout the company enjoyed high salaries and generous perks—from the private golf course at its headquarters to its fleet of corporate jets and private yachts.

Bank of America, in contrast, grew by thrift. It was a low-cost, no-nonsense operation. Unlike MBNA, it believed that size and smarts were more important than speed. It was an acquisition machine that some likened to *Star Trek*'s relentless Borg collective.

In short, the cultures in the two companies were very, very different.

Although these cultural differences seemed a recipe for disaster, it appears, judging from the reactions of BOA and MBNA employees, that the merger has worked. How can this be?

BOA had the foresight to know which MBNA practices to attempt to change and which to keep in place. Especially critical was BOA's appreciation and respect for MBNA's culture. "On Day 1, I was directed that this was not like the ones you are used to," said Clifford Skelton, who had helped manage BOA's acquisition of FleetBoston Financial before moving on to MBNA.

To try to manage the cultural transition, executives of both companies began by comparing thousands of practices covering everything from hiring to call-center operations. In many cases, BOA chose to keep MBNA's cultural practices in place. In other cases, BOA did impose its will on MBNA. For example, because MBNA's pay rates were well above market, many MBNA managers were forced to swallow a steep pay cut. Some MBNA employees left, but most remained.

In other cases, the cultures co-adapted. For example, MBNA's dress code was much more formal than BOA's business-casual approach. In the end, a hybrid code was adopted, where business suits were expected in the credit-card division's corporate offices and in front of clients, but business causal was the norm otherwise.

While most believe the merger has been successful, there are tensions. Some BOA managers see MBNA managers as arrogant and autocratic. Some MBNA managers see their BOA counterparts as bureaucratic.

Of course, BOA made another, more recent and much larger acquisition: Merrill Lynch. After a rough start, most evidence suggests this mega-merger saved Merrill from bankruptcy and appears to be working well, which might suggest that BOA has found the secret to successful mega-mergers.

Questions

1. In what ways were the cultures of Bank of America and MBNA incompatible?

2. Why do you think their cultures appeared to mesh rather than clash?

3. Do you think culture is important to the success of a merger/acquisition? Why or why not?

4. How much of the smooth transition, if any, do you think comes from both companies glossing over real differences in an effort to make the merger work?

Sources: Based on E. Dash, "A Clash of Cultures, Averted," *The New York Times* (February 20, 2007), pp. B1, B3; L. Moyer, "Bank of America Lewis Must Wait on His Fate," *Forbes* (April 29, 2009), www.forbes.com; and K. MacFadyen, "From the People Who Brought You BofA," *Mergers and Acquisitions* (October, 2009), pp. 38–40.

CASE INCIDENT 2 Did Toyota's Culture Cause Its Problems?

You may be familiar with the problems that have recently plagued Toyota. However, you may not know the whole story. First the facts. In 2010 Toyota issued a series of recalls for various models. The most serious was for a defect called "unintended acceleration," which occurs when a car accelerates with no apparent input from the driver. Investigations revealed that unintended acceleration in Toyota cars has been the cause of 37 deaths since 2000. When the problems first surfaced, however, Toyota denied it was the cause. Eventually, Toyota apologized and recalled more than 9 million cars.

To many, the root cause of Toyota's problems was its insular, arrogant culture. *Fortune* argued: "Like GM before it, Toyota has gotten smug. It believes the Toyota Way is the only way." *Time* reported "a Toyota management team

that had fallen in love with itself and become too insular to properly handle something like the current crisis." Transportation Secretary Ray LaHood described Toyota's culture as "safety-deaf."

But is this the reality? Increasingly, evidence suggests that Toyota's culture—or even the cars it produces—is not the source of the problem.

A 2011 report released by the U.S. National Highway Traffic Safety Administration (NHTSA) concluded that unintended acceleration was not caused by problems in the electronic circuitry. *The Wall Street Journal* wrote that "safety regulators, human-error experts and auto makers say driver error is the primary cause of sudden acceleration." *Forbes* and *The Atlantic* commented that most of the incidents of sudden acceleration in Toyota cars occurred with elderly drivers, and elderly drivers are known to be more prone to confusing pedals. Many other independent investigations, including ones conducted by automobile experts at *Popular Mechanics* and *Car and Driver*, reached the same conclusion: the main cause of unintended acceleration was drivers mistaking the gas pedal for the brake pedal.

There's a long history of misreporting on this issue. Audi was nearly driven into bankruptcy when *60 Minutes* aired a report, "Out of Control," purportedly proving that defects in the car were behind six fatal sudden-acceleration accidents. As it turns out, *60 Minutes* paid sometime to tamper with the car—filling a canister of compressed air linked to the transmission—to cause the sudden acceleration shown in the segment. Further investigations never uncovered evidence that defects in Audi's cars were behind the incidents.

Does Toyota have an insular and inbred corporate culture? Probably. But it's been that way for a long time, and it's far from clear that the culture, or even the company's cars, is responsible for the sudden acceleration problems.

Questions

1. If Toyota is not the cause of unintended acceleration, why was it blamed for it?

2. Investigations have shown that after stories of unintended acceleration are publicized, report of incidents increase for all automakers. Why is this the case?

3. Is it possible to have a strong—even arrogant—culture and still produce safe and high-quality vehicles?

4. If you were the CEO of Toyota when the story was first publicized, how would you have reacted?

Sources: A. Taylor, "How Toyota Lost Its Way," *Fortune* (July 26, 2010), pp. 108–117; P. Allen, "Anatomy of Toyota's Problem Pedal: Mechanic's Diary," *Popular Mechanics* (March 3, 2010), downloaded July 11, 2011 from www.popularmechanics.com/; B. Saporito, "Behind the Troubles at Toyota," *Time* (February 11, 2010), downloaded July 11, 2011, from www.time.com/; and B. Simon, "LaHood Voices Concerns Over Toyota Culture," *Financial Times* (February 24, 2010), downloaded July 11, 2011, from www.ft.com/.

ENDNOTES

1. See, for example, E. H. Schein, "Culture: The Missing Concept in Organization Studies," *Administrative Science Quarterly* 41, no. 2 (1996), pp. 229–240.

2. This seven-item description is based on C. A. O'Reilly III, J. Chatman, and D. F. Caldwell, "People and Organizational Culture: A Profile Comparison Approach to Assessing Person-Organization Fit," *Academy of Management Journal* (September 1991), pp. 487–516; and J. A. Chatman and K. A. Jehn, "Assessing the Relationship Between Industry Characteristics and Organizational Culture: How Different Can You Be?" *Academy of Management Journal* (June 1994), pp. 522–553.

3. K. S. Cameron, R. E. Quinn, J. DeGraff, and A. V. Thakor, *Competing Values Leadership: Creating Value in Organizations* (Cheltenham, UK and Northampton, MA: Edward Elgar, 2006).

4. C. A. Hartnell, A. Y. Ou, and A. Kinicki, "Organizational Culture and Organizational Effectiveness: A Meta-Analytic Investigation of the Competing Values Framework's Theoretical Suppositions," *Journal of Applied Psychology,* Online first publication (January 17, 2011), doi: 10.1037/a0021987.

5. The view that there will be consistency among perceptions of organizational culture has been called the "integration" perspective. For a review of this perspective and conflicting approaches, see D. Meyerson and J. Martin, "Cultural Change: An Integration of Three Different Views," *Journal of Management Studies* (November 1987), pp. 623–647; and P. J. Frost, L. F. Moore, M. R. Louis, C. C. Lundberg, and J. Martin (eds.), *Reframing Organizational Culture* (Newbury Park, CA: Sage, 1991).

6. See J. M. Jermier, J. W. Slocum Jr., L. W. Fry, and J. Gaines, "Organizational Subcultures in a Soft Bureaucracy: Resistance Behind the Myth and Facade of an Official Culture," *Organization Science* (May 1991), pp. 170–194; and P. Lok, R. Westwood, and J. Crawford, 'Perceptions of Organisational Subculture and their Significance for Organisational Commitment," *Applied Psychology: An International Review* 54, no. 4 (2005), pp. 490–514.

7. D. A. Hoffman and L. M. Jones, "Leadership, Collective Personality, and Performance," *Journal of Applied Psychology* 90, no. 3 (2005), pp. 509–522.

8. T. Hsieh, "Zappos's CEO on Going to Extremes for Customers." *Harvard Business Review* (July/August 2010), pp. 41–45.

9. See, for example, G. G. Gordon and N. DiTomaso, "Predicting Corporate Performance from Organizational Culture," *Journal of Management Studies* (November 1992), pp. 793–798; J. B. Sorensen, "The Strength of Corporate Culture and the Reliability of Firm Performance," *Administrative Science Quarterly* (March 2002), pp. 70–91; and J. Rosenthal and M. A. Masarech, "High-Performance Cultures: How Values Can Drive Business Results," *Journal of Organizational Excellence* (Spring 2003), pp. 3–18.

10. Y. Wiener, "Forms of Value Systems: A Focus on Organizational Effectiveness and Cultural Change and Maintenance," *Academy of Management Review* (October 1988), p. 536; and B. Schneider, A. N. Salvaggio, and M. Subirats, "Climate Strength: A New Direction for Climate Research," *Journal of Applied Psychology* 87 (2002), pp. 220–229.

11. R. T. Mowday, L. W. Porter, and R. M. Steers, *Employee Linkages: The Psychology of Commitment, Absenteeism, and Turnover* (New York: Academic Press, 1982); C. Vandenberghe, "Organizational Culture, Person-Culture Fit, and Turnover: A Replication in the Health Care Industry," *Journal of Organizational Behavior* (March 1999), pp. 175–184; and M. Schulte, C. Ostroff, S. Shmulyian, and A. Kinicki, "Organizational Climate Configurations: Relationships to Collective Attitudes, Customer Satisfaction, and Financial Performance," *Journal of Applied Psychology* 94, no. 3 (2009), pp. 618–634.

12. J. W. Grizzle, A. R. Zablah, T. J. Brown, J. C. Mowen, and J. M. Lee, "Employee Customer Orientation in Context: How the Environment Moderates the Influence of Customer Orientation on Performance Outcomes," *Journal of Applied Psychology* 94, no. 5 (2009), pp. 1227–1242.

13. M. R. Bashshur, A. Hernández, and V. González-Romá, "When Managers and Their Teams Disagree: A Longitudinal Look at the Consequences of Differences in Perceptions of Organizational Support," *Journal of Applied Psychology* 96, no. 3 (2011), pp. 558–573.

14. S. L. Dolan and S. Garcia, "Managing by Values: Cultural Redesign for Strategic Organizational Change at the Dawn of the Twenty-First Century," *Journal of Management Development* 21, no. 2 (2002), pp. 101–117.

15. See C. A. O'Reilly and J. A. Chatman, "Culture as Social Control: Corporations, Cults, and Commitment," in B. M. Staw and L. L. Cummings (eds.), *Research in Organizational Behavior*, vol. 18 (Greenwich, CT: JAI Press, 1996), pp. 157–200. See also M. Pinae Cunha, "The 'Best Place to Be': Managing Control and Employee Loyalty in a Knowledge-Intensive Company," *Journal of Applied Behavioral Science* (December 2002), pp. 481–495.

16. Y. Ling, Z. Simsek, M. H. Lubatkin, and J. F. Veiga, "Transformational Leadership's Role in Promoting Corporate Entrepreneurship: Examining the CEO-TMT Interface," *Academy of Management Journal* 51, no. 3 (2008), pp. 557–576; and A. Malhotra, A. Majchrzak, and B. Rosen, Benson, "Leading Virtual Teams," *Academy of Management Perspectives* 21, no. 1 (2007), pp. 60–70.

17. D. Denison, "What Is the Difference Between Organizational Culture and Organizational Climate? A Native's Point of View on a Decade of Paradigm Wars," *Academy of Management Review* 21 (1996) pp. 519–654; and L. R. James, C. C. Choi, C. E. Ko, P. K. McNeil, M. K. Minton, M. A. Wright, and K. Kim, "Organizational and Psychological Climate: A Review of Theory and Research," *European Journal of Work and Organizational Psychology* 17, no. 1 (2008), pp. 5–32.

18. J. Z. Carr, A. M. Schmidt, J. K. Ford, and R. P. DeShon, "Climate Perceptions Matter: A Meta-Analytic Path Analysis Relating Molar Climate, Cognitive and Affective States, and Individual Level Work Outcomes," *Journal of Applied Psychology* 88, no. (2003), pp. 605–619.

19. Schulte, Ostroff, Shmulyian, and Kinicki, "Organizational Climate Configurations: Relationships to Collective Attitudes, Customer Satisfaction, and Financial Performance."

20. See, for example, Z. S. Byrne, J. Stoner, K. R. Thompson, and W. Hochwarter, "The Interactive Effects of Conscientiousness, Work Effort, and Psychological Climate on Job Performance," *Journal of Vocational Behavior* 66,

no. 2 (2005), pp. 326–338; D. S. Pugh, J. Dietz, A. P. Brief, and J. W. Wiley, "Looking Inside and Out: The Impact of Employee and Community Demographic Composition on Organizational Diversity Climate," *Journal of Applied Psychology* 93, no. 6 (2008), pp. 1422–1428; J. C. Wallace, E. Popp, and S. Mondore, "Safety Climate as a Mediator Between Foundation Climates and Occupational Accidents: A Group-Level Investigation," *Journal of Applied Psychology* 91, no. 3 (2006), pp. 681–688; and K. H. Ehrhart, L. A. Witt, B. Schneider, and S. J. Perry, "Service Employees Give as They Get: Internal Service as a Moderator of the Service Climate-Service Outcomes Link," *Journal of Applied Psychology* 96, no. 2 (2011), pp. 423–431.

21. J C. Wallace, P. D. Johnson, K. Mathe, and J. Paul, "Structural and Psychological Empowerment Climates, Performance, and the Moderating Role of Shared Felt Accountability: A Managerial Perspective," *Journal of Applied Psychology* 96, no. 3 (2011), pp. 840–850.

22. J. M. Beus, S. C. Payne, M. E. Bergman, and W. Arthur, "Safety Climate and Injuries: An Examination of Theoretical and Empirical Relationships," *Journal of Applied Psychology* 95, no. 4 (2010), pp. 713–727.

23. R. L. Jepperson, "Institutions, Institutional Effects, and Institutionalism," in W. W. Powell and P. J. DiMaggio (eds.), *The New Institutionalism in Organizational Analysis* (Chicago: University of Chicago Press, 1991), pp. 143–163; G. F. Lanzara and G. Patriotta, "The Institutionalization of Knowledge in an Automotive Factory: Templates, Inscriptions, and the Problems of Durability," *Organization Studies* 28, no. 5 (2007), pp. 635–660; and T. B. Lawrence, M. K. Mauws, B. Dyck, and R. F. Kleysen, "The Politics of Organizational Learning: Integrating Power into the 4I Framework," *Academy of Management Review* (January 2005), pp. 180–191.

24. Sorensen, "The Strength of Corporate Culture and the Reliability of Firm Performance."

25. See T. Cox Jr., *Cultural Diversity in Organizations: Theory, Research & Practice* (San Francisco: Berrett-Koehler, 1993), pp. 162–170; L. Grensing-Pophal, "Hiring to Fit Your Corporate Culture," *HRMagazine* (August 1999), pp. 50–54; and D. L. Stone, E. F. Stone-Romero, and K. M. Lukaszewski, "The Impact of Cultural Values on the Acceptance and Effectiveness of Human Resource Management Policies and Practices," *Human Resource Management Review* 17, no. 2 (2007), pp. 152–165.

26. S. Cartwright and C. L. Cooper, "The Role of Culture Compatibility in Successful Organizational Marriages," *Academy of Management Executive* (May 1993), pp. 57–70; R. A. Weber and C. F. Camerer, "Cultural Conflict and Merger Failure: An Experimental Approach," *Management Science* (April 2003), pp. 400–412; and I. H. Gleibs, A. Mummendey, and P. Noack, "Predictors of Change in Postmerger Identification During a Merger Process: A Longitudinal Study," *Journal of Personality and Social Psychology* 95, no. 5 (2008), pp. 1095–1112.

27. P. Gumbel, "Return of the Urge to Merge," *Time Europe Magazine* (July 13, 2003), www.time.com/time/europe/magazine/article/0,13005,901030721-464418,00.html.

28. S. F. Gale, "Memo to AOL Time Warner: Why Mergers Fail—Case Studies," *Workforce Management* (February 2003),

www.workforce.com; and W. Bock, "Mergers, Bubbles, and Steve Case," *Wally Bock's Monday Memo*, January 20, 2003, www.mondaymemo.net/030120feature.htm.

29. E. H. Schein, "The Role of the Founder in Creating Organizational Culture," *Organizational Dynamics* (Summer 1983), pp. 13–28.

30. E. H. Schein, "Leadership and Organizational Culture," in F. Hesselbein, M. Goldsmith, and R. Beckhard (eds.), *The Leader of the Future* (San Francisco: Jossey-Bass, 1996), pp. 61–62.

31. See, for example, J. R. Harrison and G. R. Carroll, "Keeping the Faith: A Model of Cultural Transmission in Formal Organizations," *Administrative Science Quarterly* (December 1991), pp. 552–582; and D. E. Bowen and C. Ostroff, "The 'Strength' of the HRM System, Organizational Climate Formation, and Firm Performance," *Academy of Management Review* 29 (2004), pp. 203–221.

32. B. Schneider, H. W. Goldstein, and D. B. Smith, "The ASA Framework: An Update," *Personnel Psychology* (Winter 1995), pp. 747–773; D. M. Cable and T. A. Judge, "Interviewers' Perceptions of Person-Organization Fit and Organizational Selection Decisions," *Journal of Applied Psychology* (August 1997), pp. 546–561; M. L. Verquer, T. A. Beehr, and S. H. Wagner, "A Meta-Analysis of Relations Between Person-Organization Fit and Work Attitudes," *Journal of Vocational Behavior* (December 2003), pp. 473–489; and W. Li, Y. Wang, P. Taylor, K. Shi, and D. He, "The Influence of Organizational Culture on Work-Related Personality Requirement Ratings: A Multilevel Analysis," *International Journal of Selection and Assessment* 16, no. 4 (2008), pp. 366–384.

33. R. Levering and M. Moskowitz, "And the Winners Are . . . ," *Fortune* (January 20, 2011), http://money.cnn.com/magazines/fortune/bestcompanies/2011/full_list/.

34. D. C. Hambrick and P. A. Mason, "Upper Echelons: The Organization as a Reflection of Its Top Managers," *Academy of Management Review* (April 1984), pp. 193–206; M. A. Carpenter, M. A. Geletkanycz, and W. G. Sanders, "Upper Echelons Research Revisited: Antecedents, Elements, and Consequences of Top Management Team Composition," *Journal of Management* 30, no. 6 (2004), pp. 749–778, and H. Wang, A. S. Tsui, and K. R. Xin, "CEO Leadership Behaviors, Organizational Performance, and Employees' Attitudes," *The Leadership Quarterly* 22, no. 1 (2011), pp. 92–105.

35. See, for instance, J. P. Wanous, *Organizational Entry*, 2nd ed. (New York: Addison-Wesley, 1992); D. M. Cable and C. K. Parsons, "Socialization Tactics and Person-Organization Fit," *Personnel Psychology* (Spring 2001), pp. 1–23; and T. N. Bauer, T. Bodner, B. Erdogan, D. M. Truxillo, and J. S. Tucker, "Newcomer Adjustment During Organizational Socialization: A Meta-Analytic Review of Antecedents, Outcomes, and Methods," *Journal of Applied Psychology* 92, no. 3 (2007), pp. 707–721.

36. G. Kranz, "Training That Starts Before the Job Begins," *Workforce Management Online* (July 2009), www.workforce.com.

37. D. C. Feldman, "The Multiple Socialization of Organization Members," *Academy of Management Review* (April 1981), p. 310.

38. C. J. Collins, "The Interactive Effects of Recruitment Practices and Product Awareness on Job Seekers' Employer Knowledge and Application Behaviors," *Journal of Applied Psychology* 92, no. 1 (2007), pp. 180–190.

39. J. D. Kammeyer-Mueller and C. R. Wanberg, "Unwrapping the Organizational Entry Process: Disentangling Multiple Antecedents and Their Pathways to Adjustment," *Journal of Applied Psychology* 88 (2003), pp. 779–794; E. W. Morrison, "Longitudinal Study of the Effects of Information Seeking on Newcomer Socialization," *Journal of Applied Psychology* 78 (2003), pp. 173–183; and M. Wangm Y. Zhan, E. McCune, and D. Truxillo, "Understanding Newcomers' Adaptability and Work-Related Outcomes: Testing the Mediating Roles of Perceived P-E Fit Variables," *Personnel Psychology* 64, no. 1 (2011), pp. 163–189.

40. Van Maanen and Schein, "Career Development," p. 59. J. Van Maanen and E. H. Schein, "Career development." In J. R. Hackman and J. L. Suttle (eds.) *Improving Life at Work.* (Santa Monica, Calif.: Goodyear Publishing, 1977), pp. 30–95.

41. E. W. Morrison, "Newcomers' Relationships: The Role of Social Network Ties During Socialization," *Academy of Management Journal* 45 (2002), pp. 1149–1160.

42. T. N. Bauer, T. Bodner, B. Erdogan, D. M. Truxillo, and J. S. Tucker, "Newcomer Adjustment During Organizational Socialization: A Meta-Analytic Review of Antecedents, Outcomes, and Methods," *Journal of Applied Psychology* 92, no. 3 (2007), pp. 707–721.

43. W. R. Boswell, A. J. Shipp, S. C., Payne, and S. S. Culbertson, "Changes in Newcomer Job Satisfaction Over Time: Examining the Pattern of Honeymoons and Hangovers," *Journal of Applied Psychology* 94, no. 4 (2009), pp. 844–858.

44. C Vandenberghe, A. Panaccio, K. Bentein, K. Mignonac, and P. Roussel, "Assessing Longitudinal Change of and Dynamic Relationships Among Role Stressors, Job Attitudes, Turnover Intention, and Well-Being in Neophyte Newcomers," *Journal of Organizational Behavior* 32, no. 4 (2011), pp. 652–671.

45. E. Ransdell, "The Nike Story? Just Tell It!" *Fast Company* (January–February 2000), pp. 44–46; and A. Muccino, "Exclusive Interview with Chuck Eichten," *Liquid Brand Summit Blog,* (February 4, 2011), http://blog.liquidbrandsummit.com/.

46. D. M. Boje, "The Storytelling Organization: A Study of Story Performance in an Office-Supply Firm," *Administrative Science Quarterly* (March 1991), pp. 106–126; and M. Ricketts and J. G. Seiling, "Language, Metaphors, and Stories: Catalysts for Meaning Making in Organizations," *Organization Development Journal* (Winter 2003), pp. 33–43l.

47. A. J. Shipp and K. J. Jansen, "Reinterpreting Time in Fit Theory: Crafting and Recrafting Narratives of Fit in Medias Res," *Academy of Management Review* 36, no. 1 (2011), pp. 76–101.

48. See G. Islam and M. J. Zyphur, "Rituals in Organizations: A Review and Expansion of Current Theory," *Group and Organization Management* 34, no. 1 (2009), pp. 114–139.

49. V. Matthews, "Starting Every Day with a Shout and a Song," *Financial Times* (May 2, 2001), p. 11; and M. Gimein, "Sam Walton Made Us a Promise," *Fortune* (March 18, 2002), pp. 121–130.

50. M. G. Pratt and A. Rafaeli "Artifacts and Organizations: Understanding Our Objective Reality," in A. Rafaeli and

M. G. Pratt, *Artifacts and Organizations: Beyond Mere Symbolism* (Mahwah, NJ: Lawrence Erlbaum, 2006), pp. 279–288.

51. See B. Victor and J. B. Cullen, "The Organizational Bases of Ethical Work Climates," *Administrative Science Quarterly* (March 1988), pp. 101–125; R. L. Dufresne, "An Action Learning Perspective on Effective Implementation of Academic Honor Codes," *Group & Organization Management* (April 2004), pp. 201–218; and A. Ardichvilli, J. A. Mitchell, and D. Jondle, "Characteristics of Ethical Business Cultures," *Journal of Business Ethics* 85, no. 4 (2009), pp. 445–451.

52. J. P. Mulki, J. F. Jaramillo, and W. B. Locander, "Critical Role of Leadership on Ethical Climate and Salesperson Behaviors," *Journal of Business Ethics* 86, no. 2 (2009), pp. 125–141; M. Schminke, M. L. Ambrose, and D. O. Neubaum, "The Effect of Leader Moral Development on Ethical Climate and Employee Attitudes," *Organizational Behavior and Human Decision Processes* 97, no. 2 (2005), pp. 135–151; and M. E. Brown, L. K. Treviño, and D. A. Harrison, "Ethical Leadership: A Social Learning Perspective for Construct Development and Testing," *Organizational Behavior and Human Decision Processes* 97, no. 2 (2005), pp. 117–134.

53. D. M. Mayer, M. Kuenzi, R. Greenbaum, M. Bardes, and S. Salvador, "How Low Does Ethical Leadership Flow? Test of a Trickle-Down Model," *Organizational Behavior and Human Decision Processes* 108, no. 1 (2009), pp. 1–13.

54. B. Sweeney, D. Arnold, and B. Pierce, "The Impact of Perceived Ethical Culture of the Firm and Demographic Variables on Auditors' Ethical Evaluation and Intention to Act Decisions," *Journal of Business Ethics* 93, no. 4 (2010), pp. 531–551.

55. M. L. Gruys, S. M. Stewart, J. Goodstein, M. N. Bing, and A. C. Wicks, "Values Enactment in Organizations: A Multi-Level Examination," *Journal of Management* 34, no. 4 (2008), pp. 806–843.

56. D. L. Nelson and C. L. Cooper (eds.), *Positive Organizational Behavior* (London: Sage, 2007); K. S. Cameron, J. E. Dutton, and R. E. Quinn (eds.), *Positive Organizational Scholarship: Foundations of a New Discipline* (San Francisco: Berrett-Koehler, 2003); and F. Luthans and C. M. Youssef, "Emerging Positive Organizational Behavior," *Journal of Management* (June 2007), pp. 321–349.

57. J. Robison, "Great Leadership Under Fire," *Gallup Leadership Journal* (March 8, 2007), pp. 1–3.

58. R. Wagner and J. K. Harter, *12: The Elements of Great Managing* (New York: Gallup Press, 2006).

59. R. Wagner and J. K. Harter, "Performance Reviews Without the Anxiety," *Gallup Leadership Journal* (July 12, 2007), pp. 1–4; and Wagner and Harter, *12: The Elements of Great Managing*.

60. S. Fineman, "On Being Positive: Concerns and Counterpoints," *Academy of Management Review* 31, no. 2 (2006), pp. 270–291.

61. D. P. Ashmos and D. Duchon, "Spirituality at Work: A Conceptualization and Measure," *Journal of Management Inquiry* (June 2000), p. 139; and E. Poole, "Organisational

Spirituality: A Literature Review," *Journal of Business Ethics* 84, no. 4 (2009), pp. 577–588.

62. L. W. Fry and J. W. Slocum, "Managing the Triple Bottom Line Through Spiritual Leadership," *Organizational Dynamics* 37, no. 1 (2008), pp. 86–96.

63. This section is based on I. A. Mitroff and E. A. Denton, *A Spiritual Audit of Corporate America: A Hard Look at Spirituality, Religion, and Values in the Workplace* (San Francisco: Jossey-Bass, 1999); E. H. Burack, "Spirituality in the Workplace," *Journal of Organizational Change Management* 12, no. 3 (1999), pp. 280–291; and C. L. Jurkiewicz and R. A. Giacalone, "A Values Framework for Measuring the Impact of Workplace Spirituality on Organizational Performance," *Journal of Business Ethics* 49, no. 2 (2004), pp. 129–142.

64. See, for example, B. S. Pawar, "Workplace Spirituality Facilitation: A Comprehensive Model," *Journal of Business Ethics* 90, no. 3 (2009), pp. 375–386; and L. Lambert, *Spirituality Inc.: Religion in the American Workplace* (New York: New York University Press, 2009).

65. M. Lips-Miersma, K. L. Dean, and C. J. Fornaciari, "Theorizing the Dark Side of the Workplace Spirituality Movement," *Journal of Management Inquiry* 18, no. 4 (2009), pp. 288–300.

66. J.-C. Garcia-Zamor, "Workplace Spirituality and Organizational Performance," *Public Administration Review* (May–June 2003), pp. 355–363; and L. W. Fry, S. T. Hannah, M. Noel, and F. O. Walumbwa, "Impact of Spiritual Leadership on Unit Performance," *Leadership Quarterly* 22, no. 2 (2011), pp. 259–270.

67. A. Rego and M. Pina e Cunha, "Workplace Spirituality and Organizational Commitment: An Empirical Study," *Journal of Organizational Change Management* 21, no. 1 (2008), pp. 53–75; and R. W. Kolodinsky, R. A. Giacalone, and C. L. Jurkiewicz, "Workplace Values and Outcomes: Exploring Personal, Organizational, and Interactive Workplace Spirituality," *Journal of Business Ethics* 81, no. 2 (2008), pp. 465–480.

68. D. J. McCarthy and S. M. Puffer, "Interpreting the Ethicality of Corporate Governance Decision in Russia: Utilizing Integrative Social Contracts Theory to Evaluate the Relevance of Agency Theory Norms," *Academy of Management Review* 33, no. 1 (2008), pp. 11–31.

69. P. Dvorak, "A Firm's Culture Can Get Lost in Translation," *The Wall Street Journal* (April 3, 2006), pp. B1, B3; K. Kranhold, "The Immelt Era, Five Years Old, Transforms GE," *The Wall Street Journal* (September 11, 2006), pp. B1, B3; and S. McCartney, "Teaching Americans How to Behave Abroad," *The Wall Street Journal* (April 11, 2006), pp. D1, D4.

70. J. A. Chatman, "Matching People and Organizations: Selection and Socialization in Public Accounting Firms," *Administrative Science Quarterly* (September 1991), pp. 459–484; and A. E. M. Van Vianen, "Person-Organization Fit: The Match Between Newcomers' and Recruiters' Preferences for Organizational Cultures," *Personnel Psychology* (Spring 2000), pp. 113–149.

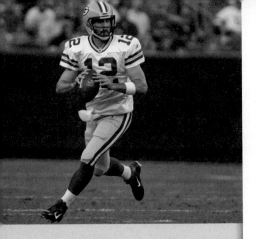

LEARNING OBJECTIVES

After studying this chapter, you should be able to:

1 Define *initial selection*, and identify the most useful methods.

2 Define *substantive selection*, and identify the most useful methods.

3 Define *contingent selection*, and contrast the arguments for and against drug testing.

4 Compare the four main types of training.

5 Contrast formal and informal training methods.

6 Contrast on-the-job and off-the-job training.

7 Describe the purposes of performance evaluation, and list the methods by which it can be done.

8 Show how managers can improve performance evaluations.

9 Describe how organizations can manage work–family conflicts.

MyManagementLab

Access a host of interactive learning aids to help strengthen your understanding of the chapter concepts at **www.mymanagementlab.com.**

TESTING NFL QUARTERBACKS

It's often said that the entire human resources function in organizations is meant to fix mistakes made at the time of hiring. There is an element of truth in that, but it's also true that making accurate hiring decisions is itself the most important aspect of human resources. And perhaps no aspect of selection is more interesting or surprising than this: a 12-minute paper-and-pencil test may well be the single best method for selecting employees in most occupations, including, perhaps, National Football League (NFL) quarterbacks.

We're talking about the Wonderlic Cognitive Ability Test, one of the most extensively validated tests ever. (We first discussed it in Chapter 2.) The Wonderlic has been applied to hundreds of occupations, but nowhere is its use more intriguing than in the NFL. As NFL fans know, prior to the football draft every year, potential draftees go through a "combine" where their skills are tested: they run, they bench-press, they scrimmage—and they also take the Wonderlic. Although players and members of the media often express skepticism about the validity of the test, evidence suggests it works.

Scores range from 0 to 50. The average chemist scores 31, compared to 26 for a journalist, 22 for a bank teller, and 15 for a warehouse worker. Among football players, scores vary by position. Offensive linemen and quarterbacks generally have much higher scores than running backs, cornerbacks, or middle linebackers.

Here's a select sample of how some NFL quarterbacks scored on the Wonderlic (scores for others like Matt Cassel, Troy Smith, and Jon Kitna were unavailable):

30 and higher (very intelligent) Ryan Fitzpatrick: 48, Alex Smith: 40, Eli Manning: 39, Matthew Stafford: 38, Tony Romo: 37, Sam Bradford: 36, Aaron Rodgers: 35, Christian Ponder: 35, Tom Brady: 33, Matt Ryan: 32, Brian Brohm: 32, Matt Schaub: 30, Philip Rivers: 30

25–29 (intelligent) Matt Hasselbeck: 29, Marc Bulger: 29, Peyton Manning: 28, Drew Brees: 28, Mark Sanchez: 28, Joe Flacco: 27, Jason Campbell: 27, Josh Freeman: 27, Jay Cutler: 26, Carson Palmer: 26, Kyle Orton: 26, Colt McCoy: 25, Shaun Hill: 25, Ben Roethlisberger: 25

20–24 (above average) Jimmy Clausen: 23, Chad Henne: 22, Brett Favre: 22, Tim Tebow: 22, Cam Newton: 21, Michael Vick: 20, Jake Locker: 20

Less than 20 (average to below average) Derek Anderson: 19, Bruce Gradkowski: 19, Vince Young: 16, Donovan McNabb: 16, David Garrard: 14, Seneca Wallace: 12

It's clear NFL quarterbacks are smart—most score well above average relative to the U.S. population (the population average is 19). But do differences among the quarterbacks predict success? It's not clear. In the past several

Human Resource Policies and Practices

To manage people well, companies should . . . elevate HR to a position of power and primacy in the organization. —Jack Welch seasons, there has not been a strong correlation between Wonderlic scores and quarterback ratings (a composite index assessing quarterback performance). One reporter looking at these results called it a "useless exam."

On the other hand, if you take an average of the Wonderlic scores of the quarterbacks for the past eight Super Bowl winners, you get a rather lofty average of 31.

Sources: M. Mirabile, "NFL Quarterback Wonderlic Scores," www.macmirabile.com/Wonderlic .htm; E. Thompson, "Wonderlic Scores of 2010 NFL Starting Quarterbacks and NFL Draft QB Prospects," *Palm Beach Post* (March 10, 2010), www.palmbeachpost.com/sports/; J. Saraceno, "Who Knows if This Longhorn Is Short on IQ," *USA Today* (March 1, 2006), p. 2C; and S. Smith, "Wonderlic Test: NFL Should Sack Useless Exam," *CBS News Sports* (February 28, 2011), downloaded on July 3, 2011, from www.cbsnews.com/.

The message of this chapter is that human resource (HR) policies and practices—such as employee selection, training, and performance management—influence an organization's effectiveness.[1] However, studies show managers—even HR managers—often don't know which HR practices work and which don't. To see how much you know (before learning the right answers in this chapter), take the self-assessment.

SELF-ASSESSMENT LIBRARY

How Much Do I Know About Human Resource Management (HRM)?

In the Self-Assessment Library (available on CD and online), take assessment IV.G.2 (How Much Do I Know About HRM?) and answer the following questions:

1. How did you score compared to your classmates'? Did the results surprise you?
2. How much of effective HRM is common sense?
3. Do you think your score will improve after you read this chapter?

Selection Practices

We just suggested that the most important HR function is hiring the right people. How do you figure out who they are? Identifying the right people is the objective of the selection process, which matches individual characteristics (ability, experience, and so on) with the requirements of the job.[2] When management fails to get a proper match, employee performance and satisfaction both suffer. As a result of the Great Recession and the continued high unemployment rate, there are now many applicants for almost every open job position. This makes it more important than ever to ensure that your organization has an effective method for separating the most qualified candidates from the large number of applicants.

How the Selection Process Works

Exhibit 17-1 shows how the selection process works in most organizations. Having decided to apply for a job, applicants go through several stages—three

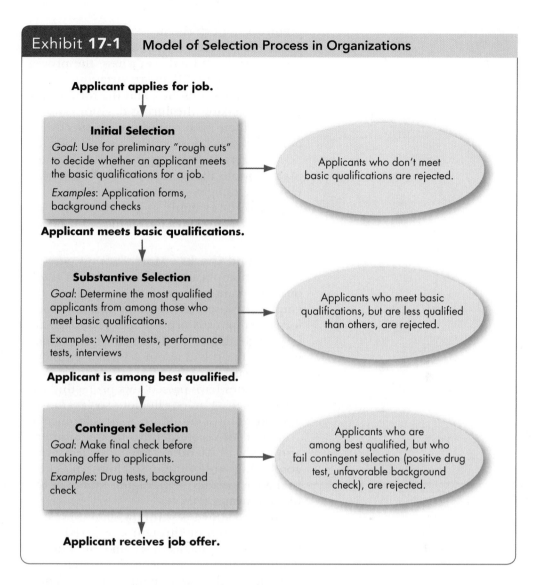

Exhibit **17-1**   Model of Selection Process in Organizations

Applicant applies for job.

Initial Selection

Goal: Use for preliminary "rough cuts" to decide whether an applicant meets the basic qualifications for a job.

Examples: Application forms, background checks

Applicants who don't meet basic qualifications are rejected.

Applicant meets basic qualifications.

Substantive Selection

Goal: Determine the most qualified applicants from among those who meet basic qualifications.

Examples: Written tests, performance tests, interviews

Applicants who meet basic qualifications, but are less qualified than others, are rejected.

Applicant is among best qualified.

Contingent Selection

Goal: Make final check before making offer to applicants.

Examples: Drug tests, background check

Applicants who are among best qualified, but who fail contingent selection (positive drug test, unfavorable background check), are rejected.

Applicant receives job offer.

are shown in the exhibit—during which they can be rejected at any time. In practice, some organizations forgo some of these steps in the interests of time. (A meat-packing plant may hire someone who walks in the door, but there is not a long line of people who want to "thread" a pig's intestines for a living.) But most organizations follow a process that looks something like this exhibit. Let's go into a bit more detail about each stage.

Initial Selection

Initial selection devices are the first information applicants submit and are used for preliminary rough cuts to decide whether the applicant meets the basic qualifications for a job. Application forms (including letters of recommendation) are initial selection devices. We list background checks as either an initial selection device or a contingent selection device, depending on how the organization handles them. Some organizations prefer to look into an applicant's background right away. Others wait until the applicant is about ready to be hired, contingent on everything else checking out.

Application Forms   You've no doubt submitted your fair share of applications. By itself, the information submitted on an application form is not a very useful

1   Define *initial selection,* and identify the most useful methods.

predictor of performance. However, it can be a good initial screen. For example, there's no sense spending time interviewing an applicant for a registered nurse position if he doesn't have the proper credentials (education, certification, experience). Many organizations encourage applicants to apply online. It takes only a few minutes, and the form can be forwarded to the people responsible for making the hiring decision. Most major corporations have a career page on their Web site where prospective employees can search for available positions by location or job type and then apply online.

Managers must be careful about the questions they ask on applications. It's pretty obvious that questions about race, gender, and nationality are disallowed. However, it might surprise you that other questions also put companies in legal jeopardy. For example, it generally is not permissible to ask about prior arrest records or even convictions unless the answer is job related.

Background Checks   More than 80 percent of employers conduct reference checks on applicants at some point in the hiring process. The reason is obvious: they want to know how an applicant did in past jobs and whether former employers would recommend hiring the person. The problem is that rarely do former employers provide useful information. In fact, nearly two-thirds refuse to provide detailed references because they are afraid of being sued for saying something bad about a former employee. Although this concern is often unfounded (employers are safe as long as they stick to documented facts, and several states have passed laws protecting truthful information provided in reference checks), in our litigious society most employers play it safe. The result is a paradox: most employers want reference information, but few will give it out.

Letters of recommendation are another form of background check. These also aren't as useful as they may seem. Applicants select those who will write good things about them, so almost all letters of recommendation are positive. In the end, readers either ignore them or read "between the lines" to try to find hidden meaning there.

Many employers will now search for candidates online through a general Internet search or through a targeted search on social networking sites. The legality of this practice has come into question, but there is no doubt that many employers include an electronic search to see whether candidates have any history that might make them a dubious choice for employment. For some potential employees, an embarrassing or incriminating photo circulated through Facebook may make it hard to get a job.

Finally, some employers check credit histories or criminal records. A bank hiring tellers, for example, would probably want to know about an applicant's criminal and credit histories. Increasingly, credit checks are being used for nonbanking jobs. Kevin Palmer's offer of a job with a property management company evaporated after the company performed a credit check on him that revealed a bankruptcy in his past.[3] Despite the trend, because of the invasive nature of such checks, employers need to be sure there is a need for them. To further complicate matters, however, *not* checking can carry a legal cost. Manor Park Nursing Home in Texas failed to do a criminal background check of an employee who later sexually assaulted a resident of the home. The jury awarded the plaintiff $1.1 million, concluding the nursing home was negligent for failing to conduct a background check.[4]

Substantive Selection

2 Define *substantive selection*, and identify the most useful methods.

If an applicant passes the initial screens, next are substantive selection methods. These are the heart of the selection process and include written tests, performance tests, and interviews.

Written tests are the heart of the selection process at Cabela's, a specialty retailer of hunting, fishing, camping, and other outdoor merchandise. Job applicants for Cabela's contact center and retail stores are given a difficult 150-question test that measures the depth of their knowledge of outdoor sports. Cabela's management believes that the written tests are helpful in determining who will succeed in providing customers with exceptional service and product knowledge.

Source: William Thomas Cain/Getty Images.

Written Tests   Long popular as selection devices, written tests—called "paper-and-pencil" tests, though most are now available online—declined in use between the late 1960s and mid-1980s, especially in the United States. They were frequently characterized as discriminatory, and many organizations had not validated them as job related. The past 20 years, however, have seen a resurgence, and today more than 60 percent of all U.S. organizations and most of the *Fortune* 1,000 use some type of employment test.[5] Managers recognize that valid tests can help predict who will be successful on the job.[6] Applicants, however, tend to view written tests as less valid and fair than interviews or performance tests.[7] Typical written tests include (1) intelligence or cognitive ability tests, (2) personality tests, (3) integrity tests, and (4) interest inventories.

Tests of intellectual ability, spatial and mechanical ability, perceptual accuracy, and motor ability have long proven valid predictors for many skilled, semiskilled, and unskilled operative jobs organizations.[8] Intelligence tests have proven to be particularly good predictors for jobs that include cognitively complex tasks (like learning the ever-more-complex playbooks in the NFL).[9] Many experts say intelligence tests are the *single best* selection measure across jobs, and that they are at least as valid in the European Union (EU) nations as in the United States.[10]

Personality tests are inexpensive and simple to administer, and in the past decade, their use has grown. The traits that best predict job performance are conscientiousness and positive self-concept.[11] This makes sense in that conscientious people tend to be motivated and dependable, and positive people are "can-do" oriented and persistent. However, concerns about applicant faking remain, because it's fairly easy for applicants to claim they are hard-working, motivated, and dependable when asked in a job application setting.[12] Two reviews of studies comparing self-reported personality to observer-rated personality found that observer ratings are better predictors of job performance and other behaviors.[13] Thus, employers might want to consider asking employment references about applicant personality as part of the screening process.

As ethical problems have increased in organizations, integrity tests have gained popularity. These paper-and-pencil tests measure factors such as dependability, carefulness, responsibility, and honesty; they have proven to be powerful predictors of supervisory ratings of job performance and of theft, discipline problems, and excessive absenteeism.[14]

Performance-Simulation Tests   What better way to find out whether applicants can do a job successfully than by having them do it? That's precisely the logic of performance-simulation tests.

Although they are more complicated to develop and administer than written tests, performance-simulation tests have higher *face validity* (which measures whether applicants perceive the measures to be accurate), and their popularity has increased. The three best-known are work samples, assessment centers, and situational judgment tests.

Work sample tests are hands-on simulations of part or all of the work that applicants for routine jobs must perform. Each work sample element is matched with a job-performance element to measure applicants' knowledge, skills, and abilities with more validity than written aptitude and personality tests.[15] Work samples are widely used in the hiring of skilled workers, such as welders, machinists, carpenters, and electricians. Job candidates for production jobs often have a limited period of time to perform a variety of typical work tasks on a specially built simulated assembly line.[16]

A more elaborate set of performance-simulation tests, specifically designed to evaluate a candidate's managerial potential, is administered in **assessment centers**. Line executives, supervisors, and/or trained psychologists evaluate candidates as they go through one to several days of exercises that simulate real problems they would confront on the job.[17] A candidate might be required to play the role of a manager who must decide how to respond to ten memos in an in-basket within a 2-hour period.

To reduce the costs of job simulations, many organizations have started to use situational judgment tests, which ask applicants how they would perform in a variety of job situations and compare their answers to those of high-performing employees.[18] One study comparing situational judgment tests to assessment centers found the assessment center was a better predictor of job performance, although the difference was not large.[19] Ultimately, the lower cost of the situational judgment test may make it a better choice for some organizations than a more elaborate work sample or assessment center.

Interviews   Of all the selection devices organizations around the globe use to differentiate candidates, the interview remains the most common.[20] It also tends to have a disproportionate amount of influence. Over-reliance on interviews is problematic, because extensive evidence shows that impression management techniques like self-promotion have a strong effect on interviewer preferences even when unrelated to the job.[21] Conversely, the candidate who performs poorly in the employment interview is likely to be cut from the applicant pool regardless of experience, test scores, or letters of recommendation.

These findings are relevant because of the interview's typical nature.[22] The popular unstructured interview—short, casual, and made up of random questions—is simply not a very effective selection device.[23] The data it gathers are typically biased and often only modestly related to future job performance. Still, managers are reluctant to use *structured interviews* in place of their favorite questions, such as "If you could be any animal, what would you be, and why?"[24]

Without structure, interviewers tend to favor applicants who share their attitudes, give undue weight to negative information, and allow the order in which applicants are interviewed to influence their evaluations.[25] To reduce such bias

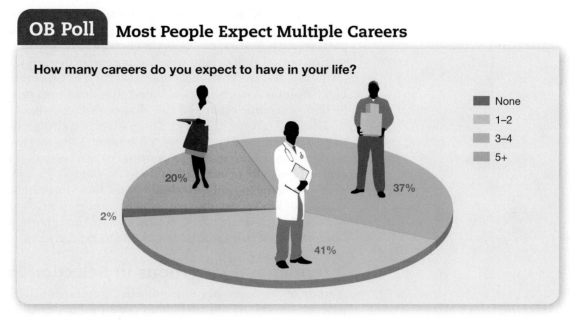

OB Poll   **Most People Expect Multiple Careers**

How many careers do you expect to have in your life?

None
1–2
3–4
5+

20%

2%

37%

41%

Source: Based on J. Yang and A. Gonzalez, "Charles Schwab Survey of 1,000 Adults," *USA Today* (March 9, 2011), p. 1B.

and improve the validity of interviews, managers should adopt a standardized set of questions, a uniform method of recording information, and standardized ratings of applicants' qualifications. Training interviewers to focus on specific dimensions of job performance, practicing evaluation of sample candidates, and giving interviewers feedback on how well they were focused on job-relevant characteristics significantly improves the accuracy of their ratings.[26] Interview effectiveness also improves when employers use *behavioral structured interviews*, probably because these assessments are less influenced by interviewer biases.[27] They require applicants to describe how they handled specific problems and situations in previous jobs, based on the assumption that past behavior offers the best predictor of future behavior. Panel interviews also minimize the influence of individual biases and have higher validity.

In practice, most organizations use interviews as more than a prediction-of-performance device.[28] Companies as diverse as Southwest Airlines, Disney, Bank of America, Microsoft, Procter & Gamble, and Harrah's Entertainment use them to assess applicant–organization fit. So, in addition to evaluating specific, job-related skills, managers are looking at personality characteristics and personal values to find individuals who fit the organization's culture and image.

Contingent Selection

3 Define *contingent selection*, and contrast the arguments for and against drug testing.

If applicants pass the substantive selection methods, they are ready to be hired, contingent on a final check. One common contingent method is a drug test. Publix grocery stores make a tentative offer to applicants contingent on their passing such a test and checking out as drug-free.

work sample tests *Hands-on simulations of part or all of the work that applicants for routine jobs must perform.*

assessment centers *A set of performance-simulation tests designed to evaluate a candidate's managerial potential.*

Drug testing is controversial. Many applicants think testing without reasonable suspicion is invasive or unfair and say they should be tested on job-performance factors, not lifestyle choices that may not be relevant. Employers might counter that drug use and abuse are extremely costly, not just in financial terms but also in terms of people's safety. They have the law on their side. The U.S. Supreme Court has concluded that drug tests are "minimally invasive" selection procedures that as a rule do not violate individuals' rights.

Under the Americans with Disabilities Act, firms may not require employees to pass a medical exam before a job offer is made. However, they can conduct medical exams *after* making a contingent offer—to determine whether an applicant is physically or mentally able to do the job. Employers also sometimes use medical exams to find out whether and how they can accommodate employees with disabilities. For jobs requiring exposure to heavy physical or psychological demands, such as air traffic controllers or firefighters, medical exams are obviously an important indicator of ability to perform.

International Variations in Selection Processes

A study of 300 large organizations in 22 countries demonstrated that selection practices differ by nation.[29] The use of educational qualifications in screening candidates seems to be a universal practice, but aside from this, different countries emphasize different selection techniques. Structured interviews were popular in some countries and nonexistent in others. The study authors suggested that "certain cultures may find structured interviews antithetical to beliefs about how one should conduct an interpersonal interaction or the extent to which one should trust the judgment of the interviewer."[30] Other research shows that across the Netherlands, the United States, France, Spain, Portugal, and Singapore, most applicants prefer interviews and work sample tests and dislike use of personal contacts and integrity tests.[31] There was little variation in preferences across these countries.

Executives of ImageNet Company (in red jackets), a Japanese Internet retailer, conducted job interviews atop Mount Fuji, Japan's highest mountain. Of the 20 candidates who applied for one of four job openings, 11 succeeded in reaching the summit of the 12,388-foot mountain for the interview. ImageNet said that the unique interview was to ensure that job applicants "have what it takes to scale the heights of business" and would identify candidates who are highly motivated, determined to succeed, and prepared for unusual challenges. Requiring applicants to climb a mountain to attend an interview would run afoul of equal employment laws in the United States and most European nations.

Source: Yuriko Nakao/Reuters/Landov Media.

Competent employees don't remain competent forever. Skills deteriorate and can become obsolete, and new skills need to be learned. That's why U.S. corporations with a hundred or more employees spent more than $125 billion on formal training in a recent year.[32]

Types of Training

4 Compare the four main types of training.

Training can include everything from teaching employees basic reading skills to conducting advanced courses in executive leadership. Here we discuss four general skill categories—basic literacy, technical skills, interpersonal skills, and problem-solving skills—and ethics training.

Basic Skills   One survey of more than 400 human resources professionals found that 40 percent of employers believe high school graduates lack basic skills in reading comprehension, writing, and math.[33] As work has become more sophisticated, the need for these basic skills has grown significantly, leading to a gap between employer demands for skills and the available skills in the workforce.[34] The challenge isn't unique to the United States. It's a worldwide problem—from the most developed countries to the least.[35] For many undeveloped countries, widespread illiteracy means there is almost no hope of competing in a global economy.

Organizations increasingly have to teach employees basic reading and math skills. A literacy audit showed that employees at gun manufacturer Smith & Wesson needed at least an eighth-grade reading level to do typical workplace tasks.[36] Yet 30 percent of the company's 676 workers with no degree scored below eighth-grade levels in either reading or math. After the first round of basic-skills classes, company-paid and on company time, 70 percent of attendees brought their skills up to the target level, allowing them to do a better job. They displayed increased abilities to use fractions and decimals, better overall communication, greater ease in writing and reading charts, graphs, and bulletin boards—and a significant increase in confidence.

Technical Skills   Most training is directed at upgrading and improving an employee's technical skills, increasingly important for two reasons: new technology and new structural designs in the organization.

Indian companies have faced a dramatic increase in demand for skilled workers in areas like engineering for emerging technologies, but many recent engineering graduates lack up-to-date knowledge required to perform these technical tasks.[37] Companies like Tata and Wipro provide new hires with up to 3 months of training to ensure they have the knowledge to perform the technical work demanded. In addition, these organizations are attempting to form partnerships with engineering schools to ensure their curricula meet the needs of contemporary employers.

As organizations flatten their structures, expand their use of teams, and break down traditional departmental barriers, employees need mastery of a wider variety of tasks and increased knowledge of how their organization operates. The restructuring of jobs around empowered teams at Miller Brewing led management to introduce a comprehensive business literacy program to help employees better understand competition, the state of the beer industry, where the company's revenues come from, how costs are calculated, and where employees fit into the company's value chain.[38]

Problem-Solving Skills   Problem-solving training for managers and other employees can include activities to sharpen their logic, reasoning, and problem-defining skills as well as their abilities to assess causation, develop and analyze alternatives, and select solutions. Problem-solving training has become a part of almost every organizational effort to introduce self-managed teams or implement quality-management programs.

Interpersonal Skills   Almost all employees belong to a work unit, and their work performance depends on their ability to effectively interact with their co-workers and boss. Some employees have excellent interpersonal abilities, but others require training to improve listening, communicating, and team-building skills. Although professionals are greatly interested in interpersonal skills training, most evidence suggests that skills learned in such training do not readily transfer back to the workplace.[39]

Civility Training   As human resource managers have become increasingly aware of the effects of social behavior in the workplace, they have paid more attention to the problems of incivility, bullying, and abusive supervision in organizations. Examples of incivility include being ignored, being excluded from social situations, having your reputation undermined in front of others, and experiencing other actions meant to demean or disparage. Researchers have shown that these forms of negative behavior can decrease satisfaction, reduce job performance, increase perceptions of unfair treatment, increase depression, and lead to psychological withdrawal from the workplace.[40]

Is there anything managers can do to minimize incivility, bullying, and abusive supervision? One possibility is training specifically targeted to building civility by having directed conversations about it and supporting the reduction of incivility on an ongoing process. Following a training intervention based on these principles, co-worker civility, respect, job satisfaction, and management trust have increased, while supervisor incivility, cynicism, and absences

There's a heavy focus on teamwork and unit cohesion for this squad of midshipmen during their 18-hour-long Sea Trials training at the U.S. Naval Academy. Learning how to become a team player and recognizing the value of teamwork are part of the interpersonal skills training for cadets who are finishing their freshman year at the academy. Working together to complete a challenge, such as transporting the log shown here, is the objective of the training, because the tasks cannot be completed alone. The training also teaches cadets the skills of encouraging and motivating peers to succeed as part of building unity among squad members.

decreased.[41] Thus, the evidence suggests that deliberate interventions to improve the workplace climate for positive behavior can indeed minimize the problems of incivility.

Ethics Training   A large percentage of employees working in the 1,000 largest U.S. corporations receive ethics training[42] either during new-employee orientation, as part of ongoing developmental programs, or as periodic reinforcement of ethical principles.[43] But the jury is still out on whether you can actually teach ethics.[44]

Critics argue that ethics are based on values, and value systems are learned by example at an early age. By the time employees are hired, their ethical values are fixed. Some research does suggest ethics training does not have a significant long-term effect on participants' values and even that exposure to business and law school programs *decreases* students' level of prosocial ethical values.[45]

Supporters of ethics training say values *can* be learned and changed after early childhood. And even if they couldn't, ethics training helps employees recognize ethical dilemmas and become more aware of the ethical issues underlying their actions. It also reaffirms an organization's expectations that members will act ethically. Individuals who have greater exposure to organizational ethics codes and ethics training do tend to be more satisfied and perceive their organizations as more socially responsible, so ethics training does have some positive effects.[46]

Training Methods

5   Contrast formal and informal training methods.

Historically, *training* meant "formal training," planned in advance and having a structured format. However, evidence indicates 70 percent of workplace learning takes place in *informal training*—unstructured, unplanned, and easily adapted to situations and individuals—for teaching skills and keeping employees current.[47] In reality, most informal training is nothing other than employees helping each other out, sharing information, and solving work-related problems together. Thus, many managers are now supportive of what used to be considered "idle chatter."

6   Contrast on-the-job and off-the-job training.

On-the-job training methods include job rotation, apprenticeships, understudy assignments, and formal mentoring programs. But because they often disrupt the workplace, organizations also invest in *off-the-job training*. The $125 billion figure we cited for training was largely spent on the formal off-the-job variety, the most popular method being live classroom lectures. But it also encompasses public seminars, self-study programs, Internet courses, Webinars, podcasts, and group activities that use role-plays and case studies.

MyManagementLab
For an interactive application of this topic, check out this chapter's simulation activity at **www.mymanagementlab.com.**

The fastest-growing training medium is probably computer-based training, or e-training.[48] E-learning systems emphasize learner control over the pace and content of instruction, allow e-learners to interact through online communities, and incorporate other techniques such as simulations and group discussions. Computer-based training that lets learners actively participate in exercises and quizzes was more effective than traditional classroom instruction.[49] Recent research has also highlighted the ways in which computer-based training can be improved by providing learners with regular prompts to set goals for learning, use effective study strategies, and measure progress toward their learning goals.[50]

On the positive side, e-training increases flexibility because organizations can deliver materials anywhere, any time. It also seems fast and efficient. On the other hand, it's expensive to design self-paced online materials, employees miss the social interaction of a classroom, online learners are more susceptible to distractions, and "clicking through" training without engaging in practice activities provides no assurance that employees have actually learned anything.[51]

Videogame training is widely used in the technology industry and is gaining popularity in low-tech firms. Cold Stone Creamery, for example, has developed a proprietary game called "Stone City" to help new employees like the young man shown here learn about products, portion sizes, and customer service. As one element of computerized training, Internet games are intrinsically motivating and result in employees choosing to repeatedly engage in game play and mastering skills. Computer-based training is fast and efficient and gives learners control over the pace and content of instruction.

Source: Abel Uribe/MCT/Newscom.

Evaluating Effectiveness

The *effectiveness* of a training program can refer to the level of student satisfaction, the amount students learn, the extent to which they transfer the material from training to their jobs, or the financial return on investments in training.[52] These results are not always related. Some people who have a positive experience in an upbeat, fun class learn very little; some who learn a great deal have difficulty figuring out how to use their knowledge at work; and changes in employee behavior are often not large enough to justify the expense of training. This means rigorous measurement of multiple training outcomes should be a part of every training effort.

The success of training also depends on the individual. If individuals are unmotivated, they will learn very little. What creates training motivation? Personality is important: those with an internal locus of control, high conscientiousness, high cognitive ability, and high self-efficacy learn more. The climate also is important: when trainees believe there are opportunities and resources to let them apply their newly learned skills, they are more motivated and do better in training programs.[53] Finally, after-training support from supervisors and co-workers has a strong influence on whether employees transfer their learning into new behavior.[54] For a training program to be effective requires not just teaching the skills but also changing the work environment to support the trainees.

Performance Evaluation

7 Describe the purposes of performance evaluation, and list the methods by which it can be done.

Would you study differently or exert a different level of effort for a college course graded on a pass–fail basis than for one that awarded letter grades A to F? Students typically tell us they study harder when letter grades are at stake. When they take a course on a pass–fail basis, they tend to do just enough to ensure a passing grade.

What applies in the college context also applies to employees at work. In this section, we show how the choice of a performance evaluation system and the way it's administered can be an important force influencing employee behavior.

What Is Performance?

In the past, most organizations assessed only how well employees performed the tasks listed on a job description, but today's less hierarchical and more service-oriented organizations require more. Researchers now recognize three major types of behavior that constitute performance at work:

1. **Task performance.** Performing the duties and responsibilities that contribute to the production of a good or service or to administrative tasks. This includes most of the tasks in a conventional job description.
2. **Citizenship.** Actions that contribute to the psychological environment of the organization, such as helping others when not required, supporting organizational objectives, treating co-workers with respect, making constructive suggestions, and saying positive things about the workplace.
3. **Counterproductivity.** Actions that actively damage the organization. These behaviors include stealing, damaging company property, behaving aggressively toward co-workers, and taking avoidable absences.

Most managers believe good performance means doing well on the first two dimensions and avoiding the third.[55] A person who does core job tasks very well but is rude and aggressive toward co-workers is not going to be considered a good employee in most organizations, and even the most pleasant and upbeat worker who can't do the main job tasks well is not going to be a good employee.

Purposes of Performance Evaluation

Performance evaluation serves a number of purposes.[56] One is to help management make general *human resource decisions* about promotions, transfers, and terminations. Evaluations also *identify training and development needs*. They *pinpoint employee skills and competencies* for which remedial programs can be developed. Finally, they *provide feedback to employees* on how the organization views their performance and are often the *basis for reward allocations,* including merit pay increases.

Because our interest is in organizational behavior, here we emphasize performance evaluation as a mechanism for providing feedback and determining reward allocations.

What Do We Evaluate?

The criteria management choose to evaluate will have a major influence on what employees do. The three most popular sets of criteria are individual task outcomes, behaviors, and traits.

Individual Task Outcomes If ends count rather than means, management should evaluate an employee's task on outcomes such as quantity produced, scrap generated, and cost per unit of production for a plant manager or on

task performance *The combination of effectiveness and efficiency at doing your core job tasks.*

citizenship *Actions that contribute to the psychological environment of the organization, such as helping others when not required*

counterproductivity *Actions that actively damage the organization, including stealing, behaving aggressively toward co-workers, or being late or absent*

Behavior is an important element in evaluating the performance of caregivers in nursing homes and retirement facilities. In addition to individual task outcomes, the caregiver shown here attending to a resident at a nursing home for the elderly in Yokohama, Japan, is evaluated on behaviors such as helping others and building caring and trusting relationships with residents and their family members. These subjective factors contribute to the effectiveness of the nursing home and its reputation as a place where older people are treated with love and respect.

Source: Kyodo via AP Images.

overall sales volume in the territory, dollar increase in sales, and number of new accounts established for a salesperson.

Behaviors   It is difficult to attribute specific outcomes to the actions of employees in advisory or support positions or employees whose work assignments are part of a group effort. We may readily evaluate the group's performance, but if it is hard to identify the contribution of each group member, management will often evaluate the employee's behavior. A plant manager might be evaluated on promptness in submitting monthly reports or leadership style, and a salesperson on average number of contact calls made per day or sick days used per year.

Measured behaviors needn't be limited to those directly related to individual productivity. As we pointed out in discussing organizational citizenship behavior (see Chapters 1 and 3), helping others, making suggestions for improvements, and volunteering for extra duties make work groups and organizations more effective and often are incorporated into evaluations of employee performance.

Traits   The weakest criteria, because they're furthest removed from actual job performance, are individual traits.[57] Having a good attitude, showing confidence, being dependable, looking busy, or possessing a wealth of experience may or may not be highly correlated with positive task outcomes, but it's naïve to ignore the reality that organizations still use such traits to assess job performance.

Who Should Do the Evaluating?

Who should evaluate an employee's performance? By tradition, the task has fallen to managers, because they are held responsible for their employees' performance. But others may do the job better.

With many of today's organizations using self-managed teams, telecommuting, and other organizing devices that distance bosses from employees, the immediate superior may not be the most reliable judge of an employee's performance. Peers and even subordinates are being asked to take part in the process, and employees are participating in their own evaluation. One survey found about half of executives and 53 percent of employees now have input into their performance evaluations.[58] As you might expect, self-evaluations often suffer from overinflated assessment and self-serving bias, and they seldom agree with superiors' ratings.[59] They are probably better suited to developmental than evaluative purposes and should be combined with other sources of information to reduce rating errors.

In most situations, in fact, it is highly advisable to use multiple sources of ratings. Any individual performance rating may say as much about the rater as about the person being evaluated. By averaging across raters, we can obtain a more reliable, unbiased, and accurate performance evaluation.

Another popular approach to performance evaluation is 360-degree evaluations.[60] These provide performance feedback from the employee's full circle of daily contacts, from mailroom workers to customers to bosses to peers (see Exhibit 17-2). The number of appraisals can be as few as 3 or 4 or as many as 25; most organizations collect 5 to 10 per employee.

What's the appeal of the 360-degree appraisal? By relying on feedback from co-workers, customers, and subordinates, organizations are hoping to give everyone a sense of participation in the review process and gain more accurate readings on employee performance.

Evidence on the effectiveness of the 360-degree evaluation is mixed.[61] It provides employees with a wider perspective on their performance, but many organizations don't spend the time to train evaluators in giving constructive

Exhibit 17-2   360-Degree Evaluations

The primary objective of the 360-degree performance evaluation is to pool feedback from all of the employee's customers.

Top management (Internal customer)

Manager (Internal customer)

Suppliers (External customer)

Subordinates (Internal customer)

Employee

Clients (External customer)

Co-workers or team members (Internal customer)

Other department representatives (Internal customer)

Source: Adapted from *Personnel Journal* (November 1994), p. 100.

glOBalization!

Performance Appraisal Around the World

The process of appraising performance is complicated and requires both assessing what employees are doing and communicating this information back to the employees. These are two highly social, context-dependent processes, so we might expect performance appraisal to vary dramatically depending on the country. Preliminary research suggests that management practices related to performance appraisal do indeed vary across borders.

A structured interview study examined Chinese managers' beliefs about performance appraisal. Most respondents found it a good way to build communication and believed performance levels are a function of each person's individual attributes. These attitudes were fairly similar to those of managers in the United States, where most research on performance appraisal has been performed. However, the Chinese managers believed a person in a position of power and control should run the appraisal meeting, unlike the more informal preferences of U.S. managers.

One larger-scale study compared appraisal practices in the United States, Canada, the United Kingdom, Finland, Sweden, Hong Kong, and Singapore using the dimensions of culture identified in the GLOBE survey. Appraisals were more frequently used for communication and development in countries like Sweden and Finland that were low in assertiveness and power distance. Formal feedback was more frequent in highly assertive, low collectivist, and uncertainty avoidant cultures like the United States, the United Kingdom, and Canada. Finally, appraisals were more collaborative in nature in the United States and Canada, and more formal and top-down in Hong Kong and Singapore.

Source: Based on K. H. C. Cheng and W. Cascio, "Performance-Appraisal Beliefs of Chinese Employees in Hong Kong and the Pearl River Delta," *International Journal of Selection and Assessment* 17, no. 3 (2009), pp. 329–333; and F. F. T. Chiang and T. A. Birtch, "Appraising Performance across Borders: An Empirical Examination of the Purposes and Practices of Performance Appraisal in a Multi-Country Context," *Journal of Management Studies* 47, no. 7 (2010), pp. 1365–1393.

criticism. Some allow employees to choose the peers and subordinates who evaluate them, which can artificially inflate feedback. It's also difficult to reconcile disagreements between rater groups. There is clear evidence that peers tend to give much more lenient ratings that supervisors or subordinates, and peers also tend to make more errors in appraising performance.

Methods of Performance Evaluation

We've discussed *what* we evaluate and *who* should do the evaluating. Now we ask: *How* do we evaluate an employee's performance? What are the specific techniques for evaluation?

Written Essays   Probably the simplest method is to write a narrative describing an employee's strengths, weaknesses, past performance, potential, and suggestions for improvement. The written essay requires no complex forms or extensive training to complete. But, in this method, a useful appraisal may be determined as much by the evaluator's writing skill as by the employee's actual level of performance. It's also difficult to compare essays for different employees (or for the same employees written by different managers) because there is no standardized scoring key.

Critical Incidents   **Critical incidents** focus the evaluator's attention on the difference between executing a job effectively and executing it ineffectively. The appraiser describes what the employee did that was especially effective or ineffective in a situation, citing only specific behaviors. A list of such critical incidents provides a rich set of examples to show the employee desirable behaviors and those that call for improvement.

Graphic Rating Scales   One of the oldest and most popular methods of evaluation is **graphic rating scales**. The evaluator goes through a set of performance factors—such as quantity and quality of work, depth of knowledge, cooperation, attendance, and initiative—and rates each on incremental scales. The scales may specify, say, five points, so *job knowledge* might be rated 1 ("is poorly informed about work duties") to 5 ("has complete mastery of all phases of the job"). Although they don't provide the depth of information that essays or critical incidents do, graphic rating scales are less time consuming to develop and administer and allow for quantitative analysis and comparison.

Behaviorally Anchored Rating Scales   Behaviorally anchored rating scales **(BARS)** combine major elements from the critical incident and graphic rating scale approaches. The appraiser rates employees on items along a continuum, but the items are examples of actual behavior on the job rather than general descriptions or traits. To develop the BARS, participants first contribute specific illustrations of effective and ineffective behavior, which are translated into a set of performance dimensions with varying levels of quality.

Forced Comparisons   **Forced comparisons** evaluate one individual's performance against the performance of another or others. It is a relative rather than an absolute measuring device. The two most popular comparisons are group order ranking and individual ranking.

Group order ranking requires the evaluator to place employees into a particular classification, such as top one-fifth or second one-fifth. If a rater has 20 employees, only 4 can be in the top fifth and, of course, 4 must also be relegated to the bottom fifth. This method is often used in recommending students to graduate schools.

The **individual ranking** approach rank-orders employees from best to worst. If the manager is required to appraise 30 employees, the difference between the 1st and 2nd employee is assumed to be the same as that between the 21st and 22nd. Some employees may be closely grouped, but no ties are permitted. The result is a clear ordering from the highest performer to the lowest.

One parallel to forced ranking is forced distribution of college grades. Why would universities do this? As shown in Exhibit 17-3, average GPAs have gotten much higher over time.[62] In recent years, nearly 43 percent of all letter grades given were A's, whereas there was a decrease in the number of C's. Although it is not exactly clear why this increase has occurred over time, many attribute the rise in high letter grades to the popularity of student evaluations as a means of assessing professor performance. Generous grades might produce

critical incidents   *A way of evaluating the behaviors that are key in making the difference between executing a job effectively and executing it ineffectively.*

graphic rating scales   *An evaluation method in which the evaluator rates performance factors on an incremental scale.*

behaviorally anchored rating scales (BARS)   *Scales that combine major elements from the critical incident and graphic rating scale approaches. The appraiser rates the employees based on items along a continuum, but the points are examples of actual behavior on the given job rather than general descriptions or traits.*

forced comparison   *Method of performance evaluation where an employee's performance is made in explicit comparison to others (e.g., an employee may rank third out of 10 employees in her work unit.*

group order ranking   *An evaluation method that places employees into a particular classification, such as quartiles.*

individual ranking   *An evaluation method that rank-orders employees from best to worst.*

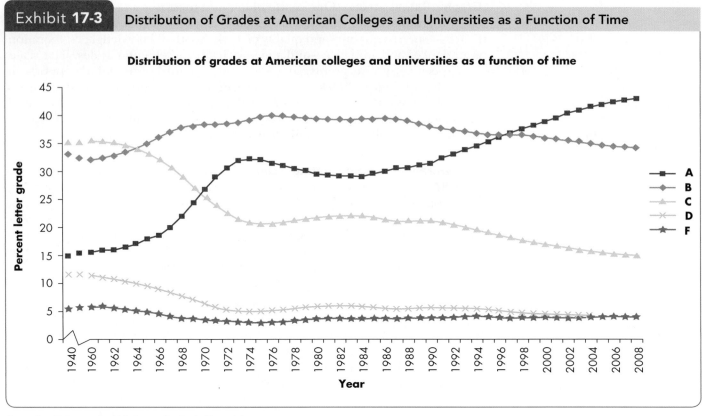

Exhibit 17-3   Distribution of Grades at American Colleges and Universities as a Function of Time

Source: Stuart Rojstaczer, Gradeinflation.com. Reprinted with permission.

higher student evaluations. It's also the case that giving higher grades can help students become more competitive candidates for graduate school and jobs.

In response to grade inflation, some colleges have instituted forced grade distributions, whereby professors must give a certain percentage of A's, B's, and C's. This is exactly what Princeton recently did; each department can now give A's to no more than 35 percent of its students. Natasha Gopaul, a Princeton senior, commented, "You do feel you might be one of the ones they just cut off."

Suggestions for Improving Performance Evaluations

8 Show how managers can improve performance evaluations.

The performance evaluation process is a potential minefield. Evaluators can unconsciously inflate evaluations (positive leniency), understate performance (negative leniency), or allow the assessment of one characteristic to unduly influence the assessment of others (the halo error). Some appraisers bias their evaluations by unconsciously favoring people who have qualities and traits similar to their own (the similarity error). And, of course, some evaluators see the evaluation process as a political opportunity to overtly reward or punish employees they like or dislike. A review of the literature and several studies on performance appraisals demonstrates that many managers deliberately distort performance ratings in order to maintain a positive relationship with their subordinates or to achieve a positive image of themselves by showing that all their

Recruiting the Unemployed

As the economy has continued to perform poorly since the start of the Great Recession, a large number of individuals have joined the ranks of the long-term unemployed. The difficulties of unemployment are compounded because many employers either overtly or covertly prefer candidates who do not have gaps in their work history. For example, *New York Times* reporter Catherine Rampell found in hundreds of job postings on Monster.com, CareerBuilder, and Craigslist that employers prefer people who are either currently employed or only recently laid off. This makes it extremely difficult for qualified individuals to find work because it constitutes a bias against the unemployed.

Although federal regulators in the Equal Employment Opportunity Commission have voiced concerns about the practice, unemployment is not a protected status like age, race, or gender. Due to gaps in the law, some states like New Jersey, New York, and Michigan have considered or implemented laws prohibiting advertisements that discourage unemployed workers from applying.

What can employers do to ensure they are giving qualified individuals who have been unemployed a fair shot at open positions? A few principles can help ensure they are recruiting ethically:

1. Always try to evaluate the whole candidate, including prior experience, ability, and personality. Don't get overly focused on a single detail of their employment history.

2. If you are concerned about an employment gap in the résumé, ask about it directly. Don't assume it reflects a lack of initiative or interest in work.

3. Consider offering additional training to those who may have missed out on certain developments in the field during their spell of unemployment. Although it can add expense, your organization might benefit from securing someone other employers would overlook.

Sources: Based on C. Rampell, "The Help-Wanted Sign Comes with a Frustrating Asterisk," *The New York Times* (July 25, 2011), www.nytimes.com; and S. Kelly, "Unemployed Not Wanted? The EEOC Scrutinizes Whether Companies' Recruiting Only Already Employed Applications Could Be Discrimination." *Treasury and Risk* (April 2011), www.treasuryandrisk.com.

employees are performing well.[63] Although no protections *guarantee* accurate performance evaluations, the following suggestions can make the process more objective and fair.

Use Multiple Evaluators   As the number of evaluators increases, the probability of attaining more accurate information increases, as does the likelihood that the employee will accept the feedback as valid.[64] We often see multiple evaluators in competitions in such sports as diving and gymnastics. A set of evaluators judges a performance, the highest and lowest scores are dropped, and the final evaluation is made up of those remaining. The logic of multiple evaluators applies to organizations as well. If an employee has had ten supervisors, nine having rated her excellent and one poor, we can safely discount the one poor evaluation. By moving employees around within the organization to gain a number of evaluations, or by using multiple assessors (as in 360-degree appraisals), we increase the probability of achieving more valid and reliable evaluations.

Evaluate Selectively   To increase agreement among them, appraisers should evaluate only where they have some expertise.[65] They should thus be as close as possible, in organizational level, to the individual being evaluated. The more levels that separate them, the less opportunity the evaluator has to observe the individual's behavior and, not surprisingly, the greater the possibility for inaccuracies.

Train Evaluators   If you can't *find* good evaluators, *make* them. Training evaluators can produce more accurate raters.[66] Most rater training courses emphasize changing the raters' frame of reference by teaching them what to look for, so everyone in the organization defines *good performance* in the same way. Another effective training technique is to encourage raters to describe the employee's behavior in as much detail as possible. Providing more detail encourages raters to remember more about the employee's performance, rather than just acting on their feelings about the employee at the moment.

Provide Employees with Due Process   The concept of *due process* can be applied to appraisals to increase the perception that employees are being treated fairly.[67] Three features characterize due process systems: (1) Individuals are provided with adequate notice of what is expected of them; (2) all evidence relevant to a proposed violation is aired in a fair hearing so the individuals affected can respond; and (3) the final decision is based on the evidence and free of bias.

One technique organizations might consider to enhance due process is posting appraisals online so employees can see their own performance scores exactly as the supervisor enters them. One company that did so found employees believed rater accountability and employee participation were higher when appraisal information was available online prior to appraisal interviews.[68] It might be that raters were more sensitive to providing accurate ratings when they knew employees would be able to see their own information directly.

Providing Performance Feedback

Few activities are more unpleasant for many managers than providing performance feedback to employees. In fact, unless pressured by organizational policies and controls, managers are likely to ignore this responsibility.

Why? First, even though almost every employee could stand to improve in some areas, managers fear confrontation when presenting negative feedback. Second, many employees do tend to become defensive when their weaknesses are pointed out. Instead of accepting the feedback as constructive and a basis for improving performance, some criticize the manager or redirect blame to someone else. Finally, employees tend to have an inflated assessment of their own performance. Statistically speaking, half of all employees must be below-average performers. But the average employee's estimate of his or her own performance level generally falls around the 75th percentile.[69] So even when managers are providing good news, employees are likely to perceive it as not good enough.

The solution to the problem is not to ignore it but to train managers to conduct constructive feedback sessions. An effective review—in which the employee perceives the appraisal as fair, the manager as sincere, and the climate as constructive—can leave the employee feeling upbeat, informed about areas needing improvement, and determined to correct them.[70] It probably won't surprise you that employees in a bad mood are much less likely to take advice than employees in a good mood.[71] Appraisals should also be as specific as possible. People are most likely to overrate their own performance when asked about overall job performance, but they can be more objective when feedback is about a specific area.[72] It's also hard to figure out how to improve your performance globally—it's much easier to improve in specific areas. In addition, the performance review should be a counseling activity more than a judgment process, best accomplished by allowing it to evolve from the employee's own self-evaluation.

International Variations in Performance Appraisal

Let's examine performance evaluation globally in the context of four cultural dimensions: individualism/collectivism, a person's relationship to the environment, time orientation, and focus of responsibility.

Individual-oriented cultures such as the United States emphasize formal performance evaluation systems more than informal systems. They advocate written evaluations performed at regular intervals, the results of which managers share with employees and use in the determination of rewards. On the other hand, the collectivist cultures that dominate Asia and much of Latin America are characterized by more informal systems—downplaying formal feedback and disconnecting reward allocations from performance ratings. Some of these differences may be narrowing, however. In Korea, Singapore, and even Japan, the use of performance evaluation has increased dramatically in the past decade, though not always smoothly or without controversy. One survey of Korean employees revealed that a majority questioned the validity of their performance evaluation results.[73]

One recent study focused on the banking industry found significant differences across countries in performance appraisal practices.[74] Formal performance appraisals were used more frequently in countries that were high in assertiveness, high in uncertainty avoidance, and low in in-group collectivism. In other words, assertive countries that see performance as an individual responsibility, and that desire certainty about where people stand, were more likely to use formal performance appraisals. On the other hand, in high uncertainty avoidance cultures performance appraisals were also used more frequently for communication and development purposes (as opposed to being used for rewards and promotion). Another study found that individuals who were high in power distance and high in collectivism tend to give more lenient performance appraisals.[75]

SELF-ASSESSMENT LIBRARY

How Good Am I at Giving Performance Feedback?

In the Self-Assessment Library (available on CD and online), take assessment III.A.3 (How Good Am I at Giving Performance Feedback?).

Managing Work–Life Conflicts in Organizations

9 Describe how organizations can manage work–family conflicts.

We introduced work–life balance in Chapter 1 and discussed the blurring lines between work life and personal life. Here, we specifically focus on what organizations can do to help employees reduce conflicts.

Work–life conflicts grabbed management's attention in the 1980s, largely as a result of the increased entry into the workforce of women with dependent children. In response, most major organizations took actions to make their workplaces more family-friendly.[76] They introduced on-site child care, summer day camps, flextime, job sharing, leaves for school functions, telecommuting, and part-time employment. But organizations quickly realized work–life conflicts were not limited to female employees with children. Male workers and women without children were also facing this problem. Heavy workloads and increased travel demands, for instance, made it increasingly hard for many employees to meet both work and personal responsibilities. A Boston College survey of nearly 1,000 fathers who have professional careers showed that the participants put more importance on job security and flexible, family-friendly working schedules than on high income and advancement opportunities.[77]

Organizations are modifying their workplaces with scheduling options and benefits to accommodate the varied needs of a diverse workforce. Employees at NestléPurina can bring their dogs into the office, SAS Institute has on-site childcare, a health care center, and a fitness center; and other firms offer perks ranging from on-site laundry to food services and free child care.[78] Exhibit 17-4 lists some initiatives to help employees reduce work–life conflicts.

Time pressures aren't the primary problem underlying these conflicts.[79] It's the psychological incursion of work into the family domain—and vice versa—when people are worrying about personal problems at work and thinking about work problems at home. So, dad may make it home in time for dinner, but his mind is elsewhere. This suggests organizations should spend less effort helping employees with time-management issues and more helping them clearly segment their lives. Keeping workloads reasonable, reducing work-related travel,

---

Myth or Science?

"Work Is Making Us Fat"

This statement is true. Let's explain.

Two-thirds of U.S. adults are overweight or even obese, and the changing nature of work is a major reason. Indeed, it might be the main explanation for why obesity has become the number-one public health problem in the United States and many other advanced economies.

Our work has evolved to be more mental than physical. That tends to make it more interesting, but also more sedentary. Why is that a problem? The changes in work are estimated to mean that, on average, workers burn 120 to 150 fewer calories a day than they did 50 years ago. That may not seem like a lot, but it equates to 25 pounds of potential weight gain per year.

Interestingly, research indicates that our physical activity in leisure time hasn't changed much in the past 50 years. So we burn as many calories in nonwork activities as before—it's work that is killing us.

Fifty years ago, about half of all private-sector jobs included some kind of physical labor (farming, mining, construction, manufacturing). Today, fewer than 20 percent do, thanks to the growth of jobs in retailing, information technology, education, and business.

What is the implication? "We need to encourage physical activity even more, especially given that we sit more during the day than we did 100 years ago," said Keri Gans, a spokesperson for the American Dietetic Association.

Some ways to do that are taking the stairs when you can, parking your car a good distance from work, and going for a walk at lunchtime. And, of course, exercising more off the job. As one expert noted when commenting on the increasingly sedentary nature of work, "We just have to make time for it."

Sources: T. Parker-Hope, "Sedentary Work Cited as Factor in Rising Obesity," *The New York Times* (May 26, 2011), pp. A1, A3; A. Gardner, "Sedentary Jobs Helping to Drive Obesity Epidemic," *US News & World Report* (May 26, 2011), downloaded July 11, 2011, from http://health.usnews.com/; and T. S. Church et al., "Trends Over 5 Decades in U.S. Occupation-Related Physical Activity and Their Associations with Obesity," *PLoS ONE* 6, no. 5 (2011), doi:10.1371/journal.pone.0019657.

Exhibit **17-4**	**Work–Life Initiatives**

Time based strategies	• Flextime • Job sharing • Leave for new parents • Transportation • Telecommuting • Paid time off	At Abbott, 89% of employees held jobs that permitted them to flex their schedules; at Lego 90% of employees do. Cisco provides job-sharing and videoconferencing facilities to minimize needs for travel away from family. Deloitte offers employees 4 unpaid weeks sabbatical, or 3 to 6 partially paid months off to volunteer. Deutsche Bank offers parents 20 days of free backup care per child per year, which they can redeem at local child care centers. At DuPont, 15% of employees telecommute; at Eli Lilly 30% of employees telecommute.
Information based strategies	• Work–life support • Relocation assistance • Elder care resources • Counseling services	Blue Cross Blue Shield of North Carolina provides ParentLife classes and seminars. Capital One provides a networking and counseling group for parents of children with autism. Genetech offers a CareerLab, which provides career counseling, skills workshops, and networking sessions. Hallmark offers employees monthly meetings to talk about career management for women. Johnson and Johnson offers work–life Webinars covering topics like single parenting, fatherhood, and elder care.
Money-based strategies	• Insurance subsidies • Flexible benefits • Adoption assistance • Discounts for child care tuition • Direct financial assistance • Domestic partner benefits • Scholarships, tuition reimbursement	Accenture offers a $5,000 adoption assistance benefit. Carlson companies offers employees scholarships of up to $20,000 to attend the University of Minnesota's Carlson School of Management. Citi employees can save up to $5,000 per year in pretax dependent care accounts, with a match of up to 30% from the company. Colgate-Palmolive provides up to $10,000 per year in annual tuition aid for job-related courses. IBM provides medical testing and therapy for children with special needs, up to a lifetime maximum of $50,000. Prudential employees can receive up to 15% off child care discounts.
Direct services	• On-site child care • Fitness center • Summer child care • On-site conveniences • Concierge services • Free or discounted company products	Allstate and SAS provide on-site child care center at company headquarters. Companies like AOL and Verizon have on-site fitness centers and discounts at gyms nationwide. Bristol-Myers Squibb offers full-time, part-time, and backup care for kids up to age 5, and summer camps for older children. Discovery Communications provides low-cost concierge services to help with to-do lists. Turner Broadcasting has a wellness center at headquarters that provides free exams, vaccinations, allergy shots, and health coaching. REI employees can participate in a program that offers large discounts on company products.
Culture-change strategies	• Establishing work–life balanced culture; training managers to help employees deal with work–life conflicts • Tie manager pay to employee satisfaction • Focus on employees' actual performance, not "face time"	At American Express, 80% of managers received training on how to supervise employees with flexible work arrangements. Bank of America's My Work program allows mothers to log in from home or a satellite office. General Mills has a flexibility manager to enhance work–life balance. Pearson developed a Flexible Work Options. Accountability Guide that trains managers in the use of flextime for their employees.

Sources: "2010 100 Best Companies" *Working Mother* (August 17, 2011), www.workingmother.com; "100 Best Companies to Work For," *CNNMoney,* (August 17, 2011), www.money.cnn.com; and J. Goudreau, "Top Companies for Work-Life Balance," *Forbes* (May 13, 2011), www.forbes.com.

and offering on-site quality child care are examples of practices that can help in this endeavor.

Not surprisingly, people differ in their preference for scheduling options and benefits.[80] Some prefer organizational initiatives that better segment work from their personal lives, as flextime, job sharing, and part-time hours do by allowing employees to schedule work hours less likely to conflict with personal responsibilities. Others prefer ways to integrate work and personal life, such as on-site child care, gym facilities, and company-sponsored family picnics. On average, though, most people do prefer an organization that provides more support for work–life balance. One study even found that potential employees, particularly women, are more attracted to organizations that have a reputation for supporting employee work–life balance.[81]

MyManagementLab

Now that you have finished this chapter, go back to **www.mymanagementlab.com** to continue practicing and applying the concepts you've learned.

Summary and Implications for Managers

An organization's human resource policies and practices create important forces that shape employee behavior and attitudes. In this chapter, we specifically discussed the influence of selection practices, training and development programs, and performance evaluation systems.

- If properly designed, an organization's selection practices will identify competent candidates and accurately match them to the job and the organization. Although employee selection is far from a science, some organizations fail to design a selection system that can achieve the right person–job fit.
- The most obvious effect of training programs is direct improvement in the skills necessary to successfully complete the job. Increased ability thus improves potential, but whether that potential becomes realized is largely an issue of motivation.
- A second benefit of training is that it increases an employee's self-efficacy—that is, a person's expectation that he or she can successfully execute the behaviors required to produce an outcome (see Chapter 7). Employees with high self-efficacy have strong expectations about their abilities to perform in new situations. They're confident and expect to be successful. Training, then, is a means to positively affect self-efficacy because employees may be more willing to undertake job tasks and exert a high level of effort.
- A major goal of performance evaluation is to assess an individual's performance accurately as a basis for allocating rewards. If evaluation is inaccurate or emphasizes the wrong criteria, employees will be over- or underrewarded. As demonstrated in Chapter 7 in our discussion of equity theory, evaluations perceived as unfair can result in reduced effort, increases in absenteeism, or a search for alternative job opportunities.

Social Media Is a Great Source of New Hires

ocial media sites such as Facebook, LinkedIn, and Twitter, and job boards like Monster.com, are indispensable in today's marketplace for top talent.

It's true that an online presence with social media sites is a good way to sniff out fraud. Studies reveal that 45 percent of today's résumés contain at least one piece of false information. Mining social media sites is great at gaining a fuller—and more accurate—picture of a candidate.

One survey found that today 63 percent of employers use social media sites in recruitment and hiring decisions. Another revealed that 80 percent of employers plan to increase their presence on Facebook and LinkedIn in the future.

Not only can social media sites help you make a more informed selection decisions, they can be a great help in recruiting more and better candidates to apply in the first place. Dawn Mitchell, a recruiter for business software company Red Hat, says it's about "living where the candidates are." She says that nearly all her recent hires have come from social media contacts.

Increasingly, recruiting firms that link applicants to companies are finding social media critical for their business too. "Social media is the heart of everything we do," said Bill Peppler of Kavaliro Staffing Services. "We make numerous job placements that we never would have been able to do without Facebook," he said.

Accenture—the New York–based consulting firm—has mastered the art of using social media in hiring. John Campagnino, Accenture's global director of recruitment, says it has become "a centerpiece of our talent acquisition strategy." Campagnino says that Accenture interacts with potential hires on Facebook, LinkedIn, and Twitter; posts jobs on these sites daily; and creates "talent communities" by joining professional groups.

Hiring without heavy reliance on social media is backward-looking, and a missed opportunity.

lot of employers are scaling back their presence on online job boards like Monster.com and social media sites like Facebook and LinkedIn, because there is just too much chaff for the wheat. For example, McLean, Virginia–based Science Applications International Corporate (SAIC) reduced the number of job boards it uses from 15 to 6. SAIC found that it simply wasn't getting to enough of the right candidates early enough to staff its engineering and analyst positions. "We need to reach candidates earlier, before they're being pursued by competitors," the company said.

Paris-owned food services company Sodexo has slashed its online presence in half. Why? Because while recruiting via social media increased the number of applications, nearly all the increase was in unqualified applicants. "Recruiters had to put in all this extra time to read applications but we didn't get benefit from it," said Arie Ball, the company's talent acquisition vice president.

PNC also is scaling back due to the low signal-to-noise ratio. "We used to post everything," said the online banking company. "But you have to think strategically."

There is also the nontrivial issue of mistaken identity. A lot of mistaken hiring decisions have been made because a company used the wrong Facebook or LinkedIn profile. Applicants can post false information on social media sites, too.

Perhaps the biggest issue of all is objectivity. Says one employment expert, "Once an HR recruiter or administrator has been exposed to an applicant's social networking profile, it's difficult to remain objective and consider only the information that is relevant to the job."

Another recruiting manager voiced his skepticism regarding social media: "I'd love to drink the Kool-Aid if it did anything for me."

Sources: J. Light, "Recruiters Rethink Online Playbook," *The Wall Street Journal* (January 18, 2011), p. B7; R. Pyrillis, "The Bait Debate," *Workforce Management* (February 2011), pp. 16–22; and J. Bos, "Five Trends in Employee Screening: Is Your Company Prepared?" *Workforce Management* (March 2010), pp. 28–30.

- The content of the performance evaluation also influences employee performance and satisfaction. Specifically, performance and satisfaction are increased when the evaluation is based on behavioral and results-oriented criteria, when career issues as well as performance issues are discussed, and when the employee has an opportunity to participate in the evaluation.

QUESTIONS FOR REVIEW

1 What is *initial selection*? What are the most useful methods?

2 What is *substantive selection*? What are the most useful methods?

3 What is *contingent selection*? What are the arguments for and against drug testing?

4 What are the similarities and differences among the four main types of training?

5 What are the similarities and differences between formal and informal training methods?

6 What are the similarities and differences between on-the-job and off-the-job training?

7 What are the purposes of performance evaluation? What are the methods by which it can be done?

8 How can managers improve performance evaluations?

9 How can organizations manage work-family conflicts?

EXPERIENTIAL EXERCISE Evaluating Performance and Providing Feedback

Objective
To experience the assessment of performance and observe the provision of performance feedback.

Time
Approximately 30 minutes.

Procedure
Select a class leader—either a volunteer or someone chosen by your instructor. The class leader will preside over the class discussion and perform the role of manager in the evaluation review.

Your instructor will leave the room. The class leader is then to spend up to 15 minutes helping the class to evaluate your instructor. Your instructor understands that this is only a class exercise and is prepared to accept criticism (and, of course, any praise you may want to convey). Your instructor also recognizes that the leader's evaluation is actually a composite of many students' input. So, be open and honest in your evaluation and have confidence that your instructor will not be vindictive.

Research has identified seven performance dimensions to the college instructor's job: (1) instructor knowledge, (2) testing procedures, (3) student–teacher relations, (4) organizational skills, (5) communication skills, (6) subject relevance, and (7) utility of assignments. The discussion of your instructor's performance should focus on these seven dimensions. The leader may want to take notes for personal use but will not be required to give your instructor any written documentation.

When the 15-minute class discussion is complete, the leader will invite the instructor back into the room. The performance review will begin as soon as the instructor walks through the door, with the class leader becoming the manager and the instructor playing himself or herself.

When completed, class discussion will focus on performance evaluation criteria and how well your class leader did in providing performance feedback.

ETHICAL DILEMMA Credit Checking

Is it unethical—or illegal—for a hiring organization to check an applicant's credit history? The Equal Employment Opportunity Commission (EEOC) seems to think so. It is suing Kaplan Higher Education

Corporation for its use of credit checks, alleging that relying on poor credit histories to reject applicants has adverse impact on minority applicants, with no legitimate purpose justifying its use. Justine Lisser, an EEOC spokesperson, said, "Credit histories were not compiled to show responsibility. They were compiled to show whether or not someone was paying the bills, which is not always the same thing."

In its defense, Kaplan maintained that it typically conducted credit checks: "The checks are job-related and necessary for our organization to ensure that staffing handling financial matters, including financial aid, are properly screened."

A 2011 survey of employers revealed that 21 percent conducted credit checks on all applicants. That was up from 15 percent the year before. Two-thirds conduct credit checks on some applicants, up from 61 percent in 2010.

Joey Price, with BL Seamon, thought she had found the perfect candidate for a conference planner position. The candidate was fresh out of college but had experience planning conferences and a good academic record. But when Price found out that the candidate had multiple car repossessions, extremely high credit card bills, and collection agencies after her, she rejected her. "A credit report doesn't lie," Price said.

Questions

1. Do you think organizations should be allowed to investigate applicants' credit histories in the hiring process? Why or why not?

2. Do you think Seamon's Joey Price was within her rights to reject the applicant with the poor credit history? Do you think this candidate's financial problems might be job relevant?

3. Some employers chose to disclose their reasoning to applicants rejected for poor credit. Says one hiring manager, "If a credit check comes back poor, the potential employee has a week to dispute and correct the errors." What are the advantages and disadvantages of such a policy?

Sources: J. Zappe, "Survey Finds More Companies Credit-Checking Candidates," *ERE.net* (May 16, 2011), downloaded on July 11, 2011, from www.ere.net/2011/; S. Greenhouse, "Hiring Suit Takes on Bias Based on Credit," *The New York Times* (December 22, 2010), pp. B1, B4; J. Fairley, "Employers Face Challenges in Screening Candidates," *Workforce Management* (November 2010), pp. 7–9; and B. Roberts, "Close-Up on Screening," *HR Magazine* (February 2011), p. 23–29.

CASE INCIDENT 1 The End of the Performance Appraisal?

As we discussed in the chapter, organizations measure employee performance for a variety of reasons, including determining which employees need training, who is performing well enough to earn a performance reward, and who deserves a promotion. Performance appraisal information can also help determine where problems lie in the company's overall training and selection systems and defend HR decisions such as firings in court.

In light of these multiple uses, it might surprise you to learn that some companies are moving away from formal appraisal processes. Business scholar Jeffery Pfeffer describes how HR managers at companies like Apple had to bribe managers to complete assigned reviews with free tickets to San Francisco Giants games, and the head of HR at SAS received cheers from employees when he had a bonfire to burn performance appraisal forms. Clearly, appraisals are not popular with the managers asked to perform them. Pfeffer notes that the subjective nature of these reviews is troubling to many managers, leading employees to spend much of their time ingratiating themselves with the boss rather than doing their jobs. Moreover, appraisals put the focus on individual performance rather than on the performance of whole teams. Research conducted by Globoforce found that more than half the 631 survey respondents believed appraisals did not accurately reflect their performance on the job.

So what is the alternative? Zappos now rates employees not on how well they accomplish tasks but rather on how well they embody the company's core values. This feedback is delivered much more frequently during the year than the traditional annual performance meeting. Nor are the ratings used for disciplinary actions or promotions, though employees who get low scores are invited to take developmental classes to improve the fit between their behavior and the company culture. Apple has also eliminated annual performance reviews as neither timely nor helpful. Other companies have developed performance management software that automates and streamlines a more continuous performance review, allowing employees to track their performance in real time.

Questions

1. Have you ever been through a performance appraisal? Do the reactions to appraisal systems described here match your experience? Why or why not?

2. What are some potential advantages of providing employees with more regular developmental feedback than an annual meeting?

3. Are there potential drawbacks to eliminating conventional performance appraisal systems? What systems would need to be put in place to replace formal appraisals?

4. Would you feel comfortable providing others with performance feedback? What are some of the possible reasons managers often prefer not to give employees critiques of their performance?

Sources: Based on R. Pyrillis, "Is Your Performance Review Underperforming?" *Workforce Management* (May 2011), pp. 20–25; S. A. Culbert and L. Rout, *Get Rid of the Performance Review!* (New York: Business Plus, 2010); and J. Pfeffer, "Low Grades for Performance Reviews," *BusinessWeek* (August 3, 2009), p. 68.

CASE INCIDENT 2 Job Candidates Without Strong SAT Scores Need Not Apply

Many high school students probably believe that once they get into college, their SAT scores are a thing of the past. However, many job seekers are discovering their would-be employers are asking for their SAT scores as part of the selection process. Donna Chan, a 23-year-old graduate of New York's Wagner College, learned that one of the minimum requirements for many of the entry-level financial services jobs she was seeking was a combined SAT score of 1300. According to the College Board, the organization that administers the exam, the average combined math and verbal score of the freshman class of 2005 (the last class to take the old version of the SAT) was 1028. Donna Chan's score was "in the 1200s"—a good score to be sure, but not good enough to obtain any of the positions she was seeking, even though she earned a 3.9 GPA in college. "I think it's asking a bit much," says Chan. "That's something high school kids have to worry about. After four years of working hard, I think you've paid your dues, and unless you're applying to *Princeton Review* or some math-related, analytical job, I don't see the relevance."

Apparently, however, some recruiters do. Alan Sage, a vice president at systems management software company Configuresoft Inc., says SAT scores are a good predictor of success in his company, and he regularly has applicants submit their scores when applying for sales positions. He set the mark at a combined score of 1200—lower than Donna Chan faced but nonetheless well above average. Says Sage, "In my experience, people with high SAT scores tend to do better." He adds, however, that "we wouldn't exclude someone from an interview if he or she didn't score high." Similarly, Google has used SAT scores to identify individuals with higher levels of cognitive ability in the hiring process, but it also does not use an absolute cutoff.

Some individuals, such as Kristin Carnahan, a spokesperson for the College Board, feel companies should use other measures of cognitive ability, such as college grades, which are also more recent indicators than SAT scores. Google uses grades in addition to SAT scores because it believes grades reflect motivation and discipline as well as intellectual ability. However, grades aren't standardized across institutions, so they can't be compared like SAT scores can. Grade inflation also may make it more difficult for recruiters to assess an applicant's GPA. Because OB research has shown cognitive ability is a strong predictor of job performance—and the SAT is supposedly a measure of cognitive ability—many companies may continue to use it as a benchmark for job applicants.

Questions

1. Is it fair for hiring organizations to require minimum scores on standardized tests such as the SAT? Why or why not?

2. As a recruiter choosing between two individuals with different SAT scores, would you have difficulty giving the job to the applicant with the lower score? On what additional factors might your choice depend?

3. What other indicators of job performance, besides SAT scores, could you use to screen job applicants? What are the advantages and disadvantages of each?

4. Suppose you worked at a company that used SAT scores for hiring purposes. How would you handle diverse applicants, such as those from a foreign country who may not have taken the SAT?

Sources: Based on S. Foss, "Background Check—Background Search," *American Chronicle* (July 12, 2007); K. J. Dunham, "Career Journal: More Employers Ask Job Seekers for SAT Scores," *The Wall Street Journal* (October 28, 2003), p. B1; and M. LaChapelle, "Do You Hire People the Google Way?" *Times Union* (July 13, 2011), www.timesunion.com.

ENDNOTES

1. See B. Becker and B. Gerhart, "The Impact of Human Resource Management on Organizational Performance: Progress and Prospects," *Academy of Management Journal* (August 1996), pp. 779–801; M. A. Huselid, S. E. Jackson, and R. S. Schuler, "Technical and Strategic Human Resource Management Effectiveness as Determinants of Firm Performance," *Academy of Management Journal* (February 1997), pp. 171–188; C. J. Collins, and K. D. Clark, "Strategic Human Resource Practices, Top Management Team Social Networks, and Firm Performance: The Role of Human Resource Practices in Creating Organizational Competitive Advantage," *Academy of Management Journal* (December 2003), pp. 740–751; D. E. Bowen and C. Ostroff, "Understanding HRM–Firm Performance Linkages: The Role of the 'Strength' of the HRM System," *Academy of Management Review* (April 2004), pp. 203–221; and K. Birdi, C. Clegg, M. Patterson, A. Robinson, C. B. Stride, T. D. Wall, and S. J. Wood, "The Impact of Human Resource and Operational Management Practices on Company Productivity: A Longitudinal Study," *Personnel Psychology* 61, no. 3 (2008), pp. 467–501.

2. See, for instance, A. L. Kristof-Brown, R. D. Zimmerman, and E. C. Johnson, "Consequences of Individual's Fit at Work: A Meta-Analysis of Person-Job, Person-Organization, Person-Group, and Person-Supervisor Fit," *Personnel Psychology* 58, no. 2 (2005), pp. 281–342; and D. S. DeRue and F. P. Morgeson, "Stability and Change in Person-Team and Person-Role Fit over Time: The Effects of Growth Satisfaction, Performance, and General Self-Efficacy," *Journal of Applied Psychology* 92, no. 5 (2007), pp. 1242–1253.

3. J. D. Glater, "Another Hurdle for the Jobless: Credit Inquiries," *The New York Times* (August 6, 2009), www.nytimes.com.

4. C. Lachnit, "The Cost of Not Doing Background Checks," *Workforce Management,* www.workforce.com.

5. Cited in J. H. Prager, "Nasty or Nice: 56-Question Quiz," *The Wall Street Journal* (February 22, 2000), p. A4; see also H. Wessel, "Personality Tests Grow Popular," *Seattle Post-Intelligencer* (August 3, 2003), p. G1; and E. Frauenheim, "Personality Tests Adapt to the Times," *Workforce Management* (February 2010), p. 4.

6. E. Maltby, "To Find Best Hires, Firms Become Creative," *The Wall Street Journal* (November 17, 2009), p. B6.

7. J. P. Hausknecht, D. V. Day, and S. C. Thomas, "Applicant Reactions to Selection Procedures: An Updated Model and Meta-Analysis," *Personnel Psychology* (September 2004), pp. 639–683.

8. E. E. Ghiselli, "The Validity of Aptitude Tests in Personnel Selection," *Personnel Psychology* (Winter 1973), p. 475; J. E. Hunter, "Cognitive Ability, Cognitive Aptitudes, Job Knowledge, and Job Performance," *Journal of Vocational Behavior* 29, no. 3 (1986), pp. 340–362.

9. F. L. Schmidt, and J. Hunter, "General Mental Ability in the World of Work: Occupational Attainment and Job Performance," *Journal of Personality and Social Psychology* 86, no. 1 (2004), pp. 162–173; and F. L. Schmidt, J. A. Shaffer, and I. Oh, "Increased Accuracy for Range Restriction Corrections: Implications for the Role of Personality and General Mental Ability in Job and Training Performance," *Personnel Psychology* 61, no. 4 (2008), pp. 827–868.

10. J. F. Salgado, N. Anderson, S. Moscoso, C. Bertua, F. de Fruyt, and J. P. Rolland, "A Meta-Analytic Study of General Mental Ability Validity for Different Occupations in the European Community," *Journal of Applied Psychology* (December 2003), pp. 1068–1081.

11. M. R. Barrick, M. K. Mount, and T. A. Judge, "Personality and Performance at the Beginning of the New Millennium: What Do We Know and Where Do We Go Next?" *International Journal of Selection & Assessment* (March–June 2001), pp. 9–30; M. R. Barrick, G. L. Stewart, and M. Piotrowski, "Personality and Job Performance: Test of the Mediating Effects of Motivation Among Sales Representatives," *Journal of Applied Psychology* (February 2002), pp. 43–51; and C. J. Thoresen, J. C. Bradley, P. D. Bliese, and J. D. Thoresen, "The Big Five Personality Traits and Individual Job Performance and Growth Trajectories in Maintenance and Transitional Job Stages," *Journal of Applied Psychology* (October 2004), pp. 835–853.

12. R. N. Landers, P. R. Sackett, and K. A. Tuzinski, "Retesting after Initial Failure, Coaching Rumors, and Warnings against Faking in Online Personality Measures for Selection," *Journal of Applied Psychology* 96, no. 1 (2011), pp. 202–210; and J. P. Hausknecht, "Candidate Persistence and Personality Test Practice Effects: Implications for Staffing System Management," *Personnel Psychology* 63, no. 2 (2010), pp. 299–324.

13. I. Oh, G. Wang, and M. K. Mount, "Validity of Observer Ratings of the Five-Factor Model of Personality Traits: A Meta-Analysis," *Journal of Applied Psychology* 96, no. 4 (2011), pp. 762–773; and B. S. Connelly and D. S. Ones, "An Other Perspective on Personality: Meta-Analytic Integration of Observers' Accuracy and Predictive Validity," *Psychological Bulletin* 136, no. 6 (2010), pp. 1092–1122.

14. D. S. Ones, C. Viswesvaran, and F. L. Schmidt, "Comprehensive Meta-Analysis of Integrity Test Validities: Findings and Implications for Personnel Selection and Theories of Job Performance," *Journal of Applied Psychology* (August 1993), pp. 679–703; D. S. Ones, C. Viswesvaran, and F. L. Schmidt, "Personality and Absenteeism: A Meta-Analysis of Integrity Tests," *European Journal of Personality* (March–April 2003), Supplement 1, pp. S19–S38; and C. M. Berry, P. R. Sackett, and S. Wiemann, "A Review of Recent Developments in Integrity Test Research," *Personnel Psychology* 60, no. 2 (2007), pp. 271–301.

15. P. L. Roth, P. Bobko, and L. A. McFarland, "A Meta-Analysis of Work Sample Test Validity: Updating and Integrating Some Classic Literature," *Personnel Psychology* 58, no. 4 (2005), pp. 1009–1037.

16. P. Carbonara, "Hire for Attitude, Train for Skill," *Fast Company*, Greatest Hits, vol. 1 (1997), p. 68.

17. See, for instance, A. C. Spychalski, M. A. Quinones, B. B. Gaugler, and K. Pohley, "A Survey of Assessment Center Practices in Organizations in the United States, *Personnel Psychology* (Spring 1997), pp. 71–90; C. Woodruffe, *Development and Assessment Centres: Identifying and Assessing Competence* (London: Institute of Personnel and Development, 2000); and J. Schettler, "Building Bench Strength," *Training* (June 2002), pp. 55–58.

18. F. Lievens, H. Peeters, and E. Schollaert, "Situational Judgment Tests: A Review of Recent Research," *Personnel Review* 37, no. 4 (2008), pp. 426–441.

19. F. Lievens, and F. Patterson, "The Validity and Incremental Validity of Knowledge Tests, Low-Fidelity Simulations, and High-Fidelity Simulations for Predicting Job Performance in Advanced-Level High-Stakes Selection," *Journal of Applied Psychology*, Online First Publication (April 11, 2011), doi: 10.1037/a0023496.

20. R. A. Posthuma, F. P. Moregeson, and M. A. Campion, "Beyond Employment Interview Validity: A Comprehensive Narrative Review of Recent Research and Trend Over Time," *Personnel Psychology* (Spring 2002), p. 1; and S. L. Wilk and P. Cappelli, "Understanding the Determinants of Employer Use of Selection Methods," *Personnel Psychology* (Spring 2003), p. 111.

21. B. W. Swider, M. R. Barrick, T. B. Harris, and A. C. Stoverink, "Managing and Creating an Image in the Interview; The Role of Interviewee Initial Impressions," *Journal of Applied Psychology*, Online First Publication, (May 30, 2011), doi: 10.1037/a0024005.

22. K. I. van der Zee, A. B. Bakker, and P. Bakker, "Why Are Structured Interviews So Rarely Used in Personnel Selection?" *Journal of Applied Psychology* (February 2002), pp. 176–184.

23. See M. A. McDaniel, D. L. Whetzel, F. L. Schmidt, and S. D. Maurer, "The Validity of Employment Interviews: A Comprehensive Review and Meta-Analysis," *Journal of Applied Psychology* (August 1994), pp. 599–616; M. A. Campion, D. K. Palmer, and J. E. Campion, "A Review of Structure in the Selection Interview," *Personnel Psychology* (Autumn 1997), pp. 655–702; A. I. Huffcutt and D. J. Woehr, "Further Analysis of Employment Interview Validity: A Quantitative Evaluation of Interviewer-Related Structuring Methods," *Journal of Organizational Behavior* (July 1999), pp. 549–560; and M. Ziegler, E. Dietl, E. Danay, M. Vogel, and M. Bühner, "Predicting Training Success with General Mental Ability, Specific Ability Tests, and (Un)Structured Interviews: A Meta-Analysis with Unique Samples," *International Journal of Selection and Assessment* 19, no. 2 (2011), pp. 170–182.

24. van der Zee, Bakker, and Bakker, "Why Are Structured Interviews So Rarely Used in Personnel Selection?"

25. T. W. Dougherty, D. B. Turban, and J. C. Callender, "Confirming First Impressions in the Employment Interview: A Field Study of Interviewer Behavior," *Journal of Applied Psychology* (October 1994), pp. 659–665; and M. R. Barrick, B. W. Swider, and G. L. Stewart, "Initial Evaluations in the Interview: Relationships with Subsequent Interviewer Evaluations and Employment Offers," *Journal of Applied Psychology* 95, no. 6 (2010), pp. 1163–1172.

26. K. G. Melchers, N. Lienhardt, M. von Aarburg, and M. Kleinmann, "Is More Structure Really Better? A Comparison of Frame-of-Reference Training and Descriptively Anchored Rating Scales to Improve Interviewers' Rating Quality," *Personnel Psychology* 64, no. 1 (2011), pp. 53–87.

27. F. L. Schmidt and R. D. Zimmerman, "A Counterintuitive Hypothesis About Employment Interview Validity and Some Supporting Evidence," *Journal of Applied Psychology* 89, no. 3 (2004), pp. 553–561.

28. See G. A. Adams, T. C. Elacqua, and S. M. Colarelli, "The Employment Interview as a Sociometric Selection Technique," *Journal of Group Psychotherapy* (Fall 1994), pp. 99–113; R. L. Dipboye, "Structured and Unstructured Selection Interviews: Beyond the Job-Fit Model," *Research in Personnel Human Resource Management* 12 (1994), pp. 79–123; B. Schneider, D. B. Smith, S. Taylor, and J. Fleenor, "Personality and Organizations: A Test of the Homogeneity of Personality Hypothesis," *Journal of Applied Psychology* (June 1998), pp. 462–470; and M. Burke, "Funny Business," *Forbes* (June 9, 2003), p. 173.

29. A. M. Ryan, L. McFarland, H. Baron, and R. Page, "An International Look at Selection Practices: Nation and Culture as Explanations for Variability in Practice," *Personnel Psychology* (Summer 1999), pp. 359–392.

30. Ibid., p. 386.

31. N. Anderson and C. Witvliet, "Fairness Reactions to Personnel Selection Methods: An International Comparison Between the Netherlands, the United States, France, Spain, Portugal, and Singapore," *International Journal of Selection and Assessment* 16, no. 1 (2008), pp. 1–13.

32. American Society for Training and Development, *2010 State of the Industry Report*, www.astd.org/content/research.

33. T. Minton-Eversole and K. Gurchiek, "New Workers Not Ready for Prime Time," *HR Magazine* (December 2006), pp. 28–34.

34. P. Galagan, "Bridging the Skills Gap: New Factors Compound the Growing Skills Shortage," *T+D*, (February 2010), pp. 44–49.

35. M. Smulian, "England Fails on Numeracy and Literacy," *Public Finance* (February 6, 2009), p. 13; E. K. Sharma, "Growing a New Crop of Talent: India Inc. Is Increasingly Going Rural," *Business Today* (June 28, 2009), http://businesstoday.intoday.in/; and G. Paton, "Almost Half of Employers Forced to Teach Teenagers Basic Literacy and Numeracy Skills," *Telegraph* (May 9, 2011), www.telegraph.com.

36. D. Baynton, "America's $60 Billion Problem," Training, (May 2001) p. 52.

37. G. Anand, "India Graduates Millions, But Few Are Fit to Hire," *The Wall Street Journal* (April 5, 2011), www.online.wsj.com.

38. J. Barbarian, "Mark Spear: Director of Management and Organizational Development, Miller Brewing Co.," *Training* (October 2001), pp. 34–38.

39. See, for example, P. J. Taylor, D. F. Russ-Eft, and H. Taylor, "Transfer of Management Training from Alternative Perspectives," *Journal of Applied Psychology* 94, no. 1 (2009), pp. 104–121.

40. See, for example, S. Lim and A. Lee, "Work and Nonwork Outcomes of Workplace Incivility: Does Family Support Help?" *Journal of Occupational Health Psychology* 16, no. 1 (2011), pp. 95–111; C. L. Porath and C. M. Pearson, "The Cost of Bad Behavior," *Organizational Dynamics* 39, no. 1 (2010), pp. 64–71; and B. Estes and J. Wang, "Workplace Incivility: Impacts on Individual and Organizational Performance," *Human Resource Development Review* 7, no. 2 (2008), pp. 218–240.

41. M. P. Leiter, H. K. S. Laschinger, A. Day, and D. G. Oore, "The Impact of Civility Interventions on Employee Social Behavior, Distress, and Attitudes," *Journal of Applied Psychology*, Advance online publication (July 11, 2011), doi: 10.1037/a0024442.

42. G. R. Weaver, L. K. Trevino, and P. L. Cochran, "Corporate Ethics Practices in the Mid-1990's: An Empirical Study of the Fortune 1000," *Journal of Business Ethics* (February 1999), pp. 283–294.

43. M. B. Wood, *Business Ethics in Uncertain Times* (Upper Saddle River, NJ: Prentice Hall, 2004), p. 61.

44. See, for example, D. Seligman, "Oxymoron 101," *Forbes* (October 28, 2002), pp. 160–164; and R. B. Schmitt, "Companies Add Ethics Training; Will It Work?" *The Wall Street Journal* (November 4, 2002), p. B1; A. Becker, "Can You Teach Ethics to MBAs?" *BNet* (October 19, 2009), www.bnet.com.

45. W. R. Allen, P. Bacdayan, K. B. Kowalski, and M. H. Roy, "Examining the Impact of Ethics Training on Business Student Values," *Education and Training* 47, no. 3 (2005), pp. 170–182; A. Lämsä, M. Vehkaperä, T. Puttonen, and H. Pesonen, "Effect of Business Education on Women and Men Students' Attitudes on Corporate Responsibility in Society," *Journal of Business Ethics* 82, no. 1 (2008), pp. 45–58; and K. M. Sheldon and L. S. Krieger, "Understanding the Negative Effects of Legal Education on Law Students: A Longitudinal Test of Self-Determination Theory," *Personality and Social Psychology Bulletin* 33, no. 6 (2007), pp. 883–897.

46. S. Valentine and G. Fleischman, "Ethics Programs, Perceived Corporate Social Responsibility, and Job Satisfaction," *Journal of Business Ethics* 77, no. 2 (2008), pp. 159–172.

47. K. Dobbs, "The U.S. Department of Labor Estimates That 70 Percent of Workplace Learning Occurs Informally," *Sales & Marketing Management* (November 2000), pp. 94–98.

48. See, for instance, R. E. Derouin, B. A. Fritzsche, and E. Salas, "E-Learning in Organizations," *Journal of Management* 31, no. 3 (2005), pp. 920–940; and K. A. Orvis, S. L. Fisher, and M. E. Wasserman, "Power to the People: Using Learner Control to Improve Trainee Reactions and Learning in Web-Based Instructional Environments," *Journal of Applied Psychology* 94, no 4 (2009), pp. 960–971.

49. T. Sitzman, K. Kraiger, D. Stewart, and R. Wisher, "The Comparative Effectiveness of Web-Based and Classroom Instruction: A Meta-Analysis," *Personnel Psychology* 59, no. 3 (2006), pp. 623–664.

50. T. Sitzmann, B. S. Bell, K. Kraiger, and A. M. Kanar, "A Multilevel Analysis of the Effect of Prompting Self-Regulation in Technology-Delivered Instruction," *Personnel Psychology* 62 no. 4 (2009), pp. 697–734.

51. E. A. Ensher, T. R. Nielson, and E. Grant-Vallone, "Tales from the Hiring Line: Effects of the Internet and Technology on HR Processes," *Organizational Dynamics* 31, no. 3 (2002), pp. 232–233; and J. B. Arbaugh, "Do Undergraduates and MBAs Differ Online? Initial Conclusions from the Literature," *Journal of Leadership and Organizational Studies* 17, no. 2 (2010), pp. 129–142.

52. G. M. Alliger, S. I. Tannenbaum, W. Bennett, H. Traver, and A. Shotland, "A Meta-Analysis of the Relations Among Training Criteria," *Personnel Psychology* 50, no. 2 (1997), pp. 341–358; and T. Sitzmann, K. G. Brown, W. J. Casper, K. Ely, and R. D. Zimmerman, "A Review and Meta-Analysis of the Nomological Network of Trainee Reactions," *Journal of Applied Psychology* 93, no. 2 (2008), pp. 280–295.

53. J. A. Colquitt, J. A. LePine, and R. A. Noe, "Toward an Integrative Theory of Training Motivation: A Meta-Analytic Path Analysis of 20 Years of Research," *Journal of Applied Psychology* (October 2000), pp. 678–707.

54. See L. A. Burke and H. S. Hutchins, "Training Transfer: An Integrative Literature Review," *Human Resource Development Review* 6 (2007), pp. 263–296; and D. S. Chiaburu and S. V. Marinova, "What Predicts Skill Transfer? An Exploratory Study of Goal Orientation, Training Self-Efficacy, and Organizational Supports," *International Journal of Training and Development* 9, no. 2 (2005), pp. 110–123.

55. M. Rotundo and P. R. Sackett, "The Relative Importance of Task, Citizenship, and Counterproductive Performance to Global Ratings of Job Performance: A Policy Capturing Approach," *Journal of Applied Psychology* 87, no. 1 (2002), pp. 66–80; and S. W. Whiting, P. M. Podsakoff, and J. R. Pierce, "Effects of Task Performance, Helping, Voice, and Organizational Loyalty on Performance Appraisal Ratings," *Journal of Applied Psychology* 93, no. 1 (2008), pp. 125–139.

56. W. F. Cascio and H. Aguinis, *Applied Psychology in Human Resource Management*, 7th ed. (Upper Saddle River, NJ: Prentice Hall, 2010).

57. A. H. Locher and K. S. Teel, "Appraisal Trends," *Personnel Journal* (September 1988), pp. 139–145.

58. Cited in S. Armour, "Job Reviews Take on Added Significance in Down Times," *USA Today* (July 23, 2003), p. 4B.

59. D. J. Woehr, M. K. Sheehan, and W. Bennett, "Assessing Measurement Equivalence Across Rating Sources: A Multitrait-Multirater Approach," *Journal of Applied Psychology* 90, no. 3 (2005), pp. 592–600; and H. Heidemeier and K. Moser, "Self–Other Agreement in Job Performance Ratings: A Meta-Analytic Test of a Process Model," *Journal of Applied Psychology* 94, no. 2 (March 2009), pp. 353–370.

60. See, for instance, J. D. Facteau and S. B. Craig, "Are Performance Appraisal Ratings from Different Rating Sources Compatible?" *Journal of Applied Psychology* (April 2001), pp. 215–227; J. F. Brett and L. E. Atwater, "360-Degree Feedback: Accuracy, Reactions, and Perceptions of Usefulness," *Journal of Applied Psychology* (October 2001), pp. 930–942; F. Luthans and S. J. Peterson, "360 Degree Feedback with Systematic Coaching: Empirical Analysis Suggests a Winning Combination," *Human Resource Management* (Fall 2003), pp. 243–256; and B. I. J. M. van der Heijden and A. H. J. Nijhof, "The Value of Subjectivity: Problems and Prospects for 360-Degree Appraisal Systems," *International Journal of Human Resource Management* (May 2004), pp. 493–511.

61. M. K. Mount and S. E. Scullen, "Multisource Feedback Ratings: What Do They Really Measure?" in M. London (Ed.), *How People Evaluate Others in Organizations* (Mahwah, NJ: Lawrence Erlbaum, 2001), pp. 155–176; and K. Ng, C. Koh, S. Ang, J. C. Kennedy, and K. Chan, "Rating Leniency and Halo in Multisource Feedback Ratings: Testing Cultural Assumptions of Power Distance and Individualism-Collectivism," *Journal of Applied Psychology*, Online First Publication (April 11, 2011), doi: 10.1037/a0023368.

62. Catherine Rampell, "A History of College Grade Inflation," The New York Times, July 14, 2011, accessed at http://economix.blogs.nytimes.com/2011/07/14/the-history-of-college-grade-inflation/?scp=1&sq=grade%20inflation&st=cse.

63. X. M. Wang, K. F. E. Wong, and J. Y. Y. Kwong, "The Roles of Rater Goals and Ratee Performance Levels in the Distortion of Performance Ratings," *Journal of Applied Psychology* 95, no. 3 (2010), pp. 546–561; J. R. Spence and L. M. Keeping, "The Impact of Non-Performance Information on Ratings of Job Performance: A Policy-Capturing Approach," *Journal of Organizational Behavior* 31 (2010), pp. 587–608; and J. R Spence and L. Keeping, "Conscious Rating Distortion in Performance Appraisal: A Review, Commentary, and Proposed Framework for Research," *Human Resource Management Review* 21, no. 2 (2011), pp. 85–95.

64. L. E. Atwater, J. F. Brett, and A. C. Charles, "Multisource Feedback: Lessons Learned and Implications for Practice," *Human Resource Management* 46, no. 2 (2007), pp. 285–307; and R. Hensel, F. Meijers, R. van der Leeden, and J. Kessels, "360 Degree Feedback: How Many Raters Are Needed for Reliable Ratings on the Capacity to Develop Competences, with Personal Qualities as Developmental Goals?" *International Journal of Human Resource Management* 21, no. 15 (2010), pp. 2813–2830.

65. See, for instance, J. W. Hedge and W. C. Borman, "Changing Conceptions and Practices in Performance Appraisal," in A. Howard (ed.), *The Changing Nature of Work* (San Francisco, CA: Jossey-Bass, 1995), pp. 453–459.

66. See, for instance, K. L. Uggerslev and L. M. Sulsky, "Using Frame-of-Reference Training to Understand the Implications of Rater Idiosyncrasy for Rating Accuracy," *Journal of Applied Psychology* 93, no. 3 (2008), pp. 711–719; and R. F. Martell and D. P. Evans, "Source-Monitoring Training: Toward Reducing Rater Expectancy Effects in Behavioral Measurement," *Journal of Applied Psychology* 90, no. 5 (2005), pp. 956–963.

67. B. Erdogan, "Antecedents and Consequences of Justice Perceptions in Performance Appraisals," *Human Resource Management Review* 12, no. 4 (2002), pp. 555–578; and I M. Jawahar, "The Mediating Role of Appraisal Feedback Reactions on the Relationship Between Rater Feedback-Related Behaviors and Ratee Performance," *Group and Organization Management* 35, no. 4 (2010), pp. 494–526.

68. S. C. Payne, M. T. Horner, W. R. Boswell, A. N. Schroeder, and K. J. Stine-Cheyne, "Comparison of Online and Traditional Performance Appraisal Systems," *Journal of Managerial Psychology* 24, no. 6 (2009), pp. 526–544.

69. R. J. Burke, "Why Performance Appraisal Systems Fail," *Personnel Administration* (June 1972), pp. 32–40.

70. B. D. Cawley, L. M. Keeping, and P. E. Levy, "Participation in the Performance Appraisal Process and Employee Reactions: A Meta-Analytic Review of Field Investigations," *Journal of Applied Psychology* (August 1998), pp. 615–633; and P. E. Levy and J. R. Williams, "The Social Context of Performance Appraisal: A Review and Framework for the Future," *Journal of Management* 30, no. 6 (2004), pp. 881–905.

71. F. Gino and M. E. Schweitzer, "Blinded by Anger or Feeling the Love: How Emotions Influence Advice Taking," *Journal of Applied Psychology* 93, no. 3 (2008), pp. 1165–1173.

72. Heidemeier and Moser, "Self–Other Agreement in Job Performance Ratings."

73. J. Han, "Does Performance-Based Salary System Suit Korea?" *The Korea Times* (January 15, 2008), www.koreatimes.co.kr.

74. F. F. T. Chiang and T. A. Birtch, "Appraising Performance across Borders: An Empirical Examination of the Purposes and Practices of Performance Appraisal in a Multi-Country Context," *Journal of Management Studies* 47, no. 7 (2010), pp. 1365–1393.

75. K. Ng, C. Koh, S. Ang, J. C. Kennedy, and K. Chan, "Rating Leniency and Halo in Multisource Feedback Ratings: Testing Cultural Assumptions of Power Distance and Individualism-Collectivism," *Journal of Applied Psychology*, Online First Publication (April 11, 2011), doi: 10.1037/a0023368.

76. See, for instance, *Harvard Business Review on Work and Life Balance* (Boston: Harvard Business School Press, 2000); R. Rapoport, L. Bailyn, J. K. Fletcher, and B. H. Pruitt, *Beyond Work-Family Balance* (San Francisco: Jossey-Bass, 2002); and E. E. Kossek, S. Pichler, T. Bodner, and L. B. Hammer, "Workplace Social Support and Work-Family Conflict: A Meta-Analysis Clarifying the Influence of General and Work-Family Specific Supervisor and Organizational Support," *Personnel Psychology* 64, no. 2 (2011), pp. 289–313.

77. B. Harrington, F. Van Deusen, and B. Humberd, *The New Dad: Caring Committed and Conflicted.* (Boston: Boston College Center for Work and Family, 2011).

78. A. Grant, "Top 25 Companies for Work-Life Balance," *US News and World Report* (May 11, 2011), www.money.usnews.com.

79. C. P. Maertz and S. L. Boyar, "Work-Family Conflict, Enrichment, and Balance Under 'Levels' and 'Episodes' Approaches," *Journal of Management* 37, no. 1 (2011), pp. 68–98.

80. J. S. Michel and M. B. Hargis, "Linking Mechanisms of Work-Family Conflict and Segmentation," *Journal of Vocational Behavior* 73, no. 3 (2008), pp. 509–522; G. E. Kreiner, "Consequences of Work-Home Segmentation or Integration: A Person-Environment Fit Perspective," *Journal of Organizational Behavior* 27, no. 4 (2006), pp. 485–507; and C. A. Bulger, R. A. Matthews, and M. E. Hoffman, "Work and Personal Life Boundary Management: Boundary Strength, Work/Personal Life Balance, and the Segmentation-Integration Continuum," *Journal of Occupational Health Psychology* 12, no. 4 (2007), pp. 365–375.

81. D. Catanzaro, H. Moore, and T. R. Marshall, "The Impact of Organizational Culture on Attraction and Recruitment of Job Applicants," *Journal of Business and Psychology* 25, (2010), pp. 649–662.

LEARNING OBJECTIVES

After studying this chapter, you should be able to:

1 Identify forces that act as stimulants to change, and contrast planned and unplanned change.

2 Describe the sources of resistance to change.

3 Compare the four main approaches to managing organizational change.

4 Demonstrate two ways of creating a culture for change.

5 Define *stress*, and identify its potential sources.

6 Identify the consequences of stress.

7 Contrast the individual and organizational approaches to managing stress.

MyManagementLab

Access a host of interactive learning aids to help strengthen your understanding of the chapter concepts at **www.mymanagementlab.com**.

SWEET CHANGES AT CADBURY?

Hostile takeovers are never easy, especially for those in the company being acquired. But some takeovers are more hostile than others.

Kraft's acquisition of Cadbury is a case in point. After its initial offer to acquire the UK confectioner was deemed "derisory," Kraft sweetened the deal, and Cadbury's CEO declared it "good value for Cadbury shareholders." Cadbury managers and employees, however, continue to have difficulty adjusting to the change.

One problem was the way Kraft handled the acquisition. Shortly after signing the deal, Kraft reneged on its pledge to keep Cadbury's Somerdale, England, plant open. The British, infuriated, demanded that Kraft CEO Irene Rosenfeld appear before Parliament. Rosenfeld refused, saying, it "was not the best use of my personal time." Members of Parliament, in turn, threatened to bring charges of contempt. Rosenfeld retorted: "The continued assault has been somewhat surprising."

The public relations aspect of the plant closing will probably blow over with time. However, a deeper and potentially more serious issue is the difference in cultures between the two organizations.

Kraft, by far the larger, is known for its formal and relatively hierarchical culture. Its meetings tend to be lengthy, with most decisions requiring the approval of top-level executives.

Cadbury was known for its more informal and more egalitarian culture. Its former CEO was often seen on the shop floor talking informally with workers. Its managers felt they were given the autonomy to be creative. Its marketing team won awards for producing the "Cadbury Gorilla" ad (available on YouTube).

Some employees who had been part of Cadbury have complained of Kraft's "Orwellian" management. Cadbury managers complain that Kraft "runs the show with military precision . . . directives or proposals pass through a hierarchy of layers." Says another anonymous manager: "That more entrepreneurial side of things got quashed because there are so many more layers of input and discussion." And according to a former employee, "Cadbury has a cutting edge understanding of the shopper and its retail customers. We spent years building that at Cadbury, and that's been lost."

The *Financial Times* commented: "The tension reaches all levels of former Cadbury staff, from the commercial division to the factory floor." On the other hand, some argue that Cadbury has reacted in a childish manner. *Bloomberg Businessweek* commented, "For many Brits, complaining is a national sport."

Is this a story of culture clash where a sympathetic, entrepreneurial company is devoured by an arrogant, bureaucratic one? Or is it a case of

Organizational Change and Stress Management

It is not the strongest of the species that survives, nor the most intelligent, but the one most responsive to change. —Charles Darwin employees of a proud, smaller company refusing to adapt to new business conditions and a new culture?

The answer you favor appears to depend upon which side of the Atlantic you reside on.

Sources: L. Lucas, "Cadbury People Still Chewing on Kraft Culture," *Financial Times* (January 15, 2011), p. 13; L. Lucas and A. Rappeport, "Mergers and Acquisitions: A Bitter Taste," *Financial Times* (May 23, 2011), downloaded on July 19, 2011, from www.ft.com/; and M. Scott, "Why Britain Will Survive Kraft's Takeover of Cadbury," *Bloomberg Businessweek* (January 21, 2010), downloaded on July 8, 2011, from www.businessweek.com/.

This chapter is about change and stress. We describe environmental forces that require firms to change, why people and organizations often resist change, and how this resistance can be overcome. We review processes for managing organizational change. Then we move to the topic of stress and its sources and consequences. In closing, we discuss what individuals and organizations can do to better manage stress levels.

First, see how well you handle change by taking the following self-assessment.

SELF-ASSESSMENT LIBRARY

How Well Do I Respond to Turbulent Change?

In the Self-Assessment Library (available on CD and online), take assessment III.C.1 (How Well Do I Respond to Turbulent Change?) and answer the following questions.

1. How did you score? Are you surprised by your score?
2. During what time of your life have you experienced the most change? How did you deal with it? Would you handle these changes in the same way today? Why or why not?
3. Are there ways you might reduce your resistance to change?

Forces for Change

1 Identify forces that act as stimulants to change, and contrast planned and unplanned change.

No company today is in a particularly stable environment. Even those with dominant market share must change, sometimes radically. Even though Apple has been successful with its iPad, the growing number of competitors in the field of tablet computers suggests that Apple will need to continually update and innovate to keep ahead of the market.

"Change or die!" is thus the rallying cry among today's managers worldwide. Exhibit 18-1 summarizes six specific forces stimulating change.

In a number of places in this book, we've discussed the *changing nature of the workforce.* Almost every organization must adjust to a multicultural environment, demographic changes, immigration, and outsourcing. *Technology* is continually changing jobs and organizations. It is not hard to imagine the very idea of an office becoming an antiquated concept in the near future.

The housing and financial sectors recently have experienced extraordinary *economic shocks,* leading to the elimination, bankruptcy, or acquisition of some of

Exhibit **18-1**	**Forces for Change**

Force	Examples
Nature of the workforce	More cultural diversity
	Aging population
	Increased immigration and outsourcing
Technology	Faster, cheaper, and more mobile computers and handheld devices
	Emergence and growth of social networking sites
	Deciphering of the human genetic code
Economic shocks	Rise and fall of global housing market
	Financial sector collapse
	Global recession
Competition	Global competitors
	Mergers and consolidations
	Increased government regulation of commerce
Social trends	Increased environmental awareness
	Liberalization of attitudes toward gay, lesbian, and transgender employees
	More multitasking and connectivity
World politics	Rising health care costs
	Negative social attitudes toward business and executives
	Opening of markets in China

the best-known U.S. companies, including Bear Stearns, Merrill Lynch, Lehman Brothers, Countrywide Financial, Washington Mutual, and Ameriquest. Tens of thousands of jobs were lost and may never return. After years of declining numbers of bankruptcies, the global recession caused the bankruptcy of auto manufacturers General Motors and Chrysler, retailers Borders and Sharper Image, and myriad other organizations.

Competition is changing. Competitors are as likely to come from across the ocean as from across town. Successful organizations will be fast on their feet, capable of developing new products rapidly and getting them to market quickly. In other words, they'll be flexible and will require an equally flexible and responsive workforce. Increasingly, in the United States and Europe, the government regulates business practices, including executive pay.

Social trends don't remain static either. Consumers who are otherwise strangers now meet and share product information in chat rooms and blogs. Companies must continually adjust product and marketing strategies to be sensitive to changing social trends, as Liz Claiborne did when it sold off fashion brands (such as Ellen Tracy), deemphasized large vendors such as Macy's, and streamlined operations and cut staff. Consumers, employees, and organizational leaders are more sensitive to environmental concerns. "Green" practices are quickly becoming expected rather than optional.

Not even globalization's strongest proponents could have imagined how *world politics* would change in recent years. We've seen a major set of financial crises that have rocked global markets, a dramatic rise in the power and influence of China, and dramatic shakeups in government across the Arab world. Throughout the industrialized world, businesses—particularly in the banking and financial sectors—have come under new scrutiny.

Planned Change

Source: Emmanuel Dunand/AFP/Getty Images/Newscom

Jeff Bezos is the change agent at Amazon.com. He founded the company as an online bookstore in 1994 and then built it into the largest retailer on the Web that sells everything from groceries to electronics. Amazon changed from a seller of electronics to also become a product developer when it created the Kindle reading device and the Kindle service for downloading books in less than 60 seconds. In his drive for change at Amazon, Bezos combines a long-term orientation with identifying a customer need. Bezos is shown here unveiling the Kindle DX, a large-screen version of the original Kindle designed for reading newspapers, magazines, and textbooks.

A group of housekeeping employees who work for a small hotel confronted the owner: "It's very hard for most of us to maintain rigid 7-to-4 work hours," said their spokeswoman. "Each of us has significant family and personal responsibilities. And rigid hours don't work for us. We're going to begin looking for someplace else to work if you don't set up flexible work hours." The owner listened thoughtfully to the group's ultimatum and agreed to its request. The next day, a flextime plan for these employees was introduced.

A major automobile manufacturer spent several billion dollars to install state-of-the-art robotics. One area that would receive the new equipment was quality control, where sophisticated computers would significantly improve the company's ability to find and correct defects. Because the new equipment would dramatically change the jobs in the quality-control area, and because management anticipated considerable employee resistance to it, executives were developing a program to help people become familiar with it and deal with any anxieties they might be feeling.

Both these scenarios are examples of **change**, or making things different. However, only the second scenario describes a **planned change**. Many changes are like the one that occurred at the hotel: they just happen. Some organizations treat all change as an accidental occurrence. In this chapter, we address change as an intentional, goal-oriented activity.

What are the goals of planned change? First, it seeks to improve the ability of the organization to adapt to changes in its environment. Second, it seeks to change employee behavior.

Who in organizations is responsible for managing change activities? The answer is **change agents**.[1] They see a future for the organization that others have not identified, and they are able to motivate, invent, and implement this vision. Change agents can be managers or nonmanagers, current or new employees, or outside consultants.

DuPont has two primary change agents in CEO Ellen Kullman and Chief Innovation Officer Thomas Connelly.[2] Taking the reins of the company in 2010, Kullman has pushed the organization toward a higher level of achievement by focusing on a principle Connelly calls "launch hard and ramp fast." This means the organization will seek to derive as much of its revenues from new products as possible. The goal is to move DuPont from a comparatively placid culture to one that focuses on market-driven science and delivers products customers need. The process has not always been easy, but it is necessary to keep DuPont ahead of the competitive marketplace.

Many change agents fail because organizational members resist change. In the next section, we discuss resistance to change and what managers can do about it.

Resistance to Change

2 Describe the sources of resistance to change.

Our egos are fragile, and we often see change as threatening. One recent study showed that even when employees are shown data that suggest they need to change, they latch onto whatever data they can find that suggests they are okay and don't need to change.[3] Employees who have negative feelings about a

MyManagementLab
For an interactive application of this topic, check out this chapter's simulation activity at **www.mymanagementlab.com.**

change cope by not thinking about it, increasing their use of sick time, and quitting. All these reactions can sap the organization of vital energy when it is most needed.[4]

Resistance to change can be positive if it leads to open discussion and debate.[5] These responses are usually preferable to apathy or silence and can indicate that members of the organization are engaged in the process, providing change agents an opportunity to explain the change effort. Change agents can also use resistance to modify the change to fit the preferences of other members of the organization. When they treat resistance only as a threat, rather than a point of view to be discussed, they may increase dysfunctional conflict.

Resistance doesn't necessarily surface in standardized ways. It can be overt, implicit, immediate, or deferred. It's easiest for management to deal with overt and immediate resistance, such as complaints, a work slowdown, or a strike threat. The greater challenge is managing resistance that is implicit or deferred. These responses—loss of loyalty or motivation, increased errors or absenteeism—are more subtle and more difficult to recognize for what they are. Deferred actions also cloud the link between the change and the reaction to it and may surface weeks, months, or even years later. Or a single change of little inherent impact may be the straw that breaks the camel's back because resistance to earlier changes has been deferred and stockpiled.

Exhibit 18-2 summarizes major forces for resistance to change, categorized by their sources. Individual sources reside in human characteristics such as perceptions, personalities, and needs. Organizational sources reside in the structural makeup of organizations themselves.

It's worth noting that not all change is good. Speed can lead to bad decisions, and sometimes those initiating change fail to realize the full magnitude of the effects or their true costs. Rapid, transformational change is risky, and

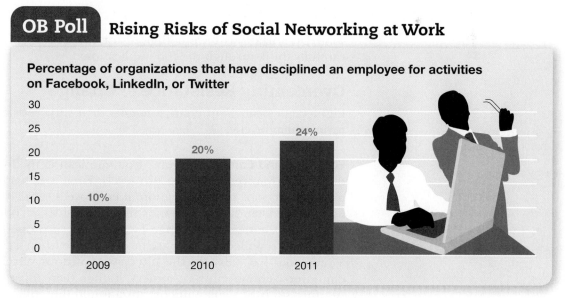

OB Poll   **Rising Risks of Social Networking at Work**

Percentage of organizations that have disciplined an employee for activities on Facebook, LinkedIn, or Twitter

- 2009: 10%
- 2010: 20%
- 2011: 24%

Source: Based on J. Yang and P. Trap, "Society for Human Resource Management Survey," *USA Today* (June 2, 2011), p. 1B.

---

change   *Making things different.*

planned change   *Change activities that are intentional and goal oriented.*

change agents   *Persons who act as catalysts and assume the responsibility for managing change activities.*

Exhibit 18-2	Sources of Resistance to Change

Individual Sources

Habit—To cope with life's complexities, we rely on habits or programmed responses. But when confronted with change, this tendency to respond in our accustomed ways becomes a source of resistance.

Security—People with a high need for security are likely to resist change because it threatens their feelings of safety.

Economic factors—Changes in job tasks or established work routines can arouse economic fears if people are concerned that they won't be able to perform the new tasks or routines to their previous standards, especially when pay is closely tied to productivity.

Fear of the unknown—Change substitutes ambiguity and uncertainty for the unknown.

Selective information processing—Individuals are guilty of selectively processing information in order to keep their perceptions intact. They hear what they want to hear, and they ignore information that challenges the world they've created.

Organizational Sources

Structural inertia—Organizations have built-in mechanisms—such as their selection processes and formalized regulations—to produce stability. When an organization is confronted with change, this structural inertia acts as a counterbalance to sustain stability.

Limited focus of change—Organizations consist of a number of interdependent subsystems. One can't be changed without affecting the others. So limited changes in subsystems tend to be nullified by the larger system.

Group inertia—Even if individuals want to change their behavior, group norms may act as a constraint.

Threat to expertise—Changes in organizational patterns may threaten the expertise of specialized groups.

Threat to established power relationships—Any redistribution of decision-making authority can threaten long-established power relationships within the organization.

some organizations have collapsed for this reason.[6] Change agents need to carefully think through the full implications.

Overcoming Resistance to Change

Eight tactics can help change agents deal with resistance to change.[7] Let's review them briefly.

Education and Communication   Communicating the logic of a change can reduce employee resistance on two levels. First, it fights the effects of misinformation and poor communication: if employees receive the full facts and clear up misunderstandings, resistance should subside. Second, communication can help "sell" the need for change by packaging it properly.[8] A study of German companies revealed changes are most effective when a company communicates a rationale that balances the interests of various stakeholders (shareholders, employees, community, customers) rather than those of shareholders only.[9] Another study of a changing organization in the Philippines found that formal change information sessions decreased employee anxiety about the change, while providing high-quality information about the change increased commitment to it.[10]

Participation   It's difficult to resist a change decision in which we've participated. Assuming participants have the expertise to make a meaningful contribution, their involvement can reduce resistance, obtain commitment, and increase the quality of the change decision. However, against these advantages are the negatives: potential for a poor solution and great consumption of time.

Building Support and Commitment   When employees' fear and anxiety are high, counseling and therapy, new-skills training, or a short paid leave of absence may facilitate adjustment. When managers or employees have low emotional commitment to change, they favor the status quo and resist it.[11] Employees are also more accepting of changes when they are committed to the organization as a whole.[12] So, firing up employees and emphasizing their commitment to the organization overall can also help them emotionally commit to the change rather than embrace the status quo.

Develop Positive Relationships   People are more willing to accept changes if they trust the managers implementing them.[13] One study surveyed 235 employees from a large housing corporation in the Netherlands that was experiencing a merger. Those who had a more positive relationship with their supervisors, and who felt that the work environment supported development, were much more positive about the change process.[14] Another set of studies found that individuals who were dispositionally resistant to change felt more positive about the change if they trusted the change agent.[15] This research suggests that if managers are able to facilitate positive relationships, they may be able to overcome resistance to change even among those who ordinarily don't like changes.

Implementing Changes Fairly   One way organizations can minimize negative impact is to make sure change is implemented fairly. As we saw in Chapter 7, procedural fairness is especially important when employees perceive an outcome as negative, so it's crucial that employees see the reason for the change and perceive its implementation as consistent and fair.[16]

Manipulation and Cooptation   *Manipulation* refers to covert influence attempts. Twisting facts to make them more attractive, withholding information, and creating false rumors to get employees to accept change are all examples of manipulation. If management threatens to close a manufacturing plant whose employees are resisting an across-the-board pay cut, and if the threat is actually untrue, management is using manipulation. *Cooptation*, on the other hand, combines manipulation and participation. It seeks to "buy off" the leaders of a resistance group by giving them a key role, seeking their advice not to find a better solution but to get their endorsement. Both manipulation and cooptation are relatively inexpensive ways to gain the support of adversaries, but they can backfire if the targets become aware they are being tricked or used. Once that's discovered, the change agent's credibility may drop to zero.

Selecting People Who Accept Change   Research suggests the ability to easily accept and adapt to *change* is related to personality—some people simply have more positive attitudes about change than others.[17] Such individuals are open to experience, take a positive attitude toward change, are willing to take risks, and are flexible in their behavior. One study of managers in the United States, Europe, and Asia found those with a positive self-concept and high risk tolerance coped better with organizational change. A study of 258 police officers found those higher in growth-needs strength, internal locus of control, and internal work motivation had more positive attitudes about organizational change efforts.[18] Individuals higher in general mental ability are also better able to learn and adapt to changes in the workplace.[19] In sum, an impressive body of evidence shows organizations can facilitate change by selecting people predisposed to accept it.

Besides selecting individuals who are willing to accept changes, it is also possible to select teams that are more adaptable. Studies have shown that teams that are strongly motivated by learning about and mastering tasks are better able to adapt to changing environments.[20] This research suggests that it may be necessary to consider not just individual motivation, but also group motivation when trying to implement changes.

Coercion   Last on the list of tactics is *coercion,* the application of direct threats or force on the resisters. If management really is determined to close a manufacturing plant whose employees don't acquiesce to a pay cut, the company is using coercion. Other examples are threats of transfer, loss of promotions, negative performance evaluations, and a poor letter of recommendation. The advantages and drawbacks of coercion are approximately the same as for manipulation and cooptation.

The Politics of Change

No discussion of resistance would be complete without a brief mention of the politics of change. Because change invariably threatens the status quo, it inherently implies political activity.

Politics suggests the impetus for change is more likely to come from outside change agents, employees new to the organization (who have less invested in the status quo), or managers slightly removed from the main power structure. Managers who have spent their entire careers with a single organization and achieved a senior position in the hierarchy are often major impediments to change. It is a very real threat to their status and position. Yet they may be expected to implement changes to demonstrate they're not merely caretakers. By acting as change agents, they can convey to stockholders, suppliers, employees, and customers that they are addressing problems and adapting to a dynamic environment. Of course, as you might guess, when forced to introduce change, these longtime power holders tend to implement incremental changes. Radical change is too threatening. This explains why boards of directors that recognize the imperative for rapid and radical change frequently turn to outside candidates for new leadership.[21]

Approaches to Managing Organizational Change

3 Compare the four main approaches to managing organizational change.

Now we turn to several approaches to managing change: Lewin's classic three-step model of the change process, Kotter's eight-step plan, action research, and organizational development.

Lewin's Three-Step Model

Kurt Lewin argued that successful change in organizations should follow three steps: **unfreezing** the status quo, **movement** to a desired end state, and **refreezing** the new change to make it permanent.[22] (See Exhibit 18-3.)

The status quo is an equilibrium state. To move from equilibrium—to overcome the pressures of both individual resistance and group conformity—unfreezing

Exhibit **18-3**   Lewin's Three-Step Change Model

Unfreezing → Movement → Refreezing

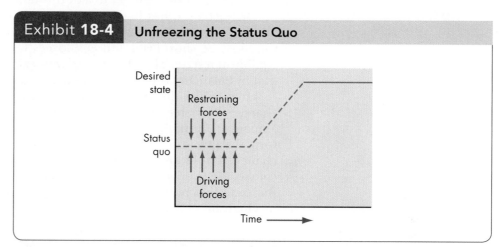

Exhibit **18-4**   Unfreezing the Status Quo

must happen in one of three ways (see Exhibit 18-4.) The **driving forces**, which direct behavior away from the status quo, can be increased. The **restraining forces**, which hinder movement away from equilibrium, can be decreased. A third alternative is to combine the first two approaches. Companies that have been successful in the past are likely to encounter restraining forces because people question the need for change.[23] Similarly, research shows that companies with strong cultures excel at incremental change but are overcome by restraining forces against radical change.[24]

Consider a large oil company that decided to consolidate its three divisional marketing offices in Seattle, San Francisco, and Los Angeles into a single regional San Francisco office. The decision was made in New York and the people affected had no say whatsoever in the choice. The reorganization meant transferring more than 150 employees, eliminating some duplicate managerial positions, and instituting a new hierarchy of command.

The oil company's management could expect employee resistance to the consolidation. Those in Seattle or Los Angeles may not want to transfer to another city, pull youngsters out of school, make new friends, adapt to new co-workers, or undergo the reassignment of responsibilities. Positive incentives such as pay increases, liberal moving expenses, and low-cost mortgage funds for new homes in San Francisco might encourage employees to accept the change. Management might also unfreeze acceptance of the status quo by removing restraining forces. It could counsel employees individually, hearing and clarifying each employee's specific concerns and apprehensions. Assuming most are

unfreezing   *Changing to overcome the pressures of both individual resistance and group conformity.*

movement   *A change process that transforms the organization from the status quo to a desired end state.*

refreezing   *Stabilizing a change intervention by balancing driving and restraining forces.*

driving forces   *Forces that direct behavior away from the status quo.*

restraining forces   *Forces that hinder movement from the existing equilibrium.*

unjustified, the counselor could assure employees there was nothing to fear and offer tangible evidence that restraining forces are unwarranted. If resistance is extremely high, management may have to resort to both reducing resistance and increasing the attractiveness of the alternative if the unfreezing is to be successful.

Research on organizational change has shown that, to be effective, the actual change has to happen quickly.[25] Organizations that build up to change do less well than those that get to and through the movement stage quickly.

Once change has been implemented, to be successful the new situation must be refrozen so it can be sustained over time. Without this last step, change will likely be short-lived and employees will attempt to revert to the previous equilibrium state. The objective of refreezing, then, is to stabilize the new situation by balancing the driving and restraining forces.

How could the oil company's management refreeze its consolidation change? By systematically replacing temporary forces with permanent ones. Management might impose a permanent upward adjustment of salaries. The formal rules and regulations governing behavior of those affected by the change should also be revised to reinforce the new situation. Over time, of course, the work group's own norms will evolve to sustain the new equilibrium. But until that point is reached, management will have to rely on more formal mechanisms.

Kotter's Eight-Step Plan for Implementing Change

John Kotter of the Harvard Business School built on Lewin's three-step model to create a more detailed approach for implementing change.[26] Kotter began by listing common mistakes managers make when trying to initiate change. They may fail to create a sense of urgency about the need for change, to create a coalition for managing the change process, to have a vision for change and effectively communicate it, to remove obstacles that could impede the vision's achievement, to provide short-term and achievable goals, and to anchor the changes into the organization's culture. They may also declare victory too soon.

Kotter then established eight sequential steps to overcome these problems. They're listed in Exhibit 18-5.

Notice how Kotter's first four steps essentially extrapolate Lewin's "unfreezing" stage. Steps 5, 6 and 7 represent "movement," and the final step works on

---

Exhibit 18-5   Kotter's Eight-Step Plan for Implementing Change

1. Establish a sense of urgency by creating a compelling reason for why change is needed.
2. Form a coalition with enough power to lead the change.
3. Create a new vision to direct the change and strategies for achieving the vision.
4. Communicate the vision throughout the organization.
5. Empower others to act on the vision by removing barriers to change and encouraging risk taking and creative problem solving.
6. Plan for, create, and reward short-term "wins" that move the organization toward the new vision.
7. Consolidate improvements, reassess changes, and make necessary adjustments in the new programs.
8. Reinforce the changes by demonstrating the relationship between new behaviors and organizational success.

Source: Based on J. P. Kotter, *Leading Change* (Boston: Harvard Business School Press, 1996).

"refreezing." So Kotter's contribution lies in providing managers and change agents with a more detailed guide for successfully implementing change.

Action Research

Action research is a change process based on the systematic collection of data and selection of a change action based on what the analyzed data indicate.[27] Its value is in providing a scientific methodology for managing planned change. Action research consists of five steps (note how they closely parallel the scientific method): diagnosis, analysis, feedback, action, and evaluation.

The change agent, often an outside consultant in action research, begins by gathering information about problems, concerns, and needed changes from members of the organization. This *diagnosis* is analogous to the physician's search to find specifically what ails a patient. In action research, the change agent asks questions, reviews records, and interviews employees and listens to their concerns.

Diagnosis is followed by *analysis.* What problems do people key in on? What patterns do these problems seem to take? The change agent synthesizes this information into primary concerns, problem areas, and possible actions.

Action research requires the people who will participate in any change program to help identify the problem and determine the solution. So the third step—*feedback*—requires sharing with employees what has been found from the first and second steps. The employees, with the help of the change agent, develop action plans for bringing about any needed change.

Now the *action* part of action research is set in motion. The employees and the change agent carry out the specific actions they have identified to correct the problem.

The final step, consistent with the scientific underpinnings of action research, is *evaluation* of the action plan's effectiveness, using the initial data gathered as a benchmark.

Action research provides at least two specific benefits. First, it's problem focused. The change agent objectively looks for problems, and the type of problem determines the type of change action. Although this may seem intuitively obvious, many change activities are not handled this way. Rather, they're solution centered. The change agent has a favorite solution—for example, implementing flextime, teams, or a process reengineering program—and then seeks out problems that the solution fits.

Second, because action research engages employees so thoroughly in the process, it reduces resistance to change. Once employees have actively participated in the feedback stage, the change process typically takes on a momentum of its own under their sustained pressure to bring it about.

Organizational Development

Organizational development (OD) is a collection of change methods that try to improve organizational effectiveness and employee well-being.[28]

OD methods value human and organizational growth, collaborative and participative processes, and a spirit of inquiry.[29] Contemporary OD borrows

action research *A change process based on systematic collection of data and then selection of a change action based on what the analyzed data indicate.*

organizational development (OD) *A collection of planned change interventions, built on humanistic-democratic values, that seeks to improve organizational effectiveness and employee well-being.*

These retirement center employees participate in a simulated training program to help them understand the diminishing abilities of the older population that is growing in developing nations worldwide. While wearing glasses that blurred their vision, they collaborated in an activity of devising a driving route. Called Xtreme Aging, the training program has become a regular part of many nursing and medical school curricula and corporate training programs and is designed to help participants grow in their understanding of and sensitivity to the needs of older customers and fellow workers.

Source: Kirk Irwin/The New York Times/Redux Pictures.

heavily from postmodern philosophy in placing heavy emphasis on the subjective ways in which people see their environment. The focus is on how individuals make sense of their work environment. The change agent may take the lead in OD, but there is a strong emphasis on collaboration. These are the underlying values in most OD efforts:

1. **Respect for people.** Individuals are perceived as responsible, conscientious, and caring. They should be treated with dignity and respect.
2. **Trust and support.** An effective and healthy organization is characterized by trust, authenticity, openness, and a supportive climate.
3. **Power equalization.** Effective organizations deemphasize hierarchical authority and control.
4. **Confrontation.** Problems should be openly confronted, not swept under the rug.
5. **Participation.** The more engaged in the decisions they are, the more people affected by a change will be committed to implementing them.

What are some OD techniques or interventions for bringing about change? Here are six.

Sensitivity Training A variety of names—**sensitivity training**, laboratory training, encounter groups, and T-groups (training groups)—all refer to an early method of changing behavior through unstructured group interaction.[30] Members were brought together in a free and open environment in which participants discuss themselves and their interactive processes, loosely directed by a professional behavioral scientist who created the opportunity to express ideas, beliefs, and attitudes without taking any leadership role. The group was process-oriented, which means individuals learned through observing and participating rather than being told.

Many participants found these unstructured groups intimidating, chaotic, and damaging to work relationships. Although extremely popular in the 1960s, they diminished in use during the 1970s and have essentially disappeared. However, organizational interventions such as diversity training, executive coaching, and team-building exercises are descendants of this early OD intervention technique.

Survey Feedback   One tool for assessing attitudes held by organizational members, identifying discrepancies among member perceptions, and solving these differences is the **survey feedback** approach.[31]

Everyone in an organization can participate in survey feedback, but of key importance is the organizational "family"—the manager of any given unit and the employees who report directly to him or her. All usually complete a questionnaire about their perceptions and attitudes on a range of topics, including decision-making practices; communication effectiveness; coordination among units; and satisfaction with the organization, job, peers, and immediate supervisor.

Data from this questionnaire are tabulated with data pertaining to an individual's specific "family" and to the entire organization and then distributed to employees. These data become the springboard for identifying problems and clarifying issues that may be creating difficulties for people. Particular attention is given to encouraging discussion and ensuring it focuses on issues and ideas and not on attacking individuals. For instance, are people listening? Are new ideas being generated? Can decision making, interpersonal relations, or job assignments be improved? Answers should lead the group to commit to various remedies for the problems identified.

Process Consultation   Managers often sense their unit's performance can be improved but are unable to identify what to improve and how. The purpose of **process consultation (PC)** is for an outside consultant to assist a client, usually a manager, "to perceive, understand, and act upon process events" with which the manager must deal.[32] These events might include work flow, informal relationships among unit members, and formal communication channels.

PC is similar to sensitivity training in assuming we can improve organizational effectiveness by dealing with interpersonal problems and in emphasizing involvement. But PC is more task directed, and consultants are there to "give the client 'insight' into what is going on around him, within him, and between him and other people."[33] They do not solve the organization's problems but rather guide or coach the client to solve his or her own problems after *jointly* diagnosing what needs improvement. The client develops the skill to analyze processes within his or her unit and can continue to call on it long after the consultant is gone. Because the client actively participates in both the diagnosis and the development of alternatives, he or she arrives at greater understanding of the process and the remedy and is less resistant to the action plan chosen.

Team Building   We've noted throughout this book that organizations increasingly rely on teams to accomplish work tasks. **Team building** uses high-interaction group activities to increase trust and openness among team members, improve coordinative efforts, and increase team performance.[34] Here, we emphasize the intragroup level, meaning organizational families (command groups) as well as committees, project teams, self-managed teams, and task groups.

---

sensitivity training   *Training groups that seek to change behavior through unstructured group interaction.*

survey feedback   *The use of questionnaires to identify discrepancies among member perceptions; discussion follows, and remedies are suggested.*

process consultation (PC)   *A meeting in which a consultant assists a client in understanding process events with which he or she must deal and identifying processes that need improvement.*

team building   *High interaction among team members to increase trust and openness.*

ServiceMaster, a provider of lawn care, cleaning, disaster restoration, and other services, is a sponsoring company of Habitat for Humanity. As a sponsor, ServiceMaster provides employee volunteers and the funds to buy building materials for constructing homes for families in need. For ServiceMaster, the building project also serves as a team-building activity, with employees spending their workdays at the building site rather than on their regular jobs. Serving as a high-interaction group activity, the Habitat build increases trust and openness among employees and translates into better communication and greater cooperation in the workplace.

Source: c51/ZUMA Press/Newscom.

Team building typically includes goal-setting, development of interpersonal relations among team members, role analysis to clarify each member's role and responsibilities, and team process analysis. It may emphasize or exclude certain activities, depending on the purpose of the development effort and the specific problems with which the team is confronted. Basically, however, team building uses high interaction among members to increase trust and openness.

Intergroup Development   A major area of concern in OD is dysfunctional conflict among groups. **Intergroup development** seeks to change groups' attitudes, stereotypes, and perceptions about each other. Here, training sessions closely resemble diversity training (in fact, diversity training largely evolved from intergroup development in OD), except rather than focusing on demographic differences, they focus on differences among occupations, departments, or divisions within an organization.

In one company, the engineers saw the accounting department as composed of shy and conservative types and the human resources department as having a bunch of "ultra-liberals more concerned that some protected group of employees might get their feelings hurt than with the company making a profit." Such stereotypes can have an obvious negative impact on coordination efforts among departments.

Among several approaches for improving intergroup relations, a popular one emphasizes problem solving.[35] Each group meets independently to list its perceptions of itself and of the other group and how it believes the other group perceives it. The groups share their lists, discuss similarities and differences, and look for the causes of disparities. Are the groups' goals at odds? Were perceptions distorted? On what basis were stereotypes formulated? Have some differences been caused by misunderstanding of intentions? Have words and concepts been defined differently by each group? Answers to questions like these clarify the exact nature of the conflict.

Once they have identified the causes of the difficulty, the groups move to the integration phase—developing solutions to improve relations between them.

Subgroups can be formed of members from each of the conflicting groups to conduct further diagnosis and formulate alternative solutions.

Appreciative Inquiry   Most OD approaches are problem centered. They identify a problem or set of problems, then look for a solution. **Appreciative inquiry (AI)** instead accentuates the positive.[36] Rather than looking for problems to fix, it seeks to identify the unique qualities and special strengths of an organization, which members can build on to improve performance. That is, AI focuses on an organization's successes rather than its problems.

The AI process consists of four steps—discovery, dreaming, design, and discovery—often played out in a large-group meeting over a 2- or 3-day time period and overseen by a trained change agent. *Discovery* sets out to identify what people think are the organization's strengths. Employees recount times they felt the organization worked best or when they specifically felt most satisfied with their jobs. In *dreaming*, employees use information from the discovery phase to speculate on possible futures, such as what the organization will be like in 5 years. In *design*, participants find a common vision of how the organization will look in the future and agree on its unique qualities. For the fourth step, participants seek to define the organization's *destiny* or how to fulfill their dream, and they typically write action plans and develop implementation strategies.

AI has proven an effective change strategy in organizations such as GTE, Roadway Express, and the U.S. Navy. American Express used AI to revitalize its culture during a lean economy. In workshops, employees described how they already felt proud of working at American Express and were encouraged to create a change vision by describing how it could be better in the future. The efforts led to some very concrete improvements. Senior managers were able to use employees' information to better their methods of making financial forecasts, improve IT investments, and create new performance-management tools for managers. The end result was a renewed culture focused on winning attitudes and behaviors.[37]

Creating a Culture for Change

4 Demonstrate two ways of creating a culture for change.

We've considered how organizations can *adapt* to change. But recently, some OB scholars have focused on a more proactive approach—how organizations can *embrace* change by transforming their cultures. In this section, we review two such approaches: stimulating an innovative culture and creating a learning organization.

Stimulating a Culture of Innovation

How can an organization become more innovative? An excellent model is W. L. Gore, the $2.6-billion-per-year company best known as the maker of Gore-Tex fabric.[38] Gore has developed a reputation as one of the most innovative

intergroup development   *OD efforts to change the attitudes, stereotypes, and perceptions that groups have of each other.*

appreciative inquiry (AI)   *An approach that seeks to identify the unique qualities and special strengths of an organization, which can then be built on to improve performance.*

U.S. companies by developing a stream of diverse products—including guitar strings, dental floss, medical devices, and fuel cells.

What's the secret of Gore's success? What can other organizations do to duplicate its track record for innovation? Although there is no guaranteed formula, certain characteristics surface repeatedly when researchers study innovative organizations. We've grouped them into structural, cultural, and human resource categories. Change agents should consider introducing these characteristics into their organization to create an innovative climate. Before we look at these characteristics, however, let's clarify what we mean by innovation.

Definition of *Innovation*   We said change refers to making things different. **Innovation**, a more specialized kind of change, is a new idea applied to initiating or improving a product, process, or service.[39] So all innovations imply change, but not all changes necessarily introduce new ideas or lead to significant improvements. Innovations can range from small incremental improvements, such as netbook computers, to radical breakthroughs, such as Nissan's electric Leaf car.

Sources of Innovation   *Structural variables* have been the most studied potential source of innovation.[40] A comprehensive review of the structure–innovation relationship leads to the following conclusions:[41]

1. Organic structures positively influence innovation. Because they're lower in vertical differentiation, formalization, and centralization, organic organizations facilitate the flexibility, adaptation, and cross-fertilization that make the adoption of innovations easier.
2. Long tenure in management is associated with innovation. Managerial tenure apparently provides legitimacy and knowledge of how to accomplish tasks and obtain desired outcomes.
3. Innovation is nurtured when there are slack resources. Having an abundance of resources allows an organization to afford to purchase innovations, bear the cost of instituting them, and absorb failures.

Innovation is a specialized kind of change whereby a new idea is applied to initiating or improving a product, process, or service. Twitter, for example, is an innovation in the distribution of information. Twitter's founders Evan Williams (left) and Biz Stone shown in this photo along with Jack Dorsey launched their new communication tool for sending 140-character messages, or tweets, from a computer or mobile device. As a social network, Twitter allows users to have live digital conversations. By using Twitter's search feature, users can have a real-time view into other people's conversations.

Source: Peter DaSilva/The New York Times/Redux.

4. Interunit communication is high in innovative organizations.[42] These organizations are high users of committees, task forces, cross-functional teams, and other mechanisms that facilitate interaction across departmental lines.

Innovative organizations tend to have similar *cultures*. They encourage experimentation. They reward both successes and failures. They celebrate mistakes. Unfortunately, in too many organizations, people are rewarded for the absence of failures rather than for the presence of successes. Such cultures extinguish risk taking and innovation. People will suggest and try new ideas only when they feel such behaviors exact no penalties. Managers in innovative organizations recognize that failures are a natural by-product of venturing into the unknown.

Within the *human resources* category, innovative organizations actively promote the training and development of their members so they keep current, offer high job security so employees don't fear getting fired for making mistakes, and encourage individuals to become champions of change. Once a new idea is developed, **idea champions** actively and enthusiastically promote it, build support, overcome resistance, and ensure it's implemented.[43] Champions have common personality characteristics: extremely high self-confidence, persistence, energy, and a tendency to take risks. They also display characteristics associated with transformational leadership—they inspire and energize others with their vision of an innovation's potential and their strong personal conviction about their mission. Idea champions are good at gaining the commitment of others, and their jobs provide considerable decision-making discretion; this autonomy helps them introduce and implement innovations.[44]

Do successful idea champions do things differently in different cultures? Yes.[45] People in collectivist cultures prefer appeals for cross-functional support for innovation efforts; people in high power distance cultures prefer champions to work closely with those in authority to approve innovative activities before work is begun; and the higher the uncertainty avoidance of a society, the more champions should work within the organization's rules and procedures to develop the innovation. These findings suggest that effective managers will alter their organization's championing strategies to reflect cultural values. So, for instance, although idea champions in Russia might succeed by ignoring budgetary limitations and working around confining procedures, champions in Austria, Denmark, Germany, or other cultures high in uncertainty avoidance will be more effective by closely following budgets and procedures.

Sergio Marcchione, CEO of Fiat-Chrysler, has acted as idea champion for the single objective of updating the pipeline of vehicles for Chrysler. To facilitate this change, he has radically dismantled the bureaucracy, tearing up Chrysler's organization chart and introducing a flatter structure with himself at the lead. As a result, the company introduced a more innovative line of vehicles and planned to redesign or significantly refresh 75 percent of its lineup in 2010 alone.[46]

Creating a Learning Organization

Another way an organization can proactively manage change is to make continuous growth part of its culture—to become a learning organization.[47]

innovation   *A new idea applied to initiating or improving a product, process, or service.*

idea champions   *Individuals who take an innovation and actively and enthusiastically promote the idea, build support, overcome resistance, and ensure that the idea is implemented.*

What's a Learning Organization?   Just as individuals learn, so too do organizations. A **learning organization** has developed the continuous capacity to adapt and change. "All organizations learn, whether they consciously choose to or not—it is a fundamental requirement for their sustained existence."[48] Some organizations just do it better than others.

Most organizations engage in **single-loop learning**.[49] When they detect errors, their correction process relies on past routines and present policies. In contrast, learning organizations use **double-loop learning**. They correct errors by *modifying* objectives, policies, and standard routines. Double-loop learning challenges deeply rooted assumptions and norms. It provides opportunities for radically different solutions to problems and dramatic jumps in improvement.

Exhibit 18-6 summarizes the five basic characteristics of a learning organization. It's one in which people put aside their old ways of thinking, learn to be open with each other, understand how their organization really works, form a plan or vision everyone can agree on, and work together to achieve that vision.[50]

Proponents of the learning organization envision it as a remedy for three fundamental problems of traditional organizations: fragmentation, competition, and reactiveness.[51] First, *fragmentation* based on specialization creates "walls" and "chimneys" that separate different functions into independent and often warring fiefdoms. Second, an overemphasis on *competition* often undermines collaboration. Managers compete to show who is right, who knows more, or who is more persuasive. Divisions compete when they ought to cooperate and share knowledge. Team leaders compete to show who the best manager is. And third, *reactiveness* misdirects management's attention to problem solving rather than creation. The problem solver tries to make something go away, while a creator tries to bring something new into being. An emphasis on reactiveness pushes out innovation and continuous improvement and, in its place, encourages people to run around "putting out fires."

Managing Learning   What can managers do to make their firms learning organizations? Here are some suggestions:

- **Establish a strategy.**   Management needs to make explicit its commitment to change, innovation, and continuous improvement.
- **Redesign the organization's structure.**   The formal structure can be a serious impediment to learning. Flattening the structure, eliminating or combining departments, and increasing the use of cross-functional teams reinforces interdependence and reduces boundaries.

Exhibit **18-6**   Characteristics of a Learning Organization

1. There exists a shared vision that everyone agrees on.

2. People discard their old ways of thinking and the standard routines they use for solving problems or doing their jobs.

3. Members think of all organizational processes, activities, functions, and interactions with the environment as part of a system of interrelationships.

4. People openly communicate with each other (across vertical and horizontal boundaries) without fear of criticism or punishment.

5. People sublimate their personal self-interest and fragmented departmental interests to work together to achieve the organization's shared vision.

Source: Based on P. M. Senge, *The Fifth Discipline* (New York: Doubleday, 1990).

● **Reshape the organization's culture.**   To become a learning organization, managers must demonstrate by their actions that taking risks and admitting failures are desirable. That means rewarding people who take chances and make mistakes. And management needs to encourage functional conflict. "The key to unlocking real openness at work," says one expert on learning organizations, "is to teach people to give up having to be in agreement. We think agreement is so important. Who cares? You have to bring paradoxes, conflicts, and dilemmas out in the open, so collectively we can be more intelligent than we can be individually."[52]

Work Stress and Its Management

5   Define *stress* and identify its potential sources.

Friends say they're stressed from greater workloads and longer hours because of downsizing at their companies. Parents worry about the lack of job stability and reminisce about a time when a job with a large company implied lifetime security. We read surveys in which employees complain about the stress of trying to balance work and family responsibilities.[53] Indeed, as Exhibit 18-7 shows, work is, for most people, the most important source of stress in life. What are the causes and consequences of stress, and what can individuals and organizations do to reduce it?

What Is Stress?

Stress is a dynamic condition in which an individual is confronted with an opportunity, demand, or resource related to what the individual desires and for which the outcome is perceived to be both uncertain and important.[54] This is a complicated definition. Let's look at its components more closely.

Exhibit 18-7	Work Is the Biggest Source of Stress for Most

"What area of your life causes you the most stress on a regular basis?"

Area	Causes Most Stress
My job	26%
My finances	20%
My relationships	21%
My children	10%
School	8%
Fear of a disaster/terror attack	3%
Other	8%

Source: 2009 Stress Management poll of 7,807 individuals, stress.about.com/gi/pages/poll.htm?linkback5&poll_id52213421040&poll 151&poll351&submit15Submit1Vote.

---

learning organization   *An organization that has developed the continuous capacity to adapt and change.*

single-loop learning   *A process of correcting errors using past routines and present policies.*

double-loop learning   *A process of correcting errors by modifying the organization's objectives, policies, and standard routines.*

stress   *An unpleasant psychological process that occurs in response to environmental pressures.*

Although stress is typically discussed in a negative context, it is not necessarily bad in and of itself; it also has a positive value.[55] It's an opportunity when it offers potential gain. Consider, for example, the superior performance an athlete or stage performer gives in a "clutch" situation. Such individuals often use stress positively to rise to the occasion and perform at their maximum. Similarly, many professionals see the pressures of heavy workloads and deadlines as positive challenges that enhance the quality of their work and the satisfaction they get from their job.

Recently, researchers have argued that **challenge stressors**—or stressors associated with workload, pressure to complete tasks, and time urgency—operate quite differently from **hindrance stressors**—or stressors that keep you from reaching your goals (for example, red tape, office politics, confusion over job responsibilities). Although research is just starting to accumulate, early evidence suggests challenge stressors produce less strain than hindrance stressors.[56]

Researchers have sought to clarify the conditions under which each type of stress exists. It appears that employees who have a stronger affective commitment to their organization can transfer psychological stress into greater focus and higher sales performance, whereas employees with low levels of commitment perform worse under stress.[57] And when challenge stress increases, those with high levels of organizational support have higher role-based performance, but those with low levels of organizational support do not.[58]

More typically, stress is associated with **demands** and **resources**. Demands are responsibilities, pressures, obligations, and uncertainties individuals face in the workplace. Resources are things within an individual's control that he or she can use to resolve the demands. Let's discuss what this demands–resources model means.[59]

When you take a test at school or undergo your annual performance review at work, you feel stress because you confront opportunities and performance pressures. A good performance review may lead to a promotion, greater responsibilities, and a higher salary. A poor review may prevent you from getting a promotion. An extremely poor review might even result in your being fired. To the extent you can apply resources to the demands on you—such as

"Men Experience More Job Stress Than Women"

This statement is false. One recent review of the literature concluded, "Few, if any, differences exist between the respective amount of occupational stress men and women experience." Another review of 183 studies found that men and women differed to a very small degree on the burnout they experience.

While it doesn't appear that men and women differ in the work stress they report, there is more to the story.

Working women tend to report more life stress than men. The reason may be that, as surveys reliably show, when a husband and wife both work full-time outside the home, the wife carries considerably greater household responsibilities (cleaning, shopping, keeping finances). So if both spouses work the same number of hours, it's likely the wife's total load of paid work and household/family work is greater—and thus more stressful generally, even if her work stress alone is not greater. Says one expert, "A woman's major stressors come from both the work she's paid for and the work she isn't." The former doesn't differ between the genders, but the latter clearly does.

Sources: S. B. Watson, Y. W. Goh, and S. Sawang, "Gender Influences on the Work-Related Stress Coping Process," _Journal of Individual Differences_ 32, no. 1 (2011), pp. 39–46; R. K. Purvanova, and J. P. Muros, "Gender Differences in Burnout: A Meta-Analysis," _Journal of Vocational Behavior_ 77, no. 2 (2010), pp. 168–185; and M. Casserly, "Summer Burnout: Avoiding Overload This Season," _Forbes_ (May 26, 2011), downloaded on July 20, 2011, from http://blogs.forbes.com/meghancasserly/.

Exhibit **18-8**   A Model of Stress

being prepared, placing the exam or review in perspective, or obtaining social support—you will feel less stress.

Research suggests adequate resources help reduce the stressful nature of demands when demands and resources match. If emotional demands are stressing you, having emotional resources in the form of social support is especially important. If the demands are cognitive—say, information overload—then job resources in the form of computer support or information are more important. Thus, under the demands–resources perspective, having resources to cope with stress is just as important in offsetting it as demands are in increasing it.[60]

Potential Sources of Stress

What causes stress? As the model in Exhibit 18-8 shows, there are three categories of potential stressors: environmental, organizational, and personal. Let's take a look at each.[61]

Environmental Factors   Just as environmental uncertainty influences the design of an organization's structure, it also influences stress levels among employees in that organization. Indeed, uncertainty is the biggest reason people have trouble coping with organizational changes.[62] There are three main types of environmental uncertainty: economic, political, and technological.

Changes in the business cycle create *economic uncertainties*. When the economy is contracting, for example, people become increasingly anxious about

challenge stressors   *Stressors associated with workload, pressure to complete tasks, and time urgency.*
hindrance stressors   *Stressors that keep you from reaching your goals (for example, red tape, office politics, confusion over job responsibilities).*

demands   *Responsibilities, pressures, obligations, and even uncertainties that individuals face in the workplace.*

resources   *Things within an individual's control that can be used to resolve demands.*

their job security. *Political uncertainties* don't tend to create stress among North Americans as they do for employees in countries such as Haiti or Venezuela. The obvious reason is that the United States and Canada have stable political systems, in which change is typically implemented in an orderly manner. Yet political threats and changes, even in countries such as the United States and Canada, can induce stress. Threats of terrorism in developed and developing nations, or the difficulties of East Germany reintegrating with West Germany, lead to political uncertainty that becomes stressful to people in these countries.[63] Because innovations can make an employee's skills and experience obsolete in a very short time, computers, robotics, automation, and similar forms of *technological change* are also a threat to many people and cause them stress.

Organizational Factors   There is no shortage of factors within an organization that can cause stress. Pressures to avoid errors or complete tasks in a limited time, work overload, a demanding and insensitive boss, and unpleasant co-workers are a few examples. We've categorized these factors around task, role, and interpersonal demands.[64]

Task demands relate to a person's job. They include the design of the job (its degrees of autonomy, task variety, degree of automation), working conditions, and the physical work layout. Assembly lines can put pressure on people when they perceive the line's speed to be excessive. Working in an overcrowded room or a visible location where noise and interruptions are constant can increase anxiety and stress.[65] As customer service grows ever more important, emotional labor becomes a source of stress.[66] Imagine being a flight attendant for Southwest Airlines or a cashier at Starbucks. Do you think you could put on a happy face when you're having a bad day?

Role demands relate to pressures placed on a person as a function of the particular role he or she plays in the organization. Role conflicts create expectations that may be hard to reconcile or satisfy. Role overload occurs when the employee is expected to do more than time permits. Role ambiguity means role expectations are not clearly understood and the employee is not sure what to do. Individuals who face high situational constraints (such as fixed work hours or demanding job responsibilities) are also less able to engage in the proactive coping behaviors that reduce stress levels.[67] When faced with hassles at work,

Task demands are organizational factors that can cause stress. These call center employees of Encore Capital Group in Gurgaon, India, have the difficult job of collecting mostly credit card and auto debts of Americans. The nature of their job can cause stress, as the people they call may be abusive, emotional, frustrated, sad, or angry. Encore strives to reduce the on-the-job stress of its call center workers by teaching them how to empathize with the delinquent borrowers and how to handle verbal abuse. Collectors learn that the debtors respond to them when they are very polite and respectful and never raise their voice.

Source: Zack Canepari /The New York Times /Redux Pictures.

they will not only have higher levels of distress at the time, but they'll also be less likely to take steps to eliminate stressors in the future.

Interpersonal demands are pressures created by other employees. Lack of social support from colleagues and poor interpersonal relationships can cause stress, especially among employees with a high social need. A rapidly growing body of research has also shown that negative co-worker and supervisor behaviors, including fights, bullying, incivility, racial harassment, and sexual harassment, are especially strongly related to stress at work.[68]

Personal Factors   The typical individual works about 40 to 50 hours a week. But the experiences and problems people encounter in the other 120-plus can spill over to the job. Our final category, then, is factors in the employee's personal life: family issues, personal economic problems, and inherent personality characteristics.

National surveys consistently show people hold *family* and personal relationships dear. Marital difficulties, the breaking of a close relationship, and discipline troubles with children create stresses employees often can't leave at the front door when they arrive at work.[69]

Regardless of income level—people who make $100,000 per year seem to have as much trouble handling their finances as those who earn $20,000— some people are poor money managers or have wants that exceed their earning capacity. The *economic* problems of overextended financial resources create stress and siphon attention away from work.

Studies in three diverse organizations found that participants who reported stress symptoms before beginning a job accounted for most of the variance in stress symptoms reported 9 months later.[70] The researchers concluded that some people may have an inherent tendency to accentuate negative aspects of the world. If this is true, then a significant individual factor that influences stress is a person's basic disposition. That is, stress symptoms expressed on the job may actually originate in the person's *personality*.

Stressors Are Additive   When we review stressors individually, it's easy to overlook that stress is an additive phenomenon—it builds up.[71] Each new and persistent stressor adds to an individual's stress level. So a single stressor may be relatively unimportant in and of itself, but if added to an already high level of stress, it can be the straw that breaks the camel's back. To appraise the total amount of stress an individual is under, we have to sum up his or her opportunity stresses, constraint stresses, and demand stresses.

Individual Differences

Some people thrive on stressful situations, while others are overwhelmed by them. What differentiates people in terms of their ability to handle stress? What individual variables moderate the relationship between *potential* stressors and *experienced* stress? At least four—perception, job experience, social support, and personality—are relevant.

In Chapter 6, we demonstrated that employees react in response to their perception of reality, rather than to reality itself. *Perception*, therefore, will moderate the relationship between a potential stress condition and an employee's reaction to it. Layoffs may cause one person to fear losing his job, while another sees an opportunity to get a large severance allowance and start her own business. So stress potential doesn't lie in objective conditions; rather, it lies in an employee's interpretation of those conditions.

Experience on the job tends to be negatively related to work stress. Why? Two explanations have been offered.[72] First is selective withdrawal. Voluntary turnover is more probable among people who experience more stress. Therefore, people who remain with an organization longer are those with more stress-resistant traits or those more resistant to the stress characteristics of their organization. Second, people eventually develop coping mechanisms to deal with stress. Because this takes time, senior members of the organization are more likely to be fully adapted and should experience less stress.

Social support—collegial relationships with co-workers or supervisors—can buffer the impact of stress.[73] This is among the best-documented relationships in the stress literature. Social support acts as a palliative, mitigating the negative effects of even high-strain jobs.

Perhaps the most widely studied *personality* trait in stress is neuroticism, which we discussed in Chapter 5. As you might expect, neurotic individuals are more prone to experience psychological strain.[74] Evidence suggests that neurotic individuals are more prone to believe there are stressors in their work environments, so part of the problem is that they believe their environments are more threatening. They also tend to select less adaptive coping mechanisms, relying on avoidance as a way of dealing with problems rather than attempting to resolve them.[75]

Workaholism is another personal characteristic related to stress levels. Workaholics are people obsessed with their work; they put in an enormous number of hours, think about work even when not working, and create additional work responsibilities to satisfy an inner compulsion to work more. In some ways, they might seem like ideal employees. That's probably why when most people are asked in interviews what their greatest weakness is, they reflexively say, "I just work too hard." However, there is a difference between working hard and working compulsively. Workaholics are not necessarily more productive than other employees, despite their extreme efforts. The strain of putting in such a high level of work effort eventually begins to wear on the workaholic, leading to higher levels of work–life conflict and psychological burnout.[76]

Cultural Differences

Research suggests the job conditions that cause stress show some differences across cultures. One study revealed that whereas U.S. employees were stressed by a lack of control, Chinese employees were stressed by job evaluations and lack of training. It doesn't appear that personality effects on stress are different across cultures, however. One study of employees in Hungary, Italy, the United Kingdom, Israel, and the United States found Type A personality traits (see Chapter 5) predicted stress equally well across countries.[77] A study of 5,270 managers from 20 countries found individuals from individualistic countries such as the United States, Canada, and the United Kingdom experienced higher levels of stress due to work interfering with family than did individuals from collectivist countries in Asia and Latin America.[78] The authors proposed that this may occur because, in collectivist cultures, working extra hours is seen as a sacrifice to help the family, whereas in individualistic cultures, work is seen as a means to personal achievement that takes away from the family.

Evidence suggests that stressors are associated with perceived stress and strains among employees in different countries. In other words, stress is equally bad for employees of all cultures.[79]

SELF-ASSESSMENT LIBRARY

How Stressful Is My Life?

In the Self-Assessment Library (available on CD and online), take assessment III.C.2 (How Stressful Is My Life?).

Consequences of Stress

6 Identify the consequences of stress.

Stress shows itself in a number of ways, such as high blood pressure, ulcers, irritability, difficulty making routine decisions, loss of appetite, accident proneness, and the like. These symptoms fit under three general categories: physiological, psychological, and behavioral symptoms.

Physiological Symptoms   Most early concern with stress was directed at physiological symptoms because most researchers were specialists in the health and medical sciences. Their work led to the conclusion that stress could create changes in metabolism, increase heart and breathing rates and blood pressure, bring on headaches, and induce heart attacks.

Evidence now clearly suggests stress may have harmful physiological effects. One study linked stressful job demands to increased susceptibility to upper-respiratory illnesses and poor immune system functioning, especially for individuals with low self-efficacy.[80] A long-term study conducted in the United Kingdom found that job strain was associated with higher levels of coronary heart disease.[81] Still another study conducted with Danish human services workers found that higher levels of psychological burnout at the work-unit level were related to significantly higher levels of sickness absence.[82] Many other studies have shown similar results linking work stress to a variety of indicators of poor health.

Psychological Symptoms   Job dissatisfaction is "the simplest and most obvious psychological effect" of stress.[83] But stress shows itself in other psychological states—for instance, tension, anxiety, irritability, boredom, and procrastination. For example, a study that tracked physiological responses of employees over time found that stress due to high workloads was related to higher blood pressure and lower emotional well-being.[84]

An Ethical Choice

Responsibly Managing Your Own Stress

Although much of the research we've reviewed in this chapter discusses how organizations and managers can relieve stress for employees, employees also have a certain degree of responsibility for managing their own stress. Beyond the fact that high levels of stress are unpleasant, employees who experience them have difficulty concentrating at work, make more mistakes, miss more days of work, and use more health insurance. This suggests that it may be your ethical responsibility as an employee to ensure your stress levels are not high enough to interfere with your ability to work effectively for clients, customers, and co-workers. A few examples of strategies you might want to employ to reduce your level of stress from work include the following:

1. **Take breaks.** If you're feeling depleted or exhausted at work, taking some time away from your tasks can significantly reduce your level of psychological strain.
2. **Let your supervisor know you're stressed.** In many cases, managers will want to provide assistance to workers who are experiencing stress, but if they don't know there's a problem, they can't help to address it.
3. **Detach yourself from work in your off-time.** Try not to take work home with you, and make your time off a period when you can truly recover from the strains of the day. Research shows that workers who can detach themselves from their work in their off-time experience significantly less stress than those who do not.

Sources: Based on M. M. Krischer, L. M. Penney, and E. M. Hunter, "Can Counterproductive Work Behaviors Be Productive? CWB as Emotion-Focused Coping," *Journal of Occupational Health Psychology* 15, no 2 (2010), pp. 154–166; V. C. Hahn, C. Binnewies, S. Sonnentag, and E. J. Mojza, "Learning How to Recover from Job Stress: Effects of a Recovery Training Program on Recovery, Recovery Related Self-Efficacy, and Well-Being," *Journal of Occupational Health Psychology* 16, no. 2 (2011), pp. 202–216; and S. Sonnentag, C. Binnewies, and E. J. Mojza, "Staying Well and Engaged when Demands are High: The Role of Psychological Detachment," *Journal of Applied Psychology* 95, no. 5 (2010), pp. 965–976.

Jobs that make multiple and conflicting demands or that lack clarity about the incumbent's duties, authority, and responsibilities increase both stress and dissatisfaction.[85] Similarly, the less control people have over the pace of their work, the greater their stress and dissatisfaction. Jobs that provide a low level of variety, significance, autonomy, feedback, and identity appear to create stress and reduce satisfaction and involvement in the job.[86] Not everyone reacts to autonomy in the same way, however. For those with an external locus of control, increased job control increases the tendency to experience stress and exhaustion.[87]

Behavioral Symptoms   Research on behavior and stress has been conducted across several countries and over time, and the relationships appear relatively consistent. Behavior-related stress symptoms include reductions in productivity, absence, and turnover, as well as changes in eating habits, increased smoking or consumption of alcohol, rapid speech, fidgeting, and sleep disorders.[88]

A significant amount of research has investigated the stress–performance relationship. The most widely studied pattern of this relationship is the inverted U shown in Exhibit 18-9.[89] The logic underlying the figure is that low to moderate levels of stress stimulate the body and increase its ability to react. Individuals then often perform their tasks better, more intensely, or more rapidly. But too much stress places unattainable demands on a person, which result in lower performance. In spite of the popularity and intuitive appeal of the inverted-U model, it doesn't get a lot of empirical support.[90] So we should be careful of assuming it accurately depicts the stress–performance relationship.

As we mentioned earlier, researchers have begun to differentiate challenge and hindrance stressors, showing that these two forms of stress have opposite effects on job behaviors, especially job performance. A meta-analysis of responses from more than 35,000 individuals showed role ambiguity, role conflict, role overload, job insecurity, environmental uncertainty, and situational constraints were all consistently negatively related to job performance.[91] There is also evidence that challenge stress improves job performance in a supportive work environment, whereas hindrance stress reduces job performance in all work environments.[92]

7   Contrast the individual and organizational approaches to managing stress.

Managing Stress

Because low to moderate levels of stress can be functional and lead to higher performance, management may not be concerned when employees experience

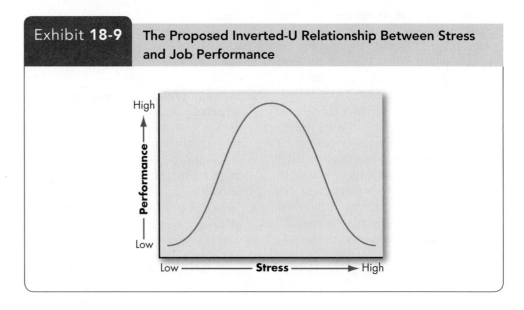

Exhibit 18-9   **The Proposed Inverted-U Relationship Between Stress and Job Performance**

them. Employees, however, are likely to perceive even low levels of stress as undesirable. It's not unlikely, therefore, for employees and management to have different notions of what constitutes an acceptable level of stress on the job. What management may consider to be "a positive stimulus that keeps the adrenaline running" is very likely to be seen as "excessive pressure" by the employee. Keep this in mind as we discuss individual and organizational approaches toward managing stress.[93]

Individual Approaches   An employee can take personal responsibility for reducing stress levels. Individual strategies that have proven effective include time-management techniques, increased physical exercise, relaxation training, and expanded social support networks. Also see the Ethical Choice box in this chapter for additional suggestions.

Many people manage their time poorly. The well-organized employee, like the well-organized student, can often accomplish twice as much as the person who is poorly organized. So an understanding and utilization of basic time-management principles can help individuals better cope with tensions created by job demands.[94] A few of the best-known time-management principles are (1) making daily lists of activities to be accomplished, (2) prioritizing activities by importance and urgency, (3) scheduling activities according to the priorities set, (4) knowing your daily cycle and handling the most demanding parts of your job when you are most alert and productive, and (5) avoiding electronic distractions like frequently checking e-mail, which can limit attention and reduce efficiency.[95] These time-management skills can help minimize procrastination by focusing efforts on immediate goals and boosting motivation even in the face of tasks that are less desirable.[96]

Physicians have recommended noncompetitive *physical exercise*, such as aerobics, walking, jogging, swimming, and riding a bicycle, as a way to deal with excessive stress levels. These activities increase lung capacity, lower the at-rest heart rate, and provide a mental diversion from work pressures, effectively reducing work-related levels of stress.[97]

Individuals can also teach themselves to reduce tension through *relaxation techniques* such as meditation, hypnosis, and deep breathing. The objective is to reach a state of deep physical relaxation, in which you focus all your energy on release

This group of Chinese working women participate in a yoga class in Beijing as a way to deal with excessive stress levels caused by long working hours and trying to achieve a work/life balance. Working women in China have high levels of stress because in Chinese culture women are expected to take more responsibility for family matters than in other cultures. As an individual approach to managing stress, yoga is a noncompetitive physical exercise that combines stretching, mental imagery, breathing control, physical postures, and meditation. Yoga reduces stress, anxiety, and muscle tension, provides a mental diversion from work pressures, and promotes physical well-being by lowering blood pressure and heart rate.

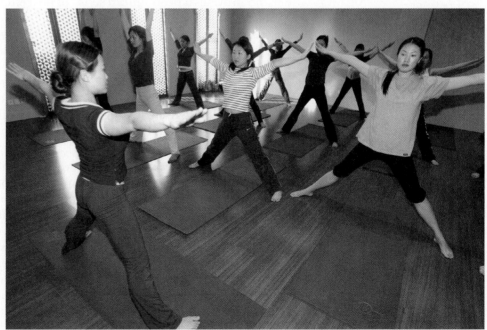

Source: AFP Photo/Getty Images/Newscom.

Work–Family Stress in Different Cultures

Studies repeatedly show that conflicts between work life and nonwork life, especially conflicts between work and family responsibilities, are significant stressors. Examples of work–life conflicts include nights and weekends spent at work rather than with family, work schedules so full that vacations cannot happen, and work obligations that require arranging for child care at the last minute. As we noted in Chapter 17, many organizations have experimented with policies like flexible scheduling or working from home to reduce work–life conflicts and help employees reduce their levels of stress. The question is, do these policies have the same effects in different cultures, which have different values and norms regarding family and life responsibilities?

Reviewers have critiqued the literature on strain related to work–life conflict for failing to take culture into account. And, in fact, the great majority of studies on stress due to work–life conflict have been conducted entirely within the United States. Research that included multiple cultures suggests that collectivist cultures have lower levels of work–life conflict because collectivists are more likely to obtain social support from others. Differences in cultural expectations for men and women in different cultures also mean that women in some countries will experience greater work–life conflict because they have more responsibilities in the family domain, whereas in more egalitarian cultures men and women will experience similar levels of work–life conflict.

Do these cultural differences mean organizations should use different policies to combat work–life conflicts? One study of nearly 25,000 IBM employees in 75 countries investigated how policies like flexibility about where and when work is performed were related to employee stress levels. The results clearly showed that both forms of flexibility (such as work-at-home arrangements and flexible schedules) were linked to lower levels of work–life conflict in affluent and developing countries in the East and the West. In other words, it appears that flexible scheduling can help reduce employee stress levels around the world. This is good news for organizations attempting to develop policies and procedures that apply equally to all their employees.

Sources: Based on E. J. Hill, J. J. Erickson, E. K. Holmes, and M. Ferris, "Workplace Flexibility, Work Hours, and Work-Life Conflict: Finding an Extra Day or Two," *Journal of Family Psychology* 24, no. 3 (2010), pp. 349–358; and G. N. Powell, A. M. Francesco, and Y. Ling, "Toward Culture-Sensitive Theories of the Work-Family Interface," *Journal of Organizational Behavior* 30, no. 5 (2009), pp. 597–616.

of muscle tension.[98] Deep relaxation for 15 or 20 minutes a day releases strain and provides a pronounced sense of peacefulness, as well as significant changes in heart rate, blood pressure, and other physiological factors. A growing body of research shows that simply taking breaks from work at routine intervals can facilitate psychological recovery and reduce stress significantly and may improve job performance, and these effects are even greater if relaxation techniques are employed.[99]

As we have noted, friends, family, or work colleagues can provide an outlet when stress levels become excessive. Expanding your *social support network* provides someone to hear your problems and offer a more objective perspective on a stressful situation than your own.

Organizational Approaches   Several organizational factors that cause stress—particularly task and role demands—are controlled by management and thus can be modified or changed. Strategies to consider include improved employee selection and job placement, training, realistic goal-setting, redesign of jobs, increased employee involvement, improved organizational communication, employee sabbaticals, and corporate wellness programs.

Certain jobs are more stressful than others but, as we've seen, individuals differ in their response to stressful situations. We know individuals with little experience or an external locus of control tend to be more prone to stress. *Selection and placement* decisions should take these facts into consideration. Obviously, management shouldn't restrict hiring to only experienced individuals with an internal locus, but such individuals may adapt better to high-stress jobs and perform those jobs more effectively. Similarly, *training* can increase an individual's self-efficacy and thus lessen job strain.

We discussed *goal-setting* in Chapter 7. Individuals perform better when they have specific and challenging goals and receive feedback on their progress toward these goals. Goals can reduce stress as well as provide motivation.[100] Employees who are highly committed to their goals and see purpose in their jobs experience less stress because they are more likely to perceive stressors as challenges rather than hindrances. Specific goals perceived as attainable clarify performance expectations. In addition, goal feedback reduces uncertainties about actual job performance. The result is less employee frustration, role ambiguity, and stress.

Redesigning jobs to give employees more responsibility, more meaningful work, more autonomy, and increased feedback can reduce stress because these factors give employees greater control over work activities and lessen dependence on others. But as we noted in our discussion of work design, not all employees want enriched jobs. The right redesign for employees with a low need for growth might be less responsibility and increased specialization. If individuals prefer structure and routine, reducing skill variety should also reduce uncertainties and stress levels.

Role stress is detrimental to a large extent because employees feel uncertain about goals, expectations, how they'll be evaluated, and the like. By giving these employees a voice in the decisions that directly affect their job performance, management can increase employee control and reduce role stress. Thus, managers should consider *increasing employee involvement* in decision making, because evidence clearly shows that increases in employee empowerment reduce psychological strain.[101]

Increasing formal *organizational communication* with employees reduces uncertainty by lessening role ambiguity and role conflict. Given the importance that perceptions play in moderating the stress–response relationship, management can also use effective communications as a means to shape employee perceptions. Remember that what employees categorize as demands, threats, or opportunities at work is an interpretation and that interpretation can be affected by the symbols and actions communicated by management.

Some employees need an occasional escape from the frenetic pace of their work. Companies including Genentech, American Express, Intel, General Mills, Microsoft, Morningstar, DreamWorks Animation, and Adobe Systems have begun to provide extended voluntary leaves.[102] These *sabbaticals*—ranging in length from a few weeks to several months—allow employees to travel, relax, or pursue personal projects that consume time beyond normal vacations. Proponents say they can revive and rejuvenate workers who might otherwise be headed for burnout.

Our final suggestion is organizationally supported **wellness programs**. These typically provide workshops to help people quit smoking, control alcohol use, lose weight, eat better, and develop a regular exercise program; they focus on the employee's total physical and mental condition.[103] Some help employees improve their psychological health as well. A meta-analysis of 36 programs designed to reduce stress (including wellness programs) showed that interventions to help employees reframe stressful situations and use active coping strategies appreciably reduced stress levels.[104] Most wellness programs assume employees need to take personal responsibility for their physical and mental health and that the organization is merely a means to that end.

wellness programs *Organizationally supported programs that focus on the employee's total physical and mental condition.*

Cindy Russell poses with her assembled gear in preparation for a one-month sabbatical to go fly fishing in the South Pacific. Russell is a paralegal with the law firm Alters, Boldt, Brown, Rash, and Culmo in Miami. Like many small companies, the law firm does not have a formal sabbatical program. But Russell approached her boss with the idea, saying that she worked long hours in preparing for trials and desired a longer time away from work than her vacation time allowed. She explained how the fishing trip would help her to decompress and return to work energized and refreshed. Russell was granted the leave, some of it unpaid, after convincing her boss how it would benefit both her and the firm.

Source: C.W. Griffin/Miami Herald/MCT/Newscom.

Most firms that have introduced wellness programs have found significant benefits. A study of eight Canadian organizations found that every dollar spent on comprehensive wellness programs generated a return of $1.64, and for high-risk employees, such as smokers, the return was nearly $4.00.[105]

MyManagementLab

Now that you have finished this chapter, go back to **www.mymanagementlab.com** to continue practicing and applying the concepts you've learned.

Summary and Implications for Managers

The need for change has been implied throughout this text. "A casual reflection on change should indicate that it encompasses almost all of our concepts in the organizational behavior literature."[106] For instance, think about attitudes, motivation, work teams, communication, leadership, organizational structures, human resource practices, and organizational cultures. Change was an integral part in our discussion of each. If environments were perfectly static, if employees' skills and abilities were always up to date and incapable of deteriorating, and if tomorrow were always exactly the same as today, organizational change would have little or no relevance to managers. But the real world is turbulent, requiring organizations and their members to undergo dynamic change if they are to perform at competitive levels.

- Managers are the primary change agents in most organizations. By the decisions they make and their role-modeling behaviors, they shape the organization's change culture.

Responsible Managers Relieve Stress on Their Employees

POINT

One of the reasons the economic recovery has been sluggish is that employers have been reluctant to replace those they laid off. If you can produce the same amount or provide the same service with fewer employees, that's efficient, of course. But is it a short-sighted way to manage? Evidence suggests that employees are at their breaking point—and employers will pay a price just like the employees they are stressing.

Employees are really stressed. More work is being done with fewer people. Workers wonder whether they will be the "next shoe to fall" in layoffs. In a recent survey of managers, 81 percent agreed worker stress and fatigue is a greater problem than in the past.

Says one Sacramento, California, employee, "I can't remember the last time I went out for lunch. I bring my lunch and eat at my desk," she says. She can't even complain to her husband, since he's the same boat—working 10-hour days and "coming home late and exhausted."

Some employers are long-sighted enough to address the problem.

Tony Schwartz, CEO of a consulting firm, decided to institute a program he called "Take Back Your Lunch." He encourages his employees to take a lunch break and even urges them to organize midday gatherings with social networking site Meetup.com.

Another company with progressive management is the accounting firm Ernst & Young. Of the company's 23,000 employees, about 10 percent work under flexible arrangements where they can work less or adopt a more flexible schedule during nonpeak times.

These companies have found that taking the long view and emphasizing balance helps good employees be more productive over the long-term—and more likely to stick around. "We listen to our people and they tell us very consistently that flexibility in incredibly important to them and to their family," said James Turley, Ernst & Young's CEO.

COUNTERPOINT

It is not hard to find employees who think they're overworked and underpaid. If a company managed according to worker complaints, the squeakiest wheel would always get the grease. Sure, people might work fewer hours and feel less stressed, but that would compromise an organization's ability to be competitive and to reward its hardest-working and most productive employees.

Labor is often the largest single cost for an employer, which means that if it is to be competitive, the firm needs to earn more revenue per employee. It doesn't take a math genius to realize that one way of accomplishing that is to pay attention to the denominator. It's that magical thing we call "productivity," a central metric by which we can measure the organization's performance. Organizations that are productive today enjoy higher earnings later.

Take Deutsche Bank as an example. The number of front-office employees in Deutsche Bank's investment banking division has fallen 12 percent from pre-crisis levels, while net revenue per employee has increased 20 percent. That sounds like a well-managed company, doesn't it? Yet Deutsche Bank employees probably do feel they're working harder. They are. What would you think of a company if the story instead was, "Net revenue per employee has fallen 20 percent, but employees feel much less stressed at work"? We don't live in a world where companies have the luxury of doing less with more.

Managers shouldn't go out of their way to stress out their employees. Nor should they turn a blind eye toward burnout. But realistically, in today's globally competitive business environment, the organizations that will survive are those that can do more with less. If that means employees are stressed by higher workloads, well, it beats the unemployment line, doesn't it?

Sources: S. Greenhouse, "The Retention Bonus? Time," *The New York Times* (January 8, 2011), pp. B1, B7; M. V. Rafter, "The Yawning of a New Era," *Workforce Management* (December 2010), pp. 3–4; and M. Turner, "Deutsche Says It Does More with Less," *Financial News* (June 2, 2011), downloaded on July 19, 2011, from www.efinancialnews.com/.

- Management decisions related to structural design, cultural factors, and human resource policies largely determine the level of innovation within the organization.
- Management policies and practices will determine the degree to which the organization learns and adapts to changing environmental factors.
- The existence of work stress, in and of itself, need not imply lower performance. The evidence indicates that stress can be either a positive or a negative influence on employee performance.
- Low to moderate amounts of stress enable many people to perform their jobs better by increasing their work intensity, alertness, and ability to react. This is especially true if stress arises due to challenges on the job rather than hindrances that prevent employees from doing their jobs effectively.
- However, a high level of stress, or even a moderate amount sustained over a long period, eventually takes its toll, and performance declines.

QUESTIONS FOR REVIEW

1 What forces act as stimulants to change, and what is the difference between planned and unplanned change?

2 What forces act as sources of resistance to change?

3 What are the four main approaches to managing organizational change?

4 How can managers create a culture for change?

5 What is stress, and what are the possible sources of stress?

6 What are the consequences of stress?

7 What are the individual and organizational approaches to managing stress?

EXPERIENTIAL EXERCISE Power and the Changing Environment

Objectives
1. To describe the forces for change influencing power differentials in organizational and interpersonal relationships.
2. To understand the effect of technological, legal/political, economic, and social changes on the power of individuals within an organization.

The Situation
Your organization manufactures golf carts and sells them to country clubs, golf courses, and consumers. Your team is faced with the task of assessing how environmental changes will affect individuals' organizational power. Read each of the five scenarios and then, for each, identify the five members in the organization whose power will increase most in light of the environmental condition(s). [*Note:* m = male, (f) = female.]

Accountant/CPA (m)

Advertising expert (m)

Chemist (m)

Chief financial officer (f)

Computer programmer (f)

Corporate trainer (m)

General manager (m)

Human resource manager (f)

Industrial engineer (m)

In-house counsel (m)

Marketing manager (f)

Operations manager (f)

Product designer (m)

Public relations expert (m)

Securities analyst (m)

1. New computer-aided manufacturing technologies are being introduced in the workplace during the next 2 to 18 months.
2. New federal emission standards are being legislated by the government that will essentially make gas-powered golf carts (40 percent of your current business) obsolete.
3. Sales are way down for two reasons: (a) a decline in the number of individuals playing golf and (b) your competitor was faster to embrace lithium batteries, which allow golf carts to run longer without another charge.

4. Given the growth of golf courses in other places (especially India, China, and Southeast Asia), the company is planning to go international in the next 12 to 18 months.

5. The U.S. Equal Employment Opportunity Commission is applying pressure to balance the male–female population in the organization's upper hierarchy by threatening to publicize the predominance of men in upper management.

The Procedure
1. Divide the class into teams of three to four students each.

2. Teams should read each scenario and identify the five members whose power will increase most in light of the external environmental conditions described.

3. Teams should then address this question: assuming that the five environmental changes are taking place at once, which five members of the organization will now have the most power?

4. After 20 to 30 minutes, representatives of each team will be selected to present and justify their conclusions to the entire class. Discussion will begin with scenario 1 and proceed through scenario 5 and the "all at once" scenario.

Source: Adapted from J. E. Barbuto Jr., "Power and the Changing Environment," *Journal of Management Education* (April 2000), pp. 288–296.

ETHICAL DILEMMA   Changes at WPAC

WPAC—a television station based in Yuma, Arizona—had been experiencing a ratings decline for several years. In 2009, the station switched from a CBS to NBC affiliate. That has explained some of the ratings decline. However, in recent months, the ratings have continued to slide. Eventually, the station manager, Lucien Stone, decided he had to make a change to the local newscast.

After meeting with the programming manager, Stone called a meeting of WPAC employees and announced his intention to "spice things up" during the 5 P.M. and 10 P.M. local news. The 30-minute broadcasts would still include the traditional "top stories," "sports," and "weather" segments. However, on slow news days, more attention-getting material would be used. Stone also indicated some programming decisions would probably be revisited. "The days of *Little House on the Prairie* are over," he said.

Madison Devereaux, 29, had been the chief meteorologist for WPAC since 2010. After receiving her degree in meteorology from the University of Oklahoma in 2007, she joined WPAC and quickly worked her way up the ranks, impressing viewers and WPAC management alike with her extension knowledge and articulate, professional, mistake-free delivery.

Though she was Christian, Devereaux never was one to go around "thumping Bibles in the newsroom," as she put it. Most of those at WPAC weren't even aware of Madison's religious views.

Devereaux was troubled by the announced changes to WPAC's programming but didn't speak up at the time. One Monday during a pre-production meeting, she learned that on Thursday of that week, WPAC reporter Sam Berkshow would present a segment called "Dancing Around the Economy," which would focus on how local strip clubs were doing well despite the sluggish economy.

Devereaux didn't think it was appropriate to air the segment during the 5 P.M. newcast and asked both her producer and Stone to reconsider the piece, or at least air it in the 10 P.M. time slot. When they refused, she asked whether she could take the day off when the segment aired. Stone again refused. This was "sweeps week" (when ratings are calculated), Stone wanted to air the story now, and Devereaux's contract prohibited her from taking time off during sweeps week.

When Devereaux didn't show up for work that Thursday, WPAC fired her, arguing she had breached her contract.

For her part, Devereaux said, "I'm not angry with the station, but I am sorry about the changes that have taken place."

Questions
1. Do you think either party behaved unethically in this case?
2. If you shared Devereaux's views, would you have handled the situation differently? How?
3. Drawing on Kotter's eight-step plan for implementing change, how might WPAC have handled its planned change differently?

Sources: Based on C. Edelhart, "Weatherman's Stand Against Story Costs Job," *Californian* (May 16, 2011), downloaded July 7, 2011, from www.bakersfield.com/; and K. T. Phan, "ABC Affiliate Fires Christian over Strip Club Segment," *Fox News* (May 10, 2011), www.nation.foxnews.com.

CASE INCIDENT 1 Starbucks Returns to Its Roots

You are probably so used to seeing Starbucks coffee shops everywhere that you might not realize the company went from just 11 stores in 1987 to 2,600 in the year 2000. This incredibly rapid growth sprang from the company's ability to create a unique experience for customers who wanted to buy its distinct brand of lattes and mochas wherever they found themselves. At Starbucks' core, there was also a culture of treating each customer as a valued guest who should feel comfortable relaxing and taking in the ambience of the store. Whether you were in the company's founding location in Seattle, Washington, or at the other end of the country in Miami, Florida, you knew what to expect when you went to a Starbucks.

This uniform culture was truly put to the test in the face of massive expansion, however, and by 2006 Starbucks' chairman and former CEO Howard Schultz knew something had gone wrong. He noted that "As I visited hundreds of Starbucks stores in cities around the world, the entrepreneurial merchant in me sensed that something intrinsic to Starbucks' brand was missing. An aura. A spirit. The stores were lacking a certain soul." Starbucks' performance had become lackluster, with hundreds of planned store openings being canceled and hundreds more stores being closed.

So, Schultz took the dramatic step of coming back as CEO and engaging in a companywide effort to change the corporate culture back to what it had been before its expansion. All 7,000 Starbucks stores were closed for a single afternoon as part of a training effort of 135,000 baristas. Quality control was a primary mission; baristas were instructed to pour every glass of espresso like honey from a spoon, to preserve the flavor. This emphasis on quality over speed ran counter to the principles of mass production, but it was just what the company needed to ensure it could retain its culture. Espresso machines that obscured the customers' view were replaced with lower-profile machines that allowed baristas to look directly at guests while making beverages. And "assembly-line production," like making several drinks at once, was discouraged in favor of slowly making each drink for each customer.

Schultz is convinced his efforts to take the culture back to its roots as a neighborhood coffee shop—one entranced with the "romance of coffee" and treating every customer as an old friend—has saved the company. Today, Starbucks earns more than $10 billion in annual revenue and serves more than 50 million customers a week around the globe.

Questions

1. What factors are most likely to change when a company grows very rapidly, as Starbucks did? How can these changes threaten the culture of an organization?

2. Why might this type of radical change process be easier for Starbucks to implement than it would be for other companies?

3. A great deal of the return to an original culture has been credited to Howard Schultz, who acted as an idea champion. Explain how Schultz's efforts to change the Starbucks culture fit with our discussion of culture change earlier in the chapter.

4. Schultz's change initiative might succeed at another company that values customization and high levels of customer service, but how would it need to differ at a firm that emphasizes speed and efficiency of service?

Sources: Based on H. Schultz, "How Starbucks Got Its Mojo Back," *Newsweek*, (March 21, 2011), www .newsweek.com; A. Ignatius, "We Had to Own the Mistakes," *Harvard Business Review* (July/August 2010), pp. 108–115; and R. Baker, "Starbucks Demonstrates Power of Brand," *Marketing Week* (April 28, 2011), www.marketingweek.co.uk.

CASE INCIDENT 2 The Rise of Extreme Jobs

Before Barbara Agoglia left her job at American Express, she was spending 13 hours a day working and commuting. She also had to be available via cell phone 24/7. The last straw came when she didn't have time to wait with her school-age son at his bus stop. Carolyn Buck also has an extreme job. She usually works more than 60 hours a week for Ernst & Young and often has to travel to India and China.

Agoglia and Buck are not alone. Most U.S. adults are working more hours than ever, but one group in particular stands out: those with extreme jobs—people who spend more than half their time working and commuting to and from work. More than 1.7 million people consider their jobs *too* extreme, according to a recent study.

What accounts for the rise in extreme jobs? It's not entirely clear, but the usual suspects of globalization, technology, and competitiveness are high on everyone's lists.

As extreme as Agoglia and Buck's jobs may seem, U.S. workers may have it comparatively easy. Most surveys indicate extreme jobs are worse in developing counties. A 2006 *Harvard Business Review* study of managers in 33 global companies indicated that compared to U.S. managers, managers in developing countries were more than twice as likely to have extreme jobs.

For those who hold extreme jobs, personal life often takes a back seat. Forty-four percent take fewer than 10 vacation days per year. Many individuals with extreme jobs see society changing into a "winner takes all" mode, where those who are willing to go the extra mile will reap a disproportionate share of the intrinsic and extrinsic rewards.

Why do people take extreme jobs (or allow their jobs to become extreme)? A 2006 study suggested that for both men and women, the number-one reason for working long, stressful hours is not pay. Rather, it's the rush they get from doing stimulating or challenging work. As one Asian manager said, "Building this business in markets where no one has done anything like this before is enormously exciting. And important. We've built distribution centers that are vital to China's growth—they contribute to the overall prospects of our economy."

Although this sounds all good, the situation is more complicated when you ask holders of extreme jobs about what their jobs cost them. Among them, 66 percent of men and 77 percent of women say their job interferes with their ability to maintain a home. For those with extreme jobs who have children, 65 percent of men and 33 percent of women say it keeps them from having a relationship with their children. And 46 percent of male and female extreme job holders say their jobs interfere with having a strong relationship with their spouse. About half the members of each group say it interferes with their sex life. "I can't even fathom having a boyfriend," says one extreme job holder. Another, Chris Cicchinelli, was so concerned about being out of touch with work during his honeymoon that he got a satellite phone. Even that didn't help. He ended up cutting his 10-day honeymoon to 5 days. "I had major anxiety," he said.

The problem of overwork has become so pronounced in South Korea that many employers are forcing employees to take time off and locking them out of their computer systems during scheduled vacation times. Managers complain that Korean workers have become comparatively unproductive during their work hours, in part because they are so exhausted they cannot perform effectively. One authority on Korean society opines that employees are worried that if they do not work extreme hours, their employers will see them as expendable.

Questions

1. Do you think you will ever have an extreme job? Are you sure? Explain.

2. Why do you think the number of extreme jobs has risen?

3. Do you think organizations should encourage extreme jobs, discourage them, or completely leave them to an employee's discretion?

4. Why do you think people take extreme jobs in the first place?

Sources: Based on T. Weiss, "How Extreme Is Your Job?" *Forbes* (February 1, 2007), p. 1; S. A. Hewlett and C. B. Luce, "Extreme Jobs," *Harvard Business Review* (December 2006), pp. 49–58; S. Armour, "Hi, I'm Joan, and I'm a Workaholic," *USA Today* (May 23, 2007), pp. 1B, 2B; and C. Oliver, "Workaholics Forced to Take Time Off," *Financial Times* (July 5, 2011), www.ft.com.

ENDNOTES

1. See, for instance, J. Birkinshaw, G. Hamel, and M. J. Mol, "Management Innovation," *Academy of Management Review* 33, no. 4 (2008), pp. 825–845; and J. Welch and S. Welch, "What Change Agents Are Made Of," *BusinessWeek* (October 20, 2008), p. 96.
2. C. J. Loomis and D. Burke, "Can Ellen Kullman Make DuPont Great Again?" *Fortune* (May 3, 2010), pp. 156–163.
3. P. G. Audia and S. Brion, "Reluctant to Change: Self-Enhancing Responses to Diverging Performance Measures," *Organizational Behavior and Human Decision Processes* 102 (2007), pp. 255–269.
4. M. Fugate, A. J. Kinicki, and G. E. Prussia, "Employee Coping with Organizational Change: An Examination of Alternative Theoretical Perspectives and Models," *Personnel Psychology* 61, no. 1 (2008), pp. 1–36.
5. J. D. Ford, L. W. Ford, and A. D'Amelio, "Resistance to Change: The Rest of the Story," *Academy of Management Review* 33, no. 2 (2008), pp. 362–377.
6. M. T. Hannan, L. Pólos, and G. R. Carroll, "The Fog of Change: Opacity and Asperity in Organizations," *Administrative Science Quarterly* (September 2003), pp. 399–432.
7. J. P. Kotter and L. A. Schlesinger, "Choosing Strategies for Change," *Harvard Business Review* (March–April 1979), pp. 106–114.
8. J. E. Dutton, S. J. Ashford, R. M. O'Neill, and K. A. Lawrence, "Moves That Matter: Issue Selling and Organizational Change," *Academy of Management Journal* (August 2001), pp. 716–736.
9. P. C. Fiss and E. J. Zajac, "The Symbolic Management of Strategic Change: Sensegiving via Framing and Decoupling," *Academy of Management Journal* 49, no. 6 (2006), pp. 1173–1193.
10. A. E. Rafferty and S. L. D. Restubog, "The Impact of Change Process and Context on Change Reactions and Turnover

During a Merger," *Journal of Management* 36, no. 5 (2010), pp. 1309–1338.

11. Q. N. Huy, "Emotional Balancing of Organizational Continuity and Radical Change: The Contribution of Middle Managers," *Administrative Science Quarterly* (March 2002), pp. 31–69; D. M. Herold, D. B. Fedor, and S. D. Caldwell, "Beyond Change Management: A Multilevel Investigation of Contextual and Personal Influences on Employees' Commitment to Change," *Journal of Applied Psychology* 92, no. 4 (2007), pp. 942–951; and G. B. Cunningham, "The Relationships Among Commitment to Change, Coping with Change, and Turnover Intentions," *European Journal of Work and Organizational Psychology* 15, no. 1 (2006), pp. 29–45.

12. R. Peccei, A. Giangreco, and A. Sebastiano, "The Role of Organizational Commitment in the Analysis of Resistance to Change: Co-predictor and Moderator Effects," *Personnel Review* 40, no. 2 (2011), pp. 185–204.

13. J. P. Kotter, "Leading Change: Why Transformational Efforts Fail," *Harvard Business Review* 85 (January 2007), p. 96–103.

14. K. van Dam, S. Oreg, and B. Schyns, "Daily Work Contexts and Resistance to Organisational Change: The Role of Leader-Member Exchange, Development Climate, and Change Process Characteristics," *Applied Psychology: An International Review* 57, no. 2 (2008), pp. 313–334.

15. S. Oreg and N. Sverdlik, "Ambivalence toward Imposed Change: The Conflict between Dispositional Resistance to Change and the Orientation toward the Change Agent," *Journal of Applied Psychology* 96, no. 2 (2011), pp. 337–349.

16. D. B. Fedor, S. Caldwell, and D. M. Herold, "The Effects of Organizational Changes on Employee Commitment: A Multilevel Investigation," *Personnel Psychology* 59 (2006), pp. 1–29; and R. D. Foster, "Resistance, Justice, and Commitment to Change," *Human Resource Development Quarterly* 21, no. 1 (2010), pp. 3–39.

17. S. Oreg, "Personality, Context, and Resistance to Organizational Change," *European Journal of Work and Organizational Psychology* 15, no. 1 (2006), pp. 73–101.

18. S. M. Elias, "Employee Commitment in Times of Change: Assessing the Importance of Attitudes Toward Organizational Change," *Journal of Management* 35, no. 1 (2009), pp. 37–55.

19. J. W. B. Lang and P. D. Bliese, "General Mental Ability and Two Types of Adaptation to Unforeseen Change: Applying Discontinuous Growth Models to the Task-Change Paradigm," *Journal of Applied Psychology* 94, no. 2 (2009), pp. 411–428.

20. C. O. L. H. Porter, J. W. Webb, and C. I Gogus, "When Goal Orientations Collide: Effects of Learning and Performance Orientation on Team Adaptability in Response to Workload Imbalance," *Journal of Applied Psychology* 95, no. 5 (2010), pp. 935–943.

21. See, for instance, A. Karaevli, "Performance Consequences for New CEO 'Outsiderness': Moderating Effects of Pre- and Post-Succession Contexts," *Strategic Management Journal* 28, no. 7 (2007), pp. 681–706.

22. K. Lewin, *Field Theory in Social Science* (New York: Harper & Row, 1951).

23. P. G. Audia, E. A. Locke, and K. G. Smith, "The Paradox of Success: An Archival and a Laboratory Study of Strategic Persistence Following Radical Environmental Change," *Academy of Management Journal* (October 2000), pp. 837–853; and P. G. Audia and S. Brion, "Reluctant to Change: Self-Enhancing Responses to Diverging Performance Measures,"

Organizational Behavior and Human Decision Processes 102, no. 2 (2007), pp. 255–269.

24. J. B. Sorensen, "The Strength of Corporate Culture and the Reliability of Firm Performance," *Administrative Science Quarterly* (March 2002), pp. 70–91.

25. J. Amis, T. Slack, and C. R. Hinings, "The Pace, Sequence, and Linearity of Radical Change," *Academy of Management Journal* (February 2004), pp. 15–39; and E. Autio, H. J. Sapienza, and J. G. Almeida, "Effects of Age at Entry, Knowledge Intensity, and Imitability on International Growth," *Academy of Management Journal* (October 2000), pp. 909–924.

26. J. P. Kotter, "Leading Changes: Why Transformation Efforts Fail," *Harvard Business Review* (March–April 1995), pp. 59–67; and J. P. Kotter, *Leading Change* (Harvard Business School Press, 1996).

27. See, for example, C. Eden and C. Huxham, "Action Research for the Study of Organizations," in S. R. Clegg, C. Hardy, and W. R. Nord (eds.), *Handbook of Organization Studies* (London: Sage, 1996); and L. S. Lüscher and M. W. Lewis, "Organizational Change and Managerial Sensemaking: Working Through Paradox," *Academy of Management Journal* 51, no. 2 (2008), pp. 221–240.

28. For a sampling of various OD definitions, see H. K. Sinangil and F. Avallone, "Organizational Development and Change," in N. Anderson, D. S. Ones, H. K. Sinangil, and C. Viswesvaran (eds.), *Handbook of Industrial, Work and Organizational Psychology*, vol. 2 (Thousand Oaks, CA: Sage, 2001), pp. 332–335; and R. J. Marshak and D. Grant, "Organizational Discourse and New Organization Development Practices," *British Journal of Management* 19, no. 1 (2008), pp. S7–S19.

29. See, for instance, R. Lines, "Influence of Participation in Strategic Change: Resistance, Organizational Commitment and Change Goal Achievement," *Journal of Change Management* (September 2004), pp. 193–215.

30. S. Highhouse, "A History of the T-Group and Its Early Application in Management Development," *Group Dynamics: Theory, Research, & Practice* (December 2002), pp. 277–290.

31. J. E. Edwards and M. D. Thomas, "The Organizational Survey Process: General Steps and Practical Considerations," in P. Rosenfeld, J. E. Edwards, and M. D. Thomas (eds.), *Improving Organizational Surveys: New Directions, Methods, and Applications* (Newbury Park, CA: Sage, 1993), pp. 3–28.

32. E. H. Schein, *Process Consultation: Its Role in Organizational Development*, 2nd ed. (Reading, MA: Addison-Wesley, 1988), p. 9. See also E. H. Schein, *Process Consultation Revisited: Building Helpful Relationships* (Reading, MA: Addison-Wesley, 1999).

33. Schein, *Process Consultation*.

34. W. W. G. Dyer, W. G. Dyer, and J. H. Dyer, *Team Building: Proven Strategies for Improving Team Performance* (Hoboken, NJ: Jossey-Bass, 2007).

35. U. Wagner, L. Tropp, G. Finchilescu, and C. Tredoux (Eds), *Improving Intergroup Relations* (New York: Wiley-Blackwell, 2008).

36. See, for example, R. Fry, F. Barrett, J. Seiling, and D. Whitney (eds.), *Appreciative Inquiry & Organizational Transformation: Reports from the Field* (Westport, CT: Quorum, 2002); J. K. Barge and C. Oliver, "Working with Appreciation in Managerial Practice," *Academy of Management Review* (January 2003), pp. 124–142; and D. van der Haar and D. M. Hosking, "Evaluating Appreciative Inquiry: A Relational Constructionist Perspective," *Human Relations* (August 2004), pp. 1017–1036.

37. G. Giglio, S. Michalcova, and C. Yates, "Instilling a Culture of Winning at American Express," *Organization Development Journal* 25, no. 4 (2007), pp. P33–P37.

38. A. Harrington, "Who's Afraid of a New Product?" *Fortune* (November 10, 2003), pp. 189–192; C. C. Manz, F. Shipper, and G. L. Stewart, "Everyone a Team Leader: Shared Influence at W. L. Gore and Associates," *Organizational Dynamics* 38, no. 3 (2009), pp. 239–244.

39. See, for instance, R. M. Kanter, "When a Thousand Flowers Bloom: Structural, Collective and Social Conditions for Innovation in Organizations," in B. M. Staw and L. L. Cummings (eds.), *Research in Organizational Behavior,* vol. 10 (Greenwich, CT: JAI Press, 1988), pp. 169–211.

40. F. Damanpour, "Organizational Innovation: A Meta-Analysis of Effects of Determinants and Moderators," *Academy of Management Journal* (September 1991), p. 557.

41. Ibid., pp. 555–590; and G. Westerman, F. W. McFarlan, and M. Iansiti, "Organization Design and Effectiveness over the Innovation Life Cycle," *Organization Science* 17, no. 2 (2006), pp. 230–238.

42. See P. R. Monge, M. D. Cozzens, and N. S. Contractor, "Communication and Motivational Predictors of the Dynamics of Organizational Innovation," *Organization Science* (May 1992), pp. 250–274; P. Schepers and P. T. van den Berg, "Social factors of work-environment creativity," *Journal of Business and Psychology* 21, no. 3 (2007), pp. 407–428.

43. D. L. Day, "Raising Radicals: Different Processes for Championing Innovative Corporate Ventures," *Organization Science* (May 1994), pp. 148–172; and M. E. Mullins, S. W. J. Kozlowski, N. Schmitt, and A. W. Howell, "The Role of the Idea Champion in Innovation: The Case of the Internet in the Mid-1990s," *Computers in Human Behavior* 24, no. 2 (2008), pp. 451–467.

44. Howell and Higgins, "Champions of Change." J. M. Howell and C. A. Higgins "Champions of change: Identifying, understanding, and supporting champions of technological innovations." *Organizational Dynamics* 19, (1990), pp. 40–55.

45. See S. Shane, S. Venkataraman, and I. MacMillan, "Cultural Differences in Innovation Championing Strategies," *Journal of Management* 21, no. 5 (1995), pp. 931–952.

46. A. Taylor, "Chrysler's Speed Merchant," *Fortune* (September 6, 2010), pp. 77–82.

47. See, for example, T. B. Lawrence, M. K. Mauws, B. Dyck, and R. F. Kleysen, "The Politics of Organizational Learning: Integrating Power into the 4I Framework," *Academy of Management Review* (January 2005), pp. 180–191.

48. D. H. Kim, "The Link Between Individual and Organizational Learning," *Sloan Management Review* (Fall 1993), p. 37.

49. C. Argyris and D. A. Schon, *Organizational Learning* (Reading, MA: Addison-Wesley, 1978).

50. B. Dumaine, "Mr. Learning Organization," *Fortune* (October 17, 1994), p. 148.

51. F. Kofman and P. M. Senge, "Communities of Commitment: The Heart of Learning Organizations," *Organizational Dynamics* (Autumn 1993), pp. 5–23.

52. Dumaine, "Mr. Learning Organization," p. 154.

53. See, for instance, S. Armour, "Rising Job Stress Could Affect Bottom Line," *USA Today* (July 29, 2003), p. 1B; and J. Schramm, "Work/Life on Hold," *HRMagazine* 53 (October 2008), p. 120.

54. Adapted from R. S. Schuler, "Definition and Conceptualization of Stress in Organizations," *Organizational Behavior and Human Performance* (April 1980), p. 189. For an updated review of definitions, see C. L. Cooper, P. J. Dewe, and M. P. O'Driscoll, *Organizational Stress: A Review and Critique of Theory, Research, and Applications* (Thousand Oaks, CA: Sage, 2002).

55. See, for instance, M. A. Cavanaugh, W. R. Boswell, M. V. Roehling, and J. W. Boudreau, "An Empirical Examination of Self-Reported Work Stress Among U.S. Managers," *Journal of Applied Psychology* (February 2000), pp. 65–74.

56. N. P. Podsakoff, J. A. LePine, and M. A. LePine, "Differential Challenge-Hindrance Stressor Relationships with Job Attitudes, Turnover Intentions, Turnover, and Withdrawal Behavior: A Meta-Analysis," *Journal of Applied Psychology* 92, no. 2 (2007), pp. 438–454; and J. A. LePine, M. A. LePine, and C. L. Jackson, "Challenge and Hindrance Stress: Relationships with Exhaustion, Motivation to Learn, and Learning Performance," *Journal of Applied Psychology* (October 2004), pp. 883–891.

57. L. W. Hunter and S. M. B. Thatcher, "Feeling the Heat: Effects of Stress, Commitment, and Job Experience on Job Performance," *Academy of Management Journal* 50, no. 4 (2007), pp. 953–968.

58. J. C. Wallace, B. D. Edwards, T. Arnold, M. L. Frazier, and D. M. Finch, "Work Stressors, Role-Based Performance, and the Moderating Influence of Organizational Support," *Journal of Applied Psychology* 94, no. 1 (2009), pp. 254–262.

59. N. W. Van Yperen and O. Janssen, "Fatigued and Dissatisfied or Fatigued but Satisfied? Goal Orientations and Responses to High Job Demands," *Academy of Management Journal* (December 2002), pp. 1161–1171; and N. W. Van Yperen and M. Hagedoorn, "Do High Job Demands Increase Intrinsic Motivation or Fatigue or Both? The Role of Job Control and Job Social Support," *Academy of Management Journal* (June 2003), pp. 339–348.

60. J. de Jonge and C. Dormann, "Stressors, Resources, and Strain at Work: A Longitudinal Test of the Triple-Match Principle," *Journal of Applied Psychology* 91, no. 5 (2006), pp. 1359–1374.

61. This section is adapted from C. L. Cooper and R. Payne, *Stress at Work* (London: Wiley, 1978); S. Parasuraman and J. A. Alutto, "Sources and Outcomes of Stress in Organizational Settings: Toward the Development of a Structural Model," *Academy of Management Journal* 27, no. 2 (June 1984), pp. 330–350; and P. M. Hart and C. L. Cooper, "Occupational Stress: Toward a More Integrated Framework," in N. Anderson, D. S. Ones, H. K. Sinangil, and C. Viswesvaran (eds.), *Handbook of Industrial, Work and Organizational Psychology,* vol. 2 (London: Sage, 2001), pp. 93–114.

62. A. E. Rafferty and M. A. Griffin, "Perceptions of Organizational Change: A Stress and Coping Perspective," *Journal of Applied Psychology* 71, no. 5 (2007), pp. 1154–1162.

63. H. Garst, M. Frese, and P. C. M. Molenaar, "The Temporal Factor of Change in Stressor-Strain Relationships: A Growth Curve Model on a Longitudinal Study in East Germany," *Journal of Applied Psychology* (June 2000), pp. 417–438.

64. See, for example, M. L. Fox, D. J. Dwyer, and D. C. Ganster, "Effects of Stressful Job Demands and Control of Physiological and Attitudinal Outcomes in a Hospital Setting," *Academy of Management Journal* (April 1993), pp. 289–318.

65. T. L. Smith-Jackson and K. W. Klein, "Open-Plan Offices: Task Performance and Mental Workload," *Journal of Environmental Psychology* 29, no. 2 (2009), pp. 279–289.

66. T. M. Glomb, J. D. Kammeyer-Mueller, and M. Rotundo, "Emotional Labor Demands and Compensating Wage Differentials," *Journal of Applied Psychology* (August 2004), pp. 700–714; and A. A. Grandey, "When 'The Show Must Go On': Surface Acting and Deep Acting as Determinants of Emotional Exhaustion and Peer-Rated Service Delivery," *Academy of Management Journal* (February 2003), pp. 86–96.

67. C. Fritz and S. Sonnentag, "Antecedents of Day-Level Proactive Behavior: A Look at Job Stressors and Positive Affect During the Workday," *Journal of Management* 35, no. 1 (2009), pp. 94–111.

68. S. Lim, L. M. Cortina, and V. J. Magley, "Personal and Workgroup Incivility: Impact on Work and Health Outcomes," *Journal of Applied Psychology* 93, no. 1 (2008), pp. 95–107; N. T. Buchanan, and L. F. Fitzgerald, "Effects of Racial and Sexual Harassment on Work and the Psychological Well-Being of African American Women," *Journal of Occupational Health Psychology* 13, no. 2 (2008), pp. 137–151; C. R. Willness, P. Steel, and K. Lee, "A Meta-Analysis of the Antecedents and Consequences of Workplace Sexual Harassment," *Personnel Psychology* 60, no. 1 (2007), pp. 127–162; and B. Moreno-Jiménez, A. Rodríguez-Muñoz, J. C. Pastor, A. I. Sanz-Vergel, and E. Garrosa, "The Moderating Effects of Psychological Detachment and Thoughts of Revenge in Workplace Bullying," *Personality and Individual Differences* 46, no. 3 (2009), pp. 359–364.

69. V. S. Major, K. J. Klein, and M. G. Ehrhart, "Work Time, Work Interference with Family, and Psychological Distress," *Journal of Applied Psychology* (June 2002), pp. 427–436. See also P. E. Spector, C. L. Cooper, S. Poelmans, T. D. Allen, M. O'Driscoll, J. I. Sanchez, et al., "A Cross-National Comparative Study of Work-Family Stressors, Working Hours, and Well-Being: China and Latin America Versus the Anglo World," *Personnel Psychology* (Spring 2004), pp. 119–142.

70. D. L. Nelson and C. Sutton, "Chronic Work Stress and Coping: A Longitudinal Study and Suggested New Directions," *Academy of Management Journal* (December 1990), pp. 859–869.

71. H. Selye, *The Stress of Life,* rev. ed. (New York: McGraw-Hill, 1976); and Q. Hu, W. B. Schaufeli, and T. W. Taris, "The Job Demands–Resources Model: An Analysis of Additive and Joint Effects of Demands and Resources," *Journal of Vocational Behavior* 79, no. 1 (2011), pp. 181–190.

72. S. J. Motowidlo, J. S. Packard, and M. R. Manning, "Occupational Stress: Its Causes and Consequences for Job Performance," *Journal of Applied Psychology* (November 1987), pp. 619–620; and E. R. Crawford, J. A. LePine, and B. L. Rich, "Linking Job Demands and Resources to Employee Engagement and Burnout: A Theoretical Extension and Meta-Analytic test," Journal of Applied Psychology 95, no. 5 (2010), pp. 834–848.

73. See J. B. Halbesleben, "Sources of Social Support and Burnout: A Meta-Analytic Test of the Conservation of Resources Model," *Journal of Applied Psychology* 91, no. 5 (2006), pp. 1134–1145; N. Bolger and D. Amarel, "Effects of Social Support Visibility on Adjustment to Stress: Experimental Evidence," *Journal of Applied Psychology* 92, no. 3 (2007), pp. 458–475; and C. Fernet, M. Gagné and S. Austin, "When Does Quality of Relationships with Coworkers Predict Burnout over Time? The Moderating Role of Work Motivation" *Journal of Organizational Behavior* 31 (2010), pp. 1163–1180.

74. See, for example, C. M. Middeldorp, D. C. Cath, A. L. Beem, G. Willemsen, and D. I. Boomsma, "Life Events, Anxious Depression, and Personality: A Prospective and Genetic Study," *Psychological Medicine* 38, no. 11 (2008), pp. 1557–1565; A. A. Uliaszek, R. E. Zinbarg, S. Mineka, M. G. Craske, J. M. Sutton, J. W. Griffith, R. Rose, A. Waters, and C. Hammen, "The Role of Neuroticism and Extraversion in the Stress-Anxiety and Stress-Depression Relationships," *Anxiety, Stress, and Coping* 23, no. 4 (2010), pp. 363–381.

75. J. D. Kammeyer-Mueller, T. A. Judge, and B. A. Scott, "The Role of Core Self-Evaluations in the Coping Process," *Journal of Applied Psychology* 94, no. 1 (2009), pp. 177–195.

76. R. J. Burke, A. M. Richardson, and M. Mortinussen, "Workaholism Among Norwegian Managers: Work and Well-Being Outcomes," *Journal of Organizational Change Management* 7 (2004), pp. 459–470; and W. B. Schaufeli, T. W. Taris, and W. van Rhenen, "Workaholism, Burnout, and Work Engagement: Three of a Kind or Three Different Kinds of Employee Well-Being," *Applied Psychology: An International Review* 57, no. 2 (2008), pp. 173–203.

77. J. Chen, C. Silverthorne, and J. Hung, "Organization Communication, Job Stress, Organizational Commitment, and Job Performance of Accounting Professionals in Taiwan and America," *Leadership & Organization Development Journal* 27, no. 4 (2006), pp. 242–249; and C. Liu, P. E. Spector, and L. Shi, "Cross-National Job Stress: A Quantitative and Qualitative Study," *Journal of Organizational Behavior* (February 2007), pp. 209–239.

78. P. E. Spector, T. D. Allen, S. A. Y. Poelmans, L. M. Lapierre, C. L. Cooper, M. O'Driscoll, et al., "Cross National Differences in Relationships of Work Demands, Job Satisfaction, and Turnover Intention with Work-Family Conflict," *Personnel Psychology* 60, no. 4 (2007), pp. 805–835.

79. H. M. Addae and X. Wang, "Stress at Work: Linear and Curvilinear Effects of Psychological-, Job-, and Organization-Related Factors: An Exploratory Study of Trinidad and Tobago," *International Journal of Stress Management* (November 2006), pp. 476–493.

80. J. Schaubroeck, J. R. Jones, and J. L. Xie, "Individual Differences in Utilizing Control to Cope with Job Demands: Effects on Susceptibility to Infectious Disease," *Journal of Applied Psychology* (April 2001), pp. 265–278.

81. M. Kivimäki, J. Head, J. E. Ferrie, E. Brunner, M. G. Marmot, J. Vahtera, and M. J. Shipley, "Why Is Evidence on Job Strain and Coronary Heart Disease Mixed? An Illustration of Measurement Challenges in the Whitehall II Study," *Psychosomatic Medicine* 68, no. 3 (2006), pp. 398–401.

82. M. Borritz, K. B. Christensen, U. Bültmann, R. Rugulies, T. Lund, I Andersen, E. Villadsen, F. Didreichsen, and T. S. Krisensen, "Impact on Burnout and Psychosocial Work Characteristics on Future Long-Term Sickness Absence, Prospective Results of the Danish PUMA Study Among Human Service Workers," *Journal of Occupational and Environmental Medicine* 52, no. 10 (2010), pp. 964–970.

83. B. D. Steffy and J. W. Jones, "Workplace Stress and Indicators of Coronary-Disease Risk," *Academy of Management Journal* 31, no. 3 (1988), pp. 686–698.

84. R. Illies, N. Dimotakis, and I. E. DePater, "Psychological and Physiological Reactions to High Workloads: Implications

for Well-Being," *Personnel Psychology* 63, no. 2 (2010), pp. 407–463.

85. D. Örtqvist and J. Wincent, "Prominent Consequences of Role Stress: A Meta-Analytic Review," *International Journal of Stress Management*, 13, no. 4 (2006), pp. 399–422.

86. J. R. Hackman and G. R. Oldham, "Development of the Job Diagnostic Survey," *Journal of Applied Psychology* (April 1975), pp. 159–170; J. J. Hakanen, A. B. Bakker, and M. Jokisaari, "A 35-Year Follow-Up Study on Burnout Among Finnish Employees," *Journal of Occupational Health Psychology* 16, no. 3 (2011), pp. 345–360; Crawford, LePine, and Rich, "Linking Job Demands and Resources to Employee Engagement and Burnout; and G. A. Chung-Yan, "The Nonlinear Effects of Job Complexity and Autonomy on Job Satisfaction, Turnover, and Psychological Well-Being," *Journal of Occupational Health Psychology* 15, no. 3 (2010), pp. 237–251.

87. L. L. Meier, N. K. Semmer, A. Elfering, and N. Jacobshagen, "The Double Meaning of Control: Three-Way Interactions Between Internal Resources, Job Control, and Stressors at Work," *Journal of Occupational Health Psychology* 13, no. 3 (2008), pp. 244–258.

88. E. M. de Croon, J. K. Sluiter, R. W. B. Blonk, J. P. J. Broersen, and M. H. W. Frings-Dresen, "Stressful Work, Psychological Job Strain, and Turnover: A 2-Year Prospective Cohort Study of Truck Drivers," *Journal of Applied Psychology* (June 2004), pp. 442–454; R. Cropanzano, D. E. Rupp, and Z. S. Byrne, "The Relationship of Emotional Exhaustion to Work Attitudes, Job Performance, and Organizational Citizenship Behaviors," *Journal of Applied Psychology* (February 2003), pp. 160–169; and S. Diestel and K. Schmidt, "Costs of Simultaneous Coping with Emotional Dissonance and Self-Control Demands at Work: Results from Two German Samples," *Journal of Applied Psychology* 96, no. 3 (2011), pp. 643–653.

89. See, for instance, S. Zivnuska, C. Kiewitz, W. A. Hochwarter, P. L. Perrewe, and K. L. Zellars, "What Is Too Much or Too Little? The Curvilinear Effects of Job Tension on Turnover Intent, Value Attainment, and Job Satisfaction," *Journal of Applied Social Psychology* (July 2002), pp. 1344–1360.

90. L. A. Muse, S. G. Harris, and H. S. Field, "Has the Inverted-U Theory of Stress and Job Performance Had a Fair Test?" *Human Performance* 16, no. 4 (2003), pp. 349–364.

91. S. Gilboa, A. Shirom, Y. Fried, and C. Cooper, "A Meta-Analysis of Work Demand Stressors and Job Performance: Examining Main and Moderating Effects," *Personnel Psychology* 61, no. 2 (2008), pp. 227–271.

92. J. C. Wallace, B. D. Edwards, T. Arnold, M. L. Frazier, and D. M. Finch, "Work Stressors, Role-Based Performance, and the Moderating Influence of Organizational Support," *Journal of Applied Psychology* 94, no. 1 (2009), pp. 254–262.

93. The following discussion has been influenced J. M. Ivancevich, M. T. Matteson, S. M. Freedman, and J. S. Phillips, "Worksite Stress Management Interventions," *American Psychologist* (February 1990), pp. 252–261; R. Schwarzer, "Manage Stress at Work Through Preventive and Proactive Coping," in E. A. Locke (ed.), *Handbook of Principles of Organizational Behavior* (Malden, MA: Blackwell, 2004), pp. 342–355; and K. M. Richardson and H. R. Rothstein, "Effects of Occupational Stress Management Intervention Programs: A Meta-Analysis," *Journal of Occupational Health Psychology* 13, no. 1 (2008), pp. 69–93.

94. T. H. Macan, "Time Management: Test of a Process Model," *Journal of Applied Psychology* (June 1994), pp. 381–391; and B. J. C. Claessens, W. Van Eerde, C. G. Rutte, and R. A. Roe, "Planning Behavior and Perceived Control of Time at Work," *Journal of Organizational Behavior* (December 2004), pp. 937–950.

95. See, for example, G. Lawrence-Ell, *The Invisible Clock: A Practical Revolution in Finding Time for Everyone and Everything* (Seaside Park, NJ: Kingsland Hall, 2002); and B. Tracy, *Time Power* (New York: AMACOM, 2004).

96. R. W. Renn, D. G. Allen, and T. M. Huning, "Empirical Examination of Individual-Level Personality-Based Theory of Self-Management Failure," *Journal of Organizational Behavior* 32, no. 1 (2011), pp. 25–43; and P. Gröpel and P. Steel, "A Mega-Trial Investigation of Goal Setting, Interest Enhancement, and Energy on Procrastination," *Personality and Individual Differences* 45, no. 5 (2008), pp. 406–411.

97. P. Salmon, "Effects of Physical Exercise on Anxiety, Depression, and Sensitivity to Stress: A Unifying Theory," *Clinical Psychology Review* 21, no. 1 (2001), pp. 33–61.

98. K. M. Richardson and H. R. Rothstein, "Effects of Occupational Stress Management Intervention Programs: A Meta-Analysis," *Journal of Occupational Health Psychology* 13, no. 1 (2008), pp. 69–93.

99. V. C. Hahn, C. Binnewies, S. Sonnentag, and E. J. Mojza, "Learning How to Recover From Job Stress: Effects of a Recovery Training Program on Recovery, Recovery-Related Self-Efficacy, and Well-Being," *Journal of Occupational Health Psychology* 16, no. 2 (2011), pp. 202–216; and C. Binnewies, S. Sonnentag, and E. J. Mojza, "Recovery During the Weekend and Fluctuations in Weekly Job Performance: A Week-Level Study Examining Intra-Individual Relationships," *Journal of Occupational and Organizational Psychology* 83, no. 2 (2010), pp. 419–441.

100. E. R. Greenglass and L. Fiksenbaum, "Proactive Coping, Positive Affect, and Well-Being: Testing for Mediation Using Path Analysis," *European Psychologist* 14, no. 1 (2009), pp. 29–39; and P. Miquelon and R. J. Vallerand, "Goal Motives, Well-Being, and Physical Health: Happiness and Self-Realization as Psychological Resources under Challenge," *Motivation and Emotion* 30, no. 4 (2006), pp. 259–272.

101. M. M. Butts, R. J. Vandenberg, D. M. DeJoy, B. S. Schaffer, and M. G. Wilson, "Individual Reactions to High Involvement Work Processes: Investigating the Role of Empowerment and Perceived Organizational Support," *Journal of Occupational Health Psychology* 14, no. 2 (2009), pp. 122–136.

102. "100 Best Companies to Work For," *Fortune* (August 17, 2011), http://money.cnn.com/magazines/fortune.

103. L. Blue, "Making Good Health Easy," *Time* (November 12, 2009), www.time.com; and M. Andrews, "Americas Best Health Plans," *US News and World Report* (November 5, 2007), pp. 54–60.

104. K. M. Richardson and H. R. Rothstein, "Effects of Occupational Stress Management Intervention Programs: A Meta-Analysis," *Journal of Occupational Health Psychology* 13, no. 1 (2008), pp. 69–93.

105. D. Brown, "Wellness Programs Bring Healthy Bottom Line," *Canadian HR Reporter* (December 17, 2001), pp. 1ff.

106. P. S. Goodman and L. B. Kurke, "Studies of Change in Organizations: A Status Report," in P. S. Goodman (ed.), *Change in Organizations* (San Francisco: Jossey-Bass, 1982), p. 1.

For every complex problem, there is a solution that is simple, neat, and wrong.

—H. L. Mencken

A number of years ago, a friend of mine was excited because he had read about the findings from a research study that finally, once and for all, resolved the question of what it takes to make it to the top in a large corporation. I doubted there was any simple answer to this question but, not wanting to dampen his enthusiasm, I asked him to tell me of what he had read. The answer, according to my friend, was *participation in college athletics.* To say I was skeptical of his claim is a gross understatement, so I asked him to tell me more.

The study encompassed 1,700 successful senior executives at the 500 largest U.S. corporations. The researchers found that half of these executives had played varsity-level college sports.[1] My friend, who happens to be good with statistics, informed me that since fewer than 2 percent of all college students participate in intercollegiate athletics, the probability of this finding occurring by mere chance is less than 1 in 10 million! He concluded his analysis by telling me that, based on this research, I should encourage my management students to get into shape and to make one of the varsity teams.

My friend was somewhat perturbed when I suggested that his conclusions were likely to be flawed. These executives were all males who attended college in the 1940s and 1950s. Would his advice be meaningful to females in the twenty-first century? These executives also weren't your typical college students. For the most part, they had attended elite private colleges such as Princeton and Amherst, where a large proportion of the student body participates in intercollegiate sports. And these "jocks" hadn't necessarily played football or basketball; many had participated in golf, tennis, baseball, cross-country running, crew, rugby, and similar minor sports. Moreover, maybe the researchers had confused the direction of causality. That is, maybe individuals with the motivation and ability to make it to the top of a large corporation are drawn to competitive activities like college athletics.

My friend was guilty of misusing research data. Of course, he is not alone. We are all continually bombarded with reports of experiments that link certain substances to cancer in mice and surveys that show changing attitudes toward sex among college students, for example. Many of these studies are carefully designed, with great caution taken to note the implications and limitations of the findings. But some studies are poorly designed, making their conclusions at best suspect, and at worst meaningless.

Rather than attempting to make you a researcher, the purpose of this appendix is to increase your awareness as a consumer of behavioral research. A knowledge of research methods will allow you to appreciate more fully the care in data collection that underlies the information and conclusions presented in this text. Moreover, an understanding of research methods will make you a more skilled evaluator of the OB studies you will encounter in business and professional journals. So an appreciation of behavioral research is important because (1) it's the foundation on which the theories in this text are built, and (2) it will benefit you in future years when you read reports of research and attempt to assess their value.

Purposes of Research

Research is concerned with the systematic gathering of information. Its purpose is to help us in our search for the truth. Although we will never find ultimate truth—in our case, that would be to know precisely how any person or group would behave in any organizational context—ongoing research adds to our body of OB knowledge by supporting some theories, contradicting others, and suggesting new theories to replace those that fail to gain support.

Research Terminology

Researchers have their own vocabulary for communicating among themselves and with outsiders. The following briefly defines some of the more popular terms you're likely to encounter in behavioral science studies.[2]

Variable

A *variable* is any general characteristic that can be measured and that changes in amplitude, intensity, or both. Some examples of OB variables found in this textbook are job satisfaction, employee productivity, work stress, ability, personality, and group norms.

Hypothesis

A tentative explanation of the relationship between two or more variables is called a *hypothesis*. My friend's statement that participation in college athletics leads to a top executive position in a large corporation is an example of a hypothesis. Until confirmed by empirical research, a hypothesis remains only a tentative explanation.

Dependent Variable

A *dependent variable* is a response that is affected by an independent variable. In terms of the hypothesis, it is the variable that the researcher is interested in explaining. Referring back to our opening example, the dependent variable in my friend's hypothesis was executive succession. In organizational behavior research, the most popular dependent variables are productivity, absenteeism, turnover, job satisfaction, and organizational commitment.[3]

Independent Variable

An *independent variable* is the presumed cause of some change in the dependent variable. Participating in varsity athletics was the independent variable in my friend's hypothesis. Popular independent variables studied by OB researchers include intelligence, personality, job satisfaction, experience, motivation, reinforcement patterns, leadership style, reward allocations, selection methods, and organization design.

You may have noticed we said that job satisfaction is frequently used by OB researchers as both a dependent and an independent variable. This is not an error. It merely reflects that the label given to a variable depends on its place in the hypothesis. In the statement "Increases in job satisfaction lead to reduced turnover," job satisfaction is an independent variable. However, in the statement "Increases in money lead to higher job satisfaction," job satisfaction becomes a dependent variable.

Moderating Variable

A *moderating variable* abates the effect of the independent variable on the dependent variable. It might also be thought of as the contingency variable: If *X* (independent variable), then *Y* (dependent variable) will occur, but only under conditions *Z* (moderating variable). To translate this into a real-life example, we might say that if we increase the amount of direct supervision in the work area (*X*), then there will be a change in worker productivity (*Y*), but this effect will be moderated by the complexity of the tasks being performed (*Z*).

Causality

A hypothesis, by definition, implies a relationship. That is, it implies a presumed cause and effect. This direction of cause and effect is called *causality*. Changes in the independent variable are assumed to cause changes in the dependent variable. However, in behavioral research, it's possible to make an incorrect assumption of causality when relationships are found. For example, early behavioral scientists found a relationship between employee satisfaction and productivity. They concluded that a happy worker was a productive worker. Follow-up research has supported the relationship, but disconfirmed the direction of the arrow. The evidence more correctly suggests that high productivity leads to satisfaction rather than the other way around.

Correlation Coefficient

It's one thing to know that there is a relationship between two or more variables. It's another to know the *strength* of that relationship. The term *correlation coefficient* is used to indicate that strength, and is expressed as a number between −1.00 (a perfect negative relationship) and +1.00 (a perfect positive correlation).

When two variables vary directly with one another, the correlation will be expressed as a positive number. When they vary inversely—that is, one increases as the other decreases—the correlation will be expressed as a negative number. If the two variables vary independently of each other, we say that the correlation between them is zero.

For example, a researcher might survey a group of employees to determine the satisfaction of each with his or her job. Then, using company absenteeism reports, the researcher could correlate the job satisfaction scores against individual attendance records to determine whether employees who are more satisfied with their jobs have better attendance records than their counterparts who indicated lower job satisfaction. Let's suppose the researcher found a correlation coefficient of +0.50 between satisfaction and attendance. Would that be a strong association? There is, unfortunately, no precise numerical cutoff separating strong and weak relationships. A standard statistical test would need to be applied to determine whether the relationship was a significant one.

A final point needs to be made before we move on: A correlation coefficient measures only the strength of association between two variables. A high value does *not* imply causality. The length of women's skirts and stock market prices, for instance, have long been noted to be highly correlated, but one should be careful not to infer that a causal relationship between the two exists. In this instance, the high correlation is more happenstance than predictive.

Theory

The final term we introduce in this section is *theory*. Theory describes a set of systematically interrelated concepts or hypotheses that purports to explain and predict phenomena. In OB, theories are also frequently referred to as *models*. We use the two terms interchangeably.

There are no shortages of theories in OB. For instance, we have theories to describe what motivates people, the most effective leadership styles, the best way to resolve conflicts, and how people acquire power. In some cases, we have half a dozen or more separate theories that purport to explain and predict a given phenomenon. In such cases, is one right and the others wrong? No! They tend to reflect science at work—researchers testing previous theories, modifying them, and, when appropriate, proposing new models that may prove to have higher explanatory and predictive powers. Multiple theories attempting to explain common phenomena merely attest that OB is an active discipline, still growing and evolving.

Evaluating Research

As a potential consumer of behavioral research, you should follow the dictum of *caveat emptor*—let the buyer beware! In evaluating any research study, you need to ask three questions.[4]

Is it valid? Is the study actually measuring what it claims to be measuring? A number of psychological tests have been discarded by employers in recent years because they have not been found to be valid measures of the applicants' ability to do a given job successfully. But the validity issue is relevant to all research studies. So, if you find a study that links cohesive work teams with higher productivity, you want to know how each of these variables was measured and whether it is actually measuring what it is supposed to be measuring.

Is it reliable? Reliability refers to consistency of measurement. If you were to have your height measured every day with a wooden yardstick, you'd get highly reliable results. On the other hand, if you were measured each day by an elastic tape measure, there would probably be considerable disparity between your height measurements from one day to the next. Your height, of course, doesn't change from day to day. The variability is due to the unreliability of the measuring device. So if a company asked a group of its employees to complete a reliable job satisfaction questionnaire, and then repeat the questionnaire six

months later, we'd expect the results to be very similar—provided nothing changed in the interim that might significantly affect employee satisfaction.

Is it generalizable? Are the results of the research study generalizable to groups of individuals other than those who participated in the original study? Be aware, for example, of the limitations that might exist in research that uses college students as subjects. Are the findings in such studies generalizable to full-time employees in real jobs? Similarly, how generalizable to the overall work population are the results from a study that assesses job stress among 10 nuclear power plant engineers in the hamlet of Mahone Bay, Nova Scotia?

Research Design

Doing research is an exercise in trade-offs. Richness of information typically comes with reduced generalizability. The more a researcher seeks to control for confounding variables, the less realistic his or her results are likely to be. High precision, generalizability, and control almost always translate into higher costs. When researchers make choices about whom they'll study, where their research will be done, the methods they'll use to collect data, and so on, they must make some concessions. Good research designs are not perfect, but they do carefully reflect the questions being addressed. Keep these facts in mind as we review the strengths and weaknesses of five popular research designs: case studies, field surveys, laboratory experiments, field experiments, and aggregate quantitative reviews.

Case Study

You pick up a copy of Soichiro Honda's autobiography. In it he describes his impoverished childhood; his decisions to open a small garage, assemble motorcycles, and eventually build automobiles; and how this led to the creation of one of the largest and most successful corporations in the world. Or you're in a business class and the instructor distributes a 50-page handout covering two companies: Wal-Mart and Kmart. The handout details the two firms' histories; describes their corporate strategies, management philosophies, and merchandising plans; and includes copies of their recent balance sheets and income statements. The instructor asks the class members to read the handout, analyze the data, and determine why Wal-Mart has been so much more successful than Kmart in recent years.

Soichiro Honda's autobiography and the Wal-Mart and Kmart handouts are case studies. Drawn from real-life situations, case studies present an in-depth analysis of one setting. They are thorough descriptions, rich in details about an individual, a group, or an organization. The primary source of information in case studies is obtained through observation, occasionally backed up by interviews and a review of records and documents.

Case studies have their drawbacks. They're open to the perceptual bias and subjective interpretations of the observer. The reader of a case is captive to what the observer/case writer chooses to include and exclude. Cases also trade off generalizability for depth of information and richness of detail. Because it's always dangerous to generalize from a sample of one, case studies make it difficult to prove or reject a hypothesis. On the other hand, you can't ignore the in-depth analysis that cases often provide. They are an excellent device for initial exploratory research and for evaluating real-life problems in organizations.

Field Survey

A lengthy questionnaire was created to assess the use of ethics policies, formal ethics structures, formalized activities such as ethics training, and executive involvement in ethics programs among billion-dollar corporations. The public affairs or corporate communications office of all *Fortune* 500 industrial firms and 500 service corporations were contacted to get the name and address of the "officer most responsible for dealing with ethics and conduct issues" in each firm. The questionnaire, with a cover letter explaining the nature of the study, was mailed to these 1,000 officers. Of the total, 254 returned a completed questionnaire, for a response rate just above 25 percent. The results of the survey found, among other things, that 77 percent had formal codes of ethics and 54 percent had a single officer specifically assigned to deal with ethics and conduct issues.[5]

The preceding study illustrates a typical field survey. A sample of respondents (in this case, 1,000 corporate officers in the largest U.S. publicly held corporations) was selected to represent a larger group that was under examination (billion-dollar U.S. business firms). The respondents were then surveyed using a questionnaire or interviewed to collect data on particular characteristics (the content and structure of ethics programs and practices) of interest to the researchers. The standardization of response items allows for data to be easily quantified, analyzed, and summarized, and for the researchers to make inferences from the representative sample about the larger population.

The field survey provides economies for doing research. It's less costly to sample a population than to obtain data from every member of that population. (There are, for instance, more than 5,000 U.S. business firms with sales in excess of a billion dollars; and since some of these are privately held and don't release financial data to the public, they are excluded from the *Fortune* list). Moreover, as the ethics study illustrates, field surveys provide an efficient way to find out how

people feel about issues or how they say they behave. These data can then be easily quantified.

But the field survey has a number of potential weaknesses. First, mailed questionnaires rarely obtain 100 percent returns. Low response rates call into question whether conclusions based on respondents' answers are generalizable to nonrespondents. Second, the format is better at tapping respondents' attitudes and perceptions than behaviors. Third, responses can suffer from social desirability; that is, people saying what they think the researcher wants to hear. Fourth, since field surveys are designed to focus on specific issues, they're a relatively poor means of acquiring depth of information. Finally, the quality of the generalizations is largely a factor of the population chosen. Responses from executives at *Fortune* 500 firms, for instance, tell us nothing about small- or medium-sized firms or not-for-profit organizations. In summary, even a well-designed field survey trades off depth of information for breadth, generalizability, and economic efficiencies.

Laboratory Experiment

The following study is a classic example of the laboratory experiment. A researcher, Stanley Milgram, wondered how far individuals would go in following commands. If subjects were placed in the role of a teacher in a learning experiment and told by an experimenter to administer a shock to a learner each time that learner made a mistake, would the subjects follow the commands of the experimenter? Would their willingness to comply decrease as the intensity of the shock was increased?

To test these hypotheses, Milgram hired a set of subjects. Each was led to believe that the experiment was to investigate the effect of punishment on memory. Their job was to act as teachers and administer punishment whenever the learner made a mistake on the learning test.

Punishment was administered by an electric shock. The subject sat in front of a shock generator with 30 levels of shock—beginning at zero and progressing in 15-volt increments to a high of 450 volts. The demarcations of these positions ranged from "Slight Shock" at 15 volts to "Danger: Severe Shock" at 450 volts. To increase the realism of the experiment, the subjects received a sample shock of 45 volts and saw the learner—a pleasant, mild-mannered man about 50 years old—strapped into an "electric chair" in an adjacent room. Of course, the learner was an actor, and the electric shocks were phony, but the subjects didn't know this.

Taking his seat in front of the shock generator, the subject was directed to begin at the lowest shock level and to increase the shock intensity to the next level each time the learner made a mistake or failed to respond.

When the test began, the shock intensity rose rapidly because the learner made many errors. The subject got verbal feedback from the learner: At 75 volts, the learner began to grunt and moan; at 150 volts, he demanded to be released from the experiment; at 180 volts, he cried out that he could no longer stand the pain; and at 300 volts, he insisted that he be let out, yelled about his heart condition, screamed, and then failed to respond to further questions.

Most subjects protested and, fearful they might kill the learner if the increased shocks were to bring on a heart attack, insisted they could not go on with their job. Hesitations or protests by the subject were met by the experimenter's statement, "You have no choice, you must go on! Your job is to punish the learner's mistakes." Of course, the subjects did have a choice. All they had to do was stand up and walk out.

The majority of the subjects dissented. But dissension isn't synonymous with disobedience. Sixty-two percent of the subjects increased the shock level to the maximum of 450 volts. The average level of shock administered by the remaining 38 percent was nearly 370 volts.[6]

In a laboratory experiment such as that conducted by Milgram, an artificial environment is created by the researcher. Then the researcher manipulates an independent variable under controlled conditions. Finally, since all other things are held equal, the researcher is able to conclude that any change in the dependent variable is due to the manipulation or change imposed on the independent variable. Note that, because of the controlled conditions, the researcher is able to imply causation between the independent and dependent variables.

The laboratory experiment trades off realism and generalizability for precision and control. It provides a high degree of control over variables and precise measurement of those variables. But findings from laboratory studies are often difficult to generalize to the real world of work. This is because the artificial laboratory rarely duplicates the intricacies and nuances of real organizations. In addition, many laboratory experiments deal with phenomena that cannot be reproduced or applied to real-life situations.

Field Experiment

The following is an example of a field experiment. The management of a large company is interested in determining the impact that a four-day workweek would have on employee absenteeism. To be more specific, management wants to know if employees working four 10-hour days have lower absence rates than similar employees working the traditional five-day week of 8 hours each day. Because the company is large, it has a number of manufacturing plants that employ essentially similar workforces. Two of these are chosen for the experiment, both located in the greater Cleveland area. Obviously, it would not be appropriate to compare two similar-sized plants if one is in rural Mississippi and the other is in urban Copenhagen because factors such as national culture, transportation, and weather might be more likely to explain any differences found than changes in the number of days worked per week.

In one plant, the experiment was put into place—workers began the four-day week. At the other plant, which became the control group, no changes were made in the employees' five-day week. Absence data were gathered from the company's records at both locations for a period of 18 months. This extended time period lessened the possibility that any results would be distorted by the mere novelty of changes being implemented in the experimental plant. After 18 months, management found that absenteeism had dropped by 40 percent at the experimental plant, and by only 6 percent in the control plant. Because of the design of this study, management believed that the larger drop in absences at the experimental plant was due to the introduction of the compressed workweek.

The field experiment is similar to the laboratory experiment, except it is conducted in a real organization. The natural setting is more realistic than the laboratory setting, and this enhances validity but hinders control. In addition, unless control groups are maintained, there can be a loss of control if extraneous forces intervene—for example, an employee strike, a major layoff, or a corporate restructuring. Maybe the greatest concern with field studies has to do with organizational selection bias. Not all organizations are going to allow outside researchers to come in and study their employees and operations. This is especially true of organizations that have serious problems. Therefore, since most published studies in OB are done by outside researchers, the selection bias might work toward the publication of studies conducted almost exclusively at successful and well-managed organizations.

Our general conclusion is that, of the four research designs we've discussed to this point, the field experiment typically provides the most valid and generalizable findings and, except for its high cost, trades off the least to get the most.[7]

Aggregate Quantitative Reviews

What's the overall effect of organizational behavior modification (OB Mod) on task performance? There have been a number of field experiments that have sought to throw light on this question. Unfortunately, the wide range of effects from these various studies makes it hard to generalize.

To try to reconcile these diverse findings, two researchers reviewed all the empirical studies they could find on the impact of OB Mod on task performance over a 20-year period.[8] After discarding reports that had inadequate information, had nonquantitative data, or didn't meet all conditions associated with principles of behavioral modification, the researchers narrowed their set to 19 studies that included data on 2,818 individuals. Using an aggregating technique called *meta-analysis,* the researchers were able to synthesize the studies quantitatively and to conclude that the average person's task performance will rise from the 50th percentile to the 67th percentile after an OB Mod intervention.

The OB Mod–task performance review done by these researchers illustrates the use of meta-analysis, a quantitative form of literature review that enables researchers to look at validity findings from a comprehensive set of individual studies, and then apply a formula to them to determine if they consistently produced similar results.[9] If results prove to be consistent, it allows researchers to conclude more confidently that validity is generalizable. Meta-analysis is a means for overcoming the potentially imprecise interpretations of qualitative reviews and to synthesize variations in quantitative studies. In addition, the technique enables researchers to identify potential moderating variables between an independent and a dependent variable.

In the past 25 years, there's been a surge in the popularity of this research method. Why? It appears to offer a more objective means for doing traditional literature reviews. Although the use of meta-analysis requires researchers to make a number of judgment calls, which can introduce a considerable amount of subjectivity into the process, there is no arguing that meta-analysis reviews have now become widespread in the OB literature.

Ethics in Research

Researchers are not always tactful or candid with subjects when they do their studies. For instance, questions in field surveys may be perceived as embarrassing by respondents or as an invasion of privacy. Also, researchers in laboratory studies have been known to deceive participants about the true purpose of their experiment "because they felt deception was necessary to get honest responses."[10]

The "learning experiments" conducted by Stanley Milgram, which were conducted more than 30 years ago, have been widely criticized by psychologists on ethical grounds. He lied to subjects, telling them his study was investigating learning, when, in fact, he was concerned with obedience. The shock machine he used was a fake. Even the "learner" was an accomplice of Milgram's who had been trained to act as if he were hurt and in pain. Yet ethical lapses continue. For instance, in 2001, a professor of organizational behavior at Columbia University sent out a common letter on university letterhead to 240 New York City restaurants in which he detailed how he had eaten at this restaurant with his wife in celebration of their wedding anniversary, how he had gotten food poisoning, and that he had spent the night in his bathroom throwing up.[11] The letter closed with: "Although it is not my intention to file any reports with the Better Business Bureau or the Department of Health, I want you to understand what I went through in anticipation that you will respond accordingly. I await your response." The fictitious letter was part of the professor's study to determine how restaurants responded to complaints. But it created culinary chaos among many of the restaurant owners, managers, and chefs as they reviewed menus and produce deliveries for possibly spoiled food, and questioned kitchen workers about possible lapses. A follow-up letter of apology from the university for "an egregious error in judgment by a junior faculty member" did little to offset the distress it created for those affected.

Professional associations like the American Psychological Association, the American Sociological Association, and the Academy of Management have published formal guidelines for the conduct of research. Yet the ethical debate continues. On one side are those who argue that strict ethical controls can damage the scientific validity of an experiment and cripple future research. Deception, for example, is often necessary to avoid contaminating results. Moreover, proponents of minimizing ethical controls note that few subjects have been appreciably harmed by deceptive experiments. Even in Milgram's highly manipulative experiment, only 1.3 percent of the subjects reported negative feelings about their experience. The other side of this debate focuses on the rights of participants. Those favoring strict ethical controls argue that no procedure should ever be emotionally or physically distressing to subjects, and that, as professionals, researchers are obliged to be completely honest with their subjects and to protect the subjects' privacy at all costs.

Summary

The subject of organizational behavior is composed of a large number of theories that are research based. Research studies, when cumulatively integrated, become theories, and theories are proposed and followed by research studies designed to validate them. The concepts that make up OB, therefore, are only as valid as the research that supports them.

The topics and issues in this book are for the most part research-derived. They represent the result of systematic information gathering rather than merely hunch, intuition, or opinion. This doesn't mean, of course, that we have all the answers to OB issues. Many require far more corroborating evidence. The generalizability of others is limited by the research methods used. But new information is being created and published at an accelerated rate. To keep up with the latest findings, we strongly encourage you to regularly review the latest research in organizational behavior. More academic work can be found in journals such as the *Academy of Management Journal, Academy of Management Review, Administrative Science Quarterly, Human Relations, Journal of Applied Psychology, Journal of Management, Journal of Organizational Behavior,* and *Leadership Quarterly.* For more practical interpretations of OB research findings, you may want to read the *Academy of Management Executive, California Management Review, Harvard Business Review, Organizational Dynamics,* and the *Sloan Management Review.*

Endnotes

1. J. A. Byrne, "Executive Sweat," *Forbes,* May 20, 1985, pp. 198–200.

2. See D. P. Schwab, *Research Methods for Organizational Behavior* (Mahwah, NJ: Lawrence Erlbaum Associates, 1999); and S. G. Rogelberg (ed.), *Blackwell Handbook of Research Methods in Industrial and Organizational Psychology* (Malden, MA: Blackwell, 2002).

3. B. M. Staw and G. R. Oldham, "Reconsidering Our Dependent Variables: A Critique and Empirical Study," *Academy of Management Journal,* December 1978, pp. 539–559; and B. M. Staw, "Organizational Behavior: A Review and Reformulation of the Field's Outcome Variables," in M. R. Rosenzweig and L. W. Porter (eds.), *Annual Review of Psychology,* vol. 35 (Palo Alto, CA: Annual Reviews, 1984), pp. 627–666.

4. R. S. Blackburn, "Experimental Design in Organizational Settings," in J. W. Lorsch (ed.), *Handbook of Organizational Behavior* (Upper Saddle River, NJ: Prentice Hall, 1987), pp. 127–128; and F. L. Schmidt, C. Viswesvaran, D. S. Ones, "Reliability Is Not Validity and Validity Is Not Reliability," *Personnel Psychology,* Winter 2000, pp. 901–912.

5. G. R. Weaver, L. K. Trevino, and P. L. Cochran, "Corporate Ethics Practices in the Mid-1990's: An Empirical Study of the Fortune 1000," *Journal of Business Ethics,* February 1999, pp. 283–294.

6. S. Milgram, *Obedience to Authority* (New York: Harper & Row, 1974). For a critique of this research, see T. Blass, "Understanding Behavior in the Milgram Obedience Experiment: The Role of Personality, Situations, and Their Interactions," *Journal of Personality and Social Psychology,* March 1991, pp. 398–413.

7. See, for example, W. N. Kaghan, A. L. Strauss, S. R. Barley, M. Y. Brannen, and R. J. Thomas, "The Practice and Uses of Field Research in the 21st Century Organization," *Journal of Management Inquiry,* March 1999, pp. 67–81.

8. A. D. Stajkovic and F. Luthans, "A Meta-Analysis of the Effects of Organizational Behavior Modification on Task Performance, 1975–1995," *Academy of Management Journal,* October 1997, pp. 1122–1149.

9. See, for example, K. Zakzanis, "The Reliability of Meta Analytic Review," *Psychological Reports,* August 1998, pp. 215–222; C. Ostroff and D. A. Harrison, "Meta-Analysis, Level of Analysis, and Best Estimates of Population Correlations: Cautions for Interpreting Meta-Analytic Results in Organizational Behavior," *Journal of Applied Psychology,* April 1999, pp. 260–270; R. Rosenthal and M. R. DiMatteo, "Meta-Analysis: Recent Developments in Quantitative Methods for Literature Reviews," in S. T. Fiske, D. L. Schacter, and C. Zahn-Wacher (eds.), *Annual Review of Psychology,* vol. 52 (Palo Alto, CA: Annual Reviews, 2001), pp. 59–82; and F. L. Schmidt and J. E. Hunter, "Meta-Analysis," in N. Anderson, D. S. Ones, H. K. Sinangil, and C. Viswesvaran (eds.), *Handbook of Industrial, Work & Organizational Psychology,* vol. 1 (Thousand Oaks, CA: Sage, 2001), pp. 51–70.

10. For more on ethical issues in research, see T. L. Beauchamp, R. R. Faden, R. J. Wallace, Jr., and L. Walters (eds.), *Ethical Issues in Social Science Research* (Baltimore, MD: Johns Hopkins University Press, 1982); and J. G. Adair, "Ethics of Psychological Research: New Policies, Continuing Issues, New Concerns," *Canadian Psychology,* February 2001, pp. 25–37.

11. J. Kifner, "Scholar Sets Off Gastronomic False Alarm," *New York Times,* September 8, 2001, p. A1.

Comprehensive Cases

Managing Motivation in a Difficult Economy

Learning Goals

In this case, you'll have an opportunity to assess a motivational program designed to reenergize a troubled company's workforce. Acting on behalf of the company's executive board, you'll evaluate the board's current strategy based on survey data. You'll also advise board members about improving the effectiveness of this program based on what you've learned about goal-setting and motivation in organizations.

Major Topic Areas

- Changing nature of work
- Diversity and age
- Goal-setting
- Organizational downsizing
- Organizational justice

The Scenario

Morgan-Moe's drug stores are in trouble. A major regional player in the retail industry, the company has hundreds of stores in the upper Midwest. Unfortunately, a sharp decline in the region's manufacturing economy has put management in a serious financial bind. Revenues have been consistently dwindling. Customers spend less, and the stores have had to switch their focus to very low-margin commodities, such as milk and generic drugs, rather than the high-margin impulse-buy items that used to be the company's bread and butter. The firm has had to close quite a few locations, reversing its expansion plans for the first time since it incorporated.

Being that this is uncharted territory for the company, Jim Claussen, vice president for human relations, had been struggling with how to address the issue with employees. As the company's fortunes worsened, he could see that employees were becoming more and more disaffected. Their insecurity about their jobs was taking a toll on attitudes. The company's downsizing was big news, and the employees didn't like what they were hearing.

Media reports of Morgan-Moe's store closings have focused on the lack of advance notice or communication from the company's corporate offices, as well as the lack of severance payments for departing employees. In the absence of official information, rumors and gossip have spread like wildfire among remaining employees. A few angry blogs developed by laid-off employees, like IHateMorganMoe.blogspot.com, have made the morale and public relations picture even worse.

Morgan-Moe is changing in other ways as well. The average age of its workforce is increasing rapidly. A couple of factors have contributed to this shift. First, fewer qualified young people are around because many families have moved south to find jobs. Second, stores have been actively encouraged to hire older workers, such as retirees looking for some supplemental income. Managers are very receptive to these older workers because they are more mature, miss fewer days of work, and do not have child care responsibilities. They are also often more qualified than younger workers because they have more experience, sometimes in the managerial or executive ranks.

These older workers have been a great asset to the company in troubled times, but they are especially likely to leave if things get bad. If these older workers start to leave the company, taking their hard-earned experience with them, it seems likely that Morgan-Moe will sink deeper toward bankruptcy.

The System

Claussen wasn't quite sure how to respond to employees' sense of hopelessness and fear until a friend gave him a book entitled *Man's Search for Meaning*. The book was written by a psychologist named Victor Frankl, who survived the concentration camps at Auschwitz. Frankl found that those who had a clear sense of purpose, a reason to live, were more likely to persevere in the face of nearly unspeakable suffering. Something about this book, and its advocacy of finding meaning and direction as a way to triumph over adversity, really stuck with Claussen. He thought he might be able to apply its lessons to his workforce. He proposed the idea of a new direction for management to the company's executive committee, and they reluctantly agreed to try his suggestions.

Over the last 6 months, stores throughout the company have used a performance management system that, as Claussen says, "gets people to buy into the idea of performing so that they can see some real results in their stores. It's all about seeing that your work serves a broader purpose. I read about how some companies have been sharing store performance information with employees to get them to understand what their jobs really mean and participate in making changes, and I thought that was something we'd be able to do."

The HR team came up with five options for the management system. Corporate allowed individual managers to choose the option they thought would work best with their employees so that managers wouldn't feel too much like a rapid change was being forced on them. Program I is opting out of the new idea, continuing to stay the course and providing employees with little to no information or opportunities for participation. Program II tracks employee absence and sick leave and shares that information with individual employees, giving them feedback about things they can control. Management takes no further action. Program III tracks sales and inventory replacement rates across shifts. As in Program II, information is shared with employees, but without providing employee feedback about absence and sick leave. Program IV, the most comprehensive, tracks the same information as Programs II and III. Managers communicate it in weekly brainstorming sessions, during which employees try to determine what they can do better in the future and make suggestions for improving store performance. Program V keeps the idea of brainstorming but doesn't provide employees with information about their behavior or company profits.

Since implementing the system, Claussen has spoken with several managers about what motivated them to choose the program they did. Artie Washington, who chose Program IV, said, "I want to have my employees' input on how to keep the store running smoothly. Everybody worries about their job security in this economy. Letting them know what's going on and giving them ways to change things keeps them involved."

Betty Alvarez couldn't disagree more. She selected Program I. "I would rather have my employees doing their jobs than going to meetings to talk about doing their jobs. That's what management is for." Michael

Ostremski, another proponent of Program I, added, "It's okay for the employees to feel a little uncertain—if they think we're in the clear, they'll slack off. If they think we're in trouble, they'll give up."

Cal Martins also questions the need to provide information to the whole team, but he chose Program II. "A person should know where he or she stands in the job, but they don't have to know about everyone else. It creates unnecessary tension."

This is somewhat similar to Cindy Ang's reason for picking Program V. "When we have our brainstorming meetings, I learn what they [the employees] think is most pressing, not what some spreadsheet says. It gives me a better feel for what's going on in my store. Numbers count, of course, but they don't tell you everything. I was also a little worried that employees would be upset if they saw that we aren't performing well."

Results to Date

Claussen is convinced the most elaborate procedure (Program IV) is the most effective, but not everyone in the executive committee is won over by his advocacy. Although they have supported the test implementation of the system because it appears to have relatively low costs, others on the committee want to see results. CEO Jean Masterson has asked for a complete breakdown of the performance of the various stores over the past 4 years. She's especially interested in seeing how sales figures and turnover rates have been affected by the new program.

The company has been collecting data in spreadsheets on sales and turnover rates, and it prepared the following report, which also estimates the dollar cost of staff time taken up in each method. These costs are based on the number of hours employees spend working on the program multiplied by their wage rate. Estimates of turnover, profit, and staff time are collected per store. Profit and turnover data include means and standard deviations across locations; profit is net of the monthly time cost. Turnover information refers to the percentage of employees who either quit or are terminated in a month.

To see if any patterns emerged in managers' selection of programs, the company calculated relationships between program selection and various attributes of the stores. Program I was selected most frequently by the oldest stores and those in the most economically distressed areas. Programs II and III were selected most frequently by stores in urban areas and in areas where the workforce was younger on average. Programs IV and V were selected most frequently in stores in rural areas, and especially where the workforce is older on average.

Program	Methods	Number of Stores	Average Turnover	Weekly Profit per Month	Monthly Staff Time Cost
Program I	Traditional management	83	Mean = 30% SD = 10%	Mean = $5,700 SD = $3,000	None
Program II	Share absence and sick leave	27	Mean = 23% SD = 14%	Mean = $7,000 SD = $5,800	$1,960
Program III	Share sales and inventory	35	Mean = 37% SD = 20%	Mean = $11,000 SD = $2,700	$2,440
Program IV	Share information and brainstorm	67	Mean = 17% SD = 20%	Mean = $13,000 SD = $3,400	$3,420
Program V	Brainstorm without sharing information	87	Mean = 21% SD = 12%	Mean = $14,000 SD = $2,400	$2,750

Your Assignment

Your task is to prepare a report for the company's executive committee on the effectiveness of these programs. Make certain it is in the form of a professional business document. Your audience won't necessarily know about the organizational principles you're describing, so make sure you provide detailed explanations that someone in a real business can understand.

When you write, make sure you touch on the following points:

1. Consider the five management systems as variables in an experiment. Identify the independent and dependent variables, and explain how they are related to one another.
2. Based on the discussion of independent and dependent variables in the textbook, is there anything else you'd like to measure as an outcome?
3. Look over the data and decide which method of management appears most effective in generating revenues and reducing turnover, and why. Which methods appear least effective, and why?
4. Are there any concerns you have about these data?
   a. Does a comparison of the number of stores using each method influence your conclusions at all?
   b. Does the fact that managers are selecting the specific program to use (including Program I,

which continues the status quo) affect the inferences you can draw about program success?
   c. What are the advantages of randomly assigning different conditions to the stores instead of using this self-selection process?
5. How does the changing nature of the workforce and the economy, described in your textbook and in the case, affect your conclusions about how to manage retail employees? Does the participation of a more experienced workforce help or hurt these programs? Why might these programs work differently in an economy that isn't doing so poorly?
6. Claussen essentially designed the program on his own, with very little research into goal-setting and motivation. Based on your textbook, how well has he done? Which parts of the program appear to fit well with research evidence on goal-setting? What parts would you change to get more substantial improvements in employee motivation?
7. Describe the feelings employees might have when these systems are implemented that could help or hinder the program's success. What advice would you give managers about how to implement the programs so they match the principles of organizational justice described in your textbook?

Repairing Jobs That Fail to Satisfy

Learning Goals

Companies often divide up work as a way to improve efficiency, but specialization can lead to negative consequences. DrainFlow is a company that has effectively used specialization to reduce costs relative to its competitors' costs for years, but rising customer complaints suggest the firm's strong position may be slipping. After reading the case, you will suggest some ways it can create more interesting work for employees. You'll also tackle the problem of finding people qualified and ready to perform the multiple responsibilities required in these jobs.

Major Topic Areas

- Job design
- Job satisfaction
- Personality
- Emotional labor

The Scenario

DrainFlow is a large residential and commercial plumbing maintenance firm that operates around the United States. It has been a major player in residential plumbing for decades, and its familiar rhyming motto, "When Your Drain Won't Go, Call DrainFlow," has been plastered on billboards since the 1960s.

Lee Reynaldo has been a regional manager at DrainFlow for about 2 years. She used to work for a newer competing chain, Lightning Plumber, that has been drawing more and more customers from DrainFlow. Although her job at DrainFlow pays more, Lee isn't happy with the way things are going. She's noticed the work environment just isn't as vital or energetic as the environment she saw at Lightning.

Lee thinks the problem is that employees aren't motivated to provide the type of customer service Lightning Plumber employees offer. She recently sent surveys to customers to collect information about performance, and the data confirmed her fears. Although 60 percent of respondents said they were satisfied with their experience and would use DrainFlow again, 40 percent felt their experience was not good, and 30 percent said

they would use a competitor the next time they had a plumbing problem.

Lee is wondering whether DrainFlow's job design might be contributing to its problems in retaining customers. DrainFlow has about 2,000 employees in four basic job categories: plumbers, plumber's assistants, order processors, and billing representatives. This structure is designed to keep costs as low as possible. Plumbers make very high wages, whereas plumber's assistants make about one-quarter of what a licensed plumber makes. Using plumber's assistants is therefore a very cost-effective strategy that has enabled DrainFlow to easily undercut the competition when it comes to price. Order processors make even less than assistants but about the same as billing processors. All work is very specialized, but employees are often dependent on another job category to perform at their most efficient level.

Like most plumbing companies, DrainFlow gets business mostly from the Yellow Pages and the Internet. Customers either call in to describe a plumbing problem or submit an online request for plumbing services, receiving a return call with information within 24 hours. In either case, DrainFlow's order processors listen to the customer's description of the problem to determine whether a plumber or a plumber's assistant should make the service call. The job is then assigned accordingly, and a service provider goes to the location. When the job has been completed, via cell phone a billing representative relays the fee to the service rep, who presents a bill to the customer for payment. Billing representatives can take customers' credit card payments by phone or e-mail an invoice for online payment.

The Problem

Although specialization does cut costs significantly, Lee is worried about customer dissatisfaction. According to her survey, about 25 percent of customer contacts ended in no service call because customers were confused by the diagnostic questions the order processors asked and because the order processors did not have sufficient knowledge or skill to explain the situation. That means fully one in four people who call DrainFlow to hire a plumber are worse than dissatisfied: they aren't customers at all! The remaining 75 percent of calls that did end in a customer service encounter resulted in other problems.

The most frequent complaints Lee found in the customer surveys were about response time and cost, especially when the wrong person was sent to a job. A plumber's assistant cannot complete a more technically complicated job. The appointment has to be rescheduled, and the customer's time and the staff's time have been wasted. The resulting delay often caused customers in these situations to decline further contact with DrainFlow—many of them decided to go with Lightning Plumber.

"When I arrive at a job I can't take care of," says plumber's assistant Jim Larson, "the customer gets ticked off. They thought they were getting a licensed plumber, since they were calling for a plumber. Telling them they have to have someone else come out doesn't go over well."

On the other hand, when a plumber responds to a job easily handled by a plumber's assistant, the customer is still charged at the plumber's higher pay rate. Licensed plumber Luis Berger also does not like being in the position of giving customers bad news. "If I get called out to do something like snake a drain, the customer isn't expecting a hefty bill. I'm caught between a rock and a hard place—I don't set the rates or make the appointments, but I'm the one who gets it from the customer." Plumbers also resent being sent to do such simple work.

Susie McCarty is one of DrainFlow's order processors. She's frustrated too when the wrong person is sent to a job but feels she and the other order processors are doing the best they can. "We have a survey we're supposed to follow with the calls to find out what the problem is and who needs to take the job," she explains. "The customers don't know that we have a standard form, so they think we can answer all their questions. Most of us don't know any more about plumbing than the caller. If they don't use the terms on the survey, we don't understand what they're talking about. A plumber would, but we're not plumbers; we just take the calls."

Customer service issues also involve the billing representatives. They are the ones who have to keep contacting customers about payment. "It's not my fault the wrong guy was sent," says Elizabeth Monty. "If two guys went out, that's two trips. If a plumber did the work, you pay plumber rates. Some of these customers don't get that I didn't take their first call, and so I get yelled at." The billing representatives also complain that they see only the tail end of the process, so they don't know what the original call entailed. The job is fairly impersonal, and much of the work is recording customer complaints. Remember—40 percent of customers aren't satisfied, and it's the billing representatives who take the brunt of their negative reactions on the phone.

As you can probably tell, all employees have to engage in emotional labor, as described in your textbook, and many lack the skills or personality traits to complete the customer interaction component of their jobs. They aren't trained to provide customer service, and they see their work mostly in technical, or mechanical, terms. Quite a few are actually anxious about speaking directly with customers. The office staff (order processors and billing representatives) realize customer service is part of their job, but they also find dealing with negative feedback from customers and co-workers taxing.

A couple of years ago a management consulting company was hired to survey DrainFlow worker attitudes. The results showed they were less satisfied than workers in other comparable jobs. The following table provides a breakdown of respondent satisfaction levels across a number of categories:

	DrainFlow Plumbers	DrainFlow Plumber Assistants	DrainFlow Office Workers	Average Plumber	Average Office Workers
I am satisfied with the work I am asked to do.	3.7	2.5	2.5	4.3	3.5
I am satisfied with my working conditions.	3.8	2.4	3.7	4.1	4.2
I am satisfied with my interactions with co-workers.	3.5	3.2	2.7	3.8	3.9
I am satisfied with my interactions with my supervisor.	2.5	2.3	2.2	3.5	3.4

The information about average plumbers and average office workers is taken from the management consulting company's records of other companies. They aren't exactly surprising, given some of the complaints DrainFlow employees have made. Top management is worried about these results, but they haven't been able to formulate a solution. The traditional DrainFlow culture has been focused on cost containment, and the "soft stuff" like employee satisfaction hasn't been a major issue.

The Proposed Solution

The company is in trouble, and as revenues shrink and the cost savings that were supposed to be achieved by dividing up work fail to materialize, a change seems to be in order.

Lee is proposing using cash rewards to improve performance among employees. She thinks if employees were paid based on work outcomes, they'd work harder to satisfy customers. Because it's not easy to measure how satisfied people are with the initial call-in, Lee would like to give the order processors a small reward for every 20 calls successfully completed. For the hands-on work, she'd like to have each billing representative collect information about customer satisfaction for each completed call. If no complaints are made and the job is handled promptly, a moderate cash reward would be given to the plumber or plumber's assistant. If the customer indicates real satisfaction with the service, a larger cash reward would be provided.

Lee also wants to find people who are a better fit with the company's new goals. Current hiring procedure relies on unstructured interviews with each location's general manager, and little consistency is found in the way these managers choose employees. Most lack training in customer service and organizational behavior. Lee thinks it would be better if hiring methods were standardized across all branches in her region to help managers identify recruits who can actually succeed in the job.

Your Assignment

Your task is to prepare a report for Lee on the potential effectiveness of her cash reward and structured-interview programs. Make certain it is in the form of a professional business document that you'd actually give to an experienced manager at this level of a fairly large corporation. Lee is very smart when it comes to managing finances and running a plumbing business, but she won't necessarily know about the organizational behavior principles you're describing. Because any new proposals must be passed through top management, you should also address their concerns about cost containment. You'll need to make a strong evidence-based financial case that changing the management style will benefit the company.

When you write, make sure you touch on the following points:

1. Although it's clear employees are not especially satisfied with their work, do you think this is a reason for concern? Does research suggest satisfied workers are actually better at their jobs? Are any other behavioral outcomes associated with job satisfaction?
2. Using job characteristics theory, explain why the present system of job design may be contributing to employee dissatisfaction. Describe some ways you could help employees feel more satisfied with their work by redesigning their jobs.
3. Lee has a somewhat vague idea about how to implement the cash rewards system. Describe some of the specific ways you would make the reward system work better, based on the case.
4. Explain the advantages and disadvantages of using financial incentives in a program of this nature. What, if any, potential problems might arise if people are given money for achieving customer satisfaction goals? What other types of incentives might be considered?
5. Create a specific plan to assess whether the reward system is working. What are the dependent variables that should change if the system works? How will you go about measuring success?
6. What types of hiring recommendations would you make to find people better suited for these jobs? Which Big Five personality traits would be useful for the customer service responsibilities and emotional labor?

Building a Coalition

Learning Goals

Many of the most important organizational behavior challenges require coordinating plans and goals among groups. This case describes a multiorganizational effort, but the same principles of accommodation and compromise also apply when trying to work with multiple divisions within a single organization. You'll create a blueprint for managing a complex development team's progress, steering team members away from negative conflicts and toward productive discussion. You'll also be asked to help create a new message for executives so they can lead effectively.

Major Topic Areas

- Group dynamics
- Maximizing team performance
- Organizational culture
- Integrative bargaining

The Scenario

The Woodson Foundation, a large nonprofit social service agency, is teaming up with the public school system in Washington, D.C., to improve student outcomes. There's ample room for improvement. The schools have problems with truancy, low student performance, and crime. New staff quickly burn out as their initial enthusiasm for helping students is blunted by the harsh realities they encounter in the classroom. Turnover among new teachers is very high, and many of the best and brightest are the most likely to leave for schools that aren't as troubled.

The plan is to create an experimental after-school program that will combine the Woodson Foundation's skill in raising private money and coordinating community leaders with the educational expertise of school staff. Ideally, the system will be financially self-sufficient, which is important because less money is available for schools than in the past. After several months of negotiation, the leaders of the Woodson Foundation and the school system have agreed that the best course is to develop a new agency that will draw on resources from both organizations. The Woodson foundation will provide logistical support and program development and measurement staff; the school system will provide classrooms and teaching staff.

The first stage in bringing this new plan to fruition is the formation of an executive development team. This team will span multiple functional areas and establish the operating plan for improving school performance. Its cross-organizational nature means representatives from both the Woodson Foundation and the school district must participate. The National Coalition for Parental Involvement in Education (NCPIE) is also going to be a major partner in the program, acting as a representative for parents on behalf of the PTA.

Conflict and Agreement in the Development Team

While it would be perfect if all the groups could work together easily to improve student outcomes, there is little doubt some substantive conflicts will arise. Each group has its own interests, and in some cases these are directly opposed to one another.

School district representatives want to ensure the new jobs will be unionized and will operate in a way consistent with current school board policies. They are very concerned that if Woodson assumes too dominant a role, the school board won't be able to control the operations of the new system. The complexity of the school system has led to the development of a highly complex bureaucratic structure over time, and administrators want to make sure their policies and procedures will still hold for teachers in these programs even outside the regular school day. They also worry that jobs going into the new system will take funding from other school district jobs.

Woodson, founded by entrepreneur Theodore Woodson around 1910, still bears the hallmarks of its founder's way of doing business. Woodson emphasized efficiency and experimentation in everything he did. Many of the foundation's charities have won awards for minimizing costs while still providing excellent services. Their focus on using hard data to measure performance for all their initiatives is not consistent with the school district culture.

Finally, the NCPIE is driven by a mission to increase parental control. The organization believes that when communities are able to drive their own educational methods, students and parents are better able to achieve success together. The organization is strongly committed to celebrating diversity along racial, gender, ethnic, and disability status categories. Its members are most interested in the process by which changes are made, ensuring everyone has the ability to weigh in.

Some demographic diversity issues complicate the team's situation. Most of the students served by the Washington, D.C., school district are African American, along with large populations of Caucasians and Hispanics. The NCPIE makeup generally matches the demographic diversity of the areas served by the public schools. The Woodson foundation, based in northern Virginia, is predominantly staffed by Caucasian professionals. There is some concern with the idea that a new group that does not understand the demographic concerns of the community will be so involved in a major change in educational administration. The leadership of the new program will have to be able to present an effective message for generating enthusiasm for the program across diverse stakeholder groups.

Although the groups differ in important ways, it's also worth considering what they have in common. All are interested in meeting the needs of students. All would like to increase student learning. The school system does benefit from anything that increases student test scores. And the Woodson Foundation and NCPIE are united in their desire to see more parents engaged in the system.

Candidates for the Development Team

The development team will consist of three individuals—HR representatives from the Woodson Foundation, the schools, and the NCPIE—who have prepared the following list of potential candidates for consideration.

Victoria Adams is the superintendent of schools for Washington, D.C. She spearheaded the initial communication with the Woodson Foundation and has been building support among teachers and principals. She thinks the schools and the foundation need to have larger roles than the parents and communities. "Of course we want their involvement and support, but as the professionals, we should have more say when it comes to making decisions and implementing programs. We don't want to shut anyone out, but we have to be realistic about what the parents can do."

Duane Hardy has been a principal in the Washington area for more than 15 years. He also thinks the schools should have the most power. "We're the ones who work with these kids every day. I've watched class sizes get bigger, and scores and graduation rates go down. Yes, we need to fix this, but these outside groups can't understand the limitations we're dealing with. We have the community, the politicians, the taxpayers—everyone watching what we're doing, everyone thinking

they know what's best. The parents, at least, have more of a stake in this."

"The most important thing is the kids," says second-year teacher Ari Kaufman. He is well liked by his students but doesn't get along well with other faculty members. He's seen as a "squeaky wheel." "The schools need change so badly. And how did they get this way? From too little outside involvement."

Community organizer Mason Dupree doesn't like the level of bureaucracy either. He worries that the school's answer to its problems is to throw more money at them. "I know these kids. I grew up in these neighborhoods. My parents knew every single teacher I had. The schools wanted our involvement then. Now all they want is our money. And I wouldn't mind giving it to them if I thought it would be used responsibly, not spent on raises for people who haven't shown they can get the job done."

Meredith Watson, with the Woodson Foundation, agrees the schools have become less focused on the families. A former teacher, she left the field of education after being in the classroom for 6 years. "There is so much waste in the system," she complains. "Jobs are unnecessarily duplicated, change processes are needlessly convoluted. Unless you're an insider already, you can't get anything done. These parents want to be involved. They know their kids best."

Unlike her NCPIE colleagues, Candace Sharpe thinks the schools are doing the best they can. She is a county social worker, relatively new to the D.C. area. "Parents say they want to be involved but then don't follow through. *We* need to step it up, *we* need to lead the way. Lasting change doesn't come from the outside, it comes from the home."

Victor Martinez has been at the Woodson Foundation for 10 years, starting as an intern straight out of college. "It's sometimes hard to see a situation when you're in the thick of it," he explains. "Nobody likes to be told they're doing something wrong, but sometimes it has to be said. We all know there are flaws in the system. We can't keep the status quo. It just isn't cutting it."

Strategies for the Program Team

Once the basic membership and principles for the development team have been established, the program team would also like to develop a handbook for those who will be running the new program. Ideally, this set of principles can help train new leaders to create an inspirational message that will facilitate success. The actual content of the program and the nature of the message will be hammered out by the development team, but it is still possible to generate some overriding principles for the program team in advance of these decisions.

Your Assignment

The Woodson Foundation, the NCPIE, and the schools have asked you to provide some information about how to form teams effectively. They would like your response to explain what should be done at each step of the way, from the selection of appropriate team members to setting group priorities and goals, setting deadlines, and describing effective methods for resolving conflicts that arise. After this, they'd like you to prepare a brief set of principles for leaders of the newly established program. That means you will have two audiences: the development team, which will receive one report on how it can effectively design the program, and the program team, which will receive one report on how it can effectively lead the new program.

The following points should help you form a comprehensive message for the development team:

1. The development team will be more effective if members have some idea about how groups and teams typically operate. Review the dominant perspectives on team formation and performance from the chapters in the book for the committee so it can know what to expect.
2. Given the profiles of candidates for the development team, provide suggestions for who would likely be a good group member and who might be less effective in this situation. Be sure you are using the research on groups and teams in the textbook to defend your choices.
3. Using principles from the chapters on groups and teams, describe how you will advise the team to manage conflict effectively.
4. Describe how integrative negotiation strategies might achieve joint goals for the development team.

The following points should help you form a message for the program team:

1. Leaders of the new combined organization should have a good idea of the culture of the school district, the NCPIE, and the Woodson Foundation because they will need to manage relationships with all three groups on an ongoing basis. How would you describe the culture of these various stakeholder organizations? Use concepts from the chapter on organizational culture to describe how they differ and how they are similar.
2. Consider how leaders of the new program can generate a transformational message and encourage employee and parent trust. Using material from the chapter on leadership, describe how you would advise leaders to accomplish these ends.
3. Given the potential for demographic fault lines in negotiating these changes, what would you advise as a strategy for managing diversity issues for program leaders? ❧

CASE 4 Boundaryless Organizations

Learning Goals

The multinational organization is an increasingly common and important part of the economy. This case takes you into the world of a cutting-edge music software business seeking success across three very different national and organizational cultures. Its managers need to make important decisions about how to structure work processes so employees can be satisfied and productive doing very different tasks.

Major Topic Areas

*   Organizational structure and boundaryless organizations
*   Organizational culture
*   Human resources
*   Organizational socialization

The Scenario

Newskool Grooves is a transnational company developing music software. The software is used to compose music, play recordings in clubs, and produce albums. Founder and CEO Gerd Finger is, understandably, the company's biggest fan. "I started this company from nothing, from just me, my ideas, and my computer. I love music—love playing music, love writing programs for making music, love listening to music—and the money is nice, too." Gerd says he never wanted to work for someone else, to give away his ideas and let someone else profit from them. He wanted to keep control over them, and their image. "Newskool Grooves is always ahead of the pack. In this business, if you can't keep up, you're out. And we are the company everyone else must keep up with. Everyone knows when they get something from us, they're getting only the best and the newest."

The company headquarters are in Berlin, the nerve center for the organization, where new products are developed and the organizational strategy is established. Newskool outsources a great deal of its coding work to programmers in Kiev, Ukraine. Its marketing efforts are increasingly based in its Los Angeles offices. This division of labor is at least partially based on technical expertise and cost issues. The German team excels at design and production tasks. Because most of Newskool's customers are English speakers, the Los Angeles office has been the best group to write ads and market products. The Kiev offices are filled with outstanding programmers who don't require the very high rates of compensation you'd find in German or U.S. offices. The combination of high-tech software, rapid reorganization, and outsourcing makes Newskool the very definition of a boundaryless organization.

Gerd also makes the final decision on hiring every employee for the company and places a heavy emphasis on independent work styles. "Why would I want to put my company in the hands of people I can't count on?" he asks with a laugh. "They have to believe in what we're doing here, really understand our direction and be able to go with it. I'm not the babysitter, I'm not the school master handing out homework. School time is over. This is the real world."

The Work Culture

Employees want to work at this company because it's cutting edge. Newskool's software is used by a number of dance musicians and DJs, who have been the firm's core market, seeing it as a relatively expensive but very high-quality and innovative brand. Whenever the rest of the market for music software goes in one direction, it seems like Newskool heads in a completely different direction in an effort to keep itself separate from the pack. This strategy has tended to pay off. While competitors develop similar products and therefore need to continually lower their prices to compete with one another, Newskool has kept revenues high by creating completely new types of products that don't face this type of price competition.

Unfortunately, computer piracy has eroded Newskool's ability to make money with just software-based music tools, and it has had to move into the production of hardware, such as drum machines and amplifiers that incorporate its computer technology. Making this massive market change might be challenging for some companies, but for an organization that reinvents itself every 2 or 3 years like Newskool does, the bigger fight is a constant war against stagnation and rigidity.

The organization has a very decentralized culture. With only 115 employees, the original management philosophy of allowing all employees to participate in decision making and innovation is still the lifeblood of the company's culture. One developer notes, "At Newskool, they want you to be part of the process. If you are a person who wants to do what you're told at work, you're in trouble. Most times, they can't tell you what they want you to do next—they don't even know what comes next! That's why they hire employees who are creative, people who can try to make the next thing happen. It's challenging, but a lot of us think it's very much an exciting environment."

The Boundaryless Environment

Because so much of the work can be performed on computers, Gerd decided early to allow employees to work outside the office. The senior management in Berlin and Los Angeles are both quite happy with this arrangement. Because some marketing work does require face-to-face contact, the Los Angeles office has weekly in-person meetings. Employees who like Newskool are happiest when they can work through the night and sleep most of the day, firing up their computers to get work done at the drop of a hat. Project discussions often happen via social networking on the company's intranet.

The Kiev offices have been less eager to work with the boundaryless model. Managers say their computer programmers find working with so little structure rather uncomfortable. They are more used to the idea of a strong leadership structure and well-defined work processes.

"When I started," says one manager, "Gerd said getting in touch with him would be no problem, getting in touch with L.A. would be no problem. We're small, we're family, he said. Well, it is a problem. When I call L.A., they say to wait until their meeting day. I can't always wait until they decide to get together. I call Gerd—he says, 'Figure it out.' Then when I do, he says it isn't right and we have to start again. If he just told me in the first place, we would have done it."

Some recent events have also shaken up the company's usual way of doing business. Developers in the corporate offices had a major communications breakdown about their hardware DJ controller, which required many hours of discussion to resolve. It seems that people who seldom met face to face had all made progress—but had moved in opposite directions! To test and design the company's hardware products, employees apparently need to do more than send each other code; sometimes they need to collaborate face to face. Some spirited disagreements have been voiced within the organization about how to move forward in this new environment.

The offices are experiencing additional difficulties. Since the shift to newer products, Sandra Pelham in the Los Angeles office has been more critical of the company. "With the software, we were more limited in the kinds of advertising media we could access. So now, with the hardware—real instruments—we finally thought, 'All right, this is something we can work with!' We had a whole slate of musicians and DJs and producers to contact for endorsements, but Gerd said, 'No way.' He didn't want customers who only cared that a celebrity liked us. He scrapped the whole campaign. He says we're all about creativity and doing our own thing—until we don't want to do things his way."

Although the organization is not without problems, there is little question Newskool has been a standout success in the computer music software industry. While many are shuttering their operations, Newskool is using its market power to push forward the next generation of electronic music-making tools. As Gerd Finger puts it, "Once the rest of the industry has gotten together and figured out how they're all going to cope with change, they'll look around and see that we're already three miles ahead of them down the road to the future."

Your Assignment

Gerd has asked for your advice on how to keep his organization successful. He wants to have some sort of benchmark for how other boundaryless organizations in the tech sector stay competitive despite the challenges of so many workers heading in so many different directions. You will need to prepare a report for the company's executive committee. Your report should read like a proposal to a corporate executive who has a great deal of knowledge about the technical aspects of his company but might not have much knowledge of organizational behavior.

When you write, make sure you touch on the following points:

1. Identify some of the problems likely to occur in a boundaryless organization like Newskool Grooves. What are the advantages of boundaryless organizations?

2. Consider some of the cultural issues that will affect a company operating in such different parts of the world and whose employees may not be representative of the national cultures of each country. Are the conflicts you observe a function of the different types of work people have to perform?

3. Based on what you know about motivation and personality, what types of people are likely to be satisfied in each area of the company? Use concepts from job characteristics theory and the emerging social relationships perspective on work to describe what might need to change to increase employee satisfaction in all areas.

4. What types of human resources practices need to be implemented in this sort of organization? What principles of selection and hiring are likely to be effective? Which Big Five traits and abilities might Newskool supervisors want to use for selection?

5. What kind of performance measures might you want to see for each office?

6. How can the company establish a socialization program that will maximize employee creativity and independence? Do employees in all its locations need equal levels of creativity?

The Stress of Caring

Learning Goals

One of the most consistent changes in the structure of work over the past few decades has been a shift from a manufacturing economy to a service economy. More workers are now engaged in jobs that include providing care and assistance, especially in education and medicine. This work is satisfying for some people, but it can also be highly stressful. In the following scenario, consider how a company in the nursing care industry is responding to the challenges of the new environment.

Major Topic Areas

- Stress
- Organizational change
- Emotions
- Leadership

The Scenario

Parkway Nursing Care is an organization facing a massive change. The company was founded in 1972 with just two nursing homes in Phoenix, Arizona. The company was very successful, and throughout the 1980s it continued to turn a consistent profit while slowly acquiring or building 30 more units. This low-profile approach changed forever in 1993 when venture capitalist Robert Quine decided to make a major investment in expanding Parkway in return for a portion of its profits over the coming years. The number of nursing homes exploded, and Parkway was operating 180 homes by the year 2000.

The company now has 220 facilities in the southwestern United States, with an average of 115 beds per facility and a total of nearly 30,000 employees. In addition to health care facilities, it also provides skilled in-home nursing care. Parkway is seen as one of the best care facilities in the region, and it has won numerous awards for its achievements in the field.

As members of the Baby Boom generation become senior citizens, the need for skilled care will only increase. Parkway wants to make sure it is in a good position to meet this growing need. This means the company must continue expanding rapidly.

The pressure for growth is one significant challenge, but it's not the only one. The nursing home industry has come under increasing government scrutiny following investigations that turned up widespread patient abuse and billing fraud. Parkway has always had outstanding patient care, and no substantiated claim of abuse or neglect in any of its homes has ever been made, but the need for increased documentation will still affect the company. As the federal government tries to trim Medicare expenses, Parkway may face a reduction in funding.

The Problem

As growth has continued, Parkway has remained committed to providing dignity and health to all residents in its facilities. The board of directors wants to see renewed commitment to the firm's mission and core values, not a diffusion of its culture. Its members are worried there might be problems to address. Interviews with employees suggest there's plenty to worry about.

Shift leader Maxine Vernon has been with Parkway for 15 years. "Now that the government keeps a closer eye on our staffing levels, I've seen management do what it can to keep positions filled, and I don't always agree with who is hired. Some of the basic job skills can be taught, sure, but how to *care* for our patients—a lot of these new kids just don't pick up on that."

"The problem isn't with staff—it's with Parkway's focus on filling the beds," says nurse's aide Bobby Reed. "When I started here, Parkway's reputation was still about the service. Now it's about numbers. No one is intentionally negligent—there just are too many patients to see."

A recent college graduate with a B.A. in psychology, Dalton Manetti is more stressed than he expected he would be. "These aren't the sweet grannies you see in the movies. Our patients are demanding. They complain about everything, even about being called patients, probably because most of them think they shouldn't be here in the first place. A lot of times, their gripes amount to nothing, but we have to log them in anyway."

Carmen Frank has been with Parkway almost a year and is already considering finding a new job. "I knew there were going to be physical parts to this job, and I thought I'd be able to handle that. It's not like I was looking for a desk job, you know? I go home after every

Year	Patients	Injuries per Staff Member	Incidents per Patient	Certified Absences per Staff	Other Absence per Staff	Turnover Rate
2000	21,200	3.32	4.98	4.55	3.14	0.31
2001	22,300	3.97	5.37	5.09	3.31	0.29
2002	22,600	4.87	5.92	4.71	3.47	0.28
2003	23,100	4.10	6.36	5.11	3.61	0.35
2004	23,300	4.21	6.87	5.66	4.03	0.31
2005	23,450	5.03	7.36	5.33	3.45	0.28
2006	23,600	5.84	7.88	5.28	4.24	0.36
2007	24,500	5.62	8.35	5.86	4.06	0.33
2008	24,100	7.12	8.84	5.63	3.89	0.35
2009	25,300	6.95	9.34	6.11	4.28	0.35

shift with aches all over—my back, my arms, my legs. I've never had to take so much time off from a job because I hurt. And then when I come back, I feel like the rest of the staff thinks I'm weak."

"I started working here right out of high school because it was the best-paid of the jobs I could get," says Niecey Wilson. "I had no idea what I was getting myself into. Now I really like my job. Next year I'm going to start taking some night classes so I can move into another position. But some of the staff just think of this as any other job. They don't see the patients as people, more like inventory. If they want to work with inventory, they should get a job in retail."

Last month, the company's human resources department pulled the following information from its records at the request of the board of directors. The numbers provide some quantitative support for the concerns voiced by staff.

Injuries to staff occur mostly because of back strain from lifting patients. Patient incidents reflect injuries due to slips, falls, medication errors, or other accidents. Certified absences are days off from work due to medically verified illnesses or injuries. Other absences are days missed that are not due to injuries or illnesses; these are excused absences (unexcused absences are grounds for immediate firing).

Using Organizational Development to Combat Stress and Improve Performance

The company wants to use such organizational development methods as appreciative inquiry (AI) to create change and reenergize its sense of mission. As the chapter on organizational change explains, AI procedures systematically collect employee input and then use this information to create a change message everyone can support. The human resources department conducted focus groups, asking employees to describe some of their concerns and suggestions for the future. The focus groups highlighted a number of suggestions, although they don't all suggest movement in the same direction.

Many suggestions concerned schedule flexibility. One representative comment was this: "Most of the stress on this job comes because we can't take time off when we need it. The LPNs [licensed practical nurses, who do much of the care] and orderlies can't take time off when they need to, but a lot of them are single parents or primary caregivers for their own children. When they have to leave for child care responsibilities, the work suffers and there's no contingency plan to help smooth things over. Then everyone who is left has to work extra hard. The person who takes time off feels guilty, and there can be fights over taking time off. If we had some way of covering these emergency absences, we'd all be a lot happier, and I think the care would be a lot better."

Other suggestions proposed a better method for communicating information across shifts. Most of the documentation for shift work is done in large spiral notebooks. When a new shift begins, staff members say they don't have much time to check on what happened in the previous shift. Some younger caregivers would like to have a method that lets them document patient outcomes electronically because they type faster than they can write. The older caregivers are more committed to the paper-based process, in part because they think switching systems would require a lot of work. (Government regulations on health care reporting require that any documentation be made in a form that cannot be altered after the fact, to prevent covering up abuse, so specialized software systems must be used for electronic documentation.)

Finally, the nursing care staff believes its perspectives on patient care are seldom given an appropriate hearing. "We're the ones who are with the patients most of the time, but when it comes to doing this the right way, our point of view gets lost. We really could save a lot of money by eliminating some of these unnecessary routines and programs, but it's something management always just says it will consider." Staff members seem to want some way to provide suggestions for improvement, but it isn't clear what method they would prefer.

Your Assignment

Parkway has taken some initial steps toward a new direction, but clearly it has a lot of work left to do. You've been brought in as a change management consultant to help the company change its culture and respond to the stress that employees experience. Remember to create your report as if for the leadership of a major corporation.

When you write your recommendations, make sure you touch on the following points:

1. What do the data on employee injuries, incidents, absences, and turnover suggest to you? Is there reason for concern about the company's direction?
2. The company is going to be making some significant changes based on the AI process, and most change efforts are associated with resistance. What are the most common forms of resistance, and which would you expect to see at Parkway?
3. Given the board of directors' desire to reenergize the workforce, what advice would you provide for creating a leadership strategy? What leader behaviors should nursing home directors and nurse supervisors demonstrate?
4. What are the major sources of job stress at Parkway? What does the research on employee stress suggest you should do to help minimize the experience of psychological strain for employees? Create a plan for how to reduce stress among employees.
5. Based on the information collected in the focus groups, design a survey to hand out to employees. What sort of data should the survey gather? What types of data analysis methods would you like to employ for these data?

Indexes

Name Index

References followed by b indicate boxes;
e, exhibits; f, figure; n, notes

A

A. T. Kearney, 519
Abelson, M., 336n
Abosch, K. S., 268n
Abrams, D., 302n
Abramson, L. Y., 195n, 198n
Ackerman, P. L., 234n
Ackman, William, 448f
Acton, Lord, 436b
Adair, W. L., 365n, 477n
Adam, H., 467n
Adams, G. A., 572n
Adams, G. L., 441n, 443n
Adams, J. S., 235n
Adams, J. Stacy, 220
Addae, H. M., 614n
Addison, J. T., 268n
Adegbesan, J. A., 508n
Aditya, R. N., 402n, 403n, 404n
Adkins, B., 163n
Adler, N., 365n
Adler, N. J., 199n
Agle, B. R., 408n
Agnvall, E., 364n
Aguinis, H., 329n, 573n
Aguirre, F., 35n
Ahearne, M., 304n, 402n
Ahlburg, D., 93n
Ahlfinger, N. Richardson, 305n
Ahmad, A. S., 66n
Aiken, M., 509n
Ailon, G., 162n
Aime, F., 330n
AirAsia, 347f, 532
Ajzen, I., 92n
Akerlof, G. A., 198n
Akst, D., 402n
Albarracín, D., 92n, 197n
Aleandri, Emelise, 232
Alge, B. J., 364n
Algesheimer, R. L., 291n
Allen, D., 330n
Allen, D. G., 615n
Allen, N. J., 129n, 331n
Allen, P., 538n
Allen, T. D., 266n, 407n, 408n, 614n
Allen, W. R., 573n
Alliger, G. M., 402n, 408n, 573n
Allison, M., 363n
Allouf, M., 442n
Alloy, L. B., 128n
Allport, G. W., 159n
Allport, Gordon, 133

Almeida, J. G., 612n
Almond, S., 66n
Almor, T., 509n
Alsop, R., 36n
Alutto, J. A., 613n
Amabile, T. M., 199n
Amanatullah, E. T., 477n
Amankwah-Amoah, J., 328n
Amarel, D., 614n
Ambady, N., 65n, 125n, 127n, 128n
Ambrose, M. L., 235n, 509n, 541n
Amburgey, T. L., 509n
Ames, D. R., 161n, 401n, 476n
Amis, J., 612n
Amstad, F. T., 303n
Anand, G., 573n
Anand, N., 508n
Anand, R., 67n
Anand, V., 365n
Andersen, I., 614n
Andersen, J. A., 197n
Anderson, C., 441n, 475n, 477n, 509n
Anderson, N., 65n, 66n, 129n, 163n, 266n, 363n, 403n, 571n, 572n, 612n, 613n
Andersson, L. M., 303n
Ando, J., 160n
Andrews, J. P., 403n
Andrews, M., 615n
Andrews, M. C., 441n, 442n
Andrews, S., 412n
Ang, S., 378n, 401n, 574n
Angell, L. C., 331n
Ansberry, C., 266n
Anstey, K. J., 65n
Anthony, S. D., 507n
Anthony, W. P., 442n
Antonakis, J., 401n
Applebaum, E., 267n
Applebaum, S. H., 283e
Aquino, K., 423n
Aranya, N., 509n
Arbaugh, J. B., 573n
Ardena, R., 181n
Ardichvili, A., 37n, 541n
Argyris, C., 613n
Ariely, D., 36n
Arita, E., 268n
Arkani, S., 87n
Armeli, S., 93n
Armenakis, A. A., 305n, 330n
Armour, S., 37n, 574n, 611n, 613n
Arnau, R. C., 159n
Arnold, D., 541n
Arnold, J., 475n
Arnold, J. A., 129n
Arnold, T., 613n, 615n

Arnold, T. J., 509n
Arnst, C., 191n
Arrington, K., 267n
Arthur, M. B., 404n
Arthur, W., 539n
Arthur, W., Jr., 162n, 332n
Arum, R., 230n
Arvey, R. D., 159n, 508n
Aryee, S., 267n, 407n, 442n
Asch, S. E., 196n, 303n
Asch, Solomon, 282, 293
Ash, Mary Kay, 379
Ashford, J., 36n
Ashford, S. J., 365n, 611n
Ashforth, B. E., 125n, 126n, 129n, 302n, 365n, 442n
Ashkanasy, N. M., 111e, 125n, 127n, 162n, 401n
Ashkenas, R., 508n
Ashmos, D. P., 267n, 541n
Aspinwall, L. G., 126n
Aspinwall, Lisa, 534b
Atkinson, J. W., 233n
Atwater, L., 234n, 402n
Atwater, L. E., 196n, 235n, 408n, 574n
Au, W., 515n
Audia, P. G., 611n, 612n
Augier, M., 197n
Austin, N., 35n
Austin, S., 614n
Autio, E., 612n
Avallone, F., 612n
Avery, D. R., 65n, 66n, 67n, 302n
Avolio, B. J., 92n, 233n, 404n, 405n, 406n, 408n, 409n
Awamleh, R., 403n
Awong, T., 210n
Axelrod, J., 262n
Axtell, R. E., 365n
Aycan, Z., 93n, 236n, 267n
Ayman, R., 402n
Azar, B., 534n

B

Baas, M., 128n, 199n
Babcock, L., 476n, 477n
Babkoff, H., 126n
Bacdayan, P., 573n
Bacharach, S. B., 441n
Bachiochi, P. D., 93n
Bachrach, D. G., 94n, 406n, 442n
Backstrom, I., 35n
Badal, J., 440n
Bader, P., 408n
Baer, M., 160n
Bagsby, P. G., 128n
Bailey, D. E., 330n, 476n

Organization Index

*References followed by b indicate boxes;
e, exhibits; f, figure; n, notes*

Index A Combined Glossary/Subject Index

Enhancement, 432e

Entrepreneur roles, 7, 142b

Environment, *Institutions or forces outside an organization that potentially affect the organization's performance,* 499–500

Equity theory, *A theory that says that individuals compare their job inputs and outcomes with those of others and then respond to eliminate any inequities,* 219–222

Escalation of commitment, *An increased commitment to a previous decision in spite of negative information,* 180, 181

Essays, written, 558

Esteem, need for, 203

Ethical dilemmas and ethical choices, *Situations in which individuals are required to define right and wrong conduct,* 22–23

in decision-making, 187–188

decision-making and, 185f

of downsizing, 496

gossip as an, 345b

leadership and, 386–387

motivation and, 209b

rewards as, 258b

workplace romances as, 423b

Ethics

emotions and, 103

failure and, 24b

global virtual teams and, 315b

during negotiation, 468b

in organizational culture, 525–527

in political behavior, 434–435

training in, 553

Ethnicity, 48

E-training, 553, 554f

Evidence-based management (EBM), *The basing of managerial decisions on the best available scientific evidence,* 11

Exchange, as power tactic, 418

Exclusion, 43e

Excuses, 432e

Exemplification, 432e

Exercise, as emotion, mood source, 107

Exit, *Dissatisfaction expressed through behavior directed toward leaving the organization,* 82–84

Expectancy theory, *A theory that says that the strength of a tendency to act in a certain way depends on the strength of an expectation that the act will be followed by a given outcome and on the attractiveness of that outcome to the individual,* 224–226

Expectations, 173

Expertise, creativity and, 189

Expert power, *Influence based on special skills or knowledge,* 415

Explanations, 222

Explosive strength, 55e

Extent flexibility, 55e

Extraversion, *A personality dimension describing someone who is sociable, gregarious, and assertive,* 136, 137–138, 370

Extrinsic rewards and motivation, 208–211

F

Face culture, 515b

Facial expressions, 100

Failure, 24b

Fairness, perception of, 58, 84, 222, 416, 434

Favors, 432e

Fear, as motivator, 228b

Feedback, *The degree to which carrying out the work activities required by a job results in the individual obtaining direct and clear information about the effectiveness of his or her performance,* 213, 241, 340–341, 562–563

Felt conflict, *Emotional involvement in a conflict that creates anxiety, tenseness, frustration, or hostility,* 452, 453

Felt emotions, *An individual's actual emotions,* 109, 110

Femininity, *A national culture attribute that indicates little differentiation between male and female roles; a high rating indicates that women are treated as the equals of men in all aspects of the society,* 151

Fiedler contingency model, *The theory that effective groups depend on a proper match between a leader's style of interacting with subordinates and the degree to which the situation gives control and influence to the leader,* 372–375

Figurehead roles, 6, 7e

Filtering, *A sender's manipulation of information so that it will be seen more favorably by the receiver,* 353

Five-stage group-development model, *The five distinct stages groups go through: forming, storming, norming, performing, and adjourning,* 275–276

Fixed pie, *The belief that there is only a set amount of goods or services to be divvied up between the parties,* 459

Fixed vs. variable socialization, 522e

Flattery, 432e

Flexibility, physical, 55e

Flexible benefits, *A benefits plan that allows each employee to put together a benefits package individually tailored to his or her own needs and situation,* 257–258

Flexible spending plans, for benefits, 259

Flextime, *Flexible work hours,* 245–247, 248f

Forced comparison, *Method of performance evaluation where an employee's performance is made in explicit comparison to others (e.g., an employee may rank third out of 10 employees in her work unit),* 559

Formal channels, *Communication channels established by an organization to transmit messages related to the professional activities of members,* 338, 339

Formal group, *A designated work group defined by an organization's structure,* 272, 273

Formalization, *The degree to which jobs within an organization are standardized,* 486, 487, 515–516

Formal regulations, 186

Formal small-group networks, 343

Forming stage, *The first stage in group development, characterized by much uncertainty,* 275

Functional conflict, *Conflict that supports the goals of the group and improves its performance,* 447–448, 455–456

Functions, of managers, 6

Fundamental attribution error, *The tendency to underestimate the influence of external factors and overestimate the influence of internal factors when making judgments about the behavior of others,* 169

G

Gainsharing, *A formula-based group incentive plan,* 256, 257

Galatea effect, 217

Gender

bullying differences by, 12

as emotion, mood source, 107–108

influence on decision-making, 184

in negotiation, 466

stress and, 596b

in the workforce, 46–47

Gender identity, 51–52

General mental ability (GMA), *An overall factor of intelligence, as suggested by the positive correlations among specific intellectual ability dimensions,* 53

Generation Nexters, 146, 155

attempt to agree on the exchange rate for them, 117–118, 458, 459
anger in, 118
cross-cultural differences in, 462b
global implications of, 469–470
process of, 463–467
in sports, 471
third-party, 467–468
See also Conflict
Negotiator role, 7e, 8
Netters, 146, 155
Networking
as a managerial activity, 8
as organizational challenge, 20–21
social, 347–348, 359
Networks, formal communication, 343
Neutralizers, *Attributes that make it impossible for leader behavior to make any difference to follower outcomes,* 394–395
Nexters, 146, 155
Nominal group technique, *A group decision-making method in which individual members meet face to face to pool their judgments in a systematic but independent fashion,* 295–296
Nonsanctioned leadership, 368
Norming stage, *The third stage in group development, characterized by close relationships and cohesiveness,* 275
Norms, *Acceptable standards of behavior within a group that are shared by the group's members,* 280, 281, 285–286
Number aptitude, 53e

O

Offers, in distributive bargaining, 460
Offshoring, 500b
Off-the-job training, 553
On-the-job training, 553
Openness to experience, *A personality dimension that characterizes someone in terms of imagination, sensitivity, and curiosity,* 136, 137, 138, 370
Operant conditioning theory, 218
Organic model, *A structure that is flat, uses cross-hierarchical and cross-functional teams, has low formalization, possesses a comprehensive information network, and relies on participative decision making,* 496–498
Organization, *A consciously coordinated social unit, composed of two or more people, that functions on a relatively continuous basis to achieve a common goal or set of goals,* 5
Organizational behavior (OB), *A field of study that investigates the impact that individuals, groups, and structure have on behavior within*

organizations, for the purpose of applying such knowledge toward improving an organization's effectiveness, 10
applications for emotions and moods, 115–120
Big Five Model and, 138e
challenges, opportunities for, 15–23
developing model of, 22–30
disciplines of, 13–14
global implications of, 30, 32
literature about, 31
model, 25e
variables in, 14–15
Organizational change, 584–586
action research process for, 587
creating a culture for, 591–595
global implications of, 606
Kotter's eight-step plan for, 586–587
Lewin's three-step model for, 584–586
See also Change
Organizational citizenship behavior (OCB). *See Citizenship behavior*
Organizational climate, *The shared perceptions organizational members have about their organization and work environment,* 516–518
Organizational commitment, *The degree to which an employee identifies with a particular organization and its goals and wishes to maintain membership in the organization,* 74–75, 78
Organizational culture, *A system of shared meaning held by members that distinguishes the organization from other organizations,* 420, 427
creating and sustaining, 519–523
defining, 512–514
ethical considerations for, 525–527
face and dignity cultures in, 515b
functions of, 516–519
global implications of, 533
as a liability, 517–518
positive environment for, 527
workplace spirituality and, 529–532
Organizational demography, *The degree to which members of a work unit share a common demographic attribute, such as age, sex, race, educational level, or length of service in an organization, and the impact of this attribute on turnover,* 318, 320
Organizational development (OD), *A collection of planned change interventions, built on humanistic–democratic values, that seeks to improve organizational effectiveness and employee well-being,* 587–591
Organizational justice, *An overall perception of what is fair in the*

workplace, composed of distributive, procedural, and interactional justice, 222, 223
Organizational politics, 424–426, 429
Organizational structure, *The way in which job tasks are formally divided, grouped, and coordinated,* 480
designs of, 486–496
differences in, 496–501
global, 489b
global implications of, 502
as source of conflict, 450–451
Organizational survival, *The degree to which an organization is able to exist and grow over the long term,* 29
Organizing, *Determining what tasks are to be done, who is to do them, how the tasks are to be grouped, who reports to whom, and where decisions are to be made,* 6, 9
Other-inside/outside referent, 220–221
Other-orientation, 142–143
Outcomes, *Key factors that are affected by some other variables*
in conflict process, 455–458
in OB model, 25
in organizational culture, 513
in performance evaluation, 555–556
Outsourcing, 500b
Overconfidence bias, 177–178, 182–183

P

Participative management, *A process in which subordinates share a significant degree of decision-making power with their immediate superiors,* 251
Path–goal theory, *A theory that states that it is the leader's job to assist followers in attaining their goals and to provide the necessary direction and/or support to ensure that leader–member exchange (LMX) theory A theory that supports leaders' creation of in-groups and out-groups,* 376, 377
Pay. *See Compensation*
Peer pressure, 294b
People skills, improving, 19–20
Perceived conflict, *Awareness by one or more parties of the existence of conditions that create opportunities for conflict to arise,* 451–452
Perceived organizational support (POS), *The degree to which employees believe an organization values their contribution and cares about their well-being,* 76–77, 78
Perceivers, 167
Perception, *A process by which individuals organize and interpret their sensory impressions in order to give meaning to their environment,* 166–173, 190, 192